2012 | WORLD DEVELOPMENT INDICATORS

Photo credits: World Bank photo library, except page 282, David Cieslikowski/World Bank.

If you have questions or comments about this product, please contact:

Development Data Group
The World Bank
1818 H Street NW, Room MC2-812, Washington, D.C. 20433 USA
Hotline: 800 590 1906 or 202 473 7824; fax 202 522 1498
Email: data@worldbank.org
Web site: www.worldbank.org or data.worldbank.org

ISBN 978-0-8213-8985-0

ECO-AUDIT
Environmental Benefits Statement
The World Bank is committed to preserving endangered forests and natural resources. The Office of the Publisher
has chosen to print World Development Indicators 2012 on recycled paper with 50 percent postconsumer fiber in
accordance with the recommended standards for paper usage set by the Green Press Initiative, a nonprofit program
supporting publishers in using fiber that is not sourced from endangered forests. For more information, visit www.
greenpressinitiative.org.

Saved:
64 trees
26 million Btu of total energy
6,503 pounds of net greenhouse gases
29,321 gallons of waste water
1,859 pounds of solid waste

2012 | WORLD DEVELOPMENT INDICATORS

THE WORLD BANK

PREFACE

World Development Indicators 2012 is a compilation of relevant, high-quality, and internationally comparable statistics about development and the quality of people's lives. Organized around six themes—world view, people, the environment, the economy, states and markets, and global links—it aims to put data into the hands of policy makers, development specialists, students, and the public. We encourage and applaud the use of the data presented here to help reduce poverty and to solve the world's most pressing development challenges.

The full dataset used to produce *World Development Indicators* contains more than 1,000 indicators for 216 economies, with many time series extending back to 1960. Highly visual, interactive, and multilingual presentations of the data are available at the popular website http://data.worldbank.org and through the DataFinder application for mobile devices. And, as a major part of the World Bank's Open Data Initiative, the data are freely available for use and reuse under an open license. A companion printed volume, *The Little Data Book 2012*, presents a selection of indicators for each economy, and the biennial *Statistics for Small States* presents data for less-populated developing countries.

This 16th edition of *World Development Indicators* relies heavily on statistics produced by national authorities and agencies. Since the first edition in 1997, there has been a substantial increase in the availability and quality of the data, thanks to improvements in statistical capacity in many countries. More remains to be done: the capacity to use statistical data remains weak; demand is growing for greater disaggregation of indicators (for instance by sex, age, or geography); and data in some key areas, such as agriculture, are often missing or outdated. A new global statistical action plan (www.paris21.org/busan-action-plan), endorsed in November 2011 at the highest political levels at the Fourth High Level Forum on Aid Effectiveness in Busan, Republic of Korea, provides an important framework to address remaining challenges, to integrate statistics into decision making, to promote open access to data and improve their use, and to increase resources for statistical systems.

World Development Indicators is possible only through the excellent collaboration of many partners who provide the data for this collection, and I would like to thank them all: the United Nations family, the International Monetary Fund, the International Telecommunication Union, the Organisation for Economic Co-operation and Development, the statistical offices of more than 200 economies, and countless others whose support and advice have made this unique product possible.

As always, we welcome your ideas for making the data in *World Development Indicators* useful and relevant for improving the lives of people around the world.

Shaida Badiee
Director
Development Economics Data Group

ACKNOWLEDGMENTS

This book was prepared by a team led by Soong Sup Lee under the management of Neil Fantom and comprising Awatif Abuzeid, Azita Amjadi, Maja Bresslauer, David Cieslikowski, Liu Cui, Mahyar Eshragh-Tabary, Shota Hatakeyama, Masako Hiraga, Wendy Ven-dee Huang, Bala Bhaskar Naidu Kalimili, Buyant Khaltarkhuu, Elysee Kiti, Alison Kwong, Ibrahim Levent, Hiroko Maeda, Johan Mistiaen, Maurice Nsabimana, Sulekha Patel, Beatriz Prieto-Oramas, William Prince, Premi Rathan Raj, Evis Rucaj, Emi Suzuki, Eric Swanson, Jomo Tariku, and Estela Zamora, working closely with other teams in the Development Economics Vice Presidency's Development Data Group. *World Development Indicators* electronic products were prepared by a team led by Reza Farivari and comprising Ramvel Chandrasekaran, Ying Chi, Jean-Pierre Djomalieu, Ramgopal Erabelly, Federico Escaler, Shelley Fu, Gytis Kanchas, Ugendran Makhachkala, Vilas Mandlekar, Nacer Megherbi, Shanmugam Natarajan, Parastoo Oloumi, Atsushi Shimo, Maryna Taran, Malarvizhi Veerappan, and Vera Wen. The work was carried out under the direction of Shaida Badiee. Valuable advice was provided by Zia M. Qureshi and David Rosenblatt.

The choice of indicators and text content was shaped through close consultation with and substantial contributions from staff in the World Bank's four thematic networks—Financial and Private Sector Development, Human Development, Poverty Reduction and Economic Management, and Sustainable Development—and staff of the International Finance Corporation and the Multilateral Investment Guarantee Agency. Most important, the team received substantial help, guidance, and data from external partners. For individual acknowledgments of contributions to the book's content, please see *Credits*. For a listing of our key partners, see *Partners*.

Communications Development Incorporated provided overall design direction, editing, and layout, led by Meta de Coquereaumont, Bruce Ross-Larson, and Christopher Trott and assisted by Rob Elson. Elaine Wilson created the cover and graphics and typeset the book. Joseph Caponio provided production assistance. Peter Grundy, of Peter Grundy Art & Design, designed the report. Staff from External Affairs oversaw printing and dissemination of the book.

TABLE OF CONTENTS

FRONT

1. WORLD VIEW

2. PEOPLE

3. ENVIRONMENT

TABLE OF CONTENTS

 ## 4. ECONOMY

 ## 5. STATES AND MARKETS

6. GLOBAL LINKS

BACK

PARTNERS

Defining, gathering, and disseminating international statistics is a collective effort of many people and organizations. The indicators presented in *World Development Indicators* are the fruit of decades of work at many levels, from the field workers who administer censuses and household surveys to the committees and working parties of the national and international statistical agencies that develop the nomenclature, classifications, and standards fundamental to an international statistical system. Nongovernmental organizations and the private sector have also made important contributions, both in gathering primary data and in organizing and publishing their results. And academic researchers have played a crucial role in developing statistical methods and carrying on a continuing dialogue about the quality and interpretation of statistical indicators. All these contributors have a strong belief that available, accurate data will improve the quality of public and private decisionmaking.

The organizations listed here have made *World Development Indicators* possible by sharing their data and their expertise with us. More important, their collaboration contributes to the World Bank's efforts, and to those of many others, to improve the quality of life of the world's people. We acknowledge our debt and gratitude to all who have helped to build a base of comprehensive, quantitative information about the world and its people.

For easy reference, Web addresses are included for each listed organization. The addresses shown were active on March 1, 2012. Information about the World Bank is also provided.

International and government agencies

Carbon Dioxide Information Analysis Center

The Carbon Dioxide Information Analysis Center (CDIAC) is the primary global climate change data and information analysis center of the U.S. Department of Energy. The CDIAC's scope includes anything that would potentially be of value to those concerned with the greenhouse effect and global climate change, including concentrations of carbon dioxide and other radiatively active gases in the atmosphere, the role of the terrestrial biosphere and the oceans in the biogeochemical cycles of greenhouse gases, emissions of carbon dioxide to the atmosphere, long-term climate trends, the effects of elevated carbon dioxide on vegetation, and the vulnerability of coastal areas to rising sea levels.

For more information, see http://cdiac.ornl.gov.

Centre for Research on the Epidemiology of Disasters

Since 1988 the World Health Organization Collaborating Centre for Research on the Epidemiology of Disasters has maintained the Emergency Events Database, which was created with support from the Belgian government. The main objective of the database is to serve the purposes of humanitarian action at the national and international levels. It aims to rationalize decisionmaking for disaster preparedness and provide an objective base for vulnerability assessment and priority setting. The database contains essential core data—compiled from various sources, including UN agencies, nongovernmental organizations, insurance companies, research institutes, and press agencies—on the occurrence and effects of more than 18,000 mass disasters since 1900.

For more information, see www.emdat.be.

Deutsche Gesellschaft für Internationale Zusammenarbeit

The Deutsche Gesellschaft für Internationale Zusammenarbeit (GIZ) GmbH is a German government-owned corporation for international cooperation with worldwide operations. GIZ's aim is to positively shape political, economic, ecological, and social development in partner countries, thereby improving people's living conditions and prospects.

For more information, see www.giz.de.

Food and Agriculture Organization

The Food and Agriculture Organization, a specialized agency of the United Nations, was founded in October 1945 with a mandate to raise nutrition levels and living standards, to increase agricultural productivity, and to better the condition of rural populations. The organization provides direct development assistance; collects, analyzes, and disseminates information; offers policy and planning advice to governments; and serves as an international forum for debate on food and agricultural issues.

For more information, see www.fao.org.

Internal Displacement Monitoring Centre

The Internal Displacement Monitoring Centre was established in 1998 by the Norwegian Refugee Council and is the leading international body monitoring conflict-induced internal displacement worldwide. The center contributes to improving national and international capacities to protect and assist the millions of people around the globe who have been displaced within their own country as a result of conflicts or human rights violations.

For more information, see www.internal-displacement.org.

International Civil Aviation Organization

The International Civil Aviation Organization (ICAO), a specialized agency of the United Nations, is responsible for establishing international standards and recommended practices and procedures for the technical, economic, and legal aspects of international civil aviation operations. ICAO's strategic objectives include enhancing global aviation safety and security and the efficiency of aviation operations, minimizing the adverse effect of global civil aviation on the environment, maintaining the continuity of aviation operations, and strengthening laws governing international civil aviation.

For more information, see www.icao.int.

International Energy Agency

Founded in 1974, the International Energy Agency's (IEA) mandate is to facilitate cooperation among member countries in order to increase energy efficiency, promote use of clean energy and technology, and diversify energy sources while protecting the environment. The IEA publishes annual and quarterly statistical publications covering both Organisation for Economic Co-operation and Development (OECD) and non-OECD countries' data on oil, gas, coal, electricity, and renewable sources of energy; energy supply and consumption; and energy prices and taxes. The IEA also analyzes all aspects of sustainable development globally and provides policy recommendations.

For more information, see www.iea.org.

PARTNERS

International Labour Organization

The International Labour Organization (ILO), a specialized agency of the United Nations, seeks the promotion of social justice and internationally recognized human and labor rights. ILO helps advance the creation of decent jobs and the kinds of economic and working conditions that give working people and business people a stake in lasting peace, prosperity, and progress. As part of its mandate, the ILO maintains an extensive statistical publication program.

For more information, see www.ilo.org.

International Monetary Fund

The International Monetary Fund (IMF) is an international organization of 187 member countries established to promote international monetary cooperation, a stable system of exchange rates, and the balanced expansion of international trade and to foster economic growth and high levels of employment. The IMF reviews national, regional, and global economic and financial developments; provides policy advice to member countries; and serves as a forum where they can discuss the national, regional, and global consequences of their policies.

The IMF also makes financing temporarily available to member countries to help them address balance of payments problems. Among the IMF's core missions are the collection and dissemination of high-quality macroeconomic and financial statistics as an essential prerequisite for formulating appropriate policies. The IMF provides technical assistance and training to member countries in areas of its core expertise, including the development of economic and financial data in accordance with international standards.

For more information, see www.imf.org.

International Telecommunication Union

The International Telecommunication Union (ITU) is the leading UN agency for information and communication technologies. ITU's mission is to enable the growth and sustained development of telecommunications and information networks and to facilitate universal access so that people everywhere can participate in, and benefit from, the emerging information society and global economy. A key priority lies in bridging the so-called Digital Divide by building information and communication infrastructure, promoting adequate capacity building, and developing confidence in the use of cyberspace through enhanced online security. ITU also concentrates on strengthening emergency communications for disaster prevention and mitigation.

For more information, see www.itu.int.

National Science Foundation

The National Science Foundation (NSF) is an independent U.S. government agency whose mission is to promote the progress of science; to advance the national health, prosperity, and welfare; and to secure the national defense. NSF's goals—discovery, learning, research infrastructure, and stewardship—provide an integrated strategy to advance the frontiers of knowledge, cultivate a world-class, broadly inclusive science and engineering workforce, expand the scientific literacy of all citizens, build the nation's research capability through investments in advanced instrumentation and facilities, and support excellence in science and engineering research and education through a capable and responsive organization.

For more information, see www.nsf.gov.

The Office of U.S. Foreign Disaster Assistance

On November 3, 1961, U.S. President John F. Kennedy established the U.S. Agency for International Development (USAID), the first U.S. foreign assistance organization whose primary emphasis was long-range economic and social development assistance to foreign countries. The Office of U.S. Foreign Disaster Assistance is the office within USAID responsible for providing nonfood humanitarian assistance in response to international crises and disasters. The USAID administrator is designated as the president's special coordinator for international disaster assistance, which the Office of U.S. Foreign Disaster Assistance assists in coordinating.

For more information see www.globalcorps.com/ofda.html and www.usaid.gov/our_work/humanitarian_assistance/disaster_assistance.

Organisation for Economic Co-operation and Development

The Organisation for Economic Co-operation and Development (OECD) includes 34 member countries sharing a commitment to democratic government and the market economy to support sustainable economic growth, boost employment, raise living standards, maintain financial stability, assist other countries' economic development, and contribute to growth in world trade. With active relationships with some 100 other countries, it has a global reach. It is best known for its publications and statistics, which cover economic and social issues from macroeconomics to trade, education, development, and science and innovation.

The Development Assistance Committee (DAC, www.oecd.org/dac) is one of the principal bodies through which the OECD deals with issues related to cooperation with developing countries. The DAC is a key forum of major bilateral donors, who work together to increase the effectiveness of their common efforts to support sustainable development. The DAC concentrates on two key areas: the contribution of international development to the capacity of developing countries to participate in the global economy and the capacity of people to overcome poverty and participate fully in their societies.

For more information, see www.oecd.org.

Stockholm International Peace Research Institute

The Stockholm International Peace Research Institute (SIPRI) conducts research on questions of conflict and cooperation of importance for international peace and security, with the aim of contributing to an understanding of the conditions for peaceful solutions to international conflicts and for a stable peace. SIPRI's main publication, *SIPRI Yearbook,* is an authoritative and independent source on armaments and arms control and other conflict and security issues.

For more information, see www.sipri.org.

Understanding Children's Work

As part of broader efforts to develop effective and long-term solutions to child labor, the International Labour Organization, the United Nations Children's Fund (UNICEF), and the World Bank initiated the joint interagency research program "Understanding Children's Work and Its Impact" in December 2000. The Understanding Children's Work (UCW) project was located at UNICEF's Innocenti Research Centre in Florence, Italy, until June 2004, when it moved to the Centre for International Studies on Economic Growth in Rome.

The UCW project addresses the crucial need for more and better data on child labor. UCW's online database contains data by country on child labor and the status of children.

For more information, see www.ucw-project.org.

PARTNERS

United Nations

The United Nations currently has 193 member states. The purposes of the United Nations, as set forth in its charter, are to maintain international peace and security; to develop friendly relations among nations; to cooperate in solving international economic, social, cultural, and humanitarian problems and in promoting respect for human rights and fundamental freedoms; and to be a center for harmonizing the actions of nations in attaining these ends.

For more information, see www.un.org.

United Nations Centre for Human Settlements, Global Urban Observatory

The Urban Indicators Programme of the United Nations Human Settlements Programme was established to address the urgent global need to improve the urban knowledge base by helping countries and cities design, collect, and apply policy-oriented indicators related to development at the city level.

With the Urban Indicators and Best Practices programs, the Global Urban Observatory is establishing a worldwide information, assessment, and capacity-building network to help governments, local authorities, the private sector, and nongovernmental and other civil society organizations.

For more information, see www.unhabitat.org.

United Nations Children's Fund

The United Nations Children's Fund (UNICEF) works with other UN bodies and with governments and nongovernmental organizations to improve children's lives in more than 190 countries through various programs in education and health. UNICEF focuses primarily on five areas: child survival and development, basic education and gender equality (including girls' education), child protection, HIV/AIDS, and policy advocacy and partnerships.

For more information, see www.unicef.org.

United Nations Conference on Trade and Development

The United Nations Conference on Trade and Development (UNCTAD) is the principal organ of the United Nations General Assembly in the field of trade and development. Its mandate is to accelerate economic growth and development, particularly in developing countries. UNCTAD discharges its mandate through policy analysis; intergovernmental deliberations, consensus building, and negotiation; monitoring, implementation, and follow-up; and technical cooperation.

For more information, see www.unctad.org.

United Nations Department of Peacekeeping Operations

The United Nations Department of Peacekeeping Operations contributes to the most important function of the United Nations—maintaining international peace and security. The department helps countries torn by conflict to create the conditions for lasting peace. The first peacekeeping mission was established in 1948 and has evolved to meet the demands of different conflicts and a changing political landscape. Today's peacekeepers undertake a wide variety of complex tasks, from helping build sustainable institutions of governance, to monitoring human rights, to assisting in security sector reform, to disarming, demobilizing, and reintegrating former combatants.

For more information, see www.un.org/en/peacekeeping.

United Nations Educational, Scientific, and Cultural Organization, Institute for Statistics

The United Nations Educational, Scientific, and Cultural Organization (UNESCO) is a specialized agency of the United Nations that promotes international cooperation among member states and associate members in education, science, culture, and communications. The UNESCO Institute for Statistics is the organization's statistical branch, established in July 1999 to meet the growing needs of UNESCO member states and the international community for a wider range of policy-relevant, timely, and reliable statistics on these topics.

For more information, see www.uis.unesco.org.

United Nations Environment Programme

The mandate of the United Nations Environment Programme is to provide leadership and encourage partnership in caring for the environment by inspiring, informing, and enabling nations and people to improve their quality of life without compromising that of future generations.

For more information, see www.unep.org.

United Nations Industrial Development Organization

The United Nations Industrial Development Organization was established to act as the central coordinating body for industrial activities and to promote industrial development and cooperation at the global, regional, national, and sectoral levels. Its mandate is to help develop scientific and technological plans and programs for industrialization in the public, cooperative, and private sectors.

For more information, see www.unido.org.

United Nations International Strategy for Disaster Reduction

Created in December 1999 as the successor to the International Decade for Natural Disaster Reduction, the mandate of the secretariat of the United Nations International Strategy for Disaster Reduction is to serve as the focal point in the UN system for coordination of disaster reduction and to ensure synergies among disaster relief activities.

For more information, see www.unisdr.org.

United Nations Office on Drugs and Crime

The United Nations Office on Drugs and Crime was established in 1977 and is a global leader in the fight against illicit drugs and international crime. The office assists member states in their struggle against illicit drugs, crime, and terrorism by helping build capacity, conducting research and analytical work, and assisting in the ratification and implementation of relevant international treaties and domestic legislation related to drugs, crime, and terrorism.

For more information, see www.unodc.org.

United Nations Office of the High Commissioner for Refugees

The United Nations Office of the High Commissioner for Refugees (UNHCR) is mandated to lead and coordinate international action to protect refugees and resolve refugee problems worldwide. Its primary purpose is to safeguard the rights and well-being of refugees. UNHCR also collects and disseminates statistics on refugees.

For more information, see www.unhcr.org.

PARTNERS

Upsalla Conflict Data Program

The Upsalla Conflict Data Program has collected information on armed violence since 1946 and is one of the most accurate and well used data sources on global armed conflicts. Its definition of armed conflict is becoming a standard in how conflicts are systematically defined and studied. In addition to data collection on armed violence, its researchers conduct theoretically and empirically based analyses of the causes, escalation, spread, prevention, and resolution of armed conflict.

For more information, see www.pcr.uu.se/research/UCDP.

World Bank

The World Bank is a vital source of financial and technical assistance for developing countries. The World Bank is made up of two unique development institutions owned by 187 member countries—the International Bank for Reconstruction and Development (IBRD) and the International Development Association (IDA). These institutions play different but collaborative roles to advance the vision of an inclusive and sustainable globalization. The IBRD focuses on middle-income and creditworthy poor countries, while IDA focuses on the poorest countries. Together they provide low-interest loans, interest-free credits, and grants to developing countries for a wide array of purposes, including investments in education, health, public administration, infrastructure, financial and private sector development, agriculture, and environmental and natural resource management. The World Bank's work focuses on achieving the Millennium Development Goals by working with partners to alleviate poverty.

For more information, see http://data.worldbank.org.

World Health Organization

The objective of the World Health Organization (WHO), a specialized agency of the United Nations, is the attainment by all people of the highest possible level of health. It is responsible for providing leadership on global health matters, shaping the health research agenda, setting norms and standards, articulating evidence-based policy options, providing technical support to countries, and monitoring and assessing health trends.

For more information, see www.who.int.

World Intellectual Property Organization

The World Intellectual Property Organization (WIPO) is a specialized agency of the United Nations dedicated to developing a balanced and accessible international intellectual property (IP) system, which rewards creativity, stimulates innovation, and contributes to economic development while safeguarding the public interest. WIPO carries out a wide variety of tasks related to the protection of IP rights. These include developing international IP laws and standards, delivering global IP protection services, encouraging the use of IP for economic development, promoting better understanding of IP, and providing a forum for debate.

For more information, see www.wipo.int.

World Tourism Organization

The World Tourism Organization is an intergovernmental body entrusted by the United Nations with promoting and developing tourism. It serves as a global forum for tourism policy issues and a source of tourism know-how.

For more information, see www.unwto.org.

World Trade Organization

The World Trade Organization (WTO) is the only international organization dealing with the global rules of trade between nations. Its main function is to ensure that trade flows as smoothly, predictably, and freely as possible. It does this by administering trade agreements, acting as a forum for trade negotiations, settling trade disputes, reviewing national trade policies, assisting developing countries in trade policy issues—through technical assistance and training programs—and cooperating with other international organizations. At the heart of the system—known as the multilateral trading system—are the WTO's agreements, negotiated and signed by a large majority of the world's trading nations and ratified by their parliaments.

For more information, see www.wto.org.

Private and nongovernmental organizations

Center for International Earth Science Information Network

The Center for International Earth Science Information Network, a center within the Earth Institute at Columbia University, works at the intersection of the social, natural, and information sciences and specializes in online data and information management, spatial data integration and training, and interdisciplinary research related to human interactions in the environment.

For more information, see www.ciesin.org.

Containerisation International

Containerisation International Yearbook is one of the most authoritative reference books on the container industry. The information can be accessed on the Containerisation International Web site, which also provides a comprehensive online daily business news and information service for the container industry.

For more information, see www.ci-online.co.uk.

DHL

DHL provides shipping and customized transportation solutions for customers in more than 220 countries and territories. It offers expertise in express, air, and ocean freight; overland transport; contract logistics solutions; and international mail services.

For more information, see www.dhl.com.

International Institute for Strategic Studies

The International Institute for Strategic Studies (IISS) provides information and analysis on strategic trends and facilitates contacts between government leaders, business people, and analysts that could lead to better public policy in international security and international relations. The IISS is a primary source of accurate, objective information on international strategic issues.

For more information, see www.iiss.org.

PARTNERS

International Road Federation

The International Road Federation (IRF) is a nongovernmental, not-for-profit organization whose mission is to encourage and promote development and maintenance of better, safer, and more sustainable roads and road networks. Working together with its members and associates, the IRF promotes social and economic benefits that flow from well planned and environmentally sound road transport networks. It helps put in place technological solutions and management practices that provide maximum economic and social returns from national road investments. The IRF works in all aspects of road policy and development worldwide with governments and financial institutions, members, and the community of road professionals.

For more information, see www.irfnet.org.

Netcraft

Netcraft provides Internet security services such as antifraud and antiphishing services, application testing, code reviews, and automated penetration testing. Netcraft also provides research data and analysis on many aspects of the Internet and is a respected authority on the market share of web servers, operating systems, hosting providers, Internet service providers, encrypted transactions, electronic commerce, scripting languages, and content technologies on the Internet.

For more information, see http://news.netcraft.com.

PwC

PwC provides industry-focused services in the fields of assurance, tax, human resources, transactions, performance improvement, and crisis management services to help address client and stakeholder issues.

For more information, see www.pwc.com.

Standard & Poor's

Standard & Poor's is the world's foremost provider of independent credit ratings, indexes, risk evaluation, investment research, and data. S&P's *Global Stock Markets Factbook* draws on data from S&P's Emerging Markets Database (EMDB) and other sources covering data on more than 100 markets with comprehensive market profiles for 82 countries. Drawing a sample of stocks in each EMDB market, Standard & Poor's calculates indexes to serve as benchmarks that are consistent across national boundaries.

For more information, see www.standardandpoors.com.

World Conservation Monitoring Centre

The World Conservation Monitoring Centre provides information on the conservation and sustainable use of the world's living resources and helps others to develop information systems of their own. It works in close collaboration with a wide range of people and organizations to increase access to the information needed for wise management of the world's living resources.

For more information, see www.unep-wcmc.org.

World Economic Forum

The World Economic Forum (WEF) is an independent international organization committed to improving the state of the world by engaging leaders in partnerships to shape global, regional, and industry agendas. Economic research at the WEF—led by the Global Competitiveness Programme—focuses on identifying the impediments to growth so that strategies to achieve sustainable economic progress, reduce poverty, and increase prosperity can be developed. The WEF's competitiveness reports range from global coverage, such as *Global Competitiveness Report,* to regional and topical coverage, such as *Africa Competitiveness Report, The Lisbon Review,* and *Global Information Technology Report.*

For more information, see: www.weforum.org.

World Resources Institute

The World Resources Institute is an independent center for policy research and technical assistance on global environmental and development issues. The institute provides—and helps other institutions provide—objective information and practical proposals for policy and institutional change that will foster environmentally sound, socially equitable development. The institute's current areas of work include trade, forests, energy, economics, technology, biodiversity, human health, climate change, sustainable agriculture, resource and environmental information, and national strategies for environmental and resource management.

For more information, see www.wri.org.

USERS GUIDE

Tables

The tables are numbered by section and display the identifying icon of the section. Countries and economies are listed alphabetically (except for Hong Kong SAR, China, which appears after China). Data are shown for 158 economies with a population of more than 1 million, as well as for Taiwan, China, in selected tables. Table 1.6 presents selected indicators for 58 other economies—small economies with a population between 30,000 and 1 million and smaller economies if they are members of the International Bank for Reconstruction and Development or, as it is commonly known, the World Bank. Data for these economies are included on the *World Development Indicators* CD-ROM and the World Bank's Open Data website (http://data.worldbank.org). The term *country,* used interchangeably with *economy,* does not imply political independence but refers to any territory for which authorities report separate social or economic statistics. When available, aggregate measures for income and regional groups appear at the end of each table.

Indicators are shown for the most recent year or period for which data are available and, in most tables, for an earlier year or period (usually 1990 or 2000 in this edition). Time series data for all 216 economies are available on the *World Development Indicators* CD-ROM and the World Bank's Open Data website (http://data.worldbank.org).

Known deviations from standard definitions or breaks in comparability over time or across countries are either footnoted in the tables or noted in *About the data.* When available data are deemed to be too weak to provide reliable measures of levels and trends or do not adequately adhere to international standards, the data are not shown.

Aggregate measures for income groups

The aggregate measures for income groups include 216 economies (the economies listed in the main tables plus those in table 1.6) whenever data are available. To maintain consistency in the aggregate measures over time and between tables, missing data are imputed where possible. The aggregates are totals (designated by a *t* if the aggregates include gap-filled estimates for missing data and by an *s,* for simple totals, where they do not), median values (*m*), weighted averages (*w*), or simple averages (*u*). Gap filling of amounts not allocated to countries may result in discrepancies between subgroup aggregates and overall totals. For further discussion of aggregation methods, see *Statistical methods.*

Aggregate measures for regions

The aggregate measures for regions cover only low- and middle-income economies, including economies with populations of less than 1 million listed in table 1.6.

The country composition of regions is based on the World Bank's analytical regions and may differ from common geographic usage. For regional classifications, see the map on the inside back cover and the list on the back cover flap. For further discussion of aggregation methods, see *Statistical methods.*

Statistics

Data are shown for economies as they were constituted in 2010, and historical data are revised to reflect current political arrangements. Exceptions are noted throughout the tables.

Additional information about the data is provided in *Primary data documentation,* which summarizes national and international efforts to improve basic data collection and gives country-level information on primary sources, census years, fiscal years, statistical methods and concepts used, and other background information. *Statistical methods* provides technical information on some of the general calculations and formulas used throughout the book.

Data consistency, reliability, and comparability

Considerable effort has been made to standardize the data, but full comparability cannot be assured, and care must be taken in interpreting the indicators. Many factors affect data availability, comparability, and reliability: statistical systems in many developing economies are still weak; statistical methods, coverage, practices, and definitions differ widely; and cross-country and intertemporal comparisons involve complex technical and conceptual problems that cannot be resolved unequivocally. Data coverage may not be complete because of special circumstances affecting the collection and reporting of data, such as problems stemming from conflicts.

For these reasons, although data are drawn from the sources thought to be most authoritative, they should be construed only as indicating trends and characterizing major differences among economies rather than as offering precise quantitative measures of those differences. Discrepancies in data presented in different editions of *World Development Indicators* reflect updates by countries as well as revisions to historical series and changes in methodology. Thus readers are advised not to compare data series across editions of *World Development Indicators* or across World Bank publications. Consistent time series data for 1960–2010 are available on the *World Development Indicators* CD-ROM and the World Bank's Open Data website (http://data.worldbank.org).

Except where otherwise noted, growth rates are in real terms. (See *Statistical methods* for information on the methods used to calculate growth rates.) Data for some economic indicators for some economies are presented in fiscal years rather than calendar years; see *Primary data documentation.* The methods used for converting national currencies are described in *Statistical methods.*

Country notes

- Unless otherwise noted, data for China do not include data for Hong Kong SAR, China; Macao SAR, China; or Taiwan, China.
- Data for Indonesia include Timor-Leste through 1999 unless otherwise noted.
- Montenegro declared independence from Serbia and Montenegro on June 3, 2006. When available, data for each country are shown separately. However, some indicators for Serbia continue to include data for Montenegro through 2005; these data are footnoted in the tables. Moreover, data for most indicators from 1999

onward for Serbia exclude data for Kosovo, which in 1999 became a territory under international administration pursuant to UN Security Council Resolution 1244 (1999); any exceptions are noted. Kosovo became a World Bank member on June 29, 2009, and its data are shown in the tables when available.

· Netherlands Antilles, for which data were listed in previous editions, ceased to exist on October 10, 2010. Data for Curaçao and Sint Maarten, which became countries within the Kingdom of the Netherlands, are now listed separately. Data for Bonaire, Saba, and St. Eustatius, which became special municipalities of the Netherlands, are included in data for the Netherlands.

· South Sudan declared its independence on July 9, 2011. When available, data are shown separately for South Sudan; data for Sudan include South Sudan unless otherwise noted.

Classification of economies

For operational and analytical purposes the World Bank's main criterion for classifying economies is gross national income (GNI) per capita (calculated by the *World Bank Atlas* method). Every economy is classified as low income, middle income (subdivided into lower middle and upper middle), or high income. For income classifications see the map on the inside front cover and the list on the front cover flap. Low- and middle-income economies are sometimes referred to as developing economies. The term is used for convenience; it is not intended to imply that all economies in the group are experiencing similar development or that other economies have reached a preferred or final stage of development. Note that classification by income does not necessarily reflect development status. Because GNI per capita changes over time, the country composition of income groups may change from one edition of *World Development Indicators* to the next. Once the classification is fixed for an edition, based on GNI per capita in the most recent year for which data are available (2010 in this edition), all historical data presented are based on the same country grouping.

Low-income economies are those with a GNI per capita of $1,005 or less in 2010. Middle-income economies are those with a GNI per capita of $1,006–$12,275. Lower middle-income and upper middle-income economies are separated at a GNI per capita of $3,976. High-income economies are those with a GNI per capita of $12,276 or more. The 17 participating member countries of the euro area are presented as a subgroup under high-income economies.

Symbols

..

means that data are not available or that aggregates cannot be calculated because of missing data in the years shown.

0 or 0.0

means zero or small enough that the number would round to zero at the displayed number of decimal places.

/

in dates, as in 2009/10, means that the period of time, usually 12 months, straddles two calendar years and refers to a crop year, a survey year, or a fiscal year.

$

means current U.S. dollars unless otherwise noted.

>

means more than.

<

means less than.

Data presentation conventions

· A blank means not applicable or, for an aggregate, not analytically meaningful.
· A billion is 1,000 million.
· A trillion is 1,000 billion.
· Figures in italics refer to years or periods other than those specified or to growth rates calculated for less than the full period specified.

· Data for years that are more than three years from the range shown are footnoted.

The cutoff date for data is February 1, 2012.

WORLD VIEW

We now have data to monitor the first 10 years of the Millennium Development Goals. Results are starting to appear, and we have a better view of where we will be in 2015. We will not achieve all the targets we set for ourselves, but progress measured against 1990 benchmarks accelerated in the last decade, lifting millions of people out of poverty, enrolling millions of children in school, and sharply reducing loss of life from preventable causes. We know this because we have access to greatly improved statistics.

The need for reliable and timely statistics was recognized long before the Millennium Development Goals were proposed in 2000, but the widespread attention given to their quantitative targets has increased demand for regular and uniform reporting of key indicators. The International Development Goals proposed by the Organisation for Economic Co-operation and Development in 1996 (OECD DAC 1996) included 21 indicators under seven headings that anticipated the Millennium Development Goals. The World Bank's 1992 *Poverty Reduction Handbook* (World Bank 1992) noted the need for an overall strategy for country statistical capacity and institution building.

Faced with large gaps in the international database, the Partnership in Statistics for Development in the 21st Century (PARIS21) was established in 1999 to coordinate efforts to increase developing countries' statistical capacity. In 2004 the Second Roundtable on Managing for Development Results endorsed the Marrakech Action Plan for Statistics, creating an international agenda for support to statistics in developing countries. Subsequently the Accra Agenda for Action made broad commitments on behalf of donors and developing countries to strengthen national statistical systems; provide more data disaggregated by sex, region, and economic status; and "invest in strengthening developing countries' national statistical capacity and information systems, including those for managing aid" (OECD 2008a). More recently, the 2009 Dakar Declaration on the Development of Statistics reaffirmed that "concerted and co-ordinated actions are required to make more effective use of statistical data to support poverty reduction policies and programs and to strengthen and sustain the capacity of statistical systems especially in developing countries" (PARIS21 2009a).

Much progress has been made. When the current round of censuses concludes in 2014, 98 percent of the world's population will have been counted. Since donors began reporting support for statistical capacity development in 2008, financial commitments to statistics have increased 60 percent to $1.6 billion over 2008–10. More than 55 developing countries have improved the data collection, management, and dissemination of household surveys. The United Nations Inter-Agency and Expert Group on the Millennium Development Goal Indicators has conducted a series of regional workshops aimed at improving the MDG monitoring and has reported annually on progress. The quality of statistics as measured by the World Bank's statistical capacity indicator has improved from its benchmark level of 54 in 1999 to 67 in 2011. The availability of data for monitoring the Millennium Development Goals has improved commensurately: in 2003 only 4 countries had two data points for at least 16 of 22 principal Millennium Development Goals indicators; by 2009 this had risen to 118 countries (PARIS21 2009b).

Any assessment of the Millennium Development Goals must acknowledge that amid all the signs of progress, there are gaps. Shortcomings. Disappointments. Some targets will not be reached in this decade or the next. Likewise the statistical record is still incomplete, Continuing progress will require renewed commitment and careful monitoring.

1

Eradicate extreme poverty and hunger

Goal 1

Poverty and hunger remain, but fewer people live in extreme poverty. The proportion of people living on less than $1.25 a day fell from 43.1 percent in 1990 to 22.2 percent in 2008. While the food, fuel, and financial crises over the past four years have worsened the situation of vulnerable populations and slowed poverty reduction in some countries, global poverty rates have continued to fall. Between 2005 and 2008 both the poverty rate and the number of people living in extreme poverty fell in all six developing country regions, the first time that has happened. Preliminary estimates for 2010 show that the extreme poverty rate fell further, reaching the global target of the Millennium Development Goals of halving world poverty five years early.

Further progress is possible and likely before the 2015 target date of the Millennium Development Goals, if developing countries maintain the robust growth rates achieved over much of the past decade. But even then, hundreds of millions of people will remain mired in poverty, especially in Sub-Saharan Africa and South Asia and wherever poor health and lack of education deprive people of productive employment; environmental resources have been depleted or spoiled; and corruption, conflict, and misgovernance waste public resources and discourage private investment.

Poverty rates fell sharply in the new millennium   **1a**

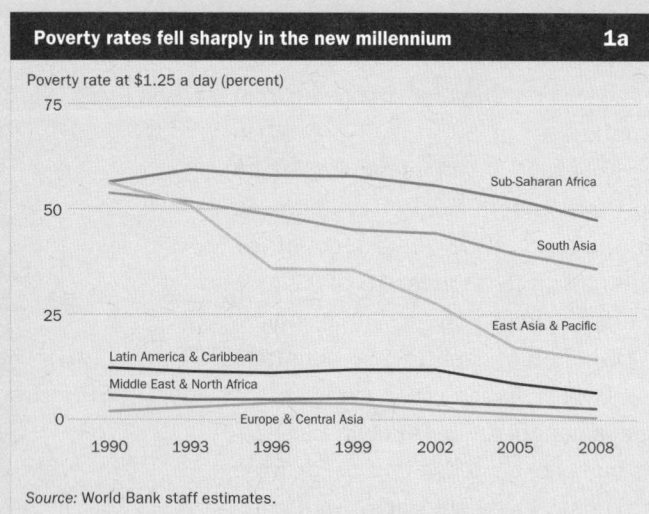

Poverty rate at $1.25 a day (percent)

Source: World Bank staff estimates.

Fewer people living in extreme poverty   **1b**

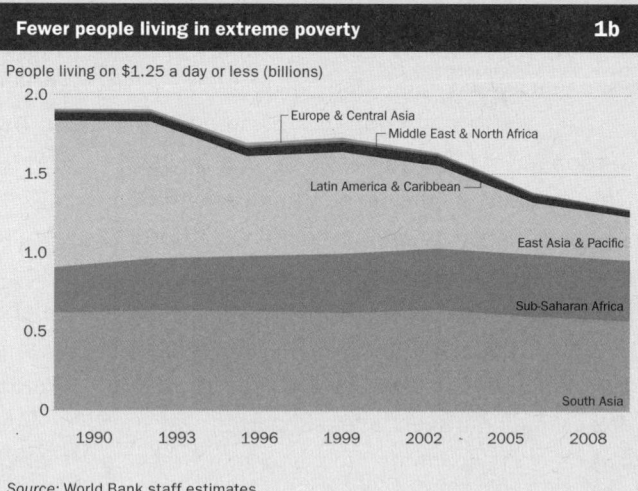

People living on $1.25 a day or less (billions)

Source: World Bank staff estimates.

The most rapid decline in poverty occurred in East Asia and the Pacific, where extreme poverty in China fell from 60 percent in 1990 to 13 percent. In developing countries outside China, the poverty rate fell from 37 percent to 25 percent. Poverty remains widespread in Sub-Saharan Africa and South Asia, but progress has been substantial. In South Asia the poverty rate fell from 54 percent in 1990 to 36 percent in 2008. And over 2005–2008 the poverty rate in Sub-Saharan Africa fell 4.8 percentage points to less than 50 percent, the largest drop in Sub-Saharan Africa since international poverty rates have been computed.

In 2008, 1.28 billion people lived on less than $1.25 a day. Since 1990 the number of people living in extreme poverty has fallen in all regions except Sub-Saharan Africa, where the rate of population growth exceeded the rate of poverty reduction, increasing the number of extremely poor people from 290 million in 1990 to 356 million in 2008. The largest number of poor people remain in South Asia, where 571 million people live on less than $1.25 a day, down from a peak of 641 million in 2002.

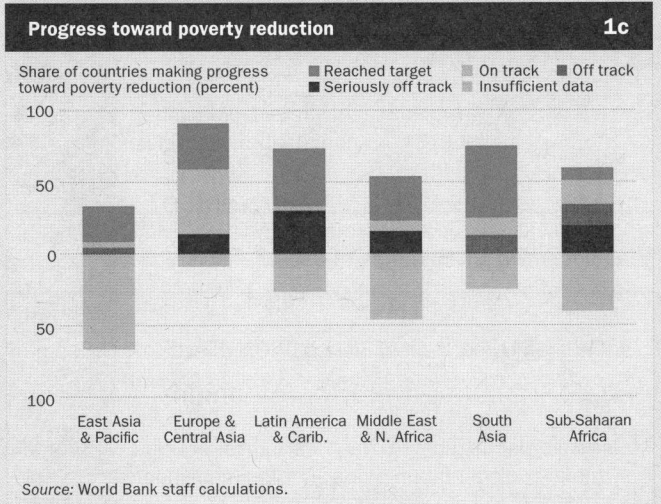

Progress toward poverty reduction — 1c

Share of countries making progress toward poverty reduction (percent)

■ Reached target ■ On track ■ Off track
■ Seriously off track ■ Insufficient data

East Asia & Pacific | Europe & Central Asia | Latin America & Carib. | Middle East & N. Africa | South Asia | Sub-Saharan Africa

Source: World Bank staff calculations.

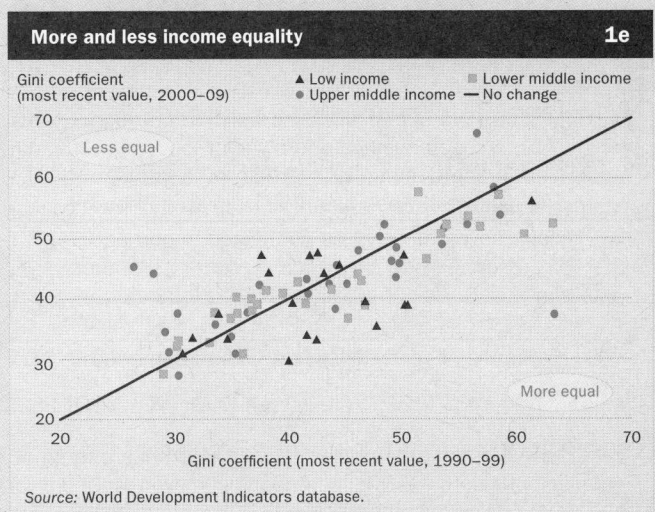

More and less income equality — 1e

Gini coefficient (most recent value, 2000–09)

▲ Low income ■ Lower middle income
● Upper middle income — No change

Less equal

More equal

Gini coefficient (most recent value, 1990–99)

Source: World Development Indicators database.

Individual country progress is assessed by comparing the rate of poverty reduction with the average rate required to achieve a 50 percent reduction in 25 years. Countries that have already reached the target are listed as "achieved." Those matching the required rate are listed as "on track." Countries that will take longer but could reach the target by 2040, based on past performance, are listed as "off track." And those that would need still longer or where poverty rates have increased are listed as "seriously off track."

Is income inequality improving or getting worse? At any level of income per person, the less equal the distribution of income the greater the poverty rate. The Gini coefficient is a common measure of inequality. A higher value indicates greater inequality. Poor countries often have less equal distributions of income than do rich countries, but there are significant regional differences as well. Data for 81 countries with values measured before and after 2000 show Gini coefficients fell in 44, including many low-income economies.

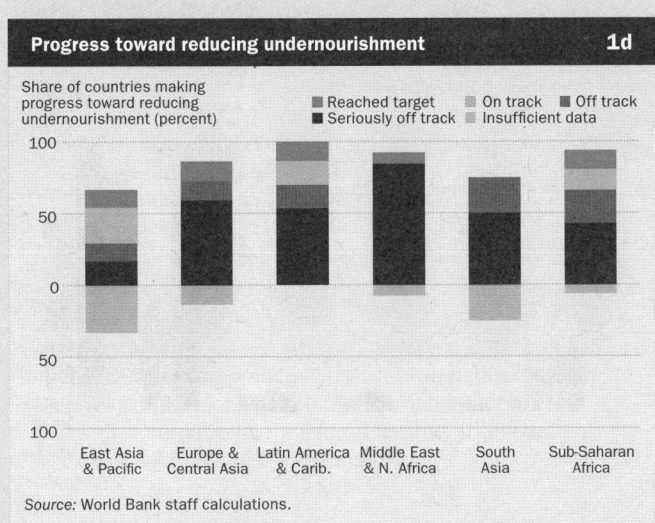

Progress toward reducing undernourishment — 1d

Share of countries making progress toward reducing undernourishment (percent)

■ Reached target ■ On track ■ Off track
■ Seriously off track ■ Insufficient data

East Asia & Pacific | Europe & Central Asia | Latin America & Carib. | Middle East & N. Africa | South Asia | Sub-Saharan Africa

Source: World Bank staff calculations.

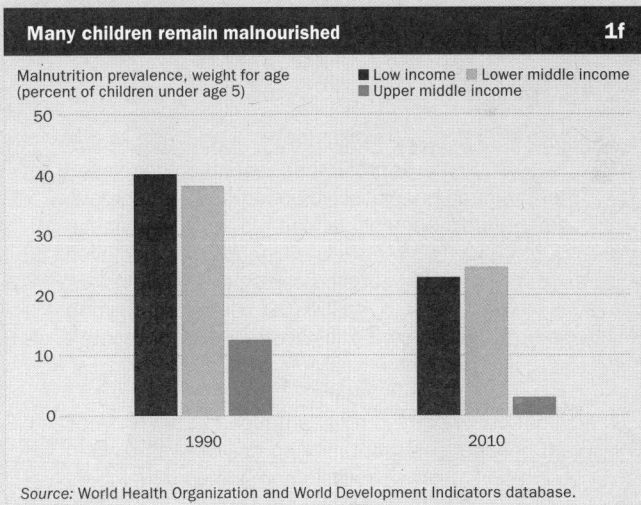

Many children remain malnourished — 1f

Malnutrition prevalence, weight for age (percent of children under age 5)

■ Low income ■ Lower middle income
■ Upper middle income

1990   2010

Source: World Health Organization and World Development Indicators database.

Undernourishment measures the availability of food to meet people's basic energy needs. The Millennium Development Goals call for halving the proportion of undernourished people, but few countries will reach that target by 2015. Rising agricultural production has kept ahead of population growth, but increasing food prices and the diversion of food crops to fuel production have reversed the declining rate of undernourishment since 2004–06. The Food and Agriculture Organization estimated that there were 739 million people without adequate daily food intake in 2008.

Malnutrition rates have dropped substantially since 1990, but more than 100 million children under age 5 remain malnourished. Only 40 of 90 countries with adequate data to monitor trends are on track to reach the Millennium Development Goal target of halving the number of people who suffer from hunger. Malnutrition in children often begins at birth, when poorly nourished mothers give birth to underweight babies. Malnourished children develop more slowly, enter school later, and perform less well. Programs to encourage breastfeeding and improve the diets of mothers and children can help.

Achieve universal primary education

Goal 2

The commitment to provide primary education to every child is the oldest of the Millennium Development Goals, having been set at the first Education for All conference in Jomtien, Thailand, more than 20 years ago. Achieving this goal has often seemed tantalizingly near, but only Latin America and the Caribbean has reached the goal, although East Asia and Pacific and Europe and Central Asia are close.

Progress among the poorest countries, slow in the 1990s, has accelerated since 2000, particularly in South Asia and Sub-Saharan Africa, but full enrollment remains elusive. Many children start school but drop out before completing the primary stage, discouraged by cost, distance, physical danger, and failure to progress. Even as countries approach the target of Millennium Development Goal 2, the education demands of modern economies expand. In the 21st century primary education will be of value only as a stepping stone toward secondary and higher education.

The last step toward education for all	1g

Primary school completion rate (percent)

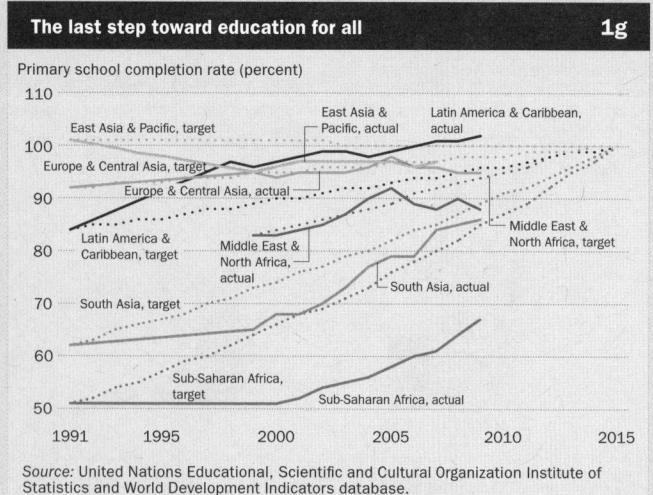

Source: United Nations Educational, Scientific and Cultural Organization Institute of Statistics and World Development Indicators database.

64 million children out of school	1h

Number of children not attending primary school (millions)

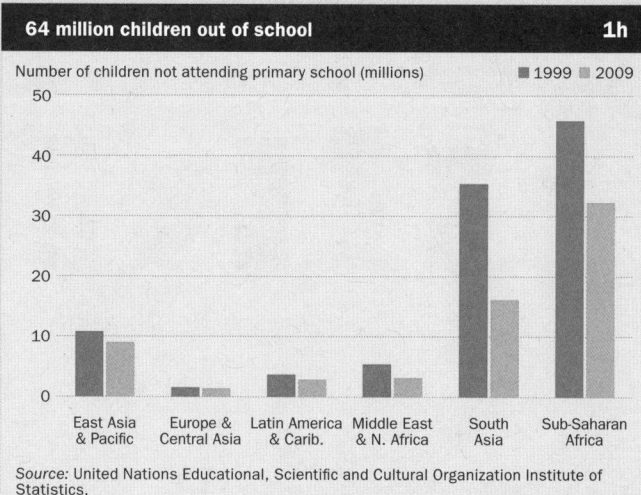

Source: United Nations Educational, Scientific and Cultural Organization Institute of Statistics.

In 2009, 87 percent of children in developing countries completed primary school. In most regions school enrollment picked up after the Millennium Development Goals were promulgated in 2000, when the completion rate was 80 percent. Sub-Saharan Africa and South Asia, which started out farthest behind, have made substantial progress but will still fall short of the goal. The Middle East and North Africa has stalled at completion rates of around 90 percent, while Europe and Central Asia and East Asia and Pacific are within striking distance but have made little progress in the last five years.

Many children enroll in primary school but attend intermittently or drop out entirely. This is particularly the case for girls whose work is needed at home. In rural areas the work of children of both sexes may be needed during planting and harvest. Other obstacles, including the lack of suitable facilities, absence of teachers, and school fees, discourage parents from sending their children to school. The problem is worst in South Asia and Sub-Saharan Africa, where more than 48 million children of primary school age are not in school.

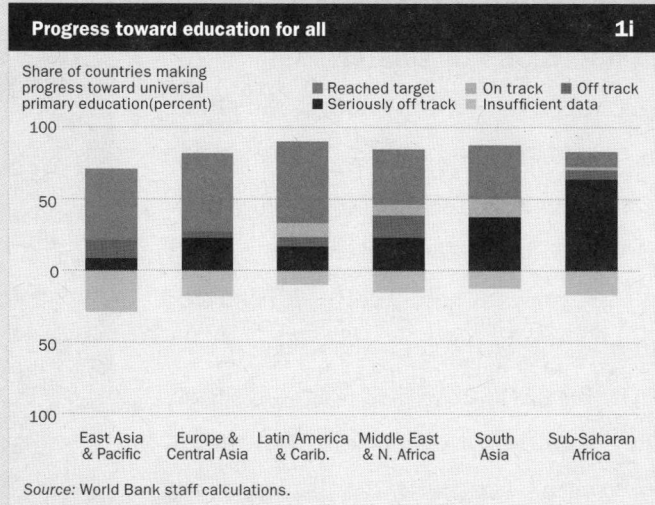

Progress toward education for all 1i

Share of countries making progress toward universal primary education(percent)

Legend: ■ Reached target ■ On track ■ Off track ■ Seriously off track ■ Insufficient data

Source: World Bank staff calculations.

Sixty developing countries, half the countries for which adequate data are available, have achieved or are on track to achieve the Millennium Development Goal target of a full course of primary schooling for all children. Twelve more will miss the 2015 deadline. At their current rate of progress they will achieve full enrollment sometime after 2015. That leaves at least 48 countries seriously off track, making little or no progress, 30 of them in Sub-Saharan Africa.

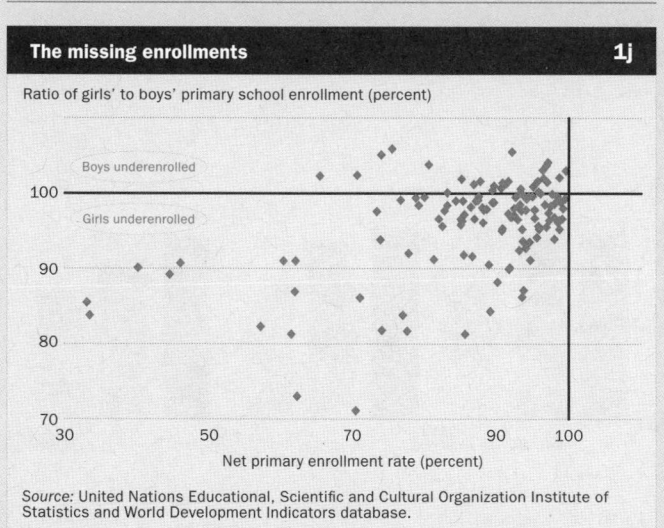

The missing enrollments 1j

Ratio of girls' to boys' primary school enrollment (percent)

Net primary enrollment rate (percent)

Source: United Nations Educational, Scientific and Cultural Organization Institute of Statistics and World Development Indicators database.

A major obstacle to achieving universal primary education is the shortfall in girls' enrollments. Almost all school systems with low enrollment rates show underenrollment of girls in primary school. In only a few places are boys' enrollment rates lower than girls'. Starting at such a disadvantage, most girls will never catch up. Achieving the Millennium Development Goal target to enroll and keep girls in school is essential.

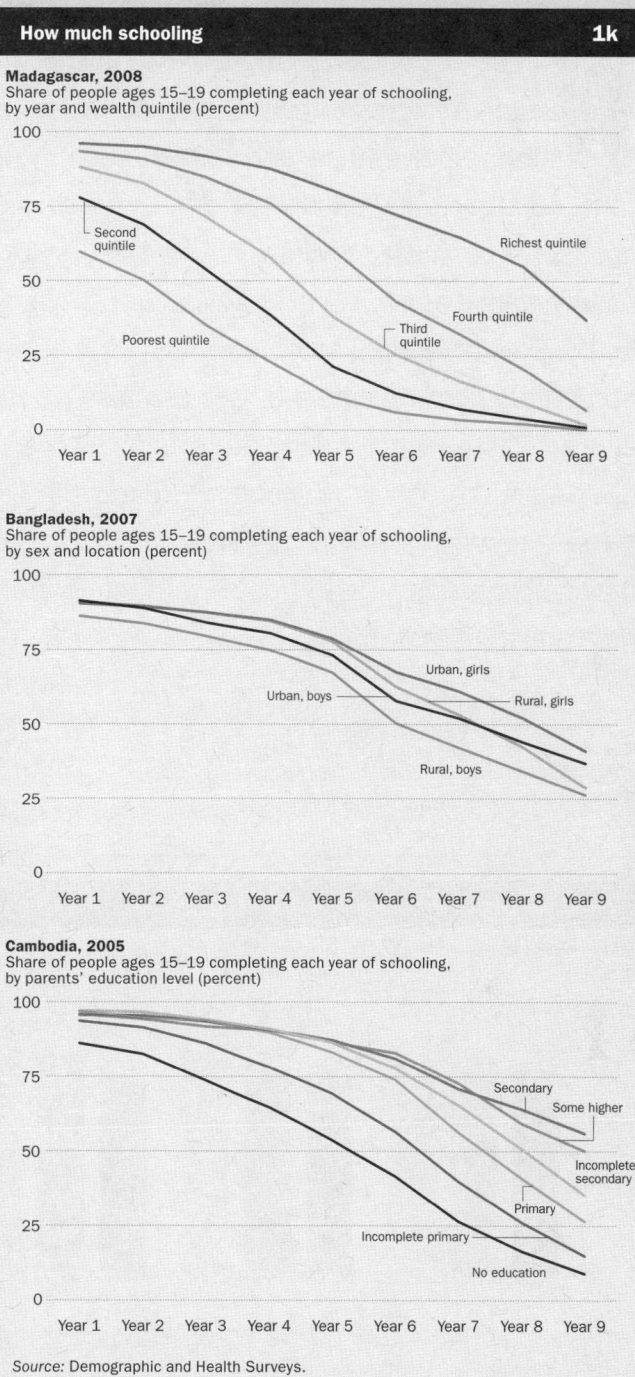

How much schooling 1k

Source: Demographic and Health Surveys.

Many factors affect how long students stay in school. Children from poor families are less likely to attend or stay in school. In most countries girls and children from rural areas are also less likely to attend, but Bangladesh has used targeted incentives to raise girls' attendance rates. In Cambodia and everywhere else parents with lower levels of education are less likely to keep their children in school. Achieving the Millennium Development Goal target will require breaking the cycle of lack of education–poverty–low enrollment.

Promote gender equity and empower women

Goal 3

Women are making progress along the three dimensions of gender equality and women's empowerment that the Millennium Development Goals monitor: education, employment, and participation in public decisionmaking. These are important, but there are others. Efforts are under way to improve monitoring of women's access to financial services, entrepreneurship, and migration and remittances as well as of violence against women. Time-use surveys, for example, can illuminate differences in the roles of women and men within the household and the workplace. Disaggregating other statistical indicators by sex can also reveal patterns of disadvantage or, occasionally, advantage for women. Whatever the case, women make important contributions to economic and social development. Expanding opportunities for them in the public and private sectors is a core development strategy. And good statistics are essential for developing policies that effectively promote gender equity and increase the welfare and productivity of women.

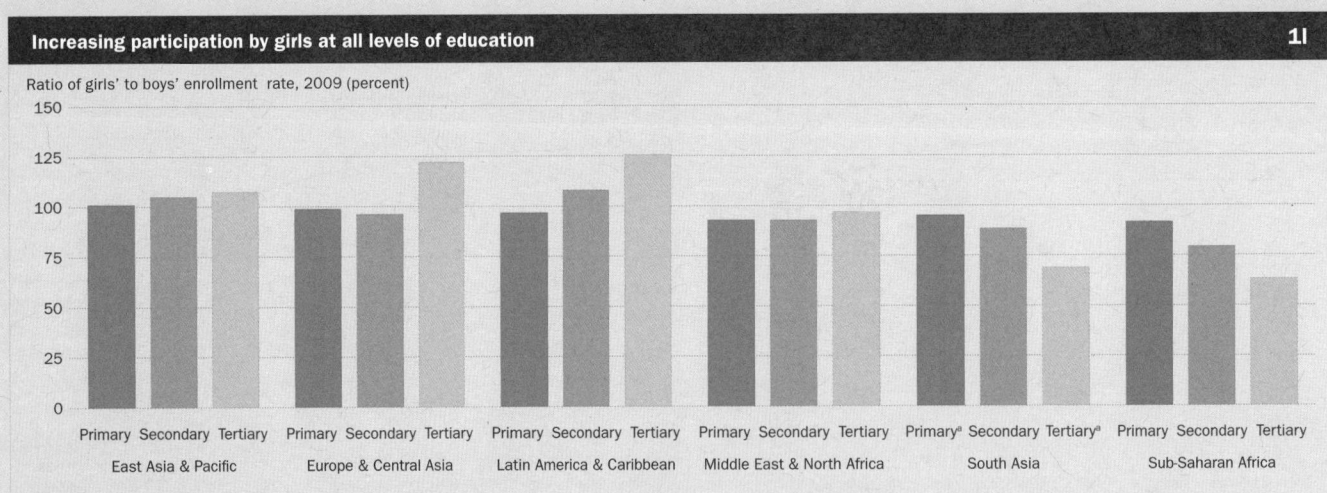

Increasing participation by girls at all levels of education 1l

Ratio of girls' to boys' enrollment rate, 2009 (percent)

a. Data are for 2008.
Source: United Nations Educational, Scientific and Cultural Organization Institute of Statistics and World Development Indicators database.

Girls have made substantial gains in primary and secondary school enrollment. In many countries girls' enrollment rates outnumber boys', particularly in secondary school. And more girls are staying in school. In 1991 only 73 percent of girls in developing countries finished primary school; by 2010 the completion rate stood at 86 percent. But this comparison obscures the underlying problem of underenrollment. Girls are still less likely to enroll in primary school or to stay through the end of primary school. In some countries the situation changes at the secondary level. Girls who complete primary school may be more likely to stay in school, while boys drop out. In Europe and Central Asia and Latin American and the Caribbean the differences in higher education enrollment are substantial. This is an unsatisfactory path to equity. Rapid growth and poverty reduction truly require education for all.

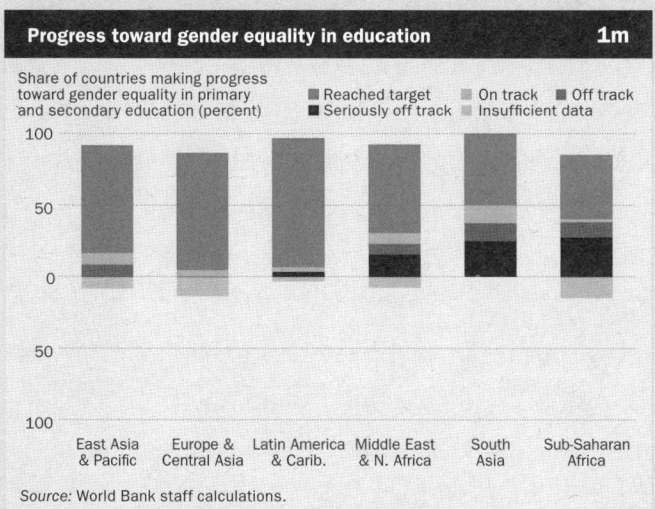

Progress toward gender equality in education | **1m**

Share of countries making progress toward gender equality in primary and secondary education (percent)

- ■ Reached target
- □ On track
- ■ Off track
- ■ Seriously off track
- □ Insufficient data

Source: World Bank staff calculations.

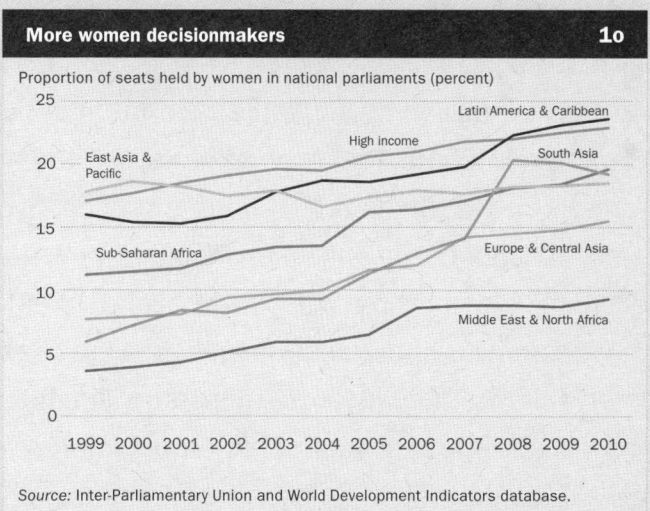

More women decisionmakers | **1o**

Proportion of seats held by women in national parliaments (percent)

Source: Inter-Parliamentary Union and World Development Indicators database.

Substantial progress has been made toward increasing the proportion of girls enrolled in primary and secondary education. By the end of the 2009/10 school year, 96 countries had achieved equality in enrollment rates and 7 more were on track to do so by 2015. That leaves only 27 countries off track or seriously off track, mostly low- and lower middle-income economies in the Middle East and North Africa, South Asia, and Sub-Saharan Africa. Fourteen countries lacked adequate data to assess progress.

The proportion of parliamentary seats held by women has increased everywhere. In Latin America and the Caribbean women now hold 24 percent of all parliamentary seats. The most impressive gains have been made in South Asia, where the number of seats held by women tripled between 1999 and 2000. In Sub-Saharan Africa Rwanda leads the way, making history in 2008 when it elected a parliament composed 56 percent of women. The Middle East and North Africa lags far behind.

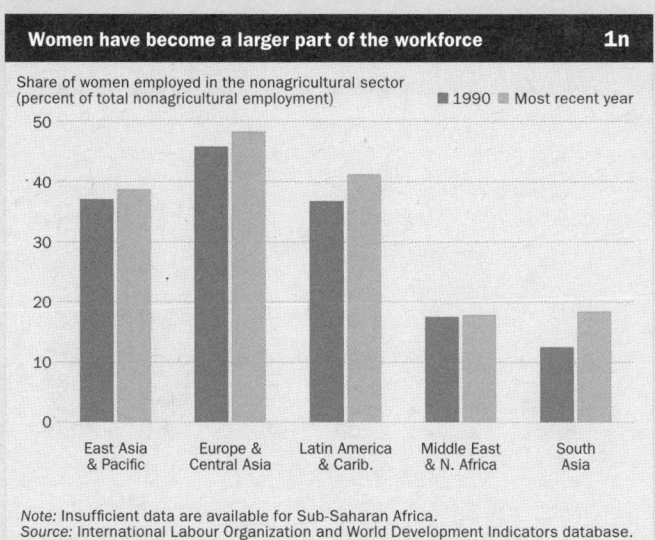

Women have become a larger part of the workforce | **1n**

Share of women employed in the nonagricultural sector (percent of total nonagricultural employment)

- ■ 1990
- □ Most recent year

Note: Insufficient data are available for Sub-Saharan Africa.
Source: International Labour Organization and World Development Indicators database.

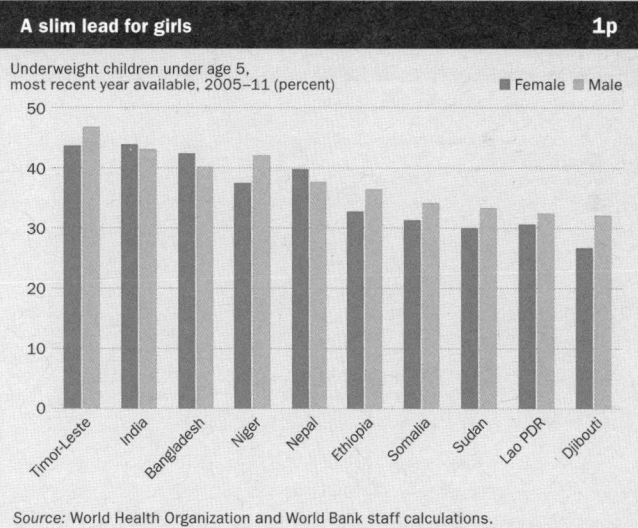

A slim lead for girls | **1p**

Underweight children under age 5, most recent year available, 2005–11 (percent)

- ■ Female
- □ Male

Source: World Health Organization and World Bank staff calculations.

Women's share in paid employment in the nonagricultural sector has risen marginally but remains less than 20 percent in the Middle East and North Africa and South Asia. In many countries the majority of women who work hold insecure jobs outside the formal sector. Overall labor force participation rates of women follow a similar pattern, but they are highest in Sub-Saharan Africa, where 60 percent of women ages 15 and older are in the labor force, although many are employed as unpaid family workers.

Girls are less likely to attend school, have secure jobs, or hold public office. But by most measures, they have an advantage in one area: malnutrition. Out of 99 countries with data for 2005–11, 19 had a larger proportion of underweight girls than of underweight boys; 74 had a larger proportion of underweight boys than of underweight girls, and 6 had no difference. The chart shows the 10 countries with the highest proportion of underweight children during the period.

Reduce child mortality

Goal 4

In 1990, 12 million children died before their fifth birthday. By 1999 there were fewer than 10 million child deaths, and the number has continued to fall to just over 7.5 million in 2010. That is good news, but the ambitious Millennium Development Goal target of a two-thirds reduction in the under-five mortality rate will be met by no more than 40 countries. Only Latin America and the Caribbean and upper middle-income economies as a whole will, on average, reach the target.

Most children die from causes that are readily preventable or curable with existing interventions, such as acute respiratory infections, diarrhea, measles, and malaria. And most die in the first year of life. Rapid improvements prior to 1990 in a few countries gave hope that mortality rates for infants and children could be cut further in the following 25 years, but progress slowed almost everywhere after 1990, leaving most countries far behind the target before the goals were announced. Was the target too challenging? Perhaps. But the more important question is whether it encouraged countries to use their resources wisely to achieve the fastest possible progress.

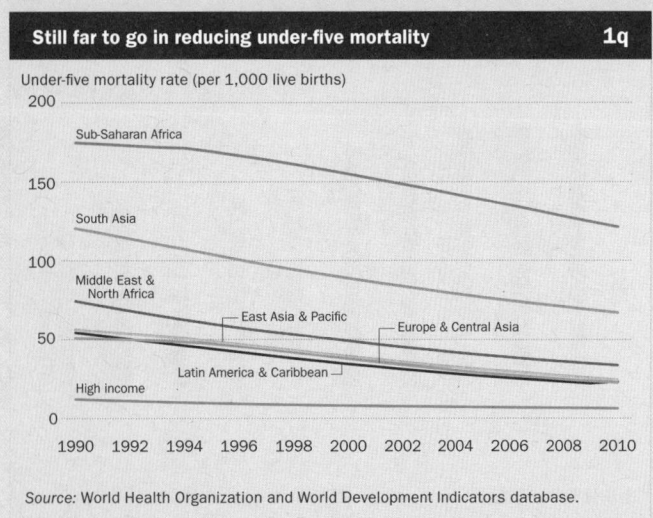

Still far to go in reducing under-five mortality   **1q**

Under-five mortality rate (per 1,000 live births)

Source: World Health Organization and World Development Indicators database.

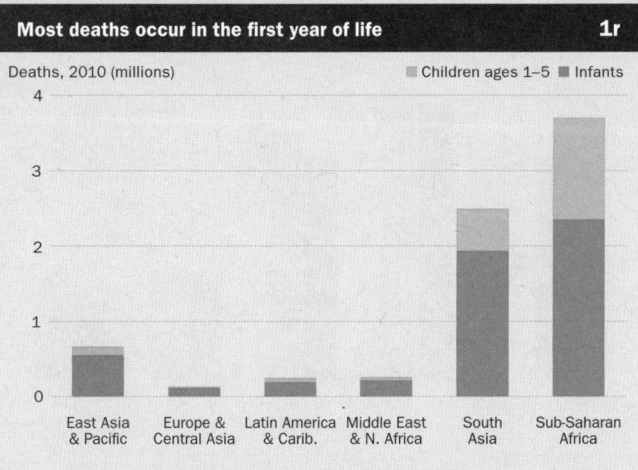

Most deaths occur in the first year of life   **1r**

Deaths, 2010 (millions)   ■ Children ages 1–5   ■ Infants

Source: World Health Organization and World Development Indicators database.

Mortality rates have been falling everywhere. In developing countries the mortality rate fell from an average of 98 per 1,000 live births in 1990 to 63 in 2010. But rates remain much higher in many countries, especially in Sub-Saharan Africa and parts of South Asia. In Sub-Saharan Africa one child in eight dies before his or her fifth birthday. The odds are somewhat better in South Asia, where 1 child in 15 dies. But even in these regions there are countries exhibiting rapid progress.

Almost 70 percent of deaths of children under age 5 occur in the first year of life, and half in the first month. Therefore, reducing child mortality requires addressing the causes of neonatal and infant deaths: inadequate care at birth and afterward, malnutrition, poor sanitation, and exposure to acute and chronic disease. Improvements in infant and child mortality are, in turn, the largest contributors to increased life expectancy in most countries.

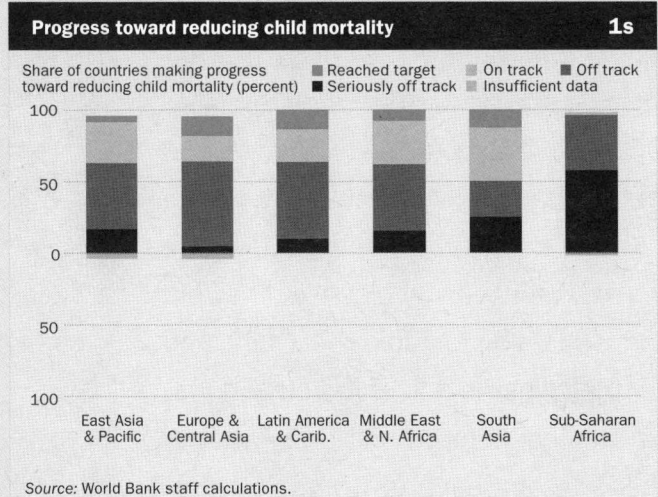

Progress toward reducing child mortality   **1s**

Share of countries making progress toward reducing child mortality (percent)

■ Reached target   ■ On track   ■ Off track
■ Seriously off track   ■ Insufficient data

Source: World Bank staff calculations.

A concerted effort by academic researchers and international statistical agencies has greatly improved measurement of infant and child mortality. Therefore, few countries lack estimates of child mortality rates, although many are derived from statistical models. Ten countries have already achieved a two-thirds reduction in under-five mortality rates since 1990, and 26 are on track to do so by 2015. But that leaves 105 countries, with half of developing countries' population, off track or seriously off track.

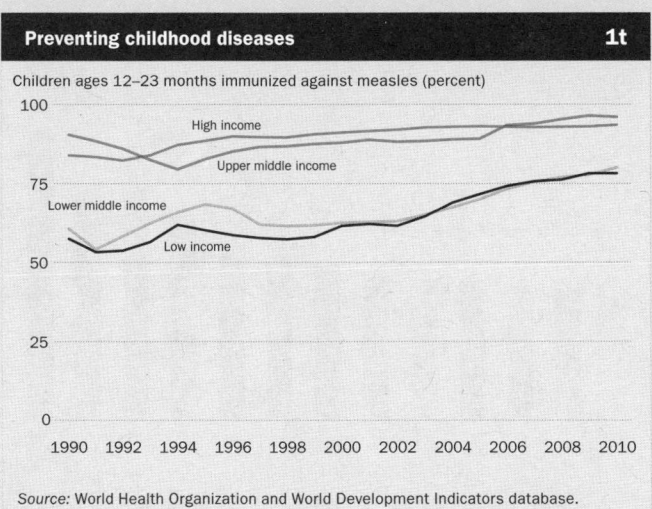

Preventing childhood diseases   **1t**

Children ages 12–23 months immunized against measles (percent)

Source: World Health Organization and World Development Indicators database.

Illnesses that could be prevented by early childhood vaccinations still account for many child deaths. Despite years of vaccination campaigns, many children in low- and lower middle-income economies remain unprotected. Measles is one example. Other recommended immunizations include diphtheria, pertussis, tetanus, and the BCG immunization for tuberculosis. To be successful, vaccination campaigns must reach all children and be sustained over time.

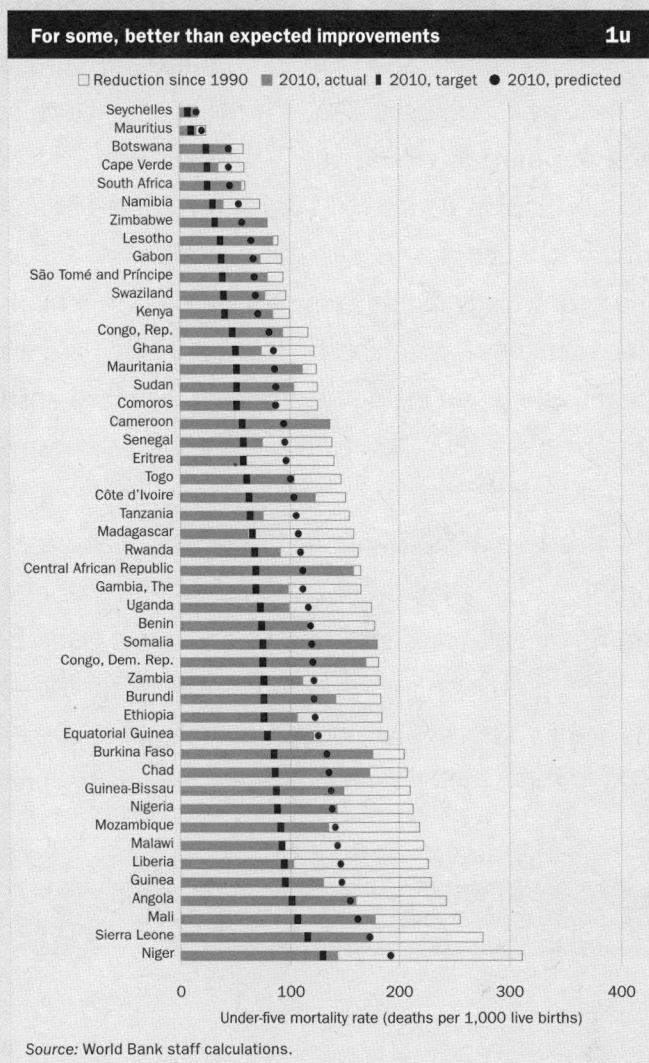

For some, better than expected improvements   **1u**

□ Reduction since 1990   ■ 2010, actual   ▌2010, target   ● 2010, predicted

Under-five mortality rate (deaths per 1,000 live births)

Source: World Bank staff calculations.

In 1990 the under-five mortality rate in Niger stood at 311 per 1,000 live births, the worst in the world. In the same year, Seychelles, with an under-five mortality rate of 16, was the best in Sub-Saharan Africa. How have they fared since? In the 20 years from the Millennium Development Goals baseline, Niger's mortality rate fell by 168, the greatest in the region, while Seychelles's fell by 3. In proportional terms Niger experienced a 54 percent reduction—second greatest in the region—and Seychelles a 16 percent reduction. Both are short of the Millennium Development Goal target, but Niger, having started in last place, has progressed faster. Has this been the general rule? On average, countries in Sub-Saharan Africa that started in worse positions have done better. But experience has been mixed: conflict-affected countries such as the Democratic Republic of the Congo and Somalia have made almost no progress, while similarly situated countries such as Uganda and Zambia have done much better. Two countries, Madagascar and Malawi, are on track to achieve the Millennium Development Goal target. Several others, including Eritrea, Niger, and Tanzania, are close. Only one country, Zimbabwe, moved backward from 1990 to 2010.

Reduce maternal mortality

Goal 5

An estimated 358,000 maternal deaths occurred worldwide in 2008, a 34 percent decrease since 1990. The Millennium Development Goals call for reducing the maternal mortality ratio by 75 percent between 1990 and 2015, but few countries and no developing country region on average will achieve this target. What makes maternal mortality such a compelling problem is that it strikes young women experiencing a natural life event. They die because they are poor. Malnourished. Weakened by disease. They die because they lack access to trained health care workers and modern medical facilities. And because women in poor countries have more children, their lifetime risk of maternal death may be more than 200 times greater than for women in Western Europe and North America.

Reducing maternal mortality requires a comprehensive approach to women's reproductive health, starting with family planning and access to contraception. Many health problems among pregnant women are preventable or treatable through visits with trained health workers before childbirth. Good nutrition, vaccinations, and treatment of infections can improve outcomes for mother and child. Skilled attendants at time of delivery and access to hospital treatments are essential for dealing with life-threatening emergencies such as severe bleeding and hypertensive disorders.

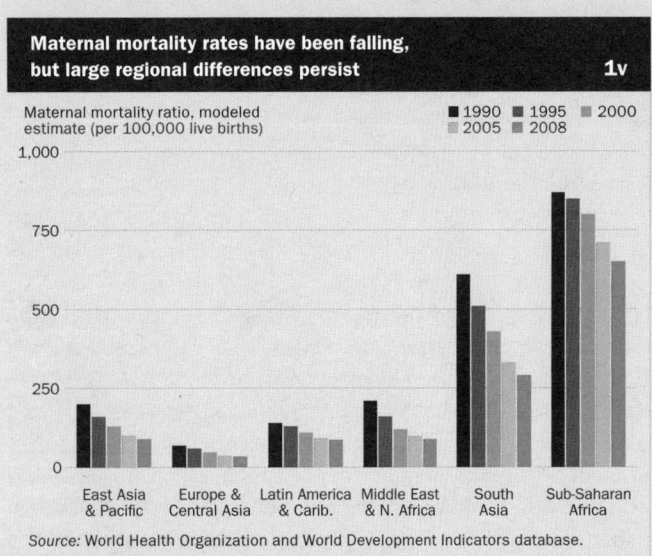
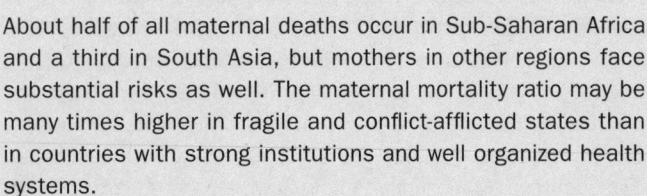

Maternal mortality rates have been falling, but large regional differences persist 1v

Maternal mortality ratio, modeled estimate (per 100,000 live births)

■ 1990 ■ 1995 ■ 2000 ■ 2005 ■ 2008

Source: World Health Organization and World Development Indicators database.

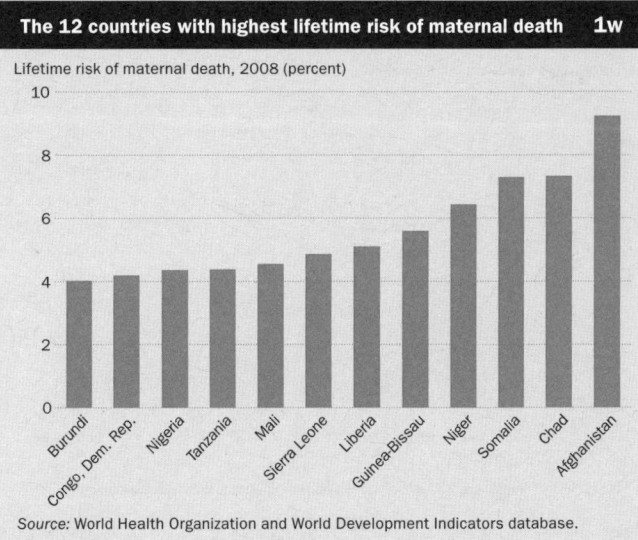

The 12 countries with highest lifetime risk of maternal death 1w

Lifetime risk of maternal death, 2008 (percent)

Burundi, Congo, Dem. Rep., Nigeria, Tanzania, Mali, Sierra Leone, Liberia, Guinea-Bissau, Niger, Somalia, Chad, Afghanistan

Source: World Health Organization and World Development Indicators database.

About half of all maternal deaths occur in Sub-Saharan Africa and a third in South Asia, but mothers in other regions face substantial risks as well. The maternal mortality ratio may be many times higher in fragile and conflict-afflicted states than in countries with strong institutions and well organized health systems.

In high-fertility countries women are repeatedly exposed to the risk of maternal mortality. In Afghanistan in 2008, where the lifetime risk of maternal death was over 9 percent, one woman in 11 is expected to die in childbirth; in Burundi one woman in 25 is at risk. In high-income economies the lifetime risk is less than 0.03 percent, or less than 1 woman in 3,500.

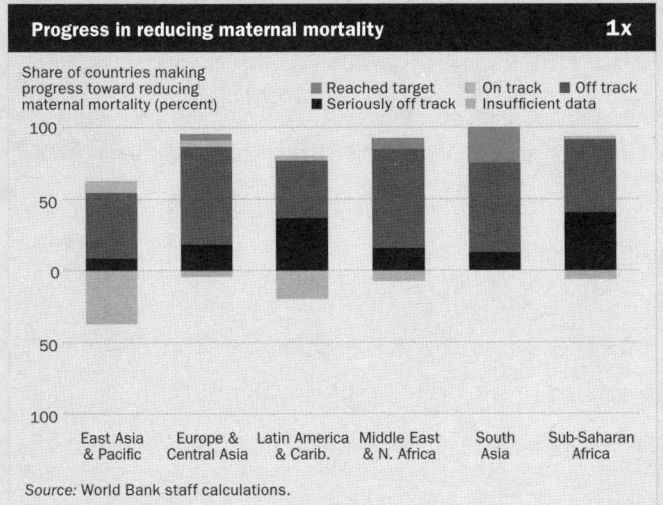

Progress in reducing maternal mortality 1x

Share of countries making progress toward reducing maternal mortality (percent)

- Reached target
- Seriously off track
- On track
- Off track
- Insufficient data

Source: World Bank staff calculations.

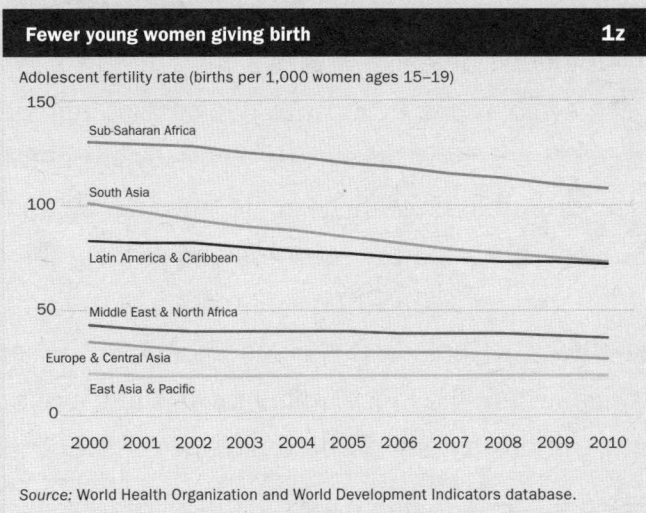

Fewer young women giving birth 1z

Adolescent fertility rate (births per 1,000 women ages 15–19)

Sub-Saharan Africa
South Asia
Latin America & Caribbean
Middle East & North Africa
Europe & Central Asia
East Asia & Pacific

Source: World Health Organization and World Development Indicators database.

Progress in reducing maternal mortality ratios has been slow, far slower than imagined by the Millennium Development Goal target of a 75 percent reduction from 1990 levels. Only four countries have achieved this target, and five more are on track. Accurately measuring maternal mortality is difficult and requires specialized surveys and good reporting of vital events. Recent efforts by statisticians have improved estimates, but for many countries the need for improved monitoring of maternal health will continue long past 2015.

The adolescent fertility rate is highest in Sub-Saharan Africa and is declining slowly. Women who give birth at an early age are likely to bear more children and are at greater risk of death or serious complications from pregnancy. In many developing countries the number of women ages 15–19 is still increasing. Preventing unintended pregnancies and delaying childbirth among young women increase the chances of their attending school and eventually obtaining paid employment.

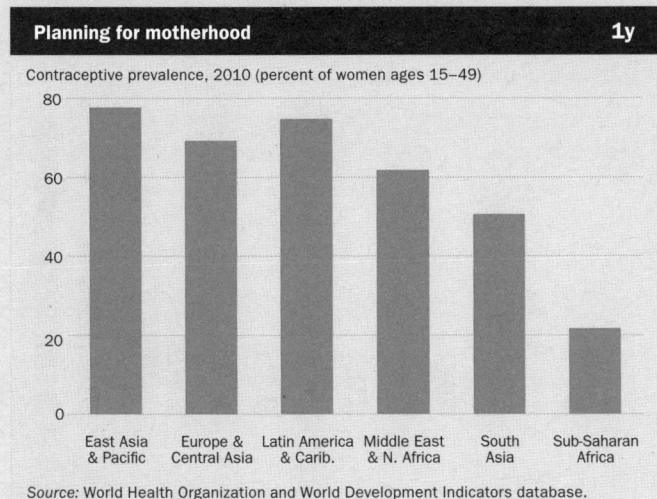

Planning for motherhood 1y

Contraceptive prevalence, 2010 (percent of women ages 15–49)

Source: World Health Organization and World Development Indicators database.

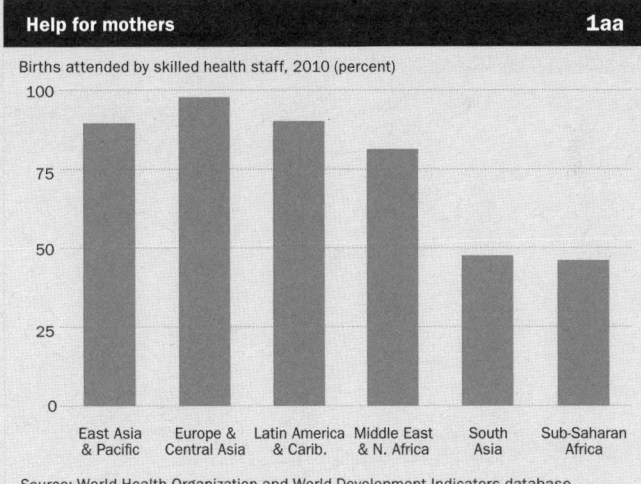

Help for mothers 1aa

Births attended by skilled health staff, 2010 (percent)

Source: World Health Organization and World Development Indicators database.

Contraceptive use has increased in most developing countries for which data are available. In almost all regions more than half of women who are married or in union use some method of birth control. More than 200 million women want to delay or cease childbearing, and a substantial proportion say that their last birth was unwanted or mistimed. Worldwide an estimated 120 million women have an unmet need for family planning.

In South Asia and Sub-Saharan Africa less than half of all births are attended by doctors, nurses, or trained midwives. Having skilled health workers present for deliveries is key to reducing maternal mortality. In many places women have only untrained caregivers or family members to attend them during childbirth. Skilled health workers are trained to give necessary care before, during, and after delivery; they can conduct deliveries on their own, summon additional help in emergencies, and provide care for newborns.

Combat HIV/AIDS, malaria, and other diseases

Goal 6

Epidemic diseases exact a huge toll in human suffering and lost opportunities for development. Poverty, armed conflict, and natural disasters contribute to the spread of disease and are made worse by it. In Africa the spread of HIV/AIDS has reversed decades of improvement in life expectancy and left millions of children orphaned. It is draining the supply of teachers and eroding the quality of education.

There are 300–500 million cases of malaria each year, leading to more than 1 million deaths. Malaria is a disease of poverty. Nearly all the cases occur in Sub-Saharan Africa, where the most lethal form of the malaria parasite is abundant. Most deaths from malaria are among children under age 5, but the disease can be debilitating in adults as well.

Tuberculosis kills some 2 million people a year, most of them ages 15–45. The disease, once controlled by antibiotics, is spreading again because of the emergence of drug-resistant strains. People living with HIV/AIDS, which reduces resistance to tuberculosis, are particularly vulnerable, as are refugees, displaced persons, and prisoners living in close quarters and unsanitary conditions. Well managed medical intervention using appropriate drug therapy is the key to stopping the spread of tuberculosis.

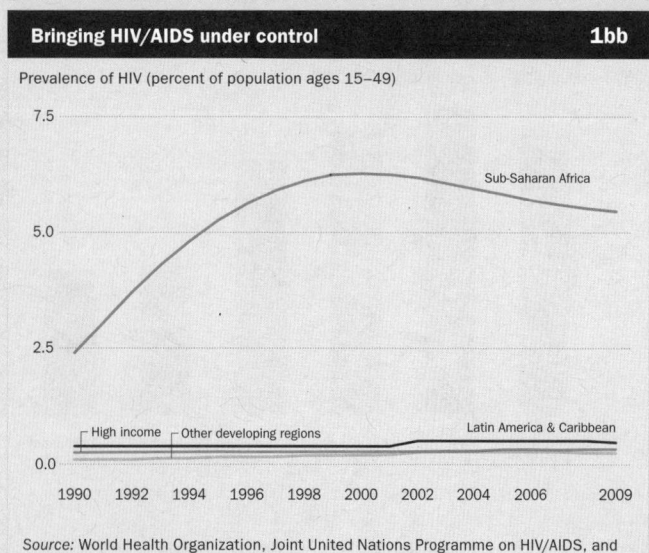

Bringing HIV/AIDS under control   **1bb**

Prevalence of HIV (percent of population ages 15–49)

Source: World Health Organization, Joint United Nations Programme on HIV/AIDS, and World Development Indicators database.

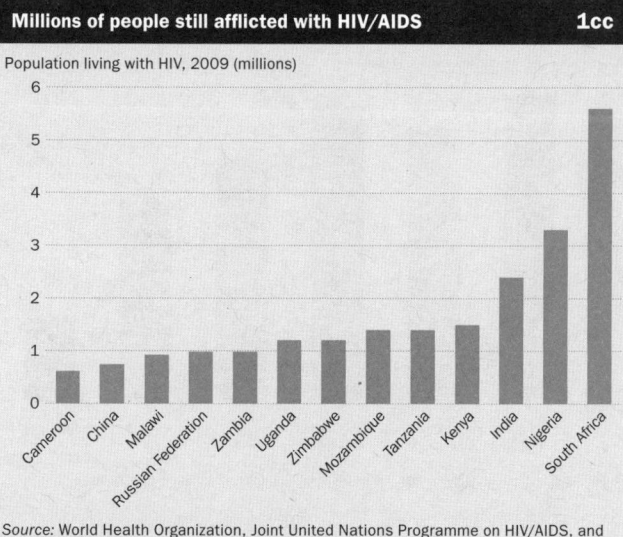

Millions of people still afflicted with HIV/AIDS   **1cc**

Population living with HIV, 2009 (millions)

Source: World Health Organization, Joint United Nations Programme on HIV/AIDS, and World Development Indicators database.

Sub-Saharan Africa remains the center of the HIV/AIDS epidemic, but the proportion of adults living with AIDS has begun to fall even as the survival rate of those with access to antiretroviral drugs has increased. In Africa 58 percent of adults with HIV/AIDS are women. Among young people ages 15–24, the prevalence rate among women is more than twice that among men. Latin America and the Caribbean, where 0.5 percent of adults are infected, has the next highest prevalence rate.

In 2009, 31–33 million people were living with HIV/AIDS, and approximately 1.5 million of them were under age 15. Another 16.9 million children, 14.8 million of them in Sub-Saharan Africa, have lost one or both parents to AIDS. By the end of 2009, 5.25 million people were receiving antiretroviral drugs, or 36 percent of the population for which the World Health Organization recommends treatment.

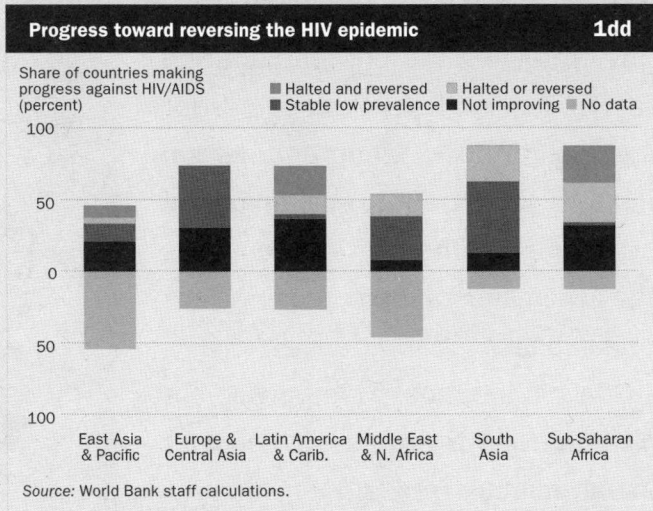

Progress toward reversing the HIV epidemic `1dd`

Share of countries making progress against HIV/AIDS (percent)

Legend: Halted and reversed | Halted or reversed | Stable low prevalence | Not improving | No data

Source: World Bank staff calculations.

The Millennium Development Goals call for halting and then reversing the spread of HIV/AIDS by 2015. The progress assessment shown here is based on prevalence rates for adults ages 15–49. Countries that have a declining prevalence rate since 2005 are assessed to have halted the epidemic; those that have a prevalence rate less than their earliest measured rate have reversed the epidemic. Countries that have a prevalence rate of less than 0.2 percent are considered stable. Countries that have a prevalence rate greater than 0.2 percent and that have neither halted nor reversed the epidemic are shown as not improving.

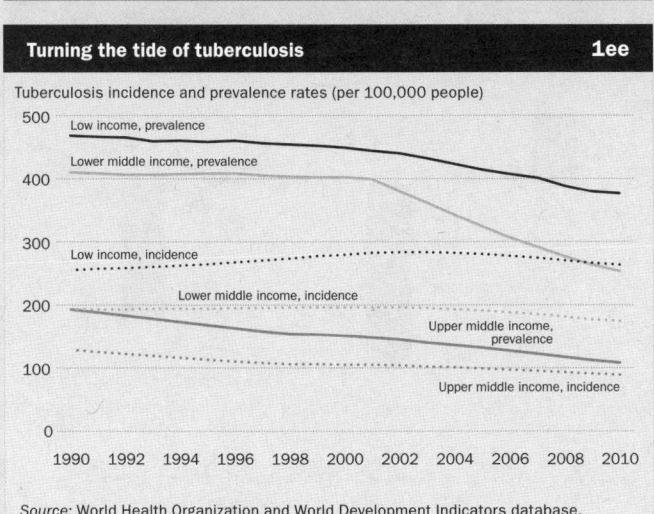

Turning the tide of tuberculosis `1ee`

Tuberculosis incidence and prevalence rates (per 100,000 people)

Source: World Health Organization and World Development Indicators database.

Tuberculosis is one of the main causes of adult deaths from a single infectious agent in developing countries. The data shown here illustrate the association of tuberculosis with poverty. The incidence rate is three times higher in low-income economies than in upper middle-income economies. The number of new tuberculosis cases peaked in 2004, and prevalence rates are also declining, but the targets of halving the 1990 prevalence and death rates by 2015 are unlikely to be met.

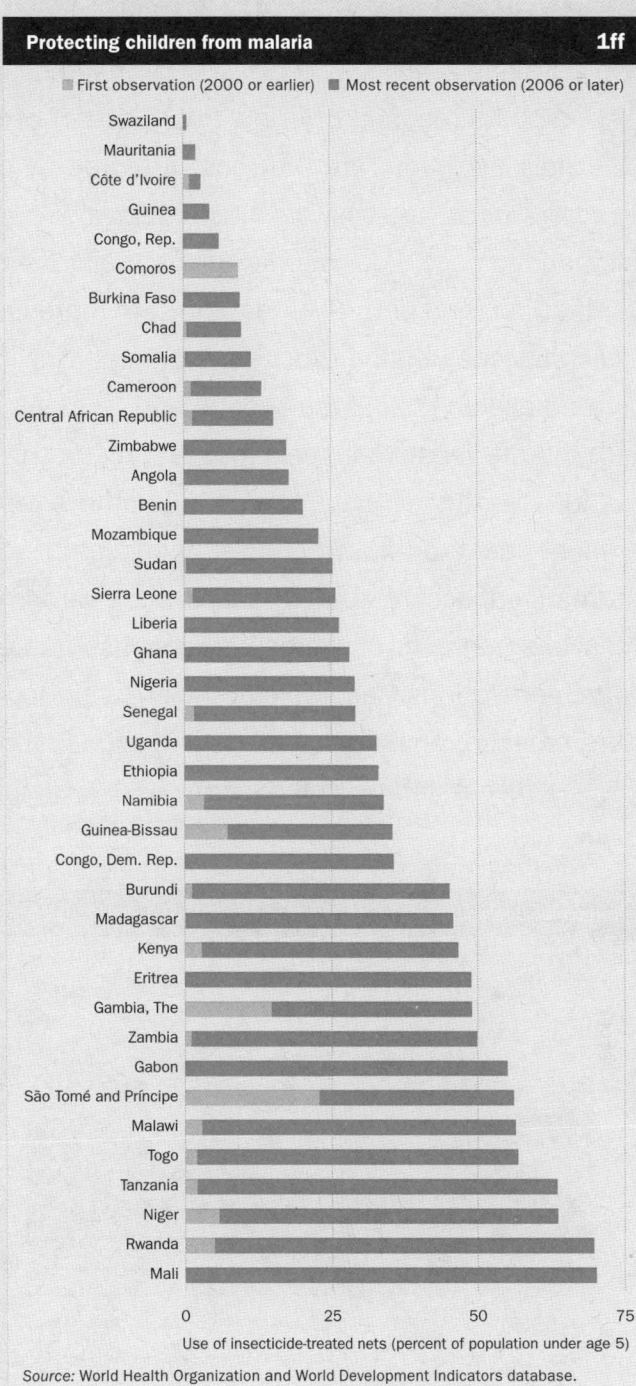

Protecting children from malaria `1ff`

First observation (2000 or earlier) | Most recent observation (2006 or later)

Use of insecticide-treated nets (percent of population under age 5)

Source: World Health Organization and World Development Indicators database.

Malaria is endemic in most tropical and subtropical regions, but 90 percent of malaria deaths occur in Sub-Saharan Africa. Those most severely affected are children under age 5. Even those who survive malaria do not escape unharmed. Repeated episodes of fever and anemia take a toll on mental and physical development. Insecticide-treated nets have proved to be an effective preventative, and their use has grown rapidly. Between 2008 and 2010, 290 million nets were distributed in Sub-Saharan Africa. But coverage remains uneven. In some countries with large numbers of reported cases, use of nets for children remains at less than 20 percent.

Ensure environmental sustainability

Goal 7

S ustainable development can be ensured only by protecting the environment and using its resources wisely. Poor people, often dependent on natural resources for their livelihood, are the most affected by environmental degradation and natural disasters (fires, storms, earthquakes), whose effects are worsened by environmental mismanagement. Poor people also suffer from shortcomings in the built environment: whether in urban or rural areas, they are more likely to live in substandard housing, lack basic services, and be exposed to unhealthy living conditions.

The seventh goal of the Millennium Development Goals is the most wide ranging but perhaps the least well specified. Among its 10 indicators, only 3 are associated with quantified and timebound targets. For others we can only monitor trends.

Most countries have adopted principles of sustainable development and agreed to international accords on protecting the environment. But the failure to reach a comprehensive agreement on limiting greenhouse gas emissions leaves billions of people and future generations vulnerable to the impacts of climate change. Growing populations put more pressure on marginal lands and expose more people to hazardous conditions that will be exacerbated by global warming.

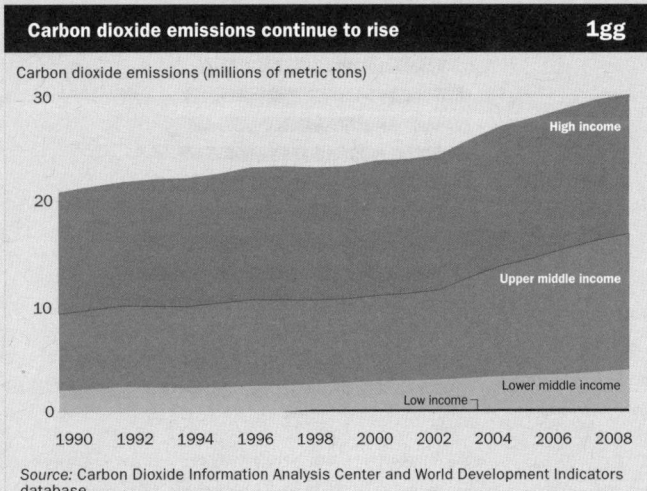

Carbon dioxide emissions continue to rise   **1gg**

Carbon dioxide emissions (millions of metric tons)

Source: Carbon Dioxide Information Analysis Center and World Development Indicators database.

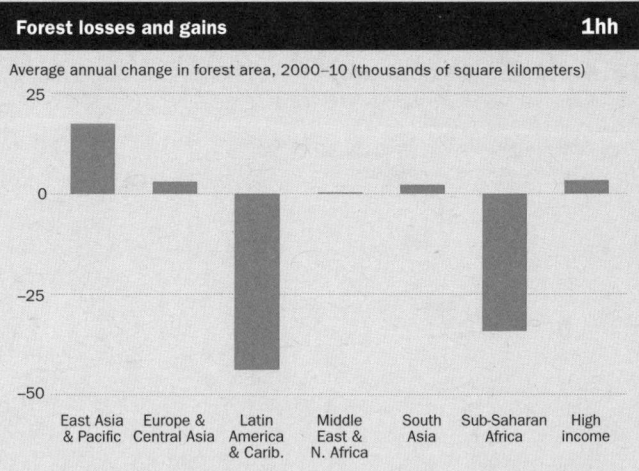

Forest losses and gains   **1hh**

Average annual change in forest area, 2000–10 (thousands of square kilometers)

Source: Food and Agriculture Organization and World Development Indicators database.

Annual emissions of carbon dioxide reached 32 million metric tons in 2008 and are still rising. High-income economies remain the largest emitters, but the rapidly growing upper middle-income economies are not far behind. Measured by emissions per capita, however, emissions by high-income economies are more than three times higher than average emissions by low- and middle-income economies.

Loss of forests threatens the livelihood of poor people, destroys habitat that harbors biodiversity, and eliminates an important carbon sink that helps moderate climate change. Net losses since 1990 have been substantial, especially in Latin American and the Caribbean and Sub-Saharan Africa, and only partially compensated for by net gains in Asia and high-income economies.

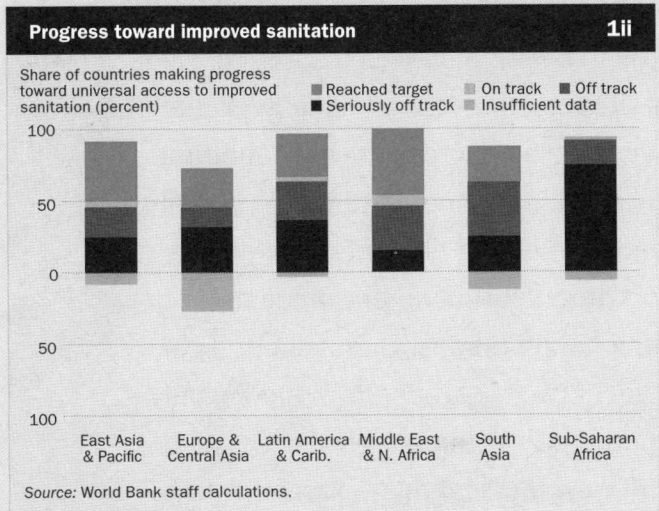

Progress toward improved sanitation **1ii**

Share of countries making progress toward universal access to improved sanitation (percent)

■ Reached target   ■ On track   ■ Off track
■ Seriously off track   ■ Insufficient data

East Asia & Pacific | Europe & Central Asia | Latin America & Carib. | Middle East & N. Africa | South Asia | Sub-Saharan Africa

Source: World Bank staff calculations.

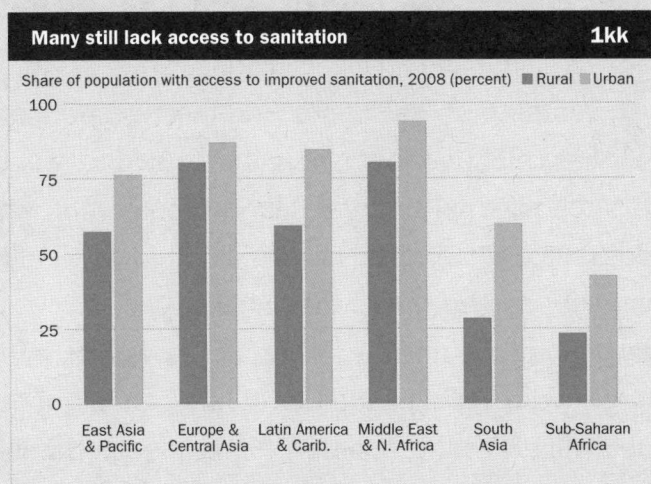

Many still lack access to sanitation **1kk**

Share of population with access to improved sanitation, 2008 (percent) ■ Rural ■ Urban

East Asia & Pacific | Europe & Central Asia | Latin America & Carib. | Middle East & N. Africa | South Asia | Sub-Saharan Africa

Source: World Health Organization and World Development Indicators database.

The Millennium Development Goals call for cutting the proportion of the population without access to improved sanitation and water sources in half by 2015. By 2010, 2.7 billion people still lacked access to improved sanitation, and more than 1 billion people practiced open defecation, posing enormous health risks. At the present pace only 37 countries are likely to reach the target—an increase of two since 2008. East Asia and Pacific and Middle East and North Africa are the only developing regions on track to reach the target by 2015.

In 1990, 63 percent of the people living in low- and middle-income economies lacked access to a flush toilet or other form of improved sanitation. By 2010 the access rate had improved 19 percentage points to 44 percent. The situation is worse in rural areas, where 57 percent of the population lack access to improved sanitation. The large urban–rural disparity, especially in Sub-Saharan Africa and South Asia, is the principal reason the sanitation target of the Millennium Development Goals will not be reached.

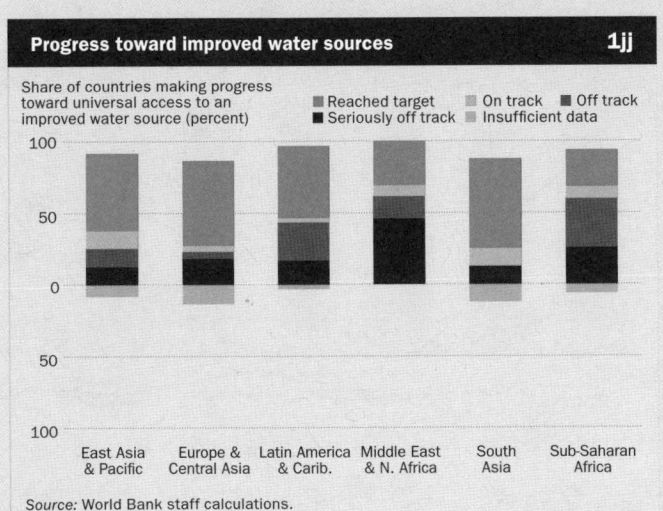

Progress toward improved water sources **1jj**

Share of countries making progress toward universal access to an improved water source (percent)

■ Reached target   ■ On track   ■ Off track
■ Seriously off track   ■ Insufficient data

East Asia & Pacific | Europe & Central Asia | Latin America & Carib. | Middle East & N. Africa | South Asia | Sub-Saharan Africa

Source: World Bank staff calculations.

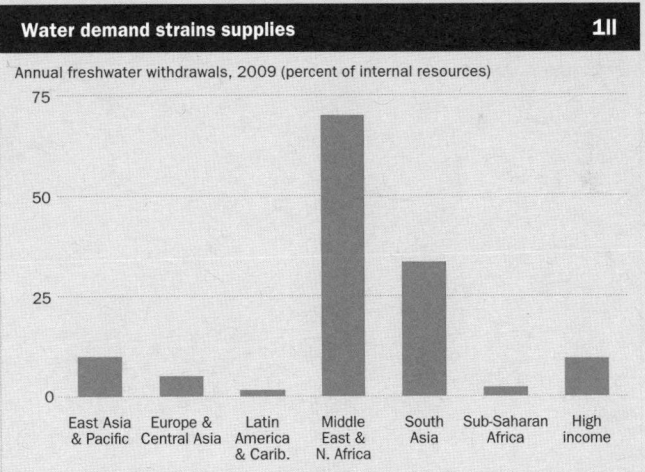

Water demand strains supplies **1ll**

Annual freshwater withdrawals, 2009 (percent of internal resources)

East Asia & Pacific | Europe & Central Asia | Latin America & Carib. | Middle East & N. Africa | South Asia | Sub-Saharan Africa | High income

Source: Food and Agriculture Organization and World Development Indicators database.

In 1990 more than 1 billion people lacked access to drinking water from a convenient, protected source, but the situation is improving. The proportion of people in developing countries with access to an improved water source increased from 71 percent in 1990 to 86 percent in 2008, reaching the Millennium Development Goal target of halving the proportion of people without access to an improved water source. Seventy-three countries have reached or are on track to reach the target. At this rate, only Middle East and North Africa and Sub-Saharan Africa will fall short.

Worldwide more than 70 percent of freshwater withdrawals go to agricultural and 20 percent to industrial uses. Only 10 percent go to households, many of which are underserved. The potential impacts of global warming and increased demand for water will require more efficient use of available resources. As pressure grows on internal water resources, conflicts over shared, external resources may also increase.

Develop a global partnership for development

Goal 8

The eighth and final goal distinguishes the Millennium Development Goals from previous sets of resolutions and targeted programs. It recognizes the multidimensional nature of development and the need for wealthy countries and developing countries to work together to create an environment in which rapid, sustainable development is possible. Following the Millennium Summit, world leaders meeting at Monterrey, Mexico, in 2002 agreed to provide financing for development through a coherent process that recognized the need for domestic as well as international resources. Subsequent high-level meetings expanded on these commitments. Along with increased aid flows and debt relief for the poorest, highly indebted countries, goal 8 recognizes the need to reduce barriers to trade and to share the benefits of new medical and communication technologies. Goal 8 also reminds us that development challenges differ for large and small countries and for those that are landlocked or isolated by large expanses of ocean. Building and sustaining a partnership is an ongoing process that does not stop at a specific date or when a target is reached. However it is measured, a strong commitment to partnership should be the continuing legacy of the Millennium Development Goals.

Most donors have maintained their aid levels	1mm

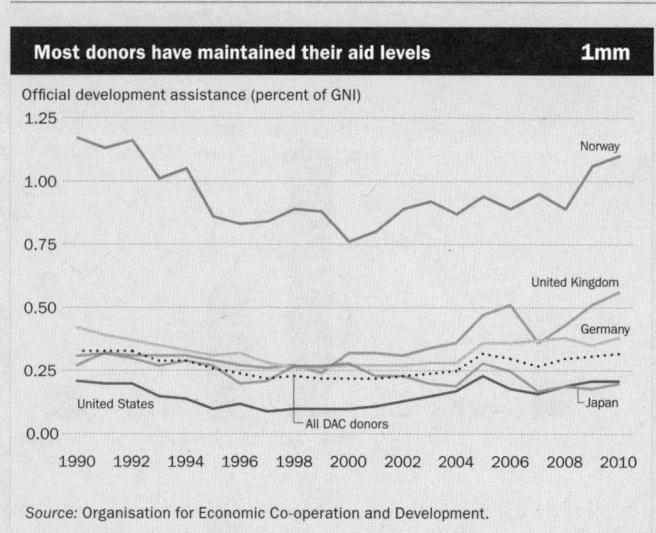

Source: Organisation for Economic Co-operation and Development.

But their domestic subsidies to agricultural are greater	1nn

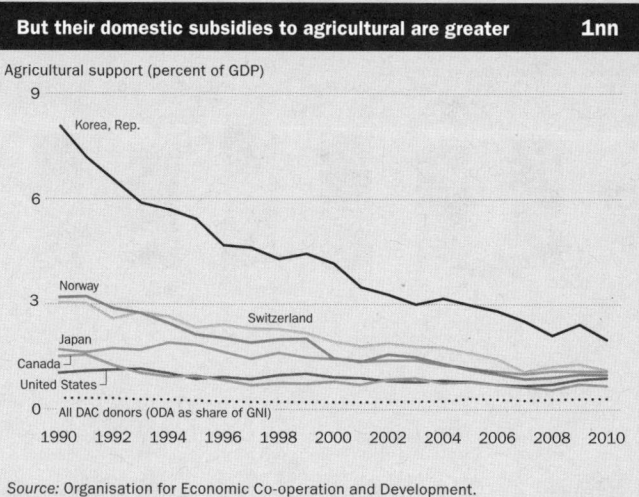

Source: Organisation for Economic Co-operation and Development.

The financial crisis that began in 2008 and fiscal austerity in many high-income economies have threatened to undermine commitments to increase official development assistance. So far leading donors have maintained their level of support. Total disbursements by members of the Organisation for Economic Co-operation and Development's Development Assistance Committee reached $130 billion in 2010, a real increase of 4.3 percent over 2008.

Organisation for Economic Co-operation and Development (OECD) members (which include some upper middle-income economies such as Chile and Mexico) spend more on support to domestic agricultural producers than on official development assistance. In 2010 the OECD producer support estimate was $227 billion, down about 10 percent from the previous three years.

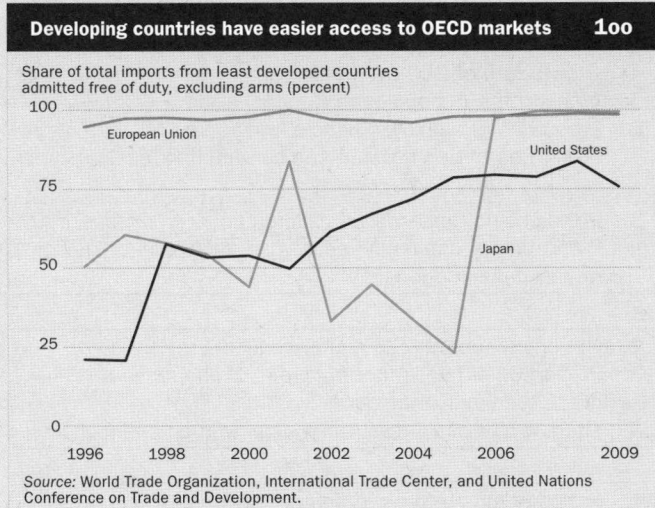

Developing countries have easier access to OECD markets   **1oo**

Share of total imports from least developed countries
admitted free of duty, excluding arms (percent)

Source: World Trade Organization, International Trade Center, and United Nations Conference on Trade and Development.

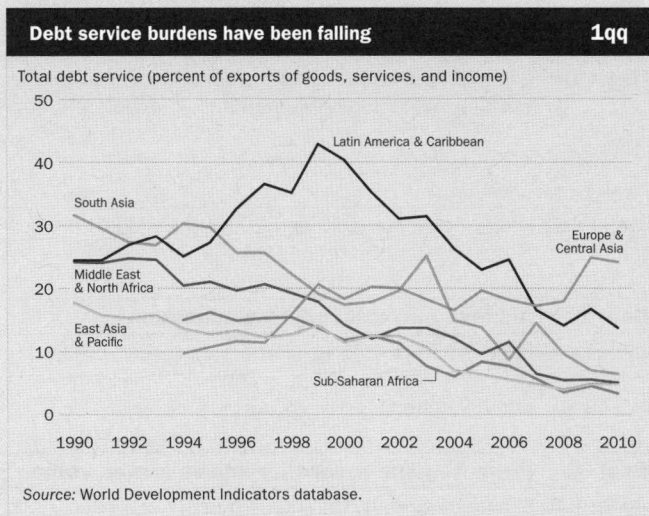

Debt service burdens have been falling   **1qq**

Total debt service (percent of exports of goods, services, and income)

Source: World Development Indicators database.

Many rich countries have pledged to admit the exports of the least developed countries duty free. However, arcane rules of origin and phytosanitary standards keep many countries from qualifying for duty-free access. And uncertainty over market access may inhibit development of export industries. Compared with the European Union, the large U.S. market retains many barriers to the exports of the poorest countries.

Growing economies, better debt management, and debt relief for the poorest countries have allowed developing countries to substantially reduce their debt burdens. Despite the financial crisis and a 2.3 percent contraction in the global economy in 2009, debt service ratios continued to fall in most developing country regions. Only in Europe and Central Asia has the ratio of debt service to exports risen since 2008, although rising export earnings have helped moderate the trend.

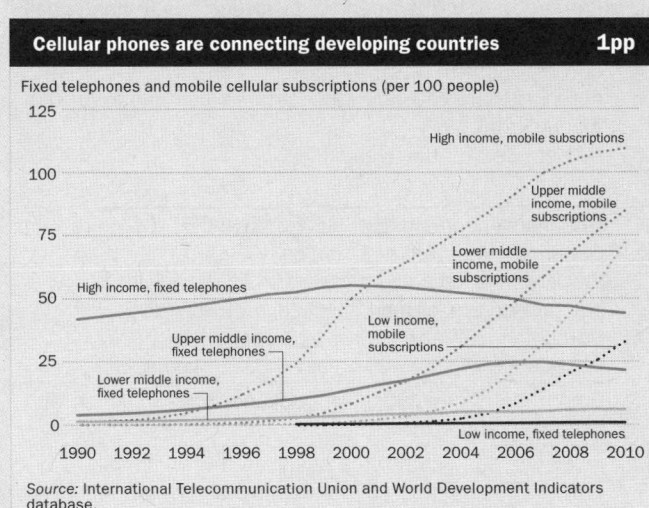

Cellular phones are connecting developing countries   **1pp**

Fixed telephones and mobile cellular subscriptions (per 100 people)

Source: International Telecommunication Union and World Development Indicators database.

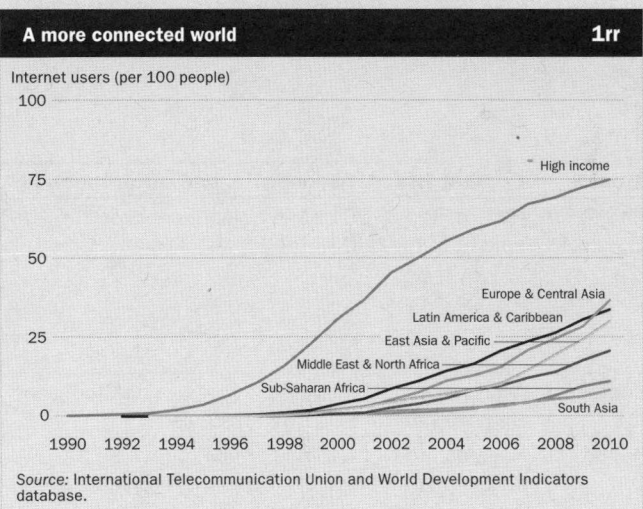

A more connected world   **1rr**

Internet users (per 100 people)

Source: International Telecommunication Union and World Development Indicators database.

Telecommunications is an essential tool for development, and new technologies are creating new opportunities everywhere. The growth of fixed-telephone systems has peaked in high-income economies and will never reach the same level of use in developing countries, where mobile cellular subscriptions continue to grow rapidly. In high-income economies, with more than one subscription per person, the pace of growth appears to be slowing. Gradually the world is becoming more connected.

In 2000 Internet use was spreading rapidly in high-income economies but was barely under way in developing country regions. Now developing countries are beginning to catch up. By 2010 there were an average of 34 internet users per 100 people in upper middle-income economies. Like telephones, Internet use is strongly correlated with income. In low-income economies there were only 5.4 users per 100 people in 2010. But growth is picking up.

Millennium Development Goals

Goals and targets from the Millennium Declaration   Indicators for monitoring progress

Goal 1	Eradicate extreme poverty and hunger		
Target 1.A	Halve, between 1990 and 2015, the proportion of people whose income is less than $1 a day	1.1	Proportion of population below $1 purchasing power parity (PPP) a day[a]
		1.2	Poverty gap ratio [incidence × depth of poverty]
		1.3	Share of poorest quintile in national consumption
Target 1.B	Achieve full and productive employment and decent work for all, including women and young people	1.4	Growth rate of GDP per person employed
		1.5	Employment to population ratio
		1.6	Proportion of employed people living below $1 (PPP) a day
		1.7	Proportion of own-account and contributing family workers in total employment
Target 1.C	Halve, between 1990 and 2015, the proportion of people who suffer from hunger	1.8	Prevalence of underweight children under five years of age
		1.9	Proportion of population below minimum level of dietary energy consumption

Goal 2	Achieve universal primary education		
Target 2.A	Ensure that by 2015 children everywhere, boys and girls alike, will be able to complete a full course of primary schooling	2.1	Net enrollment ratio in primary education
		2.2	Proportion of pupils starting grade 1 who reach last grade of primary education
		2.3	Literacy rate of 15- to 24-year-olds, women and men

Goal 3	Promote gender equality and empower women		
Target 3.A	Eliminate gender disparity in primary and secondary education, preferably by 2005, and in all levels of education no later than 2015	3.1	Ratios of girls to boys in primary, secondary, and tertiary education
		3.2	Share of women in wage employment in the nonagricultural sector
		3.3	Proportion of seats held by women in national parliament

Goal 4	Reduce child mortality		
Target 4.A	Reduce by two-thirds, between 1990 and 2015, the under-five mortality rate	4.1	Under-five mortality rate
		4.2	Infant mortality rate
		4.3	Proportion of one-year-old children immunized against measles

Goal 5	Improve maternal health		
Target 5.A	Reduce by three-quarters, between 1990 and 2015, the maternal mortality ratio	5.1	Maternal mortality ratio
		5.2	Proportion of births attended by skilled health personnel
Target 5.B	Achieve by 2015 universal access to reproductive health	5.3	Contraceptive prevalence rate
		5.4	Adolescent birth rate
		5.5	Antenatal care coverage (at least one visit and at least four visits)
		5.6	Unmet need for family planning

Goal 6	Combat HIV/AIDS, malaria, and other diseases		
Target 6.A	Have halted by 2015 and begun to reverse the spread of HIV/AIDS	6.1	HIV prevalence among population ages 15–24 years
		6.2	Condom use at last high-risk sex
		6.3	Proportion of population ages 15–24 years with comprehensive, correct knowledge of HIV/AIDS
		6.4	Ratio of school attendance of orphans to school attendance of nonorphans ages 10–14 years
Target 6.B	Achieve by 2010 universal access to treatment for HIV/AIDS for all those who need it	6.5	Proportion of population with advanced HIV infection with access to antiretroviral drugs
Target 6.C	Have halted by 2015 and begun to reverse the incidence of malaria and other major diseases	6.6	Incidence and death rates associated with malaria
		6.7	Proportion of children under age five sleeping under insecticide-treated bednets
		6.8	Proportion of children under age five with fever who are treated with appropriate antimalarial drugs
		6.9	Incidence, prevalence, and death rates associated with tuberculosis
		6.10	Proportion of tuberculosis cases detected and cured under directly observed treatment short course

The Millennium Development Goals and targets come from the Millennium Declaration, signed by 189 countries, including 147 heads of state and government, in September 2000 (www. un.org/millennium/declaration/ares552e.htm) as updated by the 60th UN General Assembly in September 2005. The revised Millennium Development Goal (MDG) monitoring framework shown here, including new targets and indicators, was presented to the 62nd General Assembly, with new numbering as recommended by the Inter-agency and Expert Group on MDG Indicators at its 12th meeting on November 14, 2007. The goals and targets are interrelated and should be seen as a whole. They represent a partnership between the developed countries and the developing countries "to create an environment—at the national and global levels alike—which is conducive to development and the elimination of poverty." All indicators should be disaggregated by sex and urban-rural location as far as possible.

Goals and targets from the Millennium Declaration | Indicators for monitoring progress

Goal 7	Ensure environmental sustainability	
Target 7.A	Integrate the principles of sustainable development into country policies and programs and reverse the loss of environmental resources	7.1 Proportion of land area covered by forest 7.2 Carbon dioxide emissions, total, per capita and per $1 GDP (PPP) 7.3 Consumption of ozone-depleting substances
Target 7.B	Reduce biodiversity loss, achieving, by 2010, a significant reduction in the rate of loss	7.4 Proportion of fish stocks within safe biological limits 7.5 Proportion of total water resources used 7.6 Proportion of terrestrial and marine areas protected 7.7 Proportion of species threatened with extinction
Target 7.C	Halve by 2015 the proportion of people without sustainable access to safe drinking water and basic sanitation	7.8 Proportion of population using an improved drinking water source 7.9 Proportion of population using an improved sanitation facility
Target 7.D	Achieve by 2020 a significant improvement in the lives of at least 100 million slum dwellers	7.10 Proportion of urban population living in slums[b]

Goal 8	Develop a global partnership for development	
Target 8.A	Develop further an open, rule-based, predictable, nondiscriminatory trading and financial system (Includes a commitment to good governance, development, and poverty reduction—both nationally and internationally.)	Some of the indicators listed below are monitored separately for the least developed countries (LDCs), Africa, landlocked developing countries, and small island developing states. **Official development assistance (ODA)** 8.1 Net ODA, total and to the least developed countries, as percentage of OECD/DAC donors' gross national income 8.2 Proportion of total bilateral, sector-allocable ODA of OECD/DAC donors to basic social services (basic education, primary health care, nutrition, safe water, and sanitation)
Target 8.B	Address the special needs of the least developed countries (Includes tariff and quota-free access for the least developed countries' exports; enhanced program of debt relief for heavily indebted poor countries (HIPC) and cancellation of official bilateral debt; and more generous ODA for countries committed to poverty reduction.)	8.3 Proportion of bilateral official development assistance of OECD/DAC donors that is untied 8.4 ODA received in landlocked developing countries as a proportion of their gross national incomes 8.5 ODA received in small island developing states as a proportion of their gross national incomes
Target 8.C	Address the special needs of landlocked developing countries and small island developing states (through the Programme of Action for the Sustainable Development of Small Island Developing States and the outcome of the 22nd special session of the General Assembly)	**Market access** 8.6 Proportion of total developed country imports (by value and excluding arms) from developing countries and least developed countries, admitted free of duty 8.7 Average tariffs imposed by developed countries on agricultural products and textiles and clothing from developing countries 8.8 Agricultural support estimate for OECD countries as a percentage of their GDP 8.9 Proportion of ODA provided to help build trade capacity
Target 8.D	Deal comprehensively with the debt problems of developing countries through national and international measures in order to make debt sustainable in the long term	**Debt sustainability** 8.10 Total number of countries that have reached their HIPC decision points and number that have reached their HIPC completion points (cumulative) 8.11 Debt relief committed under HIPC Initiative and Multilateral Debt Relief Initiative (MDRI) 8.12 Debt service as a percentage of exports of goods and services
Target 8.E	In cooperation with pharmaceutical companies, provide access to affordable essential drugs in developing countries	8.13 Proportion of population with access to affordable essential drugs on a sustainable basis
Target 8.F	In cooperation with the private sector, make available the benefits of new technologies, especially information and communications	8.14 Telephone lines per 100 population 8.15 Cellular subscribers per 100 population 8.16 Internet users per 100 population

a. Where available, indicators based on national poverty lines should be used for monitoring country poverty trends.

b. The proportion of people living in slums is measured by a proxy, represented by the urban population living in households with at least one of these characteristics: lack of access to improved water supply, lack of access to improved sanitation, overcrowding (3 or more persons per room), and dwellings made of nondurable material.

1.1 Size of the economy

	Population	Surface area	Population density	Gross national income, *Atlas* method		Gross national income per capita, *Atlas* method		Purchasing power parity gross national income			Gross domestic product	
	millions	thousand sq. km	people per sq. km	$ billions	Rank	$	Rank	$ billions	Per capita $	Rank	% growth	Per capita % growth
	2010	**2010**	**2010**	**2010**	**2010**	**2010**	**2010**	**2010**	**2010**	**2010**	**2009–10**	**2009–10**
Afghanistan	34	652	53	14.3	109	410	204	36.5[a]	1,060[a]	199	8.2	5.2
Albania	3	29	117	12.7	117	3,960[b]	124	27.3	8,520	114	3.5	3.1
Algeria	35	2,382	15	155.7	49	4,390	119	287.2[a]	8,100[a]	117	3.3	1.8
Angola	19	1,247	15	75.2	62	3,940	125	103.1	5,410	135	2.3	3.0
Argentina	40	2,780	15	348.4	26	8,620	85	629.3	15,570	78	9.2	8.2
Armenia	3	30	109	9.9	127	3,200	135	17.5	5,660	133	2.1	1.9
Australia	22	7,741	3	1,030.3	13	46,200	20	823.0	36,910	32	2.3	0.7
Austria	8	84	102	394.6	25	47,030	18	333.9	39,790	24	2.3	2.0
Azerbaijan	9	87	110	48.3	74	5,330	109	83.9	9,270	108	5.0	3.8
Bahrain	1	1	1,661	19.7	99	18,730[c]	62	26.0	24,710[c]	55	6.3	−6.5
Bangladesh	149	144	1,142	104.7	57	700	187	269.7	1,810	182	6.1	4.9
Belarus	9	208	47	56.5	67	5,950	104	129.0	13,590	88	7.6	7.8
Belgium	11	31	360	499.5	20	45,840	21	417.3	38,290	28	2.3	1.3
Benin	9	113	80	7.0	139	780	184	14.0	1,590	186	3.0	0.1
Bolivia	10	1,099	9	17.9	104	1,810	158	46.0	4,640	142	4.1	2.5
Bosnia and Herzegovina	4	51	74	17.9	105	4,770	112	33.5	8,910	113	0.8	1.0
Botswana	2	582	4	13.6	113	6,790	95	27.5	13,700	86	7.2	5.9
Brazil	195	8,515	23	1,830.4	8	9,390	82	2,144.9	11,000	98	7.5	6.6
Bulgaria	8	111	69	47.3	75	6,280	101	101.2	13,440	89	0.2	0.9
Burkina Faso	16	274	60	9.0	131	550	193	20.7	1,250	190	9.2	6.0
Burundi	8	28	326	1.4	184	170	215	3.4	400	213	3.9	1.3
Cambodia	14	181	80	10.6	121	750	185	29.4	2,080	174	6.0	4.8
Cameroon	20	475	41	23.2	95	1,180	168	44.4	2,270	170	2.6	1.0
Canada	34	9,985	4	1,475.9	10	43,250	23	1,309.5	38,370	27	3.2	2.0
Central African Republic	4	623	7	2.1	177	470	199	3.5	790	209	3.3	1.4
Chad	11	1,284	9	6.9	140	620	189	13.7	1,220	193	4.3	1.6
Chile	17	756	23	173.2	47	10,120	78	250.5	14,640	80	5.2	4.2
China	1,338	9,600	143	5,720.8	2	4,270	121	10,221.7	7,640	120	10.4	9.8
Hong Kong SAR, China	7	1	6,783	231.7	37	32,780	36	335.6	47,480	15	7.0	6.0
Colombia	46	1,142	42	255.3	34	5,510	108	419.6	9,060	109	4.3	2.9
Congo, Dem. Rep.	66	2,345	29	12.0	119	180	214	21.4	320	215	7.2	4.3
Congo, Rep.	4	342	12	8.7	135	2,150	152	13.0	3,220	160	8.8	6.0
Costa Rica	5	51	91	31.7	87	6,810	94	52.5[a]	11,270[a]	96	4.2	2.7
Côte d'Ivoire	20	322	62	23.0	96	1,160	171	35.8	1,810	182	3.0	1.0
Croatia	4	57	79	61.4	66	13,890	67	83.4	18,890	73	−1.2	−0.9
Cuba	11	110	106	62.2	64	5,520	107	..	..		4.3	4.3
Cyprus	1	9	119	23.7[c]	93	29,430[c]	40	24.4[c]	30,300[c]	42	1.0[c]	0.6[c]
Czech Republic	11	79	136	188.3	43	17,890	59	241.0	22,910	63	2.3	2.0
Denmark	6	43	131	329.5	29	59,400	10	228.0	41,100	23	1.3	0.9
Dominican Republic	10	49	205	49.9	72	5,030	110	89.6[a]	9,030[a]	111	7.8	6.3
Ecuador	14	256	58	55.7	69	3,850[b]	126	114.0	7,880	118	3.6	2.1
Egypt, Arab Rep.	81	1,001	81	196.2	41	2,420	148	491.3	6,060	129	5.1	3.3
El Salvador	6	21	299	21.0	97	3,380	131	40.6[a]	6,550[a]	126	1.4	0.9
Eritrea	5	118	52	1.8	180	340	209	2.8[a]	540[a]	212	2.2	−0.8
Estonia	1	45	32	19.4	101	14,460	66	26.5	19,810	68	3.1	3.1
Ethiopia	83	1,104	83	32.4	85	390	207	86.1	1,040	200	10.1	7.8
Finland	5	338	18	255.2	35	47,570	16	198.9	37,070	31	3.7	3.2
France	65	549	118	2,749.8	5	42,370	26	2,254.9	34,750	34	1.5	0.9
Gabon	2	268	6	11.7	120	7,740	89	19.8	13,180	90	5.7	3.8
Gambia, The	2	11	173	0.8	198	450	201	2.2	1,300	189	5.0	2.1
Georgia	4[d]	70	78[d]	12.0[d]	118	2,690[d]	145	22.2[d]	4,990[d]	139	6.4[d]	5.4[d]
Germany	82	357	235	3,522.0	4	43,070	25	3,115.4	38,100	29	3.7	3.8
Ghana	24	239	107	30.1	88	1,230	166	40.5	1,660	185	6.6	5.2
Greece	11	132	88	305.0	31	26,950	44	312.7	27,630	51	−3.5	−3.8
Guatemala	14	109	134	39.4	79	2,740	142	66.8[a]	4,650[a]	141	2.8	0.2
Guinea	10	246	41	4.0	160	400	206	10.2	1,020	202	1.9	−0.3
Guinea-Bissau	2	36	54	0.9	194	590	191	1.8	1,180	196	3.5	1.4
Haiti	10	28	363	6.6	141	670	188	11.6[a]	1,180[a]	195	−5.1	−6.3

	Population	Surface area	Population density	Gross national income, *Atlas* method		Gross national income per capita, *Atlas* method		Purchasing power parity gross national income			Gross domestic product	
									Per capita			Per capita
	millions	thousand sq. km	people per sq. km	$ billions	Rank	$	Rank	$ billions	$	Rank	% growth	% growth
	2010	2010	2010	2010	2010	2010	2010	2010	2010	2010	2009–10	2009–10
Honduras	8	112	68	14.2	110	1,870	155	28.6[a]	3,770[a]	151	2.8	0.7
Hungary	10	93	110	128.6	53	12,860	69	195.5	19,550	69	1.3	1.5
India	1,225	3,287	412	1,553.9	9	1,270	164	4,159.7	3,400	157	8.8	7.3
Indonesia	240	1,905	132	599.2	18	2,500	147	1,008.2	4,200	148	6.1	5.0
Iran, Islamic Rep.	74	1,745	45	330.4	27	4,520	116	840.0	11,490	95	1.8	0.6
Iraq	32	435	74	74.9	63	2,340	149	108.1	3,370	158	0.8	–2.1
Ireland	4	70	65	187.1	44	41,820	29	150.1	33,540	37	–0.4	–0.8
Israel	8	22	352	207.2	39	27,180	43	210.8	27,660	50	4.7	2.8
Italy	60	301	206	2,159.3	7	35,700	33	1,923.7	31,810	39	1.5	1.1
Jamaica	3	11	249	13.0	115	4,800	111	19.7[a]	7,310[a]	122	–0.6	–0.8
Japan	127	378	350	5,334.4	3	41,850	28	4,411.7	34,610	35	4.0	4.1
Jordan	6	89	68	26.3	90	4,340	120	35.1	5,800	130	3.1	0.9
Kazakhstan	16	2,725	6	123.8	56	7,580	90	175.7	10,770	103	7.3	5.8
Kenya	41	580	71	31.8	86	790	183	68.1	1,680	184	5.3	2.8
Korea, Dem. Rep.	24	121	202	..		..[e]		..	..		..	..
Korea, Rep.	49	100	503	972.3	15	19,890	55	1,422.7	29,110	43	6.2	5.9
Kosovo	2	11	167	6.0	147	3,290	132	..	..		4.0	3.4
Kuwait	3	18	154	..		..[f]		..	..		..	..
Kyrgyz Republic	5	200	28	4.5	157	830	181	11.3	2,070	175	–1.4	–2.5
Lao PDR	6	237	27	6.5	144	1,050	176	15.3	2,460	168	9.4	7.9
Latvia	2	65	36	26.1	91	11,640	74	36.7	16,380	76	–0.3	0.4
Lebanon	4	10	413	37.5	82	8,880	84	59.5	14,090	84	7.0	6.2
Lesotho	2	30	72	2.3	174	1,040	178	4.3	1,960	177	3.3	2.6
Liberia	4	111	41	0.8	197	200	213	1.4	340	214	5.5	1.3
Libya	6	1,760	4	77.1	61	12,320	72	105.7[a]	16,880[a]	75	2.1	0.3
Lithuania	3	65	52	37.8	81	11,510	76	59.4	18,060	74	1.3	2.9
Macedonia, FYR	2	26	82	9.4	128	4,570	115	22.5	10,920	100	1.8	1.6
Madagascar	21	587	36	8.8	134	430	203	19.9	960	204	1.6	–1.3
Malawi	15	118	158	4.9	156	330	211	12.7	850	207	7.1	3.8
Malaysia	28	331	86	220.4	38	7,760	87	403.9	14,220	83	7.2	5.5
Mali	15	1,240	13	9.2	130	600	190	15.8	1,030	201	4.5	1.4
Mauritania	3	1,031	3	3.6	162	1,030	179	6.6	1,910	180	5.0	2.7
Mauritius	1	2	631	9.9	126	7,750	88	17.9	13,960	85	4.0	3.7
Mexico	113	1,964	58	1,008.0	14	8,890	83	1,627.0	14,340	81	5.4	4.1
Moldova	4[g]	34	124[g]	6.5[g]	145	1,810[g]	158	12.0[g]	3,360[g]	159	6.9[g]	7.1[g]
Mongolia	3	1,564	2	5.2	153	1,870	155	10.1	3,670	152	6.4	4.7
Morocco	32	447	72	92.6[h]	59	2,850[h]	140	149.3[h]	4,600[h]	143	3.7[h]	2.6[h]
Mozambique	23	799	30	10.3	123	440	202	21.7	930	205	7.2	4.8
Myanmar	48	677	73	..		..[e]		93.5[a]	1,950[a]	178	10.4	9.6
Namibia	2	824	3	10.3	124	4,510	118	14.7	6,420	127	4.8	2.9
Nepal	30	147	209	14.5	108	490	197	36.2	1,210	194	4.6	2.7
Netherlands	17	42	493	814.8	16	49,030	14	694.7	41,810	22	1.7	1.2
New Zealand	4	268	17	124.2	54	28,770	42	121.3	28,100	46	–0.5	–1.6
Nicaragua	6	130	48	6.4	146	1,110	173	16.1[a]	2,790[a]	164	7.6	6.1
Niger	16	1,267	12	5.7	149	370	208	11.2	720	210	8.8	5.0
Nigeria	158	924	174	186.4	45	1,180	168	344.2	2,170	172	7.9	5.2
Norway	5	324	16	427.1	24	87,350	4	286.3	58,570	6	0.7	–0.6
Oman	3	310	9	49.5	71	18,260	58	68.3	25,190	56	1.1	–1.7
Pakistan	174	796	225	182.8	46	1,050	176	484.4	2,790	164	4.1	2.3
Panama	4	75	47	24.5	92	6,970	92	44.9[a]	12,770[a]	91	4.8	3.2
Papua New Guinea	7	463	15	8.9	133	1,300	161	16.6[a]	2,420[a]	169	8.0	5.6
Paraguay	6	407	16	17.6	106	2,720	144	32.8	5,080	137	15.0	13.0
Peru	29	1,285	23	136.7	52	4,700	114	259.6	8,930	112	8.8	7.6
Philippines	93	300	313	192.2	42	2,060	153	370.7	3,980	149	7.6	5.8
Poland	38	313	126	474.9	21	12,440	71	731.5	19,160	71	3.9	3.9
Portugal	11	92	116	232.7	36	21,870	48	261.6	24,590	59	1.4	1.3
Puerto Rico	4	9	448	61.7	65	15,500	63	..	..		–2.1	–2.3
Qatar	2	12	152	..		..[f]		..	..		8.6	–5.1

	Population	Surface area	Population density	Gross national income, *Atlas* method		Gross national income per capita, *Atlas* method		Purchasing power parity gross national income			Gross domestic product	
	millions	thousand sq. km	people per sq. km	$ billions	Rank	$	Rank	$ billions	Per capita $	Rank	% growth	Per capita % growth
	2010	2010	2010	2010	2010	2010	2010	2010	2010	2010	2009–10	2009–10
Romania	21	238	93	168.2	48	7,850	86	306.4	14,290	82	0.9	1.1
Russian Federation	142	17,098	9	1,403.9	12	9,900	79	2,726.8	19,240	70	4.0	4.1
Rwanda	11	26	431	5.5	151	520	195	12.3	1,150	197	7.5	4.3
Saudi Arabia	27	2,150[i]	13	*434.1*	23	*16,190*	61	609.8	22,750	64	3.8	1.3
Senegal	12	197	65	13.5	114	1,090	174	23.8	1,910	180	4.2	1.4
Serbia	7	88	83	41.0	78	5,630	106	80.8	11,090	97	1.0	1.4
Sierra Leone	6	72	82	2.0	178	340	209	4.9	830	208	4.9	2.7
Singapore	5	1	7,253	203.4	40	40,070	30	283.3	55,790	7	14.5	12.5
Slovak Republic	5	49	113	91.5	60	16,840	60	124.8	22,980	62	4.2	4.0
Slovenia	2	20	102	49.0	73	23,900	47	54.4	26,530	54	1.4	0.9
Somalia	9	638	15	..		..[e]		..	..		..	..
South Africa	50	1,219	41	304.6	32	6,090	102	517.9	10,360	105	2.8	1.5
South Sudan	..	..	..	..		..[j]		..	..		..	..
Spain	46	505	92	1,462.9	11	31,750	39	1,465.2	31,800	40	–0.1	–0.5
Sri Lanka	21	66	333	46.7	76	2,240	150	104.6	5,010	138	8.0	7.0
Sudan	44	2,506	18	55.3	70	1,270	164	88.6	2,030	176	4.5	1.9
Swaziland	1	17	61	3.1	168	2,950	138	5.7	5,430	134	1.1	0.8
Sweden	9	450	23	469.8	22	50,100	13	372.6	39,730	25	5.6	4.7
Switzerland	8	41	196	559.7	19	71,520	7	391.0	49,960	14	2.7	1.6
Syrian Arab Republic	20	185	111	56.3	68	2,750	141	104.6	5,120	136	3.2	1.1
Tajikistan	7	143	49	5.5	152	800	182	14.7	2,140	173	3.8	2.4
Tanzania	45	947	51	23.4[k]	94	530[k]	194	62.6[k]	1,430[k]	187	7.0[k]	3.9[k]
Thailand	69	513	135	286.6	33	4,150	123	565.8	8,190	115	7.8	7.2
Timor-Leste	1	15	76	2.5	171	2,220	151	4.0[a]	3,600[a]	153	7.4	5.1
Togo	6	57	111	3.0	169	490	197	5.4	890	206	3.4	1.2
Trinidad and Tobago	1	5	261	20.6	98	15,380	64	32.3[a]	24,050[a]	60	0.1	–0.2
Tunisia	11	164	68	43.9	77	4,160	122	95.6	9,060	109	3.7	2.6
Turkey	73	784	95	719.9	17	9,890	80	1,129.9	15,530	79	9.0	7.6
Turkmenistan	5	488	11	19.1	103	3,790	128	37.8[a]	7,490[a]	121	9.2	7.9
Uganda	33	242	167	16.6	107	500	196	41.8	1,250	190	5.2	1.9
Ukraine	46	604	79	137.8	51	3,000	136	303.8	6,620	125	4.2	4.6
United Arab Emirates	8	84	90	*290.9*	30	*41,930*	27	*351.0*	50,580	11	1.4	–6.3
United Kingdom	62	244	257	2,377.2	6	38,200	31	2,230.6	35,840	33	2.1	1.4
United States	309	9,832	34	14,645.6	1	47,340	17	14,635.6	47,310	16	3.0	2.1
Uruguay	3	176	19	34.3	84	10,230	77	45.7	13,620	87	8.5	8.1
Uzbekistan	28	447	66	36.1	83	1,280	162	87.7[a]	3,110[a]	161	8.5	6.7
Venezuela, RB	29	912	33	334.1	28	11,590	75	350.2	12,150	93	–1.5	–3.0
Vietnam	87	331	280	101.1	58	1,160	171	267.0	3,070	162	6.8	5.7
West Bank and Gaza	4	6	690	..		..[j]		..	..		..	..
Yemen, Rep.	24	528	46	28.1	89	1,170	170	60.1	2,500	166	8.0	4.8
Zambia	13	753	17	13.8	111	1,070	175	17.8	1,380	188	7.6	5.9
Zimbabwe	13	391	32	5.8	148	460	200	..	..		9.0	8.2
World	**6,895 s**	**134,222 s**	**53 w**	**62,525.2 t**		**9,069 w**		**76,295.6 t**	**11,066 w**		**4.2 w**	**3.0 w**
Low income	796	15,551	53	420.2		528		1,040.5	1,307		5.9	3.7
Middle income	4,971	82,896	62	18,508.7		3,723		33,538.4	6,747		7.6	6.4
Lower middle income	2,519	23,568	111	4,077.7		1,619		9,147.8	3,632		6.9	5.3
Upper middle income	2,452	59,328	42	14,429.0		5,884		24,447.4	9,970		7.8	7.1
Low & middle income	5,767	98,447	60	18,948.9		3,286		34,577.9	5,996		7.6	6.2
East Asia & Pacific	1,962	16,302	124	7,249.4		3,696		13,058.0	6,657		9.7	8.9
Europe & Central Asia	405	23,603	18	2,946.7		7,272		5,428.2	13,396		5.7	5.3
Latin America & Carib.	583	20,394	29	4,505.0		7,733		6,365.1	10,926		6.2	5.0
Middle East & N. Africa	331	8,775	38	1,283.5		3,874		*2,627.3*	8,068		4.3	2.5
South Asia	1,633	5,131	342	1,920.1		1,176		5,101.4	3,124		8.1	6.6
Sub-Saharan Africa	853	24,243	36	1,003.6		1,176		1,833.4	2,148		4.8	2.3
High income	1,127	35,774	33	43,682.7		38,745		42,072.5	37,317		3.1	2.5
Euro area	332	2,628	130	12,794.4		38,565		11,399.6	34,360		2.0	1.6

a. Based on regression; others are extrapolated from the 2005 International Comparison Program benchmark estimates. b. Included in the aggregates for upper middle-income economies based on earlier data. c. Refers to the area controlled by the government of the Republic of Cyprus. d. Excludes Abkhazia and South Ossetia. e. Estimated to be low income ($1,005 or less). f. Estimated to be high income ($12,276 or more). g. Excludes Transnistria. h. Includes Former Spanish Sahara. i. Provisional estimate. j. Estimated to be lower middle income ($1,006–$3,975). k. Covers mainland Tanzania only.

About the data

Population, land area, income, and output are basic measures of the size of an economy. They also provide a broad indication of actual and potential resources. Population, land area, income (as measured by gross national income, GNI), and output (as measured by gross domestic product, GDP) are therefore used throughout *World Development Indicators* to normalize other indicators.

Population estimates are generally based on extrapolations from the most recent national census. For further discussion of the measurement of population and population growth, see *About the data* for table 2.1.

The surface area of an economy includes inland bodies of water and some coastal waterways. Surface area thus differs from land area, which excludes bodies of water, and from gross area, which may include offshore territorial waters. Land area is particularly important for understanding an economy's agricultural capacity and the environmental effects of human activity. (For measures of land area and data on rural population density, land use, and agricultural productivity, see tables 3.1–3.3.) Innovations in satellite mapping and computer databases have resulted in more precise measurements of land and water areas.

GNI measures total domestic and foreign value added claimed by residents. GNI comprises GDP plus net receipts of primary income (compensation of employees and property income) from nonresident sources. The World Bank uses GNI per capita in U.S. dollars to classify countries for analytical purposes and to determine borrowing eligibility. For definitions of the income groups in *World Development Indicators,* see *Users guide.* For discussion of the usefulness of national income and output as measures of productivity or welfare, see *About the data* for tables 4.1 and 4.2.

When calculating GNI in U.S. dollars from GNI reported in national currencies, the World Bank follows the *World Bank Atlas* conversion method, using a three-year average of exchange rates to smooth the effects of transitory fluctuations in exchange rates. (For further discussion of the *World Bank Atlas* method, see *Statistical methods.*)

Because exchange rates do not always reflect differences in price levels between countries, the table also converts GNI and GNI per capita estimates into international dollars using purchasing power parity (PPP) rates. PPP rates provide a standard measure allowing comparison of real levels of expenditure between countries, just as conventional price indexes allow comparison of real values over time.

PPP rates are calculated by simultaneously comparing the prices of similar goods and services among a large number of countries. In the most recent round of price surveys conducted by the International Comparison Program (ICP), 146 countries and territories participated in the data collection, including China for the first time, India for the first time since 1985, and almost all African countries. The PPP conversion factors presented in the table come from three sources. For 47 high- and upper middle-income countries conversion factors are provided by Eurostat and the Organisation for Economic Co-operation and Development (OECD), with PPP estimates for 35 European countries incorporating new price data collected since 2005. For the remaining 2005 ICP countries the PPP estimates are extrapolated from the 2005 ICP benchmark results, which account for relative price changes between each economy and the United States. For countries that did not participate in the 2005 ICP round, the PPP estimates are imputed using a statistical model. More information on the results of the 2005 ICP is available at www.worldbank.org/data/icp.

All 216 economies shown in *World Development Indicators* are ranked by size, including those that appear in table 1.6. The ranks are shown only in table 1.1. No rank is shown for economies for which numerical estimates of GNI per capita are not published. Economies with missing data are included in the ranking at their approximate level, so that the relative order of other economies remains consistent.

Definitions

• **Population** is based on the de facto definition of population, which counts all residents regardless of legal status or citizenship—except for refugees not permanently settled in the country of asylum, who are generally considered part of the population of their country of origin. The values shown are midyear estimates. See also table 2.1. • **Surface area** is a country's total area, including areas under inland bodies of water and some coastal waterways. • **Population density** is midyear population divided by land area in square kilometers. • **Gross national income (GNI)** is the sum of value added by all resident producers plus any product taxes (less subsidies) not included in the valuation of output plus net receipts of primary income (compensation of employees and property income) from abroad. Data are in current U.S. dollars converted using the *World Bank Atlas* method (see *Statistical methods*). • **Gross national income per capita** is GNI divided by midyear population. GNI per capita in U.S. dollars is converted using the *World Bank Atlas* method. • **Purchasing power parity (PPP) gross national income** is GNI converted to international dollars using PPP rates. An international dollar has the same purchasing power over GNI that a U.S. dollar has in the United States. • **Gross domestic product (GDP)** is the sum of value added by all resident producers plus any product taxes (less subsidies) not included in the valuation of output. Growth is calculated from constant price GDP data in local currency. • **Gross domestic product per capita** is GDP divided by midyear population.

Data sources

Population estimates are prepared by World Bank staff from a variety of sources (see *Data sources* for table 2.1). Data on surface and land area are from the Food and Agriculture Organization (see *Data sources* for table 3.1). GNI, GNI per capita, GDP growth, and GDP per capita growth are estimated by World Bank staff based on national accounts data collected by World Bank staff during economic missions or reported by national statistical offices to other international organizations such as the OECD. PPP conversion factors are estimates by Eurostat/OECD and by World Bank staff based on data collected by the ICP.

	Eradicate extreme poverty and hunger					Achieve universal primary education		Promote gender equality		Reduce child mortality	
	Share of poorest quintile in national consumption or income %	Vulnerable employment Unpaid family workers and own-account workers % of total employment		Prevalence of malnutrition Underweight % of children under age 5		Primary completion rate %		Ratio of girls to boys enrollments in primary and secondary education %		Under-five mortality rate per 1,000 live births	
	2000–11[a,b]	1990	2007–10[a]	1990	2005–10[a]	1991	2010	1991	2010[c]	1990	2010
Afghanistan	9.4	..	..	..	..	28	..	54	64	209	149
Albania	8.1	..	..	..	6.3	..	86	96	98	41	18
Algeria	..	..	..	9.2	3.7	80	96	83	98	68	36
Angola	2.0[d]	..	..	..	15.6	33	47	..	79	243	161
Argentina	4.4[d]	26[e]	20[e]	..	2.3	100	106	107	104	27	14
Armenia	8.8	..	38	..	4.2	105	101	..	102	55	20
Australia	..	10	9	..	..	..	..	100	98	9	5
Austria	8.6	..	9	..	..	..	99	95	97	9	4
Azerbaijan	8.0	..	55	..	8.4	95	90	100	99	93	46
Bahrain	..	..	2	6.3	..	97	..	101	..	17	10
Bangladesh	8.9	..	..	61.5	41.3	41	65	75	107	143	48
Belarus	9.2	..	..	..	1.3	94	103	..	101	17	6
Belgium	8.5	17	10	..	..	79	90	101	98	10	4
Benin	7.0	..	..	..	20.2	22	63	..	..	178	115
Bolivia	2.1	40[e]	57	9.7	4.5	71	99	..	99	121	54
Bosnia and Herzegovina	6.7	..	..	..	1.6	..	70	..	102	19	8
Botswana	..	..	..	..	11.2	90	94	109	100	59	48
Brazil	2.9	29[e]	25	..	2.2	93	..	..	102	59	19
Bulgaria	8.5	..	9	..	..	90	95	99	97	22	13
Burkina Faso	6.7	..	..	29.6	26.0	20	45	..	89[f]	205	176
Burundi	9.0	..	..	30.2	35.2	46	56	82	94	183	142
Cambodia	7.5	..	83	..	28.8	45	87	..	94	121	51
Cameroon	6.7	..	..	18	16.6	53	79	83	85	137	136
Canada	7.2	..	..	..	..	..	..	99	99	8	6
Central African Republic	3.4	..	..	..	..	28	41	61	69	165	159
Chad	6.3	94	..	..	..	18	33	41	65	207	173
Chile	4.3	..	26	..	0.5	..	96	100	99	19	9
China	5.0	..	..	12.6	3.4	107	..	86	103	48	18
Hong Kong SAR, China	..	6	7	..	..	102	96	102	102	..	..
Colombia	3.0	28	49	8.8	3.4	73	114	108	104	37	22
Congo, Dem. Rep.	5.5	..	..	..	28.2	48	59	70	79	181	170
Congo, Rep.	5.0	..	..	21.1	11.8	54	71	89	..	116	93
Costa Rica	3.9	25	20	2.5	1.1	79	96	101	102	17	10
Côte d'Ivoire	5.6	..	..	..	29.4	42	59[f]	..	..	151	123
Croatia	8.1	..	18	..	1.0	85	95	103	102	13	6
Cuba	..	..	..	..	..	99	98	106	98	13	6
Cyprus	..	..	14	..	..	90	103	100	100	11	4
Czech Republic	..	7	14	0.9	..	92	101	98	101	14	4
Denmark	..	7	5	..	..	98	97	101	101	9	4
Dominican Republic	4.7	39	42	8.4	3.4	61	92	..	97	62	27
Ecuador	4.3	36[e]	43	..	..	91	106	100	103	52	20
Egypt, Arab Rep.	9.2	28	27	10.5	6.8	..	98	81	..	94	22
El Salvador	3.7	35	38	11.1	6.6	65	96	101	98	62	16
Eritrea	..	..	..	36.9	..	18	40	82	80	141	61
Estonia	6.8	2	5	..	..	..	98	103	101	21	5
Ethiopia	9.3	92	..	..	34.6	23	72	68	89	184	106
Finland	9.6	..	9	..	..	97	98	109	102	7	3
France	..	11	7	..	..	106	..	102	100	9	4
Gabon	6.2	48	..	..	..	62	..	96	..	93	74
Gambia, The	4.8	..	..	..	15.8	45	71	65	99	165	98
Georgia	5.3	..	63	..	1.1	..	116	98	97	47	22
Germany	8.5	5	7	..	1.1	100	100	99	96	9	4
Ghana	5.2	..	..	24.1	14.3	64	94[f]	78	96[f]	122	74
Greece	6.7	42	28	..	..	99	101	99	97	13	4
Guatemala	3.1	..	..	27.8	13.0	..	84	87	95	78	32
Guinea	6.4	..	..	..	20.8	17	64	45	77	229	130
Guinea-Bissau	7.3	..	..	..	17.2	5	68	55	..	210	150
Haiti	2.4	..	..	23.7	18.9	27	..	..	..	151	165

	Eradicate extreme poverty and hunger					Achieve universal primary education		Promote gender equality		Reduce child mortality	
	Share of poorest quintile in national consumption or income %	Vulnerable employment Unpaid family workers and own-account workers % of total employment		Prevalence of malnutrition Underweight % of children under age 5		Primary completion rate %		Ratio of girls to boys enrollments in primary and secondary education %		Under-five mortality rate per 1,000 live births	
	2000–11[a,b]	1990	2007–10[a]	1990	2005–10[a]	1991	2010	1991	2010[c]	1990	2010
Honduras	2.0	49[e]	50	15.8	8.6	64	99	104	107	58	24
Hungary	8.4	7	7	2.3	..	82	98	100	99	19	6
India	8.6	..	..	59.5	43.5	64	96	73	92	115	63
Indonesia	8.3	..	64	31.0	17.5	93	105	93	101	85	35
Iran, Islamic Rep.	6.4	..	42	..	..	88	104	85	96	65	26
Iraq	8.7	..	..	10.4	7.1	58	65	79	81	46	39
Ireland	7.4	20	12	..	..	103	..	104	103	9	4
Israel	5.7	..	7	..	..	..	103	105	101	12	5
Italy	6.5	27	19	..	..	98	103	100	99	10	4
Jamaica	5.4	42	37	4.0	1.9	94	73	103	99	38	24
Japan	..	19	10	..	..	102	102	101	100	6	3
Jordan	7.7	..	10	4.8	1.9	101	101	101	102	38	22
Kazakhstan	9.1	..	32	..	4.9	103	116[f]	..	98[f]	57	33
Kenya	4.8	..	..	20.1	16.4	..	..	92	95	99	85
Korea, Dem. Rep.	..	..	..	..	18.8	..	..	..	..	45	33
Korea, Rep.	..	..	24	..	..	99	101	99	99	8	5
Kosovo	..	..	..	..	..	..	..	..	..	..	..
Kuwait	..	..	..	..	1.7	57	112[f]	100	105	15	11
Kyrgyz Republic	6.8	..	..	..	2.7	..	97	102	99	72	38
Lao PDR	7.6	..	..	39.8	31.6	41	79	77	87	145	54
Latvia	6.6	..	8	..	..	..	92	101	98	21	10
Lebanon	..	..	28	..	..	..	87	101	104	38	22
Lesotho	3.0	..	..	13.8	13.5	59	70	124	106	89	85
Liberia	6.4	..	79	..	20.4	..	62	..	..	227	103
Libya	..	..	..	..	5.6	..	..	..	..	45	17
Lithuania	6.6	..	9	..	..	..	96	96	99	17	7
Macedonia, FYR	5.1	..	23	..	1.8	98	92	99	99	39	12
Madagascar	5.4	84	..	35.5	..	36	72	96	97	159	62
Malawi	7.0	84	..	24.4	13.8	31	67	82	101	222	92
Malaysia	4.5	29	22	22.1	12.9	91	..	101	..	18	6
Mali	8.0	..	83	29.0	27.9	9	55[f]	58	83[f]	255	178
Mauritania	6.0	..	..	43.3	15.9	33	75	71	101	124	111
Mauritius	..	12	16	..	..	115	96	102	100	24	15
Mexico	4.4	26	30	13.9	3.4	88	104	97	102	49	17
Moldova	7.8	..	29	..	3.2	..	93	105	101	37	19
Mongolia	7.1	..	58	10.8	5.3	..	108	109	103	107	32
Morocco	6.5	..	51	8.1	..	48	85	70	89	86	36
Mozambique	5.2	..	..	..	18.3	26	61	71	89	219	135
Myanmar	..	..	..	28.8	..	..	104	95	102	112	66
Namibia	3.2	..	..	21.5	17.5	74	84	106	104	73	40
Nepal	8.3	..	..	..	38.8	51	..	59	..	141	50
Netherlands	..	9	11	..	..	..	..	97	99	8	4
New Zealand	..	13	11	..	..	..	..	100	103	11	6
Nicaragua	6.2	43[e]	45	9.6	5.7	42	81	119	102	68	27
Niger	8.1	..	..	41.0	39.9	17	46[f]	53	78	311	143
Nigeria	4.4	..	..	35.1	26.7	..	74	77	90	213	143
Norway	9.6	..	6	..	..	100	100	102	99	9	3
Oman	..	..	..	21.4	8.6	74	101	89	98	47	9
Pakistan	9.6	..	63	39.0	..	..	67	48	80	124	87
Panama	3.3	34	31	..	..	86	97	99	101	33	20
Papua New Guinea	..	..	..	..	18.1	46	..	80	..	90	61
Paraguay	3.3	23[e]	45	2.8	3.4	68	94	98	100	50	25
Peru	3.9	36[e]	40[e]	8.8	4.5	..	102	96	99	78	19
Philippines	6.0	..	44	29.8	20.7	88	92	99	101	59	29
Poland	7.7	28	19	..	..	96	95	101	99	17	6
Portugal	..	24	18	..	..	..	..	103	100	15	4
Puerto Rico	..	..	..	..	..	..	..	..	104	..	..
Qatar	3.9	..	0	..	..	71	100	98	109	21	8

	Eradicate extreme poverty and hunger					Achieve universal primary education		Promote gender equality		Reduce child mortality	
	Share of poorest quintile in national consumption or income %	Vulnerable employment Unpaid family workers and own-account workers % of total employment		Prevalence of malnutrition Underweight % of children under age 5		Primary completion rate %		Ratio of girls to boys enrollments in primary and secondary education %		Under-five mortality rate per 1,000 live births	
	2000–11[a,b]	1990	2007–10[a]	1990	2005–10[a]	1991	2010	1991	2010[c]	1990	2010
Romania	8.3	27	33	5.0	..	96	91	99	99	37	14
Russian Federation	6.5	1	6	..	..	92	98	105	98	27	12
Rwanda	5.2	..	..	24.3	18.0	50	70	95	102	163	91
Saudi Arabia	..	..	..	..	5.3	..	93	..	97	45	18
Senegal	6.2	83	..	19.0	14.5	39	59	69	100	139	75
Serbia	8.9	..	28	..	1.8	..	96	..	101	29	7
Sierra Leone	6.1	..	..	25.4	21.3	..	74[f]	64	..	276	174
Singapore	..	8	10	..	..	..	..	..	..	8	3
Slovak Republic	10.1	..	12	..	..	95	98	102	101	18	8
Slovenia	8.2	12	14	..	..	95	95	103	99	10	3
Somalia	..	..	..	..	32.8	..	..	..	53	180	180
South Africa	2.7	..	10	..	8.7	76	..	..	104	60	57
South Sudan	..	..	..	..	..	..	..	..	..	..	..
Spain	7.0	23	11	..	..	104	102	104	102	11	5
Sri Lanka	6.9	43[e]	40[e]	29.3	21.6	101	101	102	..	32	17
Sudan	6.8	..	..	31.8	31.7	..	58	78	90	125	103
Swaziland	4.1	..	..	..	7.3	61	77	..	94	96	78
Sweden	9.1	..	7	..	..	96	94	102	99	7	3
Switzerland	7.6	9	9	..	..	53	95	97	98	8	5
Syrian Arab Republic	7.7	..	33	11.5	10.1	89	104	85	99	38	16
Tajikistan	8.3	..	..	..	15.0	..	104	..	90	116	63
Tanzania	6.8	91[e]	..	25.1	16.2	55	90	97	96	155	92
Thailand	6.7	70	53	16.3	7.0	..	..	99	103	32	13
Timor-Leste	9.0	..	..	..	45.3	..	65	..	98	169	81
Togo	7.6	..	..	21.2	20.5	35	74	59	75	147	103
Trinidad and Tobago	..	22	..	4.7	..	102	91	101	101	37	27
Tunisia	5.9	..	..	8.5	3.3	74	91	86	101	49	16
Turkey	5.7	..	34	8.7	..	90	99	81	95	80	18
Turkmenistan	..	..	..	..	..	..	..	..	..	98	56
Uganda	5.8	..	..	19.7	16.4	..	57	77	99	175	99
Ukraine	9.7	..	..	..	..	92	98	102	99	21	13
United Arab Emirates	..	..	1	..	..	103	..	104	..	22	7
United Kingdom	..	10	11	..	..	..	..	102	101	9	5
United States	5.4	..	..	..	..	..	104	100	100	11	8
Uruguay	4.9	..	23[e]	6.5	..	94	106	107	104	23	11
Uzbekistan	7.1	..	..	..	4.4	80	93[f]	..	98[f]	77	52
Venezuela, RB	4.3	..	31	6.7	3.7	81	94	105	102	33	18
Vietnam	7.4	..	..	40.7	20.2	..	..	..	102	51	23
West Bank and Gaza	7.4	..	28	..	2.2	..	95	..	104	45	22
Yemen, Rep.	7.2	..	..	29.6	..	..	63	..	75	128	77
Zambia	3.6	65	..	21.2	14.9	..	103	87	96	183	111
Zimbabwe	..	..	..	..	8.0	14.0	97	..	92	..	78	80
World	..	.. w	.. w	.. w	.. w	79 w	88 w	87 w	96 w	90 w	58 w
Low income	..	..	..	40.2	23.0	44	65	80	91	165	108
Middle income	..	..	..	..	..	83	92	85	97	85	51
Lower middle income	..	..	73	38.1	24.6	68	88	81	93	113	69
Upper middle income	..	..	..	12.5	3.0	97	98	98	103	49	20
Low & middle income	..	..	..	28.7	17.9	78	87	84	96	98	63
East Asia & Pacific	..	..	..	20.4	5.8	101	97	89	103	56	24
Europe & Central Asia	..	..	19	8.5	1.9	92	95	98	97	51	23
Latin America & Carib.	..	29	31	7.5	3.0	84	102	99	102	54	23
Middle East & N. Africa	..	..	36	11.8	7.9	..	88	80	93	74	34
South Asia	..	..	81	52.2	32.9	62	86	69	92	120	67
Sub-Saharan Africa	..	..	..	29.0	22.0	51	67	82	89	175	121
High income	..	..	..	..	..	..	97	100	100	12	6
Euro area	..	15	11	..	..	101	101	..	99	10	4

a. Data are for the most recent year available. b. See table 2.9 for survey year and whether share is based on income or consumption expenditure. c. Provisional data. d. Covers urban areas only. e. Limited coverage. f. Data are for 2011.

Millennium Development Goals: eradicating poverty and saving lives

1.2

About the data

About the data

Tables 1.2–1.4 present indicators for 17 of the 21 targets specified by the Millennium Development Goals. Each of the eight goals includes one or more targets, and each target has several associated indicators for monitoring progress toward the target. Most of the targets are set as a value of a specific indicator to be attained by a certain date. In some cases the target value is set relative to a level in 1990. In others it is set at an absolute level. Some of the targets for goals 7 and 8 have not yet been quantified.

The indicators in this table relate to goals 1–4. Goal 1 has three targets between 1990 and 2015: to halve the proportion of people whose income is less than $1.25 a day, to achieve full and productive employment and decent work for all, and to halve the proportion of people who suffer from hunger. Estimates of poverty rates are in tables 2.7 and 2.8. The indicator shown here, the share of the poorest quintile in national consumption or income, is a distributional measure. Countries with more unequal distributions of consumption (or income) have a higher rate of poverty for a given average income. Vulnerable employment measures the portion of the labor force that receives the lowest wages and least security in employment. No single indicator captures the concept of suffering from hunger. Child malnutrition is a symptom of inadequate food supply, lack of essential nutrients, illnesses that deplete these nutrients, and undernourished mothers who give birth to underweight children.

Progress toward universal primary education is measured by the primary completion rate. Because many school systems do not record school completion on a consistent basis, it is estimated from the gross enrollment rate in the final grade of primary education, adjusted for repetition. Official enrollments sometimes differ significantly from attendance, and even school systems with high average enrollment ratios may have poor completion rates.

Eliminating gender disparities in education would help increase the status and capabilities of women. The ratio of female to male enrollments in primary and secondary education provides an imperfect measure of the relative accessibility of schooling for girls.

The targets for reducing under-five mortality rates are among the most challenging. Under-five mortality rates are harmonized estimates produced by a weighted least squares regression model and are available at regular intervals for most countries.

Most of the 60 indicators relating to the Millennium Development Goals can be found in *World Development Indicators*. Table 1.2a shows where to find the indicators for the first four goals. For more information about data collection methods and limitations, see *About the data* for the tables listed there. For information about the indicators for goals 5–8, see *About the data* for tables 1.3 and 1.4.

Definitions

• **Share of poorest quintile in national consumption or income** is the share of the poorest 20 percent of the population in consumption or, in some cases, income. • **Vulnerable employment** is the sum of unpaid family workers and own-account workers as a percentage of total employment. • **Prevalence of malnutrition** is the percentage of children under age 5 whose weight for age is more than two standard deviations below the median for the international reference population ages 0–59 months. The data are based on the new international child growth standards for infants and young children, called the Child Growth Standards, released in 2006 by the World Health Organization. • **Primary completion rate** is the percentage of students completing the last year of primary education. It is calculated as the total number of students in the last grade of primary education, minus the number of repeaters in that grade, divided by the total number of children of official graduation age. • **Ratio of girls to boys enrollments in primary and secondary education** is the ratio of the female to male gross enrollment rate in primary and secondary education. • **Under-five mortality rate** is the probability of a child born in a specific year dying before reaching age 5, if subject to the age-specific mortality rate of that year. The probability is derived from life tables and is expressed as a rate per 1,000 live births.

Location of indicators for Millennium Development Goals 1–4 — 1.2a

Goal 1. Eradicate extreme poverty and hunger	Table
1.1 Proportion of population below $1.25 a day	2.8
1.2 Poverty gap ratio	2.8
1.3 Share of poorest quintile in national consumption	1.2, 2.9
1.4 Growth rate of GDP per person employed	2.4
1.5 Employment to population ratio	2.4
1.6 Proportion of employed people living below $1 per day	—
1.7 Proportion of own-account and unpaid family workers in total employment	1.2, 2.4
1.8 Prevalence of underweight in children under age 5	1.2, 2.20
1.9 Proportion of population below minimum level of dietary energy consumption	2.20
Goal 2. Achieve universal primary education	
2.1 Net enrollment ratio in primary education	2.12
2.2 Proportion of pupils starting grade 1 who reach last grade of primary	2.13
2.3 Literacy rate of 15- to 24-year-olds	2.14
Goal 3. Promote gender equality and empower women	
3.1 Ratio of girls to boys in primary, secondary, and tertiary education	1.2, 2.12*
3.2 Share of women in wage employment in the nonagricultural sector	1.5, 2.3*
3.3 Proportion of seats held by women in national parliament	1.5
Goal 4. Reduce child mortality	
4.1 Under-five mortality rate	1.2, 2.23, 5.8
4.2 Infant mortality rate	2.23
4.3 Proportion of one-year-old children immunized against measles	2.18

— No data are available in the World Development Indicators database. * Table shows information on related indicators.

Data sources

The indicators here and throughout this book have been compiled by World Bank staff from primary and secondary sources. Efforts have been made to harmonize the data series used to compile this table with those published on the United Nations Millennium Development Goals Web site (www.un.org/millenniumgoals), but some differences in timing, sources, and definitions remain. For more information see the data sources for the indicators listed in table 1.2a.

1.3 Millennium Development Goals: protecting our common environment

	Improve maternal health			Combat HIV/AIDS and other diseases		Ensure environmental sustainability					Develop a global partnership for development
	Maternal mortality ratio Modeled estimate per 100,000 live births	Contraceptive prevalence rate % of married women ages 15–49		HIV prevalence % of population ages 15–49	Incidence of tuberculosis per 100,000 people	Carbon dioxide emissions per capita metric tons		Nationally protected terrestrial and marine areas % of total land area	Access to improved sanitation facilities % of population		Internet users[a] per 100 people
	2008	**1990**	**2005–10[b]**	**2009**	**2010**	**1990**	**2008**	**2010**	**1990**	**2010**	**2010**
Afghanistan	1,400	..	23	..	189	0.1	0.0	0.4	..	37	3.7
Albania	31	..	69	..	14	2.3	1.3	8.4	76	94	45.0
Algeria	120	51	61	0.1	90	3.1	3.2	6.2	88	95	12.5
Angola	610	..	..	2.0	304	0.4	1.4	12.1	29	58	10.0
Argentina	70	..	78	0.5	27	3.4	4.8	5.3	90	..	36.0
Armenia	29	56	55	0.1	73	..	1.8	8.0	..	90	44.0
Australia	8	..	..	0.1	6	16.8	18.6	12.5	100	100	75.9
Austria	5	..	..	0.3	5	7.9	8.1	22.9	100	100	72.7
Azerbaijan	38	..	51	0.1	110	..	5.4	7.1	..	82	46.7
Bahrain	19	54	..	..	23	24.1	21.4	0.7	..	..	55.0
Bangladesh	340	40	53	<0.1[c]	225	0.1	0.3	1.6	39	56	3.7
Belarus	15	..	73	0.3	70	..	6.5	7.2	93	93	32.1
Belgium	5	78	..	0.2	9	10.9	9.8	13.2	100	100	73.7
Benin	410	..	17	1.2	94	0.1	0.5	23.3	5	13	3.1
Bolivia	180	30	61	0.2	135	0.8	1.3	18.5	18	27	20.0
Bosnia and Herzegovina	9	..	36	..	50	..	8.3	0.6	..	95	52.0
Botswana	190	33	53	24.8	503	1.6	2.5	30.9	38	62	6.0
Brazil	58	59	81	..	43	1.4	2.1	26.0	68	79	40.7
Bulgaria	13	..	..	0.1	40	8.9	6.6	8.9	99	100	46.0
Burkina Faso	560	..	17	1.2	55	0.1	0.1	14.2	8	17	1.4
Burundi	970	..	22	3.3	129	0.1	0.0	4.8	44	46	2.1
Cambodia	290	..	51	0.5	437	0.0	0.3	23.4	9	31	1.3
Cameroon	600	16	29	5.3	177	0.1	0.3	9.0	48	49	4.0
Canada	12	..	..	0.2	5	16.2	16.3	6.2	100	100	81.3
Central African Republic	850	..	19	4.7	319	0.1	0.1	17.7	11	34	2.3
Chad	1,200	..	5	3.4	276	0.0	0.0	9.4	8	13	1.7
Chile	26	56	58	0.4	19	2.6	4.4	13.3	84	96	45.0
China	38	85	85	0.1[c]	78	2.2	5.3	16.0	24	64	34.4
Hong Kong SAR, China	..	86	80	..	80	4.8	5.5	41.8	..	..	71.8
Colombia	85	66	79	0.5	34	1.7	1.5	20.5	67	77	36.5
Congo, Dem. Rep.	670	8	17	..	327	0.1	0.0	10.0	9	24	0.7
Congo, Rep.	580	..	44	3.4	372	0.5	0.5	9.7	..	18	5.0
Costa Rica	44	..	80	0.3	13	1.0	1.8	17.6	93	95	36.5
Côte d'Ivoire	470	..	13	3.4	139	0.5	0.4	21.8	20	24	2.6
Croatia	14	..	..	<0.1	21	..	5.3	9.5	99	99	60.1
Cuba	53	..	78	0.1	9	3.2	2.8	5.3	80	91	15.9
Cyprus	10	..	..	..	4	6.1	7.9	4.5	100	100	53.0
Czech Republic	8	78	..	<0.1	7	..	11.2	15.1	100	98	68.6
Denmark	5	78	..	0.2	6	9.8	8.4	4.1	100	100	88.8
Dominican Republic	100	56	73	0.9	67	1.3	2.2	24.1	73	83	39.5
Ecuador	140	53	..	0.4	65	1.6	1.9	38.0	69	92	29.0
Egypt, Arab Rep.	82	48	60	<0.1	18	1.3	2.7	6.1	72	95	26.7
El Salvador	110	47	73	0.8	28	0.5	1.0	1.4	75	87	15.9
Eritrea	280	..	..	0.8	100	..	0.1	3.8	9	..	5.4
Estonia	12	..	..	1.2	25	..	13.6	22.6	95	95	74.2
Ethiopia	470	5	15	..	261	0.1	0.1	18.4	3	21	0.7
Finland	8	77	..	0.1	7	10.2	10.6	8.5	100	100	86.9
France	8	81	71	0.4	9	6.9	5.9	17.1	100	100	77.5
Gabon	260	..	..	5.2	553	5.2	1.7	14.6	..	33	7.2
Gambia, The	400	12	..	2.0	273	0.2	0.3	1.3	..	68	9.2
Georgia	48	..	53	0.1	107	..	1.2	3.4	96	95	26.3
Germany	7	70	..	0.1	5	..	9.6	42.3	100	100	82.5
Ghana	350	17	24	1.8	86	0.3	0.4	14.0	7	14	9.5
Greece	2	..	..	0.1	5	7.2	8.7	9.9	97	98	44.6
Guatemala	110	..	54	0.8	62	0.6	0.9	29.5	62	78	10.5
Guinea	680	..	9	1.3	334	0.2	0.1	6.4	10	18	1.0
Guinea-Bissau	1,000	..	14	2.5	233	0.2	0.2	26.9	..	20	2.5
Haiti	300	10	32	1.9	230	0.1	0.3	0.1	26	17	8.4

	Improve maternal health			Combat HIV/AIDS and other diseases		Ensure environmental sustainability					Develop a global partnership for development
	Maternal mortality ratio Modeled estimate per 100,000 live births	Contraceptive prevalence rate % of married women ages 15–49		HIV prevalence % of population ages 15–49	Incidence of tuberculosis per 100,000 people	Carbon dioxide emissions per capita metric tons		Nationally protected terrestrial and marine areas % of total land area	Access to improved sanitation facilities % of population		Internet users[a] per 100 people
	2008	**1990**	**2005–10**[b]	**2009**	**2010**	**1990**	**2008**	**2010**	**1990**	**2010**	**2010**
Honduras	110	*47*	65	0.8	51	0.5	1.2	13.9	50	77	11.1
Hungary	13	..	..	<0.1	15	6.1	5.4	5.1	100	100	65.2
India	230	*45*	54	0.3	185	0.8	1.5	4.8	18	34	7.5
Indonesia	240	*50*	56	0.2	189	0.8	1.7	6.4	32	54	9.9
Iran, Islamic Rep.	30	*49*	79	0.2	17	4.1	7.4	6.9	79	100	13.0
Iraq	75	*14*	50	..	64	2.9	3.4	0.1	..	73	2.5
Ireland	3	..	65	0.2	8	8.7	9.9	1.2	99	99	69.8
Israel	7	*68*	..	0.2	5	7.2	5.2	15.1	100	100	65.4
Italy	5	..	..	0.3	5	7.5	7.4	15.9	..	..	53.7
Jamaica	89	*55*	72	1.7	7	3.3	4.5	7.3	80	80	26.5
Japan	6	*58*	54	<0.1	21	8.9	9.5	10.9	100	100	77.6
Jordan	59	*40*	59	..	5	3.3	3.7	1.9	97	98	38.9
Kazakhstan	45	..	51	0.1	151	..	15.1	2.5	96	97	33.4
Kenya	530	*27*	46	6.3	298	0.2	0.3	11.7	25	32	25.9
Korea, Dem. Rep.	250	*62*	..	..	345	..	3.2	3.9	..	80	0.0
Korea, Rep.	18	*79*	80	<0.1	97	5.7	10.5	3.0	100	100	82.5
Kosovo	..	..	..	..	..	..	..	..	..	..	..
Kuwait	9	..	..	..	41	21.8	30.1	1.1	100	100	38.3
Kyrgyz Republic	81	..	48	0.3	159	..	1.2	6.9	..	93	19.6
Lao PDR	580	..	38	0.2	90	0.1	0.3	16.6	..	63	7.0
Latvia	20	..	..	0.7	39	..	3.3	16.4	..	..	71.5
Lebanon	26	..	..	0.1	17	3.1	4.1	0.4	..	..	31.0
Lesotho	530	*23*	47	23.6	633	..	..	0.5	..	26	3.9
Liberia	990	..	11	1.5	293	0.2	0.2	1.6	..	18	7.0
Libya	64	..	..	..	40	9.3	9.5	0.1	97	97	14.0
Lithuania	13	..	..	0.1	69	..	4.5	14.4	..	..	62.8
Macedonia, FYR	9	..	14	..	21	..	5.8	4.9	..	88	51.9
Madagascar	440	*17*	40	0.2	266	0.1	0.1	2.5	9	15	1.7
Malawi	510	*13*	41	11.0	219	0.1	0.1	15.0	39	51	2.3
Malaysia	31	*50*	..	0.5	82	3.1	7.6	13.7	84	96	56.3
Mali	830	..	8	1.0	68	0.0	0.0	2.4	15	22	2.7
Mauritania	550	*4*	9	0.7	337	1.3	0.6	1.1	16	26	3.0
Mauritius	36	*75*	..	1.0	22	1.4	3.1	0.7	89	89	28.7
Mexico	85	*63*	73	0.3	16	3.9	4.3	11.9	64	85	31.1
Moldova	32	..	68	0.4	182	..	1.3	1.4	..	85	40.1
Mongolia	65	..	55	<0.1	224	4.6	4.1	13.4	..	51	12.9
Morocco	110	*42*	..	0.1	91	1.0	1.5	1.5	53	70	49.0
Mozambique	550	..	16	11.5	544	0.1	0.1	14.8	11	18	4.2
Myanmar	240	*17*	41	0.6	384	0.1	0.3	5.2	..	76	0.2
Namibia	180	*41*	55	13.1	603	0.0	1.8	14.7	24	32	6.5
Nepal	380	*24*	48	0.4	163	0.0	0.1	17.0	10	31	7.9
Netherlands	9	*76*	69	0.2	7	11.0	10.6	15.2	100	100	90.7
New Zealand	14	..	..	0.1	8	7.0	7.8	20.0	..	..	83.0
Nicaragua	100	..	72	0.2	42	0.6	0.8	36.8	43	52	10.0
Niger	820	*4*	18	0.8	185	0.1	0.1	7.1	5	9	0.8
Nigeria	840	*6*	15	3.6	133	0.5	0.6	12.6	37	31	28.4
Norway	7	*74*	88	0.1	6	7.4	10.5	10.9	100	100	93.3
Oman	20	*9*	24	0.1	13	5.5	17.3	9.3	82	99	62.0
Pakistan	260	*15*	27	0.1	231	0.6	1.0	9.8	27	48	16.8
Panama	71	..	52	0.9	48	1.3	2.0	11.5	58	69	42.7
Papua New Guinea	250	..	32	0.9	303	0.5	0.3	1.4	47	45	1.3
Paraguay	95	*48*	79	0.3	46	0.5	0.7	5.4	37	71	19.8
Peru	98	*59*	74	0.4	106	1.0	1.4	13.1	54	71	34.3
Philippines	94	*36*	51	<0.1	275	0.7	0.9	5.0	57	74	25.0
Poland	6	*73*	..	0.1	23	9.6	8.3	21.8	..	90	62.5
Portugal	7	..	67	0.6	29	4.4	5.3	6.1	92	100	51.3
Puerto Rico	18	..	..	..	2	..	..	4.4	..	..	42.7
Qatar	8	..	..	<0.1	38	24.9	49.1	1.4	100	100	81.6

	Improve maternal health			Combat HIV/AIDS and other diseases		Ensure environmental sustainability					Develop a global partnership for development
	Maternal mortality ratio Modeled estimate per 100,000 live births	Contraceptive prevalence rate % of married women ages 15–49		HIV prevalence % of population ages 15–49	Incidence of tuberculosis per 100,000 people	Carbon dioxide emissions per capita metric tons		Nationally protected terrestrial and marine areas % of total land area	Access to improved sanitation facilities % of population		Internet users[a] per 100 people
	2008	**1990**	**2005–10[b]**	**2009**	**2010**	**1990**	**2008**	**2010**	**1990**	**2010**	**2010**
Romania	27	..	..	0.1	116	6.8	4.4	7.8	71	..	40.0
Russian Federation	39	..	80	1.0	106	..	12.0	9.2	74	70	43.4
Rwanda	540	21	52	2.9	106	0.1	0.1	10.0	36	55	13.0
Saudi Arabia	24	..	24	..	18	13.3	16.6	29.9	..	..	41.0
Senegal	410	..	12	0.9	288	0.4	0.4	23.5	38	52	16.0
Serbia	8	..	41	0.1	18	..	6.8	6.0	..	92	43.1
Sierra Leone	970	3	8	1.6	682	0.1	0.2	4.3	11	13	0.3
Singapore	9	65	..	0.1	35	15.4	6.7	3.4	99	100	71.1
Slovak Republic	6	74	..	<0.1	8	..	6.9	23.2	100	100	79.9
Slovenia	18	..	..	<0.1	11	..	8.5	13.1	100	100	69.3
Somalia	1,200	..	15	0.7	286	0.0	0.1	0.5	..	23	1.2
South Africa	410	57	..	17.8	981	9.5	8.9	6.9	71	79	12.3
South Sudan	..	..	..	..	..	..	..	..	..	..	..
Spain	6	..	66	0.4	16	5.9	7.2	7.6	100	100	65.8
Sri Lanka	39	..	68	<0.1	66	0.2	0.6	15.0	70	92	12.0
Sudan	750	9	8	1.1	119	0.2	0.3	4.2	27	26	10.2
Swaziland	420	20	49	25.9	1,287	0.5	1.1	3.0	48	57	9.0
Sweden	5	..	..	0.1	7	6.0	5.3	10.0	100	100	90.0
Switzerland	10	..	..	0.4	8	6.4	5.3	24.9	100	100	82.2
Syrian Arab Republic	46	..	54	..	20	3.0	3.6	0.6	85	95	20.7
Tajikistan	64	..	37	0.2	206	..	0.5	4.1	..	94	11.5
Tanzania	790	10	34	5.6	177	0.1	0.2	26.9	7	10	11.0
Thailand	48	66	80	1.3	137	1.7	4.2	17.3	84	96	21.2
Timor-Leste	370	25	22	..	498	..	0.2	6.4	..	47	0.2
Togo	350	34	15	3.2	455	0.2	0.2	11.0	13	13	5.4
Trinidad and Tobago	55	..	43	1.5	19	14.0	37.4	9.6	93	92	48.5
Tunisia	60	50	60	<0.1	25	1.6	2.4	1.3	74	..	36.6
Turkey	23	63	73	<0.1	28	2.8	4.0	1.9	84	90	39.8
Turkmenistan	77	..	48	..	66	..	9.7	3.0	98	98	2.2
Uganda	430	5	24	6.5	209	0.0	0.1	10.3	27	34	12.5
Ukraine	26	..	67	1.1	101	..	7.0	3.6	..	94	44.6
United Arab Emirates	10	..	..	..	3	28.8	25.0	4.7	97	98	78.0
United Kingdom	12	70	84	0.2	13	10.0	8.5	18.1	100	100	84.7
United States	24	71	79	0.6	4	19.5	18.0	13.7	100	100	74.2
Uruguay	27	..	78	0.5	21	1.3	2.5	0.3	94	100	47.9
Uzbekistan	30	..	65	0.1	128	..	4.6	2.3	84	100	19.4
Venezuela, RB	68	..	..	..	33	6.2	6.1	50.2	82	..	35.9
Vietnam	56	53	80	0.4	199	0.3	1.5	4.6	37	76	27.9
West Bank and Gaza	..	..	50	..	5	..	0.5	0.6	..	92	36.4
Yemen, Rep.	210	10	28	..	49	0.8	1.0	0.7	24	53	12.3
Zambia	470	15	41	13.5	462	0.3	0.2	36.0	46	48	10.1
Zimbabwe	790	43	59[d]	14.3	633	1.5	0.7	28.0	41	40	11.5
World	**260 w**	**58 w**	**62 w**	**0.8 w**	**128 w**	**4.2[e] w**	**4.8[e] w**	**11.9 w**	**47 w**	**62 w**	**30.2 w**
Low income	590	22	34	2.6	264	..	0.3	10.6	21	37	5.6
Middle income	210	59	65	0.7	132	2.4	3.4	11.9	39	59	23.8
Lower middle income	300	40	50	0.7	174	1.1	1.5	8.5	29	47	13.5
Upper middle income	60	75	81	0.7	89	3.6	5.3	13.2	46	73	34.1
Low & middle income	290	56	61	0.9	150	2.2	3.0	11.6	37	56	21.5
East Asia & Pacific	89	75	78	0.2	123	1.8	4.3	13.3	30	66	29.8
Europe & Central Asia	34	..	69	0.6	90	9.8	7.8	7.7	80	84	39.3
Latin America & Carib.	86	58	75	0.5	43	2.3	2.8	19.8	68	79	34.0
Middle East & N. Africa	88	42	62	0.1	42	2.6	3.8	4.0	73	88	20.9
South Asia	290	42	51	0.3	192	0.7	1.2	5.6	22	38	8.1
Sub-Saharan Africa	650	15	22	5.5	271	0.9	0.8	11.6	26	31	11.3
High income	15	70	..	0.3	14	11.8	11.9	12.7	100	100	73.4
Euro area	7	..	..	0.3	..	8.9	8.0	16.5	100	100	71.2

a. Data are from the International Telecommunication Union's (ITU) World Telecommunication/ICT Indicators database. Please cite ITU for third-party use of these data. b. Data are for the most recent year available. c. Includes Hong Kong SAR, China. d. Data are for 2011. e. Includes emissions not allocated to specific countries.

About the data

The Millennium Development Goals address concerns common to all economies. Diseases and environmental degradation do not respect national boundaries. Epidemic diseases, wherever they occur, pose a threat to people everywhere. And environmental damage in one location may affect the well-being of plants, animals, and humans far away. The indicators in the table relate to goals 5, 6, and 7 and the targets of goal 8 that address access to new technologies. For the other targets of goal 8, see table 1.4.

The target of achieving universal access to reproductive health has been added to goal 5 to address the importance of family planning and health services in improving maternal health and preventing maternal death. Women with multiple pregnancies are more likely to die in childbirth. Access to contraception is an important way to limit and space births.

Measuring disease prevalence or incidence can be difficult. Most developing economies lack reporting systems for monitoring diseases. Estimates are often derived from survey data and report data from sentinel sites, extrapolated to the general population. Tracking diseases such as HIV/AIDS, which has a long latency between contraction of the virus and the appearance of symptoms, or malaria, which has periods of dormancy, can be particularly difficult. The table shows the estimated prevalence of HIV among adults ages 15–49. Prevalence among older populations can be affected by life-prolonging treatment. The incidence of tuberculosis is based on case notifications and estimates of cases detected in the population.

Carbon dioxide emissions are the primary source of greenhouse gases, which contribute to global warming, threatening human and natural habitats. In recognition of the vulnerability of animal and plant species, a new target of reducing biodiversity loss has been added to goal 7. Increasing the proportion of terrestrial and marine areas protected helps defend vulnerable plant and animal species and safeguard biodiversity.

Access to reliable supplies of safe drinking water and sanitary disposal of excreta are two of the most important means of improving human health and protecting the environment. Improved sanitation facilities prevent human, animal, and insect contact with excreta.

Internet use includes narrowband and broadband Internet. Narrowband is often limited to basic applications; broadband is essential to promote e-business, e-learning, e-government, and e-health.

Definitions

• **Maternal mortality ratio** is the number of women who die from pregnancy-related causes during pregnancy and childbirth, per 100,000 live births. Data are from various years and adjusted to a common 2008 base year. The values are modeled estimates (see *About the data* for table 2.19). • **Contraceptive prevalence rate** is the percentage of women ages 15–49 married or in union who are practicing, or whose sexual partners are practicing, any form of contraception. • **HIV prevalence** is the percentage of people ages 15–49 who are infected with HIV. • **Incidence of tuberculosis** is the estimated number of new tuberculosis cases (pulmonary, smear positive, and extrapulmonary). • **Carbon dioxide emissions** are those stemming from the burning of fossil fuels and the manufacture of cement. They include emissions produced during consumption of solid, liquid, and gas fuels and gas flaring (see table 3.9). • **Nationally protected terrestrial and marine areas** are terrestrial and marine protected areas as a percentage of total territorial area, where all nationally designated protected areas with known location and extent are included. All overlaps between different designations and categories, buffered points, and polygons are removed, and all the undated protected areas are dated. • **Access to improved sanitation facilities** is the percentage of the population with at least adequate access to excreta disposal facilities (private or shared, but not public) that can effectively prevent human, animal, and insect contact with excreta (facilities do not have to include treatment to render sewage outflows innocuous). Improved facilities range from simple but protected pit latrines to flush toilets with a sewerage connection. To be effective, facilities must be correctly constructed and properly maintained. • **Internet users** are people with access to the worldwide network.

Location of indicators for Millennium Development Goals 5–7	**1.3a**
Goal 5. Improve maternal health	**Table**
5.1 Maternal mortality ratio	1.3, 2.19
5.2 Proportion of births attended by skilled health personnel	2.19
5.3 Contraceptive prevalence rate	1.3, 2.19
5.4 Adolescent fertility rate	2.19
5.5 Antenatal care coverage	1.5, 2.19
5.6 Unmet need for family planning	2.19
Goal 6. Combat HIV/AIDS, malaria, and other diseases	
6.1 HIV prevalence among pregnant women ages 15–24	1.3*, 2.22*
6.2 Condom use at last high-risk sex	—
6.3 Proportion of population ages 15–24 with comprehensive, correct knowledge of HIV/AIDS	—
6.4 Ratio of school attendance of orphans to school attendance of nonorphans ages 10–14	—
6.5 Proportion of population with advanced HIV infection with access to antiretroviral drugs	2.22
6.6 Incidence and death rates associated with malaria	—
6.7 Proportion of children under age 5 sleeping under insecticide-treated bednets	2.18
6.8 Proportion of children under age 5 with fever who are treated with appropriate antimalarial drugs	2.18
6.9 Incidence, prevalence, and death rates associated with tuberculosis	1.3, 2.22
6.10 Proportion of tuberculosis cases detected and cured under directly observed treatment, short course	2.18
Goal 7. Ensure environmental sustainability	
7.1 Proportion of land area covered by forest	3.1
7.2 Carbon dioxide emissions, total, per capita, and per $1 purchasing power parity GDP	3.9
7.3 Consumption of ozone-depleting substances	3.10*
7.4 Proportion of fish stocks within safe biological limits	—
7.5 Proportion of total water resources used	3.5
7.6 Proportion of terrestrial and marine areas protected	1.3
7.7 Proportion of species threatened with extinction	—
7.8 Proportion of population using an improved drinking water source	2.18, 3.5
7.9 Proportion of population using an improved sanitation facility	1.3, 2.18, 3.13
7.10 Proportion of urban population living in slums	—

— No data are available in the World Development Indicators database. * Table shows information on related indicators.

Data sources

The indicators here and throughout this book have been compiled by World Bank staff from primary and secondary sources. Efforts have been made to harmonize the data series used to compile this table with those published on the United Nations Millennium Development Goals Web site (www.un.org/millenniumgoals), but some differences in timing, sources, and definitions remain. For more information see the data sources for the indicators listed in tables 1.3a and 1.4a.

Development Assistance Committee members

	Net official development assistance (ODA) by donor		Least developed countries' access to high-income markets								Support to agriculture
	% of donor GNI	For basic social services[a] % of total sector-allocable ODA	Goods (excluding arms) admitted free of tariffs % of exports from least developed countries		Agricultural products		Average tariff on exports of least developed countries % Textiles		Clothing		% of GDP
	2010	2010	2003	2009	2003	2009	2003	2009	2003	2009	2010
Australia	0.32	14.6	99.9	100.0	0.2	0.0	0.1	0.0	1.2	0.0	0.12
Canada	0.33	18.1	97.5	100.0	0.2	0.1	0.2	0.2	1.7	1.7	0.67
European Union			96.6	98.4	1.8	0.5	0.1	0.1	1.2	1.2	0.72
Austria	0.32	3.1									
Belgium	0.64	11.7									
Denmark	0.90	10.4									
Finland	0.55	8.4									
France	0.50	8.6									
Germany	0.38	5.9									
Greece	0.17	6.6									
Ireland	0.53	22.9									
Italy	0.15	12.5									
Luxembourg	1.09	34.5									
Netherlands	0.81	7.6									
Portugal	0.29	6.6									
Spain	0.43	13.6									
Sweden	0.97	12.4									
United Kingdom	0.56	12.7									
Japan	0.20	2.5	44.8	99.4	4.7	1.2	2.7	2.6	0.1	0.1	1.09
Korea, Rep.[b]	0.12	4.3	25.1[c]	48.2	27.6[c]	50.2	10.9[c]	6.4	11.3[c]	6.2	2.01
New Zealand[b]	0.26	16.6	97.7	98.8	4.0	0.0	0.3	0.0	0.4	0.0	0.23
Norway	1.10	11.1	98.6	100.0	4.7	0.2	0.0	0.0	1.2	1.0	0.99
Switzerland	0.41	11.0	96.3	100.0	5.4	0.0	0.0	0.0	0.0	0.0	1.11
United States	0.21	31.0	67.2	75.8	6.3	5.7	6.4	5.7	12.3	11.3	0.91

Heavily indebted poor countries (HIPCs)

	HIPC decision point[d]	HIPC completion point[d]	HIPC Initiative assistance end-2010 net present value $ millions	MDRI assistance end-2010 net present value $ millions		HIPC decision point[d]	HIPC completion point[d]	HIPC Initiative assistance end-2010 net present value $ millions	MDRI assistance end-2010 net present value $ millions
Afghanistan	Jul. 2007	Jan. 2010	653	20	Haiti	Nov. 2006	Jun. 2009	163	674
Benin	Jul. 2000	Mar. 2003	384	756	Honduras	Jul. 2000	Apr. 2005	814	1,884
Bolivia[e]	Feb. 2000	Jun. 2001	1,948	1,956	Liberia	Mar. 2008	Jun. 2010	2,957	241
Burkina Faso[e,f]	Jul. 2000	Apr. 2002	810	765	Madagascar	Dec. 2000	Oct. 2004	1,224	1,584
Burundi	Aug. 2005	Jan. 2009	1,008	91	Malawi[f]	Dec. 2000	Aug. 2006	1,375	914
Cameroon	Oct. 2000	Apr. 2006	1,856	885	Mali[e]	Sep. 2000	Mar. 2003	789	1,313
Central African Republic	Sep. 2007	Jun. 2009	674	231	Mauritania	Feb. 2000	Jun. 2002	911	563
Chad	May 2001	Floating	240	669	Mozambique[e]	Apr. 2000	Sep. 2001	3,140	1,318
Comoros	Jun. 2010	Floating	150	45	Nicaragua	Dec. 2000	Jan. 2004	4,847	1,178
Congo, Dem. Rep.	Jul. 2003	Jul. 2010	9,474	528	Niger[f]	Dec. 2000	Apr. 2004	944	646
Congo, Rep.	Mar. 2006	Jan. 2010	1,903	130	Rwanda[f]	Dec. 2000	Apr. 2005	953	286
Côte d'Ivoire	Mar. 2009	Floating	3,243	1,095	São Tomé & Príncipe[f]	Dec. 2000	Mar. 2007	171	38
Ethiopia[f]	Nov. 2001	Apr. 2004	2,728	1,865	Senegal	Jun. 2000	Apr. 2004	715	1,696
Gambia, The	Dec. 2000	Dec. 2007	98	244	Sierra Leone	Mar. 2002	Dec. 2006	917	423
Ghana	Feb. 2002	Jul. 2004	3,083	2,549	Tanzania	Apr. 2000	Nov. 2001	2,969	2,503
Guinea	Dec. 2000	Floating	799	862	Togo	Nov. 2008	Dec. 2010	305	466
Guinea-Bissau	Dec. 2000	Dec. 2010	744	79	Uganda[e]	Feb. 2000	May 2000	1,505	2,263
Guyana[e]	Nov. 2000	Dec. 2003	894	488	Zambia	Dec. 2000	Apr. 2005	3,662	1,871

a. Includes primary education, basic life skills for youth, adult and early childhood education, basic health care, basic health infrastructure, basic nutrition, infectious disease control, health education, health personnel development, population policy and administrative management, reproductive health care, family planning, sexually transmitted disease control including HIV/AIDS, personnel development for population and reproductive health, basic drinking water supply and basic sanitation, and multisector aid for basic social services.
b. Calculated by World Bank staff using the World Integrated Trade Solution based on the United Nations Conference on Trade and Development's Trade Analysis and Information Systems database. c. Data are for 2004. d. Refers to the Enhanced HIPC Initiative. e. Also reached completion point under the original HIPC Initiative. The assistance includes original debt relief.
f. Assistance includes topping up at completion point.

Achieving the Millennium Development Goals requires an open, rule-based global economy in which all countries, rich and poor, participate. Many poor countries, lacking the resources to finance development, burdened by unsustainable debt, and unable to compete globally, need assistance from rich countries. For goal 8—develop a global partnership for development—many indicators therefore monitor the actions of members of the Organisation for Economic Co-operation and Development's (OECD) Development Assistance Committee (DAC).

Official development assistance (ODA) has risen in recent years as a share of donor countries' gross national income (GNI), but the poorest economies need additional assistance to achieve the Millennium Development Goals. In 2010 net ODA from OECD DAC members rose 3.2 percent in real terms, to $131.1 billion or 0.33 percent of OECD DAC members' combined GNI.

One important action that high-income economies can take is to reduce barriers to exports from low- and middle-income economies. The European Union has begun to eliminate tariffs on imports of "everything but arms" from least developed countries, and the United States offers special concessions to imports from Sub-Saharan Africa. However, these programs still have many restrictions.

Average tariffs in the table reflect high-income OECD member tariff schedules for exports of countries designated least developed countries by the United Nations. Although average tariffs have been falling, averages may disguise high tariffs on specific goods (see table 6.7 for each country's share of tariff lines with "international peaks"). The averages in the table include ad valorem duties and equivalents.

Subsidies to agricultural producers and exporters in OECD countries are another barrier to developing economies' exports. Agricultural subsidies in OECD economies are estimated at $366 billion in 2010.

The Debt Initiative for Heavily Indebted Poor Countries (HIPCs), an important step in placing debt relief within the framework of poverty reduction, is the first comprehensive approach to reducing the external debt of the world's poorest, most heavily indebted countries. A 1999 review led to an enhancement of the framework. In 2005, to further reduce the debt of HIPCs and provide resources for meeting the Millennium Development Goals, the Multilateral Debt Relief Initiative (MDRI), proposed by the Group of Eight countries, was launched.

Under the MDRI four multilateral institutions—the International Development Association (IDA), International Monetary Fund (IMF), African Development Fund (AfDF), and Inter-American Development Bank (IDB)—provide 100 percent debt relief on eligible debts due to them from countries having completed the HIPC Initiative process. Data in the table refer to status as of September 2011 and might not show countries that have since reached the decision or completion point. Debt relief under the HIPC Initiative has reduced future debt payments by $59 billion (in end-2010 net present value terms) for 36 countries that have reached the decision point. And 32 countries that have reached the completion point have received additional assistance of $33 billion (in end-2010 net present value terms) under the MDRI.

• **Net official development assistance (ODA)** is grants and loans (net of repayments of principal) that meet the DAC definition of ODA and are made to countries on the DAC list of recipients. • **ODA for basic social services** is aid commitments by DAC donors for basic education, primary health care, nutrition, population policies and programs, reproductive health, and water and sanitation services. • **Goods admitted free of tariffs** are exports of goods (excluding arms) from least developed countries admitted without tariff. • **Average tariff** is the unweighted average of the effectively applied rates for all products subject to tariffs. • **Agricultural products** are plant and animal products, including tree crops but excluding timber and fish products. • **Textiles** and **clothing** are natural and synthetic fibers and fabrics and articles of clothing made from them. • **Support to agriculture** is gross transfers from taxpayers and consumers arising from policy measures, net of associated budgetary receipts, regardless of their objectives and impacts on farm production and income or consumption of farm products. • **HIPC decision point** is when a heavily indebted poor country with an established track record of good performance under adjustment programs supported by the IMF and the World Bank commits to additional reforms and a poverty reduction strategy and starts receiving debt relief. • **HIPC completion point** is when a country successfully completes the key structural reforms agreed on at the decision point, including implementing a poverty reduction strategy. The country then receives full debt relief under the HIPC Initiative without further policy conditions. • **HIPC Initiative assistance** is the debt relief committed as of the decision point (assuming full participation of creditors). Topping-up assistance and assistance provided under the original HIPC Initiative were committed in net present value terms as of the decision point and are converted to end-2010 terms. • **MDRI assistance** is 100 percent debt relief on eligible debt from IDA, IMF, AfDF, and IDB, delivered in full to countries having reached the HIPC completion point.

Location of indicators for Millennium Development Goal 8	1.4a
Goal 8. Develop a global partnership for development	**Table**
8.1 Net ODA as a percentage of DAC donors' gross national income	1.4
8.2 Proportion of ODA for basic social services	1.4
8.3 Proportion of ODA that is untied	—
8.4 Proportion of ODA received in landlocked countries as a percentage of GNI	—
8.5 Proportion of ODA received in small island developing states as a percentage of GNI	—
8.6 Proportion of total developed country imports (by value, excluding arms) from least developed countries admitted free of duty	1.4
8.7 Average tariffs imposed by developed countries on agricultural products and textiles and clothing from least developed countries	1.4, 6.7*
8.8 Agricultural support estimate for OECD countries as a percentage of GDP	1.4
8.9 Proportion of ODA provided to help build trade capacity	—
8.10 Number of countries reaching HIPC decision and completion points	1.4
8.11 Debt relief committed under new HIPC initiative	1.4
8.12 Debt services as a percentage of exports of goods and services	6.9*
8.13 Proportion of population with access to affordable, essential drugs on a sustainable basis	—
8.14 Fixed telephone lines per 100 people	5.11
8.15 Mobile cellular subscribers per 100 people	5.11
8.16 Internet users per 100 people	1.3, 5.12

— No data are available in the World Development Indicators database. * Table shows information on related indicators.

Data on ODA are from the OECD. Data on goods admitted free of tariffs and average tariffs are from the World Trade Organization in collaboration with the United Nations Conference on Trade and Development and the International Trade Centre (www. mdg-trade.org). Data on support to agriculture are from the OECD's *Producer and Consumer Support Estimates, OECD Database 1986–2010*. Data on the HIPC Initiative and MDRI are from the World Bank's Economic Policy and Debt Department.

Women in development

	Female population	Life expectancy at birth		Pregnant women receiving prenatal care	Teenage mothers	Women in wage employment in nonagricultural sector	Unpaid family workers		Female part-time employment	Female legislators, senior officials, and managers	Women in parliaments	
			years		% of women ages 15–19	% of nonagricultural wage employment	Male % of male employment	Female % of female employment				
	% of total	Male	Female	%					% of total	% of total	% of total seats	
	2010	2010	2010	2005–10[a]	2005–10[a]	2009	2010	2010	2005–10[a]	2005–10[a]	1990	2011
Afghanistan	48.3	48	48	36	..	18	..	..	..	..	4	28
Albania	49.9	74	80	97	3	..	..	..	..	..	29	16
Algeria	49.5	71	74	89	..	15	..	..	..	5	2	8
Angola	50.5	49	52	80	29	..	..	..	..	..	15	39
Argentina	51.1	72	79	99	..	..	0.4[b]	1.2[b]	65[b]	23[b]	6	39
Armenia	53.5	71	77	99	5	40	7.6	17.1	56	22	36	9
Australia	50.2	80	84	98	..	47	0.2	0.3	70[b]	37	6	25
Austria	51.2	78	83	..	..	48	1.9	2.4	80	29	12	28
Azerbaijan	50.5	68	74	77	6	43	..	..	..	7	..	16
Bahrain	37.6	74	76	100	..	10	0.5	0.8	..	12	..	3
Bangladesh	49.4	68	69	53	33	..	..	..	..	10	10	19
Belarus	53.5	65	77	99	..	56	..	..	..	..	..	32
Belgium	51.0	77	83	..	..	47	0.3	1.8	80	34	9	39
Benin	50.7	54	57	84	21	..	..	..	..	..	3	8
Bolivia	50.1	64	69	86	18	38	..	..	56	29	9	25
Bosnia and Herzegovina	51.9	73	78	99	..	36	2.6	10.4	..	..	..	17
Botswana	49.6	54	52	94	..	45	..	..	55	30	5	8
Brazil	50.8	70	77	98	..	42	3.4	6.3	68	36	5	9
Bulgaria	51.7	70	77	..	..	51	0.7	1.5	52	34	21	21
Burkina Faso	50.4	54	56	85	..	27	..	..	..	31	..	15
Burundi	50.9	49	51	99	..	..	..	..	..	..	..	32
Cambodia	51.1	61	64	89	8	..	25.2	60.8	..	21	..	21
Cameroon	50.1	50	52	82	..	..	..	..	..	..	14	14
Canada	50.4	79	83	100	..	51	0.1	0.2	67[b]	36[b]	13	25
Central African Republic	50.7	46	49	69	..	..	..	..	..	..	4	13
Chad	50.3	48	51	53	..	..	..	..	..	..	..	13
Chile	50.6	76	82	..	..	37	1.1	2.5	58	24	..	14
China	48.1[c]	72[c]	75[c]	92	..	..	..	..	..	17	21	21
Hong Kong SAR, China	52.6	80	86	..	..	50	0.1	1.0	..	29	..	..
Colombia	50.8	70	77	97	20	48	3.7	7.1	60	38	5	13
Congo, Dem. Rep.	50.3	47	50	86	24	..	..	..	..	..	5	10
Congo, Rep.	49.9	56	58	86	27	..	..	..	..	..	14	7
Costa Rica	49.2	77	82	90	..	41	0.9	2.6	64	30	11	39
Côte d'Ivoire	49.0	54	56	85	..	..	..	..	..	..	6	9
Croatia	51.9	74	80	100	4	46	1.1	4.6	60	27	..	24
Cuba	49.7	77	81	100	..	43	..	..	..	29	34	43
Cyprus	49.0	77	82	99	..	48	1.3	2.9	64	13	2	11
Czech Republic	51.0	74	81	..	..	46	0.3	1.0	69	28	..	22
Denmark	50.4	77	81	..	..	50	0.1	0.5	63	22	31	38
Dominican Republic	49.8	70	76	99	21	39	..	..	50	31	8	21
Ecuador	49.9	73	78	..	..	..	7.4	19.9	54	28[b]	5	32
Egypt, Arab Rep.	49.8	71	75	74	10	18	..	..	..	11	4	2
El Salvador	52.5	67	77	94	23	48	7.1	7.2	55	25	12	19
Eritrea	50.7	59	63	..	..	..	..	..	..	..	..	22
Estonia	53.9	71	81	..	..	54	0.2	0.2	67	37	..	20
Ethiopia	50.2	57	60	28	17	..	..	..	..	16[b]	..	28
Finland	50.9	77	83	..	..	52	0.6	0.5	62	30	32	43
France	51.3	78	85	..	..	49	0.3	0.9	78	39	7	19
Gabon	49.8	61	63	..	..	..	..	..	..	..	13	15
Gambia, The	50.6	57	59	98	..	..	..	..	..	..	8	8
Georgia	52.9	70	77	98	10	48	19.6	37.9	..	34	..	7
Germany	51.0	78	83	..	..	48	0.3	0.9	80	30	..	33
Ghana	49.1	63	65	90	13	..	..	..	..	..	..	8
Greece	50.5	78	83	..	..	43	3.3	9.2	66	30	7	17
Guatemala	51.3	67	74	93	22	..	..	..	..	..	7	12
Guinea	49.5	52	55	88	32	29	..	..	..	..	..	..
Guinea-Bissau	50.4	46	49	93	..	..	..	..	..	..	20	10
Haiti	50.4	61	63	85	14	..	..	..	..	..	..	11

	Female population	Life expectancy at birth		Pregnant women receiving prenatal care	Teenage mothers	Women in wage employment in nonagricultural sector	Unpaid family workers		Female part-time employment	Female legislators, senior officials, and managers	Women in parliaments	
		years			% of women ages 15–19	% of nonagricultural wage employment	Male % of male employment	Female % of female employment			% of total seats	
	% of total	Male	Female	%					% of total	% of total		
	2010	2010	2010	2005–10[a]	2005–10[a]	2009	2010	2010	2005–10[a]	2005–10[a]	1990	2011
Honduras	50.0	71	75	92	22	42	..	..	..	41	10	18
Hungary	52.5	71	78	..	..	49	0.2	0.4	66	36	21	9
India	48.3	64	67	75	16	..	..	..	..	..	5	11
Indonesia	50.1	67	71	95	9	32	8.1	32.4	..	22	12	18
Iran, Islamic Rep.	49.3	71	75	98	..	..	4.8	29.7	..	13	2	3
Iraq	49.8	65	72	84	..	12	..	..	..	..	11	25
Ireland	50.0	78	83	..	..	52	0.7	0.7	76	33	8	15
Israel	50.7	80	83	..	..	50	0.1	0.3	74	32	7	19
Italy	51.1	79	84	..	..	44	1.2	2.3	77	33	13	21
Jamaica	50.8	70	76	99	14	48	0.4	2.1	..	..	5	13
Japan	51.3	80	86	..	..	42	1.1	6.9	70	10	1	11
Jordan	48.6	72	75	99	5	16	0.5	0.5	..	..	0	11
Kazakhstan	52.0	64	73	100	7	50	0.6	0.9	..	38	..	18
Kenya	50.1	55	58	92	18	..	..	..	..	..	1	10
Korea, Dem. Rep.	50.9	65	72	100	..	..	..	..	..	..	21	15
Korea, Rep.	50.1	77	84	..	..	42	1.2	12.5	60	10	2	16
Kosovo	..	68	72	..	..	..	..	..	..	..	..	..
Kuwait	40.3	74	76	100	..	..	..	..	..	14	..	8
Kyrgyz Republic	50.7	65	73	97	..	51	..	..	..	35	..	23
Lao PDR	50.1	66	68	71	17	..	..	..	..	..	6	25
Latvia	54.0	69	78	..	..	55	1.3	1.4	61	41	..	20
Lebanon	51.2	70	75	..	..	..	..	..	..	8	0	3
Lesotho	50.9	48	47	92	..	..	..	..	..	52	..	24
Liberia	49.8	55	57	79	38	..	12.5	19.7	..	..	..	13
Libya	49.3	72	77	93	..	..	..	..	..	..	..	8
Lithuania	53.5	68	79	..	..	53	1.5	1.9	61	41	..	19
Macedonia, FYR	49.9	73	77	94	..	42	6.3	16.6	49	28	..	31
Madagascar	50.2	65	68	86	32	..	..	..	..	22	7	13
Malawi	50.0	53	54	92	..	..	..	..	..	..	10	21
Malaysia	49.3	72	76	79	..	39	2.6	8.1	..	24	5	10
Mali	50.0	50	52	70	36	..	..	..	..	..	..	10
Mauritania	49.7	57	60	75	..	..	..	..	..	..	..	22
Mauritius	50.6	69	77	..	..	37	1.0	4.9	..	23	7	19
Mexico	50.7	74	79	96	..	39	4.8	9.7	54	31	12	26
Moldova	52.6	65	73	98	6	54	1.3	3.5	..	38	..	19
Mongolia	50.6	64	72	100	..	51	10.3	35.1	..	47	25	4
Morocco	51.0	70	74	..	..	21	15.0	48.6	..	13	0	11
Mozambique	51.3	49	51	92	..	..	..	..	..	..	16	39
Myanmar	50.7	63	66	80	..	..	..	..	..	..	..	4
Namibia	50.3	62	63	95	15	..	..	..	..	36	7	24
Nepal	50.4	68	69	44	19	..	..	..	..	14	6	33
Netherlands	50.4	79	83	..	..	48	0.3	1.1	75	29	21	39
New Zealand	50.9	79	83	..	..	51	0.7	1.3	72[b]	40[b]	14	34
Nicaragua	50.5	71	77	90	25	38	..	..	51	41	15	21
Niger	49.7	54	55	46	39	36	..	..	..	..	5	13
Nigeria	49.4	51	52	58	23	..	..	..	..	..	..	4
Norway	50.0	79	83	..	..	50	0.2	0.3	70	34	36	40
Oman	41.3	71	76	99	..	22	..	..	..	9	..	0
Pakistan	49.2	64	66	61	9	13	19.7	65.0	..	3	10	22
Panama	49.6	73	79	96	..	42	3.0	6.8	48	48	8	9
Papua New Guinea	49.0	60	65	79	..	..	..	..	..	..	0	1
Paraguay	49.5	70	74	96	12	40	10.4	11.0	55	34	6	13
Peru	49.9	71	76	95	26	38	4.5[b]	8.7[b]	61[b]	19[b]	6	22
Philippines	49.8	65	72	91	10	42	9.0	17.4	..	55	9	22
Poland	51.8	72	81	..	..	48	2.5	5.5	68	36	14	20
Portugal	51.6	76	82	..	..	49	0.7	1.2	66	32	8	27
Puerto Rico	51.9	75	83	..	..	42	0.0	0.0	..	43	..	..
Qatar	24.3	78	78	100	..	10	..	..	..	7	..	0

	Female population	Life expectancy at birth		Pregnant women receiving prenatal care	Teenage mothers	Women in wage employment in nonagricultural sector	Unpaid family workers		Female part-time employment	Female legislators, senior officials, and managers	Women in parliaments	
		years			% of women ages 15–19	% of nonagricultural wage employment	Male % of male employment	Female % of female employment			% of total seats	
	% of total 2010	Male 2010	Female 2010	% 2005–10[a]	2005–10[a]	2009	2010	2010	% of total 2005–10[a]	% of total 2005–10[a]	1990	2011
Romania	51.5	70	77	..	..	46	6.9	20.0	47	32	34	11
Russian Federation	53.7	63	75	..	..	53	*0.1*	*0.1*	62	37	..	14
Rwanda	50.9	54	56	98	6	..	..	..	..	0	17	56
Saudi Arabia	44.6	73	75	97	..	*15*	..	..	..	8	..	0
Senegal	50.4	58	60	94	18	..	..	..	..	..	13	23
Serbia	50.5	71	77	98	..	44	*4.1*	*15.6*	..	36	..	22
Sierra Leone	51.2	47	48	87	34	..	..	..	..	..	..	13
Singapore	49.6	79	84	..	..	45	*0.3*	*1.0*	..	31	5	22
Slovak Republic	51.4	72	79	..	..	48	0.1	0.2	59	35	..	16
Slovenia	51.1	76	83	..	..	48	3.8	6.2	59	35	..	14
Somalia	50.4	49	53	26	..	..	..	..	..	..	4	7
South Africa	50.5	51	53	97	..	45	*0.4*	*1.4*	..	30	3	45
South Sudan	..	62	61								..	..
Spain	50.6	79	85	..	..	47	0.7	1.0	78	34	15	37
Sri Lanka	50.6	72	78	99	..	31	4.5[b]	22.3[b]	..	24[b]	5	6
Sudan	49.6	59	63	64	..	..	..	..	..	..	..	26
Swaziland	50.8	49	48	97	23	..	..	..	..	..	4	14
Sweden	50.2	80	84	..	..	50	0.3	0.2	63	31	38	45
Switzerland	50.9	80	85	..	..	48	1.6	2.4	80	33	14	29
Syrian Arab Republic	49.4	74	77	88	..	15	3.3	12.4	27	10	9	12
Tajikistan	50.8	64	71	80	..	..	..	..	..	..	..	19
Tanzania	50.1	57	58	88	23	..	..	..	..	16	..	36
Thailand	50.9	71	77	99	..	46	*13.6*	*28.5*	..	24	3	13
Timor-Leste	49.0	61	63	84	7	..	..	..	..	..	..	29
Togo	50.5	55	58	87	..	..	..	..	..	..	5	11
Trinidad and Tobago	51.5	66	73	96	..	..	..	..	..	43	17	29
Tunisia	50.0	73	77	96	..	..	..	..	..	..	4	28
Turkey	50.1	71	76	95	..	24	5.1	35.2	58	10	1	14
Turkmenistan	50.8	61	69	99	..	..	..	..	..	..	26	17
Uganda	50.0	53	54	94	25	..	..	..	..	33	12	35
Ukraine	54.0	65	76	99	4	55	*0.4*	*0.3*	..	39	..	8
United Arab Emirates	30.5	76	78	100	..	*20*	*0.0*	*0.0*	..	10	0	23
United Kingdom	50.8	79	82	..	..	47	0.2	0.4	75	36	6	22
United States	50.7	76	81	..	..	48	*0.1*	*0.1*	67	43	7	17
Uruguay	51.7	73	80	96	..	*46*	2.1[b]	0.8[b]	64[b]	40	6	15
Uzbekistan	50.3	65	71	99	..	*39*	..	..	..	..	..	22
Venezuela, RB	49.8	71	77	..	..	*42*	0.5	1.2	64	27	10	17
Vietnam	50.6	73	77	91	..	..	..	..	..	22	18	24
West Bank and Gaza	49.2	71	74	99	..	*18*	5.5	19.8	..	10	..	..
Yemen, Rep.	49.7	64	67	47	..	6	..	..	..	4	4	0
Zambia	49.9	48	49	94	28	..	..	..	..	19	7	14
Zimbabwe	50.7	51	49	90[d]	21	..	..	..	..	..	11	15
World	**49.6 w**	**68 w**	**72 w**	**84 w**	**.. w**	**.. w**	**.. w**	**.. w**	**.. w**		**13 w**	**19 w**
Low income	50.1	58	60	69	..	..	..	..	..	..	..	20
Middle income	49.3	67	71	86	..	..	..	..	..	..	13	18
Lower middle income	49.2	64	67	78	..	..	..	..	..	..	11	15
Upper middle income	49.4	71	75	94	..	..	..	..	..	..	14	19
Low & middle income	49.4	66	70	83	..	..	..	..	..	..	13	18
East Asia & Pacific	48.8	70	74	92	..	..	..	..	..	..	17	18
Europe & Central Asia	52.3	66	75	..	..	48	1.9	5.3	..	..	..	16
Latin America & Carib.	50.6	71	77	97	..	*41*	3.5	6.8	62	..	12	23
Middle East & N. Africa	49.7	70	74	85	..	..	..	..	..	..	4	9
South Asia	48.6	64	67	71	16	..	..	..	..	..	6	20
Sub-Saharan Africa	50.0	53	55	74	..	..	..	..	..	..	..	20
High income	50.5	77	83	..	..	47	0.6	2.2	71	..	12	23
Euro area	51.0	78	84	..	..	47	0.7	1.5	77	..	12	26

a. Data are for the most recent year available. b. Limited coverage. c. Includes Taiwan, China. d. Data are for 2011.

About the data

Despite much progress in recent decades, gender inequalities remain pervasive in many dimensions of life—worldwide. But while disparities exist throughout the world, they are most prevalent in developing countries. Gender inequalities in the allocation of such resources as education, health care, nutrition, and political voice matter because of the strong association with well-being, productivity, and economic growth. These patterns of inequality begin at an early age, with boys routinely receiving a larger share of education and health spending than do girls, for example.

Because of biological differences girls are expected to experience lower infant and child mortality rates and to have a longer life expectancy than boys. This biological advantage may be overshadowed, however, by gender inequalities in nutrition and medical interventions and by inadequate care during pregnancy and delivery, so that female rates of illness and death sometimes exceed male rates. Gender bias can be seen in child mortality rates (table 2.23) and life expectancy at birth. Female child mortality rates that are as high as or higher than male child mortality rates may indicate discrimination against girls.

Having a child during the teenage years limits girls' opportunities for better education, jobs, and income. Pregnancy is more likely to be unintended during the teenage years, and births are more likely to be premature and are associated with greater risks of complications during delivery and of death. In many countries maternal mortality (tables 1.3 and 2.19) is a leading cause of death among women of reproductive age, although most of those deaths are preventable.

Data on women in wage employment in the nonagricultural sector show the extent to which women have access to paid employment—which affects their integration into the monetary economy—and indicate the degree to which labor markets are open to women in industry and services—which affects not only equal employment opportunity for women, but also economic efficiency through flexibility of the labor market and the economy's capacity to adapt to changes over time. In many developing countries nonagricultural wage employment accounts for only a small portion of total employment. As a result, the contribution of women to the national economy is underestimated and therefore misrepresented. The indicator is difficult to interpret without additional information on the share of women in total employment, which allows an assessment to be made of whether women are under- or overrepresented in nonagricultural wage employment. The indicator does not reveal differences in the quality of nonagricultural wage employment in terms of earnings, work conditions, or legal and social protection. The indicator also does not reflect whether women reap the economic benefits of such employment. Finally, female employment and the employment share of the agricultural sector for both men and women tend to be underreported.

Women's wage work is important for economic growth and the well-being of families. But women often face such obstacles as restricted access to credit markets, capital, land, and training and education; time constraints due to traditional family responsibilities; and labor market bias and discrimination. These obstacles force women to limit their full participation in paid economic activities, to be less productive, and to receive lower wages. More women than men are in unpaid family employment and part-time employment. And men and women have different occupational distributions. There is no official International Labour Organization definition of full-time work, so the definition of part-time workers differs across countries, and thus comparisons should be made with caution.

The female share of high-skilled occupations such as legislators, senior officials, and managers indicates gender segregation of employment. Women are vastly underrepresented in decisionmaking positions in government, although there is some evidence of recent improvement. Gender parity in parliamentary representation is still far from being realized. Without representation at this level, it is difficult for women to influence policy.

For information on other aspects of gender, see tables 1.2 (Millennium Development Goals: eradicating poverty and saving lives), 1.3 (Millennium Development Goals: protecting our common environment), 2.3 (Employment by economic activity), 2.4 (Decent work and productive employment), 2.5 (Unemployment), 2.6 (Children at work), 2.10 (Assessing vulnerability and security), 2.13 (Education efficiency), 2.14 (Education completion and outcomes), 2.15 (Education gaps by income and gender), 2.19 (Reproductive health), 2.22 (Health risk factors and future challenges), and 2.23 (Mortality).

Definitions

• **Female population** is the percentage of the population that is female. • **Life expectancy at birth** is the number of years a newborn infant would live if prevailing patterns of mortality at the time of its birth were to stay the same throughout its life. • **Pregnant women receiving prenatal care** are women attended at least once during pregnancy by skilled health personnel for reasons related to pregnancy. • **Teenage mothers** are women ages 15–19 who already have children or are currently pregnant. • **Women in wage employment in nonagricultural sector** are female wage employees in the nonagricultural sector as a percentage of total nonagricultural wage employment. • **Unpaid family workers** are those who work without pay in a market-oriented establishment or activity operated by a related person living in the same household. There is no official International Labour Organization definition of full-time work, so the definition of part-time workers differs across countries and thus comparisons should be made with caution. • **Female part-time employment** is the percentage of part-time workers who are female. Part-time workers are employed people whose normal hours of work are less than those of comparable full-time workers. The definition of part-time varies across countries. • **Female legislators, senior officials, and managers** are the percentage of legislators, senior officials, and managers (International Standard Classification of Occupations–88 category 1) who are female. • **Women in parliaments** are parliamentary seats in a single or lower chamber held by women.

Data sources

Data on female population are from the United Nations Population Division's *World Population Prospects: The 2010 Revision,* and data on life expectancy for more than half the countries in the table (most of them developing countries) are from its *World Population Prospects: The 2010 Revision,* with additional data from census reports, other statistical publications from national statistical offices, Eurostat's *Demographic Statistics,* the Secretariat of the Pacific Community's Statistics and Demography Programme, and the U.S. Bureau of the Census International Data Base. Data on pregnant women receiving prenatal care are from the United Nations Children's Fund's (UNICEF) *The State of the World's Children 2012* based on household surveys, including MEASURE DHS Demographic and Health Surveys by ICF International and Multiple Indicator Cluster Surveys by UNICEF. Data on teenage mothers are from MEASURE DHS Demographic and Health Surveys by ICF International. Data on labor force, employment, and occupation are from the International Labour Organization's *Key Indicators of the Labour Market,* 7th edition. Data on women in parliaments are from the Inter-Parliamentary Union.

	Population	Surface area	Population density	Gross national income				Gross domestic product		Life expectancy at birth	Adult literacy rate	Carbon dioxide emissions
				Atlas method		Purchasing power parity						
	thousands 2010	thousand sq. km 2010	people per sq. km 2010	$ millions 2010	Per capita $ 2010	$ millions 2010	Per capita $ 2010	% growth 2009–10	Per capita % growth 2009–10	years 2010	% ages 15 and older 2005–10[a]	thousand metric tons 2008
American Samoa	68	0.2	342	..	..[b]	..	..	..	..	..	..	..
Andorra	85	0.5	181	3,447	41,750	..	..	3.6	2.1	..	..	539
Antigua and Barbuda	88	0.4	200	1,169	13,280[c]	1,795[d]	20,400[d]	–5.2	–5.4	..	99	447
Aruba	108	0.2	600	..	..[e]	..	..	..	..	75	98	2,288
Bahamas, The	343	13.9	34	6,973	20,610	8,392[d]	24,800[d]	0.9	–0.5	75	..	2,156
Barbados	274	0.4	637	3,454	12,660	5,183	19,000	–5.3	–5.5	77	..	1,353
Belize	345	23.0	15	1,313	3,810	2,139[d]	6,200[d]	2.9	–0.6	76	..	425
Bermuda	65	0.1	1,292	..	..[e]	..	..	–8.1	–8.4	79	..	389
Bhutan	726	38.4	19	1,361	1,870	3,622	4,990	7.4	5.6	67	53	733
Brunei Darussalam	399	5.8	76	12,461	31,800	19,661	50,180	–1.8	–3.6	78	95	10,594
Cape Verde	496	4.0	123	1,620	3,270	1,893	3,820	5.4	4.5	74	85	308
Cayman Islands	56	0.3	234	..	..[e]	..	..	..	..	..	99	557
Channel Islands	153	0.2	807	..	..[e]	..	..	..	..	80	..	..
Comoros	735	1.9	395	550	750	802	1,090	2.1	–0.6	61	74	125
Curaçao	143	0.4	321	..	..[e]	..	..	..	..	..	..	..
Djibouti	889	23.2	38	1,105	1,270	2,149	2,460	5.0	3.0	58	..	524
Dominica	68	0.8	91	458	6,740	812[d]	11,940[d]	0.1	–0.1	..	..	128
Equatorial Guinea	700	28.1	25	10,182	14,550	16,635	23,760	0.9	–1.8	51	93	4,815
Faeroe Islands	49	1.4	35	..	..[e]	..	..	..	..	80	..	708
Fiji	860	18.3	47	3,123	3,630	3,880	4,510	0.3	–0.6	69	..	1,254
French Polynesia	271	4.0	74	..	..[e]	..	..	..	..	75	..	891
Gibraltar	29	0.0	2,924	..	..[e]	..	..	..	..	..	..	422
Greenland	57	410.5	0[f]	1,466	26,020	..	..	–5.4	–5.4	68	..	576
Grenada	104	0.3	306	724	6,960	1,033[d]	9,930[d]	–0.8	–0.7	76	..	246
Guam	179	0.5	331	..	..[e]	..	..	..	..	76	..	..
Guyana	755	215.0	4	2,164	2,870	2,606[d]	3,450[d]	3.6	3.3	70	..	1,525
Iceland	318	103.0	3	10,381	32,640	8,991	28,270	–4.0	–3.8	81	..	2,230
Isle of Man	83	0.6	145	..	..[e]	..	..	..	..	..	..	..
Kiribati	100	0.8	123	200	2,000	352[d]	3,520[d]	1.8	–0.2	..	..	29

About the data

The table shows data for economies with a population between 30,000 and 1 million and for smaller economies if they are members of the World Bank. Where data on gross national income (GNI) per capita are not available, the estimated range is given. For more information on the calculation of GNI and purchasing power parity (PPP) conversion factors, see *About the data* for table 1.1. Additional data for the economies in the table are available on the *World Development Indicators* CD-ROM or at http://data.worldbank.org.

Definitions

• **Population** is based on the de facto definition of population, which counts all residents regardless of legal status or citizenship—except for refugees not permanently settled in the country of asylum, who are generally considered part of the population of their country of origin. The values shown are midyear estimates. For more information, see *About the data* for table 2.1. • **Surface area** is a country's total area, including areas under inland bodies of water and some coastal waterways. • **Population density** is midyear population divided by land area in square kilometers. • **Gross national income (GNI), *Atlas* method,** is the sum of value added by all resident producers plus any product taxes (less subsidies) not included in the valuation of output plus net receipts of primary income (compensation of employees and property income) from abroad. Data are in current U.S. dollars converted using the *World Bank Atlas* method (see *Statistical methods*). • **Purchasing power parity (PPP) GNI** is GNI converted to international dollars using PPP rates. An international dollar has the same purchasing power over GNI that a U.S. dollar has in the United States. • **GNI per capita** is GNI divided by midyear population. • **Gross domestic product (GDP)** is the sum of value added by all resident producers plus any product taxes (less subsidies) not included in the valuation of output. Growth is calculated from constant price GDP data in local

Key indicators for other economies

	Population	Surface area	Population density	Gross national income				Gross domestic product		Life expectancy at birth	Adult literacy rate	Carbon dioxide emissions
				Atlas method		Purchasing power parity						
		thousand sq. km	people per sq. km	$ millions	Per capita $	$ millions	Per capita $	% growth	Per capita % growth	years	% ages 15 and older	thousand metric tons
	thousands 2010	2010	2010	2010	2010	2010	2010	2009–10	2009–10	2010	2005–10[a]	2008
Liechtenstein	36	0.2	225	*4,903*	*137,070*	..	..	–1.2	–1.9	..	..	..
Luxembourg	507	2.6	196	39,030	76,980	31,050	61,240	2.7	0.8	80	..	10,502
Macao SAR, China	544	0.0	19,429	*18,527*	*34,880*	*24,020*	*45,220*	26.4	23.4	81	93	1,335
Maldives	316	0.3	1,053	1,818	5,750	2,563	8,110	9.9	8.4	77	98	920
Malta	416	0.3	1,300	7,958	19,130	10,258	24,660	3.1	2.6	81	92	2,560
Marshall Islands	54	0.2	300	197	3,640	..	..	5.2	4.0	..	..	99
Mayotte	204	0.4	551	..	..[b]	..	..	..	..	78	..	..
Micronesia, Fed. Sts.	111	0.7	159	304	2,740	388[d]	3,490[d]	3.1	2.8	69	..	62
Monaco	35	0.0	17,704	*6,479*	*183,150*	..	..	–2.6	–2.7	..	..	..
Montenegro	632	13.8	47	4,260	6,740	8,073	12,770	2.5	2.2	74	..	1,951
New Caledonia	247	18.6	14	..	..[e]	..	..	..	..	76	96	3,150
Northern Mariana Islands	61	0.5	132	..	..[e]	..	..	..	..	..	..	..
Palau	20	0.5	45	134	6,560	225[d]	11,000[d]	2.0	1.4	..	..	213
Samoa	184	2.8	65	549	2,980	782[d]	4,250[d]	1.7	0.8	72	99	161
San Marino	32	0.1	526	*1,572*	*50,400*	..	..	*1.9*	*1.3*	83	..	..
São Tomé and Príncipe	165	1.0	172	199	1,200	318	1,930	4.5	2.9	64	89	128
Seychelles	87	0.5	189	845	9,710	1,835[d]	21,090[d]	6.2	6.6	73	92	682
Sint Maarten	38	0.0	1,113	..	..[e]	..	..	..	..	..	..	..
Solomon Islands	538	28.9	19	552	1,030	1,192[d]	2,220[d]	7.0	4.2	67	..	198
St. Kitts and Nevis	52	0.3	200	615	11,830	831[d]	15,970[d]	–5.0	–5.5	..	..	249
St. Lucia	174	0.6	285	1,142	6,560	1,830[d]	10,520[d]	3.1	2.1	74	..	396
St. Martin	30	0.1	556	..	..[e]	..	..	..	..	..	..	..
St. Vincent & Grenadines	109	0.4	279	688	6,320	1,184[d]	10,870[d]	–1.3	–1.0	72	..	202
Suriname	525	163.8	3	*3,077*	*5,920*	3,991[d]	7,680[d]	*3.1*	*2.1*	70	95	2,439
Tonga	104	0.8	144	342	3,290	477[d]	4,580[d]	–0.5	–0.9	72	99	176
Turks and Caicos Islands	38	1.0	40	..	..[e]	..	..	..	..	..	..	158
Tuvalu	10	0.0	328	47	4,760[g]	..	..	–1.9	–2.1	..	..	..
Vanuatu	240	12.2	20	633	2,640	1,035[d]	4,310[d]	3.0	0.4	71	82	92
Virgin Islands (U.S.)	110	0.4	314	..	..[e]	..	..	..	..	79	..	..

a. Data are for the most recent year available. b. Estimated to be upper middle income ($3,976–$12,275). c. Included in the aggregates for upper middle-income economies based on earlier data. d. Based on regression; others are extrapolated from the 2005 International Comparison Program benchmark estimates. e. Estimated to be high income ($12,276 or more). f. Less than 0.5. g. Included in the aggregates for lower middle-income economies based on earlier data.

currency. • **GDP per capita** is GDP divided by midyear population. • **Life expectancy at birth** is the number of years a newborn infant would live if prevailing patterns of mortality at the time of its birth were to stay the same throughout its life. • **Adult literacy rate** is the percentage of adults ages 15 and older who can, with understanding, read and write a short, simple statement about their everyday life. • **Carbon dioxide emissions** are those stemming from the burning of fossil fuels and the manufacture of cement. They include carbon dioxide produced during consumption of solid, liquid, and gas fuels and gas flaring.

Data sources

The indicators here and throughout the book are compiled by World Bank staff from primary and secondary sources. More information about the indicators and their sources can be found in the *About the data*, *Definitions*, and *Data sources* entries that accompany each table in subsequent sections.

PEOPLE

The *People* section documents demographic trends, labor force structure, poverty incidence, income distribution, education inputs and outcomes, and health services and status. Together these indicators provide a multidimensional portrait of human development and social welfare. For 2012 a new table has been added, and the contents of others have changed. Table 2.20 now shows data by sex for three measures of the prevalence of child malnutrition—underweight, stunting, and wasting—and for the proportion of overweight children. Data on antiretroviral therapy coverage and cause of death have been added to table 2.22. And table 2.23 now includes neonatal mortality rates computed with the same methodology used to estimate infant and under-five mortality rates. Also new is table 2.24, which presents selected health indicators by income quintile. These subnational data highlight substantial within-country disparities between the poor and rich in mortality and fertility rates and in child and reproductive health outcomes.

Table 2.8 provides more recent data on poverty at international poverty lines for more countries, including global and regional poverty estimates released by the World Bank in February 2012. In 2008, 1.29 billion people, or 22 percent of developing countries' population, lived below the extreme poverty line of $1.25 a day, down from 1.94 billion people, or 52 percent of developing countries' population, in 1981. In 1990, the benchmark year for the Millennium Development Goals, the extreme poverty rate was 43.1 percent.

Progress has been slower at the $2 a day poverty line, around which many people in lower middle-income economies live. The number of people living below $2 a day fell from 2.59 billion in 1981 to 2.47 billion in 2008—a decrease of only 120 million—and the number of people living on $1.25–$2 a day almost doubled

to 1.18 billion in 2008. This bunching up just above the extreme poverty line indicates the vulnerabilities faced by a great many people in the world.

Looking at the trend from 2005 to 2008, both the absolute number and the proportion of people living in extreme poverty declined in every developing country region. This across-the-board reduction over a three-year monitoring cycle is the first since the World Bank began monitoring extreme poverty. Since 2008 food, fuel, and financial crises have had sharp negative impacts on vulnerable populations and slowed poverty reduction in some countries, but global poverty kept falling. In fact, a preliminary survey-based estimate for 2010—based on a much smaller sample than the global update—indicates that the global poverty rate at $1.25 a day fell to less than half its 1990 value. If these results are confirmed by follow-up studies, the first target of the Millennium Development Goals—cutting the extreme poverty rate to half its 1990 level—may have been achieved on a global level before the 2015 target date.

The World Bank's database of international poverty measures now includes income or consumption data collected by national statistical offices drawn from 850 household surveys and interviews with 1.23 million randomly sampled households in nearly 130 countries. The most recent year for which a reliable global estimate can be calculated is 2008, because for many low-income countries more recent data are either not available or not comparable with previous estimates. The availability, frequency, and quality of poverty monitoring data remain low, especially in small states and in countries and territories with fragile situations. The need to improve household survey programs for poverty monitoring in these countries is urgent. But institutional, political, and financial obstacles continue to hamper data collection, analysis, and public access.

	Population			Average annual population growth		Population age composition			Dependency ratio		Crude death rate	Crude birth rate
	millions			%		%			% of working-age population		per 1,000 people	per 1,000 people
						Ages 0–14	Ages 15–64	Ages 65+	Young	Old		
	2000	2010	2020	2000–10	2010–20	2010	2010	2010	2010	2010	2010	2010
Afghanistan	26.0	34.4	44.8	2.8	2.6	46	51	2	91	4	16	44
Albania	3.1	3.2	3.3	0.4	0.2	23	68	10	34	14	6	13
Algeria	30.5	35.5	40.1	1.5	1.2	27	68	5	40	7	5	20
Angola	13.9	19.1	24.8	3.1	2.6	47	51	2	91	5	14	42
Argentina	36.9	40.4	43.7	0.9	0.8	25	65	11	39	16	8	17
Armenia	3.1	3.1	3.1	0.1	0.1	20	69	11	29	16	9	15
Australia	19.2	22.3	25.2	1.5	1.2	19	68	13	28	20	6	13
Austria	8.0	8.4	8.5	0.5	0.1	15	68	18	22	26	9	9
Azerbaijan	8.0	9.1	10.1	1.2	1.1	21	73	7	29	9	6	19
Bahrain	0.6	1.3	1.5	6.8	1.9	20	78	2	26	3	3	20
Bangladesh	129.6	148.7	167.1	1.4	1.2	31	64	5	49	7	6	20
Belarus	10.0	9.5	9.2	−0.5	−0.4	15	71	14	21	19	15	11
Belgium	10.3	10.9	11.1	0.6	0.2	17	66	17	26	27	10	12
Benin	6.5	8.9	11.5	3.1	2.6	44	53	3	82	6	12	40
Bolivia	8.3	9.9	11.6	1.8	1.5	36	59	5	61	8	7	26
Bosnia and Herzegovina	3.7	3.8	3.6	0.2	−0.4	15	71	14	21	20	10	9
Botswana	1.8	2.0	2.2	1.3	0.9	33	63	4	51	6	13	24
Brazil	174.4	194.9	209.6	1.1	0.7	25	68	7	38	10	6	15
Bulgaria	8.2	7.5	7.0	−0.8	−0.7	14	69	18	20	25	15	10
Burkina Faso	12.3	16.5	22.1	2.9	2.9	45	52	2	86	4	12	43
Burundi	6.4	8.4	10.1	2.7	1.8	38	59	3	64	5	14	34
Cambodia	12.4	14.1	15.9	1.3	1.2	32	64	4	50	6	8	22
Cameroon	15.7	19.6	24.1	2.2	2.1	41	56	4	73	6	14	36
Canada	30.8	34.1	37.1	1.0	0.8	16	69	14	24	20	8	11
Central African Republic	3.7	4.4	5.3	1.7	1.9	40	56	4	73	7	16	35
Chad	8.2	11.2	14.4	3.1	2.5	45	52	3	88	6	16	45
Chile	15.4	17.1	18.4	1.0	0.8	22	69	9	32	13	6	14
China	1,262.6	1,338.3	1,381.6	0.6	0.3	19	72	8	27	11	7	12
Hong Kong SAR, China	6.7	7.1	7.8	0.6	0.9	12	76	13	15	17	6	13
Colombia	39.8	46.3	52.1	1.5	1.2	29	66	6	44	9	5	20
Congo, Dem. Rep.	49.6	66.0	85.0	2.8	2.5	46	51	3	91	5	16	43
Congo, Rep.	3.1	4.0	5.0	2.5	2.1	41	56	4	73	7	11	35
Costa Rica	3.9	4.7	5.3	1.7	1.2	25	69	7	36	10	4	16
Côte d'Ivoire	16.6	19.7	24.5	1.7	2.2	41	55	4	74	7	12	34
Croatia	4.4	4.4	4.3	0.0	−0.3	15	68	17	22	25	12	10
Cuba	11.1	11.3	11.1	0.1	−0.1	17	70	12	25	18	7	10
Cyprus	0.9	1.1	1.2	1.6	1.0	18	71	12	25	16	7	12
Czech Republic	10.3	10.5	10.7	0.2	0.2	14	71	15	20	21	10	11
Denmark	5.3	5.5	5.7	0.4	0.3	18	66	16	27	25	10	11
Dominican Republic	8.6	9.9	11.1	1.4	1.1	31	63	6	49	10	6	22
Ecuador	12.3	14.5	16.3	1.6	1.2	30	63	6	48	10	5	21
Egypt, Arab Rep.	67.6	81.1	94.8	1.8	1.6	32	63	5	50	8	5	23
El Salvador	5.9	6.2	6.6	0.4	0.6	32	61	7	52	11	7	20
Eritrea	3.7	5.3	6.8	3.6	2.6	42	56	2	74	4	8	36
Estonia	1.4	1.3	1.3	−0.2	−0.1	15	67	17	23	25	12	12
Ethiopia	65.6	83.0	100.9	2.3	2.0	41	55	3	75	6	10	31
Finland	5.2	5.4	5.5	0.4	0.2	17	66	17	25	26	10	11
France	60.8	64.9	67.6	0.7	0.4	18	65	17	28	26	8	13
Gabon	1.2	1.5	1.8	2.0	1.9	35	60	4	59	7	9	27
Gambia, The	1.3	1.7	2.2	2.9	2.6	44	54	2	82	4	9	38
Georgia	4.4[a]	4.5[a]	4.2[a]	0.1[a]	−0.7[a]	17	69	14	24	21	11	12
Germany	82.2	81.8	79.8	−0.1	−0.2	13	66	20	20	31	11	8
Ghana	19.2	24.4	30.3	2.4	2.2	39	58	4	67	7	8	32
Greece	10.9	11.3	11.5	0.4	0.1	15	67	19	22	28	9	10
Guatemala	11.2	14.4	18.3	2.5	2.4	41	54	4	77	8	5	32
Guinea	8.3	10.0	12.8	1.8	2.4	43	54	3	80	6	13	39
Guinea-Bissau	1.2	1.5	1.9	2.0	2.1	41	55	3	75	6	17	38
Haiti	8.6	10.0	11.3	1.4	1.2	36	60	4	60	7	9	27

Population dynamics 2.1

	Population (millions)			Average annual population growth (%)		Population age composition (%)			Dependency ratio (% of working-age population)		Crude death rate (per 1,000 people)	Crude birth rate (per 1,000 people)
						Ages 0–14	Ages 15–64	Ages 65+	Young	Old		
	2000	2010	2020	2000–10	2010–20	2010	2010	2010	2010	2010	2010	2010
Honduras	6.2	7.6	9.2	2.0	1.9	37	59	4	62	7	5	27
Hungary	10.2	10.0	9.8	–0.2	–0.2	15	69	17	21	24	13	9
India	1,053.9	1,224.6	1,385.2	1.5	1.2	31	64	5	47	8	8	22
Indonesia	213.4	239.9	262.1	1.2	0.9	27	67	6	40	8	7	18
Iran, Islamic Rep.	65.3	74.0	80.9	1.2	0.9	23	72	5	32	7	5	17
Iraq	24.3	32.0	42.3	2.8	2.8	43	54	3	81	6	6	35
Ireland	3.8	4.5	5.0	1.6	1.0	21	67	12	32	17	6	17
Israel	6.3	7.6	8.9	1.9	1.5	27	62	10	44	17	5	22
Italy	56.9	60.5	60.8	0.6	0.1	14	66	20	21	31	10	9
Jamaica	2.6	2.7	2.8	0.4	0.3	29	63	8	46	12	7	16
Japan	126.9	127.5	123.6	0.0	–0.3	13	64	23	21	35	10	9
Jordan	4.8	6.0	7.2	2.3	1.8	38	59	4	64	7	4	25
Kazakhstan	14.9	16.3	18.0	0.9	1.0	24	69	7	36	10	9	22
Kenya	31.3	40.5	52.5	2.6	2.6	42	55	3	77	5	11	38
Korea, Dem. Rep.	22.9	24.3	25.3	0.6	0.4	23	68	10	34	14	10	14
Korea, Rep.	47.0	48.9	50.2	0.4	0.3	16	72	11	23	15	5	9
Kosovo	1.7	1.8	1.9	0.7	0.7	..	..	..	..	..	7	19
Kuwait	1.9	2.7	3.4	3.4	2.2	27	71	3	38	4	3	18
Kyrgyz Republic	4.9	5.4	6.1	1.1	1.2	30	66	4	46	7	7	27
Lao PDR	5.3	6.2	7.0	1.5	1.3	35	62	4	56	6	6	23
Latvia	2.4	2.2	2.1	–0.6	–0.4	14	68	18	20	26	13	9
Lebanon	3.7	4.2	4.5	1.2	0.6	25	68	7	36	11	7	15
Lesotho	2.0	2.2	2.4	1.0	1.0	37	58	4	64	7	16	28
Liberia	2.8	4.0	5.2	3.4	2.6	43	54	3	81	5	11	39
Libya	5.2	6.4	7.0	1.9	1.0	30	65	4	47	7	4	23
Lithuania	3.5	3.3	3.1	–0.6	–0.5	15	69	16	22	23	13	11
Macedonia, FYR	2.0	2.1	2.1	0.3	0.0	18	71	12	25	17	9	11
Madagascar	15.4	20.7	27.3	3.0	2.8	43	54	3	80	6	6	35
Malawi	11.2	14.9	20.7	2.8	3.3	46	51	3	90	6	13	44
Malaysia	23.4	28.4	33.0	1.9	1.5	30	65	5	47	7	5	20
Mali	11.3	15.4	20.5	3.1	2.9	47	51	2	93	4	15	46
Mauritania	2.6	3.5	4.3	2.7	2.2	40	57	3	69	5	10	34
Mauritius	1.2	1.3	1.3	0.8	0.4	22	71	7	31	10	7	12
Mexico	100.0	113.4	125.7	1.3	1.0	29	65	6	45	10	5	20
Moldova	3.6[b]	3.6[b]	3.3[b]	–0.2[b]	–0.6[b]	17	72	11	23	15	13	12
Mongolia	2.4	2.8	3.2	1.3	1.4	28	68	4	40	6	6	23
Morocco	28.8	32.0	35.0	1.0	0.9	28	66	5	42	8	6	20
Mozambique	18.2	23.4	29.1	2.5	2.2	44	53	3	84	6	15	38
Myanmar	45.0	48.0	51.7	0.6	0.7	26	69	5	37	7	9	17
Namibia	1.9	2.3	2.7	1.9	1.6	36	60	4	61	6	8	26
Nepal	24.4	30.0	35.1	2.1	1.6	36	60	4	61	7	6	24
Netherlands	15.9	16.6	17.0	0.4	0.2	18	67	15	26	23	8	11
New Zealand	3.9	4.4	4.8	1.2	1.0	20	67	13	31	20	7	15
Nicaragua	5.1	5.8	6.6	1.3	1.3	34	61	5	57	8	5	24
Niger	10.9	15.5	22.0	3.5	3.5	49	49	2	100	4	13	49
Nigeria	123.7	158.4	203.7	2.5	2.5	43	54	3	80	6	14	40
Norway	4.5	4.9	5.2	0.8	0.7	19	67	15	28	22	9	13
Oman	2.3	2.8	3.3	2.1	1.8	27	70	3	39	4	4	18
Pakistan	144.5	173.6	205.2	1.8	1.7	35	60	4	59	7	7	27
Panama	3.0	3.5	4.0	1.7	1.4	29	64	7	45	10	5	20
Papua New Guinea	5.4	6.9	8.5	2.4	2.1	39	58	3	67	5	8	30
Paraguay	5.3	6.5	7.6	1.9	1.6	34	61	5	55	8	5	24
Peru	25.9	29.1	32.3	1.2	1.1	30	64	6	47	10	5	20
Philippines	77.3	93.3	109.6	1.9	1.6	35	61	4	58	6	6	25
Poland	38.5	38.2	38.1	–0.1	0.0	15	72	14	21	19	10	11
Portugal	10.2	10.6	10.5	0.4	–0.1	15	67	18	23	27	10	10
Puerto Rico	3.8	4.0	4.0	0.4	–0.1	21	66	13	32	19	8	13
Qatar	0.6	1.8	2.3	10.9[c]	2.6	13	85	1	16	1	2	13

2.1 Population dynamics

	Population			Average annual population growth		Population age composition			Dependency ratio		Crude death rate	Crude birth rate
							%		% of working-age population			
						Ages 0–14	Ages 15–64	Ages 65+	Young	Old	per 1,000 people	per 1,000 people
	millions			%								
	2000	2010	2020	2000–10	2010–20	2010	2010	2010	2010	2010	2010	2010
Romania	22.4	21.4	20.9	−0.5	−0.3	15	70	15	22	21	12	10
Russian Federation	146.3	141.8	139.3	−0.3	−0.2	15	72	13	21	18	14	13
Rwanda	8.1	10.6	14.0	2.7	2.8	43	55	3	78	5	12	41
Saudi Arabia	20.0	27.4	33.1	3.1	1.9	30	67	3	46	4	4	22
Senegal	9.5	12.4	16.0	2.7	2.5	44	54	2	81	4	9	37
Serbia	7.5	7.3	7.2	−0.3	−0.2	18[d]	68[d]	14[d]	26[d]	21[d]	14	9
Sierra Leone	4.1	5.9	7.2	3.5	2.0	43	55	2	78	3	16	39
Singapore	4.0	5.1	5.6	2.3	0.9	17	74	9	24	12	4	9
Slovak Republic	5.4	5.4	5.5	0.1	0.1	15	73	12	21	17	10	11
Slovenia	2.0	2.0	2.1	0.3	0.1	14	70	16	20	24	9	11
Somalia	7.4	9.3	12.2	2.3	2.7	45	52	3	86	5	15	44
South Africa	44.0	50.0	52.4	1.3	0.5	30	65	5	46	7	15	21
South Sudan	..	..	..	..	..	..	..	..	..	..	21	30
Spain	40.3	46.1	48.4	1.3	0.5	15	68	17	22	25	8	11
Sri Lanka	18.7	20.9	22.3	1.1	0.7	25	67	8	37	12	7	18
Sudan	34.2[e]	43.6[e]	54.9[e]	2.4[e]	2.3[e]	40[e]	56[e]	4[e]	71[e]	6[e]	9[e]	33[e]
Swaziland	1.0	1.1	1.2	0.4	1.2	38	58	3	66	6	14	29
Sweden	8.9	9.4	9.9	0.6	0.5	17	65	18	25	28	10	12
Switzerland	7.2	7.8	8.0	0.9	0.3	15	68	17	22	25	8	10
Syrian Arab Republic	16.0	20.4	24.3	2.5	1.7	37	59	4	62	7	4	23
Tajikistan	6.2	6.9	7.9	1.1	1.4	37	60	3	62	6	6	28
Tanzania	34.0	44.8	61.0	2.8	3.1	45	52	3	86	6	10	41
Thailand	63.2	69.1	71.9	0.9	0.4	21	71	9	29	13	7	12
Timor-Leste	0.8	1.1	1.5	3.0	2.8	46	51	3	91	6	8	38
Togo	4.8	6.0	7.3	2.3	2.0	40	57	3	70	6	11	32
Trinidad and Tobago	1.3	1.3	1.4	0.4	0.2	21	72	7	28	10	8	15
Tunisia	9.6	10.5	11.6	1.0	0.9	23	70	7	34	10	6	18
Turkey	63.6	72.8	80.7	1.3	1.0	26	68	6	39	9	5	18
Turkmenistan	4.5	5.0	5.7	1.1	1.2	29	67	4	44	6	8	22
Uganda	24.2	33.4	45.3	3.2	3.0	48	49	3	99	5	12	45
Ukraine	49.2	45.9	43.3	−0.7	−0.6	14	70	15	20	22	15	11
United Arab Emirates	3.0	7.5	9.2	9.1	2.0	17	83	0	21	1	1	13
United Kingdom	58.9	62.2	65.7	0.6	0.5	17	66	17	26	25	9	13
United States	282.2	309.3	334.9	0.9	0.8	20	67	13	30	20	8	14
Uruguay	3.3	3.4	3.5	0.2	0.3	23	64	14	35	22	9	14
Uzbekistan	24.7	28.2	31.6	1.4	1.1	29	66	4	44	7	5	23
Venezuela, RB	24.3	28.8	33.1	1.7	1.4	29	65	6	45	9	5	21
Vietnam	77.6	86.9	95.2	1.1	0.9	24	70	6	34	9	5	17
West Bank and Gaza	3.0	4.2	5.5	3.2	2.7	42	55	3	78	5	4	33
Yemen, Rep.	17.7	24.1	32.2	3.1	2.9	44	53	3	83	5	6	38
Zambia	10.2	12.9	17.7	2.4	3.1	46	51	3	92	6	16	46
Zimbabwe	12.5	12.6	15.5	0.0	2.1	39	57	4	68	7	13	29
World	**6,117.8 s**	**6,894.6 s**	**7,635.2 s**	**1.2 w**	**1.0 w**	**27 w**	**66 w**	**8 w**	**41 w**	**12 w**	**8 w**	**20 w**
Low income	643.7	796.3	979.1	2.1	2.1	39	57	4	69	6	11	33
Middle income	4,424.5	4,970.8	5,478.1	1.2	1.0	27	67	6	40	10	8	19
Lower middle income	2,146.7	2,518.7	2,901.8	1.6	1.4	32	63	5	51	8	8	24
Upper middle income	2,277.9	2,452.1	2,576.2	0.7	0.5	22	70	8	31	11	7	14
Low & middle income	5,068.2	5,767.2	6,457.2	1.3	1.1	29	65	6	44	9	8	21
East Asia & Pacific	1,813.8	1,961.6	2,068.9	0.8	0.5	22	71	7	31	10	7	14
Europe & Central Asia	398.5	405.2	414.4	0.2	0.2	19	70	11	28	15	11	15
Latin America & Carib.	514.3	582.6	642.4	1.2	1.0	28	65	7	43	10	6	19
Middle East & N. Africa	277.4	331.3	386.5	1.8	1.6	31	64	5	48	7	5	23
South Asia	1,398.0	1,633.1	1,860.8	1.6	1.3	32	64	5	50	8	8	23
Sub-Saharan Africa	666.3	853.4	1,084.2	2.5	2.4	42	54	3	78	6	13	37
High income	1,049.6	1,127.4	1,178.1	0.7	0.4	17	67	16	26	23	8	12
Euro area	315.0	331.8	336.7	0.5	0.1	15	66	18	23	28	9	10

a. Excludes Abkhazia and South Ossetia. b. Excludes Transnistria. c. Increase is due to a surge in the number of migrants since 2004. d. Includes Kosovo. e. Includes South Sudan.

Population dynamics | **2.1**

About the data

Population estimates are usually based on national population censuses. Estimates for the years before and after the census are interpolations or extrapolations based on demographic models. Errors and undercounting occur even in high-income countries; in developing countries errors may be substantial because of limits in the transport, communications, and other resources required to conduct and analyze a full census.

The quality and reliability of official demographic data are also affected by public trust in the government, government commitment to full and accurate enumeration, confidentiality and protection against misuse of census data, and census agencies' independence from political influence. Moreover, comparability of population indicators is limited by differences in the concepts, definitions, collection procedures, and estimation methods used by national statistical agencies and other organizations that collect the data.

Of the 158 economies in the table and the 58 economies in table 1.6, 180 (about 86 percent) conducted a census during the 2000 census round (1995–2004). As of January 2012, 141 countries have completed a census for the 2010 census round (2005–14). The currentness of a census and the availability of complementary data from surveys or registration systems are objective ways to judge demographic data quality. Some European countries' registration systems offer complete information on population in the absence of a census. See table 2.17 and *Primary data documentation* for the most recent census or survey year and for the completeness of registration.

Current population estimates for developing countries that lack recent census data and pre- and post-census estimates for countries with census data are provided by the United Nations Population Division and other agencies. The cohort component method—a standard method for estimating and projecting population—requires fertility, mortality, and net migration data, often collected from sample surveys, which can be small or limited in coverage. Population estimates are from demographic modeling and so are susceptible to biases and errors from shortcomings in the model and in the data. Because the five-year age group is the cohort unit and five-year period data are used, interpolations to obtain annual data or single age structure may not reflect actual events or age composition.

The growth rate of the total population conceals age-group differences in growth rates. In many developing countries the once rapidly growing under-15 population is shrinking. Previously high fertility rates

and declining mortality rates are now reflected in the larger share of the working-age population.

Dependency ratios capture variations in the proportions of children, elderly people, and working-age people in the population that imply the dependency burden that the working-age population bears in relation to children and the elderly. But dependency ratios show only the age composition of a population, not economic dependency. Some children and elderly people are part of the labor force, and many working-age people are not.

Vital rates are based on data from birth and death registration systems, censuses, and sample surveys by national statistical offices and other organizations, or on demographic analysis. Data for 2010 for some high-income countries are provisional estimates based on vital registers. The estimates for many countries are projections based on extrapolations of levels and trends from earlier years or interpolations of population estimates and projections from the United Nations Population Division.

Vital registers are the preferred source for these data, but in many developing countries systems for registering births and deaths are absent or incomplete because of deficiencies in the coverage of events or geographic areas. Many developing countries carry out special household surveys that ask respondents about recent births and deaths. Estimates derived in this way are subject to sampling errors and recall errors.

The United Nations Statistics Division monitors the completeness of vital registration systems. Some countries have made progress over the last 60 years, but others still have deficiencies in civil registration systems. For example, only 57 percent of countries and areas register at least 90 percent of births, and only 53 percent register at least 90 percent of deaths. Some of the most populous developing countries—Bangladesh, Brazil, China, India, Indonesia, Nigeria, Pakistan—lack complete vital registration systems.

International migration is the only other factor besides birth and death rates that directly determines a country's population growth. From 1990 to 2005 the number of migrants in high-income countries rose 40 million. About 195 million people (3 percent of the world population) live outside their home country. Estimating migration is difficult. At any time many people are located outside their home country as tourists, workers, or refugees or for other reasons. Standards for the duration and purpose of international moves that qualify as migration vary, and estimates require information on flows into and out of countries that is difficult to collect.

Definitions

- **Population** is based on the de facto definition of population, which counts all residents regardless of legal status or citizenship—except for refugees not permanently settled in the country of asylum, who are generally considered part of the population of their country of origin. The values shown are mid-year estimates for 2000 and 2010 and projections for 2020. • **Average annual population growth** is the exponential change for the period indicated. See *Statistical methods* for more information. • **Population age composition** is the percentage of the total population that is in specific age groups. • **Dependency ratio** is the ratio of dependents—people younger than 15 or older than 64—to the working-age population—those ages 15–64. • **Crude death rate** and **crude birth rate** are the number of deaths and the number of live births occurring during the year, per 1,000 people, estimated at midyear. Subtracting the crude death rate from the crude birth rate provides the rate of natural increase, which is equal to the population growth rate in the absence of migration.

Data sources

The World Bank's population estimates are compiled and produced by its Development Data Group in consultation with its Human Development Network, operational staff, and country offices. The United Nations Population Division's *World Population Prospects: The 2010 Revision* is a source of the demographic data for more than half the countries, most of them developing countries, and the source of data on age composition and dependency ratios for all countries. Other important sources are census reports and other statistical publications from national statistical offices; household surveys by national agencies, ICF International (for MEASURE DHS), and the U.S. Centers for Disease Control and Prevention; Eurostat's *Demographic Statistics;* Secretariat of the Pacific Community, Statistics and Demography Programme; and U.S. Bureau of the Census, International Data Base.

	Labor force participation rate				Labor force				
	% ages 15 and older				Total millions		Ages 15 and older average annual % growth	Female % of labor force	
	Male		Female						
	2000	2010	2000	2010	2000	2010	2000–10	2000	2010
Afghanistan	81	80	13	16	6.5	9.1	3.3	13.3	15.2
Albania	73	71	51	50	1.3	1.5	1.2	41.7	41.6
Algeria	76	72	12	15	8.8	11.2	2.4	13.7	16.9
Angola	75	77	67	63	5.2	7.1	3.1	48.4	45.9
Argentina	74	75	43	47	15.4	18.4	1.8	38.1	40.2
Armenia	73	70	58	49	1.5	1.4	−0.2	48.8	46.5
Australia	72	73	55	59	9.6	11.8	2.1	43.8	45.3
Austria	69	68	48	54	3.9	4.3	1.1	43.5	45.9
Azerbaijan	71	68	57	61	3.5	4.6	2.6	47.0	49.1
Bahrain	86	87	35	39	0.3	0.7	8.6	21.4	19.3
Bangladesh	86	84	54	57	57.3	72.3	2.3	37.5	39.9
Belarus	65	62	53	50	4.7	4.5	−0.6	48.9	49.0
Belgium	61	61	44	48	4.4	4.9	1.0	42.9	45.3
Benin	81	78	64	67	2.6	3.6	3.5	46.5	47.5
Bolivia	82	81	60	64	3.5	4.6	2.6	43.2	44.8
Bosnia and Herzegovina	58	59	33	35	1.3	1.5	1.1	39.1	40.0
Botswana	80	82	70	72	0.8	1.0	2.4	46.9	46.3
Brazil	82	81	55	59	83.7	101.6	1.9	41.2	43.7
Bulgaria	57	60	48	49	3.6	3.5	−0.3	47.1	46.8
Burkina Faso	91	91	77	78	5.5	7.5	3.2	48.2	47.6
Burundi	84	82	86	84	2.9	4.3	3.9	53.2	52.1
Cambodia	83	87	77	79	5.8	8.0	3.2	51.2	49.9
Cameroon	77	77	62	64	6.2	8.2	2.8	45.1	45.7
Canada	72	72	59	62	16.3	19.0	1.6	45.8	47.1
Central African Republic	86	85	71	73	1.7	2.1	2.1	46.4	47.1
Chad	80	80	65	65	3.2	4.4	3.2	45.5	45.3
Chile	75	74	35	47	6.1	8.0	2.8	33.1	39.6
China	83	80	71	68	724.5	799.8	1.0	45.0	44.6
Hong Kong SAR, China	73	68	49	51	3.3	3.7	1.0	41.9	46.0
Colombia	82	80	49	55	17.3	22.1	2.5	38.7	42.5
Congo, Dem. Rep.	73	72	71	70	18.5	25.3	3.1	50.1	49.9
Congo, Rep.	71	73	65	68	1.3	1.7	3.0	48.1	48.6
Costa Rica	81	79	37	46	1.6	2.2	3.2	30.8	36.2
Côte d'Ivoire	82	81	49	52	6.4	7.8	2.0	35.0	37.4
Croatia	63	60	45	46	2.0	2.0	0.0	44.1	45.9
Cuba	70	70	38	43	4.7	5.3	1.1	35.0	38.0
Cyprus	72	71	50	57	0.4	0.6	2.7	40.8	43.5
Czech Republic	70	68	52	49	5.2	5.3	0.2	44.4	43.3
Denmark	72	69	60	60	2.9	2.9	0.3	46.6	47.2
Dominican Republic	80	79	46	51	3.5	4.4	2.2	36.6	39.4
Ecuador	84	83	50	54	5.4	6.9	2.4	37.4	39.7
Egypt, Arab Rep.	73	74	20	24	20.1	27.1	3.0	21.5	24.2
El Salvador	79	79	45	47	2.2	2.6	1.6	39.6	41.4
Eritrea	90	90	75	80	1.7	2.6	4.5	47.3	48.6
Estonia	67	68	52	57	0.7	0.7	0.6	48.7	50.4
Ethiopia	91	90	73	78	29.0	40.8	3.4	45.2	47.2
Finland	67	65	57	56	2.6	2.7	0.3	47.5	47.8
France	63	62	48	51	27.2	29.9	0.9	45.5	47.1
Gabon	67	65	55	56	0.4	0.6	2.8	45.5	46.3
Gambia, The	83	83	71	72	0.5	0.8	3.2	47.0	47.9
Georgia	74	74	55	56	2.2[a]	2.4[a]	0.8[a]	46.2	47.0
Germany	68	67	49	53	40.3	42.2	0.4	43.7	45.6
Ghana	77	72	73	67	8.4	10.4	2.1	48.1	47.6
Greece	65	65	40	45	4.9	5.3	0.8	39.1	41.5
Guatemala	86	88	42	49	4.0	5.7	3.6	34.6	38.1
Guinea	78	78	63	65	3.3	4.1	2.2	44.6	45.2
Guinea-Bissau	79	78	63	68	0.5	0.6	2.6	45.5	47.3
Haiti	69	71	57	60	3.2	4.2	2.5	46.5	47.0

Labor force structure

	Labor force participation rate				Labor force				
	% ages 15 and older				Total millions		Ages 15 and older average annual % growth	Female % of labor force	
	Male		Female						
	2000	2010	2000	2010	2000	2010	2000–10	2000	2010
Honduras	88	83	44	42	2.4	3.0	2.4	34.1	34.1
Hungary	58	58	41	44	4.2	4.3	0.3	44.7	46.0
India	83	81	34	29	409.4	472.6	1.4	27.8	25.3
Indonesia	85	84	50	51	99.6	118.0	1.7	37.7	38.2
Iran, Islamic Rep.	73	72	14	16	18.5	25.3	3.1	16.0	17.9
Iraq	69	69	13	14	5.5	7.5	3.1	16.0	17.5
Ireland	71	68	47	52	1.8	2.1	1.9	40.6	43.7
Israel	61	62	48	53	2.5	3.2	2.6	45.7	47.1
Italy	61	60	35	38	23.3	25.1	0.8	38.7	40.3
Jamaica	78	72	59	56	1.2	1.2	0.3	44.3	45.1
Japan	76	72	49	50	67.6	66.7	–0.1	40.7	42.3
Jordan	68	65	13	15	1.2	1.6	2.5	14.3	18.0
Kazakhstan	76	77	65	66	7.5	8.8	1.5	49.2	49.4
Kenya	73	72	63	61	11.9	15.5	2.7	46.8	46.5
Korea, Dem. Rep.	88	84	74	72	13.6	14.6	0.7	47.5	47.7
Korea, Rep.	73	72	49	49	22.7	24.6	0.8	40.5	41.3
Kosovo	..	..	..	..	..	..	..	..	..
Kuwait	82	82	44	43	1.0	1.4	3.5	25.1	23.9
Kyrgyz Republic	74	78	56	55	2.1	2.5	2.0	44.6	42.7
Lao PDR	81	79	79	77	2.5	3.2	2.5	49.9	49.8
Latvia	65	66	49	55	1.1	1.2	0.6	48.1	50.1
Lebanon	71	71	19	23	1.1	1.5	2.4	22.9	25.5
Lesotho	80	73	68	59	0.8	0.9	0.5	49.1	46.0
Liberia	62	64	58	58	1.0	1.4	3.6	49.0	47.7
Libya	73	77	27	30	1.8	2.4	2.8	26.1	28.0
Lithuania	67	63	55	54	1.7	1.6	–0.3	49.5	50.3
Macedonia, FYR	66	69	41	43	0.8	0.9	1.3	38.8	38.6
Madagascar	90	89	84	84	7.3	10.1	3.3	48.7	48.9
Malawi	81	81	77	85	4.8	6.7	3.3	49.7	51.5
Malaysia	82	77	45	44	9.9	12.0	1.9	34.7	35.8
Mali	66	70	37	37	3.1	4.3	3.4	37.5	35.5
Mauritania	78	79	23	28	0.8	1.1	3.8	23.3	26.5
Mauritius	81	76	41	44	0.5	0.6	1.2	34.5	37.7
Mexico	83	81	39	44	40.3	49.6	2.1	32.9	36.5
Moldova	64	45	55	38	1.6[b]	1.2[b]	–3.0[b]	49.7	49.2
Mongolia	66	65	56	54	0.9	1.2	2.2	46.8	46.4
Morocco	79	75	29	26	10.2	11.4	1.1	27.9	27.1
Mozambique	83	83	88	86	8.7	11.1	2.4	55.0	53.6
Myanmar	81	82	74	75	24.2	28.0	1.5	48.3	48.9
Namibia	65	70	49	58	0.6	0.9	3.8	44.4	46.3
Nepal	90	88	82	80	12.4	16.0	2.6	48.9	49.2
Netherlands	73	72	53	58	8.2	8.9	0.8	43.1	45.6
New Zealand	73	74	57	62	1.9	2.4	2.0	45.2	46.7
Nicaragua	83	80	38	46	1.8	2.4	2.8	32.5	37.9
Niger	88	90	38	40	3.5	5.1	3.7	30.9	31.2
Nigeria	67	63	45	48	39.2	50.3	2.5	40.1	42.8
Norway	72	70	60	62	2.4	2.6	1.0	46.5	46.9
Oman	78	80	23	28	0.8	1.2	4.4	17.1	17.9
Pakistan	84	83	16	22	43.0	59.7	3.3	15.3	20.7
Panama	82	83	45	49	1.3	1.6	2.5	35.4	37.3
Papua New Guinea	74	74	71	71	2.3	3.0	2.7	48.5	48.3
Paraguay	87	86	51	57	2.3	3.1	3.0	36.6	39.7
Peru	83	85	58	67	12.0	15.5	2.6	41.2	44.6
Philippines	82	79	49	50	30.9	38.7	2.2	37.5	38.8
Poland	64	64	49	48	17.4	18.2	0.5	45.8	45.1
Portugal	70	68	53	56	5.2	5.6	0.7	45.3	47.4
Puerto Rico	60	54	35	35	1.4	1.4	0.3	39.5	42.3
Qatar	92	95	39	52	0.3	1.3	13.7	15.6	12.4

	Labor force participation rate				Labor force				
	% ages 15 and older				Total millions		Ages 15 and older average annual % growth	Female % of labor force	
	Male		Female						
	2000	2010	2000	2010	2000	2010	2000–10	2000	2010
Romania	71	65	58	48	11.8	10.2	−1.5	46.6	44.7
Russian Federation	69	71	55	56	73.3	75.5	0.3	48.6	48.9
Rwanda	85	85	86	86	3.8	5.2	3.2	52.3	51.8
Saudi Arabia	74	74	16	17	6.0	9.6	4.7	14.7	14.8
Senegal	89	88	64	66	3.9	5.4	3.1	42.9	43.9
Serbia	..	67	..	51	..	3.5ᶜ	..	..	43.9
Sierra Leone	63	69	67	66	1.6	2.3	3.7	53.2	50.7
Singapore	78	77	53	57	2.1	2.8	3.0	40.6	42.3
Slovak Republic	68	68	53	51	2.6	2.7	0.5	45.6	44.6
Slovenia	64	65	51	53	1.0	1.0	0.8	46.3	46.3
Somalia	78	77	37	38	2.3	2.9	2.2	32.8	33.6
South Africa	61	60	44	44	15.2	18.2	1.8	43.1	42.8
South Sudan	..	..	..	..	..	..	..	..	..
Spain	66	67	41	52	18.2	23.2	2.4	39.5	44.3
Sri Lanka	77	76	37	35	7.8	8.6	0.9	33.1	32.2
Sudan	76	77	29	31	10.3	14.0	3.0	27.9	28.7
Swaziland	72	71	43	44	0.3	0.4	2.2	40.3	39.7
Sweden	68	68	58	59	4.6	5.0	0.9	47.1	47.0
Switzerland	78	75	58	61	4.0	4.5	1.2	44.3	45.8
Syrian Arab Republic	80	72	20	13	4.8	5.5	1.2	20.2	15.2
Tajikistan	75	75	58	57	2.4	2.8	1.8	44.1	45.2
Tanzania	91	90	87	88	16.7	22.1	2.8	49.7	49.8
Thailand	81	80	65	64	34.8	39.4	1.2	46.1	45.7
Timor-Leste	75	74	38	38	0.2	0.3	3.6	32.6	33.3
Togo	82	81	76	80	2.2	2.9	3.1	49.0	50.5
Trinidad and Tobago	77	78	47	55	0.6	0.7	1.8	39.9	43.2
Tunisia	72	70	24	25	3.2	3.8	1.8	24.9	26.9
Turkey	74	71	27	28	21.9	26.5	1.9	26.9	28.7
Turkmenistan	74	76	48	46	1.7	2.2	2.2	40.6	39.3
Uganda	83	80	81	76	10.1	13.4	2.8	50.0	49.3
Ukraine	65	66	52	53	23.4	23.2	−0.1	49.1	49.3
United Arab Emirates	92	92	34	44	1.7	4.9	10.5	12.0	14.8
United Kingdom	70	69	54	56	29.5	31.8	0.8	45.2	45.9
United States	74	70	59	58	147.1	157.5	0.7	45.8	46.1
Uruguay	76	77	52	55	1.6	1.7	0.8	43.2	44.5
Uzbekistan	72	74	48	48	9.2	12.1	2.8	40.6	39.8
Venezuela, RB	82	80	48	52	10.5	13.4	2.4	37.2	39.3
Vietnam	83	81	74	73	41.3	51.1	2.1	49.1	48.5
West Bank and Gaza	67	66	11	15	0.6	1.0	4.6	13.4	17.8
Yemen, Rep.	71	72	22	25	4.2	6.5	4.3	24.0	25.8
Zambia	85	86	75	73	4.5	5.5	2.1	47.2	46.1
Zimbabwe	82	90	69	83	5.5	6.6	1.9	46.4	49.3
World	**79 w**	**77 w**	**52 w**	**51 w**	**2,770.2 t**	**3,223.0 t**	**1.5 w**	**39.9 w**	**39.9 w**
Low income	83	83	66	68	279.3	363.5	2.6	44.9	45.6
Middle income	80	79	51	49	1,987.5	2,308.6	1.5	38.4	38.0
Lower middle income	81	79	39	37	828.5	994.1	1.8	32.1	31.5
Upper middle income	80	78	60	59	1,159.1	1,314.4	1.3	42.8	43.0
Low & middle income	81	79	52	51	2,266.8	2,672.1	1.6	39.2	39.1
East Asia & Pacific	83	81	68	65	991.2	1,118.0	1.2	44.3	44.1
Europe & Central Asia	69	70	50	50	176.8	191.8	0.8	45.0	44.8
Latin America & Carib.	81	80	48	53	224.6	278.2	2.1	38.3	41.2
Middle East & N. Africa	74	72	18	20	80.3	104.9	2.7	20.0	21.5
South Asia	83	81	35	32	536.8	638.8	1.7	28.2	27.1
Sub-Saharan Africa	77	76	61	63	257.2	340.4	2.8	44.9	45.6
High income	71	69	51	52	503.4	550.9	0.9	43.2	43.9
Euro area	65	65	45	50	144.9	159.6	1.0	42.6	44.8

a. Excludes Abkhazia and South Ossetia. b. Excludes Transnistria. c. Includes Kosovo.

The labor force is the supply of labor available for producing goods and services in an economy. It includes people who are currently employed and people who are unemployed but seeking work as well as first-time job-seekers. Not everyone who works is included, however. Unpaid workers, family workers, and students are often omitted, and some countries do not count members of the armed forces. Labor force size tends to vary during the year as seasonal workers enter and leave.

Data on the labor force are compiled by the International Labour Organization (ILO) from labor force surveys, censuses, establishment censuses and surveys, and administrative records such as employment exchange registers and unemployment insurance schemes. For some countries a combination of these sources is used. Labor force surveys are the most comprehensive source for internationally comparable labor force data. They can cover all non-institutionalized civilians, all branches and sectors of the economy, and all categories of workers, including people holding multiple jobs. By contrast, labor force data from population censuses are often based on a limited number of questions on the economic characteristics of individuals, with little scope to probe. The resulting data often differ from labor force survey data and vary considerably by country, depending on the census scope and coverage. Establishment censuses and surveys provide data only on the employed population, not unemployed workers, workers in small establishments, or workers in the informal sector (ILO, *Key Indicators of the Labour Market 2001–2002).*

The reference period of a census or survey is another important source of differences: in some countries data refer to people's status on the day of the census or survey or during a specific period before the inquiry date, while in others data are recorded without reference to any period. In developing countries, where the household is often the basic unit of production and all members contribute to output, but some at low intensity or irregularly, the estimated labor force may be much smaller than the numbers actually working.

Differing definitions of employment age also affect comparability. For most countries the working age is 15 and older, but in some countries children younger than 15 work full- or part-time and are included in the estimates. Similarly, some countries have an upper age limit. As a result, calculations may systematically over- or underestimate actual rates. For further information on source, reference period, or definition, consult the original source.

The labor force participation rates in the table are from the ILO's Key Indicators of the Labour Market, 7th edition, database. These harmonized estimates use strict data selection criteria and enhanced methods to ensure comparability across countries and over time to avoid the inconsistencies mentioned above. Estimates are based mainly on labor force surveys, with other sources (population censuses and nationally reported estimates) used only when no survey data are available.

The labor force estimates in the table were calculated by applying labor force participation rates from the ILO database to World Bank population estimates to create a series consistent with these population estimates. This procedure sometimes results in labor force estimates that differ slightly from those in the ILO's *Yearbook of Labour Statistics* and its database Key Indicators of the Labour Market.

Estimates of women in the labor force and employment are generally lower than those of men and are not comparable internationally, reflecting that demographic, social, legal, and cultural trends and norms determine whether women's activities are regarded as economic. In many countries many women work on farms or in other family enterprises without pay, and others work in or near their homes, mixing work and family activities during the day.

• **Labor force participation rate** is the proportion of the population ages 15 and older that engages actively in the labor market, by either working or looking for work during a reference period. • **Total labor force** is people ages 15 and older who engage actively in the labor market, either by working or looking for work during a reference period. It includes both the employed and the unemployed. • **Average annual percentage growth of the labor force** is calculated using the exponential endpoint method (see *Statistical methods* for more information). • **Female labor force as a percentage of the labor force** shows the share of women active in the total labor force.

Data on labor force participation rates are from the ILO's Key Indicators of the Labour Market, 7th edition, database. Labor force numbers were calculated by World Bank staff, applying labor force participation rates from the ILO database to population estimates.

Employment by economic activity

	Agriculture				Industry				Services			
	Male % of male employment		Female % of female employment		Male % of male employment		Female % of female employment		Male % of male employment		Female % of female employment	
	1990–92[a]	2007–10[a]	1990–92[a]	2007–10[a]	1990–92[a]	2007–10[a]	1990–92[a]	2007–10[a]	1990–92[a]	2007–10[a]	1990–92[a]	2007–10[a]
Afghanistan	..	..	..	..	..	..	..	..	..	..	..	..
Albania	..	..	..	..	..	..	..	..	..	..	..	..
Algeria	..	..	..	..	..	..	..	..	..	..	..	..
Angola	..	..	..	..	..	..	..	..	..	..	..	..
Argentina	0[b]	2[b]	0[b]	0[b]	40[b]	33[b]	18[b]	10[b]	59[b]	65[b]	81[b]	89[b]
Armenia	..	39	..	49	..	25	..	8	..	35	..	43
Australia	6	4	4	2	32	32	12	9	61	64	84	88
Austria	6	5	8	5	47	37	20	12	46	58	72	84
Azerbaijan	..	37	..	40	..	19	..	7	..	44	..	53
Bahrain	3	..	0	..	33	..	7	..	64	..	92	..
Bangladesh	54	..	85	..	16	..	9	..	25	..	2	..
Belarus	..	15	..	9	..	33	..	24	..	37	..	64
Belgium	3	2	3	1	41	34	16	10	56	64	82	89
Benin	..	..	..	..	..	..	..	..	..	..	..	..
Bolivia	3[b]	34	1[b]	38	42[b]	28	17[b]	9	55[b]	38	83[b]	53
Bosnia and Herzegovina	..	..	..	..	..	..	..	..	..	..	..	..
Botswana	..	..	..	..	..	..	..	..	..	..	..	..
Brazil	31[b]	21	25[b]	12	27[b]	29	10[b]	13	43[b]	50	65[b]	75
Bulgaria	..	8	..	5	..	41	..	25	..	51	..	70
Burkina Faso	..	..	..	..	..	..	..	..	..	..	..	..
Burundi	..	..	..	..	..	..	..	..	..	..	..	..
Cambodia	..	69	..	75	..	8	..	9	..	23	..	16
Cameroon	..	..	..	..	..	..	..	..	..	..	..	..
Canada	6[b]	3[b]	2[b]	1[b]	31[b]	32[b]	11[b]	10[b]	64[b]	65[b]	87[b]	89[b]
Central African Republic	..	..	..	..	..	..	..	..	..	..	..	..
Chad	..	..	..	..	..	..	..	..	..	..	..	..
Chile	24	15	6	6	32	31	15	11	45	54	79	83
China	..	..	..	..	..	..	..	..	..	..	..	..
Hong Kong SAR, China	1	0	0	0	37	19	27	4	63	80	73	96
Colombia	2[b]	26	1[b]	5	35[b]	23	25[b]	16	63[b]	51	74[b]	79
Congo, Dem. Rep.	..	..	..	..	..	..	..	..	..	..	..	..
Congo, Rep.	..	..	..	..	..	..	..	..	..	..	..	..
Costa Rica	32	17	5	4	27	27	25	13	41	51	69	82
Côte d'Ivoire	..	..	..	..	..	..	..	..	..	..	..	..
Croatia	..	14	..	16	..	38	..	15	..	48	..	69
Cuba	..	25	..	9	..	22	..	12	..	53	..	80
Cyprus	11	5	13	3	31	30	23	9	56	65	63	88
Czech Republic	..	4	..	2	..	49	..	23	..	47	..	75
Denmark	7	4	3	1	37	29	16	9	56	67	81	90
Dominican Republic	26	21	3	2	23	26	21	14	52	48	76	83
Ecuador	10[b]	33	2[b]	22	29[b]	24	17[b]	11	62[b]	43	81[b]	67
Egypt, Arab Rep.	35	28	52	46	25	27	10	6	41	44	37	49
El Salvador	48[b]	33	15[b]	5	23[b]	22	23[b]	18	29[b]	45	63[b]	77
Eritrea	..	..	..	..	..	..	..	..	..	..	..	..
Estonia	23	6	13	3	42	43	30	18	36	50	57	78
Ethiopia	..	9	..	10	..	25	..	20	..	76	..	64
Finland	11	6	6	3	38	36	15	10	51	58	78	87
France	7	4	5	2	39	33	17	10	54	63	78	88
Gabon	..	..	..	..	..	..	..	..	..	..	..	..
Gambia, The	..	..	..	..	..	..	..	..	..	..	..	..
Georgia	..	51	..	57	..	17	..	4	..	33	..	40
Germany	4	2	4	1	50	40	24	14	46	58	73	84
Ghana	66	..	59	..	10	..	10	..	23	..	32	..
Greece	20	12	26	13	29	28	17	8	51	60	57	79
Guatemala	19[b]	..	3[b]	..	36[b]	..	27[b]	..	45[b]	..	70[b]	..
Guinea	..	..	..	..	..	..	..	..	..	..	..	..
Guinea-Bissau	..	..	..	..	..	..	..	..	..	..	..	..
Haiti	76	..	50	..	9	..	9	..	13	..	38	..

Employment by economic activity

	Agriculture				Industry				Services			
	Male % of male employment		Female % of female employment		Male % of male employment		Female % of female employment		Male % of male employment		Female % of female employment	
	1990–92[a]	2007–10[a]	1990–92[a]	2007–10[a]	1990–92[a]	2007–10[a]	1990–92[a]	2007–10[a]	1990–92[a]	2007–10[a]	1990–92[a]	2007–10[a]
Honduras	53[b]	48	6[b]	10	18[b]	22	25[b]	22	29[b]	30	69[b]	68
Hungary	19	6	13	2	43	40	29	20	38	53	58	78
India	..	46[b]	..	65[b]	..	24[b]	..	18[b]	..	30[b]	..	17[b]
Indonesia	54	39	57	38	15	22	13	15	31	40	31	47
Iran, Islamic Rep.	..	19	..	31	..	33	..	27	..	47	..	42
Iraq	..	17	..	51	..	22	..	4	..	61	..	46
Ireland	17	8	3	1	35	29	18	9	49	63	79	90
Israel	5	3	2	1	38	30	15	10	57	67	83	89
Italy	8	5	9	3	41	39	23	14	52	57	68	83
Jamaica	36	28	16	10	25	24	12	7	39	48	72	83
Japan	6	4	7	4	40	33	27	15	54	62	65	80
Jordan	..	2	..	1	..	21	..	9	..	77	..	90
Kazakhstan	..	31	..	29	..	26	..	12	..	43	..	59
Kenya	..	..	..	..	..	..	..	..	..	..	..	..
Korea, Dem. Rep.	..	..	..	..	..	..	..	..	..	..	..	..
Korea, Rep.	14	6	18	7	40	20	28	13	46	73	54	81
Kosovo	..	..	..	..	..	..	..	..	..	..	..	..
Kuwait	..	..	..	..	..	..	..	..	..	..	..	..
Kyrgyz Republic	..	..	..	..	..	..	..	..	..	..	..	..
Lao PDR	..	..	..	..	..	..	..	..	..	..	..	..
Latvia	..	12	..	6	..	34	..	14	..	53	..	80
Lebanon	..	..	..	..	..	..	..	..	..	..	..	..
Lesotho	..	..	..	..	..	..	..	..	..	..	..	..
Liberia	..	50	..	48	..	14	..	5	..	37	..	47
Libya	..	..	..	..	..	..	..	..	..	..	..	..
Lithuania	..	12	..	7	..	33	..	16	..	55	..	77
Macedonia, FYR	..	20	..	20	..	33	..	28	..	47	..	52
Madagascar	..	..	..	..	..	..	..	..	..	..	..	..
Malawi	..	..	..	..	..	..	..	..	..	..	..	..
Malaysia	23	17	20	9	31	32	32	23	46	51	48	68
Mali	..	..	..	..	..	..	..	..	..	..	..	..
Mauritania	..	..	..	..	..	..	..	..	..	..	..	..
Mauritius	15	10	13	8	36	32	48	22	48	58	39	70
Mexico	34	19	11	4	25	30	19	18	41	51	70	78
Moldova	..	34	..	28	..	26	..	14	..	41	..	58
Mongolia	..	41[b]	..	39[b]	..	19[b]	..	11[b]	..	40[b]	..	50[b]
Morocco	4[b]	34	3[b]	59	33[b]	24	46[b]	15	63[b]	42	51[b]	25
Mozambique	..	..	..	..	..	..	..	..	..	..	..	..
Myanmar	..	..	..	..	..	..	..	..	..	..	..	..
Namibia	45	23	52	8	21	24	8	9	34	53	40	83
Nepal	75	..	91	..	4	..	1	..	20	..	8	..
Netherlands	5	4	2	2	33	24	10	6	60	61	81	84
New Zealand	13[b]	9	8[b]	4	31[b]	31	13[b]	10	56[b]	61	79[b]	86
Nicaragua	..	42	..	8	..	21	..	19	..	37	..	72
Niger	..	..	..	..	..	..	..	..	..	..	..	..
Nigeria	..	..	..	..	..	..	..	..	..	..	..	..
Norway	7	4	3	1	34	31	10	7	58	65	86	92
Oman	..	..	..	..	..	..	..	..	..	..	..	..
Pakistan	45	37	69	75	20	22	15	12	35	41	16	13
Panama	36	24	3	7	19	24	11	10	45	52	86	82
Papua New Guinea	..	..	..	..	..	..	..	..	..	..	..	..
Paraguay	3[b]	31	0[b]	19	33[b]	25	19[b]	10	64[b]	44	80[b]	71
Peru	1[b]	1[b]	0[b]	1[b]	30[b]	32[b]	13[b]	14[b]	69[b]	67[b]	87[b]	86[b]
Philippines	53	42	32	24	17	18	14	10	29	40	55	66
Poland	..	13	..	13	..	42	..	16	..	45	..	71
Portugal	10	11	13	11	39	38	24	16	51	51	63	73
Puerto Rico	5	2	0	1	27	25	19	10	67	73	80	90
Qatar	..	3	..	0	..	58	..	5	..	39	..	95

	Agriculture				Industry				Services			
	Male % of male employment		Female % of female employment		Male % of male employment		Female % of female employment		Male % of male employment		Female % of female employment	
	1990–92[a]	2007–10[a]	1990–92[a]	2007–10[a]	1990–92[a]	2007–10[a]	1990–92[a]	2007–10[a]	1990–92[a]	2007–10[a]	1990–92[a]	2007–10[a]
Romania	29	29	38	31	44	36	30	20	28	35	33	49
Russian Federation	..	11	..	7	..	38	..	19	..	51	..	74
Rwanda	..	..	..	..	..	..	..	..	..	..	..	..
Saudi Arabia	..	5	..	0	..	23	..	2	..	72	..	98
Senegal	..	..	..	..	..	..	..	..	..	..	..	..
Serbia	..	25	..	23	..	32	..	16	..	43	..	61
Sierra Leone	..	..	..	..	..	..	..	..	..	..	..	..
Singapore	1	2	0	1	36	26	32	17	63	73	68	83
Slovak Republic	..	4	..	2	..	50	..	21	..	46	..	77
Slovenia	..	9	..	9	..	43	..	21	..	48	..	71
Somalia	..	..	..	..	..	..	..	..	..	..	..	..
South Africa	..	6	..	4	..	35	..	13	..	59	..	83
South Sudan	..	..	..	..	..	..	..	..	..	..	..	..
Spain	11	6	8	3	41	34	17	10	49	60	75	88
Sri Lanka	..	30[b]	..	37[b]	..	25[b]	..	25[b]	..	27[b]	..	27[b]
Sudan	..	..	..	..	..	..	..	..	..	..	..	..
Swaziland	..	..	..	..	..	..	..	..	..	..	..	..
Sweden	5	3	2	1	40	31	12	8	55	66	86	91
Switzerland	5	4	4	2	39	30	15	10	57	61	81	82
Syrian Arab Republic	23	14	54	24	28	36	8	9	49	51	38	67
Tajikistan	..	..	..	..	..	..	..	..	..	..	..	..
Tanzania	78[b]	..	90[b]	..	7[b]	..	1[b]	..	15[b]	..	8[b]	..
Thailand	60	44	62	39	18	21	13	18	22	35	25	43
Timor-Leste	..	..	..	..	..	..	..	..	..	..	..	..
Togo	..	..	..	..	..	..	..	..	..	..	..	..
Trinidad and Tobago	15	5	6	2	34	44	14	15	51	51	80	82
Tunisia	..	..	..	..	..	..	..	..	..	..	..	..
Turkey	33	18	72	39	26	30	11	16	41	52	17	45
Turkmenistan	..	..	..	..	..	..	..	..	..	..	..	..
Uganda	..	..	..	..	..	..	..	..	..	..	..	..
Ukraine	..	..	..	..	..	..	..	..	..	..	..	..
United Arab Emirates	..	5	..	0	..	28	..	7	..	66	..	93
United Kingdom	3	2	1	1	41	29	16	7	55	68	82	91
United States	4	2	1	1	34	25	14	7	62	72	85	92
Uruguay	7[b]	16	1[b]	5	36[b]	29	21[b]	13	57[b]	56	78[b]	83
Uzbekistan	..	..	..	..	..	..	..	..	..	..	..	..
Venezuela, RB	17	13	2	2	32	31	16	11	52	57	82	87
Vietnam	..	..	..	..	..	..	..	..	..	..	..	..
West Bank and Gaza	..	10	..	28	..	29	..	11	..	61	..	61
Yemen, Rep.	44	..	83	..	14	..	2	..	38	..	13	..
Zambia	47	..	56	..	15	..	3	..	22	..	18	..
Zimbabwe	..	..	..	..	..	..	..	..	..	..	..	..
World	.. w	.. w	.. w	.. w	.. w	.. w	.. w	.. w	.. w	.. w	.. w	.. w
Low income	..	..	..	..	..	..	..	..	..	..	..	..
Middle income	..	..	..	..	..	..	..	..	..	..	..	..
Lower middle income	..	..	..	..	..	..	..	..	..	..	..	..
Upper middle income	..	..	..	..	..	..	..	..	..	..	..	..
Low & middle income	..	..	..	..	..	..	..	..	..	..	..	..
East Asia & Pacific	..	..	..	..	..	..	..	..	..	..	..	..
Europe & Central Asia	..	16	..	15	..	35	..	18	..	49	..	66
Latin America & Carib.	21	19	15	8	30	29	14	14	49	52	71	78
Middle East & N. Africa	..	23	..	43	..	29	..	14	..	48	..	43
South Asia	..	46	..	65	..	24	..	18	..	30	..	17
Sub-Saharan Africa	..	..	..	..	..	..	..	..	..	..	..	..
High income	6	4	5	3	38	31	19	11	56	64	76	86
Euro area	7	4	6	3	42	36	20	12	50	59	73	85

Note: Data across sectors may not sum to 100 percent because of workers not classified by sector.
a. Data are for the most recent year available. b. Limited coverage.

Employment by economic activity | 2.3

The International Labour Organization (ILO) classifies economic activity using the International Standard Industrial Classification (ISIC) of All Economic Activities, revision 2 (1968), revision 3 (1990), and revision 4 (2008). Because this classification is based on where work is performed (industry) rather than type of work performed (occupation), all of an enterprise's employees are classified under the same industry, regardless of their trade or occupation. The categories should sum to 100 percent. Where they do not, the differences are due to workers who are not classified by economic activity.

Data on employment are drawn from labor force surveys, household surveys, official estimates, censuses and administrative records of social insurance schemes, and establishment surveys when no other information is available. The concept of employment generally refers to people above a certain age who worked, or who held a job, during a reference period. Employment data include both full-time and part-time workers.

There are many differences in how countries define and measure employment status, particularly members of the armed forces, self-employed workers, and unpaid family workers. Where members of the armed forces are included, they are allocated to the service sector, causing that sector to be somewhat overstated relative to the service sector in economies where they are excluded. Where data are obtained from establishment surveys, data cover only employees; thus self-employed and unpaid family workers are excluded. In such cases the employment share of the agricultural sector is severely underreported. Caution should be also used where the data refer only to urban areas, which record little or no agricultural work. Moreover, the age group and area covered could differ by country or change over time within a country. For detailed information, consult the original source.

Countries also take different approaches to the treatment of unemployed people. In most countries unemployed people with previous job experience are classified according to their last job. But in some countries the unemployed and people seeking their first job are not classifiable by economic activity. Because of these differences, the size and distribution of employment by economic activity may not be fully comparable across countries.

The ILO reports data by major divisions of the ISIC revision 2, revision 3, or revision 4. In the table the reported divisions or categories are aggregated into three broad groups: agriculture, industry, and services. Such broad classification may obscure fundamental shifts within countries' industrial patterns. A slight majority of countries report economic activity according to the ISIC revision 2 instead of revision 3 or revision 4. The use of one classification or the other should not have a significant impact on the information for the three broad sectors presented in the table.

The distribution of economic wealth in the world remains strongly correlated with employment by economic activity. The wealthier economies are those with the largest share of total employment in services, whereas the poorer economies are largely agriculture based.

The distribution of economic activity by gender reveals some clear patterns. Men still make up the majority of people employed in all three sectors, but the gender gap is biggest in industry. Employment in agriculture is also male-dominated, although not as much as industry. Segregating one sex in a narrow range of occupations significantly reduces economic efficiency by reducing labor market flexibility and thus the economy's ability to adapt to change. This segregation is particularly harmful for women, who have a much narrower range of labor market choices and lower levels of pay than men. But it is also detrimental to men when job losses are concentrated in industries dominated by men and job growth is centered in service occupations, where women have better chances, as has been the recent experience in many countries.

There are several explanations for the rising importance of service jobs for women. Many service jobs—such as nursing and social and clerical work—are considered "feminine" because of a perceived similarity to women's traditional roles. Women often do not receive the training needed to take advantage of changing employment opportunities. And the greater availability of part-time work in service industries may lure more women, although it is unclear whether this is a cause or an effect.

• **Agriculture** corresponds to division 1 (ISIC revision 2), tabulation categories A and B (ISIC revision 3), or tabulation category A (ISIC revision 4) and includes hunting, forestry, and fishing. • **Industry** corresponds to divisions 2–5 (ISIC revision 2), tabulation categories C–F (ISIC revision 3), or tabulation categories B–F (ISIC revision 4) and includes mining and quarrying (including oil production), manufacturing, construction, and public utilities (electricity, gas, and water). • **Services** correspond to divisions 6–9 (ISIC revision 2), tabulation categories G–P (ISIC revision 3), or tabulation categories G–U (ISIC revision 4) and include wholesale and retail trade and restaurants and hotels; transport, storage, and communications; financing, insurance, real estate, and business services; and community, social, and personal services.

Data on employment are from the ILO's Key Indicators of the Labour Market, 7th edition, database.

2.4 Decent work and productive employment

	Employment to population ratio				Gross enrollment ratio, secondary		Vulnerable employment				Labor productivity	
	Total % ages 15 and older		Youth % ages 15–24		% of relevant age group		Unpaid family workers and own-account workers				GDP per person employed % growth	
							Male % of male employment		Female % of female employment			
	1991	2010	1991	2010	1991	2010a	1990	2007–10b	1990	2007–10b	1990–92	2008–10
Afghanistan	46	45	32	31	16	46	..	..	..	..	..	..
Albania	52	52	40	36	89	89	..	..	..	..	–16.6	6.6
Algeria	34	39	22	22	60	95	..	..	..	..	–4.6	0.8
Angola	66	64	47	46	12	31	..	..	..	..	–5.6	0.8
Argentina	55	56	48	34	74	89	25c	22c	27c	17c	9.0	0.2
Armenia	46	41	26	18	..	92	..	36	..	40	–24.4	–6.5
Australia	57	62	58	61	132	129	12	11	9	7	3.0	0.7
Austria	54	58	61	54	102	100	..	9	..	9	1.3	–0.9
Azerbaijan	56	60	37	31	88	..	..	47	..	62	–12.6	5.5
Bahrain	61	65	32	32	100	..	..	2	..	1	0.8	1.9
Bangladesh	73	68	64	53	18	49	..	..	..	..	2.3	3.4
Belarus	59	50	39	31	93	..	..	..	..	..	–4.0	3.2
Belgium	46	50	31	25	101	111	18	11	17	8	1.6	–0.4
Benin	72	72	66	57	..	..	..	..	..	..	..	..
Bolivia	63	69	48	49	..	80	32c	49	50c	67	2.6	1.3
Bosnia and Herzegovina	39	35	21	17	..	90	..	..	..	..	–14.7	–1.9
Botswana	56	63	36	41	49	..	..	..	..	..	..	..
Brazil	60	65	54	53	..	101	29c	27	30c	22	–0.3	1.8
Bulgaria	47	49	30	24	98	88	..	10	..	8	3.1	1.5
Burkina Faso	82	81	76	73	7	21	..	..	..	..	1.6	0.3
Burundi	83	77	70	56	5	25	..	..	..	..	..	..
Cambodia	80	81	71	70	25	46	..	79	..	86	4.0	–1.2
Cameroon	64	68	42	43	26	42	..	..	..	..	–6.6	–0.3
Canada	59	61	57	55	101	101	..	..	..	..	0.8	0.2
Central African Republic	72	73	56	54	12	13	..	..	..	..	..	..
Chad	67	67	49	49	6	26	..	..	..	..	..	..
Chile	50	55	33	31	97	88	..	26	..	25	6.6	0.4
China	75	71	72	57	41	81	..	..	..	..	6.8	8.8
Hong Kong SAR, China	63	57	54	31	..	83	..	10	..	5	5.4	1.7
Colombia	46	59	35	35	53	96	30c	48	26c	49	–0.7	0.6
Congo, Dem. Rep.	66	66	40	39	21	38	..	..	..	..	–13.0	0.4
Congo, Rep.	62	66	40	39	46	..	..	..	..	..	..	..
Costa Rica	55	60	48	42	45	100	26	19	21	20	2.4	–0.7
Côte d'Ivoire	63	64	50	48	..	..	..	..	..	..	–4.1	0.7
Croatia	51	46	27	25	83	95	..	17	..	19	–7.7	–0.6
Cuba	53	56	41	40	94	89	..	..	..	..	..	..
Cyprus	57	60	41	34	72	98	..	16	..	12	–0.9	0.2
Czech Republic	60	54	49	25	91	90	..	17	..	10	–5.2	0.2
Denmark	62	60	65	58	109	117	8	7	6	4	2.5	0.8
Dominican Republic	52	56	37	37	..	76	42	49	30	30	0.9	2.0
Ecuador	57	64	45	44	55	80	33c	37	41c	51	–0.1	–0.9
Egypt, Arab Rep.	43	44	22	25	69	..	..	22	..	49	–1.3	2.6
El Salvador	57	57	46	42	38	65	..	33	..	46	..	..
Eritrea	75	78	69	67	11	32	..	..	..	..	..	..
Estonia	67	51	50	27	100	104	2	6	3	4	–8.0	1.9
Ethiopia	76	80	70	71	14	36	..	..	..	..	–7.9	5.8
Finland	60	55	49	40	116	108	..	12	..	7	1.7	–1.3
France	50	51	33	31	100	113	11	8	11	6	1.4	0.1
Gabon	52	50	20	15	40	..	..	..	..	..	..	..
Gambia, The	71	72	58	56	19	54	..	..	..	..	..	..
Georgia	55	54	23	20	95	86	..	62	..	65	–25.4	0.3
Germany	56	55	58	47	98	103	5	8	6	6	3.7	–0.9
Ghana	68	67	43	36	35	58d	..	..	..	..	0.7	1.9
Greece	46	48	31	21	94	..	40	29	46	27	2.1	–1.6
Guatemala	62	65	54	58	23	59	..	..	..	..	1.0	–2.5
Guinea	69	70	51	52	11	38	..	..	..	..	..	..
Guinea-Bissau	64	68	44	48	5	..	..	..	..	..	..	..
Haiti	58	60	32	29	..	..	..	..	..	..	..	..

Decent work and productive employment

	Employment to population ratio				Gross enrollment ratio, secondary		Vulnerable employment				Labor productivity	
	Total % ages 15 and older		Youth % ages 15–24		% of relevant age group		Unpaid family workers and own-account workers				GDP per person employed % growth	
							Male % of male employment		Female % of female employment			
	1991	2010	1991	2010	1991	2010ᵃ	1990	2007–10ᵇ	1990	2007–10ᵇ	1990–92	2008–10
Honduras	57	60	49	47	33	73	48ᶜ	49	50ᶜ	52	..	..
Hungary	49	45	38	18	86	98	8	8	7	5	0.3	−1.3
India	58	54	46	34	46	60	..	..	..	..	1.0	5.6
Indonesia	63	63	46	40	46	77	..	62	..	67	6.2	3.2
Iran, Islamic Rep.	40	40	28	24	53	84	..	40	..	52	5.7	−0.9
Iraq	32	34	20	17	40	..	..	..	..	..	−32.8	0.3
Ireland	45	52	38	31	100	117	25	18	10	5	2.6	2.1
Israel	46	54	24	27	92	91	..	9	..	5	1.6	0.3
Italy	45	44	33	20	79	99	29	21	24	15	0.6	−1.0
Jamaica	63	56	43	25	70	93	46	41	37	31	0.7	−3.1
Japan	63	57	43	39	97	102	15	10	26	11	0.5	0.0
Jordan	32	36	17	20	82	91	..	11	..	3	−5.0	0.1
Kazakhstan	64	67	45	44	98	97	..	30	..	34	−15.1	−0.9
Kenya	67	60	45	33	..	60	..	..	..	..	−3.9	0.6
Korea, Dem. Rep.	79	74	73	57	..	..	..	..	..	..	..	..
Korea, Rep.	59	58	36	24	91	97	..	23	..	27	5.1	2.7
Kosovo	..	..	..	..	..	..	..	..	..	..	..	..
Kuwait	58	66	26	31	53	101	..	..	..	..	−0.2	−4.4
Kyrgyz Republic	60	61	41	40	100	84	..	..	..	..	−13.1	−2.0
Lao PDR	80	77	72	62	21	45	..	..	..	..	..	..
Latvia	59	49	43	27	92	95	..	8	..	7	−19.6	−0.2
Lebanon	39	42	26	23	61	81	..	32	..	16	..	..
Lesotho	49	47	38	28	24	46	..	..	..	..	..	..
Liberia	57	59	34	33	..	..	..	69	..	89	..	..
Libya	44	49	25	29	..	..	..	..	..	..	..	..
Lithuania	56	48	35	20	92	98	..	10	..	8	−13.9	−0.9
Macedonia, FYR	38	38	18	15	76	83	..	24	..	22	−6.9	−2.0
Madagascar	83	84	71	71	19	31	..	..	..	..	−5.8	−6.1
Malawi	72	77	47	51	17	32	..	..	..	..	−2.1	3.7
Malaysia	60	59	46	35	57	68	31	23	25	20	6.0	0.3
Mali	47	48	35	36	7	38	..	77	..	89	1.3	1.9
Mauritania	32	36	15	16	13	24	..	..	..	..	..	..
Mauritius	53	55	41	31	55	89	13	17	7	14	..	..
Mexico	57	58	50	43	54	87	29	27	15	32	1.0	−1.2
Moldova	59	38	38	18	90	88	..	34	..	28	−23.1	−2.2
Mongolia	51	57	35	32	82	93	..	60	..	54	..	..
Morocco	46	45	39	30	36	..	..	47	..	65	−1.6	2.7
Mozambique	77	78	64	57	7	25	..	..	..	..	−3.6	4.2
Myanmar	73	76	51	53	23	54	..	..	..	..	2.0	..
Namibia	45	40	24	11	43	..	..	..	..	..	..	..
Nepal	84	82	79	73	34	..	..	..	..	..	..	..
Netherlands	53	62	53	63	120	120	7	13	12	10	0.4	−0.3
New Zealand	57	63	54	50	92	119	15	15	10	9	0.6	1.1
Nicaragua	55	60	47	46	43	69	..	45	..	45	..	..
Niger	54	61	47	53	7	13	..	..	..	..	−5.9	−2.5
Nigeria	53	51	29	32	24	44	..	..	..	..	−2.8	4.6
Norway	59	64	49	52	103	110	..	8	..	3	3.9	−0.3
Oman	52	55	28	32	45	100	..	..	..	..	0.6	1.4
Pakistan	47	51	38	41	23	34	..	59	..	78	6.4	−0.1
Panama	49	62	34	42	62	74	44	33	19	28	..	..
Papua New Guinea	70	71	57	54	12	..	..	..	..	..	..	..
Paraguay	68	69	64	57	31	67	17ᶜ	42	31ᶜ	48	..	..
Peru	53	71	35	55	67	92	30ᶜ	34ᶜ	46ᶜ	47ᶜ	−0.8	2.4
Philippines	60	60	42	39	70	85	..	42	..	46	−3.3	1.4
Poland	54	51	32	27	87	97	..	20	..	17	1.1	1.9
Portugal	59	55	53	29	66	107	22	18	28	17	2.1	1.3
Puerto Rico	38	37	20	18	..	82	..	..	..	..	..	..
Qatar	79	86	51	66	84	94	..	0	..	0	−0.3	11.1

	Employment to population ratio				Gross enrollment ratio, secondary		Vulnerable employment				Labor productivity	
							Unpaid family workers and own-account workers				GDP per person employed	
	Total % ages 15 and older		Youth % ages 15–24		% of relevant age group		Male % of male employment		Female % of female employment		% growth	
	1991	2010	1991	2010	1991	2010ᵃ	1990	2007–10ᵇ	1990	2007–10ᵇ	1990–92	2008–10
Romania	57	52	49	24	92	95	21	33	33	33	–9.3	–3.2
Russian Federation	59	58	41	36	93	89	1	6	1	5	–7.9	–1.4
Rwanda	88	85	80	73	18	32	..	..	..	..	..	..
Saudi Arabia	51	47	25	12	..	101	..	..	..	..	4.8	–0.7
Senegal	68	69	59	57	15	37	77	..	91	..	–1.1	0.0
Serbia	48ᵉ	46ᵉ	28ᵉ	19ᵉ	..	91	..	30	..	29	..	..
Sierra Leone	64	65	39	42	16	..	..	..	..	..	..	..
Singapore	64	63	56	34	..	..	10	12	6	7	–2.0	5.0
Slovak Republic	59	51	46	21	88	89	..	17	..	7	–0.8	1.6
Slovenia	50	55	28	34	89	97	..	15	..	12	–2.3	–1.6
Somalia	52	53	42	39	..	..	..	..	..	..	..	..
South Africa	37	39	15	13	69	94	..	8	..	12	–5.3	–0.4
South Sudan	..	..	..	..	..	..	..	..	..	..	..	..
Spain	42	47	35	25	105	119	21	13	25	9	1.8	2.5
Sri Lanka	49	52	28	30	72	..	..	38ᶜ	..	44ᶜ	5.5	4.8
Sudan	47	49	32	27	20	39	..	..	..	..	1.4	1.7
Swaziland	44	44	27	26	49	58	..	..	..	..	..	..
Sweden	64	58	58	38	90	100	..	9	..	5	1.9	–0.1
Switzerland	67	65	69	61	98	95	8	9	11	9	–0.6	–1.1
Syrian Arab Republic	46	39	38	24	48	72	..	34	..	25	6.3	1.5
Tajikistan	58	58	38	38	102	87	..	..	..	..	–20.4	5.8
Tanzania	79	79	70	69	5	27	86ᶜ	..	96ᶜ	..	–2.3	3.3
Thailand	77	71	70	46	31	77	67	50	74	55	6.8	0.7
Timor-Leste	58	54	46	41	..	56	..	..	..	..	..	..
Togo	70	75	56	57	20	..	..	..	..	..	..	..
Trinidad and Tobago	45	63	33	48	82	90	22	..	21	..	–3.5	0.6
Tunisia	41	41	29	23	45	90	..	..	..	..	2.5	1.7
Turkey	53	44	48	32	48	78	..	28	..	48	1.0	–1.5
Turkmenistan	53	54	34	35	..	..	..	..	..	..	–13.0	4.9
Uganda	79	75	61	55	10	28	..	..	..	..	–0.8	3.1
Ukraine	58	54	36	34	94	96	..	..	..	..	–7.9	–4.3
United Arab Emirates	71	76	44	43	68	..	..	1	..	0	–3.6	–5.2
United Kingdom	58	57	63	48	87	102	13	15	6	8	6.1	–0.9
United States	61	58	54	42	92	96	..	..	..	..	1.7	2.3
Uruguay	55	61	45	44	84	90	..	22ᶜ	..	24ᶜ	5.2	3.9
Uzbekistan	52	54	33	35	99	105	..	..	..	..	–7.7	5.4
Venezuela, RB	55	61	38	40	56	83	..	30	..	32	4.5	–3.9
Vietnam	78	75	73	58	35	77	..	..	..	..	4.6	3.4
West Bank and Gaza	31	31	20	16	..	86	..	26	..	31	..	..
Yemen, Rep.	39	42	24	27	..	44	..	..	..	..	0.9	2.2
Zambia	65	67	47	51	21	..	56	..	81	..	–2.7	3.6
Zimbabwe	69	83	48	73	49	..	..	..	..	..	–4.3	5.4
World	**62 w**	**60 w**	**52 w**	**43 w**	**50 w**	**68 w**	**.. w**	**.. w**	**.. w**	**.. w**	**0.9 w**	**2.0 w**
Low income	72	71	58	55	26	39	..	..	..	..	–3.4	–2.3
Middle income	63	60	52	41	47	69	..	..	..	..	1.2	4.2
Lower middle income	58	55	43	36	42	58	..	70	..	77	0.4	3.7
Upper middle income	67	65	60	48	67	83	..	..	..	..	1.5	4.4
Low & middle income	64	61	53	43	44	64	..	..	..	..	1.0	4.3
East Asia & Pacific	73	70	67	53	41	76	..	..	..	..	6.4	7.9
Europe & Central Asia	57	54	41	34	85	89	..	18	..	19	–9.3	–0.7
Latin America & Carib.	57	62	47	45	57	90	30	31	29	31	1.3	0.1
Middle East & N. Africa	40	41	27	24	54	72	..	33	..	48	1.0	1.1
South Asia	59	55	47	37	37	55	..	78	..	86	3.2	4.8
Sub-Saharan Africa	63	64	46	46	22	36	..	..	..	..	–4.8	1.5
High income	57	55	46	38	91	100	..	..	..	..	2.8	0.7
Euro area	50	51	42	34	..	107	16	13	14	9	2.3	–0.1

a. Provisional data. b. Data are for the most recent year available. c. Limited coverage. d. Data are for 2011. e. Includes Montenegro.

Decent work and productive employment | 2.4

Four targets were added to the UN Millennium Declaration at the 2005 World Summit High-Level Plenary Meeting of the 60th Session of the UN General Assembly. One was full and productive employment and decent work for all, which is seen as the main route for people to escape poverty. The four indicators for this target have an economic focus, and three of them are presented in the table.

The employment to population ratio indicates how efficiently an economy provides jobs for people who want to work. A high ratio means that a large proportion of the population is employed. But a lower employment to population ratio can be seen as a positive sign, especially for young people, if it is caused by an increase in their education. This indicator has a gender bias because women who do not consider their work employment or who are not perceived as working tend to be undercounted. This bias has different effects across countries and reflects demographic, social, legal, and cultural trends and norms.

Comparability of employment ratios across countries is also affected by variations in definitions of employment and population (see *About the data* for table 2.3). The biggest difference results from the age range used to define labor force activity. The population base for employment ratios can also vary (see table 2.1). Most countries use the resident, noninstitutionalized population of working age living in private households, which excludes members of the armed forces and individuals residing in mental, penal, or other types of institutions. But some countries include members of the armed forces in the population base of their employment ratio while excluding them from employment data (International Labour Organization, *Key Indicators of the Labour Market,* 7th edition).

The proportion of unpaid family workers and own-account workers in total employment is derived from information on status in employment. Each status group faces different economic risks, and unpaid family workers and own-account workers are the most vulnerable—and therefore the most likely to fall into poverty. They are the least likely to have formal work arrangements, are the least likely to have social protection and safety nets to guard against economic shocks, and often are incapable of generating sufficient savings to offset these shocks. A high proportion of unpaid family workers in a country indicates weak development, little job growth, and often a large rural economy.

Data on employment by status are drawn from labor force surveys and household surveys, supplemented by official estimates and censuses for a small group of countries. The labor force survey is the most comprehensive source for internationally comparable employment, but there are still some limitations for comparing data across countries and over time even within a country. Information from labor force surveys is not always consistent in what is included in employment. For example, information provided by the Organisation for Economic Cooperation and Development relates only to civilian employment, which can result in an underestimation of "employees" and "workers not classified by status," especially in countries with large armed forces. While the categories of unpaid family workers and self-employed workers, which include own-account workers, would not be affected, their relative shares would be. Geographic coverage is another factor that can limit cross-country comparisons. The employment by status data for many Latin American countries covers urban areas only. Similarly, in some countries in Sub-Saharan Africa, where limited information is available anyway, the members of producer cooperatives are usually excluded from the self-employed category. For detailed information on definitions and coverage, consult the original source.

Labor productivity is used to assess a country's economic ability to create and sustain decent employment opportunities with fair and equitable remuneration. Productivity increases obtained through investment, trade, technological progress, or changes in work organization can increase social protection and reduce poverty, which in turn reduce vulnerable employment and working poverty. Productivity increases do not guarantee these improvements, but without them—and the economic growth they bring—improvements are highly unlikely. For comparability of individual sectors labor productivity is estimated according to national accounts conventions. However, there are still significant limitations on the availability of reliable data. Information on consistent series of output in both national currencies and purchasing power parity dollars is not easily available, especially in developing countries, because the definition, coverage, and methodology are not always consistent across countries. For example, countries employ different methodologies for estimating the missing values for the nonmarket service sectors and use different definitions of the informal sector.

• **Employment to population ratio** is the proportion of a country's population that is employed. People ages 15 and older are generally considered the working-age population. People ages 15–24 are generally considered the youth population. • **Gross enrollment ratio, secondary,** is the ratio of total enrollment in secondary education, regardless of age, to the population of the age group that officially corresponds to secondary education. • **Vulnerable employment** is unpaid family workers and own-account workers as a percentage of total employment. • **Labor productivity** is the growth rate of gross domestic product (GDP) divided by the number of people engaged in the production of goods and services.

Data sources

Data on employment to population ratio, vulnerable employment, and labor productivity are from the International Labour Organization's Key Indicators of the Labour Market, 7th edition, database. Data on gross enrollment ratios are from the United Nations Educational, Scientific, and Cultural Organization Institute for Statistics.

	Unemployment						Long-term unemployment			Unemployment by educational attainment		
	Total % of total labor force		Male % of male labor force		Female % of female labor force		% of total unemployment			% of total unemployment		
	1990–92[a]	2007–10[a]	1990–92[a]	2007–10[a]	1990–92[a]	2007–10[a]	Total 2007–10[a]	Male 2007–10[a]	Female 2007–10[a]	Primary 2007–10[a]	Secondary 2007–10[a]	Tertiary 2007–10[a]
Afghanistan	..	..	..	..	..	..	..	..	..	..	..	..
Albania	..	13.8	..	12.2	..	15.9	..	..	..	..	..	..
Algeria	23.0	11.4	24.2	10.0	20.3	20.0	..	..	..	..	..	..
Angola	..	..	..	..	..	..	..	..	..	..	..	..
Argentina	6.7[b]	8.6[b]	6.4[b]	7.8[b]	7.0[b]	9.8[b]	..	..	..	48.1	36.7	15.3
Armenia	..	28.6	..	21.9	..	35.0	58.2	52.2	63.8	11.1	68.3	20.6
Australia	10.8	5.2[b]	11.4	5.1[b]	10.0	5.4[b]	18.5[b]	20.3[b]	16.4[b]	47.4	33.6	19.0
Austria	3.6	4.4	3.5	4.6	3.8	4.2	25.2	27.8	22.0	37.5	54.5	8.0
Azerbaijan	..	6.0	..	5.2	..	6.9	..	..	..	9.9	75.8	14.3
Bahrain	6.3	..	5.2	..	11.8	..	..	..	..	22.7	38.8	31.7
Bangladesh	1.9	5.0	2.0	4.2	1.9	7.4	..	..	..	..	..	..
Belarus	..	..	..	..	..	..	..	..	..	10.8	38.6	50.6
Belgium	6.7	8.3	4.8	8.1	9.5	8.5	48.8	49.6	47.8	33.9	40.5	19.0
Benin	1.5	..	2.2	..	0.6	..	..	..	..	..	..	..
Bolivia	5.5[b]	5.2	5.5[b]	4.5	5.6[b]	6.0	..	..	..	..	..	..
Bosnia and Herzegovina	17.6	27.2	15.5	25.6	21.6	30.0	..	..	..	94.9		4.8
Botswana	13.8	..	11.7	..	17.2	..	..	..	..	..	..	..
Brazil	6.4[b]	8.3	5.4[b]	6.1	7.9[b]	11.0	..	..	..	49.3	35.7	4.1
Bulgaria	..	10.2	..	10.9	..	9.5	46.4	46.3	46.5	42.5	47.4	10.1
Burkina Faso	..	3.3	..	..	..	..	..	..	..	..	..	..
Burundi	0.5	..	0.7	..	0.3	..	..	..	..	..	..	..
Cambodia	..	1.7	..	1.5	..	1.8	..	..	..	..	..	..
Cameroon	..	2.9	..	2.5	..	3.3	..	..	..	..	..	..
Canada	11.2[b]	8.0[b]	12.0[b]	8.7[b]	10.2[b]	7.2[b]	12.0[b]	12.7[b]	11.0[b]	26.3[b]	41.0[b]	32.7[b]
Central African Republic	..	..	..	..	..	..	..	..	..	..	..	..
Chad	..	..	..	..	..	..	..	..	..	..	..	..
Chile	4.4	8.1	3.9	7.2	5.3	9.6	..	..	..	17.8	58.5	23.5
China	2.3[b]	4.3	..	..	..	..	..	..	..	..	..	..
Hong Kong SAR, China	2.0	5.2	2.0	6.0	1.9	4.3	..	..	..	38.0	43.8	17.1
Colombia	9.5[b]	11.6	6.8[b]	9.1	13.0[b]	15.0	..	..	..	21.0	53.7	23.0
Congo, Dem. Rep.	..	..	..	..	..	..	..	..	..	..	..	..
Congo, Rep.	..	..	..	..	..	..	..	..	..	..	..	..
Costa Rica	4.1	7.8	3.5	6.6	5.4	9.9	..	..	..	66.9	23.4	7.9
Côte d'Ivoire	6.7	..	..	..	..	..	..	..	..	..	..	..
Croatia	11.1	11.8	11.1	11.4	11.2	12.2	44.4	41.4	47.7	16.0	70.4	11.6
Cuba	..	1.6	..	1.4	..	2.0	..	..	..	46.6	48.5	3.6
Cyprus	2.1	6.2	2.0	6.0	2.2	6.4	20.4	21.0	19.8	26.9[b]	42.1[b]	29.7[b]
Czech Republic	2.3	7.3	2.4	6.4	2.1	8.5	43.3	43.3	43.3	29.6	64.8	5.7
Denmark	9.0	7.4	8.3	8.2	9.9	6.6	19.1	20.6	16.9	35.5	37.2	20.8
Dominican Republic	20.7	14.3	12.0	9.8	35.2	21.4	..	..	..	32.0	42.2	19.5
Ecuador	8.9[b]	6.5	6.0[b]	5.2	13.2[b]	8.4	..	..	..	..	..	..
Egypt, Arab Rep.	9.0	9.4	6.4	5.2	17.0	22.9	..	..	..	..	..	..
El Salvador	7.9[b]	7.3	8.4[b]	9.0	7.2[b]	4.9	..	..	..	..	..	..
Eritrea	..	..	..	..	..	..	..	..	..	..	..	..
Estonia	3.7	16.9	3.9	19.5	3.5	14.3	27.4	26.8	28.4	25.2	58.1	18.0
Ethiopia	1.3	20.5	1.1	12.1	1.6	29.9	..	..	..	..	..	..
Finland	11.6	8.4	13.3	9.0	9.6	7.7	23.6	27.0	19.3	36.6	45.3	17.4
France	10.2	9.3	8.1	9.0	12.8	9.7	40.1	41.5	38.7	39.5	41.7	18.3
Gabon	..	..	..	..	..	..	..	..	..	..	..	..
Gambia, The	..	..	..	..	..	..	..	..	..	..	..	..
Georgia	..	16.5	..	16.8	..	16.1	..	..	..	4.6	56.1	39.2
Germany	6.6	7.1	5.3	7.5	8.4	6.6	47.4	48.1	46.3	32.3	56.5	11.0
Ghana	4.7	..	3.7	..	5.5	..	..	..	..	..	..	..
Greece	7.8	12.5	4.9	9.9	12.9	16.2	45.0	38.8	50.3	27.7	48.9	22.4
Guatemala	..	..	..	..	..	..	..	..	..	..	..	..
Guinea	..	..	..	..	..	..	..	..	..	..	..	..
Guinea-Bissau	..	..	..	..	..	..	..	..	..	..	..	..
Haiti	12.7	..	11.9	..	13.8	..	..	..	..	..	..	..

	Unemployment						Long-term unemployment			Unemployment by educational attainment		
	Total % of total labor force		Male % of male labor force		Female % of female labor force		% of total unemployment			% of total unemployment		
							Total	Male	Female	Primary	Secondary	Tertiary
	1990–92[a]	2007–10[a]	1990–92[a]	2007–10[a]	1990–92[a]	2007–10[a]	2007–10[a]	2007–10[a]	2007–10[a]	2007–10[a]	2007–10[a]	2007–10[a]
Honduras	3.2[b]	2.9	3.3[b]	2.9	3.0[b]	2.9	..	..	..	..	..	..
Hungary	9.9	11.2	11.0	11.6	8.7	10.7	50.6	51.2	49.9	33.8	58.4	7.8
India	..	..	..	..	..	..	..	..	..	..	..	..
Indonesia	2.8	7.1	2.7	6.1	3.0	8.7	..	..	..	43.4	40.6	10.2
Iran, Islamic Rep.	11.1	10.5	9.5	9.1	24.4	16.8	..	..	..	40.4	31.0	25.5
Iraq	..	..	..	..	..	..	..	..	..	..	..	..
Ireland	15.0	13.5	14.9	16.7	15.3	9.5	49.0	53.9	38.2	38.3	39.0	18.5
Israel	11.2	6.6	9.2	6.8	13.9	6.5	22.4	25.7	18.5	22.1	48.0	28.1
Italy	9.3	8.4	6.7	7.6	13.9	9.7	48.5	47.2	49.9	47.2	40.3	11.2
Jamaica	15.4	11.4	9.4	8.5	22.2	14.8	..	..	..	12.0	4.5	3.9
Japan	2.2	5.0	2.1	5.4	2.2	4.5	37.6	44.8	25.2	66.8	..	33.2
Jordan	..	12.9	..	10.3	..	24.1	..	..	..	..	..	..
Kazakhstan	..	6.6	..	5.6	..	7.5	..	..	..	45.1	39.7	15.2
Kenya	..	..	..	..	..	..	..	..	..	..	..	..
Korea, Dem. Rep.	..	..	..	..	..	..	..	..	..	..	..	..
Korea, Rep.	2.5	3.7	2.8	4.0	2.1	3.3	0.3	0.5	0.3	15.3	63.7	21.1
Kosovo	..	45.4	..	40.7	..	56.4	81.7	82.8	79.8	64.0	46.0	15.0
Kuwait	..	..	..	..	..	..	..	..	..	..	..	..
Kyrgyz Republic	..	8.6	..	7.3	..	9.4	..	..	..	..	..	..
Lao PDR	..	..	..	..	..	..	..	..	..	..	..	..
Latvia	..	18.7	..	21.7	..	15.7	45.0	48.2	40.6	23.3	62.2	14.5
Lebanon	..	9.0	..	8.6	..	10.1	..	..	..	45.5	19.7	29.7
Lesotho	..	25.3	..	23.0	..	28.0	..	..	..	57.2	33.5	0.4
Liberia	..	3.7	..	3.4	..	4.1	..	..	..	..	..	..
Libya	..	..	..	..	..	..	..	..	..	..	..	..
Lithuania	..	17.8	..	21.2	..	14.4	41.4	42.3	40.2	15.0	67.7	17.3
Macedonia, FYR	..	32.0	..	31.9	..	32.2	83.1	83.5	82.4	..	..	..
Madagascar	..	..	..	..	..	..	..	..	..	..	..	..
Malawi	..	..	..	..	..	..	..	..	..	..	..	..
Malaysia	3.7	3.7	3.4	3.6	4.2	3.8	..	..	..	10.4	60.9	24.9
Mali	..	..	..	..	..	..	..	..	..	..	..	..
Mauritania	..	..	..	..	..	..	..	..	..	..	..	..
Mauritius	3.3	7.7	3.2	4.6	3.6	12.8	..	..	..	43.5	29.6	7.9
Mexico	3.1	5.3	2.7	5.3	4.0	5.3	2.4	2.7	2.0	51.5	25.2	21.0
Moldova	..	6.4	..	7.8	..	4.9	..	..	..	..	..	..
Mongolia	..	..	..	..	..	..	..	..	..	28.2	49.0	22.1
Morocco	16.0[b]	10.0	13.0[b]	9.8	25.3[b]	10.5	..	..	..	..	..	..
Mozambique	..	..	..	..	..	..	..	..	..	..	..	..
Myanmar	6.0	..	4.7	..	8.8	..	..	..	..	..	..	..
Namibia	19.0	37.6	20.0	32.5	19.0	43.0	..	..	..	..	..	..
Nepal	..	2.7	..	3.1	..	2.4	..	..	..	..	..	..
Netherlands	5.6	4.5	4.0	4.4	7.8	4.5	27.6	27.7	27.4	42.0	36.6	18.7
New Zealand	10.6[b]	6.5[b]	11.4[b]	6.2[b]	9.7[b]	6.8[b]	9.0[b]	8.9[b]	9.0[b]	30.6	39.2	25.7
Nicaragua	14.4	5.0	11.3	4.9	19.5	5.1	..	..	..	..	..	..
Niger	..	..	..	..	..	..	..	..	..	..	..	..
Nigeria	..	..	..	..	..	..	..	..	..	..	..	..
Norway	5.9	3.6	6.6	4.1	5.1	3.0	9.5	10.6	7.7	29.9	49.3	17.9
Oman	..	..	..	..	..	..	..	..	..	..	..	..
Pakistan	5.2	5.0	3.8	4.0	14.0	8.7	..	..	..	14.7	10.1	28.0
Panama	14.7	6.5	10.8	5.3	22.3	8.5	..	..	..	35.8	39.8	23.8
Papua New Guinea	7.7	..	9.0	..	5.9	..	..	..	..	..	..	..
Paraguay	5.0[b]	5.6	6.0[b]	4.4	3.7[b]	7.5	..	..	..	53.5	31.4	13.4
Peru	9.4[b]	6.3[b]	7.5[b]	4.4[b]	12.5[b]	8.8[b]	..	..	..	31.5[b]	30.5[b]	37.3[b]
Philippines	8.6	7.4	7.9	7.6	9.9	6.9	..	..	..	13.1	45.2	41.2
Poland	13.3	9.6	12.2	9.3	14.7	10.0	25.5	25.3	25.8	15.9	71.8	12.1
Portugal	4.1[b]	10.8	3.5[b]	9.8	5.0[b]	11.9	52.3	51.7	52.8	67.3	15.9	13.5
Puerto Rico	16.9	13.4	19.1	14.9	13.3	11.6	..	..	..	..	..	..
Qatar	..	0.5	..	0.2	..	2.6	38.5	35.3	40.3	19.0	52.7	24.0

	Unemployment						Long-term unemployment			Unemployment by educational attainment		
	Total % of total labor force		Male % of male labor force		Female % of female labor force		% of total unemployment			% of total unemployment		
	1990–92[a]	2007–10[a]	1990–92[a]	2007–10[a]	1990–92[a]	2007–10[a]	Total 2007–10[a]	Male 2007–10[a]	Female 2007–10[a]	Primary 2007–10[a]	Secondary 2007–10[a]	Tertiary 2007–10[a]
Romania	..	7.3	..	7.9	..	6.5	34.9	36.9	32.0	28.2	62.7	6.7
Russian Federation	5.2	7.5	5.2	8.0	5.2	6.9	35.2	32.7	38.0	13.1	52.8	34.1
Rwanda	0.3	..	0.6	..	0.2	..	..	..	..	..	..	..
Saudi Arabia	..	5.4	..	3.5	..	15.9	..	..	..	7.5	48.6	43.6
Senegal	..	..	..	..	..	..	..	..	..	..	..	..
Serbia	..	19.2	..	18.4	..	20.2	71.1	70.1	72.1	20.3	68.4	11.2
Sierra Leone	..	..	..	..	..	..	..	..	..	..	..	..
Singapore	2.7	5.9	2.7	5.4	2.6	6.5	..	..	..	27.2	22.7	50.1
Slovak Republic	..	14.4	..	14.2	..	14.6	59.3	58.3	60.5	27.8	66.2	5.9
Slovenia	7.1	7.2	8.1	7.4	6.0	7.0	43.3	45.0	41.2	23.3	58.1	16.3
Somalia	..	..	..	..	..	..	..	..	..	..	..	..
South Africa	..	23.8	..	22.0	..	25.9	14.4	..	..	15.4	80.7	0.8
South Sudan	..	..	..	..	..	..	..	..	..	..	..	..
Spain	18.1	20.1	13.9	19.7	25.8	20.5	45.1	44.6	45.6	58.4	22.6	17.7
Sri Lanka	14.2[b]	4.9	..	3.5	..	7.7	..	..	..	45.4[b]	22.8[b]	31.8[b]
Sudan	..	..	..	..	..	..	..	..	..	..	..	..
Swaziland	..	..	..	..	..	..	..	..	..	..	..	..
Sweden	5.7	8.4	6.7	8.5	4.6	8.2	16.6	18.1	14.8	32.5	44.9	16.4
Switzerland	2.8	4.2	2.3	3.8	3.5	4.8	34.3	28.3	39.8	27.9	53.7	17.7
Syrian Arab Republic	6.8	8.4	5.2	5.7	14.0	22.5	..	..	..	46.1	28.0	4.9
Tajikistan	..	..	..	..	..	..	..	..	..	66.5	28.8	4.6
Tanzania	3.6[b]	..	2.8[b]	..	4.3[b]	..	..	..	..	..	..	..
Thailand	1.4	1.2	1.3	1.2	1.5	1.1	..	..	..	41.5	49.3	0.2
Timor-Leste	..	..	..	..	..	..	..	..	..	..	..	..
Togo	..	..	..	..	..	..	..	..	..	..	..	..
Trinidad and Tobago	19.6	5.3	17.0	3.5	23.9	6.2	..	..	..	27.9	65.9	5.2
Tunisia	..	14.2	..	..	..	..	..	..	..	..	..	..
Turkey	8.5	11.9	8.8	11.4	7.8	13.0	28.6	24.7	37.0	52.5	26.0	13.9
Turkmenistan	..	..	..	..	..	..	..	..	..	..	..	..
Uganda	1.0	4.2	1.3	3.1	0.6	5.1	..	..	..	..	..	..
Ukraine	..	8.8	..	6.6	..	6.1	..	..	..	7.4	52.9	39.7
United Arab Emirates	..	4.0	..	2.0	..	12.0	..	..	..	19.7	42.6	33.2
United Kingdom	9.7	7.8	11.5	8.6	7.3	6.7	32.6	37.2	26.0	37.1	46.5	14.3
United States	7.5[b]	9.6[b]	7.9[b]	10.5[b]	7.0[b]	8.6[b]	29.0[b]	29.9[b]	27.7[b]	17.9	35.5	46.5
Uruguay	9.0[b]	7.3	6.8[b]	5.3	11.8[b]	9.7	..	..	..	59.1	27.0	13.8
Uzbekistan	..	..	..	..	..	..	..	..	..	..	..	..
Venezuela, RB	7.7	7.6	8.2	7.2	6.8	8.1	..	..	..	..	..	..
Vietnam	..	2.4	..	..	..	..	..	..	..	..	..	..
West Bank and Gaza	..	24.5	..	17.7	..	38.6	..	..	..	53.8	14.3	24.5
Yemen, Rep.	..	14.6	..	11.5	..	40.9	..	..	..	..	..	..
Zambia	18.9	..	16.3	..	22.4	..	..	..	..	..	..	..
Zimbabwe	..	..	..	..	..	..	..	..	..	..	..	..
World	.. w	.. w	.. w	.. w	.. w	.. w	.. w	.. w	.. w	.. w	.. w	.. w
Low income	..	..	..	..	..	..	..	..	..	..	..	..
Middle income	..	..	..	..	..	..	..	..	..	..	..	..
Lower middle income	..	..	..	..	..	..	..	..	..	..	..	..
Upper middle income	3.5	5.8	..	..	..	..	..	..	..	..	..	..
Low & middle income	..	..	..	..	..	..	..	..	..	..	..	..
East Asia & Pacific	2.5	4.7	..	..	..	..	..	..	..	..	..	..
Europe & Central Asia	..	9.5	..	10.3	..	8.8	..	..	..	26.1	47.8	25.6
Latin America & Carib.	6.6	7.8	5.4	6.4	8.3	9.8	..	..	..	42.3	38.1	13.0
Middle East & N. Africa	12.7	10.6	10.8	8.8	21.5	18.4	..	..	..	..	..	..
South Asia	..	..	..	..	..	..	..	..	..	..	..	..
Sub-Saharan Africa	..	..	..	..	..	..	..	..	..	..	..	..
High income	7.5	8.5	7.1	8.7	8.0	8.1	32.6	34.2	31.3	33.9	42.2	26.8
Euro area	9.1	10.0	7.2	9.8	11.9	10.2	44.0	44.2	43.3	42.9	41.3	14.8

a. Data are for the most recent year available. b. Limited coverage.

Unemployment | 2.5

Unemployment and total employment are the broadest indicators of economic activity as reflected by the labor market. The International Labour Organization (ILO) defines the unemployed as members of the economically active population who are without work but available for and seeking work, including people who have lost their jobs or who have voluntarily left work. Some unemployment is unavoidable. At any time some workers are temporarily unemployed—between jobs as employers look for the right workers and workers search for better jobs. Such unemployment, often called frictional unemployment, results from the normal operation of labor markets.

Changes in unemployment over time may reflect changes in the demand for and supply of labor; they may also reflect changes in reporting practices. Paradoxically, low unemployment rates can disguise substantial poverty in a country, while high unemployment rates can occur in countries with a high level of economic development and low rates of poverty. In countries without unemployment or welfare benefits people eke out a living in vulnerable employment. In countries with well developed safety nets workers can afford to wait for suitable or desirable jobs. But high and sustained unemployment indicates serious inefficiencies in resource allocation.

The ILO definition of unemployment notwithstanding, reference periods, the criteria for people considered to be seeking work, and the treatment of people temporarily laid off or seeking work for the first time vary across countries. In many developing countries it is especially difficult to measure employment and unemployment in agriculture. The timing of a survey, for example, can maximize the effects of seasonal unemployment in agriculture. And informal sector employment is difficult to quantify where informal activities are not tracked.

Data on unemployment are drawn from labor force sample surveys and general household sample surveys, censuses, and official estimates, which are generally based on information from different sources and can be combined in many ways. Administrative records, such as social insurance statistics and employment office statistics, are not included in the table because of their limitations in coverage. Labor force surveys generally yield the most comprehensive data because they include groups not covered in other unemployment statistics, particularly people seeking work for the first time. These surveys generally use a definition of unemployment that follows the international recommendations more closely than that used by other sources and therefore generate statistics that are more comparable internationally. But the age group, geographic coverage, and collection methods could differ by country or change over time within a country. For detailed information, consult the original source.

Women tend to be excluded from the unemployment count for various reasons. Women suffer more from discrimination and from structural, social, and cultural barriers that impede them from seeking work. Also, women are often responsible for the care of children and the elderly and for household affairs. They may not be available for work during the short reference period, as they need to make arrangements before starting work. Furthermore, women are considered to be employed when they are working part-time or in temporary jobs, despite the instability of these jobs or their active search for more secure employment.

Long-term unemployment is measured by the length of time that an unemployed person has been without work and looking for a job. The data in the table are from labor force surveys. The underlying assumption is that shorter periods of joblessness are of less concern, especially when the unemployed are covered by unemployment benefits or similar forms of support. The length of time that a person has been unemployed is difficult to measure, because the ability to recall that time diminishes as the period of joblessness extends. Women's long-term unemployment is likely to be lower in countries where women constitute a large share of the unpaid family workforce.

Unemployment by level of educational attainment provides insights into the relation between the educational attainment of workers and unemployment and may be used to draw inferences about changes in employment demand. Information on educational attainment is the best available indicator of skill levels of the labor force. Besides the limitations to comparability raised for measuring unemployment, the different ways of classifying the education level may also cause inconsistency. Education level is supposed to be classified according to International Standard Classification of Education 1997 (ISCED97). For more information on ISCED97, see *About the data* for table 2.11.

• **Unemployment** is the share of the labor force without work but available for and seeking employment. Definitions of labor force and unemployment may differ by country (see *About the data*). • **Long-term unemployment** is the number of people with continuous periods of unemployment extending for a year or longer, expressed as a percentage of the total unemployed. • **Unemployment by educational attainment** is the unemployed by level of educational attainment as a percentage of the total unemployed. The levels of educational attainment accord with the ISCED97 of the United Nations Educational, Scientific, and Cultural Organization.

Data sources

Data on unemployment are from the ILO's Key Indicators of the Labour Market, 7th edition, database.

	Survey year	Children in employment					Employment by economic activity[a]			Status in employment[a]		
		% of children ages 7–14			% of children ages 7–14 in employment		% of children ages 7–14 in employment			% of children ages 7–14 in employment		
		Total	Male	Female	Work only	Study and work	Agriculture	Manufacturing	Services	Self-employed	Wage	Unpaid family
Afghanistan		..	..	..	..	..	..	..	..	..	..	..
Albania	2005	25.0	18.8	22.0	6.7	93.3	..	..	..	..	1.4	94.5
Algeria		..	..	..	..	..	..	..	..	..	..	..
Angola[b]	2001	30.1	30.0	30.1	26.6	73.4	..	..	..	..	6.2	80.1
Argentina	2004	12.9	15.7	9.8	4.8	95.2	..	..	..	34.2	8.1	56.2
Armenia		..	..	..	..	..	..	..	..	..	..	..
Australia		..	..	..	..	..	..	..	..	..	..	..
Austria		..	..	..	..	..	..	..	..	..	..	..
Azerbaijan	2005	5.2	5.8	4.5	6.3	93.7	91.7	0.7	7.4	4.1	3.8	92.1
Bahrain		..	..	..	..	..	..	..	..	..	..	..
Bangladesh	2006	16.2	25.7	6.4	37.8	62.2	..	..	..	–	17.0	77.8
Belarus	2005	11.7	12.1	11.2	0.0	100.0	..	..	..	..	9.2	78.8
Belgium		..	..	..	..	..	..	..	..	..	..	..
Benin	2006	74.4	72.8	76.1	36.1	63.9	..	..	..	..	..	..
Bolivia	2008	32.1	33.0	31.1	5.2	94.8	73.2	6.1	19.2	0.9	9.2	89.9
Bosnia and Herzegovina	2006	10.6	11.7	9.5	0.1	99.9	..	..	..	..	1.6	92.1
Botswana		..	..	..	..	..	..	..	..	..	..	..
Brazil	2008	5.2	6.9	3.5	4.8	95.2	54..7	7.6	34.6	5.5	24.7	69.8[c]
Bulgaria		..	..	..	..	..	..	..	..	..	..	..
Burkina Faso	2006	42.1	49.0	34.5	67.7	32.3	70.9	1.4	24.9	1.9	2.2	95.8
Burundi	2005	11.7	12.5	11.0	38.9	61.1	..	..	..	25.9	68.6	
Cambodia[d]	2003–04	48.9	49.6	48.1	13.8	86.2	82.3	4.2	12.9	6.0	4.1	89.4
Cameroon	2007	43.4	43.5	43.4	21.9	78.1	88.5	3.1	8.2	2.5	9.5	87.6
Canada		..	..	..	..	..	..	..	..	..	..	..
Central African Republic	2000	67.0	66.5	67.6	54.9	45.1	..	..	..	..	2.0	56.4
Chad	2004	60.4	64.4	56.2	49.1	50.9	..	..	..	..	1.8	77.2
Chile	2003	4.1	5.1	3.1	3.2	96.8	24.1	6.9	66.9	..	..	..
China		..	..	..	..	..	..	..	..	..	..	..
Hong Kong SAR, China		..	..	..	..	..	..	..	..	..	..	..
Colombia	2007	3.9	5.3	2.3	24.8	75.2	41.2	10.8	46.1	22.7	29.1	45.6
Congo, Dem. Rep.[d]	2000	39.8	39.9	39.8	35.7	64.3	..	..	..	..	6.6	76.7
Congo, Rep	2005	30.1	29.9	30.2	9.9	90.1	..	..	..	..	4.2	84.5
Costa Rica[d]	2004	5.7	8.1	3.5	44.6	55.4	40.3	9.5	49.0	15.8	57.7	26.6
Côte d'Ivoire	2006	45.7	47.7	43.6	46.8	53.2	..	..	..	..	2.4	88.0
Croatia		..	..	..	..	..	..	..	..	..	..	..
Cuba		..	..	..	..	..	..	..	..	..	..	..
Cyprus		..	..	..	..	..	..	..	..	..	..	..
Czech Republic		..	..	..	..	..	..	..	..	..	..	..
Denmark		..	..	..	..	..	..	..	..	..	..	..
Dominican Republic[d]	2005	5.8	9.0	2.7	6.2	93.8	18.5	9.8	57.5	23.8	19.5	56.2[e]
Ecuador	2006	14.3	16.9	11.6	21.0	79.0	69.3	6.3	22.8	3.6	15.2	81.2
Egypt, Arab Rep.	2005	7.9	11.5	4.3	21.0	79.0	..	..	..	..	11.4	87.4
El Salvador	2007	7.1	10.1	3.8	24.9	75.1	50.1	13.3	35.2	2.2	23.6	74.2
Eritrea		..	..	..	..	..	..	..	..	..	..	..
Estonia		..	..	..	..	..	..	..	..	..	..	..
Ethiopia	2005	56.0	64.3	47.1	69.4	30.6	94.6	1.5	3.7	1.7	2.4	95.8
Finland		..	..	..	..	..	..	..	..	..	..	..
France		..	..	..	..	..	..	..	..	..	..	..
Gabon		..	..	..	..	..	..	..	..	..	..	..
Gambia, The	2005	43.5	33.9	52.3	32.1	67.9	..	..	..	..	1.1	87.3
Georgia	2006	31.8	33.6	29.9	1.0	99.0	..	..	..	..	4.3	77.0
Germany		..	..	..	..	..	..	..	..	..	..	..
Ghana	2006	48.9	49.9	48.0	18.7	81.3	..	..	..	..	6.1	76.2
Greece		..	..	..	..	..	..	..	..	..	..	..
Guatemala	2006	18.2	24.5	11.7	28.4	71.6	63.7	9.7	24.7	2.0	18.8	79.2
Guinea	1994	48.3	47.2	49.5	98.6	1.4	..	..	..	..	..	..
Guinea-Bissau	2006	50.5	52.8	48.1	36.4	63.6	..	..	..	..	4.0	87.7
Haiti	2005	33.4	37.3	29.6	17.7	82.3	..	..	..	..	1.8	79.4

	Survey year	Children in employment					Employment by economic activity[a]			Status in employment[a]		
		% of children ages 7–14			% of children ages 7–14 in employment		% of children ages 7–14 in employment			% of children ages 7–14 in employment		
		Total	Male	Female	Work only	Study and work	Agriculture	Manufacturing	Services	Self-employed	Wage	Unpaid family
Honduras	2007	8.7	13.3	4.1	45.1	54.9	61.6	10.4	25.1	3.5	23.0	73.5
Hungary		..	..	..	..	..	..	..	..	..	..	..
India	2004–05	4.2	4.2	4.2	84.9	15.2	69.4	16.0	12.4	7.1	6.8	59.3
Indonesia	2000	8.9	8.8	9.1	24.9	75.1	..	..	..	..	17.8	75.8[e]
Iran, Islamic Rep.		..	..	..	..	..	..	..	..	..	..	..
Iraq	2006	14.7	17.9	11.3	32.4	67.6	..	..	..	..	7.0	85.3
Ireland		..	..	..	..	..	..	..	..	..	..	..
Israel		..	..	..	..	..	..	..	..	..	..	..
Italy		..	..	..	..	..	..	..	..	..	..	..
Jamaica	2005	9.8	11.3	8.3	2.5	97.5	..	..	..	..	16.3	74.9
Japan		..	..	..	..	..	..	..	..	..	..	..
Jordan		..	..	..	..	..	..	..	..	..	..	..
Kazakhstan	2006	3.6	4.4	2.8	1.6	98.4	..	..	..	–	4.0	75.0
Kenya	2000	37.7	40.1	35.2	14.1	85.9	..	..	..	..	..	..
Korea, Dem. Rep.		..	..	..	..	..	..	..	..	..	..	..
Korea, Rep.		..	..	..	..	..	..	..	..	..	..	..
Kosovo		..	..	..	..	..	..	..	..	..	..	..
Kuwait		..	..	..	..	..	..	..	..	..	..	..
Kyrgyz Republic	2006	5.2	5.8	4.6	7.9	92.1	..	..	..	–	3.7	81.9
Lao PDR		..	..	..	..	..	..	..	..	..	..	..
Latvia		..	..	..	..	..	..	..	..	..	..	..
Lebanon		..	..	..	..	..	..	..	..	..	..	..
Lesotho	2002	2.6	4.0	1.3	74.4	25.6	58.0	0.0	10.4	3.7	36.6	59.7[c]
Liberia	2007	37.4	37.8	37.1	45.0	55.0	..	..	..	..	1.7	79.3
Libya		..	..	..	..	..	..	..	..	..	..	..
Lithuania		..	..	..	..	..	..	..	..	..	..	..
Macedonia, FYR	2005	11.8	14.8	8.6	2.8	97.2	..	..	..	..	3.9	89.5
Madagascar	2007	26.0	27.7	24.2	40.9	59.1	87.6	2.9	8.2	0.1	10.0	89.9
Malawi	2006	40.3	41.3	39.4	10.5	89.5	..	..	..	..	6.7	75.5
Malaysia		..	..	..	..	..	..	..	..	..	..	..
Mali	2006	49.5	55.0	44.1	59.5	40.5	..	..	..	..	1.6	80.4
Mauritania		..	..	..	..	..	..	..	..	..	..	..
Mauritius		..	..	..	..	..	..	..	..	..	..	..
Mexico[f]	2009	12.2	16.5	7.6	22.6	77.4	38.2	11.7	47.0	2.7	34.3	63.1
Moldova	2000	33.5	34.1	32.8	3.8	96.2	..	..	..	..	2.9	82.0
Mongolia	2006–07	10.1	11.4	8.6	16.4	83.6	91.3	0.3	6.3	5.1	0.1	94.7
Morocco	1998–99	13.2	13.5	12.8	93.2	6.8	60.6	8.3	10.1	2.1	10.0	81.7
Mozambique[d]	1996	1.8	1.9	1.7	100.0	0.0	..	..	..	..	..	..
Myanmar		..	..	..	..	..	..	..	..	..	..	..
Namibia	1999	15.4	16.2	14.7	9.5	90.5	91.5	0.4	8.0	0.1	4.5	95.0
Nepal	1999	47.2	42.2	52.4	35.6	64.4	87.0	1.4	11.1	4.2	3.3	92.4
Netherlands		..	..	..	..	..	..	..	..	..	..	..
New Zealand		..	..	..	..	..	..	..	..	..	..	..
Nicaragua	2005	10.1	16.2	3.9	30.8	69.2	70.5	9.7	19.3	1.2	13.8	85.0[c]
Niger	2006	47.1	49.2	45.0	66.5	33.5	..	..	..	4.8	74.5	..
Nigeria		..	..	..	..	..	..	..	..	..	..	..
Norway		..	..	..	..	..	..	..	..	..	..	..
Oman		..	..	..	..	..	..	..	..	..	..	..
Pakistan		..	..	..	..	..	..	..	..	..	..	..
Panama	2008	8.9	12.1	5.4	14.6	85.4	73.3	2.9	22.9	12.6	11.3	76.1[c]
Papua New Guinea		..	..	..	..	..	..	..	..	..	..	..
Paraguay[c]	2005	15.3	22.6	7.7	24.2	75.7	60.8	6.2	32.1	9.3	24.8	65.8
Peru	2007	42.2	44.8	39.5	4.0	96.0	62.6	5.0	31.1	3.8	7.6	88.6
Philippines	2001	13.3	16.3	10.0	14.8	85.2	64.3	4.1	30.6	4.1	22.8	73.1
Poland		..	..	..	..	..	..	..	..	..	..	..
Portugal	2001	3.6	4.6	2.6	3.6	96.4	48.5	11.2	33.3	..	..	..
Puerto Rico		..	..	..	..	..	..	..	..	..	..	..
Qatar		..	..	..	..	..	..	..	..	..	..	..

	Survey year	Children in employment					Employment by economic activity[a]			Status in employment[a]		
		% of children ages 7–14			% of children ages 7–14 in employment		% of children ages 7–14 in employment			% of children ages 7–14 in employment		
		Total	Male	Female	Work only	Study and work	Agriculture	Manufacturing	Services	Self-employed	Wage	Unpaid family
Romania	2000	1.4	1.7	1.1	20.7	79.3	97.1	0.0	2.3	4.5	92.9[e]	..
Russian Federation		..	..	..	..	..	..	..	..	..	..	..
Rwanda	2008	7.5	8.0	7.0	18.5	81.5	85.5	0.7	10.5	14.8	12.8	72.3
Saudi Arabia		..	..	..	..	..	..	..	..	..	..	..
Senegal	2005	18.5	24.4	12.6	61.9	38.1	79.1	5.0	14.0	6.3	4.4	84.1
Serbia	2005	6.9	7.2	6.6	2.1	97.9	..	..	..	..	5.2	89.4
Sierra Leone	2007	14.9	14.9	14.9	57.7	42.3	83.8	0.8	13.4	9.7	0.9	87.8
Singapore		..	..	..	..	..	..	..	..	..	..	..
Slovak Republic		..	..	..	..	..	..	..	..	..	..	..
Slovenia		..	..	..	..	..	..	..	..	..	..	..
Somalia	2006	43.5	45.5	41.5	53.5	46.5	..	..	..	..	1.6	94.8
South Africa	1999	27.7	29.0	26.4	5.1	94.9	..	..	..	7.1	7.1	85.8
South Sudan		..	..	..	..	..	..	..	..	..	..	..
Spain		..	..	..	..	..	..	..	..	..	..	..
Sri Lanka	1999	17.0	20.4	13.4	5.4	94.6	71.2	13.1	15.0	2.9	8.3	88.0
Sudan[g]	2000	19.1	21.5	16.8	55.9	44.1	..	..	..	..	7.3	81.3
Swaziland	2000	11.2	11.4	10.9	14.0	86.0	..	..	..	..	10.4	85.9
Sweden		..	..	..	..	..	..	..	..	..	..	..
Switzerland		..	..	..	..	..	..	..	..	..	..	..
Syrian Arab Republic	2006	6.6	8.8	4.3	34.6	65.4	..	..	..	..	21.5	68.8
Tajikistan	2005	8.9	8.7	9.1	9.0	91.0	..	..	..	..	24.2	71.3
Tanzania	2005–06	31.1	35.0	27.1	28.2	71.8	85.3	0.7	14.0	56.3[h]	0.9	42.8[e]
Thailand	2005	15.1	15.7	14.4	4.2	95.8	..	..	..	..	13.5	80.0
Timor-Leste		..	..	..	..	..	..	..	..	..	..	..
Togo	2006	38.7	39.8	37.4	29.8	70.2	82.9	1.3	15.1	5.0	1.6	93.4
Trinidad and Tobago	2000	3.9	5.2	2.8	12.8	87.2	..	..	..	..	29.8	64.9
Tunisia		..	..	..	..	..	..	..	..	..	..	..
Turkey[i]	2006	2.6	3.3	1.8	38.8	61.2	57.1	14.3	27.1	2.1	34.1	63.8
Turkmenistan		..	..	..	..	..	..	..	..	..	..	..
Uganda	2005–06	38.2	39.8	36.5	7.7	92.3	95.5	1.4	3.0	1.4	1.5	97.1
Ukraine	2005	17.3	18.0	16.6	0.1	99.9	..	..	..	..	3.1	79.3
United Arab Emirates		..	..	..	..	..	..	..	..	..	..	..
United Kingdom		..	..	..	..	..	..	..	..	..	..	..
United States		..	..	..	..	..	..	..	..	..	..	..
Uruguay		..	..	..	..	..	..	..	..	..	..	..
Uzbekistan	2005	5.1	5.3	4.9	1.0	99.0	..	..	..	..	3.8	78.6
Venezuela, RB[d]	2006	5.1	6.9	3.3	19.8	80.2	32.3	7.2	55.7	31.6	33.1	35.3
Vietnam	2006	21.3	21.0	21.6	11.9	88.1	..	..	..	..	5.9	91.2
West Bank and Gaza		..	..	..	..	..	..	..	..	..	..	..
Yemen, Rep.	2006	18.3	20.7	15.9	30.9	69.1	..	..	..	..	6.1	86.1
Zambia	2008	34.4	35.4	33.3	18.6	81.4	91.9	0.7	7.0	2.9	3.9	93.1
Zimbabwe	1999	14.3	15.3	13.3	12.0	88.0	..	..	..	3.4	28.4	68.2

a. Shares may not sum to 100 percent because of a residual category not included in the table. b. Covers only Angola-secured territory. c. Refers to unpaid workers, regardless of whether they are family workers. d. Covers children ages 10–14. e. Refers to family workers, regardless of whether they are paid. f. Covers children ages 12–14. g. Covers northern Sudan only. h. Covers mainly workers working on their own shamba. i. Covers children ages 6–14.

About the data

The data in the table refer to children's work in the sense of "economic activity"—that is, children in employment, a broader concept than child labor (see ILO 2009a for details on this distinction).

In line with the definition of economic activity adopted by the 13th International Conference of Labour Statisticians, the threshold set by the 1993 UN System of National Accounts for classifying a person as employed is to have been engaged at least one hour in any activity relating to the production of goods and services during the reference period. Children seeking work are thus excluded. Economic activity covers all market production and certain nonmarket production, including production of goods for own use. It excludes unpaid household services (commonly called "household chores")—that is, the production of domestic and personal services by household members for a household's own consumption.

Data are from household surveys by the International Labor Organization (ILO), the United Nations Children's Fund (UNICEF), the World Bank, and national statistical offices. The surveys yield data on education, employment, health, expenditure, and consumption indicators related to children's work.

Household survey data generally include information on work type—for example, whether a child is working for payment in cash or in kind or is involved in unpaid work, working for someone who is not a member of the household, or involved in any type of family work (on the farm or in a business). Country surveys define the ages for child labor as 5–17. The data in the table have been recalculated to present statistics for children ages 7–14.

Although efforts are made to harmonize the definition of employment and the questions on employment in survey questionnaires, significant differences remain in the survey instruments that collect data on children in employment and in the sampling design underlying the surveys. Differences exist not only across different household surveys in the same country but also across the same type of survey carried out in different countries, so estimates of working children are not fully comparable across countries.

The table aggregates the distribution of children in employment by the industrial categories of the International Standard Industrial Classification (ISIC): agriculture, manufacturing, and services. A residual category—which includes mining and quarrying; electricity, gas, and water; construction; extraterritorial organization; and other inadequately defined activities—is not presented. ISIC revision 2 and revision 3 are both used, depending on the country's codification for describing economic activity. This does not affect the definition of the groups in the table.

The table also aggregates the distribution of children in employment by three major categories of status in employment, based on the International Classification of Status in Employment (1993): self-employed workers, wage workers (also known as employees), and unpaid family workers. A residual category—which includes those not classifiable by status—is not presented.

In most countries more boys are involved in employment, or the gender difference is small. However, girls are often more present in hidden or underreported forms of employment such as domestic service, and in almost all societies girls bear greater responsibility for household chores in their own homes, work that lies outside the System of National Accounts production boundary and is thus not considered in estimates of children's employment.

Definitions

• **Survey year** is the year in which the underlying data were collected. • **Children in employment** are children involved in any economic activity for at least one hour in the reference week of the survey. • **Work only** refers to children who are employed and not attending school. • **Study and work** refer to children attending school in combination with employment. • **Employment by economic activity** is the distribution of children in employment by the major industrial categories (ISIC revision 2 or revision 3). • **Agriculture** corresponds to division 1 (ISIC revision 2) or categories A and B (ISIC revision 3) and includes agriculture and hunting, forestry and logging, and fishing. • **Manufacturing** corresponds to division 3 (ISIC revision 2) or category D (ISIC revision 3). • **Services** correspond to divisions 6–9 (ISIC revision 2) or categories G–P (ISIC revision 3) and include wholesale and retail trade, hotels and restaurants, transport, financial intermediation, real estate, public administration, education, health and social work, other community services, and private household activity. • **Self-employed workers** are people whose remuneration depends directly on the profits derived from the goods and services they produce, with or without other employees, and include employers, own-account workers, and members of producers cooperatives. • **Wage workers** (also known as employees) are people who hold explicit (written or oral) or implicit employment contracts that provide basic remuneration that does not depend directly on the revenue of the unit for which they work. • **Unpaid family workers** are people who work without pay in a market-oriented establishment operated by a related person living in the same household.

Data sources

Data on children at work are estimates produced by the Understanding Children's Work project based on household survey data sets made available by the ILO's International Programme on the Elimination of Child Labour under its Statistical Monitoring Programme on Child Labour, UNICEF under its Multiple Indicator Cluster Survey program, the World Bank under its Living Standards Measurement Study program, and national statistical offices. Information on how the data were collected and some indication of their reliability can be found at www.ilo.org/public/english/standards/ipec/simpoc/, www.childinfo.org, and www.worldbank.org/lsms. Detailed country statistics can be found at www.ucw-project.org.

	Population below national poverty line							Poverty gap at national poverty line			
	Survey year[a]	Rural %	Urban %	National %	Survey year[a]	Rural %	Urban %	National %	Survey year[a]	Rural %	Urban %	National %
Afghanistan[b]	..	..	..	..	2008[c]	37.5	29.0	36.0	2008[c]	8.3	6.2	7.9
Albania[b]	2005	24.2	11.2	18.5	2008	14.6	10.1	12.4	2008	2.6	1.9	2.3
Angola		..	..	..	2000[c]	..	62.3	..		..	..	..
Argentina	2009[d]	..	13.2	..	2010[d]	..	9.9			..	..	..
Armenia[b]	2009	34.9	33.7	34.1	2010	36.0	36.0	35.8		..	..	..
Azerbaijan[b]	2001	42.5	55.7	49.6	2008	18.5	14.8	15.8		..	..	..
Bangladesh	2005	43.8	28.4	40.0	2010	35.2	21.3	31.5	2010	7.4	4.3	6.5
Belarus	2008	..	..	6.1	2009	..	..	5.4		..	..	..
Benin		..	..	..	2003[c]	46.0	29.0	39.0	2003[c]	14.0	8.0	12.0
Bhutan		..	..	..	2007[c]	30.9	1.7	23.2	2007[c]	8.1	0.4	6.1
Bolivia	2006[d]	76.5	50.3	59.9	2007[d]	77.3	50.9	60.1		..	..	..
Bosnia and Herzegovina[b]	2004	22.0	11.3	17.7	2007	17.8	8.2	14.0		..	..	..
Botswana	1993	40.4	24.7	32.9	2003	44.8	19.4	30.6	2003	18.4	6.5	11.7
Brazil	2008[d]	..	..	22.6	2009[d]	..	..	21.4		..	..	..
Bulgaria[b]	2001	..	..	12.8	2007	..	..	10.6	2007	..	..	3.0
Burkina Faso	2003	65.5	22.1	51.0	2009	52.6	27.9	46.7	2009	17.4	7.8	15.1
Burundi		..	..	..	2006[c]	68.9	34.0	66.9	2006[c]	24.2	10.3	23.4
Cambodia[b]	2004	37.8	17.6	34.7	2007	34.5	11.8	30.1	2007	8.3	2.8	7.2
Cameroon		..	..	..	2007[c]	55.0	12.2	39.9	2007[c]	17.5	2.8	12.3
Cape Verde		..	..	..	2007[c]	44.3	13.2	26.6	2007[c]	14.3	3.3	8.1
Central African Republic		..	..	..	2008[c]	69.4	49.6	62.0	2008[c]	35.0	29.8	33.1
Chad		..	..	..	2003[c]	58.6	24.6	55.0	2003[c]	23.3	7.4	21.6
Chile	2006[d]	12.3	13.9	13.7	2009[d]	12.9	15.5	15.1		..	..	..
China	2004[d]	2.8			2005[d]	2.5				..	..	..
Colombia	2009[d]	54.3	35.8	40.2	2010[d]	50.3	33.0	37.2		..	..	..
Comoros		..	..	..	2004[c]	48.7	34.5	44.8	2004[c]	17.8	12.1	16.3
Congo, Dem. Rep.		..	..	..	2006	75.7	61.5	71.3	2006	34.9	26.2	32.2
Congo, Rep.		..	..	..	2005	57.7	..	50.1	2005	20.6	..	18.9
Costa Rica	2009[d]	23.0	20.7	21.7	2010[d]	..	..	24.2		..	..	..
Côte d'Ivoire[b]	2002	45.8	32.3	40.2	2008	54.2	29.4	42.7	2008	20.3	9.5	15.3
Croatia[b]	2002	..	..	11.2	2004	..	..	11.1	2004	..	..	2.6
Dominican Republic	2009[d]	47.0	28.6	34.6	2010[d]	..	..	34.4		..	..	..
Ecuador	2009[d]	57.5	25.0	36.0	2010[d]	53.0	22.5	32.8		..	..	..
Egypt, Arab Rep.	2005	26.8	10.1	19.6	2008	30.0	10.6	22.0		..	..	..
El Salvador	2008[d,e]	49.0	35.7	39.9	2009[d,e]	46.5	33.3	37.8		..	..	..
Ethiopia	2000	45.4	36.9	44.2	2005	39.3	35.1	38.9	2005	8.5	7.7	8.3
Fiji	2003	40.0	28.0	35.0	2009	43.3	18.6	31.0	2009	14.8	5.4	10.1
Gabon		..	..	..	2005	44.6	29.8	32.7	2005	16.0	8.5	10.0
Gambia, The[b]		..	..	..	2010[c]	73.9	32.7	48.4		..	..	..
Georgia[b]	2008	27.8	17.5	22.7	2009	30.7	18.4	24.7		..	..	..
Ghana	1998	49.6	19.4	39.5	2006	39.2	10.8	28.5	2006	13.5	3.1	9.6
Guatemala	2000	74.5	27.1	56.2	2006	70.5	30.0	51.0		..	..	..
Guinea		..	..	..	2007[c]	63.0	30.5	53.0	2007[c]	22.0	7.7	17.6
Guinea-Bissau		..	..	..	2002	69.1	51.6	64.7	2002	27.8	16.9	25.0
Haiti		..	..	..	2001[d]	88.0	45.0	77.0		..	..	..
Honduras	2009[d,e]	64.4	52.8	58.8	2010[d,e]	65.4	54.3	60.0		..	..	..
India	2005	41.8	25.7	37.2	2010	33.8	20.9	29.8	2010	6.8	4.5	6.2
Indonesia	2010	16.6	9.9	13.3	2011	15.7	9.2	12.5	2011	2.6	1.5	2.1
Iraq		..	..	..	2007	39.3	16.1	22.9	2007	9.0	2.7	4.5
Jamaica	2006[d]	..	..	14.3	2007[d]	..	..	9.9		..	..	..
Jordan		..	..	..	2006	19.0	12.0	13.0	2006	..	..	2.8
Kazakhstan[b]	2008	..	..	12.1	2009	..	..	8.2	2009	..	..	1.3
Kenya		..	..	..	2005[c]	49.1	33.7	45.9	2005[c]	17.5	11.4	16.3
Kosovo[b]	2005	49.2	37.4	45.1	2009	35.3	33.1	34.5	2009	..	..	9.6
Kyrgyz Republic[b]	2009	..	..	31.7	2010	..	..	33.7		..	..	..
Lao PDR[b]	2002	..	..	33.5	2008	31.7	17.4	27.6		..	..	..
Latvia[b]	2002	11.6	..	7.5	2004	12.7	..	5.9		..	..	..

Poverty rates at national poverty lines

	Population below national poverty line								Poverty gap at national poverty line			
	Survey year[a]	Rural %	Urban %	National %	Survey year[a]	Rural %	Urban %	National %	Survey year[a]	Rural %	Urban %	National %
Lesotho[b]	1994	68.9	36.7	66.6	2003	60.5	41.5	56.6	..	..	..	..
Liberia[b]	..	..	..	..	2007	67.7	55.1	63.8	2007	26.3	20.2	24.4
Macedonia, FYR[b]	2005	21.2	19.8	20.4	2006	21.3	17.7	19.0	2006	7.7	6.9	7.2
Madagascar	2004	77.3	53.7	72.1	2005	73.5	52.0	68.7	2005	28.9	19.3	26.8
Malawi	..	..	..	..	2004	55.9	25.4	52.4	2004	8.6	2.8	8.0
Malaysia[b]	2007	7.1	2.0	3.6	2009	8.4	1.7	3.8	2009	1.8	0.3	0.8
Mali	2006	57.0	18.5	47.5	2010	50.6	18.8	43.6	2010	15.6	4.7	13.2
Mauritania	2004	59.0	28.9	46.7	2008	59.4	20.8	42.0	2008	22.3	4.9	14.5
Mexico	2008[d]	60.3	40.1	47.7	2010[d]	60.8	45.5	51.3		..	..	..
Moldova[b]	2009	36.3	12.6	26.3	2010	30.3	10.4	21.9	2010	6.5	1.8	4.5
Mongolia	..	..	..		2008[c]	46.6	26.9	35.2	2008[c]	13.4	7.7	10.1
Montenegro	2009	14.8	2.6	6.8	2010	11.3	4.0	6.6	2010	1.7	0.7	1.1
Morocco	2001	25.1	7.6	15.3	2007	14.5	4.8	9.0		..	..	..
Mozambique	2003	55.3	51.5	54.1	2008	56.9	49.6	54.7	2008	22.2	19.1	21.2
Namibia	1994	69.0	31.0	58.0	2004	49.0	17.0	38.0	2004	16.0	6.0	13.0
Nepal	..	..	..		2010	27.4	15.5	25.2	2010[c]	6.0	3.2	5.4
Nicaragua	2001	67.8	30.1	45.8	2005	67.9	29.1	46.2		..	..	..
Niger	..	..	..		2007[c]	63.9	36.7	59.5	2007[c]	21.2	11.3	19.6
Nigeria	..	..	..		2004[c]	63.8	43.1	54.7	2004[c]	26.6	16.2	22.8
Pakistan	2005	28.1	14.9	23.9	2006	27.0	13.1	22.3		..	..	..
Panama	2003	62.7	20.0	36.8	2008	59.8	17.7	32.7		..	..	..
Paraguay	2009[d]	49.8	24.7	35.1	2010[d]	48.9	24.7	34.7		..	..	..
Peru	2009	60.3	21.1	34.8	2010	54.2	19.1	31.3		..	..	..
Philippines	2006	..	..	26.4	2009	..	..	26.5	2009	..	..	7.2
Poland[b]	2007	..	..	14.6	2008	..	..	10.6		..	..	..
Romania[b]	2005	23.5	8.1	15.1	2006	22.3	6.8	13.8	2006	5.3	1.4	3.2
Russian Federation	2005	22.7	8.1	11.9	2006	21.2	7.4	11.1	2006	5.5	1.7	2.7
Rwanda	2006	64.2	23.2	58.5	2011	48.7	22.1	44.9	2011	..	..	14.8
São Tomé and Príncipe	..	..	..		2009[c]	..	..	66.2	2009[c]	..	..	24.8
Senegal[b]	..	..	..		2005[c]	61.9	35.1	50.8	2005[c]	21.5	9.3	16.4
Serbia[b]	2009	9.6	4.9	6.9	2010	13.6	5.7	9.2		..	..	..
Sierra Leone	..	..	..		2003[c]	78.5	47.0	66.4	2003[c]	34.6	16.3	27.5
South Africa	2000	..	..	38.0	2006	..	..	23.0	2006	..	..	7.0
South Sudan	..	..	..		2009	55.4	24.2	50.6	2009	26.5	8.8	23.7
Sri Lanka	2007	15.7	6.7	15.2	2010	9.4	5.3	8.9	2010	1.8	1.2	1.7
Sudan	..	..	..		2009	57.6	26.5	46.5	2009	21.3	7.1	16.2
Swaziland	..	..	..		2001[c]	75.0	49.0	69.2	2001[c]	37.0	20.0	32.9
Tajikistan[b]	2007	55.0	49.4	53.5	2009	..	..	46.7		..	..	..
Tanzania	2000	38.6	23.7	35.6	2007	37.4	21.8	33.4	2007	11.0	6.5	9.9
Thailand	2008	11.5	3.0	9.0	2009	10.4	3.0	8.1		..	..	..
Timor-Leste	2001	..	..	39.7	2007	..	..	49.9		..	..	..
Togo	..	..	..		2006	74.3	36.8	61.7	2006	29.3	10.3	22.9
Turkey	2008	34.6	9.4	17.1	2009	38.7	8.9	18.1		..	..	..
Uganda	2005	34.2	13.7	31.1	2009	27.2	9.1	24.5	2009	7.6	1.8	6.8
Ukraine[b]	2007	8.1	2.9	4.6	2008	4.7	2.0	2.9	2008	0.7	0.3	0.4
Uruguay	2009[d]	9.6	21.4	20.9	2010[d]	6.2	18.7	18.6		..	..	..
Venezuela, RB	2008[d]	..	..	32.6	2009[d]	..	..	28.5		..	..	..
Vietnam	2006	20.4	3.9	16.0	2008	18.7	3.3	14.5	2008	4.6	0.5	3.5
West Bank and Gaza	2007	..	..	31.2	2009	..	..	21.9	2009	..	..	4.9
Yemen, Rep.	1998	42.5	32.3	40.1	2005	40.1	20.7	34.8	2005	10.6	4.5	8.9
Zambia	2004	77.3	29.1	58.4	2006	76.8	26.7	59.3	2006	38.8	9.4	28.5
Zimbabwe	..	..	..		2003[c]	..	..	72.0		..	..	..

Note: Poverty rates are based on per capita consumption estimated from household survey data, unless otherwise noted.
a. Refers to the year in which the underlying household survey data were collected or, when the data collection period bridged two calendar years, the year in which most of the data were collected. b. World Bank estimates. c. Estimates based on survey data from earlier years are available but are not comparable with the most recent year reported here; these are available at http://data.worldbank.org and http://povertydata.worldbank.org. d. Based on income per capita estimated from household survey data. e. Measured as share of households.

Estimates of poverty rates and gaps at national poverty lines are useful for comparing poverty across time within but not across countries. Table 2.8 shows poverty indicators at international poverty lines that allow for comparisons across countries.

For countries with an active poverty monitoring program, the World Bank—in collaboration with national institutions, other development agencies, and civil society—periodically prepares poverty assessments and other analytical reports to assess the extent and causes of poverty. These reports review levels and changes in poverty indicators over time and across regions within countries, assess the impact of growth and public policy on poverty and inequality, review the adequacy of monitoring and evaluation, and contain detailed technical overviews of the underlying household survey data and poverty measurement methods used. The reports are a key source of comprehensive information on poverty indicators at national poverty lines and generally feed into country-owned processes to reduce poverty, build in-country capacity, and support joint work.

An increasing number of countries have their own national programs to monitor and disseminate official poverty estimates at national poverty lines along with well documented household survey data sources and estimation methodology. Estimates from national poverty monitoring programs and the underlying methods used are periodically reviewed by the World Bank and included in the table.

The complete online database of poverty estimates at national poverty lines (http://data. worldbank.org/topic/poverty) is regularly updated and may contain more recent data or revisions not incorporated in the table. In addition, the poverty and equity data portal (http://povertydata.worldbank.org/poverty/home/) provides access to both the database and user-friendly dashboards with graphs and interactive maps that visualize trends in key poverty and inequality indicators for different regions and countries. The database is maintained by the Global Poverty Working Group, a team of poverty experts from the Poverty Reduction and Equity Network, the Development Research Group, and the Development Data Group.

Data quality

Poverty estimates at national poverty lines are computed from household survey data collected from nationally representative samples of households. These data must contain sufficiently detailed information to compute a comprehensive estimate of total household income or consumption (including consumption or income from own production), from which it is possible to construct a correctly weighted distribution of per capita consumption or income.

As with any indicator measured from household surveys, data quality can affect the precision of poverty estimates and their comparability over time. These include selective survey nonresponse, seasonality effects, differences in the number of income or consumption items in the questionnaire, and the time period over which respondents are asked to recall their expenditures.

National poverty lines

National poverty lines are the benchmark for estimating poverty indicators that are consistent with the country's specific economic and social circumstances. National poverty lines reflect local perceptions of the level and composition of consumption or income needed to be nonpoor. The perceived boundary between poor and nonpoor typically rises with the average income of a country and thus does not provide a uniform measure for comparing poverty rates across countries. While poverty rates at national poverty lines should not be used for comparing poverty rates across countries, they are appropriate for guiding and monitoring the results of country-specific national poverty reduction strategies.

Almost all national poverty lines are anchored to the cost of a food bundle—based on the prevailing national diet of the poor—that provides adequate nutrition for good health and normal activity, plus an allowance for nonfood spending. National poverty lines must be adjusted for inflation between survey years to remain constant in real terms and thus allow for meaningful comparisons of poverty over time. Because diets and consumption baskets change over time, countries periodically recalculate the poverty line based on new survey data. In such cases the new poverty lines should be deflated to obtain comparable poverty estimates from earlier years. The table reports indicators based on the two most recent years for which survey data are available. Countries for which the most recent indicators reported are not comparable to those based on survey data from an earlier year are footnoted in the table.

• **Survey year** is the year in which the underlying household survey data were collected or, when the data collection period bridged two calendar years, the year in which most of the data were collected.
• **Population below national poverty line** is the percentage of the rural, urban, or national population living below the corresponding rural, urban, or national poverty line, based on consumption estimated from household survey data, unless otherwise noted.
• **Poverty gap at national poverty line** is the mean shortfall from the rural, urban, or national poverty line (counting the nonpoor as having zero shortfall) as a percentage of the corresponding rural, urban, or national poverty line, based on consumption estimated from household survey data, unless otherwise noted. This measure reflects the depth of poverty as well as its incidence.

Data on poverty rates at national poverty lines are compiled by the Global Poverty Working Group, based on data from World Bank's country poverty assessments and analytical reports as well as country Poverty Reduction Strategies and official poverty estimates. Further documentation of the data, measurement methods and tools, and research, as well as poverty assessments and analytical reports, are available at http://data.worldbank.org/topic/poverty, www.worldbank.org/poverty, and http://povertydata.worldbank.org/poverty/home/.

Poverty rates at international poverty lines

	International poverty line in local currency		International poverty line[a]									
	$1.25 a day 2005	$2 a day 2005	Survey year[b]	Population below $1.25 a day %	Poverty gap at $1.25 a day %	Population below $2 a day %	Poverty gap at $2 a day %	Survey year[b]	Population below $1.25 a day %	Poverty gap at $1.25 a day %	Population below $2 a day %	Poverty gap at $2 a day %
Albania	75.5	120.8	2005	<2	<0.5	7.9	1.5	2008	<2	<0.5	4.3	0.9
Algeria	48.4[c]	77.5[c]	1988	7.6	1.2	24.6	6.7	1995	6.8	1.4	23.6	6.5
Angola	88.1	141.0	..	..	..	..	..	2000[d]	54.3	29.9	70.2	42.4
Argentina	1.7	2.7	2009[d,e]	2.0	1.2	3.4	1.7	2010[d,e]	<2	0.7	<2	0.9
Armenia	245.2	392.4	2007	3.5	0.7	20.5	4.5	2008	<2	<0.5	12.4	2.3
Azerbaijan	2,170.9	3,473.5	2001	6.3	1.1	27.1	6.8	2008	<2	<0.5	2.8	0.6
Bangladesh	31.9	51.0	2005	50.5	14.2	80.3	34.3	2010	43.3	11.2	76.5	30.4
Belarus	949.5	1,519.2	2007	<2	<0.5	<2	<0.5	2008	<2	<0.5	<2	<0.5
Belize	1.8[c]	2.9[c]	1998[f]	11.3	4.7	26.3	10.0	1999[f]	12.2	5.5	22.0	9.9
Benin	344.0	550.4	..	..	..	..	..	2003	47.3	15.7	75.3	33.5
Bhutan	23.1	36.9	2003	26.2	7.0	49.5	18.8	2007	10.2	1.8	29.8	8.5
Bolivia	3.2	5.1	2007[e]	13.1	6.6	24.7	10.9	2008[e]	15.6	8.6	24.9	13.1
Bosnia and Herzegovina	1.1	1.7	2004	<2	<0.5	<2	<0.5	2007	<2	<0.5	<2	<0.5
Botswana	4.2	6.8	1986	35.6	13.8	54.7	25.8	1994	31.2	11.0	49.4	22.3
Brazil	2.0	3.1	2008[f]	6.0	3.4	11.3	5.3	2009[f]	6.1	3.6	10.8	5.4
Bulgaria	0.9	1.5	2003	<2	<0.5	<2	<0.5	2007	<2	<0.5	<2	<0.5
Burkina Faso	303.0	484.8	2003	56.5	20.3	81.2	39.3	2009	44.6	14.7	72.6	31.7
Burundi	558.8	894.1	1998	86.4	47.3	95.4	64.1	2006	81.3	36.4	93.5	56.1
Cambodia	2,019.1	3,230.6	2007	32.2	7.7	60.1	22.6	2008	22.8	4.9	53.3	17.4
Cameroon	368.1	589.0	2001	10.8	2.3	32.5	9.5	2007	9.6	1.2	30.4	8.2
Cape Verde	97.7	156.3	..	..	..	..	..	2002	21.0	6.1	40.9	15.2
Central African Republic	384.3	614.9	2003	62.4	28.3	81.9	45.3	2008	62.8	31.3	80.1	46.8
Chad	409.5	655.1	..	..	..	..	..	2003	61.9	25.6	83.3	43.9
Chile	484.2	774.7	2006[f]	<2	0.5	3.2	1.1	2009[f]	<2	0.7	2.7	1.2
China	5.1[g]	8.2[g]	2005[h]	16.3	4.0	36.9	12.5	2008[h]	13.1	3.2	29.8	10.1
Colombia	1,489.7	2,383.5	2009[f]	9.7	4.7	18.5	8.2	2010[f]	8.2	3.8	15.8	6.8
Comoros	368.0	588.8	..	..	..	..	..	2004	46.1	20.8	65.0	34.2
Congo, Dem. Rep.	395.3	632.5	..	..	..	..	..	2006	87.7	52.8	95.2	67.6
Congo, Rep.	469.5	751.1	..	..	..	..	..	2005	54.1	22.8	74.4	38.8
Costa Rica	348.7[c]	557.9[c]	2008[f]	2.4	1.5	5.0	2.3	2009[f]	3.1	1.8	6.0	2.7
Croatia	5.6	8.9	2004	<2	<0.5	<2	<0.5	2008	<2	<0.5	<2	<0.5
Czech Republic	19.0	30.4	1993[e]	<2	<0.5	<2	<0.5	1996[e]	<2	<0.5	<2	<0.5
Côte d'Ivoire	407.3	651.6	2002	23.3	6.8	46.8	17.6	2008	23.8	7.5	46.3	17.8
Djibouti	134.8	215.6	..	..	..	..	..	2002	18.8	5.3	41.2	14.6
Dominican Republic	25.5[c]	40.8[c]	2009[f]	3.0	0.7	10.0	2.7	2010[f]	2.2	0.5	9.9	2.4
Ecuador	0.6	1.0	2009[f]	6.4	2.9	13.5	5.5	2010[f]	4.6	2.1	10.6	4.1
Egypt, Arab Rep.	2.5	4.0	2005	2.0	<0.5	18.5	3.5	2008	<2	<0.5	15.4	2.8
El Salvador	6.0[c]	9.6[c]	2008[f]	5.4	1.9	14.0	4.8	2009[f]	9.0	4.4	16.9	7.6
Estonia	11.0	17.7	2003	<2	<0.5	2.6	<0.5	2004	<2	<0.5	<2	0.5
Ethiopia	3.4	5.5	2000	55.6	16.2	86.4	37.9	2005	39.0	9.6	77.6	28.9
Fiji	1.9	3.1	2003	29.2	11.3	48.7	21.8	2009	5.9	1.1	22.9	6.0
Gabon	554.7	887.5	..	..	..	..	..	2005	4.8	0.9	19.6	5.0
Gambia, The	12.9	20.7	1998	65.6	33.8	81.2	49.1	2003	33.6	11.7	55.9	24.4
Georgia	1.0	1.6	2007	15.2	4.1	34.9	11.8	2008	15.3	4.6	32.2	11.7
Ghana	5,594.8	8,951.6	1998	39.1	14.4	63.3	28.5	2006	28.6	9.9	51.8	21.3
Guatemala	5.7[c]	9.1[c]	2004[f]	24.4	13.2	39.2	20.2	2006[f]	13.5	4.7	26.3	10.5
Guinea	1,849.5	2,959.1	2003	56.3	21.3	80.8	39.7	2007	43.3	15.0	69.6	31.0
Guinea-Bissau	355.3	568.6	1993	52.1	20.6	75.7	37.4	2002	48.9	16.6	78.0	34.9
Guyana	131.5[c]	210.3[c]	1993[e]	6.9	1.5	17.1	5.4	1998[e]	8.7	2.8	18.0	6.7
Haiti	24.2[c]	38.7[c]	..	..	..	..	..	2001[e]	61.7	32.3	77.5	46.7
Honduras	12.1[c]	19.3[c]	2008[f]	21.4	11.8	32.6	17.5	2009[f]	17.9	9.4	29.8	14.9
Hungary	171.9	275.0	2004	<2	<0.5	<2	<0.5	2007	<2	<0.5	<2	<0.5
India	19.5[i]	31.2[i]	2005[h]	41.6	10.5	75.6	29.5	2010[h]	32.7	7.5	68.7	24.5
Indonesia	5,241.0[i]	8,385.7[i]	2009[h]	20.4	4.1	52.7	16.5	2010[h]	18.1	3.3	46.1	14.3
Iran, Islamic Rep.	3,393.5	5,429.6	1998	<2	<0.5	8.3	1.8	2005	<2	<0.5	8.0	1.8
Iraq	799.8	1,279.7	..	..	..	..	..	2007	2.8	<0.5	21.4	4.4
Jamaica	54.2[c]	86.7[c]	2002	<2	<0.5	8.5	1.5	2004	<2	<0.5	5.4	0.8

	International poverty line in local currency			International poverty line[a]								
	$1.25 a day 2005	$2 a day 2005	Survey year[b]	Population below $1.25 a day %	Poverty gap at $1.25 a day %	Population below $2 a day %	Poverty gap at $2 a day %	Survey year[b]	Population below $1.25 a day %	Poverty gap at $1.25 a day %	Population below $2 a day %	Poverty gap at $2 a day %
Jordan	0.6	1.0	2008	<2	<0.5	2.1	<0.5	2010	<2	<0.5	<2	<0.5
Kazakhstan	81.2	129.9	2008	<2	<0.5	<2	<0.5	2009	<2	<0.5	<2	<0.5
Kenya	40.9	65.4	1997	19.6	4.6	42.7	14.7	2005	43.4	16.9	67.2	31.8
Kyrgyz Republic	16.2	26.0	2008	6.4	1.5	20.7	5.9	2009	6.2	1.4	21.7	6.0
Lao PDR	4,677.0	7,483.2	2002	44.0	12.1	76.9	31.1	2008	33.9	9.0	66.0	24.8
Latvia	0.4	0.7	2007	<2	<0.5	<2	<0.5	2008	<2	<0.5	<2	<0.5
Lesotho	4.3	6.9	1994	46.2	25.6	59.7	36.1	2003	43.4	20.8	62.3	33.1
Liberia	0.6	1.0		..	..	..	..	2007	83.8	40.9	94.9	59.6
Lithuania	2.1	3.3	2004	<2	<0.5	<2	0.5	2008	<2	<0.5	<2	<0.5
Macedonia, FYR	29.5	47.2	2008	<2	<0.5	4.3	0.7	2009	<2	<0.5	5.9	0.9
Madagascar	945.5	1,512.8	2005	67.8	26.5	89.6	46.9	2010	81.3	43.3	92.6	60.1
Malawi	71.2	113.8	1998	83.1	46.0	93.5	62.3	2004	73.9	32.3	90.5	51.8
Malaysia	2.6	4.2	2007[e]	<2	<0.5	2.9	<0.5	2009[e]	<2	<0.5	2.3	<0.5
Mali	362.1	579.4	2006	51.4	18.8	77.1	36.5	2010	50.4	16.4	78.7	35.2
Mauritania	157.1	251.3	2004	25.4	7.0	52.6	19.2	2008	23.4	6.8	47.7	17.7
Mexico	9.6	15.3	2006	<2	<0.5	4.9	1.0	2008	<2	<0.5	5.2	1.3
Micronesia, Fed. Sts.	0.8[c]	1.3[c]		..	..	..	..	2000	31.2	16.3	44.7	24.5
Moldova	6.0	9.7	2009	<2	<0.5	7.1	1.2	2010	<2	<0.5	4.4	0.7
Montenegro	0.6	1.0	2007	<2	<0.5	<2	<0.5	2008	<2	<0.5	<2	<0.5
Morocco	6.9	11.0	2001	6.3	0.9	24.3	6.3	2007	2.5	0.5	14.0	3.2
Mozambique	14,532.1	23,251.4	2003	74.7	35.4	90.0	53.6	2008	59.6	25.1	81.8	42.9
Namibia	6.3	10.1	1993	49.1	24.6	62.2	36.5	2004[e]	31.9	9.5	51.1	21.8
Nepal	33.1	52.9	2003	53.1	18.4	77.3	36.6	2010	24.8	5.6	57.3	19.0
Nicaragua	9.1[c]	14.6[c]	2001[e]	14.4	3.7	34.4	11.5	2005[e]	11.9	2.4	31.7	9.6
Niger	334.2	534.7	2005	50.2	18.3	75.3	35.6	2008	43.6	12.4	75.2	30.8
Nigeria	98.2	157.2	2004	63.1	28.7	83.1	45.9	2010	68.0	33.7	84.5	50.2
Pakistan	25.9	41.4	2006	22.6	4.1	61.0	18.8	2008	21.0	3.5	60.2	17.9
Panama	0.8[c]	1.2[c]	2009[f]	5.9	1.8	14.6	4.9	2010[f]	6.6	2.1	13.8	5.1
Papua New Guinea	2.1[c]	3.4[c]		..	..	..	..	1996	35.8	12.3	57.4	25.5
Paraguay	2,659.7	4,255.6	2009[f]	7.6	3.2	14.2	6.0	2010[f]	7.2	3.0	13.2	5.7
Peru	2.1	3.3	2009[f]	5.5	1.6	14.0	4.6	2010[f]	4.9	1.3	12.7	4.1
Philippines	30.2	48.4	2006	22.6	5.5	45.0	16.4	2009	18.4	3.7	41.5	13.8
Poland	2.7	4.3	2008	<2	<0.5	<2	<0.5	2009	<2	<0.5	<2	<0.5
Romania	2.1	3.4	2008	<2	<0.5	2.0	0.6	2009	<2	<0.5	<2	0.5
Russian Federation	16.7	26.8	2008	<2	<0.5	<2	<0.5	2009	<2	<0.5	<2	<0.5
Rwanda	295.9	473.5	2006	72.1	34.8	87.4	52.2	2011	63.2	26.6	82.4	44.6
São Tomé and Príncipe	7,953.9	12,726.3		..	..	..	..	2001	28.2	7.9	54.2	20.6
Senegal	372.8	596.5	2001	44.2	14.3	71.3	31.2	2005	33.5	10.8	60.4	24.7
Serbia	42.9	68.6	2008	<2	<0.5	<2	<0.5	2009	<2	<0.5	<2	<0.5
Seychelles	5.6[c]	9.0[c]	2000	<2	<0.5	<2	<0.5	2007	<2	<0.5	<2	<0.5
Sierra Leone	1,745.3	2,792.4	1990	62.8	44.8	75.0	54.0	2003	53.4	20.3	76.1	37.5
Slovak Republic	23.5	37.7	2008[e]	<2	<0.5	<2	<0.5	2009[e]	<2	<0.5	<2	<0.5
Slovenia	198.2	317.2	2003	<2	<0.5	<2	<0.5	2004	<2	<0.5	<2	<0.5
South Africa	5.7	9.1	2006	17.4	3.3	35.7	12.3	2009	13.8	2.3	31.3	10.2
Sri Lanka	50.0	80.1	2002	14.0	2.6	39.7	11.9	2007	7.0	1.0	29.1	7.4
St. Lucia	2.4[c]	3.8[c]		..	..	..	..	1995[e]	20.9	7.2	40.6	15.5
Sudan	154.4	247.0		..	..	..	..	2009	19.8	5.5	44.1	15.4
Suriname	2.3[c]	3.7[c]		..	..	..	..	1999[e]	15.5	5.9	27.2	11.7
Swaziland	4.7	7.5	2001	62.9	29.4	81.0	45.8	2010	40.6	16.0	60.4	29.3
Syrian Arab Republic	30.8	49.3		..	..	..	..	2004	<2	<0.5	16.9	3.3
Tajikistan	1.2	1.9	2007	14.7	4.4	37.0	12.2	2009	6.6	1.2	27.7	7.0
Tanzania	603.1	964.9	2000	84.6	41.6	95.3	60.3	2007	67.9	28.1	87.9	47.5
Thailand	21.8	34.9	2008[j]	<2	<0.5	5.0	0.8	2009[j]	<2	<0.5	4.6	0.8
Timor-Leste	0.6[c]	1.0[c]	2001	52.9	19.1	77.5	37.1	2007	37.4	8.9	72.8	27.0
Togo	352.8	564.5		..	..	..	..	2006	38.7	11.4	69.3	27.9
Trinidad and Tobago	5.8[c]	9.2[c]	1988[e]	<2	<0.5	8.6	1.9	1992[e]	4.2	1.1	13.5	3.9

	International poverty line in local currency			International poverty line[a]									
	$1.25 a day 2005	$2 a day 2005	Survey year[b]	Population below $1.25 a day %	Poverty gap at $1.25 a day %	Population below $2 a day %	Poverty gap at $2 a day %	Survey year[b]	Population below $1.25 a day %	Poverty gap at $1.25 a day %	Population below $2 a day %	Poverty gap at $2 a day %
Tunisia	0.9	1.4	2000	2.6	0.5	12.8	3.0	2005	<2	<0.5	8.1	1.8
Turkey	1.3	2.0	2007	<2	<0.5	4.5	1.2	2008	<2	<0.5	4.2	0.7
Turkmenistan	5,961.1[c]	9,537.7[c]	1993[e]	63.5	25.8	85.7	44.9	1998	24.8	7.0	49.7	18.4
Uganda	930.8	1,489.2	2006	51.5	19.1	75.6	36.4	2009	38.0	12.2	64.7	27.4
Ukraine	2.1	3.4	2008	<2	<0.5	<2	<0.5	2009	<2	<0.5	<2	<0.5
Uruguay	19.1	30.6	2009[f]	<2	<0.5	<2	<0.5	2010[f]	<2	<0.5	<2	<0.5
Venezuela, RB	1,563.9	2,502.2	2005[f]	13.4	8.2	21.9	11.6	2006[f]	6.6	3.7	12.9	5.9
Vietnam	7,399.9	11,839.8	2006	21.4	5.3	48.1	16.3	2008	16.9	3.8	43.4	13.5
West Bank and Gaza	2.7[c]	4.3[c]	2007	<2	<0.5	2.5	0.5	2009	<2	<0.5	<2	<0.5
Yemen, Rep.	113.8	182.1	1998	12.9	3.0	36.4	11.1	2005	17.5	4.2	46.6	14.8
Zambia	3,537.9	5,660.7	2004	64.3	32.8	81.5	48.3	2006	68.5	37.0	82.6	51.8

a. Based on nominal per capita consumption averages and distributions estimated parametrically from grouped household survey data, unless otherwise noted. b. Refers to the year in which the underlying household survey data were collected or, when the data collection period bridged two calendar years, the year in which most of the data were collected. c. Based on purchasing power parity (PPP) dollars imputed using regression. d. Covers urban areas only. e. Based on per capita income averages and distributions estimated parametrically from grouped household survey data. f. Estimated nonparametrically from nominal income per capita distributions based on unit-record household survey data. g. PPP conversion factor based on urban prices. h. Population-weighted average of urban and rural estimates. i. Based on benchmark national PPP estimate rescaled to account for cost-of-living differences in urban and rural areas. j. Estimated nonparametrically from nominal consumption per capita distributions based on unit-record household survey data.

Regional poverty estimates and progress toward the Millennium Development Goals

Global poverty measured at the $1.25 a day poverty line has been decreasing since the 1980s. The share of population living on less than $1.25 a day fell almost 10 percentage points, to 43 percent, in 1990 and then fell about 20 percentage points between 1990 and 2008. The number of people living in extreme poverty fell from 1.9 billion in 1990 to about 1.3 billion in 2008 (figure 2.8a). This substantial reduction in extreme poverty over the past quarter century, however, disguises large regional differences.

The greatest reduction in poverty occurred in East Asia and Pacific, where the poverty rate declined from 77 percent in 1981 to 14 percent in 2008 and the number of people living on less than $1.25 a day dropped more than 800 million (figure 2.8b). Much of this decline was in China, where the poverty rate fell from 84 percent to 13 percent, leaving about 660 million fewer people poor. Over the same period the poverty rate in South Asia fell from 61 percent to 36 percent (table 2.8c). In contrast, the poverty rate fell only slightly in Sub-Saharan Africa—from less than 52 percent in 1981 to more than 59 percent in 1993 then down to 47.5 percent in 2008. But the number of people living below the poverty line has nearly doubled over this period and started declining slightly only from 2005 onward.

Most of the people who have escaped extreme poverty remain very poor by the standards of middle-income countries. The median poverty line for developing countries in 2005 was $2 a day. The poverty rate for all developing countries measured at this line fell from nearly 70 percent in 1981 to 43 percent in 2008, but the number of people living on less than $2 a day has remained nearly constant at around 2.5 billion. The largest decrease, in both number and proportion, occurred in East Asia and Pacific, led by China. By contrast in Sub-Saharan Africa and South Asia, particularly India, the number of people living on less than $2 a day increased. And globally the number of people living on $1.25–$2 a day nearly doubled, to 1.2 billion (see figure 2.8a).

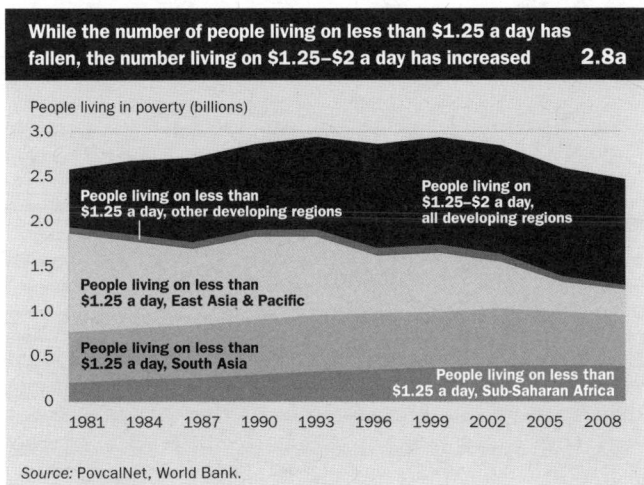

While the number of people living on less than $1.25 a day has fallen, the number living on $1.25–$2 a day has increased **2.8a**

People living in poverty (billions)

People living on less than $1.25 a day, other developing regions

People living on $1.25–$2 a day, all developing regions

People living on less than $1.25 a day, East Asia & Pacific

People living on less than $1.25 a day, South Asia

People living on less than $1.25 a day, Sub-Saharan Africa

Source: PovcalNet, World Bank.

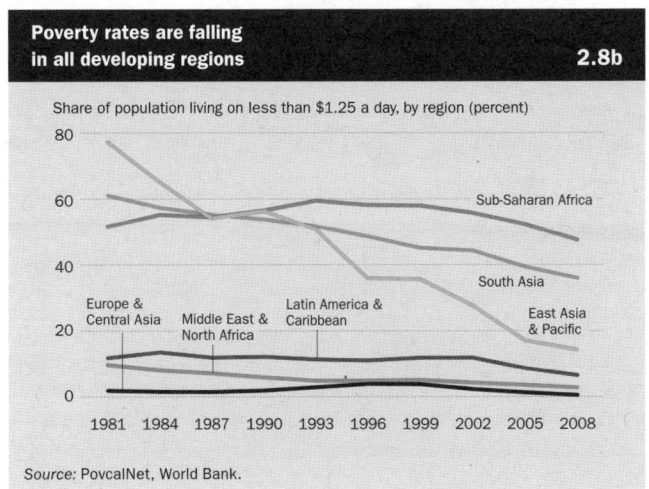

Poverty rates are falling in all developing regions **2.8b**

Share of population living on less than $1.25 a day, by region (percent)

Sub-Saharan Africa

South Asia

Europe & Central Asia

Middle East & North Africa

Latin America & Caribbean

East Asia & Pacific

Source: PovcalNet, World Bank.

2.8 Poverty rates at international poverty lines

Regional poverty estimates										2.8c
Region or country	1981	1984	1987	1990	1993	1996	1999	2002	2005	2008
People living on less than 2005 PPP $1.25 a day (millions)										
East Asia & Pacific	1,097	970	848	926	871	640	656	523	332	284
China	835	720	586	683	633	443	446	363	212	173
Europe & Central Asia	8	7	7	9	14	18	18	11	6	2
Latin America & Caribbean	43	53	49	53	53	54	60	63	48	37
Middle East & North Africa	16	15	15	13	12	12	14	12	10	9
South Asia	568	574	593	617	632	631	619	640	598	571
India	429	427	443	448	462	463	473	484	466	445
Sub-Saharan Africa	205	239	257	290	330	349	376	390	395	386
Total	1,938	1,858	1,768	1,909	1,910	1,704	1,743	1,639	1,389	1,289
Share of people living on less than 2005 PPP $1.25 a day (percent)										
East Asia & Pacific	77.2	65.0	54.1	56.2	50.7	35.9	35.6	27.6	17.1	14.3
China	84.0	69.4	54.0	60.2	53.7	36.4	35.6	28.4	16.3	13.1
Europe & Central Asia	1.9	1.6	1.5	1.9	2.9	3.9	3.8	2.3	1.3	0.5
Latin America & Caribbean	11.9	13.6	12.0	12.2	11.4	11.1	11.9	11.9	8.7	6.5
Middle East & North Africa	9.6	8.0	7.1	5.8	4.8	4.8	5.0	4.2	3.5	2.7
South Asia	61.1	57.4	55.3	53.8	51.7	48.6	45.1	44.3	39.4	36.0
India	59.8	55.7	54.1	51.3	49.7	47.2	45.6	44.5	40.8	37.4
Sub-Saharan Africa	51.5	55.2	54.4	56.5	59.4	58.1	57.9	55.7	52.3	47.5
Total	52.2	47.1	42.3	43.1	41.0	34.8	34.1	30.8	25.1	22.4
People living on less than 2005 PPP $2 a day (millions)										
East Asia & Pacific	1,313	1,316	1,279	1,334	1,301	1,140	1,138	984	758	659
China	972	963	907	961	926	792	770	655	482	395
Europe & Central Asia	36	30	29	32	43	53	57	37	22	10
Latin America & Caribbean	87	104	92	98	100	102	111	118	92	71
Middle East & North Africa	52	51	54	53	53	57	60	57	53	44
South Asia	811	855	906	959	1,010	1,047	1,069	1,120	1,113	1,125
India	621	651	689	722	760	788	818	848	857	862
Sub-Saharan Africa	288	324	350	389	434	466	503	533	559	562
Total	2,585	2,680	2,710	2,864	2,941	2,865	2,937	2,848	2,596	2,471
Share of people living on less than 2005 PPP $2 a day (percent)										
East Asia & Pacific	92.4	88.3	81.6	81.0	75.8	64.0	61.7	51.9	39.0	33.2
China	97.8	92.9	83.7	84.6	78.6	65.1	61.4	51.2	36.9	29.8
Europe & Central Asia	8.3	6.7	6.3	6.9	9.2	11.2	12.1	7.9	4.6	2.2
Latin America & Caribbean	23.8	26.8	22.4	22.4	21.7	21.0	22.0	22.2	16.7	12.4
Middle East & North Africa	30.1	27.1	26.1	23.5	22.1	22.2	22.0	19.7	17.4	13.9
South Asia	87.2	85.6	84.5	83.6	82.7	80.7	77.8	77.4	73.4	70.9
India	86.6	84.9	84.1	82.6	81.9	80.2	78.9	77.9	75.0	72.4
Sub-Saharan Africa	72.2	74.7	74.3	76.0	78.1	77.5	77.4	76.1	74.1	69.2
Total	69.6	68.0	64.8	64.6	63.1	58.6	57.4	53.5	46.9	43.0

Source: World Bank PovcalNet.

The World Bank produced its first global poverty estimates for developing countries for *World Development Report 1990: Poverty* (World Bank 1990) using household survey data for 22 countries (Ravallion, Datt, and van de Walle 1991). Since then there has been considerable expansion in the number of countries that field household income and expenditure surveys. The World Bank's Development Research Group maintains a database that is updated annually as new survey data become available (and thus may contain more recent data or revisions that are not incorporated into the table) and conducts a major reassessment of progress against poverty about every three years. PovcalNet (http://iresearch.worldbank.org/Povcal-Net/) is an interactive computational tool that allows users to replicate these internationally comparable $1.25 and $2 a day global, regional, and country-level poverty estimates and to compute poverty measures for custom country groupings and for different poverty lines. The Poverty and Equity Data portal (http://povertydata.worldbank.org/poverty/home/) provides access to the database and user-friendly dashboards with graphs and interactive maps that visualize trends in key poverty and inequality indicators for different regions and countries. The country dashboards display trends in poverty measures based on the national poverty lines (see table 2.7) alongside the internationally comparable estimates in the table, produced from and consistent with PovcalNet.

Data availability

The World Bank's internationally comparable poverty monitoring database now draws on income or detailed consumption data collected from interviews with 1.23 million randomly sampled households through more than 850 household surveys collected by national statistical offices in nearly 130 countries. Despite progress in the last decade, the challenges of measuring poverty remain. The timeliness, frequency, quality, and comparability of household surveys need to increase substantially, particularly in the poorest countries. The availability and quality of poverty monitoring data remains low in small states, countries with fragile situations, and low-income countries and even some middle-income countries. The low frequency and lack of comparability of the data available in some countries create uncertainty over the magnitude of poverty reduction. The need to improve household survey programs for monitoring poverty is clearly urgent. But institutional, political, and financial obstacles continue to limit data collection, analysis, and public access.

Data quality

Besides the frequency and timeliness of survey data, other data quality issues arise in measuring household living standards. The surveys ask detailed questions on sources of income and how it was spent, which must be carefully recorded by trained personnel.

Income is generally more difficult to measure accurately, and consumption comes closer to the notion of living standards. And income can vary over time even if living standards do not. But consumption data are not always available: the latest estimates reported here use consumption data for about two-thirds of countries.

However, even similar surveys may not be strictly comparable because of differences in timing or in the quality and training of enumerators. Comparisons of countries at different levels of development also pose a potential problem because of differences in the relative importance of the consumption of nonmarket goods. The local market value of all consumption in kind (including own production, particularly important in underdeveloped rural economies) should be included in total consumption expenditure but may not be. Most survey data now include valuations for consumption or income from own production, but valuation methods vary.

The statistics reported here are based on consumption data or, when unavailable, on income surveys. Analysis of some 20 countries for which income and consumption expenditure data were both available from the same surveys found income to yield a higher mean than consumption but also higher inequality. When poverty measures based on consumption and income were compared, the two effects roughly cancelled each other out: there was no significant statistical difference.

International poverty lines

International comparisons of poverty estimates entail both conceptual and practical problems. Countries have different definitions of poverty, and consistent comparisons across countries can be difficult. Local poverty lines tend to have higher purchasing power in rich countries, where more generous standards are used, than in poor countries.

Poverty measures based on international poverty lines attempt to hold the real value of the poverty line constant across countries, as is done when making comparisons over time. Since *World Development Report 1990* the World Bank has aimed to apply a common standard in measuring extreme poverty, anchored to what *poverty* means in the world's poorest countries. The welfare of people living in different countries can be measured on a common scale by adjusting for differences in the purchasing power of currencies. The commonly used $1 a day standard, measured in 1985 international prices and adjusted to local currency using purchasing power parities (PPPs), was chosen for *World Development Report 1990* because it was typical of the poverty lines in low-income countries at the time.

Early editions of *World Development Indicators* used PPPs from the Penn World Tables to convert values in local currency to equivalent purchasing power measured in U.S dollars. Later editions used

1993 consumption PPP estimates produced by the World Bank. International poverty lines were recently revised using the new data on PPPs compiled in the 2005 round of the International Comparison Program, along with data from an expanded set of household income and expenditure surveys. The new extreme poverty line is set at $1.25 a day in 2005 PPP terms, which represents the mean of the poverty lines found in the poorest 15 countries ranked by per capita consumption. The new poverty line maintains the same standard for extreme poverty—the poverty line typical of the poorest countries in the world—but updates it using the latest information on the cost of living in developing countries.

• **International poverty line in local currency** is the international poverty lines of $1.25 and $2.00 a day in 2005 prices, converted to local currency using the PPP conversion factors estimated by the International Comparison Program. • **Survey year** is the year in which the underlying data were collected or, when the data collection period bridged two calendar years, the year in which most of the data were collected. • **Population below $1.25 a day** and **population below $2 a day** are the percentages of the population living on less than $1.25 a day and $2 a day at 2005 international prices. As a result of revisions in PPP exchange rates, poverty rates for individual countries cannot be compared with poverty rates reported in earlier editions. • **Poverty gap** is the mean shortfall from the poverty line (counting the nonpoor as having zero shortfall), expressed as a percentage of the poverty line. This measure reflects the depth of poverty as well as its incidence.

The poverty measures are prepared by the World Bank's Development Research Group. The international poverty lines are based on nationally representative primary household surveys by national statistical offices or by private agencies under the supervision of government or international agencies and obtained from government statistical offices and World Bank Group country departments. Detailed information on the methodology adopted by the Socio-Economic Database for Latin America and the Caribbean to process the income data used for countries in this region is available at http://sedlac.econo.unlp.edu.ar/eng/methodology.php. The World Bank Group has prepared an annual review of its poverty work since 1993. For details on data sources and methods used in deriving the World Bank's latest estimates, see http://iresearch.worldbank.org/povcalnet. For further discussion of the results, see Ravallion, Chen, and Sangraula (2009) and Chen and Ravallion (2011).

Distribution of income or consumption

	Survey year	Gini index		Lowest 10%	Lowest 20%	Second 20%	Third 20%	Fourth 20%	Highest 20%	Highest 10%
						Percentage share of income or consumption[a]				
Afghanistan	2008[b]	27.8		4.1	9.4	13.6	17.4	22.1	37.5	23.2
Albania	2008[b]	34.5		3.5	8.1	12.1	15.9	20.9	43.0	29.0
Algeria	1995[b]	35.3		2.9	7.0	11.6	16.2	22.6	42.6	26.9
Angola[c]	2000[b]	58.6		0.6	2.0	5.7	10.8	19.7	61.9	44.7
Argentina[c]	2010[d]	44.5		1.5	4.4	9.3	14.8	22.2	49.4	32.3
Armenia	2008[b]	30.9		3.7	8.8	12.8	16.7	21.9	39.8	25.4
Australia	1994[d]	35.2		2.0	5.9	12.0	17.2	23.6	41.3	25.4
Austria	2000[d]	29.1		3.3	8.6	13.3	17.4	22.9	37.8	23.0
Azerbaijan	2008[b]	33.7		3.4	8.0	12.1	16.2	21.7	42.1	27.4
Bangladesh	2010[b]	32.1		4.0	8.9	12.4	16.1	21.3	41.4	27.0
Belarus	2008[b]	27.2		3.8	9.2	13.8	17.8	22.9	36.4	21.9
Belgium	2000[d]	33.0		3.4	8.5	13.0	16.3	20.8	41.4	28.1
Belize	1999[d]	53.1		0.9	3.3	8.6	11.2	19.4	57.5	42.2
Benin	2003[b]	38.6		3.0	7.0	10.8	15.0	21.0	46.1	31.2
Bhutan	2007[b]	38.1		2.8	6.6	10.8	15.4	22.0	45.2	29.4
Bolivia	2007[d]	56.3		0.5	2.1	6.8	11.9	19.9	59.3	43.3
Bosnia and Herzegovina	2007[b]	36.2		2.7	6.7	11.3	16.1	22.7	43.2	27.3
Botswana	1994[b]	61.0		1.3	3.1	5.8	9.6	16.4	65.0	51.2
Brazil	2009[d]	54.7		0.8	2.9	7.1	12.4	19.0	58.6	42.9
Bulgaria	2007[b]	28.2		3.3	8.5	13.7	17.9	23.1	36.7	22.2
Burkina Faso	2009[b]	39.8		2.9	6.7	10.6	14.8	20.9	47.0	32.2
Burundi	2006[b]	33.3		4.1	9.0	11.9	15.4	21.0	42.8	28.0
Cambodia	2008[b]	37.9		3.3	7.5	11.0	14.9	20.6	45.9	31.4
Cameroon	2007[b]	38.9		2.9	6.7	10.5	14.9	21.7	46.2	30.4
Canada	2000[d]	32.6		2.6	7.2	12.7	17.2	23.0	39.9	24.8
Cape Verde	2002[b]	50.5		1.9	4.5	7.9	12.3	19.4	55.9	40.6
Central African Republic	2008[b]	56.3		1.2	3.4	6.9	11.1	18.0	60.6	46.1
Chad	2003[b]	39.8		2.6	6.3	10.4	15.0	21.8	46.6	30.8
Chile	2009[d]	52.1		1.5	4.3	7.9	11.7	18.4	57.7	42.8
China	2005[d]	42.5		1.8	5.0	9.9	15.0	22.2	47.9	32.0
Hong Kong SAR, China	1996[d]	43.4		2.0	5.3	9.4	13.9	20.7	50.7	34.9
Colombia	2010[d]	55.9		0.9	3.0	6.8	11.2	18.8	60.2	44.4
Comoros	2004[b]	64.3		0.9	2.6	5.4	8.9	15.1	68.0	55.2
Congo, Dem. Rep.	2006[b]	44.4		2.3	5.5	9.2	13.8	20.9	50.6	34.7
Congo, Rep.	2005[b]	47.3		2.1	5.0	8.4	13.0	20.5	53.1	37.1
Costa Rica	2009[d]	50.7		1.2	3.9	8.0	12.4	19.9	55.9	39.5
Côte d'Ivoire	2008[b]	41.5		2.2	5.6	10.1	14.9	21.8	47.6	31.8
Croatia	2008[b]	33.7		3.3	8.1	12.2	16.2	21.6	42.0	27.5
Czech Republic	1996[d]	25.8		4.3	10.2	14.3	17.5	21.7	36.2	22.7
Denmark	1997[d]	24.7		2.6	8.3	14.7	18.2	22.9	35.8	21.3
Djibouti	2002[b]	40.0		2.4	6.0	10.5	15.2	21.8	46.5	30.9
Dominican Republic	2010[d]	47.2		1.8	4.7	8.6	13.2	20.8	52.8	36.4
Ecuador	2010[d]	49.3		1.4	4.3	8.2	13.0	20.7	53.8	38.3
Egypt, Arab Rep.	2008[b]	30.8		4.0	9.2	13.0	16.4	21.0	40.3	26.6
El Salvador	2009[d]	48.3		1.0	3.7	8.8	13.7	20.7	53.1	37.0
Estonia	2004[b]	36.0		2.7	6.8	11.6	16.2	22.2	43.2	28.0
Ethiopia	2005[b]	29.8		4.1	9.3	13.2	16.8	21.3	39.4	25.6
Finland	2000[d]	26.9		4.0	9.6	14.1	17.5	22.1	36.7	22.6
Fiji	2009[b]	42.8		2.6	6.2	9.9	14.1	20.3	49.6	34.9
France	1995[d]	32.7		2.8	7.2	12.6	17.2	22.8	40.2	25.1
Gabon	2005[b]	41.5		2.6	6.2	10.1	14.5	21.0	48.2	33.0
Gambia, The	2003[b]	47.3		2.0	4.8	8.6	13.2	20.6	52.8	36.9
Georgia	2008[b]	41.3		2.0	5.3	10.3	15.2	22.1	47.2	31.3
Germany	2000[d]	28.3		3.2	8.5	13.7	17.8	23.1	36.9	22.1
Ghana	2006[b]	42.8		2.0	5.2	9.8	14.7	21.6	48.6	32.8
Greece	2000[d]	34.3		2.5	6.7	11.9	16.8	23.0	41.5	26.0
Guatemala	2006[d]	55.9		1.1	3.1	6.9	11.4	18.5	60.3	44.9

	Survey year	Gini index	Percentage share of income or consumption[a]						
			Lowest 10%	Lowest 20%	Second 20%	Third 20%	Fourth 20%	Highest 20%	Highest 10%
Guinea	2007[b]	39.4	2.7	6.4	10.5	15.1	21.9	46.2	30.3
Guinea-Bissau	2002[b]	35.5	3.1	7.3	11.6	16.0	21.9	43.2	28.1
Guyana	1998[d]	44.5	1.3	4.5	9.8	14.7	21.6	49.5	34.0
Haiti	2001[d]	59.2	0.7	2.4	6.3	10.4	17.6	63.4	47.7
Honduras	2009[d]	57.0	0.4	2.0	6.1	11.4	20.5	59.9	42.4
Hungary	2007[b]	31.2	3.5	8.4	12.9	16.9	22.0	39.9	25.4
India	2005[b]	33.4	3.8	8.6	12.2	15.8	21.0	42.4	28.3
Indonesia	2005[b]	34.0	3.7	8.3	12.0	15.8	21.0	42.8	28.5
Iran, Islamic Rep.	2005[b]	38.3	2.6	6.4	10.9	15.5	22.0	45.2	29.6
Iraq	2007[b]	30.9	3.8	8.7	12.8	16.7	22.0	39.9	25.2
Ireland	2000[d]	34.3	2.9	7.4	12.3	16.3	21.9	42.0	27.2
Israel	2001[d]	39.2	2.1	5.7	10.5	15.9	23.0	44.9	28.8
Italy	2000[d]	36.0	2.3	6.5	12.0	16.8	22.8	42.0	26.8
Jamaica	2004[b]	45.5	2.3	5.4	9.0	13.5	20.6	51.6	35.9
Japan	1993[d]	24.9	4.8	10.6	14.2	17.6	22.0	35.7	21.7
Jordan	2010[b]	35.4	3.4	7.7	11.6	15.7	21.5	43.6	28.7
Kazakhstan	2009[b]	29.0	4.0	9.1	13.2	17.1	22.3	38.4	23.8
Kenya	2005[b]	47.7	2.0	4.8	8.7	13.2	20.1	53.2	38.0
Korea, Rep.	1998[d]	31.6	2.9	7.9	13.6	18.0	23.1	37.5	22.5
Kyrgyz Republic	2009[b]	36.2	2.8	6.8	11.4	16.0	22.4	43.4	27.8
Lao PDR	2008[b]	36.7	3.3	7.6	11.3	15.3	20.9	44.8	30.3
Latvia	2008[b]	36.6	2.6	6.6	11.4	16.1	22.3	43.6	28.1
Lesotho	2003[b]	52.5	1.0	3.0	7.2	12.5	21.0	56.4	39.4
Liberia	2007[b]	38.2	2.4	6.4	11.4	15.7	21.6	45.0	30.1
Lithuania	2008[b]	37.6	2.6	6.6	11.1	15.7	22.1	44.4	29.1
Macedonia, FYR	2009[b]	43.2	2.0	5.1	9.5	14.5	22.0	48.9	32.4
Madagascar	2010[b]	44.1	2.2	5.4	9.5	14.1	20.9	50.1	34.7
Malawi	2004[b]	39.0	3.0	7.0	10.8	14.9	20.8	46.5	31.9
Malaysia	2009[d]	46.2	1.8	4.5	8.7	13.7	21.6	51.5	34.7
Mali	2010[b]	33.0	3.5	8.0	12.0	16.3	22.4	41.3	25.8
Mauritania	2008[b]	40.5	2.4	6.0	10.4	15.1	21.5	47.0	31.6
Mexico	2010[d]	47.7	1.4	4.4	8.9	13.3	20.4	53.0	37.2
Micronesia, Fed. Sts.[c]	2000[b]	61.1	0.4	1.6	5.2	10.2	19.1	64.0	47.1
Moldova	2010[b]	33.0	3.3	7.8	12.2	16.5	22.3	41.2	26.0
Mongolia	2008[b]	36.5	3.0	7.1	11.2	15.6	22.1	44.0	28.4
Montenegro	2008[b]	30.0	3.6	8.5	13.1	17.2	22.4	38.8	24.1
Morocco	2007[b]	40.9	2.7	6.5	10.5	14.5	20.6	47.9	33.2
Mozambique	2008[b]	45.7	1.9	5.2	9.5	13.7	20.1	51.5	36.7
Namibia	2004[d]	63.9	1.4	3.2	5.0	8.2	15.0	68.6	54.8
Nepal	2010[b]	32.8	3.6	8.3	12.2	16.2	21.9	41.5	26.5
Netherlands	1999[d]	30.9	2.5	7.6	13.2	17.2	23.3	38.7	22.9
New Zealand	1997[d]	36.2	2.2	6.4	11.4	15.8	22.6	43.8	27.8
Nicaragua	2005[b]	40.5	2.6	6.2	10.2	14.8	21.5	47.2	31.5
Niger	2008[b]	34.6	3.6	8.1	11.8	15.8	21.3	43.1	28.5
Nigeria	2010[b]	48.8	1.8	4.4	8.3	13.0	20.3	54.0	38.2
Norway	2000[d]	25.8	3.9	9.6	14.0	17.2	22.0	37.2	23.4
Pakistan	2008[b]	30.0	4.4	9.6	12.9	16.4	21.1	40.0	26.1
Panama	2010[d]	51.9	1.1	3.3	7.8	12.5	20.1	56.4	40.1
Papua New Guinea	1996[b]	50.9	1.9	4.5	7.7	12.1	19.3	56.4	40.9
Paraguay	2010[d]	52.4	1.0	3.3	7.8	12.8	19.8	56.4	41.1
Peru	2010[d]	48.1	1.4	3.9	8.3	13.6	21.5	52.6	36.1
Philippines	2009[b]	43.0	2.6	6.0	9.4	13.9	21.0	49.7	33.6
Poland	2009[b]	34.1	3.3	7.7	12.0	16.2	22.0	42.1	27.1
Portugal	1997[d]	38.5	2.0	5.8	11.0	15.5	21.9	45.9	29.8
Qatar	2007[b]	41.1	1.3	3.9	..	..	..	52.0	35.9
Romania	2009[b]	30.0	3.4	8.3	13.1	17.4	22.9	38.3	23.5
Russian Federation	2009[b]	40.1	2.8	6.5	10.4	14.8	21.3	47.1	31.7

	Survey year	Gini index	Percentage share of income or consumption[a]						
			Lowest 10%	Lowest 20%	Second 20%	Third 20%	Fourth 20%	Highest 20%	Highest 10%
Rwanda	2011[b]	50.8	2.1	5.2	8.3	11.9	17.8	56.8	43.2
São Tomé and Príncipe	2001[b]	50.8	2.2	5.2	8.5	12.2	17.7	56.4	43.6
Senegal	2005[b]	39.2	2.5	6.2	10.6	15.3	22.0	45.9	30.1
Serbia	2009[b]	27.8	3.7	8.9	13.7	17.8	22.8	36.9	22.2
Seychelles	2007[b]	65.8	1.6	3.7	5.7	8.3	12.7	69.6	60.2
Sierra Leone	2003[b]	42.5	2.6	6.1	9.7	14.0	20.9	49.3	33.6
Singapore	1998[d]	42.5	1.9	5.0	9.4	14.6	22.0	49.0	32.8
Slovak Republic	2009[d]	26.0	4.4	10.1	14.1	17.5	22.0	36.2	22.4
Slovenia	2004[b]	31.2	3.4	8.2	12.8	17.0	22.6	39.4	24.6
South Africa	2009[b]	63.1	1.2	2.7	4.6	8.2	16.3	68.2	51.7
South Sudan	2009[b]	45.5	..	..	..	..	..	..	..
Spain	2000[d]	34.7	2.6	7.0	12.1	16.4	22.5	42.0	26.6
Sri Lanka	2007[b]	40.3	3.1	6.9	10.4	14.4	20.5	47.8	32.9
St. Lucia	1995[d]	42.6	2.0	5.2	9.9	14.8	21.8	48.3	32.5
Sudan	2009[b]	35.3	2.7	6.8	11.7	16.4	22.7	42.4	26.7
Suriname	1999[d]	52.9	1.1	3.2	7.2	12.3	20.4	56.9	40.6
Swaziland	2010[b]	51.5	1.7	4.1	7.4	12.0	20.0	56.6	40.1
Sweden	2000[d]	25.0	3.6	9.1	14.0	17.6	22.7	36.6	22.2
Switzerland	2000[d]	33.7	2.9	7.6	12.2	16.3	22.6	41.3	25.9
Syrian Arab Republic	2004[b]	35.8	3.4	7.7	11.4	15.5	21.4	43.9	28.9
Tajikistan	2009[b]	30.8	3.5	8.3	12.8	17.0	22.6	39.4	24.3
Tanzania	2007[b]	37.6	2.8	6.8	11.1	15.6	21.7	44.8	29.6
Thailand	2009[b]	40.0	2.8	6.7	10.3	14.5	21.4	47.2	31.5
Timor-Leste	2007[b]	31.9	4.0	9.0	12.5	16.1	21.2	41.3	27.0
Togo	2006[b]	34.4	3.3	7.6	11.7	16.1	22.2	42.4	27.1
Trinidad and Tobago	1992[d]	40.3	2.1	5.5	10.3	15.5	22.7	45.9	29.9
Tunisia	2005[b]	41.4	2.4	5.9	10.1	14.7	21.3	47.9	32.5
Turkey	2008[b]	39.0	2.1	5.7	10.9	15.9	22.4	45.1	29.4
Turkmenistan	1998[b]	40.8	2.6	6.1	10.2	14.7	21.5	47.5	31.7
Uganda	2009[b]	44.3	2.4	5.8	9.6	13.8	20.0	50.7	36.1
Ukraine	2009[b]	26.4	4.2	9.7	14.0	17.7	22.4	36.3	22.0
United Kingdom	1999[d]	36.0	2.1	6.1	11.4	16.0	22.5	44.0	28.5
United States	2000[d]	40.8	1.9	5.4	10.7	15.7	22.4	45.8	29.9
Uruguay	2010[d]	45.3	1.9	4.9	9.0	13.7	21.5	50.9	34.4
Uzbekistan	2003[b]	36.7	2.9	7.1	11.5	15.7	21.5	44.2	29.5
Venezuela, RB	2006[d]	44.8	1.2	4.3	9.5	14.6	22.2	49.4	33.2
Vietnam	2008[b]	35.6	3.2	7.4	11.5	15.8	21.8	43.4	28.2
West Bank and Gaza	2009[b]	35.5	3.2	7.4	11.5	15.8	21.8	43.4	28.2
Yemen, Rep.	2005[b]	37.7	2.9	7.2	11.3	15.3	21.0	45.3	30.8
Zambia	2006[b]	54.6	1.5	3.6	6.7	11.2	19.2	59.4	43.1
Zimbabwe	1995[b]	50.1	1.8	4.6	8.1	12.2	19.3	55.7	40.3

a. Percentage shares by quintile may not sum to 100 percent because of rounding. b. Refers to expenditure shares by percentiles of population, ranked by per capita expenditure. c. Covers urban areas only. d. Refers to income shares by percentiles of population, ranked by per capita income.

Distribution of income or consumption | 2.9

Inequality in the distribution of income is reflected in the percentage shares of income or consumption accruing to portions of the population ranked by income or consumption levels. The portions ranked lowest by personal income receive the smallest shares of total income. The Gini index provides a convenient summary measure of the degree of inequality. Data on the distribution of income or consumption come from nationally representative household surveys. Where the original data from the household survey were available, they have been used to directly calculate the income or consumption shares by quintile. Otherwise, shares have been estimated from the best available grouped data.

The distribution data have been adjusted for household size, providing a more consistent measure of per capita income or consumption. No adjustment has been made for spatial differences in cost of living within countries, because the data needed for such calculations are generally unavailable. For further details on the estimation method for low- and middle-income economies, see Ravallion and Chen (1996).

Because the underlying household surveys differ in method and type of data collected, the distribution data are not strictly comparable across countries. These problems are diminishing as survey methods improve and become more standardized, but achieving strict comparability is still impossible (see *About the data* for tables 2.7 and 2.8).

Two sources of noncomparability should be noted in particular. First, the surveys can differ in many respects, including whether they use income or consumption expenditure as the living standard indicator. The distribution of income is typically more unequal than the distribution of consumption. In addition, the definitions of income used differ more often among surveys. Consumption is usually a much better welfare indicator, particularly in developing countries. Second, households differ in size (number of members) and in the extent of income sharing among members. And individuals differ in age and consumption needs. Differences among countries in these respects may bias comparisons of distribution.

World Bank staff have made an effort to ensure that the data are as comparable as possible. Wherever possible, consumption has been used rather than income. Income distribution and Gini indexes for high-income economies are calculated directly from the Luxembourg Income Study database, using an estimation method consistent with that applied for developing countries.

• **Survey year** is the year in which the underlying data were collected. • **Gini index** measures the extent to which the distribution of income (or consumption expenditure) among individuals or households within an economy deviates from a perfectly equal distribution. A Lorenz curve plots the cumulative percentages of total income received against the cumulative number of recipients, starting with the poorest individual. The Gini index measures the area between the Lorenz curve and a hypothetical line of absolute equality, expressed as a percentage of the maximum area under the line. Thus a Gini index of 0 represents perfect equality, while an index of 100 implies perfect inequality. • **Percentage share of income or consumption** is the share of total income or consumption that accrues to subgroups of population indicated by deciles or quintiles.

Data on distribution are compiled by the World Bank's Development Research Group using PovcalNet (http://iresearch.worldbank.org/PovcalNet) based on household survey data obtained from government statistical agencies and World Bank country departments. Detailed information on the methodology adopted by the Socio-Economic Database for Latin America and the Caribbean to process the income data used for countries in this region is available at http://sedlac.econo.unlp.edu.ar/eng/methodology.php. Data for high-income economies are computed based on data from the Luxembourg Income Study database.

Assessing vulnerability and security

	Youth unemployment		Female-headed households	Pension contributors			Public expenditure on pensions			
	Male % of male labor force ages 15–24 2007–10[a]	Female % of female labor force ages 15–24 2007–10[a]	% of total 2007–10[a]	Year	% of labor force	% of working-age population	Year	% of GDP	Year	Average pension % of average wage
Afghanistan	..	..	..	2006	3.7	2.3	2005	0.5		..
Albania	26	28	16	2007	37.9	25.7	2009	6.1		..
Algeria	..	..	..	2002	36.7	22.0	2002	3.2		..
Angola	..	..	25		..	..		..		..
Argentina	19[b]	25[b]	34	2008	42.3	33.1	2010	7.4	2000	43.8
Armenia	37	55	36	2008	32.1	24.6	2006	3.2	2007	20.3
Australia	12[b]	11[b]	..	2005	90.7	69.7	2007	3.4		..
Austria	9	9	..	2005	93.7	68.5	2007	12.3		..
Azerbaijan	13	16	25	2007	35.4	24.7	2007	3.8	2006	24.3
Bahrain	..	..	..	2007	20.2	13.4	2004	0.9		..
Bangladesh	..	..	13	2004	2.5	1.9	2006	0.3		..
Belarus	..	..	54	2008	93.5	66.8	2008	10.2	2002	41.6
Belgium	22	22	..	2005	91.4	61.5	2007	8.9		..
Benin	..	..	23	2005	5.5	4.2	2006	1.5		..
Bolivia	..	..	23	2008	12.2	9.4	2009	1.5		..
Bosnia and Herzegovina	45	52	..	2009	24.5	29.0	2009	9.4		..
Botswana	..	..	..	2006	9.0	7.2	2009	1.3		..
Brazil	14	23	..	2008	55.2	45.7	2010	6.1		..
Bulgaria	24	22	..	2008	78.7	54.7	2008	8.5	2004	42.9
Burkina Faso	..	..	..	2004	1.2	1.1	2004	0.7		..
Burundi	..	..	..	2006	3.5	3.3	2006	0.7		..
Cambodia	4	3	27		..	..	2005	0.6		..
Cameroon	..	..	..	2006	16.2	11.5	2005	0.4		..
Canada	17[b]	12[b]	..	2007	66.9	53.6	2007	4.2		..
Central African Republic	..	..	..	2004	1.5	1.3	2004	0.8		..
Chad	..	..	..	2005	2.7	2.0		..		..
Chile	17	22	..	2008	59.6	39.5	2009	5.0	2006	53.5
China	..	..	..	2007	26.9	27.7	2006	2.5		..
Hong Kong SAR, China	15	10	..	2008	78.9	55.4	2006	1.6		..
Colombia	18	30	34	2008	31.5	20.2	2010	3.5		..
Congo, Dem. Rep.	..	..	21	2008	14.2	10.5				
Congo, Rep.	..	..	23	2008	9.7	7.5		..		
Costa Rica	10	13	..	2004	55.5	40.2	2009	2.8		..
Côte d'Ivoire	..	..	..	2004	12.8	9.1	2006	0.7		..
Croatia	30	34	24	2010	82.9	50.0	2009	10.3	2005	32.4
Cuba	3	4	46		..	..		..		..
Cyprus	16	17	..		..	..		..		..
Czech Republic	18	19	..	2007	95.4	67.5	2007	8.5	2005	40.7
Denmark	16	12	..	2007	92.9	86.7	2007	5.6		..
Dominican Republic	21	45	35	2008	25.6	19.1	2009	0.7		..
Ecuador	12[b]	18[b]	..	2004	26.4	18.0	2010	1.8		..
Egypt, Arab Rep.	17	48	13	2009	55.1	27.9	2004	4.1		..
El Salvador	13	8	..	2008	22.9	15.7	2010	1.7		..
Eritrea	..	..	..		..	..	2001	0.3		..
Estonia	35	30	..	2004	94.5	68.7	2007	10.9	2007	35.4
Ethiopia	..	..	23		..	..	2006	0.3		..
Finland	22	19	..	2005	89.7	67.4	2007	8.3		..
France	22	23	..	2005	87.3	61.4	2007	12.5		..
Gabon	..	..	..		..	..		..		..
Gambia, The	..	..	..	2006	2.7	2.2	2003	0.1		..
Georgia	32	41	..	2004	29.2	22.6	2004	3.0	2003	13.0
Germany	10	9	..	2005	86.9	65.6	2007	10.7		..
Ghana	..	..	34	2004	8.1	6.4	2002	1.3		..
Greece	27	41	..	2005	86.0	58.3	2010	13.5		..
Guatemala	..	..	..	2008	20.3	14.7	2009	1.2		..
Guinea	..	..	17	1993	12.1	10.8		..		..
Guinea-Bissau	..	..	..	2004	2.0	1.5	2005	2.1		..
Haiti	..	..	44		..	..		..		..

	Youth unemployment		Female-headed households	Pension contributors			Public expenditure on pensions			
	Male % of male labor force ages 15–24 2007–10[a]	Female % of female labor force ages 15–24 2007–10[a]	% of total 2007–10[a]	Year	% of labor force	% of working-age population	Year	% of GDP	Year	Average pension % of average wage
Honduras	..	..	26	2008	17.3	11.1	2010	0.0		..
Hungary	28	25	..	2008	92.0	56.7	2008	10.5	2005	39.8
India	..	..	14	2006	10.3	6.4	2007	2.2		..
Indonesia	22	23	13	2008	7.1	8.0	2010	1.0		..
Iran, Islamic Rep.	20	34	..	2001	34.2	18.9	2000	1.1		..
Iraq	..	..	11	2009	35.6	19.0	2009	3.9		..
Ireland	34	21	..	2005	88.9	64.1	2007	3.6		..
Israel	15	13	..	2008	..	89.1	2007	4.8		..
Italy	27	29	..	2005	90.1	57.1	2007	14.1		..
Jamaica	23	33	41	2004	17.2	12.7	2004	0.7		..
Japan	10	8	..	2005	95.4	75.0	2007	8.8		..
Jordan	23	46	11	2006	38.4	19.9	2005	2.0		..
Kazakhstan	7	8	..	2004	62.5	48.4	2009	3.2	2003	24.9
Kenya	..	..	34	2006	7.5	6.4	2003	1.1		..
Korea, Dem. Rep.	..	..	..		..	..		..		..
Korea, Rep.	11	9	..	2005	49.5	34.3	2005	1.6		..
Kosovo	..	..	..				2009	2.7[c]		..
Kuwait	..	..	..		..	..		..		..
Kyrgyz Republic	..	..	25	2006	40.4	29.6	2010	2.7	2003	27.5
Lao PDR	..	..	..	2004	..	6.0	2005	0.2		..
Latvia	35	34	..	2003	91.7	70.6	2009	8.5	2005	33.1
Lebanon	22	22	..	2003	34.5	17.3	2003	2.1		..
Lesotho	29	42	..	2005	4.4	3.5		..		..
Liberia	4	8	30		..	..		..		..
Libya	..	..	..	2004	68.5	37.5	2001	2.1		..
Lithuania	38	31	..	2007	82.9	56.9	2010	8.6	2005	30.9
Macedonia, FYR	35	38	8	2008	52.3	33.2	2008	9.4	2006	55.0
Madagascar	..	..	22	2009	5.3	4.9		..		..
Malawi	..	..	..		..	..	2004	0.3		..
Malaysia	10	12	..	2008	49.0	32.5	2004	0.3		..
Mali	..	..	12	2010	7.3	4.4	2010	1.6		..
Mauritania	..	..	..	2000	13.1	9.4	2003	0.6		..
Mauritius	19	29	..	2000	53.4	34.5	2007	2.9		..
Mexico	9	10	..	2008	27.4	19.0	2007	1.4		..
Moldova	16	15	34	2009	56.7	32.1	2009	9.1	2003	20.9
Mongolia	..	..	29	2005	33.5	25.6	2009	4.9		..
Morocco	23	19	..	2007	23.8	13.5	2003	1.9		..
Mozambique	..	..	..	2006	1.9	1.7	2006	0.3		..
Myanmar	..	..	..		..	..		..		..
Namibia	..	..	44	2008	9.6	5.8	2004	1.3		..
Nepal	..	..	23	2008	3.4	2.6	2006	0.2		..
Netherlands	9	9	..	2005	90.7	70.7	2007	4.7		..
New Zealand	17[b]	17[b]	..		..	..	2007	4.3		..
Nicaragua	..	..	..	2008	21.7	14.6		..		..
Niger	..	..	19	2006	1.9	1.3	2006	0.7		..
Nigeria	..	..	19	2004	8.1	4.8	2004	0.9		..
Norway	11	8	..	2005	93.2	75.2	2007	4.7		..
Oman	..	..	..		..	..		..		..
Pakistan	7	11	10	2008	3.9	2.2	2004	0.5		..
Panama	12	21	..		..	..		..		..
Papua New Guinea	..	..	..	2009	4.4	3.3	2005	0.2		..
Paraguay	9	17	..	2004	12.4	9.4	2001	1.2		..
Peru	13[b]	16[b]	22	2008	21.7	15.6	2010	2.5		..
Philippines	17	20	17	2007	25.0	17.0	2003	1.5		..
Poland	22	25	..	2005	81.4	52.7	2009	10.0	2007	47.1
Portugal	21	24	..	2005	92.0	71.6	2007	10.8		..
Puerto Rico	29	22	..		..	..		..		..
Qatar	1	8	..		..	..		..		..

	Youth unemployment		Female-headed households	Pension contributors			Public expenditure on pensions			
	Male % of male labor force ages 15–24 2007–10[a]	Female % of female labor force ages 15–24 2007–10[a]	% of total 2007–10[a]	Year	% of labor force	% of working-age population	Year	% of GDP	Year	Average pension % of average wage
Romania	22	22	..	2007	67.9	45.0	2009	8.3	2005	41.5
Russian Federation	17	18	..	2007	66.8	49.9	2010	8.3	2003	29.2
Rwanda	..	..	31	2004	4.6	4.1	2005	0.7		..
Saudi Arabia	24	46	..		..	..		..		..
Senegal	..	..	20	2003	5.1	4.1	2006	1.4		..
Serbia	31	41	29	2003	45.0	40.2	2010	14.0		..
Sierra Leone	..	..	22	2004	5.5	3.8		..		..
Singapore	10	17	..	2008	62.1	44.6		..		..
Slovak Republic	35	32	..	2003	78.9	55.3	2007	9.3	2005	44.7
Slovenia	15	14	..	2008	87.4	63.8	2007	12.7	2005	44.3
Somalia	..	..	..		..	..		..		..
South Africa	45	53	..	2007	6.3	3.7	2010	2.2		..
South Sudan	..	..	..		..	..		..		..
Spain	43	40	..	2005	69.4	48.7	2007	8.0	2006	58.6
Sri Lanka	17	28	..	2006	24.1	14.9	2007	2.0		..
Sudan	..	..	19	2005	5.2	2.9		..		..
Swaziland	..	..	48	2009	15.4	10.3		..		..
Sweden	27	24	..	2005	88.8	72.2	2007	7.2		..
Switzerland	7	8	..	2005	95.4	78.7	2007	6.4	2000	40.0
Syrian Arab Republic	15	40	..	2008	26.8	14.3	2004	1.3		..
Tajikistan	..	..	..		..	..		..	2003	25.7
Tanzania	..	..	24	2006	4.3	4.0	2006	0.9		..
Thailand	4	5	30	2008	22.8	18.3	2006	0.8		..
Timor-Leste	..	..	12		..	..		..		..
Togo	..	..	..	2003	7.3	5.7	2003	0.8		..
Trinidad and Tobago	9	13	..	2008	71.1	51.2	2010	2.8		..
Tunisia	..	..	..	2004	48.6	25.5	2003	4.3		..
Turkey	21	23	..	2007	58.6	30.5	2008	6.2	2007	61.3
Turkmenistan	..	..	..		..	..		..		..
Uganda	..	..	30	2004	10.3	9.2	2003	0.3		..
Ukraine	..	..	49	2010	65.3	44.7	2010	17.8	2007	48.3
United Arab Emirates	8	22	..		..	..		..		..
United Kingdom	21	17	..	2005	93.2	71.5	2007	5.4		..
United States	21[b]	16[b]	..	2005	92.2	71.4	2007	6.0	2006	29.2
Uruguay	16	25	..	2007	78.5	61.2	2010	8.8		..
Uzbekistan	..	..	18	2005	..	86.3	2005	6.5	2005	40.0
Venezuela, RB	12	16	..	2008	33.9	24.2	2010	5.0		..
Vietnam	..	..	..	2008	19.3	15.2	2004	2.5		..
West Bank and Gaza	39	47	..	2009	14.0	6.5	2009	4.0		..
Yemen, Rep.	..	..	..	2006	10.4	5.0	2004	1.5		..
Zambia	..	..	24	2006	10.9	8.0	2008	1.4		..
Zimbabwe	..	..	38		..	..	2002	2.3		..
World	.. w	.. w								
Low income	..	..								
Middle income	..	..								
Lower middle income	..	..								
Upper middle income	..	..								
Low & middle income										
East Asia & Pacific	..									
Europe & Central Asia	17	18								
Latin America & Carib.	12	18								
Middle East & N. Africa	19	36								
South Asia	..									
Sub-Saharan Africa		..								
High income	19	17								
Euro area	22	22								

a. Data are for the most recent year available. b. Limited coverage. c. Includes expenditure on old-age and survivors benefits only.

As traditionally measured, poverty is a static concept, and vulnerability a dynamic one. Vulnerability reflects a household's resilience in the face of shocks and the likelihood that a shock will lead to a decline in well-being. Thus, it depends primarily on the household's assets and insurance mechanisms. Because poor people have fewer assets and less diversified sources of income than do the better-off, fluctuations in income affect them more.

Enhancing security for poor people means reducing their vulnerability to such risks as ill health, providing them the means to manage risk themselves, and strengthening market or public institutions for managing risk. Tools include microfinance programs, public provision of education and basic health care, and old age assistance (see tables 2.11 and 2.16).

Poor households face many risks, and vulnerability is thus multidimensional. The indicators in the table focus on individual risks—youth unemployment, female-headed households, income insecurity in old age—and the extent to which publicly provided services may be capable of mitigating some of these risks. Poor people face labor market risks, often having to take up precarious, low-quality jobs and to increase their household's labor market participation by sending their children to work (see tables 2.4 and 2.6). Income security is a prime concern for the elderly.

Youth unemployment is an important policy issue for many economies. Experiencing unemployment may permanently impair a young person's productive potential and future employment opportunities. The table presents unemployment among youth ages 15–24, but the lower age limit for young people in a country could be determined by the minimum age for leaving school, so age groups could differ across countries. Also, since this age group is likely to include school leavers, the level of youth unemployment varies considerably over the year as a result of different school opening and closing dates. The youth unemployment rate shares similar limitations on comparability as the general unemployment rate. For further information, see *About the data* for table 2.5 and the original source.

The definition of female-headed household differs greatly across countries, making cross-country comparison difficult. In some cases it is assumed that a woman cannot be the head of any household with an adult male, because of sex-biased stereotype. Caution should be used in interpreting the data.

Pension scheme coverage may be broad or even universal where eligibility is determined by citizenship, residency, or income status. In contribution-related schemes, however, eligibility is usually restricted to individuals who have contributed for a minimum number of years. Definitional issues—relating to the labor force, for example—may arise in comparing coverage by contribution-related schemes over time and across countries (for country-specific information, see Hinz and others 2011). The share of the labor force covered by a pension scheme may be overstated in countries that do not try to count informal sector workers as part of the labor force.

Public interventions and institutions can provide services directly to poor people, although whether these interventions and institutions work well for the poor is debated. State action is often ineffective, in part because governments can influence only a few of the many sources of well-being and in part because of difficulties in delivering goods and services. The effectiveness of public provision is further constrained by the fiscal resources at governments' disposal and the fact that state institutions may not be responsive to the needs of poor people.

The data on public pension spending cover the pension programs of the social insurance schemes for which contributions had previously been made. In many cases noncontributory pensions or social assistance targeted to the elderly and disabled are also included. A country's pattern of spending is correlated with its demographic structure—spending increases as the population ages.

• **Youth unemployment** is the share of the labor force ages 15–24 without work but available for and seeking employment. • **Female-headed households** are households with a female head. • **Pension contributors** are members of the labor force or working-age population (here defined as ages 15 and older) covered by a pension scheme. • **Public expenditure on pensions** is all government expenditures on cash transfers to the elderly, the disabled, and survivors and the administrative costs of these programs. • **Average pension** is the average pension payment of all pensioners of the main pension schemes (including old-age, survivors, disability, military, and work accident or disease pensions) divided by the average wage of all formal sector workers.

Data sources

Data on youth unemployment are from the ILO's Key Indicators of the Labour Market, 7th edition, database. Data on female-headed households are from MEASURE DHS Demographic and Health Surveys by ICF International. Data on pension contributors and public expenditure on pensions are from Hinz and others (2011).

	Public expenditure per student						Public expenditure on education		Trained teachers in primary education	Primary school pupil–teacher ratio
			% of GDP per capita				% of GDP	% of total government expenditure	% of total	pupils per teacher
	Primary		Secondary		Tertiary					
	1999	2010[a]	1999	2010[a]	1999	2010[a]	2010[a]	2010[a]	2010[a]	2010[a]
Afghanistan	..	..	..	..	..	..	..	..	..	44
Albania	..	..	..	..	..	..	..	..	..	20
Algeria	12.0	..	..	..	..	..	4.3	20.3	..	23
Angola	..	..	..	..	..	..	..	..	..	46
Argentina	12.9	16.8	18.2	27.1	17.7	19.1	6.0	14.0	..	16
Armenia	..	16.5	..	17.8	..	7.5	3.2	13.0	..	..
Australia	16.4	20.2	15.0	18.8	26.6	20.7	5.1	12.9	..	..
Austria	24.9	24.1	30.0	27.4	51.8	43.5	5.5	11.2	..	11
Azerbaijan	6.9	..	17.0	..	19.1	22.3	3.2	10.9	100.0	11
Bahrain	..	..	..	..	..	..	2.9	11.7	..	..
Bangladesh	..	8.8	11.5	12.0	46.6	27.7	2.2	14.1	58.4	43
Belarus	..	..	..	..	..	14.7	4.5	8.9	99.8	15
Belgium	18.2	22.4	23.7	36.5	38.2	36.6	6.4	12.9	..	11
Benin	11.8	13.0	24.0	..	208.2	..	4.5	18.2	42.6	46
Bolivia	14.2	..	11.7	..	44.1	..	..	..	..	..
Bosnia and Herzegovina	..	..	..	..	..	..	..	..	..	..
Botswana	..	..	..	..	..	..	7.8	16.2	..	..
Brazil	10.8	18.5	9.5	19.5	57.2	27.6	5.4	..	..	23
Bulgaria	15.2	24.4	18.4	24.2	17.6	24.8	4.4	12.3	..	17
Burkina Faso	..	..	..	..	..	..	..	..	85.7[b]	48[b]
Burundi	14.4	19.0	67.8	64.1	1,036.1	477.4	9.2	25.1	91.2	51
Cambodia	5.8	6.8	11.5	6.8	42.5	..	2.6	..	99.1	48
Cameroon	..	6.6	..	28.0	..	28.0	3.5	17.9	57.1	46
Canada	..	..	..	..	44.0	..	4.8	..	..	..
Central African Republic	..	4.4	..	14.5	..	96.0	1.2	12.0	..	84
Chad	..	9.6	..	19.1	..	279.1	2.8	10.1	45.3	56
Chile	14.4	17.4	14.8	17.7	19.4	13.7	4.5	..	..	23
China	..	..	11.5	..	90.0	..	..	..	..	17
Hong Kong SAR, China	12.4	15.1	17.7	18.0	..	26.8	3.6	20.2	95.6	15
Colombia	15.2	15.7	16.1	15.3	37.7	29.4	4.8	14.9	100.0	28
Congo, Dem. Rep.	..	..	..	..	..	..	..	..	91.7	37
Congo, Rep.	..	11.1	..	..	..	134.2	6.2	..	86.8	49
Costa Rica	15.5	14.6	21.4	14.4	..	..	6.3	23.1	89.5	18
Côte d'Ivoire	14.3	..	41.3	..	141.0	..	4.6	24.6	100.0[b]	49[b]
Croatia	..	21.8	..	25.2	35.8	29.2	4.3	..	..	15
Cuba	25.0	44.2	37.1	51.9	77.6	61.1	13.4	18.3	100.0	9
Cyprus	17.1	28.7	28.2	38.3	47.9	57.0	7.4	17.4	..	14
Czech Republic	11.2	13.6	21.7	22.8	33.7	25.7	4.1	9.5	..	19
Denmark	24.6	24.9	38.1	31.5	65.9	52.1	7.7	15.0	..	..
Dominican Republic	..	7.5	..	6.7	..	..	..	..	84.9	26
Ecuador	4.4	..	9.6	..	..	..	..	..	82.6	17
Egypt, Arab Rep.	..	..	..	..	..	..	3.8	11.9	..	27
El Salvador	8.6	8.8	7.5	9.4	8.9	11.7	3.2	..	92.7	31
Eritrea	15.0	..	37.4	..	430.8	..	..	..	93.8	38
Estonia	20.9	25.9	27.2	29.6	31.8	22.1	5.7	14.2	..	12
Ethiopia	..	18.2	..	9.8	..	31.0	4.7	25.4	39.4	54
Finland	17.4	18.5	25.9	32.2	40.5	32.5	6.1	12.4	..	14
France	17.9	18.0	29.5	27.8	30.7	37.0	5.6	10.6	..	19
Gabon	..	..	..	..	..	..	..	..	..	25[b]
Gambia, The	..	24.6	..	16.2	..	94.4	5.0	22.8	..	37
Georgia	..	14.8	..	15.5	..	11.4	3.2	7.7	94.6	8
Germany	..	15.6	..	21.8	..	..	4.6	10.4	..	13
Ghana	17.6	11.4	40.4	27.2	..	171.7	5.5	24.4	50.6[b]	31[b]
Greece	11.7	..	15.6	..	26.5	..	..	..	..	..
Guatemala	6.7	10.4	4.3	6.2	..	..	3.2	..	..	28
Guinea	..	7.0	..	6.1	..	100.0	2.4	19.2	65.2	42
Guinea-Bissau	..	..	..	..	..	..	..	..	38.9	52
Haiti	..	..	..	..	..	..	..	..	..	..

Education inputs | 2.11

	Public expenditure per student						Public expenditure on education		Trained teachers in primary education	Primary school pupil–teacher ratio
			% of GDP per capita				% of GDP	% of total government expenditure	% of total	pupils per teacher
	Primary		Secondary		Tertiary					
	1999	2010[a]	1999	2010[a]	1999	2010[a]	2010[a]	2010[a]	2010[a]	2010[a]
Honduras	..	18.7	..	279.7	..	..	..	..	36.4	33
Hungary	17.9	21.9	19.0	23.0	34.1	24.8	5.1	10.4	..	10
India	11.9	..	24.7	..	95.0	..	..	..	..	..
Indonesia	..	11.4	..	12.9	..	16.8	4.6	26.0	..	16
Iran, Islamic Rep.	9.3	15.2	10.1	21.1	35.5	19.2	4.7	19.8	98.4	20
Iraq	..	..	..	..	..	..	..	..	..	..
Ireland	11.0	18.6	16.8	27.5	28.6	32.7	5.7	13.4	..	16
Israel	20.5	19.5	21.9	20.4	30.9	21.3	5.9	13.7	..	13
Italy	24.0	24.5	27.7	26.7	27.6	25.0	4.6	9.4	..	..
Jamaica	13.4	19.9	21.0	22.6	70.4	50.2	6.1	11.5	..	21
Japan	21.1	21.5	20.9	22.3	15.1	20.9	3.8	9.4	..	18
Jordan	13.7	11.9	15.8	14.3	..	..	..	..	..	..
Kazakhstan	..	..	..	..	..	10.1	3.1	..	..	16[b]
Kenya	21.4	..	14.4	..	207.9	..	6.7	17.2	96.8[b]	47
Korea, Dem. Rep.	..	..	..	..	..	..	..	..	..	..
Korea, Rep.	18.4	19.4	15.7	23.2	8.4	10.1	4.8	15.8	..	22
Kosovo	..	..	..	..	..	..	4.3	17.4	..	..
Kuwait	17.0	10.0	..	13.7	..	..	..	..	100.0	8
Kyrgyz Republic	..	..	..	..	24.3	17.6	6.0	18.6	68.4	24
Lao PDR	2.2	..	4.4	..	67.7	..	3.3	13.2	96.9	30
Latvia	19.5	31.4	23.7	32.3	27.9	14.2	5.6	14.7	..	12
Lebanon	..	..	..	..	13.8	10.0	1.8	7.2	..	14
Lesotho	37.0	24.8	82.4	55.7	939.7	..	13.1	23.7	63.4	34
Liberia	..	..	..	..	..	..	2.8	12.1	40.2	24
Libya	..	..	..	..	23.4	..	..	..	..	..
Lithuania	..	18.1	..	22.6	34.2	17.0	4.9	13.1	..	13
Macedonia, FYR	..	..	..	..	..	..	..	..	..	16
Madagascar	5.7	7.8	..	11.5	..	144.8	3.2	13.4	90.4	40
Malawi	13.4	6.8	9.6	23.3	2,503.9	1,937.6	5.7[b]	14.7[b]	95.9	79
Malaysia	12.6	14.6	21.9	20.2	81.6	60.7	5.8	18.9	..	13
Mali	15.3	15.0	59.7	37.5	256.8	135.3	4.5	22.0	50.0	48[b]
Mauritania	11.6	13.4	36.4	31.2	80.1	193.9	4.3	15.2	100.0	37
Mauritius	9.3	9.0	14.2	14.3	25.4	16.1	3.1	11.4	100.0	21
Mexico	11.9	13.7	14.5	13.6	48.8	38.9	4.9	..	95.6	28
Moldova	..	41.4	..	39.4	..	44.8	9.1	22.3	..	16
Mongolia	..	14.6	..	..	..	6.0	5.4	14.6	97.6	30
Morocco	17.4	16.9	45.5	..	97.1	83.3	5.4	25.7	100.0[b]	26[b]
Mozambique	..	..	..	..	1,408.9	..	..	..	75.9	58
Myanmar	..	..	6.6	..	27.0	..	..	..	99.9	28
Namibia	22.2	17.8	36.3	16.4	157.3	..	8.1	22.4	95.6	30
Nepal	9.1	17.8	13.1	11.3	141.3	39.3	4.7	20.2	80.7[b]	30[b]
Netherlands	15.2	17.2	22.2	25.0	47.4	41.5	5.5	11.9	..	..
New Zealand	20.0	21.9	23.7	23.6	39.5	31.4	7.2	16.1	..	14
Nicaragua	..	..	..	..	..	..	..	..	74.9	30
Niger	..	21.1	..	41.9	..	438.8	3.8	16.9	96.4[b]	39[b]
Nigeria	..	..	..	..	..	..	..	..	66.1	36
Norway	21.8	18.3	30.4	25.6	45.8	46.8	6.5	16.1	..	..
Oman	10.7	12.8	20.9	14.6	..	41.6	4.4	..	100.0	12
Pakistan	..	..	..	..	..	..	2.4	9.9	84.2	40
Panama	13.7	7.5	19.1	9.9	33.7	21.6	3.8	..	91.6	23
Papua New Guinea	..	..	..	..	..	..	..	..	..	..
Paraguay	13.6	..	18.4	..	58.9	..	..	..	..	..
Peru	7.6	7.8	10.8	8.9	21.1	..	2.6	16.4	..	20
Philippines	12.0	9.0	10.2	9.1	14.4	..	2.7	16.9	..	31
Poland	..	25.3	10.9	22.9	21.1	18.4	5.1	11.8	..	10
Portugal	18.8	19.9	26.6	31.6	27.1	26.7	4.9	11.0	..	11
Puerto Rico	..	..	..	..	..	..	..	..	6.6	12
Qatar	..	10.3	..	11.0	..	337.7	2.4	8.2	42.9	12

2.11 Education inputs

	Public expenditure per student						Public expenditure on education		Trained teachers in primary education	Primary school pupil–teacher ratio
			% of GDP per capita				% of GDP	% of total government expenditure	% of total	pupils per teacher
	Primary		Secondary		Tertiary					
	1999	2010a	1999	2010a	1999	2010a	2010a	2010a	2010a	2010a
Romania	..	..	..	..	32.6	..	..	..	..	16
Russian Federation	..	..	..	..	10.9	14.2	4.1	..	..	18
Rwanda	11.2	8.2	42.7	37.1	1,228.1	186.8	4.7b	16.9b	91.5	65
Saudi Arabia	..	..	..	..	..	..	5.6	19.3	..	11
Senegal	13.6	16.4	..	28.0	..	186.9	5.6	24.0	47.9	34
Serbia	..	61.6	..	14.4	..	43.3	5.0	9.5	94.2	16
Sierra Leone	..	..	..	..	..	..	4.3	18.1	48.0b	31b
Singapore	..	11.5	..	17.5	..	28.7	3.3	10.3	94.3	17
Slovak Republic	10.2	15.6	18.4	15.1	32.8	18.3	3.6	10.3	..	16
Slovenia	26.1	..	25.6	..	27.8	21.2	5.2	11.8	..	17
Somalia	..	..	..	..	..	..	..	..	..	..
South Africa	14.2	17.6	20.0	19.8	..	..	6.0	19.2	87.4	31
South Sudan	..	..	..	..	..	..	..	..	..	..
Spain	18.0	20.3	24.4	25.8	19.6	27.3	4.6	11.2	..	13
Sri Lanka	..	7.4	..	..	..	..	2.1	8.1	..	24
Sudan	..	..	..	..	..	..	..	..	59.7	38
Swaziland	8.3	17.7	23.2	37.1	434.9	..	7.4	16.0	73.1	32
Sweden	22.3	26.2	26.1	30.9	51.7	41.3	6.8	12.9	..	9
Switzerland	22.7	20.5	27.3	31.1	53.8	43.8	5.4	16.7	..	..
Syrian Arab Republic	10.8	16.8	21.0	14.2	..	..	..	..	..	18
Tajikistan	..	..	..	..	..	17.5	4.0	14.7	92.9	25
Tanzania	..	21.5	..	18.8	..	873.3	6.2	18.3	94.5	51
Thailand	18.1	24.4	16.2	15.4	36.5	17.6	3.8	22.3	..	16
Timor-Leste	..	..	..	..	..	83.9	14.0	11.7	..	30
Togo	7.7	10.8	27.7	..	..	..	4.5	17.6	76.7	41
Trinidad and Tobago	11.5	14.9	12.2	16.1	148.3	..	..	..	88.0	18
Tunisia	14.2	17.3	24.6	24.3	81.1	46.1	6.3	22.7	..	17
Turkey	9.8	..	9.6	..	35.3	..	..	..	..	..
Turkmenistan	..	..	..	..	..	..	..	..	..	..
Uganda	..	7.2	..	20.5	..	104.3	3.2	15.0	89.4	49
Ukraine	..	..	..	..	..	36.5	..	..	99.9	16
United Arab Emirates	5.4	6.2	7.2	8.6	26.2	19.9	1.0	23.4	100.0	17
United Kingdom	13.9	23.3	23.8	28.9	25.6	22.2	5.4	11.1	..	18
United States	17.7	22.5	22.3	24.8	26.8	21.2	5.5	13.8	..	14
Uruguay	7.2	..	9.9	..	..	..	..	..	..	14
Uzbekistan	..	..	..	..	..	..	..	..	100.0b	16b
Venezuela, RB	..	..	..	..	..	..	..	..	88.4	12
Vietnam	..	19.4	..	17.0	..	60.6	5.3	19.8	98.3	20
West Bank and Gaza	..	..	..	..	..	..	..	..	100.0	28
Yemen, Rep.	..	..	..	..	..	..	5.2	16.0	..	31
Zambia	7.0	..	19.4	..	160.4	..	1.3	..	..	58
Zimbabwe	12.7	..	19.3	..	..	75.4	2.5	8.3	..	..
World	.. m	16.4 m	.. m	22.7 m	.. m	.. m	4.6 m	15.6 m	.. w	24 w
Low income	..	..	..	..	..	..	3.8	18.7	82.9	45
Middle income	..	..	..	..	..	..	4.4	..	..	..
Lower middle income	..	..	..	..	..	..	4.0	..	..	..
Upper middle income	13.8	15.9	..	15.4	..	..	4.8	..	..	19
Low & middle income	..	..	..	..	..	..	4.1	..	..	26
East Asia & Pacific	..	..	..	..	37.8	..	3.8	17.2	..	17
Europe & Central Asia	..	..	..	..	..	17.3	4.4	14.0	..	17
Latin America & Carib.	12.6	12.4	12.9	13.6	..	..	4.4	..	..	24
Middle East & N. Africa	..	..	..	..	..	..	4.8	20.0	..	24
South Asia	..	8.8	13.1	..	95.0	..	2.5	12.6	..	..
Sub-Saharan Africa	..	..	..	..	..	..	5.0	18.9	..	46
High income	17.9	19.7	22.3	25.1	31.8	27.3	5.1	12.7	..	15
Euro area	17.9	19.9	25.9	27.5	30.7	32.5	5.5	11.5	..	14

a. Provisional data. b. Data are for 2011.

About the data

Data on education are collected by the United Nations Educational, Scientific, and Cultural Organization (UNESCO) Institute for Statistics from official responses to its annual education survey. The data are used for monitoring, policymaking, and resource allocation. While international standards ensure comparable datasets, data collection methods may vary by country and within countries over time.

For most countries the data on education spending in the table refer to public spending—government spending on education at all levels plus subsidies provided to households and other private entities—and generally exclude foreign aid for education that is not included in the government budget. The data may also exclude spending by religious schools, which play a significant role in many developing countries. Data are gathered from ministries of education and from other ministries or agencies involved in education spending.

The share of public expenditure devoted to education allows an assessment of the priority a government assigns to education relative to other public investments, as well as a government's commitment to investing in human capital development. However, returns on investment to education, especially primary and lower secondary education, cannot be understood simply by comparing current education indicators with national income. It takes a long time before currently enrolled children can productively contribute to the national economy (Hanushek 2002).

High-quality data on education finance are scarce. Improving their quality is a priority of the UNESCO Institute for Statistics. Additional resources are being allocated for technical assistance to countries in need, especially in Sub-Saharan Africa. Interagency partnerships and collaborations with national ministries in charge of education finance data are improving, and actual expenditure data are increasingly being collected. Tracking private education spending is still a challenge for all countries.

The share of trained teachers in primary education reveals a country's commitment to investing in the development of its human capital engaged in teaching, but it does not take into account differences in teachers' experiences and status, teaching methods, teaching materials, and classroom conditions—all factors that affect the quality of teaching and learning. Some teachers without formal training may have acquired equivalent pedagogical skills through professional experience.

The pupil–teacher ratio reflects the average number of pupils per teacher. It differs from the average class size because of the different practices countries employ, such as part-time teachers, school shifts, and multigrade classes. The comparability of pupil–teacher ratios across countries is further affected by the definition of teachers and by differences in class size by grade and in the number of hours taught, as well as the different practices mentioned above. Moreover, the underlying enrollment levels are subject to a variety of reporting errors (for further discussion of enrollment data, see *About the data* for table 2.12).While the pupil–teacher ratio is often used to compare the quality of schooling across countries, it is often weakly related to student learning and quality of education.

All education data published by the UNESCO Institute for Statistics are mapped to the International Standard Classification of Education 1997 (ISCED97). This classification system ensures the comparability of education programs at the international level. UNESCO developed the ISCED to facilitate comparisons of education statistics and indicators of different countries on the basis of uniform and internationally agreed definitions. First developed in the 1970s, the current version was formally adopted in November 1997.

The reference years in the table reflect the school year for which the data are presented. In some countries the school year spans two calendar years (for example, from September 2009 to June 2010); in these cases the reference year refers to the year in which the school year ended (2010 in the example).

Definitions

• **Public expenditure per student** is public current and capital spending on education divided by the number of students by level as a percentage of gross domestic product (GDP) per capita. • **Public expenditure on education** is current and capital expenditures on education by local (including municipalities), regional, and national governments as a percentage of GDP and as a percentage of total government expenditure. • **Trained teachers in primary education** are the percentage of primary school teachers who have received the minimum organized teacher training (pre-service or in-service) required for teaching at the specified level of education in their country. • **Primary school pupil–teacher ratio** is the number of pupils enrolled in primary school divided by the number of primary school teachers (regardless of their teaching assignment).

Data sources

Data on education inputs are from the UNESCO Institute for Statistics.

2.12 Participation in education

	Gross enrollment ratio				Net enrollment rate				Adjusted net enrollment rate, primary		Children out of school	
		% of relevant age group				% of relevant age group			% of primary school–age children		thousand primary school–age children	
	Preprimary	Primary	Secondary	Tertiary	Primary		Secondary		Male	Female	Male	Female
	2010[a]	2010[a]	2010[a]	2010[a]	1991	2010[a]	1999	2010[a]	2010[a]	2010[a]	2010[a]	2010[a]
Afghanistan	..	97	46	3	28	..	..	..	..	..	..	..
Albania	56	87	89	..	..	80	68	..	79	79	23	20
Algeria	77	110	95	31	89	96	..	..	98	96	28	53
Angola	104	124	31	4	..	86	..	12	93	78	119	373
Argentina	74	118	89	71	..	..	74	82	..	..	..	..
Armenia	31	103	92	52	..	..	86	86	78	81	13	10
Australia	81	104	129	76	98	97	90	85	97	98	31	23
Austria	96	100	100	60	90	..	..	..	..	..	..	..
Azerbaijan	25	94	..	19	89	84	75	..	85	84	40	38
Bahrain	..	..	..	..	99	..	86	..	..	..	..	..
Bangladesh	13	103	49	11	64	92	44	46	91	100	718	1
Belarus	99	100	..	83	..	92	82	87	95	97	9	5
Belgium	118	105	111	67	96	99	..	..	99	99	4	3
Benin	18	126	..	..	51	94	18	..	..	..	..	..
Bolivia	45	105	80	..	..	..	68	68	..	..	..	..
Bosnia and Herzegovina	17	88	90	36	..	85	..	..	86	88	14	11
Botswana	..	..	..	..	89	..	53	..	..	..	..	..
Brazil	65	127	101	36	..	94	66	82	96	94	290	396
Bulgaria	79	103	88	53	..	98	85	83	99	100	1	0[b]
Burkina Faso	3[c]	79[c]	23[c]	3	27	63[c]	8	18[c]	65	58	452	531
Burundi	9	156	25	3	50	..	..	16	98	100	10	1
Cambodia	13	127	46	8	..	96	14	..	96	95	32	40
Cameroon	28	120	42	11	69	92	..	..	100	88	6	171
Canada	71	99	101	..	98	..	95	..	..	..	..	..
Central African Republic	4	93	13	3	53	71	..	11	81	61	63	135
Chad	2	90	26	2	..	..	7	..	..	..	..	..
Chile	56	106	88	59	..	94	..	83	94	94	46	48
China	54	111	81	26	97	..	..	..	..	..	..	..
Hong Kong SAR, China	..	102	83	60	..	94	70	75	96	98	7	4
Colombia	49	115	96	39	71	88	56	74	92	91	187	188
Congo, Dem. Rep.	3	94	38	6	56	..	..	..	..	..	..	..
Congo, Rep.	13	115	..	6	..	91	..	..	92	89	24	32
Costa Rica	71	110	100	..	87	..	..	..	..	..	..	..
Côte d'Ivoire	4[c]	88[c]	..	..	46	61	19	..	67	56	497	664
Croatia	58	93	95	49	..	87	81	92	93	93	7	6
Cuba	100	103	89	95	94	99	75	86	100	100	0[b]	1
Cyprus	81	105	98	52	87	99	88	96	99	99	0[b]	0[b]
Czech Republic	106	106	90	61	..	..	81	84	..	..	..	..
Denmark	96	99	117	74	98	96	88	89	95	97	11	6
Dominican Republic	38	108	76	..	..	90	39	62	96	90	28	57
Ecuador	126	114	80	40	..	97	46	..	..	..	..	..
Egypt, Arab Rep.	24	106	..	30	..	96	77	..	100	96	15	184
El Salvador	64	114	65	23	..	94	44	58	94	95	26	21
Eritrea	14	45	32	2	20	33	18	29	37	33	203	215
Estonia	96	99	104	63	..	94	84	92	96	96	1	1
Ethiopia	5	102	36	5	30	81	12	..	85	80	1,023	1,367
Finland	66	99	108	92	99	97	95	94	98	98	5	4
France	110	111	113	55	100	99	93	98	..	..	..	..
Gabon	42[c]	182[c]	..	..	..	..	..	..	..	..	..	..
Gambia, The	30	83	54	4	50	66	..	..	68	71	44	41
Georgia	58	109	86	28	..	100	76	79	..	..	..	..
Germany	114	102	103	..	84	97	..	..	..	..	..	..
Ghana	69	107[c]	58[c]	9	..	84[c]	34	49[c]	84[c]	85[c]	298[c]	270[c]
Greece	..	..	..	..	95	..	82	..	..	..	..	..
Guatemala	71	116	59	..	..	97	24	50	100	98	5	27
Guinea	14	94	38	9	27	77	12	29	83	70	131	224
Guinea-Bissau	7	123	..	..	..	74	9	..	77	73	26	30
Haiti	..	..	..	..	21	..	..	..	..	..	..	..

	Gross enrollment ratio				Net enrollment rate				Adjusted net enrollment rate, primary		Children out of school	
		% of relevant age group				% of relevant age group			% of primary school–age children		thousand primary school–age children	
	Preprimary	Primary	Secondary	Tertiary	Primary		Secondary		Male	Female	Male	Female
	2010[a]	2010[a]	2010[a]	2010[a]	1991	2010[a]	1999	2010[a]	2010[a]	2010[a]	2010[a]	2010[a]
Honduras	44	116	73	19	88	96	..	..	96	98	23	8
Hungary	85	102	98	62	..	92	83	91	98	98	4	3
India	54	118	60	16	..	92	..	..	..	..	..	..
Indonesia	43	118	77	23	95	96	47	67	..	..	..	..
Iran, Islamic Rep.	43	108	84	43	97	..	..	..	..	..	..	..
Iraq	..	..	..	..	76	..	30	..	..	..	..	..
Ireland	..	108	117	61	90	95	91	98	97	99	6	3
Israel	106	113	91	62	..	97	87	88	97	97	13	10
Italy	97	103	99	66	..	98	85	93	100	99	5	11
Jamaica	113	89	93	29	97	82	83	84	84	82	28	32
Japan	90	103	102	59	100	100	99	99	..	..	..	..
Jordan	36	97	91	42	..	90	77	84	93	95	30	21
Kazakhstan	66[c]	111[c]	100[c]	41[c]	..	88[c]	88	90[c]	99[c]	100[c]	3[c]	1[c]
Kenya	52	113	60	4	..	83	33	50	84	85	523	486
Korea, Dem. Rep.	..	..	..	..	..	..	..	..	..	..	..	..
Korea, Rep.	121	104	97	104	99	99	96	96	100	99	0[b]	14
Kosovo	..	..	..	..	..	..	..	..	..	..	..	..
Kuwait	82	106	101	..	47	92	98	89	97	100	3	0[b]
Kyrgyz Republic	19	100	84	49	..	87	..	79	95	95	9	9
Lao PDR	16	121	45	13	59	89	26	37	91	87	35	47
Latvia	84	101	95	60	..	95	..	84	94	95	3	3
Lebanon	81	105	81	54	..	92	..	75	94	93	15	15
Lesotho	33	103	46	..	72	73	17	30	72	75	53	46
Liberia	..	96	..	..	..	..	18	..	..	..	..	..
Libya	..	..	..	..	..	..	..	..	..	..	..	..
Lithuania	75	97	98	77	..	93	90	91	97	97	2	2
Macedonia, FYR	25	89	83	40	..	87	..	..	93	95	5	3
Madagascar	9	149	31	4	72	..	..	24	..	..	..	..
Malawi	..	135	32	1	..	97	30	28	..	..	..	..
Malaysia	67	..	68	40	..	..	66	68	..	..	..	..
Mali	3[c]	82[c]	39[c]	6	..	63[c]	..	31[c]	71	61	377	481
Mauritania	..	102	24	4	..	74	14	..	73	76	72	61
Mauritius	96	99	89	25	93	93	67	..	92	94	5	3
Mexico	103	115	87	27	98	98	56	70	99	100	39	11
Moldova	76	94	88	38	..	88	78	79	90	90	8	7
Mongolia	77	100	93	53	..	95	58	83	98	98	2	3
Morocco	63[c]	114[c]	..	13	56	96[c]	30	..	97[c]	96[c]	58[c]	75[c]
Mozambique	..	115	25	..	42	92	3	16	95	89	124	243
Myanmar	10	126	54	..	..	..	32	51	..	..	..	..
Namibia	..	107	..	9	82	85	39	..	84	89	31	21
Nepal	..	..	..	..	..	..	..	..	..	..	..	..
Netherlands	96	108	120	63	95	100	91	87	..	..	..	..
New Zealand	93	101	119	83	100	99	90	95	99	100	1	1
Nicaragua	55	118	69	..	70	92	35	46	93	95	27	21
Niger	6[c]	71[c]	13	1	23	62[c]	6	10	64	52	478	607
Nigeria	14	83	44	..	..	..	..	..	..	..	..	..
Norway	98	99	110	74	100	99	95	95	99	99	3	2
Oman	45	105	100	24	69	94	61	90	98	98	3	2
Pakistan	..	95	34	5	..	74	..	34	81	67	1,884	3,241
Panama	67	108	74	45	92	98	59	69	99	98	2	4
Papua New Guinea	..	60	..	..	65	..	..	..	..	..	..	..
Paraguay	35	100	67	37	94	85	45	60	86	86	62	60
Peru	78	109	92	..	86	95	63	78	97	97	54	43
Philippines	51	107	82	29	96	89	50	61	88	90	799	662
Poland	66	97	97	71	..	96	91	91	96	96	47	47
Portugal	82	114	107	62	98	99	80	..	99	100	3	2
Puerto Rico	96	93	82	86	..	86	..	..	83	88	28	18
Qatar	55	103	94	10	89	92	74	83	96	97	2	1

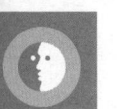

2.12 Participation in education

	Gross enrollment ratio				Net enrollment rate				Adjusted net enrollment rate, primary		Children out of school	
	% of relevant age group				% of relevant age group				% of primary school–age children		thousand primary school–age children	
	Preprimary	Primary	Secondary	Tertiary	Primary		Secondary		Male	Female	Male	Female
	2010a	2010a	2010a	2010a	1991	2010a	1999	2010a	2010a	2010a	2010a	2010a
Romania	77	96	95	64	73	87	77	82	92	93	35	32
Russian Federation	90	99	89	76	..	93	..	..	95	96	128	93
Rwanda	10	143	32	5	..	99	..	..	89	92	84	60
Saudi Arabia	11	106	101	37	..	90	..	81	90	89	154	164
Senegal	13	87	37	8	45	75	..	..	76	80	238	191
Serbia	53	96	91	49	..	93	..	90	95	94	8	8
Sierra Leone	7c	125c	..	..	..	..	..	..	..	..	..	..
Singapore	..	..	..	..	..	..	..	..	..	..	..	..
Slovak Republic	91	102	89	54	..	..	..	..	..	..	..	..
Slovenia	86	98	97	87	..	97	90	92	97	97	2	2
Somalia	..	..	..	..	..	..	..	..	..	..	..	..
South Africa	65	102	94	..	90	85	62	..	89	91	372	326
South Sudan	..	..	..	..	..	..	..	..	..	..	..	..
Spain	126	107	119	73	100	100	88	94	100	100	2	1
Sri Lanka	42	99	..	15	..	94	..	..	94	94	56	51
Sudan	27	73	39	..	..	..	..	..	..	..	..	..
Swaziland	23	116	58	..	74	86	32	33	86	85	15	15
Sweden	95	100	100	71	100	99	96	96	100	99	1	3
Switzerland	102	102	95	51	84	94	84	83	99	99	4	2
Syrian Arab Republic	10	118	72	..	91	93	39	67	100	98	2	16
Tajikistan	9	102	87	20	..	97	63	85	99	96	2	13
Tanzania	33	102	27	2	51	98	5	..	91	93	359	290
Thailand	100c	91	79c	48c	..	90	..	74c	90	89	304	307
Timor-Leste	..	117	56	17	..	85	..	37	86	86	14	14
Togo	9	140	..	..	65	92	21	..	..	..	..	..
Trinidad and Tobago	..	105	90	..	90	94	69	..	97	94	2	4
Tunisia	..	109	90	34	94	98	64	..	..	..	..	..
Turkey	22	102	78	46	89	97	56	74	98	97	59	103
Turkmenistan	..	..	..	..	..	..	..	..	..	..	..	..
Uganda	14	121	28	4	..	91	13	..	90	92	357	266
Ukraine	97	99	96	79	..	91	91	86	91	91	73	64
United Arab Emirates	..	..	..	..	97	..	75	..	..	..	..	..
United Kingdom	81	106	102	59	97	100	94	96	100	100	3	6
United States	69	102	96	95	97	95	87	89	96	98	498	247
Uruguay	89	113	90	63	91	99	..	70	100	99	0b	1
Uzbekistan	26c	95c	106c	9c	..	90c	..	92	94c	91c	62c	86c
Venezuela, RB	73	103	83	78	..	93	48	72	95	95	91	80
Vietnam	82	106	77	22	..	98	58	..	..	..	..	..
West Bank and Gaza	39	91	86	50	..	87	75	84	90	88	23	25
Yemen, Rep.	1	87	44	..	..	78	31	..	86	70	290	568
Zambia	..	115	..	..	..	91	16	..	91	94	108	76
Zimbabwe	..	..	..	6	..	..	40	..	..	..	..	..
World	50 w	107 w	68 w	27 w	.. w	88 w	51 w	60 w	91 w	89 w		
Low income	12	104	39	7	..	80	24	32	82	80		
Middle income	52	109	69	24	..	89	50	60	92	90		
Lower middle income	50	107	58	16	..	85	41	50	90	86		
Upper middle income	51	111	83	33	..	94	63	74	95	96		
Low & middle income	46	108	64	21	..	87	47	56	90	88		
East Asia & Pacific	48	111	76	25	96	..	56	..	..	..		
Europe & Central Asia	55	98	89	55	90	92	78	81	94	93		
Latin America & Carib.	71	117	90	37	..	94	59	73	95	95		
Middle East & N. Africa	..	102	72	27	..	90	58	64	94	89		
South Asia	54	110	55	11	68	86	..	..	93	89		
Sub-Saharan Africa	17	100	36	6	..	75	19	27	78	74		
High income	78	101	100	70	95	95	88	90	95	96		
Euro area	107	105	107	60	..	98	86	92	..	..		

a. Provisional data. b. Less than 0.5. c. Data are for 2011.

About the data

School enrollment data are reported to the United Nations Educational, Scientific, and Cultural Organization (UNESCO) Institute for Statistics by national education authorities and statistical offices. Enrollment indicators help monitor whether a country is on track to achieve the Millennium Development Goal of universal primary education by 2015, and whether an education system has the capacity to meet the needs of universal primary education.

Enrollment indicators are based on annual school surveys, but do not necessarily reflect actual attendance or dropout rates during the year. Also, the length of primary education differs across countries and can influence enrollment rates and ratios, although the International Standard Classification of Education (ISCED) tries to minimize the difference. A shorter duration for primary education tends to increase the ratio; a longer one to decrease it (in part because older children are more at risk of dropping out).

Overage or underage enrollments are frequent, particularly when parents prefer children to start school at other than the official age. Age at enrollment may be inaccurately estimated or misstated, especially in communities where registration of births is not strictly enforced.

Population data used to calculate population-based indicators are drawn from the United Nations Population Division. Using a single source for population data standardizes definitions, estimations, and interpolation methods, ensuring a consistent methodology across countries and minimizing potential enumeration problems in national censuses.

Gross enrollment ratios indicate the capacity of each level of the education system, but a high ratio may reflect a substantial number of overage children enrolled in each grade because of repetition or late entry rather than a successful education system. The net enrollment rate excludes overage and underage students and more accurately captures the system's coverage and internal efficiency. Differences between the gross enrollment ratio and the net enrollment rate show the incidence of overage and underage enrollments.

The adjusted net enrollment rate in primary education captures primary school–age children who have progressed to secondary education faster than their peers have and who are not counted in the traditional net enrollment rate.

Data on children out of school (primary school–age children not enrolled in primary or secondary school—dropouts, children never enrolled, and children of primary age enrolled in preprimary education) are compiled from administrative data. Large numbers of children out of school create pressure to enroll children and provide classrooms, teachers, and educational materials, a task made difficult in many countries by limited education budgets. However, getting children into school is a high priority for countries and crucial for achieving the Millennium Development Goal of universal primary education.

The reference years in the table reflect the school year for which the data are presented. In some countries the school year spans two calendar years (for example, from September 2009 to June 2010); in these cases the reference year refers to the year in which the school year ended (2010 in the example).

Definitions

• **Gross enrollment ratio** is the ratio of total enrollment, regardless of age, to the population of the age group that officially corresponds to the level of education shown. • **Preprimary education (ISCED 0)** refers to programs at the initial stage of organized instruction, designed primarily to introduce very young children, usually age 3, to a school-type environment and to provide a bridge between the home and school. On completing these programs, children continue their education at the primary level. • **Primary education (ISCED 1)** refers to programs normally designed to give students a sound basic education in reading, writing, and mathematics along with an elementary understanding of other subjects such as history, geography, natural science, social science, art, and music. Religious instruction may also be featured. It is sometimes called elementary education. • **Secondary education** refers to programs of lower (ISCED 2) and upper (ISCED 3) secondary education. Lower secondary education continues the basic programs of the primary level, but the teaching is typically more subject focused, requiring more specialized teachers for each subject area. In upper secondary education instruction is often organized even more along subject lines, and teachers typically need a higher or more subject-specific qualification. • **Tertiary education** refers to a wide range of programs with more advanced educational content. The first stage of tertiary education (ISCED 5) refers to theoretically based programs intended to provide sufficient qualifications to enter advanced research programs or professions with high-skill requirements and programs that are practical, technical, or occupationally specific. The second stage of tertiary education (ISCED 6) refers to programs devoted to advanced study and original research and leading to an advanced research qualification. • **Net enrollment rate** is the ratio of total enrollment of children of official school age to the population of the age group that officially corresponds to the level of education shown. • **Adjusted net enrollment rate, primary,** is the ratio of total enrollment of children of official school age for primary education who are enrolled in primary or secondary education to the total primary school–age population. • **Children out of school** are the number of primary school–age children not enrolled in primary or secondary school.

Data sources

Data on gross enrollment ratios, net enrollment rates, and out of school children are from the UNESCO Institute for Statistics.

2.13 | Education efficiency

	Gross intake ratio in first grade of primary education		Cohort survival rate						Repeaters in primary education		Transition rate to secondary education	
					% of grade 1 students							
	% of relevant age group		Reaching grade 5				Reaching last grade of primary education		% of enrollment		%	
	Male	Female	Male		Female		Male	Female	Male	Female	Male	Female
	2010[a]	2010[a]	1991	2009[a]	1991	2009[a]	2009[a]	2009[a]	2010[a]	2010[a]	2009[a]	2009[a]
Afghanistan	124	91	89	..	89	..	..	..	..	..	..	..
Albania	87	87	..	95	..	95	95	95	1	1	97	97
Algeria	107	105	82	93	79	97	93	97	9	6	90	92
Angola	182	148	..	53	..	37	37	27	10	12	26	45
Argentina	114	115	..	96	..	95	..	..	6	4	96	97
Armenia	91	93	..	..	..	..	..	..	0	0	100	98
Australia	..	..	98	..	99	..	..	..	..	..	..	..
Austria	103	101	..	..	..	..	96	99	0	0	100	100
Azerbaijan	91	88	..	..	..	..	100	97	0	0	98	99
Bahrain	..	..	88	98	87	98	98	98	2	2	98	99
Bangladesh	110	115	..	62	..	71	67	66	13	12	..	..
Belarus	96	96	..	..	..	..	96	100	0	0	98	100
Belgium	94	95	87	96	90	97	86	88	3	3	99	97
Benin	159	147	30	62	31	59	..	..	13	13	..	..
Bolivia	113	111	57	86	51	85	85	82	1	1	89	91
Bosnia and Herzegovina	99	100	..	73	..	73	73	73	0	0	..	..
Botswana	..	..	73	..	81	..	..	..	..	..	..	..
Brazil	..	..	..	..	..	..	..	..	..	..	..	..
Bulgaria	100	99	..	..	..	..	94	94	2	1	95	96
Burkina Faso	91[b]	86[b]	61	73	58	78	71	72	10	10	43[c]	62[c]
Burundi	164	158	66	59	61	66	56	64	34	34	41	31
Cambodia	143	144	..	60	..	65	52	57	10	8	80	81
Cameroon	144	123	67	76	66	77	67	65	14	13	42	45
Canada	99	98	..	..	..	..	..	..	0	0	..	..
Central African Republic	118	96	52	61	39	50	53	39	21	21	43	45
Chad	134	104	43	32	22	32	24	23	23	26	77	66
Chile	97	96	..	..	..	..	..	..	1	1	84	98
China	95	99	..	..	..	..	..	..	0	0	..	..
Hong Kong SAR, China	114	119	..	100	..	100	..	..	1	1	100	100
Colombia	113	107	53	84	59	85	..	..	2	2	97	96
Congo, Dem. Rep.	117	105	66	62	55	58	78	73	14	14	83	76
Congo, Rep.	109	108	66	75	68	79	71	71	20	18	69	67
Costa Rica	98	98	70	90	73	92	88	90	7	5	93	89
Côte d'Ivoire	88[b]	78[b]	68	66	61	66	..	..	19	19	47	45
Croatia	92	92	..	..	..	..	97	99	0	0	100	99
Cuba	98	98	..	97	..	97	96	95	1	0	98	99
Cyprus	107	106	96	94	97	97	..	..	0	0	100	100
Czech Republic	107	108	..	99	..	100	99	100	1	1	99	99
Denmark	100	100	98	100	99	100	99	100	0	0	99	100
Dominican Republic	113	101	..	..	..	..	..	..	9	5	82	90
Ecuador	..	..	..	..	..	..	..	..	..	..	..	..
Egypt, Arab Rep.	105	103	..	..	..	..	..	..	4	2	..	..
El Salvador	117	110	54	89	57	90	86	87	7	5	95	94
Eritrea	44	40	..	71	..	67	71	67	16	13	82	82
Estonia	100	100	..	99	..	99	98	99	1	0	99	98
Ethiopia	145	129	..	50	..	51	47	48	4	4	91	87
Finland	99	99	96	100	97	100	100	99	1	0	100	100
France	..	..	..	..	..	..	..	..	..	..	..	..
Gabon	..	..	47	..	46	..	..	..	..	..	..	..
Gambia, The	88	88	59	67	53	63	..	..	6	5	80	82
Georgia	100	102	..	94	..	99	94	99	0	0	100	100
Germany	100	99	..	..	..	..	98	99	1	1	99	99
Ghana	109[b]	111[b]	72	80	65	77	..	..	2[b]	3[b]	91	92
Greece	..	..	..	..	..	..	..	..	..	..	..	..
Guatemala	131	131	..	71	..	70	65	64	12	10	93	90
Guinea	112	96	43	74	35	62	74	56	16	18	62	51
Guinea-Bissau	169	164	..	..	..	..	..	..	14	14	..	..
Haiti	..	..	47	..	46	..	..	..	..	..	..	..

	Gross intake ratio in first grade of primary education		Cohort survival rate						Repeaters in primary education		Transition rate to secondary education	
			% of grade 1 students									
	% of relevant age group		Reaching grade 5				Reaching last grade of primary education		% of enrollment		%	
	Male	Female	Male		Female		Male	Female	Male	Female	Male	Female
	2010[a]	2010[a]	1991	2009[a]	1991	2009[a]	2009[a]	2009[a]	2010[a]	2010[a]	2009[a]	2009[a]
Honduras	125	120	50	75	43	80	74	79	1	1	..	..
Hungary	103	102	..	..	..	..	98	98	2	2	97	98
India	129	125	..	..	..	..	..	..	..	..	81	81
Indonesia	121	118	..	83	..	89	..	..	4	3	91	93
Iran, Islamic Rep.	107	108	75	94	67	94	94	94	2	2	96	97
Iraq	..	..	75	..	70	..	..	..	..	..	..	..
Ireland	106	107	..	99	..	100	..	..	1	1	..	..
Israel	98	101	..	100	..	98	100	98	2	1	70	69
Italy	101	100	..	99	..	100	99	100	0	0	100	100
Jamaica	81	78	92	96	94	96	94	96	3	2	92	91
Japan	103	103	100	100	100	100	100	100	0	0	..	..
Jordan	98	98	93	..	89	..	..	..	1	1	99	99
Kazakhstan	112[b]	111[b]	..	..	..	..	..	..	0[b]	0[b]	100[c]	100[c]
Kenya	..	..	..	..	..	..	..	..	..	..	..	..
Korea, Dem. Rep.	..	..	..	..	..	..	..	..	..	..	..	..
Korea, Rep.	100	98	92	99	92	99	99	99	0	0	100	100
Kosovo	..	..	..	..	..	..	..	..	..	..	..	..
Kuwait	101	103	..	96	..	96	96	96	1	1	99	99
Kyrgyz Republic	106	104	..	..	..	..	98	97	0	0	100	99
Lao PDR	136	126	34	66	32	68	..	..	18	16	80	77
Latvia	100	102	..	96	..	96	95	95	3	2	94	98
Lebanon	108	106	..	90	..	91	..	..	9	7	84	91
Lesotho	103	94	53	76	77	85	..	..	23	17	75	73
Liberia	120	112	..	64	..	56	49	43	6	7	64	60
Libya	..	..	..	..	..	..	..	..	..	..	..	..
Lithuania	93	94	..	..	..	..	98	99	1	0	99	99
Macedonia, FYR	97	97	..	..	..	..	..	..	0	0	98	98
Madagascar	184	184	31	34	31	35	..	..	21	19	65	63
Malawi	150	159	37	60	33	62	63	57	19	19	78	76
Malaysia	..	..	86	98	87	98	97	98	..	..	100	99
Mali	82[b]	76[b]	48	89[c]	42	87[c]	81	77	13[b]	13[b]	74	72
Mauritania	104	107	52	74	47	75	71	70	3	4	38	31
Mauritius	95	99	..	99	..	97	94	98	4	3	65	76
Mexico	117	117	81	95	82	97	93	95	4	3	95	94
Moldova	98	97	..	..	..	..	95	96	0	0	99	98
Mongolia	145	138	..	93	..	95	..	..	0	0	96	98
Morocco	110[b]	109[b]	70	94	64	94	78	78	13	9	84[c]	80[c]
Mozambique	168	159	42	56	34	51	37	34	8	7	52	55
Myanmar	152	151	..	72	..	77	..	..	0	0	77	77
Namibia	93	95	52	90	57	93	..	..	18	14	80	83
Nepal	..	..	44	60	32	64	..	..	12[b]	12[b]	81	81
Netherlands	100	99	..	99	..	100	..	..	..	..	..	..
New Zealand	..	..	96	..	95	..	..	..	..	..	..	..
Nicaragua	146	138	39	48	48	55	..	..	9	7	..	..
Niger	100[b]	90[b]	68	74[c]	65	69[c]	63	60	4[b]	4[b]	63[c]	59[c]
Nigeria	93	83	..	84	..	90	77	83	..	..	100	100
Norway	97	98	99	100	100	99	100	99	1	2	..	..
Oman	108	103	77	..	78	..	..	..	1	2	..	..
Pakistan	129	108	..	64	..	59	64	59	5	4	73	74
Panama	103	101	..	95	..	94	94	94	7	4	98	96
Papua New Guinea	..	..	55	..	52	..	..	..	..	..	..	..
Paraguay	101	98	58	81	60	84	76	80	6	4	89	89
Peru	103	102	..	..	..	..	88	88	7	6	96	93
Philippines	129	121	..	75	..	82	72	80	3	2	99	97
Poland	99	99	..	98	..	98	97	98	1	1	99	98
Portugal	103	103	..	..	..	..	..	..	..	..	..	..
Puerto Rico	97	94	..	..	..	..	..	..	..	..	..	..
Qatar	107	107	98	92	99	99	91	97	0	0	99	99

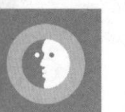

	Gross intake ratio in first grade of primary education		Cohort survival rate						Repeaters in primary education		Transition rate to secondary education	
	% of relevant age group		% of grade 1 students						% of enrollment		%	
			Reaching grade 5				Reaching last grade of primary education					
	Male	Female	Male		Female		Male	Female	Male	Female	Male	Female
	2010a	2010a	1991	2009a	1991	2009a	2009a	2009a	2010a	2010a	2009a	2009a
Romania	97	95	..	..	..	..	95	96	2	1	98	97
Russian Federation	..	..	..	..	..	..	..	..	..	..	..	..
Rwanda	186	182	49	45	51	50	..	..	14	14	73	72
Saudi Arabia	104	106	80	97	76	91	97	90	3	3	91	97
Senegal	100	106	78	73	68	75	58	61	6	6	71	66
Serbia	92	92	..	..	..	..	98	99	1	0	97	99
Sierra Leone	133b	121b	..	..	..	..	..	..	15b	16b	..	..
Singapore	..	..	..	99	..	99	99	99	0	0	86	92
Slovak Republic	95	95	..	..	..	..	98	98	3	3	97	97
Slovenia	99	98	..	100	..	99	100	99	1	0	99	98
Somalia	..	..	..	..	..	..	..	..	..	..	..	..
South Africa	94	88	61	..	67	..	..	..	..	..	..	..
South Sudan	..	..	..	..	..	..	..	..	..	..	..	..
Spain	102	102	..	99	..	100	99	100	3	2	92	95
Sri Lanka	94	95	97	..	98	..	..	..	1	1	95	97
Sudan	83	75	..	89	..	100	..	..	4	4	96	92
Swaziland	123	113	58	95	64	97	81	87	17	13	90	92
Sweden	104	103	99	99	99	99	99	99	0	0	100	100
Switzerland	92	94	72	..	72	..	..	..	2	1	..	..
Syrian Arab Republic	116	117	87	..	85	..	94	95	9	6	94	95
Tajikistan	102	98	..	..	..	..	99	99	0	0	99	98
Tanzania	96	97	69	87	71	93	76	87	3	2	45	37
Thailand	..	..	..	..	..	..	..	..	..	..	..	..
Timor-Leste	141	141	..	68	..	74	63	70	19	15	84	87
Togo	157	150	55	78	38	77	..	..	22	22	73	67
Trinidad and Tobago	104	101	98	90	99	94	87	92	7	5	87	89
Tunisia	106	106	76	95	70	97	..	..	8	5	81	87
Turkey	99	97	93	91	92	93	..	..	2	2	97	97
Turkmenistan	..	..	..	..	..	..	..	..	..	..	..	..
Uganda	153	157	..	56	..	58	..	..	11	11	60	58
Ukraine	103	104	..	..	..	..	..	..	0	0	100	100
United Arab Emirates	..	..	78	..	80	..	..	..	2	2	94	99
United Kingdom	..	..	..	..	..	..	..	..	0	0	..	..
United States	101	98	..	98	..	89	..	..	0	0	..	..
Uruguay	106	106	98	94	100	97	94	97	7	4	75	87
Uzbekistan	97b	94b	..	..	..	..	98c	98c	0b	0b	100c	98c
Venezuela, RB	100	98	69	93	80	95	90	94	5	3	96	97
Vietnam	..	..	..	..	..	..	..	..	..	..	..	..
West Bank and Gaza	91	91	..	..	..	..	..	..	0	0	96	98
Yemen, Rep.	109	96	..	..	..	..	..	..	7	6	..	..
Zambia	114	117	..	71	..	70	55	52	6	6	65	68
Zimbabwe	..	..	70	..	72	..	..	..	..	..	..	..
World	116 w	113 w	.. w	.. w	.. w	.. w			.. w	.. w	.. w	.. w
Low income	130	123	..	62	..	63			11	11	..	..
Middle income	114	111	..	..	..	..			..	..	..	..
Lower middle income	122	116	..	..	..	..			..	..	82	83
Upper middle income	99	101	..	..	..	..			2	1	..	..
Low & middle income	117	114	..	..	..	..			..	..	..	..
East Asia & Pacific	99	102	..	..	..	..			1	1	..	..
Europe & Central Asia	..	..	..	..	..	..			..	..	..	..
Latin America & Carib.	..	..	..	..	..	..			..	..	..	..
Middle East & N. Africa	105	104	..	..	..	..			7	4	..	..
South Asia	127	121	..	..	..	..			..	..	80	80
Sub-Saharan Africa	122	114	..	67	..	68			..	..	..	..
High income	101	103	..	..	..	..			0	0	..	..
Euro area	101	100	..	..	..	..			1	1	..	..

a. Provisional data. b. Data are for 2011. c. Data are for 2010.

About the data

The United Nations Educational, Scientific, and Cultural Organization (UNESCO) Institute for Statistics calculates indicators of students' progress through school. These indicators measure an education system's success in reaching students and efficiently moving them from one grade to the next.

The gross intake ratio in the first grade of primary education indicates the level of access to primary education and the education system's capacity to provide access to primary education. A low gross intake ratio in the first grade of primary education reflects the fact that many children do not enter primary education even though school attendance, at least through the primary level, is mandatory in most countries. Because the gross intake ratio includes all new entrants regardless of age, it can exceed 100 percent in some situations, such as immediately after fees have been abolished or when the number of reenrolled children is large. The indicator is not calculated when new entrants and repeaters are not correctly distinguished in the first grade of primary education.

The cohort survival rate to grade 5 and to the last grade of primary education shows the percentage of students entering primary school who are expected to reach the specified grade. It measures an education system's holding power and internal efficiency. Cohort survival rates are calculated based on the reconstructed cohort method, which uses data on enrollment by grade for the two most recent years and data on repeaters by grade for the most recent of those two years to reflect current patterns of grade transition. Rates approaching 100 percent indicate high retention and low dropout levels.

Data on repeaters are often used to indicate an education system's internal efficiency. Repeaters not only increase the cost of education for the family and the school system, but also use limited school resources. Country policies on repetition and promotion differ. In some cases the number of repeaters is controlled because of limited capacity. In other cases the number of repeaters is almost 0 because of automatic promotion—suggesting a system that is highly efficient but that may not be endowing students with enough cognitive skills.

The transition rate from primary to secondary education conveys the degree of access or transition between the two levels. As completing primary education is a prerequisite for participating in lower secondary education, growing numbers of primary completers will inevitably create pressure for more available places at the secondary level. A low transition rate can signal such problems as an inadequate examination and promotion system or insufficient secondary education capacity. The quality of data on the transition rate is affected when new entrants and repeaters are not correctly distinguished in the first grade of secondary education. Students who interrupt their studies after completing primary education could also affect data quality.

The reference years in the table reflect the school year for which the data are presented. In some countries the school year spans two calendar years (for example, from September 2009 to June 2010); in these cases the reference year refers to the year in which the school year ended (2010 in the example).

Definitions

• **Gross intake ratio in first grade of primary education** is the number of new entrants in grade 1 regardless of age as a percentage of the population of the official primary school entrance age. • **Cohort survival rate** is the percentage of children enrolled in the first grade of primary education who eventually reach grade 5 or the last grade of primary education. The estimate is based on the reconstructed cohort method (see *About the data*). • **Repeaters in primary education** are the number of students enrolled in the same grade as in the previous year as a percentage of all students enrolled in primary education. • **Transition rate to secondary education** is the number of new entrants to the first grade of secondary education (general programs only) in a given year as a percentage of the number of students enrolled in the final grade of primary education in the previous year.

Data sources

Data on education efficiency are from the UNESCO Institute for Statistics.

Education completion and outcomes

	Primary completion rate						Youth literacy rate				Adult literacy rate	Students at lowest proficiency on PISA mathematics
	% of relevant age group						% ages 15–24				% ages 15 and older	%
	Total		Male		Female		Male		Female			
	1991	2010[a]	1991	2010[a]	1991	2010[a]	1985–94[b]	2005–10[b]	1985–94[b]	2005–10[b]	2005–10[b]	2009
Afghanistan	28	..	41	..	14	..	..	..	..	..	..	..
Albania	..	86	..	86	..	86	..	99	..	99	96	40
Algeria	80	96	86	96	73	96	86	94	62	89	73	..
Angola	33	47	..	53	..	40	..	81	..	66	70	..
Argentina	100	106	..	104	..	108	98	99	99	99	98	37
Armenia	105	101	..	100	..	103	100	100	100	100	100	..
Australia	..	..	..	..	..	..	..	..	..	..	..	5
Austria	..	99	..	99	..	100	..	..	..	..	..	8
Azerbaijan	95	90	96	90	94	89	..	100	..	100	100	11
Bahrain	97	..	96	..	98	..	97	100	97	100	91	..
Bangladesh	41	65	..	62	..	69	52	74	38	77	56	..
Belarus	94	103	95	95	95	95	100	100	100	100	100	..
Belgium	79	90	76	89	82	92	..	..	..	..	..	8
Benin	22	63	30	74	14	53	55	65	27	43	42	..
Bolivia	71	99	78	100	64	99	96	99	92	99	91	..
Bosnia and Herzegovina	..	70	..	69	..	71	..	100	..	100	98	..
Botswana	90	94	83	92	98	96	86	94	92	97	84	..
Brazil	93	..	..	..	..	..	..	97	..	99	90	38
Bulgaria	90	95	88	95	92	96	..	98	..	97	98	24
Burkina Faso	20	45	25	48	15	42	27	47	14	33	29	..
Burundi	46	56	49	57	43	55	59	77	48	76	67	..
Cambodia	45	87	..	87	..	87	..	89	..	86	78	..
Cameroon	53	79	57	85	49	72	..	89	..	77	71	..
Canada	..	..	..	..	..	..	..	..	..	..	..	3
Central African Republic	28	41	37	52	20	30	63	72	35	57	55	..
Chad	18	33	29	41	7	24	26	54	9	39	34	..
Chile	..	96	..	102	..	89	98	99	99	99	99	22
China	107	..	..	..	..	..	97	99	91	99	94	..
Hong Kong SAR, China	102	96	..	95	..	96	..	..	..	..	..	3
Colombia	73	114	70	113	76	115	89	97	92	98	93	39
Congo, Dem. Rep.	48	59	61	67	36	50	..	73	..	62	67	..
Congo, Rep.	54	71	59	73	49	69	..	87	..	78	..	..
Costa Rica	79	96	77	95	81	97	..	98	..	99	96	..
Côte d'Ivoire	42	59[c]	53	65[c]	32	52[c]	60	72	38	61	55	..
Croatia	85	95	..	95	..	95	100	100	100	100	99	12
Cuba	99	98	..	98	..	99	..	100	..	100	100	..
Cyprus	90	103	89	103	90	103	100	100	100	100	98	..
Czech Republic	92	101	91	101	93	101	..	..	..	..	..	7
Denmark	98	97	98	97	98	98	..	..	..	..	..	5
Dominican Republic	61	92	..	93	..	91	..	95	..	97	88	..
Ecuador	91	106	91	105	92	106	97	97	96	97	84	..
Egypt, Arab Rep.	..	98	..	100	..	97	71	88	54	82	66	..
El Salvador	65	96	64	96	66	96	85	95	85	95	84	..
Eritrea	18	40	21	43	15	36	..	92	..	86	67	..
Estonia	..	98	..	97	..	98	100	100	100	100	100	3
Ethiopia	23	72	28	75	18	69	39	56	28	33	30	..
Finland	97	98	98	98	97	97	..	..	..	..	..	2
France	106	..	..	..	..	..	..	..	..	..	..	9
Gabon	62	..	59	..	65	..	94	99	92	97	88	..
Gambia, The	45	71	56	69	34	72	..	71	..	60	46	..
Georgia	..	116	..	116	..	116	..	100	..	100	100	..
Germany	100	100	99	100	100	100	..	..	..	..	..	6
Ghana	64	94[c]	71	97[c]	56	91[c]	..	81	..	79	67	..
Greece	99	101	99	101	98	100	99	99	99	99	97	11
Guatemala	..	84	..	87	..	81	82	89	71	84	74	..
Guinea	17	64	24	75	9	53	..	68	..	54	39	..
Guinea-Bissau	5	68	7	75	3	60	..	78	..	64	52	..
Haiti	27	..	29	..	26	..	..	..	..	..	49	..

Education completion and outcomes

	Primary completion rate						Youth literacy rate				Adult literacy rate	Students at lowest proficiency on PISA mathematics
	% of relevant age group						% ages 15–24				% ages 15 and older	%
	Total		Male		Female		Male		Female			
	1991	2010[a]	1991	2010[a]	1991	2010[a]	1985–94[b]	2005–10[b]	1985–94[b]	2005–10[b]	2005–10[b]	2009
Honduras	64	99	67	96	61	102	..	93	..	95	84	..
Hungary	82	98	89	98	90	97	99	99	99	99	99	8
India	64	96	76	96	52	95	74	88	49	74	63	..
Indonesia	93	105	..	104	..	105	97	100	95	99	92	44
Iran, Islamic Rep.	88	104	93	104	82	104	92	99	81	99	85	..
Iraq	58	65	63	74	52	55	..	85	..	80	78	..
Ireland	103	..	103	..	103	..	..	..	..	..	..	7
Israel	..	103	..	102	..	105	..	..	..	..	..	21
Italy	98	103	98	103	97	103	..	100	..	100	99	9
Jamaica	94	73	90	74	98	73	..	92	..	98	86	..
Japan	102	102	102	103	102	102	..	..	..	..	..	4
Jordan	101	101	101	101	101	101	..	99	..	99	92	35
Kazakhstan	103	116[c]	103	116[c]	103	116[c]	100	100	100	100	100	30
Kenya	..	..	..	..	..	..	..	92	..	94	87	..
Korea, Dem. Rep.	..	..	..	..	..	..	..	100	..	100	100	..
Korea, Rep.	99	101	99	100	100	101	..	..	..	..	..	2
Kosovo	..	..	..	..	..	..	..	..	..	..	..	..
Kuwait	57	112	58	110	56	114	91	99	84	99	94	..
Kyrgyz Republic	..	97	..	96	..	97	..	100	..	100	99	65
Lao PDR	41	79	46	83	36	75	..	89	..	79	73	..
Latvia	..	92	..	94	..	90	100	100	100	100	100	6
Lebanon	..	87	..	85	..	89	..	98	..	99	90	..
Lesotho	59	70	42	60	76	79	..	86	..	98	90	..
Liberia	..	62	..	67	..	57	66	70	54	81	59	..
Libya	..	..	..	..	..	..	99	100	96	100	89	..
Lithuania	..	96	..	97	..	94	100	100	100	100	100	9
Macedonia, FYR	98	92	..	92	..	93	99	99	99	99	97	..
Madagascar	36	72	35	72	37	73	..	66	..	64	64	..
Malawi	31	67	35	65	27	68	70	87	49	86	74	..
Malaysia	91	..	91	..	91	..	96	98	95	99	92	..
Mali	9	55[c]	12	61[c]	7	50[c]	..	47	..	31	26	..
Mauritania	33	75	39	74	26	76	..	71	..	64	57	..
Mauritius	115	96	115	96	115	96	91	96	92	98	88	..
Mexico	88	104	91	104	92	104	96	99	95	98	93	22
Moldova	..	93	..	94	..	91	100	99	100	100	98	..
Mongolia	..	108	..	107	..	109	..	95	..	97	97	..
Morocco	48	85	57	87	39	82	71	87	46	72	56	..
Mozambique	26	61	32	66	21	55	..	78	..	64	55	..
Myanmar	..	104	..	101	..	106	..	96	..	95	92	..
Namibia	74	84	67	80	81	88	86	91	90	95	89	..
Nepal	51	..	70	..	41	..	68	87	33	77	59	..
Netherlands	..	..	..	..	..	..	..	..	..	..	..	3
New Zealand	..	..	..	..	..	..	..	..	..	..	..	5
Nicaragua	42	81	43	78	53	84	..	85	..	89	78	..
Niger	17	46[c]	21	52[c]	13	40[c]	..	52	..	23	29	..
Nigeria	..	74	..	79	..	70	81	78	62	65	61	..
Norway	100	100	100	101	100	100	..	..	..	..	..	6
Oman	74	101	78	102	70	100	..	98	..	98	87	..
Pakistan	..	67	..	75	..	59	..	79	..	61	56	..
Panama	86	97	86	97	86	97	95	97	95	96	94	51
Papua New Guinea	46	..	51	..	42	..	..	65	..	70	60	..
Paraguay	68	94	68	92	69	95	96	99	95	99	95	..
Peru	..	102	..	102	..	102	97	98	94	97	90	48
Philippines	88	92	85	89	86	94	96	97	97	98	95	..
Poland	96	95	..	95	..	95	100	100	100	100	100	6
Portugal	..	..	..	..	..	..	99	100	99	100	95	8
Puerto Rico	..	..	..	..	..	..	92	87	94	88	90	..
Qatar	71	100	71	99	72	100	89	98	91	98	95	51

2.14 Education completion and outcomes

	Primary completion rate						Youth literacy rate				Adult literacy rate	Students at lowest proficiency on PISA mathematics
	% of relevant age group						% ages 15–24				% ages 15 and older	%
	Total		Male		Female		Male		Female			
	1991	2010[a]	1991	2010[a]	1991	2010[a]	1985–94[b]	2005–10[b]	1985–94[b]	2005–10[b]	2005–10[b]	2009
Romania	96	91	96	91	96	91	99	97	99	98	98	20
Russian Federation	92	98	92	..	93	..	100	100	100	100	100	10
Rwanda	50	70	51	65	50	74	75	77	75	77	71	..
Saudi Arabia	..	93	..	94	..	92	94	99	81	97	86	..
Senegal	39	59	48	58	31	61	49	74	28	56	50	..
Serbia	..	96	..	96	..	97	..	..	..	..	..	18
Sierra Leone	..	74[c]	..	78[c]	..	71[c]	..	68	..	48	41	..
Singapore	..	..	..	..	..	..	99	100	99	100	95	3
Slovak Republic	95	98	95	98	96	99	..	..	..	..	..	7
Slovenia	95	95	..	95	..	95	100	100	100	100	100	7
Somalia	..	..	..	..	..	..	..	..	..	..	..	..
South Africa	76	..	72	..	80	..	..	97	..	98	89	..
South Sudan	..	..	..	..	..	..	..	..	..	..	..	..
Spain	104	102	104	102	103	102	100	100	100	100	98	9
Sri Lanka	101	101	101	101	101	101	..	97	..	99	91	..
Sudan	..	58	..	61	..	55	..	..	..	..	..	..
Swaziland	61	77	57	76	64	78	83	92	84	95	87	..
Sweden	96	94	96	93	96	94	..	..	..	..	..	8
Switzerland	53	95	53	94	54	97	..	..	..	..	..	4
Syrian Arab Republic	89	104	94	104	84	103	..	96	..	93	84	..
Tajikistan	..	104	..	106	..	102	100	100	100	100	100	..
Tanzania	55	90	56	88	55	92	86	78	78	76	73	..
Thailand	..	..	..	..	..	..	..	98	..	98	94	22
Timor-Leste	..	65	..	64	..	67	..	..	..	..	51	..
Togo	35	74	48	84	22	64	..	85	..	68	57	..
Trinidad and Tobago	102	91	99	91	105	91	99	100	99	100	99	30
Tunisia	74	91	79	90	70	92	..	98	..	96	78	43
Turkey	90	99	93	100	86	98	97	99	88	97	91	18
Turkmenistan	..	..	..	..	..	..	..	100	..	100	100	..
Uganda	..	57	..	58	..	56	77	90	63	85	73	..
Ukraine	92	98	99	97	99	98	..	100	..	100	100	..
United Arab Emirates	103	..	104	..	103	..	81	94	85	97	90	..
United Kingdom	..	..	..	..	..	..	..	..	..	..	..	6
United States	..	104	..	103	..	104	..	..	..	..	..	8
Uruguay	94	106	91	105	96	106	98	98	99	100	98	23
Uzbekistan	80	93[c]	..	94[c]	..	92[c]	..	100	..	100	99	..
Venezuela, RB	81	94	76	93	86	95	95	98	96	99	95	..
Vietnam	..	..	..	..	..	..	94	97	93	96	93	..
West Bank and Gaza	..	95	..	97	..	93	..	99	..	99	95	..
Yemen, Rep.	..	63	..	73	..	53	83	96	35	72	62	..
Zambia	..	103	..	98	..	108	67	82	66	67	71	..
Zimbabwe	97	..	99	..	96	..	97	98	94	99	92	..
World	**79 w**	**88 w**	**86 w**	**90 w**	**75 w**	**87 w**	**88 w**	**92 w**	**79 w**	**87 w**	**84 w**	
Low income	44	65	..	68	..	63	66	75	52	68	61	
Middle income	83	92	89	93	77	91	89	94	79	88	83	
Lower middle income	68	88	76	90	60	86	87	89	75	79	71	
Upper middle income	97	98	101	96	94	99	94	99	93	99	93	
Low & middle income	78	87	85	89	73	86	86	91	75	85	80	
East Asia & Pacific	101	97	105	96	97	98	97	99	92	99	94	
Europe & Central Asia	92	95	93	96	92	94	99	99	98	99	98	
Latin America & Carib.	84	102	84	101	85	102	91	97	92	97	91	
Middle East & N. Africa	..	88	..	91	..	85	84	93	67	87	74	
South Asia	62	86	75	87	52	84	71	85	47	72	61	
Sub-Saharan Africa	51	67	57	71	47	63	73	77	58	67	62	
High income	..	97	..	98	..	97	99	99	99	99	98	
Euro area	101	101	100	100	100	101	..	..	..	..	..	

a. Provisional data. b. Data are for the most recent year available. c. Data are for 2011.

About the data

Many governments publish statistics that indicate how their education systems are working and developing—statistics on enrollment and such efficiency indicators as repetition rates, pupil–teacher ratios, and cohort progression. The World Bank and the United Nations Educational, Scientific, and Cultural Organization (UNESCO) Institute for Statistics jointly developed the primary completion rate indicator. Increasingly used as a core indicator of an education system's performance, it reflects an education system's coverage and the educational attainment of students. The indicator is a key measure of education outcome at the primary level and of progress toward the Millennium Development Goals and the Education for All initiative. However, a high primary completion rate does not necessarily mean high levels of student learning.

The primary completion rate reflects the primary cycle as defined by the International Standard Classification of Education (ISCED97), ranging from three or four years of primary education (in a very small number of countries) to five or six years (in most countries) and seven (in a small number of countries).

The primary completion rate is also called the gross intake ratio to last grade of primary education. It is the number of new entrants in the last grade of primary education, regardless of age, divided by the population at the entrance age for the last grade of primary education. Data limitations preclude adjusting for students who drop out during the final year of primary education. Thus this rate is a proxy that should be taken as an upper estimate of the actual primary completion rate.

There are many reasons why the primary completion rate can exceed 100 percent. The numerator may include late entrants and overage children who have repeated one or more grades of primary education as well as children who entered school early, while the denominator is the number of children at the entrance age for the last grade of primary education.

Basic student outcomes include achievements in reading and mathematics judged against established standards. The UNESCO Institute for Statistics has established literacy as an outcome indicator based on an internationally agreed definition.

The literacy rate is the percentage of the population who can, with understanding, both read and write a short, simple statement about their everyday life. In practice, literacy is difficult to measure. To estimate literacy using such a definition requires census or survey measurements under controlled conditions. Many countries estimate the number of literate people from self-reported data. Some use educational attainment data as a proxy but apply different lengths of school attendance or levels of completion. Because definitions and methodologies of data collection differ across countries, data should be used cautiously.

The reported literacy data are compiled by the UNESCO Institute for Statistics based on national censuses and household surveys during 1985–2010. For countries without recent literacy data, the UNESCO Institute for Statistics estimates literacy rates with the Global Age-Specific Literacy Projection Model. For detailed information on sources, definitions, and methodology, see www.uis.unesco.org.

Literacy statistics for most countries cover the population ages 15 and older, but some include younger ages or are confined to age ranges that tend to inflate literacy rates. The youth literacy rate for ages 15–24 reflects recent progress in education. It measures the accumulated outcomes of primary education over the previous 10 years or so by indicating the proportion of the population who have passed through the primary education system and acquired basic literacy and numeracy skills. Generally, literacy also encompasses numeracy, the ability to make simple arithmetic calculations.

In many countries national assessments enable ministries of education to monitor progress in learning outcomes. Of the handful of internationally or regionally comparable assessments, one of the largest is the Programme for International Student Assessment (PISA). Coordinated by the Organisation for Economic Co-operation and Development (OECD), it measures the knowledge and skills of 15-year-olds, the age at which students in most countries are nearing the end of their compulsory time in school. The assessment tests reading, mathematical, and scientific literacy in terms of general competencies—that is, how well students can apply the knowledge and skills they have learned at school to real-life challenges. It does not test how well a student has mastered a school's specific curriculum.

The table presents the percentage of students at the lowest level of proficiency on the PISA mathematics scale. Student achievement is benchmarked in terms of levels of proficiency, ranging from level 1 (lowest) to level 6 (highest), as demonstrated through ability to analyze, reason, and communicate effectively while posing, solving, and interpreting mathematical problems that involve quantitative, spatial, probabilistic, or other mathematical concepts. The average score is 496. Because the figures are derived from samples, the data reflect a small measure of statistical uncertainty.

Definitions

• **Primary completion rate,** or the gross intake ratio to last grade of primary education, is the number of new entrants in the last grade of primary education, regardless of age, divided by the population at the entrance age for the last grade of primary education. • **Youth literacy rate** is the percentage of the population ages 15–24 that can, with understanding, both read and write a short simple statement about their everyday life. • **Adult literacy rate** is the percentage of the population ages 15 and older that can, with understanding, both read and write a short simple statement about their everyday life. • **Students at lowest proficiency on PISA mathematics** is the percentage of students whose mathematics score are below 357.77 (level 1) on the PISA.

Data sources

Data on primary completion rates and literacy rates are from the UNESCO Institute for Statistics. Data on PISA mathematics results are from the OECD.

2.15 | Education gaps by income and gender

	Survey year	Gross intake rate in first grade of primary education		Gross primary participation rate		Average years of schooling		Primary completion rate				Children out of school	
		% of relevant age group		% of relevant age group		Ages 15–19		% of relevant age group				% of relevant age group	
		Poorest quintile	Richest quintile	Poorest quintile	Richest quintile	Poorest quintile	Richest quintile	Poorest quintile	Richest quintile	Male	Female	Poorest quintile	Richest quintile
Armenia	2005	93	80	106	102	9	10	119	116	113	112	2	1
Azerbaijan	2006	92	118	100	108	9	11	94	109	103	105	20	11
Bangladesh	2006	144	147	96	105	8	13	65	97	83	86	12	6
Belize	2006	80	89	106	113	8	11	59	130	107	72	5	7
Benin	2006	67	107	61	114	6	8	31	95	67	52	57	12
Bolivia	2003	92	95	108	129	6	9	76	98	90	81	22	5
Burundi	2005	201	191	91	144	4	7	20	70	44	39	5	3
Cambodia	2005	208	151	113	134	5	8	42	121	88	85	37	13
Cameroon	2006	108	75	93	116	6	14	43	111	90	74	3	2
Colombia	2005	161	84	127	99	6	10	94	109	100	103	11	2
Côte d'Ivoire	2006	51	77	57	110	5	8	47	127	88	71	4	3
Dominican Republic	2007	130	112	113	107	7	11	69	109	88	106	12	4
Egypt, Arab Rep.	2005	107	97	95	99	9	12	84	92	92	88	12	1
Ethiopia	2005	86	124	47	112	3	6	14	90	46	33	74	30
Georgia	2006	90	104	101	103	15	14	102	102	106	104	2	1
Ghana	2006	107	121	81	117	5	8	62	88	93	86	22	12
Guatemala	2000	176	124	81	114	4	8	15	80	34	36	7	3
Guinea	2005	55	119	52	121	5	7	32	93	76	48	60	16
Guinea-Bissau	2006	135	184	94	166	4	7	34	125	80	54	12	11
Guyana	2006	74	76	105	101	10	10	109	118	91	112	2	1
Haiti	2005	177	188	87	159	4	7	31	136	73	82	69	24
Kazakhstan	2006	118	101	106	103	9	9	102	115	102	97	0ª	1
Kenya	2003	134	125	92	106	6	9	40	76	71	72	38	11
Kosovo	2000	104	119	95	104	9	11	82	94	98	83	1	4
Lesotho	2004	169	111	116	124	5	8	36	122	69	85	18	3
Macedonia, FYR	2005	102	190	89	97	8	10	120	119	133	78	0ª	0ª
Madagascar	2003–04	250	153	118	145	3	8	42	141	77	77	33	3
Malawi	2006	234	207	133	169	5	7	30	80	49	52	0ª	0ª
Mali	2006	41	98	46	110	5	8	36	79	55	41	67	20
Mauritania	2007	67	96	62	116	5	9	17	89	48	52	2	2
Moldova	2005	96	84	99	95	9	12	97	100	96	98	2	1
Mozambique	2003	128	143	75	143	3	6	13	100	57	43	46	7
Namibia	2006	112	104	118	109	7	10	81	109	94	90	11	2
Nepal	2001	184	141	109	139	5	8	49	96	69	62	33	6
Nicaragua	2001	149	106	85	105	4	9	34	124	78	83	40	4
Niger	2006	50	90	35	89	4	7	31	71	60	30	74	28
Nigeria	2003	78	101	70	108	7	10	48	71	70	54	52	6
Panama	2003	125	116	108	102	7	11	100	94	105	88	1	1
Peru	2004	121	90	118	96	7	11	106	99	100	97	6	1
Rwanda	2005	274	195	131	151	3	5	31	88	48	42	13	8
Serbia	2005	90	98	98	100	9	10	86	96	94	89	1	0ª
Somalia	2005	13	44	8	93	8	10	2	58	26	20	87	46
Swaziland	2006	147	117	117	114	6	9	69	110	85	98	17	4
Syrian Arab Republic	2006	110	149	102	107	7	8	92	93	93	92	0ª	0ª
Tanzania	2004	123	123	82	119	5	7	32	108	58	60	44	15
Togo	2006	115	148	99	128	6	7	40	82	67	56	1	1
Turkey	2003	108	111	97	97	6	7	95	85	100	81	20	5
Uganda	2006	180	144	107	124	5	8	27	68	50	42	25	7
Vietnam	2006	99	100	108	100	13	18	99	104	96	103	3	2
Yemen, Rep.	2006	66	109	50	101	7	10	25	103	84	31	2	2
Zambia	2007	135	123	105	112	5	9	50	101	88	73	22	3
Zimbabwe	1999	106	111	144	144	7	10	36	80	51	57	22	8

a. Less than 0.5.

Education gaps by income and gender

The data in the table describe basic information on school participation and educational attainment by individuals in different socioeconomic groups within countries. The data are from Demographic and Health Surveys by Macro International with the support of the U.S. Agency for International Development, Multiple Indicator Cluster Surveys by the United Nations Children's Fund (UNICEF), and Living Standards Measurement Studies by the World Bank's Development Economics Research Group. These large-scale household sample surveys, conducted periodically in developing countries, collect information on a large number of health, nutrition, and population measures as well as on respondents' social, demographic, and economic characteristics using detailed questionnaires. The data presented here draw on responses to individual and household questionnaires.

Typically, the surveys collect basic information on educational attainment and enrollment levels from every household member ages 5 and older as part of household socioeconomic characteristics. The surveys are not intended for the collection of detailed education data; thus the education section of the surveys is not as detailed as, for instance, the health section of the Demographic and Health Survey or the Multiple Indicator Cluster Survey, and the data obtained from them do not replace other data on education flows. Still, the education data provide micro-level information on education that cannot be obtained from administrative data, such as information on children not attending school.

Socioeconomic status as displayed in the table is based on household assets, including ownership of consumer items, features of the household dwelling, and other characteristics related to wealth. Each household asset on which information was collected was assigned a weight generated through principal-component analysis, which was used to create breakpoints defining wealth quintiles, expressed as quintiles of individuals in the population.

The selection of the asset index for defining socioeconomic status was based on pragmatic rather than conceptual considerations: Demographic and Health Surveys do not collect consumption data but do have detailed information on household ownership of consumer goods and access to a variety of goods and services. Like income or consumption, the asset index defines disparities primarily in economic terms. It therefore excludes other possibilities of disparities among groups, such as those based on gender, education, ethnic background, or other

facets of social exclusion. To that extent the index provides only a partial view of the multidimensional concepts of poverty, inequality, and inequity.

Creating one index that includes all asset indicators limits the types of analysis that can be performed. In particular, the use of a unified index does not permit a disaggregated analysis to examine which asset indicators have a more or less important association with education status. In addition, some asset indicators may reflect household wealth better in some countries than in others—or reflect different degrees of wealth in different countries. Taking such information into account and creating country-specific asset indexes with country-specific choices of asset indicators might produce a more effective and accurate index for each country. The asset index used in the table does not have this flexibility.

The analysis was carried out for about 80 countries. The table shows the most recent estimates for the poorest and richest quintiles by gender only; the full set of estimates for all indicators, other subgroups, including by urban and rural location, and older data are available in the country reports (see *Data sources*). The data in the table differ from data for similar indicators in preceding tables either because the indicator refers to a period a few years preceding the survey date or because the indicator definition or methodology is different. Findings should be used with caution because of measurement error inherent in the use of survey data.

• **Survey year** is the year in which the underlying data were collected. • **Gross intake rate in first grade of primary education** is the number of students in grade 1 regardless of age as a percentage of the population of the official primary school entrance age. These data may differ from those in table 2.13. • **Gross primary participation rate** is the ratio of total students attending primary school regardless of age to the population of the age group that officially corresponds to primary education. • **Average years of schooling** are the years of formal schooling received, on average, by youths and adults ages 15–19. • **Primary completion rate** is the number of students, regardless of age, in the last grade of primary school minus the number of repeaters in that grade, divided by the number of students of official graduation age. These data differ from those in table 2.14 because the source is different. • **Children out of school** are children of official primary school age who are not attending primary or secondary education. Children of official primary school age who are attending preprimary education are considered out of school. These data differ from those in table 2.12 because the source is different.

Data sources

Data on education gaps by income and gender are from an analysis using the ADePT Education software tool (http://go.worldbank.org/X385KNDXM0) of MEASURE DHS Demographic and Health Surveys by ICF International, Multiple Indicator Cluster Surveys by UNICEF, and Living Standards Measurement Studies by the World Bank. Country reports and further updates are available at www.worldbank.org/education/edstats/.

2.16 | Health systems

	Health expenditure						Health workers			Hospital beds
	Total % of GDP	Public % of total	Out of pocket % of total	External resources % of total	Per capita $	Per capita PPP $	Physicians	per 1,000 people Nurses and midwives	Community health workers	per 1,000 people
	2010	**2010**	**2010**	**2010**	**2010**	**2010**	**2005–10**[a]	**2005–10**[a]	**2005–10**[a]	**2005–10**[a]
Afghanistan	7.6[b]	11.7[b]	83.0[b]	32.0[b]	38[b]	44[b]	0.2	0.5	..	0.4
Albania	6.5	39.0	60.8	1.8	241	577	1.2	3.9	..	2.8
Algeria	4.2	77.9	20.9	0.0	178	330	1.2	1.9	..	..
Angola	2.9[c]	82.5[c]	17.5[c]	2.9[c]	123[c]	168[c]	..	..	..	0.8
Argentina	8.1	54.6	29.9	0.1	742	1,287	3.2	..	..	4.5
Armenia	4.4	40.6	55.1	14.3	133	239	3.8	4.8	..	3.7
Australia	8.7[d]	68.0[d]	20.5[d]	0.0[d]	4,775[d]	3,441[d]	3.0	9.6	0.0	3.8
Austria	11.0	77.5	14.6	0.0	4,958	4,388	4.9	7.9	..	7.7
Azerbaijan	5.9	20.3	69.5	0.8	332	579	3.8	8.3	..	7.5
Bahrain	5.0	73.3	14.5	0.0	864	1,083	1.4	3.7	..	1.8
Bangladesh	3.5	33.6	64.1	8.0	23	57	0.3	0.3	0.3	0.3
Belarus	5.6	77.7	19.8	0.5	320	786	5.2	13.1	..	11.1
Belgium	10.7	74.7	20.2	0.0	4,618	4,025	3.0	0.5	..	6.5
Benin	4.1	49.5	46.8	35.9	31	65	0.1	0.8	..	0.5
Bolivia	4.8	62.8	28.7	5.3	97	233	..	..	..	1.1
Bosnia and Herzegovina	11.1	61.4	38.6	1.8	499	972	1.6	5.0	..	3.4
Botswana	8.3	72.5	8.1	18.3	615	1,145	0.3	2.8	0.5	1.8
Brazil	9.0	47.0	30.6	0.0	990	1,028	1.8	6.4	..	2.4
Bulgaria	6.9	54.5	44.2	0.0	435	947	3.7	4.7	..	6.6
Burkina Faso	6.7	51.0	36.2	22.9	40	93	0.1	0.7	0.1	0.4
Burundi	11.6[c]	38.2[c]	37.9[c]	45.8[c]	21[c]	47[c]	..	..	..	1.9[e]
Cambodia	5.6	37.2	40.4	23.9	45	121	0.2	0.9	..	0.8
Cameroon	5.1[c]	29.6[c]	66.5[c]	13.2[c]	61[c]	122[c]	..	..	..	1.3
Canada	11.3	70.5	14.7	0.0	5,222	4,404	2.0	10.4	..	3.2
Central African Republic	4.0	35.4	61.4	13.4	18	31	..	..	..	1.0[e]
Chad	4.5	25.0	72.5	7.9	31	62	..	..	..	0.4
Chile	8.0	48.2	33.3	0.0	947	1,199	1.0	0.1	..	2.1
China	5.1	53.6	36.6	0.1	221	379	1.4	1.4	0.8	4.2
Hong Kong SAR, China	..	..	..	..	..	..	..	..	..	..
Colombia	7.6	72.7	19.5	0.0	472	713	0.1	0.6	..	1.0
Congo, Dem. Rep.	7.9	42.5	35.9	32.7	16	27	..	..	..	0.8
Congo, Rep.	2.5	46.7	53.3	4.1	72	104	0.1	0.8	..	1.6
Costa Rica	10.9	68.1	27.8	0.6	811	1,242	..	..	..	1.2
Côte d'Ivoire	5.3	21.6	77.5	9.8	60	98	0.1	0.5	..	0.4
Croatia	7.8	84.9	14.5	0.0	1,067	1,514	2.6	5.3	..	5.4
Cuba	10.6	91.5	8.5	0.0	607	431	6.7	9.1	..	5.9
Cyprus	6.0	41.5	48.8	0.0	1,705	1,842	2.6	4.3	..	3.8
Czech Republic	7.9	83.7	14.7	0.0	1,480	2,051	3.7	8.7	..	7.1
Denmark	11.4	85.1	13.1	0.0	6,422	4,537	3.4	16.1	..	3.5
Dominican Republic	6.2	43.4	37.2	0.7	323	578	..	..	..	1.6
Ecuador	8.1	37.2	49.0	0.4	328	653	1.7	2.0	..	1.5
Egypt, Arab Rep.	4.7	37.4	61.2	0.6	123	289	2.8	3.5	..	1.7
El Salvador	6.9	61.7	33.9	1.9	237	450	1.6	0.4	..	1.0
Eritrea	2.7[c]	48.2[c]	51.8[c]	38.0[c]	12[c]	16[c]	..	..	..	0.7[e]
Estonia	6.0	78.7	19.6	60.7	853	1,226	3.3	6.6	..	5.4
Ethiopia	4.9	53.5	37.2	39.4	16	51	0.0	0.2	0.3	0.2
Finland	9.0	75.1	18.8	0.0	3,984	3,281	2.9	24.0	..	6.2
France	11.9	77.8	7.3	0.0	4,691	4,021	3.4	0.3	..	6.9
Gabon	3.5[c]	52.9[c]	47.1[c]	2.4[c]	302[c]	522[c]	..	..	..	6.3
Gambia, The	5.7	50.8	23.8	41.2	26	80	0.0	0.6	0.1	1.1[e]
Georgia	10.1	23.6	68.3	2.8	272	522	4.8	3.2	..	3.1
Germany	11.6	77.1	13.0	0.0	4,668	4,332	3.6	11.1	..	8.2
Ghana	5.2	59.5	26.9	16.9	67	85	0.1	1.0	0.2	0.9[e]
Greece	10.2	59.4	38.4	0.0	2,729	2,853	6.2	0.2	..	4.8
Guatemala	6.9	35.8	53.9	1.7	196	325	..	..	..	0.6
Guinea	4.9	11.3	88.1	10.8	23	56	0.1	0.0	..	0.3
Guinea-Bissau	8.5[c]	10.0[c]	66.4[c]	23.3[c]	47[c]	100[c]	0.0	0.6	..	1.0
Haiti	6.9	21.4	40.2	38.3	46	76	..	..	..	1.3

	Health expenditure						Health workers			Hospital beds
	Total % of GDP	Public % of total	Out of pocket % of total	External resources % of total	Per capita		Physicians	per 1,000 people Nurses and midwives	Community health workers	per 1,000 people
					$	PPP $				
	2010	2010	2010	2010	2010	2010	2005–10[a]	2005–10[a]	2005–10[a]	2005–10[a]
Honduras	6.8	65.2	31.1	6.3	137	263	..	..	..	0.8
Hungary	7.3	69.4	24.0	0.0	942	1,469	3.0	6.4	..	7.1
India	4.1	29.2	61.2	1.2	54	132	0.6	1.0	0.0	0.9
Indonesia	2.6	49.1	38.3	1.3	77	112	0.3	2.0	..	0.6
Iran, Islamic Rep.	5.6	40.1	57.8	0.0	317	836	0.9	1.4	..	1.7
Iraq	8.4[c,f]	81.2[c,f]	18.8[c,f]	0.8[c,f]	247[c,f]	340[c,f]	0.7	1.4	..	1.3
Ireland	9.2	69.2	15.2	0.0	4,242	3,704	3.2	15.7	..	4.9
Israel	7.6	60.3	29.2	0.0	2,183	2,186	3.7	5.2	..	3.5
Italy	9.5	77.6	19.6	0.0	3,248	3,022	3.5	0.3	..	3.6
Jamaica	4.8	53.5	33.0	2.1	247	372	..	..	..	1.9
Japan	9.5	82.5	14.3	0.0	4,065	3,204	2.1	4.1	..	13.7
Jordan	8.0	67.7	25.1	3.7	357	448	2.5	4.0	..	1.8
Kazakhstan	4.3	59.4	40.1	0.6	393	541	4.1	8.3	..	7.6
Kenya	4.8	44.3	42.7	36.1	37	78	..	..	..	1.4
Korea, Dem. Rep.	..	..	..	..	..	..	..	..	..	..
Korea, Rep.	6.9	59.0	31.4	0.0	1,439	2,023	2.0	5.3	..	10.3
Kosovo	..	..	..	..	..	..	..	..	..	..
Kuwait	2.6	80.4	17.8	0.0	1,223	1,133	1.8	4.6	..	2.0
Kyrgyz Republic	6.2	56.2	37.8	12.8	53	140	2.3	5.7	..	5.1
Lao PDR	4.5	33.3	51.2	15.1	46	97	0.3	1.0	..	0.7
Latvia	6.7	61.1	37.8	0.0	718	1,093	3.0	4.8	..	6.4
Lebanon	7.0	39.2	44.7	4.7	651	980	3.5	2.2	..	3.5
Lesotho	11.1	76.2	16.4	19.5	109	170	..	..	..	1.3
Liberia	11.8	32.5	35.2	55.1	29	49	0.0	0.3	..	0.8
Libya	3.9[c]	68.8[c]	31.2[c]	0.6[c]	484[c]	713[c]	1.9	6.8	..	3.7
Lithuania	7.0	73.5	25.8	1.1	781	1,299	3.6	7.2	..	6.8
Macedonia, FYR	7.1	63.8	35.9	0.8	317	791	2.6	0.6	..	4.5
Madagascar	3.8	60.3	27.1	9.0	16	36	0.2	..	..	0.2
Malawi	6.6	60.2	11.1	63.8	26	65	0.0	0.3	0.7	1.3[e]
Malaysia	4.4	55.5	34.2	0.0	368	641	0.9	2.7	..	1.8
Mali	5.0	46.6	53.2	27.4	32	56	0.0	0.3	..	0.1
Mauritania	4.4[c]	53.1[c]	44.3[c]	10.1[c]	43[c]	79[c]	0.1	0.7	..	0.4
Mauritius	6.0	41.7	51.7	2.0	449	803	..	..	..	3.4[e]
Mexico	6.3	48.9	47.1	0.0	604	959	2.0	..	..	1.6
Moldova	11.7[g]	45.8[g]	44.9[g]	9.6[g]	190[g]	360[g]	2.7	6.6	..	6.2
Mongolia	5.4	55.1	41.4	3.9	120	218	2.8	3.5	0.0	5.8
Morocco	5.2	38.0	53.6	0.4	148	246	0.6	0.9	..	1.1
Mozambique	5.2	71.7	13.7	24.2	21	49	0.0	0.3	..	0.8
Myanmar	2.0	12.2	81.1	8.7	17	34	0.5	0.8	0.1	0.6
Namibia	6.8	58.4	7.4	19.0	361	436	0.4	2.8	..	2.7
Nepal	5.5	33.2	48.3	11.3	30	66	..	..	..	5.0
Netherlands	11.9	79.2	5.2	0.0	5,593	5,038	2.9	0.2	..	4.7
New Zealand	10.1	83.2	10.5	0.0	3,279	3,020	2.7	10.9	..	..
Nicaragua	9.1	53.3	43.3	14.6	103	253	..	..	..	0.8
Niger	5.2	50.9	41.3	29.4	18	37	0.0	0.1	..	0.3
Nigeria	5.1[c]	37.9[c]	59.2[c]	9.2[c]	63[c]	121[c]	0.4	1.6	0.1	..
Norway	9.5	83.9	15.3	0.0	8,091	5,426	4.2	31.9	..	3.3
Oman	2.8	80.1	12.3	0.0	574	598	1.9	4.1	..	1.8
Pakistan	2.2	38.5	50.5	4.8	22	59	0.8	0.6	0.1	0.6
Panama	8.1	75.1	19.9	0.1	616	1,123	..	..	..	2.2
Papua New Guinea	3.6	71.5	15.9	24.0	49	88	0.1	0.5	0.6	..
Paraguay	5.9	36.4	57.1	2.4	163	302	..	..	..	1.3
Peru	5.1	54.0	39.5	1.7	269	481	0.9	1.3	..	1.5
Philippines	3.6	35.3	54.0	1.3	77	142	..	..	..	0.5
Poland	7.5	72.6	22.1	0.1	917	1,476	2.2	5.8	..	6.7
Portugal	11.0	68.1	24.8	0.0	2,367	2,818	3.9	5.3	..	3.3
Puerto Rico	..	..	..	..	..	..	..	..	..	..
Qatar	1.8	77.5	16.0	0.0	1,489	1,622	2.8	7.4	..	1.2

	Health expenditure						Health workers			Hospital beds
	Total % of GDP	Public % of total	Out of pocket % of total	External resources % of total	Per capita $	Per capita PPP $	Physicians	per 1,000 people Nurses and midwives	Community health workers	per 1,000 people
	2010	2010	2010	2010	2010	2010	2005–10[a]	2005–10[a]	2005–10[a]	2005–10[a]
Romania	5.6	78.1	21.5	0.0	428	811	2.3	5.9	..	6.6
Russian Federation	5.1	62.1	31.4	0.0	525	998	4.3	8.5	..	9.7
Rwanda	10.5	50.1	22.2	47.0	56	121	0.0	0.4	..	1.6
Saudi Arabia	4.3	62.9	18.6	0.0	680	968	0.9	2.1	..	2.2
Senegal	5.7	55.5	35.0	18.5	59	109	0.1	0.4	..	0.3
Serbia	10.4	61.9	36.4	0.8	546	1,169	2.1	4.5	..	5.4
Sierra Leone	13.1	11.3	79.4	20.6	43	107	0.0	0.2	0.0	0.4
Singapore	4.0	36.3	54.0	0.0	1,733	2,273	1.8	5.9	..	3.1
Slovak Republic	8.8	65.9	30.5	0.0	1,413	2,060	3.0	0.3	..	6.5
Slovenia	9.4	73.7	12.6	0.0	2,154	2,552	2.5	8.4	..	4.6
Somalia	..	..	..	..	..	..	0.0	0.1	..	..
South Africa	8.9	44.1	16.6	2.2	649	935	..	..	..	2.8
South Sudan	..	..	..	..	..	..	..	..	..	..
Spain	9.5	72.8	20.7	0.0	2,883	3,027	4.0	5.1	..	3.2
Sri Lanka	2.9	44.7	44.9	3.0	70	148	0.5	1.9	..	..
Sudan	6.3	29.8	67.2	3.3	84	141	0.3	0.8	..	0.7
Swaziland	6.6	63.7	15.4	17.2	203	333	..	..	..	2.1[e]
Sweden	9.6	81.1	17.0	0.0	4,710	3,757	3.8	11.9	..	2.8
Switzerland	11.5	59.0	30.9	0.0	7,812	5,394	4.1	16.5	..	5.2
Syrian Arab Republic	3.4	46.0	54.0	0.7	97	174	1.5	1.9	..	1.5
Tajikistan	6.0	26.7	66.5	6.1	49	128	2.1	5.3	..	5.2
Tanzania	6.0	67.3	13.6	48.8	31	83	0.0	0.2	..	0.7
Thailand	3.9	75.0	13.9	0.3	179	330	0.3	..	..	2.1
Timor-Leste	9.1	55.8	11.3	33.7	57	84	..	..	..	5.9
Togo	7.7	44.2	46.9	15.2	41	77	0.1	0.3	..	0.9
Trinidad and Tobago	5.7	59.9	32.8	0.1	861	1,449	1.2	3.6	..	2.6
Tunisia	6.2	54.3	39.8	0.3	238	483	1.2	3.3	..	2.1
Turkey	6.7	75.2	16.0	0.0	678	1,029	1.5	0.6	..	2.5
Turkmenistan	2.5[c]	59.4[c]	40.6[c]	0.3[c]	106[c]	199[c]	2.4	4.4	..	4.0
Uganda	9.0	21.7	49.8	25.9	47	124	0.1	1.3	..	0.5
Ukraine	7.7	56.6	40.5	0.4	234	519	3.2	8.6	..	8.7
United Arab Emirates	3.7	74.4	18.8	0.0	1,450	1,544	1.9	4.1	..	1.9
United Kingdom	9.6	83.9	10.0	0.0	3,503	3,480	2.7	10.1	..	3.3
United States	17.9	53.1	11.8	0.0	8,362	8,362	2.4	9.8	..	3.0
Uruguay	8.4	67.1	13.0	0.0	998	1,188	3.7	5.5	..	1.2
Uzbekistan	5.8	47.5	42.7	0.9	82	184	2.6	11.1	..	4.6
Venezuela, RB	4.9	34.9	59.0	0.0	663	589	..	..	..	1.1
Vietnam	6.8	37.8	57.6	3.4	83	215	1.2	1.0	..	3.1
West Bank and Gaza	..	..	..	..	..	..	..	..	..	..
Yemen, Rep.	5.2	24.2	74.8	4.3	63	122	0.3	..	..	0.7
Zambia	5.9	60.3	26.5	39.2	73	90	0.1	0.7	..	2.0
Zimbabwe	..	..	..	..	..	..	..	..	..	3.0
World	10.5 w	62.8 w	17.7 w	0.2 w	949 w	1,023 w	1.4 w	2.8 w	.. w	2.9 w
Low income	5.4	38.7	48.1	25.9	27	61	0.2	0.5	..	..
Middle income	5.7	52.0	36.4	0.6	225	369	1.2	2.0	..	2.4
Lower middle income	4.2	40.2	52.3	2.8	71	149	0.8	1.5	..	1.4
Upper middle income	6.1	54.3	33.4	0.2	382	594	1.7	2.6	..	3.7
Low & middle income	5.7	51.8	36.6	1.1	199	329	1.1	1.9	..	2.2
East Asia & Pacific	4.7	53.4	36.7	0.4	183	316	1.2	1.5	0.8	3.9
Europe & Central Asia	5.8	65.0	29.0	0.3	439	797	3.2	6.7	..	7.4
Latin America & Carib.	7.8	50.2	34.3	0.2	670	854	1.8	..	..	1.9
Middle East & N. Africa	4.7	50.1	47.0	0.7	203	425	1.4	2.3	..	1.6
South Asia	3.8	30.0	60.5	2.3	47	115	0.6	0.9	0.1	0.9
Sub-Saharan Africa	6.5	45.1	31.8	10.5	84	143	0.2	0.8	..	..
High income	12.7	65.1	13.7	0.0	4,879	4,660	2.8	7.1	..	5.7
Euro area	10.8	76.2	14.3	0.1	3,969	3,685	3.6	4.7	..	5.8

a. Data are for the most recent year available. b. Nonprofit institutions (such as nongovernmental organizations) serving households are accounted for in external resources, which are recorded under government expenditure. GDP includes both licit and illicit activity (for example, opium production). Public expenditures include external assistance. c. Derived from incomplete data. d. Excludes expenditure on residential facilities for care of the aged. e. Data are for 2011. f. Excludes northern Iraq. g. Excludes Transnistria.

Health systems—the combined arrangements of institutions and actions whose primary purpose is to promote, restore, or maintain health (World Health Organization, *World Health Report 2000*)—are increasingly being recognized as key to combating disease and improving the health status of populations. The World Bank's (2007a) *Healthy Development: Strategy for Health, Nutrition, and Population Results* emphasizes the need to strengthen health systems, which are weak in many countries, in order to increase the effectiveness of programs aimed at reducing specific diseases and further reduce morbidity and mortality. To evaluate health systems, the World Health Organization (WHO) has recommended that key components—such as financing, service delivery, workforce, governance, and information—be monitored using several key indicators (WHO 2008b). The data in the table are a subset of the first four indicators. Monitoring health systems allows the effectiveness, efficiency, and equity of different health system models to be compared. Health system data also help identify weaknesses and strengths and areas that need investment, such as additional health facilities, better health information systems, or better trained human resources.

Health expenditure data are broken down into public and private expenditures. In general, low-income economies have a higher share of private health expenditure than do middle- and high-income countries, and out-of-pocket expenditure (direct payments by households to providers) makes up the largest proportion of private expenditures. High out-of-pocket expenditures may discourage people from accessing preventive or curative care and can impoverish households that cannot afford needed care. Health financing data are collected through national health accounts, which systematically, comprehensively, and consistently monitoring health system resource flows. To establish a national health account, countries must define the boundaries of the health system and classify health expenditure information along several dimensions, including sources of financing, providers of health services, functional use of health expenditures, and beneficiaries of expenditures. The accounting system can then provide an accurate picture of resource envelopes and financial flows and allow analysis of the equity and efficiency of financing to inform policy.

This year's table, like last year's, presents out-of-pocket expenditure as a percentage of total health expenditure; editions before 2011 presented out-of-pocket expenditure as a percentage of private health expenditure. Thus data for this indicator from 2011 onward should not be compared with data from editions before 2011.

External resources for health are disbursements to recipient countries as reported by donors, lagged one year to account for the delay between disbursement and expenditure. Except where a reliable full national health account study has been done, most data are from the Organisation for Economic Co-operation and Development Development Assistance Committee's Creditor Reporting System database, which compiles data from government expenditure accounts, government records on external assistance, routine surveys of external financing assistance, and special services. Because of the variety of sources, caution should be used in interpreting the data.

In countries where the fiscal year spans two calendar years, expenditure data have been allocated to the later year (for example, 2009 data cover fiscal year 2008/09). Many low-income countries use Demographic and Health Surveys or Multiple Indicator Cluster Surveys funded by donors to obtain health system data.

Data on health worker (physicians, nurses and midwives, and community health workers) density show the availability of medical personnel. The WHO estimates that at least 2.5 physicians, nurses, and midwives per 1,000 people are needed to provide adequate coverage with primary care interventions associated with achieving the Millennium Development Goals (WHO, *World Health Report 2006*). The WHO compiles data from household and labor force surveys, censuses, and administrative records. Data comparability is limited by differences in definitions and training of medical personnel varies. In addition, human resources tend to be concentrated in urban areas, so that average densities do not provide a full picture of health personnel available to the entire population.

Availability and use of health services, such as hospital beds per 1,000 people, reflect both demand- and supply-side factors. In the absence of a consistent definition this is a crude indicator of the extent of physical, financial, and other barriers to health care.

• **Total health expenditure** is the sum of public and private health expenditure. It covers the provision of health services (preventive and curative), family planning and nutrition activities, and emergency aid for health but excludes provision of water and sanitation. • **Public health expenditure** is recurrent and capital spending from central and local governments, external borrowing and grants (including donations from international agencies and nongovernmental organizations), and social (or compulsory) health insurance funds. • **Out-of-pocket health expenditure** is direct household outlays, including gratuities and in-kind payments, for health practitioners and pharmaceutical suppliers, therapeutic appliances, and other goods and services whose primary intent is to restore or enhance health. • **External resources for health** are funds or services in kind provided by entities that are not part of the country. The resources may come from international organizations, other countries through bilateral arrangements, or foreign nongovernmental organizations and are part of public and private health expenditure. • **Health expenditure per capita** is total health expenditure divided by population in U.S. dollars and in international dollars converted using 2005 purchasing power parity (PPP) rates from the World Bank's International Comparison Project. • **Physicians** include generalist and specialist medical practitioners. • **Nurses and midwives** include professional nurses and midwives, auxiliary nurses and midwives, enrolled nurses and midwives, and other personnel, such as dental nurses and primary care nurses. • **Community health workers** include traditional medicine practitioners, faith healers, assistant or community health education workers, community health officers, family health workers, lady health visitors, health extension package workers, community midwives, and traditional birth attendants. • **Hospital beds** are inpatient beds for both acute and chronic care available in public, private, general, and specialized hospitals and rehabilitation centers.

Data on health expenditure are from the WHO's National Global Health Expenditure database (see http://apps.who.int/nha/database for the most recent updates), supplemented by country data. Data on physicians, nurses and midwives, and community health workers are from the WHO's Global Atlas of the Health Workforce database (http://apps.who.int/globalatlas). Data on hospital beds are from the WHO, supplemented by country data.

	Year last national health account completed	Number of national health accounts completed	Year of last health survey	Year of last census	Completeness		
						%	
					Birth registration 2005–10[a]	Infant death reporting 2005–10[a]	Total death reporting 2005–10[a]
		1995–2010		2001–11			
Afghanistan	2008	1	2010		..	..	..
Albania	2009	2	2008/09	2001	99	30	85
Algeria	2003	3	2006	2008	99	..	91
Angola		0	2006/07		..	..	..
Argentina	1997	1		2010	..	100	99
Armenia	2010	7	2005	2001	96	43	100
Australia	2008	14		2006	..	92	96
Austria	2009	15		2011	..	100	100
Azerbaijan		0	2006	2009	94	26	79
Bahrain	2000	1		2010		84	79
Bangladesh	2008	13	2007	2011	10	..	..
Belarus	2010	1	2005	2009	..	62	100
Belgium	2009	7		2011	..	96	99
Benin	2008	4	2006	2002	60	..	..
Bolivia	2008	14	2008	2001	..	..	31
Bosnia and Herzegovina	2010	7	2006		100	48	93
Botswana	2002	3	2000	2011	72	32	43
Brazil	2009	10	1996	2010	91	50	88
Bulgaria	2009	9		2011	..	98	97
Burkina Faso	2009	7	2006	2006	64	31	90
Burundi	2007	1	2005	2008	60	..	..
Cambodia		0	2010	2008	66	..	..
Cameroon	1995	1	2006	2005	70	..	..
Canada	2010	16		2011	..	99	98
Central African Republic		0	2006	2003	49	..	..
Chad		0	2004	2009	..	..	..
Chile	2010	8		2002	99	100	100
China	2009	15		2010	..	..	97
Hong Kong SAR, China		0		2006	..	66	94
Colombia	2009	12	2010	2006	97	55	77
Congo, Dem. Rep.	2009	7	2010		28	..	..
Congo, Rep.	2005	1	2009	2007	81	..	..
Costa Rica	2003	2	1993	2011	..	96	98
Côte d'Ivoire	2008	2	2006		55	..	..
Croatia	2010	2		2011	..	94	99
Cuba		0	2006	2002	100	100	100
Cyprus	2008	6		2001		56	72
Czech Republic	2009	15	1993	2011	..	89	100
Denmark	2009	15		2011	..	86	97
Dominican Republic	2008	8	2007	2010	78	1	54
Ecuador	2008	9	2004	2010	90	54	84
Egypt, Arab Rep.	2008	3	2008	2006	99	56	100
El Salvador	2010	16	2008	2007	99	35	79
Eritrea		0	2002		..	..	..
Estonia	2010	12			..	76	95
Ethiopia	2008	4	2005	2007	7	..	100
Finland	2010	16		2010	..	84	99
France	2010	16		2006	..	100	98
Gabon		0	2000	2003	..	..	..
Gambia, The	2004	3	2005/06	2003	55	..	..
Georgia	2010	10	2005	2002	92	49	97
Germany	2009	15		2011	..	97	100
Ghana	2002	1	2008	2010	71	100	..
Greece		0		2011	..	69	91
Guatemala	2008	14	2002	2002	..	63	92
Guinea		0	2005		43	..	..
Guinea-Bissau		0	2010	2009	24	..	..

Health information | 2.17

	Year last national health account completed	Number of national health accounts completed	Year of last health survey	Year of last census	Completeness		
						%	
					Birth registration	Infant death reporting	Total death reporting
		1995–2010		2001–11	2005–10[a]	2005–10[a]	2005–10[a]
Haiti	2006	1	2005/06	2003	81	..	..
Honduras	2005	3	2005/06	2001	94	100	100
Hungary	2009	15		2001	..	89	98
India	2004	2	2005/06	2011	41	..	..
Indonesia	2008	8	2007	2010	53	..	..
Iran, Islamic Rep.	2007	4	2000	2006	..	..	100
Iraq	2010	3	2006		95	100	100
Ireland	2009	16		2011	..	86	98
Israel	2007	2		2009	..	100	96
Italy	2009	4		2012	..	99	98
Jamaica	2000	1	2005	2011	89	73	88
Japan	2008	14		2010	..	92	100
Jordan	2009	6	2009	2004	..	..	82
Kazakhstan	2010	2	2006	2009	99	83	88
Kenya	2010	3	2010	2009	60	43	42
Korea, Dem. Rep.		0	2010	2009	100	73	93
Korea, Rep.	2010	16		2010	..	82	98
Kosovo		0			..	..	..
Kuwait		0	1996	2010	..	100	73
Kyrgyz Republic	2010	6	2005/06	2009	94	76	91
Lao PDR		0	2006	2005	72	..	..
Latvia	2008	5		2011	..	65	96
Lebanon	2008	11	2000		..	..	87
Lesotho		0	2009/10	2006	45	..	..
Liberia	2008	1	2009	2008	4	..	..
Libya		0	2000	2006	..	..	..
Lithuania	2009	8		2011	..	71	93
Macedonia, FYR		0	2005	2010	94	61	100
Madagascar	2007	2	2008/09		80	..	..
Malawi	2006	5	2010	2008	..	..	71
Malaysia	2009	13		2010	..	80	99
Mali	2004	6	2010	2009	81	..	..
Mauritania	2008	1	2007	2000	56	..	..
Mauritius	2004	2		2011	..	90	100
Mexico	2010	16	1995	2010	..	82	100
Moldova	2010	2	2005	2004	..	73	91
Mongolia	2003	5	2010	2010	98	60	98
Morocco	2006	3	2006	2004	..	..	..
Mozambique	2006	4	2009	2007	31	..	..
Myanmar	2007	10	2000		72	58	100
Namibia	2008	11	2009	2001	67	..	100
Nepal	2010	11	2010	2001	35	..	..
Netherlands	2010	16		2011	..	89	99
New Zealand	2009	15		2006	..	97	96
Nicaragua	2008	14	2006/07	2005	..	66	68
Niger	2009	6	2006	2001	32	..	..
Nigeria	2005	8	2008	2006	30	..	3
Norway	2009	13		2001	..	97	99
Oman	1998	1	1995	2010	..	100	70
Pakistan	2006	1	2010		27	88	80
Panama	1997	1	2003	2010	..	68	90
Papua New Guinea	2000	3	1996		..	..	..
Paraguay	2008	14	2004	2002	..	34	71
Peru	2005	11	2008	2007	93	45	59
Philippines	2007	13	2008	2010	..	38	84
Poland	2009	15		2011	..	89	97
Portugal	2008	9		2011	..	57	99

	Year last national health account completed	Number of national health accounts completed	Year of last health survey	Year of last census	Completeness		
						%	
					Birth registration	Infant death reporting	Total death reporting
	1995–2010			2001–11	2005–10[a]	2005–10[a]	2005–10[a]
Puerto Rico		0	1996	2010	..	100	100
Qatar	2010	2		2010	..	77	78
Romania	2009	12	1999	2011	..	73	100
Russian Federation	2008	13	1996	2010	..	76	100
Rwanda	2006	5	2007/08	2002	82	..	100
Saudi Arabia	2008	1	2007	2010	..	100	98
Senegal	2005	2	2008/09	2002	55	100	100
Serbia	2010	8	2005/06	2011	99	37	89
Sierra Leone	2006	3	2008	2004	51	13	..
Singapore		0	2005	2010	..	100	74
Slovak Republic	2009	13		2011	..	100	100
Slovenia	2010	16		2011	..	79	97
Somalia		0	2006		3	..	..
South Africa	1998	3	2003	2001	92	78	82
South Sudan		0		2008			
Spain	2009	15		2001	..	84	94
Sri Lanka	2008	14	2006/07	2001	97	67	94
Sudan	2010	2	2010	2008	33	..	..
Swaziland		0	2010	2010	30	..	100
Sweden	2009	9			..	100	98
Switzerland	2010	16		2010	..	100	100
Syrian Arab Republic		0	2006	2004	95	..	100
Tajikistan	2010	4	2005	2010	88	24	72
Tanzania	2006	3	2010	2002	16	..	..
Thailand	2007	13	2005/06	2010	99	53	79
Timor-Leste		0	2009/10	2010	55	..	..
Togo	2002	1	2010	2010	78	..	..
Trinidad and Tobago	2000	1	2006	2011	96	49	94
Tunisia	2005	5	2006	2004	..	..	99
Turkey	2008	11	2003		94	60	100
Turkmenistan		0	2006		96	..	..
Uganda	2007	6	2009/10	2002	21	..	..
Ukraine	2008	6	2007	2001	100	75	93
United Arab Emirates		0		2010	..	96	91
United Kingdom	2009	13		2011	..	100	96
United States	2009	15	2009	2010	..	100	98
Uruguay	2008	13		2004	..	77	100
Uzbekistan	2010	1	2006		100	..	..
Venezuela, RB		0	2000	2001	..	62	87
Vietnam	2007	10	2006	2009	88	71	86
West Bank and Gaza	2005	1	2006	2007	96	28	73
Yemen, Rep.	2007	4	2006	2004	22	..	16
Zambia	2006	12	2007	2010	14	..	73
Zimbabwe	2001	3	2005/06	2002	38	..	..

a. Data are for the most recent year available.

About the data

According to the World Health Organization (WHO), health information systems are crucial for monitoring and evaluating health systems, which are increasingly recognized as important for combating disease and improving health status. Health information systems underpin decisionmaking through four data functions: generation, compilation, analysis and synthesis, and communication and use. The health information system collects data from the health sector and other relevant sectors; analyzes the data and ensures their overall quality, relevance, and timeliness; and converts data into information for health-related decisionmaking (WHO 2008b).

Numerous indicators have been proposed to assess a country's health information system. They can be grouped into two broad types: indicators related to data generation using core sources and methods (health surveys, civil registration, censuses, facility reporting, health system resource tracking) and indicators related to capacity for data synthesis, analysis, and validation. Indicators related to data generation reflect a country's capacity to collect relevant data at suitable intervals using the most appropriate data sources. Benchmarks include periodicity, timeliness, contents, and availability. Indicators related to capacity for synthesis, analysis, and validation measure the dimensions of the institutional frameworks needed to ensure data quality, including independence, transparency, and access. Benchmarks include the availability of independent coordination mechanisms and micro- and meta-data (WHO 2008a).

The indicators in the table are all related to data generation, including the years the last national health account, last health survey, and latest population census were completed. Frequency of data collection, a benchmark of data generation, is shown as the number of years for which a national health account was completed during the specified years. National health account data may be collected using different approaches such as Organisation for Economic Co-operation and Development (OECD) System of Health Accounts, WHO National Health Account producers guide approach, local national health accounting methods, or Pan American Health Organization/WHO satellite health accounts approach.

Indicators related to data generation include completeness of birth registration, infant death reporting, and total death reporting.

Definitions

- **Year last national health account completed** is the latest year for which the health expenditure data are available using the national health account approach. • **Number of national health accounts completed** is the number of national health accounts completed during the specified years. • **Year of last health survey** is the latest year the national survey that collects health information was conducted. • **Year of last census** is the latest year a census was conducted in the last 10 years. • **Completeness of birth registration** is the percentage of children under age 5 whose births were registered at the time of the survey. The numerator of completeness of birth registration includes children whose birth certificate was seen by the interviewer or whose mother or caretaker says the birth has been registered. • **Completeness of infant death reporting** is the number of infant deaths reported by national statistical authorities to the United Nations Statistics Division's *Demographic Yearbook* divided by the number of infant deaths estimated by the United Nations Population Division. • **Completeness of total death reporting** is the number of total deaths from civil registration systems reported by national statistical authorities to the United Nations Statistics Division's *Demographic Yearbook* divided by the number of total deaths estimated by the United Nations Population Division.

Data sources

Data on year last national health account completed and number of national health accounts completed were compiled by the World Bank's Health, Nutrition, and Population Unit using information on the health expenditures provided by the WHO National Health Accounts staff and the OECD. Data on year of last health survey are from ICF International and the United Nations Children's Fund (UNICEF). Data on year of last census are from United Nations Statistics Division's 2011 World Population and Housing Census Program (http://unstats.un.org/unsd/demographic/sources/census/2010_PHC/default.htm). Data on completeness of birth registration are compiled by UNICEF in *State of the World's Children 2012* based mostly on household surveys and ministry of health data. Data used to calculate completeness of infant death reporting and total death reporting are from the United Nations Statistics Division's *Population and Vital Statistics Report* and the United Nations Population Division's *World Population Prospects: The 2010 Revision.*

Disease prevention coverage and quality

	Access to an improved water source		Access to improved sanitation facilities		Child immunization rate		Children with acute respiratory infection (ARI) taken to health provider	Children with diarrhea who received oral rehydration and continuous feeding	Children sleeping under treated nets[a]	Children with fever receiving antimalarial drugs	Tuberculosis	
											Treatment success rate	Case detection rate
	% of population		% of population		% of children ages 12–23 months[b]		% of children under age 5 with ARI	% of children under age 5 with diarrhea	% of children under age 5	% of children under age 5 with fever	% of new registered cases	% of new estimated cases
	1990	2010	1990	2010	Measles 2010	DTP3 2010	2005–10[c]	2005–10[c]	2005–10[c]	2005–10[c]	2009	2010
Afghanistan	..	50	..	37	62	66	..	..	..	..	86	47
Albania	97	95	76	94	99	99	70	63	..	..	89	97
Algeria	94	83	88	95	95	95	53	24	..	..	91	70
Angola	42	51	29	58	93	91	..	..	17.7	29.3	72	77
Argentina	94	97	90	90	99	94	..	..	..	..	46	66
Armenia	..	98	..	90	97	94	57	59	..	..	73	62
Australia	100	100	100	100	94	92	..	..	..	..	80	84
Austria	100	100	100	100	76	83	..	..	..	..	66	84
Azerbaijan	70	80	..	82	67	72	33	31	..	..	62	63
Bahrain	..	..	..	..	99	99	..	..	..	..	98	84
Bangladesh	77	81	39	56	94	95	37	68	..	..	92	46
Belarus	100	100	93	93	99	98	90	54	..	..	64	74
Belgium	100	100	100	100	94	99	..	..	..	..	76	87
Benin	57	75	5	13	69	83	36	42	20.1	54.0	90	45
Bolivia	70	88	18	27	79	80	51	29	..	..	86	62
Bosnia and Herzegovina	97	99	..	95	93	90	91	53	..	..	99	71
Botswana	93	96	38	62	94	96	..	..	..	..	79	70
Brazil	89	98	68	79	99	98	50	..	..	..	72	88
Bulgaria	100	100	99	100	97	94	..	..	..	..	85	79
Burkina Faso	43	79	8	17	94	95	39	42	9.6	48.0	76	53
Burundi	70	72	44	46	92	96	38	23	45.2	17.2	90	70
Cambodia	31	64	9	31	93	92	64	50	4.2	0.2	95	65
Cameroon	49	77	48	49	79	84	35	22	13.1	57.8	78	69
Canada	100	100	100	100	93	80	..	..	..	..	75	83
Central African Republic	58	67	11	34	62	54	32	47	15.1	57.0	53	47
Chad	39	51	8	13	46	59	26	23	9.8	35.7	76	31
Chile	90	96	84	96	93	92	..	..	..	..	72	75
China	67	91	24	64	99	99	..	..	..	..	95	87
Hong Kong SAR, China	..	..	..	..	..	..	..	..	..	..	70	87
Colombia	89	92	67	77	88	88	64	52	..	..	77	72
Congo, Dem. Rep.	45	45	9	24	68	63	40	37	35.7	39.1	88	53
Congo, Rep.	..	71	..	18	76	90	48	39	6.1	48.0	78	68
Costa Rica	93	97	93	95	83	88	..	..	..	..	54	78
Côte d'Ivoire	76	80	20	24	70	85	35	45	3.0	36.0	79	83
Croatia	99	99	99	99	95	96	..	..	..	..	63	73
Cuba	82	94	80	91	99	96	..	..	..	..	90	79
Cyprus	100	100	100	100	87	99	..	..	..	..	29	68
Czech Republic	100	100	100	98	98	99	..	..	..	..	67	88
Denmark	100	100	100	100	85	90	..	..	..	..	53	93
Dominican Republic	88	86	73	83	79	88	70	55	..	0.6	85	59
Ecuador	72	94	69	92	98	99	..	..	..	..	75	51
Egypt, Arab Rep.	93	99	72	95	96	97	73	19	..	..	88	64
El Salvador	74	88	75	87	92	92	67	..	..	..	89	96
Eritrea	43	61	9	14	99	99	..	..	48.9	13.1	85	55
Estonia	98	98	95	95	95	94	..	..	..	..	59	85
Ethiopia	14	44	3	21	81	86	19	15	33.1	9.5	84	72
Finland	100	100	100	100	98	99	..	..	..	..	68	87
France	100	100	100	100	90	99	..	..	..	..	..	47
Gabon	..	87	..	33	55	45	..	..	55.1	..	55	42
Gambia, The	74	89	..	68	97	98	69	38	49.0	63.0	89	44
Georgia	81	98	96	95	94	91	74	37	..	..	75	100
Germany	100	100	100	100	96	93	..	..	..	..	77	89
Ghana	53	86	7	14	93	94	51	45	28.2	43.0	87	70
Greece	96	100	97	98	99	99	..	..	..	..	..	68
Guatemala	81	92	62	78	93	94	..	..	..	..	83	37
Guinea	51	74	10	18	51	57	42	38	4.5	73.9	79	33
Guinea-Bissau	36	64	..	20	61	76	52	53	35.5	51.2	67	62
Haiti	59	69	26	17	59	59	31	43	..	5.1	79	62

Disease prevention coverage and quality

	Access to an improved water source		Access to improved sanitation facilities		Child immunization rate		Children with acute respiratory infection (ARI) taken to health provider	Children with diarrhea who received oral rehydration and continuous feeding	Children sleeping under treated nets[a]	Children with fever receiving antimalarial drugs	Tuberculosis	
											Treatment success rate	Case detection rate
	% of population		% of population		% of children ages 12–23 months[b]		% of children under age 5 with ARI	% of children under age 5 with diarrhea	% of children under age 5	% of children under age 5 with fever	% of new registered cases	% of new estimated cases
	1990	2010	1990	2010	Measles 2010	DTP3 2010	2005–10[c]	2005–10[c]	2005–10[c]	2005–10[c]	2009	2010
Honduras	76	87	50	77	99	98	56	49	..	0.5	86	74
Hungary	96	100	100	100	99	99	..	..	..	..	57	100
India	69	92	18	34	74	72	69	33	..	8.2	88	59
Indonesia	70	82	32	54	89	83	66	54	3.3	0.8	91	66
Iran, Islamic Rep.	90	96	79	100	99	99	..	..	..	..	83	81
Iraq	81	79	..	73	73	65	82	64	..	..	90	48
Ireland	100	100	99	99	90	94	..	..	..	..	67	88
Israel	100	100	100	100	98	96	..	..	..	..	86	93
Italy	100	100	..	..	90	96	..	..	..	..	..	57
Jamaica	93	93	80	80	88	99	75	39	..	..	70	72
Japan	100	100	100	100	94	98	..	..	..	..	52	84
Jordan	97	97	97	98	98	98	75	32	..	..	75	100
Kazakhstan	96	95	96	97	99	99	71	48	..	..	62	82
Kenya	44	59	25	32	86	83	56	43	46.7	23.2	86	82
Korea, Dem. Rep.	100	98	..	80	99	93	80	67	..	..	89	100
Korea, Rep.	..	98	100	100	98	94	..	..	..	..	83	90
Kosovo	..	..	..	..	..	..	..	..	..	..	..	..
Kuwait	99	99	100	100	98	98	..	..	..	..	85	86
Kyrgyz Republic	..	90	..	93	99	96	62	22	..	..	82	66
Lao PDR	..	67	..	63	64	74	32	49	40.5	8.2	93	72
Latvia	99	99	..	78	93	89	..	..	..	..	75	100
Lebanon	100	100	..	..	53	74	..	..	..	..	82	71
Lesotho	80	78	..	26	85	83	66	48	..	..	70	85
Liberia	..	73	..	18	64	64	62	47	26.4	67.2	83	56
Libya	54	..	97	97	98	98	..	..	..	..	69	84
Lithuania	..	..	..	..	96	95	..	..	..	..	73	76
Macedonia, FYR	100	100	..	88	98	95	93	45	..	..	90	89
Madagascar	29	46	9	15	67	74	42	49	45.8	19.7	82	44
Malawi	41	83	39	51	93	93	52	27	56.5	30.9	88	65
Malaysia	88	100	84	96	96	94	..	..	..	..	78	80
Mali	28	64	15	22	63	76	38	38	70.2	31.7	78	51
Mauritania	30	50	16	26	67	64	45	32	..	20.7	63	21
Mauritius	99	99	89	89	99	99	..	..	..	..	88	44
Mexico	85	96	64	85	95	95	..	..	..	..	86	110
Moldova	..	96	..	85	97	90	60	48	..	..	54	63
Mongolia	54	82	..	51	97	96	63	47	..	..	88	72
Morocco	73	83	53	70	98	99	..	..	..	..	84	97
Mozambique	36	47	11	18	70	74	65	47	22.8	36.7	85	34
Myanmar	56	83	..	76	88	90	..	..	..	..	85	71
Namibia	64	93	24	32	75	83	72	48	34.0	20.3	85	82
Nepal	76	89	10	31	86	82	43	37	..	0.1	90	72
Netherlands	100	100	100	100	96	97	..	..	..	..	80	85
New Zealand	100	100	..	..	91	93	..	..	..	..	76	90
Nicaragua	74	85	43	52	99	98	..	..	..	..	85	100
Niger	35	49	5	9	71	70	47	34	63.7	33.0	79	35
Nigeria	47	58	37	31	71	69	45	25	29.1	49.1	83	40
Norway	100	100	100	100	93	93	..	..	..	..	82	93
Oman	80	89	82	99	97	99	..	..	..	..	98	85
Pakistan	85	92	27	48	86	88	69	37	..	3.3	91	65
Panama	84	93	58	69	95	94	..	..	..	..	80	89
Papua New Guinea	41	40	47	45	55	56	63	..	..	..	72	70
Paraguay	52	86	37	71	94	90	..	..	..	..	80	77
Peru	75	85	54	71	94	93	68	60	..	..	81	100
Philippines	85	92	57	74	88	87	50	60	..	0.0	89	65
Poland	..	100	..	90	98	99	..	..	..	..	67	80
Portugal	96	99	92	100	96	98	..	..	..	..	84	79
Puerto Rico	..	..	..	..	..	..	..	..	..	..	81	96
Qatar	100	100	100	100	99	97	..	..	..	..	80	87

2.18 Disease prevention coverage and quality

	Access to an improved water source		Access to improved sanitation facilities		Child immunization rate		Children with acute respiratory infection (ARI) taken to health provider	Children with diarrhea who received oral rehydration and continuous feeding	Children sleeping under treated nets[a]	Children with fever receiving antimalarial drugs	Tuberculosis	
					% of children ages 12–23 months[b]						Treatment success rate	Case detection rate
	% of population		% of population		Measles	DTP3	% of children under age 5 with ARI	% of children under age 5 with diarrhea	% of children under age 5	% of children under age 5 with fever	% of new registered cases	% of new estimated cases
	1990	2010	1990	2010	2010	2010	2005–10[c]	2005–10[c]	2005–10[c]	2005–10[c]	2009	2010
Romania	75	..	71	72	95	97	..	..	..	..	85	74
Russian Federation	93	97	74	70	98	97	..	..	..	..	55	78
Rwanda	66	65	36	55	82	80	28	24	69.8	10.8	85	60
Saudi Arabia	89	..	..	..	98	98	..	..	..	..	65	88
Senegal	61	72	38	52	60	70	47	43	29.2	9.1	85	31
Serbia	99	99	..	92	95	91	93	71	..	..	86	130
Sierra Leone	38	55	11	13	82	90	46	57	25.8	30.1	79	32
Singapore	100	100	99	100	95	97	..	..	..	..	82	87
Slovak Republic	100	100	100	100	98	99	..	..	..	..	82	88
Slovenia	100	99	100	100	95	96	..	..	..	..	87	79
Somalia	..	29	..	23	46	45	13	7	11.4	7.9	85	38
South Africa	83	91	71	79	65	63	..	..	..	..	73	72
South Sudan	..	..	..	..	..	..	..	..	..	..	..	..
Spain	100	100	100	100	95	97	..	..	..	..	..	87
Sri Lanka	67	91	70	92	99	99	58	67	2.9	0.3	86	69
Sudan	65	58	27	26	90	90	90	56	25.3	35.8	80	50
Swaziland	39	71	48	57	94	89	73	22	0.6	0.6	69	66
Sweden	100	100	100	100	96	98	..	..	..	..	85	87
Switzerland	100	100	100	100	90	96	..	..	..	..	..	55
Syrian Arab Republic	86	90	85	95	82	80	77	34	..	..	88	90
Tajikistan	..	64	..	94	94	93	64	22	1.3	1.9	81	44
Tanzania	55	53	7	10	92	91	71	50	63.6	59.1	88	77
Thailand	86	96	84	96	98	99	84	46	..	..	86	70
Timor-Leste	..	69	..	47	66	72	71	63	41.0	6.0	85	87
Togo	49	61	13	13	84	92	23	24	56.9	33.8	81	10
Trinidad and Tobago	88	94	93	92	92	90	74	32	..	..	69	87
Tunisia	81	94	74	85	97	98	59	62	..	..	83	91
Turkey	85	100	84	90	97	96	..	22	..	..	91	77
Turkmenistan	..	..	98	98	99	99	83	25	..	..	84	96
Uganda	43	72	27	34	55	60	73	39	32.8	59.6	67	61
Ukraine	..	98	..	94	94	90	..	..	..	..	60	73
United Arab Emirates	100	100	97	98	94	94	..	..	..	..	73	57
United Kingdom	100	100	100	100	93	96	..	..	..	..	82	91
United States	99	99	100	100	92	95	..	..	..	..	60	88
Uruguay	96	100	94	100	95	95	..	..	..	..	80	97
Uzbekistan	90	87	84	100	98	99	68	28	..	..	81	48
Venezuela, RB	90	..	82	..	79	78	..	..	..	..	84	66
Vietnam	57	95	37	76	98	93	83	65	5.0	2.6	92	54
West Bank and Gaza	..	85	..	92	..	..	..	..	..	..	82	16
Yemen, Rep.	67	55	24	53	73	87	..	48	..	..	88	76
Zambia	49	61	46	48	91	82	..	68	56	49.9	90	90
Zimbabwe	79	80	41	40	84	83	43	35	17.3	23.6	78	56
World	**76 w**	**88 w**	**47 w**	**62 w**	**85 w**	**85 w**	**.. w**	**.. w**	**.. w**	**.. w**	**86 w**	**65 w**
Low income	54	65	21	37	78	80	..	39	..	31.9	86	58
Middle income	73	90	39	59	86	85	..	..	..	..	87	67
Lower middle income	70	87	29	47	80	79	67	37	..	13.8	87	61
Upper middle income	76	93	46	73	96	96	..	..	..	..	86	81
Low & middle income	71	86	37	56	84	84	..	..	..	..	87	65
East Asia & Pacific	68	90	30	66	95	94	..	..	..	..	92	76
Europe & Central Asia	90	96	80	84	96	95	..	..	..	..	65	73
Latin America & Carib.	86	94	68	79	93	93	..	..	..	..	77	80
Middle East & N. Africa	86	89	73	88	88	89	..	..	..	..	87	73
South Asia	71	90	22	38	77	76	67	37	..	7.2	88	58
Sub-Saharan Africa	49	61	26	31	75	77	..	35	34.0	37.8	79	60
High income	99	100	100	100	93	95	..	..	..	..	68	85
Euro area	100	100	100	100	93	96	..	..	..	..	..	..

a. For malaria prevention only. b. Refers to children who were immunized before age 12 months or in some cases at any time before the survey (12–23 months). c. Data are for the most recent year available.

Disease prevention coverage and quality

People's health is influenced by the environment in which they live. Lack of clean water and basic sanitation is the main reason diseases transmitted by feces are so common in developing countries. Access to drinking water from an improved source and access to improved sanitation do not ensure safety or adequacy, as these characteristics are not tested at the time of the surveys. But improved drinking water technologies and improved sanitation facilities are more likely than those characterized as unimproved to provide safe drinking water and to prevent contact with human excreta. The data are derived by the Joint Monitoring Programme of the World Health Organization (WHO) and United Nations Children's Fund (UNICEF) based on national censuses and nationally representative household surveys. The coverage rates for water and sanitation are based on information from service users on the facilities their households actually use rather than on information from service providers, which may include nonfunctioning systems. While the estimates are based on use, the Joint Monitoring Programme reports use as access, because access is the term used in the Millennium Development Goal target for drinking water and sanitation.

Governments in developing countries usually finance immunization against measles and diphtheria, pertussis (whooping cough), and tetanus (DTP) as part of the basic public health package. In many developing countries lack of precise information on the size of the cohort of one-year-old children makes immunization coverage difficult to estimate from program statistics. The data shown here are based on an assessment of national immunization coverage rates by the WHO and UNICEF. The assessment considered both administrative data from service providers and household survey data on children's immunization histories. Based on the data available, consideration of potential biases, and contributions of local experts, the most likely true level of immunization coverage was determined for each year.

Acute respiratory infection continues to be a leading cause of death among young children, killing nearly 1.5 million children under age 5 globally each year. Data are drawn mostly from household health surveys in which mothers report on number of episodes and treatment for acute respiratory infection.

Most diarrhea-related deaths are due to dehydration, and many of these deaths can be prevented with the use of oral rehydration salts at home. However, recommendations for the use of oral rehydration therapy have changed over time based on scientific progress, so it is difficult to accurately compare use rates across countries. Until the current recommended method for home management of diarrhea is adopted and applied in all countries, the data should be used with caution. Also, the prevalence of diarrhea may vary by season. Since country surveys are administered at different times, data comparability is further affected.

Malaria is endemic to the poorest countries in the world, mainly in tropical and subtropical regions of Africa, Asia, and the Americas. Insecticide-treated nets, properly used and maintained, are one of the most important malaria-preventive strategies to limit human-mosquito contact.

Prompt and effective treatment of malaria is a critical element of malaria control. It is vital that sufferers, especially children under age 5, start treatment within 24 hours of the onset of symptoms, to prevent progression—often rapid—to severe malaria and death. Data on malaria are from national-level surveys, including Multiple Indicator Cluster Surveys, Demographic and Health Surveys, and Malaria Indicator Surveys.

Data on the success rate of tuberculosis treatment are provided for countries that have submitted data to the WHO. The treatment success rate for tuberculosis provides a useful indicator of the quality of health services. A low rate suggests that infectious patients may not be receiving adequate treatment. An important complement to the tuberculosis treatment success rate is the case detection rate, which indicates whether there is adequate coverage by the recommended case detection and treatment strategy. Uncertainty bounds for the case detection rate, not shown in the table, are available at http://data.worldbank.org and from the original source.

The table shows the tuberculosis detection rate for all detection methods. Editions before 2010 included the tuberculosis detection rates by DOTS, the internationally recommended strategy for tuberculosis control. Thus data on the case detection rate from 2010 onward cannot be compared with data in previous editions.

For indicators that are from household surveys, the year in the table refers to the survey year. For more information, consult the original sources.

• **Access to an improved water source** refers to people with access to at least 20 liters of water a person a day from an improved source, such as piped water into a dwelling, public tap, tubewell, protected dug well, and rainwater collection, within 1 kilometer of the dwelling. • **Access to improved sanitation facilities** refers to people with at least adequate access to excreta disposal facilities that can effectively prevent human, animal, and insect contact with excreta. Improved facilities range from protected pit latrines to flush toilets. • **Child immunization rate** refers to children ages 12–23 months who, before 12 months or at any time before the survey, had received one dose of measles vaccine and three doses of diphtheria, pertussis (whooping cough), and tetanus (DTP3) vaccine. • **Children with acute respiratory infection (ARI) taken to health provider** are children under age 5 with ARI in the two weeks before the survey who were taken to an appropriate health provider. • **Children with diarrhea who received oral rehydration and continuous feeding** are children under age 5 with diarrhea in the two weeks before the survey who received either oral rehydration therapy or increased fluids, with continuous feeding. • **Children sleeping under treated nets** are children under age 5 who slept under an insecticide-treated net to prevent malaria the night before the survey. • **Children with fever receiving antimalarial drugs** are children under age 5 who were ill with fever in the two weeks before the survey and received any appropriate (locally defined) antimalarial drugs. • **Tuberculosis treatment success rate** is new registered infectious tuberculosis cases that were cured or that completed a full course of treatment as a percentage of smear-positive cases registered for treatment outcome evaluation. • **Tuberculosis case detection rate** is newly identified tuberculosis cases (including relapses) as a percentage of estimated incident cases (case detection, all forms).

Data on access to water and sanitation are from the WHO and UNICEF's *Progress on Drinking Water and Sanitation* (2012). Data on immunization are from WHO and UNICEF estimates (www.who.int/immunization_monitoring). Data on children with ARI, with diarrhea, sleeping under treated nets, and receiving antimalarial drugs are from UNICEF's *State of the World's Children 2012*, Childinfo, and MEASURE DHS Demographic and Health Surveys by ICF International. Data on tuberculosis are from the WHO's *Global Tuberculosis Control: A Short Update to the 2011 Report*.

Reproductive health

	Total fertility rate		Adolescent fertility rate	Unmet need for contraception	Contraceptive prevalence rate	Pregnant women receiving prenatal care	Births attended by skilled health staff		Maternal mortality ratio			Lifetime risk of maternal mortality
					Any method					per 100,000 live births		
	births per woman		births per 1,000 women ages 15–19	% of married women ages 15–49	% of married women ages 15–49	%	% of total		National estimates	Modeled estimates		Probability 1 woman in:
	1990	2010	2010	2005–10ᵃ	2005–10ᵃ	2005–10ᵃ	1990	2005–10ᵃ	2005–10ᵃ	1990	2008	2008
Afghanistan	8.0	6.3	107	..	23	36	..	24	..	1,700	1,400	11
Albania	3.2	1.5	16	13	69	97	93	99	21	48	31	1,700
Algeria	4.7	2.3	7	11	61	89	77	95	..	250	120	340
Angola	7.2	5.4	157	..	..	80	..	47	..	1,000	610	29
Argentina	3.0	2.2	55	..	78	99	96	98	55	72	70	600
Armenia	2.5	1.7	34	13	55	99	100	100	27	51	29	1,900
Australia	1.9	1.9	14	..	..	98	100	..	..	10	8	7,400
Austria	1.5	1.4	11	..	..	..	..	..	..	10	5	14,300
Azerbaijan	2.7	2.3	32	23	51	77	97	88	24	64	38	1,200
Bahrain	3.7	2.5	15	..	..	100	..	97	..	25	19	2,200
Bangladesh	4.5	2.2	73	17	53	53	..	27	190	870	340	110
Belarus	1.9	1.4	21	..	73	99	100	100	1	37	15	5,100
Belgium	1.6	1.8	12	..	..	..	..	..	..	7	5	10,900
Benin	6.7	5.3	103	30	17	84	..	74	400	790	410	43
Bolivia	4.9	3.3	76	20	61	86	43	71	310	510	180	150
Bosnia and Herzegovina	1.7	1.1	15	23	36	99	97	100	3	18	9	9,300
Botswana	4.7	2.8	47	..	53	94	78	95	200	83	190	180
Brazil	2.8	1.8	76	..	81	98	70	97	75	120	58	860
Bulgaria	1.8	1.5	39	..	..	..	99	100	5	24	13	5,800
Burkina Faso	6.8	5.9	120	31	17	85	..	54	310	770	560	28
Burundi	6.5	4.3	20	..	22	99	..	60	620	1,200	970	25
Cambodia	5.7	2.6	36	17	51	89	..	71	206	690	290	110
Cameroon	5.9	4.5	120	3	29	82	64	63	..	680	600	35
Canada	1.8	1.7	12	..	..	100	..	100	..	6	12	5,600
Central African Republic	5.8	4.6	102	..	19	69	..	44	540	880	850	27
Chad	6.7	6.0	149	..	5	53	..	23	..	1,300	1,200	14
Chile	2.6	1.9	57	..	58	..	..	100	17	56	26	2,000
China	2.3	1.6	9	..	85	92	94	99	32	110	38	1,500
Hong Kong SAR, China	1.3	1.1	4	..	80	..	..	100	..	..	..	..
Colombia	3.1	2.1	71	7	79	97	94	98	76	140	85	460
Congo, Dem. Rep.	7.1	5.8	183	24	17	88	..	79	550	900	670	24
Congo, Rep.	5.4	4.5	115	16	44	86	..	83	780	460	580	39
Costa Rica	3.2	1.8	63	..	80	90	98	99	21	35	44	1,100
Côte d'Ivoire	6.3	4.4	115	29	13	85	..	57	540	690	470	44
Croatia	1.6	1.5	13	..	..	100	100	100	13	8	14	5,200
Cuba	1.8	1.5	44	8	78	100	..	100	43	63	53	1,400
Cyprus	2.4	1.5	6	..	..	99	..	..	..	17	10	6,600
Czech Republic	1.9	1.5	10	..	..	..	100	100	2	15	8	8,500
Denmark	1.7	1.9	5	..	..	..	..	..	..	7	5	10,900
Dominican Republic	3.5	2.6	106	11	73	99	92	98	160	220	100	320
Ecuador	3.7	2.5	81	..	..	..	..	..	61	230	140	270
Egypt, Arab Rep.	4.4	2.7	43	9	60	74	37	79	55	220	82	380
El Salvador	4.0	2.3	79	..	73	94	90	96	59	200	110	350
Eritrea	6.2	4.5	59	..	..	..	..	..	..	930	280	72
Estonia	2.0	1.6	19	..	..	..	99	100	7	48	12	5,300
Ethiopia	7.1	4.2	58	34	15	28	..	6	670	990	470	40
Finland	1.8	1.9	9	..	..	..	..	..	..	7	8	7,600
France	1.8	2.0	6	..	71	..	..	..	..	13	8	6,600
Gabon	5.2	3.3	85	..	..	..	..	..	..	260	260	110
Gambia, The	6.1	4.9	71	..	..	98	44	57	..	750	400	49
Georgia	2.2	1.6	42	..	53	98	97	100	52	58	48	1,300
Germany	1.5	1.4	7	..	..	..	..	100	..	13	7	11,100
Ghana	5.6	4.2	66	35	24	90	40	57	450	630	350	66
Greece	1.4	1.4	10	..	..	..	..	..	..	6	2	31,800
Guatemala	5.6	4.0	104	..	54	93	..	51	130	140	110	210
Guinea	6.7	5.2	143	21	9	88	31	46	980	1,200	680	26
Guinea-Bissau	6.6	5.1	102	25	14	93	..	44	410	1,200	1,000	18
Haiti	5.4	3.3	43	38	32	85	23	26	630	670	300	93

	Total fertility rate		Adolescent fertility rate	Unmet need for contraception	Contraceptive prevalence rate	Pregnant women receiving prenatal care	Births attended by skilled health staff		Maternal mortality ratio			Lifetime risk of maternal mortality
			births per 1,000 women ages 15–19	% of married women ages 15–49	Any method % of married women ages 15–49	%	% of total		per 100,000 live births			Probability 1 woman in:
									National estimates	Modeled estimates		
	births per woman											
	1990	2010	2010	2005–10a	2005–10a	2005–10a	1990	2005–10a	2005–10a	1990	2008	2008
Honduras	5.1	3.1	89	17	65	92	47	67	..	210	110	240
Hungary	1.8	1.3	15	..	..	..	99	100	19	23	13	5,500
India	3.9	2.6	79	13	54	75	..	53	250	570	230	140
Indonesia	3.1	2.1	43	15	56	95	41	82	230	620	240	190
Iran, Islamic Rep.	4.8	1.7	27	..	79	98	..	97	25	150	30	1,500
Iraq	6.0	4.7	91	..	50	84	54	80	84	93	75	300
Ireland	2.1	2.1	12	..	65	..	..	..	..	6	3	17,800
Israel	2.8	3.0	14	..	..	..	..	..	..	12	7	5,100
Italy	1.3	1.4	5	..	..	..	..	..	..	10	5	15,200
Jamaica	2.9	2.3	73	..	72	99	92	98	..	66	89	450
Japan	1.5	1.4	6	..	54	..	100	..	..	12	6	12,200
Jordan	5.8	3.8	25	11	59	99	87	99	19	110	59	510
Kazakhstan	2.7	2.6	27	..	51	100	99	100	37	78	45	950
Kenya	6.0	4.7	99	26	46	92	50	44	488	380	530	38
Korea, Dem. Rep.	2.4	2.0	1	..	..	100	..	100	77	270	250	230
Korea, Rep.	1.6	1.2	4	..	80	..	..	..	..	18	18	4,700
Kosovo	3.9	2.3	..	..	..	..	..	..	..	..	..	..
Kuwait	2.6	2.3	14	..	..	100	..	100	..	10	9	4,500
Kyrgyz Republic	3.7	2.9	33	1	48	97	99	99	64	77	81	450
Lao PDR	6.2	2.7	34	..	38	71	..	37	410	1,200	580	49
Latvia	2.0	1.2	15	..	..	..	100	100	32	57	20	3,600
Lebanon	3.1	1.8	16	..	..	..	..	..	..	52	26	2,000
Lesotho	4.9	3.2	66	..	47	92	..	62	1,200	370	530	62
Liberia	6.5	5.2	131	36	11	79	..	46	990	1,100	990	20
Libya	4.8	2.6	3	..	..	93	..	100	..	100	64	540
Lithuania	2.0	1.6	18	..	..	..	100	100	9	34	13	5,800
Macedonia, FYR	2.1	1.4	19	34	14	99	89	100	4	16	9	7,300
Madagascar	6.3	4.7	127	19	40	86	57	44	500	710	440	45
Malawi	6.8	6.0	111	..	41	92	55	54	810	910	510	36
Malaysia	3.5	2.6	12	..	..	79	93	99	29	56	31	1,200
Mali	7.1	6.3	176	31	8	70	..	49	460	1,200	830	22
Mauritania	5.9	4.5	75	25	9	75	40	61	690	780	550	41
Mauritius	2.3	1.5	33	..	..	..	91	99	..	72	36	1,600
Mexico	3.4	2.3	68	..	73	96	84	95	54	93	85	500
Moldova	2.4	1.5	31	7	68	98	100	100	45	62	32	2,000
Mongolia	4.1	2.5	20	14	55	100	..	100	47	130	65	730
Morocco	4.0	2.3	13	..	..	..	31	..	130	270	110	360
Mozambique	6.2	4.9	134	..	16	92	..	55	500	1,000	550	37
Myanmar	3.4	2.0	14	..	41	80	46	64	320	420	240	180
Namibia	5.2	3.2	62	21	55	95	68	81	450	180	180	160
Nepal	5.2	2.7	93	25	48	44	7	19	280	870	380	80
Netherlands	1.6	1.8	5	..	69	..	..	..	..	10	9	7,100
New Zealand	2.2	2.2	24	..	..	..	..	..	..	18	14	3,800
Nicaragua	4.8	2.6	108	8	72	90	..	74	67	190	100	300
Niger	7.8	7.1	199	16	18	46	15	18	650	1,400	820	16
Nigeria	6.4	5.5	114	20	15	58	31	39	550	1,100	840	23
Norway	1.9	2.0	8	..	..	88	100	..	..	9	7	7,600
Oman	7.2	2.3	9	..	24	99	..	99	17	49	20	1,600
Pakistan	6.0	3.4	30	25	27	61	19	39	250	490	260	93
Panama	3.0	2.5	79	..	52	96	86	89	60	86	71	520
Papua New Guinea	4.8	4.0	64	..	32	79	..	53	730	340	250	94
Paraguay	4.5	3.0	69	..	79	96	66	82	130	130	95	310
Peru	3.8	2.5	51	8	74	95	53	84	93	250	98	370
Philippines	4.3	3.1	50	22	51	91	..	62	160	180	94	320
Poland	2.0	1.4	13	..	..	..	100	100	2	17	6	13,300
Portugal	1.4	1.3	14	..	67	..	98	..	..	15	7	9,800
Puerto Rico	2.2	1.8	52	..	..	..	..	..	..	29	18	3,000
Qatar	4.2	2.3	16	..	..	100	..	100	..	15	8	4,400

2.19 Reproductive health

	Total fertility rate		Adolescent fertility rate	Unmet need for contraception	Contraceptive prevalence rate	Pregnant women receiving prenatal care	Births attended by skilled health staff		Maternal mortality ratio			Lifetime risk of maternal mortality
					Any method					per 100,000 live births		Probability 1 woman in:
	births per woman		births per 1,000 women ages 15–19	% of married women ages 15–49	% of married women ages 15–49	%	% of total		National estimates	Modeled estimates		
	1990	2010	2010	2005–10a	2005–10a	2005–10a	1990	2005–10a	2005–10a	1990	2008	2008
Romania	1.8	1.4	30	..	..	..	100	99	21	170	27	2,700
Russian Federation	1.9	1.5	26	..	80	..	99	100	17	74	39	1,900
Rwanda	7.0	5.4	37	38	52	98	26	69	..	1,100	540	35
Saudi Arabia	5.8	2.8	18	..	24	97	..	97	14	41	24	1,300
Senegal	6.6	4.8	96	32	12	87	..	52	400	750	410	46
Serbia	1.8	1.4	20	29	41	98	..	99	9	13	8	7,500
Sierra Leone	5.7	5.0	120	28	8	87	..	42	860	1,300	970	21
Singapore	1.9	1.2	6	..	..	..	..	..	..	6	9	10,000
Slovak Republic	2.1	1.4	18	..	..	..	100	100	10	15	6	13,300
Slovenia	1.5	1.6	5	..	..	..	100	100	10	11	18	4,100
Somalia	6.6	6.3	69	26	15	26	..	33	1,000	1,100	1,200	14
South Africa	3.7	2.5	54	..	..	97	..	..	400	230	410	100
South Sudan	..	3.9	..	..	..	40	..	19	..	..	..	..
Spain	1.3	1.4	12	..	66	..	..	..	..	7	6	11,400
Sri Lanka	2.5	2.3	23	..	68	99	..	99	39	91	39	1,100
Sudan	6.0	4.4	57	6	8	56	69	49	1,100	830	750	32
Swaziland	5.7	3.4	74	24	49	97	..	82	589	260	420	75
Sweden	2.1	2.0	6	..	..	..	..	..	..	7	5	11,400
Switzerland	1.6	1.5	4	..	..	..	..	100	..	8	10	7,600
Syrian Arab Republic	5.3	2.9	39	11	54	88	..	96	..	120	46	610
Tajikistan	5.2	3.3	27	24	37	80	90	83	86	120	64	430
Tanzania	6.2	5.5	129	25	34	88	44	49	450	880	790	23
Thailand	2.1	1.6	40	..	80	99	..	99	12	50	48	1,200
Timor-Leste	5.3	5.6	58	31	22	84	..	29	560	650	370	44
Togo	6.3	4.1	59	41	15	87	31	60	..	650	350	67
Trinidad and Tobago	2.4	1.6	33	27	43	96	..	98	..	86	55	1,100
Tunisia	3.6	2.0	5	..	60	96	69	95	..	130	60	860
Turkey	3.0	2.1	34	18	73	95	..	95	29	68	23	1,900
Turkmenistan	4.3	2.4	18	..	48	99	..	100	12	91	77	500
Uganda	7.1	6.1	136	41	24	94	38	42	440	670	430	35
Ukraine	1.8	1.4	28	10	67	99	100	99	16	49	26	3,000
United Arab Emirates	4.4	1.7	25	..	..	100	..	100	0	28	10	4,200
United Kingdom	1.8	1.9	30	..	84	..	..	..	..	10	12	4,700
United States	2.1	2.1	33	..	79	..	99	..	13	12	24	2,100
Uruguay	2.5	2.0	60	..	78	96	..	100	34	39	27	1,700
Uzbekistan	4.1	2.5	13	8	65	99	..	100	21	53	30	1,400
Venezuela, RB	3.4	2.5	88	..	..	..	..	..	57	84	68	540
Vietnam	3.6	1.8	24	..	80	91	..	88	69	170	56	850
West Bank and Gaza	6.5	4.5	50	..	50	99	..	99	..	..	..	..
Yemen, Rep.	8.7	5.2	71	24	28	47	16	36	..	540	210	91
Zambia	6.5	6.3	142	27	41	94	51	47	590	390	470	38
Zimbabwe	5.2	3.3	58	13	59b	93b	70	60b	730	390	790	42
World	**3.2 w**	**2.5 w**	**53 w**	**.. w**	**62 w**	**84 w**	**62 w**	**66 w**		**400 w**	**260 w**	**140 w**
Low income	5.7	4.1	94	25	34	69	..	44		860	590	39
Middle income	3.3	2.3	51	..	65	86	60	71		350	210	190
Lower middle income	4.2	2.9	68	14	50	78	38	57		540	300	100
Upper middle income	2.6	1.8	29	..	81	94	89	98		110	60	880
Low & middle income	3.6	2.6	58	..	61	83	58	65		440	290	120
East Asia & Pacific	2.6	1.8	19	..	78	92	82	91		200	89	580
Europe & Central Asia	2.3	1.8	27	..	69	..	93	98		69	34	1,700
Latin America & Carib.	3.2	2.2	72	..	75	97	74	90		140	86	480
Middle East & N. Africa	4.9	2.7	37	..	62	85	47	81		210	88	380
South Asia	4.2	2.7	73	15	51	71	32	48		610	290	110
Sub-Saharan Africa	6.2	4.9	108	25	22	74	..	46		870	650	31
High income	1.8	1.8	18	..	..	..	..	..		15	15	3,900
Euro area	1.5	1.6	8	..	..	..	..	..		11	7	10,100

a. Data are for most recent year available. b. Data are for 2011.

Reproductive health is a state of physical and mental well-being in relation to the reproductive system and its functions and processes. Means of achieving reproductive health include education and services during pregnancy and childbirth, safe and effective contraception, and prevention and treatment of sexually transmitted diseases. Complications of pregnancy and childbirth are the leading cause of death and disability among women of reproductive age in developing countries.

Total and adolescent fertility rates are based on data on registered live births from vital registration systems or, in the absence of such systems, from censuses or sample surveys. The estimated rates are generally considered reliable measures of fertility in the recent past. Where no empirical information on age-specific fertility rates is available, a model is used to estimate the share of births to adolescents. For countries without vital registration systems fertility rates are generally based on extrapolations from trends observed in censuses or surveys from earlier years.

More couples in developing countries want to limit or postpone childbearing but are not using effective contraception. These couples have an unmet need for contraception. Common reasons are lack of knowledge about contraceptive methods and concerns about possible side effects. This indicator excludes women not exposed to the risk of unintended pregnancy because of menopause, infertility, or postpartum anovulation.

Contraceptive prevalence reflects all methods—ineffective traditional methods as well as highly effective modern methods. Contraceptive prevalence rates are obtained mainly from household surveys, including Demographic and Health Surveys, Multiple Indicator Cluster Surveys, and contraceptive prevalence surveys (see *Primary data documentation* for the most recent survey year). Unmarried women are often excluded from such surveys, which may bias the estimates.

Good prenatal and postnatal care improves maternal health and reduces maternal and infant mortality. However, indicators on use of antenatal care services provide no information on the content or quality of the services. Data on antenatal care are obtained mostly from household surveys, which ask women who have had a live birth whether and from whom they received antenatal care.

The share of births attended by skilled health staff is an indicator of a health system's ability to provide adequate care for pregnant women.

Maternal mortality ratios are generally of unknown reliability, as are many other cause-specific mortality indicators. Household surveys such as Demographic and Health Surveys attempt to measure maternal mortality by asking respondents about survivorship of sisters. The main disadvantage of this method is that the estimates of maternal mortality that it produces pertain to 12 years or so before the survey, making them unsuitable for monitoring recent changes or observing the impact of interventions. In addition, measurement of maternal mortality is subject to many types of errors. Even in high-income countries with reliable vital registration systems, misclassification of maternal deaths has been found to lead to serious underestimation.

The national estimates of maternal mortality ratios in the table are based on national surveys, vital registration records, and surveillance data or are derived from community and hospital records. The modeled estimates are based on an exercise by the World Health Organization (WHO), United Nations Children's Fund (UNICEF), United Nations Population Fund (UNFPA), and World Bank and include country-level time series data. For countries with complete vital registration systems with good attribution of cause of death, the data are used directly to estimate maternal mortality. For countries without complete registration data but with other types of data and for countries with no data, maternal mortality is estimated with a multilevel regression model using available national maternal mortality data and socio-economic information, including fertility, birth attendants, and GDP. The methodology differs from that used for previous estimates, so data should not be compared across editions. For further information on methodology, see the original source. Neither set of ratios can be assumed to provide an exact estimate of maternal mortality for any of the countries in the table.

In countries with a high risk of maternal death, many girls die before reaching reproductive age. Lifetime risk of maternal mortality refers to the probability that a 15-year-old girl will eventually die due to a maternal cause.

For the indicators that are from household surveys, the year in the table refers to the survey year. For more information, consult the original sources.

• **Total fertility rate** is the number of children that would be born to a woman if she were to live to the end of her childbearing years and bear children in accordance with the age-specific fertility rate of the specified year. • **Adolescent fertility rate** is the number of births per 1,000 women ages 15–19. • **Unmet need for contraception** is the percentage of fertile, married women of reproductive age who do not want to become pregnant and are not using contraception. • **Contraceptive prevalence rate** is the percentage of women married or in union ages 15–49 who are practicing, or whose sexual partners are practicing, any form of contraception. • **Pregnant women receiving prenatal care** are women attended at least once during pregnancy by skilled health personnel for pregnancy-related reasons. • **Births attended by skilled health staff** are live births attended by personnel trained to give women the necessary care during pregnancy, labor, and postpartum; to conduct deliveries on their own; and to care for newborns. • **Maternal mortality ratio** is the number of women who die from pregnancy-related causes while pregnant or within 42 days of pregnancy termination per 100,000 live births. • **Lifetime risk of maternal death** is the probability (1 in the number of women likely to die due to a maternal cause) that a 15-year-old girl will eventually die due to a maternal cause, if throughout her lifetime she experiences the maternal death risk and overall fertility and mortality rates of the specified year for a given population.

Data on total fertility are from the United Nations Population Division's *World Population Prospects: The 2010 Revision;* census reports and other statistical publications from national statistical offices; household surveys by national agencies, ICF International (for MEASURE DHS), and the U.S. Centers for Disease Control and Prevention; Eurostat's *Demographic Statistics;* and the U.S. Bureau of the Census International Data Base. Data on adolescent fertility are from *World Population Prospects: The 2010 Revision,* with annual data linearly interpolated by the World Bank's Development Data Group. Data on unmet need for contraception and contraceptive prevalence are from household surveys, including MEASURE DHS Demographic and Health Surveys by ICF International and Multiple Indicator Cluster Surveys by UNICEF. Data on pregnant women receiving prenatal care, births attended by skilled health staff, and national estimates of maternal mortality are from UNICEF's *State of the World's Children 2012* and Childinfo and MEASURE DHS Demographic and Health Surveys by ICF International. Modeled estimates of maternal mortality and lifetime risk of maternal mortality are from WHO, UNICEF, UNFPA, and the World Bank's *Trends in Maternal Mortality: 1990–2008* (2010).

2.20 | Nutrition and growth

	Prevalence of undernourishment		Prevalence of child malnutrition						Prevalence of overweight children	
					% of children under age 5				% of children under age 5	
			Underweight		Stunting		Wasting			
	% of population		Male	Female	Male	Female	Male	Female	Male	Female
	1990–92	2006–08	2005–10[a]	2005–10[a]	2005–10[a]	2005–10[a]	2005–10[a]	2005–10[a]	2005–10[a]	2005–10[a]
Afghanistan	..	..	..	..	..	..	..	..	..	..
Albania	<5	<5	6.6	6.0	22.8	23.4	11.5	7.3	23.3	23.4
Algeria	<5	<5	3.7	3.7	16.7	15.0	3.9	4.1	13.4	12.4
Angola	67	41	16.6	14.6	32.4	26.1	8.2	8.1	..	..
Argentina	<5	<5	2.4	2.2	8.2	8.1	1.1	1.4	10.2	9.5
Armenia	45	21	3.4	5.2	18.8	17.4	5.8	5.1	13.9	9.1
Australia	<5	<5	..	..	..	..	..	..	..	..
Austria	<5	<5	..	..	..	..	..	..	..	..
Azerbaijan	27	<5	8.7	8.0	28.5	24.9	7.8	5.7	14.9	12.7
Bahrain	..	..	..	..	..	..	..	..	..	..
Bangladesh	38	26	40.2	42.4	43.8	42.6	18.4	16.5	1.2	1.0
Belarus	<5	<5	1.5	1.0	4.7	4.2	2.8	1.6	11.3	8.1
Belgium	<5	<5	..	..	..	..	..	..	..	..
Benin	20	12	22.7	17.6	47.9	41.6	9.0	7.8	11.6	11.3
Bolivia	29	27	4.9	4.0	28.1	26.2	2.0	0.8	9.2	8.1
Bosnia and Herzegovina	<5	<5	2.2	1.0	12.8	10.7	3.8	4.3	27.4	23.9
Botswana	19	25	12.1	10.2	34.0	28.7	7.5	6.8	11.3	11.1
Brazil	11	6	2.2	2.1	8.3	5.8	1.8	1.4	6.9	7.7
Bulgaria	<5	<5	..	..	..	..	..	..	..	..
Burkina Faso	14	8	27.1	24.7	37.9	32.0	11.9	10.7	7.9	7.6
Burundi	44	62	..	..	..	..	..	..	..	..
Cambodia	38	25	28.8[b]	29.1[b]	42.3[b]	39.4[b]	11.2[b]	10.5[b]	1.9[b]	1.9[b]
Cameroon	33	22	18.9	14.3	39.1	33.7	8.2	6.4	9.8	9.5
Canada	<5	<5	..	..	..	..	..	..	..	..
Central African Republic	44	40	..	..	..	..	..	..	..	..
Chad	60	39	..	..	..	..	..	..	..	..
Chile	7	<5	0.6	0.5	2.2	1.8	0.3	0.2	9.8	9.1
China	18[c]	10[c]	3.5	3.3	9.9	8.9	2.4	2.1	7.5	5.6
Hong Kong SAR, China	..	..	..	..	..	..	..	..	..	..
Colombia	15	9	3.5	3.3	13.7	11.6	0.9	0.9	5.4	4.2
Congo, Dem. Rep.	..	..	30.4	26.1	48.5	43.3	15.5	12.5	6.5	7.2
Congo, Rep.	42	13	12.9	10.6	33.2	29.0	8.4	7.7	8.4	8.6
Costa Rica	<5	<5	0.6	1.8	4.8	6.6	0.6	1.5	8.3	7.9
Côte d'Ivoire	15	14	30.3	28.4	40.1	37.8	15.3	12.4	5.0	4.9
Croatia	<5	<5	..	..	..	..	..	..	..	..
Cuba	6	<5	..	..	..	..	..	..	..	..
Cyprus	<5	<5	..	..	..	..	..	..	..	..
Czech Republic	<5	<5	..	..	..	..	..	..	..	..
Denmark	<5	<5	..	..	..	..	..	..	..	..
Dominican Republic	28	24	3.2	3.7	11.2	8.9	2.5	2.1	9.0	7.5
Ecuador	23	15	..	..	..	..	..	..	..	..
Egypt, Arab Rep.	<5	<5	8.1	5.4	33.0	28.4	8.8	7.1	19.8	21.2
El Salvador	13	9	6.5	6.7	21.3	19.8	2.4	0.7	6.3	5.0
Eritrea	67	65	..	..	..	..	..	..	..	..
Estonia	<5	<5	..	..	..	..	..	..	..	..
Ethiopia	69	41	36.5	32.8	51.8	49.6	13.7	10.8	5.7	4.5
Finland	<5	<5	..	..	..	..	..	..	..	..
France	<5	<5	..	..	..	..	..	..	..	..
Gabon	6	<5	..	..	..	..	..	..	..	..
Gambia, The	14	19	16.7	15.0	28.6	26.6	8.1	6.6	2.9	2.5
Georgia	58	6	1.3	1.0	12.3	10.2	1.8	1.5	21.3	18.3
Germany	<5	<5	0.9	1.3	1.5	1.2	1.2	0.8	3.6	3.3
Ghana	28	5	15.7	12.9	30.5	26.7	9.7	7.7	5.8	5.9
Greece	<5	<5	..	..	..	..	..	..	..	..
Guatemala	15	22	13.9	12.1	48.7	47.3	1.1	1.1	5.3	4.6
Guinea	20	16	21.9	19.7	41.5	38.5	8.9	7.8	5.2	5.0
Guinea-Bissau	22	22	16.6	17.8	29.7	26.3	5.3	5.8	17.6	16.5
Haiti	63	57	20.4	17.4	33.2	26.5	10.2	10.4	4.4	3.5

	Prevalence of undernourishment		Prevalence of child malnutrition						Prevalence of overweight children	
			Underweight		% of children under age 5 Stunting		Wasting		% of children under age 5	
	% of population		Male	Female	Male	Female	Male	Female	Male	Female
	1990–92	2006–08	2005–10[a]	2005–10[a]	2005–10[a]	2005–10[a]	2005–10[a]	2005–10[a]	2005–10[a]	2005–10[a]
Honduras	19	12	8.9	8.3	31.5	28.3	1.6	1.1	6.3	5.2
Hungary	<5	<5	..	..	..	..	..	..	..	..
India	20	19	43.1	43.9	47.9	48.0	20.7	19.3	2.2	1.7
Indonesia	16	13	20.7	18.6	41.3	38.8	15.7	13.8	11.3	11.2
Iran, Islamic Rep.	<5	<5	..	..	..	..	..	..	..	..
Iraq	..	..	7.7	6.6	28.7	26.2	6.2	5.4	15.6	14.3
Ireland	<5	<5	..	..	..	..	..	..	..	..
Israel	<5	<5	..	..	..	..	..	..	..	..
Italy	<5	<5	..	..	..	..	..	..	..	..
Jamaica	11	5	1.9	2.6	3.0	4.4	1.9	2.2	..	..
Japan	<5	<5	..	..	..	..	..	..	..	..
Jordan	<5	<5	1.6	2.1	7.9	8.7	1.6	1.6	7.9	5.2
Kazakhstan	<5	<5	5.4	4.3	17.9	16.9	4.5	2.8	15.1	14.5
Kenya	33	33	17.3	15.5	37.3	33.1	8.2	5.8	4.7	5.3
Korea, Dem. Rep.	21	35	18.8	18.8	32.4	32.4	5.0	5.3	0.0	0.0
Korea, Rep.	<5	<5	..	..	..	..	..	..	..	..
Kosovo	..	..	..	..	..	..	..	..	..	..
Kuwait	20	5	2.0	1.5	4.2	3.4	1.5	2.1	10.0	8.0
Kyrgyz Republic	17	11	2.9	2.5	18.7	17.5	3.5	3.2	12.7	8.6
Lao PDR	31	22	32.5	30.6	48.3	46.8	7.8	6.8	1.5	1.0
Latvia	<5	<5	..	..	..	..	..	..	..	..
Lebanon	<5	<5	..	..	..	..	..	..	..	..
Lesotho	15	14	16.0	11.1	43.1	35.0	4.2	3.5	7.7	6.9
Liberia	30	32	21.9	18.7	41.9	36.7	7.9	7.8	4.9	3.5
Libya	<5	<5	6.3	4.8	22.2	19.6	6.8	6.1	23.2	21.6
Lithuania	<5	<5	..	..	..	..	..	..	..	..
Macedonia, FYR	<5	<5	1.7	1.9	13.5	9.2	2.4	4.5	16.6	15.8
Madagascar	21	25	..	..	51.6	46.7	..	..	..	..
Malawi	43	27	15.2	12.6	51.8	44.1	4.4	3.8	10.3	8.2
Malaysia	<5	<5	13.2	12.7	17.2	17.2	..	..	..	..
Mali	27	12	29.7	26.0	40.7	36.2	16.2	14.3	4.9	4.6
Mauritania	12	8	17.8	13.9	25.8	20.0	9.4	6.8	1.3	0.6
Mauritius	7	5	..	..	..	..	..	..	..	..
Mexico	<5	<5	4.3	2.6	16.0	15.0	2.5	1.5	8.4	6.7
Moldova	<5	<5	3.0	3.4	11.0	11.5	6.0	5.6	8.9	9.3
Mongolia	28	27	5.3	5.3	29.2	25.6	2.6	2.8	15.6	12.6
Morocco	6	<5	..	..	..	..	..	..	..	..
Mozambique	59	38	20.6	16.0	46.8	40.7	4.9	3.5	4.1	3.2
Myanmar	..	..	..	..	..	..	..	..	..	..
Namibia	32	18	18.5	16.5	32.0	27.1	7.3	7.8	4.9	4.4
Nepal	21	17	37.7	39.8	49.1	49.6	13.0	12.4	0.6	0.6
Netherlands	<5	<5	..	..	..	..	..	..	..	..
New Zealand	<5	<5	..	..	..	..	..	..	..	..
Nicaragua	50	19	5.6	5.9	24.0	21.9	1.5	1.4	6.7	5.6
Niger	37	16	42.1	37.5	56.8	52.6	13.8	10.9	3.6	3.5
Nigeria	16	6	28.6	24.8	43.1	38.8	14.8	14.0	10.3	10.7
Norway	<5	<5	..	..	..	..	..	..	..	..
Oman	..	..	8.9	8.3	11.3	8.5	8.1	6.0	1.5	2.0
Pakistan	25	25	..	..	..	..	..	..	..	..
Panama	18	15	..	..	..	..	..	..	..	..
Papua New Guinea	..	..	21.0	14.6	47.4	39.6	4.8	4.0	4.2	2.5
Paraguay	16	10	..	..	..	..	..	..	..	..
Peru	27	16	4.5	4.5	30.5	25.9	0.9	0.8	9.8	9.8
Philippines	24	13	20.9	20.6	33.5	31.1	7.4	6.4	3.6	2.9
Poland	<5	<5	..	..	..	..	..	..	..	..
Portugal	<5	<5	..	..	..	..	..	..	..	..
Puerto Rico	..	..	..	..	..	..	..	..	..	..
Qatar	..	..	..	..	..	..	..	..	..	..

	Prevalence of undernourishment		Prevalence of child malnutrition						Prevalence of overweight children	
			Underweight		% of children under age 5 Stunting		Wasting		% of children under age 5	
	% of population		Male	Female	Male	Female	Male	Female	Male	Female
	1990–92	2006–08	2005–10[a]	2005–10[a]	2005–10[a]	2005–10[a]	2005–10[a]	2005–10[a]	2005–10[a]	2005–10[a]
Romania	<5	<5	..	..	..	..	..	1.8	..	..
Russian Federation	<5	<5	..	..	..	..	..	..	..	..
Rwanda	44	32	18.9	17.2	53.1	50.3	5.0	4.7	7.2	6.3
Saudi Arabia	<5	<5	6.1	4.5	10.8	7.8	12.7	10.8	6.3	6.0
Senegal	22	19	14.4	14.6	21.3	18.8	8.8	8.5	3.0	1.8
Serbia	<5[d]	<5[d]	2.2	1.3	8.2	8.0	4.8	4.2	20.4	18.2
Sierra Leone	45	35	24.2	18.5	39.5	35.4	10.4	10.6	10.3	9.9
Singapore	..	..								
Slovak Republic	<5	<5	..	..	..	..	..	..	..	..
Slovenia	<5	<5	..	..	..	..	..	..	..	..
Somalia	..	..	34.2	31.3	42.7	41.3	14.4	11.9	4.9	4.5
South Africa	<5	<5	..	..	..	..	..	..	..	..
South Sudan	..	..	..	..	..	..	..	..	..	..
Spain	<5	<5	..	..	..	..	..	..	..	..
Sri Lanka	28	20	21.6	21.6	19.8	18.7	12.1	11.5	0.7	1.0
Sudan	39	22	33.4	30.0	39.8	35.8	21.9	20.1	5.1	5.5
Swaziland	12	19	6.3	5.9	33.0	26.1	3.5	2.4	11.8	10.9
Sweden	<5	<5	..	..	..	..	..	..	..	..
Switzerland	<5	<5	..	..	..	..	..	..	..	..
Syrian Arab Republic	<5	<5	11.5	8.7	28.4	26.5	12.5	10.5	17.8	18.1
Tajikistan	34	26	15.9	14.0	41.1	37.2	6.8	6.7	7.2	6.2
Tanzania	29	34	17.8	14.6	45.9	39.2	5.8	4.0	6.0	5.0
Thailand	26	16	6.9	7.1	16.5	15.0	4.6	4.8	8.8	7.2
Timor-Leste	39	31	46.8	43.7	59.8	55.6	20.4	17.4	6.0	5.7
Togo	43	30	20.5	20.5	28.4	25.2	6.1	5.9	4.2	5.1
Trinidad and Tobago	11	11	..	..	..	..	..	..	..	..
Tunisia	<5	<5	3.7	2.9	9.9	8.0	3.6	3.3	8.5	9.2
Turkey	<5	<5	..	..	..	..	..	..	..	..
Turkmenistan	9	7	..	..	..	..	..	..	..	..
Uganda	19	22	18.2	14.6	41.2	36.1	7.7	4.9	5.0	4.7
Ukraine	<5	<5	..	..	..	..	..	..	..	..
United Arab Emirates	<5	<5	..	..	..	..	..	..	..	..
United Kingdom	<5	<5	..	..	..	..	..	..	..	..
United States	<5	<5	..	..	..	..	..	..	..	..
Uruguay	5	<5	..	..	..	..	..	..	..	..
Uzbekistan	5	11	4.6	4.3	19.5	19.7	5.3	3.7	13.1	12.5
Venezuela, RB	10	7	..	..	..	..	..	..	..	..
Vietnam	31	11	20.5	19.9	31.9	29.0	10.2	9.1	3.4	2.5
West Bank and Gaza	10	21	2.2	2.3	12.3	11.2	1.7	1.8	13.4	9.4
Yemen, Rep.	30	30	..	..	..	..	..	..	..	..
Zambia	35	44	16.9	13.0	48.8	42.9	6.0	5.2	8.6	8.2
Zimbabwe	40	30	15.1	12.9	38.6	33.1	7.6	6.9	9.5	8.7
World	**16 w**	**13 w**								
Low income	38	29								
Middle income	17	12								
Lower middle income	20	17								
Upper middle income	14	9								
Low & middle income	19	14								
East Asia & Pacific	19	11								
Europe & Central Asia	7	6								
Latin America & Carib.	12	9								
Middle East & N. Africa	7	7								
South Asia	22	20								
Sub-Saharan Africa	32	22								
High income	<5	<5								
Euro area	<5	<5								

a. Data are for the most recent year available. b. Data are for 2011. c. Includes Hong Kong SAR, China; Macao SAR, China; and Taiwan, China. d. Includes Montenegro.

About the data

Good nutrition is the cornerstone for survival, health and development. Well nourished children perform better in school, grow into healthy adults, and in turn give their children a better start in life. Well nourished women face fewer risks during pregnancy and childbirth, and their children set off on firmer developmental paths, both physically and mentally (United Nations Children's Fund [UNICEF], www. childinfo.org).

Data on undernourishment are from the Food and Agriculture Organization (FAO) of the United Nations and measure food deprivation based on average food available for human consumption per person, the level of inequality in access to food, and the minimum calories required for an average person.

From a policy and program standpoint, however, this measure has its limits. First, food insecurity exists even where food availability is not a problem because of inadequate access of poor households to food. Second, food insecurity is an individual or household phenomenon, and the average food available to each person, even corrected for possible effects of low income, is not a good predictor of food insecurity among the population. And third, nutrition security is determined not only by food security but also by the quality of care of mothers and children and the quality of the household's health environment (Smith and Haddad 2000).

Undernourished children have lower resistance to infection and are more likely to die from common childhood ailments such as diarrheal diseases and respiratory infections. Frequent illness saps the nutritional status of those who survive, locking them into a vicious cycle of recurring sickness and faltering growth (UNICEF, www.childinfo.org). Estimates of child malnutrition, based on prevalence of underweight and stunting, are from national survey data. The proportion of underweight children is the most common malnutrition indicator. Being even mildly underweight increases the risk of death and inhibits cognitive development in children. And it perpetuates the problem across generations, as malnourished women are more likely to have low-birthweight babies. Stunting, or being below median height for age, is often used as a proxy for multifaceted deprivation and as an indicator of long-term changes in malnutrition.

Estimates of overweight children are also from national survey data. Once considered only a high-income economy problem, overweight children have become a growing concern in developing countries. Research shows an association between childhood obesity and a high prevalence of diabetes, respiratory disease, high blood pressure, and psychosocial and orthopedic disorders (de Onis and Blössner 2003). Childhood obesity is associated with a higher chance of obesity, premature death, and disability in adulthood. In addition to increased future risks, obese children experience breathing difficulties and increased risk of fractures, hypertension, early markers of cardiovascular disease, insulin resistance, and psychological effects. Children in low- and middle-income countries are more vulnerable to inadequate nutrition before birth and in infancy and early childhood. Many of these children are exposed to high-fat, high-sugar, high-salt, calorie-dense, micronutrient-poor foods, which tend to be lower in cost than more nutritious foods. These dietary patterns, in conjunction with low levels of physical activity, result in sharp increases in childhood obesity, while undernutrition continues (World Health Organization [WHO]).

New international growth reference standards for infants and young children were released in 2006 by the WHO to monitor children's nutritional status. Differences in growth to age 5 are influenced more by nutrition, feeding practices, environment, and healthcare than by genetics or ethnicity. The previously reported data were based on the U.S. National Center for Health Statistics–WHO growth reference. Because of the change in standards, the data in this edition should not be compared with data in editions prior to 2008.

For indicators from household surveys, the year in the table refers to the survey year. For more information, consult the original sources.

Definitions

• **Prevalence of undernourishment** is the percentage of the population whose dietary energy consumption is continuously below a minimum requirement for maintaining a healthy life and carrying out light physical activity with an acceptable minimum weight for height. • **Prevalence of child malnutrition** is the percentage of children under age 5 whose weight for age (underweight) or height for age (stunting) is more than two standard deviations below the median for the international reference population ages 0–59 months. Height is measured by recumbent length for children up to two years old and by stature while standing for older children. Data are based on the WHO child growth standards released in 2006. • **Prevalence of overweight children** is the percentage of children under age 5 whose weight for height is more than two standard deviations above the median for the international reference population of the corresponding age as established by the WHO child growth standards released in 2006.

Data sources

Data on undernourishment are from the FAO's *The State of Food Insecurity in the World*. Data on malnutrition and overweight children are from the WHO's Global Database on Child Growth and Malnutrition (www.who.int/nutgrowthdb).

	Low-birthweight babies	Exclusive breastfeeding	Consumption of iodized salt	Vitamin A supplementation	Prevalence of anemia	
					%	
	% of births 2005–10[a]	% of children under 6 months 2005–10[a]	% of households 2005–10[a]	% of children 6–59 months 2010	Children under age 5 2005–10[a]	Pregnant women 2005–10[a]
Afghanistan	..	83	..	96	..	61
Albania	7	39	76	..	31	34
Algeria	6	7	61	..	43	43
Angola	..	..	45	28	..	57
Argentina	7	..	..	..	17	31
Armenia	7	35	97	..	37	..
Australia	..	..	..	..	8	12
Austria	..	..	..	..	11	15
Azerbaijan	10	12	54	89[b]	..	..
Bahrain	..	..	..	..	25	28
Bangladesh	22	43	84	100	..	..
Belarus	4	9	94	..	27	26
Belgium	..	..	..	..	9	13
Benin	15	43	67	100	78	75
Bolivia	6	60	89	24	..	..
Bosnia and Herzegovina	5	18	62	..	27	35
Botswana	13	20	..	91	..	21
Brazil	8	40	96	..	55	29
Bulgaria	9	..	100	..	27	30
Burkina Faso	16	16	34	100	..	..
Burundi	11	69	98	73	56	47
Cambodia	8	74	83	95	55	44
Cameroon	11	21	49	89	..	..
Canada	..	..	..	..	8	12
Central African Republic	13	23	62	0	..	..
Chad	..	3	..	68	71	60
Chile	6	85	..	..	24	28
China	3	28	97	..	..	..
Hong Kong SAR, China	..	..	..	..	..	..
Colombia	6	43	..	..	28	31
Congo, Dem. Rep.	10	37	59	83	71	67
Congo, Rep.	13	19	82	84	66	55
Costa Rica	7	15	..	..	..	..
Côte d'Ivoire	17	4	..	100	69	55
Croatia	5	98	88	..	23	28
Cuba	5	26	88	..	27	39
Cyprus	..	..	..	..	19	25
Czech Republic	..	..	..	..	18	22
Denmark	..	..	..	..	9	12
Dominican Republic	11	9	19	..	35	40
Ecuador	8	..	..	..	38	38
Egypt, Arab Rep.	13	53	79	68[b]	49	34
El Salvador	..	31	..	..	..	..
Eritrea	..	..	..	44	70	55
Estonia	..	..	..	..	23	23
Ethiopia	20	49	20	84	54	31
Finland	..	..	..	..	11	15
France	..	..	..	..	8	11
Gabon	..	..	..	0	44	46
Gambia, The	11	36	21	100	..	..
Georgia	5	11	100	..	41	42
Germany	..	..	..	..	8	12
Ghana	13	63	32	93	..	..
Greece	..	..	..	..	12	19
Guatemala	11	50	76	36	..	..
Guinea	12	48	41	97	76	..
Guinea-Bissau	11	38	12	100	75	58
Haiti	25	41	3	21	..	50

	Low-birthweight babies	Exclusive breastfeeding	Consumption of iodized salt	Vitamin A supplementation	Prevalence of anemia	
					%	
	% of births 2005–10[a]	% of children under 6 months 2005–10[a]	% of households 2005–10[a]	% of children 6–59 months 2010	Children under age 5 2005–10[a]	Pregnant women 2005–10[a]
Honduras	10	30	..	..	..	21
Hungary	..	..	..	..	19	21
India	28	46	51	34	74	50
Indonesia	11	15	62	80	44	44
Iran, Islamic Rep.	7	23	99	..	35	..
Iraq	15	25	28	..	56	38
Ireland	..	..	..	..	10	15
Israel	..	..	..	..	12	17
Italy	..	..	..	..	11	15
Jamaica	14	15	..	..	..	..
Japan	..	..	..	..	11	15
Jordan	13	22	..	..	..	..
Kazakhstan	6	17	92	..	..	26
Kenya	8	32	98	62	..	..
Korea, Dem. Rep.	6	..	25	99	..	..
Korea, Rep.	..	..	..	..	..	23
Kosovo	..	..	..	..	..	..
Kuwait	..	..	..	..	..	31
Kyrgyz Republic	5	32	76	97	..	34
Lao PDR	11	26	84	83	..	56
Latvia	..	..	..	..	27	25
Lebanon	..	..	..	..	..	32
Lesotho	..	54	84	..	49	25
Liberia	14	34	..	97	..	..
Libya	..	..	..	..	34	34
Lithuania	..	..	..	..	24	24
Macedonia, FYR	6	16	94	..	..	32
Madagascar	16	51	53	95	..	..
Malawi	13	72	50	96	73	47
Malaysia	11	..	18	..	32	..
Mali	19	38	79	99	..	..
Mauritania	34	46	23	97	68	53
Mauritius	..	..	..	..	..	..
Mexico	7	..	..	..	24	21
Moldova	6	46	60	..	41	36
Mongolia	5	57	83	61	..	37
Morocco	..	..	21	..	..	..
Mozambique	16	37	25	100	..	52
Myanmar	9	24	93	94	63	50
Namibia	16	24	..	13	41	31
Nepal	21	53	..	91	48	42
Netherlands	..	..	..	..	9	13
New Zealand	..	..	..	..	11	18
Nicaragua	9	31	..	7	20	..
Niger	27	27	32	98	84	61
Nigeria	12	13	..	91	..	..
Norway	..	..	..	..	6	9
Oman	12	..	..	..	..	..
Pakistan	32	37	..	87	..	..
Panama	..	..	..	..	..	..
Papua New Guinea	10	56	92	14	60	55
Paraguay	6	24	94	..	30	39
Peru	8	68	..	..	..	..
Philippines	21	34	81	91	21	43
Poland	..	..	..	..	23	25
Portugal	..	..	..	..	13	17
Puerto Rico	..	..	..	..	..	..
Qatar	..	..	..	..	..	29

2.21 Nutrition intake and supplements

	Low-birthweight babies	Exclusive breastfeeding	Consumption of iodized salt	Vitamin A supplementation	Prevalence of anemia	
					%	
	% of births 2005–10[a]	% of children under 6 months 2005–10[a]	% of households 2005–10[a]	% of children 6–59 months 2010	Children under age 5 2005–10[a]	Pregnant women 2005–10[a]
Romania	..	..	..	..	40	30
Russian Federation	6	..	..	..	27	21
Rwanda	6	85	88	92	56	..
Saudi Arabia	..	..	..	..	33	32
Senegal	19	34	41	97	83	58
Serbia	6	15	32	..	..	..
Sierra Leone	14	11	58	100	83	60
Singapore	..	..	..	..	19	24
Slovak Republic	..	..	..	..	23	25
Slovenia	..	..	..	..	14	19
Somalia	11	9	1	62	..	..
South Africa	..	..	..	39	..	22
South Sudan	..	..	..	..	..	..
Spain	..	..	..	..	13	18
Sri Lanka	17	76	92	85	..	..
Sudan	..	34	11	82	85	58
Swaziland	9	44	52	38	47	24
Sweden	..	..	..	..	9	13
Switzerland	..	..	..	..	6	..
Syrian Arab Republic	10	43	79	33[b]	41	39
Tajikistan	10	25	62	95	..	45
Tanzania	10	50	59	99	72	58
Thailand	7	15	47	..	..	..
Timor-Leste	..	52	60	48	..	..
Togo	11	63	32	100	52	50
Trinidad and Tobago	19	13	28	..	30	30
Tunisia	5	6	..	..	..	..
Turkey	11	42	69	..	33	40
Turkmenistan	4	11	87	..	..	30
Uganda	14	60	96	64	73	64
Ukraine	4	18	18	..	..	27
United Arab Emirates	6	..	..	..	28	28
United Kingdom	..	..	..	..	..	15
United States	..	..	..	..	..	6
Uruguay	9	57	..	..	19	27
Uzbekistan	5	26	53	94	..	..
Venezuela, RB	8	..	..	..	33	40
Vietnam	5	17	93	95[b]	..	..
West Bank and Gaza	7	27	86	..	..	..
Yemen, Rep.	..	..	..	..	68	58
Zambia	11	61	..	92	..	..
Zimbabwe	11	32[c]	91	49	58	47
World	**15 w**	**37 w**	**70 w**	**.. w**	**.. w**	**.. w**
Low income	15	44	62	88	..	..
Middle income	15	35	71	..	..	..
Lower middle income	21	37	54	56	65	48
Upper middle income	5	30	91	..	..	..
Low & middle income	15	37	70	..	..	..
East Asia & Pacific	6	26	86	..	..	..
Europe & Central Asia	7	..	..	..	30	30
Latin America & Carib.	8	..	..	..	36	..
Middle East & N. Africa	11	34	69	..	48	..
South Asia	27	47	55	50	74	50
Sub-Saharan Africa	13	35	50	86	..	..
High income	..	..	..	..	..	13
Euro area	..	..	..	..	10	14

a. Data are for the most recent year available. b. Country's vitamin A supplementation programs do not target children all the way up to 59 months of age. c. Data are for 2011.

Low birthweight, which is associated with maternal malnutrition, raises the risk of infant mortality and stunts growth in infancy and childhood. There is also emerging evidence that low-birthweight babies are more prone to noncommunicable diseases such as diabetes and cardiovascular diseases. Low birthweight can arise as a result of a baby being born too soon or too small for gestational age. Babies born prematurely who are also small for their gestational age have the worst prognosis. In low- and middle-income countries low birthweight stems primarily from poor maternal health and nutrition. Three factors have the most impact: poor maternal nutritional status before conception, mother's short stature (due mostly to undernutrition and infections during childhood), and poor nutrition during pregnancy (United Nations Children's Fund [UNICEF], www.childinfo.org). Estimates of low-birthweight infants are drawn mostly from hospital records and household surveys. Many births in developing countries take place at home and are seldom recorded. A hospital birth may indicate higher income and therefore better nutrition, or it could indicate a higher risk birth. Caution should therefore be used in interpreting the data.

For optimal infant and young child feeding, mothers initiate breastfeeding within one hour of birth, breastfeed exclusively for the first six months, and continue to breastfeed for two years or more while providing nutritionally adequate, safe, and age-appropriate solid, semisolid, and soft foods (UNICEF, www.childinfo.org). Optimal breastfeeding can save an estimated 1.4 million children a year. Breast milk alone contains all the nutrients, antibodies, hormones, and antioxidants an infant needs to thrive. It protects babies from diarrhea and acute respiratory infections, stimulates their immune systems and response to vaccination, and may confer cognitive benefits. The data on breastfeeding are derived from household surveys.

Iodine deficiency is the single most important cause of preventable mental retardation, it contributes significantly to the risk of stillbirth and miscarriage, and it increases infant mortality. A diet low in iodine is the main cause of iodine deficiency. It usually occurs among populations living in areas where the soil has been depleted of iodine. If soil is deficient in iodine, so are the plants grown in it, including the grains and vegetables that people and animals consume. There are almost no countries in the world where iodine deficiency has not been a public health problem. Every year about 40 million

newborns in low- and middle-income countries remain unprotected from the lifelong consequences of brain damage associated with iodine deficiency disorders, which affect a child's ability to learn and to earn a living as an adult, thereby preventing children, communities, and countries from fulfilling their potential (UNICEF, www.childinfo.org). Widely used and inexpensive, iodized salt is the best source of iodine, and a global campaign to iodize edible salt is significantly reducing the risks. The data on consumption of iodized salt are derived from household surveys.

Vitamin A is essential for immune system functioning. Vitamin A deficiency, a leading cause of blindness, also causes a greater risk of dying from a range of childhood ailments such as measles, malaria, and diarrhea. In low- and middle-income countries, where vitamin A is consumed largely in fruits and vegetables, daily per capita intake is often insufficient to meet dietary requirements. Providing young children with two high-dose vitamin A capsules a year is a safe, cost-effective, efficient strategy for eliminating vitamin A deficiency and improving child survival. Giving vitamin A to new breastfeeding mothers helps protect their children during the first months of life. Food fortification with vitamin A is being introduced in many developing countries.

Anemia is a condition in which the number of red blood cells or their oxygen-carrying capacity is insufficient to meet physiologic needs, which vary by age, sex, altitude, smoking status, and pregnancy status. In its severe form it is associated with fatigue, weakness, dizziness, and drowsiness (World Health Organization [WHO], www.who.int/topics/anaemia/). Children under age 5 and pregnant women have the highest risk for anemia. Data on anemia are compiled by the WHO based mainly on nationally representative surveys between 1993 and 2005, which measured hemoglobin in the blood. WHO's hemoglobin thresholds were then used to determine anemia status based on age, sex, and physiological status. Data should be used with caution because surveys differ in quality, coverage, age group interviewed, and treatment of missing values across countries and over time.

For indicators from household surveys, the year in the table refers to the survey year. For more information, consult the original sources.

• **Low-birthweight babies** are newborns weighing less than 2.5 kilograms within the first hours of life, before significant postnatal weight loss has occurred. • **Exclusive breastfeeding** is the percentage of children less than six months old who were fed breast milk alone (no other liquids) in the past 24 hours. • **Consumption of iodized salt** is the percentage of households that use edible salt fortified with iodine. • **Vitamin A supplementation** is the percentage of children ages 6–59 months old who received at least two doses of vitamin A in the previous year. • **Prevalence of anemia, children under age 5,** is the percentage of children under age 5 whose hemoglobin level is less than 110 grams per liter at sea level. • **Prevalence of anemia, pregnant women,** is the percentage of pregnant women whose hemoglobin level is less than 110 grams per liter at sea level.

Data sources

Data on low-birthweight babies, breastfeeding, consumption of iodized salt, and vitamin A supplementation are from the United Nations Children's Fund's *The State of the World's Children 2012* and Childinfo. Data on anemia are from the WHO's *Worldwide Prevalence of Anemia 1993–2005* (2008c) and Integrated WHO Nutrition Global Databases.

	Prevalence of smoking		Incidence of tuberculosis	Prevalence of diabetes	Prevalence of HIV[a]					Antiretroviral therapy coverage	Cause of death		
	% of adults		per 100,000 people	% of population ages 20–79	Total % of population ages 15–49		Female % of total population with HIV	Youth % of population ages 15–24		% of population with advanced HIV infection	% of population		
											Communicable diseases and maternal, prenatal, and nutrition conditions	Non-communicable diseases	Injuries
	Male	Female						Male	Female				
	2009	2009	2010	2011	1990	2009	2009	2009	2009	2005–10[b]	2005–10[b]	2005–10[b]	2005–10[b]
Afghanistan	..	..	189	7.8	..	..	..	..	..	..	63	29	8
Albania	60	19	14	2.9							5	89	5
Algeria	..	..	90	7.0	<0.1	0.1	30	0.1	<0.1	25	30	63	8
Angola	..	..	304	3.0	0.5	2.0	60	0.6	1.6	24	69	25	7
Argentina	32	22	27	5.7	0.3	0.5	32	0.3	0.2	70	14	80	6
Armenia	51	2	73	8.7	<0.1	0.1	<43	<0.1	<0.1	24	6	90	4
Australia	22	19	6	6.8	0.1	0.1	31	0.1	0.1	..	4	90	6
Austria	47	45	5	6.8	<0.1	0.3	29	0.3	0.2	..	3	91	6
Azerbaijan	41	..	110	2.8	<0.1	0.1	60	<0.1	0.1	21	11	85	4
Bahrain	34	8	23	19.9	..	..	..	..	..	..	10	79	11
Bangladesh	46	2	225	10.7	<0.1	<0.1	30	<0.1	<0.1	23	38	52	10
Belarus	49	9	70	8.2	<0.1	0.3	50	<0.1	0.1	29	2	87	11
Belgium	30	22	9	4.9	<0.1	0.2	31	<0.1	<0.1	..	8	86	6
Benin	15	1	94	2.0	0.2	1.2	58	0.3	0.7	53	60	33	6
Bolivia	42	18	135	6.8	0.2	0.2	32	0.1	0.1	19	35	57	8
Bosnia and Herzegovina	47	36	50	7.7	..	..	..	..	..	..	2	95	4
Botswana	..	..	503	11.1	3.5	24.8	57	5.2	11.8	83	60	31	9
Brazil	22	13	43	10.4	..	..	..	..	..	60	14	74	12
Bulgaria	48	27	40	6.9	<0.1	0.1	29	<0.1	<0.1	23	3	94	4
Burkina Faso	18	8	55	3.0	3.9	1.2	60	0.5	0.8	46	73	21	7
Burundi	..	..	129	2.8	3.9	3.3	60	1.0	2.1	19	67	26	7
Cambodia	49[c]	5[c]	437	2.9	0.5	0.5	63	0.1	0.1	94	47	46	7
Cameroon	14	2	177	6.2	0.6	5.3	58	1.6	3.9	28	63	31	6
Canada	24	17	5	8.7	0.1	0.2	21	0.1	0.1	..	5	89	6
Central African Republic	..	..	319	3.2	3.1	4.7	61	1.0	2.2	19	65	27	7
Chad	22	3	276	3.9	1.1	3.4	59	1.0	2.5	36	73	21	5
Chile	38	33	19	9.8	<0.1	0.4	31	0.2	0.1	63	9	83	8
China	51	2	78	9.0	..	0.1[d]	..	..	..	..	7	83	10
Hong Kong SAR, China	..	..	80	7.8	..	..	..	..	..	..	..	..	..
Colombia	..	..	34	10.0	0.2	0.5	33	0.2	0.1	17	13	66	21
Congo, Dem. Rep.	10	2	327	3.2	..	..	..	..	..	..	72	21	7
Congo, Rep.	10	1	372	5.6	5.2	3.4	59	1.2	2.6	23	58	33	9
Costa Rica	24	8	13	9.9	<0.1	0.3	29	0.2	0.1	68	7	81	13
Côte d'Ivoire	17	4	139	5.0	2.4	3.4	58	0.7	1.5	28	58	33	9
Croatia	36	30	21	5.3	<0.1	<0.1	<33	<0.1	<0.1	80	3	92	6
Cuba	..	..	9	9.8	<0.1	0.1	31	0.1	0.1	<95	8	84	8
Cyprus	..	..	4	9.5	..	..	..	..	..	..	4	90	6
Czech Republic	43	31	7	5.5	<0.1	<0.1	<42	<0.1	<0.1	..	4	90	6
Denmark	30	28	6	5.7	<0.1	0.2	27	0.1	0.1	..	6	90	5
Dominican Republic	17	13	67	8.3	0.4	0.9	59	0.3	0.7	47	22	68	10
Ecuador	..	..	65	6.8	0.3	0.4	31	0.2	0.2	30	20	65	15
Egypt, Arab Rep.	40	1	18	16.9	<0.1	<0.1	23	<0.1	<0.1	11	12	82	6
El Salvador	..	..	28	9.7	0.1	0.8	34	0.4	0.3	53	17	67	16
Eritrea	10	2	100	3.6	0.3	0.8	60	0.2	0.4	37	49	40	12
Estonia	46	23	25	7.2	<0.1	1.2	31	0.3	0.2	..	2	90	8
Ethiopia	8	1	261	3.4	..	..	..	..	..	..	57	34	9
Finland	28	22	7	6.0	<0.1	0.1	<36	0.1	<0.1	..	2	89	9
France	36	27	9	5.6	0.3	0.4	32	0.2	0.1	..	6	87	7
Gabon	19	3	553	10.6	0.9	5.2	58	1.4	3.5	47	52	41	7
Gambia, The	31	3	273	2.0	0.1	2.0	58	0.9	2.4	18	60	34	6
Georgia	57	6	107	2.8	<0.1	0.1	43	<0.1	<0.1	65	5	91	4
Germany	33	25	5	5.5	0.1	0.1	18	0.1	<0.1	..	5	92	4
Ghana	11	3	86	5.1	0.3	1.8	59	0.5	1.3	24	53	39	8
Greece	63	41	5	5.3	0.1	0.1	31	0.1	0.1	..	6	91	4
Guatemala	22	4	62	9.5	0.1	0.8	33	0.5	0.3	44	35	47	18
Guinea	25	2	334	4.4	1.1	1.3	59	0.4	0.9	40	60	32	7
Guinea-Bissau	..	..	233	3.1	0.3	2.5	60	0.8	2.0	30	67	28	6
Haiti	..	..	230	6.8	1.3	1.9	60	0.6	1.3	43	54	41	5

Health risk factors and future challenges

	Prevalence of smoking		Incidence of tuberculosis	Prevalence of diabetes	Prevalence of HIV[a]					Antiretroviral therapy coverage	Cause of death		
							Female % of total population with HIV	Youth % of population ages 15–24			% of population		
	% of adults		per 100,000 people	% of population ages 20–79	Total % of population ages 15–49					% of population with advanced HIV infection	Communicable diseases and maternal, prenatal, and nutrition conditions	Non-communicable diseases	Injuries
	Male	Female						Male	Female				
	2009	2009	2010	2011	1990	2009	2009	2009	2009	2005–10[b]	2005–10[b]	2005–10[b]	2005–10[b]
Honduras	..	3	51	6.8	1.1	0.8	32	0.3	0.2	33	23	69	8
Hungary	43	33	15	6.2	0.1	<0.1	<33	<0.1	<0.1	27	1	93	6
India	26	4	185	9.2	0.1	0.3	39	0.1	0.1	..	37	53	10
Indonesia	61	5	189	5.2	<0.1	0.2	30	0.1	<0.1	21	28	64	9
Iran, Islamic Rep.	26	2	17	11.3	<0.1	0.2	29	<0.1	<0.1	4	13	72	14
Iraq	31	4	64	9.3	..	..	..	..	..	..	24	44	31
Ireland	..	..	8	5.4	<0.1	0.2	29	0.1	0.1	..	7	87	6
Israel	29	13	5	7.6	<0.1	0.2	29	0.1	<0.1	..	8	87	5
Italy	33	19	5	5.3	0.3	0.3	33	<0.1	<0.1	..	3	92	4
Jamaica	..	..	7	16.0	2.1	1.7	33	1.0	0.7	46	21	68	11
Japan	42	12	21	7.9	<0.1	<0.1	34	<0.1	<0.1	..	14	80	6
Jordan	47	6	5	12.4	..	..	..	..	..	..	15	74	11
Kazakhstan	40	9	151	7.9	<0.1	0.1	60	0.1	0.2	27	8	78	14
Kenya	26	1	298	5.2	3.9	6.3	59	1.8	4.1	48	63	28	9
Korea, Dem. Rep.	..	..	345	8.6	..	..	..	..	..	0	29	65	6
Korea, Rep.	49	7	97	7.7	<0.1	<0.1	31	<0.1	<0.1	..	6	82	12
Kosovo	..	..	..	..	..	..	..	..	..	..	..	..	..
Kuwait	35	4	41	21.1	..	..	..	..	..	..	11	76	13
Kyrgyz Republic	45	2	159	6.5	<0.1	0.3	29	0.1	0.1	12	14	77	9
Lao PDR	51	4	90	3.3	<0.1	0.2	42	0.1	0.2	67	41	48	10
Latvia	50	22	39	8.1	<0.1	0.7	30	0.2	0.1	12	3	90	8
Lebanon	46	31	17	20.2	<0.1	0.1	31	0.1	<0.1	18	7	84	9
Lesotho	..	..	633	3.5	0.8	23.6	62	5.4	14.2	48	63	29	7
Liberia	14	..	293	3.4	0.3	1.5	61	0.3	0.7	14	68	28	4
Libya	47	1	40	14.2	..	..	..	..	..	..	12	78	11
Lithuania	50	22	69	8.0	<0.1	0.1	<33	<0.1	<0.1	27	3	86	11
Macedonia, FYR	..	..	21	7.9	..	..	..	..	..	..	2	95	3
Madagascar	..	..	266	4.8	0.2	0.2	31	0.1	0.1	2	52	42	6
Malawi	26	4	219	5.7	7.2	11.0	59	3.1	6.8	46	63	28	9
Malaysia	50	2	82	12.3	0.1	0.5	11	0.1	<0.1	23	24	67	9
Mali	28	2	68	2.0	0.4	1.0	62	0.2	0.5	50	75	20	5
Mauritania	29	4	337	4.4	0.2	0.7	31	0.4	0.3	25	60	32	8
Mauritius	31	2	22	15.1	<0.1	1.0	29	0.3	0.2	22	7	87	6
Mexico	24	8	16	15.9	0.4	0.3	27	0.2	0.1	54	12	78	10
Moldova	43	5	182	2.8	<0.1	0.4	42	0.1	0.1	17	5	87	8
Mongolia	48	6	224	7.2	<0.1	<0.1	<29	<0.1	<0.1	8	14	72	13
Morocco	33	2	91	7.0	<0.1	0.1	32	0.1	0.1	27	19	75	6
Mozambique	18	2	544	3.1	1.2	11.5	61	3.1	8.6	30	64	28	8
Myanmar	40	8	384	7.2	0.2	0.6	35	0.3	0.3	18	33	40	27
Namibia	30	9	603	8.0	1.6	13.1	59	2.3	5.8	76	51	38	12
Nepal	36	29	163	3.7	0.2	0.4	33	0.2	0.1	11	43	50	7
Netherlands	31	26	7	5.4	0.1	0.2	30	0.1	<0.1	..	7	89	4
New Zealand	27	24	8	8.8	0.1	0.1	<37	<0.1	<0.1	..	3	91	6
Nicaragua	..	..	42	11.2	<0.1	0.2	31	0.1	0.1	40	20	69	11
Niger	9	1	185	4.1	0.1	0.8	53	0.2	0.5	22	81	16	3
Nigeria	10	3	133	4.9	1.3	3.6	59	1.2	2.9	21	68	27	5
Norway	31	28	6	4.8	<0.1	0.1	30	<0.1	<0.1	..	7	87	6
Oman	12	1	13	10.8	<0.1	0.1	<33	<0.1	<0.1	<95	6	83	11
Pakistan	34	6	231	8.0	<0.1	0.1	29	0.1	<0.1	4	46	46	8
Panama	17	4	48	9.8	0.2	0.9	31	0.4	0.3	37	19	69	12
Papua New Guinea	58	31	303	7.7	<0.1	0.9	58	0.3	0.8	52	47	44	9
Paraguay	30	14	46	6.7	<0.1	0.3	31	0.2	0.1	37	20	69	12
Peru	..	9	106	6.1	0.4	0.4	25	0.2	0.1	37	30	60	10
Philippines	47	10	275	10.0	<0.1	<0.1	30	<0.1	<0.1	37	31	61	8
Poland	36	25	23	9.2	<0.1	0.1	31	<0.1	<0.1	22	4	89	7
Portugal	32	16	29	9.8	0.1	0.6	31	0.3	0.2	..	9	86	4
Puerto Rico	..	..	2	13.3	..	..	..	..	..	..	..	..	..
Qatar	..	..	38	20.2	<0.1	<0.1	<50	<0.1	<0.1	..	8	69	23

	Prevalence of smoking		Incidence of tuberculosis	Prevalence of diabetes	Prevalence of HIV[a]					Antiretroviral therapy coverage	Cause of death		
	% of adults		per 100,000 people	% of population ages 20–79	Total % of population ages 15–49		Female % of total population with HIV	Youth % of population ages 15–24 with HIV		% of population with advanced HIV infection	% of population		
											Communicable diseases and maternal, prenatal, and nutrition conditions	Non-communicable diseases	Injuries
	Male 2009	Female 2009	2010	2011	1990	2009	2009	Male 2009	Female 2009	2005–10[b]	2005–10[b]	2005–10[b]	2005–10[b]
Romania	46	24	116	7.9	<0.1	0.1	30	0.1	<0.1	81	4	91	5
Russian Federation	59	24	106	10.0	<0.1	1.0	49	0.2	0.3	..	5	82	12
Rwanda	..	..	106	3.2	5.2	2.9	61	1.3	1.9	88	63	29	8
Saudi Arabia	24	1	18	20.0	..	..	..	..	..	..	13	71	15
Senegal	16	1	288	3.3	0.2	0.9	59	0.3	0.7	51	65	30	5
Serbia	38	27	18	7.9	0.1	0.1	24	0.1	0.1	38	2	95	4
Sierra Leone	39	8	682	3.2	<0.1	1.6	60	0.6	1.5	18	77	18	5
Singapore	35	6	35	9.8	<0.1	0.1	30	<0.1	<0.1	..	16	79	5
Slovak Republic	39	19	8	5.9	<0.1	<0.1	<17	<0.1	<0.1	62	5	90	6
Slovenia	30	22	11	7.8	<0.1	<0.1	<29	<0.1	<0.1	..	4	87	8
Somalia	..	..	286	4.3	0.1	0.7	47	0.4	0.6	6	62	27	11
South Africa	24	8	981	7.1	0.7	17.8	62	4.5	13.6	37	67	29	5
South Sudan	..	..	..	..	..	..	..	..	..	..	..	..	..
Spain	36	27	16	6.5	0.4	0.4	24	0.2	0.1	..	5	91	4
Sri Lanka	27	1	66	7.6	<0.1	<0.1	<32	<0.1	<0.1	20	9	65	26
Sudan	24	2	119	8.7	0.1	1.1	58	0.5	1.3	5	43	44	13
Swaziland	16	2	1,287	3.1	2.3	25.9	58	6.5	15.6	59	62	28	11
Sweden	..	..	7	4.4	0.1	0.1	31	<0.1	<0.1	..	5	90	5
Switzerland	31	21	8	6.0	0.2	0.4	32	0.2	0.1	..	4	90	6
Syrian Arab Republic	42	..	20	10.2	..	..	..	..	..	..	13	77	10
Tajikistan	..	..	206	6.5	<0.1	0.2	30	<0.1	<0.1	11	37	59	4
Tanzania	21	3	177	2.8	4.8	5.6	59	1.7	3.9	30	66	27	8
Thailand	45	3	137	7.7	1.0	1.3	40	..	..	61	17	71	12
Timor-Leste	..	..	498	7.6	..	..	..	..	..	..	60	34	5
Togo	..	..	455	3.3	0.6	3.2	59	0.9	2.2	29	61	34	5
Trinidad and Tobago	27	11	19	13.1	0.2	1.5	33	1.0	0.7	..	12	78	10
Tunisia	58	5	25	9.7	<0.1	<0.1	<37	<0.1	<0.1	53	22	72	7
Turkey	47	15	28	8.1	<0.1	<0.1	30	<0.1	<0.1	62	9	85	6
Turkmenistan	..	..	66	2.8	..	..	..	..	..	..	19	73	8
Uganda	16	3	209	2.9	10.2	6.5	58	2.3	4.8	39	64	25	10
Ukraine	50	13	101	2.9	0.1	1.1	49	0.2	0.3	10	6	86	8
United Arab Emirates	19	2	3	19.2	..	..	..	..	..	..	13	67	21
United Kingdom	25	23	13	5.4	0.1	0.2	31	0.2	0.1	..	8	88	4
United States	33	25	4	9.6	0.5	0.6	25	0.3	0.2	..	6	87	7
Uruguay	31	22	21	5.9	0.1	0.5	32	0.3	0.2	49	8	87	6
Uzbekistan	22	3	128	6.7	<0.1	0.1	29	<0.1	<0.1	..	15	79	6
Venezuela, RB	..	..	33	10.5	..	..	..	..	..	..	13	66	21
Vietnam	48	2	199	3.2	<0.1	0.4	30	0.1	0.1	34	16	75	9
West Bank and Gaza	..	..	5	9.4	..	..	..	..	..	..	..	..	..
Yemen, Rep.	35	11	49	9.9	..	..	..	..	..	..	44	45	11
Zambia	24	4	462	4.8	12.7	13.5	57	4.2	8.9	64	64	27	9
Zimbabwe	30	4	633	9.9	10.1	14.3	60	3.3	6.9	34	75	21	4
World	**37 w**	**8 w**	**128 w**	**8.3 w**	**0.3 w**	**0.8 w**	**37 w**	**0.4 w**	**0.7 w**		**27 w**	**63 w**	**9 w**
Low income	28	4	264	5.9	1.8	2.6	46	0.9	1.9		58	33	9
Middle income	39	6	132	8.7	0.2	0.7	..	..	..		26	65	10
Lower middle income	32	4	174	8.0	0.3	0.7	38	0.2	0.5		38	53	9
Upper middle income	46	7	89	9.4	0.2	0.7	..	..	..		11	79	10
Low & middle income	38	5	150	8.4	0.3	0.9	39	..	..		31	59	10
East Asia & Pacific	52	3	123	8.3	0.1	0.2	..	..	..		13	76	10
Europe & Central Asia	50	18	90	7.7	0.1	0.6	42	0.1	0.2		6	84	9
Latin America & Carib.	25	13	43	10.5	0.4	0.5	..	..	..		16	72	12
Middle East & N. Africa	35	3	42	11.6	0.1	0.1	28	0.1	0.1		19	69	12
South Asia	29	4	192	9.0	0.1	0.3	37	0.1	0.1		39	51	10
Sub-Saharan Africa	16	3	271	4.6	2.4	5.5	58	1.5	3.8		65	28	7
High income	34	21	14	7.9	0.2	0.3	28	0.2	0.1		7	87	6
Euro area	35	25	..	5.8	0.2	0.3	27	0.1	0.1		5	90	5

a. See http://data.worldbank.org or the original source for uncertainty bands. b. Data are for the most recent year available. c. Data are for 2010. d. Includes Hong Kong SAR, China.

About the data

The limited availability of data on health status is a major constraint in assessing the health situation in developing countries. Surveillance data are lacking for many major public health concerns. Estimates of prevalence and incidence are available for some diseases but are often unreliable and incomplete. National health authorities differ widely in capacity and willingness to collect or report information. To compensate for this and improve reliability and international comparability, the World Health Organization (WHO) prepares estimates in accordance with epidemiological models and statistical standards.

Smoking is the most common form of tobacco use and the prevalence of smoking is therefore a good measure of the tobacco epidemic (Corrao and others 2000). Tobacco use causes heart and other vascular diseases and cancers of the lung and other organs. Given the long delay between starting to smoke and the onset of disease, the health impact of smoking will increase rapidly only in the next few decades. The data presented in the table are age-standardized rates for adults ages 15 and older from the WHO.

Tuberculosis is one of the main causes of adult deaths from a single infectious agent in developing countries. In developed countries tuberculosis has reemerged largely as a result of cases among immigrants. Since tuberculosis incidence cannot be directly measured, estimates are obtained by eliciting expert opinion or are derived from measurements of prevalence or mortality. These estimates include uncertainty intervals, which are not shown in the table but are available at http://data.worldbank.org and from the original source.

Diabetes, an important cause of ill health and a risk factor for other diseases in developed countries, is spreading rapidly in developing countries. Highest among the elderly, prevalence rates are rising among younger and productive populations in developing countries. Economic development has led to the spread of Western lifestyles and diet to developing countries, resulting in a substantial increase in diabetes. Without effective prevention and control programs, diabetes will likely continue to increase. Data are estimated based on sample surveys.

Adult HIV prevalence rates reflect the rate of HIV infection in each country's population. Low national prevalence rates can be misleading, however. They often disguise epidemics that are initially concentrated in certain localities or population groups and threaten to spill over into the wider population. In many developing countries most new infections occur in young adults, with young women especially vulnerable.

Data on HIV are from the Joint United Nations Programme on HIV/AIDS's (UNAIDS) *Global Report: UNAIDS Report on the Global AIDS Epidemic 2010.* Changes in procedures and assumptions for estimating the data and better coordination with countries have resulted in improved estimates of HIV and AIDS. For example, improved software was used to model the course of HIV epidemics and their impacts, making full use of information on HIV prevalence trends from surveillance data as well as survey data. The software explicitly includes the effect of antiretroviral therapy when calculating HIV incidence and models reduced infectivity among people receiving antiretroviral therapy, which is having a larger impact on HIV prevalence and allowing HIV-positive people to live longer. The software also allows for changes in urbanization over time—important because prevalence is higher in urban areas and because many countries have seen rapid urbanization over the past two decades. The estimates include plausible bounds, not shown in the table, which reflect the certainty associated with each of the estimates. The bounds are available at http://data.worldbank.org and from the original source.

Standard antiretroviral therapy consists of the use of at least three antiretroviral drugs to maximally suppress HIV and stop the progression of HIV disease. Antiretroviral therapy has led to huge reductions in death and suffering of people with advanced HIV infection. Data are collected through three international monitoring and reporting processes: country responses to the WHO; research by the Interagency Task Team on Prevention of HIV Infection in Women, Mothers and their Children; and country report to UNAIDS through the United Nations General Assembly Special Session Declaration of Commitment on HIV/AIDS.

Data on cause of death are compiled by the WHO, based mainly on data from national vital registry systems, as well as sample registration systems, population laboratories, and epidemiological analysis of specific conditions. Data are classified based on the International Statistical Classification of Diseases and Related Health Problems, 10th revision. Data have been carefully analyzed to take into account incomplete coverage of vital registration and the likely differences in cause of death patterns that would be expected in undercovered and often poorer subpopulations. Special attention has also been paid to misattribution or miscoding of causes of death in cardiovascular diseases, cancer, injuries, and general ill-defined categories. For further information, consult the original source.

For indicators from household surveys, the year in the table refers to the survey year. For more information, consult the original sources.

Definitions

• **Prevalence of smoking** is the percentage of the population ages 15 and older who smoke any tobacco products. It includes daily and nondaily smoking. Estimates are adjusted and age-standardized prevalence • **Incidence of tuberculosis** is the number of new and relapse cases of tuberculosis (all types) per 100,000 people. • **Prevalence of diabetes** is the percentage of people ages 20–79 who have type 1 or type 2 diabetes. • **Prevalence of HIV** is the percentage of people who are infected with HIV. Total and youth rates are percentages of the relevant age group. Female rate is as a percentage of the total population living with HIV. • **Antiretroviral therapy coverage** is the percentage of adults and children with advanced HIV infection currently receiving antiretroviral therapy according to nationally approved treatment protocols (or WHO/UNAIDS standards) among the estimated number of people with advanced HIV infection. • **Cause of death** is the share of all deaths due to the specified underlying cause. • **Communicable diseases and maternal, perinatal, and nutrition conditions** are infectious and parasitic diseases, respiratory infections, and nutritional deficiencies such as underweight and stunting. • **Noncommunicable diseases** are cancer, diabetes mellitus, cardiovascular diseases, digestive diseases, skin diseases, musculoskeletal diseases, and congenital anomalies. • **Injuries** include unintentional and intentional injuries.

Data sources

Data on smoking are from the WHO's *Report on the Global Tobacco Epidemic 2011.* Data on tuberculosis are from the WHO's *Global Tuberculosis Control Report 2011.* Data on diabetes are from the International Diabetes Federation's *Diabetes Atlas,* 5th edition. Data on HIV are from UNAIDS's *Global Report: UNAIDS Report on the Global AIDS Epidemic 2010.* Data on antiretroviral therapy coverage are from the WHO. Data on cause of death are from the WHO's Health Statistics and Health Information Systems database (www.who.int/healthinfo/global_burden_disease/estimates_country).

	Life expectancy at birth (years)		Neonatal mortality rate (per 1,000 live births)		Infant mortality rate (per 1,000 live births)		Under-five mortality rate (per 1,000 live births)		Child mortality rate per 1,000 Male 2005–10[a,b]	Female 2005–10[a,b]	Adult mortality rate per 1,000 Male 2006–10[a]	Female 2006–10[a]
	1990	2010	1990	2010	1990	2010	1990	2010				
Afghanistan	42	48	53	45	140	103	209	149	..	..	409	377
Albania	72	77	17	9	36	16	41	18	3	1	95	46
Algeria	67	73	29	18	55	31	68	36	..	..	126	102
Angola	41	51	51	41	144	98	243	161	..	..	386	337
Argentina	71	76	15	7	24	12	27	14	..	..	160	74
Armenia	68	74	26	11	46	18	55	20	8	3	162	79
Australia	77	82	5	3	8	4	9	5	..	..	82	47
Austria	76	80	4	2	8	4	9	4	..	..	99	50
Azerbaijan	65	71	31	19	74	39	93	46	9	5	181	74
Bahrain	72	75	6	4	15	9	17	10	..	..	95	73
Bangladesh	59	69	55	27	99	38	143	48	16	20	163	137
Belarus	71	70	7	3	14	4	17	6	..	..	334	112
Belgium	76	80	4	2	9	4	10	4	..	..	107	61
Benin	49	56	40	32	107	73	178	115	64	65	332	276
Bolivia	59	66	39	23	84	42	121	54	18	20	225	167
Bosnia and Herzegovina	67	75	12	5	17	8	19	8	..	..	134	69
Botswana	64	53	22	19	46	36	59	48	..	..	535	579
Brazil	66	73	28	12	50	17	59	19	..	..	218	114
Bulgaria	72	74	11	7	18	11	22	13	..	..	205	86
Burkina Faso	48	55	41	38	103	93	205	176	..	..	300	249
Burundi	46	50	49	42	110	88	183	142	65	65	418	381
Cambodia	55	63	38	22	87	43	121	51	20	20	262	222
Cameroon	53	51	34	34	85	84	137	136	..	..	410	378
Canada	77	81	4	4	7	5	8	6	..	..	92	55
Central African Republic	49	48	43	42	110	106	165	159	74	82	469	436
Chad	51	49	45	41	113	99	207	173	..	..	372	316
Chile	74	79	9	5	16	8	19	9	..	..	123	57
China	69[c]	73[c]	24	11	38	16	48	18	..	..	138	88
Hong Kong SAR, China	77	83	..	..	..	..	..	..	..	..	74	37
Colombia	68	73	20	12	30	18	37	22	4	3	194	89
Congo, Dem. Rep.	47	48	48	46	117	112	181	170	70	64	407	354
Congo, Rep.	56	57	33	29	74	61	116	93	49	43	335	301
Costa Rica	76	79	10	6	15	9	17	10	..	..	110	58
Côte d'Ivoire	53	55	46	41	105	86	151	123	..	..	377	349
Croatia	72	76	8	3	11	5	13	6	1	1	140	57
Cuba	74	79	7	3	11	5	13	6	..	..	108	68
Cyprus	77	79	5	2	10	3	11	4	..	..	77	38
Czech Republic	71	77	9	2	12	3	14	4	..	..	138	63
Denmark	75	79	4	2	7	3	9	4	..	..	107	65
Dominican Republic	68	73	29	15	48	22	62	27	6	4	200	131
Ecuador	69	75	20	10	41	18	52	20	..	..	161	84
Egypt, Arab Rep.	62	73	28	9	68	19	94	22	5	5	140	85
El Salvador	66	72	18	6	48	14	62	16	..	..	281	119
Eritrea	48	61	31	18	87	42	141	61	..	..	345	261
Estonia	69	75	13	3	17	4	21	5	..	..	234	77
Ethiopia	47	59	48	35	111	68	184	106	56	56	304	259
Finland	75	80	4	2	6	2	7	3	..	..	123	56
France[d]	77	81	3	2	7	3	9	4	..	..	118	55
Gabon	61	62	31	26	68	54	93	74	..	..	288	263
Gambia, The	53	58	42	31	78	57	165	98	46	39	299	244
Georgia	70	73	27	15	40	20	47	22	5	4	177	67
Germany	75	80	4	2	7	3	9	4	..	..	101	54
Ghana	57	64	38	28	77	50	122	74	38	28	255	225
Greece	77	80	9	2	11	3	13	4	..	..	101	46
Guatemala	62	71	28	15	56	25	78	32	..	..	226	122
Guinea	44	54	51	38	135	81	229	130	89	86	352	303
Guinea-Bissau	43	48	48	40	125	92	210	150	110	88	410	358
Haiti	55	62	38	27	104	70	151	165	33	36	264	236

	Life expectancy at birth (years)		Neonatal mortality rate (per 1,000 live births)		Infant mortality rate (per 1,000 live births)		Under-five mortality rate (per 1,000 live births)		Child mortality rate per 1,000		Adult mortality rate per 1,000	
									Male	Female	Male	Female
	1990	2010	1990	2010	1990	2010	1990	2010	2005–10[a,b]	2005–10[a,b]	2006–10[a]	2006–10[a]
Honduras	66	73	23	12	45	20	58	24	8	9	164	115
Hungary	69	74	12	4	17	5	19	6	..	..	229	99
India	58	65	47	32	81	48	115	63	9	12	253	168
Indonesia	62	69	31	17	56	27	85	35	13	12	205	169
Iran, Islamic Rep.	62	73	28	14	50	22	65	26	..	..	163	80
Iraq	68	68	23	20	37	31	46	39	6	7	281	125
Ireland	75	80	5	2	8	3	9	4	..	..	97	57
Israel	77	82	6	2	10	4	12	5	..	..	79	45
Italy	77	82	6	2	8	3	10	4	..	..	78	41
Jamaica	71	73	13	9	31	20	38	24	5	6	189	117
Japan	79	83	3	1	5	2	6	3	..	..	85	42
Jordan	70	73	20	13	32	18	38	22	3	7	143	99
Kazakhstan	68	68	26	17	48	29	57	33	5	4	366	147
Kenya	59	56	31	28	64	55	99	85	27	25	380	358
Korea, Dem. Rep.	70	69	22	18	23	26	45	33	..	..	194	124
Korea, Rep.	71	81	3	2	6	4	8	5	..	..	90	41
Kosovo	68	70	..	..	..	..	..	..	..	..	..	..
Kuwait	73	75	9	6	13	10	15	11	..	..	102	62
Kyrgyz Republic	68	69	30	19	59	33	72	38	8	4	304	132
Lao PDR	54	67	39	21	100	42	145	54	..	..	207	167
Latvia	69	73	12	5	16	8	21	10	..	..	247	94
Lebanon	69	72	18	12	31	19	38	22	..	..	150	101
Lesotho	59	47	36	35	72	65	89	85	..	..	578	613
Liberia	42	56	53	34	151	74	227	103	62	64	349	314
Libya	68	75	22	10	33	13	45	17	..	..	137	85
Lithuania	71	73	10	3	14	5	17	7	..	..	275	95
Macedonia, FYR	71	75	17	8	34	10	39	12	2	1	126	78
Madagascar	51	66	40	22	97	43	159	62	30	31	215	169
Malawi	47	53	44	27	131	58	222	92	52	54	409	411
Malaysia	70	74	9	3	15	5	18	6	..	..	147	75
Mali	44	51	57	48	131	99	255	178	117	114	361	297
Mauritania	56	58	42	39	80	75	124	111	53	44	290	220
Mauritius	69	73	16	9	21	13	24	15	..	..	206	102
Mexico	71	77	17	7	38	14	49	17	..	..	133	73
Moldova	67	69	15	9	30	16	37	19	7	4	302	146
Mongolia	61	68	27	12	76	26	107	32	11	10	294	141
Morocco	64	72	36	19	67	30	86	36	..	..	144	91
Mozambique	43	50	51	39	146	92	219	135	..	..	482	444
Myanmar	57	65	44	32	79	50	112	66	..	..	235	187
Namibia	61	62	25	17	49	29	73	40	24	19	345	343
Nepal	54	68	54	28	97	41	141	50	21	18	186	160
Netherlands	77	81	5	3	7	4	8	4	..	..	75	56
New Zealand	75	81	4	3	9	5	11	6	..	..	87	58
Nicaragua	64	74	25	12	52	23	68	27	..	..	197	111
Niger	41	54	48	32	132	73	311	143	138	135	313	271
Nigeria	46	51	49	40	126	88	213	143	91	93	393	365
Norway	77	81	4	2	7	3	9	3	..	..	82	50
Oman	71	73	22	5	36	8	47	9	..	..	138	76
Pakistan	61	65	51	41	96	70	124	87	14	22	189	158
Panama	72	76	14	9	26	17	33	20	..	..	133	70
Papua New Guinea	56	62	30	23	65	47	90	61	..	..	315	239
Paraguay	68	72	24	14	40	21	50	25	..	..	168	121
Peru	66	74	27	9	55	15	78	19	13	4	158	97
Philippines	65	68	23	14	42	23	59	29	10	9	262	145
Poland	71	76	11	4	15	5	17	6	..	..	198	76
Portugal	74	79	7	2	11	3	15	4	..	..	122	53
Puerto Rico	74	79	..	..	..	..	..	..	..	..	133	51
Qatar	74	78	10	4	17	7	21	8	..	..	69	59

	Life expectancy at birth		Neonatal mortality rate		Infant mortality rate		Under-five mortality rate		Child mortality rate		Adult mortality rate	
	years		per 1,000 live births		per 1,000 live births		per 1,000 live births		per 1,000 Male	Female	per 1,000 Male	Female
	1990	2010	1990	2010	1990	2010	1990	2010	2005–10[a,b]	2005–10[a,b]	2006–10[a]	2006–10[a]
Romania	70	73	15	8	29	11	37	14	..	..	185	76
Russian Federation	69	69	12	6	22	9	27	12	..	..	372	139
Rwanda	33	55	41	29	99	59	163	91	69	55	348	315
Saudi Arabia	69	74	20	10	36	15	45	18	3	4	126	96
Senegal	53	59	40	27	70	50	139	75	43	39	291	239
Serbia	71	74	16	4	25	6	29	7	4	3	150[e]	82[e]
Sierra Leone	39	47	57	45	162	114	276	174	67	61	464	444
Singapore	76	82	4	1	6	2	8	3	..	..	77	45
Slovak Republic	71	75	12	4	15	7	18	8	..	..	184	74
Slovenia	73	79	5	2	9	2	10	3	..	..	124	54
Somalia	45	51	52	52	108	108	180	180	53	54	368	312
South Africa	62	52	18	18	47	41	60	57	..	..	567	560
South Sudan	..	62	..	..	..	..	..	..	..	..	..	..
Spain	77	82	6	3	9	4	11	5	..	..	94	43
Sri Lanka	70	75	18	10	26	14	32	17	..	..	186	78
Sudan	53	61	39	35	78	66	125	103	38	30	265	211
Swaziland	59	48	24	21	70	55	96	78	32	30	562	580
Sweden	78	81	3	2	6	2	7	3	..	..	69	41
Switzerland	77	82	4	3	7	4	8	5	..	..	76	42
Syrian Arab Republic	71	76	18	9	31	14	38	16	5	3	110	72
Tajikistan	63	67	37	25	91	52	116	63	18	13	224	128
Tanzania	51	57	40	26	95	60	155	92	..	..	362	343
Thailand	72	74	17	8	26	11	32	13	..	..	205	101
Timor-Leste	46	62	48	24	127	56	169	81	..	..	259	223
Togo	53	57	40	32	87	66	147	103	55	43	340	297
Trinidad and Tobago	69	70	23	18	32	24	37	27	5	8	233	136
Tunisia	70	75	23	9	39	14	49	16	..	..	123	69
Turkey	63	74	33	10	66	14	80	18	6	6	136	77
Turkmenistan	63	65	33	23	78	47	98	56	..	..	304	159
Uganda	47	54	36	26	106	63	175	99	75	62	400	385
Ukraine	70	70	9	6	18	11	21	13	4	1	385	142
United Arab Emirates	72	77	12	4	18	6	22	7	..	..	90	68
United Kingdom	76	80	5	3	8	5	9	5	..	..	95	58
United States	75	78	6	4	9	7	11	8	..	..	139	80
Uruguay	72	76	11	6	20	9	23	11	..	..	133	60
Uzbekistan	67	68	30	23	63	44	77	52	11	7	243	139
Venezuela, RB	71	74	17	10	28	16	33	18	..	..	171	89
Vietnam	65	75	23	12	37	19	51	23	5	4	132	89
West Bank and Gaza	68	73	..	..	36	20	45	22	3	3	142	105
Yemen, Rep.	56	65	43	32	90	57	128	77	10	11	231	186
Zambia	47	48	40	30	109	69	183	111	66	55	491	493
Zimbabwe	61	50	27	27	52	51	78	80	21	21	543	594
World	**65 w**	**70 w**	**32 w**	**23 w**	**62 w**	**41 w**	**90 w**	**58 w**	**.. w**	**.. w**	**210 w**	**150 w**
Low income	53	59	46	33	103	70	165	108	53	51	297	260
Middle income	64	69	33	22	61	38	85	51	..	..	202	136
Lower middle income	59	65	41	29	78	50	113	69	21	22	244	175
Upper middle income	69	73	23	11	39	17	49	20	..	..	161	100
Low & middle income	63	68	35	25	68	45	98	63	..	..	213	152
East Asia & Pacific	68	72	25	13	42	20	56	24	..	..	157	105
Europe & Central Asia	68	71	21	11	42	19	51	23	..	..	273	116
Latin America & Carib.	68	74	23	11	43	18	54	23	..	..	181	98
Middle East & N. Africa	64	72	29	16	56	27	74	34	..	..	160	95
South Asia	59	65	48	33	86	52	120	67	11	15	239	166
Sub-Saharan Africa	50	54	43	35	105	76	175	121	68	65	379	346
High income	75	80	6	3	10	5	12	6	..	..	117	62
Euro area	76	81	5	2	8	3	10	4	..	..	107	53

a. Data are for the most recent year available. b. Refers to a survey year. Values were estimated directly from surveys and cover the 5 or 10 years preceding the survey. c. Includes Taiwan, China. d. Excludes the French overseas departments of French Guiana, Guadeloupe, Martinique, and Réunion. e. Includes Kosovo.

About the data

Mortality rates for different age groups (infants, children, and adults) and overall mortality indicators (life expectancy at birth or survival to a given age) are important indicators of health status in a country. Because data on the incidence and prevalence of diseases are frequently unavailable, mortality rates are often used to identify vulnerable populations. And they are among the indicators most frequently used to compare socioeconomic development across countries.

The main sources of mortality data are vital registration systems and direct or indirect estimates based on sample surveys or censuses. A "complete" vital registration system—covering at least 90 percent of vital events in the population—is the best source of age-specific mortality data. Where reliable age-specific mortality data are available, life expectancy at birth is directly estimated from the life table constructed from age-specific mortality data.

But complete vital registration systems are fairly uncommon in developing countries. Thus estimates must be obtained from sample surveys or derived by applying indirect estimation techniques to registration, census, or survey data (see table 2.17 and *Primary data documentation*). Survey data are subject to recall error, and surveys estimating infant deaths require large samples because households in which a birth has occurred during a given year cannot ordinarily be preselected for sampling. Indirect estimates rely on model life tables that may be inappropriate for the population concerned. Because life expectancy at birth is estimated using infant mortality data and model life tables for many developing countries, similar reliability issues arise for this indicator. Extrapolations based on outdated surveys may not be reliable for monitoring changes in health status or for comparative analytical work.

Estimates of neonatal, infant, and under-five mortality tend to vary by source and method for a given time and place. Years for available estimates also vary by country, making comparison across countries and over time difficult. To make neonatal, infant, and under-five mortality estimates comparable and to ensure consistency across estimates by different agencies, the United Nations Inter-agency Group for Child Mortality Estimation, which comprises the United Nations Children's Fund (UNICEF), the United Nations Population Division, the World Health Organization (WHO), the World Bank, and other universities and research institutes, developed and adopted a statistical method that uses all available information to reconcile differences. The method uses a locally

weighted polynomial regression to obtain a best estimate trend line by fitting a set of local regressions of mortality rates against their reference dates. (For further discussion of childhood mortality estimates, see UN Inter-agency Group for Child Mortality Estimation 2011; for a graphic presentation and detailed background data, see www.childmortality.org).

Neonatal, infant, and child mortality rates are higher for boys than for girls in countries in which parental gender preferences are insignificant. Under-five and child mortality rates capture the effect of gender discrimination better than neonatal and infant mortality rates do, as malnutrition and medical interventions are more important in this age group. Where female child mortality is higher, as in some countries in South Asia, girls probably have unequal access to resources. Child mortality rates in the table are not compatible with neonatal, infant, and under-five mortality rates because of differences in methodology and reference year. Child mortality data were estimated directly from surveys and cover the 10 years preceding the survey. In addition to estimates from Demographic Health Surveys, estimates derived from Multiple Indicator Cluster Surveys have been added to the table; they cover the 5 years preceding the survey.

Rates for adult mortality come from life tables. Adult mortality rates increased notably in a dozen countries in Sub-Saharan Africa in the early 2000s and in several countries in Europe and Central Asia in the first half of the 1990s. In Sub-Saharan Africa the increase stems from AIDS-related mortality and affects both sexes, though women are more affected. In Europe and Central Asia the causes are more diverse (high prevalence of smoking, high-fat diet, excessive alcohol use, stressful conditions related to the economic transition) and affect men more.

Annual data series from the United Nations are interpolated based on five-year estimates and thus may not reflect actual events.

Definitions

• **Life expectancy at birth** is the number of years a newborn infant would live if prevailing patterns of mortality at the time of its birth were to stay the same throughout its life. • **Neonatal mortality rate** is the number of neonatal infants dying before reaching 28 days of age, per 1,000 live births. • **Infant mortality rate** is the number of infants dying before reaching one year of age, per 1,000 live births. • **Under-five mortality rate** is the probability of a child born in a specific year dying before reaching age 5, if subject to the age-specific mortality rate of that year. The probability is derived from life tables and is expressed as a rate per 1,000 live births. • **Child mortality rate** is the probability per 1,000 of dying between ages 1 and 5—that is, the probability of a 1-year-old dying before reaching age 5—if subject to current age-specific mortality rates. • **Adult mortality rate** is the probability per 1,000 of dying between the ages of 15 and 60—that is, the probability of a 15-year-old dying before reaching age 60—if subject to current age-specific mortality rates between those ages.

Data sources

Data on life expectancy at birth are World Bank calculations based on male and female data from *World Population Prospects: The 2010 Revision* (for more than half of countries, most of them developing countries), census reports and other statistical publications from national statistical offices, Eurostat's *Demographic Statistics,* and the U.S. Bureau of the Census International Data Base. Data on neonatal, infant, and under-five mortality are from the UN Inter-agency Group for Child Mortality Estimation's *Levels and Trends in Child Mortality: Report 2011* and are based mainly on household surveys, censuses, and vital registration data. Data on child mortality are from MEASURE DHS Demographic and Health Surveys by ICF International and World Bank calculations based on infant and under-five mortality from Multiple Indicator Cluster Surveys by UNICEF. Most data on adult mortality are linear interpolations of five-year data from *World Population Prospects: The 2010 Revision.* Remaining data on adult mortality are from the Human Mortality Database by the University of California, Berkeley, and the Max Planck Institute for Demographic Research (www.mortality.org).

2.24 Health gaps by income

	Survey year	Infant mortality rate		Under-five mortality rate		Total fertility rate		Teenage mothers	
		per 1,000 live births		per 1,000 live births		births per woman		% of women ages 15–19	
		Poorest quintile	Richest quintile	Poorest quintile	Richest quintile	Poorest quintile	Richest quintile	Poorest quintile	Richest quintile
Algeria		..	..	..	..	..	..	..	..
Armenia	2005	42	14	52	23	1.8	1.5	5	0
Azerbaijan	2006	52	37	63	41	2.3	1.6	6	3
Bangladesh	2007	66	36	86	43	3.2	2.2	42	20
Bolivia	2008	89	26	116	31	6.2	1.9	31	8
Bosnia and Herzegovina		..	..	..	..	..	..	..	..
Burkina Faso	2006	97	78	196	111	6.6	3.6	26	12
Cambodia	2005	101	34	127	43	4.9	2.4	11	5
Cameroon	2006	101	51	189	88	6.5	3.2	36	14
Colombia	2010	22	12	29	13	3.2	1.4	29	7
Congo, Dem. Rep.	2007	113	58	184	97	7.4	4.2	29	12
Congo, Rep.	2005	92	56	135	85	6.7	2.9	35	13
Côte d'Ivoire	2006	147	59	229	83	7.4	2.9	52	12
Dominican Republic	2007	43	26	53	28	3.8	1.7	37	8
Egypt, Arab Rep.	2008	42	17	49	19	3.4	2.7	12	5
Ethiopia	2005	80	60	130	92	6.6	3.2	24	8
Gambia, The	2006	106	58	158	72	..	..	..	..
Ghana	2008	59	47	103	60	6.5	2.3	18	4
Guinea	2005	127	68	217	113	6.5	4.2	39	20
Guinea-Bissau		..	..	..	..	..	..	..	..
Haiti	2006	78	45	125	55	6.6	2.0	22	7
Honduras	2006	37	19	50	20	5.6	2.1	31	10
India	2006	82	34	118	39	3.9	1.8	25	5
Indonesia	2007	56	26	77	32	3.0	2.7	6	10
Jordan	2009	32	29	36	32	4.9	2.7	5	3
Kazakhstan	2006	68	42	82	45	3.4	1.2	8	5
Kenya	2009	66	57	98	69	7.0	2.9	24	16
Kyrgyz Republic		..	..	..	..	..	..	..	..
Lao PDR		..	..	..	..	..	..	..	..
Liberia	2009	121	95	176	137	8.0	3.2	53	20
Madagascar	2009	61	37	106	48	6.8	2.7	51	14
Malawi	2006	72	62	123	99	7.1	4.1	43	20
Mali	2006	124	80	233	124	7.6	4.9	37	23
Mauritania	2007	89	57	144	87	5.4	3.6	14	11
Moldova	2005	20	16	29	17	2.1	1.4	8	1
Namibia	2007	60	24	92	30	5.1	2.4	22	5
Nepal	2006	71	40	98	47	4.7	1.9	18	14
Niger	2006	91	67	206	157	7.9	6.4	40	24
Nigeria	2008	100	58	219	87	7.1	4.0	46	5
Pakistan	2007	94	53	121	60	5.8	3.0	16	4
Philippines	2008	40	15	59	17	5.2	1.9	19	4
Rwanda	2008	99	45	161	84	5.8	4.4	5	4
Senegal	2005	77	43	143	56	6.7	3.3	34	8
Serbia		..	..	..	..	..	..	..	..
Sierra Leone	2008	148	93	211	145	6.3	3.2	49	16
Somalia		..	..	..	..	..	..	..	..
Swaziland	2007	84	84	118	101	5.5	2.6	33	15
Syrian Arab Republic	2006	18	16	22	20	..	..	..	..
Tanzania	2010	61	63	103	84	7.0	3.2	28	13
Thailand		..	..	..	..	..	..	..	..
Timor-Leste	2009/10	62	38	87	52	7.3	4.2	9	3
Togo	2006	92	43	150	62	7.3	2.9	36	7
Ukraine	2007	19	9	23	9	1.7	1.0	8	1
Uzbekistan	2006	59	36	72	42	..	..	..	..
Yemen, Rep.	2006	94	36	118	118	..	..	..	..
Zambia	2007	69	74	124	124	8.4	3.4	37	14
Zimbabwe	2006	48	45	72	72	5.5	2.3	32	7

Child health

	Survey year	Diarrhea				Acute respiratory infection (ARI)				Prevalence of child malnutrition (underweight)		Child immunization	
		Prevalence % of children under age 5		Treatment % of children under age 5 with diarrhea		Prevalence % of children under age 5		Treatment Children with ARI taken to health provider % of children under age 5 with ARI		Old standards % of children under age 5		All vaccinations % of children ages 12–23 months	
		Poorest quintile	Richest quintile	Poorest quintile	Richest quintile	Poorest quintile	Richest quintile	Poorest quintile	Richest quintile	Poorest quintile	Richest quintile	Poorest quintile	Richest quintile
Algeria	2006	10	8	..	..	7	5	38	68	5	3	81	95
Armenia	2005	20	13	65	80	11	11	30	42	5	1	66	68
Azerbaijan	2006	13	10	66	55	4	2	15	11	17	4	7	32
Bangladesh	2007	10	8	79	88	6	3	45	73	55	31	80	88
Bolivia	2008	30	20	58	75	24	17	40	70	11	2	78	81
Bosnia and Herzegovina	2006	4	5	..	..	5	3	97	96	2	4	66	71
Burkina Faso	2006	19	16	57	73	6	2	45	73	44	24	64	81
Cambodia	2005	22	14	66	40	12	3	41	58	43	23	56	76
Cameroon	2006	30	10	46	73	10	6	20	50	35	6	42	72
Colombia	2010	16	7	67	82	7	4	54	67	12	3	64	67
Congo, Dem. Rep.	2007	17	14	65	55	9	6	32	48	33	19	20	50
Congo, Rep.	2005	15	12	54	54	..	..	..	..	20	5	29	73
Côte d'Ivoire	2006	20	13	55	77	8	3	21	71	26	10	58	92
Dominican Republic	2007	16	13	64	63	9	4	63	65	7	2	48	76
Egypt, Arab Rep.	2008	10	7	39	32	10	8	70	82	9	7	89	94
Ethiopia	2005	18	14	24	55	12	11	19	33	43	29	14	36
Gambia, The	2006	21	15	..	..	6	5	68	68	26	14	83	74
Ghana	2008	25	10	58	69	6	3	45	87	23	11	75	84
Guinea	2005	18	17	47	73	10	8	30	59	28	21	29	45
Guinea-Bissau	2006	13	14	..	..	4	7	32	82	21	10	43	64
Haiti	2006	25	18	48	67	10	5	21	37	27	7	34	56
Honduras	2006	19	11	64	68	14	6	46	74	21	2	77	68
India	2006	9	8	25	49	6	4	61	80	61	25	24	71
Indonesia	2007	18	10	60	57	8	5	48	74	..	..	39	75
Jordan	2009	18	14	56	64	5	3	66	78	4	0	82	89
Kazakhstan	2006	1	2	46	71	1	2	37	53	5	1	98	96
Kenya	2009	20	13	80	79	11	5	57	63	31	12	61	70
Kyrgyz Republic	2006	3	4	..	..	..	..	..	..	3	3	..	..
Lao PDR	2006	17	9	..	..	6	3	28	12	44	18	18	45
Liberia	2007	19	19	63	83	8	9	59	89	26	17	23	56
Madagascar	2009	8	10	52	67	3	3	33	68	47	28	41	82
Malawi	2006	26	20	65	76	9	8	51	65	25	16	66	77
Mali	2006	13	8	41	68	10	11	9	50	37	22	49	56
Mauritania	2007	25	19	29	29	7	7	33	64	40	13	39	25
Moldova	2005	7	12	50	70	5	10	42	68	..	..	82	59
Namibia	2007	13	11	57	74	7	1	65	94	27	9	59	82
Nepal	2006	13	12	27	59	6	5	36	54	54	24	68	94
Niger	2006	22	18	50	66	10	11	19	59	48	30	20	48
Nigeria	2008	14	5	25	61	4	1	32	66	40	13	5	53
Pakistan	2007	23	20	52	59	15	13	67	92	..	..	26	64
Philippines	2008	10	7	68	82	7	3	42	64	..	..	64	87
Rwanda	2008	16	13	32	49	16	14	16	43	30	10	82	83
Senegal	2005	24	23	51	52	10	15	35	61	25	7	59	65
Serbia	2006	7	5	..	..	3	2	89	..	4	2	50	54
Sierra Leone	2008	13	9	74	86	7	4	39	46	27	15	39	40
Somalia	2006	26	14	..	..	18	12	5	28	..	..	5	22
Swaziland	2007	23	9	89	85	10	8	66	75	9	3	82	79
Syrian Arab Republic	2006	9	6	..	..	4	6	72	86	13	8	51	77
Tanzania	2010	15	16	56	68	4	5	18	62	25	12	69	85
Thailand	2006	10	6	..	..	7	3	85	78	15	4	92	86
Timor-Leste	2009/10	13	17	81	76	2	2	53	80	..	..	43	45
Togo	2006	15	9	..	..	7	8	17	28	37	15	39	63
Ukraine		..	..	..	..	..	..	..	..	..	..	..	..
Uzbekistan	2006	..	..	..	..	..	..	..	..	6	3	90	80
Yemen, Rep.	2006	35	27	..	..	..	..	..	..	..	..	18	73
Zambia	2007	14	16	71	79	5	6	78	56	21	14	71	78
Zimbabwe	2006	15	15	65	79	7	2	9	51	18	6	43	64

Reproductive and women's health

	Survey year	Knowledge of contraception		Contraceptive prevalence rate		Pregnant women receiving prenatal care		Births attended by skilled health staff[a]		Problem accessing health care	
		Any method % of married women ages 15–49		Any method % of married women ages 15–49		%		%		%	
		Poorest quintile	Richest quintile	Poorest quintile	Richest quintile	Poorest quintile	Richest quintile	Poorest quintile	Richest quintile	Poorest quintile	Richest quintile
Algeria	2006	..	..	56	65	76	98	88	98	..	..
Armenia	2005	97	100	51	60	86	99	98	100	92	67
Azerbaijan	2006	96	99	55	57	56	98	76	100	94	65
Bangladesh	2007	100	100	55	60	32	85	7	57	26	17
Bolivia	2008	90	100	46	71	79	97	39	99	95	78
Bosnia and Herzegovina	2006	..	..	35	35	98	100	99	100	..	..
Burkina Faso	2006	85	99	9	41	79	98	56	65	88	65
Cambodia	2005	98	100	31	54	58	91	22	92	93	72
Cameroon	2006	72	99	11	44	48	98	19	96	92	69
Colombia	2010	100	100	76	80	92	99	86	99	..	..
Congo, Dem. Rep.	2007	79	98	14	39	78	95	62	98	95	70
Congo, Rep.	2005	97	100	40	46	75	98	69	99	..	..
Côte d'Ivoire	2006	75	99	9	24	69	97	29	95	..	..
Dominican Republic	2007	99	100	68	73	87	98	90	98	75	43
Egypt, Arab Rep.	2008	100	100	55	65	57	93	58	97	87	45
Ethiopia	2005	76	96	4	37	..	..	..	..	98	82
Gambia, The	2006	..	..	6	13	98	98	28	89	..	..
Ghana	2008	93	100	14	31	93	100	23	96	78	48
Guinea	2005	87	97	5	17	68	98	15	87	93	71
Guinea-Bissau	2006	..	..	6	23	76	89	19	79	..	..
Haiti	2006	100	100	20	38	72	97	8	71	98	75
Honduras	2006	100	100	53	73	88	99	38	98	94	69
India	2006	99	100	42	68	58	97	21	90	67	15
Indonesia	2007	96	100	53	64	83	99	47	96	62	25
Jordan	2009	100	100	54	65	97	100	99	100	81	62
Kazakhstan	2006	99	100	42	59	100	100	100	100	..	..
Kenya	2009	86	99	20	55	84	97	23	82	39	27
Kyrgyz Republic	2006	..	..	50	51	94	99	93	100	..	..
Lao PDR	2006	..	..	..	..	16	88	3	81	..	..
Liberia	2007	72	99	4	20	68	96	30	82	91	45
Madagascar	2009	87	100	20	57	73	97	22	90	75	37
Malawi	2006	98	100	38	46	90	95	43	77	90	53
Mali	2006	70	93	4	19	20	80	9	76	74	47
Mauritania	2007	53	93	2	19	53	94	21	95	..	..
Moldova	2005	99	100	67	70	97	98	99	100	85	56
Namibia	2007	97	100	32	71	90	97	61	98	89	33
Nepal	2006	100	100	33	61	50	92	9	64	91	63
Niger	2006	68	89	11	21	37	82	5	60	87	59
Nigeria	2008	41	96	3	35	24	94	9	86	86	49
Pakistan	2007	92	99	16	43	38	92	18	79	..	..
Philippines	2008	96	100	41	50	91	99	98	99	88	50
Rwanda	2008	99	99	28	50	95	97	49	76	89	65
Senegal	2005	89	99	4	25	86	99	21	91	88	54
Serbia	2006	..	..	33	49	96	100	98	100	..	..
Sierra Leone	2008	65	89	4	20	84	97	28	72	96	69
Somalia	2006	..	..	12	19	8	51	11	77	..	..
Swaziland	2007	100	100	37	62	96	99	51	93	70	22
Syrian Arab Republic	2006	..	..	42	68	68	94	78	99	..	..
Tanzania	2010	97	100	23	51	82	95	31	88	56	16
Thailand	2006	..	..	74	69	96	100	93	100	..	..
Timor-Leste	2009/10	66	93	15	34	75	96	12	71	94	70
Togo	2006	94	99	12	19	69	100	30	97	..	..
Ukraine	2007	99	100	62	71	98	99	99	100	..	..
Uzbekistan	2006	..	..	66	63	98	99	100	100	..	..
Yemen, Rep.	2006	..	..	15	44	32	79	17	74	..	..
Zambia	2007	98	100	41	54	90	98	26	92	77	42
Zimbabwe	2006	99	100	48	72	92	98	44	97	89	46

About the data

Health survey data at the national level do not reveal within-country inequalities associated with socioeconomic status. The data in the table describe the health and demographic status as well as use of health services by individuals in different socioeconomic groups within countries. The data are from MEASURE DHS Demographic and Health Surveys by ICF International and Multiple Indicator Cluster Surveys by the United Nations Children's Fund.

Obtaining reliable data on a household's or individual's socioeconomic status is challenging, and methods have evolved over time. Earlier measurements relied on indicators such as household income and consumption, which are prone to bias and are time and labor intensive when included in survey questionnaires. The wealth index, developed by MEASURE DHS with partial funding from the World Bank, is calculated using easy-to-collect data on a household's ownership of selected assets, such as televisions and bicycles; materials used for housing construction; and types of water access and sanitation facilities. A single asset index is developed on the basis of data from the entire country sample and used. Generated with a statistical procedure known as principal components analysis, the wealth index places individual households on a continuous scale of relative wealth. Demographic and Health Surveys and Multiple Indicator Cluster Surveys separate all interviewed households into five wealth quintiles to compare the influence of wealth on various population, health and nutrition indicators. The wealth index is presented in the final reports of these surveys.

Data disaggregated by wealth quintile provide insights into health differentials by socioeconomic status and allow problems particular to the poor, such as unequal access to health care to be identified. If the poor have a greater disease burden than the rich, programs should focus on reaching the poor. But this is rare. Health services too often fail poor people in access, quality, and affordability. In low-income countries the poor are particularly disadvantaged in using health care and experience worse health outcomes than the rich. The table shows the estimates for the poorest and richest quintiles only; the full set of estimates for up to 70 indicators is available at http://data.worldbank.org and http://data.worldbank.org/data-catalog/health-nutrition-population-statistics. The estimates in the table are based on household survey data, which may refer to a period preceding the survey date or use a definition or methodology different from the estimates in the other tables. Thus the estimates may differ, and caution should be exercised in using the data.

Definitions

• **Survey year** is the year in which the underlying data were collected. The reference year of the data may be preceding the survey year. • **Infant mortality rate** is the number of infants dying before reaching one year of age, per 1,000 live births. • **Under-five mortality rate** is the probability that a child born in a specific year will die before reaching age 5, if subject to the age-specific mortality rate of that year. The probability is derived from life tables and expressed as a rate per 1,000 live births. • **Total fertility rate** is the number of children that would be born to a woman if she were to live to the end of her childbearing years and bear children in accordance with age-specific fertility rates of a reference period. • **Teenage mothers** are women ages 15–19 who are mothers or pregnant with their first child. • **Diarrhea prevalence** is the percentage of children under age 5 who had diarrhea in the two weeks preceding the survey. • **Diarrhea treatment** is the percentage of children under age 5 with diarrhea in the two weeks preceding the survey who received oral rehydration salts, recommended homemade fluids (rehydration salts or recommended home solution), or increased fluids. • **Acute respiratory infection (ARI) prevalence** is the percentage of children under age 5 who were ill with a cough accompanied by rapid breathing in the two weeks preceding the survey. • **Children with ARI taken to health provider** are children under age 5 with ARI in the two weeks preceding the survey who were taken to a health facility. • **Prevalence of child malnutrition (underweight)** is the percentage of children under age 5 whose weight for age is more than two standard deviations below the median for the international reference population. Data are based on the old standards of the U.S. Centers for Disease Control National Center for Health Statistics and World Health Organization international reference population. • **Child immunization (all vaccinations)** is the percentage of children ages 12–23 months who have received vaccines for Bacillus Calmette-Guérin and measles; three doses each of diphtheria, pertussis, and tetanus; and polio vaccine (excluding polio 0) by the time of the survey, according to the vaccination card or the mother's report. • **Knowledge of contraception** is the percentage of currently married women who know at least one contraceptive method. • **Contraceptive prevalence rate** is the percentage of women ages 15-49 married or in union who are practicing, or whose sexual partners are practicing, any form of contraception. • **Pregnant women receiving prenatal care** are women with one or more live births in the one, two, or three years preceding the survey who have received at least one antenatal care during pregnancy before the most recent birth from any skilled personnel. • **Births attended by skilled health staff** are live births in the one, two, or three years preceding the survey attended by any skilled personnel. • **Problem accessing health care** is the percentage of women who report they have a big problem accessing health care when they are sick due to inadequate knowledge of where to go for treatment, need to get permission or money for treatment, distance to health facility, need to take transport, desire not to go alone, or concern that a female provider may not be available.

Data sources

Data on health gaps by income are from MEASURE DHS Demographic and Health Surveys, by ICF International, downloaded through STATcompiler, and from Multiple Indicator Cluster Surveys by UNICEF through their final reports.

ENVIRONMENT

The indicators in the *Environment* section measure the use of resources and the way human activities affect the natural and built environment. They include measures of environmental goods (forests, water, cultivatable land) and of degradation (pollution, deforestation, loss of habitat, and loss of biodiversity). Sustainable development and poverty reduction require efficient use of environmental resources. These indicators show that growing populations and expanding economies have placed greater demands on land, water, forests, minerals, and energy resources. But new technologies, increasing productivity, and better policies can ensure that future development is environmentally and socially sustainable.

Nowhere are these risks and opportunities more intertwined than in the global effort to mitigate the effects of climate change. At the December 2011 United Nations Conference on Climate Change in Durban, South Africa, all 194 participating countries adopted the Durban Platform for Enhanced Action, which sets the direction of climate negotiations. The platform calls for parties to negotiate a legal agreement on climate change no later than 2015 that would apply to all countries and be effective by 2020. Negotiators also launched a Green Climate Fund that will eventually channel billions of dollars a year to developing countries for adaptation to and mitigation of climate change.

As documented in *World Development Report 2010: Development and Climate Change* (World Bank 2009j), climate change is already eroding development gains and causing disruptions to social and economic systems in some countries. Continued rise in temperature, accompanied by changes in precipitation patterns, is projected for this century, and more frequent, severe, and prolonged climate-related events such as floods and droughts are also projected—posing risks for agriculture, food production, and water supplies. Poor countries and the poorest people in all countries are the most vulnerable to the impacts. Understanding climate change is thus key for development policy. Because uncertainty increases with climate change, better climate information is critical for wise development decisions.

This year's *Environment* section includes two new tables on information related to climate change. Table 3.11 presents data on carbon dioxide emissions by economic sector, which shows how differences in industrial structure and production technologies affect the production of carbon dioxide and how these patterns have changed. Table 3.12 presents data on climate variability, exposure to impact, and resilience.

Other indicators in this section describe land use, agriculture and food production, forests and biodiversity, water resources, energy use and efficiency, natural resource rents, urbanization, environmental impacts, government commitments, and threatened species. Table 3.8 adds newly available data on the share of the population with access to electricity.

Where possible, the indicators come from international sources and are standardized to facilitate comparison across countries. But ecosystems span national boundaries, and access to natural resources may vary within countries. For example, water may be abundant in some parts of a country but scarce in others, and countries often share water resources. Land productivity and optimal land use may be location specific, but widely separated regions can have common characteristics. Greenhouse gas emissions and climate change are measured globally, but their effects are experienced locally, shaping people's lives and opportunities. Measuring environmental phenomena and their effects at the subnational, national, and supranational levels and incorporating these values in national income accounts and other statistical frameworks remain major challenges for economists, environmentalists, and statisticians.

3

Rural population and land use

	Rural population			Land area	Land use							
	% of total		average annual % growth	thousand sq. km	Forest area		Permanent cropland		Arable land		Arable land hectares per 100 people	
	1990	2010	1990–2010	2010	1990	2010	1990	2009	1990	2009	1990	2009
Afghanistan	82	75	2.3	652.2	2.1	2.1	0.2	0.2	12.1	11.9	41.6	23.3
Albania	64	52	–0.9	27.4	28.8	28.3	4.6	3.2	21.1	22.3	17.6	19.2
Algeria	48	34	–0.4	2,381.7	0.7	0.6	0.2	0.4	3.0	3.1	28.0	21.5
Angola	63	42	0.7	1,246.7	48.9	46.9	0.4	0.2	2.3	3.2	28.1	21.6
Argentina	13	8	–1.7	2,736.7	12.7	10.7	0.4	0.4	9.6	11.3	80.9	77.4
Armenia	33	36	0.5	28.5	12.2	9.2	2.1	1.9	14.9	16.0	12.3	14.8
Australia	15	11	0.1	7,682.3	20.1	19.4	0.0	0.0	6.2	6.1	280.7	214.8
Austria	34	32	–0.4	82.5	45.8	47.1	1.0	0.8	17.3	16.6	18.6	16.4
Azerbaijan	46	48	0.8	82.6	11.2	11.3	3.7	2.7	20.5	22.7	23.1	20.9
Bahrain	12	11	7.2	0.8	0.3	1.3	2.9	2.6	2.9	1.3	0.4	0.1
Bangladesh	80	72	0.5	130.2	11.5	11.1	2.5	7.5	72.6	58.1	9.0	5.2
Belarus	34	26	–1.8	202.9	38.4	42.5	0.9	0.6	30.0	27.3	59.6	58.3
Belgium	4	3	0.0	30.3	22.4	22.4	0.5[a]	0.7	23.3[a]	27.7	0.2	7.8
Benin	66	58	2.2	110.6	52.1	41.2	0.9	2.7	14.6	22.1	33.8	28.5
Bolivia	44	34	0.2	1,083.3	58.0	52.8	0.1	0.2	1.9	3.4	31.5	38.2
Bosnia and Herzegovina	61	51	–1.3	51.2	43.3	42.7	2.9	2.0	16.7	19.5	21.6	26.5
Botswana	58	39	–0.7	566.7	24.2	20.0	0.0	0.0	0.7	0.4	30.4	12.6
Brazil	25	14	–2.5	8,459.4	68.0	61.4	0.8	0.9	6.0	7.2	33.9	31.7
Bulgaria	34	28	–1.6	108.6	30.1	36.2	2.7	1.6	34.9	28.9	44.2	41.4
Burkina Faso	86	80	2.5	273.6	25.0	20.6	0.2	0.2	12.9	21.6	37.8	36.9
Burundi	94	89	2.2	25.7	11.3	6.7	14.0	13.6	36.2	35.0	16.6	11.0
Cambodia	87	77	0.3	176.5	73.3	57.2	0.6	0.9	20.9	22.1	38.8	27.9
Cameroon	59	42	0.2	472.7	51.4	42.1	2.6	3.0	12.6	12.6	48.8	31.1
Canada	23	19	0.6	9,093.5	34.1	34.1	0.7	0.8	5.0	5.0	163.7	133.7
Central African Republic	63	61	1.6	623.0	37.2	36.3	0.1	0.1	3.1	3.1	65.4	45.2
Chad	79	72	2.0	1,259.2	10.4	9.2	0.0	0.0	2.6	3.4	54.5	39.3
Chile	17	11	–1.6	743.5	20.5	21.8	0.3	0.6	3.8	1.7	21.3	7.5
China	73	55	–1.1	9,327.5	16.8	22.2	0.8	1.5	13.3	11.8	10.9	8.3
Hong Kong SAR, China	1	..	..	1.0	..	..	..	..	..	..	..	..
Colombia	32	25	0.2	1,109.5	56.3	54.5	1.5	1.4	3.0	1.6	10.0	3.9
Congo, Dem. Rep.	72	65	1.8	2,267.1	70.7	68.0	0.5	0.3	2.9	3.0	18.3	10.4
Congo, Rep.	46	38	1.5	341.5	66.5	65.6	0.1	0.2	1.4	1.5	20.1	12.7
Costa Rica	49	36	0.0	51.1	50.2	51.0	4.9	5.9	5.1	3.9	8.5	4.4
Côte d'Ivoire	60	50	0.7	318.0	32.1	32.7	11.0	13.5	7.6	8.8	19.4	14.5
Croatia	46	42	–0.7	56.0	33.1	34.3	2.0	1.6	21.7	15.5	27.1	19.6
Cuba	27	24	–0.1	106.4	19.2	27.0	4.2	3.5	31.6	34.3	32.1	32.4
Cyprus	33	30	0.5	9.2	17.4	18.7	5.5	3.6	11.5	9.4	13.8	8.0
Czech Republic	25	27	0.4	77.3	34.0	34.4	3.1	1.0	41.1	41.2	32.1	30.3
Denmark	15	13	–1.6	42.4	10.5	12.8	0.2	0.1	60.4	57.3	49.8	44.0
Dominican Republic	45	30	–1.2	48.3	40.8	40.8	9.3	9.7	18.6	16.6	12.5	8.2
Ecuador	45	33	–0.6	248.4	49.9	39.7	4.8	5.4	5.8	4.8	15.6	8.4
Egypt, Arab Rep.	57	57	1.7	995.5	0.0	0.1	0.4	0.8	2.3	2.9	4.0	3.6
El Salvador	51	39	–0.2	20.7	18.2	13.9	12.5	11.1	26.5	32.7	10.3	11.0
Eritrea	84	78	2.4	101.0	16.0	15.2	0.0	0.0	4.9	6.8	0.1	13.5
Estonia	29	31	–0.1	42.4	49.3	52.3	0.3	0.2	26.3	14.1	72.7	44.5
Ethiopia	87	82	1.8	1,000.0	13.7	12.3	0.5	1.0	10.0	13.9	1.4	17.2
Finland	39	36	–0.4	303.9	71.9	72.9	0.0	0.0	7.4	7.4	45.5	42.3
France	26	22	–0.5	547.7	26.5	29.1	2.2	1.9	32.9	33.5	30.9	28.4
Gabon	31	14	–1.5	257.7	85.4	85.4	0.6	0.6	1.1	1.3	31.8	22.0
Gambia, The	62	42	0.8	10.0	44.2	48.0	0.5	0.5	18.2	40.0	18.8	23.8
Georgia	45	47	0.8	69.5	40.0	39.5	4.8	1.7	11.4	6.4	16.3	10.2
Germany	27	26	–0.5	348.6	30.8	31.8	1.3	0.6	34.3	34.3	15.1	14.6
Ghana	64	49	0.8	227.5	32.7	21.7	6.6	12.3	11.9	19.3	18.3	18.5
Greece	41	39	–0.2	128.9	25.6	30.3	8.3	8.9	22.5	19.8	28.5	22.6
Guatemala	59	51	1.6	107.2	44.3	34.1	4.5	8.8	12.1	14.0	14.6	10.7
Guinea	72	65	1.5	245.7	29.6	26.6	2.0	2.8	11.6	11.6	49.5	29.2
Guinea-Bissau	72	70	2.0	28.1	78.8	71.9	4.2	8.9	8.9	10.7	24.6	20.2
Haiti	72	50	–1.4	27.6	4.2	3.7	11.6	10.9	28.3	38.1	11.0	10.6

	Rural population			Land area	Land use							
	% of total		average annual % growth	thousand sq. km	Forest area		Permanent cropland		Arable land		Arable land hectares per 100 people	
					% of land area							
	1990	2010	1990–2010	2010	1990	2010	1990	2009	1990	2009	1990	2009
Honduras	60	51	1.1	111.9	72.7	46.4	3.2	3.7	13.1	9.1	29.9	13.7
Hungary	34	32	–1.4	89.6	20.0	22.6	2.6	2.1	56.2	50.6	48.7	45.8
India	75	70	0.9	2,973.2	21.5	23.0	2.2	3.9	54.8	53.1	18.6	13.1
Indonesia	69	46	–1.4	1,811.6	65.4	52.1	6.5	10.5	11.2	13.0	11.0	9.9
Iran, Islamic Rep.	44	31	–0.6	1,628.6	6.8	6.8	0.8	1.1	9.3	10.6	27.7	23.5
Iraq	30	34	3.3	437.4	1.8	1.9	0.7	0.6	13.3	10.4	31.9	14.5
Ireland	43	38	–0.2	68.9	6.7	10.7	0.0	0.0	15.1	15.8	29.6	24.4
Israel	10	8	1.6	21.6	6.1	7.1	4.1	3.6	15.9	14.0	7.4	4.1
Italy	33	32	0.0	294.1	25.8	31.1	10.1	8.9	30.6	23.4	15.9	11.4
Jamaica	51	46	–0.2	10.8	31.9	31.1	9.2	9.2	11.0	11.1	5.0	4.5
Japan	37	33	–0.6	364.5	68.4	68.5	1.3	0.9	13.1	11.8	3.9	3.4
Jordan	28	22	2.0	88.2	1.1	1.1	0.8	0.9	2.0	2.3	5.7	3.4
Kazakhstan	44	42	1.8	2,699.7	1.3	1.2	0.1	0.0	13.0	8.7	213.2	145.4
Kenya	82	78	2.2	569.1	6.5	6.1	0.8	1.1	8.8	9.5	21.3	13.7
Korea, Dem. Rep.	42	37	–0.5	120.4	68.1	47.1	1.5	1.7	19.0	22.0	11.4	10.9
Korea, Rep.	26	18	–0.9	96.9	64.5	64.2	1.6	2.1	19.8	16.4	4.6	3.3
Kosovo	..	..	..	10.9[b]	..	..	..	..	..	27.6	..	16.8
Kuwait	2	2	2.1	17.8	0.2	0.3	0.1	0.2	0.2	0.6	0.2	0.4
Kyrgyz Republic	62	63	0.6	191.8	4.4	5.0	0.4	0.4	6.9	6.7	29.0	24.0
Lao PDR	85	67	–0.3	230.8	75.0	68.2	0.3	0.5	3.5	5.9	19.1	22.3
Latvia	31	32	–0.7	62.2	51.0	53.9	0.4	0.1	27.1	18.8	64.6	51.8
Lebanon	17	13	–0.2	10.2	12.8	13.4	11.9	14.0	17.9	14.2	6.2	3.5
Lesotho	86	73	0.0	30.4	1.3	1.4	0.1	0.1	10.4	11.0	19.3	15.6
Liberia	55	39	2.3	96.3	51.2	44.9	1.6	2.2	3.6	4.2	16.5	10.4
Libya	24	22	0.7	1,759.5	0.1	0.1	0.2	0.2	1.0	1.0	41.6	27.9
Lithuania	32	33	–0.9	62.7	31.0	34.5	0.7	0.4	46.0	32.8	78.0	61.5
Macedonia, FYR	42	32	–1.4	25.2	35.9	39.6	2.2	1.4	23.8	16.7	31.3	20.4
Madagascar	76	70	2.4	581.5	23.5	21.6	1.0	1.0	4.7	5.1	24.1	14.7
Malawi	88	80	2.5	94.1	41.3	34.4	1.4	1.3	23.9	38.2	24.0	24.9
Malaysia	50	28	–1.7	328.6	68.1	62.3	16.0	17.6	5.2	5.5	9.3	6.4
Mali	77	67	2.2	1,220.2	11.5	10.2	0.1	0.1	1.7	5.2	23.7	42.7
Mauritania	60	59	2.1	1,030.7	0.4	0.2	0.0	0.0	0.4	0.4	20.0	11.6
Mauritius	56	57	0.4	2.0	19.2	17.2	3.0	2.0	49.3	42.9	9.4	6.8
Mexico	29	22	–0.1	1,944.0	36.2	33.3	1.0	1.4	12.5	12.9	28.8	22.4
Moldova	53	59	0.4	32.9	9.7	11.7	14.2	9.2	52.8	55.2	46.8	51.0
Mongolia	43	43	1.2	1,553.6	8.1	7.0	0.0	0.0	0.9	0.6	62.5	35.4
Morocco	52	43	0.2	446.3	11.3	11.5	1.6	2.2	19.5	18.0	35.1	25.5
Mozambique	79	62	1.0	786.4	55.2	49.6	0.3	0.3	4.4	6.4	25.5	22.1
Myanmar	75	66	–0.2	653.5	60.0	48.6	0.8	1.7	14.6	16.9	24.4	23.2
Namibia	72	62	0.9	823.3	10.6	8.9	0.0	0.0	0.8	1.0	46.7	35.7
Nepal	91	82	1.2	143.4	33.7	25.4	0.5	0.8	16.0	16.7	12.0	8.2
Netherlands	31	17	–2.6	33.8	10.2	10.8	0.9	1.0	26.0	31.2	5.9	6.4
New Zealand	15	13	0.3	263.3	29.3	31.4	0.2	0.3	10.0	1.8	76.7	10.9
Nicaragua	48	43	0.7	120.3	37.5	25.9	1.6	1.9	10.8	15.8	31.6	33.3
Niger	85	83	3.4	1,266.7	1.5	1.0	0.0	0.0	8.7	11.8	141.7	99.8
Nigeria	65	50	1.1	910.8	18.9	9.9	2.8	3.3	32.4	37.3	30.3	22.0
Norway	28	22	0.9	305.5	30.0	32.9	0.0	0.0	2.8	2.7	20.3	17.3
Oman	34	28	2.4	309.5	0.0	0.0	0.1	0.1	0.1	0.3	1.9	3.7
Pakistan	69	63	1.1	770.9	3.3	2.2	0.6	1.1	26.6	26.5	18.3	12.0
Panama	46	25	–1.6	74.3	51.0	43.7	2.1	2.0	6.7	7.4	20.7	15.8
Papua New Guinea	85	88	2.3	452.9	69.6	63.4	1.2	1.5	0.4	0.6	4.6	3.9
Paraguay	51	39	0.2	397.3	53.3	44.3	0.2	0.3	5.3	9.6	49.7	59.9
Peru	31	28	0.7	1,280.0	54.8	53.1	0.3	0.6	2.7	2.9	16.1	12.7
Philippines	51	34	–0.5	298.2	22.0	25.7	14.8	16.9	18.4	18.1	8.9	5.9
Poland	39	39	0.2	304.2	29.2	30.7	1.1	1.3	47.3	41.2	37.8	32.9
Portugal	52	39	–1.5	91.5	36.4	37.8	8.5	8.5	25.6	12.3	23.5	10.6
Puerto Rico	28	1	–17.9	8.9	32.4	62.2	5.6	4.5	7.3	6.8	1.8	1.5
Qatar	8	4	7.7	11.6	0.0	0.0	0.1	0.3	0.9	1.0	2.1	0.8

	Rural population			Land area	Land use							
	% of total		average annual % growth	thousand sq. km	Forest area		Permanent cropland		Arable land		Arable land hectares per 100 people	
	1990	2010	1990–2010	2010	1990	2010	1990	2009	1990	2009	1990	2009
Romania	47	45	−0.6	229.9	27.8	28.6	2.6	1.6	41.2	38.2	40.7	40.9
Russian Federation	27	27	0.0	16,376.9	49.4	49.4	0.1	0.1	8.1	7.4	88.8	85.8
Rwanda	95	81	2.6	24.7	12.9	17.6	12.4	11.3	35.7	52.7	12.4	12.6
Saudi Arabia	23	16	−5.5	2,000.0c	0.5	0.5	0.0	0.1	1.6	1.5	21.0	11.9
Senegal	61	57	2.2	192.5	48.6	44.0	0.2	0.3	16.1	20.0	42.7	31.8
Serbia	50	48	−0.8	88.4	26.4	30.7	26.2	3.4	..	37.7	..	45.1
Sierra Leone	67	62	1.7	71.6	43.5	38.1	1.9	1.8	6.8	15.1	12.2	18.9
Singapore	–	–	..	0.7	3.0	2.9	1.5	0.0	1.5	0.0	0.0	0.0
Slovak Republic	44	43	0.0	48.1	40.0	40.2	1.0	0.5	32.5	28.7	31.0	25.5
Slovenia	50	52	1.2	20.1	59.0	62.2	1.8	1.3	9.9	8.7	10.0	8.6
Somalia	70	63	1.6	627.3	13.2	10.8	0.0	0.0	1.6	1.6	15.5	11.0
South Africa	48	38	0.1	1,214.5	6.8	4.7	0.7	0.8	11.1	11.8	38.2	29.1
South Sudan	..	..	..	..	..	..	..	..	..	..	..	..
Spain	25	23	−0.2	499.1	27.7	36.4	9.7	9.5	30.7	25.1	39.5	27.2
Sri Lanka	83	85	0.9	62.7	37.5	29.7	15.9	15.5	14.4	19.1	5.2	5.8
Sudan	73	55	0.9	2,376.0	32.1	29.4	0.0	0.1	5.4	8.5	48.3	47.5
Swaziland	77	75	1.1	17.2	27.4	32.7	0.7	0.9	10.5	10.2	20.9	15.0
Sweden	17	15	0.3	410.3	66.5	68.7	0.0	0.0	6.9	6.4	33.2	28.3
Switzerland	27	26	0.8	40.0	28.8	31.0	0.6	0.6	10.3	10.2	6.1	5.3
Syrian Arab Republic	51	45	1.3	183.6	2.0	2.7	4.0	5.4	26.6	25.4	39.6	23.3
Tajikistan	68	74	1.4	140.0	2.9	2.9	0.9	1.0	6.1	5.3	15.6	10.9
Tanzania	81	74	2.4	885.8	46.8	37.7	1.1	1.7	10.2	11.3	35.3	23.0
Thailand	71	66	0.1	510.9	38.3	37.1	6.1	7.2	34.2	29.9	30.7	22.3
Timor-Leste	79	72	1.6	14.9	65.0	49.9	3.9	4.0	7.4	11.1	14.8	15.0
Togo	70	57	0.9	54.4	12.6	5.3	1.7	3.3	38.6	40.4	57.3	37.3
Trinidad and Tobago	92	86	0.0	5.1	47.0	44.1	6.8	4.3	7.0	4.9	3.0	1.9
Tunisia	42	33	−0.2	155.4	4.1	6.5	12.5	14.3	18.7	17.4	35.7	25.9
Turkey	41	30	−0.2	769.6	12.6	14.7	3.9	3.8	32.0	27.7	45.5	29.7
Turkmenistan	55	51	0.4	469.9	8.8	8.8	0.1	0.1	2.9	3.9	34.8	37.2
Uganda	89	87	3.0	197.1	23.8	15.2	9.3	11.3	25.0	33.0	28.3	20.4
Ukraine	33	32	−0.6	579.3	16.0	16.8	1.9	1.6	57.6	56.1	64.0	70.5
United Arab Emirates	21	22	7.7	83.6	2.9	3.8	0.2	2.4	0.4	0.8	1.9	0.9
United Kingdom	11	10	−0.1	241.9	10.8	11.9	0.3	0.2	27.4	25.0	11.6	9.8
United States	25	18	−1.0	9,147.4	32.4	33.2	0.2	0.3	20.3	17.8	74.4	53.1
Uruguay	11	8	−1.0	175.0	5.3	10.0	0.3	0.2	7.2	10.7	40.5	56.2
Uzbekistan	60	63	1.3	425.4	7.2	7.7	0.9	0.8	10.5	10.1	20.9	15.5
Venezuela, RB	16	6	−3.9	882.1	59.0	52.5	0.9	0.7	3.2	3.1	14.3	9.7
Vietnam	80	71	0.4	310.1	28.8	44.5	3.2	10.8	16.4	20.3	8.1	7.3
West Bank and Gaza	32	28	2.3	6.0	1.5	1.5	19.1	19.4	18.1	16.6	5.5	2.5
Yemen, Rep.	79	68	2.2	528.0	1.0	1.0	0.2	0.5	2.9	2.2	12.8	5.0
Zambia	61	64	1.4	743.4	71.0	66.5	0.0	0.0	3.9	4.5	36.8	26.3
Zimbabwe	71	62	0.0	386.9	57.3	40.4	0.3	0.3	7.5	10.8	27.6	33.5
World	**57 w**	**49 w**	**0.3 w**	**129,561.0 s**	**32.0 w**	**31.1 w**	**1.1 w**	**1.2 w**	**10.9 w**	**10.7 w**	**23.7 w**	**20.4 w**
Low income	79	72	1.5	15,043.5	31.2	27.6	0.7	0.9	7.7	9.6	23.8	18.5
Middle income	62	51	0.1	80,675.5	33.9	32.8	1.4	1.4	11.1	10.9	18.8	17.8
Lower middle income	68	60	0.8	22,789.9	30.7	27.9	1.9	2.7	14.8	16.4	18.7	15.1
Upper middle income	56	43	−0.9	57,885.6	35.2	34.6	1.1	0.9	9.2	8.7	18.9	20.6
Low & middle income	64	54	0.3	95,718.9	33.5	31.9	1.2	1.3	10.5	10.7	19.3	17.9
East Asia & Pacific	71	54	−0.9	15,853.7	29.0	29.6	2.2	3.4	12.1	11.5	12.0	9.4
Europe & Central Asia	37	36	0.1	22,748.9	38.4	38.6	0.4	0.4	11.6	10.5	68.5	59.2
Latin America & Carib.	29	21	−0.6	20,116.2	51.6	47.0	0.9	1.0	6.6	7.4	30.3	25.9
Middle East & N. Africa	48	42	1.1	8,643.6	2.4	2.4	0.8	1.0	5.9	5.9	22.5	15.6
South Asia	75	70	1.0	4,771.2	16.6	17.1	1.8	3.1	42.7	41.4	17.8	12.3
Sub-Saharan Africa	72	63	1.7	23,585.4	31.1	28.0	0.8	1.0	6.6	8.5	32.1	24.2
High income	27	22	−0.5	33,842.1	27.9	28.8	0.7	0.7	11.7	10.8	42.5	33.2
Euro area	29	26	−0.4	2,552.0	33.8	37.3	4.8	4.2	27.1	24.4	22.9	18.8

a. Includes Luxembourg. b. Data are from national sources. c. Provisional estimate.

About the data

With more than 3 billion people, including 70 percent of the world's poor people, living in rural areas, adequate indicators to monitor progress in rural areas are essential. However, few indicators are disaggregated between rural and urban areas (for some that are, see tables 2.7, 3.5, and 3.13). The table shows indicators of rural population and land use. Rural population is approximated as the midyear nonurban population. While a practical means of identifying the rural population, it is not precise (see box 3.1a for further discussion).

The data in the table show that land use patterns are changing. They also indicate major differences in resource endowments and uses among countries. True comparability of the data is limited, however, by variations in definitions, statistical methods, and quality of data. Countries use different definitions of rural and urban population and land use. The Food and Agriculture Organization of the United Nations (FAO), the primary compiler of the data, occasionally adjusts its definitions of land use categories and revises earlier data. Because the data reflect changes in reporting procedures as well as actual changes in land use, apparent trends should be interpreted cautiously.

Satellite images show land use that differs from that of ground-based measures in area under cultivation and type of land use. Moreover, land use data in some countries (India is an example) are based on reporting systems designed for collecting tax revenue. With land taxes no longer a major source of government revenue, the quality and coverage of land use data have declined. Data on forest area may be particularly unreliable because of irregular surveys and differences in definitions (see About the data for table 3.4). Forest area statistics released by the FAO between 1948 and 1963 were based mostly on data from country questionnaires. Remote sensing, statistical monitoring, and expert analysis of country surveys have been applied since 1980 to improve forest coverage estimates. The FAO's Global Forest Resources Assessment 2010 covers 230 countries and is the most comprehensive assessment of forests, forestry, and the benefits of forest resources in both scope and number of countries and people involved. It examines status and trends for about 90 variables on the extent, condition, uses, and values of forests and other wooded land.

What is rural? Urban? 3.1a

The rural population identified in table 3.1 is approximated as the difference between total population and urban population, calculated using the urban share reported by the United Nations Population Division. There is no universal standard for distinguishing rural from urban areas, and any urban-rural dichotomy is an oversimplification (see About the data for table 3.13). The two distinct images—isolated farm, thriving metropolis—represent poles on a continuum. Life changes along a variety of dimensions, moving from the most remote forest outpost through fields and pastures, past tiny hamlets, through small towns with weekly farm markets, into intensively cultivated areas near large towns and small cities, eventually reaching the center of a megacity. Along the way access to infrastructure, social services, and nonfarm employment increase, and with them population density and income. Because rurality has many dimensions, for policy purposes the rural-urban dichotomy presented in tables 3.1, 3.5, and 3.13 is inadequate.

A 2005 World Bank Policy Research Paper proposes an operational definition of rurality based on population density and distance to large cities (Chomitz, Buys, and Thomas 2005). The report argues that these criteria are important gradients along which economic behavior and appropriate development interventions vary substantially. Where population densities are low, markets of all kinds are thin, and the unit cost of delivering most social services and many types of infrastructure is high. Where large urban areas are distant, farm-gate or factory-gate prices of outputs will be low and input prices will be high, and it will be difficult to recruit skilled people to public service or private enterprises. Thus, low population density and remoteness together define a set of rural areas that face special development challenges.

Using these criteria and the Gridded Population of the World (CIESIN 2005), the authors' estimates of the rural population for Latin America and the Caribbean differ substantially from those in table 3.1. Their estimates range from 13 percent of the population, based on a population density of less than 20 people per square kilometer, to 64 percent, based on a population density of more than 500 people per square kilometer. Taking remoteness into account, the estimated rural population would be 13–52 percent. The estimate for Latin America and the Caribbean in table 3.1 is 21 percent.

Data sources

Data on urban population shares used to estimate rural population are from the United Nations Population Division's World Urbanization Prospects: The 2009 Revision, and data on total population are World Bank estimates. Data on land area, permanent cropland, and arable land are from the FAO's electronic files. The FAO gathers these data from national agencies through annual questionnaires and by analyzing the results of national agricultural censuses. Data on forest area are from the FAO's Global Forest Resources Assessment 2010.

	Agricultural land[a]			Average annual precipitation	Land under cereal production		Fertilizer consumption		Agricultural employment		Agricultural machinery	
	% of land area		% irrigated	millimeters	thousand hectares		% of fertilizer production	kilograms per hectare of arable land	% of total employment		Tractors per 100 sq. km of arable land	
	1990–92	2007–09	2007–09	2007–09	1990–92	2008–10	2007–09	2007–09	1990–92	2007–09	1990	2009
Afghanistan	58	58	4.8	327	2,250.0	3,122.0	146.8	3.2	..	..	0.2	0.1
Albania	41	44	16.8	1,485	189.5	145.7	..	45.5	..	44.1	212.4	121.9
Algeria	16	17	2.1	89	3,530.5	2,988.8	487.9	7.8	..	..	129.1	139.6
Angola	46	47	..	1,010	1,012.0	1,670.0	..	1.1	5.1	..	..	..
Argentina	47	51	..	591	8,372.5	9,358.1	153.3	25.4	0.4	1.2	100.2	86.9
Armenia	41	62	8.9	562	162.8	156.7	..	29.3	..	44.2	345.5	291.6
Australia	61	53	0.4	534	13,319.8	19,476.4	151.7	29.0	5.3	3.3	..	..
Austria	42	38	1.4	1,110	837.7	994.8	..	83.1	7.1	5.3	2,373.6	2,390.3
Azerbaijan	53	58	29.5	447	627.0	954.6	..	13.6	34.7	38.6	194.8	148.2
Bahrain	13	9	..	83	..	..	5.9	..	2.4	..	45.0	75.0
Bangladesh	73	70	..	2,666	10,860.8	12,349.1	231.5	281.7	66.4	..	2.3	1.2
Belarus	46	44	0.5	618	2,603.0	2,380.3	46.3	281.1	22.3	..	206.9	86.8
Belgium	44[b]	45	0.4	847	386.2[b]	329.5	..	..	2.9	1.5	1,523.3[b]	1,127.0
Benin	21	30	..	1,039	667.3	1,109.3	..	..	..	..	1.0	..
Bolivia	33	34	..	1,146	680.2	931.6	..	6.0	2.1	36.1	24.8	20.0
Bosnia and Herzegovina	43	42	..	1,028	304.1	286.2	..	24.5	..	..	235.3	..
Botswana	46	46	..	416	77.9	111.3	..	..	..	..	140.5	134.8
Brazil	29	31	..	1,782	20,564.1	18,674.3	245.0	124.9	28.3	17.0	143.8	129.2
Bulgaria	56	46	1.4	608	2,231.6	1,917.5	115.1	167.4	21.2	7.1	135.8	172.3
Burkina Faso	35	44	..	748	2,844.0	4,290.2	..	9.1	..	..	2.4	..
Burundi	83	84	..	1,274	220.0	232.7	..	0.9	..	..	1.8	..
Cambodia	26	31	..	1,904	1,733.4	3,106.8	..	7.1	..	72.2	3.2	5.9
Cameroon	19	20	..	1,604	950.3	1,639.9	..	7.4	..	..	0.9	..
Canada	7	7	..	537	20,176.4	13,013.6	22.2	46.8	4.1	2.4	164.8	162.5
Central African Republic	8	8	..	1,343	95.4	163.1	..	..	..	..	..	..
Chad	38	39	..	322	1,337.6	2,467.1	..	..	..	..	..	..
Chile	21	21	5.6	1,522	694.3	523.1	94.7	595.8	18.0	11.2	127.6	425.9
China	57	56	..	645	92,582.2	90,131.6	96.8	488.4	58.5	39.6	66.6	81.8
Hong Kong SAR, China	..	..	..	..	..	..	..	..	0.7	0.2	..	..
Colombia	41	38	..	2,612	1,440.7	1,047.7	227.0	496.8	1.4	19.7	96.8	..
Congo, Dem. Rep.	10	10	..	1,543	1,921.1	1,980.4	..	0.5	..	..	..	..
Congo, Rep.	31	31	..	1,646	9.9	31.8	..	1.1	..	..	..	..
Costa Rica	42	35	1.5	2,926	76.3	76.0	..	826.6	24.1	12.3	..	..
Côte d'Ivoire	60	64	..	1,348	1,451.0	851.0	..	15.9	..	..	19.9	32.1
Croatia	43	23	0.4	1,113	592.7	550.0	48.7	246.8	..	13.9	35.2	49.4
Cuba	63	63	..	1,335	252.3	401.6	445.3	14.2	25.3	18.6	226.2	203.2
Cyprus	17	14	20.8	498	65.1	35.7	..	181.9	12.0	3.9	1,377.4	1,460.1
Czech Republic	..	55	0.3	677	..	1,467.2	112.4	123.3	..	3.1	252.0	262.3
Denmark	65	62	9.6	703	1,611.9	1,489.4	..	103.2	5.1	2.5	634.7	486.3
Dominican Republic	54	51	..	1,410	153.1	225.4	..	27.2	18.7	14.5	25.9	21.5
Ecuador	29	30	12.6	2,087	918.4	875.7	..	187.3	6.6	28.7	54.2	90.7
Egypt, Arab Rep.	3	4	..	51	2,477.1	2,967.1	48.5	502.8	38.4	31.6	249.6	390.6
El Salvador	70	75	2.1	1,724	486.3	354.3	..	107.4	35.8	20.9	..	..
Eritrea	..	75	..	384	..	461.7	..	3.5	..	..	5.0	8.3
Estonia	32	22	..	626	453.6	274.1	378.1	69.5	18.1	4.0	455.3	604.7
Ethiopia	..	35	0.5	848	..	9,340.5	..	7.9	..	..	..	..
Finland	8	8	..	536	914.5	954.2	75.8	108.0	8.9	4.6	916.5	784.0
France	55	53	5.1	867	9,346.0	9,258.8	437.6	148.3	5.9	2.9	800.0	635.3
Gabon	20	20	..	1,831	16.1	22.9	..	6.1	..	..	..	..
Gambia, The	61	67	..	836	78.3	322.7	..	6.8	..	..	2.4	..
Georgia	46	36	4.0	1,026	248.5	173.2	14.3	43.0	..	53.4	295.6	216.9
Germany	49	48	..	700	6,514.4	6,612.9	60.8	181.4	3.7	1.7	1,309.4	838.3
Ghana	56	68	..	1,187	1,203.5	1,602.1	..	11.9	62.0	..	7.1	4.5
Greece	71	64	16.9	652	1,396.1	916.8	333.5	83.7	21.9	11.9	744.2	1,004.7
Guatemala	40	41	..	1,996	822.7	923.3	..	106.8	13.6	..	..	..
Guinea	57	58	..	1,651	819.8	2,028.7	..	0.6	..	..	12.7	25.1
Guinea-Bissau	51	58	..	1,577	117.2	152.5	..	..	..	..	0.8	..
Haiti	57	67	..	1,440	462.9	446.2	..	..	65.6	..	2.6	..

	Agricultural land[a]			Average annual precipitation	Land under cereal production		Fertilizer consumption		Agricultural employment		Agricultural machinery	
	% of land area		% irrigated	millimeters	thousand hectares		% of fertilizer production	kilograms per hectare of arable land	% of total employment		Tractors per 100 sq. km of arable land	
	1990–92	2007–09	2007–09	2007–09	1990–92	2008–10	2007–09	2007–09	1990–92	2007–09	1990	2009
Honduras	30	29	..	1,976	516.8	538.5	..	62.3	38.2	34.6	30.9	48.7
Hungary	68	64	1.8	589	2,746.0	2,585.7	154.0	80.0	11.3	4.6	97.7	261.8
India	61	61	35.1	1,083	99,499.5	92,610.0	166.3	167.8	..	..	60.7	128.5
Indonesia	23	30	..	2,702	14,732.7	17,387.5	110.9	181.4	54.9	39.7	2.2	2.0
Iran, Islamic Rep.	39	30	19.0	228	9,787.4	9,440.3	125.4	69.7	..	21.2	141.5	152.8
Iraq	23	20	..	216	3,919.5	2,555.5	118.6	37.2	..	23.4	65.8	92.2
Ireland	64	61	..	1,118	295.3	276.4	..	477.3	11.6	5.0	1,623.4	1,476.4
Israel	27	24	28.4	435	104.9	79.1	2.5	189.5	3.5	1.7	798.8	695.3
Italy	54	47	18.8	832	4,225.4	3,494.3	186.5	135.5	8.0	3.7	1,586.5	2,117.1
Jamaica	44	41	..	2,051	2.9	2.0	..	58.2	27.3	20.2	..	..
Japan	15	13	35.2	1,668	2,430.9	1,941.8	114.3	235.1	6.4	3.9	4,492.9	4,532.1
Jordan	13	12	9.2	111	121.1	44.5	32.3	2,444.2	..	3.0	340.8	301.7
Kazakhstan	82	77	..	250	22,152.4	15,068.4	34.1	2.4	..	29.4	62.0	24.2
Kenya	48	48	0.0	630	1,804.8	2,542.4	..	32.4	..	..	20.0	25.2
Korea, Dem. Rep.	21	24	..	1,054	1,517.6	1,268.2	..	..	..	..	295.4	..
Korea, Rep.	22	19	51.6	1,274	1,293.2	970.4	87.8	388.8	15.8	7.0	211.0	1,115.4
Kosovo	..	52	..				..	..	..	..	..	..
Kuwait	8	8	..	121	0.3	1.1	0.2	54.5	..	..	220.0	89.0
Kyrgyz Republic	53	55	9.4	533	578.0	579.8	..	21.0	38.2	34.0	189.4	188.1
Lao PDR	7	10	..	1,834	597.9	1,090.6	..	..	..	..	8.5	..
Latvia	41	29	0.0	641	696.7	531.2	..	64.9	..	8.7	363.7	501.4
Lebanon	59	67	19.9	661	42.1	64.9	3.1	19.9	..	..	174.9	..
Lesotho	77	77	..	788	153.1	190.5	..	..	..	..	57.7	..
Liberia	26	27	..	2,391	120.0	251.2	..	..	..	47.6	..	..
Libya	9	9	..	56	287.7	329.0	28.2	40.3	..	..	184.3	218.9
Lithuania	54	43	..	656	1,134.0	1,037.6	8.5	45.4	..	9.2	256.0	631.8
Macedonia, FYR	51	40	7.3	619	235.2	161.8	..	56.9	..	19.7	730.2	1,243.8
Madagascar	63	70	2.2	1,513	1,340.2	1,729.0	..	2.6	..	..	4.9	1.9
Malawi	45	59	0.5	1,181	1,430.2	1,831.2	53,107.2	26.6	..	..	152.9	..
Malaysia	23	24	..	2,875	693.8	680.1	126.3	769.8	21.8	13.5	10.2	2.2
Mali	26	34	..	282	2,451.6	3,975.1	..	3.2	..	..	8.4	9.8
Mauritania	38	38	..	92	123.6	291.5	..	..	..	..	..	..
Mauritius	56	48	21.4	2,041	0.5	0.1	..	209.4	14.3	9.0	..	..
Mexico	54	53	5.5	752	9,928.3	9,980.0	328.9	51.7	26.8	13.5	123.5	97.7
Moldova	78	75	9.2	450	675.6	884.7	..	9.4	40.0	31.1	310.1	197.6
Mongolia	80	75	..	241	592.6	259.1	..	7.9	..	40.0	80.3	40.0
Morocco	69	67	4.6	346	5,019.6	5,059.7	12.5	20.8	3.6	40.9	45.0	..
Mozambique	61	63	..	1,032	1,376.9	2,490.7	..	2.9	..	..	..	..
Myanmar	16	19	24.8	2,091	5,577.5	8,732.4	185.8	5.4	69.1	..	13.6	10.7
Namibia	47	47	..	285	195.2	309.9	..	1.6	48.2	16.3	..	..
Nepal	29	30	27.7	1,500	2,840.0	3,383.2	..	1.4	81.2	..	21.9	111.7
Netherlands	59	57	10.6	778	180.9	210.4	16.3	240.9	3.7	2.5	2,073.1	1,301.5
New Zealand	61	44	..	1,732	135.3	135.5	238.3	1,231.7	10.8	6.6	315.1	..
Nicaragua	34	43	..	2,391	295.1	464.9	..	22.2	38.9	29.5	20.0	..
Niger	28	35	..	151	7,554.6	10,629.4	..	0.1	..	..	0.2	..
Nigeria	80	82	..	1,150	16,836.0	13,808.9	..	2.1	..	..	4.7	6.6
Norway	3	3	..	1,414	359.2	300.6	29.3	191.3	5.5	2.7	1,779.1	1,539.1
Oman	3	6	4.0	125	2.8	3.1	2.5	236.4	..	..	41.1	58.1
Pakistan	34	34	73.9	494	11,758.2	13,288.7	150.7	217.2	48.3	44.7	129.7	153.4
Panama	29	30	..	2,692	183.6	154.9	..	46.8	26.3	17.9	102.0	147.2
Papua New Guinea	2	3	..	3,142	2.1	3.4	..	119.8	..	..	59.4	..
Paraguay	44	53	..	1,130	501.0	1,439.3	..	66.4	1.9	26.5	71.6	69.1
Peru	17	17	..	1,738	609.0	1,248.7	98,094.6	104.5	0.8	0.8	36.3	..
Philippines	37	40	..	2,348	6,719.2	6,853.3	1,408.8	140.5	45.4	35.2	65.2	116.8
Poland	62	53	0.4	600	8,321.1	8,423.6	101.4	144.6	25.0	13.3	823.6	1,257.9
Portugal	42	40	11.4	854	751.9	324.7	91.8	159.1	11.5	11.2	563.1	1,397.7
Puerto Rico	46	21	8.5	2,054	0.4	0.2	..	..	3.4	1.5	438.5	525.0
Qatar	6	6	..	74	1.2	2.1	2.8	3,191.7	..	2.3	84.0	63.1

	Agricultural land[a]			Average annual precipitation	Land under cereal production		Fertilizer consumption		Agricultural employment		Agricultural machinery	
	% of land area		% irrigated	millimeters	thousand hectares		% of fertilizer production	kilograms per hectare of arable land	% of total employment		Tractors per 100 sq. km of arable land	
	1990–92	2007–09	2007–09	2007–09	1990–92	2008–10	2007–09	2007–09	1990–92	2007–09	1990	2009
Romania	64	59	2.2	637	5,773.9	5,016.9	69.0	48.5	33.0	29.1	140.6	201.2
Russian Federation	14	13	2.0	460	59,541.3	32,331.0	13.0	15.6	15.4	9.7	97.8	27.1
Rwanda	74	81	..	1,212	249.5	386.3	..	1.1	..	..	1.0	0.5
Saudi Arabia	58	81	..	59	1,121.9	317.4	8.8	43.8	..	4.1	19.2	..
Senegal	46	49	..	686	1,087.2	1,477.5	601.1	4.9	..	..	1.6	2.1
Serbia	..	58	0.6	..	..	1,873.4	294.0	133.8	..	24.0	..	17.7
Sierra Leone	39	48	..	2,526	432.9	649.1	..	..	..	..	4.1	..
Singapore	1	0	..	2,497	..	..	..	..	0.3	1.1	..	..
Slovak Republic	..	40	1.0	824	..	701.3	59.6	95.5	..	3.6	197.5	154.6
Slovenia	28	23	0.9	1,162	112.5	95.7	..	241.9	..	9.1	4,000.0	5,895.2
Somalia	70	70	..	282	401.6	596.3	..	..	..	..	15.9	12.0
South Africa	81	82	..	495	5,352.0	3,540.2	168.3	49.2	..	5.1	107.9	43.0
South Sudan	..	..	..	..	..	..	..	..	..	..	..	..
Spain	61	55	11.9	636	7,402.0	5,984.2	106.1	96.9	9.7	4.2	483.1	831.2
Sri Lanka	37	42	..	1,712	802.6	1,124.7	2,970.1	257.9	43.6	32.6	163.1	..
Sudan	52	58	1.0	416	8,258.8	7,886.4	..	7.9	..	..	7.2	13.8
Swaziland	71	71	..	788	61.5	56.2	..	..	..	..	228.9	87.1
Sweden	8	8	..	624	1,119.2	959.1	264.4	69.4	3.3	2.2	601.9	592.4
Switzerland	40	38	..	1,537	201.2	151.8	..	190.4	4.3	3.1	2,783.1	2,602.9
Syrian Arab Republic	74	76	8.9	252	3,712.6	2,620.6	153.2	65.4	28.2	15.2	128.1	215.0
Tajikistan	32	34	14.8	691	273.5	443.5	493.4	47.2	46.8	..	415.4	310.2
Tanzania	38	40	..	1,071	3,253.6	5,018.9	..	8.7	84.2	..	8.2	23.3
Thailand	42	39	..	1,622	10,586.6	12,339.5	1,397.2	125.1	60.8	41.5	33.0	280.5
Timor-Leste	22	25	..	1,500	77.8	106.8	..	..	..	..	8.5	..
Togo	59	62	..	1,168	573.2	880.8	..	3.3	..	..	0.5	0.6
Trinidad and Tobago	16	11	..	2,200	7.1	2.2	0.7	85.2	11.5	3.8	1,238.9	1,972.7
Tunisia	60	63	4.1	207	1,469.9	651.8	10.3	42.3	..	..	82.4	142.6
Turkey	52	51	13.4	593	13,731.1	12,005.1	208.5	96.5	44.7	22.9	279.8	395.3
Turkmenistan	69	69	..	161	331.3	983.6	..	..	..	..	464.7	..
Uganda	60	70	..	1,180	1,139.0	1,842.5	..	2.1	..	65.6	..	..
Ukraine	72	71	5.3	565	12,542.3	14,184.5	44.7	29.7	20.8	15.8	153.3	102.7
United Arab Emirates	4	7	..	78	1.4	0.0	30.8	1,033.0	..	4.2	51.4	63.3
United Kingdom	75	72	..	1,220	3,488.6	3,008.4	183.2	239.2	2.2	1.1	760.6	..
United States	46	44	..	715	65,850.8	57,488.4	103.6	109.3	2.9	1.5	238.4	271.3
Uruguay	85	85	1.2	1,265	569.8	785.8	2,741.0	131.1	4.5	11.0	260.3	219.5
Uzbekistan	65	63	..	206	1,225.3	1,642.1	77.5	193.3	..	..	..	..
Venezuela, RB	24	24	..	1,875	763.1	1,256.3	80.7	200.2	11.8	8.5	..	..
Vietnam	22	33	..	1,821	6,953.4	8,641.7	403.5	402.3	..	..	47.0	262.5
West Bank and Gaza	61	61	4.6	402	0.0	32.5	..	..	..	13.4	442.2	737.3
Yemen, Rep.	44	44	..	167	730.0	927.3	..	12.0	52.6	..	39.0	41.0
Zambia	28	31	..	1,020	797.8	1,216.2	..	27.3	49.8	..	21.9	..
Zimbabwe	35	42	..	657	1,168.5	1,901.8	185.2	28.0	..	..	60.1	..
World	**38 w**	**38 w**	**..**	**..**	**699,721.0 s**	**681,889.9 s**	**94.7 w**	**122.1 w**	**.. w**	**.. w**	**202.4 w**	**.. w**
Low income	35	38	..	..	57,506.1	90,727.2	236.5	25.9	..	..	8.4	..
Middle income	38	38	..	..	486,828.8	448,296.9	101.7	142.2	..	..	84.1	109.4
Lower middle income	45	47	..	..	208,267.4	209,263.7	135.8	118.9	..	..	53.0	..
Upper middle income	35	34	..	..	278,561.3	239,033.1	89.6	159.4	48.5	31.3	111.9	114.5
Low & middle income	37	38	..	..	544,334.9	539,024.0	102.9	128.6	..	..	75.8	..
East Asia & Pacific	48	49	..	..	142,379.2	150,606.8	105.4	..	57.8	39.6	53.2	..
Europe & Central Asia	29	28	..	..	125,257.0	92,762.3	35.7	38.8	23.2	16.3	135.9	115.6
Latin America & Carib.	34	36	..	..	48,465.9	49,996.0	212.8	92.2	18.9	14.3	120.9	..
Middle East & N. Africa	24	23	..	..	31,097.6	27,682.0	46.8	79.5	..	27.2	114.6	155.8
South Asia	55	55	..	..	128,100.5	125,939.2	168.5	176.0	..	..	62.1	120.7
Sub-Saharan Africa	42	45	..	..	69,034.7	92,037.8	192.9	10.5	..	..	19.8	..
High income	38	37	..	..	155,386.1	142,865.9	74.3	104.3	6.2	3.3	472.1	..
Euro area	49	46	..	..	32,498.0	30,496.6	98.7	143.4	6.7	3.6	986.1	841.4

a. Includes permanent pastures, arable land, and land under permanent crops. b. Includes Luxembourg.

About the data

Agriculture is still a major sector in many economies, and agricultural activities provide developing countries with food and revenue. But agricultural activities also can degrade natural resources. Poor farming practices can cause soil erosion and loss of soil fertility. Efforts to increase productivity by using chemical fertilizers, pesticides, and intensive irrigation have environmental costs and health impacts. Excessive use of chemical fertilizers can alter the chemistry of soil. Pesticide poisoning is common in developing countries. And salinization of irrigated land diminishes soil fertility. Thus, inappropriate use of inputs for agricultural production has far-reaching effects.

The table provides indicators of major inputs to agricultural production: land, fertilizer, labor, and machinery. There is no single correct mix of inputs: appropriate levels and application rates vary by country and over time and depend on the type of crops, the climate and soils, and the production process used.

The agriculture sector is the most water-intensive sector, and water delivery in agriculture is increasingly important. The table shows irrigated agricultural land as share of total agricultural land area and data on average precipitation to illustrate how countries obtain water for agricultural use.

The data here and in table 3.3 are collected by the Food and Agriculture Organization of the United Nations (FAO) through annual questionnaires. The FAO tries to impose standard definitions and reporting methods, but complete consistency across countries and over time is not possible. Thus, data on agricultural land in different climates may not be comparable. For example, permanent pastures are quite different in nature and intensity in African countries and dry Middle Eastern countries. Data on agricultural employment, in particular, should be used with caution. In many countries much agricultural employment is informal and unrecorded, including substantial work performed by women and children. To address some of these concerns, this indicator is heavily footnoted in the database in sources, definition, and coverage.

Fertilizer consumption measures the quantity of plant nutrients. Consumption is calculated as production plus imports minus exports. Because some chemical compounds used for fertilizers have other industrial applications, the consumption data may overstate the quantity available for crops. Fertilizer consumption as a share of production shows the agriculture sector's vulnerability to import and energy price fluctuation. The FAO recently revised the time series for fertilizer consumption and irrigation for 2002 onward, but recent data are not available for all countries. FAO collects fertilizer statistics for production, imports, exports, and consumption through the new FAO fertilizer resources questionnaire. In the previous release, the data were based on total consumption of fertilizers, but the data in the recent release are based on the nutrients in fertilizers. Some countries compile fertilizer data on a calendar year basis, while others do so on a crop year basis (July–June). Previous editions of *World Development Indicators* reported data on a crop year basis, but this edition uses the calendar year, as adopted by the FAO. Caution should thus be used when comparing data over time.

Definitions

• **Agricultural land** is permanent pastures, arable land, and land under permanent crops. Permanent pasture is land used for five or more years for forage, including natural and cultivated crops. Arable land includes land defined by the FAO as land under temporary crops (double-cropped areas are counted once), temporary meadows for mowing or for pasture, land under market or kitchen gardens, and land temporarily fallow. Land abandoned as a result of shifting cultivation is excluded. Land under permanent crops is land cultivated with crops that occupy the land for long periods and need not be replanted after each harvest, such as cocoa, coffee, and rubber. Land under flowering shrubs, fruit trees, nut trees, and vines is included, but land under trees grown for wood or timber is not. • **Irrigated land** refers to areas purposely provided with water, including land irrigated by controlled flooding. • **Average annual precipitation** is the long-term average in depth (over space and time) of annual precipitation in the country. Precipitation is defined as any kind of water that falls from clouds as a liquid or a solid. • **Land under cereal production** refers to harvested areas, although some countries report only sown or cultivated area. • **Fertilizer consumption** is the quantity of plant nutrients applied to arable land. Fertilizer products cover nitrogen, potash, and phosphate fertilizers (including ground rock phosphate). Traditional nutrients—animal and plant manures—are not included. • **Fertilizer production** is fertilizer consumption, exports, and nonfertilizer use of fertilizer products minus fertilizer imports. • **Agricultural employment** is employment in agriculture, forestry, hunting, and fishing (see table 2.3). • **Agricultural machinery** refers to wheel and crawler tractors (excluding garden tractors) in use in agriculture at the end of the calendar year specified or during the first quarter of the following year.

Data sources

Data on agricultural inputs are from the FAO's electronic files. Data on agricultural employment are from the International Labour Organization's Key Indicators of the Labour Market, 7th edition, database.

	Crop production index 2004–06 = 100		Food production index 2004–06 = 100		Livestock production index 2004–06 = 100		Cereal yield kilograms per hectare		Agricultural productivity Agriculture value added per worker 2000 $	
	1990	**2009**	**1990**	**2009**	**1990**	**2009**	**1990**	**2010**	**1990**	**2010**
Afghanistan	67.0	125.0	68.0	114.0	70.0	101.0	1,201	1,908	..	..
Albania	85.0	121.0	69.0	110.0	58.0	99.0	2,794	4,762	764	..
Algeria	41.0	121.0	50.0	117.0	69.0	109.0	688	1,568	1,702	2,254
Angola	33.0	153.0	42.0	144.0	74.0	110.0	321	617	206	340
Argentina	53.0	83.0	63.0	95.0	84.0	113.0	2,232	4,937	6,683	12,957
Armenia	67.0	125.0	74.0	131.0	84.0	134.0	1,843	2,074	1,607	4,723
Australia	67.0	101.0	74.0	103.0	85.0	101.0	1,716	1,721	19,447	35,208
Austria	89.0	103.0	93.0	101.0	95.0	99.0	5,577	5,358	13,413	25,771
Azerbaijan	95.0	110.0	82.0	115.0	79.0	118.0	2,113	2,019	1,001	1,241
Bahrain	61.0	116.0	90.0	117.0	137.0	117.0	..	..	..	..
Bangladesh	66.0	122.0	63.0	121.0	56.0	113.0	2,491	4,144	275	507
Belarus	77.0	111.0	110.0	120.0	127.0	129.0	2,741	2,827	2,042	5,700
Belgium	..	100.0	..	97.0	..	98.0	5,755[a]	9,231	..	..
Benin	45.0	117.0	48.0	122.0	70.0	100.0	848	1,402	427	..
Bolivia	53.0	106.0	61.0	113.0	68.0	119.0	1,361	2,333	683	716
Bosnia and Herzegovina	75.0	99.0	87.0	110.0	92.0	128.0	3,553	3,858	..	15,028
Botswana	83.0	122.0	95.0	116.0	98.0	114.0	266	544	761	447
Brazil	59.0	117.0	51.0	116.0	44.0	113.0	1,755	4,055	1,625	4,118
Bulgaria	149.0	98.0	179.0	103.0	248.0	96.0	3,954	3,665	3,983	10,923
Burkina Faso	44.0	95.0	50.0	105.0	53.0	109.0	600	1,054	107	..
Burundi	98.0	61.0	98.0	65.0	103.0	136.0	1,349	1,346	118	..
Cambodia	46.0	147.0	46.0	137.0	53.0	92.0	1,362	3,108	..	434
Cameroon	58.0	113.0	61.0	114.0	79.0	103.0	1,259	1,711	420	..
Canada	82.0	109.0	73.0	107.0	68.0	95.0	2,636	3,490	28,898	44,619
Central African Republic	76.0	113.0	61.0	111.0	54.0	110.0	810	1,465	321	..
Chad	51.0	105.0	56.0	112.0	74.0	110.0	559	775	170	..
Chile	60.0	101.0	58.0	101.0	55.0	101.0	3,620	6,822	3,457	6,267
China	56.0	116.0	48.0	115.0	39.0	112.0	4,325	5,521	258	545
Hong Kong SAR, China	..	..	..	..	..	..	..	..	..	..
Colombia	80.0	108.0	70.0	112.0	68.0	117.0	2,475	3,895	3,123	2,874
Congo, Dem. Rep.	125.0	98.0	120.0	99.0	99.0	102.0	800	771	213	173
Congo, Rep.	66.0	112.0	63.0	116.0	53.0	126.0	624	785	..	..
Costa Rica	62.0	109.0	59.0	113.0	70.0	116.0	3,097	3,730	2,993	5,596
Côte d'Ivoire	68.0	103.0	66.0	108.0	80.0	111.0	887	1,717	658	1,056
Croatia	93.0	110.0	105.0	114.0	106.0	106.0	3,975	5,486	5,552	16,423
Cuba	136.0	88.0	160.0	98.0	185.0	136.0	2,342	1,940	4,117	3,618
Cyprus	136.0	73.0	98.0	87.0	69.0	95.0	1,886	1,595	5,808	7,927
Czech Republic	..	99.0	..	98.0	..	95.0	..	4,691	..	6,415
Denmark	115.0	112.0	94.0	107.0	81.0	101.0	6,118	5,889	14,588	53,407
Dominican Republic	98.0	107.0	78.0	116.0	58.0	126.0	3,996	4,234	1,974	5,083
Ecuador	66.0	114.0	56.0	115.0	48.0	114.0	1,724	3,117	2,109	2,040
Egypt, Arab Rep.	56.0	116.0	54.0	118.0	53.0	114.0	5,703	6,541	1,767	3,265
El Salvador	92.0	112.0	75.0	109.0	62.0	107.0	1,939	2,806	1,742	2,752
Eritrea	..	84.0	..	99.0	..	111.0	..	536	..	66
Estonia	129.0	126.0	157.0	115.0	175.0	109.0	1,304	2,444	3,288	3,156
Ethiopia	..	126.0	..	122.0	..	113.0	..	1,674	..	226
Finland	110.0	109.0	108.0	101.0	107.0	97.0	3,543	3,136	17,163	47,514
France	96.0	100.0	99.0	98.0	98.0	96.0	6,083	7,093	21,454	57,973
Gabon	78.0	118.0	91.0	115.0	86.0	102.0	1,750	1,782	1,216	1,972
Gambia, The	56.0	119.0	60.0	119.0	76.0	106.0	1,004	1,127	253	282
Georgia	138.0	73.0	105.0	72.0	78.0	68.0	1,998	1,271	2,359	1,817
Germany	93.0	106.0	107.0	105.0	114.0	103.0	5,411	6,716	13,730	32,866
Ghana	34.0	119.0	37.0	119.0	78.0	120.0	989	1,814	..	..
Greece	80.0	81.0	86.0	86.0	99.0	95.0	3,036	4,908	..	..
Guatemala	57.0	125.0	57.0	122.0	70.0	103.0	1,998	2,299	2,241	2,803
Guinea	59.0	105.0	59.0	107.0	43.0	120.0	1,455	1,409	166	242
Guinea-Bissau	60.0	94.0	62.0	98.0	70.0	115.0	1,531	1,555	..	..
Haiti	107.0	109.0	96.0	106.0	59.0	102.0	1,027	980	..	..

Agricultural output and productivity

	Crop production index		Food production index		Livestock production index		Cereal yield		Agricultural productivity	
									Agriculture value added per worker 2000 $	
							kilograms per hectare			
	2004–06 = 100		2004–06 = 100		2004–06 = 100					
	1990	2009	1990	2009	1990	2009	1990	2010	1990	2010
Honduras	70.0	105.0	65.0	103.0	51.0	105.0	1,468	1,094	1,184	2,041
Hungary	100.0	89.0	118.0	94.0	161.0	96.0	4,521	4,759	4,177	8,522
India	73.0	113.0	71.0	114.0	62.0	115.0	1,891	2,537	357	489
Indonesia	61.0	121.0	62.0	120.0	62.0	114.0	3,800	4,876	493	730
Iran, Islamic Rep.	55.0	99.0	54.0	104.0	51.0	115.0	1,445	2,359	1,988	..
Iraq	102.0	87.0	118.0	92.0	153.0	100.0	1,061	1,687	..	..
Ireland	91.0	82.0	97.0	91.0	96.0	93.0	6,577	7,409	..	13,931
Israel	95.0	97.0	72.0	104.0	56.0	109.0	3,486	3,015	..	..
Italy	84.0	91.0	89.0	97.0	96.0	106.0	3,945	5,436	10,435	31,254
Jamaica	98.0	105.0	81.0	106.0	61.0	106.0	1,116	1,172	2,224	2,758
Japan	123.0	94.0	114.0	98.0	107.0	101.0	5,846	5,852	19,563	48,794
Jordan	66.0	106.0	57.0	110.0	44.0	115.0	1,220	1,963	1,976	3,401
Kazakhstan	144.0	131.0	142.0	126.0	147.0	115.0	1,338	804	1,781	1,782
Kenya	72.0	105.0	68.0	110.0	67.0	114.0	1,562	1,613	400	337
Korea, Dem. Rep.	99.0	101.0	92.0	100.0	96.0	100.0	3,916	3,582	..	..
Korea, Rep.	91.0	106.0	79.0	108.0	62.0	110.0	5,853	6,196	5,338	19,807
Kosovo	..	..	..	..	..	..	..	..	..	..
Kuwait	39.0	106.0	48.0	110.0	54.0	112.0	3,653	3,415	..	..
Kyrgyz Republic	64.0	106.0	76.0	101.0	107.0	102.0	2,772	2,604	685	996
Lao PDR	52.0	129.0	50.0	125.0	49.0	118.0	2,268	3,751	388	532
Latvia	106.0	114.0	194.0	118.0	253.0	114.0	1,641	2,667	1,896	3,837
Lebanon	96.0	101.0	83.0	104.0	54.0	112.0	1,878	2,740	..	41,013
Lesotho	127.0	81.0	106.0	100.0	91.0	112.0	1,037	909	255	202
Liberia	62.0	97.0	77.0	121.0	79.0	124.0	1,029	1,179	..	..
Libya	77.0	103.0	75.0	104.0	73.0	106.0	674	662	..	..
Lithuania	81.0	136.0	133.0	110.0	154.0	95.0	1,938	2,667	..	5,996
Macedonia, FYR	102.0	110.0	102.0	114.0	97.0	114.0	2,652	3,329	2,413	5,946
Madagascar	79.0	110.0	80.0	112.0	99.0	113.0	1,945	2,987	213	187
Malawi	50.0	131.0	47.0	127.0	64.0	151.0	992	2,206	89	169
Malaysia	59.0	109.0	53.0	114.0	58.0	109.0	2,740	3,800	3,826	6,680
Mali	54.0	134.0	61.0	146.0	75.0	135.0	726	1,615	406	..
Mauritania	63.0	124.0	76.0	107.0	79.0	104.0	870	946	651	404
Mauritius	107.0	95.0	89.0	98.0	45.0	109.0	4,191	10,000	3,446	6,401
Mexico	74.0	99.0	65.0	101.0	59.0	105.0	2,424	3,499	2,250	3,302
Moldova	121.0	90.0	139.0	91.0	196.0	91.0	2,928	2,696	1,349	1,610
Mongolia	230.0	216.0	134.0	146.0	132.0	142.0	1,098	1,370	1,477	1,524
Morocco	68.0	116.0	68.0	117.0	71.0	116.0	1,120	1,548	1,807	3,315
Mozambique	60.0	101.0	63.0	98.0	47.0	95.0	477	1,006	132	234
Myanmar	42.0	122.0	41.0	126.0	25.0	138.0	2,762	3,989	..	..
Namibia	56.0	100.0	82.0	90.0	89.0	86.0	457	373	1,267	881
Nepal	62.0	112.0	64.0	110.0	70.0	107.0	1,920	2,295	248	238
Netherlands	91.0	106.0	103.0	108.0	106.0	109.0	6,959	8,574	23,743	47,805
New Zealand	74.0	105.0	64.0	98.0	67.0	97.0	5,034	7,387	19,767	26,556
Nicaragua	59.0	111.0	51.0	115.0	45.0	119.0	1,524	2,086	..	2,779
Niger	49.0	138.0	46.0	132.0	42.0	122.0	310	479	239	..
Nigeria	47.0	88.0	49.0	92.0	61.0	112.0	1,148	1,413	..	..
Norway	135.0	84.0	110.0	103.0	103.0	106.0	4,399	3,810	17,454	46,480
Oman	63.0	112.0	52.0	97.0	40.0	77.0	2,160	18,987	1,029	..
Pakistan	67.0	108.0	60.0	115.0	56.0	117.0	1,766	2,592	769	947
Panama	123.0	88.0	91.0	102.0	64.0	114.0	1,867	2,131	2,303	4,109
Papua New Guinea	72.0	117.0	69.0	108.0	66.0	91.0	2,603	3,839	559	683
Paraguay	70.0	92.0	64.0	110.0	72.0	117.0	1,979	3,457	1,660	2,710
Peru	46.0	117.0	49.0	123.0	55.0	128.0	2,603	3,899	911	1,607
Philippines	72.0	111.0	67.0	112.0	49.0	114.0	2,065	3,232	854	1,119
Poland	133.0	109.0	110.0	104.0	114.0	102.0	3,284	3,220	1,619	2,994
Portugal	110.0	91.0	98.0	98.0	84.0	106.0	1,878	3,463	4,516	7,019
Puerto Rico	138.0	100.0	133.0	103.0	132.0	104.0	1,080	1,878	..	..
Qatar	56.0	138.0	66.0	168.0	73.0	192.0	2,897	4,795	..	..

	Crop production index 2004–06 = 100		Food production index 2004–06 = 100		Livestock production index 2004–06 = 100		Cereal yield kilograms per hectare		Agricultural productivity Agriculture value added per worker 2000 $	
	1990	**2009**	**1990**	**2009**	**1990**	**2009**	**1990**	**2010**	**1990**	**2010**
Romania	82.0	85.0	94.0	93.0	116.0	99.0	3,011	3,331	2,351	9,700
Russian Federation	100.0	107.0	117.0	106.0	143.0	97.0	1,743	1,844	1,915	2,731
Rwanda	76.0	122.0	72.0	121.0	59.0	122.0	1,043	1,930	174	..
Saudi Arabia	83.0	95.0	70.0	102.0	56.0	111.0	4,245	5,621	7,863	20,233
Senegal	78.0	143.0	76.0	136.0	71.0	113.0	795	1,196	262	256
Serbia	78.0[b]	106.0	99.0[b]	99.0	109.0[b]	98.0	2,926[b]	4,959	..	2,057
Sierra Leone	69.0	101.0	68.0	104.0	81.0	116.0	1,202	1,554	..	..
Singapore	90.0	149.0	492.0	98.0	535.0	93.0	..	..	21,392	29,145
Slovak Republic	..	93.0	..	92.0	..	86.0	..	3,754	..	9,924
Slovenia	74.0	87.0	76.0	93.0	75.0	93.0	3,279	5,973	13,217	76,633
Somalia	122.0	100.0	92.0	100.0	88.0	100.0	793	432	..	..
South Africa	83.0	108.0	78.0	109.0	79.0	110.0	1,877	4,162	2,287	3,662
South Sudan	..	..	..	..	..	..	..	..	..	..
Spain	89.0	105.0	83.0	104.0	72.0	98.0	2,485	3,231	8,938	22,035
Sri Lanka	87.0	111.0	85.0	112.0	75.0	107.0	2,965	3,974	672	966
Sudan	50.0	106.0	47.0[c]	103.0	47.0	99.0	456	452	512	929
Swaziland	99.0	97.0	90.0	101.0	85.0	110.0	1,284	1,226	1,025	1,217
Sweden	130.0	106.0	109.0	101.0	103.0	97.0	4,964	4,518	23,307	51,585
Switzerland	118.0	106.0	104.0	103.0	102.0	104.0	5,984	6,084	20,556	27,066
Syrian Arab Republic	51.0	93.0	51.0	96.0	54.0	99.0	750	1,789	2,698	..
Tajikistan	83.0	115.0	99.0	118.0	132.0	117.0	994	2,721	370	577
Tanzania	61.0	110.0	62.0	106.0	61.0	101.0	1,507	1,332	219	292
Thailand	64.0	111.0	69.0	112.0	73.0	112.0	2,009	2,938	443	706
Timor-Leste	81.0	136.0	95.0	129.0	104.0	109.0	1,608	2,451	..	..
Togo	67.0	104.0	64.0	114.0	68.0	123.0	747	1,187	376	..
Trinidad and Tobago	141.0	113.0	84.0	107.0	50.0	104.0	3,326	2,727	1,825	1,024
Tunisia	74.0	101.0	69.0	101.0	58.0	107.0	1,145	1,702	2,383	3,050
Turkey	78.0	103.0	79.0	108.0	83.0	112.0	2,214	2,727	2,254	3,770
Turkmenistan	73.0	92.0	51.0	113.0	49.0	126.0	2,210	3,289	1,275	..
Uganda	72.0	106.0	71.0	105.0	64.0	100.0	1,498	1,608	189	200
Ukraine	98.0	118.0	128.0	106.0	166.0	95.0	2,834	2,727	1,231	2,500
United Arab Emirates	28.0	100.0	29.0	113.0	43.0	143.0	2,216	2,667	..	..
United Kingdom	104.0	102.0	107.0	101.0	107.0	99.0	6,171	6,957	19,880	25,681
United States	79.0	105.0	77.0	109.0	78.0	105.0	4,755	6,988	18,703	51,120
Uruguay	48.0	134.0	60.0	109.0	70.0	100.0	2,183	4,251	5,648	8,682
Uzbekistan	83.0	118.0	76.0	123.0	82.0	114.0	1,777	4,516	1,427	2,782
Venezuela, RB	76.0	108.0	71.0	106.0	71.0	110.0	2,486	4,038	4,458	7,667
Vietnam	45.0	110.0	47.0	114.0	38.0	133.0	3,073	5,161	222	367
West Bank and Gaza	..	109.0	..	101.0	..	85.0	..	1,163	..	..
Yemen, Rep.	61.0	121.0	56.0	126.0	50.0	134.0	908	1,092	621	749
Zambia	61.0	129.0	74.0	115.0	77.0	96.0	1,352	2,547	213	214
Zimbabwe	118.0	91.0	94.0	92.0	75.0	105.0	1,625	752	270	160
World	**70.0[c] w**	**122.2 w**	**70.0[c] w**	**123.0 w**	**74.0[c] w**	**120.3 w**	**2,756[c] w**	**3,568 w**	**781 w**	**992 w**
Low income	78.4	132.2	78.3	133.2	78.0	131.7	1,565	2,075	240	288
Middle income	73.4	128.4	68.7	130.3	62.5	131.4	2,556	3,312	481	786
Lower middle income	74.8	127.2	72.8	128.2	69.4	131.8	1,928	2,718	472	677
Upper middle income	72.6	129.1	66.5	131.4	59.6	131.2	3,177	3,831	487	871
Low & middle income	73.8	128.7	69.4	130.5	63.3	131.4	2,429	3,103	455	728
East Asia & Pacific	69.9	133.1	62.7	135.1	48.8	135.2	3,796	4,925	305	585
Europe & Central Asia	111.4	129.4	118.2	126.3	137.7	119.2	2,596	2,239	2,245	3,204
Latin America & Carib.	75.8	128.1	71.2	131.2	69.7	132.6	2,089	3,919	2,221	3,663
Middle East & N. Africa	74.7	127.3	72.8	131.6	69.3	134.7	1,471	2,379	1,796	..
South Asia	78.0	119.3	74.5	122.7	69.2	132.9	1,926	2,691	373	521
Sub-Saharan Africa	71.1	128.7	72.9	130.0	80.1	125.1	1,033	1,335	307	322
High income	90.7	103.9	90.4	106.3	90.7	104.0	4,138	5,319	14,129	24,483
Euro area	90.9	96.9	95.6	97.7	98.2	100.0	4,490	5,685	12,590	25,752

a. Includes Luxembourg. b. Includes Montenegro. c. Food and Agriculture Organization estimate.

About the data

The agricultural production indexes in the table are prepared by the Food and Agriculture Organization of the United Nations (FAO). The FAO obtains data from official and semiofficial reports of crop yields, area under production, and livestock numbers. If data are unavailable, the FAO makes estimates. The indexes are calculated using the Laspeyres formula: production quantities of each commodity are weighted by average international commodity prices in the base period and summed for each year. Because the FAO's indexes are based on the concept of agriculture as a single enterprise, estimates of the amounts retained for seed and feed are subtracted from the production data to avoid double counting. The aggregates are net production available for any use except as seed and feed. The FAO's indexes may differ from those from other sources because of differences in coverage, weights, concepts, time periods, calculation methods, and use of international prices.

To facilitate cross-country comparisons, the FAO uses international commodity prices to value production. These prices, expressed in international dollars (equivalent in purchasing power to the U.S. dollar), are derived using a Geary-Khamis formula applied to agricultural outputs (see Inter-Secretariat Working Group on National Accounts 1993, sections 16.93–96). This method assigns a single price to each commodity so that, for example, one metric ton of wheat has the same price regardless of where it was produced. The use of international prices eliminates fluctuations in the value of output due to transitory movements of nominal exchange rates unrelated to the purchasing power of the domestic currency.

Data on cereal yield may be affected by a variety of reporting and timing differences. Millet and sorghum, which are grown as feed for livestock and poultry in Europe and North America, are used as food in Africa, Asia, and countries of the former Soviet Union. So some cereal crops are excluded from the data for some countries and included elsewhere, depending on their use.

Definitions

• **Crop production index** is agricultural production for the period specified relative to the base period 2004–06. It includes all crops except fodder crops. The regional and income group aggregates for the FAO's production indexes are calculated from the underlying values in international dollars, normalized to the base period 2004–06. • **Food production index** covers food crops that are considered edible and that contain nutrients. Coffee and tea are excluded because, although edible, they have no nutritive value. • **Livestock production index** includes meat and milk from all sources, dairy products such as cheese, and eggs, honey, raw silk, wool, and hides and skins. • **Cereal yield,** measured in kilograms per hectare of harvested land, includes wheat, rice, maize, barley, oats, rye, millet, sorghum, buckwheat, and mixed grains. Production data on cereals refer to crops harvested for dry grain only. Cereal crops harvested for hay or harvested green for food, feed, or silage, and those used for grazing, are excluded. The FAO allocates production data to the calendar year in which the bulk of the harvest took place. But most of a crop harvested near the end of a year will be used in the following year. • **Agricultural productivity** is the ratio of agricultural value added, measured in 2005 U.S. dollars, to the number of workers in agriculture. Agricultural productivity is measured by value added per unit of input. (For further discussion of the calculation of value added in national accounts, see *About the data* for tables 4.1 and 4.2.) Agricultural value added includes that from forestry and fishing. Thus interpretations of land productivity should be made with caution.

Data sources

Data on agricultural production indexes, cereal yield, and agricultural employment are from the FAO's electronic files, available on the FAO website (www.fao.org). Data on agricultural value added are from the World Bank's national accounts files.

	Forest area		Average annual deforestation[a]		Threatened species				GEF benefits index for biodiversity	Nationally protected areas			
	thousand sq. km		%		Mammals	Birds	Fish	Higher plants[b]	0–100 (no biodiversity to maximum biodiversity)	Terrestrial % of land area		Marine % of territorial waters	
	1990	2010	1990–2000	2000–10	2011	2011	2011	2011	2008	1990	2010	1990	2010
Afghanistan	14	14	0.00	0.00	11	14	5	2	3.4	0.4	0.4	..	..
Albania	8	8	0.26	−0.10	3	5	39	0	0.2	3.4	9.8	0.2	1.6
Algeria	17	15	0.54	0.57	14	9	36	12	2.9	6.3	6.3	0.2	0.3
Angola	610	585	0.21	0.21	15	23	39	34	8.3	12.4	12.4	0.1	0.1
Argentina	348	294	0.88	0.81	38	49	37	35	17.7	4.6	5.5	0.8	1.1
Armenia	3	3	1.31	1.48	9	12	3	1	0.2	6.9	8.0	..	..
Australia	1,545	1,493	−0.03	0.37	55	52	103	27	87.7	7.5	10.6	10.9	28.3
Austria	38	39	−0.16	−0.13	3	7	11	9	0.3	20.1	22.9	..	..
Azerbaijan	9	9	0.00	0.00	7	14	10	0	0.8	6.2	7.1	..	..
Bahrain	0c	0c	−5.56	−3.55	3	3	8	0	0.0	1.3	1.3	0.0	0.7
Bangladesh	15	14	0.18	0.18	34	30	18	15	1.4	1.7	1.8	0.4	0.8
Belarus	78	86	−0.62	−0.43	4	4	2	0	0.0	6.5	7.2	..	..
Belgium	7	7	0.15	−0.16	3	2	11	0	0.0	3.2	13.8	0.0	0.0
Benin	58	46	1.29	1.04	11	6	27	13	0.2	23.8	23.8	0.0	0.0
Bolivia	628	572	0.44	0.50	20	34	0	72	12.5	8.8	18.5	..	..
Bosnia and Herzegovina	22	22	0.11	0.00	4	5	31	0	0.4	0.5	0.6	0.7	0.7
Botswana	137	114	0.90	0.99	7	10	2	0	1.4	30.3	30.9	..	..
Brazil	5,748	5,195	0.51	0.50	81	122	84	389	100.0	9.0	26.3	8.2	16.5
Bulgaria	33	39	−0.14	−1.53	7	11	19	5	0.8	2.0	9.2	0.2	3.2
Burkina Faso	68	56	0.91	1.01	9	7	4	3	0.3	13.7	14.2	..	..
Burundi	3	2	3.71	1.40	11	11	17	2	0.3	3.8	4.8	..	..
Cambodia	129	101	1.14	1.34	37	24	42	29	3.5	0.0	25.8	0.0	0.4
Cameroon	243	199	0.94	1.05	38	20	112	378	12.5	7.0	9.2	0.4	0.4
Canada	3,101	3,101	0.00	0.00	12	15	35	1	21.5	4.7	7.5	0.6	1.2
Central African Republic	232	226	0.13	0.13	8	9	3	17	1.5	17.5	17.7	..	..
Chad	131	115	0.62	0.66	13	9	1	2	2.2	9.4	9.4	..	..
Chile	153	162	−0.37	−0.25	20	34	20	34	15.3	16.0	16.6	3.5	3.7
China	1,571	2,069	−1.20	−1.57	75	86	113	374	66.6	13.5	16.6	0.4	1.3
Hong Kong SAR, China	..	..	..	..	2	20	13	6	..	41.1	41.8	..	..
Colombia	625	605	0.16	0.17	52	94	54	215	51.5	19.3	20.9	0.9	15.5
Congo, Dem. Rep.	1,604	1,541	0.20	0.20	30	35	83	80	19.9	10.0	10.0	3.8	4.4
Congo, Rep.	227	224	0.08	0.07	11	2	46	37	3.6	5.4	9.4	0.0	32.8
Costa Rica	26	26	0.76	−0.93	9	19	50	112	9.7	18.7	20.9	11.9	12.2
Côte d'Ivoire	102	104	−0.10	−0.15	23	15	45	106	3.4	22.6	22.6	0.1	0.1
Croatia	19	19	−0.19	−0.19	7	10	60	5	0.6	7.8	13.0	1.3	3.4
Cuba	21	29	−1.70	−1.66	14	17	34	155	12.5	4.3	6.4	1.3	4.4
Cyprus	2	2	−0.63	−0.09	5	4	19	16	0.5	7.1	10.5	0.3	0.6
Czech Republic	26	27	−0.03	−0.08	2	5	2	8	0.1	13.6	15.1	..	..
Denmark	4	5	−0.89	−1.14	2	2	15	1	0.2	4.2	4.9	3.0	3.2
Dominican Republic	20	20	0.00	0.00	6	14	21	27	6.0	22.2	22.2	30.4	30.4
Ecuador	138	99	1.53	1.81	43	73	50	1,714	29.3	21.6	25.1	0.2	75.4
Egypt, Arab Rep.	0c	1	−2.98	−1.73	17	9	39	2	2.9	1.9	5.9	4.4	9.3
El Salvador	4	3	1.26	1.45	5	5	14	24	0.9	0.4	0.8	3.1	3.1
Eritrea	16	15	0.28	0.28	10	12	18	4	0.8	4.9	5.0	0.0	0.0
Estonia	21	22	−0.71	0.12	1	3	5	0	0.1	17.7	20.4	25.3	26.5
Ethiopia	151	123	0.97	1.08	33	24	14	24	8.4	17.7	18.4	..	..
Finland	219	222	−0.26	0.14	1	4	6	1	0.2	4.2	9.0	3.5	5.0
France	145	160	−0.55	−0.39	9	6	44	27	5.3	10.2	16.5	0.3	21.3
Gabon	220	220	0.00	0.00	14	4	61	120	3.0	4.6	15.1	0.2	7.3
Gambia, The	4	5	−0.42	−0.41	10	8	23	4	0.1	1.5	1.5	0.1	0.1
Georgia	28	27	0.04	0.09	10	10	9	0	0.6	2.8	3.7	0.2	0.4
Germany	107	111	−0.31	0.00	6	5	23	13	0.6	31.9	42.4	35.7	40.3
Ghana	74	49	1.99	2.08	16	13	44	117	1.9	14.6	14.7	0.0	0.0
Greece	33	39	−0.88	−0.81	10	10	75	52	2.8	5.7	16.2	0.5	2.6
Guatemala	47	37	1.20	1.40	16	10	25	72	8.0	25.9	30.6	0.3	12.5
Guinea	73	65	0.51	0.54	22	13	65	22	2.3	6.8	6.8	0.0	0.0
Guinea-Bissau	22	20	0.44	0.48	12	5	32	4	0.6	7.6	16.1	2.7	45.8
Haiti	1	1	0.62	0.76	5	13	20	26	5.2	0.3	0.3	0.0	0.0

	Forest area		Average annual deforestation[a]		Threatened species				GEF benefits index for biodiversity	Nationally protected areas			
	thousand sq. km		%		Mammals	Birds	Fish	Higher plants[b]	0–100 (no biodiversity to maximum biodiversity)	Terrestrial % of land area		Marine % of territorial waters	
	1990	2010	1990–2000	2000–10	2011	2011	2011	2011	2008	1990	2010	1990	2010
Honduras	81	52	2.38	2.06	7	9	27	107	7.2	13.6	18.2	0.0	1.9
Hungary	18	20	−0.57	−0.62	2	8	9	8	0.2	4.6	5.1	..	..
India	639	684	−0.22	−0.46	94	78	212	291	39.9	4.7	5.0	1.6	1.7
Indonesia	1,185	944	1.75	0.51	184	119	140	385	81.0	10.0	14.1	0.5	2.0
Iran, Islamic Rep.	111	111	0.00	0.00	16	20	29	1	7.3	5.2	7.1	1.0	1.7
Iraq	8	8	−0.17	−0.09	13	16	11	0	1.6	0.1	0.1	0.0	0.0
Ireland	5	7	−3.16	−1.53	5	1	20	1	0.6	0.6	1.8	0.1	0.2
Israel	1	2	−1.49	−0.07	15	13	36	0	0.8	16.3	17.8	0.4	0.4
Italy	76	91	−0.98	−0.90	7	7	47	61	3.8	5.0	15.1	0.5	17.4
Jamaica	3	3	0.11	0.11	5	10	21	206	4.4	10.2	18.9	0.2	4.2
Japan	250	250	0.03	−0.05	28	39	64	6	36.0	13.4	16.5	2.0	5.5
Jordan	1	1	0.00	0.00	13	10	13	1	0.4	0.7	1.9	0.0	30.0
Kazakhstan	34	33	0.17	0.17	16	20	14	16	5.1	2.4	2.5	..	..
Kenya	37	35	0.35	0.33	28	31	68	126	8.8	11.6	11.8	5.2	10.5
Korea, Dem. Rep.	82	57	1.67	2.00	9	24	13	5	0.7	4.3	5.9	0.1	0.1
Korea, Rep.	64	62	0.13	0.11	9	29	19	3	1.7	2.2	2.4	3.5	3.9
Kosovo	..	..	..	..	..	..	..	..	..	..	..	..	..
Kuwait	0[c]	0[c]	−3.46	−2.57	6	8	11	0	0.1	1.6	1.6	0.0	0.0
Kyrgyz Republic	8	10	−0.26	−1.07	6	12	3	14	1.1	6.4	6.9	..	..
Lao PDR	173	158	0.46	0.49	45	23	46	17	5.0	1.5	16.6	..	..
Latvia	32	34	−0.21	−0.34	1	4	6	0	0.0	6.5	18.0	4.6	6.7
Lebanon	1	1	0.00	−0.45	10	8	22	1	0.2	0.5	0.5	0.0	0.1
Lesotho	0[c]	0[c]	−0.49	−0.47	2	7	1	4	0.3	0.5	0.5	..	..
Liberia	49	43	0.63	0.67	18	11	53	47	2.6	1.6	1.8	0.0	0.0
Libya	2	2	0.00	0.00	12	3	24	2	1.6	0.1	0.1	0.0	0.1
Lithuania	19	22	−0.38	−0.68	3	4	6	0	0.0	2.0	14.5	0.8	10.7
Macedonia, FYR	9	10	−0.49	−0.41	5	9	13	0	0.2	4.2	4.9	..	..
Madagascar	137	126	0.42	0.45	65	35	85	273	29.2	2.2	3.1	0.0	0.1
Malawi	39	32	0.88	0.97	7	15	101	12	3.5	15.0	15.0	..	..
Malaysia	224	205	0.36	0.54	70	45	64	674	13.9	17.1	18.1	1.5	2.0
Mali	141	125	0.58	0.61	12	9	3	7	1.5	2.3	2.4	..	..
Mauritania	4	2	2.66	2.66	15	11	32	0	1.3	0.5	0.5	32.1	32.1
Mauritius	0[c]	0[c]	0.03	1.00	6	11	13	88	3.3	1.7	4.5	0.3	0.3
Mexico	703	648	0.52	0.30	100	56	152	191	68.7	2.2	11.1	1.1	16.7
Moldova	3	4	−0.16	−1.77	4	8	8	2	0.0	0.9	1.4	..	..
Mongolia	125	109	0.67	0.73	11	20	1	0	4.2	4.1	13.4	..	..
Morocco	50	51	0.06	−0.23	18	10	47	28	3.5	1.2	1.5	0.8	1.3
Mozambique	434	390	0.52	0.54	12	24	55	40	7.2	14.8	15.8	1.8	3.3
Myanmar	392	318	1.17	0.93	45	43	39	37	10.0	3.1	6.3	0.3	0.3
Namibia	88	73	0.87	0.97	12	25	27	25	5.2	14.4	14.9	0.5	8.2
Nepal	48	36	2.09	0.70	31	31	7	2	2.1	7.7	17.0	..	..
Netherlands	3	4	−0.43	−0.14	4	2	13	0	0.2	11.2	12.4	12.8	22.1
New Zealand	77	83	−0.69	−0.01	9	70	23	19	20.2	25.4	26.2	0.4	10.8
Nicaragua	45	31	1.67	2.01	6	12	30	40	3.3	15.4	36.7	0.6	37.2
Niger	19	12	3.74	0.98	12	7	4	2	0.9	7.1	7.1	..	..
Nigeria	172	90	2.68	3.67	26	14	59	171	6.0	11.6	12.8	0.2	0.2
Norway	91	101	−0.19	−0.80	7	2	19	2	1.3	7.0	14.6	1.2	2.4
Oman	0[c]	0[c]	0.00	0.00	9	11	26	6	3.7	0.0	10.7	0.0	1.3
Pakistan	25	17	1.76	2.24	23	27	34	2	4.9	10.1	10.1	1.8	1.8
Panama	38	33	1.18	0.36	15	17	41	192	10.9	17.2	18.7	3.1	4.0
Papua New Guinea	315	287	0.45	0.48	39	37	42	142	25.4	1.9	3.1	0.3	0.3
Paraguay	212	176	0.88	0.97	8	27	0	9	2.8	2.9	5.4	..	..
Peru	702	680	0.14	0.18	54	98	20	268	33.4	4.7	13.6	2.8	2.8
Philippines	66	77	−0.80	−0.75	38	74	71	210	32.3	8.7	10.9	0.5	2.5
Poland	89	93	−0.20	−0.31	5	6	7	8	0.5	15.3	22.4	3.4	4.1
Portugal	33	35	−0.28	−0.11	11	8	53	68	5.5	5.8	8.3	2.1	3.1
Puerto Rico	3	6	−4.92	−1.76	3	8	19	51	4.0	10.0	10.1	1.5	1.6
Qatar	0[c]	0[c]	0.00	0.00	3	4	11	0	0.1	1.7	2.5	0.0	0.3

3.4 Deforestation and biodiversity

	Forest area (thousand sq. km)		Average annual deforestation[a] (%)		Threatened species				GEF benefits index for biodiversity (0–100 (no biodiversity to maximum biodiversity))	Nationally protected areas Terrestrial % of land area		Marine % of territorial waters	
	1990	2010	1990–2000	2000–10	Mammals 2011	Birds 2011	Fish 2011	Higher plants[b] 2011	2008	1990	2010	1990	2010
Romania	64	66	0.01	−0.32	7	11	19	4	0.7	2.9	7.1	1.6	33.3
Russian Federation	8,090	8,091	0.00	0.00	32	49	35	8	34.1	5.0	9.1	2.2	10.8
Rwanda	3	4	−0.79	−2.38	20	12	9	4	0.9	9.9	10.0	..	..
Saudi Arabia	10	10	0.00	0.00	9	15	23	3	3.2	7.6	31.3	0.6	3.4
Senegal	93	85	0.49	0.49	16	10	45	9	1.0	24.1	24.1	5.8	12.4
Serbia	23	27	−0.62	−0.99	6	9	11	2	0.2	5.3	6.0	..	..
Sierra Leone	31	27	0.65	0.69	17	10	47	48	1.3	4.9	4.9	0.0	0.0
Singapore	0[c]	0[c]	0.00	0.00	11	15	25	57	0.1	5.0	5.4	0.0	1.4
Slovak Republic	19	19	0.01	−0.06	3	6	5	5	0.1	19.3	23.2	..	..
Slovenia	12	13	−0.37	−0.16	4	2	29	7	0.2	7.6	13.2	0.0	0.7
Somalia	83	67	0.97	1.07	15	12	27	21	6.1	0.6	0.6	0.0	0.0
South Africa	82	57	0.00	0.00	24	40	87	65	20.7	6.5	6.9	0.7	6.5
South Sudan	..	..	..	..	..	..	..	..	..	..	..	..	..
Spain	138	182	−2.09	−0.68	16	9	71	205	6.8	7.7	8.6	0.6	3.5
Sri Lanka	24	19	1.20	1.12	29	15	44	282	7.9	20.3	21.5	0.1	1.1
Sudan	764	699	0.80	0.08	15	15	19	16	5.1	4.2	4.2	0.0	0.0
Swaziland	5	6	−0.93	−0.84	5	11	4	3	0.1	3.0	3.0	..	..
Sweden	273	282	−0.04	−0.30	1	2	12	4	0.3	6.0	10.9	3.9	5.3
Switzerland	12	12	−0.37	−0.38	2	1	9	2	0.2	14.5	24.9	..	..
Syrian Arab Republic	4	5	−1.51	−1.29	16	14	34	2	0.9	0.3	0.6	0.0	0.6
Tajikistan	4	4	−0.05	0.00	8	12	5	13	0.7	1.9	4.1	..	..
Tanzania	415	334	1.02	1.13	35	42	174	290	14.8	26.6	27.5	3.7	10.0
Thailand	195	190	0.28	0.02	57	46	97	86	8.0	14.7	20.1	4.0	4.4
Timor-Leste	10	7	1.22	1.40	4	7	5	0	0.6	..	6.1	0.0	6.7
Togo	7	3	3.37	5.13	11	5	24	9	0.3	11.3	11.3	0.0	0.0
Trinidad and Tobago	2	2	0.30	0.32	2	2	24	1	2.2	30.5	31.2	0.2	2.8
Tunisia	6	10	−2.67	−1.86	13	6	35	6	0.5	1.3	1.3	1.1	1.2
Turkey	97	113	−0.47	−1.11	17	14	70	5	6.2	1.7	1.9	2.4	2.4
Turkmenistan	41	41	0.00	0.00	9	16	11	3	1.8	3.0	3.0	..	..
Uganda	48	30	2.03	2.56	22	21	61	36	2.8	7.9	10.3	..	..
Ukraine	93	97	−0.25	−0.21	11	11	21	16	0.5	1.8	3.5	4.1	4.9
United Arab Emirates	2	3	−2.38	−0.24	7	9	13	0	0.2	0.3	5.6	0.3	2.6
United Kingdom	26	29	−0.68	−0.31	5	2	43	11	3.5	22.0	26.4	4.9	5.7
United States	2,963	3,040	−0.13	−0.13	37	76	183	219	94.2	12.4	12.4	21.0	28.6
Uruguay	9	17	−4.38	−2.14	11	24	36	0	1.2	0.3	0.3	0.2	0.3
Uzbekistan	30	33	−0.54	−0.20	10	15	7	15	1.1	2.1	2.3	..	..
Venezuela, RB	520	463	0.57	0.60	32	27	37	68	25.3	40.1	53.8	7.0	15.3
Vietnam	94	138	−2.28	−1.65	54	43	68	119	12.1	4.5	6.2	0.3	1.7
West Bank and Gaza	0[c]	0[c]	0.00	−0.10	3	9	0	0	..	0.6	0.6	..	..
Yemen, Rep.	5	5	0.00	0.00	9	15	23	158	3.2	0.0	0.5	0.0	1.8
Zambia	528	495	0.32	0.33	9	14	20	9	3.8	36.0	36.0	..	..
Zimbabwe	222	156	1.58	1.88	9	14	3	14	1.9	18.0	28.0	..	..
World	**41,582 s**	**40,204 s**	**0.18 w**	**0.11 w**	**3,105 s**	**3,401 s**	**6,213 s**	**10,987 s**	..	**8.4 w**	**12.3 w**	**4.6 w**	**10.0 w**
Low income	4,721	4,155	0.63	0.61	..	..	..	..	..	9.6	10.7	..	..
Middle income	27,387	26,420	0.22	0.08	..	..	..	..	..	7.9	12.3	2.6	7.5
Lower middle income	7,003	6,364	0.59	0.30	..	..	..	..	..	7.3	9.4	2.7	4.4
Upper middle income	20,384	20,056	0.10	0.01	..	..	..	..	..	8.2	13.4	2.6	8.5
Low & middle income	32,108	30,575	0.28	0.15	..	..	..	..	..	8.2	12.0	2.6	7.2
East Asia & Pacific	4,602	4,698	0.08	−0.44	..	..	..	..	..	10.8	15.0	0.5	1.4
Europe & Central Asia	8,735	8,784	−0.02	−0.04	..	..	..	..	..	4.3	7.5	2.2	10.4
Latin America & Carib.	10,389	9,460	0.47	0.45	..	..	..	..	..	9.7	20.2	5.0	13.1
Middle East & N. Africa	207	211	−0.10	−0.15	..	..	..	..	..	3.3	3.9	0.8	2.0
South Asia	795	817	−0.01	−0.29	..	..	..	..	..	5.3	5.9	1.5	1.7
Sub-Saharan Africa	7,379	6,605	0.55	0.48	..	..	..	..	..	11.1	11.7	3.3	5.8
High income	9,474	9,629	−0.14	−0.04	..	..	..	..	..	8.9	12.9	9.3	16.5
Euro area	859	952	−0.76	−0.31	..	..	..	..	..	11.3	17.0	6.7	15.1

a. Negative values indicate an increase in forest area. b. Flowering plants only. c. Less than 0.5.

As threats to biodiversity mount, the international community is increasingly focusing on conserving diversity. Deforestation is a major cause of loss of biodiversity, and habitat conservation is vital for stemming this loss. Conservation efforts have focused on protecting areas of high biodiversity.

The Food and Agriculture Organization of the United Nations (FAO) *Global Forest Resources Assessment 2010* provides detailed information on forest cover in 2010 and adjusted estimates of forest cover in 1990 and 2000. The current survey uses a uniform definition of forest. Because of space limitations, the table does not break down forest cover between natural forest and plantation, a breakdown the FAO provides for developing countries. Thus the deforestation data in the table may underestimate the rate at which natural forest is disappearing in some countries.

The number of threatened species is an important measure of the immediate need for conservation in an area. Global analyses of the status of threatened species have been carried out for few groups of organisms. Only for mammals, birds, and amphibians has the status of virtually all known species been assessed. Threatened species are defined using the International Union for Conservation of Nature's (IUCN) classification: *endangered* (in danger of extinction and unlikely to survive if causal factors continue operating) and *vulnerable* (likely to move into the endangered category in the near future if causal factors continue operating).

The Global Environment Facility's (GEF) benefits index for biodiversity is a comprehensive indicator of national biodiversity status and is used to guide its biodiversity priorities. For each country the bio-diversity indicator incorporates the best available and comparable information in four relevant dimensions: represented species, threatened species, represented ecoregions, and threatened ecoregions. To combine these dimensions into one measure, the indicator uses dimensional weights that reflect the consensus of conservation scientists at the GEF, IUCN, WWF International, and other nongovernmental organizations.

The World Conservation Monitoring Centre (WCMC) compiles data on protected areas, numbers of certain species, and numbers of those species under threat from various sources. Because of differences in definitions, reporting practices, and reporting periods, cross-country comparability is limited.

Nationally protected areas are defined using the six IUCN management categories for areas of at least 1,000 hectares: scientific reserves and strict nature reserves with limited public access; national parks of national or international significance and not materially affected by human activity; natural monuments and natural landscapes with unique aspects; managed nature reserves and wildlife sanctuaries; protected landscapes (which may include cultural landscapes); and areas managed mainly for the sustainable use of natural systems to ensure long-term protection and maintenance of biological diversity. The data in the table cover these six categories as well as terrestrial protected areas that are not assigned to a category by the IUCN. Designating an area as protected does not mean that protection is in force. And for small countries that have only protected areas smaller than 1,000 hectares, the size limit in the definition leads to an underestimate of protected areas.

Due to variations in consistency and methods of collection, data quality is highly variable across countries. Some countries update their information more frequently than others, some have more accurate data on extent of coverage, and many underreport the number or extent of protected areas.

• **Forest area** is land spanning more than 0.5 hectare with trees higher than 5 meters and a canopy cover of more than 10 percent or with trees able to reach these thresholds in situ. It excludes land that is predominantly under agricultural or urban land use. • **Average annual deforestation** is the permanent conversion of natural forest area to other uses, including agriculture, ranching, settlements, and infrastructure. Deforested areas exclude areas logged but intended for regeneration and areas degraded by fuelwood gathering, acid precipitation, or forest fires. • **Threatened species** are species classified by the IUCN as endangered, vulnerable, rare, indeterminate, out of danger, or insufficiently known. Mammals exclude whales and porpoises. Birds are listed for the country where their breeding or wintering ranges are located. Fish are cold-blooded aquatic vertebrates of the superclass *Pisces*. Higher plants are native vascular plant species. • **GEF benefits index for biodiversity** is a composite index of relative biodiversity potential based on the species in each country and their threat status and diversity of habitat types. • **Nationally protected areas** are totally or partially protected areas of at least 1,000 hectares that are designated as scientific reserves with limited public access, national parks, natural monuments, nature reserves or wildlife sanctuaries, and protected landscapes. Terrestrial protected areas exclude marine areas, unclassified areas, littoral (intertidal) areas, and sites protected under local or provincial law. Marine protected areas are areas of intertidal or subtidal terrain—and overlying water and associated flora and fauna and historical and cultural features—that have been reserved to protect part of or the entire enclosed environment.

Data sources

Data on forest area are from the FAO's *Global Forest Resources Assessment 2010* and website. Data on threatened species are from the electronic files of the United Nations Environment Programme (UNEP) and WCMC and the *2011 IUCN Red List of Threatened Species*. The GEF benefits index for biodiversity is from Pandey and others (2006a). Data on nationally protected areas are from the UNEP and WCMC, based on data from national authorities, national legislation, and international agreements.

	Internal renewable freshwater resources[a]		Annual freshwater withdrawals					Water productivity	Access to an improved water source	
	Flows billion cu. m **2009**	Per capita cu. m **2009**	billion cu. m **2009**[b]	% of internal resources **2009**[b]	% for agriculture **2009**[b]	% for industry **2009**[b]	% for domestic **2009**[b]	GDP/water use 2000 $ per cu. m **2009**[b]	% of urban population **2010**	% of rural population **2010**
Afghanistan	55	1,645	23.1	35.6	99	1	1	..	42	78
Albania	27	8,425	1.8	4.4	58	12	30	3	94	96
Algeria	11	322	6.2	52.7	64	14	23	12	79	85
Angola	148	7,976	0.6	0.4	33	29	38	40	38	60
Argentina	276	6,889	32.6	4.0	66	12	22	12	80	98
Armenia	7	2,223	2.8	36.4	66	4	30	1	97	99
Australia	492	22,413	22.6	4.6	74	11	16	24	100	100
Austria	55	6,575	3.7	4.7	3	79	18	60	100	100
Azerbaijan	8	907	12.2	35.2	76	19	4	2	71	88
Bahrain	0[c]	3	0.4	219.8	45	6	50	35	..	100
Bangladesh	105	714	35.9	2.9	88	2	10	2	80	85
Belarus	37	3,913	4.3	7.5	19	54	27	6	99	100
Belgium	12	1,111	6.2	34.0	1	88	12	42	100	100
Benin	10	1,197	0.1	0.5	45	23	32	25	68	84
Bolivia	304	31,054	2.0	0.3	57	15	28	6	71	96
Bosnia and Herzegovina	36	9,422	0.3	0.9	..	..	..	24	98	100
Botswana	2	1,211	0.2	1.6	41	18	41	40	92	99
Brazil	5,418	28,037	58.1	0.7	55	17	28	15	85	100
Bulgaria	21	2,769	6.1	28.7	16	68	16	3	100	100
Burkina Faso	13	782	1.0	7.9	70	2	28	4	73	95
Burundi	10	1,231	0.3	2.3	77	6	17	3	71	83
Cambodia	121	8,628	2.2	0.5	94	2	4	3	58	87
Cameroon	273	14,237	1.0	0.3	76	7	17	14	52	95
Canada	2,850	84,495	46.0	1.6	12	69	20	18	99	100
Central African Republic	141	32,653	0.1	0.0	1	16	82	15	51	92
Chad	15	1,371	0.4	0.9	52	24	24	8	44	70
Chile	884	52,136	11.3	1.2	70	20	9	9	75	99
China	2,813	2,113	554.1	19.5	65	23	12	5	85	98
Hong Kong SAR, China	..	..	..	..	..	..	..	..	..	..
Colombia	2,112	46,261	12.7	0.6	39	4	57	11	72	99
Congo, Dem. Rep.	900	14,018	0.6	0.0[c]	18	20	63	10	27	79
Congo, Rep.	222	56,324	0.0	0.0[c]	9	22	70	101	32	95
Costa Rica	112	24,484	2.7	2.4	53	17	29	9	91	100
Côte d'Ivoire	77	3,971	1.4	1.7	43	19	38	8	68	91
Croatia	38	8,512	0.6	0.6	2	14	85	45	97	100
Cuba	38	3,385	7.6	19.8	75	10	15	4	89	96
Cyprus	1	715	0.2	19.3	86	3	10	66	100	100
Czech Republic	13	1,254	1.7	13.3	2	57	42	45	100	100
Denmark	6	1,086	0.7	10.8	36	5	58	253	100	100
Dominican Republic	21	2,144	3.5	16.6	64	2	34	11	84	87
Ecuador	432	30,291	15.3	3.6	92	3	6	2	89	96
Egypt, Arab Rep.	2	23	68.3	119.0	86	6	8	2	99	100
El Salvador	18	2,881	1.4	5.5	55	17	28	11	76	94
Eritrea	3	549	0.6	9.2	95	0	5	1	57	74
Estonia	13	9,483	1.8	14.0	0[c]	97	3	5	97	99
Ethiopia	122	1,503	5.6	4.6	94	0[c]	6	3	34	97
Finland	107	20,042	1.6	1.5	3	72	25	86	100	100
France	200	3,099	31.6	15.0	12	69	18	46	100	100
Gabon	164	110,997	0.1	0.1	38	9	53	46	41	95
Gambia, The	3	1,784	0.1	0.9	28	24	48	8	85	92
Georgia	58	13,179	1.6	2.6	65	13	22	3	96	100
Germany	107	1,306	32.3	21.0	0[c]	84	16	62	100	100
Ghana	30	1,272	1.0	1.8	66	10	24	8	80	91
Greece	58	5,141	9.5	12.7	89	2	9	17	99	100
Guatemala	109	7,781	2.9	2.6	55	30	15	9	87	98
Guinea	226	23,153	1.6	0.7	84	3	13	2	65	90
Guinea-Bissau	16	10,781	0.2	0.6	82	5	13	1	53	91
Haiti	13	1,319	1.2	8.6	78	4	19	3	51	85

	Internal renewable freshwater resources[a]		Annual freshwater withdrawals					Water productivity	Access to an improved water source	
	Flows billion cu. m 2009	Per capita cu. m 2009	billion cu. m 2009[b]	% of internal resources 2009[b]	% for agriculture 2009[b]	% for industry 2009[b]	% for domestic 2009[b]	GDP/water use 2000 $ per cu. m 2009[b]	% of urban population 2010	% of rural population 2010
Honduras	96	12,877	1.2	1.2	58	25	17	9	79	95
Hungary	6	599	5.6	5.4	6	82	12	..	100	100
India	1,446	1,197	761.0	39.8	90	2	7	1	90	97
Indonesia	2,019	8,504	113.3	5.6	82	7	12	2	74	92
Iran, Islamic Rep.	129	1,757	93.3	67.7	92	1	7	2	92	97
Iraq	35	1,132	66.0	87.3	79	15	7	0[c]	56	91
Ireland	49	10,989	..	..	..	..	..	..	100	100
Israel	1	100	2.0	101.9	58	6	36	83	100	100
Italy	183	3,032	45.4	23.7	44	36	20	25	100	100
Jamaica	9	3,489	0.6	6.2	34	22	44	17	88	98
Japan	430	3,371	90.0	20.9	63	18	19	54	100	100
Jordan	1	115	0.9	99.4	65	4	31	16	92	98
Kazakhstan	75	4,686	33.1	28.9	87	12	1	1	90	99
Kenya	21	525	2.7	8.9	79	4	17	7	52	82
Korea, Dem. Rep.	67	2,764	8.7	11.2	76	13	10	..	97	99
Korea, Rep.	65	1,330	25.5	36.5	62	12	26	30	88	100
Kosovo	..	..	..	..	..	..	..	..	..	..
Kuwait	0[c]	0[c]	0.9	..	54	2	44	43	99	99
Kyrgyz Republic	49	9,199	10.1	43.7	94	3	3	0[c]	85	99
Lao PDR	190	31,151	4.3	1.3	93	4	3	1	62	77
Latvia	17	7,424	0.4	1.2	12	50	39	27	96	100
Lebanon	5	1,144	1.3	28.1	60	11	29	20	100	100
Lesotho	5	2,433	0.1	1.7	20	40	40	20	73	91
Liberia	200	52,139	0.2	0.1	34	27	40	3	60	88
Libya	1	96	4.3	718.0	83	3	14	11	..	..
Lithuania	16	4,659	2.4	9.6	3	90	7	7	..	98
Macedonia, FYR	5	2,625	1.0	16.1	12	67	21	4	99	100
Madagascar	337	16,746	14.7	4.4	97	1	2	0[c]	34	74
Malawi	16	1,118	1.0	5.6	84	4	12	3	80	95
Malaysia	580	20,752	13.2	2.3	34	36	30	10	99	100
Mali	60	4,024	6.5	6.5	90	1	9	1	51	87
Mauritania	0[c]	118	1.6	14.0	94	2	5	1	48	52
Mauritius	3	2,158	0.7	26.4	68	3	30	9	99	100
Mexico	409	3,651	79.8	17.5	77	9	14	8	91	97
Moldova	1	280	1.9	16.4	40	52	9	1	93	99
Mongolia	35	12,833	0.5	1.4	44	32	24	4	53	100
Morocco	29	917	12.6	43.4	87	3	10	5	61	98
Mozambique	100	4,388	0.7	0.3	74	3	23	11	29	77
Myanmar	1,003	21,071	33.2	2.8	89	1	10	..	78	93
Namibia	6	2,747	0.3	1.7	71	5	24	19	90	99
Nepal	198	6,734	9.8	4.7	98	0[c]	2	1	88	93
Netherlands	11	665	10.6	11.7	1	87	12	41	100	100
New Zealand	327	75,768	4.8	1.5	74	4	21	13	100	100
Nicaragua	190	33,221	1.3	0.7	84	2	14	4	68	98
Niger	4	234	2.4	7.0	88	1	11	1	39	100
Nigeria	221	1,431	10.3	3.6	53	15	31	8	43	74
Norway	382	79,110	2.9	0.8	29	43	28	66	100	100
Oman	1	516	1.3	86.6	88	1	10	23	78	93
Pakistan	55	323	183.5	79.5	94	1	5	1	89	96
Panama	147	42,578	0.5	0.3	51	3	46	44	83	97
Papua New Guinea	801	119,492	0.4	0.0	0[c]	43	57	12	33	87
Paraguay	94	14,822	0.5	0.1	71	8	20	19	66	99
Peru	1,616	56,179	19.3	1.0	85	8	7	4	65	91
Philippines	479	5,223	81.6	17.0	82	10	8	1	92	93
Poland	54	1,405	12.0	19.4	10	60	31	20	100	100
Portugal	38	3,574	8.5	12.3	73	19	8	15	100	99
Puerto Rico	7	1,790	1.0	14.0	7	2	91	65	..	..
Qatar	0[c]	35	0.4	455.2	59	2	39	122	100	100

3.5 Freshwater

	Internal renewable freshwater resources[a]		Annual freshwater withdrawals					Water productivity	Access to an improved water source	
	Flows billion cu. m	Per capita cu. m	billion cu. m	% of internal resources	% for agriculture	% for industry	% for domestic	GDP/water use 2000 $ per cu. m	% of urban population	% of rural population
	2009	2009	2009[b]	2009[b]	2009[b]	2009[b]	2009[b]	2009[b]	2010	2010
Romania	42	1,969	6.9	3.2	17	61	22	8	..	99
Russian Federation	4,313	30,405	66.2	1.5	20	60	20	6	92	99
Rwanda	10	921	0.2	1.6	68	8	24	22	63	76
Saudi Arabia	2	90	23.7	943.3	88	3	9	11	..	97
Senegal	26	2,131	2.2	5.7	93	3	4	3	56	93
Serbia	..	..	4.1	..	2	82	17	2	98	99
Sierra Leone	160	27,878	0.5	0.3	71	10	19	3	35	87
Singapore	1	120	..	..	..	..	..	..	..	100
Slovak Republic	13	2,325	0.7	1.4	3	50	47	64	100	100
Slovenia	19	9,153	0.9	3.0	0[c]	82	18	27	99	100
Somalia	6	658	3.3	22.4	99	0[c]	0[c]	..	7	66
South Africa	45	908	12.5	25.0	63	6	31	15	79	99
South Sudan	..	..	..	..	..	..	..	..	..	..
Spain	111	2,422	32.5	29.0	61	22	18	22	100	100
Sri Lanka	53	2,555	13.0	24.5	87	6	6	2	90	99
Sudan	30	706	37.1	57.6	97	1	2	1	52	67
Swaziland	3	2,260	1.0	23.1	97	1	2	2	65	91
Sweden	171	18,390	2.6	1.5	4	59	37	110	100	100
Switzerland	40	5,217	2.6	4.9	2	58	41	110	100	100
Syrian Arab Republic	7	356	16.8	99.8	88	4	9	2	86	93
Tajikistan	66	9,774	12.0	74.8	92	5	4	0[c]	54	92
Tanzania	84	1,930	5.2	5.4	89	0	10	4	44	79
Thailand	225	3,268	57.3	13.1	90	5	5	3	95	97
Timor-Leste	8	7,469	1.2	14.3	91	0[c]	8	0[c]	60	91
Togo	12	1,949	0.2	1.2	45	2	53	10	40	89
Trinidad and Tobago	4	2,874	0.2	6.0	9	25	66	61	93	98
Tunisia	4	402	2.9	61.7	76	4	13	11	84	99
Turkey	227	3,160	40.1	18.8	74	11	15	9	99	100
Turkmenistan	1	273	24.9	100.8	97	1	2	0[c]	72	97
Uganda	39	1,205	0.3	0.5	36	18	46	36	68	95
Ukraine	53	1,153	38.5	27.6	51	36	12	1	98	98
United Arab Emirates	0[c]	22	4.0	2,032.0	83	2	15	39	100	100
United Kingdom	145	2,346	13.0	8.8	10	33	57	132	100	100
United States	2,818	9,186	478.4	15.6	40	46	14	24	94	100
Uruguay	59	17,639	3.7	2.6	87	2	11	8	100	100
Uzbekistan	16	588	59.6	118.3	91	3	6	0[c]	81	98
Venezuela, RB	722	25,451	9.1	0.7	44	8	49	18	75	94
Vietnam	359	4,178	82.0	9.3	95	4	1	1	93	99
West Bank and Gaza	1	201	0.4	49.9	45	7	48	9	81	86
Yemen, Rep.	2	90	3.6	168.6	91	2	7	4	47	72
Zambia	80	6,303	1.7	1.7	76	7	17	3	46	87
Zimbabwe	12	983	4.2	21.0	79	7	14	1	69	98
World	**42,383 s**	**6,258 w**	**3,908.3 s**	**7.3 w**	**70 w**	**18 w**	**12 w**	**10 w**	**81 w**	**96 w**
Low income	4,197	5,381	188.6	4.3	90	2	8	2	57	86
Middle income	29,152	5,944	2,791.0	7.0	79	11	10	3	84	96
Lower middle income	7,995	3,227	1,607.4	12.6	88	5	7	1	83	93
Upper middle income	21,157	8,718	1,183.6	5.0	66	20	14	6	86	98
Low & middle income	33,348	5,867	2,979.6	6.7	79	11	10	3	80	95
East Asia & Pacific	8,773	4,506	952.0	9.9	73	16	10	4	84	97
Europe & Central Asia	5,076	12,887	330.4	5.0	63	26	11	3	91	99
Latin America & Carib.	13,425	23,323	269.5	1.6	68	11	21	10	81	98
Middle East & N. Africa	226	695	276.5	70.0	86	6	8	2	81	94
South Asia	1,990	1,236	1,026.6	33.4	91	2	7	1	88	95
Sub-Saharan Africa	3,858	4,634	124.6	2.2	84	4	12	4	49	83
High income	9,034	8,305	928.7	9.4	41	42	17	31	98	100
Euro area	977	2,952	185.6	16.4	32	52	17	36	100	100

a. Excludes river flows from other countries because of data unreliability. b. Data are for the most recent year available (see *Primary data documentation*). c. Less than 0.5.

About the data

The data on freshwater resources are based on estimates of runoff into rivers and recharge of groundwater. These estimates are based on different sources and refer to different years, so cross-country comparisons should be made with caution. Because the data are collected intermittently, they may hide significant variations in total renewable water resources from year to year. The data also fail to distinguish between seasonal and geographic variations in water availability within countries. Data for small countries and countries in arid and semiarid zones are less reliable than those for larger countries and countries with greater rainfall.

Caution should also be used in comparing data on annual freshwater withdrawals, which are subject to variations in collection and estimation methods. In addition, inflows and outflows are estimated at different times and at different levels of quality and precision, requiring caution in interpreting the data, particularly for water-short countries, notably in the Middle East and North Africa.

Water productivity is an indication only of the efficiency by which each country uses its water resources. Given the different economic structure of each country, these indicators should be used carefully, taking into account the countries' sectoral activities and natural resource endowments.

The data on access to an improved water source measure the percentage of the population with ready access to water for domestic purposes. The data are based on surveys and estimates provided by governments to the Joint Monitoring Programme of the World Health Organization (WHO) and the United Nations Children's Fund (UNICEF). The coverage rates are based on information from service users on actual household use rather than on information from service providers, which may include nonfunctioning systems. Access to drinking water from an improved source does not ensure that the water is safe or adequate, as these characteristics are not tested at the time of survey. While information on access to an improved water source is widely used, it is extremely subjective, and such terms as *safe, improved, adequate,* and *reasonable* may have different meaning in different countries despite official WHO definitions (see *Definitions*). Even in high-income countries treated water may not always be safe to drink. Access to an improved water source is equated with connection to a supply system; it does not take into account variations in the quality and cost (broadly defined) of the service.

Definitions

• **Internal renewable freshwater resources** are the average annual flows of rivers and groundwater from rainfall in the country. Natural incoming flows originating outside a country's borders are excluded. Overlapping water resources between surface runoff and groundwater recharge are also deducted.
• **Internal renewable freshwater resources per capita** are calculated using the World Bank's population estimates (see table 2.1). • **Annual freshwater withdrawals** are total water withdrawals, not counting evaporation losses from storage basins. Withdrawals also include water from desalination plants in countries where they are a significant source. Withdrawals can exceed 100 percent of total renewable resources where extraction from nonrenewable aquifers or desalination plants is considerable or where water reuse is significant. Withdrawals for agriculture and industry are total withdrawals for irrigation and livestock production and for direct industrial use (including for cooling thermoelectric plants). Withdrawals for domestic uses include drinking water, municipal use or supply, and use for public services, commercial establishments, and homes. • **Water productivity** is calculated as GDP in constant prices divided by annual total water withdrawal. • **Access to an improved water source** is the percentage of the population with reasonable access to an adequate amount of water from an improved source, such as piped water into a dwelling, plot, or yard; public tap or standpipe; tubewell or borehole; protected dug well or spring; and rainwater collection. Unimproved sources include unprotected dug wells or springs, carts with small tank or drum, bottled water, and tanker trucks. Reasonable access is defined as the availability of at least 20 liters a person a day from a source within 1 kilometer of the dwelling.

Data sources

Data on freshwater resources and withdrawals are from the Food and Agriculture Organization's AQUASTAT database. The GDP estimates used to calculate water productivity are from the World Bank national accounts database. Data on access to water are from WHO and UNICEF's *Progress on Drinking Water and Sanitation* (2012).

	Emissions of organic water pollutants				Industry shares of emissions of organic water pollutants							
								% of total				
	thousand kilograms per day		kilograms per day per worker		Primary metals	Paper and pulp	Chemicals	Food and beverages	Stone, ceramics, and glass	Textiles	Wood	Other
	1990	2007[a]	1990	2007[a]	2007[a]	2007[a]	2007[a]	2007[a]	2007[a]	2007[a]	2007[a]	2007[a]
Afghanistan	..	0.2	..	0.21	..	19.7	27.9	14.1	11.7	23.3	..	3.1
Albania	2.4	3.6	0.25	0.25	..	..	..	39.8	..	60.2	..	11.9
Algeria	..	..	..	..	..	..	..	..	..	..	..	..
Angola	..	..	..	..	..	..	..	..	..	..	..	..
Argentina	181.4	155.5	0.21	0.23	3.8	8.4	15.8	30.5	3.5	14.3	2.1	21.6
Armenia	..	..	..	..	..	..	..	..	..	..	..	..
Australia	..	..	..	..	..	..	..	..	..	..	..	..
Austria	90.5	84.4	0.15	0.14	5.7	7.1	9.3	12.2	5.8	4.3	6.0	49.5
Azerbaijan	41.3	20.0	0.15	0.18	8.8	3.0	18.5	19.6	8.4	11.7	1.5	28.6
Bahrain	..	..	..	..	..	..	..	..	..	..	..	..
Bangladesh	250.8	303.0	0.15	0.14	0.7	2.3	3.0	7.6	2.6	79.3	0.5	4.2
Belarus	..	..	..	..	..	..	..	..	..	..	..	..
Belgium	107.8	95.9	0.17	0.17	6.4	7.9	18.6	16.4	3.1	5.5	2.2	40.0
Benin	..	..	..	..	..	..	..	..	..	..	..	..
Bolivia	11.3	11.5	0.24	0.25	0.9	9.8	13.1	35.4	7.7	18.4	5.3	9.5
Bosnia and Herzegovina	..	..	..	..	..	..	..	..	..	..	..	..
Botswana	2.5	3.2	0.30	0.23	..	2.4	..	43.8	0.6	3.9	..	50.0
Brazil	..	..	..	..	..	..	..	..	..	..	..	..
Bulgaria	124.3	102.1	0.17	0.17	3.7	4.3	8.0	17.7	4.8	26.8	3.0	31.7
Burkina Faso	..	..	..	..	..	..	..	..	..	..	..	..
Burundi	..	..	..	..	..	..	..	..	..	..	..	..
Cambodia	3.8	..	0.17		..	..	..	..	..	..	..	..
Cameroon	..	..	..	..	..	..	..	..	..	..	..	..
Canada	300.9	306.6	0.17	0.16	4.3	8.9	10.9	14.0	2.8	7.3	6.5	45.3
Central African Republic	..	..	..	..	..	..	..	..	..	..	..	..
Chad	..	..	..	..	..	..	..	..	..	..	..	..
Chile	..	92.5	..	0.25	7.6	6.3	13.7	35.1	3.6	9.1	6.9	17.7
China	..	9,428.9	..	0.13	7.2	3.9	13.0	7.4	6.3	20.6	1.7	39.9
Hong Kong SAR, China	..	..	..	..	..	..	..	..	..	..	..	..
Colombia	..	87.0	..	0.20	2.3	8.9	17.3	21.3	5.3	24.1	0.9	19.9
Congo, Dem. Rep.	..	..	..	..	..	..	..	..	..	..	..	..
Congo, Rep.	..	..	..	..	..	..	..	..	..	..	..	..
Costa Rica	..	..	..	..	..	..	..	..	..	..	..	..
Côte d'Ivoire	..	..	..	..	..	..	..	..	..	..	..	..
Croatia	48.5	42.9	0.17	0.17	3.1	7.2	9.5	17.6	5.9	14.5	4.9	37.2
Cuba	..	..	..	..	..	..	..	..	..	..	..	..
Cyprus	7.1	8.0	0.21	0.23	0.3	8.9	9.3	36.3	9.9	5.1	8.0	22.2
Czech Republic	177.1	146.5	0.14	0.13	5.4	4.8	10.9	10.9	6.4	7.4	4.4	49.8
Denmark	84.5	61.0	0.18	0.16	1.4	11.5	13.1	16.4	4.8	1.5	4.0	47.3
Dominican Republic	88.6	..	0.18		..	..	..	..	..	..	..	..
Ecuador	28.6	44.7	0.24	0.28	1.8	7.8	12.8	46.4	4.4	12.3	2.2	12.3
Egypt, Arab Rep.	206.5		0.19		..	..	..	..	..	..	..	..
El Salvador	..	..	..	..	..	..	..	..	..	..	..	..
Eritrea	2.4	2.5	0.19	0.20	0.2	4.4	9.5	27.3	9.6	29.0	0.1	20.3
Estonia	21.7	16.0	0.15	0.14	0.4	7.3	7.1	14.6	5.5	8.0	16.4	40.8
Ethiopia	18.5	32.2	0.23	0.24	1.4	6.0	10.9	34.7	8.3	27.9	1.5	9.3
Finland	72.5	55.3	0.19	0.14	1.0	15.4	8.7	9.0	4.4	2.8	7.3	51.4
France	326.5	569.4	0.11	0.16	3.2	7.4	15.0	16.6	3.8	4.8	2.4	46.9
Gabon	..	..	..	..	..	..	..	..	..	..	..	..
Gambia, The	0.8	..	0.27		..	..	..	..	..	..	..	..
Georgia	..	..	..	..	..	..	..	..	..	..	..	..
Germany	806.6	936.2	0.13	0.14	3.8	7.1	12.4	11.4	3.4	2.4	1.9	57.6
Ghana	..	16.0	..	0.17	3.0	3.8	15.9	18.6	4.1	10.2	33.3	11.2
Greece	50.9	60.8	0.19	0.20	3.9	9.0	10.1	23.9	7.0	14.4	2.8	28.9
Guatemala	..	..	..	..	..	..	..	..	..	..	..	..
Guinea	..	..	..	..	..	..	..	..	..	..	..	..
Guinea-Bissau	..	..	..	..	..	..	..	..	..	..	..	..

Water pollution | 3.6

	Emissions of organic water pollutants				Industry shares of emissions of organic water pollutants							
	thousand kilograms per day		kilograms per day per worker					% of total				
					Primary metals	Paper and pulp	Chemicals	Food and beverages	Stone, ceramics, and glass	Textiles	Wood	Other
	1990	2007[a]	1990	2007[a]	2007[a]	2007[a]	2007[a]	2007[a]	2007[a]	2007[a]	2007[a]	2007[a]
Haiti	5.2	..	0.20	..	..	..	..	..	..	..	..	..
Honduras	..	..	..	..	..	..	..	..	..	..	..	..
Hungary	122.1	110.6	0.18	0.15	2.7	6.4	10.6	15.2	3.7	9.1	3.3	49.0
India	..	..	..	..	..	..	..	..	..	..	..	..
Indonesia	721.8	883.0	0.18	0.19	1.4	4.1	12.0	23.1	4.0	29.2	6.3	19.9
Iran, Islamic Rep.	131.6	160.8	0.16	0.15	7.1	2.8	12.8	16.1	13.8	11.2	0.7	35.5
Iraq	7.7	7.7	0.27	0.27	13.1	25.6	29.9	16.9	5.4	9.1	..	..
Ireland	36.1	28.4	0.19	0.16	1.3	10.2	17.6	14.8	5.9	0.8	3.8	45.5
Israel	54.6	52.7	0.16	0.16	1.6	8.9	13.4	16.4	2.9	7.9	1.2	47.6
Italy	378.3	479.2	0.13	0.13	3.5	5.2	10.3	9.3	5.4	13.6	2.9	49.6
Jamaica	..	..	..	..	..	..	..	..	..	..	..	..
Japan	1,455.0	1,126.9	0.14	0.15	3.3	7.0	11.2	15.0	3.6	5.3	2.0	52.5
Jordan	15.0	29.1	0.18	0.18	2.3	6.1	13.7	20.8	11.5	18.6	2.3	24.5
Kazakhstan	123.5	97.4	0.23	0.24	33.3	2.3	8.9	18.7	9.3	3.9	0.6	23.0
Kenya	..	..	..	..	..	..	..	..	..	..	..	..
Korea, Dem. Rep.	..	..	..	..	..	..	..	..	..	..	..	..
Korea, Rep.	366.9	319.6	0.12	0.11	4.2	5.4	12.1	6.3	3.0	9.3	0.9	58.9
Kosovo	..	..	..	..	..	..	..	..	..	..	..	..
Kuwait	..	..	..	..	..	..	..	..	..	..	..	..
Kyrgyz Republic	28.9	12.2	0.14	0.20	9.8	6.3	8.5	24.2	17.5	9.8	1.6	22.4
Lao PDR	4.3	4.3	0.14	0.14	1.8	2.2	3.8	9.2	7.5	49.2	21.4	4.9
Latvia	39.8	28.4	0.12	0.18	2.7	7.7	5.8	21.1	4.4	11.8	19.1	27.3
Lebanon	14.7	14.7	0.19	0.19	0.5	7.5	6.0	25.5	12.9	16.7	4.5	26.3
Lesotho	..	5.3	..	0.13	0.9	0.5	0.3	2.6	0.8	93.5	..	1.4
Liberia	..	..	..	..	..	..	..	..	..	..	..	..
Libya	..	..	..	..	..	..	..	..	..	..	..	..
Lithuania	54.0	42.2	0.15	0.17	0.9	5.7	8.3	20.5	4.7	17.6	11.4	30.8
Macedonia, FYR	27.0	20.3	0.20	0.18	5.8	4.7	6.3	15.1	3.2	44.7	2.9	17.3
Madagascar	..	92.8	..	0.14	0.3	1.6	12.4	7.6	2.8	58.9	6.3	10.0
Malawi	37.2	32.7	0.40	0.39	..	1.4	3.7	82.1	0.6	7.5	1.1	3.6
Malaysia	..	208.3	..	0.12	2.8	4.9	16.5	9.1	3.8	6.6	7.8	48.5
Mali	..	..	..	..	..	..	..	..	..	..	..	..
Mauritania	..	..	..	..	..	..	..	..	..	..	..	..
Mauritius	16.8	15.4	0.16	0.17	0.4	3.6	5.9	14.7	..	63.9	0.7	10.9
Mexico	425.0	..	0.18	..	..	..	..	..	..	..	..	..
Moldova	29.2	18.8	0.44	0.45	..	3.8	..	95.2	..	..	..	0.9
Mongolia	..	8.8	..	0.21	3.7	5.1	3.3	27.2	9.5	41.6	5.4	4.1
Morocco	..	74.0	..	0.16	1.0	2.9	7.9	16.3	6.5	43.5	2.0	19.9
Mozambique	..	..	..	..	..	..	..	..	..	..	..	..
Myanmar	..	..	..	..	..	..	..	..	..	..	..	..
Namibia	..	..	..	..	..	..	..	..	..	..	..	..
Nepal	26.4	26.8	0.14	0.16	1.6	3.9	7.2	19.2	29.9	29.4	2.0	6.8
Netherlands	142.3	128.2	0.20	0.19	3.1	13.4	14.1	18.2	4.0	2.1	2.6	42.5
New Zealand	46.7	61.6	0.24	0.23	2.0	12.2	8.6	31.1	3.1	5.8	8.0	29.3
Nicaragua	..	..	..	..	..	..	..	..	..	..	..	..
Niger	..	..	..	..	..	..	..	..	..	..	..	..
Nigeria	..	..	..	..	..	..	..	..	..	..	..	..
Norway	51.8	46.9	0.20	0.18	4.9	12.1	7.5	19.1	4.3	2.0	6.0	44.2
Oman	3.8	7.6	0.15	0.16	4.0	4.6	17.8	20.4	20.5	2.4	4.0	26.3
Pakistan	..	153.7	..	0.17	2.2	1.9	9.1	15.1	4.3	55.6	0.4	11.2
Panama	10.3	13.7	0.30	0.32	0.9	11.6	6.9	55.2	4.0	4.7	1.6	15.0
Papua New Guinea	..	..	..	..	..	..	..	..	..	..	..	..
Paraguay	15.3	10.8	0.20	0.28	3.1	9.3	16.7	42.6	5.9	11.0	4.5	6.9
Peru	..	..	..	..	..	..	..	..	..	..	..	..
Philippines	169.0	144.6	0.17	0.15	2.6	4.2	9.5	14.4	2.7	21.6	2.1	42.9
Poland	446.7	359.7	0.16	0.16	3.3	5.1	11.3	18.1	5.5	10.3	4.9	41.5
Portugal	140.6	87.7	0.14	0.17	0.2	8.1	3.4	19.8	5.2	16.3	8.5	38.5

	Emissions of organic water pollutants				Industry shares of emissions of organic water pollutants							
	thousand kilograms per day		kilograms per day per worker					% of total					
					Primary metals	Paper and pulp	Chemicals	Food and beverages	Stone, ceramics, and glass	Textiles	Wood	Other
	1990	2007[a]	1990	2007[a]	2007[a]	2007[a]	2007[a]	2007[a]	2007[a]	2007[a]	2007[a]	2007[a]
Puerto Rico	..	..	..	..								
Qatar	..	6.4	..	0.12	3.7	6.7	10.5	6.5	18.1	20.7	12.5	21.3
Romania	411.2	222.1	0.12	0.15	4.5	3.5	7.1	13.9	4.0	25.0	5.3	36.8
Russian Federation	1,521.4	1,381.7	0.16	0.17	8.4	4.9	11.6	17.9	8.3	6.3	4.2	38.4
Rwanda	8.1	8.1	0.37	0.37	*	..	9.0	77.1	4.3	1.9	2.9	4.8
Saudi Arabia	..	106.6	..	0.18	3.2	6.9	11.6	20.0	10.7	14.4	3.3	30.0
Senegal	6.1	6.6	0.30	0.29	4.9	6.3	23.8	44.6	3.9	10.5	0.8	5.3
Serbia	..	..	..	..	..	..	..	..	..	..	..	..
Sierra Leone	..	..	..	..	..	..	..	..	..	..	..	..
Singapore	33.1	38.3	0.09	0.09	0.5	5.5	11.9	5.3	1.3	2.3	0.5	72.7
Slovak Republic	72.8	47.9	0.13	0.14	7.9	5.4	9.1	10.7	6.0	5.0	4.2	51.7
Slovenia	28.1	28.8	0.13	0.13	4.6	6.1	12.2	7.7	4.1	10.8	4.9	49.6
Somalia	..	..	..	..	..	..	..	..	..	..	..	..
South Africa	260.5	229.6	0.17	0.17	9.9	6.6	10.6	15.7	5.2	10.4	4.2	37.4
South Sudan	..	..	..	..	..	..	..	..	..	..	..	..
Spain	348.0	378.8	0.16	0.15	3.1	8.0	10.8	15.3	7.9	8.4	3.8	42.7
Sri Lanka	..	266.1		0.19	2.6	4.3	9.0	22.4	6.3	43.6	2.5	9.3
Sudan	..	38.6		0.29	0.6	1.9	7.0	57.5	14.2	8.0	1.7	9.1
Swaziland	..	..	..	..	..	..	..	..	..	..	..	..
Sweden	116.8	96.9	0.15	0.14	5.3	11.9	9.9	8.6	2.6	1.2	5.6	54.9
Switzerland	..	..	..	..	..	..	..	..	..	..	..	..
Syrian Arab Republic	59.7	80.4	0.16	0.16	1.6	1.9	7.3	19.9	11.3	32.0	5.2	20.9
Tajikistan	29.1	12.8	0.17	0.24	28.2	2.7	2.0	18.0	8.9	38.4	0.3	1.8
Tanzania	..	30.3	..	0.34	2.6	4.8	8.6	61.2	1.9	12.7	2.9	5.3
Thailand	369.4	581.4	0.15	0.15	1.9	4.2	12.4	16.4	4.7	20.5	2.8	37.2
Timor-Leste	..	..	..	..	..	..	..	..	..	..	..	..
Togo	..	..	..	..	..	..	..	..	..	..	..	..
Trinidad and Tobago	7.0	7.6	0.23	0.29	4.8	18.2	21.3	39.3	8.0	7.7	8.5	5.0
Tunisia	..	..	..	..	..	..	..	..	..	..	..	..
Turkey	175.8	346.4	0.18	0.15	3.8	3.8	8.6	12.4	6.6	32.2	1.7	30.9
Turkmenistan	..	..	..	..	..	..	..	..	..	..	..	..
Uganda	3.3	2.1	0.29	0.23	..	7.8	7.3	34.8	13.3	17.2	2.3	19.6
Ukraine	..	498.2	..	0.19	13.9	4.3	11.2	19.7	6.8	5.6	2.1	36.5
United Arab Emirates	..	..	..	..	..	..	..	..	..	..	..	..
United Kingdom	599.9	521.7	0.16	0.17	2.7	12.5	13.5	14.9	3.6	4.3	2.5	46.1
United States	2,307.0	1,850.8	0.14	0.14	3.5	8.1	13.1	12.0	3.9	4.3	4.1	51.1
Uruguay	..	..	..	..	..	..	..	..	..	..	..	..
Uzbekistan	..	..	..	..	..	..	..	..	..	..	..	..
Venezuela, RB	..	..	..	..	..	..	..	..	..	..	..	..
Vietnam	141.0	544.8	0.16	0.14	1.4	3.5	6.8	12.7	6.4	40.2	3.3	25.8
West Bank and Gaza	..	..	..	..	..	..	..	..	..	..	..	..
Yemen, Rep.	12.6	46.5	0.24	0.21	..	2.1	7.4	35.9	14.6	15.5	5.1	19.4
Zambia	..	..	..	..	..	..	..	..	..	..	..	..
Zimbabwe	29.3	..	0.20	..	..	..	..	..	..	..	..	..

a. Data are derived using the United Nations Industrial Development Organization's (UNIDO) industry database four-digit International Standard Industrial Classification (ISIC). Data in italics are for the most recent year available and are derived using UNIDO's industry database at the three-digit ISIC.

About the data

Emissions of organic pollutants from industrial activities are a major cause of degradation of water quality. Water quality and pollution levels are generally measured as concentration or load—the rate of occurrence of a substance in an aqueous solution. Polluting substances include organic matter, metals, minerals, sediment, bacteria, and toxic chemicals. The table focuses on organic water pollution resulting from industrial activities. Because water pollution tends to be sensitive to local conditions, the national-level data in the table may not reflect the quality of water in specific locations.

The data in the table come from an international study of industrial emissions that may have been the first to include data from developing countries (Hettige, Mani, and Wheeler 1998). These data were updated through 2007 by the World Bank's Development Research Group. Unlike estimates from earlier studies based on engineering or economic models, these estimates are based on actual measurements of plant-level water pollution. The focus is on organic water pollution caused by organic waste, measured in terms of biochemical oxygen demand (BOD), because the data for this indicator are the most plentiful and reliable for cross-country comparisons of emissions. BOD measures the strength of an organic waste by the amount of oxygen consumed in breaking it down. A sewage overload in natural waters exhausts the water's dissolved oxygen content. Wastewater treatment, by contrast, reduces BOD.

Data on water pollution are more readily available than are other emissions data because most industrial pollution control programs start by regulating emissions of organic water pollutants. Such data are fairly reliable because sampling techniques for measuring water pollution are more widely understood and much less expensive than those for air pollution.

Hettige, Mani, and Wheeler (1998) used plant- and sector-level information on emissions and employment from 13 national environmental protection agencies and sector-level information on output and employment from the United Nations Industrial Development Organization (UNIDO). Their econometric analysis found that the ratio of BOD to employment in each industrial sector is about the same across countries. This finding allowed the authors to estimate BOD loads across countries and over time. The estimated BOD intensities per unit of employment were multiplied by sectoral employment numbers from UNIDO's industry database for 1980–98. These estimates of sectoral emissions were then used to calculate kilograms of emissions of organic water pollutants per day for each country and year. The data in the table were derived by updating these estimates through 2007.

Definitions

• **Emissions of organic water pollutants** are measured as biochemical oxygen demand, or the amount of oxygen that bacteria in water will consume in breaking down waste, a standard water treatment test for the presence of organic pollutants. Emissions per worker are total emissions divided by the number of industrial workers. • **Industry shares of emissions of organic water pollutants** are emissions from manufacturing activities as defined by two-digit divisions of the International Standard Industrial Classification revision 3.

Data sources

Data on water pollutants are from Hettige, Mani, and Wheeler (1998). The data were updated through 2007 by the World Bank Development Research Group using the same methodology as the initial study. Data on industrial sectoral employment are from UNIDO's industry database.

	Energy production		Energy use									Alternative and nuclear energy	
	Total million metric tons of oil equivalent		Total million metric tons of oil equivalent		average annual % growth	Per capita kilograms of oil equivalent		% of total				% of total energy use	
								Fossil fuel		Combustible renewables and waste			
	1990	2009	1990	2009	1990–2009	1990	2009	1990	2009	1990	2009	1990	2009
Afghanistan	..	..	..	..	..	..	..	..	..	..	..	..	..
Albania	2.4	1.3	2.7	1.7	1.6	809	538	76.5	54.1	13.6	12.4	9.2	26.4
Algeria	100.1	152.3	22.2	39.8	3.0	877	1,138	99.9	99.8	0.1	0.1	0.1	0.1
Angola	28.7	101.0	5.9	11.9	3.8	569	641	25.5	37.6	73.5	60.1	1.1	2.3
Argentina	48.4	80.8	46.1	74.2	2.5	1,411	1,853	88.7	89.4	3.7	3.1	7.5	6.8
Armenia	0.1	0.8	7.7	2.6	–2.3	2,171	843	97.2	68.4	0.0	0.0	1.7	31.7
Australia	157.5	310.7	86.2	131.1	2.3	5,053	5,971	93.9	94.4	4.6	4.4	1.5	1.2
Austria	8.1	11.4	24.8	31.7	1.7	3,228	3,784	79.2	70.2	10.0	17.6	11.0	12.0
Azerbaijan	20.6	64.6	26.2	12.0	–2.8	3,665	1,338	100.0	98.2	0.0	0.0	0.2	1.7
Bahrain	13.4	17.5	4.4	9.5	4.4	8,826	8,096	100.0	99.8	0.0	0.0	0.0	0.0
Bangladesh	10.8	24.8	12.7	29.6	4.6	121	201	45.5	69.8	53.9	29.8	0.6	0.5
Belarus	3.3	4.0	45.5	26.8	–1.7	4,470	2,815	95.6	90.3	0.4	6.0	0.0	0.0
Belgium	13.1	15.3	48.3	57.2	0.9	4,844	5,300	76.0	73.6	1.6	4.9	23.1	21.8
Benin	1.8	2.0	1.7	3.5	3.7	348	404	4.8	40.4	94.1	57.4	0.0	0.0
Bolivia	4.9	14.2	2.6	6.2	3.9	392	638	67.2	79.1	28.9	17.7	3.9	3.2
Bosnia and Herzegovina	4.6	4.5	7.0	6.0	2.9	1,629	1,580	93.9	92.2	2.3	3.1	3.7	9.0
Botswana	0.9	0.9	1.3	2.0	2.7	912	1,034	66.0	64.3	33.4	23.6	0.0	0.0
Brazil	104.2	230.3	140.2	240.2	3.0	937	1,243	51.2	51.3	34.1	31.6	13.1	15.6
Bulgaria	9.6	9.8	28.6	17.5	–1.3	3,277	2,305	84.3	73.1	0.6	4.3	13.9	24.9
Burkina Faso	..	..	..	..	..	..	..	..	..	..	..	..	..
Burundi	..	..	..	..	..	..	..	..	..	..	..	..	..
Cambodia	..	3.7	..	5.2	3.3	..	371	..	27.8	..	70.7	..	0.1
Cameroon	11.0	8.8	5.0	6.9	1.8	409	361	18.7	30.9	76.7	64.1	4.6	5.0
Canada	273.7	389.8	208.6	254.1	1.4	7,505	7,534	74.6	74.9	3.9	4.5	21.5	21.7
Central African Republic	..	..	..	..	..	..	..	..	..	..	..	..	..
Chad	..	..	..	..	..	..	..	..	..	..	..	..	..
Chile	7.5	9.3	13.6	28.8	4.3	1,028	1,698	74.6	74.5	19.7	17.5	5.7	7.6
China	886.3	2,084.9	863.0	2,257.1	5.1	760	1,695	75.5	87.4	23.2	9.0	1.3	3.7
Hong Kong SAR, China	0.0	0.1	8.7	14.9	2.5	1,518	2,133	100.0	95.1	0.6	0.4	0.0	0.0
Colombia	48.2	99.1	24.2	31.8	0.8	730	697	67.4	75.2	22.8	14.0	9.8	11.1
Congo, Dem. Rep.	12.0	23.3	11.8	22.9	3.9	324	357	11.2	3.7	84.7	93.7	4.1	2.9
Congo, Rep.	8.7	15.3	0.8	1.4	3.2	334	356	35.1	44.1	59.5	51.1	5.3	2.0
Costa Rica	1.0	2.7	2.0	4.9	5.0	660	1,067	48.4	44.7	36.6	15.8	14.4	39.5
Côte d'Ivoire	3.4	11.9	4.3	10.4	5.0	345	535	23.3	23.5	73.5	75.2	2.6	1.8
Croatia	5.1	4.1	9.0	8.7	1.3	1,884	1,965	86.5	83.4	3.5	4.2	3.6	6.8
Cuba	9.4	5.6	19.3	11.5	–1.8	1,824	1,022	55.7	84.1	44.3	15.8	0.0	0.1
Cyprus	0.0	0.1	1.4	2.5	2.9	1,775	2,298	99.5	95.7	0.5	1.8	0.0	2.5
Czech Republic	40.9	31.2	49.6	42.0	0.1	4,796	4,004	91.7	79.6	1.6	5.6	6.8	17.5
Denmark	10.1	23.9	17.4	18.6	0.1	3,377	3,369	89.6	80.4	6.6	16.2	0.3	3.3
Dominican Republic	1.0	1.9	4.1	8.1	3.6	570	826	74.9	76.6	24.4	21.8	0.7	1.6
Ecuador	16.5	27.3	6.0	11.4	3.9	584	796	79.1	86.7	13.8	5.4	7.2	7.0
Egypt, Arab Rep.	54.9	88.2	31.8	72.0	4.8	560	903	94.0	96.3	3.3	2.1	2.7	1.7
El Salvador	1.7	3.2	2.5	5.1	3.8	463	828	31.4	37.8	48.2	33.8	20.3	28.2
Eritrea	0.7	0.6	0.9	0.7	–2.0	276	142	19.4	22.6	80.6	77.4	0.0	0.0
Estonia	5.4	4.2	9.9	4.7	–2.0	6,316	3,543	100.0	83.4	1.9	14.7	0.0	0.4
Ethiopia	14.1	30.4	14.9	32.7	3.8	308	402	5.5	7.1	93.9	92.0	0.6	1.0
Finland	12.1	16.6	28.4	33.2	1.5	5,692	6,213	55.5	48.8	16.1	20.9	20.9	21.8
France	111.9	129.5	223.9	256.2	0.9	3,848	3,970	58.1	51.0	4.9	5.9	38.7	43.9
Gabon	14.6	13.6	1.2	1.8	2.7	1,272	1,214	32.0	34.0	62.9	61.8	5.1	4.2
Gambia, The	..	..	0.1	0.1	..	64	84	0.0	0.0	..	..	..	..
Georgia	2.1	1.3	12.4	3.2	–6.2	2,587	723	88.9	68.0	3.7	12.0	5.2	21.4
Germany	186.2	127.1	351.4	318.5	–0.2	4,424	3,889	86.8	79.5	1.4	7.8	11.8	13.0
Ghana	4.4	7.0	5.3	9.2	3.2	358	388	18.2	24.3	73.7	69.8	9.3	6.4
Greece	9.2	10.1	21.4	29.4	2.2	2,111	2,609	94.6	92.4	4.2	3.4	1.0	3.0
Guatemala	3.4	6.1	4.4	9.8	4.0	497	701	28.1	46.1	68.5	52.1	3.4	1.8
Guinea	..	..	..	..	..	..	..	..	..	..	..	..	..
Guinea-Bissau	..	..	0.1	0.1	..	73	67	0.0	0.0	..	..	..	..
Haiti	1.3	1.9	1.6	2.6	3.4	219	263	19.7	28.1	77.7	71.2	2.5	0.7

Energy production and use

	Energy production Total million metric tons of oil equivalent		Energy use Total million metric tons of oil equivalent		average annual % growth	Per capita kilograms of oil equivalent		% of total Fossil fuel		Combustible renewables and waste		Alternative and nuclear energy % of total energy use	
	1990	2009	1990	2009	1990–2009	1990	2009	1990	2009	1990	2009	1990	2009
Honduras	1.7	2.2	2.4	4.4	3.6	487	592	30.0	50.3	63.0	44.3	8.2	5.5
Hungary	14.6	11.0	28.7	24.9	0.0	2,762	2,480	81.5	74.2	2.3	7.1	12.8	16.8
India	291.8	502.5	316.7	675.8	3.8	362	560	55.4	73.0	42.1	24.5	2.5	2.3
Indonesia	169.1	351.8	101.3	202.0	3.5	550	851	54.7	65.6	42.9	26.0	2.4	8.4
Iran, Islamic Rep.	179.3	349.8	67.9	215.9	6.4	1,237	2,951	98.9	99.7	0.3	0.2	0.8	0.3
Iraq	104.9	119.6	18.1	32.2	3.6	994	1,035	98.6	97.6	0.1	0.1	1.2	0.9
Ireland	3.5	1.5	10.0	14.3	2.6	2,842	3,216	84.6	88.7	1.1	2.2	0.6	2.3
Israel	0.4	3.3	11.5	21.5	3.4	2,463	2,878	97.2	96.5	0.0	0.1	3.1	4.8
Italy	25.3	27.0	146.6	164.6	1.2	2,584	2,735	93.4	87.5	0.6	4.3	3.9	5.9
Jamaica	0.5	0.5	2.8	3.3	2.1	1,167	1,208	82.6	83.7	17.1	15.9	0.3	0.4
Japan	75.2	93.8	439.3	472.0	0.6	3,556	3,700	84.5	81.0	1.1	1.4	14.4	17.6
Jordan	0.2	0.3	3.3	7.5	4.3	1,028	1,260	98.1	98.0	0.1	0.1	1.8	1.7
Kazakhstan	90.5	145.8	72.7	65.8	–0.7	4,450	4,091	96.9	99.0	0.2	0.2	0.9	0.9
Kenya	9.0	15.6	10.9	18.7	2.8	467	474	17.5	16.8	77.9	76.0	4.5	7.2
Korea, Dem. Rep.	28.9	20.3	33.2	19.3	–2.0	1,649	795	93.1	89.0	2.9	5.4	4.0	5.6
Korea, Rep.	22.6	44.3	93.1	229.2	4.6	2,171	4,701	83.8	81.7	0.8	1.3	15.4	17.0
Kosovo	..	..	..	..	..	..	..	..	..	..	..	..	..
Kuwait	50.4	130.2	9.1	30.2	8.1	4,364	11,402	99.9	100.0	0.1	0.0	0.0	0.0
Kyrgyz Republic	2.5	1.2	7.5	3.0	–3.4	1,693	566	93.5	72.5	0.1	0.1	11.5	28.3
Lao PDR	..	..	..	..	..	..	..	..	..	..	..	..	..
Latvia	1.1	2.1	7.9	4.2	–2.1	2,949	1,871	81.8	59.4	8.4	30.0	4.9	7.1
Lebanon	0.1	0.2	2.0	6.6	4.2	663	1,580	92.5	95.9	5.3	1.8	2.2	0.8
Lesotho	..	..	..	0.0	..	..	9	..	0.0	..	..	..	..
Liberia	..	..	..	..	..	..	..	..	..	..	..	..	..
Libya	73.2	87.1	11.3	20.4	2.3	2,614	3,258	98.9	99.2	1.1	0.8	0.0	0.0
Lithuania	4.9	4.2	16.1	8.4	–1.9	4,357	2,512	75.8	55.7	1.8	9.8	28.2	34.9
Macedonia, FYR	1.3	1.6	2.5	2.8	0.8	1,298	1,352	98.0	84.2	0.0	7.0	1.7	4.3
Madagascar	..	..	..	..	..	..	..	..	..	..	..	..	..
Malawi	..	..	..	..	..	..	..	..	..	..	..	..	..
Malaysia	48.8	89.7	22.0	66.8	5.9	1,208	2,391	88.8	94.7	9.7	4.5	1.6	0.9
Mali	..	..	..	..	..	..	..	..	..	..	..	..	..
Mauritania	..	..	..	..	..	..	..	..	..	..	..	..	..
Mauritius	..	..	0.5	1.2	..	453	947	0.0	0.0	..	..	..	..
Mexico	194.7	220.0	122.5	174.6	2.0	1,453	1,559	87.2	88.9	7.0	4.8	5.9	6.3
Moldova	0.1	0.1	9.9	2.4	–5.2	2,669	687	100.0	91.3	0.4	3.3	0.2	0.2
Mongolia	2.7	7.7	3.4	3.2	–0.5	1,558	1,194	96.9	96.4	2.5	3.2	0.0	0.0
Morocco	0.8	0.8	6.9	15.1	4.0	280	477	93.8	92.5	4.6	3.2	1.5	1.7
Mozambique	5.6	11.9	5.9	9.8	2.9	437	427	5.5	7.7	93.9	81.8	0.4	14.9
Myanmar	10.7	22.4	10.7	15.1	2.3	271	316	14.4	27.7	84.7	69.9	1.0	2.4
Namibia	0.2	0.3	0.7	1.7	5.4	445	764	62.0	70.5	15.9	12.0	17.4	7.2
Nepal	5.5	8.8	5.8	10.0	3.0	303	338	5.1	11.1	93.7	85.8	1.3	2.7
Netherlands	60.5	63.0	65.7	78.2	0.9	4,393	4,729	95.9	93.1	1.5	4.4	1.4	2.0
New Zealand	11.5	15.2	12.8	17.4	1.5	3,720	4,032	67.0	63.7	5.7	6.3	27.1	29.8
Nicaragua	1.5	1.7	2.1	3.1	2.6	508	540	28.3	44.7	53.9	45.9	17.5	9.4
Niger	..	..	..	..	..	..	..	..	..	..	..	..	..
Nigeria	150.5	228.7	70.6	108.3	2.4	724	701	19.3	14.7	80.2	84.9	0.5	0.4
Norway	119.1	213.6	21.0	28.2	1.6	4,952	5,849	51.9	58.8	4.9	5.1	49.6	38.7
Oman	38.3	67.2	4.2	15.1	6.4	2,258	5,554	100.0	100.0	0.0	0.0	0.0	0.0
Pakistan	34.2	64.9	42.8	85.5	3.7	383	502	52.6	61.8	43.8	34.5	3.6	3.7
Panama	0.6	0.7	1.5	3.1	3.3	603	896	57.5	78.6	28.9	10.7	13.1	10.8
Papua New Guinea	..	..	..	..	..	..	..	..	..	..	..	..	..
Paraguay	4.6	7.4	3.1	4.8	1.7	724	749	21.3	28.5	72.5	53.7	76.0	99.5
Peru	10.6	15.1	9.7	15.8	2.5	449	550	63.3	73.5	27.5	15.4	9.2	11.1
Philippines	17.2	23.5	28.9	38.8	1.7	469	424	43.4	57.0	38.5	17.9	18.1	25.0
Poland	103.9	67.5	103.1	94.0	–0.5	2,705	2,464	97.8	92.8	2.2	7.1	0.1	0.3
Portugal	3.4	4.9	16.7	24.1	2.4	1,677	2,266	80.4	78.0	14.8	13.6	4.8	6.6
Puerto Rico	..	..	..	..	..	..	..	..	..	..	..	..	..
Qatar	26.6	139.9	6.2	23.8	7.5	13,098	14,911	100.0	100.0	0.0	0.0	0.0	0.0

	Energy production		Energy use									Alternative and nuclear energy	
	Total million metric tons of oil equivalent		Total million metric tons of oil equivalent		average annual % growth	Per capita kilograms of oil equivalent		% of total				% of total energy use	
							Fossil fuel		Combustible renewables and waste			
	1990	2009	1990	2009	1990–2009	1990	2009	1990	2009	1990	2009	1990	2009
Romania	40.8	28.3	62.3	34.4	–1.9	2,683	1,602	96.1	76.3	1.0	11.4	1.6	12.9
Russian Federation	1,293.1	1,181.6	879.2	646.9	–1.0	5,929	4,561	93.4	90.2	1.4	1.0	5.2	9.0
Rwanda	..	..											
Saudi Arabia	370.2	528.4	59.8	157.9	4.9	3,703	5,888	100.0	100.0	0.0	0.0	0.0	0.0
Senegal	1.0	1.3	1.7	2.9	3.4	233	243	43.3	57.8	56.7	41.1	0.0	0.7
Serbia	13.4[a]	9.4	19.3[a]	14.4	0.4	2,550[a]	1,974	90.6[a]	92.4	6.0[a]	2.0	4.2[a]	6.4
Sierra Leone	..	..											
Singapore	0.0	0.0	11.5	18.5	0.9	3,760	3,704	100.0	99.8	0.0	0.2	0.0	0.0
Slovak Republic	5.3	5.9	21.3	16.7	–0.2	4,025	3,086	81.6	69.5	0.8	5.2	15.5	24.6
Slovenia	3.1	3.5	5.7	7.0	1.8	2,858	3,417	71.3	69.3	4.7	7.2	25.5	27.3
Somalia	..	..	..	..	..	..	..	..	..	..	..	..	..
South Africa	114.5	160.6	93.9	144.0	2.3	2,667	2,921	86.6	87.8	11.1	9.8	2.4	2.4
South Sudan	..	..	..	..	..	..	..	..	..	..	..	..	..
Spain	34.6	29.7	90.1	126.5	2.7	2,319	2,756	77.4	79.9	4.5	4.9	18.1	15.8
Sri Lanka	4.2	5.1	5.5	9.3	3.2	318	449	24.1	45.3	71.0	51.1	4.9	3.6
Sudan	8.8	35.2	10.6	15.8	2.4	401	372	17.4	30.2	81.8	68.0	0.8	1.8
Swaziland	..	..	0.3	0.4	..	358	373	0.0	0.0				
Sweden	29.7	30.3	47.2	45.4	0.2	5,515	4,883	37.3	32.0	11.7	22.9	50.9	42.9
Switzerland	10.3	12.8	24.3	27.0	0.6	3,621	3,480	58.6	53.3	5.9	8.2	36.3	39.2
Syrian Arab Republic	22.3	23.6	10.5	22.5	4.8	849	1,123	97.7	99.3	0.0	0.0	2.2	0.7
Tajikistan	2.0	1.5	5.3	2.3	–2.9	1,001	342	71.3	41.2	0.0	0.0	26.7	58.6
Tanzania	9.1	18.0	9.7	19.6	4.1	382	451	6.9	11.1	91.7	87.7	1.4	1.2
Thailand	26.6	61.7	41.9	103.3	4.9	735	1,504	63.8	79.4	35.0	19.9	1.0	0.6
Timor-Leste	..	..	..	0.1	..	..	58	..	0.0	..	..	..	..
Togo	1.1	2.2	1.3	2.6	4.2	345	445	15.1	14.3	82.8	83.1	0.6	0.3
Trinidad and Tobago	12.6	44.0	6.0	20.3	8.0	4,912	15,158	99.2	99.9	0.8	0.1	0.0	0.0
Tunisia	5.7	7.8	4.9	9.2	3.6	607	881	87.0	85.7	12.9	14.1	0.1	0.2
Turkey	25.8	30.3	52.8	97.7	3.6	975	1,359	81.8	89.9	13.7	4.8	4.6	5.4
Turkmenistan	74.9	40.9	19.6	19.6	2.4	5,352	3,933	100.0	100.0	0.0	0.0	0.3	0.0
Uganda	..	..	..	..	..	..	..	..	..	..	..	..	..
Ukraine	135.8	76.9	251.8	115.5	–3.0	4,852	2,507	91.8	80.0	0.1	0.8	8.2	19.7
United Arab Emirates	110.2	168.8	20.4	59.6	5.4	11,258	8,588	100.0	100.0	0.0	0.0	0.0	0.0
United Kingdom	208.0	158.9	205.9	196.8	0.0	3,597	3,183	90.7	87.3	0.3	2.7	8.5	9.8
United States	1,652.5	1,686.4	1,915.0	2,162.9	1.0	7,672	7,051	86.4	84.1	3.3	3.9	10.3	11.9
Uruguay	1.1	1.5	2.3	4.1	2.1	724	1,224	58.7	60.3	24.2	26.0	26.8	11.1
Uzbekistan	38.6	60.7	46.4	48.8	0.5	2,261	1,758	99.2	98.4	0.0	0.0	1.2	1.6
Venezuela, RB	148.8	203.5	43.5	66.9	2.0	2,205	2,357	91.5	87.7	1.2	0.8	7.3	11.6
Vietnam	24.7	76.6	24.3	64.0	5.3	368	745	20.3	56.2	77.8	39.3	1.9	4.0
West Bank and Gaza	..	..	..	..	..	..	..	..	..	..	..	..	..
Yemen, Rep.	9.4	15.2	2.5	7.6	6.0	210	324	96.9	98.7	3.1	1.3	0.0	0.0
Zambia	4.9	7.2	5.4	7.9	2.0	687	617	15.6	7.6	74.3	80.9	12.7	11.2
Zimbabwe	8.5	8.5	9.3	9.5	–0.2	888	763	44.8	25.7	50.8	65.6	4.0	3.8
World	**8,815.9 t**	**12,241.3 t**	**8,574.0 t**	**11,787.1 t**	**1.9 w**	**1,661 w**	**1,788 w**	**80.9 w**	**80.7 w**	**10.2 w**	**10.0 w**	**8.7 w**	**9.2 w**
Low income	160.7	250.6	186.6	263.3	2.2	386	365	41.5	29.9	54.7	65.9	3.9	4.1
Middle income	4,810.5	7,351.0	3,886.6	6,158.2	2.6	1,019	1,254	78.6	81.5	17.2	13.2	4.1	5.3
Lower middle income	1,247.9	1,944.1	1,085.5	1,656.0	2.4	607	665	65.1	68.0	30.7	26.9	4.4	5.3
Upper middle income	3,564.8	5,410.7	2,803.9	4,505.9	2.7	1,375	1,848	83.7	86.3	12.0	8.3	4.0	5.3
Low & middle income	4,969.1	7,597.3	4,059.7	6,407.1	2.6	963	1,162	77.3	79.8	18.5	15.0	4.1	5.3
East Asia & Pacific	1,224.5	2,758.4	1,138.1	2,790.9	4.8	712	1,436	71.4	84.1	26.6	11.8	1.9	4.1
Europe & Central Asia	1,770.3	1,673.3	1,585.6	1,137.6	–1.0	4,067	2,831	93.0	88.9	1.5	1.9	5.3	9.3
Latin America & Carib.	613.1	937.5	457.6	716.5	2.5	1,048	1,245	70.3	71.8	20.4	17.0	9.1	11.1
Middle East & N. Africa	558.2	856.0	183.8	454.5	5.0	812	1,399	97.4	98.3	1.4	0.9	1.1	0.6
South Asia	349.4	611.2	386.8	817.1	3.8	340	514	53.5	70.7	43.9	26.8	2.5	2.4
Sub-Saharan Africa	475.6	810.5	313.9	511.2	2.6	681	689	41.7	40.1	55.9	57.3	2.2	2.5
High income	3,878.6	4,694.3	4,538.5	5,420.3	1.2	4,649	4,856	84.2	81.9	2.8	4.2	12.8	13.8
Euro area	481.9	450.2	1,069.7	1,169.7	0.9	3,509	3,536	80.0	74.2	3.1	6.7	16.5	18.6

a. Includes Kosovo and Montenegro.

Energy production and use | 3.7

In developing economies growth in energy use is closely related to growth in the modern sectors—industry, motorized transport, and urban areas—but energy use also reflects climatic, geographic, and economic factors (such as the relative price of energy). Energy use has been growing rapidly in low- and middle-income economies, but high-income economies still use almost five times as much energy on a per capita basis.

Energy data are compiled by the International Energy Agency (IEA). IEA data for economies that are not members of the Organisation for Economic Co-operation and Development (OECD) are based on national energy data adjusted to conform to annual questionnaires completed by OECD member governments.

Total energy use refers to the use of primary energy before transformation to other end-use fuels (such as electricity and refined petroleum products). It includes energy from combustible renewables and waste—solid biomass and animal products, gas and liquid from biomass, and industrial and municipal waste. Biomass is any plant matter used directly as fuel or converted into fuel, heat, or electricity. Data for combustible renewables and waste are often based on small surveys or other incomplete information and thus give only a broad impression of developments and are not strictly comparable across countries. The IEA reports include country notes that explain some of these differences (see *Data sources*). All forms of energy—primary energy and primary electricity—are converted into oil equivalents. A notional thermal efficiency of 33 percent is assumed for converting nuclear electricity into oil equivalents and 100 percent efficiency for converting hydroelectric power.

The IEA makes these estimates in consultation with national statistical offices, oil companies, electric utilities, and national energy experts. The IEA occasionally revises its time series to reflect political changes, and energy statistics undergo continual changes in coverage or methodology as more detailed energy accounts become available. Breaks in series are therefore unavoidable.

• **Energy production** refers to forms of primary energy—petroleum (crude oil, natural gas liquids, and oil from nonconventional sources), natural gas, solid fuels (coal, lignite, and other derived fuels), and combustible renewables and waste—and primary electricity, all converted into oil equivalents (see *About the data*). • **Energy use** refers to the use of primary energy before transformation to other end-use fuels, which is equal to indigenous production plus imports and stock changes, minus exports and fuels supplied to ships and aircraft engaged in international transport (see *About the data*). • **Fossil fuel** comprises coal, oil, petroleum, and natural gas products. • **Combustible renewables and waste** comprise solid biomass, liquid biomass, biogas, industrial waste, and municipal waste. • **Alternative and nuclear energy production** is noncarbohydrate energy that does not produce carbon dioxide when generated. It includes hydropower and nuclear, geothermal, and solar power, among others.

Data on energy production and use are from IEA electronic files and are published in IEA's annual publications *Energy Statistics of Non-OECD Countries, Energy Balances of Non-OECD Countries, Energy Statistics of OECD Countries,* and *Energy Balances of OECD Countries.*

	Electricity production	Sources of electricity[a]						Access to electricity
					% of total			
	billion kilowatt hours	Coal	Natural gas	Oil	Hydropower	Renewable sources[b]	Nuclear power	% of population
	2009	2009	2009	2009	2009	2009	2009	2009
Afghanistan	..	..	..	..	..	..	..	15.6
Albania	5.3	0.0	0.0	0.6	99.4	0.0	0.0	..
Algeria	42.8	0.0	97.2	2.0	0.8	0.0	0.0	99.3
Angola	4.2	0.0	0.0	23.9	76.1	0.0	0.0	26.2
Argentina	121.9	2.3	51.3	10.5	27.8	1.4	6.7	97.2
Armenia	5.7	0.0	20.3	0.0	35.6	0.1	44.0	..
Australia	260.9	77.9	13.7	1.0	4.7	2.6	0.0	..
Austria	65.6	7.7	18.8	1.7	61.4	9.6	0.0	..
Azerbaijan	18.9	0.0	85.1	2.6	12.2	0.0	0.0	..
Bahrain	12.1	0.0	100.0	0.0	0.0	0.0	0.0	99.4
Bangladesh	37.9	1.7	89.4	4.8	4.1	0.0	0.0	41.0
Belarus	30.4	0.0	81.7	17.6	0.1	0.2	0.0	..
Belgium	89.8	6.8	32.6	0.3	0.4	5.7	52.6	..
Benin	0.1	0.0	0.0	100.0	0.0	0.0	0.0	24.8
Bolivia	6.1	0.0	59.7	1.7	37.5	1.0	0.0	77.5
Bosnia and Herzegovina	15.7	59.9	0.2	0.1	39.8	0.0	0.0	..
Botswana	0.4	100.0	0.0	0.0	0.0	0.0	0.0	45.4
Brazil	466.5	2.1	2.9	3.1	83.8	5.2	2.8	98.3
Bulgaria	42.4	49.8	4.6	0.8	8.2	0.6	36.0	..
Burkina Faso	..	..	..	..	..	..	..	14.6
Burundi	..	..	..	..	..	..	..	..
Cambodia	1.2	0.0	0.0	95.6	3.9	0.5	0.0	24.0
Cameroon	5.7	0.0	7.2	22.7	70.0	0.2	0.0	48.7
Canada	603.1	15.2	6.2	1.4	60.3	1.9	15.0	..
Central African Republic	..	..	..	..	..	..	..	..
Chad	..	..	..	..	..	..	..	..
Chile	60.7	24.5	6.5	20.0	41.7	7.2	0.0	98.5
China	3,695.9	78.8	1.4	0.4	16.7	0.8	1.9	99.4
Hong Kong SAR, China	38.7	70.8	28.9	0.4	0.0	0.0	0.0	..
Colombia	57.3	7.3	19.3	0.6	71.7	1.2	0.0	93.6
Congo, Dem. Rep.	7.8	0.0	0.4	0.1	99.6	0.0	0.0	11.1
Congo, Rep.	0.5	0.0	36.0	0.0	64.0	0.0	0.0	37.1
Costa Rica	9.3	0.0	0.0	4.9	77.8	17.4	0.0	99.3
Côte d'Ivoire	5.9	0.0	61.9	0.1	35.9	2.1	0.0	47.3
Croatia	12.7	13.1	17.4	15.9	53.0	0.6	0.0	..
Cuba	17.7	0.0	13.4	82.8	0.9	2.9	0.0	97.0
Cyprus	5.2	0.0	0.0	99.2	0.0	0.1	0.0	..
Czech Republic	81.7	59.6	1.2	0.2	3.0	2.7	33.3	..
Denmark	36.4	48.6	18.5	3.2	0.1	27.6	0.0	..
Dominican Republic	15.0	12.9	13.5	63.6	9.8	0.2	0.0	95.9
Ecuador	17.2	0.0	6.9	37.5	53.5	2.1	0.0	92.2
Egypt, Arab Rep.	139.0	0.0	68.7	21.3	9.3	0.8	0.0	99.6
El Salvador	5.8	0.0	0.0	43.7	26.0	30.3	0.0	86.4
Eritrea	0.3	0.0	0.0	99.3	0.0	0.7	0.0	32.0
Estonia	8.8	91.4	1.2	0.5	0.4	5.8	0.0	..
Ethiopia	4.1	0.0	0.0	12.4	87.3	0.4	0.0	17.0
Finland	72.1	16.0	13.6	0.7	17.6	12.5	32.6	..
France	537.4	5.3	3.9	1.1	10.6	2.4	76.2	..
Gabon	1.7	0.0	26.4	20.0	53.2	0.4	0.0	36.7
Gambia, The	..	..	..	..	..	..	..	..
Georgia	8.6	0.0	12.9	0.5	86.6	0.0	0.0	..
Germany	586.4	43.8	13.5	1.6	3.2	12.8	23.0	..
Ghana	9.0	0.0	0.0	23.2	76.8	0.0	0.0	60.5
Greece	61.1	56.0	18.0	12.6	8.8	4.6	0.0	..
Guatemala	9.0	8.2	0.0	34.5	23.3	34.0	0.0	80.5
Guinea	..	..	..	..	..	..	..	..
Guinea-Bissau	..	..	..	..	..	..	..	..
Haiti	0.7	0.0	0.0	71.3	28.7	0.0	0.0	38.5

Electricity production, sources, and access

	Electricity production	Sources of electricity[a]						Access to electricity
				% of total				
	billion kilowatt hours	Coal	Natural gas	Oil	Hydropower	Renewable sources[b]	Nuclear power	% of population
	2009	2009	2009	2009	2009	2009	2009	2009
Honduras	6.6	0.0	0.0	54.9	42.5	2.6	0.0	70.3
Hungary	35.9	17.9	29.0	1.8	0.6	7.4	43.0	..
India	899.4	68.6	12.4	2.9	11.9	2.2	2.1	66.3
Indonesia	155.5	41.8	22.1	22.8	7.3	6.0	0.0	64.5
Iran, Islamic Rep.	203.2	0.2	70.4	25.8	3.6	0.1	0.0	98.4
Iraq	46.1	0.0	0.0	93.0	7.0	0.0	0.0	86.0
Ireland	27.9	14.4	58.4	3.3	3.2	11.2	0.0	..
Israel	55.0	62.5	32.8	4.0	0.0	0.1	0.0	99.7
Italy	288.3	15.1	51.1	9.0	17.0	7.0	0.0	..
Jamaica	5.5	0.0	0.0	96.4	2.0	1.6	0.0	92.0
Japan	1,041.0	26.8	27.4	7.2	7.2	2.5	26.9	..
Jordan	14.3	0.0	88.1	11.4	0.4	0.1	0.0	99.9
Kazakhstan	78.7	74.9	13.1	3.2	8.7	0.0	0.0	..
Kenya	6.9	0.0	0.0	44.1	31.6	24.4	0.0	16.1
Korea, Dem. Rep.	21.1	38.1	0.0	2.8	59.1	0.0	0.0	26.0
Korea, Rep.	451.7	46.2	15.6	4.4	0.6	0.4	32.7	..
Kosovo	..	..	..	..	..	..	..	..
Kuwait	53.2	0.0	28.8	71.2	0.0	0.0	0.0	100.0
Kyrgyz Republic	11.1	2.8	8.0	0.0	89.3	0.0	0.0	..
Lao PDR	..	..	..	..	..	..	..	55.0
Latvia	5.6	0.0	36.0	0.1	62.1	1.8	0.0	..
Lebanon	13.8	0.0	1.4	94.1	4.5	0.0	0.0	99.9
Lesotho	..	..	..	..	..	..	..	16.0
Liberia	..	..	..	..	..	..	..	..
Libya	30.4	0.0	41.0	59.0	0.0	0.0	0.0	99.8
Lithuania	14.6	0.0	14.3	5.0	2.9	1.8	74.1	..
Macedonia, FYR	6.8	77.7	0.0	3.7	18.6	0.0	0.0	..
Madagascar	..	..	..	..	..	..	..	19.0
Malawi	..	..	..	..	..	..	..	9.0
Malaysia	105.1	30.9	60.7	2.0	6.3	0.0	0.0	99.4
Mali	..	..	..	..	..	..	..	..
Mauritania	..	..	..	..	..	..	..	..
Mauritius	..	..	..	..	..	..	..	99.4
Mexico	261.0	11.3	53.1	17.5	10.2	3.9	4.0	..
Moldova	3.6	0.0	95.0	1.3	1.5	0.0	0.0	..
Mongolia	4.2	96.4	0.0	3.6	0.0	0.0	0.0	67.0
Morocco	21.4	52.4	13.3	20.3	12.1	1.8	0.0	97.0
Mozambique	17.0	0.0	0.1	0.0	99.9	0.0	0.0	11.7
Myanmar	5.9	0.0	19.6	8.9	71.5	0.0	0.0	13.0
Namibia	1.7	17.5	0.0	0.5	82.0	0.0	0.0	34.0
Nepal	3.1	0.0	0.0	0.4	99.6	0.0	0.0	43.6
Netherlands	113.5	23.4	60.5	1.3	0.1	9.5	3.7	..
New Zealand	43.5	7.6	20.6	0.0	55.7	15.9	0.0	..
Nicaragua	3.5	0.0	0.0	69.1	8.6	22.3	0.0	72.1
Niger	..	..	..	..	..	..	..	..
Nigeria	19.8	0.0	64.3	12.8	22.9	0.0	0.0	50.6
Norway	132.0	0.1	3.2	0.0	95.7	0.9	0.0	..
Oman	17.8	0.0	82.0	18.0	0.0	0.0	0.0	98.0
Pakistan	95.4	0.1	29.4	38.0	29.4	0.0	3.0	62.4
Panama	6.9	0.0	0.0	43.6	56.1	0.2	0.0	88.1
Papua New Guinea	..	..	..	..	..	..	..	..
Paraguay	55.0	0.0	0.0	0.0	100.0	0.0	0.0	96.7
Peru	35.4	2.5	34.3	4.1	57.6	1.4	0.0	85.7
Philippines	61.9	26.6	32.1	8.7	15.8	16.8	0.0	89.7
Poland	151.1	89.1	3.2	1.8	1.6	4.2	0.0	..
Portugal	49.5	26.1	29.7	6.6	16.7	20.2	0.0	..
Puerto Rico	..	..	..	..	..	..	..	..
Qatar	24.8	0.0	100.0	0.0	0.0	0.0	0.0	98.7

	Electricity production	Sources of electricity[a]						Access to electricity
				% of total				
	billion kilowatt hours	Coal	Natural gas	Oil	Hydropower	Renewable sources[b]	Nuclear power	% of population
	2009	2009	2009	2009	2009	2009	2009	2009
Romania	57.7	37.7	13.2	1.8	26.9	0.0	20.4	..
Russian Federation	990.0	16.5	47.4	1.6	17.6	0.1	16.5	..
Rwanda	..	..	..	..	..	..	..	..
Saudi Arabia	217.1	0.0	44.8	55.2	0.0	0.0	0.0	99.0
Senegal	2.9	0.0	1.7	86.4	8.4	1.9	0.0	42.0
Serbia	37.4	71.9	0.5	0.3	27.4	0.0	0.0	..
Sierra Leone	..	..	..	..	..	..	..	..
Singapore	41.8	0.0	81.0	18.8	0.0	0.1	0.0	100.0
Slovak Republic	25.9	16.5	7.6	2.4	16.9	2.1	54.3	..
Slovenia	16.4	31.3	3.6	0.2	28.7	1.2	35.0	..
Somalia	..	..	..	..	..	..	..	..
South Africa	246.8	94.1	0.0	0.0	0.6	0.1	5.2	75.0
South Sudan	..	..	..	..	..	..	..	..
Spain	291.0	12.8	36.9	6.5	9.0	16.2	18.1	..
Sri Lanka	9.9	0.0	0.0	60.3	39.5	0.2	0.0	76.6
Sudan	6.8	0.0	0.0	52.2	47.8	0.0	0.0	35.9
Swaziland	..	..	..	..	..	..	..	..
Sweden	136.6	0.7	1.1	0.5	48.2	10.2	38.2	..
Switzerland	66.7	0.0	1.0	0.2	53.6	2.0	41.5	..
Syrian Arab Republic	43.3	0.0	45.7	50.0	4.3	0.0	0.0	92.7
Tajikistan	16.1	0.0	2.0	0.0	98.0	0.0	0.0	..
Tanzania	4.6	2.7	36.2	0.9	60.2	0.0	0.0	13.9
Thailand	148.4	19.9	70.7	0.5	4.8	4.0	0.0	99.3
Timor-Leste	..	..	..	..	..	..	..	22.0
Togo	0.1	0.0	0.0	24.6	73.8	1.6	0.0	20.0
Trinidad and Tobago	7.7	0.0	99.4	0.3	0.0	0.2	0.0	99.0
Tunisia	15.7	0.0	89.7	9.2	0.5	0.6	0.0	99.5
Turkey	194.8	28.6	49.3	2.5	18.5	1.1	0.0	..
Turkmenistan	16.0	0.0	100.0	0.0	0.0	0.0	0.0	..
Uganda	..	..	..	..	..	..	..	9.0
Ukraine	173.5	36.6	8.1	0.5	6.8	0.0	48.0	..
United Arab Emirates	90.6	0.0	98.2	1.8	0.0	0.0	0.0	100.0
United Kingdom	372.0	28.5	44.5	1.2	1.4	5.4	18.6	..
United States	4,165.4	45.4	22.8	1.2	6.6	3.7	19.9	..
Uruguay	8.9	0.0	0.2	31.1	59.4	9.3	0.0	98.3
Uzbekistan	49.9	4.1	75.1	2.1	18.7	0.0	0.0	..
Venezuela, RB	123.4	0.0	14.7	12.5	72.8	0.0	0.0	99.0
Vietnam	83.2	18.0	43.4	2.5	36.0	0.0	0.0	97.6
West Bank and Gaza	..	..	..	..	..	..	..	..
Yemen, Rep.	6.7	0.0	0.0	100.0	0.0	0.0	0.0	39.6
Zambia	10.3	0.0	0.0	0.3	99.7	0.0	0.0	18.8
Zimbabwe	7.9	46.4	0.0	0.3	53.3	0.0	0.0	41.5
World	**20,079.3 w**	**40.4 w**	**21.4 w**	**4.8 w**	**16.1 w**	**3.0**	**13.4 w**	**74.1 w**
Low income	185.6	6.9	20.4	4.7	45.7	0.9	0.0	23.0
Middle income	9,255.1	47.9	19.2	5.7	20.6	1.4	4.6	81.6
Lower middle income	2,007.9	39.6	22.0	12.1	16.9	2.4	5.3	67.3
Upper middle income	7,245.8	50.2	18.5	3.9	21.6	1.2	4.4	98.0
Low & middle income	9,461.8	47.0	19.2	5.7	21.0	1.4	4.5	73.7
East Asia & Pacific	4,307.5	71.6	7.2	1.5	16.2	1.3	1.6	90.8
Europe & Central Asia	1,785.3	24.0	39.5	1.9	18.0	0.2	16.1	..
Latin America & Carib.	1,296.7	5.0	20.7	12.1	55.5	3.9	2.4	93.4
Middle East & N. Africa	584.2	2.0	58.5	32.9	4.9	0.3	0.0	92.9
South Asia	1,054.5	58.5	16.4	6.6	13.6	1.9	2.0	62.1
Sub-Saharan Africa	419.3	56.5	4.6	4.1	18.2	0.5	3.1	32.5
High income	10,673.5	34.3	23.2	4.1	11.6	4.5	21.3	..
Euro area	2,244.3	21.6	23.3	3.7	10.2	9.1	30.8	..

a. Shares may not sum to 100 percent because some sources of generated electricity are not shown. b. Excludes hydropower.

About the data

Use of energy is important in improving people's standard of living. But electricity generation also can damage the environment. Whether such damage occurs depends largely on how electricity is generated. For example, burning coal releases twice as much carbon dioxide—a major contributor to global warming—as does burning an equivalent amount of natural gas (see *About the data* for table 3.9). Nuclear energy does not generate carbon dioxide emissions, but it produces other dangerous waste products. The table provides information on electricity production by source.

The International Energy Agency (IEA) compiles data on energy inputs used to generate electricity. IEA data for countries that are not members of the Organisation for Economic Co-operation and Development (OECD) are based on national energy data adjusted to conform to annual questionnaires completed by OECD member governments. In addition, estimates are sometimes made to complete major aggregates from which key data are missing, and adjustments are made to compensate for differences in definitions. The IEA makes these estimates in consultation with national statistical offices, oil companies, electric utilities, and national energy experts. It occasionally revises its time series to reflect political changes. For example, the IEA has constructed historical energy statistics for countries of the former Soviet Union. In addition, energy statistics for other countries have undergone continuous changes in coverage or methodology in recent years as more detailed energy accounts have become available. Breaks in series are therefore unavoidable.

Data on access to electricity are collected by the IEA from industry, national surveys, and international sources.

Definitions

• **Electricity production** is measured at the terminals of all alternator sets in a station. In addition to hydropower, coal, oil, gas, and nuclear power generation, it covers generation by geothermal, solar, wind, and tide and wave energy as well as that from combustible renewables and waste. Production includes the output of electric plants designed to produce electricity only, as well as that of combined heat and power plants. • **Sources of electricity** are the inputs used to generate electricity: coal, gas, oil, hydropower, and nuclear power. • **Coal** is all coal and brown coal, both primary (including hard coal and lignite-brown coal) and derived fuels (including patent fuel, coke oven coke, gas coke, coke oven gas, and blast furnace gas). Peat is also included in this category. • **Natural gas** is natural gas but not natural gas liquids. • **Oil** is crude oil and petroleum products. • **Hydropower** is electricity produced by hydroelectric power plants. • **Renewable sources** are geothermal, solar photovoltaic, solar thermal, tide, wind, industrial waste, municipal waste, primary solid biofuels, biogases, biogasoline, biodiesels, other liquid biofuels, nonspecified primary biofuels and waste, and charcoal. • **Nuclear power** is electricity produced by nuclear power plants. • **Access to electricity** is the percentage of the population with access to electricity.

Data sources

Data on electricity production and sources are from the IEA's electronic files and its annual publications *Energy Statistics of Non-OECD Countries*, *Energy Balances of Non-OECD Countries*, *Energy Statistics of OECD Countries*, and *Energy Balances of OECD Countries*. Data on access to electricity are from the IEA's *World Energy Outlook* (2011).

| | Net energy imports[a] | | GDP per unit of energy use | | Carbon dioxide emissions | | | | | | | |
| | % of energy use | | 2005 PPP $ per kilogram of oil equivalent | | Total million metric tons | | Carbon intensity kilograms per kilogram of oil equivalent energy use | | Per capita metric tons | | kilograms per 2005 PPP $ of GDP | |
	1990	2009	1990	2009	1990	2008	1990	2008	1990	2008	1990	2008
Afghanistan	..	..	..	..	2.7	0.8	..	..	0.1	0.0	..	0.0
Albania	8	27	4.8	13.8	7.5	4.2	2.8	2.0	2.3	1.3	0.6	0.2
Algeria	−351	−283	7.1	6.5	78.9	111.3	3.6	3.0	3.1	3.2	0.5	0.4
Angola	−387	−749	5.8	8.4	4.4	24.4	0.8	2.1	0.4	1.4	0.1	0.2
Argentina	−5	−9	5.3	7.2	112.6	192.4	2.4	2.5	3.4	4.8	0.5	0.4
Armenia	98	68	1.4	5.7	3.7	5.5	0.9	1.9	1.1	1.8	0.7	0.3
Australia	−83	−137	4.7	5.7	287.3	399.2	3.3	3.1	16.8	18.6	0.7	0.5
Austria	67	64	7.9	9.2	61.0	67.7	2.5	2.0	7.9	8.1	0.3	0.2
Azerbaijan	21	−439	1.3	6.4	44.2	47.1	2.1	3.5	6.0	5.4	1.7	0.7
Bahrain	−209	−85	2.0	2.7	11.9	22.5	2.7	2.4	24.1	21.4	1.3	0.9
Bangladesh	16	16	6.2	7.0	15.5	46.5	1.2	1.7	0.1	0.3	0.2	0.2
Belarus	93	85	1.4	4.1	87.5	62.8	2.4	2.2	8.6	6.5	1.5	0.6
Belgium	73	73	5.2	6.1	108.5	104.9	2.2	1.8	10.9	9.8	0.4	0.3
Benin	−7	43	3.2	3.5	0.7	4.1	0.4	1.2	0.1	0.5	0.1	0.3
Bolivia	−89	−128	7.8	6.7	5.5	12.8	2.1	2.1	0.8	1.3	0.3	0.3
Bosnia and Herzegovina	34	25	..	4.6	3.9	31.3	0.9	5.2	1.0	8.3	..	1.1
Botswana	28	54	7.6	11.4	2.2	4.8	1.7	2.2	1.6	2.5	0.2	0.2
Brazil	26	4	7.7	7.6	208.9	393.2	1.5	1.6	1.4	2.1	0.2	0.2
Bulgaria	66	44	2.3	4.9	77.7	50.5	2.7	2.6	8.9	6.6	1.2	0.6
Burkina Faso	..	..	..	..	0.6	1.9	..	..	0.1	0.1	0.1	0.1
Burundi	..	..	..	..	0.3	0.2	..	..	0.1	0.0	0.1	0.1
Cambodia	..	29	..	5.1	0.5	4.6	..	0.9	0.0	0.3	..	0.2
Cameroon	−120	−28	5.1	5.6	1.7	5.3	0.3	0.8	0.1	0.3	0.1	0.1
Canada	−31	−53	3.6	4.6	450.1	544.1	2.2	2.0	16.2	16.3	0.6	0.5
Central African Republic	..	..	..	..	0.2	0.3	..	..	0.1	0.1	0.1	0.1
Chad	..	..	..	..	0.1	0.5	..	..	0.0	0.0	0.0	0.0
Chile	45	68	6.4	7.7	34.9	73.1	2.6	2.5	2.6	4.4	0.4	0.3
China	−3	8	1.4	3.7	2,460.7	7,031.9	2.9	3.3	2.2	5.3	2.0	0.9
Hong Kong SAR, China	99	100	15.6	18.4	27.7	38.6	3.2	2.7	4.8	5.5	0.2	0.1
Colombia	−99	−211	8.4	11.8	57.3	67.7	2.4	2.2	1.7	1.5	0.3	0.2
Congo, Dem. Rep.	−2	−2	1.9	0.8	4.1	2.8	0.3	0.1	0.1	0.0	0.2	0.2
Congo, Rep.	−997	−989	10.7	10.1	1.2	1.9	1.5	1.5	0.5	0.5	0.1	0.1
Costa Rica	49	45	9.5	9.5	3.0	8.0	1.5	1.6	1.0	1.8	0.2	0.2
Côte d'Ivoire	22	−15	5.5	3.2	5.8	7.0	1.3	0.7	0.5	0.4	0.2	0.2
Croatia	43	53	7.1	8.3	16.4	23.3	2.4	2.6	3.7	5.3	0.4	0.3
Cuba	51	52	..	..	33.3	31.4	1.7	3.0	3.2	2.8	..	..
Cyprus	100	97	7.7	8.2	4.7	8.6	3.4	3.3	6.1	7.9	0.4	0.4
Czech Republic	17	26	3.4	5.5	139.5	117.0	3.2	2.6	13.5	11.2	0.9	0.5
Denmark	42	−29	7.5	9.5	50.4	46.0	2.9	2.4	9.8	8.4	0.4	0.2
Dominican Republic	75	77	6.7	9.5	9.6	21.6	2.3	2.7	1.3	2.2	0.3	0.3
Ecuador	−175	−141	9.3	8.9	16.8	26.8	2.8	2.4	1.6	1.9	0.3	0.3
Egypt, Arab Rep.	−72	−22	5.8	5.9	75.9	210.3	2.4	3.0	1.3	2.7	0.4	0.5
El Salvador	31	38	7.9	7.2	2.6	6.1	1.1	1.2	0.5	1.0	0.1	0.2
Eritrea	19	23	1.8	3.5	..	0.4	..	0.6	..	0.1	..	0.2
Estonia	45	12	1.6	4.5	23.0	18.3	3.5	3.4	15.0	13.6	2.0	0.7
Ethiopia	5	7	1.8	2.2	3.0	7.1	0.2	0.2	0.1	0.1	0.1	0.1
Finland	57	50	4.1	4.9	50.9	56.5	1.8	1.6	10.2	10.6	0.4	0.3
France	50	49	6.3	7.4	399.0	377.0	1.8	1.4	6.9	5.9	0.3	0.2
Gabon	−1,138	−657	11.8	10.7	4.8	2.5	4.1	1.2	5.2	1.7	0.3	0.1
Gambia, The	..	..	17.6	14.0	0.2	0.4	3.1	3.0	0.2	0.3	0.2	0.2
Georgia	83	61	2.4	6.0	15.3	5.2	1.8	1.7	3.1	1.2	1.2	0.3
Germany	47	60	5.9	8.3	961.0	786.7	2.8	2.4	12.0	9.6	0.4	0.3
Ghana	17	24	2.5	3.6	3.9	8.6	0.7	0.9	0.3	0.4	0.3	0.3
Greece	57	66	8.2	9.6	72.7	97.8	3.4	3.2	7.2	8.7	0.4	0.3
Guatemala	24	39	6.7	6.1	5.1	11.9	1.1	1.5	0.6	0.9	0.2	0.2
Guinea	..	..	..	..	1.1	1.4	..	..	0.2	0.1	0.2	0.1
Guinea-Bissau	..	..	16.5	15.4	0.3	0.3	3.4	3.0	0.2	0.2	0.2	0.2
Haiti	20	28	6.4	4.0	1.0	2.4	0.6	0.9	0.1	0.3	0.1	0.2

Energy dependency and efficiency and carbon dioxide emissions | 3.9

	Net energy imports[a]		GDP per unit of energy use		Carbon dioxide emissions							
	% of energy use		2005 PPP $ per kilogram of oil equivalent		Total million metric tons		Carbon intensity kilograms per kilogram of oil equivalent energy use		Per capita metric tons		kilograms per 2005 PPP $ of GDP	
	1990	2009	1990	2009	1990	2008	1990	2008	1990	2008	1990	2008
Honduras	29	50	5.5	5.9	2.6	8.7	1.1	1.9	0.5	1.2	0.2	0.3
Hungary	49	56	4.7	6.7	63.0	54.6	2.2	2.1	6.1	5.4	0.5	0.3
India	8	26	3.3	5.1	690.6	1,742.7	2.2	2.8	0.8	1.5	0.7	0.5
Indonesia	−67	−74	3.7	4.3	149.6	406.0	1.5	2.1	0.8	1.7	0.4	0.5
Iran, Islamic Rep.	−164	−62	5.0	3.5	227.2	538.4	3.3	2.6	4.1	7.4	0.7	0.7
Iraq	−480	−272	..	3.2	52.6	102.9	2.9	3.0	2.9	3.4	..	1.1
Ireland	65	89	6.4	11.3	30.4	43.6	3.0	2.9	8.7	9.9	0.5	0.3
Israel	96	85	7.3	8.8	33.5	37.7	2.9	1.7	7.2	5.2	0.4	0.2
Italy	83	84	9.2	9.8	424.2	445.1	2.9	2.5	7.5	7.4	0.3	0.3
Jamaica	83	84	5.1	5.7	8.0	12.2	2.9	2.9	3.3	4.5	0.6	0.6
Japan	83	80	7.3	7.9	1,094.7	1,208.2	2.5	2.4	8.9	9.5	0.3	0.3
Jordan	95	96	3.2	4.1	10.4	21.4	3.2	3.0	3.3	3.7	1.0	0.7
Kazakhstan	−24	−121	1.6	2.5	261.3	237.0	3.3	3.4	15.9	15.1	2.7	1.4
Kenya	18	17	3.0	3.0	5.8	10.4	0.5	0.6	0.2	0.3	0.2	0.2
Korea, Dem. Rep.	13	−5	..	..	..	78.4	..	3.9	..	3.2	..	..
Korea, Rep.	76	81	5.2	5.4	243.8	509.2	2.6	2.2	5.7	10.5	0.5	0.4
Kosovo	..	..	..	..	..	..	..	..	..	..	..	..
Kuwait	−453	−332	2.5	4.6	45.4	76.7	5.0	2.8	21.8	30.1	0.6	0.6
Kyrgyz Republic	67	61	1.5	3.7	10.9	6.2	2.2	2.3	2.4	1.2	1.2	0.6
Lao PDR	..	..	..	..	0.2	1.5	..	..	0.1	0.3	0.1	0.1
Latvia	86	50	3.4	6.9	14.1	7.6	2.3	1.7	5.4	3.3	0.9	0.2
Lebanon	93	97	8.7	7.5	9.1	17.1	4.7	3.2	3.1	4.1	0.5	0.4
Lesotho	..	..	..	142.1	..	..	..	..	..	..	..	..
Liberia	..	..	..	..	0.5	0.6	..	..	0.2	0.2	0.5	0.4
Libya	−546	−327	..	4.7	40.3	58.3	3.6	3.0	9.3	9.5	..	0.6
Lithuania	69	50	2.9	6.0	22.2	15.1	2.0	1.6	6.0	4.5	0.6	0.3
Macedonia, FYR	49	42	6.6	6.7	10.8	11.8	4.0	3.9	5.6	5.8	0.8	0.6
Madagascar	..	..	..	..	1.0	1.9	..	..	0.1	0.1	0.1	0.1
Malawi	..	..	..	..	0.6	1.2	..	..	0.1	0.1	0.1	0.1
Malaysia	−122	−34	5.5	5.2	56.6	208.3	2.6	2.9	3.1	7.6	0.5	0.6
Mali	..	..	..	..	0.4	0.6	..	..	0.0	0.0	0.1	0.0
Mauritania	..	..	..	..	2.7	2.0	..	..	1.3	0.6	0.8	0.3
Mauritius	..	..	13.5	11.6	1.5	4.0	3.0	3.3	1.4	3.1	0.2	0.3
Mexico	−59	−26	6.9	7.7	325.6	475.8	2.7	2.6	3.9	4.3	0.4	0.3
Moldova	99	96	1.7	3.8	21.0	4.8	3.1	1.5	5.7	1.3	2.1	0.5
Mongolia	20	−138	1.6	2.9	10.0	10.9	2.9	3.5	4.6	4.1	1.9	1.1
Morocco	89	95	9.7	8.8	23.5	47.9	3.4	3.2	1.0	1.5	0.4	0.4
Mozambique	5	−22	0.9	1.9	1.0	2.3	0.2	0.2	0.1	0.1	0.2	0.1
Myanmar	0	−48	1.3	5.0	4.3	12.8	0.4	0.8	0.1	0.3	0.3	0.2
Namibia	67	81	9.4	7.4	0.0	4.0	0.0	2.2	0.0	1.8	0.0	0.3
Nepal	5	11	2.3	3.1	0.6	3.5	0.1	0.4	0.0	0.1	0.0	0.1
Netherlands	8	19	6.0	7.7	164.1	173.7	2.5	2.2	11.0	10.6	0.4	0.3
New Zealand	11	13	5.0	6.1	24.0	33.1	1.9	1.9	7.0	7.8	0.4	0.3
Nicaragua	29	45	3.7	4.6	2.6	4.3	1.3	1.4	0.6	0.8	0.3	0.3
Niger	..	..	..	..	0.8	0.9	..	..	0.1	0.1	0.2	0.1
Nigeria	−113	−111	2.0	2.9	45.4	95.8	0.6	0.9	0.5	0.6	0.3	0.3
Norway	−467	−656	6.5	8.1	31.3	50.0	1.5	1.7	7.4	10.5	0.2	0.2
Oman	−808	−346	6.5	4.4	10.4	45.7	2.5	2.8	5.5	17.3	0.4	0.7
Pakistan	20	24	4.2	4.7	68.6	163.2	1.6	2.0	0.6	1.0	0.4	0.4
Panama	58	79	10.1	13.2	3.1	6.9	2.2	2.5	1.3	2.0	0.2	0.2
Papua New Guinea	..	..	..	..	2.1	2.1	..	..	0.5	0.3	0.3	0.2
Paraguay	−49	−56	5.5	5.5	2.3	4.1	0.7	0.9	0.5	0.7	0.1	0.2
Peru	−9	4	10.0	14.4	21.2	40.5	2.2	2.7	1.0	1.4	0.2	0.2
Philippines	40	40	5.4	7.9	44.5	83.2	1.5	2.1	0.7	0.9	0.3	0.3
Poland	−1	28	3.0	6.8	366.8	316.1	3.6	3.2	9.6	8.3	1.2	0.5
Portugal	80	80	9.6	9.4	43.7	56.3	2.6	2.3	4.4	5.3	0.3	0.2
Puerto Rico	..	..	..	..	..	..	..	..	..	..	..	..
Qatar	−328	−487	..	4.9	11.8	68.5	1.9	3.0	24.9	49.1	..	0.6

3.9 | Energy dependency and efficiency and carbon dioxide emissions

	Net energy imports[a]		GDP per unit of energy use		Carbon dioxide emissions							
			2005 PPP $ per kilogram of oil equivalent		Total million metric tons		Carbon intensity kilograms per kilogram of oil equivalent energy use		Per capita metric tons		kilograms per 2005 PPP $ of GDP	
	% of energy use											
	1990	2009	1990	2009	1990	2008	1990	2008	1990	2008	1990	2008
Romania	34	18	2.9	6.7	158.9	94.7	2.6	2.4	6.8	4.4	0.9	0.4
Russian Federation	−47	−83	2.1	3.0	2,220.7	1,708.7	2.8	2.5	14.9	12.0	1.5	0.8
Rwanda	..	..	..	..	0.7	0.7	..	..	0.1	0.1	0.1	0.1
Saudi Arabia	−519	−235	5.2	3.4	215.1	433.6	3.6	2.8	13.3	16.6	0.7	0.8
Senegal	43	57	6.3	7.1	3.2	5.0	1.9	1.7	0.4	0.4	0.3	0.2
Serbia	31	35	4.6	4.8	45.3[b]	49.9	3.0[b]	3.0	5.9[b]	6.8	0.8[b]	0.7
Sierra Leone	..	..	..	..	0.4	1.3	..	..	0.1	0.2	0.1	0.3
Singapore	100	100	6.7	12.5	46.9	32.3	4.1	1.9	15.4	6.7	0.6	0.1
Slovak Republic	75	65	3.2	6.3	45.6	37.6	2.5	2.1	8.6	6.9	0.9	0.3
Slovenia	46	49	5.8	7.3	13.0	17.2	2.5	2.2	6.5	8.5	0.5	0.3
Somalia	..	..	..	..	0.0	0.6	..	..	0.0	0.1	..	..
South Africa	−22	−12	3.0	3.2	333.5	435.9	3.6	2.9	9.5	8.9	1.2	0.9
South Sudan	..	..	..	..	..	..	..	..	..	..	..	..
Spain	62	77	8.5	9.8	227.6	329.3	2.5	2.4	5.9	7.2	0.3	0.3
Sri Lanka	24	45	6.3	9.5	3.8	11.8	0.7	1.3	0.2	0.6	0.1	0.1
Sudan	17	−123	2.6	5.3	5.6	14.1	0.5	1.0	0.2	0.3	0.2	0.2
Swaziland	..	..	10.9	12.6	0.4	1.1	1.4	2.5	0.5	1.1	0.1	0.2
Sweden	37	33	4.5	6.6	51.7	49.0	1.1	1.0	6.0	5.3	0.2	0.2
Switzerland	58	53	9.2	10.6	43.0	40.4	1.8	1.5	6.4	5.3	0.2	0.1
Syrian Arab Republic	−113	−5	3.5	4.2	37.5	71.6	3.6	2.8	3.0	3.6	1.0	0.8
Tajikistan	62	35	3.0	5.5	7.2	3.1	1.7	1.3	1.3	0.5	0.7	0.3
Tanzania	7	8	2.2	2.7	2.4	6.5	0.2	0.3	0.1	0.2	0.1	0.1
Thailand	37	40	5.4	4.8	95.8	285.7	2.3	2.7	1.7	4.2	0.4	0.6
Timor-Leste	..	..	..	11.8	..	0.2	..	3.0	..	0.2	..	0.2
Togo	17	17	2.7	2.0	0.8	1.4	0.6	0.6	0.2	0.2	0.2	0.3
Trinidad and Tobago	−111	−117	2.2	1.5	17.0	49.8	2.8	2.6	14.0	37.4	1.3	1.6
Tunisia	−16	15	7.4	9.5	13.3	25.0	2.7	2.7	1.6	2.4	0.4	0.3
Turkey	51	69	8.3	8.6	150.8	284.0	2.9	2.9	2.8	4.0	0.3	0.3
Turkmenistan	−281	−109	0.7	1.7	28.1	47.8	2.5	2.1	7.2	9.7	2.3	1.5
Uganda	..	..	..	..	0.8	3.7	..	..	0.0	0.1	0.1	0.1
Ukraine	46	33	1.7	2.3	641.7	323.5	2.9	2.4	12.3	7.0	1.9	1.0
United Arab Emirates	−441	−183	6.5	5.3	52.0	155.1	2.6	2.7	28.8	25.0	0.4	0.5
United Kingdom	−1	19	6.2	10.1	570.2	522.9	2.8	2.5	10.0	8.5	0.4	0.3
United States	14	22	4.2	5.9	4,879.4	5,461.0	2.5	2.4	19.5	18.0	0.6	0.4
Uruguay	49	63	10.1	9.6	4.0	8.3	1.8	2.0	1.3	2.5	0.2	0.2
Uzbekistan	17	−24	0.9	1.5	114.0	124.9	2.5	2.5	5.3	4.6	3.1	1.9
Venezuela, RB	−242	−204	4.3	4.8	122.2	169.5	2.8	2.6	6.2	6.1	0.6	0.5
Vietnam	−2	−20	2.5	3.7	21.4	127.4	0.9	2.2	0.3	1.5	0.4	0.6
West Bank and Gaza	..	..	..	..	..	2.1	..	..	..	0.5	..	..
Yemen, Rep.	−273	−101	8.6	7.0	9.6	23.4	3.8	3.2	0.8	1.0	0.4	0.5
Zambia	9	8	1.8	2.1	2.4	1.9	0.5	0.2	0.3	0.2	0.2	0.1
Zimbabwe	8	10	..	..	15.5	9.1	1.7	1.0	1.5	0.7	..	..
World	−3[c] w	−4[c] w	4.2 w	5.5 w	22,310.9[d] w	32,082.6[d] w	2.5[d] w	2.5[d] w	4.2[d] w	4.8[d] w	0.6[d] w	0.5[d] w
Low income	14	5	2.6	3.4	..	219.1	0.6	1.0	..	0.3	..	0.3
Middle income	−24	−19	3.0	4.5	9,256.8	16,638.0	2.5	2.8	2.4	3.4	0.8	0.6
Lower middle income	−15	−17	3.0	4.6	2,001.1	3,743.9	1.8	2.4	1.1	1.5	0.6	0.5
Upper middle income	−27	−20	3.0	4.4	7,255.3	12,894.1	2.8	2.9	3.6	5.3	0.9	0.7
Low & middle income	−22	−19	3.0	4.4	9,398.8	16,856.9	2.4	2.7	2.2	3.0	0.8	0.6
East Asia & Pacific	−8	1	2.0	3.9	2,895.4	8,259.3	2.6	3.1	1.8	4.3	1.3	0.8
Europe & Central Asia	−12	−47	2.2	3.6	3,893.0	3,130.1	3.0	2.6	9.8	7.8	1.3	0.7
Latin America & Carib.	−34	−31	6.9	7.7	986.2	1,584.1	2.2	2.2	2.3	2.8	0.3	0.3
Middle East & N. Africa	−204	−88	5.7	4.7	579.0	1,230.3	3.2	2.8	2.6	3.8	0.6	0.6
South Asia	10	25	3.6	5.2	782.0	1,970.2	2.0	2.6	0.7	1.2	0.6	0.5
Sub-Saharan Africa	−52	−59	2.8	3.2	464.1	684.6	1.7	1.5	0.9	0.8	0.6	0.4
High income	15	13	5.3	6.7	11,572.3	13,284.7	2.5	2.4	11.8	11.9	0.5	0.4
Euro area	55	62	6.6	8.3	2,718.9	2,633.3	2.5	2.1	8.9	8.0	0.4	0.3

a. A negative value indicates that a country is a net exporter. b. Includes Kosovo and Montenegro. c. Deviation from zero is due to statistical errors and changes in stock. d. Includes emissions not allocated to specific countries.

About the data

Because commercial energy is widely traded, its production and use need to be distinguished. Net energy imports show the extent to which an economy's use exceeds its production. High-income economies are net energy importers; middle-income economies are their main suppliers.

The ratio of gross domestic product (GDP) to energy use indicates energy efficiency. To produce comparable and consistent estimates of real GDP across economies relative to physical inputs to GDP—that is, units of energy use—GDP is converted to 2005 international dollars using purchasing power parity (PPP) rates. Differences in this ratio over time and across economies reflect structural changes in an economy, changes in sectoral energy efficiency, and differences in fuel mixes.

Carbon dioxide emissions, largely by-products of energy production and use (see table 3.7), account for the largest share of greenhouse gases, which are associated with global warming. Anthropogenic carbon dioxide emissions result primarily from fossil fuel combustion and cement manufacturing. In combustion different fossil fuels release different amounts of carbon dioxide for the same level of energy use: oil releases about 50 percent more carbon dioxide than natural gas, and coal releases about twice as much. Cement manufacturing releases about half a metric ton of carbon dioxide for each metric ton of cement produced. Carbon intensity is the ratio of carbon dioxide per unit of energy, or the amount of carbon dioxide emitted as a result of using one unit of energy in production. Kilograms per 2005 PPP dollars of GDP shows the share of carbon dioxide per unit of GDP, a measure of how clean production processes are.

The U.S. Department of Energy's Carbon Dioxide Information Analysis Center (CDIAC) calculates annual anthropogenic emissions from data on fossil fuel consumption (from the United Nations Statistics Division's World Energy Data Set) and world cement manufacturing (from the U.S. Bureau of Mines Cement Manufacturing Data Set). Carbon dioxide emissions are often calculated and reported as elemental carbon. The values in the table were converted to actual carbon dioxide mass by multiplying them by 3.667 (the ratio of the mass of carbon to that of carbon dioxide). Although estimates of global carbon dioxide emissions are probably accurate within 10 percent (as calculated from global average fuel chemistry and use), country estimates may have larger error bounds. Trends estimated from a consistent time series tend to be more accurate than individual values. Each year the CDIAC recalculates the entire time series since 1949, incorporating recent findings and corrections. Estimates exclude fuels supplied to ships and aircraft in international transport because of the difficulty of apportioning the fuels among benefiting countries.

Definitions

- **Net energy imports** are estimated as energy use less production, both measured in oil equivalents.
- **GDP per unit of energy use** is the ratio of gross domestic product (GDP) per kilogram of oil equivalent of energy use, with GDP converted to 2005 international dollars using purchasing power parity (PPP) rates. An international dollar has the same purchasing power over GDP that a U.S. dollar has in the United States. Energy use refers to the use of primary energy before transformation to other end-use fuel, which is equal to indigenous production plus imports and stock changes minus exports and fuel supplied to ships and aircraft engaged in international transport (see *About the data* for table 3.7). • **Carbon dioxide emissions** are emissions from the burning of fossil fuels and the manufacture of cement and include carbon dioxide produced during consumption of solid, liquid, and gas fuels and gas flaring.

Data sources

Data on energy use are from the electronic files of the International Energy Agency. Data on carbon dioxide emissions are from the CDIAC, Environmental Sciences Division, Oak Ridge National Laboratory, Tennessee, United States.

	Carbon dioxide emissions		Methane emissions				Nitrous oxide emissions				Other greenhouse gas emissions	
	average annual % growth[a] 1990–2008	% change[b] 1990–2008	Total thousand metric tons of carbon dioxide equivalent 2005	% change[b] 1990–2005	% of total From energy processes 2005	Agricultural 2005	Total thousand metric tons of carbon dioxide equivalent 2005	% change[b] 1990–2005	% of total From energy processes 2005	Agricultural 2005	Total thousand metric tons of carbon dioxide equivalent 2005	% change[b] 1990–2005
Afghanistan	−6.9	−69.6	..	..	..	..	..	..	..	..	..	..
Albania	2.5	−44.2	2,407	−5.1	20.0	70.8	1,036	−18.7	7.1	78.4	62	..
Algeria	1.5	41.1	54,219	33.1	83.2	8.2	4,898	27.5	22.6	58.6	489	50.0
Angola	10.4	450.2	45,409	−8.3	15.6	27.9	38,881	−6.7	0.4	38.4	20	..
Argentina	2.6	70.8	101,821	−8.3	18.9	70.6	49,821	29.6	3.9	89.2	785	−65.8
Armenia	3.0	50.7	2,962	2.5	50.8	36.7	580	−27.6	1.2	81.6	335	..
Australia	1.7	38.9	126,488	9.7	29.7	55.1	62,966	−0.1	10.3	78.2	6,505	33.5
Austria	1.1	11.1	8,515	−15.0	21.7	48.6	4,448	−13.5	31.0	52.5	2,329	46.2
Azerbaijan	0.0	6.7	36,607	110.7	82.0	13.6	2,633	0.4	8.3	77.5	89	−49.4
Bahrain	3.0	89.1	2,766	54.9	88.7	0.6	82	70.8	39.7	16.0	279	−89.0
Bangladesh	6.7	199.5	92,414	6.5	10.0	70.5	21,386	42.1	7.5	83.1	0	..
Belarus	−1.3	−28.2	11,498	−32.8	7.6	70.9	11,680	−28.3	23.1	72.9	467	..
Belgium	−0.4	−3.3	10,063	−21.8	11.6	56.7	6,571	−27.6	38.1	44.3	2,106	583.8
Benin	9.3	468.7	4,080	−15.8	15.6	47.8	2,902	−21.5	4.0	61.5	0	..
Bolivia	3.6	133.2	30,350	30.9	25.6	34.1	15,092	3.2	0.7	36.5	0	..
Bosnia and Herzegovina	16.6	694.1	2,741	−53.5	46.7	42.4	1,196	−40.8	24.7	57.8	571	−7.5
Botswana	3.7	122.2	4,501	−22.6	8.6	84.1	3,081	−44.1	1.4	92.0	0	..
Brazil	3.3	88.2	492,160	56.4	7.6	61.1	235,987	52.6	3.4	67.0	11,816	40.5
Bulgaria	−1.9	−35.0	10,867	−24.8	13.0	18.9	4,227	−55.2	36.0	48.1	383	..
Burkina Faso	6.1	216.3	..	..	..	..	..	..	..	..	..	..
Burundi	−4.5	−41.0	..	..	..	..	..	..	..	..	..	..
Cambodia	15.3	920.4	20,215	35.0	4.9	76.1	5,794	46.9	3.5	66.1	0	..
Cameroon	4.1	205.1	18,518	37.1	39.1	42.4	9,127	−13.3	2.6	75.9	419	−55.0
Canada	1.4	20.9	89,338	30.8	32.2	29.3	40,171	−5.5	23.7	58.9	21,943	69.7
Central African Republic	1.0	31.5	..	..	..	..	..	..	..	..	..	..
Chad	11.0	237.4	..	..	..	..	..	..	..	..	..	..
Chile	4.3	109.5	18,149	49.8	24.4	39.4	8,135	57.5	16.6	73.4	13	−31.6
China	5.7	185.8	1,333,098	28.5	45.8	38.8	467,213	48.5	12.9	74.3	141,394	1,073.0
Hong Kong SAR, China	1.9	39.5	2,820	84.1	26.7	..	422	−0.9	38.5	0.0	119	−68.6
Colombia	0.0	18.1	58,100	13.5	19.9	68.0	21,288	5.2	4.4	86.1	83	97.6
Congo, Dem. Rep.	−3.1	−30.8	56,445	−41.6	10.2	23.1	54,643	−37.3	2.2	31.3	0	..
Congo, Rep.	−0.1	63.0	5,584	−10.4	32.2	31.9	3,566	−17.2	1.0	51.8	5	..
Costa Rica	5.0	171.2	2,580	−31.2	9.5	67.2	1,334	−26.2	4.5	85.4	62	..
Côte d'Ivoire	1.4	21.0	10,997	−2.2	16.9	17.4	7,364	−1.6	2.7	29.3	0	..
Croatia	2.6	41.7	3,864	−60.5	57.0	33.3	2,851	−24.5	36.6	52.4	59	−93.4
Cuba	−0.8	−5.8	9,455	−21.0	11.2	62.4	6,356	−31.8	15.1	78.7	129	..
Cyprus	3.1	83.8	616	40.0	1.8	44.0	292	19.2	13.0	65.5	190	..
Czech Republic	−0.7	−16.1	11,497	−40.3	49.4	33.6	8,878	−10.2	53.0	36.9	1,121	..
Denmark	−1.0	−8.7	7,935	−0.5	16.4	65.2	6,290	−21.5	18.0	73.4	1,422	457.6
Dominican Republic	4.5	125.9	6,081	3.8	7.8	63.7	2,255	11.0	7.8	76.8	0	..
Ecuador	3.1	59.3	17,125	31.2	31.2	57.7	4,571	42.2	3.8	84.9	63	..
Egypt, Arab Rep.	5.9	176.9	46,996	68.8	50.7	31.7	18,996	60.7	8.3	80.0	3,181	54.5
El Salvador	4.4	133.5	3,131	18.0	12.4	53.1	1,377	7.7	8.2	76.2	77	..
Eritrea	5.4	..	2,467	30.9	11.2	73.2	1,189	15.7	3.8	90.9	0	..
Estonia	−0.6	−20.6	2,108	−36.8	42.3	30.5	932	−50.7	21.5	60.5	40	1,900.0
Ethiopia	4.7	135.5	52,243	32.8	14.3	72.5	30,510	19.4	5.2	88.8	10	..
Finland	1.1	10.9	9,742	−2.8	7.4	20.7	7,124	−4.1	42.8	41.7	826	726.0
France	−0.3	−5.5	77,252	−0.3	44.3	47.7	49,058	−30.6	24.2	66.8	15,539	57.1
Gabon	−3.6	−49.0	8,218	1.4	90.4	1.1	482	58.0	10.0	23.3	9	..
Gambia, The	4.4	115.4	..	..	..	..	..	..	..	..	..	..
Georgia	−2.6	−66.1	4,410	−12.4	36.1	50.8	2,019	−26.8	35.5	56.9	12	..
Germany	−1.1	−18.1	67,582	−44.8	32.1	43.8	56,560	−23.9	38.2	52.2	31,543	8.1
Ghana	4.7	118.6	8,990	24.2	23.3	39.5	4,899	−5.6	9.3	70.5	15	−97.5
Greece	2.0	34.5	7,289	2.0	26.3	50.0	5,977	−17.1	22.1	58.2	1,842	−20.8
Guatemala	5.6	134.2	8,306	74.7	12.4	48.8	5,376	121.1	5.5	56.8	481	..
Guinea	1.5	31.9	..	..	..	..	..	..	..	..	..	..
Guinea-Bissau	−0.2	11.6	..	..	..	..	..	..	..	..	..	..
Haiti	7.6	145.0	4,006	34.8	12.1	56.2	1,438	59.6	6.2	84.2	0	..

Trends in greenhouse gas emissions

	Carbon dioxide emissions		Methane emissions				Nitrous oxide emissions				Other greenhouse gas emissions	
			Total thousand metric tons of carbon dioxide equivalent		% of total		Total thousand metric tons of carbon dioxide equivalent		% of total		Total thousand metric tons of carbon dioxide equivalent	
	average annual % growth[a] 1990–2008	% change[b] 1990–2008	2005	% change[b] 1990–2005	From energy processes 2005	Agricultural 2005	2005	% change[b] 1990–2005	From energy processes 2005	Agricultural 2005	2005	% change[b] 1990–2005
Honduras	7.4	234.5	5,191	31.5	7.2	78.4	2,865	26.0	3.8	85.9	0	..
Hungary	−0.6	−13.3	7,767	−22.9	29.1	33.6	6,961	−31.2	30.9	60.1	1,552	121.1
India	4.8	152.4	583,978	10.5	15.9	64.4	212,927	33.3	12.8	73.4	8,433	−11.9
Indonesia	4.5	171.5	208,944	18.4	25.5	46.4	123,275	43.5	3.7	71.5	1,027	−40.5
Iran, Islamic Rep.	5.0	137.0	114,585	32.5	70.6	18.2	26,644	41.1	11.4	75.3	2,569	−2.9
Iraq	3.7	95.9	15,937	−45.8	58.4	18.6	3,440	−9.9	9.7	63.3	86	−66.0
Ireland	2.4	43.4	15,331	14.3	11.9	76.7	7,486	−8.3	4.4	90.5	1,151	3,097.2
Israel	1.6	12.3	3,517	83.8	18.4	31.2	1,793	41.5	15.3	53.0	1,981	88.8
Italy	0.6	4.9	40,790	−13.4	14.7	39.8	28,620	−5.4	39.1	43.7	13,968	211.2
Jamaica	2.4	53.2	1,302	14.4	11.4	50.3	599	29.4	12.1	59.0	51	..
Japan	0.7	10.4	42,771	−36.5	8.1	71.2	29,785	−17.0	41.6	27.9	53,786	81.1
Jordan	4.2	105.5	1,796	111.5	25.0	21.8	667	39.5	8.2	55.4	112	..
Kazakhstan	0.4	−9.3	47,119	−27.3	66.2	25.3	17,594	−46.2	12.8	62.5	339	..
Kenya	3.0	78.5	22,130	23.3	16.9	65.5	10,542	14.3	5.0	88.8	0	..
Korea, Dem. Rep.	1.2	..	18,195	−15.0	58.6	23.5	3,422	−60.6	13.2	62.3	2,794	..
Korea, Rep.	3.7	108.8	32,069	2.4	19.9	38.6	13,548	34.7	41.3	35.9	10,221	66.0
Kosovo	..	..	..	..	..	..	..	..	..	..	..	..
Kuwait	7.4	69.0	14,380	119.4	93.4	1.1	650	156.9	27.7	16.9	931	254.0
Kyrgyz Republic	−1.7	−42.8	3,591	−38.2	6.8	72.3	1,510	−57.7	11.2	72.6	24	..
Lao PDR	13.1	553.1	..	..	..	..	..	..	..	..	..	..
Latvia	−3.3	−46.0	3,108	−42.1	53.6	27.7	1,253	−58.7	11.6	77.4	890	..
Lebanon	3.0	87.9	1,003	46.6	9.7	25.5	672	79.2	12.6	58.8	0	..
Lesotho	..	..	..	..	..	..	..	..	..	..	..	..
Liberia	5.0	25.8	..	..	..	..	..	..	..	..	..	..
Libya	1.8	44.7	14,682	−34.7	86.3	5.7	1,285	9.3	11.2	51.9	280	−0.7
Lithuania	−1.8	−31.7	5,516	−34.1	32.0	33.8	2,451	−45.7	5.0	86.0	656	..
Macedonia, FYR	0.4	9.6	1,403	−36.5	32.1	46.6	599	−33.9	15.9	63.9	120	..
Madagascar	3.4	93.7	..	..	..	..	..	..	..	..	..	..
Malawi	3.1	100.6	..	..	..	..	..	..	..	..	..	..
Malaysia	6.3	268.0	46,501	64.7	69.3	12.4	15,087	13.5	6.7	64.9	994	66.2
Mali	1.9	40.9	..	..	..	..	..	..	..	..	..	..
Mauritania	−3.9	−25.0	..	..	..	..	..	..	..	..	..	..
Mauritius	6.1	170.2	..	..	..	..	..	..	..	..	..	..
Mexico	1.9	46.1	128,209	26.3	40.2	42.3	42,514	8.9	10.6	75.2	4,555	53.1
Moldova	−8.5	−77.2	3,372	−17.5	45.2	29.4	849	−51.0	5.5	73.5	8	..
Mongolia	−0.2	8.5	6,067	−25.9	2.5	92.1	3,489	−30.0	2.2	93.2	0	..
Morocco	3.7	103.5	10,573	15.8	8.0	51.7	5,814	12.2	3.0	82.6	0	..
Mozambique	5.4	131.1	12,843	18.2	22.7	44.2	9,501	−12.7	3.4	71.4	282	..
Myanmar	6.6	198.8	77,211	−7.4	12.6	69.0	30,932	−23.9	2.6	42.9	0	..
Namibia	39.5	..	5,057	47.2	0.3	94.9	3,797	47.2	1.1	94.3	0	..
Nepal	7.6	458.4	22,142	9.7	5.9	82.9	4,516	26.0	13.0	76.8	0	..
Netherlands	0.0	5.9	21,259	−30.4	23.4	43.4	14,596	−10.7	52.5	39.5	3,750	−40.9
New Zealand	2.0	37.8	27,635	3.6	3.6	90.2	12,930	23.5	3.5	94.2	973	3.4
Nicaragua	4.1	63.8	6,018	26.3	6.6	74.8	3,340	10.1	3.3	91.7	0	..
Niger	−0.2	2.2	..	..	..	..	..	..	..	..	..	..
Nigeria	5.4	111.0	130,317	10.9	68.9	19.8	21,565	12.6	9.1	77.3	669	176.4
Norway	2.7	59.6	16,870	47.2	74.6	12.6	4,737	−3.1	46.5	39.0	5,202	−39.4
Oman	8.5	341.9	17,849	194.9	94.1	3.0	561	82.7	16.0	68.0	175	..
Pakistan	4.9	138.0	137,401	50.7	23.7	63.5	26,838	46.0	14.5	74.2	819	−18.8
Panama	4.0	120.5	3,219	16.5	4.0	79.2	1,204	18.0	4.9	83.7	0	..
Papua New Guinea	3.9	−1.5	..	..	..	..	..	..	..	..	..	..
Paraguay	2.7	82.0	15,388	2.0	3.9	84.1	9,067	0.6	1.7	82.6	0	..
Peru	3.7	91.5	17,187	22.7	13.5	61.3	7,560	35.4	2.9	81.9	330	..
Philippines	3.2	86.7	51,889	28.6	9.3	63.7	12,950	34.0	9.1	73.1	365	125.3
Poland	−1.1	−13.8	70,023	−36.6	62.0	21.9	30,198	4.7	33.5	57.7	2,451	360.7
Portugal	1.8	28.8	12,173	22.4	13.8	35.4	5,958	24.3	22.0	43.8	783	605.4
Puerto Rico	..	..	..	..	..	..	..	..	..	..	..	..
Qatar	6.8	481.6	15,706	387.2	96.5	0.4	200	104.1	33.9	25.0	0	..

3.10 Trends in greenhouse gas emissions

	Carbon dioxide emissions			Methane emissions				Nitrous oxide emissions				Other greenhouse gas emissions	
	average annual % growth[a] 1990–2008	% change[b] 1990–2008	Total thousand metric tons of carbon dioxide equivalent 2005	% change[b] 1990–2005	% of total — From energy processes 2005	% of total — Agricultural 2005		Total thousand metric tons of carbon dioxide equivalent 2005	% change[b] 1990–2005	% of total — From energy processes 2005	% of total — Agricultural 2005	Total thousand metric tons of carbon dioxide equivalent 2005	% change[b] 1990–2005
Romania	−2.4	−40.4	24,331	−35.1	42.7	36.0		11,537	−44.0	32.4	56.2	746	−62.8
Russian Federation	−1.0	−23.1	562,801	−18.3	79.3	9.1		76,121	−48.7	27.8	44.3	59,673	130.6
Rwanda	0.6	3.2	..	..	..	..		..	..	..	..	..	..
Saudi Arabia	2.8	101.6	48,152	67.4	83.6	4.0		6,501	17.5	14.0	46.1	2,193	−10.6
Senegal	3.0	56.3	7,129	35.1	9.9	68.3		4,083	37.2	2.7	88.5	0	..
Serbia	..	..	7,782	−58.7	41.5	43.7		4,581	−8.8	24.2	63.6	4,493	353.8
Sierra Leone	7.3	243.4	..	..	..	..		..	..	..	..	..	..
Singapore	−2.1	−31.2	2,237	136.7	60.1	1.3		1,068	163.1	77.6	2.8	2,532	396.5
Slovak Republic	−0.9	−17.7	3,911	−39.7	18.2	39.0		3,354	−37.1	52.0	37.7	395	480.9
Slovenia	1.6	32.3	3,498	0.6	30.7	32.1		1,156	−12.2	13.2	70.4	473	−38.5
Somalia	35.9	3,447.0	..	..	..	..		..	..	..	..	..	..
South Africa	1.4	30.7	63,785	24.6	45.4	31.4		24,048	12.9	12.6	59.8	2,552	71.2
South Sudan	..	..	..	..	..	..		..	..	..	..	..	..
Spain	2.7	44.7	36,338	11.9	10.4	56.8		26,529	6.5	18.7	62.6	9,080	47.7
Sri Lanka	7.1	211.8	10,210	−11.2	5.3	65.2		2,056	18.0	12.1	65.1	0	..
Sudan	7.1	152.8	67,441	55.5	7.1	85.2		49,472	34.9	1.3	92.6	0	..
Swaziland	9.2	156.9	..	..	..	..		..	..	..	..	..	..
Sweden	−0.6	−5.1	11,311	1.3	9.9	28.1		5,865	−13.1	26.8	60.2	2,078	133.7
Switzerland	−0.3	−6.0	4,748	−17.1	19.8	67.6		2,415	−15.5	20.8	59.3	2,109	97.3
Syrian Arab Republic	3.2	91.2	12,458	−10.8	53.8	28.1		5,509	33.4	9.0	78.1	0	..
Tajikistan	−2.8	−56.4	3,898	−9.3	12.8	68.6		1,378	0.2	1.4	86.9	383	−86.4
Tanzania	5.3	172.5	32,024	24.0	12.6	63.2		21,647	0.8	2.5	78.8	0	..
Thailand	5.6	198.2	83,257	5.7	16.9	66.0		22,304	15.1	21.7	65.5	1,104	−22.8
Timor-Leste	..	..	..	..	..	..		..	..	..	..	..	..
Togo	3.5	83.4	2,889	5.0	23.5	39.8		1,738	−21.3	5.6	67.5	0	..
Trinidad and Tobago	4.7	193.5	10,070	32.0	83.9	0.7		230	12.2	11.5	60.3	0	..
Tunisia	3.3	88.5	8,160	106.2	55.6	25.5		2,366	17.9	21.4	66.4	0	..
Turkey	3.4	88.3	64,251	46.4	16.0	33.6		32,781	12.8	22.7	66.4	5,066	96.9
Turkmenistan	3.3	70.4	27,984	−5.0	75.2	21.6		4,276	93.7	16.4	78.1	73	..
Uganda	8.7	358.3	..	..	..	..		..	..	..	..	..	..
Ukraine	−3.1	−49.6	70,360	−42.2	62.1	23.3		26,097	−51.3	42.8	45.6	693	209.4
United Arab Emirates	6.1	198.2	23,283	58.0	93.1	2.6		1,169	78.7	18.3	43.6	1,075	27.5
United Kingdom	−0.6	−8.3	65,788	−44.1	24.8	38.2		30,565	−44.7	24.8	60.0	10,403	96.7
United States	0.7	11.9	548,074	−14.4	41.0	34.8		317,153	1.8	30.6	56.4	239,517	158.7
Uruguay	2.3	108.5	19,589	24.1	1.5	94.3		7,017	16.1	1.4	96.9	59	..
Uzbekistan	0.6	9.6	39,602	24.0	57.3	33.7		10,003	9.4	6.2	84.2	608	..
Venezuela, RB	2.6	38.8	61,183	5.9	47.4	40.0		14,935	23.4	5.0	75.2	2,468	−24.0
Vietnam	11.3	495.0	82,978	40.1	22.7	63.9		23,030	98.3	6.1	83.0	0	..
West Bank and Gaza	17.3	..	..	..	..	..		..	..	..	..	..	..
Yemen, Rep.	4.7	143.7	6,677	73.5	17.0	54.9		3,250	57.4	11.2	72.5	0	..
Zambia	−1.3	−22.8	19,294	−28.4	6.7	59.3		25,068	−29.7	2.6	71.7	0	..
Zimbabwe	−3.4	−41.5	9,539	−5.7	11.4	73.3		6,114	−16.1	3.7	85.2	0	..
World	2.1 w	43.8 w	7,135,850 s	6.2 w	37.3 w	42.6 w		2,852,537 s	5.8 w	15.4 w	66.2 w	724,183 s	122.4 w
Low income	3.0	..	436,333	−3.0	13.7	61.2		209,159	−15.0	4.1	62.4	..	..
Middle income	3.0	79.7	5,160,313	13.6	38.8	42.6		1,830,347	17.0	10.6	70.8	260,798	207.4
Lower middle income	3.1	87.1	1,704,859	11.4	27.2	52.4		686,537	17.2	8.8	71.1	17,327	3.3
Upper middle income	3.0	77.7	3,455,454	14.7	44.6	37.8		1,143,810	16.9	11.7	70.6	243,471	257.7
Low & middle income	3.0	79.4	5,596,645	12.1	36.9	44.1		2,039,506	12.7	10.0	70.0	264,291	201.6
East Asia & Pacific	5.6	185.3	1,928,355	24.5	39.2	43.6		707,496	38.0	10.5	72.2	..	..
Europe & Central Asia	−0.8	−19.6	936,608	−17.3	67.5	17.5		214,402	−38.9	25.3	56.8	75,692	114.6
Latin America & Carib.	2.5	60.6	1,008,557	30.3	17.3	58.6		442,132	32.9	4.6	72.4	20,972	23.5
Middle East & N. Africa	4.2	112.5	287,084	20.0	64.7	20.7		73,539	36.8	10.7	74.5	6,717	20.7
South Asia	4.9	151.9	846,145	14.6	16.1	65.4		267,722	34.9	12.6	74.3	9,253	−12.5
Sub-Saharan Africa	2.2	47.5	589,897	5.4	30.5	44.0		334,216	−7.6	3.7	66.1	..	..
High income	0.8	14.8	1,539,204	−10.8	38.9	37.1		813,031	−8.2	29.1	56.8	459,891	93.3
Euro area	0.1	−3.1	317,704	−18.2	26.0	46.8		219,189	−18.1	31.7	55.4	84,230	37.2

a. Calculated using the least squares method, which accounts for ups and downs of all data points in the period (see *Statistical methods*). b. Calculated as the change in emissions since 1990, which is the baseline for Kyoto Protocol requirements.

Greenhouse gases—which include carbon dioxide, methane, nitrous oxide, hydrofluorocarbons, perfluorocarbons, and sulfur hexafluoride—contribute to climate change.

Carbon dioxide emissions, largely a by-product of energy production and use (see table 3.7), account for the largest share of greenhouse gases. Anthropogenic carbon dioxide emissions result primarily from fossil fuel combustion and cement manufacturing. Burning oil releases more carbon dioxide than burning natural gas, and burning coal releases even more for the same level of energy use. Cement manufacturing releases about half a metric ton of carbon dioxide for each metric ton of cement produced.

Methane emissions result largely from agricultural activities, industrial production landfills and wastewater treatment, and other sources such as tropical forest and other vegetation fires. The emissions are usually expressed in carbon dioxide equivalents using the global warming potential, which allows the effective contributions of different gases to be compared. A kilogram of methane is 21 times as effective at trapping heat in the earth's atmosphere as a kilogram of carbon dioxide within 100 years.

Nitrous oxide emissions are mainly from fossil fuel combustion, fertilizers, rainforest fires, and animal waste. Nitrous oxide is a powerful greenhouse gas, with an estimated atmospheric lifetime of 114 years, compared with 12 years for methane. The per kilogram global warming potential of nitrous oxide is nearly 310 times that of carbon dioxide within 100 years.

Other greenhouse gases covered under the Kyoto Protocol are hydrofluorocarbons, perfluorocarbons, and sulfur hexafluoride. Although emissions of these artificial gases are small, they are more powerful greenhouse gases than carbon dioxide, with much higher atmospheric lifetimes and high global warming potential.

For a discussion of carbon dioxide sources and the methodology behind emissions calculation, see *About the data* for table 3.9.

• **Carbon dioxide emissions** are those from the burning of fossil fuels and the manufacture of cement and include carbon dioxide produced during consumption of solid, liquid, and gas fuels and gas flaring. • **Methane emissions** are those from human activities such as agriculture and from industrial methane production. • **Methane emissions from energy processes** are those from the production, handling, transmission, and combustion of fossil fuels and biofuels. • **Agricultural methane emissions** are those from animals, animal waste, rice production, agricultural waste burning (nonenergy, on-site), and savannah burning. • **Nitrous oxide emissions** are those from agricultural biomass burning, industrial activities, and livestock management. • **Nitrous oxide emissions from energy processes** are those produced by the combustion of fossil fuels and biofuels. • **Agricultural nitrous oxide emissions** are those produced through fertilizer use (synthetic and animal manure), animal waste management, agricultural waste burning (nonenergy, on-site), and savannah burning. • **Other greenhouse gas emissions** are those of hydrofluorocarbons (used as a replacement for chlorofluorocarbons, mainly in refrigeration and semiconductor manufacturing), perfluorocarbons (a by-product of aluminum smelting and uranium enrichment, used as a replacement for chlorofluorocarbons in semiconductor manufacturing), and sulfur hexafluoride (used to insulate high-voltage electricity power equipment), all of which are to be curbed under the Kyoto Protocol.

Data sources

Data on carbon dioxide emissions are from the Carbon Dioxide Information Analysis Center, Environmental Sciences Division, Oak Ridge National Laboratory, Tennessee, United States. Data on methane, nitrous oxide, and other greenhouse gas emissions are compiled by the International Energy Agency.

Carbon dioxide emissions

	Electricity and heat production		Manufacturing industries and construction		Residential buildings and commercial and public services		Transport		Other sectors	
	1990	2008	1990	2008	1990	2008	1990	2008	1990	2008
Afghanistan	..	..	..	..	..	..	..	..	..	..
Albania	12.0	5.2	44.2	16.1	4.8	9.8	11.2	59.6	27.8	9.1
Algeria	42.9	39.2	14.1	13.6	20.3	24.9	22.6	22.4	0.0	0.0
Angola	12.5	3.7	46.1	24.1	15.7	21.7	25.2	50.3	0.7	0.3
Argentina	34.0	34.9	16.2	22.2	17.2	12.9	28.1	24.6	4.5	5.3
Armenia	29.6	19.6	22.3	37.6	30.9	0.0	14.3	15.8	2.9	26.8
Australia	54.1	62.9	17.7	12.6	3.3	3.0	23.6	20.1	1.3	1.5
Austria	35.0	34.1	17.9	18.1	20.7	14.7	24.2	31.9	2.2	1.2
Azerbaijan	44.3	50.3	24.4	7.4	7.2	22.1	5.4	17.9	18.7	2.4
Bahrain	56.2	54.2	34.3	31.1	1.0	0.9	8.5	13.8	0.0	0.0
Bangladesh	32.7	43.7	33.3	24.5	16.2	11.9	12.2	14.2	5.7	5.7
Belarus	47.4	52.9	28.1	19.9	10.3	12.4	8.1	10.2	6.2	4.6
Belgium	28.9	25.4	28.4	24.7	22.6	23.5	18.5	24.4	1.5	1.9
Benin	12.0	3.1	12.0	5.2	12.0	30.9	64.0	61.2	0.0	0.0
Bolivia	29.0	34.8	11.6	17.2	10.5	10.6	39.3	36.0	9.5	1.5
Bosnia and Herzegovina	40.6	69.5	26.4	6.6	1.2	0.6	9.2	14.2	22.6	9.0
Botswana	55.3	25.0	18.1	26.8	3.4	3.1	22.2	43.6	1.4	1.3
Brazil	14.2	19.0	29.8	29.7	8.4	5.4	41.9	41.0	5.7	4.9
Bulgaria	63.4	64.3	17.9	15.1	3.9	2.7	8.5	16.9	6.2	1.0
Burkina Faso	..	..	..	..	..	..	..	..	..	..
Burundi	..	..	..	..	..	..	..	..	..	..
Cambodia	..	36.7	..	3.7	..	26.5	..	25.0	..	7.8
Cameroon	1.1	34.3	8.2	7.0	25.5	8.4	65.2	50.6	0.0	0.0
Canada	32.9	33.5	19.8	17.8	16.8	16.4	28.6	29.4	1.9	2.9
Central African Republic	..	..	..	..	..	..	..	..	..	..
Chad	..	..	..	..	..	..	..	..	..	..
Chile	33.0	39.0	24.9	19.1	9.2	6.2	31.7	35.1	1.2	0.6
China	32.2	51.9	40.9	33.3	16.5	6.2	5.3	7.0	5.1	1.6
Hong Kong SAR, China	72.4	68.1	9.5	15.7	4.5	6.0	13.6	10.2	0.0	0.0
Colombia	24.3	18.7	27.4	31.7	8.1	8.5	37.0	38.5	3.2	2.7
Congo, Dem. Rep.	3.4	1.1	29.4	35.3	10.8	10.6	18.9	22.6	37.8	30.7
Congo, Rep.	0.0	3.4	8.6	4.1	10.0	5.4	78.6	87.2	0.0	0.0
Costa Rica	7.3	10.2	26.8	17.3	4.2	3.6	60.2	65.5	1.5	3.5
Côte d'Ivoire	22.8	43.9	16.3	9.3	11.4	12.1	44.9	24.3	4.9	10.5
Croatia	37.3	33.1	28.2	21.2	10.5	12.6	18.2	29.5	5.9	3.7
Cuba	45.2	53.3	18.4	28.3	9.1	10.0	16.0	3.0	11.2	5.4
Cyprus	45.3	51.0	20.1	15.1	4.7	4.5	29.9	26.0	0.0	3.6
Czech Republic	42.7	56.9	30.0	17.7	19.0	8.8	4.6	15.3	3.6	1.3
Denmark	51.7	50.1	10.9	10.0	12.5	7.7	20.3	28.3	4.6	3.9
Dominican Republic	41.2	50.0	10.3	6.3	12.1	13.9	35.5	29.1	1.0	0.7
Ecuador	15.2	20.7	16.9	17.5	14.5	11.4	51.7	49.2	1.8	1.2
Egypt, Arab Rep.	32.5	43.0	35.8	23.4	11.9	8.1	19.8	21.9	0.0	3.6
El Salvador	8.3	26.6	25.9	23.5	7.4	8.9	57.9	40.9	0.0	0.0
Eritrea	..	42.2	..	4.4	..	28.9	..	24.4	..	0.0
Estonia	73.2	75.8	12.4	8.2	4.1	2.3	6.6	12.9	3.8	0.9
Ethiopia	13.6	6.6	27.1	24.5	5.4	12.4	41.6	56.7	12.2	0.0
Finland	36.2	47.7	26.7	21.5	11.9	4.8	21.3	22.4	3.8	3.5
France	18.1	18.9	22.7	19.2	24.1	22.8	31.9	33.9	3.2	5.3
Gabon	34.4	28.5	15.6	38.9	13.3	9.7	35.6	21.1	2.2	1.7
Gambia, The	..	..	..	..	..	..	..	..	..	..
Georgia	46.3	19.5	22.4	15.5	16.5	18.5	13.1	37.6	1.7	8.9
Germany	42.4	45.2	18.9	14.7	20.4	20.5	16.7	18.5	1.7	1.1
Ghana	3.0	26.2	17.7	15.3	15.9	6.0	59.0	49.8	4.4	2.7
Greece	52.3	53.4	14.8	9.8	7.3	10.5	21.5	23.6	4.1	2.6
Guatemala	7.3	27.6	22.7	15.5	14.2	5.7	52.4	51.3	3.0	0.1
Guinea	..	..	..	..	..	..	..	..	..	..
Guinea-Bissau	..	..	..	..	..	..	..	..	..	..
Haiti	25.5	9.8	21.3	22.6	8.5	10.3	44.7	57.3	0.0	0.0

Carbon dioxide emissions by sector

Carbon dioxide emissions

% of total fuel combustion

	Electricity and heat production		Manufacturing industries and construction		Residential buildings and commercial and public services		Transport		Other sectors	
	1990	**2008**	**1990**	**2008**	**1990**	**2008**	**1990**	**2008**	**1990**	**2008**
Honduras	0.9	34.4	35.2	19.9	15.5	3.3	48.4	37.7	0.0	4.9
Hungary	34.8	37.6	23.2	13.2	25.2	22.7	12.5	24.2	4.4	2.2
India	44.5	59.9	28.6	19.6	9.8	6.2	13.8	9.2	3.3	5.1
Indonesia	37.3	37.7	23.7	34.0	13.7	6.3	22.7	19.7	2.7	2.3
Iran, Islamic Rep.	22.7	29.0	26.8	22.4	22.3	24.2	21.5	21.8	6.6	2.5
Iraq	28.3	35.6	27.3	24.0	9.2	9.3	35.1	31.1	0.0	0.0
Ireland	36.1	33.7	15.8	11.5	29.5	22.3	16.5	30.6	2.2	1.8
Israel	57.6	66.6	12.9	2.8	4.2	4.4	19.6	16.4	5.7	9.9
Italy	35.9	38.3	21.1	15.8	16.7	16.8	24.0	27.2	2.2	2.0
Jamaica	27.8	51.1	8.3	3.3	4.0	3.3	15.0	21.6	44.9	20.5
Japan	38.4	44.6	27.0	21.5	12.9	13.3	19.7	19.7	1.9	0.9
Jordan	38.6	48.0	14.2	14.1	11.3	10.9	28.9	24.8	7.1	2.2
Kazakhstan	47.9	47.4	34.9	22.3	0.2	0.7	6.0	7.0	11.0	22.6
Kenya	8.0	32.4	25.8	15.8	10.9	9.6	48.3	37.2	6.9	5.1
Korea, Dem. Rep.	13.9	16.2	67.4	62.9	0.5	0.1	4.1	1.7	14.2	19.1
Korea, Rep.	27.4	52.4	23.4	19.1	26.9	10.0	18.8	16.8	3.4	1.7
Kosovo	..	..	..	..	..	..	..	..	..	..
Kuwait	62.7	68.2	21.7	15.6	0.7	0.7	15.0	15.5	0.0	0.0
Kyrgyz Republic	17.3	23.1	36.9	28.5	0.0	0.0	13.3	24.2	32.6	24.3
Lao PDR	..	..	..	..	..	..	..	..	..	..
Latvia	52.3	25.8	13.6	13.8	13.4	11.4	16.6	44.9	4.1	4.2
Lebanon	43.3	49.2	5.0	11.5	22.7	10.8	28.8	28.5	0.0	0.0
Lesotho	..	..	..	..	..	..	..	..	..	..
Liberia	..	..	..	..	..	..	..	..	..	..
Libya	59.7	62.1	13.2	9.4	4.8	5.6	22.4	22.8	0.0	0.0
Lithuania	41.3	35.3	21.6	21.2	16.1	6.9	16.5	35.0	4.5	1.5
Macedonia, FYR	64.8	68.1	18.8	14.2	4.9	4.0	8.9	13.3	2.6	0.6
Madagascar	..	..	..	..	..	..	..	..	..	..
Malawi	..	..	..	..	..	..	..	..	..	..
Malaysia	35.7	49.6	30.7	24.2	4.4	2.5	29.2	23.3	0.0	0.4
Mali	..	..	..	..	..	..	..	..	..	..
Mauritania	..	..	..	..	..	..	..	..	..	..
Mauritius	..	..	..	..	..	..	..	..	..	..
Mexico	34.9	40.2	23.9	14.9	7.8	5.8	31.5	37.1	1.9	2.0
Moldova	44.8	47.7	6.7	9.8	2.9	23.5	7.9	14.7	37.6	4.4
Mongolia	51.3	62.6	22.1	13.2	6.4	7.3	12.1	13.6	8.1	3.2
Morocco	40.0	37.1	25.7	17.0	7.3	9.5	18.7	25.7	8.2	10.7
Mozambique	10.2	1.0	13.0	20.7	7.4	7.8	55.6	69.9	13.9	1.0
Myanmar	39.9	20.8	28.1	25.4	0.3	2.6	31.7	28.1	0.0	23.1
Namibia	..	22.6	..	6.6	..	0.3	..	48.6	..	21.9
Nepal	0.0	0.3	22.7	33.9	28.4	31.5	38.6	27.9	11.4	6.6
Netherlands	38.2	38.2	21.9	21.2	18.5	17.9	16.6	19.7	4.8	3.0
New Zealand	21.6	32.8	28.8	18.4	6.0	4.2	39.1	41.7	4.4	2.8
Nicaragua	30.6	40.1	18.0	14.7	7.1	6.5	40.4	35.3	3.8	3.1
Niger	..	..	..	..	..	..	..	..	..	..
Nigeria	28.5	36.5	17.3	10.1	14.3	4.8	39.9	48.6	0.0	0.0
Norway	26.9	33.4	24.5	21.3	8.7	3.2	35.1	37.3	4.9	4.8
Oman	54.8	56.7	21.8	23.1	1.9	1.3	16.8	15.3	4.7	3.6
Pakistan	27.0	32.3	34.0	32.4	14.4	11.4	23.1	23.5	1.6	0.3
Panama	22.8	27.0	21.1	18.8	9.3	5.8	46.7	47.6	0.0	0.8
Papua New Guinea	..	..	..	..	..	..	..	..	..	..
Paraguay	1.6	0.0	7.9	3.0	6.8	4.9	83.8	92.1	0.0	0.0
Peru	20.7	26.8	22.4	26.6	18.1	6.7	35.5	37.8	3.4	2.2
Philippines	35.5	44.0	21.0	18.0	6.7	5.7	34.9	31.3	2.0	1.1
Poland	65.1	55.8	13.7	12.6	12.9	13.3	6.0	14.8	2.3	3.4
Portugal	41.6	39.9	24.8	16.1	5.5	6.8	24.6	35.7	3.5	1.6
Puerto Rico	..	..	..	..	..	..	..	..	..	..
Qatar	53.3	52.1	35.9	31.5	0.6	0.4	10.1	16.0	0.0	0.0

Carbon dioxide emissions

	Electricity and heat production		Manufacturing industries and construction		Residential buildings and commercial and public services		Transport		Other sectors	
	% of total fuel combustion									
	1990	**2008**	**1990**	**2008**	**1990**	**2008**	**1990**	**2008**	**1990**	**2008**
Romania	47.3	50.4	35.8	22.3	5.2	9.1	6.9	16.6	4.8	1.6
Russian Federation	55.9	59.5	13.2	14.4	13.1	9.7	13.6	15.3	4.2	1.2
Rwanda	..	..	..	..	..	..	..	..	..	..
Saudi Arabia	50.3	51.4	17.8	22.9	1.6	1.0	30.4	24.7	0.0	0.0
Senegal	36.8	28.4	12.4	17.4	6.5	7.3	35.8	46.2	8.5	0.8
Serbia	64.6	63.3	16.6	16.9	3.3	4.9	7.2	13.1	8.3	1.8
Sierra Leone	..	..	..	..	..	..	..	..	..	..
Singapore	78.7	71.4	6.7	11.9	0.6	0.5	14.0	16.2	0.0	0.0
Slovak Republic	30.3	36.9	32.6	25.7	26.7	16.9	7.1	19.5	3.2	1.0
Slovenia	43.0	37.4	20.7	14.5	15.4	10.9	20.8	35.5	0.2	1.7
Somalia	..	..	..	..	..	..	..	..	..	..
South Africa	56.1	64.5	26.9	13.5	4.4	7.3	11.5	13.6	1.2	1.1
South Sudan	..	..	..	..	..	..	..	..	..	..
Spain	37.4	37.7	22.1	17.4	7.9	8.1	30.6	34.3	2.1	2.5
Sri Lanka	4.5	33.1	13.1	10.6	2.7	3.4	66.0	48.2	13.9	4.6
Sudan	9.1	27.0	16.9	10.0	2.5	5.7	71.3	55.6	0.2	1.5
Swaziland	..	..	..	..	..	..	..	..	..	..
Sweden	18.4	22.8	24.2	21.0	17.3	3.7	37.5	50.7	2.6	1.7
Switzerland	4.1	7.0	14.3	14.9	44.3	37.1	35.4	39.5	2.0	1.5
Syrian Arab Republic	25.2	49.9	20.6	20.9	5.0	2.9	30.6	22.2	18.6	4.2
Tajikistan	14.0	17.5	0.0	0.0	0.0	0.0	6.6	9.2	79.4	73.3
Tanzania	17.5	18.5	22.2	13.3	19.9	10.4	40.4	56.8	0.0	1.2
Thailand	36.5	41.1	18.8	29.2	3.1	2.8	34.5	22.3	7.1	4.6
Timor-Leste	..	..	..	..	..	..	..	..	..	..
Togo	12.3	1.8	3.5	7.3	10.5	12.7	73.7	78.2	0.0	0.0
Trinidad and Tobago	41.6	35.9	45.6	56.6	1.2	1.4	11.7	6.1	0.0	0.0
Tunisia	33.0	39.5	27.6	17.7	13.4	14.6	20.4	23.1	5.5	5.0
Turkey	30.2	42.7	26.6	14.6	16.8	19.3	21.9	17.1	4.6	6.3
Turkmenistan	31.6	43.4	0.0	0.0	0.0	0.0	5.2	5.9	63.3	50.8
Uganda	..	..	..	..	..	..	..	..	..	..
Ukraine	51.4	45.2	29.0	29.4	7.8	13.5	7.9	10.5	3.8	1.4
United Arab Emirates	26.4	50.8	51.4	29.8	0.6	2.3	21.6	17.1	0.0	0.0
United Kingdom	44.2	44.5	15.2	11.5	17.2	18.5	20.8	24.4	2.5	1.0
United States	43.9	47.7	14.4	11.3	11.1	9.9	29.2	30.2	1.3	0.8
Uruguay	13.9	39.8	19.5	11.4	15.5	7.1	40.0	34.3	11.2	7.5
Uzbekistan	39.1	33.3	4.9	19.0	0.0	36.6	4.7	7.8	51.3	3.3
Venezuela, RB	40.1	36.3	28.0	28.0	5.0	4.4	26.9	31.0	0.0	0.2
Vietnam	27.7	29.3	32.6	35.1	11.2	9.5	24.3	24.5	4.0	1.6
West Bank and Gaza	..	..	..	..	..	..	..	..	..	..
Yemen, Rep.	24.6	34.3	3.1	11.2	10.6	9.3	61.7	27.1	0.0	18.0
Zambia	6.2	5.0	51.5	49.1	8.5	2.5	29.6	32.1	4.2	11.9
Zimbabwe	42.8	56.8	29.4	16.1	5.9	4.0	12.9	12.5	9.0	10.6
World	**41.9 w**	**47.6 w**	**22.3 w**	**21.0 w**	**12.7 w**	**9.6 w**	**19.5 w**	**19.6 w**	**3.7 w**	**2.2 w**
Low income	18.1	25.5	50.4	36.7	2.8	6.9	10.2	17.5	18.4	13.5
Middle income	42.5	49.1	26.5	26.0	11.7	8.0	13.7	14.1	5.6	2.7
Lower middle income	42.6	48.1	25.6	23.0	8.9	8.6	14.8	16.0	8.0	4.4
Upper middle income	42.4	49.4	26.7	26.8	12.6	7.9	13.3	13.6	4.9	2.3
Low & middle income	41.9	48.8	27.0	26.1	11.5	8.0	13.6	14.1	5.9	2.9
East Asia & Pacific	32.0	50.0	39.8	33.1	14.8	6.0	8.1	8.9	5.3	1.9
Europe & Central Asia	51.7	53.4	19.2	16.9	10.1	11.1	11.3	14.1	7.7	4.4
Latin America & Carib.	29.1	31.9	24.4	22.4	9.2	6.9	33.6	35.6	3.7	3.2
Middle East & N. Africa	31.0	36.4	24.9	20.6	15.6	17.0	24.1	23.2	4.3	2.9
South Asia	42.4	56.8	29.1	20.8	10.3	6.8	14.9	10.9	3.2	4.7
Sub-Saharan Africa	48.1	53.3	25.8	13.8	6.0	7.6	18.0	23.6	2.0	1.7
High income	41.8	46.1	18.4	15.1	13.6	11.5	24.3	25.9	1.9	1.4
Euro area	36.7	37.8	21.0	16.8	18.5	17.2	21.4	25.8	2.4	2.3

Note: Shares may not sum to 100 percent because of rounding.

About the data

About the data

Carbon dioxide emissions account for the largest share of greenhouse gases, which are associated with global warming. In 2010 the International Energy Agency (IEA) released data on carbon dioxide emissions by sector for the first time, allowing a more comprehensive understanding of each sector's contribution to total emissions. The sectoral approach yields data on carbon dioxide emissions from fuel combustion (Intergovernmental Panel on Climate Change [IPCC] source/sink category 1A) as calculated using the IPCC tier 1 sectoral approach. The table does not include all sectors.

Carbon dioxide emissions from electricity and heat production are the sum of emissions from main activity producers of electricity and heat, unallocated autoproducers, and other energy industries. Main activity producers (formerly known as public supply undertakings) generate electricity or heat for sale to third parties as their primary activity and may be privately or publicly owned. Emissions from own onsite use of fuel in power plants are also included in this category. Unallocated autoproducers are undertakings that generate electricity or heat, wholly or partly for their own use as an activity that supports their primary activity and may be privately or publicly owned. In the 1996 IPCC guidelines these emissions were allocated among industry, transport, and "other" sectors. Emissions from other energy industries are emissions from fuel combusted in petroleum refineries, the manufacture of solid fuels, coal mining, oil and gas extraction, and other energy-producing industries.

Carbon dioxide emissions from manufacturing industries and construction are the emissions from fuel combustion in industry (IPCC source/sink Category 1A2). Although in the 1996 IPCC guidelines, this category included emissions from industry autoproducers that generate electricity or heat, the IEA data do not allow energy consumption to be categorized by end-use, and thus emissions from autoproducers are listed separately under unallocated autoproducers. Emissions from manufacturing industries and construction include those from coke inputs into blast furnaces, which may be reported under the transformation sector, the industry sector, or industrial processes (IPCC source/sink category 2).

Carbon emissions from residential buildings and commercial and public services are the sum of emissions from fuel combustion in households (IPCC source/sink category 1A4b) and emissions from all activities of International Standard Industrial Classification divisions 41, 50–52, 55, 63–67, 70–75, 80, 85, 90–93, and 99.

Carbon dioxide emissions from transport are emissions from fuel combustion for all transport activity (IPCC source/sink category 1A3), including domestic aviation, domestic navigation, road, rail, and pipeline transport but excluding international marine bunkers and international aviation. The IEA data do not allow energy consumption to be categorized by end-use, and thus emissions from autoproducers are listed separately under unallocated autoproducers.

Carbon dioxide emissions from other sectors are emissions from commercial and institutional activities and from residential, agriculture and forestry, fishing, and other processes not specified elsewhere that are included in IPCC source/sink categories 1A4 and 1A5. Although in the 1996 IPCC guidelines, this category included emissions from autoproducers in the commercial, residential, and agricultural sectors that generate electricity or heat, the IEA data do not allow energy consumption to be classified by end-use, and thus emissions from autoproducers are listed separately under unallocated autoproducers.

Definitions

Definitions

• **Carbon dioxide emissions from electricity and heat production** are those from main activity producers of electricity and heat, unallocated autoproducers, and other energy industries. • **Carbon dioxide emissions from manufacturing industries and construction** are those from fuel combustion in industry (IPCC source/sink category 1A2). • **Carbon dioxide emissions from residential buildings and commercial and public services** are those from fuel combustion in household and all activities of ISIC divisions 41, 50–52, 55, 63–67, 70–75, 80, 85, 90–93, and 99. • **Carbon dioxide emissions from transport** are those from fuel combustion for all transport activities (IPCC source/sink category 1A3). • **Carbon dioxide emissions from other sectors** are those from commercial and institutional activities and from residential, agriculture and forestry, fishing, and other emissions not specified elsewhere that are included in IPCC source/sink categories 1A4 and 1A5.

Data sources

Data on carbon dioxide emissions by sector are from IEA electronic files.

Climate variability, exposure to impact, and resilience

	Climate variability					Exposure to impact			Resilience
				change in average number of days/nights			% of population		
	Average daily minimum/ maximum temperature degrees Celsius **1961–1990**	Projected annual temperature degrees Celsius **2045–2065**	Projected annual cool days/ cold nights **2045–2065**	Projected annual hot days/ warm nights **2045–2065**	Projected annual precipitation millimeters **2045–2065**	Land area with an elevation of 5 meters or less % of land area **2000**	Population living in areas with an elevation of 5 meters or less **2000**	Population affected by droughts, floods, and extreme temperature **1990–2009**	Disaster risk reduction progress score 1, worst, to 5, best **2011**
Afghanistan	5.5 / 19.7	2.3 to 3.6	−1.4 / −1.5	3.1 / 7.0	−58 to 13	0.0	0.0	1.1	..
Albania	6.3 / 16.5	1.9 to 2.9	−1.5 / −1.4	3.2 / 6.5	−147 to −44	5.0	8.2	5.3	..
Algeria	15.4 / 29.6	2.4 to 3.0	−1.7 / −2.0	3.9 / 7.8	−39 to 4	0.4	3.5	0.0	3.5
Angola	14.8 / 28.3	2.1 to 2.7	−2.2 / −2.6	7.0 / 20.2	−89 to 75	0.2	2.1	1.0	..
Argentina	8.2 / 21.4	1.4 to 2.1	−1.2 / −1.3	2.9 / 6.5	−57 to 52	1.2	4.5	0.2	3.3
Armenia	1.3 / 13.0	2.1 to 3.3	−1.3 / −1.4	2.8 / 6.3	−75 to −7	0.0	0.0	0.5	3.0
Australia	14.9 / 28.4	1.7 to 2.4	−1.8 / −1.9	3.6 / 9.3	−67 to 54	1.1	7.2	3.0	4.0
Austria	2.3 / 10.4	1.9 to 2.9	−1.4 / −1.5	2.9 / 5.2	−70 to 27	0.0	0.0	0.0	..
Azerbaijan	6.7 / 17.2	1.9 to 3.1	−1.3 / −1.3	2.7 / 6.2	−58 to 3	20.0	29.8	1.1	..
Bahrain	20.5 / 33.8	2.1 to 3.0	−1.5 / −1.9	4.6 / 8.6	−19 to 4	39.0	66.6	..	..
Bangladesh	20.4 / 29.6	1.7 to 2.4	−1.7 / −2.1	3.4 / 11.8	−126 to 120	14.1	14.0	4.6	4.0
Belarus	2.0 / 10.3	2.2 to 3.1	−1.5 / −1.7	2.1 / 4.5	8 to 70	0.0	0.0	0.0	..
Belgium	5.5 / 13.6	1.4 to 2.4	−1.4 / −1.5	2.9 / 5.5	−64 to 29	9.2	14.3	0.0	..
Benin	21.7 / 33.4	2.0 to 2.5	−2.3 / −2.6	5.5 / 19.2	−207 to 97	1.2	14.1	0.9	..
Bolivia	15.2 / 27.9	2.1 to 3.0	−2.0 / −2.1	5.1 / 16.9	−91 to 137	0.0	0.0	1.3	2.3
Bosnia and Herzegovina	5.0 / 14.7	1.9 to 3.0	−1.5 / −1.5	3.1 / 6.1	−116 to −7	0.1	0.1	0.5	..
Botswana	13.6 / 29.4	2.5 to 3.3	−1.8 / −2.1	4.7 / 12.8	−106 to 24	0.0	0.0	0.7	3.0
Brazil	19.6 / 30.3	1.9 to 2.6	−2.1 / −2.5	5.6 / 19.6	−95 to 136	1.2	4.9	0.5	4.5
Bulgaria	5.6 / 15.5	1.9 to 3.1	−1.4 / −1.3	2.9 / 6.0	−127 to −21	0.4	1.5	0.0	3.5
Burkina Faso	21.5 / 35.0	2.2 to 2.8	−2.1 / −2.6	5.3 / 16.6	−229 to 88	0.0	0.0	1.3	..
Burundi	13.8 / 25.8	2.1 to 2.4	−2.1 / −2.8	7.8 / 26.2	−21 to 206	0.0	0.0	2.4	3.3
Cambodia	22.3 / 31.3	1.6 to 2.0	−1.8 / −1.7	4.5 / 18.2	−109 to 95	3.8	10.6	6.6	..
Cameroon	19.1 / 30.1	2.1 to 2.4	−2.4 / −2.4	6.2 / 22.0	−71 to 115	0.1	0.3	0.1	..
Canada	−10.1 / −0.6	2.6 to 3.5	−1.6 / −1.7	1.9 / 4.4	17 to 88	2.4	4.0	0.0	4.3
Central African Republic	18.3 / 31.5	2.1 to 2.4	−2.3 / −2.4	4.7 / 22.5	−73 to 100	0.0	0.0	0.2	..
Chad	18.6 / 34.5	2.3 to 2.6	−1.8 / −2.3	5.1 / 13.7	−79 to 41	0.0	0.0	2.7	..
Chile	3.5 / 13.4	1.2 to 1.9	−1.7 / −1.7	3.8 / 7.3	−118 to 24	3.1	1.6	0.3	2.8
China	0.9 / 13.0	2.1 to 3.0	−1.5 / −1.6	2.9 / 5.6	−37 to 86	1.4	8.1	8.0	..
Hong Kong SAR, China	19.3 / 26.0	1.4 to 1.9	−1.2 / −1.4	7.4 / 10.3	−83 to 73	24.6	26.2	0.0	..
Colombia	19.6 / 29.4	1.8 to 2.5	−2.4 / −2.9	7.9 / 26.6	−80 to 199	0.9	2.0	0.7	3.8
Congo, Dem. Rep.	18.4 / 29.6	2.1 to 2.4	−2.1 / −2.7	6.4 / 24.7	−48 to 128	0.0	0.0	0.0	..
Congo, Rep.	19.8 / 29.3	2.0 to 2.3	−2.3 / −2.7	9.1 / 26.5	−40 to 134	0.1	1.0	0.3	..
Costa Rica	19.6 / 30.0	1.6 to 2.3	−2.8 / −3.0	11.8 / 26.8	−239 to 60	2.1	0.8	0.7	4.5
Côte d'Ivoire	21.1 / 31.6	1.8 to 2.4	−2.4 / −2.5	7.1 / 22.9	−125 to 73	0.2	3.2	0.0	2.5
Croatia	6.2 / 15.6	1.9 to 2.9	−1.6 / −1.6	3.2 / 6.0	−112 to −2	3.0	3.4	0.0	..
Cuba	20.4 / 30.0	1.4 to 1.8	−1.9 / −1.8	10.5 / 17.6	−108 to 39	12.7	10.0	0.7	4.5
Cyprus	13.1 / 23.8	1.7 to 2.3	−1.9 / −1.8	4.0 / 7.3	−98 to −44	6.4	9.7	0.0	..
Czech Republic	3.3 / 11.8	1.9 to 2.8	−1.5 / −1.6	2.5 / 4.7	−43 to 55	0.0	0.0	0.2	2.8
Denmark	4.3 / 10.7	1.6 to 2.5	−1.6 / −1.7	2.6 / 5.2	21 to 87	17.7	18.5	0.0	..
Dominican Republic	19.9 / 29.2	1.5 to 1.8	−2.8 / −2.9	12.1 / 23.6	−128 to 30	4.1	3.0	0.1	3.0
Ecuador	15.6 / 28.1	1.8 to 2.3	−2.6 / −2.8	9.5 / 24.4	22 to 273	2.0	7.3	0.3	4.8
Egypt, Arab Rep.	14.8 / 29.4	1.9 to 2.4	−1.7 / −2.1	4.0 / 8.1	−20 to 1	4.0	25.6	0.0	..
El Salvador	18.4 / 30.5	1.7 to 2.9	−2.2 / −2.3	8.9 / 24.5	−205 to 14	2.5	1.7	0.4	3.3
Eritrea	18.9 / 32.1	2.1 to 2.7	−2.0 / −2.4	6.6 / 14.4	−55 to 26	3.1	1.2	7.3	..
Estonia	1.5 / 8.7	2.2 to 3.2	−1.7 / −1.8	2.1 / 4.8	33 to 93	3.4	7.2	0.0	..
Ethiopia	15.5 / 28.9	2.1 to 2.5	−2.0 / −2.7	6.6 / 21.4	−42 to 79	0.7	0.4	3.3	..
Finland	−2.4 / 5.8	2.4 to 3.7	−1.7 / −1.9	1.7 / 4.1	37 to 103	1.1	4.4	0.0	3.5
France	6.5 / 14.9	1.6 to 2.6	−1.5 / −1.5	3.6 / 6.3	−112 to 2	2.1	4.0	0.0	..
Gabon	20.9 / 29.2	1.8 to 2.2	−2.6 / −2.9	13.7 / 26.9	−51 to 148	0.5	5.9	..	..
Gambia, The	20.4 / 34.6	2.1 to 2.7	−2.3 / −2.6	6.7 / 16.8	−87 to 26	16.6	33.4	0.2	..
Georgia	0.4 / 11.2	1.9 to 3.0	−1.3 / −1.3	2.8 / 5.9	−77 to −3	1.4	3.3	0.8	2.8
Germany	4.6 / 12.4	1.7 to 2.6	−1.5 / −1.5	2.6 / 5.0	−38 to 57	4.9	4.4	0.0	4.3
Ghana	22.1 / 32.3	1.8 to 2.4	−2.4 / −2.5	6.6 / 22.1	−159 to 83	0.8	2.3	1.0	3.3
Greece	10.5 / 20.3	1.7 to 2.6	−1.7 / −1.7	3.5 / 6.5	−110 to −40	6.3	9.9	0.0	..
Guatemala	18.2 / 28.7	1.7 to 2.8	−1.7 / −1.7	7.8 / 21.6	−186 to 22	0.6	0.3	1.3	3.3
Guinea	19.6 / 31.8	2.0 to 2.6	−2.4 / −2.5	6.9 / 20.2	−122 to 104	1.1	3.6	0.2	..
Guinea-Bissau	20.9 / 32.6	1.8 to 2.2	−2.7 / −2.7	9.9 / 22.2	−69 to 130	9.5	18.8	0.5	1.0
Haiti	20.1 / 29.7	1.5 to 1.8	−2.8 / −2.8	12.6 / 23.1	−125 to 34	3.9	5.4	0.8	..

Climate variability, exposure to impact, and resilience

3.12

	Climate variability					Exposure to impact			Resilience
				change in average number of days/nights			% of population		
	Average daily minimum/ maximum temperature degrees Celsius 1961–1990	Projected annual temperature degrees Celsius 2045–2065	Projected annual cool days/ cold nights 2045–2065	Projected annual hot days/ warm nights 2045–2065	Projected annual precipitation millimeters 2045–2065	Land area with an elevation of 5 meters or less % of land area 2000	Population living in areas with an elevation of 5 meters or less 2000	Population affected by droughts, floods, and extreme temperature 1990–2009	Disaster risk reduction progress score 1, worst, to 5, best 2011
Honduras	18.9 / 28.1	1.6 to 2.6	−2.2 / −2.5	10.2 / 24.5	−204 to 15	3.0	2.2	1.3	3.8
Hungary	4.8 / 14.7	2.0 to 3.0	−1.5 / −1.7	3.0 / 5.3	−75 to 23	0.0	0.0	0.1	..
India	17.7 / 29.6	1.9 to 2.6	−2.0 / −2.2	4.6 / 13.3	−91 to 135	1.4	3.8	4.4	3.3
Indonesia	21.1 / 30.6	1.5 to 1.8	−2.8 / −2.9	16.5 / 26.7	−160 to 234	5.5	11.2	0.2	3.3
Iran, Islamic Rep.	10.1 / 24.4	2.2 to 3.3	−1.4 / −1.4	3.3 / 7.1	−51 to 6	1.6	5.0	3.1	..
Iraq	14.1 / 28.7	2.3 to 3.2	−1.5 / −1.5	3.4 / 6.8	−38 to −2	4.0	6.5	0.0	..
Ireland	5.9 / 12.7	0.9 to 1.4	−1.3 / −1.4	3.0 / 5.6	−13 to 78	4.0	6.6	0.0	..
Israel	13.4 / 25.0	1.9 to 2.7	−1.6 / −1.8	3.7 / 7.7	−41 to −11	7.8	8.3	0.0	..
Italy	9.5 / 17.4	1.8 to 2.6	−1.8 / −1.8	4.0 / 6.7	−108 to −11	5.2	7.5	0.0	3.5
Jamaica	20.6 / 29.3	1.3 to 1.8	−2.9 / −2.8	14.0 / 23.7	−102 to 28	7.1	5.8	1.1	3.8
Japan	7.0 / 15.3	1.8 to 2.3	−1.9 / −2.2	3.5 / 6.0	−47 to 80	5.9	16.2	0.0	4.5
Jordan	11.2 / 25.4	2.1 to 2.9	−1.5 / −1.6	3.7 / 7.4	−28 to −3	2.0	4.2	0.4	..
Kazakhstan	0.6 / 12.2	2.2 to 3.1	−1.2 / −1.4	2.3 / 5.0	−1 to 37	6.7	3.9	0.2	..
Kenya	18.9 / 30.6	1.9 to 2.1	−2.0 / −2.9	8.1 / 25.0	0 to 144	0.2	1.4	6.5	4.0
Korea, Dem. Rep.	0.3 / 11.1	2.1 to 2.7	−1.4 / −1.8	2.6 / 4.6	−9 to 129	2.4	5.3	2.5	..
Korea, Rep.	6.5 / 16.5	1.8 to 2.3	−1.4 / −1.8	3.2 / 5.2	0 to 181	4.3	5.0	0.1	..
Kosovo	..	2.0 to 3.1	−1.5 / −1.3	3.1 / 6.3	−148 to −34	..	..	..	..
Kuwait	18.5 / 32.2	2.2 to 3.1	−1.5 / −1.7	3.9 / 7.4	−19 to 4	8.9	22.8	0.0	..
Kyrgyz Republic	−4.6 / 7.7	2.3 to 3.2	−1.2 / −1.4	3.1 / 6.6	−32 to 35	0.0	0.0	2.1	..
Lao PDR	18.2 / 27.4	1.6 to 2.4	−1.1 / −1.3	3.1 / 12.7	−95 to 70	0.0	0.0	2.7	2.3
Latvia	1.9 / 9.3	2.1 to 3.1	−1.7 / −1.8	2.1 / 5.0	31 to 89	3.0	23.9	0.0	..
Lebanon	10.7 / 22.1	2.0 to 2.9	−1.7 / −1.6	3.6 / 7.5	−75 to −27	1.7	9.1	0.0	3.0
Lesotho	5.2 / 18.5	2.0 to 2.5	−1.6 / −1.9	3.7 / 10.1	−66 to 89	0.0	0.0	3.4	2.5
Liberia	20.0 / 30.6	1.7 to 2.2	−2.7 / −2.7	10.2 / 25.3	−115 to 81	0.4	3.3	1.9	..
Libya	14.4 / 29.2	2.0 to 2.4	−1.7 / −2.1	3.5 / 7.6	−18 to 5	0.8	4.7	0.0	..
Lithuania	2.3 / 10.1	2.0 to 3.0	−1.6 / −1.8	2.0 / 4.8	22 to 83	1.9	4.0	0.0	..
Macedonia, FYR	4.5 / 15.1	1.9 to 3.0	−1.4 / −1.3	3.2 / 6.4	−150 to −43	0.0	0.0	0.3	3.3
Madagascar	18.0 / 27.3	1.7 to 2.1	−2.5 / −2.7	7.6 / 15.7	−104 to 56	1.3	2.0	0.9	3.8
Malawi	16.6 / 27.2	2.0 to 2.5	−2.1 / −2.5	3.6 / 15.9	−53 to 91	0.0	0.0	8.8	1.8
Malaysia	21.2 / 29.6	1.6 to 1.9	−2.5 / −2.8	13.0 / 26.3	−160 to 117	3.0	9.5	0.1	3.8
Mali	20.9 / 35.6	2.5 to 3.1	−2.0 / −2.5	5.5 / 12.8	−142 to 43	0.0	0.0	0.7	..
Mauritania	20.2 / 35.1	2.4 to 3.1	−2.0 / −2.4	5.1 / 10.6	−113 to 9	1.0	20.4	3.1	..
Mauritius	18.9 / 25.9	1.3 to 1.7	−2.9 / −2.9	8.5 / 13.7	−165 to 67	7.1	5.6	0.0	3.5
Mexico	13.5 / 28.5	1.7 to 2.8	−1.6 / −1.5	5.6 / 12.1	−178 to 10	2.9	2.7	0.1	4.3
Moldova	5.0 / 13.9	2.0 to 3.3	−1.5 / −1.6	2.8 / 5.2	−72 to 11	1.3	0.9	0.3	..
Mongolia	−7.7 / 6.3	2.3 to 3.1	−1.3 / −1.4	2.2 / 4.2	1 to 50	0.0	0.0	2.6	2.8
Morocco	11.1 / 23.1	2.1 to 3.0	−1.8 / −2.0	3.6 / 7.9	−62 to −5	0.7	3.8	0.1	3.0
Mozambique	18.5 / 29.1	1.9 to 2.4	−2.2 / −2.5	5.0 / 15.0	−69 to 61	1.8	6.5	3.7	4.0
Myanmar	17.7 / 8.4	1.7 to 2.3	−1.7 / −1.8	3.8 / 13.9	−84 to 97	4.6	14.0	0.1	..
Namibia	12.7 / 27.2	2.2 to 2.9	−1.9 / −2.2	5.8 / 13.1	−67 to 23	0.3	2.9	3.4	..
Nepal	1.5 / 14.7	2.2 to 3.4	−2.1 / −2.1	2.5 / 8.0	−116 to 231	0.0	0.0	0.7	2.8
Netherlands	5.5 / 13.0	1.4 to 2.3	−1.6 / −1.6	2.9 / 5.3	−18 to 50	58.5	61.3	0.0	..
New Zealand	6.0 / 15.1	1.1 to 1.7	−2.2 / −2.1	4.1 / 7.9	−44 to 53	2.7	12.6	0.0	3.8
Nicaragua	20.3 / 29.5	1.6 to 2.4	−2.6 / −2.8	10.4 / 26.0	−220 to 19	3.6	1.5	0.8	3.8
Niger	19.4 / 34.9	2.4 to 2.8	−1.8 / −2.4	5.4 / 12.2	−71 to 36	0.0	0.0	7.5	..
Nigeria	20.8 / 32.8	2.0 to 2.5	−2.2 / −2.5	5.5 / 19.0	−128 to 89	0.5	3.0	0.1	4.0
Norway	−2.0 / 5.0	1.8 to 3.3	−1.8 / −1.8	2.2 / 4.8	41 to 131	4.9	9.3	0.0	3.8
Oman	20.8 / 30.4	2.0 to 2.4	−1.9 / −2.1	4.4 / 11.8	−16 to 31	1.1	5.5	..	..
Pakistan	13.2 / 27.2	2.4 to 3.4	−1.8 / −1.9	3.4 / 8.1	−60 to 36	1.4	1.3	1.1	3.5
Panama	21.3 / 29.5	1.6 to 2.2	−2.9 / −3.0	14.0 / 26.9	−228 to 107	3.7	4.0	0.2	3.0
Papua New Guinea	20.1 / 30.4	1.4 to 1.8	−2.8 / −2.9	15.5 / 25.5	−163 to 421	1.8	2.0	0.7	..
Paraguay	17.7 / 29.4	1.9 to 2.6	−0.8 / −1.2	3.5 / 11.8	−48 to 112	0.0	0.0	0.7	3.8
Peru	13.5 / 25.7	2.1 to 2.7	−2.5 / −2.7	7.7 / 22.9	−57 to 181	0.4	1.7	2.0	3.0
Philippines	21.6 / 30.1	1.4 to 1.8	−2.5 / −2.5	13.5 / 23.8	−136 to 140	6.0	10.5	0.8	..
Poland	3.8 / 11.9	1.9 to 2.8	−1.5 / −1.7	2.3 / 4.8	−12 to 64	1.7	2.5	0.0	3.3
Portugal	10.2 / 20.1	1.3 to 2.3	−2.0 / −1.9	4.5 / 8.7	−113 to −7	2.3	5.2	0.0	..
Puerto Rico	21.2 / 29.3	1.4 to 1.8	−3.0 / −2.9	12.8 / 24.2	−133 to 37	7.7	11.3	0.0	..
Qatar	21.3 / 33.0	2.3 to 2.9	−1.6 / −1.9	4.6 / 8.8	−23 to 8	13.4	23.1	..	..

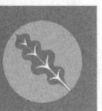

	Climate variability					Exposure to impact			Resilience
							% of population		
						Land area with an elevation of 5 meters or less	Population living in areas with an elevation of 5 meters or less	Population affected by droughts, floods, and extreme temperature	Disaster risk reduction progress score 1, worst, to 5, best
	Average daily minimum/ maximum temperature degrees Celsius	Projected annual temperature degrees Celsius	change in average number of days/nights		Projected annual precipitation millimeters				
			Projected annual cool days/ cold nights	Projected annual hot days/ warm nights		% of land area			
	1961–1990	**2045–2065**	**2045–2065**	**2045–2065**	**2045–2065**	**2000**	**2000**	**1990–2009**	**2011**
Romania	3.8 / 13.8	2.0 to 3.1	−1.5 / −1.6	3.0 / 5.5	−92 to 2	2.9	2.9	0.1	3.3
Russian Federation	−10.1 / −0.1	2.6 to 3.7	−1.6 / −1.8	1.7 / 4.0	24 to 79	1.9	2.9	0.1	..
Rwanda	11.9 / 23.8	2.1 to 2.4	−2.2 / −2.8	8.3 / 26.4	−12 to 211	0.0	0.0	1.3	..
Saudi Arabia	18.2 / 31.1	2.3 to 2.9	−1.5 / −1.7	4.6 / 9.5	−27 to 9	0.5	1.0	0.0	..
Senegal	20.8 / 34.9	2.0 to 2.7	−2.3 / −2.6	7.1 / 16.9	−124 to 37	4.5	14.8	0.6	2.8
Serbia	..	2.0 to 3.1	−1.5 / −1.4	3.2 / 6.1	−125 to −15	0.2	0.1	0.0	..
Sierra Leone	21.0 / 31.1	1.8 to 2.3	−2.7 / −2.6	9.2 / 24.0	−96 to 128	3.0	5.1	0.2	3.0
Singapore	22.6 / 30.3	1.5 to 1.8	−2.6 / −2.7	12.4 / 25.9	−134 to 49	8.1	12.1	..	..
Slovak Republic	2.1 / 11.5	2.0 to 2.9	−1.5 / −1.8	2.6 / 4.7	−44 to 45	0.0	0.0	0.0	..
Slovenia	4.2 / 13.6	2.0 to 3.0	−1.4 / −1.5	3.1 / 5.6	−93 to 5	0.2	1.3	0.0	..
Somalia	21.2 / 32.9	1.9 to 2.2	−2.2 / −2.8	9.5 / 21.2	−4 to 111	0.6	2.2	4.6	..
South Africa	10.6 / 24.9	1.9 to 2.7	−1.7 / −2.0	4.1 / 10.4	−78 to 33	0.1	0.5	1.8	..
South Sudan	..	..	..	..	..	..	..		
Spain	7.9 / 18.7	1.5 to 2.6	−1.9 / −1.8	4.0 / 8.0	−112 to −18	1.3	6.6	0.7	..
Sri Lanka	23.3 / 30.6	1.5 to 1.8	−2.8 / −2.9	7.9 / 23.9	11 to 196	3.9	5.4	2.2	3.5
Sudan	19.4 / 34.4	2.1 to 2.6	−1.8 / −2.2	5.2 / 16.6	−69 to 44	0.1	0.2	2.8	..
Swaziland	15.5 / 27.3	2.0 to 2.4	−1.6 / −2.1	3.8 / 10.9	−82 to 34	0.0	0.0	9.2	..
Sweden	−2.1 / 6.3	2.1 to 3.1	−1.7 / −1.8	2.0 / 4.4	35 to 107	1.5	6.3	0.0	3.8
Switzerland	2.0 / 9.0	1.7 to 2.8	−1.4 / −1.5	3.1 / 5.6	−89 to 11	0.0	0.0	0.0	4.8
Syrian Arab Republic	10.8 / 24.7	2.2 to 3.1	−1.6 / −1.3	3.3 / 6.7	−57 to −13	0.1	0.3	0.5	3.5
Tajikistan	−3.9 / 7.9	2.3 to 3.4	−1.4 / −1.5	3.2 / 7.0	−46 to 27	0.0	0.0	5.4	..
Tanzania	16.7 / 28.0	1.9 to 2.2	−2.1 / −2.8	6.2 / 21.6	−9 to 167	0.2	1.3	1.5	3.5
Thailand	21.2 / 31.4	1.7 to 2.1	−1.6 / −1.6	3.6 / 17.0	−109 to 76	4.2	13.8	3.8	3.8
Timor-Leste	..	1.3 to 1.7	−3.0 / −3.0	16.1 / 25.9	−123 to 206	2.9	4.4	0.0	..
Togo	21.8 / 32.5	1.9 to 2.5	−2.4 / −2.5	6.0 / 21.5	−175 to 100	0.6	6.1	0.5	..
Trinidad and Tobago	21.5 / 30.0	1.5 to 2.1	−2.9 / −3.0	14.7 / 26.5	−266 to 8	8.0	7.5	0.0	..
Tunisia	13.5 / 24.9	1.9 to 2.6	−1.9 / −2.0	3.4 / 6.8	−57 to −16	2.8	9.5	0.1	..
Turkey	5.4 / 16.8	1.9 to 2.9	−1.5 / −1.4	3.1 / 6.3	−103 to −29	1.0	2.4	0.1	..
Turkmenistan	8.7 / 21.5	1.8 to 3.0	−1.0 / −1.1	2.7 / 5.7	−32 to 12	5.3	5.6	0.0	..
Uganda	16.6 / 29.0	2.1 to 2.3	−2.1 / −2.8	6.4 / 25.6	−13 to 224	0.0	0.0	0.9	..
Ukraine	4.0 / 12.6	2.1 to 3.0	−1.4 / −1.6	2.6 / 4.8	−43 to 31	1.5	2.1	0.3	..
United Arab Emirates	21.0 / 33.0	2.2 to 2.8	−1.6 / −2.0	4.2 / 9.4	−26 to 17	4.6	7.3	..	..
United Kingdom	5.1 / 11.8	1.1 to 1.8	−1.4 / −1.5	3.0 / 5.4	−10 to 66	7.6	8.6	0.0	..
United States	2.2 / 14.9	2.0 to 3.0	−1.4 / −1.5	3.1 / 6.4	−26 to 98	1.7	4.1	0.2	3.5
Uruguay	12.2 / 22.9	1.4 to 1.8	−0.8 / −1.0	2.0 / 5.7	0 to 130	1.9	4.7	0.3	..
Uzbekistan	5.8 / 18.3	2.0 to 3.0	−1.1 / −1.3	2.6 / 5.7	−26 to 17	0.1	0.0	0.1	..
Venezuela, RB	20.3 / 30.4	1.8 to 2.9	−2.5 / −2.9	9.1 / 26.5	−150 to 85	2.3	3.7	0.2	2.8
Vietnam	20.6 / 28.3	1.4 to 2.1	−1.5 / −1.5	5.7 / 14.4	−107 to 61	17.5	42.8	1.6	..
West Bank and Gaza	..	2.0 to 2.6	−1.7 / −1.8	3.8 / 7.9	−40 to −13	14.8	11.2	..	..
Yemen, Rep.	18.6 / 29.1	2.0 to 2.6	−2.0 / −2.2	5.6 / 13.1	−24 to 51	0.6	1.8	0.1	2.3
Zambia	14.5 / 28.3	2.1 to 2.7	−2.0 / −2.5	4.0 / 17.7	−54 to 94	0.0	0.0	4.2	3.8
Zimbabwe	14.2 / 27.8	2.2 to 2.9	−1.9 / −2.3	3.8 / 13.2	−81 to 24	0.0	0.0	..	..
World						**1.8 t**	**6.5 t**	**..**	**..**
Low income						0.7	5.1	..	..
Middle income						1.8	6.5	..	..
Lower middle income						1.7	6.4	..	..
Upper middle income						1.8	6.5	..	..
Low & middle income						1.6	6.3	..	..
East Asia & Pacific						2.5	10.3	..	..
Europe & Central Asia						2.5	3.0	..	..
Latin America & Carib.						1.5	3.8	..	..
Middle East & N. Africa						1.4	9.7	..	..
South Asia						1.5	4.4	..	..
Sub-Saharan Africa						0.4	2.0	..	..
High income						2.2	7.7	..	..
Euro area						3.6	8.5	..	..

About the data

Scientists use the terms climate change and global warming to refer to the gradual increase in the Earth's surface temperature that has accelerated since the industrial revolution and especially over the past two decades. Most global warming has been caused by human activities that have changed the chemical composition of the atmosphere through a buildup of greenhouse gases—primarily carbon dioxide, methane, and nitrous oxide. Rising global temperatures will cause sea level rise and alter local climate conditions, affecting forests, crop yields, and water supplies, and may affect human health, animals, and many types of ecosystems. The 2007 Intergovernmental Panel on Climate Change's (IPCC) assessment report concluded that global warming is "unequivocal" and gave the strongest warning yet about the role of human activities. The report estimated that sea levels would rise approximately 49 centimeters over the next 100 years, with a range of uncertainty of 20–86 centimeters. That will lead to increased coastal flooding through direct inundation and a higher base for storm surges, allowing flooding of larger areas and higher elevations. Climate model simulations predict an increase in average surface air temperature of about 2.5°C by 2100 (Kattenberg and others 1996) and increase of "killer" heat waves during the warm season (Karl and others 1997).

Data in the table are categorized into three climate change topics.

· Climate variability contains such indicators as average daily minimum and maximum temperature, projected change in annual temperature, projected change in annual cool days and cold nights and hot days and warm nights, and projected change in annual precipitation. These indicators are useful for understanding critical thresholds related to heat stress in such sectors as agriculture and energy.

· Exposure to impact contains indicators that measure vulnerability to the impacts of climate change, such as land area with an elevation of 5 meters or less and population living in such areas as well as population affected by droughts, floods, and extreme temperature. A drought is an extended period of deficiency in a region's water supply as a result of below average precipitation. A drought can lead to losses in agriculture, affect inland navigation and hydropower plants, reduce access to drinking water, and cause famines. A flood is a significant rise of water level in a stream, lake, reservoir, or coastal region. Extreme temperature events are either cold waves or heat waves. A cold

wave can be both a prolonged period of excessively cold weather and the sudden invasion of very cold air over a large area. Accompanied by frost, it can damage agriculture, infrastructure, and property. A heat wave is a prolonged period of excessively hot and sometimes humid weather. Population affected by these natural disasters is the number of people injured, left homeless, or requiring immediate assistance and can include displaced or evacuated people.

· Resilience is measured by the disaster risk reduction progress score, an average of self-assessment scores submitted by countries under Priority 1 of the Hyogo Framework National Progress Reports. The Hyogo Framework is a global blueprint for disaster risk reduction efforts that was adopted by 168 countries in 2005. Assessments of Priority 1 include four indicators that reflect the degree to which countries have prioritized disaster risk reduction and the strengthening of relevant institutions.

Definitions

• **Average daily minimum and maximum temperature** are the minimum and maximum daily temperatures in the country averaged over the period specified, based on gridded climatologies from the Climatic Research Unit of the University of East Anglia. • **Projected change in annual temperature** is the projected change in annual temperature during the period specified, relative to the control period 1961–2000. • **Projected change in annual cool days and cold nights** are the projected change in the annual number of cool days and cold nights during the period specified, relative to the control period 1961–2000. Cool days are those that fall below the 10th percentile of maximum temperature in the control period, and cold nights are those that fall below the 10th percentile of minimum temperature in the control period. • **Projected change in annual hot days and warm nights** are the projected change in the annual number of hot days and warm nights during the period specified, relative to the control period 1961–2000. Hot days are those that exceed the 90th percentile of maximum temperatures in the control period, and warm nights are those that exceed the 90th percentile of minimum temperatures in the control period. • **Projected change in annual precipitation** is the projected change in annual precipitation during the period specified, relative to the control period 1961–2000. • **Land area at an elevation of 5 meters or less** is the percentage of land area with an elevation of 5 meters or less. • **Population**

at an elevation of 5 meters or less is the percentage of the population living in areas with an elevation of 5 meters or less. • **Population affected by droughts, floods, and extreme temperature** is the average annual percentage of the population that is affected by natural disasters classified as droughts, floods, or extreme temperature events. • **Disaster risk reduction progress score** is the average of self-assessment scores, ranging from 1 to 5, where 1 is the worst and 5 is the best, submitted by countries under Priority 1 of the Hyogo Framework National Progress Reports.

Data sources

Data on average daily minimum and maximum temperature are from Mitchell and others (2003). Data on projected change in annual temperature are from IPCC (2007). Data on projected change in annual cool days and cold nights and projected change in annual hot days and warm nights are from University of Cape Town Climate Systems Analysis Group calculations based on data from Meehl and others (2007). Data on projected change in annual precipitation are from Meehl and others (2007). Data on land area with an elevation of 5 meters or less and population living in areas with an elevation 5 meters or less are from CIESIN (2007). Data on population affected by droughts, floods, and extreme temperature are from the United States Agency for International Development Office of Foreign Disaster Assistance/Center for Research on the Epidemiology of Disasters International Disaster Database (www.emdat.be), Université Catholique de Louvain, and the World Bank. Data on disaster risk reduction progress score are from UNISDR (2009, 2010, 2011) Progress Reports.

3.13 | Urbanization

	Urban population					Population in urban agglomerations of more than 1 million		Population in largest city		Access to improved sanitation facilities			
	millions		% of total population		average annual % growth	% of total population		% of urban population		% of urban population		% of rural population	
	1990	2010	1990	2010	1990–2010	1990	2010	1990	2010	1990	2010	1990	2010
Afghanistan	3	9	18	25	4.3	7	11	37	44	..	60	..	30
Albania	1	2	36	48	1.7	..	..	21	29	94	95	66	93
Algeria	13	24	52	67	2.4	7	8	14	12	99	98	77	88
Angola	4	11	37	59	4.3	15	25	41	43	67	85	6	19
Argentina	28	37	87	92	1.1	39	39	37	35	93	91	73	77
Armenia	2	2	68	64	0.1	33	36	49	56	95	95	..	80
Australia	15	20	85	89	1.8	60	58	25	22	100	100	100	100
Austria	5	6	66	68	0.6	20	20	30	30	100	100	100	100
Azerbaijan	4	5	54	52	1.5	24	22	45	42	..	86	..	78
Bahrain	0	1	88	89	7.6	..	..	29	16	100	100	..	..
Bangladesh	21	42	20	28	2.8	9	14	32	35	58	57	34	55
Belarus	7	7	66	74	0.4	16	20	24	26	91	91	96	97
Belgium	10	11	96	97	0.9	17	17	17	18	100	100	100	100
Benin	2	4	35	42	3.8	..	..	31	23	14	25	0	5
Bolivia	4	7	56	67	2.3	25	33	29	25	28	35	6	10
Bosnia and Herzegovina	2	2	39	49	1.0	..	..	24	22	98	99	..	92
Botswana	1	1	42	61	2.5	..	..	21	16	61	75	22	41
Brazil	112	169	75	87	1.4	35	41	13	12	80	85	33	44
Bulgaria	6	5	66	72	–0.3	14	16	21	22	100	100	98	100
Burkina Faso	1	3	14	20	5.1	6	12	42	57	43	50	2	6
Burundi	0	1	6	11	5.3	..	..	66	52	41	49	44	46
Cambodia	1	3	13	23	3.9	6	11	51	48	36	73	5	20
Cameroon	5	11	41	58	3.6	14	20	19	19	63	58	37	36
Canada	21	28	77	81	1.3	40	44	18	20	100	100	99	99
Central African Republic	1	2	37	39	2.3	..	..	43	42	21	43	5	28
Chad	1	3	21	28	4.3	..	..	38	27	21	30	4	6
Chile	11	15	83	89	1.2	35	35	42	39	91	98	48	83
China	311	601	27	45	2.5	9	18	3	3	48	74	15	56
Hong Kong SAR, China	6	7	100	100	0.9	100	105	100	100	..	..	..	..
Colombia	23	35	68	75	1.8	31	38	21	24	79	82	40	63
Congo, Dem. Rep.	10	23	28	35	4.5	13	18	35	38	23	24	4	24
Congo, Rep.	1	3	54	62	3.2	29	33	54	53	..	20	..	15
Costa Rica	2	3	51	64	2.3	24	31	47	49	94	95	91	96
Côte d'Ivoire	5	10	40	50	3.3	17	21	42	42	38	36	8	11
Croatia	3	3	54	58	0.2	..	..	27	27	99	99	98	98
Cuba	8	9	73	76	0.0	20	19	27	25	86	94	64	81
Cyprus	1	1	67	70	1.5	..	..	33	31	100	100	100	100
Czech Republic	8	8	75	74	0.3	12	11	16	15	100	99	98	97
Denmark	4	5	85	87	0.7	20	21	24	25	100	100	100	100
Dominican Republic	4	7	55	71	2.4	21	22	38	31	83	87	61	75
Ecuador	6	10	55	67	2.4	26	31	28	28	86	96	48	84
Egypt, Arab Rep.	25	35	44	43	1.8	21	19	37	32	91	97	57	93
El Salvador	3	4	49	61	1.0	18	25	37	41	88	89	62	83
Eritrea	0	1	16	22	5.1	..	..	72	60	58	52	0	4
Estonia	1	1	71	70	0.0	..	..	43	43	96	96	94	94
Ethiopia	6	15	13	18	3.9	4	4	29	20	20	29	1	19
Finland	3	3	61	64	0.9	17	21	28	33	100	100	100	100
France	43	50	74	78	0.8	22	22	22	21	100	100	100	100
Gabon	1	1	69	86	2.4	..	..	62	49	..	33	..	30
Gambia, The	0	1	38	58	4.2	..	..	62	45	..	70	..	65
Georgia	3	2	55	53	1.1	25	25	46	48	97	96	95	93
Germany	58	60	73	74	0.0	8	8	6	6	100	100	100	100
Ghana	5	13	36	52	3.8	13	17	22	19	12	19	4	8
Greece	6	7	59	61	0.6	30	29	51	47	100	99	93	97
Guatemala	4	7	41	50	3.4	9	8	22	16	81	87	48	70
Guinea	2	4	28	35	3.6	16	17	55	47	19	32	6	11
Guinea-Bissau	0	0	28	30	2.3	..	..	54	68	..	44	4	9
Haiti	2	5	29	50	4.1	16	21	56	43	44	24	19	10

	Urban population					Population in urban agglomerations of more than 1 million		Population in largest city		Access to improved sanitation facilities			
	millions		% of total population		average annual % growth	% of total population		% of urban population		% of urban population		% of rural population	
	1990	2010	1990	2010	1990–2010	1990	2010	1990	2010	1990	2010	1990	2010
Honduras	2	4	40	49	2.9	12	14	29	28	71	85	36	69
Hungary	7	7	66	68	0.4	19	17	29	25	100	100	100	100
India	223	369	26	30	2.3	10	12	4	6	51	58	7	23
Indonesia	56	129	31	54	3.1	10	9	14	7	56	73	21	39
Iran, Islamic Rep.	31	51	56	70	1.9	24	24	21	14	83	100	74	100
Iraq	13	21	70	66	2.8	27	23	32	28	..	76	..	67
Ireland	2	3	57	62	0.8	26	25	46	40	100	100	98	98
Israel	4	7	90	92	1.8	56	57	48	47	100	100	100	100
Italy	38	41	67	68	0.7	19	17	9	8	..	..	..	..
Jamaica	1	1	49	54	0.6	..	..	49	40	78	78	81	82
Japan	78	85	63	67	0.2	46	49	42	43	100	100	100	100
Jordan	2	5	72	79	2.3	27	18	37	23	98	98	95	98
Kazakhstan	9	10	56	59	1.9	7	8	12	14	96	97	97	98
Kenya	4	9	18	22	4.0	6	9	32	39	27	32	25	32
Korea, Dem. Rep.	12	15	58	63	1.0	13	12	21	18	..	86	..	71
Korea, Rep.	32	40	74	82	0.5	51	48	33	24	100	100	100	100
Kosovo	..	..	..	..	..	..	..	..	..	..	..	..	..
Kuwait	2	3	98	98	3.4	67	84	68	86	100	100	100	100
Kyrgyz Republic	2	2	38	37	1.6	..	..	38	43	94	94	..	93
Lao PDR	1	2	15	33	5.0	..	..	70	40	..	89	..	50
Latvia	2	2	69	68	−0.6	..	..	49	46	..	82	..	71
Lebanon	2	4	83	87	0.9	44	46	53	53	100	100	..	..
Lesotho	0	1	14	27	3.7	..	..	49	39	..	32	..	24
Liberia	1	2	45	62	5.2	..	..	108	34	..	29	..	7
Libya	3	5	76	78	1.7	20	17	26	22	97	97	96	96
Lithuania	2	2	68	67	−1.4	..	..	23	24	95	95	..	..
Macedonia, FYR	1	1	58	68	0.9	..	..	40	35	92	92	..	82
Madagascar	3	6	24	30	4.0	8	9	36	30	15	21	7	12
Malawi	1	3	12	20	5.7	..	..	24	29	48	49	38	51
Malaysia	9	21	50	72	2.9	8	9	12	7	88	96	81	95
Mali	2	5	23	33	4.7	9	11	37	33	33	35	10	14
Mauritania	1	1	40	41	2.9	..	..	53	51	29	51	8	9
Mauritius	0	1	44	43	0.6	..	..	30	28	91	91	88	88
Mexico	60	88	71	78	1.6	33	35	25	22	76	87	34	79
Moldova	2	1	47	41	−0.8	..	..	38	44	..	89	..	82
Mongolia	1	2	57	58	1.9	..	..	46	61	..	64	..	29
Morocco	12	18	48	57	1.6	18	19	22	18	81	83	27	52
Mozambique	3	9	21	38	4.4	6	7	27	18	36	38	4	5
Myanmar	10	16	25	34	2.7	9	11	30	27	..	83	..	73
Namibia	0	1	28	38	3.4	..	..	36	41	62	57	9	17
Nepal	2	5	9	18	4.4	..	..	23	19	37	48	7	27
Netherlands	10	14	69	83	1.2	13	12	9	8	100	100	100	100
New Zealand	3	4	85	87	1.3	25	32	30	37	..	..	88	..
Nicaragua	2	3	52	57	1.8	18	23	34	28	59	63	26	37
Niger	1	3	15	17	4.0	6	7	36	40	19	34	2	4
Nigeria	34	79	35	50	4.0	12	15	14	13	39	35	36	27
Norway	3	4	72	78	1.3	..	..	22	23	100	100	100	100
Oman	1	2	66	72	2.6	..	..	27	33	96	100	55	95
Pakistan	34	64	31	37	2.9	15	18	21	20	72	72	7	34
Panama	1	3	54	75	2.6	35	39	65	52	73	75	40	51
Papua New Guinea	1	1	15	13	2.1	..	..	31	37	78	71	42	41
Paraguay	2	4	49	62	2.7	26	31	53	51	61	90	15	40
Peru	15	21	69	72	1.2	27	31	39	43	71	81	17	37
Philippines	30	62	49	66	2.8	14	14	27	19	69	79	45	69
Poland	23	23	61	61	0.0	4	4	7	7	96	96	..	80
Portugal	5	6	48	61	1.1	37	39	53	44	97	100	87	100
Puerto Rico	3	4	72	99	0.5	44	69	60	70	..	..	..	..
Qatar	0	2	92	96	9.7	..	..	54	28	100	100	100	100

3.13 Urbanization

	Urban population					Population in urban agglomerations of more than 1 million		Population in largest city		Access to improved sanitation facilities			
	millions		% of total population		average annual % growth	% of total population		% of urban population		% of urban population		% of rural population	
	1990	2010	1990	2010	1990–2010	1990	2010	1990	2010	1990	2010	1990	2010
Romania	12	12	53	55	0.1	9	9	17	17	88	88	52	54
Russian Federation	109	103	73	73	−0.1	17	18	8	10	80	74	58	59
Rwanda	0	2	5	19	4.5	..	..	57	57	69	52	34	56
Saudi Arabia	12	23	77	84	4.0	34	39	19	21	100	100	..	..
Senegal	3	5	39	43	3.3	19	23	50	54	62	70	22	39
Serbia	4	4	50	52	−0.1	15	15	30	29	96	96	..	88
Sierra Leone	1	2	33	38	3.0	..	..	40	40	22	23	5	6
Singapore	3	5	100	100	1.8	99	95	99	95	99	100	..	..
Slovak Republic	3	3	57	57	0.4	..	..	..	..	100	100	100	99
Slovenia	1	1	50	48	−0.2	..	..	27	26	100	100	100	100
Somalia	2	3	30	37	3.5	16	16	53	43	..	52	..	6
South Africa	18	31	52	62	2.1	28	34	10	12	82	86	60	67
South Sudan	..	..	..	..	..	..	..	..	..	..	..	..	..
Spain	29	36	75	77	0.5	22	24	15	16	100	100	100	100
Sri Lanka	3	3	17	15	0.9	..	..	21	22	85	88	67	93
Sudan	7	20	27	45	4.5	9	12	33	26	51	44	18	14
Swaziland	0	0	23	26	2.6	..	..	22	25	62	64	44	55
Sweden	7	8	83	85	0.9	12	14	15	16	100	100	100	100
Switzerland	5	6	73	74	1.1	15	15	20	20	100	100	100	100
Syrian Arab Republic	6	11	49	55	2.6	31	34	26	27	95	96	75	93
Tajikistan	2	2	32	27	1.5	..	..	35	39	93	95	..	94
Tanzania	5	12	19	26	4.7	5	7	27	28	10	20	6	7
Thailand	17	24	29	34	1.6	10	10	35	30	94	95	80	96
Timor-Leste	0	0	21	28	3.6	..	..	79	55	..	73	..	37
Togo	1	3	30	43	3.7	17	28	56	64	26	26	8	3
Trinidad and Tobago	0	0	9	14	2.9	..	..	45	32	93	92	93	92
Tunisia	5	7	58	67	1.6	..	..	14	11	95	96	44	64
Turkey	32	51	59	70	1.9	24	29	20	21	96	97	66	75
Turkmenistan	2	2	45	50	2.1	..	..	25	26	99	99	97	97
Uganda	2	4	11	13	4.4	4	5	38	36	32	34	26	34
Ukraine	35	31	67	68	−0.3	12	14	7	9	97	96	..	89
United Arab Emirates	1	6	79	78	8.0	26	21	33	27	98	98	95	95
United Kingdom	51	56	89	90	0.8	26	26	15	15	100	100	100	100
United States	188	255	75	82	1.2	42	45	9	8	100	100	99	99
Uruguay	3	3	89	93	0.5	50	49	56	53	95	100	83	99
Uzbekistan	8	10	40	37	1.8	10	8	26	21	95	100	76	100
Venezuela, RB	17	27	84	94	1.9	34	32	17	11	89	..	45	..
Vietnam	13	25	20	29	2.7	9	13	25	25	63	94	30	68
West Bank and Gaza	1	3	68	72	2.8	..	..	..	..	91	92	..	92
Yemen, Rep.	2	8	21	32	4.9	5	10	26	31	70	93	12	34
Zambia	3	5	39	36	2.0	10	11	24	31	61	57	37	43
Zimbabwe	3	5	29	38	2.0	10	13	35	34	54	52	35	32
World	**2,262 s**	**3,482 s**	**43 w**	**51 w**	**2.0 w**	**17 w**	**20 w**	**17 w**	**16 w**	**76 w**	**79 w**	**27 w**	**47 w**
Low income	108	225	21	28	3.6	8	11	34	33	38	47	17	32
Middle income	1,456	2,401	38	48	2.2	14	18	15	13	68	75	22	45
Lower middle income	560	992	32	39	2.7	12	14	16	14	61	66	17	34
Upper middle income	896	1,409	44	57	1.9	16	22	14	12	71	82	27	62
Low & middle income	1,564	2,626	36	46	2.3	13	17	16	15	66	72	21	43
East Asia & Pacific	463	901	29	46	2.7	..	..	9	7	54	76	20	57
Europe & Central Asia	246	259	63	64	0.5	16	18	15	16	88	87	68	80
Latin America & Carib.	309	462	71	79	1.6	32	35	24	22	80	84	38	59
Middle East & N. Africa	117	192	52	58	2.2	20	20	26	22	89	94	57	80
South Asia	286	492	25	30	2.5	10	13	9	11	54	60	11	28
Sub-Saharan Africa	144	319	28	37	3.9	11	14	27	26	42	42	19	23
High income	698	856	73	78	1.0	..	..	20	19	100	100	99	99
Euro area	215	244	71	74	0.6	18	18	16	15	100	100	99	100

There is no consistent and universally accepted standard for distinguishing urban from rural areas, in part because of the wide variety of situations across countries (see *About the data* for table 3.1). Most countries use an urban classification related to the size or characteristics of settlements. Some define urban areas based on the presence of certain infrastructure and services. And other countries designate urban areas based on administrative arrangements.

The population of a city or metropolitan area depends on the boundaries chosen. For example, in 1990 Beijing, China, contained 2.3 million people in 87 square kilometers of "inner city" and 5.4 million in 158 square kilometers of "core city." The population of "inner city and inner suburban districts" was 6.3 million and that of "inner city, inner and outer suburban districts, and inner and outer counties" was 10.8 million. (Most countries use the last definition.) For further discussion of urban-rural issues see box 3.1a in *About the data* for table 3.1.

Estimates of the world's urban population would change significantly if China, India, and a few other populous nations were to change their definition of urban centers. According to China's State Statistical Bureau, by the end of 1996 urban residents accounted for about 43 percent of China's population, more than double the 20 percent considered urban in 1994. In addition to the continuous migration of people from rural to urban areas, one of the main reasons for this shift was the rapid growth in the hundreds of towns reclassified as cities in recent years.

Because the estimates in the table are based on national definitions of what constitutes a city or metropolitan area, cross-country comparisons should be made with caution. To estimate urban populations, UN ratios of urban to total population were applied to the World Bank's estimates of total population (see table 2.1).

The table shows access to improved sanitation facilities for both urban and rural populations to allow comparison of access. Definitions of access and urban areas vary, however, so comparisons between countries can be misleading.

• **Urban population** is the midyear population of areas defined as urban in each country and reported to the United Nations (see *About the data*). • **Population in urban agglomerations of more than 1 million** is the percentage of a country's population living in metropolitan areas that in 2005 had a population of more than 1 million. • **Population in largest city** is the percentage of a country's urban population living in that country's largest metropolitan area. • **Access to improved sanitation facilities** is the percentage of the urban or rural population with access to at least adequate excreta disposal facilities (private or shared but not public) that can effectively prevent human, animal, and insect contact with excreta. Improved facilities range from simple but protected pit latrines to flush toilets with a sewerage connection. To be effective, facilities must be correctly constructed and properly maintained.

Data sources

Data on urban population and the population in urban agglomerations and in the largest city are from the United Nations Population Division's *World Urbanization Prospects: The 2010 Revision*. Data on total population are World Bank estimates. Data on access to sanitation are from the World Health Organization and United Nations Children's Fund's *Progress on Drinking Water and Sanitation* (2012).

	Census year	Household size		Overcrowding		Durable dwelling units		Home ownership		Multiunit dwellings		Vacancy rate	
		number of people		Households living in overcrowded dwellings[a] % of total		Buildings with durable structure % of total		Privately owned dwellings % of total		% of total		Unoccupied dwellings % of total	
		National	Urban	National	Urban	National	Urban	National	Urban	National	Urban	National	Urban
Afghanistan		..	..	..	..	..	..	..	..	..	..	..	..
Albania	2001	4.2	3.9	..	..	..	..	65[b]	30[b]	..	..	12	13
Algeria	1998	4.9	..	..	..	..	..	67	..	..	..	19	..
Angola		..	..	..	..	..	..	..	..	..	..	..	..
Argentina	2001	3.6	..	19	..	97	..	..	..	4	..	16[b]	..
Armenia	2001	4.1	4.0	4	6	93	93	95	90	1	1	..	..
Australia	2001	3.8	..	1	..	..	..	..	..	..	..	..	..
Austria	2001	2.4	..	2	..	..	..	48	..	..	..	..	..
Azerbaijan	1999	4.7	4.4	..	..	..	..	74	62	4	5	..	..
Bahrain		..	..	..	..	..	..	..	..	..	..	..	..
Bangladesh	2001	4.8	4.8	..	..	21[b]	42[b]	88[b]	61[b]	..	..	..	..
Belarus	1999			..	..	..	..	..	..	..	..	..	..
Belgium	2001	2.6	..	0[b]	..	..	..	67	..	32[b]	..	..	..
Benin	1992	5.9	..	..	..	26	..	59	..	..	..	..	..
Bolivia	2001	4.2	4.3	40	..	43	58	70	59	3[b]	5[b]	6	4
Bosnia and Herzegovina		..	..	..	..	..	..	..	..	..	..	..	..
Botswana	2001	4.2	3.9	27	47	88	90[b]	61	47	1	..	..	..
Brazil	2000	3.8	3.7	..	..	..	..	74	75	..	..	..	..
Bulgaria	2001	2.7	2.7	..	..	79	89	98	98	..	..	23	17
Burkina Faso	1996	6.2	5.8	30	53	..	..	..	..	..	..	..	..
Burundi	1990	4.7	..	..	..	..	..	..	..	..	..	..	..
Cambodia	2005	5.0	4.9	35	32	79	88	58	57	27	32	..	..
Cameroon	1987	5.2	5.1	67	77	77	..	73	48	27	42	..	..
Canada	2001	2.6	..	..	..	..	..	64	..	32	..	8	..
Central African Republic	2003	5.2	5.8	32	36[b]	78	92	85	74	..	..	..	..
Chad	1993	5.1	5.1	..	..	..	..	..	..	..	..	..	..
Chile	2002	3.4	3.5	..	..	91	92	66	65	13	15	11	10
China	2000	3.4	3.2	..	..	82	..	88	74	..	..	1	..
Hong Kong SAR, China		..	..	..	..	..	..	..	..	..	..	..	..
Colombia	1993	4.8	..	27[b]	..	83[b]	..	68[b]	..	13	..	10[b]	..
Congo, Dem. Rep.	1984	5.4	..	55	..	..	..	..	..	..	..	..	..
Congo, Rep.	1984	10.5	..	..	..	..	..	76	..	..	..	..	..
Costa Rica	2000	4.0	..	22	..	88	..	72	..	2	3	9	6
Côte d'Ivoire	1998	5.4	..	..	..	..	..	..	..	..	..	..	..
Croatia	2001	3.0	..	..	..	..	..	..	..	..	..	12	..
Cuba	2002	3.1	..	5	..	..	..	..	..	..	..	..	..
Cyprus		..	..	..	..	..	..	..	..	..	..	..	..
Czech Republic	2001	2.4	..	..	..	..	..	52	..	49	..	12	..
Denmark	2001	2.2	..	..	..	..	..	..	..	..	..	..	..
Dominican Republic	2002	3.9	..	..	..	97	..	..	..	8	..	11	..
Ecuador	2001	3.5	3.7	30	..	81	88	68[b]	58[b]	9	14	12	7
Egypt, Arab Rep.	1996	4.7	..	..	..	..	..	..	..	75	..	..	..
El Salvador	1992	..	..	63	..	67	83	70	68	3	6	11	11
Eritrea		..	..	..	..	..	..	..	..	..	..	..	..
Estonia	2000	2.4	2.3	3	..	..	..	..	..	72	..	13	..
Ethiopia	1994	4.8	4.7	..	..	..	23	..	54	..	..	..	..
Finland	2000	2.2	..	..	..	..	..	64	..	44	..	..	..
France	1999	2.5	..	..	..	..	..	55	..	..	..	7	..
Gabon	2003	5.2	..	..	..	..	..	..	..	..	..	..	..
Gambia, The	1993	8.9	..	..	..	18	..	68	..	..	..	..	..
Georgia	2002	3.5	3.5	..	..	..	..	..	..	..	..	..	..
Germany	2001	2.3	..	..	..	..	..	43	..	..	..	7	..
Ghana	2000	5.1	5.1	..	..	45	..	57	..	53	..	5	..
Greece	2001	3.0	..	1	..	..	..	..	..	..	..	..	..
Guatemala	2002	4.4	4.7	..	..	67	80	81	74	2	4	13	11
Guinea	1996	6.7	..	63	..	..	..	76	..	..	..	..	..
Guinea-Bissau		..	..	..	..	..	..	..	..	..	..	..	..
Haiti	1982	4.2	..	26	..	..	..	92	68	..	..	9	19

	Census year	Household size		Overcrowding		Durable dwelling units		Home ownership		Multiunit dwellings		Vacancy rate	
		number of people		Households living in overcrowded dwellings[a] % of total		Buildings with durable structure % of total		Privately owned dwellings % of total		% of total		Unoccupied dwellings % of total	
		National	Urban	National	Urban	National	Urban	National	Urban	National	Urban	National	Urban
Honduras	2001	4.4	..	..	..	69	85	..	..	..	..	14	..
Hungary	2001	2.6	..	2	..	..	..	..	..	..	..	4	..
India	2001	5.3	5.3	77	71	83	81	87	67	..	..	6	9
Indonesia	2000	4.0	..	..	..	..	..	..	..	..	..	..	..
Iran, Islamic Rep.	1996	4.8	4.6	33[b]	26[b]	72	76	73	67	..	..	..	..
Iraq	1997	7.7	7.2	..	..	88	96	70	66	4	5	13	15
Ireland	2002	3.0	..	..	..	..	..	..	..	8[b]	..	..	..
Israel	1995	3.5	..	..	..	..	..	..	..	..	..	..	..
Italy	2001	2.8	..	..	..	..	..	..	..	..	..	21	..
Jamaica	2001	3.5	..	..	..	98[b]	..	58[b]	..	2[b]	..	..	..
Japan	2000	2.7	..	..	..	..	..	61	..	37	..	..	..
Jordan	2004	5.3	5.1	35	34	..	..	64	60	72	80	..	..
Kazakhstan		..	..	..	..	..	..	..	..	..	..	..	..
Kenya	1999	4.6	3.4	..	..	35	72	72	25	..	..	39	17
Korea, Dem. Rep.	2000	3.8	..	23	..	..	..	50	..	15	..	..	..
Korea, Rep.	1993	4.4	..	..	..	..	..	..	..	..	..	..	..
Kosovo		..	..	..	..	..	..	..	..	9[b]	..	..	..
Kuwait	1995	6.4	..	..	..	..	..	..	..	..	..	11	..
Kyrgyz Republic	1999	4.4	3.6	..	..	..	..	..	..	..	..	..	..
Lao PDR	1995	6.1	6.1	..	..	49	77	96	86	..	..	..	..
Latvia	2000	3.0	2.6	4	..	88	..	58	..	74	..	0	..
Lebanon		..	..	..	..	..	..	..	..	..	..	..	..
Lesotho	2001	5.0	..	10[b]	..	..	..	84	..	0	..	..	..
Liberia	1974	4.8	..	31	..	20	..	1	..	..	..	..	..
Libya		6.4	..	..	..	..	..	..	..	..	..	7	..
Lithuania	2001	2.6	..	7	..	..	..	..	..	..	..	..	..
Macedonia, FYR	2002	3.6	3.6[b]	8[b]	..	95[b]	95[b]	48[b]	..	..	..	7[b]	3[b]
Madagascar	1993	4.9	4.8	64	57	..	..	81	59	..	..	..	..
Malawi	1998	4.4	4.4	30	..	48	84	86	47	..	..	..	..
Malaysia	2000	4.5	4.4	..	..	..	..	..	..	10[b]	16[b]	..	..
Mali	1998	5.6	..	..	..	..	..	..	..	..	..	..	..
Mauritania	1988	..	..	..	..	..	..	..	..	..	..	..	..
Mauritius	2000	3.9	3.8	6	7	91	94	87	81	..	..	7	6
Mexico	2005	4.0	3.9	24	20	..	..	..	..	..	..	3	2
Moldova	2003	..	..	..	..	..	..	..	..	..	..	..	..
Mongolia	2000	4.4	4.5	..	..	..	..	..	..	48	56	..	..
Morocco	1982	5.9	5.3	..	..	..	..	..	..	..	..	..	..
Mozambique	1997	4.4	4.9	37	28	7	20	92	83	1	1	0	..
Myanmar		..	..	..	..	..	..	..	..	..	..	..	..
Namibia	2001	5.3	..	..	..	..	..	..	..	..	..	..	..
Nepal	2001	5.4	4.9	..	..	..	..	88	..	..	..	0	..
Netherlands		..	..	..	..	..	..	65	..	17	..	10	..
New Zealand	2001	2.8	..	1[b]	..	..	..	84	86	0	0	8	..
Nicaragua	1995	5.3	..	..	..	79	87	77	40	..	..	..	..
Niger	2001	6.4	6.0	..	..	..	..	77	40	..	..	..	..
Nigeria	1991	5.0	4.7	..	..	..	..	..	..	..	..	..	..
Norway	1980	2.7	..	1	..	..	..	67	..	38	..	..	..
Oman	2003	7.1	..	..	..	..	..	..	..	..	..	..	..
Pakistan	1998	6.8	6.8	..	..	58	86	81	..	..	..	..	..
Panama	2000	4.1	..	28[b]	..	88	98[b]	80	66[b]	10[b]	10[b]	14	..
Papua New Guinea	1990	4.5[b]	6.5	..	..	..	..	..	44	..	8	..	..
Paraguay	2002	4.6	4.5	38[b]	..	95[b]	98[b]	79	75	1[b]	2[b]	6[b]	6[b]
Peru	2007	3.9	3.9	35	31	..	..	..	..	..	..	..	..
Philippines	2000	4.9	..	..	..	..	..	71	..	12	..	..	..
Poland	1988	3.2	..	..	..	..	..	..	..	..	..	1	..
Portugal	2001	2.8	..	..	..	..	..	76	..	86	..	..	..
Puerto Rico	2005	2.8	.	1	..	..	..	75	..	..	..	..	..
Qatar		..	..	..	..	..	..	..	..	..	..	..	..

	Census year	Household size		Overcrowding		Durable dwelling units		Home ownership		Multiunit dwellings		Vacancy rate	
		number of people		Households living in overcrowded dwellings[a] % of total		Buildings with durable structure % of total		Privately owned dwellings % of total		% of total		Unoccupied dwellings % of total	
		National	Urban	National	Urban	National	Urban	National	Urban	National	Urban	National	Urban
Romania	2002	2.9	2.8	20	20	..	..	84	72	..	..	..	..
Russian Federation	2002	2.8	2.7	7	5	..	..	..	..	73	86	..	..
Rwanda	2002	4.4	3.7	43	36	13	31	79	41	36	60	..	..
Saudi Arabia	2004	5.5	..	..	..	92[b]	..	43	..	..	..	..	..
Senegal	2002	9.2	8.0	72	68	..	..	74	54	..	..	..	..
Serbia	2001	2.9	2.2	..	..	..	..	..	..	..	..	..	..
Sierra Leone	1985	6.8	..	..	..	34	..	68	..	..	..	..	..
Singapore	2000	4.4	..	..	..	..	..	..	..	..	..	..	..
Slovak Republic	..	..	..	..	..	..	..	..	..	..	..	..	..
Slovenia	2002	2.8	2.7	14	17	..	..	91	87	33	56	..	..
Somalia	1975	..	..	..	..	..	..	..	..	..	..	..	..
South Africa	2007	3.0	2.8	16	15	..	..	43	40	..	..	..	..
South Sudan		..	..	..	..	..	..	..	..	..	..	..	..
Spain	2001	2.9	..	1	..	..	..	82	..	..	..	..	..
Sri Lanka	2001	3.8	..	..	..	93[b]	92[b]	70[b]	58[b]	1	14[b]	13	1[b]
Sudan	1993	5.8	6.0	..	..	..	..	86[b]	58[b]	0[b]	1[b]	..	..
Swaziland	1997	5.4	3.7	..	..	..	..	..	..	..	..	..	..
Sweden	1990	2.0	..	..	..	..	..	..	..	54	..	1	..
Switzerland	2000	2.2	..	1	..	..	..	34	..	77	..	..	..
Syrian Arab Republic	1981	6.3	6.0	..	..	..	..	..	..	..	..	..	..
Tajikistan	2000	..	..	..	..	..	..	..	..	..	..	..	..
Tanzania	2002	4.9	4.5[b]	33[b]	7[b]	..	..	82[b]	43[b]	..	..	..	..
Thailand	2000	3.8	..	..	..	93	93	81	62	3	..	3	..
Timor-Leste		..	..	..	..	..	..	..	..	..	..	..	..
Togo		..	..	..	..	..	..	..	..	..	..	..	..
Trinidad and Tobago	2000	3.7	..	9[b]	..	98[b]	..	74[b]	..	17[b]	..	..	..
Tunisia	1994	8.0	..	..	..	99	..	71	89[b]	6	10[b]	15	12[b]
Turkey	1990	5.0	..	..	..	..	..	70	..	..	..	..	..
Turkmenistan		..	..	..	..	..	..	..	..	..	..	..	..
Uganda	2002	4.7	3.9	..	..	19	61	76	28	37	71	..	..
Ukraine	2003	..	..	..	..	..	..	..	..	..	..	..	..
United Arab Emirates		..	..	..	..	..	..	..	..	..	..	..	..
United Kingdom	2001	..	2.4	..	..	..	..	..	69	..	19	..	..
United States	2005	2.5	..	0	..	..	..	74	..	26	..	..	..
Uruguay	1996	3.3	3.4[b]	22[b]	..	..	..	57[b]	57[b]	..	..	13[b]	13[b]
Uzbekistan		..	..	..	..	..	..	..	..	..	..	..	..
Venezuela, RB	2001	4.4	..	..	..	..	..	78	..	14	..	16	..
Vietnam	1999	4.6	4.5	..	..	77	89	95	86	..	..	..	..
West Bank and Gaza	1997	7.1	..	..	..	..	..	78	..	45	..	..	..
Yemen, Rep.	1994	6.7	6.8	54[b]	6[b]	..	..	88[b]	68[b]	3[b]	11[b]	..	..
Zambia	2000	5.3	5.9	..	..	..	..	94	30	..	..	..	..
Zimbabwe	1992	4.8	4.2	..	..	..	..	94	30	6	..	..	..

a. More than two people per room. b. Data are from a previous census.

Urbanization can yield important social benefits, improving access to public services and the job market. It also leads to significant demands for services. Inadequate living quarters and demand for housing and shelter are major concerns for policymakers.

The unmet demand for affordable housing, along with urban poverty, has led to the emergence of slums in many poor countries. Improving the shelter situation requires a better understanding of the mechanisms governing housing markets and the processes governing housing availability. That requires good data and adequate policy-oriented analysis so that housing policy can be formulated in a global comparative perspective and drawn from lessons learned in other countries. Housing policies and outcomes affect such broad socioeconomic conditions as the infant mortality rate, performance in school, household saving, productivity levels, capital formation, and government budget deficits. A good understanding of housing conditions thus requires an extensive set of indicators within a reasonable framework.

There is a strong demand for quantitative indicators that can measure housing conditions on a regular basis to monitor progress. However, data deficiencies and lack of rigorous quantitative analysis hamper informed decisionmaking on desirable policies to improve housing conditions. The data in the table are from housing and population censuses, collected using similar definitions. The table will incorporate household survey data in future editions. The table focuses attention on urban areas, where housing conditions are typically most severe. Not all the compiled indicators are presented in the table because of space limitations.

• **Census year** is the year in which the underlying data were collected. • **Household size** is the average number of people within a household, calculated by dividing total population by the number of households in the country and in urban areas. • **Overcrowding** refers to the number of households living in dwellings with two or more people per room as a percentage of total households in the country and in urban areas. • **Durable dwelling units** are the number of housing units in structures made of durable building materials (concrete, stone, cement, brick, asbestos, zinc, and stucco) expected to maintain their stability for 20 years or longer under local conditions with normal maintenance and repair, taking into account location and environmental hazards such as floods, mudslides, and earthquakes, as a percentage of total dwellings. • **Home ownership** refers to the number of privately owned dwellings as a percentage of total dwellings. When the number of private dwellings is not available from the census data, the share of households that own their housing unit is used. Privately owned and owner-occupied units are included, depending on the definition used in the census data. State- and community-owned units and rented, squatted, and rent-free units are excluded. • **Multiunit dwellings** are the number of multiunit dwellings, such as apartments, flats, condominiums, barracks, boardinghouses, orphanages, retirement houses, hostels, hotels, and collective dwellings, as a percentage of total dwellings. • **Vacancy rate** is the percentage of completed dwelling units that are currently unoccupied. It includes all vacant units, whether on the market or not (such as second homes).

Data sources

Data on urban housing conditions are from national population and housing censuses.

	Motor vehicles		Passenger cars	Road density	Road sector energy consumption				Fuel price		Particulate matter concentration	
				km. of road per 100 sq. km. of land area	% of total consumption	kilograms of oil equivalent per capita			$ per liter		Urban-population-weighted PM10 micrograms per cubic meter	
	per 1,000 people	per kilometer of road	per 1,000 people			Total	Diesel fuel	Gasoline fuel	Super grade gasoline	Diesel		
	2009	2009	2009	2009	2009	2009	2009	2009	2010	2010	1990	2009
Afghanistan	29	11	21	6	..	..	..	..	1.15	1.00	69	32
Albania	120	..	89	63	23	123	120	15	1.46	1.40	92	37
Algeria	112	35	74	5	23	265	177	67	0.32	0.19	112	75
Angola	38	..	8	4	13	85	45	36	0.65	0.43	112	56
Argentina	314	..	..	8	17	307	140	105	0.96	1.05	104	60
Armenia	103	42	94	26	22	182	38	60	1.08	0.99	367	61
Australia	688	18	550	11	18	1,103	433	610	1.27	1.23	22	14
Austria	569	45	521	127	23	878	594	208	1.63	1.55	39	27
Azerbaijan	104	13	86	61	12	155	45	109	0.75	0.56	133	29
Bahrain	537	104	451	575	12	955	369	535	0.21	0.13	75	45
Bangladesh	3	..	2	166	7	14	10	3	1.09	0.63	228	121
Belarus	282	..	240	46	7	192	107	50	1.08	0.86	24	7
Belgium	552	39	483	504	15	814	657	125	1.87	1.62	31	21
Benin	22	..	18	17	27	110	41	63	1.04	1.21	77	48
Bolivia	68	9	18	7	32	206	98	68	0.70	0.54	105	60
Bosnia and Herzegovina	138	20	121	43	15	234	148	81	1.42	1.42	36	19
Botswana	133	7	69	4	31	318	131	174	0.93	0.97	92	66
Brazil	209	18	178	21	24	298	149	73	1.58	1.14	39	19
Bulgaria	375	72	330	36	15	336	192	81	1.51	1.58	108	45
Burkina Faso	11	1	7	34	..	..	..	..	1.44	1.28	143	63
Burundi	6	..	2	44	..	..	..	..	1.43	1.42	60	28
Cambodia	21	7	18	21	7	26	13	12	1.15	0.98	107	37
Cameroon	14	..	10	6	12	42	23	18	1.20	1.10	122	58
Canada	607	15	420	14	17	1,313	405	886	1.21	1.08	25	16
Central African Republic	0	..	0	4	..	..	..	..	1.71	1.69	60	33
Chad	6	1	2	3	..	..	..	..	1.32	1.31	209	82
Chile	174	38	118	10	21	355	208	147	1.38	1.02	89	53
China	47	16	34	40	5	92	56	45	1.11	1.04	115	60
Hong Kong SAR, China	74	254	56	188	13	285	224	50	1.92	1.32	..	..
Colombia	71	25	53	15	21	144	77	54	1.41	0.95	38	20
Congo, Dem. Rep.	5	..	..	7	1	4	0	3	1.28	1.27	71	38
Congo, Rep.	27	..	16	5	27	98	68	26	1.27	0.84	130	60
Costa Rica	166	20	130	76	30	319	156	147	1.14	0.97	43	29
Côte d'Ivoire	20	5	16	25	4	21	17	6	1.68	1.30	87	29
Croatia	384	58	346	52	22	435	268	153	1.59	1.49	45	25
Cuba	38	..	21	55	4	40	16	22	1.72	1.24	31	15
Cyprus	675	48	529	134	30	682	294	351	1.47	1.47	60	28
Czech Republic	482	39	423	166	14	557	338	186	1.75	1.69	41	17
Denmark	478	36	380	170	22	727	456	292	2.00	1.79	28	16
Dominican Republic	128	..	87	26	17	144	59	78	1.23	1.03	43	16
Ecuador	57	18	36	17	38	305	174	148	0.53	0.28	36	20
Egypt, Arab Rep.	45	37	33	10	18	159	86	61	0.48	0.32	214	88
El Salvador	54	..	49	48	17	140	62	71	0.92	0.89	44	28
Eritrea	11	..	6	3	5	7	6	1	2.54	1.07	196	64
Estonia	471	11	407	129	14	493	292	218	1.54	1.57	44	9
Ethiopia	3	5	1	4	4	17	14	2	0.91	0.78	108	51
Finland	532	36	459	23	12	728	409	299	1.94	1.60	22	15
France	598	39	496	173	16	642	471	123	1.98	1.72	18	12
Gabon	..	..	..	3	6	78	53	22	..	..	9	5
Gambia, The	8	3	5	33	..	..	..	..	..	..	136	61
Georgia	151	28	126	29	22	156	69	79	1.13	1.13	224	54
Germany	564	72	510	180	16	612	323	236	1.90	1.68	27	16
Ghana	30	6	18	46	16	62	37	27	0.82	0.83	38	21
Greece	573	55	455	89	24	632	269	358	2.05	1.78	64	31
Guatemala	98	..	37	13	21	145	70	68	0.95	0.85	69	68
Guinea	..	..	..	18	..	..	..	..	0.95	0.95	103	54
Guinea-Bissau	33	..	27	12	..	..	..	..	..	..	114	45
Haiti	..	..	..	15	9	25	19	23	..	..	68	33

	Motor vehicles		Passenger cars	Road density	Road sector energy consumption				Fuel price		Particulate matter concentration	
	per 1,000 people	per kilometer of road	per 1,000 people	km. of road per 100 sq. km. of land area	% of total consumption	kilograms of oil equivalent per capita			$ per liter		Urban-population-weighted PM10 micrograms per cubic meter	
						Total	Diesel fuel	Gasoline fuel	Super grade gasoline	Diesel		
	2009	2009	2009	2009	2009	2009	2009	2009	2010	2010	1990	2009
Honduras	95	..	29	12	23	136	65	64	1.04	0.92	43	34
Hungary	347	18	301	212	17	433	259	149	1.67	1.61	34	15
India	18	5	12	125	7	37	26	11	1.15	0.82	110	57
Indonesia	79	38	45	25	14	119	44	75	0.79	0.51	132	68
Iran, Islamic Rep.	128	51	113	11	18	531	223	237	0.10	0.02	92	55
Iraq	77	55	27	9	32	334	185	134	0.78	0.56	168	110
Ireland	513	24	434	137	28	900	519	347	1.78	1.69	23	12
Israel	316	128	265	83	27	766	347	380	1.85	1.87	66	23
Italy	672	80	596	162	22	602	376	172	1.87	1.69	41	21
Jamaica	120	15	84	201	16	189	65	177	0.98	0.98	56	29
Japan	589	63	454	320	14	530	173	332	1.60	1.37	42	25
Jordan	154	117	113	9	23	290	108	173	1.04	0.73	43	17
Kazakhstan	199	33	167	4	6	235	39	205	0.71	0.51	64	30
Kenya	23	14	13	11	7	31	21	11	1.33	1.27	64	30
Korea, Dem. Rep.	..	..	..	21	2	13	7	5	..	..	169	56
Korea, Rep.	355	165	267	105	12	569	286	158	1.52	1.35	51	33
Kosovo	..	..	..	..	..	..	..	..	1.63	1.60	..	..
Kuwait	495	212	412	37	13	1,492	491	920	0.23	0.21	113	95
Kyrgyz Republic	59	9	44	17	28	160	103	51	0.85	0.79	79	35
Lao PDR	20	3	2	17	..	..	..	..	1.26	0.97	92	45
Latvia	459	15	401	107	20	370	245	137	1.48	1.49	38	12
Lebanon	..	..	..	67	26	418	5	386	1.13	0.77	39	28
Lesotho	..	..	..	20	..	..	..	..	0.97	1.07	108	43
Liberia	3	..	2	10	..	..	..	..	0.98	0.96	68	31
Libya	290	..	225	5	20	640	405	206	0.17	0.13	101	81
Lithuania	555	23	508	125	16	405	242	103	1.59	1.42	52	15
Macedonia, FYR	155	23	138	54	15	203	116	59	1.52	1.27	45	18
Madagascar	26	..	7	8	..	..	..	..	1.52	1.26	80	30
Malawi	8	..	4	13	..	..	..	..	1.71	1.54	82	33
Malaysia	350	69	313	30	21	492	178	295	0.59	0.56	35	19
Mali	14	8	8	2	..	..	..	..	1.42	1.25	258	106
Mauritania	..	..	..	1	..	..	..	..	1.16	0.99	145	68
Mauritius	166	102	129	101	..	..	..	..	1.55	1.23	21	14
Mexico	276	81	191	19	28	439	123	295	0.81	0.72	66	33
Moldova	146	41	107	38	11	75	52	23	1.21	1.08	118	33
Mongolia	72	2	48	3	11	135	42	119	1.11	1.04	181	101
Morocco	70	38	53	13	25	119	98	16	1.23	0.88	39	23
Mozambique	12	9	9	4	5	20	17	4	1.11	0.86	112	24
Myanmar	7	10	5	4	6	19	8	9	0.80	0.80	107	41
Namibia	103	5	46	5	37	281	89	174	1.06	1.09	50	45
Nepal	5	8	3	14	6	19	13	4	1.18	0.91	67	30
Netherlands	522	63	459	329	14	673	380	240	2.13	1.71	44	30
New Zealand	718	33	603	35	24	949	394	531	1.47	0.97	14	12
Nicaragua	58	15	18	17	17	90	49	38	1.09	0.99	46	24
Niger	8	6	6	1	..	..	..	..	1.07	1.16	199	92
Nigeria	31	..	31	21	8	53	4	45	0.44	0.77	195	42
Norway	578	30	465	29	12	704	549	258	2.12	2.01	22	15
Oman	215	12	166	18	13	721	59	617	0.31	0.38	133	82
Pakistan	13	8	10	32	13	63	38	11	0.86	0.92	216	101
Panama	141	35	101	19	18	162	124	151	0.85	0.77	55	33
Papua New Guinea	9	..	6	4	..	..	..	..	..	..	35	16
Paraguay	91	16	39	8	27	200	150	37	1.28	1.01	107	65
Peru	68	16	41	10	29	162	113	34	1.41	1.10	96	43
Philippines	33	..	8	67	19	79	47	29	1.05	0.84	56	17
Poland	508	50	432	123	16	400	225	105	1.57	1.50	58	34
Portugal	509	67	495	90	25	572	406	137	1.85	1.58	49	20
Puerto Rico	596	92	582	301	..	..	..	..	..	..	23	14
Qatar	532	..	335	67	9	1,331	675	591	0.19	0.19	54	31

	Motor vehicles		Passenger cars	Road density	Road sector energy consumption				Fuel price		Particulate matter concentration	
	per 1,000 people	per kilometer of road	per 1,000 people	km. of road per 100 sq. km. of land area	% of total consumption	kilograms of oil equivalent per capita			$ per liter		Urban-population-weighted PM10 micrograms per cubic meter	
						Total	Diesel fuel	Gasoline fuel	Super grade gasoline	Diesel		
	2009	2009	2009	2009	2009	2009	2009	2009	2010	2010	1990	2009
Romania	230	20	198	83	14	223	147	67	1.46	1.46	42	14
Russian Federation	271	39	233	6	7	330	114	221	0.84	0.72	41	16
Rwanda	5	..	2	53	..	..	..	..	1.63	1.62	53	23
Saudi Arabia	192	20	139	11	21	1,241	543	635	0.16	0.07	160	103
Senegal	22	16	16	8	21	50	41	9	1.57	1.34	94	80
Serbia	252	42	224	50	13	265	162	70	1.50	1.48	..	..
Sierra Leone	6	2	5	..	..	..	..	..	0.94	0.94	87	37
Singapore	156	232	121	473	15	545	347	174	1.42	1.04	108	23
Slovak Republic	348	43	293	89	11	339	194	105	1.70	1.53	46	12
Slovenia	566	30	522	192	24	836	514	288	1.67	1.62	39	26
Somalia	..	..	..	3	..	..	..	..	..	..	82	28
South Africa	162	..	110	30	11	320	134	176	1.19	1.14	39	26
South Sudan	..	..	..	..	..	..	..	..	..	..	..	..
Spain	596	41	478	132	24	660	528	126	1.56	1.47	41	25
Sri Lanka	47	..	19	148	18	79	54	22	1.19	0.66	93	71
Sudan	27	..	19	1	16	58	39	17	0.62	0.43	285	137
Swaziland	89	25	45	21	..	..	..	..	1.07	1.10	30	38
Sweden	519	8	462	129	16	773	353	357	1.87	1.82	15	10
Switzerland	563	61	519	173	21	737	286	424	1.66	1.77	34	22
Syrian Arab Republic	63	20	30	37	22	248	154	83	0.96	0.45	135	71
Tajikistan	38	..	29	19	4	14	0	12	1.02	0.91	84	30
Tanzania	7	..	4	11	6	26	19	6	1.22	1.19	56	20
Thailand	134	50	57	35	18	275	163	74	1.41	0.95	77	53
Timor-Leste	..	..	..	..	..	..	..	..	1.40	0.90	..	..
Togo	2	1	2	21	11	51	17	31	1.18	1.17	56	28
Trinidad and Tobago	353	..	..	162	5	704	313	355	..	..	136	98
Tunisia	114	61	76	12	16	145	96	41	0.94	0.82	71	23
Turkey	142	29	95	46	14	185	120	34	2.52	2.03	77	37
Turkmenistan	106	..	80	5	4	172	0	164	0.22	0.20	196	41
Uganda	8	..	3	29	..	..	..	..	1.42	1.11	29	11
Ukraine	167	45	142	28	6	153	46	102	1.01	0.92	71	17
United Arab Emirates	313	271	293	5	14	1,229	606	563	0.47	0.71	273	62
United Kingdom	523	77	460	172	19	616	351	255	1.92	1.98	24	13
United States	802	38	439	67	23	1,640	384	1,134	0.76	0.84	30	18
Uruguay	200	..	179	44	23	281	165	99	1.49	1.44	229	142
Uzbekistan	..	..	..	18	4	67	11	53	0.92	0.83	110	37
Venezuela, RB	147	..	107	11	27	626	102	459	0.02	0.01	21	9
Vietnam	13	7	13	48	14	108	59	46	0.88	0.77	123	50
West Bank and Gaza	30	22	25	93	..	..	..	..	1.71	1.54	..	..
Yemen, Rep.	35	..	16	14	24	77	2	66	0.35	0.23	133	43
Zambia	21	..	13	12	2	10	4	10	1.66	1.52	125	30
Zimbabwe	114	..	98	25	4	27	17	10	1.29	1.15	55	37
World	**170 w**	**30 w**	**125 w**	**30 w**	**15 w**	**259 w**	**110 w**	**134 w**	**1.21 w**	**1.07 w**	**79 w**	**43 w**
Low income	10	..	7	..	6	20	13	7	1.18	1.15	127	56
Middle income	66	18	54	23	11	132	65	61	1.08	0.97	96	49
Lower middle income	33	10	21	48	11	70	37	30	1.08	0.91	124	58
Upper middle income	99	25	84	17	11	195	93	92	1.13	1.02	78	43
Low & middle income	61	15	50	21	10	120	60	55	1.12	0.98	98	50
East Asia & Pacific	54	18	38	37	7	105	58	51	1.08	0.93	112	56
Europe & Central Asia	219	36	183	9	8	230	100	125	1.21	1.13	57	23
Latin America & Carib.	178	23	143	18	24	299	123	137	1.04	0.98	57	30
Middle East & N. Africa	87	40	67	9	20	283	142	115	0.94	0.56	125	66
South Asia	17	5	11	102	7	38	26	10	1.12	0.83	130	68
Sub-Saharan Africa	28	..	23	..	9	61	26	33	1.22	1.15	119	46
High income	618	37	447	46	19	939	357	519	1.63	1.55	37	23
Euro area	593	47	418	140	18	646	418	186	1.78	1.62	33	19

About the data

Traffic congestion in urban areas constrains economic productivity, damages people's health, and degrades the quality of life. In recent years ownership of passenger cars has increased, and the expansion of economic activity has led to more goods and services being transported by road over greater distances (see table 5.10). These developments have increased demand for roads and vehicles, adding to urban congestion, air pollution, health hazards, and traffic accidents and injuries.

The data in the table on motor vehicles, passenger cars, and road density are compiled by the International Road Federation (IRF) through questionnaires sent to national organizations. The IRF uses a hierarchy of sources to gather as much information as possible. Primary sources are national road associations. If they lack data or do not respond, other agencies are contacted, including road directorates, ministries of transport or public works, and central statistical offices. As a result, data quality is uneven. Coverage of each indicator may differ across countries because of different definitions. Comparability is also limited when time series data are reported. The IRF is taking steps to improve the quality of the data in its *World Road Statistics*. Because this effort covers only 2003–09, time series data may not be comparable. Another reason is coverage. Road density is a rough indicator of accessibility and does not capture road width, type, or condition. Thus comparisons over time and across countries should be made with caution.

Road sector energy consumption includes energy from petroleum products, natural gas, renewable and combustible waste, and electricity. Biodiesel and biogasoline, forms of renewable energy, are biodegradable and emit less sulfur and carbon monoxide than petroleum-derived ones. They can be produced from vegetable oils, such as soybean, corn, palm, peanut, or sunflower oil, and can be used directly only in a modified internal combustion engine.

Data on fuel prices are compiled by the German Agency for International Cooperation (GIZ), from its global network and other sources, including the Allgemeiner Deutscher Automobile Club (for Europe) and the Latin American Energy Organization (for Latin America). Local prices are converted to U.S. dollars using the exchange rate in the *Financial Times* international monetary table on the survey date. When multiple exchange rates exist, the market, parallel, or black market rate is used. Prices were compiled in mid-November 2010, based on the crude oil price of $81 a barrel Brent.

Considerable uncertainty surrounds estimates of particulate matter concentrations, and caution should be used in interpreting them. They allow for cross-country comparisons of the relative risk of particulate matter pollution facing urban residents. Major sources of urban outdoor particulate matter pollution are traffic and industrial emissions, but nonanthropogenic sources such as dust storms may also be a substantial contributor for some cities. Country technology and pollution controls are important determinants of particulate matter. Data on particulate matter for selected cities are in table 3.16.

Definitions

• **Motor vehicles** include cars, buses, and freight vehicles but not two-wheelers. Population figures are midyear population in the year for which data are available. Roads refer to motorways (a road designed and built for motor traffic that separates the traffic flowing in opposite directions), highways, main or national roads, and secondary or regional roads. • **Passenger cars** are road motor vehicles, other than two-wheelers, intended for the carriage of passengers and designed to seat no more than nine people (including the driver). • **Road density** is the ratio of the length of the country's total road network to the country's land area. The road network includes all roads in the country—motorways, highways, main or national roads, secondary or regional roads, and other urban and rural roads. • **Road sector energy consumption** is the total energy used in the road sector, including energy from petroleum products, natural gas, combustible and renewable waste, and electricity (see table 3.7). • **Total energy consumption** is the country's total energy consumption from all sources (see table 3.7). • **Diesel** is heavy oils used in internal combustion in diesel engines. • **Gasoline fuel** is light hydrocarbon oil used in internal combustion engines such as motor vehicles, excluding aircraft. • **Fuel price** is the pump price of super grade gasoline and of diesel fuel, converted from the local currency to U.S. dollars (see *About the data*). • **Particulate matter concentration** is fine suspended particulates of less than 10 microns in diameter (PM10) that are capable of penetrating deep into the respiratory tract and causing severe health damage. Data are urban-population-weighted PM10 levels in residential areas of cities with more than 100,000 residents. The estimates represent the average annual exposure level of the average urban resident to outdoor particulate matter.

Data sources

Data on vehicles and road density are from the IRF's electronic files and its annual *World Road Statistics*, except where noted. Data on road sector energy consumption are from the IRF and the International Energy Agency. Data on fuel prices are from the GIZ's electronic files. Data on particulate matter concentrations are from Pandey and others (2006b).

City		City population	Particulate matter concentration		Sulfur dioxide	Nitrogen dioxide
			Urban-population-weighted PM10 micrograms per cubic meter		micrograms per cubic meter	micrograms per cubic meter
		thousands				
		2010	1990	2009	2001[a]	2001[a]
Argentina	Buenos Aires	13,074	159	92	..	..
	Córdoba	1,493	78	45	..	97
Australia	Melbourne	3,853	17	11	..	30
	Perth	1,599	16	11	5	19
	Sydney	4,429	27	17	28	81
Austria	Vienna	1,706	45	32	14	42
Belgium	Brussels	1,904	33	23	20	48
Brazil	Rio de Janeiro	11,950	50	25	129	..
	São Paulo	20,262	57	28	43	83
Bulgaria	Sofia	1,196	118	49	39	122
Canada	Montréal	3,783	24	15	10	42
	Toronto	5,449	29	18	17	43
	Vancouver	2,220	17	11	14	37
Chile	Santiago	5,952	100	60	29	81
China	Anshan	1,663	132	68	115	88
	Beijing	12,385	141	73	90	122
	Changchun	3,597	117	61	21	64
	Chengdu	4,961	136	71	77	74
	Chongqing	9,401	194	101	340	70
	Dalian	3,306	79	41	61	100
	Foshan	4,969	107	56	..	..
	Guangzhou	8,884	99	52	57	136
	Guiyang	2,154	111	58	424	53
	Harbin	4,251	121	63	23	30
	Jinan	3,237	148	77	132	45
	Kunming	3,116	111	58	19	33
	Lanzhou	2,285	145	75	102	104
	Liupanshui	1,221[b]	94	49	102	..
	Nanchang	2,701	124	65	69	29
	Shanghai	16,575	115	60	53	73
	Shenyang	5,166	160	83	99	73
	Shenzhen	9,005	89	46	..	..
	Tianjin	7,884	198	103	82	50
	Wuhan	7,681	125	65	40	43
	Xi'an	4,747	221	115	..	..
	Zhengzhou	2,966	154	80	63	95
	Zibo	2,456	117	61	198	43
Colombia	Bogotá	8,500	51	27	..	..
Croatia	Zagreb	779[b]	48	26	31	..
Cuba	Havana	2,130	35	17	1	5
Czech Republic	Prague	1,162	42	17	14	33
Denmark	Copenhagen	1,186	30	17	7	54
Ecuador	Guayaquil	2,690	33	18	15	..
	Quito	1,846	44	24	22	..
Egypt, Arab Rep.	Cairo	11,001	274	112	69	..
Finland	Helsinki	1,117	24	17	4	35
France	Paris	10,485	14	10	14	57
Germany	Berlin	3,450	30	18	18	26
	Frankfurt	680[b]	27	16	11	45
	Munich	1,349	27	16	8	53
Ghana	Accra	2,342	37	21	..	..
Greece	Athens	3,257	69	33	34	64
Hungary	Budapest	1,706	35	16	39	51
Iceland	Reykjavik	319[b]	23	16	5	42
India	Ahmadabad	5,717	126	66	30	21
	Bengaluru	7,218	68	35	..	..

About the data

Indoor and outdoor air pollution place a major burden on world health. More than half the world's people rely on dung, wood, crop waste, or coal to meet basic energy needs. Cooking and heating with these fuels on open fires or stoves without chimneys lead to indoor air pollution, which is responsible for 1.6 million deaths a year—one every 20 seconds. In many urban areas air pollution exposure is the main environmental threat to health. Long-term exposure to high levels of soot and small particles contributes to a range of health effects, including respiratory diseases, lung cancer, and heart disease. Particulate pollution, alone or with sulfur dioxide, creates an enormous burden of ill health.

Sulfur dioxide and nitrogen dioxide emissions lead to deposition of acid rain and other acidic compounds over long distances, which can lead to the leaching of trace minerals and nutrients critical to trees and plants. Sulfur dioxide emissions can damage human health, particularly that of the young and old. Nitrogen dioxide is emitted by bacteria, motor vehicles, industrial activities, nitrogen fertilizers, fuel and biomass combustion, and aerobic decomposition of organic matter in soils and oceans.

Where coal is the primary fuel for power plants without effective dust controls, steel mills, industrial boilers, and domestic heating, high levels of urban air pollution are common—especially particulates and sulfur dioxide. Elsewhere the worst emissions are from petroleum product combustion.

Sulfur dioxide and nitrogen dioxide concentration data are based on average observed concentrations at urban monitoring sites, which not all cities have.

The data on particulate matter are estimated average annual concentrations in residential areas away from air pollution "hotspots," such as industrial districts and transport corridors. The data are from the World Bank's Development Research Group and Environment Department estimates of annual ambient concentrations of particulate matter in cities with populations exceeding 100,000 (Pandey and others 2006b). A country's technology and pollution controls are important determinants of particulate matter concentrations.

Pollutant concentrations are sensitive to local conditions, and even monitoring sites in the same city may register different levels. Thus these data should be considered only a general indication of air quality, and comparisons should be made with caution. Current World Health Organization (WHO) air quality guidelines are annual mean concentrations of 20 micrograms per cubic meter for particulate matter less than 10 microns in diameter and 40 micrograms for nitrogen dioxide and daily mean concentrations of 20 micrograms per cubic meter for sulfur dioxide.

City		City population	Particulate matter concentration		Sulfur dioxide	Nitrogen dioxide
		thousands	Urban-population-weighted PM10 micrograms per cubic meter		micrograms per cubic meter	micrograms per cubic meter
		2010	1990	2009	2001[a]	2001[a]
India (continued)	Chennai	7,547	56	29	15	17
	Delhi	22,157	227	118	24	41
	Hyderabad	6,751	62	32	12	17
	Kanpur	3,364	165	86	15	14
	Kolkata	15,552	193	101	49	34
	Lucknow	2,873	165	86	26	25
	Mumbai	20,041	95	50	33	39
	Nagpur	2,607	84	44	6	13
	Pune	5,002	71	37	..	..
Indonesia	Jakarta	9,210	137	70	..	..
Iran, Islamic Rep.	Tehran	7,241	92	55	209	..
Ireland	Dublin	1,099	24	13	20	..
Italy	Milan	2,967	46	24	31	248
	Rome	3,362	44	23	..	..
	Turin	1,665	66	35	..	..
Japan	Osaka-Kobe	11,337	48	28	19	63
	Tokyo	36,669	54	32	18	68
	Yokohama	3,654[b]	42	25	100	13
Kenya	Nairobi	3,523	67	31	..	..
Korea, Rep	Busan	3,425	52	33	60	51
	Seoul	9,773	55	35	44	60
	Daegu	2,458	59	38	81	62
Malaysia	Kuala Lumpur	1,519	36	19	24	..
Mexico	Mexico City	19,460	88	43	74	130
Netherlands	Amsterdam	1,049	45	30	10	58
New Zealand	Auckland	1,404	13	11	3	20
Norway	Oslo	888	27	19	8	43
Philippines	Manila	11,628	78	24	33	..
Poland	Katowice	309[b]	60	35	83	79
	Lódz	742[b]	60	34	21	43
	Warsaw	1,712	65	38	16	32
Portugal	Lisbon	2,824	44	18	8	52
Romania	Bucharest	1,934	47	16	10	71
Russian Federation	Moscow	10,550	42	16	109	..
	Omsk	1,124	44	17	20	34
Singapore	Singapore	4,837	108	23	20	30
Slovak Republic	Bratislava	500[b]	44	12	21	27
South Africa	Cape Town	3,405	24	16	21	72
	Durban	2,879	47	32	31	..
	Johannesburg	3,670	49	33	19	31
Spain	Barcelona	5,083	43	27	11	43
	Madrid	5,851	37	23	24	66
Sweden	Stockholm	1,285	14	9	3	20
Switzerland	Zurich	1,150	32	21	11	39
Thailand	Bangkok	6,976	88	60	11	23
Turkey	Ankara	3,906	75	35	55	46
	Istanbul	10,525	88	42	120	..
Ukraine	Kiev	2,805	91	21	14	51
United Kingdom	Birmingham	2,302	33	20	9	45
	London	8,631	27	17	25	77
	Manchester	2,253	24	12	26	49
United States	Chicago	9,204	33	20	14	57
	Los Angeles	12,762	46	28	9	74
	New York	19,425	28	17	26	79
Venezuela, RB	Caracas	3,090	31	13	33	57

a. Data are for the most recent year available. b. Data are from national sources.

Definitions

• **City population** is the number of residents of the city or metropolitan area as defined by national authorities and reported to the United Nations.
• **Particulate matter concentration** is fine suspended particulates of less than 10 microns in diameter (PM10) that are capable of penetrating deep into the respiratory tract and causing severe health damage. Data are urban-population-weighted PM10 levels in residential areas of cities with more than 100,000 residents. The estimates represent the average annual exposure level of the average urban resident to outdoor particulate matter. • **Sulfur dioxide** is an air pollutant produced when fossil fuels containing sulfur are burned. • **Nitrogen dioxide** is a poisonous, pungent gas formed when nitric oxide combines with hydrocarbons and sunlight, producing a photochemical reaction. These conditions occur in both natural and anthropogenic activities.

Data sources

Data on city population are from the United Nations Population Division's *World Urbanization Prospects: The 2010 Revision*. Data on particulate matter concentrations are from Pandey and others (2006b). Data on sulfur dioxide and nitrogen dioxide concentrations are from the WHO's Healthy Cities Air Management Information System and the World Resources Institute.

Government commitment

	Environmental strategies or action plans	Biodiversity assessments, strategies, or action plans	Participation in treaties[a]								
			Climate change[b] 1992	Ozone layer 1985	CFC control 1987	Law of the Sea[c] 1982	Biological diversity[b] 1992	Kyoto Protocol 1997	CITES 1973	CCD 1994	Stockholm Convention 2001
Afghanistan			2002	2004[d]	2004[d]		2002		1985[d]	1995[d]	
Albania	1993		1994[d]	1999[d]	1999[d]	2003	1994[d]	2005[d]	2003[d]	2000[d]	2004
Algeria	2001		1993	1992[d]	1992[d]	1996	1995	2005[d]	1983[d]	1996	2006
Angola			2000	2000[d]	2000[d]	1990	1998	2007		1997	2006[d]
Argentina	1992		1994	1990	1990	1995	1994	2001	1981	1997	2005
Armenia			1993[e]	1999[d]	1999[d]	2002	1993[e]	2003[d]	2008[d]	1997	2003
Australia	1992	1994	1992	1987[d]	1989	1994	1993	2007	1976	2000	2004
Austria			1994	1987	1989	1995	1994	2002	1982[d]	1997[d]	2002
Azerbaijan	1998		1995	1996[d]	1996[d]		2000[f]	2000[d]	1998[d]	1998[d]	2004[d]
Bahrain			1994	1990[d]	1990[d]	1985	1996	2006[d]		1997[d]	2006
Bangladesh	1991	1990	1994	1990[d]	1990[d]	2001	1994	2001[d]	1981	1996	2007
Belarus			2000[f]	1986[e]	1988[f]	2006	1993	2005[d]	1995[d]	2001[d]	2004[d]
Belgium			1996	1988	1988	1998	1996	2002	1983	1997[d]	2006
Benin	1993		1994	1993[d]	1993[d]	1997	1994	2002[d]	1984[d]	1996	2004
Bolivia	1994	1988	1994	1994[d]	1994[d]	1995	1994	1999	1979	1996	2003
Bosnia and Herzegovina			2000[d]	1993[g]	1992[g]	1994	2002[e]	2007[d]	2009[d]	2002[d]	2010
Botswana	1990	1991	1994	1991[d]	1991[d]	1990	1995	2003[d]	1977[d]	1996	2002[d]
Brazil		1988	1994	1990[d]	1990[d]	1988	1994	2002	1975	1997	2004
Bulgaria		1994	1995	1990[d]	1990[d]	1996	1996	2002	1991[d]	2001[d]	2004
Burkina Faso	1993		1993	1989	1989	2005	1993	2005[d]	1989[d]	1996	2004
Burundi	1994	1989	1997	1997[d]	1997[d]		1997	2001[d]	1988[d]	1997	2005
Cambodia	1999		1995[d]	2001[d]	2001[d]		1995[d]	2002[d]	1997	1997	2006
Cameroon		1989	1994	1989[d]	1989[d]	1985	1994	2002[d]	1981[d]	1997	2009
Canada	1990	1994	1992	1986	1988	2003	1992	2002	1975	1995	2001
Central African Republic			1995	1993[d]	1993[d]		1995	2008[d]	1980[d]	1996	2008
Chad	1990		1994	1989[d]	1994	2009	1994	2009[d]	1989[d]	1996	2004
Chile		1993	1995	1990	1990	1997	1994	2002	1975	1997	2005
China	1994	1994	1993	1989[d]	1991[d]	1996	1993	2002[f]	1981[d]	1997	2004
Hong Kong SAR, China											
Colombia	1998	1988	1995	1990[d]	1993[d]		1994	2001[d]	1981	1999	2008
Congo, Dem. Rep.		1990	1995	1994[d]	1994[d]	1989	1994	2005[d]	1976[d]	1997	2005[d]
Congo, Rep.		1990	1996	1994[d]	1994	2008	1996	2007[d]	1983[d]	1999	2007
Costa Rica	1990	1992	1994	1991[d]	1991[d]	1992	1994	2002	1975	1998	2007
Côte d'Ivoire	1994	1991	1994	1993[d]	1993[d]	1984	1994	2007[d]	1994[d]	1997	2004
Croatia	2001	2000	1996[e]	1992[g]	1992[g]	1995	1996	2007	2000[d]	2000[d]	2007
Cuba			1994	1992[d]	1992[d]	1984	1994	2002	1990[d]	1997	2007
Cyprus			1997	1992[d]	1992[d]	1988	1996	1992[d]	1974	2000[d]	2005[d]
Czech Republic	1994		1993[f]	1993[g]	1993[g]	1996	1993[f]	2001[f]	1993	2000[d]	2002
Denmark	1994		1995	1988	1988	2004	1993	2002	1977	1995	2003
Dominican Republic		1995	1998	1993[d]	1993[d]	2009	1996	2002[d]	1986[d]	1997[d]	2007
Ecuador	1993	1995	1993	1990[d]	1990[d]		1993	2000	1975	1995	2004
Egypt, Arab Rep.	1992	1988	1994	1988	1988	1983	1994	2005	1978	1995	2003
El Salvador	1994	1988	1995	1992	1992[d]		1994	1998	1987[d]	1997[d]	2008
Eritrea	1995		1995[d]	2005[d]	2005[d]		1996[d]	2005[d]	1994[d]	1996	2005[d]
Estonia	1998		1994	1996[d]	1996[d]	2005	1994	2002	1992[d]		2008[d]
Ethiopia	1994	1991	1994	1994[d]	1994[d]			2005[d]	1989[d]	1997	2003
Finland	1995		1994[e]	1986	1988	1996	1994[e]	2002	1976[d]	1995[d]	2002[d]
France	1990		1994	1987[f]	1988[f]	1996	1994	2002[f]	1978[f]	1997	2004[f]
Gabon		1990	1998	1994[d]	1994[d]	1998	1997	2006[d]	1989[d]	1996[d]	2007
Gambia, The	1992	1989	1994	1990[d]	1990[d]	1984	1994	2001[d]	1977[d]	1996	2006
Georgia	1998		1994[d]	1996[d]	1996[d]	1996	1994[d]	1999[d]	1996[d]	1999	2006
Germany			1993	1988	1988	1994	1993	2002	1976	1996	2002
Ghana	1992	1988	1995	1989[d]	1992	1983	1994	2003[d]	1975	1996	2003
Greece			1994	1988	1988	1995	1994	2002	1992[d]	1997	2006
Guatemala	1994	1988	1995	1987[d]	1989[d]	1997	1995	1999	1979	1998[d]	2008
Guinea	1994	1988	1993	1992[d]	1992[d]	1985	1993	2000[d]	1981[d]	1997	2007
Guinea-Bissau	1993	1991	1995	2002[d]	2002[d]	1986	1995	2005[d]	1990[d]	1995	2008
Haiti	1999		1996	2000[d]	2000[d]	1996	1996	2005[d]		1996	

	Environmental strategies or action plans	Biodiversity assessments, strategies, or action plans	Participation in treaties[a]								
			Climate change[b] 1992	Ozone layer 1985	CFC control 1987	Law of the Sea[c] 1982	Biological diversity[b] 1992	Kyoto Protocol 1997	CITES 1973	CCD 1994	Stockholm Convention 2001
Honduras	1993		1995	1993[d]	1993[d]	1993	1995	2000	1985[d]	1997	2005
Hungary	1995		1994	1988[d]	1989[d]	2002	1994	2002[d]	1985[d]	1999[d]	2008
India	1993	1994	1993	1991[d]	1992[d]	1995	1994	2002[d]	1976	1996	2006
Indonesia	1993	1993	1994	1992[d]	1992	1986	1994	2004	1978[d]	1998	2009
Iran, Islamic Rep.			1996	1990[d]	1990[d]		1996	2005[d]	1976	1997	2006
Iraq			2009[d]	2008[d]	2008[d]	1985	2009[d]	2009[d]		2010[d]	
Ireland			1994	1988[d]	1988	1996	1996	2002	2002	1997	2010
Israel			1996	1992[d]	1992		1995	2004	1979	1996	
Italy			1994	1988	1988	1995	1994	2002	1979	1997	
Jamaica	1994		1995	1993[d]	1993[d]	1983	1995	1999[d]	1997[d]	1997[d]	2007
Japan			1993[e]	1988[d]	1988[e]	1996	1993[e]	2002[d]	1980[e]	1998[e]	2002[d]
Jordan	1991		1993	1989[d]	1989[d]	1995	1993	2003[d]	1978[d]	1996	2004
Kazakhstan			1995	1998[d]	1998[d]		1994	2009	2000[d]	1997	2007
Kenya	1994	1992	1994	1988[d]	1988	1989	1994	2005[d]	1978	1997	2004
Korea, Dem. Rep.			1994[f]	1995[d]	1995[d]		1994[f]	2005[d]		2003[d]	2002[d]
Korea, Rep.			1993	1992[d]	1992	1996	1994	2002	1993[d]	1999	2007
Kosovo											
Kuwait			1994[d]	1992[d]	1992[d]	1986	2002	2005[d]	2002	1997	2006
Kyrgyz Republic	1995		2000	2000[d]	2000[d]		1996[d]	2003[d]	2007[d]	1997[d]	2006
Lao PDR	1995		1995[d]	1998[d]	1998[d]	1998	1996[d]	2003[d]	2004[d]	1996[d]	2006
Latvia			1995	1995[d]	1995[d]	2004	1995	2002	1997[d]	2002[d]	2004
Lebanon			1994	1993[d]	1993[d]	1995	1994	2006[d]		1996	2003
Lesotho	1989		1995	1994[d]	1994[d]	2007	1995	2000[d]	2003	1995	2002
Liberia			2002	1996[d]	1996[d]	2008	2000	2002[d]	1981[d]	1998[d]	2002[d]
Libya			1999	1990[d]	1990[d]		2001	2006[d]	2003[d]	1996	2005[d]
Lithuania			1995	1995[d]	1995[d]	2003	1996	2003	2001[d]	2003[d]	2006
Macedonia, FYR			1998[d]	1994[g]	1994[g]	1994	1997[d]	2004[d]	2000[d]	2002[d]	2004
Madagascar	1988	1991	1999	1996[d]	1996[d]	2001		2003[d]	1975	1997	2005
Malawi	1994		1994	1991[d]	1991[d]	2010	1996	2001[d]	1982[d]	1996	2009
Malaysia	1991	1988	1994	1989[d]	1989[d]	1996	1994	2002	1977[d]	1997	
Mali		1989	1995	1994[d]	1994[d]	1985	1995	2002	1994[d]	1995	2003
Mauritania	1988		1994	1994[d]	1994[d]	1996	1996	2005[d]	1998[d]	1996	2005
Mauritius	1990		1992	1992[d]	1992[d]	1994	1992	2001[d]	1975	1996	2004
Mexico		1988	1993	1987	1988[e]	1983	1993	2000	1991[d]	1995	2003
Moldova	2002		1995	1996[d]	1996[d]	2007	1995	2008[d]	2001[d]	1999[d]	2004
Mongolia	1995		1993	1996[d]	1996[d]	1996	1993	1999[d]	1996[d]	1996	2004
Morocco		1988	1995	1995	1995	2007	1995	2002[d]	1975	1996	2004
Mozambique	1994		1995	1994[d]	1994[d]	1997	1995	2005[d]	1981[d]	1997	2005
Myanmar		1989	1994	1993[d]	1993[d]	1996	1994	2003[d]	1997[d]	1997[d]	2004[d]
Namibia	1992		1995	1993[d]	1993[d]	1983	1997	2003[d]	1990[d]	1997	2005[d]
Nepal	1993		1994	1994[d]	1994[d]	1998	1993	2005[d]	1975[d]	1996	2007
Netherlands	1994		1993[e]	1988[e]	1988[e]	1996	1994[e]	2002[e]	1984	1995[e]	2002[e]
New Zealand	1994		1993	1987	1988	1996	1993	2002	1977[d]	1998	2005
Nicaragua	1994		1995	1993[d]	1993[d]	2000	1995	1999	1975	1996	2006
Niger		1991	1995	1992[d]	1992[d]		1995	2004	1975	1996	2006
Nigeria	1990	1992	1994	1988[d]	1988[d]	1986	1994	2004[d]	1974	1997	2004
Norway		1994	1993	1986	1988	1996	1993	2002	1976	1996	2002
Oman			1995	1999[d]	1999[d]	1989	1995	2005[d]	2008[d]	1996[d]	2005
Pakistan	1994	1991	1994	1992[d]	1992[d]	1997	1994	2005[d]	1976[d]	1997	2008
Panama	1990		1995	1989[d]	1989	1996	1995	1999	1978	1996	2003
Papua New Guinea	1992	1993	1993	1992[d]	1992[d]	1997	1993	2002	1975[d]	2000[d]	2003
Paraguay			1994	1992[d]	1992[d]	1986	1994	1999	1976	1997	2004
Peru		1988	1993	1989	1993[d]		1993	2002	1975	1995	2005
Philippines	1989	1989	1994	1991[d]	1991	1984	1993	2003	1981	2000	2004
Poland	1993	1991	1994	1990[d]	1990[d]	1998	1996	2002	1989	2001[d]	2008
Portugal	1995		1993	1988[d]	1988	1997	1993	2002[f]	1980	1996	2004[e]
Puerto Rico											
Qatar			1996[d]	1996[d]	1996[d]	2002	1996	2005[a]	2001[d]	1999[d]	2004[d]

3.17 | Government commitment

	Environmental strategies or action plans	Biodiversity assessments, strategies, or action plans	Participation in treaties[a]								
			Climate change[b] 1992	Ozone layer 1985	CFC control 1987	Law of the Sea[c] 1982	Biological diversity[b] 1992	Kyoto Protocol 1997	CITES 1973	CCD 1994	Stockholm Convention 2001
Romania	1995		1994	1993[d]	1993[d]	1996	1994	2001	1994[d]	1998[d]	2004
Russian Federation	1999	1994	1994	1986[e]	1988[e]	1997	1995	2008	1992[h]	2003[d]	2011
Rwanda	1991		1998	2001[d]	2001[d]		1996	2004[d]	1980[d]	1998	2002[d]
Saudi Arabia			1994[d]	1993[d]	1993[d]	1996	2001[d]	2005[d]	1996[d]	1997[d]	
Senegal	1984	1991	1994	1993[d]	1993	1984	1994	2001[d]	1977[d]	1995	2003
Serbia			2001[a]	2001[g]	2001[g]	2001	2002	2007[d]	2006[h]	2007[a]	2009
Sierra Leone	1994		1995	2001[d]	2001[d]	1994	1994[d]	2006[d]	1994[d]	1997	2003[d]
Singapore	1993	1995	1997	1989[d]	1989[d]	1994	1995	2006[d]	1986[d]	1999[d]	2005
Slovak Republic			1994[f]	1993[g]	1993[g]	1996	1994[f]	2002	1993[g]	2002[d]	2002
Slovenia	1994		1995	1992[g]	1992[g]	1995	1996	2002	2000[d]	2001[d]	2004
Somalia			2009[d]	2001[d]	2001[d]	1989	2009[d]	2010	1985[d]	2002[d]	2010[d]
South Africa	1993		1997	1990[d]	1990[d]	1997	1995	2002[d]	1975	1997	2002
South Sudan											
Spain			1993	1988[d]	1988	1997	1993	2002	1986[d]	1996	2004
Sri Lanka	1994	1991	1993	1989[d]	1989[d]	1994	1994	2002[d]	1979[d]	1998[d]	2005
Sudan			1993	1993[d]	1993[d]	1985	1995	2004[d]	1982	1995	2006
Swaziland			1996	1992[d]	1992[d]	2009	1994	2006[d]	1997[d]	1996	2006[d]
Sweden			1993	1986	1988	1996	1993	2002	1974	1995	2002
Switzerland			1993	1987	1988		1994	2003	1974	1996	2003
Syrian Arab Republic	1999		1996[d]	1989[d]	1989[d]		1996	2006[d]	2003[d]	1997	2005
Tajikistan			1998[d]	1996[d]	1998[d]		1997[d]	2008[d]		1997[d]	2007
Tanzania	1994	1988	1996	1993[d]	1993[d]	1985	1996	2002[d]	1979	1997	2004
Thailand			1994	1989[d]	1989	2011	2003	2002	1983	2001[d]	2005
Togo	1991		1995[e]	1991[d]	1991	1985	1995[e]	2004[d]	1978	1995[e]	2004
Trinidad and Tobago			1994	1989[d]	1989[d]	1986	1996	1999	1984[d]	2000[d]	2002[d]
Tunisia	1994	1988	1993	1989[d]	1989[d]	1985	1993	2003[d]	1974	1995	2004
Turkey	1998		2004[d]	1991[d]	1991[d]		1997	2006[d]	1996[d]	1998	2009
Turkmenistan			1995[d]	1993[d]	1993[d]		1996[d]	1999[d]		1996	
Uganda	1994	1988	1993	1988[d]	1988	1990	1993	2002[d]	1991[d]	1997	2004[d]
Ukraine	1999		1997	1986[e]	1988[e]	1999	1995	2004	1999[d]	2002[d]	2007
United Arab Emirates			1995[d]	1989[d]	1989[d]		2000	2005[d]	1990[d]	1998[d]	2002
United Kingdom	1995	1994	1993	1987	1988	1997	1994	2002	1976	1996	2005
United States	1995	1995	1992	1986	1988				1974	2000	
Uruguay			1994	1989[d]	1991[d]	1992	1993	2001	1975	1999[d]	2004
Uzbekistan			1993[d]	1993[d]	1993[d]		1995[d]	1999	1997[d]	1995	
Venezuela			1994	1988[d]	1989		1994	2005[d]	1977	1998[d]	2005
Vietnam		1993	1994	1994[d]	1994[d]	1994	1994	2002	1994[d]	1998[d]	2002
West Bank and Gaza											
Yemen, Rep.	1996	1992	1996	1996[d]	1996[d]	1987	1996	2004[d]	1997[d]	1997[d]	2004
Zambia	1994		1993	1990[d]	1990[d]	1983	1993	2006	1980[d]	1996	2006
Zimbabwe	1987		1992	1992[d]	1992[d]	1993	1994	2009[d]	1981[d]	1997	

a. Ratification of the treaty. b. Year the treaty entered into force in the country. c. Convention of December 10, 1982. d. Accession. e. Acceptance. f. Approval. g. Succession. h. Continuation.

National environmental strategies and participation in international treaties on environmental issues provide some evidence of government commitment to sound environmental management. But the signing of these treaties does not always imply ratification, nor does it guarantee that governments will comply with treaty obligations.

In many countries efforts to halt environmental degradation have failed, primarily because governments have neglected to make this issue a priority, a reflection of competing claims on scarce resources. To address this problem, many countries are preparing national environmental strategies—some focusing narrowly on environmental issues, and others integrating environmental, economic, and social concerns. Among such initiatives are conservation strategies and environmental action plans. Some countries have also prepared country environmental profiles and biodiversity strategies and profiles.

National conservation strategies—promoted by the World Conservation Union (IUCN)—provide a comprehensive, cross-sectoral analysis of conservation and resource management issues to help integrate environmental concerns with the development process. Such strategies discuss current and future needs, institutional capabilities, prevailing technical conditions, and the status of natural resources in a country.

National environmental action plans, supported by the World Bank and other development agencies, describe a country's main environmental concerns, identify the principal causes of environmental problems, and formulate policies and actions to deal with them. These plans are a continuing process in which governments develop comprehensive environmental policies, recommend specific actions, and outline the investment strategies, legislation, and institutional arrangements required to implement them.

Biodiversity profiles—prepared by the World Conservation Monitoring Centre and the IUCN—provide basic background on species diversity, protected areas, major ecosystems and habitat types, and legislative and administrative support. In an effort to establish a scientific baseline for measuring progress in biodiversity conservation, the United Nations Environment Programme (UNEP) coordinates global biodiversity assessments.

To address global issues, many governments have also signed international treaties and agreements launched in the wake of the 1972 United Nations Conference on the Human Environment in Stockholm and the 1992 United Nations Conference on Environment and Development (the Earth Summit) in Rio de Janeiro, which produced Agenda 21—an array of actions to address environmental challenges:

· The Framework Convention on Climate Change aims to stabilize atmospheric concentrations of greenhouse gases at levels that will prevent human activities from interfering dangerously with the global climate.
· The Vienna Convention for the Protection of the Ozone Layer aims to protect human health and the environment by promoting research on the effects of changes in the ozone layer and on alternative substances (such as substitutes for chlorofluorocarbon) and technologies, monitoring the ozone layer, and taking measures to control the activities that produce adverse effects.
· The Montreal Protocol for Chlorofluorocarbon Control requires that countries help protect the earth from excessive ultraviolet radiation by cutting chlorofluorocarbon consumption by 20 percent over their 1986 level by 1994 and by 50 percent over their 1986 level by 1999, with allowances for increases in consumption by developing countries.
· The United Nations Convention on the Law of the Sea, which became effective in November 1994, establishes a comprehensive legal regime for seas and oceans, establishes rules for environmental standards and enforcement provisions, and develops international rules and national legislation to prevent and control marine pollution.
· The Convention on Biological Diversity promotes conservation of biodiversity through scientific and technological cooperation among countries, access to financial and genetic resources, and transfer of ecologically sound technologies.

But 10 years after the Earth Summit in Rio de Janeiro the World Summit on Sustainable Development in Johannesburg recognized that many of the proposed actions had yet to materialize. To help developing countries comply with their obligations under these agreements, the Global Environment Facility (GEF) was created to focus on global improvement in biodiversity, climate change, international waters, and ozone layer depletion. The UNEP, United Nations Development Programme, and World Bank manage the GEF according to the policies of its governing body of country representatives. The World Bank is responsible for the GEF Trust Fund and chairs the GEF.

· **Environmental strategies or action plans** provide a comprehensive analysis of conservation and resource management issues that integrate environmental concerns with development. They include national conservation strategies, environmental action plans, environmental management strategies, and sustainable development strategies. The date is the year a country adopted a strategy or action plan. · **Biodiversity assessments, strategies, or action plans** include biodiversity profiles (see *About the data*). · **Participation in treaties** covers nine international treaties (see *About the data*). · **Climate change** refers to the Framework Convention on Climate Change (signed in 1992). · **Ozone layer** refers to the Vienna Convention for the Protection of the Ozone Layer (signed in 1985). · **CFC control** refers to the Protocol on Substances That Deplete the Ozone Layer (the Montreal Protocol for Chlorofluorocarbon Control) (signed in 1987). · **Law of the Sea** refers to the United Nations Convention on the Law of the Sea (signed in 1982). · **Biological diversity** refers to the Convention on Biological Diversity (signed at the Earth Summit in 1992). · **Kyoto Protocol** refers to the protocol on climate change adopted at the third conference of the parties to the United Nations Framework Convention on Climate Change in December 1997. · **CITES** is the Convention on International Trade in Endangered Species of Wild Fauna and Flora, an agreement among governments to ensure that the survival of wild animals and plants is not threatened by uncontrolled exploitation. Adopted in 1973, it entered into force in 1975. · **CCD** is the United Nations Convention to Combat Desertification, an international convention addressing the problems of land degradation in the world's drylands. Adopted in 1994, it entered into force in 1996. · **Stockholm Convention** is an international legally binding instrument to protect human health and the environment from persistent organic pollutants. Adopted in 2001, it entered into force in 2004.

Data on environmental strategies and participation in international environmental treaties are from the Secretariat of the United Nations Framework Convention on Climate Change, the Ozone Secretariat of the UNEP, the World Resources Institute, the UNEP, the Center for International Earth Science Information Network, and the United Nations Treaty Series.

	Total natural resources rents	Oil rents	Natural gas rents	Coal rents	Mineral rents	Forest rents
	% of GDP 2010	% of GDP 2010	% of GDP 2010	% of GDP 2010	% of GDP 2010	% of GDP 2010
Afghanistan	2.3	..	..	0.0	0.0	2.3
Albania	3.6	3.0	0.0	0.0	0.5	0.1
Algeria	25.7	17.6	7.8	0.0	0.3	0.1
Angola	46.3	46.1	0.1	..	0.0	0.2
Argentina	6.1	4.0	1.4	0.0	0.6	0.1
Armenia	1.7	0.0	0.0	..	1.7	0.0
Australia	8.3	0.9	0.7	1.8	6.6	0.1
Austria	0.3	0.1	0.1	0.0	0.0	0.1
Azerbaijan	46.5	42.6	3.9	..	0.0	0.0
Bahrain	23.2	16.4	6.9	..	0.0	0.0
Bangladesh	3.3	0.0	2.8	0.1	0.0	0.5
Belarus	1.9	1.3	0.0	..	0.0	0.5
Belgium	0.0	0.0	0.0	0.0	0.0	0.0
Benin	1.7	0.0	0.0	..	0.0	1.7
Bolivia	18.1	4.6	9.0	..	4.2	0.4
Bosnia and Herzegovina	2.8	0.0	0.0	2.4	2.3	0.6
Botswana	4.7	0.0	0.0	0.4	4.6	0.1
Brazil	5.3	2.2	0.1	0.0	2.7	0.3
Bulgaria	2.3	0.0	0.0	1.1	2.0	0.3
Burkina Faso	7.1	..	..	..	4.1	2.9
Burundi	13.3	..	..	..	1.3	12.0
Cambodia	1.2	0.0	0.0	..	0.0	1.2
Cameroon	9.3	7.1	0.2	0.0	0.2	1.8
Canada	3.8	2.3	0.3	0.1	0.8	0.5
Central African Republic	5.9	..	..	..	0.0	5.8
Chad	43.3	41.2	..	..	0.0	2.1
Chile	18.9	0.0	0.1	0.0	18.3	0.5
China	4.0	1.5	0.1	3.8	2.2	0.2
Hong Kong SAR, China	0.0	0.0	0.0	..	0.0	0.0
Colombia	7.9	6.5	0.5	1.4	0.8	0.1
Congo, Dem. Rep.	29.8	3.9	0.0	0.1	16.4	9.5
Congo, Rep.	64.1	61.6	0.1	..	0.0	2.5
Costa Rica	0.4	0.0	0.0	..	0.1	0.3
Côte d'Ivoire	7.1	4.3	1.0	..	0.7	1.1
Croatia	1.2	0.5	0.5	0.0	0.0	0.2
Cuba	5.1	3.0	0.6	..	1.5	0.1
Cyprus	0.0	0.0	0.0	..	0.0	0.0
Czech Republic	0.3	0.0	0.0	0.7	0.0	0.3
Denmark	2.1	1.8	0.3	0.0	0.0	0.0
Dominican Republic	0.3	0.0	0.0	..	0.2	0.0
Ecuador	20.6	20.2	0.1	..	0.0	0.3
Egypt, Arab Rep.	10.1	5.9	3.9	0.0	0.3	0.1
El Salvador	0.5	0.0	0.0	..	0.0	0.5
Eritrea	0.6	0.0	0.0	..	0.0	0.6
Estonia	1.1	0.0	0.0	1.9	0.0	1.1
Ethiopia	4.7	0.0	0.0	..	0.3	4.4
Finland	0.8	0.0	0.0	..	0.2	0.7
France	0.1	0.0	0.0	0.0	0.0	0.1
Gabon	49.8	46.4	0.2	..	0.1	3.1
Gambia, The	2.5	..	..	..	0.0	2.5
Georgia	0.8	0.2	0.0	0.1	0.6	0.1
Germany	0.1	0.0	0.0	0.1	0.0	0.1
Ghana	10.5	0.0	0.0	..	8.8	1.6
Greece	0.2	0.0	0.0	0.3	0.1	0.0
Guatemala	2.4	0.8	0.0	..	0.8	0.8
Guinea	21.2	..	..	..	17.0	4.2
Guinea-Bissau	4.6	..	..	..	0.0	4.6
Haiti	0.6	0.0	0.0	..	0.0	0.6

Contribution of natural resources to gross domestic product

3.18

	Total natural resources rents	Oil rents	Natural gas rents	Coal rents	Mineral rents	Forest rents
	% of GDP	% of GDP	% of GDP	% of GDP	% of GDP	% of GDP
	2010	2010	2010	2010	2010	2010
Honduras	1.8	0.0	0.0	..	0.7	1.1
Hungary	0.6	0.3	0.2	0.1	0.0	0.1
India	4.0	1.0	0.4	2.6	2.1	0.6
Indonesia	6.0	2.4	0.9	3.4	1.9	0.7
Iran, Islamic Rep.	31.6	23.7	6.8	0.0	1.0	0.0
Iraq	69.3	69.1	0.2	..	0.0	0.0
Ireland	0.2	0.0	0.0	0.0	0.1	0.0
Israel	0.3	0.0	0.2	0.0	0.1	0.0
Italy	0.2	0.1	0.0	0.0	0.0	0.0
Jamaica	1.1	0.0	0.0	..	1.0	0.1
Japan	0.0	0.0	0.0	0.0	0.0	0.0
Jordan	1.6	0.0	0.1	..	1.5	0.0
Kazakhstan	27.6	22.4	2.7	5.5	2.5	0.1
Kenya	1.3	0.0	0.0	..	0.1	1.2
Korea, Dem. Rep.	..	..	..	..	..	..
Korea, Rep.	0.0	0.0	0.0	0.0	0.0	0.0
Kosovo	1.5	..	..	..	1.5	..
Kuwait	43.0	41.2	1.8	..	0.0	0.0
Kyrgyz Republic	9.2	0.7	0.0	0.4	8.5	0.0
Lao PDR	14.1	..	..	0.0	12.6	1.5
Latvia	1.5	0.0	0.0	..	0.0	1.5
Lebanon	0.0	0.0	0.0	..	0.0	0.0
Lesotho	1.3	..	..	..	0.0	1.3
Liberia	14.6	..	..	..	2.1	12.5
Libya	46.1	42.3	3.8	..	0.0	0.0
Lithuania	1.8	0.1	0.0	..	0.0	1.6
Macedonia, FYR	7.4	0.0	0.0	1.5	7.3	0.1
Madagascar	3.1	..	..	..	1.3	1.8
Malawi	4.1	..	..	..	0.0	4.1
Malaysia	10.9	6.3	3.9	0.1	0.1	0.6
Mali	15.0	..	..	..	14.0	1.1
Mauritania	54.7	..	..	..	54.2	0.5
Mauritius	0.0	..	..	..	0.0	0.0
Mexico	7.3	6.0	0.5	0.1	0.6	0.1
Moldova	0.2	0.1	0.0	..	0.0	0.1
Mongolia	23.4	2.0	0.0	22.9	21.2	0.2
Morocco	2.6	0.0	0.0	0.0	2.5	0.1
Mozambique	8.5	0.0	5.0	0.0	0.1	3.3
Myanmar	..	..	..	..	..	..
Namibia	1.0	0.0	0.0	..	1.0	0.1
Nepal	3.4	0.0	0.0	0.0	0.0	3.4
Netherlands	1.2	0.1	1.1	0.0	0.0	0.8
New Zealand	2.4	0.7	0.5	0.1	0.4	1.7
Nicaragua	3.0	0.0	0.0	..	1.3	2.0
Niger	3.3	..	..	0.0	1.3	0.9
Nigeria	32.6	29.5	2.2	0.0	0.0	0.1
Norway	13.1	10.1	2.9	0.0	0.0	0.0
Oman	39.2	31.6	7.6	..	0.0	0.7
Pakistan	3.9	0.8	2.3	0.1	0.1	0.1
Panama	0.1	0.0	0.0	..	0.0	4.1
Papua New Guinea	36.3	18.4	..	..	32.2	1.3
Paraguay	1.3	0.0	0.0	..	0.0	0.1
Peru	11.3	1.1	0.7	0.0	9.3	0.2
Philippines	2.6	0.1	0.3	0.2	2.0	0.2
Poland	1.0	0.1	0.1	1.3	0.6	0.1
Portugal	0.3	0.0	0.0	0.0	0.2	..
Puerto Rico	0.0	..	..	..	0.0	..
Qatar	27.9	13.4	14.5	..	0.0	..

3.18 | Contribution of natural resources to gross domestic product

	Total natural resources rents	Oil rents	Natural gas rents	Coal rents	Mineral rents	Forest rents
	% of GDP	% of GDP	% of GDP	% of GDP	% of GDP	% of GDP
	2010	2010	2010	2010	2010	2010
Romania	2.2	1.2	0.7	0.3	0.0	0.2
Russian Federation	19.9	14.2	3.6	1.4	1.7	0.3
Rwanda	3.4	..	..	..	0.1	3.3
Saudi Arabia	53.7	50.5	3.2	..	0.0	0.0
Senegal	2.4	0.0	0.0	..	1.2	1.1
Serbia	0.9	0.8	0.1	2.0	0.0	..
Sierra Leone	4.5	..	..	..	0.9	3.6
Singapore	0.0	0.0	0.0	..	0.0	0.0
Slovak Republic	0.4	0.0	0.0	0.0	0.0	0.3
Slovenia	0.2	0.0	0.0	0.2	0.0	0.2
Somalia	..	..	..	..	..	..
South Africa	4.6	0.0	0.0	5.1	3.8	0.8
South Sudan	..	..	..	..	..	..
Spain	0.1	0.0	0.0	0.0	0.0	0.0
Sri Lanka	0.5	0.0	0.0	..	0.0	0.5
Sudan	19.3	18.5	0.0	..	0.1	0.7
Swaziland	1.7	..	..	0.0	0.0	1.7
Sweden	1.2	0.0	0.0	0.0	0.7	0.5
Switzerland	0.0	0.0	0.0	..	0.0	0.0
Syrian Arab Republic	16.5	14.4	1.9	..	0.2	0.0
Tajikistan	0.9	0.2	0.1	0.3	0.6	0.0
Tanzania	6.8	0.0	0.5	0.0	4.2	2.1
Thailand	2.7	1.1	1.2	0.1	0.1	0.3
Timor-Leste	0.3	..	..	..	0.0	0.3
Togo	3.9	0.0	0.0	0.0	1.9	2.0
Trinidad and Tobago	37.3	11.5	25.8	..	0.0	0.0
Tunisia	6.7	4.4	1.0	..	1.1	0.1
Turkey	0.5	0.2	0.0	0.2	0.2	0.1
Turkmenistan	43.9	19.7	24.2	..	0.0	..
Uganda	4.9	..	..	..	0.0	4.9
Ukraine	2.9	0.9	1.7	3.1	0.1	0.3
United Arab Emirates	20.5	18.0	2.4	..	0.0	..
United Kingdom	1.5	1.2	0.3	0.0	0.0	0.0
United States	1.0	0.7	0.1	0.4	0.1	0.1
Uruguay	1.0	0.0	0.0	..	0.2	0.9
Uzbekistan	29.4	3.3	18.1	0.2	8.1	0.0
Venezuela, RB	19.6	18.0	0.9	0.1	0.7	0.0
Vietnam	10.4	8.0	1.3	3.1	0.3	0.7
West Bank and Gaza	..	..	..	..	..	..
Yemen, Rep.	21.9	19.0	3.0	..	0.0	0.0
Zambia	28.1	0.0	0.0	0.0	26.7	1.5
Zimbabwe	3.4	0.0	0.0	2.9	1.2	2.2
World	**4.0 w**	**1.8 w**	**0.4 w**	**0.8 w**	**0.8 w**	**0.2 w**
Low income	6.5	1.2	1.3	..	1.8	2.3
Middle income	9.8	4.6	0.9	2.0	2.0	0.3
Lower middle income	11.4	5.7	1.2	2.2	1.8	0.6
Upper middle income	9.3	4.3	0.8	2.0	2.1	0.2
Low & middle income	9.8	4.5	0.9	2.0	2.0	0.3
East Asia & Pacific	7.9	1.7	0.4	3.4	2.1	0.2
Europe & Central Asia	14.2	8.9	2.5	1.3	1.2	0.3
Latin America & Carib.	8.0	4.7	0.4	0.1	2.6	0.2
Middle East & N. Africa	18.7	14.9	3.2	0.0	0.6	0.1
South Asia	6.2	0.9	0.6	2.3	1.7	0.7
Sub-Saharan Africa	16.7	12.0	0.5	..	2.8	1.3
High income	1.4	0.6	0.2	0.2	0.3	0.1
Euro area	0.3	0.0	0.1	0.0	0.0	0.1

Note: Components may not sum to 100 percent because of rounding.

Accounting for the contribution of natural resources to economic output is important in building an analytical framework for sustainable development. In some countries earnings from natural resources, especially from fossil fuels and minerals, account for a sizable share of GDP, and much of these earnings come in the form of economic rents—revenues above the cost of extracting the resources. Natural resources give rise to economic rents because they are not produced. For produced goods and services competitive forces expand supply until economic profits are driven to zero, but natural resources in fixed supply often command returns well in excess of their cost of production. Rents from nonrenewable resources—fossil fuels and minerals—as well as rents from overharvesting of forests indicate the liquidation of a country's capital stock. When countries use such rents to support current consumption rather than to invest in new capital to replace what is being used up, they are, in effect, borrowing against their future.

The estimates of natural resources rents shown in the table are calculated as the difference between the price of a commodity and the average cost of producing it. This is done by estimating the world price of units of specific commodities and subtracting estimates of average unit costs of extraction or harvesting costs (including a normal return on capital). These unit rents are then multiplied by the physical quantities countries extract or harvest to determine the rents for each commodity as a share of gross domestic product (GDP).

This definition of economic rent differs from that used in the System of National Accounts, where rents are a form of property income, consisting of payments to landowners by a tenant for the use of the land or payments to the owners of subsoil assets by institutional units permitting them to extract subsoil deposits.

The *Environment* section of previous editions of *World Development Indicators* included a table "Toward a broader measure of savings," which showed the derivation of adjusted net savings, taking into account consumption of fixed and natural capital, pollution damage, and additions to human capital. Adjusted net savings measures the net additions or subtractions from a country's stock of tangible and intangible capital. This table is included in the *Economy* section as table 4.11, along with the closely related table 4.10, "Toward a broader measure of income."

• **Total natural resources rents** are the sum of oil rents, natural gas rents, coal rents (hard and soft), mineral rents, and forest rents. • **Oil rents** are the difference between the value of crude oil production at world prices and total costs of production. • **Natural gas rents** are the difference between the value of natural gas production at world prices and total costs of production. • **Coal rents** are the difference between the value of both hard and soft coal production at world prices and their total costs of production. • **Mineral rents** are the difference between the value of production for a stock of minerals at world prices and their total costs of production. Minerals included in the calculation are tin, gold, lead, zinc, iron, copper, nickel, silver, bauxite, and phosphate. • **Forest rents** are roundwood harvest times the product of average prices and a region-specific rental rate (based on a number of reviews; World Bank 2011c).

Data on contributions of natural resources to GDP are estimates based on sources and methods described in World Bank (2011c).

ECONOMY

The data in the *Economy* section provide a picture of the global economy and the economic activity of more than 200 countries and territories that produce, trade, and consume the world's output. The indicators measure changes in the size and structure of the global economy and the effects of these changes on national economies. They include measures of macroeconomic performance (gross domestic product [GDP], consumption, investment, and international trade), stability (central government budgets, prices, the money supply, and the balance of payments), and broader measures of income and savings adjusted for pollution, depreciation, and depletion of resources.

In 2010 the world economy grew 4.2 percent, a quick rebound from 2.3 percent in 2009 and well above the annual average of 2.9 percent since 2000. Total output measured in GDP at current prices increased more than $10 trillion. Upper middle-income economies, including China, were affected by slowing investment and widespread uncertainty in financial markets but still grew 7.8 percent. Lower middle-income economies grew 6.9 percent, and low-income economies grew 5.9 percent. High-income economies, accounting for 68 percent of the world's GDP, grew 3.1 percent in 2010. Developing economies grew faster over the last decade than in the previous two and faster than high-income economies. World output in 2010 reached $63 trillion, measured in GDP at current prices—a nominal increase of 96 percent increase over 2000. Developing economies' share of global output increased from 18 percent to 31 percent. The developing economies in East Asia and Pacific grew the most, quadrupling their output and more than doubling their share of global output from 5 percent to 12 percent.

The accuracy of GDP estimates and their comparability across countries depend on timely revisions to data on GDP and its components. The frequency of revisions to GDP data varies: some countries revise numbers monthly, others quarterly or annually, and others less frequently. Such revisions are usually small and based on additional information received during the year. However, in some cases larger revisions are required because of new methodologies, changes to the base year, or changes in coverage. Comprehensive revisions of GDP data usually result in upward adjustments as improved data sources increase the coverage of the economy and as new weights for growing industries more accurately reflect their contributions to the economy. Revisions to data can lead to changes in income or lending classification, but such changes have been rare.

Revisions to GDP data may cause breaks in series unless they are applied consistently to historical data. For constant price series a break caused by rebasing can be eliminated by linking the old series to the new using historical growth rates. But for nominal GDP data a break in the time series cannot be avoided unless the statistics office revises historical series. Other data series are affected by revisions to GDP. Because rebasing real GDP and its components leaves the pre–base year current price series unchanged, the GDP deflator calculated from these two series is skewed for pre–base years. Other series affected by the break in GDP are fiscal indicators expressed as a percentage of GDP. When nominal GDP is revised upward, the ratio of revenue and expenditure to GDP look smaller than previously reported. Information on significant revisions and breaks in series will be included in the next release of the World Development Indicators database.

4.a | Recent economic performance

	Gross domestic product		Exports of goods and services		Imports of goods and services		GDP deflator		Current account balance		Gross international reserves	
	average annual % growth		average annual % growth		average annual % growth		average annual % growth		% of GDP		$ millions	months of import coverage
	2010	2011[a]	2010	2011[a]	2010	2011[a]	2010	2011[a]	2010	2011[a]	2011[a]	2011[a]
Albania	3.5	3.0	4.2	5.0	−8.5	3.2	3.5	1.9	−11.9	−11.7	2,421	4.1
Algeria	3.3	3.0	..	..	..	..	16.2	9.6	..	..	183,122	36.2
Angola	2.3	7.0	..	..	..	..	26.6	12.4	8.8	7.0	28,348	6.3
Antigua and Barbuda	−5.2	3.0	..	..	..	..	2.0	−3.9	−13.7	−13.9	148	2.5
Argentina	9.2	7.5	14.6	5.5	34.0	9.9	15.4	23.4	0.8	0.0	43,321	6.1
Armenia	2.1	4.2	21.7	6.0	13.8	7.5	9.2	6.6	−14.7	−12.8	1,959	4.8
Australia	2.3	1.7	5.3	5.2	5.1	9.2	0.1	4.1	−2.8	−2.2	42,921	1.7
Austria	2.3	2.8	8.3	6.6	8.0	5.9	1.8	2.0	3.0	2.5	11,482	0.6
Azerbaijan	5.0	0.2	24.2	1.0	1.3	2.5	11.2	17.7	29.1	26.6	10,274	9.3
Bangladesh	6.1	6.5	0.9	12.3	0.7	10.5	6.5	9.9	2.1	0.7	8,533	2.9
Belarus	7.6	3.8	7.1	7.2	11.9	2.0	10.2	35.2	−15.2	−15.7	6,076	1.7
Belgium	2.3	2.1	9.9	4.5	8.7	5.0	1.8	1.9	1.4	−0.5	18,311	0.5
Belize	2.9	2.1	..	..	..	..	0.9	5.2	−3.3	−3.3	237	3.1
Benin	3.0	3.4	..	..	..	..	1.8	1.3	..	..	976	4.3
Bolivia	4.1	4.5	9.9	5.6	11.0	5.4	8.8	11.9	4.4	4.7	9,984	17.4
Botswana	7.2	6.8	1.2	7.2	5.0	5.1	14.7	12.0	0.3	−3.3	8,337	16.7
Brazil	7.5	2.9	11.5	4.4	36.2	9.7	7.3	6.9	−2.3	−2.5	350,414	14.0
Bulgaria	0.2	2.0	16.2	5.0	4.5	5.0	2.9	−0.3	−1.5	1.3	15,321	5.6
Burkina Faso	9.2	5.8	..	..	..	..	4.0	9.5	..	..	843	3.1
Burundi	3.9	4.4	..	..	..	..	7.8	4.6	−18.7	−13.4	282	5.3
Cambodia	6.0	6.1	20.6	5.2	16.8	3.4	3.1	4.6	−7.8	−12.1	3,471	4.6
Cameroon	2.6	3.8	−0.3	7.4	4.6	7.3	3.2	4.5	−3.8	−2.9	3,199	5.2
Canada	3.2	2.3	6.4	4.2	13.1	6.0	2.9	4.1	−3.1	−2.7	65,658	1.4
Cape Verde	5.4	5.8	..	..	..	..	3.3	−4.4	−11.2	−16.7	278	2.4
Central African Republic	3.3	4.0	..	..	..	..	3.2	2.6	..	..	155	5.6
Chad	4.3	6.0	..	..	..	..	11.6	19.9	..	. ..	951	4.1
Chile	5.2	6.2	−0.3	5.7	26.3	10.5	14.4	4.6	1.8	−0.4	41,932	6.0
China	10.4	9.1	28.4	11.3	20.1	14.4	6.6	4.9	5.2	3.7	3,204,610	19.7
Hong Kong SAR, China	7.0	4.7	16.8	4.9	17.3	5.0	0.5	12.1	5.7	−0.5	285,306	6.2
Colombia	4.3	4.9	1.2	7.0	18.1	6.8	3.1	3.8	−3.1	−2.5	30,504	6.7
Comoros	2.1	2.3	..	..	..	..	3.8	5.0	..	..	161	11.6
Congo, Dem. Rep.	7.2	6.7	9.4	16.0	17.0	13.6	22.4	15.2	..	..	1,273	2.3
Congo, Rep.	8.8	5.1	..	..	..	..	19.8	14.7	..	..	5,641	6.2
Costa Rica	4.2	3.8	5.4	6.1	15.2	7.6	7.8	4.9	−4.0	−5.2	4,756	3.2
Côte d'Ivoire	3.0	−5.8	−0.5	−2.0	7.6	5.1	0.7	−6.5	..	..	4,192	4.7
Croatia	−1.2	1.2	6.0	5.8	−1.3	5.5	1.0	2.0	−1.6	−2.8	14,484	7.0
Czech Republic	2.3	2.1	18.0	5.0	18.0	6.8	−1.2	2.4	−3.1	−3.7	39,692	2.9

	Gross domestic product		Exports of goods and services		Imports of goods and services		GDP deflator		Current account balance		Gross international reserves	
	average annual % growth		average annual % growth		average annual % growth		average annual % growth		% of GDP		$ millions	months of import coverage
	2010	2011[a]	2010	2011[a]	2010	2011[a]	2010	2011[a]	2010	2011[a]	2011[a]	2011[a]
Denmark	1.3	1.3	3.2	6.6	3.5	5.4	3.9	3.2	5.5	5.8	81,794	6.1
Dominica	0.1	0.9	..	..	..	..	0.0	4.9	−15.3	−21.9	81	3.5
Dominican Republic	7.8	4.9	11.6	6.8	14.4	5.1	5.1	8.4	−8.6	−8.2	3,755	2.4
Ecuador	3.6	5.1	2.3	4.6	16.3	7.0	7.6	7.2	−3.1	−2.7	1,710	0.9
Egypt, Arab Rep.	5.1	0.5	−3.0	−4.8	−3.2	−11.7	10.1	15.1	−2.1	1.8	15,046	3.3
El Salvador	1.4	1.5	12.3	7.5	11.1	7.0	1.2	3.4	−2.3	−3.8	2,165	2.4
Equatorial Guinea	0.9	2.8	..	..	..	..	19.1	6.9	..	..	3,054	7.8
Eritrea	2.2	8.2	..	..	..	..	11.6	14.7	..	..	113	1.8
Estonia	3.1	7.6	10.7	6.1	8.8	6.5	1.5	5.4	3.5	0.9	195	0.1
Ethiopia	10.1	7.7	14.4	9.0	15.9	11.0	3.8	10.8	−1.4	−10.6	..	..
Fiji	0.3	1.3	..	..	..	..	8.1	0.4	−12.9	−7.2	832	4.6
Finland	3.7	3.1	8.6	0.0	7.4	3.5	0.4	2.2	1.9	1.0	7,942	0.9
France	1.5	1.6	9.7	5.7	8.8	5.0	0.8	1.5	−1.7	−2.0	52,819	0.8
Gabon	5.7	6.0	3.0	3.7	9.3	9.6	18.0	11.4	..	..	2,157	5.0
Gambia, The	5.0	5.3	4.1	4.7	7.0	4.3	8.4	5.5	6.5	1.9	223	8.2
Georgia	6.4	5.4	..	..	..	..	8.7	−1.7	−11.5	−10.4	2,818	4.6
Germany	3.7	3.0	13.7	5.9	11.7	6.8	0.6	1.9	5.7	5.3	72,796	0.5
Ghana	6.6	13.6	53.7	41.0	69.4	35.9	14.0	22.7	−8.6	−7.0	..	..
Greece	−3.5	−5.4	4.2	−1.0	−7.2	−10.0	1.7	2.3	−10.3	−8.6	1,442	0.2
Guatemala	2.8	2.8	4.4	4.5	12.4	5.5	5.0	8.7	−1.5	−2.2	5,847	3.8
Guinea	1.9	4.3	1.5	1.8	0.1	5.1	19.7	10.1	−7.2	−14.2	..	..
Guinea-Bissau	3.5	4.8	..	..	..	..	1.7	−9.2	..	..	225	9.4
Guyana	3.6	4.6	..	..	..	..	5.9	3.9	−7.2	−10.6	798	5.4
Haiti	−5.1	6.7	−7.3	14.5	19.7	0.2	5.4	3.2	−2.5	−13.4	1,389	3.5
Honduras	2.8	3.4	6.0	2.7	10.2	2.9	5.7	7.3	−6.2	−6.4	2,751	2.9
Hungary	1.3	3.4	14.3	8.7	12.8	7.9	3.1	5.3	1.1	2.8	48,686	5.4
Iceland	−4.0	2.8	0.4	6.2	4.0	6.7	6.9	1.7	−8.0	−8.1	8,454	14.9
India	8.8	7.0	17.9	23.0	9.2	14.0	10.5	9.1	−3.0	−3.4	272,249	5.7
Indonesia	6.1	6.5	14.9	15.9	17.3	13.6	8.0	7.1	0.8	0.4	106,665	6.4
Ireland	−0.4	2.2	6.3	7.8	2.7	6.8	−2.4	2.0	0.5	0.6	1,410	0.1
Israel	4.7	4.5	13.4	4.3	12.5	12.5	1.1	2.6	2.9	0.6	74,874	9.5
Italy	1.5	0.7	12.2	6.2	12.7	4.8	0.4	2.0	−3.5	−3.9	53,421	0.9
Jamaica	−0.6	1.3	..	..	..	..	10.6	7.3	−6.6	−11.2	2,273	3.8
Japan	4.0	−0.2	23.9	0.5	9.8	3.5	−2.2	−1.2	3.6	2.2	1,259,494	16.0
Jordan	3.1	2.5	7.6	−3.7	7.1	−0.5	6.3	1.4	−4.8	−8.5	11,489	6.8
Kazakhstan	7.3	6.6	1.9	11.0	−4.0	11.0	19.5	12.9	2.0	6.3	25,316	5.7
Kenya	5.3	4.3	6.1	8.9	3.0	8.6	3.9	10.1	−8.0	−9.2	4,264	3.4

	Gross domestic product		Exports of goods and services		Imports of goods and services		GDP deflator		Current account balance		Gross international reserves	
	average annual % growth		average annual % growth		average annual % growth		average annual % growth		% of GDP		$ millions	months of import coverage
	2010	**2011ᵃ**	**2010**	**2011ᵃ**	**2010**	**2011ᵃ**	**2010**	**2011ᵃ**	**2010**	**2011ᵃ**	**2011ᵃ**	**2011ᵃ**
Korea, Rep.	6.2	3.8	14.5	9.1	16.9	6.3	3.7	1.5	2.8	2.5	304,349	5.8
Kyrgyz Republic	−1.4	5.5	−4.2	6.5	1.6	5.5	6.9	17.8	−8.3	−6.4	1,707	4.2
Lao PDR	9.4	7.9	29.3	6.5	4.1	5.0	9.4	7.7	0.4	−14.0	..	..
Latvia	−0.3	3.8	10.3	7.0	8.6	5.0	−2.3	6.4	3.0	−0.7	6,011	4.5
Lebanon	7.0	3.0	0.4	−9.1	−7.8	−4.1	4.4	2.4	−22.8	−20.6	34,236	12.7
Lesotho	3.3	3.1	2.2	5.9	9.6	5.4	3.7	−0.7	−19.8	−24.5	..	..
Lithuania	1.3	5.8	16.3	5.8	17.6	9.0	2.0	10.0	1.5	−2.3	7,925	3.4
Luxembourg	2.7	1.9	2.8	6.0	4.6	6.2	4.9	2.4	7.7	6.1	904	0.2
Macedonia, FYR	1.8	3.8	23.4	7.2	10.9	5.8	2.2	0.7	−2.2	−5.1	2,343	4.0
Madagascar	1.6	2.6	..	..	..	..	8.1	9.2	..	..	1,279	4.2
Malawi	7.1	5.6	..	..	..	..	7.7	9.2	..	..	212	1.1
Malaysia	7.2	4.8	9.9	4.1	15.1	5.2	5.1	4.1	11.5	9.7	131,867	7.0
Mali	4.5	5.4	..	..	..	..	3.6	2.1	..	..	1,418	5.2
Mauritania	5.0	5.1	..	..	..	..	19.3	5.6	..	..	485	3.3
Mauritius	4.0	4.1	−4.2	1.9	−0.6	13.5	1.6	1.6	−8.2	−11.1	2,589	4.3
Mexico	5.4	4.0	25.6	8.6	23.5	7.2	4.4	2.7	−0.6	−0.8	144,174	4.5
Moldova	6.9	6.0	12.8	20.0	13.7	10.0	11.2	3.7	−8.3	−9.4	1,965	4.1
Morocco	3.7	4.3	16.3	7.3	3.3	8.8	0.6	−0.7	−4.3	−6.7	19,572	4.7
Mozambique	7.2	7.4	2.2	7.3	1.7	6.0	12.7	9.5	−11.6	−13.6	2,473	6.5
Namibia	4.8	3.9	−42.3	10.9	−60.0	1.9	9.3	3.9	0.3	−0.5	1,796	3.3
Nepal	4.6	4.0	−13.7	22.1	26.7	13.5	13.4	11.6	..	..	3,567	6.1
Netherlands	1.7	1.4	10.8	6.2	10.6	5.7	1.3	1.8	6.6	7.3	21,322	0.4
Nicaragua	7.6	4.1	13.2	6.1	10.8	7.9	2.9	7.9	−14.7	−16.3	1,892	3.1
Niger	8.8	6.0	..	..	..	..	1.7	3.7	..	..	659	3.3
Nigeria	7.9	7.0	..	..	..	..	7.5	23.5	1.3	14.3	35,249	4.8
Norway	0.7	1.6	1.8	6.3	9.9	6.7	6.4	6.3	12.3	16.9	49,273	4.3
Pakistan	4.1	3.2	15.8	11.7	4.4	8.8	12.0	11.2	−0.8	0.5	14,636	3.7
Panama	4.8	8.1	6.2	7.1	21.2	7.7	3.0	5.3	−10.7	−12.3	1,792	1.0
Papua New Guinea	8.0	9.0	..	..	..	..	9.3	9.8	−6.7	−24.0	4,172	6.2
Paraguay	15.0	4.9	34.3	4.0	29.3	5.1	6.7	10.6	−3.5	−3.1	4,951	4.8
Peru	8.8	6.3	2.5	7.2	23.8	9.1	6.9	4.2	−1.5	−2.7	47,266	12.9
Philippines	7.6	3.7	21.0	−7.7	22.5	1.6	4.2	5.0	4.5	2.1	67,565	9.7
Poland	3.9	4.0	12.1	6.1	13.9	7.1	1.4	2.9	−4.7	−5.1	92,824	4.6
Portugal	1.4	−1.5	8.8	6.0	5.4	−1.5	1.0	2.3	−10.0	−7.6	2,635	0.3
Romania	0.9	2.4	10.5	14.7	10.5	11.9	3.6	5.4	−4.0	−4.5	43,118	6.0
Russian Federation	4.0	4.1	7.1	5.0	25.6	10.0	11.4	11.7	4.7	5.1	455,474	13.9

Recent economic performance 4.a

	Gross domestic product		Exports of goods and services		Imports of goods and services		GDP deflator		Current account balance		Gross international reserves	
	average annual % growth		average annual % growth		average annual % growth		average annual % growth		% of GDP		$ millions	months of import coverage
	2010	2011ᵃ	2010	2011ᵃ	2010	2011ᵃ	2010	2011ᵃ	2010	2011ᵃ	2011ᵃ	2011ᵃ
Rwanda	7.5	7.2	..	..	..	..	2.1	3.8	−7.5	−6.1	825	4.8
Saudi Arabia	3.8	5.0	..	..	..	..	12.4	15.3	15.4	23.3	541,234	34.3
Senegal	4.2	4.2	5.7	5.2	3.5	4.4	1.4	4.4	..	..	2,536	4.2
Seychelles	6.2	4.0	..	..	..	..	−0.8	2.0	−24.0	−33.8	252	2.0
Sierra Leone	4.9	5.6	..	..	..	..	14.4	9.1	−16.8	−13.6	432	7.0
Singapore	14.5	4.8	19.2	4.0	16.6	5.0	−0.5	4.0	23.7	20.5	237,874	5.9
Slovak Republic	4.2	3.0	16.5	8.1	16.3	8.7	0.5	4.0	−3.4	−2.3	908	0.1
Slovenia	1.4	2.8	9.5	3.0	7.2	−2.6	−1.1	−3.0	−0.8	−0.6	836	0.3
South Africa	2.8	3.2	16.5	5.0	5.5	11.0	8.1	6.8	−2.8	−3.0	42,811	4.1
Spain	−0.1	0.7	10.3	5.9	5.4	0.5	1.0	2.1	−4.6	−3.5	33,330	0.9
Sri Lanka	8.0	7.7	5.8	15.0	13.0	16.5	7.3	7.0	−2.9	−3.8	6,095	3.8
St. Lucia	3.1	2.7	..	..	..	..	5.1	−3.5	−14.6	−21.4	213	3.0
St. Vincent & Grenadines	−1.3	−0.2	..	..	..	..	2.1	6.2	−29.2	−29.1	90	2.6
Sudan	4.5	5.3	..	..	..	..	17.6	4.1	0.3	−7.2	220	0.2
Swaziland	1.1	−2.1	−2.4	5.3	0.9	4.7	6.1	5.0	−10.7	−15.8	601	2.5
Sweden	5.6	4.1	11.1	6.8	12.7	7.0	1.2	0.9	6.6	6.6	44,243	2.3
Switzerland	2.7	1.7	8.4	7.4	7.3	5.9	0.1	−0.1	14.0	13.0	281,187	10.0
Syrian Arab Republic	3.2	−3.0	5.7	−3.5	8.3	5.8	6.3	7.5	−0.6	−2.2	16,714	9.5
Tanzania	7.0	6.4	10.7	3.9	10.9	6.7	7.7	8.3	−8.6	−9.1	3,726	4.9
Thailand	7.8	2.0	14.7	8.8	21.5	13.1	3.7	1.9	4.1	0.7	167,652	7.7
Togo	3.4	3.7	..	..	..	..	1.4	3.3	..	..	746	4.6
Trinidad and Tobago	0.1	2.8	..	..	..	..	4.4	10.3	..	..	10,106	13.7
Tunisia	3.7	−0.5	4.8	−1.2	3.8	−2.2	4.0	−5.9	−4.8	−5.8	7,652	3.5
Turkey	9.0	7.9	3.4	6.0	20.7	13.0	6.3	8.9	−6.4	−9.8	78,660	3.8
Uganda	5.2	6.3	5.6	6.4	7.8	16.0	9.1	4.3	−10.2	−12.1	2,617	4.0
Ukraine	4.2	4.5	4.5	6.5	11.1	9.0	15.0	6.5	−2.2	−4.4	30,458	4.0
United Kingdom	2.1	1.0	7.4	6.0	8.6	0.3	2.9	3.8	−3.3	−1.5	79,808	1.2
United States	3.0	1.7	11.3	6.6	12.5	3.9	0.8	2.5	−3.2	−3.4	150,964	0.7
Uruguay	8.5	5.5	8.5	7.1	16.2	7.1	5.1	6.8	−0.4	−2.0	10,289	10.3
Uzbekistan	8.5	7.5	..	..	..	..	18.5	19.6	..	..	..	..
Vanuatu	3.0	3.9	..	..	..	..	2.8	5.5	..	..	176	5.8
Venezuela, RB	−1.5	3.1	−12.9	6.1	−2.9	7.9	46.7	59.8	3.1	7.9	10,562	2.4
Vietnam	6.8	5.6	14.7	18.2	14.1	14.5	11.9	12.0	−4.0	−4.9	..	..
Yemen, Rep.	8.0	−6.0	15.8	0.2	−6.8	−1.0	24.7	19.8	−3.9	9.6	4,519	4.4
Zambia	7.6	6.8	..	..	..	..	11.7	16.9	3.8	4.9	2,324	4.3
Zimbabwe	9.0	5.0	21.5	14.1	6.6	8.0	17.5	3.3	..	..	..	..

a. Data are preliminary estimates based on World Bank staff estimates and national sources.
Source: World Development Indicators data files, the World Bank's *Global Economic Prospects 2012,* and the International Monetary Fund's *International Financial Statistics.*

	Gross domestic product		Agriculture		Industry		Manufacturing		Services	
	average annual % growth		average annual % growth		average annual % growth		average annual % growth		average annual % growth	
	1990–2000	2000–10	1990–2000	2000–10	1990–2000	2000–10	1990–2000	2000–10	1990–2000	2000–10
Afghanistan	..	11.3	..	6.3	..	14.5	..	9.5	..	14.2
Albania	3.8	5.4	4.3	1.4	–0.5	4.7	..	..	6.9	8.1
Algeria	1.9	3.9	3.6	4.2	1.8	3.2	–2.1	2.0	1.8	5.2
Angola[a]	1.6	12.9	–1.4	14.2	4.4	12.7	–0.3	19.3	–2.2	12.9
Argentina	4.3	5.6[b]	3.5	2.9	3.8	6.0	2.7	5.9	4.5	5.0
Armenia	–1.9	9.2	0.5	6.0	–7.4	9.2	–4.3	5.8	6.7	10.4
Australia	3.7	3.2	3.4	1.7	2.8	2.8	1.7	0.9	4.0	3.6
Austria	2.5	1.8	–0.1	1.3	2.5	2.0	2.5	2.6	2.7	2.0
Azerbaijan	–6.3	17.1	–1.7	4.7	–2.1	22.4	–15.7	8.3	–1.6	14.5
Bahrain	5.0	6.6	..	..	..	..	..	..	..	..
Bangladesh	4.8	5.9	2.9	3.5	7.3	7.7	7.2	7.8	4.5	6.1
Belarus	–1.6	8.0	–4.0	5.5	–1.8	12.0	–0.7	10.7	–0.4	5.4
Belgium	2.2	1.6	..	..	1.8	0.6	..	..	..	..
Benin[a]	4.8	4.0	5.8	4.6	4.1	3.8	5.8	2.7	4.2	3.2
Bolivia	4.0	4.1	2.9	2.9	4.1	5.4	3.8	4.4	4.3	3.1
Bosnia and Herzegovina	..	4.6	..	4.3	..	6.3	..	6.5	..	3.9
Botswana	5.7	4.1	–0.7	0.9	5.4	3.2	3.5	5.1	7.5	4.7
Brazil	2.7	3.7	3.6	3.6	2.4	2.8	2.0	2.5	3.8	3.9
Bulgaria	–1.1	4.8	–3.9	–2.3	–19.5	5.3	..	5.8	..	5.6
Burkina Faso	5.5	5.5	5.9	6.2	5.9	7.3	5.9	6.3	3.9	5.5
Burundi	–2.9	3.2	–1.9	–1.5	–4.3	–6.2	..	..	–2.8	10.4
Cambodia	7.0	8.7	3.7	5.6	14.3	10.6	18.6	10.2	7.1	9.2
Cameroon	1.7	3.2	5.4	3.4	–0.9	–0.4	1.4	..	0.2	6.2
Canada	3.1	2.0	1.1	1.5	3.2	0.1	4.5	–1.6	3.1	3.0
Central African Republic	2.0	1.0	3.8	0.3	0.7	–0.4	–0.2	–0.1	0.2	–2.5
Chad	2.2	9.0	4.9	..	0.6	..	..	..	0.8	..
Chile	6.6	4.0	2.2	4.2	5.6	2.3	4.4	2.7	6.9	4.4
China[a]	10.6	10.8	4.1	4.4	13.7	11.8	12.9	11.6	11.0	11.5
Hong Kong SAR, China	3.6	4.6	..	–3.9	..	–2.7	..	–3.6	..	4.9
Colombia	2.8	4.5	–2.7	2.2	1.4	4.5	–2.5	3.9	4.1	4.7
Congo, Dem. Rep.	–4.9	5.3	1.4	1.7	–8.0	8.7	–8.7	6.3	–13.0	11.2
Congo, Rep.[a]	1.0	4.3	..	..	..	..	..	..	..	..
Costa Rica	5.3	4.9	4.1	3.3	6.2	4.8	6.8	4.4	4.7	5.4
Côte d'Ivoire[a]	3.2	1.1	3.5	1.6	6.3	0.3	5.5	–1.1	2.0	1.2
Croatia	0.5	3.2	–5.5	1.9	–2.2	2.8	–3.5	1.6	2.2	3.9
Cuba	–0.7	6.7	–3.3	–0.9	–1.0	2.3	0.8	–1.5	–0.7	8.3
Cyprus	4.2	3.1	1.4	–3.3	0.6	3.0	0.2	0.1	6.5	3.9
Czech Republic	1.1	3.8	0.0	0.4	0.2	5.5	4.3	6.9	1.2	3.2
Denmark	2.7	0.9	4.6	–0.7	2.4	–0.8	2.2	0.2	2.7	1.2
Dominican Republic[a]	6.3	5.6	1.9	3.4	7.1	2.6	7.0	2.8	5.9	7.1
Ecuador	1.9	4.8	–1.7	4.4	2.6	5.4	1.5	5.2	2.4	2.8
Egypt, Arab Rep.	4.4	5.1	3.1	3.3	5.1	5.5	6.3	4.9	4.1	5.4
El Salvador	4.8	2.2	1.2	3.1	5.1	1.4	5.2	1.7	4.0	2.4
Eritrea	5.7	0.2	1.5	2.7	15.0	0.6	10.6	–6.0	5.7	0.6
Estonia	0.4	4.6	–6.2	–2.9	–2.4	8.6	7.3	8.9	3.2	7.1
Ethiopia	3.8	8.8	2.6	7.1	4.1	9.3	3.9	7.6	5.2	10.9
Finland	2.7	2.1	–0.3	2.7	3.4	3.0	6.4	3.3	2.8	1.5
France	1.9	1.3	2.0	0.3	0.9	0.5	..	0.1	2.2	1.7
Gabon[a]	2.3	2.2	2.0	1.5	1.6	0.8	3.0	3.0	3.1	3.3
Gambia, The	3.0	3.7	3.3	3.2	1.0	7.3	0.9	..	3.7	6.2
Georgia	–7.1	6.9	–11.0	0.0	–8.1	9.3	..	10.2	–0.3	8.4
Germany	1.6	1.0	0.1	–0.2	–0.1	0.1	0.1	0.5	2.6	1.7
Ghana	4.3	5.9	..	..	..	..	..	..	..	..
Greece	2.2	2.6	..	..	1.0	0.8	..	..	..	..
Guatemala	4.2	3.6	2.8	2.9	4.3	2.5	2.8	2.6	4.7	4.4
Guinea	4.4	2.9	4.3	5.0	4.9	4.6	4.0	3.1	3.6	–2.1
Guinea-Bissau	1.2	1.5	..	..	..	..	..	..	..	..
Haiti	0.5	0.6	..	..	..	..	..	..	..	..

Growth of output 4.1

	Gross domestic product		Agriculture		Industry		Manufacturing		Services	
	average annual % growth		average annual % growth		average annual % growth		average annual % growth		average annual % growth	
	1990–2000	2000–10	1990–2000	2000–10	1990–2000	2000–10	1990–2000	2000–10	1990–2000	2000–10
Honduras ·	3.2	4.6	2.2	3.2	3.6	3.6	4.0	4.1	3.8	5.9
Hungary	1.0	2.2	–1.9	3.4	3.7	2.1	7.9	3.4	0.5	2.1
India	5.9	8.0	3.2	3.0	6.1	8.5	6.7	8.7	7.7	9.6
Indonesia[a]	4.2	5.3	2.0	3.5	5.2	4.1	6.7	4.6	4.0	7.3
Iran, Islamic Rep.	3.1	5.4	3.2	5.9	2.6	6.9	5.1	9.9	3.8	5.3
Iraq	..	0.4	..	..	..	..	..	..	..	..
Ireland	7.4	2.8	0.0	–4.6	11.5	3.7	..	..	..	3.8
Israel[a]	5.5	3.6	..	..	..	..	..	..	..	..
Italy	1.5	0.5	2.1	–0.1	1.0	–0.8	1.6	–1.4	1.7	1.0
Jamaica	1.6	1.2	–0.6	–0.2	–0.8	–0.3	–1.8	–1.5	3.8	1.7
Japan	1.0	0.9	–0.4	–0.8	–0.4	0.5	0.5	1.6	1.7	1.3
Jordan	5.0	6.7	–3.0	8.2	5.2	7.9	5.6	8.9	5.0	6.1
Kazakhstan	–4.1	8.3	–8.0	3.8	–8.6	9.0	..	6.3	1.1	8.3
Kenya	2.2	4.3	1.9	1.9	1.2	4.9	1.3	4.3	3.2	4.5
Korea, Dem. Rep.	..	..	..	..	..	..	..	..	..	..
Korea, Rep.	5.8	4.1	1.6	2.0	6.0	5.4	7.3	6.3	5.6	3.6
Kosovo	..	5.3	..	..	..	..	..	..	..	..
Kuwait[a]	4.9	8.4	1.0	..	0.3	..	–0.1	..	3.5	..
Kyrgyz Republic	–4.1	4.4	1.5	0.0	–10.3	1.1	–7.5	–0.6	–5.2	10.9
Lao PDR	6.4	7.2	4.8	3.4	11.1	13.1	11.7	–0.2	6.6	7.3
Latvia	–1.5	4.8	–5.2	2.8	–8.3	3.7	–7.3	2.5	2.7	5.7
Lebanon	5.3	4.9	2.9	0.8	–0.2	4.3	1.9	0.9	1.5	4.9
Lesotho	4.0	3.5	2.8	–1.9	5.5	3.4	7.9	4.7	4.5	3.8
Liberia	4.1	0.9	..	..	..	..	..	..	..	..
Libya	..	5.4	..	..	..	..	..	..	..	..
Lithuania	–2.5	5.3	–0.4	1.9	3.3	5.8	6.6	7.1	5.8	5.3
Macedonia, FYR	–0.8	3.3	0.2	1.9	–2.3	3.3	–5.3	1.9	0.5	3.6
Madagascar	2.0	3.4	1.8	2.4	2.4	4.2	2.0	5.1	2.3	3.6
Malawi	3.7	5.2	8.6	2.9	2.0	6.2	0.5	5.7	1.6	6.5
Malaysia[a]	7.0	5.0	0.3	3.3	8.6	3.3	9.5	4.1	7.3	6.9
Mali	4.1	5.2	2.6	4.8	6.4	4.5	–1.4	5.1	3.0	6.5
Mauritania	2.9	4.4	–0.2	1.3	3.4	4.4	5.8	–0.9	4.9	5.2
Mauritius	5.2	3.9	0.0	0.1	5.4	1.8	5.3	0.6	6.3	5.6
Mexico	3.1	2.1	1.5	1.7	3.8	1.3	4.3	1.1	2.9	2.5
Moldova	–9.6	5.2	–11.2	–0.9	–13.6	–1.7	–7.1	1.0	0.7	10.1
Mongolia	1.0	7.2	0.3	4.6	1.5	5.8	–6.6	6.1	–0.9	8.9
Morocco	2.4	4.9	–0.4	5.9	3.2	3.8	2.6	3.0	3.1	4.9
Mozambique	6.1	7.8	5.2	8.3	12.3	8.5	10.2	7.1	5.0	6.9
Myanmar[a]	..	..	..	..	..	..	..	..	..	..
Namibia	4.0	5.0	3.8	–2.4	2.4	1.1	7.4	0.2	4.2	6.9
Nepal	4.9	3.8	2.5	3.2	7.1	2.5	8.9	0.7	6.2	4.4
Netherlands	3.2	1.6	1.8	1.6	1.7	0.8	2.6	1.1	3.5	2.1
New Zealand	3.3	2.6	2.9	2.0	2.5	1.1	..	..	3.6	3.1
Nicaragua	3.7	3.6	4.7	2.9	5.5	3.4	5.3	4.7	5.0	4.3
Niger[a]	2.4	4.2	3.0	..	2.0	..	2.6	..	1.9	..
Nigeria	2.5	6.7	..	..	..	..	..	..	..	..
Norway	3.9	1.7	2.6	2.6	3.8	–0.6	1.5	2.3	3.9	3.1
Oman[a]	4.5	4.7	5.0	..	3.9	..	6.0	..	5.0	..
Pakistan	3.8	5.1	4.4	3.4	4.1	6.7	3.8	8.0	4.4	5.7
Panama	4.7	6.8	3.1	2.9	6.0	6.0	2.7	1.7	4.5	7.3
Papua New Guinea	3.8	3.8	4.5	2.4	5.4	4.3	4.6	3.9	–0.6	3.9
Paraguay[a]	2.2	3.8	3.3	5.2	0.6	2.1	1.4	1.3	2.5	3.8
Peru	4.7	6.1	5.5	4.1	5.4	6.6	3.8	6.2	4.0	6.2
Philippines[a]	3.3	4.9	1.9	3.2	3.2	4.2	3.0	3.7	3.7	5.8
Poland	4.7	4.3	0.5	1.1	6.7	5.8	8.1	8.7	5.2	3.6
Portugal	2.9	0.7	–0.6	–0.2	3.1	–0.9	2.7	–0.4	2.4	1.6
Puerto Rico[a]	4.3	0.0	..	..	..	..	..	..	..	..
Qatar	..	14.2	..	..	..	..	..	..	..	..

4.1 Growth of output

	Gross domestic product		Agriculture		Industry		Manufacturing		Services	
	average annual % growth		average annual % growth		average annual % growth		average annual % growth		average annual % growth	
	1990–2000	2000–10	1990–2000	2000–10	1990–2000	2000–10	1990–2000	2000–10	1990–2000	2000–10
Romania	−0.6	5.0	−1.9	7.0	−1.2	5.8	..	..	−0.3	6.0
Russian Federation	−4.7	5.4	−4.9	1.5	−7.1	4.1	..	..	−4.7	6.5
Rwanda[a]	−0.2	7.6	2.5	..	−3.8	..	−5.8	..	−0.9	..
Saudi Arabia[a]	2.1	3.6	1.6	1.2	2.2	3.2	5.6	5.6	2.2	4.3
Senegal	3.0	4.2	2.4	2.5	3.8	3.2	3.1	1.4	3.0	5.9
Serbia	−4.2	4.1	..	1.1	..	2.0	..	..	..	5.4
Sierra Leone	−5.0	8.8	..	..	..	..	..	..	..	..
Singapore	7.2	6.0	−2.8	−3.2	7.7	5.6	7.0	6.1	7.2	6.3
Slovak Republic	1.9	5.4	0.4	6.2	4.1	7.9	..	9.7	4.4	4.2
Slovenia	2.7	3.3	0.4	−0.6	1.6	3.3	1.8	3.2	3.0	3.6
Somalia	..	..	..	..	..	..	..	..	..	..
South Africa	2.1	3.9	1.0	1.5	1.0	2.9	1.6	3.1	3.0	4.1
South Sudan	..	..	..	..	..	..	..	..	..	..
Spain	2.7	2.4	3.1	−0.1	2.2	0.8	5.2	−0.2	2.7	3.2
Sri Lanka[a]	5.3	5.6	1.9	3.1	6.9	5.7	8.1	4.6	6.0	6.2
Sudan	5.5	6.7	7.4	2.6	8.5	10.6	7.5	4.7	1.9	7.9
Swaziland	3.4	2.4	0.9	1.4	3.2	1.7	2.8	1.8	3.9	3.4
Sweden	2.3	2.2	−0.8	3.3	4.3	2.2	8.9	2.7	2.0	2.2
Switzerland	1.0	1.9	−0.9	0.5	0.2	2.0	1.0	2.3	1.2	1.9
Syrian Arab Republic	5.1	5.0	6.0	..	9.2	..	..	..	1.5	..
Tajikistan	−10.4	8.6	−6.8	7.4	−11.4	8.9	−12.6	8.2	−10.8	7.2
Tanzania[c]	3.0	7.1	3.2	4.4	3.1	9.3	2.8	8.7	2.6	7.8
Thailand[a]	4.2	4.5	1.0	2.2	5.7	5.4	6.9	5.6	3.7	4.0
Timor-Leste[a]	..	3.4	..	..	..	..	..	..	..	..
Togo[a]	3.5	2.7	4.0	2.8	1.8	8.1	1.8	7.5	3.9	−0.7
Trinidad and Tobago	3.2	6.5	2.7	−8.3	3.2	9.2	4.9	8.9	3.2	5.6
Tunisia[a]	4.7	4.7	2.6	2.5	4.4	3.0	5.7	2.8	5.5	6.6
Turkey	3.9	4.7	1.3	1.6	4.7	5.2	4.7	5.1	4.0	5.0
Turkmenistan	−4.9	13.6	−4.7	12.3	−2.7	20.2	..	..	−5.8	21.8
Uganda	7.0	7.7	3.4	2.2	12.3	9.2	14.2	6.8	8.2	8.4
Ukraine	−9.3	4.8	−5.6	2.9	−12.6	3.2	−11.2	6.2	−8.1	4.8
United Arab Emirates	4.8	5.1	..	..	..	..	..	..	..	..
United Kingdom	3.2	1.8	−0.3	0.2	1.5	−0.7	..	..	4.1	2.6
United States	3.6	1.8	3.8	1.9	3.7	0.3	..	1.9	3.6	2.2
Uruguay	3.9	3.6	3.9	2.1	1.3	3.2	−0.4	4.9	1.7	3.6
Uzbekistan	−0.2	7.1	0.5	6.4	−3.4	5.0	0.7	2.6	0.4	9.0
Venezuela, RB	1.6	4.7	1.2	2.5	1.2	2.2	4.5	2.4	−0.1	6.4
Vietnam[a]	7.9	7.5	4.3	3.7	11.9	9.3	11.2	10.9	7.5	7.5
West Bank and Gaza	7.3	−0.9	..	..	..	..	..	..	..	..
Yemen, Rep.[a]	5.6	4.1	5.1	2.7	5.2	2.0	1.8	5.1	6.1	6.0
Zambia	0.5	5.6	4.2	1.1	−4.2	9.4	0.8	5.1	2.5	5.5
Zimbabwe	2.3	−6.0	4.3	−9.6	0.4	−4.9	0.4	−5.9	3.0	−4.2
World	**2.9 w**	**2.7 w**	**2.0 w**	**2.5 w**	**2.4 w**	**2.5 w**	**.. w**	**3.1 w**	**3.1 w**	**2.8 w**
Low income	3.0	5.5	2.9	3.7	3.6	7.2	3.6	6.6	2.8	6.1
Middle income	3.9	6.4	2.4	3.5	4.4	7.2	6.2	7.5	4.0	6.6
Lower middle income	3.8	6.3	2.6	3.3	4.1	6.0	4.7	6.3	4.5	7.6
Upper middle income	3.9	6.5	2.3	3.6	4.5	7.5	6.5	7.8	3.9	6.4
Low & middle income	3.9	6.4	2.4	3.5	4.4	7.2	6.2	7.5	4.0	6.6
East Asia & Pacific	8.5	9.4	3.4	4.1	10.9	10.2	10.9	10.1	8.4	10.0
Europe & Central Asia	−1.8	5.4	−2.1	2.7	−4.4	5.4	..	..	−1.2	5.9
Latin America & Carib.	3.2	3.8	2.0	2.9	3.0	3.1	2.9	2.8	3.5	4.0
Middle East & N. Africa	3.8	4.7	2.9	4.6	4.1	3.5	4.3	5.4	3.3	5.1
South Asia	5.5	7.4	3.3	3.1	6.0	8.1	6.4	8.4	6.9	8.8
Sub-Saharan Africa	2.5	5.0	3.2	3.2	1.9	4.9	2.2	3.4	2.6	4.8
High income	2.7	1.8	1.5	0.7	1.9	0.7	..	1.9	3.0	2.1
Euro area	2.0	1.3	1.6	0.2	1.0	0.4	1.2	0.3	2.4	1.8

a. Components are at producer prices. b. Private analysts estimate that consumer price index inflation was considerably higher for 2007–09 and believe that GDP volume growth has been significantly lower than official reports indicate since the last quarter of 2008. c. Covers mainland Tanzania only.

About the data

An economy's growth is measured by the change in the volume of its output or in the real incomes of its residents. The 1993 United Nations System of National Accounts (1993 SNA) offers three plausible indicators for calculating growth: the volume of gross domestic product (GDP), real gross domestic income, and real gross national income. The volume of GDP is the sum of value added, measured at constant prices, by households, government, and industries operating in the economy.

Each industry's contribution to growth in the economy's output is measured by growth in the industry's value added. In principle, value added in constant prices can be estimated by measuring the quantity of goods and services produced in a period, valuing them at an agreed set of base year prices, and subtracting the cost of intermediate inputs, also in constant prices. This double-deflation method, recommended by the 1993 SNA and its predecessors, requires detailed information on the structure of prices of inputs and outputs.

In many industries, however, value added is extrapolated from the base year using single volume indexes of outputs or, less commonly, inputs. Particularly in the services industries, including most of government, value added in constant prices is often imputed from labor inputs, such as real wages or number of employees. In the absence of well defined measures of output, measuring the growth of services remains difficult.

Moreover, technical progress can lead to improvements in production processes and in the quality of goods and services that, if not properly accounted for, can distort measures of value added and thus of growth. When inputs are used to estimate output, as for nonmarket services, unmeasured technical progress leads to underestimates of the volume of output. Similarly, unmeasured improvements in quality lead to underestimates of the value of output and value added. The result can be underestimates of growth and productivity improvement and overestimates of inflation.

Informal economic activities pose a particular measurement problem, especially in developing countries, where much economic activity is unrecorded. A complete picture of the economy requires estimating household outputs produced for home use, sales in informal markets, barter exchanges, and illicit or deliberately unreported activities. The consistency and completeness of such estimates depend on the skill and methods of the compiling statisticians.

Rebasing national accounts

When countries rebase their national accounts, they update the weights assigned to various components to better reflect current patterns of production or uses of output. The new base year should represent normal operation of the economy—it should be a year without major shocks or distortions. Some developing countries have not rebased their national accounts for many years. Using an old base year can be misleading because implicit price and volume weights become progressively less relevant and useful.

To obtain comparable series of constant price data, the World Bank rescales GDP and value added by industrial origin to a common reference year. This year's *World Development Indicators* continues to use 2000 as the reference year. Because rescaling changes the implicit weights used in forming regional and income group aggregates, aggregate growth rates in this year's edition are not comparable with those from earlier editions with different base years.

Rescaling may result in a discrepancy between the rescaled GDP and the sum of the rescaled components. Because allocating the discrepancy would cause distortions in the growth rates, the discrepancy is left unallocated. As a result, the weighted average of the growth rates of the components generally will not equal the GDP growth rate.

Computing growth rates

Growth rates of GDP and its components are calculated using the least squares method and constant price data in the local currency. Constant price U.S. dollar series are used to calculate regional and income group growth rates. Local currency series are converted to constant U.S. dollars using an exchange rate in the common reference year. The growth rates in the table are average annual compound growth rates. Methods of computing growth are described in *Statistical methods*.

Changes in the System of National Accounts

World Development Indicators adopted the terminology of the 1993 SNA in 2001. Although many countries continue to compile their national accounts according to the SNA version 3 (referred to as the 1968 SNA), more and more are adopting the 1993 SNA. Some low-income countries still use concepts from the even older 1953 SNA guidelines, including valuations such as factor cost, in describing major economic aggregates. Countries that use the 1993 SNA are identified in *Primary data documentation*.

Definitions

• **Gross domestic product (GDP)** at purchaser prices is the sum of gross value added by all resident producers in the economy plus any product taxes (less subsidies) not included in the valuation of output. It is calculated without deducting for depreciation of fabricated capital assets or for depletion and degradation of natural resources. Value added is the net output of an industry after adding up all outputs and subtracting intermediate inputs. The industrial origin of value added is determined by the International Standard Industrial Classification (ISIC) revision 3. • **Agriculture** is the sum of gross output less the value of intermediate input used in production for industries classified in ISIC divisions 1–5 and includes forestry and fishing. • **Industry** is the sum of gross output less the value of intermediate input used in production for industries classified in ISIC divisions 10–45, which cover mining, manufacturing (also reported separately), construction, electricity, water, and gas. • **Manufacturing** is the sum of gross output less the value of intermediate input used in production for industries classified in ISIC divisions 15–37. • **Services** correspond to ISIC divisions 50–99. This sector is derived as a residual (from GDP less agriculture and industry) and may not properly reflect the sum of services output, including banking and financial services. For some countries it includes product taxes (minus subsidies) and may also include statistical discrepancies.

Data sources

Data on national accounts for most developing countries are collected from national statistical organizations and central banks by visiting and resident World Bank missions. Data for high-income economies are from Organisation for Economic Co-operation and Development (OECD) data files. The United Nations Statistics Division publishes detailed national accounts for UN member countries in *National Accounts Statistics: Main Aggregates and Detailed Tables* and publishes updates in the *Monthly Bulletin of Statistics*.

4.2 Structure of output

	Gross domestic product $ billions		Agriculture % of GDP		Industry % of GDP		Manufacturing % of GDP		Services % of GDP	
	2000	**2010**	**2000**	**2010**	**2000**	**2010**	**2000**	**2010**	**2000**	**2010**
Afghanistan	2.5	17.2	*45*	30	20	22	*15*	13	*35*	48
Albania	3.7	11.8	29	20	19	19	11	19	52	61
Algeria	54.8	162.0	9	7	59	62	7	6	33	31
Angola[a]	9.1	84.4	6	10	72	63	3	6	22	27
Argentina	284.2	368.7	5	10	28	31	18	21	67	59
Armenia	1.9	9.4	26	20	39	36	19	11	35	44
Australia	416.9	1,131.6	4	2	27	20	13	9	70	78
Austria	192.1	379.1	2	2	31	29	20	19	67	69
Azerbaijan	5.3	51.8	17	6	45	65	6	6	38	30
Bahrain	8.0	20.6	..	..	..	..	..	..	..	..
Bangladesh	47.1	100.4	26	19	25	28	15	18	49	53
Belarus	12.7	54.7	14	9	39	44	32	31	47	47
Belgium	232.7	469.4	1	1	27	22	19	*14*	72	78
Benin[a]	2.3	6.6	37	..	14	..	9	..	50	..
Bolivia	8.4	19.6	15	13	30	37	15	14	55	50
Bosnia and Herzegovina	5.5	16.6	11	8	23	28	10	14	66	64
Botswana	5.6	14.9	3	3	53	45	5	3	45	52
Brazil	644.7	2,087.9	6	6	28	27	17	16	67	67
Bulgaria	12.9	47.7	14	5	26	31	18	16	61	63
Burkina Faso	2.6	8.8	29	..	24	..	16	..	47	..
Burundi	0.7	1.6	40	..	19	..	9	..	41	..
Cambodia	3.7	11.2	38	36	23	23	17	16	39	41
Cameroon	10.1	22.4	22	..	36	..	21	..	42	..
Canada	724.9	1,577.0	2	..	33	..	19	..	65	..
Central African Republic	1.0	2.0	53	56	16	*15*	7	..	31	29
Chad	1.4	7.6	42	*14*	11	49	9	7	46	*38*
Chile	75.2	212.7	6	3	38	43	19	12	55	54
China[a]	1,198.5	5,926.6	15	10	46	47	32	30	39	43
Hong Kong SAR, China	169.1	224.5	0	*0*	12	7	3	*2*	88	93
Colombia	100.4	288.2	9	7	29	36	15	15	62	57
Congo, Dem. Rep.	4.3	13.1	50	*43*	20	*24*	5	5	30	*33*
Congo, Rep.[a]	3.2	11.9	5	4	72	80	3	4	23	16
Costa Rica	15.9	35.8	9	7	32	26	25	17	58	67
Côte d'Ivoire[a]	10.4	22.8	24	23	25	27	22	19	51	50
Croatia	21.5	60.9	6	6	29	27	20	18	65	67
Cuba	30.6	62.7	8	5	28	*20*	18	*10*	64	75
Cyprus	9.3	23.1	4	2	19	*20*	10	8	77	78
Czech Republic	56.7	192.0	4	2	38	38	27	24	58	60
Denmark	160.1	312.0	3	1	27	22	16	12	71	77
Dominican Republic[a]	24.0	51.8	7	6	36	· 32	26	24	57	62
Ecuador	15.9	58.0	9	7	*32*	38	*11*	10	59	55
Egypt, Arab Rep.	99.8	218.9	17	14	33	38	19	16	50	48
El Salvador	13.1	21.2	10	13	32	27	25	21	58	60
Eritrea	0.6	2.1	15	*15*	23	*22*	11	*6*	62	63
Estonia	5.7	19.2	5	*3*	28	29	18	*17*	68	68
Ethiopia	8.2	29.7	50	48	12	14	6	5	38	38
Finland	121.8	238.0	3	3	35	29	26	19	62	68
France	1,326.3	2,560.0	3	2	23	*19*	16	*11*	74	79
Gabon[a]	5.1	13.0	6	4	56	54	4	4	38	42
Gambia, The	0.4	0.8	36	27	13	16	5	5	51	57
Georgia	3.1	11.7	22	8	22	23	9	13	56	68
Germany	1,886.4	3,280.5	1	1	30	28	23	21	68	71
Ghana	5.0	31.3	39	30	28	19	10	6	32	51
Greece	124.4	301.1	..	..	21	18	..	..	..	..
Guatemala	19.3	41.2	*15*	13	*29*	19	*21*	19	56	68
Guinea	3.1	4.5	20	13	33	47	4	5	47	40
Guinea-Bissau	0.2	0.9	56	..	13	..	11	..	31	..
Haiti	3.7	6.7	..	..	..	..	..	..	..	..

Structure of output |4.2

	Gross domestic product		Agriculture		Industry		Manufacturing		Services	
	$ billions		% of GDP		% of GDP		% of GDP		% of GDP	
	2000	2010	2000	2010	2000	2010	2000	2010	2000	2010
Honduras	7.1	15.4	16	13	32	27	23	18	52	61
Hungary	46.4	128.6	6	4	32	31	24	23	62	65
India	460.2	1,727.1	23	19	26	26	16	14	50	55
Indonesia[a]	165.0	706.6	16	15	46	47	28	25	38	38
Iran, Islamic Rep.	101.3	331.0	14	..	37	..	13	..	50	..
Iraq	25.9	82.2	5	..	84	..	1	..	10	..
Ireland	97.5	206.6	3	1	42	32	33	24	55	67
Israel[a]	124.7	217.3	..	..	..	..	..	..	..	..
Italy	1,104.0	2,061.0	3	2	28	25	21	17	69	73
Jamaica	9.0	14.3	7	6	26	22	11	9	67	71
Japan	4,667.4	5,458.8	2	1	32	27	22	18	66	72
Jordan	8.5	27.6	2	3	26	31	16	19	72	66
Kazakhstan	18.3	149.1	9	5	40	42	18	13	51	53
Kenya	12.7	31.4	32	19	17	14	12	8	51	67
Korea, Dem. Rep.	..	..	..	..	..	..	..	..	..	..
Korea, Rep.	533.4	1,014.5	5	3	38	39	28	31	57	58
Kosovo	1.8	5.6	..	12	..	20	..	17	..	68
Kuwait[a]	37.7	109.5	0	..	59	..	3	..	40	..
Kyrgyz Republic	1.4	4.6	37	21	31	28	19	18	32	51
Lao PDR	1.7	7.3	53	33	23	30	17	8	25	37
Latvia	7.8	24.0	5	4	24	22	14	12	72	74
Lebanon	17.3	39.0	7	6	23	21	13	8	70	72
Lesotho	0.7	2.1	12	8	32	34	14	16	56	58
Liberia	0.6	1.0	72	61	12	17	9	13	16	22
Libya	33.9	62.4	5	2	66	78	3	4	29	20
Lithuania	11.4	36.3	6	4	30	28	19	16	64	68
Macedonia, FYR	3.6	9.2	12	11	34	28	21	16	54	61
Madagascar	3.9	8.7	29	29	14	16	12	14	57	55
Malawi	1.7	5.1	40	31	18	16	13	10	43	53
Malaysia[a]	93.8	237.8	9	11	48	44	31	26	43	45
Mali	2.4	9.3	42	..	21	..	4	..	38	..
Mauritania	1.1	3.6	28	20	30	37	9	4	43	43
Mauritius	4.6	9.7	7	4	31	29	23	19	62	67
Mexico	581.4	1,034.8	4	4	28	34	20	18	68	62
Moldova	1.3	5.8	29	14	22	13	16	13	49	73
Mongolia	1.1	6.2	31	16	25	38	8	7	44	46
Morocco	37.0	90.8	15	15	29	30	17	15	56	55
Mozambique	4.2	9.6	24	32	25	23	12	13	51	45
Myanmar[a]	..	..	57	36	10	26	7	20	33	38
Namibia	3.9	12.2	12	8	28	20	13	8	60	73
Nepal	5.5	15.7	41	36	22	15	9	7	37	48
Netherlands	385.1	779.4	3	2	25	24	16	13	72	74
New Zealand	51.6	126.7	9	..	25	..	17	..	66	..
Nicaragua	3.9	6.6	21	21	28	30	17	20	51	49
Niger[a]	1.8	5.5	38	..	18	..	7	..	44	..
Nigeria	46.0	193.7	49	..	31	..	3	..	21	..
Norway	168.3	417.5	2	2	42	40	11	9	56	58
Oman[a]	19.9	46.9	2	..	57	..	5	..	41	..
Pakistan	74.0	176.9	26	21	23	25	15	17	51	53
Panama	11.6	26.7	7	5	19	17	10	6	74	78
Papua New Guinea	3.5	9.5	36	36	41	45	8	6	23	19
Paraguay[a]	7.1	18.3	17	22	22	20	15	12	61	57
Peru	53.3	157.1	8	8	30	34	16	17	62	57
Philippines[a]	81.0	199.6	14	12	34	33	24	21	52	55
Poland	171.3	469.4	5	4	32	32	19	18	63	65
Portugal	117.3	228.6	4	2	28	23	18	13	68	74
Puerto Rico[a]	61.7	96.3	1	1	42	50	39	46	57	49
Qatar	17.8	98.3	..	..	..	..	..	..	..	..

	Gross domestic product		Agriculture		Industry		Manufacturing		Services	
	$ billions		% of GDP		% of GDP		% of GDP		% of GDP	
	2000	2010	2000	2010	2000	2010	2000	2010	2000	2010
Romania	37.1	161.6	13	7	36	26	15	22	51	67
Russian Federation	259.7	1,479.8	6	4	38	37	17	16	56	59
Rwanda[a]	1.7	5.6	37	34	14	14	7	6	49	52
Saudi Arabia[a]	188.4	434.7	5	3	54	62	10	10	41	35
Senegal	4.7	13.0	19	17	23	22	15	13	58	61
Serbia	6.1	38.4	20	9	30	27	24	16	50	64
Sierra Leone	0.6	1.9	58	49	28	21	4	..	13	30
Singapore	95.9	208.8	0	0	35	28	27	22	65	72
Slovak Republic	28.7	87.3	4	4	36	35	25	21	59	61
Slovenia	20.0	46.9	3	2	36	32	26	21	61	66
Somalia	..	..	..	..	..	..	..	..	..	..
South Africa	132.9	363.7	3	3	32	31	19	15	65	66
South Sudan	..	..	..	..	..	..	..	..	..	..
Spain	580.7	1,407.4	4	3	29	26	19	13	66	72
Sri Lanka[a]	16.3	49.6	20	13	27	29	17	18	53	58
Sudan	12.4	62.0	42	24	22	33	9	6	37	43
Swaziland	1.5	3.6	12	7	45	50	39	45	43	42
Sweden	247.3	458.6	2	2	29	27	22	16	69	71
Switzerland	249.9	527.9	2	1	27	27	19	19	71	72
Syrian Arab Republic	19.3	59.1	24	23	38	31	7	..	38	46
Tajikistan	0.9	5.6	27	21	39	22	34	10	34	57
Tanzania[b]	10.2	23.1	33	28	19	25	9	10	47	47
Thailand[a]	122.7	318.5	9	12	42	45	34	36	49	43
Timor-Leste[a]	0.3	0.7	26	..	19	..	3	..	56	..
Togo[a]	1.3	3.2	34	..	18	..	8	..	48	..
Trinidad and Tobago	8.2	20.6	1	1	49	52	7	5	49	47
Tunisia[a]	21.5	44.3	11	8	30	32	18	18	58	60
Turkey	266.6	734.4	11	10	31	27	23	18	57	64
Turkmenistan	2.9	20.0	24	12	44	54	11	..	31	34
Uganda	6.2	17.0	29	24	23	25	8	8	48	50
Ukraine	31.3	137.9	17	8	36	31	19	17	47	61
United Arab Emirates	104.3	297.6	2	1	50	54	13	10	48	46
United Kingdom	1,477.2	2,261.7	1	1	27	22	17	11	72	78
United States	9,898.8	14,586.7	1	1	23	20	16	13	75	79
Uruguay	22.8	39.1	7	9	25	26	14	14	69	65
Uzbekistan	13.8	39.0	34	20	23	35	9	9	43	45
Venezuela, RB	117.1	391.8	4	..	50	..	20	..	46	..
Vietnam[a]	31.2	106.4	25	21	37	41	19	20	39	38
West Bank and Gaza	4.1	..	..	..	..	..	..	..	..	..
Yemen, Rep.[a]	9.6	31.3	14	8	46	29	6	6	40	63
Zambia	3.2	16.2	22	9	25	37	11	9	52	54
Zimbabwe	6.6	7.5	18	17	25	29	16	15	57	53
World	**32,248.5 w**	**63,242.1 w**	**4 w**	**3 w**	**29 w**	**25 w**	**19 w**	**16 w**	**68 w**	**72 w**
Low income	164.8	416.5	34	25	21	25	12	14	45	50
Middle income	5,708.1	19,632.1	11	10	36	36	21	20	53	55
Lower middle income	1,258.9	4,312.3	20	17	34	31	17	16	46	52
Upper middle income	4,449.2	15,317.0	9	8	36	37	23	22	55	55
Low & middle income	5,874.8	20,071.7	12	10	35	35	21	20	53	54
East Asia & Pacific	1,727.2	7,630.5	15	11	44	45	31	29	41	43
Europe & Central Asia	709.9	3,059.0	11	7	35	32	18	17	55	61
Latin America & Carib.	2,054.4	4,980.8	6	6	30	31	18	17	65	63
Middle East & N. Africa	433.5	1,207.0	13	..	43	..	13	..	44	..
South Asia	608.2	2,090.4	24	19	26	26	15	15	50	54
Sub-Saharan Africa	342.1	1,097.9	16	13	29	30	15	13	54	57
High income	26,375.3	43,240.0	2	1	28	24	19	15	71	75
Euro area	6,256.1	12,149.1	2	2	28	26	20	16	70	72

a. Components are at producer prices. b. Covers mainland Tanzania only.

About the data

An economy's gross domestic product (GDP) represents the sum of value added by all its producers. Value added is the value of the gross output of producers less the value of intermediate goods and services consumed in production, before accounting for consumption of fixed capital in production. The United Nations System of National Accounts calls for value added to be valued at either basic prices (excluding net taxes on products) or producer prices (including net taxes on products paid by producers but excluding sales or value added taxes). Both valuations exclude transport charges that are invoiced separately by producers. Total GDP shown in the table and elsewhere in this volume is measured at purchaser prices. Value added by industry is normally measured at basic prices. When value added is measured at producer prices, this is noted in *Primary data documentation* and footnoted in the table.

While GDP estimates based on the production approach are generally more reliable than estimates compiled from the income or expenditure side, different countries use different definitions, methods, and reporting standards. World Bank staff review the quality of national accounts data and sometimes make adjustments to improve consistency with international guidelines. Nevertheless, significant discrepancies remain between international standards and actual practice. Many statistical offices, especially those in developing countries, face severe limitations in the resources, time, training, and budgets required to produce reliable and comprehensive series of national accounts statistics.

Data problems in measuring output

Among the difficulties faced by compilers of national accounts is the extent of unreported economic activity in the informal or secondary economy. In developing countries a large share of agricultural output is either not exchanged (because it is consumed within the household) or not exchanged for money.

Agricultural production often must be estimated indirectly, using a combination of methods involving estimates of inputs, yields, and area under cultivation. This approach sometimes leads to crude approximations that can differ from the true values over time and across crops for reasons other than climate conditions or farming techniques. Similarly, agricultural inputs that cannot easily be allocated to specific outputs are frequently "netted out" using equally crude and ad hoc approximations. For further discussion of the measurement of agricultural production, see *About the data* for table 3.3.

Ideally, industrial output should be measured through regular censuses and surveys of firms. But in most developing countries such surveys are infrequent, so earlier survey results must be extrapolated using an appropriate indicator. The choice of sampling unit, which may be the enterprise (where responses may be based on financial records) or the establishment (where production units may be recorded separately), also affects the quality of the data. Moreover, much industrial production is organized in unincorporated or owner-operated ventures that are not captured by surveys aimed at the formal sector. Even in large industries, where regular surveys are more likely, evasion of excise and other taxes and nondisclosure of income lower the estimates of value added. Such problems become more acute as countries move from state control of industry to private enterprise, because new firms and growing numbers of established firms fail to report. In accordance with the System of National Accounts, output should include all such unreported activity as well as the value of illegal activities and other unrecorded, informal, or small-scale operations. Data on these activities need to be collected using techniques other than conventional surveys of firms.

In industries dominated by large organizations and enterprises, such as public utilities, data on output, employment, and wages are usually readily available and reasonably reliable. But in the services industry the many self-employed workers and one-person businesses are sometimes difficult to locate, and they have little incentive to respond to surveys, let alone to report their full earnings. Compounding these problems are the many forms of economic activity that go unrecorded, including the work that women and children do for little or no pay. For further discussion of the problems of using national accounts data, see Srinivasan (1994) and Heston (1994).

Dollar conversion

To produce national accounts aggregates that are measured in the same standard monetary units, the value of output must be converted to a single common currency. The World Bank conventionally uses the U.S. dollar and applies the average official exchange rate reported by the International Monetary Fund for the year shown. An alternative conversion factor is applied if the official exchange rate is judged to diverge by an exceptionally large margin from the rate effectively applied to transactions in foreign currencies and traded products.

Definitions

• **Gross domestic product (GDP)** at purchaser prices is the sum of gross value added by all resident producers in the economy plus any product taxes (less subsidies) not included in the valuation of output. It is calculated without deducting for depreciation of fabricated assets or for depletion and degradation of natural resources. Value added is the net output of an industry after adding up all outputs and subtracting intermediate inputs. The industrial origin of value added is determined by the International Standard Industrial Classification (ISIC) revision 3. • **Agriculture** is the sum of gross output less the value of intermediate input used in production for industries classified in ISIC divisions 1–5 and includes forestry and fishing. • **Industry** is the sum of gross output less the value of intermediate input used in production for industries classified in ISIC divisions 10–45, which cover mining, manufacturing (also reported separately), construction, electricity, water, and gas. • **Manufacturing** is the sum of gross output less the value of intermediate input used in production for industries classified in ISIC divisions 15–37. • **Services** correspond to ISIC divisions 50–99. This sector is derived as a residual (from GDP less agriculture and industry) and may not properly reflect the sum of services output, including banking and financial services. For some countries it includes product taxes (minus subsidies) and may also include statistical discrepancies.

Data sources

Data on national accounts for most developing countries are collected from national statistical organizations and central banks by visiting and resident World Bank missions. Data for high-income economies are from Organisation for Economic Co-operation and Development (OECD) data files. The United Nations Statistics Division publishes detailed national accounts for UN member countries in *National Accounts Statistics: Main Aggregates and Detailed Tables* and publishes updates in the *Monthly Bulletin of Statistics*.

	Manufacturing value added		Food, beverages, and tobacco		Textiles and clothing		Machinery and transport equipment		Chemicals		Other manufacturing[a]	
	$ billions		% of total		% of total		% of total		% of total		% of total	
	2000	2010	2000	2008	2000	2008	2000	2008	2000	2008	2000	2008
Afghanistan	0.64	1.96	..	..	..	..	..	..	..	..	..	..
Albania	0.37	1.95	20	15	27	23	3	3	5	11	46	48
Algeria	3.86	7.32	..	..	..	..	..	..	..	..	..	..
Angola	0.26	4.89	..	..	..	..	..	..	..	..	..	..
Argentina	46.88	69.44	29	..	8	..	11	..	15	..	37	..
Armenia	0.32	0.89	..	..	..	..	..	..	..	..	..	..
Australia	49.08	98.34	21	19	4	3	13	14	8	7	55	58
Austria	35.36	65.50	10	9	4	2	25	26	7	7	54	56
Azerbaijan	0.28	2.81	42	15	3	1	11	6	6	4	37	75
Bahrain	..	..	..	..	..	..	..	..	..	..	..	..
Bangladesh	6.92	17.36	24	..	40	..	3	..	11	..	21	..
Belarus	3.44	14.90	..	..	..	..	..	..	..	..	..	..
Belgium	39.90	59.03	12	13	5	4	19	17	20	21	44	45
Benin	0.20	..	..	..	..	..	..	..	..	..	..	..
Bolivia	1.11	2.21	37	..	5	..	0	..	4	..	54	..
Bosnia and Herzegovina	0.47	1.87	..	..	..	..	..	..	..	..	..	..
Botswana	0.25	0.44	20	22	5	5	..	..	..	..	75	73
Brazil	96.17	280.65	17	18	7	6	19	21	12	11	45	44
Bulgaria	1.98	6.67	20	20	14	14	14	18	11	5	41	44
Burkina Faso	0.40	..	..	..	..	..	..	..	..	..	..	..
Burundi	0.05	..	..	..	..	..	..	..	..	..	..	..
Cambodia	0.59	1.65	7	..	87	..	0	..	0	..	7	..
Cameroon	1.94	..	36	..	19	..	1	..	2	..	43	..
Canada	129.47	..	12	1	4	2	32	26	8	8	45	64
Central African Republic	0.06	..	..	..	..	..	..	..	..	..	..	..
Chad	0.12	0.38	..	..	..	..	..	..	..	..	..	..
Chile	13.25	22.65	32	14	4	2	4	2	14	14	46	69
China	384.94	1,756.82	14	12	11	10	14	24	12	11	48	43
Hong Kong SAR, China	5.54	3.76	7	14	20	11	12	21	4	5	58	48
Colombia	14.44	40.07	30	..	11	..	4	..	16	..	39	..
Congo, Dem. Rep.	0.21	0.59	..	..	..	..	..	..	..	..	..	..
Congo, Rep.	0.11	0.46	..	..	..	..	..	..	..	..	..	..
Costa Rica	3.68	5.68	45	42	6	4	3	3	12	9	33	43
Côte d'Ivoire	2.26	4.38	..	..	..	..	..	..	..	..	..	..
Croatia	3.62	9.43	..	..	..	..	..	..	..	..	..	..
Cuba	4.57	4.96	..	..	..	..	..	..	..	..	..	..
Cyprus	0.85	1.66	37	32	7	3	4	5	6	6	46	54
Czech Republic	13.79	42.25	12	9	6	3	24	30	7	5	51	53
Denmark	22.25	32.86	18	16	2	2	20	19	10	12	48	51
Dominican Republic	5.64	11.49	..	..	..	..	..	..	..	..	..	..
Ecuador	2.17	5.41	60	40	3	3	1	2	5	4	31	51
Egypt, Arab Rep.	17.97	32.98	20	18	10	12	7	6	22	14	41	50
El Salvador	3.03	4.04	29	..	28	..	2	..	16	..	25	..
Eritrea	0.07	0.10	60	..	12	31	1	1	6	11	21	56
Estonia	0.90	2.39	17	14	15	8	10	18	4	6	53	55
Ethiopia	0.42	1.46	54	46	12	7	7	2	5	6	22	39
Finland	28.07	39.11	6	6	2	1	33	37	5	6	54	50
France	190.45	253.61	13	14	4	3	26	25	12	13	45	44
Gabon	0.19	0.49	..	..	..	..	..	..	..	..	..	..
Gambia, The	0.02	0.03	..	..	..	..	..	..	..	..	..	..
Georgia	0.26	1.31	37	25	1	1	12	8	7	7	43	59
Germany	392.47	614.23	8	7	2	2	33	37	10	10	47	44
Ghana	0.45	1.95	..	..	..	..	..	..	..	..	..	..
Greece	..	..	24	22	12	8	11	10	10	6	43	54
Guatemala	2.54	7.52	..	..	..	..	..	..	..	..	..	..
Guinea	0.12	0.20	..	..	..	..	..	..	..	..	..	..
Guinea-Bissau	0.02	..	..	..	..	..	..	..	..	..	..	..
Haiti	..	..	..	..	..	..	..	..	..	..	..	..

Structure of manufacturing | **4.3**

	Manufacturing value added ($ billions)		Food, beverages, and tobacco (% of total)		Textiles and clothing (% of total)		Machinery and transport equipment (% of total)		Chemicals (% of total)		Other manufacturing[a] (% of total)	
	2000	2010	2000	2008	2000	2008	2000	2008	2000	2008	2000	2008
Honduras	1.46	2.63	..	..	..	..	..	..	..	..	..	..
Hungary	9.28	25.26	15	11	5	3	27	30	10	10	43	46
India	65.75	226.79	13	9	13	8	16	16	21	14	38	54
Indonesia	45.79	175.39	18	26	17	12	20	18	11	6	35	38
Iran, Islamic Rep.	13.24	..	10	..	6	..	20	..	19	..	45	..
Iraq	0.24	..	..	..	..	..	..	..	..	..	..	..
Ireland	28.22	48.71	14	17	1	1	20	14	36	36	29	33
Israel	..	..	12	10	5	3	32	22	10	20	41	44
Italy	205.51	308.22	9	9	12	10	23	23	8	7	48	51
Jamaica	0.85	1.16	..	..	..	..	..	..	..	..	..	..
Japan	1,034.09	905.54	11	11	3	2	34	37	10	10	41	40
Jordan	1.14	4.78	30	21	7	10	3	4	18	18	43	47
Kazakhstan	3.02	18.54	..	..	..	..	..	..	..	..	..	..
Kenya	1.31	3.02	29	30	8	4	2	2	5	4	55	62
Korea, Dem. Rep.	..	..	..	..	..	..	..	..	..	..	..	..
Korea, Rep.	134.56	279.44	8	6	8	5	41	46	10	8	33	35
Kosovo		0.77	..	..	..	..	..	..	..	..	..	..
Kuwait	0.97	..	8	..	4	..	2	..	3	..	82	..
Kyrgyz Republic	0.25	0.74	33	19	2	10	1	3	1	2	63	66
Lao PDR	0.29	0.52	46	..	22	..	8	..	3	..	22	..
Latvia	0.96	2.62	27	23	11	6	8	16	3	5	51	50
Lebanon	1.97	2.85	26	..	10	..	3	..	6	..	55	..
Lesotho	0.10	0.30	..	..	..	..	..	..	..	..	..	..
Liberia	0.05	0.10	..	..	..	..	..	..	..	..	..	..
Libya	0.64	3.88	..	..	..	..	..	..	..	..	..	..
Lithuania	1.96	5.43	27	22	18	9	12	13	3	10	40	46
Macedonia, FYR	0.62	1.25	32	18	15	17	9	4	6	6	38	55
Madagascar	0.43	1.11	0	0	35	30	0	1	2	2	62	67
Malawi	0.20	0.48	71	..	5	..	0	..	9	..	15	..
Malaysia	28.95	62.10	8	9	4	2	38	30	8	12	42	47
Mali	0.09	..	..	..	..	..	..	..	..	..	..	..
Mauritania	0.09	0.12	..	..	..	..	..	..	..	..	..	..
Mauritius	0.94	1.60	20	28	52	31	1	1	..	..	26	39
Mexico	107.20	179.11	25	25	4	3	24	18	15	19	31	35
Moldova	0.18	0.62	65	40	9	14	5	5	..	..	22	41
Mongolia	0.08	0.40	49	43	40	17	0	0	2	5	9	35
Morocco	5.74	12.50	34	29	18	13	4	6	12	18	32	34
Mozambique	0.45	1.09	..	..	..	..	..	..	..	..	..	..
Myanmar	..	..	..	..	..	..	..	..	..	..	..	..
Namibia	0.46	0.88	..	..	..	..	..	..	..	..	..	..
Nepal	0.49	0.85	45	..	19	..	1	..	10	..	24	..
Netherlands	53.51	92.47	17	19	2	2	21	20	14	14	46	45
New Zealand	7.99	..	33	27	..	2	..	13	..	..	67	58
Nicaragua	0.59	1.14	..	..	..	..	..	..	..	..	..	..
Niger	0.12	..	..	..	..	..	..	..	..	..	..	..
Nigeria	1.97	..	..	..	..	..	..	..	..	..	..	..
Norway	15.70	34.12	21	20	1	1	21	25	12	9	45	45
Oman	1.08	..	12	8	5	0	1	1	5	12	76	79
Pakistan	10.10	28.24	21	22	33	29	5	8	17	14	25	26
Panama	1.10	1.57	56	..	5	..	3	..	7	..	32	..
Papua New Guinea	0.25	0.50	..	..	..	..	..	..	..	..	..	..
Paraguay	1.09	2.24	66	..	6	..	0	..	10	..	18	..
Peru	7.69	23.56	33	30	16	12	3	2	11	12	37	44
Philippines	19.83	42.80	29	22	7	5	27	33	9	6	28	33
Poland	28.21	76.44	5	17	6	4	15	19	8	8	66	53
Portugal	17.99	26.97	13	14	18	11	16	7	5	6	48	61
Puerto Rico	24.08	44.64	8	9	3	1	9	9	60	62	20	20
Qatar	..	..	4	1	8	2	0	0	21	17	67	80

4.3 | Structure of manufacturing

	Manufacturing value added		Food, beverages, and tobacco		Textiles and clothing		Machinery and transport equipment		Chemicals		Other manufacturing[a]	
	$ billions		% of total		% of total		% of total		% of total		% of total	
	2000	2010	2000	2008	2000	2008	2000	2008	2000	2008	2000	2008
Romania	4.77	32.50	32	16	12	12	13	24	5	5	38	43
Russian Federation	52.13	209.23	19	15	2	2	19	10	8	10	51	63
Rwanda	0.12	0.33	75	..	2	..	..	..	6	..	17	..
Saudi Arabia	18.21	43.85	..	19	..	5	..	6	..	27	..	43
Senegal	0.61	1.49	22	..	4	..	2	..	29	..	43	..
Serbia	1.32	5.04	..	..	..	..	..	..	..	..	..	..
Sierra Leone	0.02	..	..	..	..	..	..	..	..	..	..	..
Singapore	24.01	43.63	3	3	1	1	57	54	14	21	25	21
Slovak Republic	6.32	16.44	10	7	4	3	20	30	7	4	59	56
Slovenia	4.48	8.60	10	7	10	5	18	20	11	15	52	53
Somalia	..	..	..	..	..	..	..	..	..	..	..	..
South Africa	22.93	38.85	15	19	5	3	14	13	7	6	59	58
South Sudan	..	..	..	..	..	..	..	..	..	..	..	..
Spain	97.78	172.43	14	15	7	4	19	18	10	9	51	54
Sri Lanka	2.46	8.92	39	30	31	31	4	7	4	4	22	27
Sudan	1.02	3.30	66	..	4	..	4	..	4	..	21	..
Swaziland	0.48	1.37	..	..	..	..	..	..	..	..	..	..
Sweden	47.75	65.64	7	7	1	1	35	35	9	11	48	47
Switzerland	44.62	95.68	..	..	..	..	..	..	..	..	..	..
Syrian Arab Republic	1.29	..	..	..	..	..	..	..	..	..	..	..
Tajikistan	0.27	0.48	..	..	..	..	..	..	..	..	..	..
Tanzania[b]	0.89	2.05	45	62	0	8	2	1	7	..	46	29
Thailand	41.23	113.47	18	16	12	9	26	35	6	6	38	34
Timor-Leste	0.01	..	..	..	..	..	..	..	..	..	..	..
Togo	0.11	..	..	..	..	..	..	..	..	..	..	..
Trinidad and Tobago	0.58	1.10	21	11	1	1	0	0	27	39	51	49
Tunisia	3.50	7.27	19	17	35	24	3	..	10	9	33	49
Turkey	53.51	113.76	18	12	16	19	15	20	10	7	42	42
Turkmenistan	0.29	..	..	..	..	..	..	..	..	..	..	..
Uganda	0.44	1.33	64	..	4	..	..	..	11	..	21	..
Ukraine	5.10	21.06	..	..	..	..	..	..	..	..	..	..
United Arab Emirates	9.47	28.93	..	..	..	..	..	..	..	..	..	..
United Kingdom	226.97	230.62	14	15	4	2	25	24	10	12	47	48
United States	1,468.08	1,814.34	13	13	3	2	30	25	12	16	42	44
Uruguay	2.86	4.81	39	42	9	7	3	4	8	8	41	39
Uzbekistan	1.14	3.10	..	..	..	..	..	..	..	..	..	..
Venezuela, RB	21.71	..	22	..	2	..	..	..	34	..	41	..
Vietnam	5.79	20.94	30	..	21	..	12	..	6	..	31	..
West Bank and Gaza	..	..	32	27	21	13	1	1	4	4	41	55
Yemen, Rep.	0.55	1.88	43	60	4	9	1	0	5	4	48	27
Zambia	0.33	1.43	..	..	..	..	..	..	..	..	..	..
Zimbabwe	0.90	0.88	..	..	..	..	..	..	..	..	..	..
World	**5,737.81 t**	**9,989.14 t**	..	..	..	..	..	..	..	..	..	..
Low income	18.46	46.11	..	..	..	..	..	..	..	..	..	..
Middle income	1,188.59	3,868.14	..	..	..	..	..	..	..	..	..	..
Lower middle income	203.74	639.71	..	..	..	..	..	..	..	..	..	..
Upper middle income	985.43	3,226.81	..	..	..	..	..	..	..	..	..	..
Low & middle income	1,207.17	3,916.69	..	..	..	..	..	..	..	..	..	..
East Asia & Pacific	530.45	2,185.11	..	..	..	..	..	..	..	..	..	..
Europe & Central Asia	..	..	..	..	..	..	..	..	..	..	..	..
Latin America & Carib.	338.85	712.08	..	..	..	..	..	..	..	..	..	..
Middle East & N. Africa	51.72	115.45	..	..	..	..	..	..	..	..	..	..
South Asia	86.21	283.82	..	..	..	..	..	..	..	..	..	..
Sub-Saharan Africa	41.20	82.72	..	..	..	..	..	..	..	..	..	..
High income	4,535.77	5,562.68	..	..	..	..	..	..	..	..	..	..
Euro area	1,115.92	1,754.91	..	..	..	..	..	..	..	..	..	..

a. Includes unallocated data. b. Covers mainland Tanzania only.

Structure of manufacturing | 4.3

The data on the distribution of manufacturing value added by industry are provided by the United Nations Industrial Development Organization (UNIDO). UNIDO obtains the data from a variety of national and international sources, including the United Nations Statistics Division, the World Bank, the Organisation for Economic Co-operation and Development, and the International Monetary Fund. To improve comparability over time and across countries, UNIDO supplements these data with information from industrial censuses, statistics from national and international organizations, unpublished data that it collects in the field, and estimates by the UNIDO Secretariat. Nevertheless, coverage may be incomplete, particularly for the informal sector. When direct information on inputs and outputs is not available, estimates may be used, which may result in errors in industry totals. Moreover, countries use different reference periods (calendar or fiscal year) and valuation methods (basic or producer prices) to estimate value added. (See *About the data* for table 4.2.)

The data on manufacturing value added in U.S. dollars are from the World Bank's national accounts files and may differ from those UNIDO uses to calculate shares of value added by industry, in part because of differences in exchange rates. Thus value added in a particular industry estimated by applying the shares to total manufacturing value added will not match those from UNIDO sources. Classification of manufacturing industries in the table accords with the United Nations International Standard Industrial Classification (ISIC) revision 3. Editions of *World Development Indicators* prior to 2008 used revision 2, first published in 1948. Revision 3 was completed in 1989, and many countries now use it. But revision 2 is still widely used for compiling cross-country data. UNIDO has converted these data to accord with revision 3. Concordances matching ISIC categories to national classification systems and to related systems such as the Standard International Trade Classification are available.

In establishing classifications systems compilers must define both the types of activities to be described and the units whose activities are to be reported. There are many possibilities, and the choices affect how the statistics can be interpreted and how useful they are in analyzing economic behavior. The ISIC emphasizes commonalities in the production process and is explicitly not intended to measure outputs (for which there is a newly developed Central Product Classification). Nevertheless, the ISIC views an activity as defined by "a process

resulting in a homogeneous set of products" (United Nations 1990 [ISIC, series M, no. 4, rev. 3], p. 9).

Firms typically use multiple processes to produce a product. For example, an automobile manufacturer engages in forging, welding, and painting as well as advertising, accounting, and other service activities. Collecting data at such a detailed level is not practical, nor is it useful to record production data at the highest level of a large, multiplant, multiproduct firm. The ISIC has therefore adopted as the definition of an establishment "an enterprise or part of an enterprise which independently engages in one, or predominantly one, kind of economic activity at or from one location . . . for which data are available . . ." (United Nations 1990, p. 25). By design, this definition matches the reporting unit required for the production accounts of the United Nations System of National Accounts. The ISIC system is described in the United Nations' *International Standard Industrial Classification of All Economic Activities, Third Revision* (1990). The discussion of the ISIC draws on Ryten (1998).

• **Manufacturing value added** is the sum of gross output less the value of intermediate inputs used in production for industries classified in ISIC major division D. • **Food, beverages, and tobacco** correspond to ISIC divisions 15 and 16. • **Textiles and clothing** correspond to ISIC divisions 17–19. • **Machinery and transport equipment** correspond to ISIC divisions 29, 30, 32, 34, and 35. • **Chemicals** correspond to ISIC division 24: • **Other manufacturing,** a residual, covers wood and related products (ISIC division 20), paper and related products (ISIC divisions 21 and 22), petroleum and related products (ISIC division 23), basic metals and mineral products (ISIC division 27), fabricated metal products and professional goods (ISIC division 28), and other industries (ISIC divisions 25, 26, 31, 33, 36, and 37).

Data sources

Data on manufacturing value added are from the World Bank's national accounts files. Data used to calculate shares of industry value added are provided to the World Bank in electronic files by UNIDO. The most recent published source is UNIDO's *International Yearbook of Industrial Statistics 2011.*

4.4 Structure of merchandise exports

	Merchandise exports $ millions		Food % of total		Agricultural raw materials % of total		Fuels % of total		Ores and metals % of total		Manufactures % of total	
	2000	2010	2000	2010	2000	2010	2000	2010	2000	2010	2000	2010
Afghanistan	137	430	..	40	..	11	..	..	..	0	..	20
Albania	258	1,550	7	4	6	2	2	18	4	13	82	62
Algeria	22,031	57,053	0	1	0	0	97	97	0	0	2	2
Angola	7,921	53,500	..	..	..	..	..	..	..	..	..	..
Argentina	26,341	68,133	44	51	2	1	18	8	3	4	32	33
Armenia	294	1,011	14	17	5	1	11	3	27	52	43	24
Australia	63,870	212,554	21	11	6	2	22	31	17	34	29	17
Austria	67,710	152,313	5	7	2	2	1	3	3	4	80	80
Azerbaijan	1,745	26,476	3	3	2	0	85	95	2	0	8	2
Bahrain	6,195	13,647	1	7	0	0	0	0	16	70	10	22
Bangladesh	6,389	19,191	8	..	1	..	0	..	0	..	91	..
Belarus	7,326	25,226	7	13	4	2	20	28	1	1	65	53
Belgium	188,371	412,223	9	9	2	1	4	9	3	4	78	75
Benin	392	1,200	21	..	72	..	0	..	0	..	7	..
Bolivia	1,230	6,290	30	15	3	1	13	44	25	34	29	6
Bosnia and Herzegovina	1,069	4,803	..	7	..	6	..	15	..	12	..	57
Botswana	2,675	4,693	3	5	0	0	0	0	7	15	90	80
Brazil	55,086	201,915	23	31	5	4	2	10	10	18	58	37
Bulgaria	4,852	20,666	10	16	3	1	12	13	13	17	57	49
Burkina Faso	209	1,288	19	33	59	56	3	0	0	2	18	9
Burundi	50	100	91	81	8	5	..	2	1	5	0	6
Cambodia	1,389	5,030	1	1	3	2	0	0	0	0	96	96
Cameroon	1,833	4,000	15	24	9	15	54	50	6	3	3	8
Canada	276,635	388,019	6	10	6	4	13	26	4	8	64	49
Central African Republic	161	140	11	4	13	32	0	0	8	62	68	3
Chad	183	3,450	..	..	..	..	..	..	..	..	..	..
Chile	19,210	71,028	25	17	10	5	1	0	45	65	16	13
China[†]	249,203	1,577,824	5	3	1	0	3	2	2	1	88	94
Hong Kong SAR, China[a]	202,683	401,022	2	7	0	3	0	3	2	9	95	77
Colombia	13,040	39,820	19	12	5	4	43	60	1	2	32	23
Congo, Dem. Rep.	807	5,300	..	..	..	..	..	..	..	..	..	..
Congo, Rep.	2,489	8,200	..	..	..	..	..	..	..	..	..	..
Costa Rica	5,865	9,385	30	35	3	3	1	1	1	1	66	61
Côte d'Ivoire	3,888	10,320	50	50	14	10	21	24	0	0	14	16
Croatia	4,432	11,807	9	11	5	4	11	12	3	5	73	68
Cuba	1,676	3,900	50	..	0	..	3	..	37	..	9	..
Cyprus	951	1,412	33	34	1	2	6	0	5	14	49	50
Czech Republic	29,094	132,852	4	4	2	1	3	4	2	2	88	86
Denmark	51,292	97,681	20	18	3	3	7	8	1	2	64	60
Dominican Republic	5,737	6,598	41	27	2	1	16	2	2	4	34	65
Ecuador	4,927	17,490	37	30	4	4	49	55	0	1	10	10
Egypt, Arab Rep.	5,276	26,438	8	17	5	3	42	30	4	6	38	43
El Salvador	2,941	4,499	19	22	0	1	3	3	1	2	21	73
Eritrea	37	12	54	..	10	..	0	..	8	..	28	..
Estonia	3,830	11,605	8	10	9	5	4	16	5	3	73	62
Ethiopia	486	2,238	71	79	19	9	0	0	1	1	10	9
Finland	46,102	69,630	2	3	6	6	3	8	3	5	85	77
France	327,611	520,661	11	12	1	1	3	4	2	2	81	78
Gabon	2,598	9,371	1	1	12	9	83	83	2	3	2	4
Gambia, The	15	15	81	78	1	2	0	0	0	10	17	10
Georgia	323	1,583	28	22	3	1	8	6	29	21	31	50
Germany	551,810	1,268,874	4	5	1	1	1	2	2	3	84	82
Ghana	1,671	7,896	48	61	10	7	8	0	19	11	15	21
Greece	11,751	21,409	22	24	3	3	15	11	7	9	50	50
Guatemala	2,696	8,466	56	42	4	4	6	5	2	6	32	43
Guinea	666	1,250	3	2	3	5	0	2	63	59	30	32
Guinea-Bissau	62	125	..	..	..	..	..	..	..	..	..	..
Haiti	318	580	..	..	..	..	..	..	..	..	..	..
[†]Data for Taiwan, China	151,357	203,675	1	1	1	1	1	6	1	2	95	89

Structure of merchandise exports

	Merchandise exports		Food		Agricultural raw materials		Fuels		Ores and metals		Manufactures	
	$ millions		% of total		% of total		% of total		% of total		% of total	
	2000	2010	2000	2010	2000	2010	2000	2010	2000	2010	2000	2010
Honduras	3,343	5,742	72	54	5	1	0	4	6	4	17	35
Hungary	28,192	95,437	7	7	1	1	2	3	2	2	86	82
India	42,379	219,959	13	8	1	2	3	17	3	7	78	64
Indonesia	65,403	157,818	9	16	4	7	25	30	5	10	57	37
Iran, Islamic Rep.	28,739	100,524	3	6	0	0	89	71	1	3	7	16
Iraq	20,603	52,800	1	0	0	0	97	99	0	0	0	0
Ireland	77,413	116,801	8	9	0	1	0	1	0	1	86	85
Israel	31,404	58,393	2	3	1	1	0	1	1	1	82	93
Italy	240,518	447,535	6	8	1	1	2	5	1	2	89	82
Jamaica	1,304	1,337	23	25	0	0	0	23	4	12	73	40
Japan	479,249	769,839	0	1	0	1	0	2	1	3	94	89
Jordan	1,899	7,028	16	17	0	0	0	1	15	9	69	74
Kazakhstan	8,812	59,217	7	4	1	0	54	71	19	11	19	14
Kenya	1,734	5,151	59	48	9	11	8	4	3	2	21	35
Korea, Dem. Rep.	708	3,010	..	..	..	..	..	..	..	..	..	..
Korea, Rep.	172,267	466,384	2	1	1	1	5	7	1	2	91	89
Kosovo	..	..	..	..	..	..	..	..	..	..	..	..
Kuwait	19,436	67,014	0	0	0	0	94	93	0	0	4	6
Kyrgyz Republic	505	1,760	17	30	14	5	27	15	11	4	31	38
Lao PDR	330	1,600	..	..	..	..	..	..	..	..	..	..
Latvia	1,868	9,489	6	17	29	12	2	5	6	4	56	59
Lebanon	715	5,021	20	15	2	1	0	0	7	11	71	64
Lesotho	220	820	5	14	0	9	0	0	0	2	95	74
Liberia	329	231	..	..	..	..	..	..	..	..	..	..
Libya	13,380	47,400	1	..	0	..	93	..	0	..	7	..
Lithuania	3,810	20,835	12	17	5	2	21	23	2	1	60	54
Macedonia, FYR	1,323	3,302	15	18	2	1	5	1	9	3	69	51
Madagascar	824	1,090	38	27	3	3	4	7	2	9	52	48
Malawi	379	1,066	89	76	3	3	0	0	0	11	7	9
Malaysia	98,229	198,801	6	12	3	3	10	16	1	2	80	67
Mali	545	2,350	4	30	91	48	0	0	0	1	5	20
Mauritania	355	2,033	21	58	0	0	..	0	46	30	0	0
Mauritius	1,557	2,239	18	37	1	1	0	0	0	0	81	60
Mexico	166,367	298,305	5	6	1	0	10	14	1	3	84	76
Moldova	472	1,582	62	72	3	1	0	0	1	4	33	23
Mongolia	536	2,899	4	..	28	..	0	..	41	..	26	..
Morocco	7,432	17,579	21	19	2	2	4	1	9	12	64	66
Mozambique	364	3,200	42	16	11	4	21	20	17	54	7	2
Myanmar	1,646	8,749	..	..	..	..	..	..	..	..	..	..
Namibia	1,320	4,052	29	23	1	0	2	0	11	31	56	45
Nepal	804	860	10	19	0	4	0	0	0	5	67	72
Netherlands	233,130	573,360	13	14	3	3	8	10	2	2	59	57
New Zealand	13,272	31,396	46	56	14	11	3	5	5	4	31	21
Nicaragua	645	1,851	88	88	2	1	2	1	0	2	8	7
Niger	283	930	44	21	3	3	2	2	41	60	9	14
Nigeria	20,975	82,000	0	3	0	2	100	87	0	1	0	7
Norway	60,058	131,395	6	7	1	1	64	64	6	6	18	18
Oman	11,319	36,601	4	3	0	0	83	81	1	3	12	12
Pakistan	9,028	21,410	11	17	3	2	1	6	0	2	85	74
Panama	859	832	74	73	1	2	7	0	2	11	16	13
Papua New Guinea	2,096	5,612	15	..	2	..	29	..	51	..	2	..
Paraguay	869	4,534	65	86	15	3	0	0	0	1	19	11
Peru	7,028	35,565	30	20	3	1	7	12	39	52	20	14
Philippines	39,783	51,496	5	7	1	1	1	2	2	4	92	86
Poland	31,747	155,752	8	11	2	1	5	4	5	5	80	79
Portugal	24,363	48,748	7	11	3	3	2	6	2	4	85	74
Puerto Rico	..	..	..	..	..	..	..	..	..	..	..	..
Qatar	11,594	62,000	0	0	0	0	91	73	0	0	9	5

	Merchandise exports		Food		Agricultural raw materials		Fuels		Ores and metals		Manufactures	
	$ millions		% of total		% of total		% of total		% of total		% of total	
	2000	2010	2000	2010	2000	2010	2000	2010	2000	2010	2000	2010
Romania	10,412	49,401	3	8	5	2	7	5	7	4	77	79
Russian Federation	105,565	400,132	1	2	3	2	51	64	9	6	24	15
Rwanda	52	297	57	52	3	3	0	0	37	37	3	8
Saudi Arabia	77,583	249,700	1	1	0	0	92	87	0	0	7	11
Senegal	920	2,161	52	29	2	1	14	26	5	4	27	40
Serbia	..	9,795	17	..	6	..	0	..	16	..	61	..
Sierra Leone	13	338	19	..	1	..	..	..	1	..	10	..
Singapore[a]	137,804	351,867	2	2	0	0	7	16	1	1	86	73
Slovak Republic	11,832	65,345	3	4	2	1	7	5	3	3	84	87
Slovenia	8,770	29,446	4	4	2	2	1	4	4	4	90	85
Somalia	..	..	..	..	..	..	..	..	..	..	..	..
South Africa	29,983	81,821	8	9	3	2	10	10	11	33	54	47
South Sudan	..	..	..	..	..	..	..	..	..	..	..	..
Spain	115,251	245,637	14	15	1	1	4	5	2	3	78	73
Sri Lanka	5,430	8,500	21	27	2	4	0	0	0	1	77	67
Sudan	1,807	11,443	17	6	5	1	69	92	0	0	8	0
Swaziland	910	1,550	34	..	11	..	1	..	0	..	54	..
Sweden	87,132	158,314	2	5	5	4	3	7	2	5	82	74
Switzerland	80,500	195,392	3	4	1	0	0	3	6	4	91	89
Syrian Arab Republic	4,634	13,500	9	22	5	1	76	39	1	4	8	33
Tajikistan	785	1,195	4	..	13	..	14	..	56	..	13	..
Tanzania	734	3,687	66	32	13	7	0	3	1	34	20	24
Thailand	69,057	195,319	14	13	3	5	3	5	1	1	75	75
Timor-Leste	..	17	..	..	..	..	..	..	..	..	..	..
Togo	363	800	20	15	23	5	1	0	26	6	31	74
Trinidad and Tobago	4,274	10,590	6	3	0	0	65	66	0	0	29	31
Tunisia	5,850	16,427	9	8	1	1	12	14	2	2	77	76
Turkey	27,775	113,981	13	11	1	0	1	4	3	4	81	79
Turkmenistan	2,506	6,500	0	..	10	..	81	..	0	..	7	..
Uganda	403	1,612	71	67	15	7	6	1	5	2	3	23
Ukraine	14,573	51,478	9	19	2	1	5	7	12	7	69	65
United Arab Emirates	49,835	220,000	1	1	0	0	94	65	3	1	2	4
United Kingdom	285,425	405,666	5	6	0	1	8	13	2	4	77	70
United States	781,918	1,278,263	7	10	2	3	2	7	2	4	83	66
Uruguay	2,295	6,733	47	64	9	8	2	1	0	0	42	26
Uzbekistan	2,817	11,857	..	..	..	..	..	..	..	..	..	..
Venezuela, RB	33,529	65,786	1	0	0	0	86	93	3	2	9	4
Vietnam	14,483	72,192	25	21	2	2	26	15	0	1	43	60
West Bank and Gaza	..	..	..	..	..	..	..	..	..	..	..	..
Yemen, Rep.	4,079	8,700	2	6	0	0	97	92	0	0	0	2
Zambia	892	7,200	9	6	4	1	1	1	74	86	11	6
Zimbabwe	1,925	2,500	47	20	13	7	1	2	11	35	28	36
World	**6,456,422 t**	**15,211,311 t**	**7 w**	**8 w**	**2 w**	**2 w**	**10 w**	**12 w**	**3 w**	**5 w**	**75 w**	**69 w**
Low income	23,852	79,667	26	..	11	..	3	..	8	..	51	..
Middle income	1,350,497	4,848,882	9	10	2	2	21	22	4	6	61	59
Lower middle income	299,735	960,037	12	15	2	3	29	22	4	7	52	52
Upper middle income	1,050,746	3,889,297	9	9	2	2	19	21	5	6	63	60
Low & middle income	1,374,348	4,928,568	10	11	2	2	21	21	4	6	61	58
East Asia & Pacific	544,009	2,281,768	8	8	2	2	7	8	2	3	80	79
Europe & Central Asia	201,167	830,383	5	7	3	2	34	42	9	6	42	36
Latin America & Carib.	356,697	862,436	16	16	2	2	17	21	6	10	58	51
Middle East & N. Africa	114,670	352,565	4	..	1	..	77	..	2	..	16	..
South Asia	64,379	271,099	12	12	2	2	3	13	2	6	80	66
Sub-Saharan Africa	93,392	332,645	15	15	5	4	37	32	7	18	31	31
High income	5,082,101	10,278,808	6	8	2	2	8	9	2	4	78	72
Euro area	1,920,244	4,007,130	8	9	1	1	3	5	2	3	80	77

Note: Components may not sum to 100 percent because of unclassified trade. Exports of gold are excluded.
a. Includes re-exports.

Structure of merchandise exports | 4.4

About the data

Data on merchandise trade are from customs reports of goods moving into or out of an economy or from reports of financial transactions related to merchandise trade recorded in the balance of payments. Because of differences in timing and definitions, trade flow estimates from customs reports and balance of payments may differ. Several international agencies process trade data, each correcting unreported or misreported data, leading to other differences.

The most detailed source of data on international trade in goods is the United Nations Statistics Division's Commodity Trade Statistics (Comtrade) database. The International Monetary Fund (IMF) also collects customs-based data on trade in goods. Exports are recorded as the cost of the goods delivered to the frontier of the exporting country for shipment—the free on board (f.o.b.) value. Many countries report trade data in U.S. dollars. When countries report in local currency, the United Nations Statistics Division applies the average official exchange rate to the U.S. dollar for the period shown.

Countries may report trade according to the general or special system of trade. Under the general system exports comprise outward-moving goods that are (a) goods wholly or partly produced in the country; (b) foreign goods, neither transformed nor declared for domestic consumption in the country, that move outward from customs storage; and (c) goods previously included as imports for domestic consumption but subsequently exported without transformation. Under the special system exports comprise categories a and c. In some compilations categories b and c are classified as re-exports. Because of differences in reporting practices, data on exports may not be fully comparable across economies.

The data on total exports of goods (merchandise) are from the World Trade Organization (WTO), which obtains data from national statistical offices and the IMF's *International Financial Statistics,* supplemented by the Comtrade database and publications or databases of regional organizations, specialized agencies, economic groups, and private sources (such as Eurostat, the Food and Agriculture Organization, and country reports of the Economist Intelligence Unit). Country websites and email contact have improved collection of up-to-date statistics, reducing the proportion of estimates. The WTO database now covers most major traders in Africa, Asia, and Latin America, which together with high-income countries account for nearly 95 percent of world trade. Reliability of data for countries in Europe and Central Asia has also improved.

Export shares by major commodity group are from Comtrade. The values of total exports reported here have not been fully reconciled with the estimates from the national accounts or the balance of payments.

The classification of commodity groups is based on the Standard International Trade Classification (SITC) revision 3. Previous editions contained data based on the SITC revision 1. Data for earlier years in previous editions may differ because of this change in methodology. Concordance tables are available to convert data reported in one system to another.

Definitions

• **Merchandise exports** are the f.o.b. value of goods provided to the rest of the world. • **Food** corresponds to the commodities in SITC sections 0 (food and live animals), 1 (beverages and tobacco), and 4 (animal and vegetable oils and fats) and SITC division 22 (oil seeds, oil nuts, and oil kernels). • **Agricultural raw materials** correspond to SITC section 2 (crude materials except fuels), excluding divisions 22, 27 (crude fertilizers and minerals excluding coal, petroleum, and precious stones), and 28 (metalliferous ores and scrap). • **Fuels** correspond to SITC section 3 (mineral fuels). • **Ores and metals** correspond to the commodities in SITC divisions 27, 28, and 68 (nonferrous metals). • **Manufactures** correspond to the commodities in SITC sections 5 (chemicals), 6 (basic manufactures), 7 (machinery and transport equipment), and 8 (miscellaneous manufactured goods), excluding division 68.

Data sources

Data on merchandise exports are from the WTO. Data on shares of exports by major commodity group are from the United Nations Statistics Division's Comtrade database. The WTO publishes data on world trade in its *Annual Report.* The IMF publishes estimates of total exports of goods in its *International Financial Statistics* and *Direction of Trade Statistics,* as does the United Nations Statistics Division in its *Monthly Bulletin of Statistics.* And the United Nations Conference on Trade and Development publishes data on the structure of exports in its *Handbook of Statistics.* Tariff line records of exports are compiled in the United Nations Statistics Division's Comtrade database.

4.5 | Structure of merchandise imports

	Merchandise imports		Food		Agricultural raw materials		Fuels		Ores and metals		Manufactures	
	$ millions		% of total		% of total		% of total		% of total		% of total	
	2000	2010	2000	2010	2000	2010	2000	2010	2000	2010	2000	2010
Afghanistan	1,176	4,400	..	14	..	0	..	21	..	0	..	19
Albania	1,090	4,601	22	18	1	1	9	14	2	4	67	64
Algeria	9,171	40,212	28	16	3	2	1	2	1	2	67	78
Angola	3,040	21,500	..	..	..	..	..	..	..	..	..	..
Argentina	25,154	56,503	5	3	1	1	4	7	2	3	87	85
Armenia	882	3,783	25	18	1	1	21	18	1	3	52	56
Australia	71,529	201,640	5	5	1	1	8	14	1	2	84	75
Austria	72,394	158,752	5	7	3	2	5	11	3	5	81	74
Azerbaijan	1,172	6,746	19	19	2	2	5	1	4	2	71	76
Bahrain	4,633	10,000	10	12	1	1	1	2	3	19	41	65
Bangladesh	8,883	27,819	16	..	6	..	7	..	2	..	68	..
Belarus	8,646	34,868	12	8	2	1	30	35	4	3	48	47
Belgium	177,511	390,443	9	8	2	1	9	14	4	4	76	71
Benin	613	2,200	22	..	5	..	19	..	1	..	53	..
Bolivia	1,830	5,361	14	8	2	1	5	12	1	1	79	78
Bosnia and Herzegovina	3,107	9,223	..	18	..	2	..	19	..	2	..	58
Botswana	2,081	5,657	14	12	1	1	5	15	2	2	75	68
Brazil	59,053	191,491	7	5	2	1	15	17	3	3	73	74
Bulgaria	6,544	25,403	5	10	1	1	26	22	6	9	59	55
Burkina Faso	611	2,048	13	15	1	1	25	22	1	1	61	61
Burundi	148	509	23	14	2	1	12	2	2	1	60	82
Cambodia	1,939	7,500	10	7	3	2	13	7	0	2	73	82
Cameroon	1,489	4,850	18	18	2	2	23	27	1	1	56	52
Canada	244,786	402,280	5	7	1	1	5	10	2	3	84	77
Central African Republic	117	340	29	39	4	2	8	1	4	2	54	56
Chad	317	2,600	..	..	..	..	..	..	..	..	..	..
Chile	18,507	58,956	7	7	1	1	18	21	1	2	71	69
China†	225,094	1,395,099	4	5	5	4	9	15	6	14	75	61
Hong Kong SAR, China	214,042	442,035	4	4	1	1	2	4	2	2	91	90
Colombia	11,539	40,683	12	10	3	1	2	5	2	2	80	80
Congo, Dem. Rep.	683	4,500	..	..	..	..	..	..	..	..	..	..
Congo, Rep.	465	2,900	..	..	..	..	..	..	..	..	..	..
Costa Rica	6,372	13,570	7	9	1	1	8	12	2	2	82	73
Côte d'Ivoire	2,482	7,830	17	19	1	1	34	24	1	1	46	55
Croatia	7,887	20,054	8	10	2	1	15	19	2	2	73	67
Cuba	4,843	11,300	16	..	1	..	24	..	1	..	58	..
Cyprus	31,974	126,222	5	5	2	1	10	9	4	4	80	77
Czech Republic	3,846	8,499	19	15	1	1	13	20	1	1	65	61
Denmark	45,557	84,848	11	14	3	2	6	8	2	2	76	73
Dominican Republic	9,479	15,299	12	14	2	1	23	25	1	1	62	60
Ecuador	3,721	20,591	9	8	3	1	7	17	2	1	77	72
Egypt, Arab Rep.	14,578	52,923	25	19	5	3	8	13	2	4	56	60
El Salvador	4,947	8,498	12	17	2	2	12	16	1	1	43	64
Eritrea	471	690	37	..	1	..	2	..	1	..	58	..
Estonia	5,052	12,252	10	11	3	2	7	16	3	1	76	63
Ethiopia	1,260	8,552	7	11	1	0	20	19	1	1	71	69
Finland	34,443	68,510	5	7	2	2	12	18	6	8	73	61
France	338,940	605,706	8	8	2	1	10	14	3	3	77	73
Gabon	950	2,983	18	17	1	0	4	7	1	1	76	74
Gambia, The	187	276	35	36	1	1	12	20	1	1	51	41
Georgia	709	5,096	23	18	1	1	20	18	1	2	55	60
Germany	497,197	1,066,839	7	7	2	2	9	11	4	5	68	68
Ghana	2,973	10,703	13	15	2	1	21	1	1	1	62	81
Greece	33,480	63,173	11	12	2	1	13	24	3	3	70	60
Guatemala	4,791	13,837	12	13	2	1	13	18	1	1	72	66
Guinea	612	1,100	24	13	1	0	25	33	1	0	49	53
Guinea-Bissau	59	220	..	..	..	..	..	..	..	..	..	..
Haiti	1,036	3,150	..	..	..	..	..	..	..	..	..	..
†Data for Taiwan, China	140,642	174,371	4	5	2	1	9	21	5	7	79	65

Structure of merchandise imports

	Merchandise imports ($ millions)		Food (% of total)		Agricultural raw materials (% of total)		Fuels (% of total)		Ores and metals (% of total)		Manufactures (% of total)	
	2000	2010	2000	2010	2000	2010	2000	2010	2000	2010	2000	2010
Honduras	3,988	8,550	22	19	2	1	18	19	1	1	50	60
Hungary	32,172	88,120	3	5	1	1	5	11	3	3	84	72
India	51,523	327,230	5	4	3	2	39	36	5	5	47	51
Indonesia	43,595	131,737	10	8	7	3	19	20	3	3	61	65
Iran, Islamic Rep.	13,898	65,021	19	15	3	2	2	3	2	2	73	71
Iraq	13,384	42,500	1	..	0	..	0	..	0	..	8	..
Ireland	51,041	60,032	6	12	1	1	4	12	1	2	82	66
Israel	37,686	61,209	5	7	1	1	10	18	2	2	81	71
Italy	238,757	483,814	9	9	4	2	10	19	4	5	69	64
Jamaica	3,326	5,195	15	18	2	1	18	30	1	0	61	49
Japan	379,511	694,052	13	9	3	2	20	29	6	8	57	51
Jordan	4,597	15,402	21	16	2	1	5	22	2	2	66	56
Kazakhstan	5,040	29,760	9	9	1	1	12	10	3	1	74	80
Kenya	3,105	12,090	14	12	2	2	22	22	1	2	60	63
Korea, Dem. Rep.	1,686	4,420	..	..	..	..	..	..	..	..	..	..
Korea, Rep.	160,481	425,212	5	5	3	2	24	29	6	8	62	57
Kosovo	..	..	..	..	..	..	..	..	..	..	..	..
Kuwait	7,157	22,446	14	15	0	1	1	1	1	3	34	81
Kyrgyz Republic	554	3,223	15	17	2	1	23	27	2	1	59	54
Lao PDR	535	1,800	..	..	..	..	..	..	..	..	..	..
Latvia	3,202	11,593	12	15	2	1	12	15	2	2	71	59
Lebanon	6,230	18,460	19	16	2	1	18	21	2	2	59	59
Lesotho	809	2,200	18	20	1	2	19	11	2	1	49	53
Liberia	668	700	..	..	..	..	..	..	..	..	..	..
Libya	3,732	10,500	28	..	1	..	0	..	1	..	70	..
Lithuania	5,457	23,399	10	12	3	2	22	32	2	2	61	50
Macedonia, FYR	2,094	5,451	12	13	2	1	14	5	2	1	45	62
Madagascar	1,097	2,650	13	14	0	1	23	15	0	0	63	70
Malawi	532	1,900	10	14	2	1	16	10	1	1	72	74
Malaysia	81,963	164,733	4	8	1	2	5	10	3	5	85	74
Mali	806	2,850	15	12	1	0	24	26	1	1	59	61
Mauritania	454	1,822	19	19	0	0	23	26	0	0	41	53
Mauritius	2,093	4,402	14	21	2	2	12	19	1	1	70	56
Mexico	179,464	310,618	5	6	1	1	3	8	2	3	83	80
Moldova	777	3,855	13	15	2	1	32	21	1	1	51	62
Mongolia	615	3,278	17	..	1	..	19	..	0	..	63	..
Morocco	11,534	35,277	14	11	3	2	18	23	3	3	63	59
Mozambique	1,158	4,500	14	12	1	1	13	20	1	1	68	50
Myanmar	2,401	4,807	7	..	0	..	19	..	1	..	72	..
Namibia	1,550	5,360	17	14	1	1	3	14	1	1	78	70
Nepal	1,573	5,280	13	14	4	2	16	18	3	4	49	64
Netherlands	218,267	516,927	9	10	2	1	10	16	2	3	65	57
New Zealand	13,906	30,617	8	11	1	1	10	15	2	2	79	71
Nicaragua	1,805	4,173	16	16	1	1	18	22	1	0	65	61
Niger	395	2,150	39	15	4	2	15	13	2	1	41	69
Nigeria	8,721	44,235	20	10	1	1	2	1	2	1	75	86
Norway	34,392	77,252	6	8	2	1	4	7	5	7	81	76
Oman	5,131	19,870	22	12	1	1	2	7	3	4	70	51
Pakistan	10,864	39,044	14	13	3	5	33	30	2	3	47	49
Panama	3,379	9,145	12	8	0	0	19	1	1	0	68	90
Papua New Guinea	1,151	3,850	18	..	1	..	22	..	1	..	58	..
Paraguay	2,193	10,040	17	7	1	1	16	12	1	1	66	79
Peru	7,415	30,126	12	10	2	2	16	14	1	1	70	72
Philippines	37,027	58,229	7	11	1	1	11	17	2	4	78	67
Poland	49,029	173,648	6	8	2	2	11	11	3	3	78	74
Portugal	39,952	75,648	11	13	3	1	10	14	2	3	73	67
Puerto Rico	..	..	..	..	..	..	..	..	..	..	..	..
Qatar	3,252	23,240	12	8	1	0	0	1	3	4	84	84

	Merchandise imports		Food		Agricultural raw materials		Fuels		Ores and metals		Manufactures	
	$ millions		% of total		% of total		% of total		% of total		% of total	
	2000	2010	2000	2010	2000	2010	2000	2010	2000	2010	2000	2010
Romania	13,148	61,995	7	8	1	1	12	10	4	3	76	75
Russian Federation	44,659	248,738	20	13	2	1	4	2	3	1	59	69
Rwanda	211	1,431	21	13	3	2	14	8	2	1	60	76
Saudi Arabia	30,238	97,077	18	16	1	1	0	0	3	5	76	77
Senegal	1,519	4,782	23	22	2	2	23	30	1	2	51	44
Serbia	..	16,734	9	..	4	..	20	..	4	..	63	..
Sierra Leone	149	770	33	..	4	..	28	..	1	..	35	..
Singapore	134,545	310,791	3	3	0	0	12	26	2	2	82	66
Slovak Republic	12,760	66,557	6	6	2	1	18	13	3	4	72	76
Slovenia	10,147	30,037	6	8	4	3	9	13	5	6	76	70
Somalia	..	..	..	..	..	..	..	..	..	..	..	..
South Africa	29,695	94,040	5	6	1	1	14	20	2	2	69	65
South Sudan	..	..	..	..	..	..	..	..	..	..	..	..
Spain	156,143	314,320	9	10	2	1	12	18	3	4	73	65
Sri Lanka	7,177	13,512	14	15	1	1	9	17	1	2	74	65
Sudan	1,553	10,045	23	15	1	1	7	4	1	1	68	78
Swaziland	1,046	1,700	19	..	2	..	13	..	1	..	64	..
Sweden	72,880	148,710	6	9	2	1	9	13	3	4	74	69
Switzerland	82,521	175,933	6	6	1	1	5	8	6	4	83	81
Syrian Arab Republic	3,815	16,900	19	14	3	3	4	31	2	4	65	47
Tajikistan	675	2,900	10	..	1	..	37	..	0	..	51	..
Tanzania	1,524	7,830	15	10	3	1	19	28	1	1	63	60
Thailand	61,924	182,400	4	5	3	2	12	18	3	5	77	70
Timor-Leste	..	298	..	..	..	..	..	..	..	..	..	..
Togo	562	1,550	18	16	2	1	19	14	2	2	59	67
Trinidad and Tobago	3,308	6,575	8	11	1	1	32	33	2	5	56	50
Tunisia	8,567	22,218	8	9	3	2	11	13	2	4	76	72
Turkey	54,503	185,542	4	4	4	3	14	15	4	8	70	63
Turkmenistan	1,786	5,600	12	..	0	..	1	..	1	..	80	..
Uganda	1,536	4,550	14	12	2	1	17	20	2	1	65	65
Ukraine	13,956	60,911	6	9	2	1	43	32	5	4	41	53
United Arab Emirates	35,009	160,000	11	7	1	0	1	1	2	5	85	73
United Kingdom	348,058	560,097	8	10	2	1	4	11	3	4	78	68
United States	1,259,300	1,969,184	4	5	1	1	11	19	2	2	77	70
Uruguay	3,466	8,622	11	10	3	2	15	24	1	1	69	62
Uzbekistan	2,697	8,386	..	..	..	..	..	..	..	..	..	..
Venezuela, RB	16,213	40,800	12	15	2	1	4	1	2	1	81	81
Vietnam	15,638	84,801	5	8	3	3	14	11	2	4	73	74
West Bank and Gaza	..	..	..	..	..	..	..	..	..	..	..	..
Yemen, Rep.	2,324	9,700	36	28	2	1	12	21	1	1	49	50
Zambia	888	5,321	8	5	3	1	12	12	3	21	73	62
Zimbabwe	1,863	3,800	4	19	1	3	42	11	3	14	48	52
World	**6,659,168 t**	**15,264,186 t**	**7 w**	**7 w**	**2 w**	**1 w**	**10 w**	**16 w**	**3 w**	**4 w**	**74 w**	**68 w**
Low income	38,879	134,286	16	..	3	..	16	..	2	..	63	..
Middle income	1,250,130	4,613,566	8	8	3	2	11	15	3	6	72	68
Lower middle income	282,691	1,083,885	10	10	3	2	20	23	3	4	57	60
Upper middle income	967,323	3,529,396	7	7	3	2	9	13	3	6	76	70
Low & middle income	1,289,014	4,747,794	8	8	3	2	11	15	3	6	71	68
East Asia & Pacific	475,589	2,046,331	5	6	4	3	10	15	4	10	76	66
Europe & Central Asia	182,530	786,004	10	9	3	2	15	14	4	4	63	63
Latin America & Carib.	375,652	872,376	7	7	2	1	7	11	2	3	79	77
Middle East & N. Africa	92,037	329,532	17	15	3	2	7	13	2	3	56	66
South Asia	81,760	419,140	8	7	4	2	34	32	4	5	49	52
Sub-Saharan Africa	81,357	302,642	12	10	2	1	14	17	1	2	66	67
High income	5,370,223	10,519,458	7	7	2	1	10	16	3	4	75	68
Euro area	1,904,622	3,949,668	8	9	2	2	9	15	3	4	72	67

Note: Components may not sum to 100 percent because of unclassified trade.

Structure of merchandise imports | 4.5

About the data

Data on imports of goods are derived from the same sources as data on exports. In principle, world exports and imports should be identical. Similarly, exports from an economy should equal the sum of imports by the rest of the world from that economy. But differences in timing and definitions result in discrepancies in reported values at all levels. For further discussion of indicators of merchandise trade, see *About the data* for tables 4.4 and 6.1.

The value of imports is generally recorded as the cost of the goods when purchased by the importer plus the cost of transport and insurance to the frontier of the importing country—the cost, insurance, and freight (c.i.f.) value, corresponding to the landed cost at the point of entry of foreign goods into the country. A few countries, including Australia, Canada, and the United States, collect import data on a free on board (f.o.b.) basis and adjust them for freight and insurance costs. Many countries report trade data in U.S. dollars. When countries report in local currency, the United Nations Statistics Division applies the average official exchange rate to the U.S. dollar for the period shown.

Countries may report trade according to the general or special system of trade. Under the general system imports include goods imported for domestic consumption and imports into bonded warehouses and free trade zones. Under the special system imports comprise goods imported for domestic consumption (including transformation and repair) and withdrawals for domestic consumption from bonded warehouses and free trade zones. Goods transported through a country en route to another are excluded.

The data on total imports of goods (merchandise) in the table come from the World Trade Organization (WTO). For further discussion of the WTO's sources and methodology, see *About the data* for table 4.4. The import shares by major commodity group are from the United Nations Statistics Division's Commodity Trade Statistics (Comtrade) database. The values of total imports reported here have not been fully reconciled with the estimates of imports of goods and services from the national accounts (shown in table 4.8) or those from the balance of payments (table 4.17).

The classification of commodity groups is based on the Standard International Trade Classification (SITC) revision 3. Previous editions contained data based on the SITC revision 1. Data for earlier years in previous editions may differ because of this change in methodology. Concordance tables are available to convert data reported in one system to another.

Definitions

• **Merchandise imports** are the c.i.f. value of goods purchased from the rest of the world valued in U.S. dollars. • **Food** corresponds to the commodities in SITC sections 0 (food and live animals), 1 (beverages and tobacco), and 4 (animal and vegetable oils and fats) and SITC division 22 (oil seeds, oil nuts, and oil kernels). • **Agricultural raw materials** correspond to SITC section 2 (crude materials except fuels), excluding divisions 22, 27 (crude fertilizers and minerals excluding coal, petroleum, and precious stones), and 28 (metalliferous ores and scrap). • **Fuels** correspond to SITC section 3 (mineral fuels). • **Ores and metals** correspond to the commodities in SITC divisions 27, 28, and 68 (nonferrous metals). • **Manufactures** correspond to the commodities in SITC sections 5 (chemicals), 6 (basic manufactures), 7 (machinery and transport equipment), and 8 (miscellaneous manufactured goods), excluding division 68.

Data sources

Data on merchandise imports are from the WTO. Data on shares of imports by major commodity group are from the United Nations Statistics Division's Comtrade database. The WTO publishes data on world trade in its *Annual Report*. The International Monetary Fund publishes estimates of total imports of goods in its *International Financial Statistics* and *Direction of Trade Statistics*, as does the United Nations Statistics Division in its *Monthly Bulletin of Statistics*. And the United Nations Conference on Trade and Development publishes data on the structure of imports in its *Handbook of Statistics*. Tariff line records of imports are compiled in the United Nations Statistics Division's Comtrade database.

4.6 | Structure of service exports

	Commercial service exports		Transport		Travel		Insurance and financial services		Computer, information, communications, and other commercial services	
	$ millions		% of total		% of total		% of total		% of total	
	2000	2010	2000	2010	2000	2010	2000	2010	2000	2010
Afghanistan	..	..	..	..	..	..	..	..	..	..
Albania	429	2,192	4	11	91	74	0	0	5	15
Algeria	..	2,794	..	28	..	10	..	9	..	54
Angola	267	857	6	5	18	84	13	..	81	11
Argentina	4,775	12,931	24	16	61	38	0	0	15	46
Armenia	130	750	49	21	29	54	3	3	19	22
Australia	19,413	48,490	22	18	48	56	5	3	25	22
Austria	22,865	54,161	18	24	43	35	8	4	31	37
Azerbaijan	234	2,017	51	32	27	33	1	1	22	35
Bahrain	933	4,047	30	20	61	34	..	22	8	24
Bangladesh	283	1,209	32	14	18	7	6	4	44	75
Belarus	989	4,470	59	67	9	10	1	0	31	23
Belgium	36,285	85,339	24	30	19	12	7	5	50	53
Benin	126	204	14	9	61	64	2	2	22	24
Bolivia	207	530	24	13	33	58	22	13	21	16
Bosnia and Herzegovina	448	1,280	6	23	52	46	4	1	38	30
Botswana	306	385	17	10	73	57	4	1	7	32
Brazil	8,961	30,294	16	16	20	20	8	8	56	56
Bulgaria	2,129	6,750	30	19	50	53	1	3	18	25
Burkina Faso	28	142	13	26	67	47	0	2	19	26
Burundi	2	7	43	10	37	24	0	22	20	44
Cambodia	423	1,671	17	14	72	75	0	0	11	11
Cameroon	666	1,105	21	43	9	14	3	4	68	38
Canada	39,271	67,432	19	17	27	23	7	11	46	48
Central African Republic	..	..	..	..	..	..	..	..	..	..
Chad	..	..	..	..	..	..	..	..	..	..
Chile	3,995	10,685	55	61	21	15	3	3	22	21
China	30,146	170,249	12	20	54	27	1	2	33	51
Hong Kong SAR, China	40,362	106,432	32	27	15	19	12	14	42	40
Colombia	1,984	4,357	30	28	52	48	4	1	15	23
Congo, Dem. Rep.	..	..	..	..	..	..	..	..	..	..
Congo, Rep.	130	303	26	4	9	18	2	31	63	47
Costa Rica	1,911	4,149	13	7	68	48	0	1	18	44
Côte d'Ivoire	415	816	20	29	12	14	13	13	55	57
Croatia	4,056	11,034	14	10	68	73	1	1	17	16
Cuba	..	..	..	..	..	..	..	..	..	..
Cyprus	6,751	20,911	21	24	44	34	6	2	30	40
Czech Republic	3,798	8,044	19	24	51	27	6	15	25	34
Denmark	23,721	60,405	45	..	15	..	..	..	39	..
Dominican Republic	3,143	4,998	2	8	91	84	0	1	7	7
Ecuador	793	1,371	37	26	51	57	0	..	13	17
Egypt, Arab Rep.	9,687	23,618	27	34	45	53	1	1	27	12
El Salvador	673	944	37	32	32	41	10	3	20	23
Eritrea	54	..	18	..	64	..	1	..	17	..
Estonia	1,458	4,485	49	40	35	24	1	2	15	34
Ethiopia	387	1,991	56	59	15	26	1	0	28	14
Finland	7,669	27,729	22	11	18	10	0	2	60	76
France	82,115	143,896	22	25	40	32	3	3	34	40
Gabon	171	..	56	..	12	..	0	..	32	..
Gambia, The	73	88	27	42	67	36	1	0	6	22
Georgia	320	1,514	48	46	44	44	3	4	5	7
Germany	79,659	233,338	25	25	23	15	5	8	46	53
Ghana	490	1,344	20	27	68	46	1	1	11	26
Greece	19,181	37,336	41	55	48	33	1	2	9	10
Guatemala	702	2,192	12	13	69	63	3	2	16	22
Guinea	27	61	58	6	7	3	0	16	34	74
Guinea-Bissau	4	32	2	0	77	38	2	9	21	53
Haiti	158	183	2	..	81	91	..	..	19	9

	Commercial service exports		Transport		Travel		Insurance and financial services		Computer, information, communications, and other commercial services	
	$ millions		% of total		% of total		% of total		% of total	
	2000	2010	2000	2010	2000	2010	2000	2010	2000	2010
Honduras	487	1,003	12	5	53	65	3	2	32	28
Hungary	5,836	19,288	9	20	64	28	3	1	24	52
India	16,031	123,277	12	11	22	11	3	6	63	71
Indonesia	5,061	16,211	16	16	98	43	0	2	2	38
Iran, Islamic Rep.	1,357	..	49	..	37	..	11	..	3	..
Iraq	..	1,721	..	22	..	0	..	0	..	78
Ireland	18,326	97,833	8	5	14	4	17	19	61	72
Israel	15,619	24,209	16	18	26	20	0	0	58	63
Italy	55,998	97,368	17	15	49	39	2	6	32	40
Jamaica	1,988	2,600	17	11	67	77	1	2	15	10
Japan	68,303	138,875	37	28	5	10	4	4	53	59
Jordan	1,602	4,782	19	18	45	71	0	..	36	11
Kazakhstan	905	3,890	51	58	39	26	2	3	8	13
Kenya	727	2,920	57	54	39	27	1	5	4	14
Korea, Dem. Rep.	..	..	..	..	..	..	..	..	..	..
Korea, Rep.	30,650	81,556	45	47	22	12	3	4	31	37
Kosovo	..	..	..	..	..	..	..	..	..	..
Kuwait	1,571	7,137	88	45	6	3	6	2	0	50
Kyrgyz Republic	57	679	29	22	27	42	3	1	42	35
Lao PDR	134	489	15	10	85	78	0	2	0	9
Latvia	1,131	3,657	68	50	12	17	4	7	17	26
Lebanon	4,412	15,706	0	4	97	50	1	14	1	32
Lesotho	20	44	3	2	88	79	0	0	9	19
Liberia	..	40	..	56	..	31	..	..	..	13
Libya	119	410	13	64	63	15	17	18	7	3
Lithuania	1,052	4,064	47	60	37	25	1	1	16	14
Macedonia, FYR	290	903	42	32	13	22	2	1	44	45
Madagascar	314	..	16	..	39	..	1	..	44	..
Malawi	34	126	26	18	74	55	2	0	0	26
Malaysia	13,812	32,760	20	14	36	56	2	2	41	30
Mali	92	335	36	6	44	57	3	2	18	35
Mauritania	24	..	3	..	83	..	..	..	15	..
Mauritius	1,066	2,656	21	14	51	48	6	3	22	34
Mexico	13,291	14,935	8	7	62	79	14	12	16	2
Moldova	155	663	54	37	25	26	2	1	19	36
Mongolia	74	483	41	36	49	51	0	2	10	11
Morocco	2,854	12,138	17	18	71	55	1	2	10	25
Mozambique	325	576	30	28	23	34	3	1	47	36
Myanmar	459	334	17	45	35	22	..	..	48	34
Namibia	163	835	23	16	68	53	0	1	8	30
Nepal	410	584	15	7	38	59	0	0	47	34
Netherlands	48,361	93,361	35	27	15	14	2	2	48	57
New Zealand	4,352	8,908	28	20	52	55	1	1	19	24
Nicaragua	187	430	16	11	69	72	2	1	13	16
Niger	35	100	24	8	64	66	4	3	8	23
Nigeria	1,833	2,613	12	75	6	22	1	1	82	3
Norway	17,528	39,506	55	40	12	12	3	4	30	45
Oman	452	1,761	43	36	49	44	3	1	5	18
Pakistan	1,284	2,949	65	48	6	10	1	3	27	38
Panama	1,961	5,659	59	53	23	30	9	9	9	8
Papua New Guinea	243	279	5	7	3	1	2	3	90	89
Paraguay	573	1,324	12	17	13	16	5	2	70	64
Peru	1,445	3,816	17	22	58	60	9	6	17	12
Philippines	3,377	14,358	14	9	64	18	3	1	20	71
Poland	10,395	32,700	24	27	55	29	3	2	19	42
Portugal	8,905	22,957	16	27	59	44	3	1	22	28
Puerto Rico	..	..	..	..	..	..	..	..	..	..
Qatar	..	..	..	..	..	..	..	..	..	..

	Commercial service exports		Transport		Travel		Insurance and financial services		Computer, information, communications, and other commercial services	
	$ millions		% of total		% of total		% of total		% of total	
	2000	**2010**	**2000**	**2010**	**2000**	**2010**	**2000**	**2010**	**2000**	**2010**
Romania	1,720	8,728	37	29	21	13	8	2	35	56
Russian Federation	9,565	44,605	37	33	36	20	1	3	26	43
Rwanda	41	243	34	11	57	83	..	0	8	6
Saudi Arabia	4,779	10,346	..	20	..	65	..	12	..	3
Senegal	330	909	10	5	44	51	2	2	45	42
Serbia	..	3,525	..	22	..	23	..	2	..	53
Sierra Leone	39	60	46	40	27	43	0	1	27	15
Singapore	28,420	112,061	41	29	18	13	8	13	32	45
Slovak Republic	2,218	5,817	45	31	20	38	2	1	33	30
Slovenia	1,883	6,120	26	26	51	42	1	2	22	30
Somalia	..	..	..	..	..	..	..	..	..	..
South Africa	4,888	13,617	24	12	55	67	9	8	12	13
South Sudan	..	..	..	..	..	..	..	..	..	..
Spain	52,112	122,773	16	17	57	43	3	5	24	36
Sri Lanka	915	2,448	44	47	27	24	4	3	25	26
Sudan	24	224	63	2	22	42	8	6	15	49
Swaziland	271	250	7	8	8	20	0	16	86	55
Sweden	22,193	64,835	21	15	18	17	6	3	55	65
Switzerland	29,443	81,649	15	7	23	18	41	25	21	49
Syrian Arab Republic	1,480	7,040	17	8	73	88	2	1	10	3
Tajikistan	60	182	76	27	3	2	2	5	20	65
Tanzania	575	2,047	10	22	65	61	3	2	22	15
Thailand	13,785	34,058	24	17	54	59	1	1	22	23
Timor-Leste	..	..	..	..	..	..	..	..	..	..
Togo	46	265	23	34	18	26	9	5	51	35
Trinidad and Tobago	543	758	38	28	39	48	8	14	14	9
Tunisia	2,680	5,471	22	28	63	48	2	3	13	21
Turkey	19,267	34,247	15	28	40	61	2	4	43	8
Turkmenistan	269	..	50	..	12	..	..	..	38	..
Uganda	205	984	15	5	81	74	1	3	4	18
Ukraine	3,800	16,466	77	47	10	23	1	3	12	27
United Arab Emirates	..	..	..	..	..	..	..	..	..	..
United Kingdom	118,567	253,287	16	12	18	13	22	24	43	51
United States	275,881	522,510	16	14	37	26	7	16	40	45
Uruguay	1,249	2,458	30	18	57	61	8	5	5	16
Uzbekistan	..	..	..	..	..	..	..	..	..	..
Venezuela, RB	1,057	1,626	35	35	40	45	0	0	24	19
Vietnam	2,702	7,460	..	..	..	..	..	..	..	..
West Bank and Gaza	453	554	8	5	62	74	0	0	29	21
Yemen, Rep.	174	1,460	12	13	42	80	..	..	46	7
Zambia	114	312	37	49	58	40	4	2	0	9
Zimbabwe	..	..	..	..	..	..	..	..	..	..
World	**1,530,963 t**	**3,806,462 t**	**24 w**	**22 w**	**32 w**	**26 w**	**6 w**	**8 w**	**38 w**	**45 w**
Low income	6,240	20,076	30	24	35	26	4	4	33	47
Middle income	223,261	773,203	21	21	48	41	4	4	28	33
Lower middle income	63,035	276,733	23	23	50	32	2	3	32	42
Upper middle income	161,130	504,513	21	21	48	44	4	5	27	31
Low & middle income	229,067	792,143	22	22	48	41	4	4	28	33
East Asia & Pacific	70,928	280,031	16	17	56	38	1	2	29	43
Europe & Central Asia	44,988	144,429	39	36	33	27	2	3	27	34
Latin America & Carib.	51,355	109,176	18	17	51	57	9	8	23	19
Middle East & N. Africa	..	..	..	28	..	29	..	3	..	40
South Asia	19,358	131,836	24	19	20	13	3	5	52	63
Sub-Saharan Africa	15,245	40,508	21	31	35	50	6	5	41	14
High income	1,305,653	3,018,606	25	22	27	21	7	9	41	48
Euro area	472,024	1,145,715	23	23	32	23	4	5	40	49

Structure of service exports | 4.6

About the data

Balance of payments statistics, the main source of information on international trade in services, have many weaknesses. Disaggregation of important components may be limited and varies considerably across countries. There are inconsistencies in the methods used to report items. And the recording of major flows as net items is common (for example, insurance transactions are often recorded as premiums less claims). These factors contribute to a downward bias in the value of the service trade reported in the balance of payments.

Efforts are being made to improve the coverage, quality, and consistency of these data. Eurostat and the Organisation for Economic Co-operation and Development, for example, are working together to improve the collection of statistics on trade in services in member countries. In addition, the International Monetary Fund (IMF) has implemented the new classification of trade in services introduced in the fifth edition of its *Balance of Payments Manual* (1993).

Still, difficulties in capturing all the dimensions of international trade in services mean that the record is likely to remain incomplete. Cross-border intrafirm service transactions, which are usually not captured in the balance of payments, have increased in recent years. An example is transnational corporations' use of mainframe computers around the clock for data processing, exploiting time zone differences between their home country and the host countries of their affiliates. Another important dimension of service trade not captured by conventional balance of payments statistics is establishment trade—sales in the host country by foreign affiliates. By contrast, cross-border intrafirm transactions in merchandise may be reported as exports or imports in the balance of payments.

The data on exports of services in the table and on imports of services in table 4.7, unlike those in editions before 2000, include only commercial services and exclude the category "government services not included elsewhere." The data are compiled by the IMF based on returns from national sources. Data on total trade in goods and services from the IMF's Balance of Payments database are shown in table 4.17.

International transactions in services are defined by the IMF's *Balance of Payments Manual* (1993) as the economic output of intangible commodities that may be produced, transferred, and consumed at the same time. Definitions may vary among reporting economies. Travel services include the goods and services consumed by travelers, such as meals, lodging, and transport (within the economy visited), including car rental.

Definitions

• **Commercial service exports** are total service exports minus exports of government services not included elsewhere. • **Transport** covers all transport services (sea, air, land, internal waterway, space, and pipeline) performed by residents of one economy for those of another and involving the carriage of passengers, movement of goods (freight), rental of carriers with crew, and related support and auxiliary services. Excluded are freight insurance, which is included in insurance services; goods procured in ports by nonresident carriers and repairs of transport equipment, which are included in goods; repairs of harbors, railway facilities, and airfield facilities, which are included in construction services; and rental of carriers without crew, which is included in other services. • **Travel** covers goods and services acquired from an economy by travelers in that economy for their own use during visits of less than one year for business or personal purposes. • **Insurance and financial services** cover freight insurance on goods exported and other direct insurance such as life insurance; financial intermediation services such as commissions, foreign exchange transactions, and brokerage services; and auxiliary services such as financial market operational and regulatory services. • **Computer, information, communications, and other commercial services** cover such activities as international telecommunications and postal and courier services; computer data; news-related service transactions between residents and nonresidents; construction services; royalties and license fees; miscellaneous business, professional, and technical services; and personal, cultural, and recreational services.

Data sources

Data on commercial service exports are from the IMF, which publishes balance of payments data in its *International Financial Statistics* and *Balance of Payments Statistics Yearbook*.

	Commercial service imports		Transport		Travel		Insurance and financial services		Computer, information, communications, and other commercial services	
	$ millions		% of total		% of total		% of total		% of total	
	2000	**2010**	**2000**	**2010**	**2000**	**2010**	**2000**	**2010**	**2000**	**2010**
Afghanistan	..	..	..	..	..	..	..	..	..	..
Albania	413	1,992	23	16	66	68	8	5	3	11
Algeria	..	11,203	..	26	..	4	..	2	..	67
Angola	2,271	16,028	14	19	6	1	3	7	78	73
Argentina	8,960	13,769	27	27	49	35	4	5	20	33
Armenia	177	985	66	45	22	41	6	7	6	7
Australia	18,554	51,470	34	31	34	39	5	3	27	27
Austria	16,383	36,926	23	33	38	27	7	4	32	36
Azerbaijan	475	3,762	30	21	28	21	2	3	42	55
Bahrain	757	1,905	57	40	30	27	3	23	10	11
Bangladesh	1,523	4,128	66	83	19	6	8	2	6	9
Belarus	524	2,878	21	48	41	21	3	3	35	28
Belgium	35,288	78,377	22	25	29	24	8	4	41	47
Benin	186	488	67	59	7	11	9	5	17	25
Bolivia	450	1,128	60	41	17	28	14	13	9	18
Bosnia and Herzegovina	256	581	48	39	28	33	10	5	14	22
Botswana	538	867	42	51	37	3	4	5	17	42
Brazil	15,573	59,746	28	19	25	27	6	5	41	48
Bulgaria	1,660	4,164	44	22	32	30	5	6	18	43
Burkina Faso	132	545	64	56	15	12	18	14	3	18
Burundi	36	156	53	71	38	13	4	3	4	14
Cambodia	321	1,084	53	57	10	18	4	6	32	19
Cameroon	994	1,717	22	36	21	11	4	7	53	46
Canada	43,597	89,963	21	23	29	33	10	11	40	33
Central African Republic	..	..	..	..	..	..	..	..	..	..
Chad	..	..	..	..	..	..	..	..	..	..
Chile	4,664	11,568	47	58	13	17	9	8	31	17
China	35,858	192,174	29	33	37	29	7	9	27	30
Hong Kong SAR, China	24,588	50,869	25	28	51	36	5	9	18	27
Colombia	3,242	7,893	40	36	33	23	10	9	17	32
Congo, Dem. Rep.	..	..	..	..	..	..	..	..	..	..
Congo, Rep.	728	3,523	11	15	7	5	5	5	77	75
Costa Rica	1,261	1,769	33	38	38	24	4	8	25	30
Côte d'Ivoire	1,142	2,324	45	58	17	15	11	9	27	27
Croatia	1,782	3,389	21	16	32	25	5	6	42	53
Cuba	..	..	..	..	..	..	..	..	..	..
Cyprus	1,563	3,114	56	41	26	37	7	8	10	14
Czech Republic	5,364	16,925	13	24	24	24	9	3	54	49
Denmark	21,063	51,894	44	..	22	..	..	..	33	..
Dominican Republic	1,340	2,044	62	59	23	19	7	9	8	13
Ecuador	1,225	2,950	36	59	24	19	3	8	36	14
Egypt, Arab Rep.	7,161	12,991	31	51	15	17	7	11	48	21
El Salvador	912	1,024	44	45	18	21	17	13	21	21
Eritrea	24	..	28	..	50	..	2	..	21	..
Estonia	870	2,770	48	35	23	23	1	2	27	40
Ethiopia	479	2,534	60	65	15	6	4	4	21	25
Finland	8,323	27,650	31	20	22	15	0	3	46	61
France	64,400	131,391	28	27	35	29	2	4	36	40
Gabon	846	..	32	..	10	..	8	..	50	..
Gambia, The	32	72	78	48	11	15	10	7	1	30
Georgia	271	996	38	56	41	20	8	14	13	11
Germany	135,812	262,245	19	24	39	30	2	4	40	42
Ghana	514	2,444	53	46	20	24	6	5	22	25
Greece	10,918	19,892	37	54	42	14	3	10	18	22
Guatemala	786	2,362	54	48	23	33	8	9	15	10
Guinea	183	381	61	60	5	2	4	7	30	31
Guinea-Bissau	30	85	90	36	9	30	0	5	1	28
Haiti	270	1,223	91	47	7	5	..	0	3	47

	Commercial service imports		Transport		Travel		Insurance and financial services		Computer, information, communications, and other commercial services	
	$ millions		% of total		% of total		% of total		% of total	
	2000	2010	2000	2010	2000	2010	2000	2010	2000	2010
Honduras	688	1,312	60	45	17	24	2	8	21	23
Hungary	4,708	15,376	15	21	35	16	7	2	43	61
India	18,898	116,140	46	40	14	9	11	10	29	41
Indonesia	15,381	25,601	26	34	21	25	2	6	51	35
Iran, Islamic Rep.	1,577	..	72	..	13	..	14	..	1	..
Iraq	..	7,565	..	53	..	10	..	27	..	10
Ireland	31,212	107,270	8	2	8	7	9	13	75	78
Israel	11,849	17,787	36	33	24	19	3	2	38	46
Italy	54,632	108,616	24	24	29	25	3	8	44	44
Jamaica	1,391	1,767	42	41	15	11	8	11	35	37
Japan	115,686	155,800	30	30	28	18	3	6	39	46
Jordan	1,463	4,164	47	51	24	34	6	7	22	7
Kazakhstan	1,831	11,142	18	17	22	11	3	5	57	67
Kenya	665	1,816	51	51	20	12	10	10	19	27
Korea, Dem. Rep.	..	..	..	..	..	..	..	..	..	..
Korea, Rep.	33,128	92,936	33	31	22	19	1	2	44	48
Kosovo	..	..	..	..	..	..	..	..	..	..
Kuwait	4,115	12,260	37	40	61	55	1	3	1	2
Kyrgyz Republic	144	915	35	46	11	30	9	3	46	21
Lao PDR	13	258	38	6	62	79	–3	5	0	10
Latvia	680	2,211	31	30	36	29	10	6	22	35
Lebanon	3,340	13,262	14	14	80	36	4	10	2	41
Lesotho	247	479	7	14	78	65	3	4	12	17
Liberia	..	234	..	54	..	27	..	1	..	18
Libya	815	5,251	43	45	49	39	1	12	8	4
Lithuania	655	2,718	34	52	39	29	2	2	26	17
Macedonia, FYR	260	816	50	39	13	11	3	6	34	44
Madagascar	395	..	48	..	29	..	2	..	21	..
Malawi	167	79	53	19	30	59	0	7	17	15
Malaysia	16,603	32,216	35	37	12	25	3	4	49	38
Mali	324	813	74	57	12	12	4	6	10	25
Mauritania	130	..	37	..	33	..	..	..	30	..
Mauritius	748	1,956	35	28	24	20	7	8	34	44
Mexico	16,242	21,818	38	49	34	33	14	15	14	3
Moldova	190	729	32	39	38	36	2	3	28	21
Mongolia	158	760	54	38	33	35	1	4	13	24
Morocco	1,520	5,724	41	46	28	21	2	4	29	29
Mozambique	439	1,102	38	28	25	23	6	3	32	46
Myanmar	310	761	82	60	8	7	..	..	10	33
Namibia	308	697	29	32	24	21	6	7	40	40
Nepal	193	846	34	33	38	48	7	4	29	16
Netherlands	49,941	84,384	26	22	24	23	3	3	47	52
New Zealand	4,404	9,227	32	30	33	33	3	1	32	36
Nicaragua	334	660	46	50	23	31	7	11	23	8
Niger	125	735	67	73	21	7	3	4	9	17
Nigeria	3,144	20,163	20	43	19	28	3	3	59	26
Norway	14,832	42,358	35	28	31	33	6	3	28	36
Oman	1,758	6,525	37	41	27	15	6	11	30	33
Pakistan	2,109	6,481	72	58	12	14	4	4	12	24
Panama	1,096	2,569	55	60	17	15	8	16	20	9
Papua New Guinea	772	2,737	21	22	7	4	5	13	67	61
Paraguay	390	707	61	68	21	22	15	8	4	3
Peru	2,165	5,843	40	42	20	22	8	9	33	27
Philippines	5,175	11,188	40	44	32	31	4	3	25	21
Poland	8,862	29,473	17	21	37	29	6	4	39	46
Portugal	6,787	14,237	29	30	33	27	5	4	33	38
Puerto Rico	..	..	..	..	..	..	..	..	..	..
Qatar	..	..	..	..	..	..	..	..	..	..

	Commercial service imports		Transport		Travel		Insurance and financial services		Computer, information, communications, and other commercial services	
	$ millions		% of total		% of total		% of total		% of total	
	2000	2010	2000	2010	2000	2010	2000	2010	2000	2010
Romania	1,948	9,341	32	30	22	18	7	7	39	46
Russian Federation	16,230	72,278	14	17	55	37	3	4	28	43
Rwanda	113	442	73	73	19	17	..	1	8	9
Saudi Arabia	10,927	50,996	21	25	..	41	2	5	77	28
Senegal	396	*1,110*	61	*54*	12	*14*	10	*12*	18	*21*
Serbia	..	3,477	..	29	..	27	..	3	..	41
Sierra Leone	82	134	21	70	39	10	4	5	36	15
Singapore	29,968	96,255	42	30	16	17	7	6	34	47
Slovak Republic	1,779	6,781	24	28	17	29	5	8	54	35
Slovenia	1,423	4,305	25	22	36	28	2	4	37	46
Somalia	..	..	..	..	..	..	..	..	..	..
South Africa	5,657	18,023	43	39	37	31	7	4	13	26
South Sudan	..	..	..	..	..	..	..	..	..	..
Spain	32,837	86,752	31	24	18	19	4	7	47	49
Sri Lanka	1,592	3,084	62	66	15	15	6	6	17	13
Sudan	632	2,195	88	46	9	51	0	1	3	2
Swaziland	300	650	12	11	10	9	2	6	76	74
Sweden	24,127	47,316	14	17	34	28	3	1	50	54
Switzerland	14,533	39,435	36	21	37	28	7	7	20	43
Syrian Arab Republic	1,468	3,377	48	47	46	45	2	4	7	4
Tajikistan	*103*	389	79	51	*2*	5	6	7	*13*	37
Tanzania	620	1,840	33	39	54	45	3	4	9	12
Thailand	15,329	44,592	44	50	18	12	5	5	33	32
Timor-Leste	..	..	..	..	..	..	..	..	..	..
Togo	116	*374*	72	62	2	*13*	15	9	12	*16*
Trinidad and Tobago	363	*335*	48	*39*	41	*31*	0	7	12	*22*
Tunisia	1,119	3,165	49	50	23	17	7	9	20	23
Turkey	7,624	18,343	32	45	22	26	13	10	32	18
Turkmenistan	669	..	*23*	..	*19*	..	2	..	*57*	..
Uganda	459	1,809	33	55	*13*	14	3	13	64	18
Ukraine	2,590	12,137	15	34	18	31	6	10	61	26
United Arab Emirates	..	..	..	..	..	..	..	..	..	..
United Kingdom	96,893	162,086	25	18	39	31	6	7	30	44
United States	203,169	367,016	30	21	33	23	8	21	29	36
Uruguay	842	1,365	47	45	33	31	6	4	13	20
Uzbekistan	..	..	..	..	..	..	..	..	..	..
Venezuela, RB	4,236	10,548	43	38	25	17	5	5	27	39
Vietnam	3,252	9,921	..	..	..	..	..	..	..	..
West Bank and Gaza	459	777	12	*11*	66	62	2	2	20	25
Yemen, Rep.	757	2,263	45	47	9	8	7	10	38	35
Zambia	322	901	63	56	14	7	6	10	18	26
Zimbabwe	..	..	..	..	..	..	..	..	..	..
World	**1,485,017 t**	**3,472,677 t**	**29 w**	**27 w**	**31 w**	**25 w**	**6 w**	**9 w**	**34 w**	**39 w**
Low income	9,090	29,773	58	61	20	14	7	5	18	21
Middle income	264,736	906,395	36	39	28	26	8	8	28	27
Lower middle income	82,866	296,871	40	43	20	22	6	7	34	29
Upper middle income	182,790	613,085	35	38	30	27	8	9	27	27
Low & middle income	273,647	935,741	36	39	28	26	8	8	28	27
East Asia & Pacific	94,144	323,841	33	37	28	25	5	7	34	31
Europe & Central Asia	39,655	160,613	26	33	33	28	7	7	33	32
Latin America & Carib.	67,954	155,546	38	42	30	29	10	11	21	18
Middle East & N. Africa	23,663	70,149	48	*42*	22	*20*	..	7	23	*31*
South Asia	24,653	132,213	53	49	15	11	9	8	23	32
Sub-Saharan Africa	25,073	97,316	41	40	27	25	6	5	27	30
High income	1,211,620	2,536,783	27	24	32	25	5	10	36	42
Euro area	477,111	1,044,273	24	25	31	25	3	5	41	45

Trade in services differs from trade in goods because services are produced and consumed at the same time. Thus services to a traveler may be consumed in the producing country (for example, use of a hotel room) but are classified as imports of the traveler's country. In other cases services may be supplied from a remote location; for example, insurance services may be supplied from one location and consumed in another. For further discussion of the problems of measuring trade in services, see *About the data* for table 4.6.

The data on imports of services in the table and on exports of services in table 4.6, unlike those in editions before 2000, include only commercial services and exclude the category "government services not included elsewhere." The data are compiled by the International Monetary Fund (IMF) based on returns from national sources.

International transactions in services are defined by the IMF's *Balance of Payments Manual* (1993) as the economic output of intangible commodities that may be produced, transferred, and consumed at the same time. Definitions may vary among reporting economies.

Travel services include the goods and services consumed by travelers, such as meals, lodging, and transport (within the economy visited), including car rental.

• **Commercial service imports** are total service imports minus imports of government services not included elsewhere. • **Transport** covers all transport services (sea, air, land, internal waterway, space, and pipeline) performed by residents of one economy for those of another and involving the carriage of passengers, movement of goods (freight), rental of carriers with crew, and related support and auxiliary services. Excluded are freight insurance, which is included in insurance services; goods procured in ports by nonresident carriers and repairs of transport equipment, which are included in goods; repairs of harbors, railway facilities, and airfield facilities, which are included in construction services; and rental of carriers without crew, which is included in other services. • **Travel** covers goods and services acquired from an economy by travelers in that economy for their own use during visits of less than one year for business or personal purposes. • **Insurance and financial services** cover freight insurance on goods imported and other direct insurance such as life insurance; financial intermediation services such as commissions, foreign exchange transactions, and brokerage services; and auxiliary services such as financial market operational and regulatory services. • **Computer, information, communications, and other commercial services** cover such activities as international telecommunications, and postal and courier services; computer data; news-related service transactions between residents and nonresidents; construction services; royalties and license fees; miscellaneous business, professional, and technical services; and personal, cultural, and recreational services.

Data on commercial service imports are from the IMF, which publishes balance of payments data in its *International Financial Statistics* and *Balance of Payments Statistics Yearbook*.

4.8 | Structure of demand

	Household final consumption expenditure		General government final consumption expenditure		Gross capital formation		Exports of goods and services		Imports of goods and services		Gross savings	
	% of GDP		% of GDP		% of GDP		% of GDP		% of GDP		% of GDP	
	2000	2010	2000	2010	2000	2010	2000	2010	2000	2010	2000	2010
Afghanistan	112	111	8	11	12	16	31	15	62	54	..	..
Albania	85	88	9	8	25	26	19	30	37	52	24	13
Algeria	42	35	14	14	25	41	41	31	21	21	..	54
Angola	..	..	..	..	15	15	90	58	63	44	24	16
Argentina	71	60	14	15	16	22	11	22	12	18	13	22
Armenia	97	78	12	13	19	33	23	21	51	45	4	19
Australia	58	54	18	18	26	28	19	20	21	20	21	24
Austria	55	55	19	19	25	22	46	54	44	50	24	25
Azerbaijan	69	37	9	11	21	17	39	55	38	20	17	46
Bahrain	47	31	18	13	10	33	89	97	64	74	20	43
Bangladesh	78	77	5	5	23	24	14	18	19	25	27	38
Belarus	58	57	19	16	25	41	69	55	72	68	23	25
Belgium	53	53	21	24	23	20	78	80	75	77	25	23
Benin	82	..	12	..	19	26	15	14	28	28	10	13
Bolivia	76	62	15	14	18	17	18	41	27	34	11	25
Bosnia and Herzegovina	104	80	25	21	21	20	29	36	76	57	13	15
Botswana	31	46	25	21	32	36	53	29	41	32	41	26
Brazil	64	61	19	21	18	19	10	11	12	12	14	17
Bulgaria	68	61	19	16	18	25	50	58	56	60	12	24
Burkina Faso	79	..	21	..	17	..	9	..	25	..	5	..
Burundi	88	..	18	..	6	..	8	..	20	..	4	..
Cambodia	89	82	5	6	18	17	50	54	62	60	14	13
Cameroon	70	..	9	..	17	..	23	28	20	33	15	..
Canada	55	58	19	22	20	22	46	29	40	31	23	18
Central African Republic	81	93	14	5	10	11	20	15	24	23	..	..
Chad	87	73	8	15	23	37	17	44	35	69	..	..
Chile	64	59	12	12	22	21	32	39	30	32	21	23
China	47	35	16	13	35	48	23	30	21	26	37	53
Hong Kong SAR, China	59	62	9	8	27	24	143	223	139	217	32	30
Colombia	69	62	17	16	15	24	16	16	17	18	14	19
Congo, Dem. Rep.	88	75	8	5	3	29	22	15	21	34	..	..
Congo, Rep.	29	33	12	10	23	25	80	82	44	50	31	..
Costa Rica	67	65	13	18	17	20	49	38	46	41	13	15
Côte d'Ivoire	75	73	7	9	11	14	40	41	33	36	8	15
Croatia	60	56	24	22	19	23	42	38	45	39	18	22
Cuba	61	54	29	33	13	11	14	20	17	18	..	..
Cyprus	65	68	16	20	18	18	55	40	55	47	15	9
Czech Republic	52	51	21	22	29	23	63	79	66	75	25	21
Denmark	48	48	25	29	21	17	47	50	40	45	23	23
Dominican Republic	78	88	8	8	23	16	37	22	46	34	18	7
Ecuador	64	68	10	12	20	26	37	33	31	39	26	23
Egypt, Arab Rep.	76	75	11	11	20	19	16	21	23	26	18	18
El Salvador	88	93	10	11	17	13	27	26	42	44	14	11
Eritrea	79	..	64	..	24	..	15	5	82	20	4	..
Estonia	55	53	20	21	28	20	85	78	88	72	23	24
Ethiopia	74	89	18	10	20	21	12	11	24	32	16	17
Finland	49	55	21	25	21	19	44	40	34	39	29	21
France	56	58	23	25	20	19	29	25	28	28	22	17
Gabon	32	43	10	10	22	26	69	52	33	31	42	..
Gambia, The	78	78	14	15	17	26	48	29	57	49	..	13
Georgia	82	77	9	21	27	20	23	35	40	52	22	10
Germany	58	57	19	20	22	17	33	47	33	41	20	23
Ghana	84	80	10	11	24	22	49	25	67	38	15	20
Greece	70	75	19	18	25	16	26	22	40	30	14	5
Guatemala	84	86	7	10	18	15	20	25	29	36	12	13
Guinea	78	77	7	8	20	20	24	35	28	39	15	10
Guinea-Bissau	95	..	14	..	11	..	32	..	52	..	−15	..
Haiti	86	..	8	..	27	25	13	12	33	57	..	23

	Household final consumption expenditure		General government final consumption expenditure		Gross capital formation		Exports of goods and services		Imports of goods and services		Gross savings	
	% of GDP		% of GDP		% of GDP		% of GDP		% of GDP		% of GDP	
	2000	2010	2000	2010	2000	2010	2000	2010	2000	2010	2000	2010
Honduras	71	80	13	18	28	23	54	44	66	65	21	16
Hungary	55	53	21	22	27	18	75	87	78	80	19	20
India	64	57	13	12	24	35	13	22	14	25	25	34
Indonesia	61	57	7	9	22	32	41	25	30	23	25	32
Iran, Islamic Rep.	48	..	14	..	33	..	23	..	17	..	39	..
Iraq	..	..	..	..	..	..	..	..	..	..	..	..
Ireland	49	51	14	19	24	11	97	101	84	82	24	12
Israel	53	58	26	24	21	16	37	37	37	35	17	18
Italy	60	60	18	21	21	20	27	27	26	29	21	17
Jamaica	74	80	14	17	..	21	..	26	..	43	17	12
Japan	56	59	17	20	25	20	11	15	10	14	28	24
Jordan	81	85	24	21	22	15	42	45	68	66	23	9
Kazakhstan	62	49	12	11	19	25	57	44	49	29	21	28
Kenya	78	78	15	13	17	21	22	26	32	39	14	16
Korea, Dem. Rep.	..	..	..	..	..	..	..	..	..	..	..	..
Korea, Rep.	55	53	12	15	31	29	39	52	36	50	33	32
Kosovo	..	95	..	18	..	30	..	19	..	62	..	..
Kuwait	42	28	21	21	11	14	56	56	30	28	50	59
Kyrgyz Republic	66	84	20	19	20	28	42	58	48	89	15	20
Lao PDR	93	69	7	9	14	26	30	36	44	41	2	20
Latvia	63	63	21	17	24	21	42	53	49	54	19	24
Lebanon	84	78	17	12	20	33	14	21	36	44	–4	12
Lesotho	83	87	42	44	44	34	34	49	103	114	37	34
Liberia	89	202	14	19	5	20	21	31	26	173	..	–2
Libya	46	23	21	9	13	28	36	67	15	27	22	67
Lithuania	65	65	23	20	19	17	45	68	51	70	13	19
Macedonia, FYR	74	75	18	18	22	25	49	47	64	66	22	24
Madagascar	83	79	9	12	15	33	31	29	38	53	9	..
Malawi	82	66	15	19	14	24	26	26	35	36	10	13
Malaysia	44	48	10	13	27	21	120	97	101	79	36	33
Mali	79	..	9	..	25	..	27	..	39	..	16	..
Mauritania	83	70	26	18	19	28	46	48	74	63	21	..
Mauritius	60	76	14	14	26	22	61	45	62	58	26	16
Mexico	67	65	11	12	24	25	31	30	33	32	20	24
Moldova	91	91	10	24	24	24	50	40	75	78	16	16
Mongolia	70	53	15	14	29	41	54	55	68	62	23	27
Morocco	61	57	18	18	26	35	28	33	33	43	24	31
Mozambique	81	82	9	12	31	24	16	25	37	43	10	11
Myanmar	..	..	..	..	12	23	0	0	1	0	..	..
Namibia	63	53	24	22	17	23	41	39	45	38	25	34
Nepal	76	82	9	11	24	35	23	10	32	37	22	37
Netherlands	50	45	22	28	22	19	70	78	65	71	28	23
New Zealand	60	58	17	21	21	20	35	29	33	27	18	16
Nicaragua	84	91	12	10	30	28	24	41	51	70	8	13
Niger	83	..	13	..	11	..	18	..	26	..	5	..
Nigeria	..	..	..	..	..	..	54	39	32	27	..	..
Norway	43	43	19	22	20	22	47	41	29	29	35	36
Oman	40	40	21	20	12	30	59	53	31	41	29	38
Pakistan	75	82	9	8	17	15	13	14	15	19	20	22
Panama	60	71	13	6	24	27	73	65	70	69	23	18
Papua New Guinea	45	70	17	9	22	18	66	56	49	53	32	20
Paraguay	79	69	13	9	19	19	38	57	49	55	11	23
Peru	71	63	11	10	20	24	16	25	18	22	17	23
Philippines	72	72	11	10	18	21	51	35	53	37	23	27
Poland	64	61	17	19	25	21	27	42	34	43	19	17
Portugal	64	66	19	22	28	20	29	31	40	38	18	10
Puerto Rico	91	94	11	11	18	9	75	78	98	92	..	..
Qatar	15	21	20	25	20	39	67	47	22	31	..	..

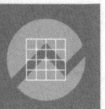

4.8 Structure of demand

	Household final consumption expenditure		General government final consumption expenditure		Gross capital formation		Exports of goods and services		Imports of goods and services		Gross savings	
	% of GDP		% of GDP		% of GDP		% of GDP		% of GDP		% of GDP	
	2000	2010	2000	2010	2000	2010	2000	2010	2000	2010	2000	2010
Romania	78	60	7	15	20	31	33	23	38	30	16	26
Russian Federation	46	49	15	19	19	23	44	30	24	22	36	28
Rwanda	88	81	11	15	18	22	9	12	26	29	13	15
Saudi Arabia	37	34	26	23	19	22	44	57	25	35	29	33
Senegal	76	82	13	9	20	29	28	25	37	44	14	19
Serbia	88	74	20	19	9	23	24	35	40	51	..	16
Sierra Leone	100	84	14	12	7	16	18	17	39	30	−4	13
Singapore	43	37	11	11	33	24	192	211	180	183	44	46
Slovak Republic	56	58	20	20	26	23	70	81	73	82	23	20
Slovenia	57	56	19	21	27	23	54	65	57	65	25	22
Somalia	..	..	..	..	..	..	..	..	..	..	..	..
South Africa	63	57	18	20	16	25	28	26	25	27	16	16
South Sudan	..	..	..	..	..	..	..	..	..	..	..	..
Spain	60	58	17	21	26	23	29	26	32	28	23	19
Sri Lanka	72	66	11	16	28	28	39	22	50	31	22	25
Sudan	76	61	8	15	18	23	15	20	18	19	9	18
Swaziland	78	77	19	25	17	17	76	58	90	77	13	3
Sweden	49	49	26	27	19	18	47	50	40	44	23	25
Switzerland	60	58	11	11	23	19	46	54	41	42	35	36
Syrian Arab Republic	64	71	12	10	17	19	35	35	29	36	22	17
Tajikistan	84	94	8	29	9	23	99	15	101	61	9	3
Tanzania[a]	78	66	12	18	17	31	13	24	20	38	13	21
Thailand	57	54	11	13	23	26	67	71	58	64	30	31
Timor-Leste	112	..	35	..	26	..	..	..	..	..	..	..
Togo	92	..	10	..	18	..	31	..	51	..	1	..
Trinidad and Tobago	57	51	9	10	20	11	59	65	45	38	26	35
Tunisia	61	63	17	16	26	26	40	49	43	54	22	20
Turkey	71	71	12	14	21	20	20	21	23	27	18	14
Turkmenistan	36	33	14	11	35	59	96	52	81	55	..	..
Uganda	77	75	15	12	19	24	11	24	22	34	14	19
Ukraine	54	63	21	20	20	19	62	50	57	53	24	17
United Arab Emirates	61	57	9	8	22	25	49	78	41	69	..	..
United Kingdom	66	64	19	23	18	15	28	30	29	33	15	12
United States	69	71	14	17	21	15	11	13	15	16	18	11
Uruguay	77	67	12	13	14	19	17	27	20	26	11	17
Uzbekistan	62	55	19	18	16	26	25	31	22	31	..	..
Venezuela, RB	52	57	12	11	24	21	30	29	18	17	34	31
Vietnam	66	65	6	7	30	39	55	78	57	88	31	32
West Bank and Gaza	95	..	27	..	33	..	16	..	71	..	9	..
Yemen, Rep.	60	81	14	12	19	12	41	30	34	34	33	9
Zambia	87	55	10	13	17	22	27	44	41	35	−1	22
Zimbabwe	60	101	24	17	14	1	39	37	36	56	..	..
World	**61 w**	**62 w**	**16 w**	**19 w**	**22 w**	**20 w**	**25 w**	**28 w**	**25 w**	**28 w**	**22 w**	**19 w**
Low income	79	80	10	10	19	23	17	20	25	32	19	27
Middle income	60	56	14	14	24	29	27	29	26	28	25	30
Lower middle income	67	64	12	11	22	28	27	28	27	31	23	28
Upper middle income	58	54	15	15	24	30	27	29	25	27	25	30
Low & middle income	61	56	14	14	24	29	27	28	25	28	25	30
East Asia & Pacific	50	42	14	13	31	41	35	37	31	33	34	46
Europe & Central Asia	60	60	14	17	20	23	37	31	31	31	26	22
Latin America & Carib.	66	63	15	15	20	22	20	22	21	22	17	21
Middle East & N. Africa	60	..	15	..	24	..	27	..	25	..	..	..
South Asia	67	62	11	11	23	32	14	20	16	25	25	33
Sub-Saharan Africa	69	64	16	17	17	24	32	30	31	32	16	17
High income	61	63	17	19	22	18	24	28	25	28	22	17
Euro area	57	58	20	22	22	19	37	41	36	39	22	20

a. Covers mainland Tanzania only.

About the data

Gross domestic product (GDP) from the expenditure side is made up of household final consumption expenditure, general government final consumption expenditure, gross capital formation (private and public investment in fixed assets, changes in inventories, and net acquisitions of valuables), and net exports (exports minus imports) of goods and services. Such expenditures are recorded in purchaser prices and include net taxes on products.

Because policymakers have tended to focus on fostering the growth of output, and because data on production are easier to collect than data on spending, many countries generate their primary estimate of GDP using the production approach. Moreover, many countries do not estimate all the components of national expenditures but instead derive some of the main aggregates indirectly using GDP (based on the production approach) as the control total. Household final consumption expenditure (private consumption in the 1968 United Nations System of National Accounts, or SNA) is often estimated as a residual, by subtracting all other known expenditures from GDP. The resulting aggregate may incorporate fairly large discrepancies. When household consumption is calculated separately, many of the estimates are based on household surveys, which tend to be one-year studies with limited coverage. Thus the estimates quickly become outdated and must be supplemented by estimates using price- and quantity-based statistical procedures. Complicating the issue, in many developing countries the distinction between cash outlays for personal business and those for household use may be blurred. *World Development Indicators* includes in household consumption the expenditures of nonprofit institutions serving households.

General government final consumption expenditure (general government consumption in the 1968 SNA) includes expenditures on goods and services for individual consumption as well as those on services for collective consumption. Defense expenditures, including those on capital outlays (with certain exceptions), are treated as current spending.

Gross capital formation (gross domestic investment in the 1968 SNA) consists of outlays on additions to the economy's fixed assets plus net changes in the level of inventories. It is generally obtained from industry reports of acquisitions and distinguishes only the broad categories of capital formation. The 1993 SNA recognizes a third category of capital formation: net acquisitions of valuables. Included in gross capital formation under the

1993 SNA guidelines are capital outlays on defense establishments that may be used by the general public, such as schools, airfields, and hospitals, and intangibles such as computer software and mineral exploration outlays. Data on capital formation may be estimated from direct surveys of enterprises and administrative records or based on the commodity flow method using data from production, trade, and construction activities. The quality of data on government fixed capital formation depends on the quality of government accounting systems (which tend to be weak in developing countries). Measures of fixed capital formation by households and corporations—particularly capital outlays by small, unincorporated enterprises—are usually unreliable.

Estimates of changes in inventories are rarely complete but usually include the most important activities or commodities. In some countries these estimates are derived as a composite residual along with household final consumption expenditure. According to national accounts conventions, adjustments should be made for appreciation of the value of inventory holdings due to price changes, but this is not always done. In highly inflationary economies this element can be substantial.

Data on exports and imports are compiled from customs reports and balance of payments data. Although the data from the payments side provide reasonably reliable records of cross-border transactions, they may not adhere strictly to the appropriate definitions of valuation and timing used in the balance of payments or correspond to the change-of-ownership criterion. This issue has assumed greater significance with the increasing globalization of international business. Neither customs nor balance of payments data usually capture the illegal transactions that occur in many countries. Goods carried by travelers across borders in legal but unreported shuttle trade may further distort trade statistics.

Gross savings represent the difference between disposable income and consumption and replace gross domestic savings, a concept used by the World Bank and included in *World Development Indicators* editions before 2006. The change was made to conform to SNA concepts and definitions. For further discussion of the problems in compiling national accounts, see Srinivasan (1994), Heston (1994), and Ruggles (1994). For an analysis of the reliability of foreign trade and national income statistics, see Morgenstern (1963).

Definitions

• **Household final consumption expenditure** is the market value of all goods and services, including durable products (such as cars and computers), purchased by households. It excludes purchases of dwellings but includes imputed rent for owner-occupied dwellings. It also includes government fees for permits and licenses. Expenditures of nonprofit institutions serving households are included, even when reported separately. Household consumption expenditure may include any statistical discrepancy in the use of resources relative to the supply of resources. • **General government final consumption expenditure** is all government current expenditures for purchases of goods and services (including compensation of employees). It also includes most expenditures on national defense and security but excludes military expenditures with potentially wider public use that are part of government capital formation. • **Gross capital formation** is outlays on additions to fixed assets of the economy, net changes in inventories, and net acquisitions of valuables. Fixed assets include land improvements (fences, ditches, drains); plant, machinery, and equipment purchases; and construction (roads, railways, schools, buildings, and so on). Inventories are goods held to meet temporary or unexpected fluctuations in production or sales, and "work in progress." • **Exports** and **imports of goods and services** are the value of all goods and other market services provided to or received from the rest of the world. They include the value of merchandise, freight, insurance, transport, travel, royalties, license fees, and other services (communication, construction, financial, information, business, personal, government services, and so on). They exclude compensation of employees and investment income (factor services in the 1968 SNA) and transfer payments. • **Gross savings** are gross national income less total consumption, plus net transfers.

Data sources

Data on national accounts indicators for most developing countries are collected from national statistical organizations and central banks by visiting and resident World Bank missions. Data for high-income economies are from Organisation for Economic Co-operation and Development (OECD) data files.

	Household final consumption expenditure				General government final consumption expenditure		Gross capital formation		Goods and services			
	average annual % growth				average annual % growth		average annual % growth		average annual % growth			
	Total		Per capita						Exports		Imports	
	1990–2000	2000–10	1990–2000	2000–10	1990–2000	2000–10	1990–2000	2000–10	1990–2000	2000–10	1990–2000	2000–10
Afghanistan	..	..	..	..	..	..	..	..	..	..	..	..
Albania	1.3	5.2	2.2	4.8	14.5	6.3	25.8	5.1	18.9	9.2	15.7	11.8
Algeria	−0.1	3.6	−1.9	2.1	3.6	4.8	−0.6	8.8	3.2	2.3	−1.0	7.8
Angola	..	..	..	..	..	..	..	..	..	..	..	..
Argentina	2.8	5.0	1.5	4.1	2.2	4.2	7.4	11.0	8.7	6.2	15.6	9.7
Armenia	−0.5	7.3	1.1	7.2	−1.5	8.2	−1.9	16.3	−18.4	5.3	−12.7	7.7
Australia	3.3	3.7	2.1	2.1	3.0	3.1	5.3	6.9	7.8	2.5	7.6	8.4
Austria	1.7	1.4	1.4	0.9	2.6	1.6	2.6	0.6	5.8	4.4	4.8	3.5
Azerbaijan	2.0	12.4	1.0	11.1	7.4	22.4	41.7	13.9	13.4	22.5	15.5	17.1
Bahrain	..	..	..	..	..	..	..	..	..	..	..	..
Bangladesh	2.6	4.6	0.5	3.2	4.7	8.5	9.2	7.7	13.1	10.6	9.7	8.0
Belarus	−0.5	11.3	−0.3	11.9	−1.9	0.1	−7.5	18.1	−4.8	5.1	−8.7	10.3
Belgium	1.9	1.4	1.6	0.8	1.6	1.5	2.4	2.1	5.3	2.6	5.0	2.7
Benin	2.6	2.3	−0.6	−0.9	4.4	8.3	12.2	7.7	1.8	2.7	2.1	1.8
Bolivia	3.6	3.4	1.3	1.6	3.6	3.5	8.5	4.8	4.5	6.9	6.0	5.4
Bosnia and Herzegovina	..	..	..	..	..	..	..	5.3	..	8.7	..	3.4
Botswana	3.2	8.5	0.8	7.1	6.1	4.8	4.6	3.1	4.4	1.6	4.3	4.8
Brazil	3.7	3.9	2.2	2.8	1.0	3.3	4.2	4.7	5.9	6.4	11.6	8.5
Bulgaria	−2.6	5.2	−2.0	5.9	−8.0	1.4	−5.3	11.2	4.3	7.6	2.9	9.0
Burkina Faso	5.7	4.5	2.8	1.5	2.9	8.7	3.1	9.0	4.4	10.9	1.9	7.2
Burundi	−4.9	..	..	..	−2.6	..	−0.5	..	−1.2	..	−1.6	..
Cambodia	6.0	8.0	3.5	6.7	7.2	9.9	10.3	12.6	21.7	14.2	14.8	13.8
Cameroon	3.1	4.5	0.6	2.2	0.7	2.8	0.4	4.4	3.2	−0.7	5.1	3.6
Canada	2.7	3.3	1.7	2.3	0.3	2.8	4.6	4.3	8.7	−0.6	7.1	3.2
Central African Republic	..	−0.9	..	−2.5	..	−1.3	..	−0.1	..	−3.6	..	−3.9
Chad	1.5	2.7	−1.7	−0.8	−8.3	2.7	4.0	−2.4	2.3	33.6	−1.8	−3.7
Chile	7.3	5.5	5.6	4.4	3.7	4.8	9.3	8.1	9.4	4.9	11.7	10.3
China	8.9	7.7	7.7	7.1	9.6	9.2	10.8	13.3	15.5	19.1	16.7	16.2
Hong Kong SAR, China	3.8	3.6	2.0	3.0	3.7	1.2	4.8	2.7	7.9	7.8	8.4	7.1
Colombia	2.4	4.0	0.6	2.4	10.9	4.1	2.1	9.6	5.0	5.2	9.3	9.6
Congo, Dem. Rep.	−1.1	..	−3.7	..	−20.4	..	2.6	..	−0.5	6.4	−2.4	15.0
Congo, Rep.	−1.8	..	..	..	−4.4	..	10.4	..	3.0	..	2.0	..
Costa Rica	5.1	4.2	2.5	2.4	2.0	2.4	5.1	5.6	10.9	5.9	9.2	4.6
Côte d'Ivoire	4.1	..	1.2	..	0.8	2.9	8.1	4.3	1.9	2.0	8.2	4.1
Croatia	1.9	2.9	2.7	2.9	2.6	2.6	7.2	7.1	6.3	3.0	4.9	4.3
Cuba	4.0	5.0	3.5	4.8	−2.9	7.6	0.7	8.8	−9.0	12.2	−2.9	10.1
Cyprus	6.1	4.3	4.2	2.6	2.3	3.6	−2.6	4.7	6.3	1.4	4.6	3.7
Czech Republic	3.0	3.3	3.0	3.1	−0.9	1.9	4.6	2.5	8.7	10.0	12.0	8.8
Denmark	2.2	1.9	1.7	1.5	2.4	1.7	5.7	0.4	5.0	3.0	6.0	4.7
Dominican Republic	6.1	6.9	4.2	5.3	7.0	4.8	11.7	2.4	8.3	1.2	9.9	2.7
Ecuador	2.1	5.2	0.2	3.5	−1.5	4.3	−0.6	8.2	5.3	5.4	2.8	8.5
Egypt, Arab Rep.	3.7	4.6	1.9	2.7	4.4	2.7	5.8	7.2	3.5	15.1	3.0	12.9
El Salvador	5.3	2.4	4.2	2.0	2.8	1.6	7.1	0.4	13.4	3.0	11.6	2.5
Eritrea	−5.0	1.6	−6.7	−2.2	22.6	1.2	19.1	−1.0	−2.5	−6.3	7.5	−3.7
Estonia	0.6	5.5	2.1	5.8	5.7	2.6	0.5	3.9	11.0	4.8	12.0	4.7
Ethiopia	3.6	10.8	0.4	8.2	9.0	1.8	6.5	11.1	7.1	9.7	5.8	16.7
Finland	1.8	2.8	1.4	2.4	0.9	1.4	3.2	1.5	10.3	3.7	6.7	4.7
France	1.6	1.7	1.2	1.0	1.4	1.6	1.9	1.4	6.8	1.4	5.7	2.7
Gabon	−0.3	4.2	−3.1	2.2	3.7	2.7	3.0	5.5	2.1	−1.8	0.1	4.0
Gambia, The	3.6	..	0.7	..	−2.2	..	1.9	..	0.1	1.6	0.1	1.7
Georgia	..	..	..	..	..	..	..	..	..	..	..	..
Germany	1.7	0.4	1.3	0.4	2.0	1.1	1.1	0.2	5.8	5.7	5.9	4.7
Ghana	..	..	..	..	..	..	..	..	..	..	..	..
Greece	2.2	3.3	1.4	2.9	2.1	2.2	4.1	0.0	7.6	2.0	7.4	1.8
Guatemala	4.2	3.7	1.9	1.2	5.1	3.9	6.1	−0.1	6.1	2.3	9.2	2.1
Guinea	5.2	4.2	1.4	2.4	−0.5	0.9	0.1	1.8	0.3	2.4	−1.1	1.2
Guinea-Bissau	..	..	..	..	..	..	..	..	..	..	..	..
Haiti	..	..	..	..	..	..	9.0	1.2	10.1	4.1	19.4	3.1

Growth of consumption and investment

	Household final consumption expenditure				General government final consumption expenditure		Gross capital formation		Goods and services			
	average annual % growth				average annual % growth		average annual % growth		average annual % growth			
	Total		Per capita						Exports		Imports	
	1990–2000	2000–10	1990–2000	2000–10	1990–2000	2000–10	1990–2000	2000–10	1990–2000	2000–10	1990–2000	2000–10
Honduras	3.0	4.6	0.6	2.5	2.0	6.0	6.9	2.8	1.6	4.1	3.8	3.8
Hungary	0.3	1.9	0.5	2.2	0.3	1.1	8.2	–0.6	9.3	9.5	11.0	7.9
India	4.8	7.1	2.8	5.5	6.6	6.2	6.9	12.9	12.3	14.7	14.4	15.9
Indonesia	6.6	4.3	5.0	3.1	0.1	8.1	–0.6	6.1	5.9	7.6	5.7	8.2
Iran, Islamic Rep.	3.2	7.4	1.5	6.1	1.6	3.6	–0.1	8.3	1.2	5.0	–6.8	13.2
Iraq	..	..	..	..	..	..	..	..	..	..	..	..
Ireland	5.6	3.1	4.8	1.2	4.1	3.5	9.7	–1.1	15.7	3.9	14.5	3.5
Israel	5.0	3.4	2.5	1.5	2.7	1.7	2.0	2.5	10.9	4.9	7.6	2.9
Italy	1.6	0.6	1.6	–0.1	–0.3	1.5	1.6	0.1	5.9	1.5	4.5	2.2
Jamaica	..	..	..	..	..	..	..	..	..	..	..	..
Japan	1.4	0.9	1.1	0.8	2.9	1.7	–0.8	–1.6	4.3	5.1	4.3	2.2
Jordan	4.9	7.6	1.1	5.2	4.7	6.7	0.3	5.1	2.6	5.0	1.5	6.3
Kazakhstan	–7.5	9.2	–6.4	8.2	–7.1	7.1	–19.0	15.2	–1.9	4.7	–12.7	4.3
Kenya	3.6	3.9	0.6	1.3	6.9	2.5	6.1	9.1	1.0	6.1	9.4	7.9
Korea, Dem. Rep.	..	..	..	..	..	..	..	..	..	..	..	..
Korea, Rep.	4.9	2.9	3.9	2.5	4.7	4.8	3.4	2.1	16.0	10.3	10.0	8.1
Kosovo	..	..	..	..	..	..	..	..	..	..	..	..
Kuwait	4.5	..	0.6	..	–2.4	..	1.0	..	–1.6	..	0.8	..
Kyrgyz Republic	–6.4	8.1	–7.3	7.0	–8.8	1.0	–4.5	9.1	–1.6	5.9	–8.2	11.4
Lao PDR	..	5.0	..	3.4	..	4.2	..	16.6	..	9.4	..	8.8
Latvia	–3.9	6.1	–2.7	6.7	1.8	1.1	–3.7	3.7	4.3	6.7	7.6	6.3
Lebanon	–0.2	3.6	–1.9	2.3	10.9	2.4	–5.8	10.3	18.6	9.6	–1.1	6.8
Lesotho	1.8	8.2	–0.1	7.1	8.1	6.3	0.2	1.6	10.3	7.9	2.7	11.3
Liberia	..	..	..	..	..	..	..	..	..	..	..	..
Libya	..	..	..	..	..	..	..	..	..	..	..	..
Lithuania	5.3	6.5	6.1	7.1	1.9	3.6	11.1	5.6	4.9	8.9	7.5	9.5
Macedonia, FYR	2.2	4.6	1.7	4.3	–0.4	0.5	3.6	4.8	4.2	2.6	7.5	3.8
Madagascar	2.2	2.2	–0.9	–0.9	0.0	5.5	3.3	14.1	3.8	6.7	4.1	9.3
Malawi	5.4	..	3.7	..	–4.4	..	–8.4	..	4.0	..	–1.1	..
Malaysia	5.3	7.4	2.6	5.3	4.8	7.4	5.3	3.0	12.0	4.8	10.3	5.8
Mali	3.0	0.9	0.3	–2.2	3.2	..	0.4	6.2	9.9	6.3	3.5	3.9
Mauritania	..	7.4	..	4.4	..	3.1	..	23.8	–1.3	–2.1	0.6	14.1
Mauritius	5.1	5.6	3.9	4.7	3.6	4.0	4.8	4.7	5.6	1.6	5.1	2.0
Mexico	3.9	2.8	2.1	1.6	1.8	1.1	4.7	0.4	14.6	4.6	12.3	4.7
Moldova	9.9	7.2	10.1	7.5	–12.4	4.9	–15.5	7.5	0.7	8.9	5.6	10.0
Mongolia	..	..	..	..	..	..	..	..	..	..	..	..
Morocco	1.8	4.7	0.3	3.5	3.9	3.9	2.5	8.3	5.9	6.0	5.1	7.8
Mozambique	5.8	5.8	2.6	3.2	3.2	–2.9	8.6	8.1	13.1	14.3	7.6	6.2
Myanmar	..	..	..	..	..	..	..	..	..	..	..	..
Namibia	4.8	4.9	1.8	3.0	3.3	4.6	7.3	8.5	3.8	2.5	5.4	5.1
Nepal	..	4.2	..	..	..	5.7	..	10.2	..	–1.6	..	6.1
Netherlands	3.1	0.5	2.5	0.1	2.0	3.3	4.4	0.8	7.3	3.9	7.6	3.7
New Zealand	3.2	3.1	2.0	1.8	2.4	3.9	6.1	3.0	5.2	2.4	6.2	4.4
Nicaragua	6.1	3.7	3.9	2.4	–1.5	1.6	11.3	4.3	9.3	8.4	12.2	5.2
Niger	1.8	..	..	..	0.8	..	4.0	..	3.1	..	–2.1	..
Nigeria	..	..	..	..	..	..	..	..	..	..	..	..
Norway	3.6	3.7	3.0	2.9	2.7	2.3	6.0	4.6	5.5	0.2	5.8	4.8
Oman	5.4	..	3.4	..	2.4	..	4.0	..	6.2	..	5.9	..
Pakistan	4.9	4.7	2.2	2.8	0.7	7.5	1.8	5.0	1.7	6.7	2.5	6.3
Panama	6.4	7.2	4.2	5.4	1.7	3.6	10.4	10.6	–0.4	7.8	1.2	7.4
Papua New Guinea	2.5	..	–0.1	..	2.5	..	1.9	..	5.1	..	3.4	..
Paraguay	2.6	3.3	0.3	1.4	2.5	4.2	0.7	3.6	3.1	7.6	2.9	6.7
Peru	4.0	5.3	2.2	4.1	5.2	5.7	7.4	10.7	8.5	7.2	9.0	9.2
Philippines	3.9	4.5	1.6	2.5	2.6	3.9	2.1	2.8	8.2	5.2	8.5	3.5
Poland	5.4	3.7	5.3	3.8	3.2	4.3	10.6	5.8	11.3	8.7	16.7	7.9
Portugal	3.0	1.3	2.7	0.9	3.0	1.6	5.9	–2.1	5.7	3.1	7.6	2.5
Puerto Rico	..	1.9	..	..	..	0.3	..	–3.6	1.6	1.1	4.5	1.6
Qatar	..	..	..	..	..	..	..	..	..	..	..	..

	Household final consumption expenditure				General government final consumption expenditure		Gross capital formation		Goods and services			
	average annual % growth				average annual % growth		average annual % growth		average annual % growth			
	Total		Per capita						Exports		Imports	
	1990–2000	2000–10	1990–2000	2000–10	1990–2000	2000–10	1990–2000	2000–10	1990–2000	2000–10	1990–2000	2000–10
Romania	1.3	6.4	1.6	6.8	0.8	3.8	−5.1	10.6	8.1	9.0	6.0	12.1
Russian Federation	−0.9	9.3	−0.7	9.7	−2.2	2.0	−19.1	7.6	0.8	6.5	−6.1	14.5
Rwanda	0.4	..	..	..	−2.6	..	0.4	..	−6.4	..	6.1	..
Saudi Arabia	..	5.3	..	1.6	..	7.6	..	11.4	..	6.9	..	16.9
Senegal	2.6	4.9	−0.2	2.1	0.9	−0.9	3.5	9.6	4.1	3.9	2.0	7.1
Serbia	..	1.0	..	1.3	..	5.9	..	18.1	..	9.7	..	8.6
Sierra Leone	−4.4	..	..	..	10.4	..	−5.6	..	−11.2	..	−0.2	..
Singapore	5.8	3.9	2.7	1.5	9.3	4.7	6.6	5.4	11.4	9.2	11.4	8.7
Slovak Republic	4.9	4.7	4.7	4.6	1.1	3.6	7.4	4.2	8.0	8.8	8.5	7.3
Slovenia	4.0	2.9	4.1	2.6	2.8	3.2	10.4	3.4	1.7	6.7	5.2	6.3
Somalia	..	..	..	..	..	..	..	..	..	..	..	..
South Africa	2.9	4.1	0.6	2.8	0.3	5.6	4.7	7.7	5.8	2.6	7.1	7.0
South Sudan	..	..	..	..	..	..	..	..	..	..	..	..
Spain	2.4	2.4	2.0	0.9	2.7	4.8	3.2	1.9	10.5	2.7	9.4	3.8
Sri Lanka	..	..	..	..	7.6	6.8	6.6	8.2	7.5	3.1	8.6	4.7
Sudan	3.7	5.9	1.1	3.4	5.5	8.4	22.0	11.2	11.6	14.3	8.4	12.0
Swaziland	7.3	2.2	5.5	1.8	7.1	6.6	−4.7	0.2	6.4	4.2	6.2	4.2
Sweden	1.5	2.2	1.2	1.7	0.6	0.9	2.0	3.0	8.6	4.2	6.4	4.0
Switzerland	1.1	1.5	0.5	0.6	0.5	1.4	0.7	0.2	4.1	4.5	4.3	3.5
Syrian Arab Republic	3.0	..	0.3	..	2.0	9.1	3.3	7.9	12.0	1.9	4.4	7.5
Tajikistan	−11.8	6.0	−13.1	4.9	−15.7	1.6	−17.6	5.8	−5.3	9.2	−6.0	10.3
Tanzania[a]	5.1	6.3	2.0	3.4	−8.8	12.8	−1.1	12.4	11.7	11.8	4.7	15.5
Thailand	3.7	3.8	2.7	2.9	5.1	5.4	−4.0	4.5	9.5	5.6	4.5	5.4
Timor-Leste	..	..	..	..	..	..	..	..	..	..	..	..
Togo	5.0	0.5	2.2	−1.9	0.0	1.3	−0.1	5.9	1.2	6.0	1.1	3.1
Trinidad and Tobago	0.7	13.3	0.1	12.9	0.3	4.3	12.5	..	6.9	5.8	9.9	9.5
Tunisia	4.2	4.5	2.5	3.5	4.5	5.1	3.1	3.9	5.3	3.4	3.7	3.0
Turkey	3.8	5.0	2.2	3.6	4.6	4.1	4.7	6.7	11.1	5.8	10.8	8.2
Turkmenistan	..	..	..	..	..	..	..	5.7	−2.4	17.5	7.2	9.4
Uganda	6.6	4.4	3.4	1.1	6.4	3.7	8.4	11.0	13.8	19.7	10.2	11.8
Ukraine	−6.9	11.2	−6.4	12.0	−4.1	2.0	−18.5	1.6	−3.6	0.9	−6.6	4.3
United Arab Emirates	..	7.0	..	..	..	4.7	..	11.9	..	12.5	..	18.7
United Kingdom	3.6	1.7	3.3	1.2	1.7	2.2	5.0	1.6	7.8	3.2	8.2	3.1
United States	3.8	2.1	2.5	1.1	0.7	2.0	7.6	−0.6	7.3	4.5	9.8	3.0
Uruguay	5.0	3.5	4.3	3.4	2.3	1.1	6.1	6.6	6.0	7.8	9.9	7.2
Uzbekistan	..	..	..	..	..	..	−2.5	4.7	2.5	4.9	−0.4	4.2
Venezuela, RB	0.6	7.6	−1.5	5.7	3.7	7.7	11.0	10.7	1.0	−2.9	8.2	12.2
Vietnam	5.4	7.8	3.8	6.6	3.2	7.9	19.8	12.0	19.2	11.2	19.5	13.2
West Bank and Gaza	5.3	−1.5	1.1	−4.9	12.7	1.3	9.2	−3.0	8.7	−3.1	7.5	−2.3
Yemen, Rep.	..	..	..	..	3.8	3.6	10.0	−0.6	22.9	1.8	11.9	5.4
Zambia	2.4	0.1	−0.3	−2.2	−8.1	24.9	3.9	6.6	6.7	21.9	15.5	15.6
Zimbabwe	..	..	..	..	..	..	..	..	3.9	−9.2	3.1	−3.8
World	**3.0 w**	**2.5 w**	**1.6 w**	**1.3 w**	**1.8 w**	**2.7 w**	**3.3 w**	**2.8 w**	**7.2 w**	**5.8 w**	**7.2 w**	**5.5 w**
Low income	2.9	5.4	0.4	3.1	−1.0	6.0	5.5	8.4	5.6	9.0	5.2	8.9
Middle income	4.0	5.6	2.5	4.4	3.3	5.7	2.6	9.6	7.5	9.9	6.5	10.2
Lower middle income	4.1	5.9	2.2	4.2	3.5	5.7	2.8	9.5	6.0	9.1	5.9	9.7
Upper middle income	4.0	5.6	2.9	4.8	3.3	5.7	2.6	9.6	7.9	10.1	6.6	10.4
Low & middle income	4.0	5.6	2.4	4.3	3.3	5.7	2.6	9.6	7.5	9.9	6.4	10.2
East Asia & Pacific	7.4	6.9	6.1	6.0	7.9	8.7	7.7	12.0	11.8	13.9	11.0	12.1
Europe & Central Asia	0.5	7.2	0.3	7.0	−0.8	3.2	−11.2	8.0	1.8	6.5	−2.3	10.6
Latin America & Carib.	3.6	4.1	1.9	2.8	1.9	3.5	5.4	5.2	8.1	4.8	10.5	6.8
Middle East & N. Africa	2.8	4.9	0.7	3.1	3.6	3.7	1.2	7.6	4.1	6.9	0.0	9.6
South Asia	4.6	6.6	2.5	4.9	5.8	6.5	6.5	11.9	10.0	13.0	11.2	13.7
Sub-Saharan Africa	3.3	4.6	0.6	2.1	0.3	5.5	4.6	7.8	..	..	5.7	8.8
High income	2.9	1.8	2.1	1.1	1.5	2.1	3.5	0.4	7.1	4.6	7.4	4.1
Euro area	1.9	1.2	1.6	0.7	1.5	1.9	2.2	0.8	6.8	3.7	6.3	3.6

a. Covers mainland Tanzania only.

Growth of consumption and investment

4.9

About the data

Measures of growth in consumption and capital formation are subject to two kinds of inaccuracy. The first stems from the difficulty of measuring expenditures at current price levels, as described in *About the data* for table 4.8. The second arises in deflating current price data to measure volume growth, where results depend on the relevance and reliability of the price indexes and weights used. Measuring price changes is more difficult for investment goods than for consumption goods because of the one-time nature of many investments and because the rate of technological progress in capital goods makes capturing change in quality difficult. (An example is computers—prices have fallen as quality has improved.) Several countries estimate capital formation from the supply side, identifying capital goods entering an economy directly from detailed production and international trade statistics. This means that the price indexes used in deflating production and international trade, reflecting delivered or offered prices, will determine the deflator for capital formation expenditures on the demand side.

Growth rates of household final consumption expenditure, household final consumption expenditure per capita, general government final consumption expenditure, gross capital formation, and exports and imports of goods and services are estimated using constant price data. (Consumption, capital formation, and exports and imports of goods and services as shares of GDP are shown in table 4.8.)

To obtain government consumption in constant prices, countries may deflate current values by applying a wage (price) index or extrapolate from the change in government employment. Neither technique captures improvements in productivity or changes in the quality of government services. Deflators for household consumption are usually calculated on the basis of the consumer price index. Many countries estimate household consumption as a residual that includes statistical discrepancies associated with the estimation of other expenditure items, including changes in inventories; thus these estimates lack detailed breakdowns of household consumption expenditures.

Definitions

• **Household final consumption expenditure** is the market value of all goods and services, including durable products (such as cars and computers), purchased by households. It excludes purchases of dwellings but includes imputed rent for owner-occupied dwellings. It also includes government fees for permits and licenses. Expenditures of nonprofit institutions serving households are included, even when reported separately. Household consumption expenditure may include any statistical discrepancy in the use of resources relative to the supply of resources. • **Household final consumption expenditure per capita** is household final consumption expenditure divided by midyear population. • **General government final consumption expenditure** is all government current expenditures for goods and services (including compensation of employees). It also includes most expenditures on national defense and security but excludes military expenditures with potentially wider public use that are part of government capital formation. • **Gross capital formation** is outlays on additions to fixed assets of the economy, net changes in inventories, and net acquisitions of valuables. Fixed assets include land improvements (fences, ditches, drains); plant, machinery, and equipment purchases; and construction (roads, railways, schools, buildings, and so on). Inventories are goods held to meet temporary or unexpected fluctuations in production or sales, and "work in progress." • **Exports** and **imports of goods and services** are the value of all goods and other market services provided to or received from the rest of the world. They include the value of merchandise, freight, insurance, transport, travel, royalties, license fees, and other services (communication, construction, financial, information, business, personal, government services, and so on). They exclude compensation of employees and investment income (factor services in the 1968 System of National Accounts) and transfer payments.

Data sources

Data on national accounts indicators for most developing countries are collected from national statistical organizations and central banks by visiting and resident World Bank missions. Data for high-income economies are from Organisation for Economic Co-operation and Development (OECD) data files.

4.10 | Toward a broader measure of national income

	Gross domestic product	Gross national income	Adjustments		Adjusted net national income	Gross domestic product	Gross national income	Adjusted net national income
			% of GNI					
			Consumption of fixed capital	Natural resource depletion				
	$ billions	$ billions			$ billions	% growth	% growth	% growth
	2010	2010	2010	2010	2010	2000–10	2000–10	2000–10
Afghanistan	17.2	15.2	8.9	2.6	13.4	..	..	..
Albania	11.8	11.7	10.6	2.5	10.1	5.4	5.8	6.6
Algeria	162.0	155.5	11.3	18.1	109.8	3.9	4.4	5.0
Angola	84.4	75.5	12.1	35.1	39.9	12.9	..	..
Argentina	368.7	358.6	12.1	4.9	297.6	5.6	5.3	5.8
Armenia	9.4	9.7	9.9	1.0	8.6	9.2	9.2	9.6
Australia	1,131.6	1,094.5	14.6	6.5	863.2	3.2	3.3	4.0
Austria	379.1	377.1	14.1	0.2	323.4	1.8	1.7	1.8
Azerbaijan	51.8	48.3	12.0	34.5	25.9	17.1	18.1	21.6
Bahrain	20.6	21.0	6.7	30.0	13.3	6.6	..	..
Bangladesh	100.4	109.7	7.5	2.3	99.0	5.9	5.3	5.9
Belarus	54.7	53.4	11.4	1.0	46.7	8.0	8.3	9.9
Belgium	469.4	477.6	13.7	0.0	412.3	1.6	1.7	1.2
Benin	6.6	6.6	8.4	0.3	6.1	4.0	3.9	3.6
Bolivia	19.6	18.8	10.2	12.3	14.6	4.1	4.2	3.2
Bosnia and Herzegovina	16.6	17.0	10.5	..	..	4.6	5.3	..
Botswana	14.9	14.8	11.6	3.4	12.6	4.1	3.5	3.5
Brazil	2,087.9	2,049.2	12.2	3.3	1,729.7	3.7	3.6	3.8
Bulgaria	47.7	46.0	14.3	2.0	38.5	4.8	5.4	4.4
Burkina Faso	8.8	8.8	7.9	4.3	7.7	5.5	6.0	5.2
Burundi	1.6	1.6	6.6	12.7	1.3	3.2	..	..
Cambodia	11.2	10.7	8.9	0.1	9.7	8.7	8.9	9.5
Cameroon	22.4	22.0	9.1	4.8	19.0	3.2	2.7	4.4
Canada	1,577.0	1,549.7	14.3	2.3	1,292.3	2.0	1.8	2.6
Central African Republic	2.0	2.0	7.7	0.0	1.9	1.0	–0.9	–1.2
Chad	7.6	6.7	9.3	29.0	4.2	9.0	20.2	–2.5
Chile	212.7	197.3	13.2	12.4	146.8	4.0	4.7	4.9
China	5,926.6	5,957.0	10.8	5.1	5,013.1	10.8	10.6	9.6
Hong Kong SAR, China	224.5	229.2	13.2	0.0	198.9	4.6	4.4	3.8
Colombia	288.2	276.1	11.8	7.7	222.2	4.5	4.7	4.5
Congo, Dem. Rep.	13.1	12.3	7.0	13.7	9.7	5.3	5.6	7.4
Congo, Rep.	11.9	8.6	14.1	59.6	2.3	4.3	..	..
Costa Rica	35.8	34.9	11.9	0.1	30.7	4.9	4.5	4.0
Côte d'Ivoire	22.8	21.7	9.4	3.9	18.8	1.1	0.9	1.1
Croatia	60.9	58.8	12.8	0.9	50.8	3.2	3.4	4.3
Cuba	62.7	61.8	11.3	3.2	52.8	6.7	6.6	6.7
Cyprus	23.1	22.5	13.3	0.0	19.5	3.1	3.0	3.3
Czech Republic	192.0	179.4	13.6	0.5	154.0	3.8	4.1	4.2
Denmark	312.0	319.3	14.0	1.7	269.3	0.9	0.4	1.7
Dominican Republic	51.8	50.0	11.4	0.2	44.2	5.6	5.5	5.4
Ecuador	58.0	56.9	10.9	12.9	43.4	4.8	4.3	5.7
Egypt, Arab Rep.	218.9	214.5	10.3	7.1	177.2	5.1	5.2	3.2
El Salvador	21.2	20.8	10.6	0.4	18.5	2.2	2.2	1.7
Eritrea	2.1	2.1	7.6	0.0	1.9	0.2	1.4	4.1
Estonia	19.2	18.4	13.0	1.6	15.7	4.6	4.6	5.3
Ethiopia	29.7	29.6	7.4	4.2	26.2	8.8	8.7	10.8
Finland	238.0	242.0	16.0	0.1	203.1	2.1	1.9	1.6
France	2,560.0	2,606.8	13.6	0.0	2,253.0	1.3	1.2	1.1
Gabon	13.0	11.5	13.3	33.1	6.1	2.2	2.3	4.3
Gambia, The	0.8	0.7	8.4	0.8	0.7	3.7	3.5	2.3
Georgia	11.7	11.5	9.7	0.6	10.3	6.9	..	..
Germany	3,280.5	3,341.4	13.6	0.1	2,883.3	1.0	0.6	1.5
Ghana	31.3	30.8	9.3	8.0	25.5	5.9	..	..
Greece	301.1	292.9	13.6	0.3	252.0	2.6	3.1	2.0
Guatemala	41.2	40.0	10.5	1.7	35.1	3.6	3.8	3.1
Guinea	4.5	4.2	8.2	14.3	3.3	2.9	3.7	0.3
Guinea-Bissau	0.9	0.9	8.0	0.5	0.8	1.5	..	..
Haiti	6.7	6.5	8.2	0.6	5.9	0.6	..	..

	Gross domestic product	Gross national income	Adjustments		Adjusted net national income	Gross domestic product	Gross national income	Adjusted net national income
			% of GNI					
			Consumption of fixed capital	Natural resource depletion				
	$ billions	$ billions			$ billions	% growth	% growth	% growth
	2010	2010	2010	2010	2010	2000–10	2000–10	2000–10
Honduras	15.4	14.8	10.1	0.5	13.2	4.6	4.6	2.5
Hungary	128.6	122.4	12.9	0.5	106.0	2.2	2.2	2.4
India	1,727.1	1,712.6	9.3	4.3	1,478.5	8.0	7.9	7.7
Indonesia	706.6	686.6	10.5	6.6	568.9	5.3	5.1	4.7
Iran, Islamic Rep.	331.0	328.6	10.9	19.9	227.5	5.4	6.2	6.7
Iraq	82.2	77.8	10.6	45.7	34.0	0.4	..	..
Ireland	206.6	171.3	16.9	0.2	142.0	2.8	2.8	1.8
Israel	217.3	210.4	13.8	0.2	180.9	3.6	2.8	3.6
Italy	2,061.0	2,051.4	13.7	0.1	1,768.9	0.5	0.5	0.3
Jamaica	14.3	13.6	11.6	0.6	11.9	1.2	..	..
Japan	5,458.8	5,601.6	13.6	0.0	4,841.4	0.9	0.7	1.2
Jordan	27.6	27.8	10.8	1.0	24.6	6.7	6.5	6.9
Kazakhstan	149.1	131.9	13.3	23.4	83.4	8.3	9.3	9.2
Kenya	31.4	31.3	7.3	1.1	28.6	4.3	4.3	4.8
Korea, Dem. Rep.	..	..	..	..	..	..	..	..
Korea, Rep.	1,014.5	1,014.8	12.9	0.0	883.5	4.1	4.0	3.3
Kosovo	5.6	5.7	10.0	..	..	5.3	..	..
Kuwait	109.5	117.2	7.2	25.1	79.3	8.4	..	..
Kyrgyz Republic	4.6	4.3	9.2	6.9	3.6	4.4	4.4	2.7
Lao PDR	7.3	7.0	9.4	8.3	5.7	7.2	7.1	6.2
Latvia	24.0	24.1	18.0	0.5	19.6	4.8	4.6	6.0
Lebanon	39.0	39.1	11.8	0.0	34.4	4.9	4.4	5.0
Lesotho	2.1	2.6	7.3	1.0	2.3	3.5	13.4	12.7
Liberia	1.0	0.8	8.4	6.4	0.7	0.9	..	..
Libya	62.4	62.0	12.0	29.0	36.6	5.4	..	..
Lithuania	36.3	35.7	12.3	0.6	31.1	5.3	5.2	6.5
Macedonia, FYR	9.2	9.0	11.1	5.9	7.5	3.3	3.4	2.6
Madagascar	8.7	8.6	7.7	1.0	7.9	3.4	3.2	2.3
Malawi	5.1	5.0	7.5	1.8	4.5	5.2	..	..
Malaysia	237.8	229.6	12.1	6.9	185.9	5.0	4.5	7.0
Mali	9.3	8.9	8.4	9.8	7.3	5.2	5.9	4.9
Mauritania	3.6	3.7	8.8	34.3	2.1	4.4	6.3	6.9
Mauritius	9.7	9.8	11.5	0.0	8.7	3.9	3.6	2.0
Mexico	1,034.8	1,020.3	12.0	5.7	839.9	2.1	2.0	1.7
Moldova	5.8	6.3	8.7	0.2	5.7	5.2	4.9	5.6
Mongolia	6.2	5.6	10.9	32.3	3.2	7.2	..	..
Morocco	90.8	88.6	10.5	1.6	77.9	4.9	4.8	4.3
Mozambique	9.6	9.4	7.7	3.3	8.4	7.8	7.4	6.5
Myanmar	..	..	..	..	..	..	..	..
Namibia	12.2	12.1	11.1	0.7	10.7	5.0	5.4	..
Nepal	15.7	15.8	7.8	2.5	14.2	3.8	..	..
Netherlands	779.4	772.7	14.2	0.8	656.9	1.6	2.0	1.2
New Zealand	126.7	121.4	14.0	1.0	103.3	2.6	2.7	2.6
Nicaragua	6.6	6.3	9.3	1.6	5.6	3.6	3.3	2.8
Niger	5.5	5.5	3.2	2.4	5.2	4.2	..	..
Nigeria	193.7	176.8	9.9	22.0	120.4	6.7	..	..
Norway	417.5	427.2	14.5	10.2	321.5	1.7	1.6	3.6
Oman	46.9	44.1	13.5	28.5	25.6	4.7	..	..
Pakistan	176.9	183.6	8.5	2.8	162.9	5.1	4.7	4.3
Panama	26.7	25.0	12.3	0.0	22.0	6.8	7.1	6.1
Papua New Guinea	9.5	9.3	9.4	22.2	6.3	3.8	..	..
Paraguay	18.3	18.0	10.4	0.0	16.1	3.8	4.0	3.9
Peru	157.1	147.0	11.8	8.1	117.7	6.1	6.7	5.3
Philippines	199.6	199.9	9.8	2.1	176.2	4.9	4.9	4.1
Poland	469.4	452.3	12.7	1.4	388.7	4.3	4.7	4.3
Portugal	228.6	221.1	18.4	0.1	180.1	0.7	0.9	0.3
Puerto Rico	96.3	63.3	20.0	..	..	0.0	0.3	..
Qatar	98.3	..	..	..	..	14.2	..	..

4.10 Toward a broader measure of national income

	Gross domestic product	Gross national income	Adjustments		Adjusted net national income	Gross domestic product	Gross national income	Adjusted net national income
			% of GNI					
			Consumption of fixed capital	Natural resource depletion				
	$ billions	$ billions			$ billions	% growth	% growth	% growth
	2010	2010	2010	2010	2010	2000–10	2000–10	2000–10
Romania	161.6	159.0	11.7	1.6	137.8	5.0	5.4	6.5
Russian Federation	1,479.8	1,431.1	12.4	14.3	1,049.8	5.4	5.6	8.4
Rwanda	5.6	5.6	8.0	3.1	5.0	7.6	..	..
Saudi Arabia	434.7	381.3	12.1	29.1	224.0	3.6	3.4	6.0
Senegal	13.0	12.9	8.9	0.8	11.6	4.2	4.1	4.3
Serbia	38.4	37.5	11.3	..	..	4.1	4.3	..
Sierra Leone	1.9	1.9	7.2	2.1	1.7	8.8	..	..
Singapore	208.8	201.1	14.4	0.0	172.1	6.0	6.1	5.4
Slovak Republic	87.3	86.1	12.7	0.4	74.8	5.4	5.5	5.6
Slovenia	46.9	46.2	13.3	0.3	40.0	3.3	3.5	3.3
Somalia	..	..	..	..	..	..	..	..
South Africa	363.7	356.5	13.5	6.0	286.8	3.9	3.9	3.8
South Sudan	..	..	..	..	..	..	..	..
Spain	1,407.4	1,388.7	13.6	0.0	1,198.9	2.4	2.5	2.2
Sri Lanka	49.6	48.9	10.1	0.3	43.8	5.6	5.6	5.5
Sudan	62.0	55.9	10.3	12.9	43.0	6.7	6.7	5.6
Swaziland	3.6	3.6	10.6	0.1	3.2	2.4	3.2	2.1
Sweden	458.6	466.9	13.2	0.4	403.3	2.2	1.9	2.3
Switzerland	527.9	568.6	13.5	0.0	491.9	1.9	2.3	1.8
Syrian Arab Republic	59.1	57.3	10.6	11.9	44.4	5.0	4.8	7.4
Tajikistan	5.6	5.6	8.6	0.8	5.0	8.6	8.1	6.2
Tanzania[a]	23.1	23.0	7.9	3.2	20.5	7.1	6.9	6.4
Thailand	318.5	304.8	11.4	2.4	263.0	4.5	4.6	4.5
Timor-Leste	0.7	2.7	2.1	..	..	3.4	..	..
Togo	3.2	2.8	8.8	3.4	2.5	2.7	..	1.1
Trinidad and Tobago	20.6	19.3	13.4	32.0	10.5	6.5	8.3	5.4
Tunisia	44.3	42.0	11.3	5.1	35.1	4.7	4.9	4.1
Turkey	734.4	727.1	12.1	0.4	636.8	4.7	4.6	3.9
Turkmenistan	20.0	18.1	11.8	..	..	13.6	16.1	..
Uganda	17.0	16.7	8.0	4.5	14.6	7.7	7.7	7.6
Ukraine	137.9	135.9	10.4	3.7	116.7	4.8	4.7	6.8
United Arab Emirates	297.6	273.5	13.6	..	..	5.1	..	..
United Kingdom	2,261.7	2,271.6	13.6	1.3	1,931.7	1.8	1.7	1.7
United States	14,586.7	14,635.6	14.0	0.9	12,453.3	1.8	1.9	1.2
Uruguay	39.1	37.7	12.6	0.6	32.7	3.6	3.9	3.1
Uzbekistan	39.0	39.0	9.2	19.2	27.9	7.1	5.0	-8.7
Venezuela, RB	391.8	389.0	12.4	12.4	292.4	4.7	4.4	8.1
Vietnam	106.4	102.0	9.4	9.4	82.8	7.5	7.8	7.3
West Bank and Gaza	..	..	..	..	..	-0.9	0.2	..
Yemen, Rep.	31.3	29.5	9.7	14.5	22.3	4.1	3.8	5.6
Zambia	16.2	14.3	10.3	18.9	10.1	5.6	7.7	5.1
Zimbabwe	7.5	7.0	8.6	2.7	6.2	-6.0	-6.0	-7.1
World	**63,242.1 w**	**63,087.6 w**	**13.0 w**	**2.6 w**	**53,010.4 w**	**2.7 w**	**2.6 w**	**2.5 w**
Low income	416.5	422.4	7.7	3.8	373.6	5.5	5.6	5.7
Middle income	19,632.1	19,525.6	11.2	6.5	16,053.8	6.4	6.4	6.2
Lower middle income	4,312.3	4,370.0	9.8	7.4	3,663.4	6.3	6.3	5.9
Upper middle income	15,317.0	15,152.4	11.6	6.2	12,388.6	6.5	6.4	6.3
Low & middle income	20,071.7	19,971.7	11.1	6.4	16,442.8	6.4	6.4	6.2
East Asia & Pacific	7,630.5	7,614.8	10.7	5.2	6,401.9	9.4	9.3	8.5
Europe & Central Asia	3,059.0	2,965.9	12.2	9.4	2,320.4	5.4	5.4	6.2
Latin America & Carib.	4,980.8	4,867.8	12.1	5.5	4,016.0	3.8	3.7	3.9
Middle East & N. Africa	1,207.0	1,334.2	10.7	12.8	1,023.9	4.7	4.9	4.9
South Asia	2,090.4	2,089.3	9.2	4.0	1,814.7	7.4	7.3	7.2
Sub-Saharan Africa	1,097.9	1,044.6	10.9	11.8	807.6	5.0	4.4	4.2
High income	43,240.0	43,247.5	13.9	0.9	36,615.4	1.8	1.7	1.5
Euro area	12,149.1	12,161.9	13.8	0.1	10,459.5	1.3	1.3	1.3

a. Covers mainland Tanzania only.

Toward a broader measure of national income

An economy's growth is typically measured by the change in the volume of its output, as shown in table 4.1. But gross domestic product (GDP), though widely tracked, may not always be the most relevant summary of aggregated economic performance for all economies, especially when production occurs at the expense of consuming capital stock. For countries with significant exhaustible natural resources and important foreign-investor presence, adjusted net national income complements GDP in assessing economic progress (Hamilton and Ley 2010).

The table presents three measures of economic progress: GDP, gross national income (GNI), and adjusted net national income. GDP accounts for all domestic production, regardless of whether the income accrues to domestic or foreign institutions. GNI accounts for the operation of foreign investors, who may be repatriating some of the income produced domestically. GNI comprises GDP plus net receipts of primary income from nonresident sources. Adjusted net national income goes a step further by subtracting from GNI a charge for the consumption of fixed capital (a calculation that yields net national income) and for the depletion of natural resources. The deduction for the depletion of natural resources, which covers net forest depletion, energy depletion, and mineral depletion, reflects the decline in asset values associated with the extraction and harvest of natural resources. For more discussion of the estimates and methodology of produced capital consumption and natural capital depletion, see *About the data* for table 4.11.

The United Nations System of National Accounts includes nonproduced natural assets (such as land, mineral resources, and forests) within the asset boundary when they are under the effective control of institutional units. The calculation of adjusted net national income, which accounts for net forest, energy, and mineral depletion, thus remains within the System of National Accounts boundaries. This point is critical because it allows for comparisons across GDP, GNI, and adjusted net national income; such comparisons reveal the impact of natural resource depletion, which is otherwise ignored by the popular economic indicators.

Adjusted net national income is particularly useful in monitoring low-income, resource-rich economies, like many countries in Sub-Saharan Africa, because such economies often see large natural resources depletion as well as substantial exports of resource rents to foreign mining companies. For recent years adjusted net national income gives a picture of

economic growth that is strikingly different from the one provided by GDP.

The key to increasing future consumption and thus the standard of living lies in increasing national wealth—including not only the traditional measures of capital (such as produced and human capital), but also natural capital. Natural capital comprises such assets as land, forests, and subsoil resources. All three types of capital are key to sustaining economic growth. By accounting for the consumption of fixed and natural capital depletion, adjusted net national income better measures the income available for consumption or for investment to increase a country's future consumption. For a measure of how comprehensive wealth is changing over time, see table 4.11.

Methods of computing growth are described in *Statistical methods*. For a detailed note on methodology, see http://data.worldbank.org.

- **Gross domestic product** is the sum of value added by all resident producers plus any product taxes (less subsidies) not included in the valuation of output.
- **Gross national income** is GDP plus net receipts of primary income (compensation of employees and property income) from abroad. • **Consumption of fixed capital** is the replacement value of capital used up in production. • **Natural resource depletion** is the sum of net forest depletion, energy depletion, and mineral depletion. Net forest depletion is unit resource rents times the excess of roundwood harvest over natural growth. Energy depletion is the ratio of the value of the stock of energy resources to the remaining reserve lifetime (capped at 25 years). It covers coal, crude oil, and natural gas. Mineral depletion is the ratio of the value of the stock of mineral resources to the remaining reserve lifetime (capped at 25 years). It covers tin, gold, lead, zinc, iron, copper, nickel, silver, bauxite, and phosphate.
- **Adjusted net national income** is GNI minus consumption of fixed capital and natural resources depletion.

GNI and GDP are estimated by World Bank staff based on national accounts data collected by World Bank staff during economic missions or reported by national statistical offices to other international organizations such as the Organisation for Economic Co-operation and Development. Data on consumption of fixed capital are from the United Nations Statistics Division's *National Accounts Statistics: Main Aggregates and Detailed Tables*, extrapolated to 2010. Data on energy, mineral, and forest depletion are estimates based on sources and methods in World Bank (2011a).

	Gross savings	Consumption of fixed capital	Education expenditure	Net forest depletion	Energy depletion	Mineral depletion	Carbon dioxide damage	Local pollution	Adjusted net savings
	% of GNI 2010	% of GNI 2010	% of GNI 2010	% of GNI 2010	% of GNI 2010	% of GNI 2010	% of GNI 2010	% of GNI 2010	% of GNI 2010
Afghanistan	..	8.9	..	2.6	0.0	0.0	0.1	0.8	..
Albania	13.6	10.6	2.8	0.0	2.2	0.3	0.3	0.2	2.7
Algeria	53.6	11.3	4.5	0.1	17.8	0.2	0.6	0.3	29.8
Angola	17.9	12.1	2.3	0.0	35.1	0.0	0.3	1.8	−29.2
Argentina	23.1	12.1	6.0	0.0	4.5	0.4	0.4	1.6	10.1
Armenia	18.1	9.9	2.2	0.0	0.0	1.0	0.4	2.2	6.8
Australia	25.1	14.6	4.5	0.0	2.2	4.3	0.3	0.0	8.2
Austria	24.9	14.1	5.3	0.0	0.1	0.0	0.1	0.2	15.6
Azerbaijan	49.5	12.0	3.4	0.0	34.5	0.0	0.9	0.4	5.1
Bahrain	45.4	6.7	3.0	0.0	30.0	0.0	0.8	0.3	10.6
Bangladesh	35.2	7.5	1.8	0.4	1.8	0.0	0.4	0.6	26.2
Belarus	25.7	11.4	4.4	0.0	1.0	0.0	1.0	0.0	16.6
Belgium	22.5	13.7	6.1	0.0	0.0	0.0	0.2	0.1	14.6
Benin	12.8	8.4	4.3	0.3	0.0	0.0	0.5	0.5	7.4
Bolivia	26.1	10.2	5.2	0.0	9.4	2.9	0.5	1.1	7.3
Bosnia and Herzegovina	14.5	10.5	..	..	1.4	1.4	1.3	0.1	..
Botswana	26.8	11.6	7.6	0.0	0.2	3.2	0.2	0.3	18.6
Brazil	16.8	12.2	5.2	0.0	1.6	1.7	0.2	0.2	6.1
Bulgaria	24.6	14.3	4.1	0.0	0.7	1.3	0.8	1.2	10.4
Burkina Faso	..	7.9	4.3	1.5	0.0	2.8	0.2	0.8	..
Burundi	..	6.6	8.7	11.8	0.0	0.9	0.1	0.1	..
Cambodia	13.2	8.9	1.6	0.1	0.0	0.0	0.3	0.4	5.1
Cameroon	..	9.1	3.1	0.0	4.6	0.1	0.2	0.7	..
Canada	18.8	14.3	4.5	0.0	1.8	0.6	0.3	0.1	6.3
Central African Republic	..	7.7	1.1	0.0	0.0	0.0	0.1	0.2	..
Chad	..	9.3	2.3	0.0	29.0	0.0	0.0	1.4	..
Chile	24.9	13.2	4.6	0.0	0.1	12.3	0.3	0.6	3.0
China	52.7	10.8	1.8	0.0	3.7	1.4	1.1	1.2	36.3
Hong Kong SAR, China	29.3	13.2	3.1	0.0	0.0	0.0	0.1	..	..
Colombia	19.8	11.8	3.9	0.0	7.2	0.5	0.2	0.1	3.8
Congo, Dem. Rep.	..	7.0	0.9	0.0	2.7	11.0	0.2	0.7	..
Congo, Rep.	..	14.1	2.5	0.0	59.6	0.0	0.2	0.9	..
Costa Rica	15.7	11.9	6.2	0.1	0.0	0.0	0.2	0.1	9.7
Côte d'Ivoire	15.4	9.4	4.3	0.0	3.4	0.5	0.3	0.3	5.3
Croatia	22.6	12.8	4.3	0.2	0.7	0.0	0.3	0.3	12.7
Cuba	..	11.3	13.4	0.0	2.3	0.9	0.4	0.0	..
Cyprus	9.5	13.3	6.9	0.0	0.0	0.0	0.3	0.3	2.5
Czech Republic	22.5	13.6	3.8	0.0	0.5	0.0	0.5	0.0	11.6
Denmark	22.4	14.0	7.3	0.0	1.7	0.0	0.1	0.0	13.9
Dominican Republic	7.5	11.4	1.9	0.0	0.0	0.2	0.4	0.0	−2.6
Ecuador	23.1	10.9	1.4	0.0	12.9	0.0	0.4	0.1	0.2
Egypt, Arab Rep.	18.2	10.3	4.4	0.1	6.8	0.2	0.8	0.7	3.6
El Salvador	11.2	10.6	3.0	0.4	0.0	0.0	0.2	0.2	2.7
Eritrea	..	7.6	1.7	0.0	0.0	0.0	0.2	0.4	..
Estonia	25.3	13.0	5.5	0.3	1.3	0.0	0.7	0.0	15.6
Ethiopia	16.7	7.4	2.9	4.0	0.0	0.2	0.2	0.2	7.5
Finland	20.3	16.0	5.7	0.0	0.0	0.1	0.2	0.0	9.7
France	17.2	13.6	5.1	0.0	0.0	0.0	0.1	0.0	8.5
Gabon	..	13.3	3.1	0.0	33.0	0.0	0.1	0.0	..
Gambia, The	13.7	8.4	3.1	0.8	0.0	0.0	0.4	0.5	6.7
Georgia	10.0	9.7	2.8	0.0	0.2	0.4	0.4	1.5	0.7
Germany	22.7	13.6	4.4	0.0	0.1	0.0	0.2	0.0	13.2
Ghana	20.8	9.3	4.7	1.5	0.0	6.5	0.3	0.0	8.6
Greece	4.8	13.6	3.2	0.0	0.2	0.1	0.2	0.5	−6.7
Guatemala	13.3	10.5	2.9	0.7	0.5	0.6	0.3	0.2	3.4
Guinea	10.5	8.2	2.3	2.3	0.0	12.0	0.3	0.6	−10.6
Guinea-Bissau	..	8.0	2.3	0.5	0.0	0.0	0.3	0.8	..
Haiti	23.2	8.2	1.5	0.6	0.0	0.0	0.3	0.5	15.1

Toward a broader measure of savings

	Gross savings	Consumption of fixed capital	Education expenditure	Net forest depletion	Energy depletion	Mineral depletion	Carbon dioxide damage	Local pollution	Adjusted net savings
	% of GNI 2010	% of GNI 2010	% of GNI 2010	% of GNI 2010	% of GNI 2010	% of GNI 2010	% of GNI 2010	% of GNI 2010	% of GNI 2010
Honduras	16.9	10.1	3.5	0.0	0.0	0.5	0.4	0.2	9.2
Hungary	21.5	12.9	5.2	0.0	0.5	0.0	0.3	0.0	12.9
India	34.0	9.3	3.1	0.5	2.5	1.3	0.9	0.7	21.8
Indonesia	32.9	10.5	4.3	0.0	5.3	1.3	0.5	0.8	18.8
Iran, Islamic Rep.	..	10.9	4.1	0.0	19.2	0.6	1.2	0.8	..
Iraq	..	10.6	..	0.0	45.7	0.0	1.1	4.0	..
Ireland	14.8	16.9	5.9	0.0	0.0	0.1	0.2	0.0	3.5
Israel	18.9	13.8	5.7	0.0	0.1	0.1	0.2	0.1	10.3
Italy	17.1	13.7	4.4	0.0	0.1	0.0	0.2	0.1	7.5
Jamaica	12.9	11.6	5.8	0.0	0.0	0.6	0.6	0.2	5.6
Japan	23.2	13.6	3.2	0.0	0.0	0.0	0.2	0.3	12.3
Jordan	9.1	10.8	5.6	0.0	0.1	0.9	0.7	0.2	2.0
Kazakhstan	31.6	13.3	4.4	0.0	21.6	1.8	1.4	0.1	−2.3
Kenya	15.6	7.3	5.9	1.1	0.0	0.1	0.3	0.1	13.1
Korea, Dem. Rep.	..	..	..	..	..	..	..	0.8	..
Korea, Rep.	31.6	12.9	4.3	0.0	0.0	0.0	0.4	0.5	22.1
Kosovo	..	10.0	..	..	0.0	0.9	..	..	..
Kuwait	54.9	7.2	3.2	0.0	25.1	0.0	0.5	0.5	14.9
Kyrgyz Republic	21.3	9.2	6.0	0.0	0.7	6.2	1.1	0.5	9.5
Lao PDR	20.5	9.4	1.1	0.0	0.0	8.3	0.2	0.8	2.9
Latvia	23.7	18.0	5.6	0.5	0.0	0.0	0.2	0.0	10.5
Lebanon	12.0	11.8	1.6	0.0	0.0	0.0	0.4	0.2	1.2
Lesotho	27.4	7.3	9.8	1.0	0.0	0.0	..	0.1	..
Liberia	−2.7	8.4	3.1	4.7	0.0	1.7	0.8	0.4	−14.0
Libya	66.8	12.0	..	0.0	29.0	0.0	0.7	1.8	..
Lithuania	18.8	12.3	4.7	0.5	0.1	0.0	0.3	0.1	10.4
Macedonia, FYR	24.8	11.1	4.9	0.1	1.0	4.8	1.0	0.1	11.6
Madagascar	..	7.7	2.7	0.2	0.0	0.8	0.2	0.1	..
Malawi	13.0	7.5	4.4	1.8	0.0	0.0	0.2	0.1	7.5
Malaysia	34.1	12.1	4.1	0.0	6.9	0.1	0.7	0.0	18.5
Mali	..	8.4	3.9	0.0	0.0	9.8	0.1	1.7	..
Mauritania	..	8.8	3.7	0.4	0.0	33.9	0.4	0.6	..
Mauritius	16.1	11.5	3.1	0.0	0.0	0.0	0.3	0.0	7.6
Mexico	24.6	12.0	4.8	0.0	5.4	0.3	0.3	0.4	11.0
Moldova	14.7	8.7	7.7	0.1	0.1	0.0	0.6	0.9	11.9
Mongolia	29.8	10.9	5.1	0.0	17.5	14.8	1.6	2.8	−12.6
Morocco	31.5	10.5	5.2	0.0	0.0	1.6	0.4	0.1	24.1
Mozambique	11.0	7.7	4.0	0.0	3.2	0.1	0.2	0.1	3.7
Myanmar	..	..	0.8	..	..	..	..	0.5	..
Namibia	34.2	11.1	8.0	0.0	0.0	0.7	0.2	0.1	30.1
Nepal	36.8	7.8	4.2	2.5	0.0	0.0	0.2	0.1	29.2
Netherlands	23.6	14.2	4.7	0.0	0.8	0.0	0.2	0.4	12.8
New Zealand	17.1	14.0	7.2	0.0	0.7	0.3	0.2	0.0	8.5
Nicaragua	13.4	9.3	3.0	0.7	0.0	0.9	0.6	0.1	4.9
Niger	..	3.2	3.5	1.5	0.0	0.9	0.1	1.4	..
Nigeria	..	9.9	0.9	0.3	21.7	0.0	0.5	0.7	..
Norway	35.2	14.5	6.0	0.0	10.2	0.0	0.1	0.0	16.4
Oman	39.7	13.5	4.2	0.0	28.5	0.0	0.8	0.0	−8.5
Pakistan	21.0	8.5	1.6	0.7	2.1	0.1	0.7	1.1	9.4
Panama	19.5	12.3	3.5	0.0	0.0	0.0	0.2	0.2	10.3
Papua New Guinea	20.8	9.4	..	0.0	0.0	22.2	0.4	0.0	..
Paraguay	23.0	10.4	3.7	0.0	0.0	0.0	0.2	1.1	15.1
Peru	24.4	11.8	2.1	0.0	1.3	6.8	0.2	0.4	5.9
Philippines	27.2	9.8	2.4	0.1	0.4	1.5	0.3	0.1	17.3
Poland	17.5	12.7	4.9	0.1	1.0	0.4	0.6	0.4	7.4
Portugal	10.8	18.4	4.9	0.0	0.0	0.1	0.2	0.0	−3.1
Puerto Rico	..	20.0	..	..	0.0	0.0	..	..	..
Qatar	..	..	1.8	..	..	..	..	0.1	..

	Gross savings	Consumption of fixed capital	Education expenditure	Net forest depletion	Energy depletion	Mineral depletion	Carbon dioxide damage	Local pollution	Adjusted net savings
	% of GNI 2010	% of GNI 2010	% of GNI 2010	% of GNI 2010	% of GNI 2010	% of GNI 2010	% of GNI 2010	% of GNI 2010	% of GNI 2010
Romania	26.7	11.7	3.4	0.0	1.6	0.0	0.5	0.0	16.2
Russian Federation	28.6	12.4	3.5	0.0	13.2	1.1	0.9	0.1	4.5
Rwanda	15.1	8.0	4.2	3.0	0.0	0.1	0.1	0.1	7.7
Saudi Arabia	32.5	12.1	7.2	0.0	29.1	0.0	0.8	1.2	–3.6
Senegal	19.7	8.9	5.2	0.0	0.0	0.8	0.3	0.7	13.7
Serbia	15.9	11.3	5.0	..	1.9	0.0	1.0	..	..
Sierra Leone	13.0	7.2	3.4	1.5	0.0	0.6	0.6	1.1	5.4
Singapore	47.7	14.4	3.0	0.0	0.0	0.0	0.2	0.4	35.7
Slovak Republic	20.4	12.7	3.5	0.3	0.0	0.0	0.4	0.0	10.4
Slovenia	22.4	13.3	4.9	0.2	0.1	0.0	0.3	0.1	13.3
Somalia	..	..	..	..	..	..	..	0.5	..
South Africa	16.8	13.5	5.4	0.2	3.3	2.6	0.9	0.2	1.6
South Sudan	..	..	..	..	..	..	..	..	..
Spain	19.1	13.6	4.2	0.0	0.0	0.0	0.2	0.2	9.2
Sri Lanka	25.1	10.1	1.7	0.3	0.0	0.0	0.2	0.3	15.9
Sudan	19.7	10.3	0.9	0.0	12.9	0.0	0.2	0.9	–3.6
Swaziland	2.7	10.6	6.9	0.1	0.0	0.0	0.2	0.1	–1.4
Sweden	24.5	13.2	6.2	0.0	0.0	0.4	0.1	0.0	17.0
Switzerland	33.4	13.5	5.3	0.0	0.0	0.0	0.1	0.1	25.0
Syrian Arab Republic	17.4	10.6	2.6	0.0	11.7	0.1	1.0	1.3	–4.8
Tajikistan	2.6	8.6	3.2	0.0	0.4	0.4	0.5	0.2	–4.3
Tanzania[a]	21.1	7.9	2.4	0.0	0.3	2.9	0.2	0.1	12.1
Thailand	32.3	11.4	4.1	0.1	2.2	0.1	0.8	0.3	21.5
Timor-Leste	..	2.1	3.3	..	0.0	0.0	0.1	..	..
Togo	..	8.8	4.4	2.1	0.0	1.3	0.4	0.1	..
Trinidad and Tobago	36.4	13.4	4.0	0.0	32.0	0.0	1.5	0.3	–26.0
Tunisia	21.4	11.3	6.0	0.1	4.1	0.9	0.5	0.1	10.3
Turkey	13.7	12.1	2.6	0.0	0.2	0.1	0.3	0.9	2.7
Turkmenistan	..	11.8	..	..	35.1	0.0	2.5	0.8	..
Uganda	19.1	8.0	3.0	4.5	0.0	0.0	0.2	0.0	9.4
Ukraine	17.5	10.4	5.9	0.0	3.7	0.0	1.7	0.1	7.4
United Arab Emirates	..	13.6	..	..	10.9	0.0	0.4	0.8	..
United Kingdom	11.9	13.6	5.1	0.0	1.3	0.0	0.2	0.0	1.8
United States	10.9	14.0	4.8	0.0	0.8	0.1	0.3	0.1	0.4
Uruguay	17.3	12.6	2.3	0.5	0.0	0.1	0.2	1.8	4.4
Uzbekistan	..	9.2	9.4	0.0	13.7	5.5	2.9	0.4	..
Venezuela, RB	31.7	12.4	3.6	0.0	12.0	0.4	0.3	0.0	10.1
Vietnam	33.2	9.4	2.8	0.2	9.0	0.2	1.0	0.5	15.8
West Bank and Gaza	..	..	..	..	..	..	..	..	..
Yemen, Rep.	9.6	9.7	4.2	0.0	14.5	0.0	0.6	0.4	–11.5
Zambia	25.4	10.3	1.3	0.0	0.0	18.9	0.1	0.3	–2.8
Zimbabwe	..	8.6	2.5	0.0	1.9	0.8	1.0	0.2	..
World	**22.5 w**	**13.0 w**	**4.2 w**	**0.0 w**	**2.1 w**	**0.5 w**	**0.4 w**	**0.3 w**	**6.4 w**
Low income	24.6	7.7	2.9	1.2	1.4	1.2	0.3	0.5	..
Middle income	33.8	11.2	3.3	0.1	5.1	1.3	0.7	0.7	14.4
Lower middle income	29.2	9.8	3.3	0.3	6.0	1.2	0.7	0.7	13.3
Upper middle income	35.1	11.6	3.3	0.0	4.8	1.3	0.7	0.7	14.7
Low & middle income	33.7	11.1	3.3	0.1	5.0	1.3	0.7	0.7	14.5
East Asia & Pacific	48.4	10.7	2.2	0.0	3.8	1.3	1.0	1.1	31.9
Europe & Central Asia	23.9	12.2	3.6	0.0	8.6	0.8	0.8	0.4	4.5
Latin America & Carib.	20.9	12.1	4.7	0.0	3.8	1.6	0.3	0.4	7.0
Middle East & N. Africa	19.2	10.7	4.3	0.1	12.4	0.4	0.7	0.9	..
South Asia	32.7	9.2	2.8	0.6	2.4	1.1	0.8	0.7	20.1
Sub-Saharan Africa	18.0	10.9	3.6	0.5	9.4	1.9	0.5	0.5	–1.0
High income	17.6	13.9	4.6	0.0	0.7	0.2	0.2	0.1	5.3
Euro area	19.4	13.8	4.7	0.0	0.1	0.0	0.2	0.1	7.3

a. Covers mainland Tanzania only.

About the data

Adjusted net savings measure the change in value of a specified set of assets, excluding capital gains. If a country's net savings are positive and the accounting includes a sufficiently broad range of assets, economic theory suggests that the present value of social welfare is increasing. Conversely, persistently negative adjusted net savings indicate that an economy is on an unsustainable path.

The table shows the extent to which today's rents from a number of natural resources and changes in human capital are balanced by net savings—that is, this generation's bequest to future generations.

Adjusted net savings are derived from standard national accounting measures of gross savings by making four adjustments. First, estimates of fixed capital consumption of produced assets are deducted to obtain net savings. Second, current public expenditures on education are added to net savings (in standard national accounting these expenditures are treated as consumption). Third, estimates of the depletion of a variety of natural resources are deducted to reflect the decline in asset values associated with their extraction and harvest. And fourth, deductions are made for damages from carbon dioxide emissions and local pollution.

The exercise treats public education expenditures as an addition to savings. However, because of the wide variability in the effectiveness of public education expenditures, these figures cannot be construed as the value of investments in human capital. A current expenditure of $1 on education does not necessarily yield $1 of human capital. The calculation should also consider private education expenditure, but data are not available for a large number of countries.

While extensive, the accounting of natural resource depletion and pollution costs still has some gaps. Key estimates missing on the resource side include the value of fossil water extracted from aquifers, net depletion of fish stocks, and depletion and degradation of soils. Important pollutants affecting human health and economic assets are excluded because no internationally comparable data are widely available on damage from ground-level ozone or sulfur oxides.

Estimates of resource depletion are based on the "change in real wealth" method described in Hamilton and Ruta (2008), which estimates depletion as the ratio between the total value of the resource and the remaining reserve lifetime. The total value of the resource is the present value of current and future rents from resource extractions. An economic rent represents an excess return to a given factor of production. Natural resources give rise to rents because they are not produced; in contrast, for produced goods and services competitive forces will expand supply until economic profits are driven to zero. For each type of resource and each country, unit resource rents are derived by taking the difference between world prices (to reflect the social opportunity cost of resource extraction) and the average unit extraction or harvest costs (including a "normal" return on capital). Unit rents are then multiplied by the physical quantity extracted or harvested to arrive at total rent. To estimate the value of the resource, rents are assumed to be constant over the life of the resource (the El Serafy approach), and the present value of the rent flow is calculated using a 4 percent social discount rate. For details on the estimation of natural wealth see World Bank (2011c).

A positive net depletion figure for forest resources implies that the harvest rate exceeds the rate of natural growth; this is not the same as deforestation, which represents a change in land use (see *Definitions* for table 3.4). In principle, there should be an addition to savings in countries where growth exceeds harvest, but empirical estimates suggest that most of this net growth is in forested areas that cannot currently be exploited economically. Because the depletion estimates reflect only timber values, they ignore all the external and nontimber benefits associated with standing forests.

Pollution damage from emissions of carbon dioxide is calculated as the marginal social cost per unit multiplied by the increase in the stock of carbon dioxide. The unit damage figure represents the present value of global damage to economic assets and to human welfare over the time the unit of pollution remains in the atmosphere.

Local pollution damage is estimated by valuing the human health effects from exposure to particulate matter pollution in urban areas. The estimates are calculated as willingness to pay to avoid illness and death from cardiopulmonary disease and lung cancer in adults and acute respiratory infections in children that is attributable to particulate emissions.

Adjusted net savings aims to be as comprehensive a measure as possible to provide a better understanding of the rate of county wealth creation or depletion. To do so, it treats education as investment and accounts for pollution damages to assets and human welfare, which goes outside the boundaries of the United Nations System of National Accounts.

For a detailed note on methodology, see http://data.worldbank.org.

Definitions

• **Gross savings** are the difference between gross national income and public and private consumption, plus net current transfers. • **Consumption of fixed capital** is the replacement value of capital used up in production. • **Education expenditure** is public current operating expenditures in education, including wages and salaries and excluding capital investments in buildings and equipment. • **Net forest depletion** is unit resource rents times the excess of roundwood harvest over natural growth. • **Energy depletion** is the ratio of the value of the stock of energy resources to the remaining reserve lifetime (capped at 25 years). It covers coal, crude oil, and natural gas. • **Mineral depletion** is the ratio of the value of the stock of mineral resources to the remaining reserve lifetime (capped at 25 years). It covers tin, gold, lead, zinc, iron, copper, nickel, silver, bauxite, and phosphate. • **Carbon dioxide damage** is estimated at $20 per ton of carbon (the unit damage in 1995 U.S. dollars) times tons of carbon emitted. • **Local pollution damage** is the willingness to pay to avoid illness and death attributable to particulate emissions. • **Adjusted net savings** are net savings plus education expenditure minus energy depletion, mineral depletion, net forest depletion, and carbon dioxide and particulate emissions damage.

Data sources

Data on gross savings are from World Bank national accounts data files (see table 4.8). Data on consumption of fixed capital are from the United Nations Statistics Division's *National Accounts Statistics: Main Aggregates and Detailed Tables,* extrapolated to 2010. Data on education expenditure are from the United Nations Educational, Scientific, and Cultural Organization Institute for Statistics online database; missing data are estimated by World Bank staff. Data on forest, energy, and mineral depletion are estimates based on sources and methods in World Bank (2011c). Data on carbon dioxide damage are from Fankhauser (1995). Data on local pollution damage are from Pandey and others (2006c). The conceptual underpinnings of the savings measure appear in Hamilton and Clemens (1999).

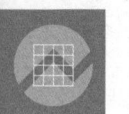

4.12 Central government finances

	Revenue[a]		Expense		Cash surplus or deficit		Net incurrence of liabilities				Debt and interest payments	
	% of GDP		% of GDP		% of GDP		% of GDP				Total debt % of GDP	Interest % of revenue
							Domestic		Foreign			
	2000	**2010**	**2000**	**2010**	**2000**	**2010**	**2000**	**2010**	**2000**	**2010**	**2010**	**2010**
Afghanistan[b]	..	10.1	..	46.1	..	1.4	..	0.2	..	0.7	..	0.0
Albania[b]	23.4	..	24.3	..	–6.7	..	3.1	..	2.6	..	..	..
Algeria	..	37.3	..	25.5	..	–4.5	..	6.0	..	0.0	..	1.0
Angola	..	..	..	..	..	..	..	..	..	..	..	..
Argentina	14.1	..	19.7	..	–5.7	..	1.9	..	2.0	..	..	..
Armenia[b]	17.7	22.4	16.4	22.7	–0.7	–4.9	0.1	0.8	2.4	2.8	..	3.7
Australia	25.8	24.6	24.0	26.6	2.0	–2.4	..	..	..	..	24.1	3.7
Austria	37.7	36.6	40.4	39.6	–2.0	–2.6	..	..	..	..	70.5	7.0
Azerbaijan[b]	..	25.8	..	14.6	..	0.3	..	0.0	..	0.2	..	0.3
Bahrain	32.9	28.8	22.6	18.8	8.5	4.0	4.8	..	0.7	..	19.2	3.2
Bangladesh[b]	9.8	11.1	9.0	11.3	–0.7	–1.7	3.3	3.1	1.1	0.4	..	21.7
Belarus[b]	28.7	31.7	25.3	31.6	0.1	–1.5	0.3	–0.2	–0.5	2.8	18.7	1.8
Belgium	42.8	40.7	42.9	44.1	0.0	–3.3	–8.2	1.8	8.9	1.7	91.8	7.8
Benin[b]	16.5	18.2	11.9	15.0	0.7	–1.0	–3.3	–0.3	3.1	2.0	..	2.7
Bolivia	18.4	23.3	28.8	21.8	–8.7	1.2	2.4	–0.2	4.2	–0.1	..	8.0
Bosnia and Herzegovina	37.1	39.7	35.6	40.6	0.7	–2.3	1.0	–1.4	0.5	3.3	..	1.1
Botswana[b]	..	..	..	..	..	..	..	..	..	..	..	..
Brazil[b]	19.9	23.1	21.7	25.6	–1.8	–3.5	..	8.3	..	–0.1	61.0	20.7
Bulgaria[b]	32.9	32.4	31.6	31.7	–0.4	–0.1	0.0	–0.4	–1.6	0.5	..	2.2
Burkina Faso	11.4	15.6	10.9	12.1	–4.5	–5.7	0.6	2.6	4.1	3.4	..	2.4
Burundi[b]	15.8	..	20.6	..	–2.4	..	3.3	..	2.9	..	..	..
Cambodia	10.3	12.2	9.4	11.3	–3.4	–3.7	–0.2	1.1	3.6	2.1	..	1.4
Cameroon[b]	14.1	..	12.0	..	0.1	..	..	..	..	..	..	..
Canada[b]	20.9	17.2	18.7	19.2	2.2	–2.0	..	..	..	..	52.6	9.8
Central African Republic[b]	..	..	..	..	..	..	..	..	..	..	..	..
Chad	..	..	..	..	..	..	..	..	..	..	..	..
Chile	21.6	22.0	21.0	21.0	–0.7	–0.4	–0.4	1.8	–0.3	0.7	..	2.1
China[b]	7.1	11.9	10.7	..	–2.6	..	4.2	2.0	0.0	0.0	..	..
Hong Kong SAR, China	14.9	20.7	21.3	19.2	–6.8	1.1	1.6	2.0	..	–0.1	34.0	0.3
Colombia	15.1	18.2	19.6	18.3	–5.8	–3.5	3.5	8.2	4.3	0.0	62.9	15.3
Congo, Dem. Rep.[b]	3.7	23.4	9.1	13.7	–4.2	3.8	4.1	–4.7	–0.1	5.5	..	1.3
Congo, Rep.[b]	28.6	..	19.9	..	1.9	..	..	..	..	..	..	..
Costa Rica	..	24.7	..	26.0	..	–3.4	..	..	..	..	..	8.8
Côte d'Ivoire	16.9	18.9	17.4	17.8	–2.5	0.9	2.2	..	1.1	..	..	7.1
Croatia[b]	35.7	32.9	39.1	36.6	–5.3	–4.3	0.5	3.9	3.9	1.3	..	5.9
Cuba	..	..	..	..	..	..	..	..	..	..	..	..
Cyprus	..	39.7	61.7	42.7	..	–5.9	..	..	..	..	97.3	7.7
Czech Republic[b]	30.5	29.6	33.4	36.7	–3.6	–4.9	2.5	2.0	0.0	2.6	36.2	3.3
Denmark	36.2	39.8	34.8	42.2	1.6	–2.1	..	..	..	..	40.8	4.9
Dominican Republic	..	14.5	..	15.6	..	–3.6	..	1.9	..	2.2	..	12.9
Ecuador[b]	..	..	..	..	..	..	..	..	..	..	..	..
Egypt, Arab Rep.[b]	24.3	24.8	27.2	28.9	–6.7	–7.7	14.4	9.2	1.7	0.2	85.8	20.5
El Salvador	16.0	19.2	17.9	21.0	–4.7	–2.7	–2.1	–0.8	9.4	2.0	50.0	11.7
Eritrea	..	..	..	..	..	..	..	..	..	..	..	..
Estonia	31.0	36.8	29.5	36.5	0.2	–1.3	..	..	..	..	9.0	0.6
Ethiopia[b]	11.9	..	14.6	..	–4.2	..	0.8	..	3.4	..	..	..
Finland	40.9	38.8	34.9	34.8	6.7	4.6	–5.2	–0.2	0.9	–0.6	36.0	3.2
France	42.9	40.9	44.9	48.1	–1.7	–7.3	..	..	..	..	83.5	5.4
Gabon	..	..	..	..	..	..	..	..	..	..	..	..
Gambia, The[b]	..	..	..	..	..	..	..	..	..	..	..	..
Georgia[b]	10.4	23.8	11.6	26.3	–1.6	–4.4	1.9	0.6	–0.8	5.5	36.7	3.7
Germany	30.6	29.7	32.0	32.0	1.4	–2.2	–0.8	3.1	0.0	–0.2	47.6	5.5
Ghana[b]	18.1	15.4	18.7	18.0	–6.5	–5.6	–0.3	2.8	5.0	2.6	..	15.2
Greece	41.9	37.1	44.7	52.0	–3.8	–15.6	..	..	..	..	142.0	14.3
Guatemala[b]	10.2	10.9	10.9	12.4	–1.8	–3.1	0.5	1.4	1.2	1.3	23.0	12.6
Guinea[b]	12.0	..	13.5	..	–2.4	..	0.2	..	2.4	..	..	..
Guinea-Bissau	..	..	..	..	..	..	..	..	..	..	..	..
Haiti	..	..	..	..	..	..	..	..	..	..	..	..

Central government finances

	Revenue[a]		Expense		Cash surplus or deficit		Net incurrence of liabilities				Debt and interest payments	
										% of GDP		Total debt % of GDP	Interest % of revenue
	% of GDP		% of GDP		% of GDP		Domestic		Foreign			
	2000	2010	2000	2010	2000	2010	2000	2010	2000	2010	2010	2010
Honduras	20.0	21.1	20.9	23.4	-3.0	-3.1	1.7	0.4	2.0	2.6	..	3.9
Hungary	38.6	41.3	42.0	46.2	-2.8	-4.1	-1.7	-1.9	2.8	6.0	83.2	10.6
India[b]	11.9	11.4	15.7	15.0	-3.9	-3.7	5.1	4.2	0.4	0.3	46.1	27.1
Indonesia[b]	18.3	15.1	16.2	14.4	-3.7	-0.6	..	1.0	1.4	0.1	26.1	9.4
Iran, Islamic Rep.[b]	23.4	31.9	16.9	24.7	1.8	0.6	1.2	..	0.0	..	..	0.6
Iraq	..	..	..	..	..	..	..	..	..	..	..	..
Ireland	33.0	31.0	27.6	44.2	4.9	-14.1	..	..	..	..	70.5	6.9
Israel	40.7	35.3	47.1	41.1	-3.5	-4.0	..	..	..	..	..	12.7
Italy	36.9	38.4	38.9	43.8	-0.7	-4.9	..	..	..	..	118.4	11.1
Jamaica	31.9	25.9	34.5	39.8	-2.4	-15.3	..	7.1	..	4.6	115.8	64.5
Japan	..	..	..	..	..	..	..	..	..	..	174.4	..
Jordan[b]	25.1	21.8	27.1	25.9	-2.0	-5.4	1.8	3.3	-1.7	2.8	59.0	8.5
Kazakhstan[b]	11.3	9.9	13.7	16.2	0.1	-1.1	-0.7	1.7	1.2	1.0	10.2	2.6
Kenya[b]	19.7	20.3	16.8	22.4	2.0	-5.9	0.1	4.9	1.2	1.9	..	10.4
Korea, Dem. Rep.	..	..	..	..	..	..	..	..	..	..	..	..
Korea, Rep.[b]	22.3	22.7	16.6	19.9	4.4	1.7	-0.9	1.4	-0.1	-0.1	..	5.0
Kosovo												
Kuwait[b]	48.3	55.5	39.4	32.6	4.9	18.7	..	..	..	..	..	0.0
Kyrgyz Republic[b]	14.2	20.2	15.8	22.0	-2.9	-5.0	..	-0.1	..	3.1	..	3.5
Lao PDR	..	14.2	..	10.8	..	-0.8	..	0.2	..	1.7	..	3.3
Latvia[b]	26.1	25.0	28.1	35.6	-2.2	-6.8	1.5	0.5	-0.2	5.9	49.9	4.5
Lebanon	16.0	22.2	30.5	29.2	-18.4	-8.2	13.3	11.6	9.3	0.3	..	48.7
Lesotho[b]	50.7	66.2	43.7	51.9	-2.8	5.7	0.0	-0.4	9.0	1.6	..	1.3
Liberia[b]	..	0.4	..	0.3	..	0.0	..	0.0	..	0.0	..	2.1
Libya	..	..	..	..	..	..	..	..	..	..	..	..
Lithuania	25.9	27.4	26.9	37.5	-2.8	-7.2	0.7	1.0	2.0	8.6	43.2	6.1
Macedonia, FYR[b]	..	32.9	..	30.3	..	-0.8	..	-0.6	..	0.2	..	1.9
Madagascar	11.7	14.2	10.6	11.8	-2.0	-1.9	1.3	0.6	1.7	3.0	..	3.9
Malawi	..	..	..	..	..	..	..	..	..	..	..	..
Malaysia[b]	17.5	20.8	16.5	19.6	-4.1	-5.4	1.6	0.5	2.1	4.8	53.1	9.8
Mali	13.4	17.1	11.6	14.7	-3.4	-2.1	-1.0	-4.4	3.0	2.6	..	1.7
Mauritania	..	..	..	..	..	..	..	..	..	..	..	..
Mauritius	..	22.7	..	22.7	..	-2.4	..	-0.2	..	1.8	37.8	10.6
Mexico[b]	14.7	..	15.4	..	-1.2	..	..	..	-0.7	..	..	..
Moldova[b]	24.5	31.6	28.9	35.0	-1.5	-2.6	1.5	0.4	-0.2	2.9	26.3	2.2
Mongolia[b]	24.4	33.7	22.4	26.6	0.2	3.0	1.3	1.2	4.3	-0.9	45.0	1.4
Morocco[b]	30.0	31.8	30.4	30.6	-3.1	-2.6	1.7	2.3	-2.8	2.1	50.3	3.8
Mozambique	..	..	..	..	..	..	..	..	..	..	..	..
Myanmar[b]	5.3	..	3.1	..	-2.7	..	2.7	..	0.0	..	..	..
Namibia[b]	30.1	29.2	28.5	24.1	-1.6	2.0	1.0	-0.8	0.7	-0.1	..	6.3
Nepal[b]	10.6	15.2	..	..	..	..	1.0	2.0	2.1	0.1	43.8	4.6
Netherlands	40.7	40.9	39.3	45.5	2.0	-4.8	..	..	..	..	58.2	4.6
New Zealand	33.7	36.1	32.1	32.1	1.7	3.1	1.4	..	-1.0	..	37.9	3.4
Nicaragua[b]	15.1	19.7	16.5	20.0	-3.6	-1.0	..	..	..	..	..	6.5
Niger	..	13.5	..	11.6	..	-0.9	..	-1.9	..	2.4	..	1.8
Nigeria[b]	..	9.7	..	7.2	..	-1.7	..	0.1	..	..	3.0	6.6
Norway	48.4	47.7	32.6	35.7	15.7	11.7	0.0	-2.5	7.1	4.7	35.4	1.8
Oman[b]	23.9	..	26.2	..	-4.4	..	-1.3	..	-0.7	..	..	..
Pakistan[b]	13.9	13.8	17.2	17.5	-4.1	-5.0	..	..	..	..	..	37.4
Panama[b]	23.1	..	22.1	..	-0.8	..	..	..	..	..	..	..
Papua New Guinea[b]	24.2	..	30.0	..	-1.9	..	1.6	..	1.8	..	..	..
Paraguay[b]	17.0	18.1	17.5	15.1	-3.9	1.4	2.7	0.1	0.9	0.3	..	2.1
Peru[b]	17.4	18.5	17.9	16.4	-2.1	0.3	0.6	1.6	2.3	-0.6	21.6	6.0
Philippines[b]	14.2	13.4	16.3	16.9	-3.7	-3.5	1.3	2.5	2.4	1.5	..	25.1
Poland	31.5	30.0	35.6	35.7	-2.8	-6.1	4.9	1.6	-1.7	3.6	48.1	8.1
Portugal	34.6	34.5	36.7	43.0	-2.6	-8.7	-0.2	3.3	2.0	5.8	84.0	7.7
Puerto Rico	..	..	..	..	..	..	..	..	..	..	..	..
Qatar[b]	..	47.2	..	19.3	..	15.2	..	..	..	..	..	3.6

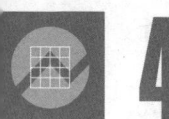

	Revenue[a]		Expense		Cash surplus or deficit		Net incurrence of liabilities				Debt and interest payments	
								% of GDP			Total debt % of GDP	Interest % of revenue
							Domestic		Foreign			
	% of GDP		% of GDP		% of GDP							
	2000	2010	2000	2010	2000	2010	2000	2010	2000	2010	2010	2010
Romania	25.8	30.9	25.9	33.8	–2.0	–4.6	0.4	2.4	1.7	0.9	..	2.0
Russian Federation	31.8	26.8	22.6	28.2	7.0	–1.9	–4.1	1.4	–1.9	0.2	9.4	1.6
Rwanda[b]	..	..	..	..	..	..	..	..	..	..	..	..
Saudi Arabia	..	..	..	..	..	..	..	..	..	..	..	..
Senegal[b]	16.9	..	12.8	..	–0.9	..	0.3	..	0.5	..	..	..
Serbia[b]	..	37.5	..	39.8	..	–3.9	..	2.3	..	1.1	38.7	2.9
Sierra Leone[b]	11.4	11.8	28.7	22.9	–9.3	–3.2	4.8	..	..	..	..	8.3
Singapore[b]	26.2	18.1	16.0	13.4	11.2	8.0	7.8	10.3	..	..	109.2	0.0
Slovak Republic	35.3	28.6	39.4	37.7	–3.2	–7.3	2.9	2.9	–0.2	3.0	38.2	4.7
Slovenia[b]	38.9	36.9	38.8	42.7	–1.1	–5.5	–0.4	3.7	1.6	–1.4	..	4.0
Somalia	..	..	..	..	..	..	..	..	..	..	..	..
South Africa	26.3	28.4	27.9	33.2	–2.0	–4.9	1.6	7.0	0.3	1.0	..	8.4
South Sudan	..	..	..	..	..	..	..	..	..	..	..	..
Spain	31.1	24.9	31.3	30.5	–0.5	–5.2	..	2.4	..	2.2	47.8	5.8
Sri Lanka[b]	16.8	14.9	23.0	19.2	–8.4	–6.6	9.5	6.9	0.0	–0.1	85.0	31.0
Sudan[b]	8.0	..	7.6	..	–0.4	..	1.0	..	..	..	..	..
Swaziland[b]	25.6	..	22.1	..	–0.8	..	..	..	..	..	..	..
Sweden	42.2	34.8	..	..	..	..	..	..	..	..	44.2	..
Switzerland[b]	24.3	18.3	25.5	17.0	2.2	1.3	–2.8	2.0	..	..	28.8	3.5
Syrian Arab Republic[b]	24.0	..	..	..	..	..	..	..	..	..	..	..
Tajikistan[b]	10.6	..	9.0	..	–0.8	..	–0.5	..	0.5	..	..	..
Tanzania	..	..	..	..	..	..	..	..	..	..	..	..
Thailand	19.5	20.3	15.9	18.6	1.5	–0.6	0.9	2.6	–0.6	–0.1	28.8	6.1
Timor-Leste	..	..	..	..	..	..	..	..	..	..	..	..
Togo	..	17.6	..	14.5	..	0.6	..	–2.7	..	1.9	..	4.5
Trinidad and Tobago[b]	27.1	33.5	23.9	32.3	2.0	–4.8	..	–0.4	..	0.3	21.4	8.4
Tunisia[b]	26.5	29.0	25.0	27.0	–2.4	–1.3	0.5	–0.6	–0.2	–0.4	40.5	6.2
Turkey[b]	..	24.4	..	25.4	..	–2.2	..	2.8	..	0.9	50.5	18.3
Turkmenistan	..	..	..	..	..	..	..	..	..	..	..	..
Uganda[b]	10.8	12.6	15.5	13.9	–1.9	–0.9	0.6	1.6	2.0	1.9	33.1	7.7
Ukraine[b]	26.8	34.6	26.9	40.7	–0.6	–5.6	1.5	6.8	–0.3	4.9	..	3.1
United Arab Emirates[b]	6.5	..	6.2	..	0.1	..	..	..	..	..	..	..
United Kingdom	37.1	36.0	36.2	46.4	1.6	–10.9	..	..	..	..	73.3	5.3
United States	20.1	16.9	19.6	26.8	0.5	–10.0	0.9	6.5	1.9	5.1	76.1	11.4
Uruguay[b]	24.7	30.9	26.6	30.3	–3.0	–0.9	–7.4	–0.8	2.7	–0.4	45.6	7.9
Uzbekistan	..	..	..	..	..	..	..	..	..	..	..	..
Venezuela, RB[b]	21.2	..	21.6	..	–1.2	..	3.9	..	–0.5	..	..	..
Vietnam	..	..	..	..	..	..	..	..	..	..	..	..
West Bank and Gaza	..	..	..	..	..	..	..	..	..	..	..	1.1
Yemen, Rep.[b]	23.4	..	21.6	..	–2.3	..	..	..	..	..	..	..
Zambia[b]	19.7	17.4	15.9	17.2	1.8	–1.5	..	..	4.6	..	..	9.0
Zimbabwe[b]	29.1	..	33.2	..	–5.2	..	–0.6	..	–0.1	..	..	..
World	**25.8 m**	**23.8 m**	**26.7 m**	**31.1 m**	**–0.2 m**	**–7.0 m**	**.. m**	**.. m**	**.. m**	**.. m**	**.. m**	**5.5 m**
Low income	10.4	..	11.0	..	–1.7	..	..	..	..	..	..	..
Middle income	14.6	18.8	18.2	..	–2.3	..	..	2.8	1.0	1.2	..	7.0
Lower middle income	13.8	14.9	18.7	17.6	–4.0	–3.6	..	..	..	..	..	6.0
Upper middle income	14.9	19.7	18.1	..	–1.8	..	0.9	3.0	0.8	0.9	..	7.0
Low & middle income	14.5	18.6	18.1	..	–2.3	..	..	0.7	..	0.4	..	5.8
East Asia & Pacific	8.2	13.5	11.6	..	–2.6	..	2.7	1.1	2.4	1.5	..	6.1
Europe & Central Asia	..	25.6	..	27.3	..	–2.2	0.7	0.7	0.4	2.9	..	3.2
Latin America & Carib.	18.1	..	19.2	..	–1.5	..	1.6	2.0	2.0	1.2	..	9.3
Middle East & N. Africa	..	30.5	..	27.2	..	–3.0	2.6	6.8	0.7	0.1	..	6.9
South Asia	12.3	11.7	16.1	15.5	–4.0	–3.8	5.1	2.0	0.4	0.3	56.5	15.9
Sub-Saharan Africa	..	24.3	..	24.2	..	–1.0	..	..	..	..	..	..
High income	27.5	24.9	27.3	32.2	0.1	–7.5	..	..	..	..	58.2	5.4
Euro area	36.3	34.7	37.5	40.0	0.1	–5.2	..	..	..	..	70.5	6.5

a. Excludes grants. b. Data were reported on a cash basis and have been adjusted to the accrual framework.

Central government finances | **4.12**

Tables 4.12–4.14 present an overview of the size and role of central governments relative to national economies. The tables are based on the concepts and recommendations of the second edition of the International Monetary Fund's (IMF) *Government Finance Statistics Manual 2001*. Before 2005 *World Development Indicators* reported data derived on the basis of the 1986 manual's cash-based method. The 2001 manual, harmonized with the 1993 United Nations System of National Accounts, recommends an accrual accounting method, focusing on all economic events affecting assets, liabilities, revenues, and expenses, not only those represented by cash transactions. It takes all stocks into account, so that stock data at the end of an accounting period equal stock data at the beginning of the period plus flows over the period. The 1986 manual considered only the debt stock data. Further, the new manual no longer distinguishes between current and capital revenue or expenditures, and it introduces the concepts of nonfinancial and financial assets. Most countries still follow the 1986 manual, however. The IMF has reclassified historical *Government Finance Statistics Yearbook* data to conform to the 2001 manual's format. Because of reporting differences, the reclassified data understate both revenue and expense.

The 2001 manual describes government's economic functions as the provision of goods and services on a nonmarket basis for collective or individual consumption, and the redistribution of income and wealth through transfer payments. Government activities are financed mainly by taxation and other income transfers, though other financing such as borrowing for temporary periods can also be used. *Government* excludes public corporations and quasi corporations (such as the central bank).

Units of government at many levels meet this definition, from local administrative units to the national government, but inadequate statistical coverage precludes presenting subnational data. Although data for general government under the 2001 manual are available for a few countries, only data for the central government are shown to minimize disparities. Still, different accounting concepts of central government make cross-country comparisons potentially misleading.

Central government can refer to consolidated or budgetary accounting. For most countries central government finance data have been consolidated into one account, but for others only budgetary central government accounts are available. Countries reporting budgetary data are noted in *Primary*

data documentation. Because budgetary accounts may not include all central government units (such as social security funds), they usually provide an incomplete picture.

Data on government revenue and expense are collected by the IMF through questionnaires to member countries and by the Organisation for Economic Co-operation and Development. Despite IMF efforts to standardize data collection, statistics are often incomplete, untimely, and not comparable across countries.

Government finance statistics are reported in local currency. The indicators here are shown as percentages of GDP. Many countries report government finance data by fiscal year; see *Primary data documentation* for information on fiscal year end by country.

• **Revenue** is cash receipts from taxes, social contributions, and other revenues such as fines, fees, rent, and income from property or sales. Grants, usually considered revenue, are excluded. • **Expense** is cash payments for government operating activities in providing goods and services. It includes compensation of employees, interest and subsidies, grants, social benefits, and other expenses such as rent and dividends. • **Cash surplus or deficit** is revenue (including grants) minus expense, minus net acquisition of nonfinancial assets. In editions before 2005 nonfinancial assets were included under revenue and expenditure in gross terms. This cash surplus or deficit is close to the earlier overall budget balance (still missing is lending minus repayments, which are included as a financing item under net acquisition of financial assets). • **Net incurrence of liabilities** is domestic financing (obtained from residents) and foreign financing (obtained from nonresidents), or the means by which a government provides financial resources to cover a budget deficit or allocates financial resources arising from a budget surplus. The net incurrence of liabilities should be offset by the net acquisition of financial assets (a third financing item). The difference between the cash surplus or deficit and the three financing items is the net change in the stock of cash. • **Total debt** is the entire stock of direct government fixed-term contractual obligations to others outstanding on a particular date. It includes domestic and foreign liabilities such as currency and money deposits, securities other than shares, and loans. It is the gross amount of government liabilities reduced by the amount of equity and financial derivatives held by the government. Because debt is a stock rather than a flow, it is measured as of a given date, usually the last day of the fiscal year. • **Interest payments** are interest payments on government debt—including long-term bonds, long-term loans, and other debt instruments —to domestic and foreign residents.

Data on central government finances are from the IMF's Government Finance Statistics database. Each country's accounts are reported using the system of common definitions and classifications in the IMF's *Government Finance Statistics Manual 2001*. See these sources for complete and authoritative explanations of concepts, definitions, and data sources.

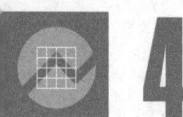

4.13 Central government expenses

	Goods and services		Compensation of employees		Interest payments		Subsidies and other transfers		Other expense	
	% of expense		% of expense		% of expense		% of expense		% of expense	
	2000	2010	2000	2010	2000	2010	2000	2010	2000	2010
Afghanistan[a]	..	75	..	23	..	0	..	2	..	0
Albania[a]	15	..	31	..	16	..	36	..	3	..
Algeria	..	11	..	34	..	1	..	45	..	8
Angola	..	..	..	..	..	..	..	..	..	..
Argentina	4	..	11	..	34	..	43	..	7	..
Armenia[a]	53	13	5	24	4	4	34	39	4	20
Australia	11	10	11	10	7	3	67	73	6	6
Austria	5	6	13	14	9	7	70	71	5	5
Azerbaijan[a]	..	9	..	12	..	1	..	18	..	61
Bahrain	8	26	58	54	7	5	8	10	..	5
Bangladesh[a]	14	12	27	19	18	22	26	35	14	12
Belarus[a]	14	10	11	12	3	2	68	69	4	7
Belgium	3	3	7	7	14	7	74	82	3	3
Benin[a]	33	16	38	48	6	4	2	30	21	2
Bolivia	16	14	25	22	8	10	45	47	6	7
Bosnia and Herzegovina	26	24	31	28	2	1	38	42	3	5
Botswana[a]	..	..	..	..	..	..	..	..	..	..
Brazil[a]	18	13	21	19	17	19	45	49	0	0
Bulgaria[a]	24	9	9	19	12	2	53	64	2	6
Burkina Faso	25	17	41	46	7	4	8	12	19	21
Burundi[a]	..	..	..	..	..	..	..	..	14	..
Cambodia	35	29	37	39	2	2	15	19	11	11
Cameroon[a]	23	..	37	..	22	..	17	..	..	..
Canada[a]	8	8	11	12	22	9	59	69	1	4
Central African Republic[a]	..	..	..	..	..	..	..	..	..	..
Chad	..	..	..	..	..	..	..	..	..	..
Chile	9	10	21	20	6	2	59	51	10	19
China[a]	..	..	..	..	5	..	65	..	0	..
Hong Kong SAR, China	23	28	26	23	0	0	27	19	26	33
Colombia	7	1	21	11	20	15	3	61	1	16
Congo, Dem. Rep.[a]	56	19	27	43	6	3	1	34	16	1
Congo, Rep.[a]	26	..	28	..	35	..	11	..	1	..
Costa Rica	..	11	..	46	..	8	..	21	..	14
Côte d'Ivoire	30	29	39	38	16	9	16	16	..	7
Croatia[a]	24	8	26	26	4	5	43	55	3	6
Cuba	..	..	..	..	..	..	..	..	..	..
Cyprus	11	12	36	35	15	7	30	33	1	1
Czech Republic[a]	7	6	10	8	3	3	74	74	7	10
Denmark	9	9	14	13	10	5	24	17	2	2
Dominican Republic	..	17	..	36	..	12	..	28	..	7
Ecuador[a]	..	..	..	..	..	..	..	..	..	..
Egypt, Arab Rep.[a]	8	8	30	25	20	18	24	42	18	8
El Salvador	15	17	43	38	11	11	3	24	27	12
Eritrea	..	..	..	..	..	..	..	..	..	..
Estonia	19	13	26	21	0	1	42	48	3	4
Ethiopia[a]	22	..	23	..	11	..	44	..	0	..
Finland	9	10	11	10	8	4	68	71	8	8
France	7	6	23	21	6	5	60	54	6	2
Gabon	..	..	..	..	..	..	..	..	..	..
Gambia, The[a]	..	..	..	..	..	..	..	..	..	..
Georgia[a]	17	16	11	18	24	4	48	51	..	11
Germany	4	5	6	5	7	5	81	81	4	4
Ghana[a]	14	16	36	40	39	16	4	28	..	12
Greece	13	12	22	24	17	10	42	50	10	7
Guatemala[a]	15	15	31	29	10	11	22	33	21	12
Guinea[a]	15	..	30	..	32	..	12	..	1	..
Guinea-Bissau	..	..	..	..	..	..	..	..	..	..
Haiti	..	..	..	..	..	..	..	..	..	..

Central government expenses

	Goods and services		Compensation of employees		Interest payments		Subsidies and other transfers		Other expense	
	% of expense		% of expense		% of expense		% of expense		% of expense	
	2000	2010	2000	2010	2000	2010	2000	2010	2000	2010
Honduras	13	14	51	56	7	4	18	6	12	21
Hungary	9	10	13	13	13	10	57	63	13	8
India[a]	12	10	10	9	30	21	43	60	7	1
Indonesia[a]	11	11	11	16	24	10	53	55	0	9
Iran, Islamic Rep.[a]	18	11	57	40	0	1	24	34	1	14
Iraq	..	..	..	..	..	..	..	..	..	..
Ireland	6	10	14	23	7	5	29	40	1	1
Israel	24	26	23	24	17	11	30	31	7	9
Italy	4	4	16	15	16	10	61	66	5	6
Jamaica	16	6	33	14	47	43	2	6	2	31
Japan	..	..	..	..	..	..	..	..	..	..
Jordan[a]	6	9	70	52	13	8	8	29	3	2
Kazakhstan[a]	25	22	9	7	10	3	55	66	1	2
Kenya[a]	21	14	55	38	18	10	3	37	2	1
Korea, Dem. Rep.	..	..	..	..	..	..	..	..	..	..
Korea, Rep.[a]	14	11	11	10	7	6	53	58	15	15
Kosovo	..	..	..	..	..	..	..	..	..	..
Kuwait[a]	23	15	32	24	1	0	32	30	11	19
Kyrgyz Republic[a]	40	25	37	28	9	4	14	42	..	2
Lao PDR	..	29	..	43	..	6	..	13	..	9
Latvia[a]	13	9	12	12	3	4	67	72	4	3
Lebanon	3	3	24	21	50	38	21	36	3	2
Lesotho[a]	30	42	38	35	8	2	21	14	..	6
Liberia[a]	..	37	..	36	..	2	..	24	..	..
Libya	..	..	..	..	..	..	..	..	..	..
Lithuania	16	10	21	15	6	5	55	68	2	6
Macedonia, FYR[a]	..	28	..	17	..	2	..	49	..	4
Madagascar	18	15	41	40	13	7	10	25	19	14
Malawi	..	..	..	..	..	..	..	..	..	..
Malaysia[a]	15	16	28	31	15	10	48	42	3	1
Mali	38	31	37	34	8	2	0	15	17	17
Mauritania	..	..	..	..	..	..	..	..	..	..
Mauritius	..	12	..	35	..	11	..	31	..	10
Mexico[a]	8	..	17	..	13	..	..	..	..	..
Moldova[a]	10	20	10	14	22	2	55	59	3	5
Mongolia[a]	23	20	13	29	7	2	56	42	2	7
Morocco[a]	13	9	42	40	13	4	29	33	3	14
Mozambique	..	..	..	..	..	..	..	..	..	..
Myanmar[a]	..	..	..	..	..	..	..	..	..	..
Namibia[a]	21	20	51	45	7	8	10	13	11	14
Nepal[a]	..	..	..	..	..	..	..	..	..	..
Netherlands	7	8	8	7	8	4	76	79	4	4
New Zealand	31	30	25	25	6	4	37	38	4	7
Nicaragua[a]	17	13	23	38	13	7	35	37	12	5
Niger	..	30	..	30	..	3	..	9	..	28
Nigeria[a]	..	15	..	24	..	9	..	53	..	..
Norway	10	11	11	16	3	2	74	68	4	5
Oman[a]	50	..	34	..	5	..	11	..	0	..
Pakistan[a]	48	22	4	4	36	31	3	25	..	17
Panama[a]	15	..	37	..	22	..	26	..	1	..
Papua New Guinea[a]	37	..	25	..	14	..	24	..	..	..
Paraguay[a]	8	10	54	53	7	3	31	27	1	7
Peru[a]	23	22	22	18	13	7	37	48	5	6
Philippines[a]	26	27	31	31	24	20	19	20	2	3
Poland	7	5	11	12	8	7	70	71	8	7
Portugal	9	7	32	24	8	6	46	51	7	1
Puerto Rico	..	..	..	..	..	..	..	..	..	..
Qatar[a]	..	28	..	28	..	7	..	16	..	22

4.13 Central government expenses

	Goods and services		Compensation of employees		Interest payments		Subsidies and other transfers		Other expense	
	% of expense		% of expense		% of expense		% of expense		% of expense	
	2000	2010	2000	2010	2000	2010	2000	2010	2000	2010
Romania	22	13	16	19	8	2	43	60	12	8
Russian Federation	19	13	17	16	9	2	54	67	1	9
Rwanda[a]	..	..	..	..	..	..	..	..	..	..
Saudi Arabia	..	..	..	..	..	..	..	..	..	..
Senegal[a]	26	..	41	..	11	..	19	..	..	..
Serbia[a]	..	13	..	25	..	3	..	58	..	1
Sierra Leone[a]	15	24	23	28	22	7	5	23	34	18
Singapore[a]	33	36	29	30	2	0	36	0	..	..
Slovak Republic	11	7	12	12	6	4	64	68	12	14
Slovenia[a]	16	13	18	19	4	4	59	62	3	3
Somalia	..	..	..	..	..	..	..	..	..	..
South Africa	11	13	16	13	18	7	53	63	2	4
South Sudan	..	..	..	..	..	..	..	..	..	..
Spain	4	4	11	8	9	5	44	81	2	5
Sri Lanka[a]	22	14	24	28	25	25	21	23	9	10
Sudan[a]	41	..	41	..	10	..	8	..	..	..
Swaziland[a]	26	..	45	..	2	..	27	..	21	..
Sweden	..	..	..	..	..	..	..	..	..	..
Switzerland[a]	23	6	5	6	3	4	67	83	2	3
Syrian Arab Republic[a]	..	..	..	..	..	..	..	..	..	..
Tajikistan[a]	31	..	22	..	4	..	43	..	0	..
Tanzania	..	..	..	..	..	..	..	..	..	..
Thailand	27	32	35	40	7	7	24	21	6	3
Timor-Leste	..	..	..	..	..	..	..	..	..	..
Togo	..	26	..	36	..	7	..	26	..	4
Trinidad and Tobago[a]	15	19	37	26	18	9	29	45	1	2
Tunisia[a]	9	6	40	36	12	7	36	39	5	12
Turkey[a]	..	10	..	25	..	18	..	44	..	6
Turkmenistan	..	..	..	..	..	..	..	..	..	..
Uganda[a]	55	31	12	14	5	9	27	45	..	1
Ukraine[a]	19	12	15	13	9	3	56	70	1	2
United Arab Emirates[a]	46	..	36	..	..	..	..	..	..	..
United Kingdom	17	18	14	14	7	4	55	53	9	12
United States	13	15	12	12	13	7	62	64	2	4
Uruguay[a]	12	13	15	23	7	8	66	46	0	10
Uzbekistan	..	..	..	..	..	..	..	..	..	..
Venezuela, RB[a]	6	..	21	..	12	..	59	..	2	..
Vietnam	..	..	..	..	..	..	..	..	..	..
West Bank and Gaza	..	12	..	67	..	1	..	18	..	1
Yemen, Rep.[a]	17	..	49	..	11	..	21	..	..	..
Zambia[a]	35	24	39	43	7	10	3	15	16	8
Zimbabwe[a]	13	..	38	..	21	..	28	..	..	..
World	**15 m**	**12 m**	**21 m**	**23 m**	**8 m**	**5 m**	**43 m**	**45 m**	**6 m**	**6 m**
Low income	..	..	..	..	..	..	..	..	..	..
Middle income	15	13	22	26	12	7	41	44	4	7
Lower middle income	15	15	29	31	15	8	29	33	..	8
Upper middle income	13	11	21	22	9	7	48	46	5	6
Low & middle income	17	14	27	28	10	6	34	36	..	7
East Asia & Pacific	23	27	31	31	10	7	44	21	0	7
Europe & Central Asia	19	13	17	17	6	3	50	58	5	6
Latin America & Carib.	13	13	23	29	13	9	43	33	4	12
Middle East & N. Africa	8	9	41	36	12	7	..	36	..	9
South Asia	22	22	10	9	30	21	26	25	7	1
Sub-Saharan Africa	..	..	..	..	..	..	..	..	..	..
High income	9	10	13	15	7	5	58	57	4	5
Euro area	7	7	14	17	8	5	60	64	4	4

Note: Components may not sum to 100 percent because of rounding or missing data.

a. Data were reported on a cash basis and have been adjusted to the accrual framework.

Central government expenses | 4.13

The term *expense* has replaced *expenditure* in the table since the 2005 edition of *World Development Indicators* in accordance with use in the International Monetary Fund's (IMF) *Government Finance Statistics Manual 2001*. Government expenses include all nonrepayable payments, whether current or capital, requited or unrequited. The concept of total central government expense as presented in the IMF's *Government Finance Statistics Yearbook* is comparable to the concept used in the 1993 United Nations System of National Accounts.

Expenses can be measured either by function (health, defense, education) or by economic type (interest payments, wages and salaries, purchases of goods and services). Functional data are often incomplete, and coverage varies by country because functional responsibilities stretch across levels of government for which no data are available. Defense expenses, usually the central government's responsibility, are shown in table 5.7. For more information on education expenses, see table 2.11; for more on health expenses, see table 2.16.

The classification of expenses by economic type in the table shows whether the government produces goods and services and distributes them, purchases the goods and services from a third party and distributes them, or transfers cash to households to make the purchases directly. When the government produces and provides goods and services, the cost is reflected in compensation of employees, use of goods and services, and consumption of fixed capital. Purchases from a third party and cash transfers to households are shown as subsidies and other transfers, and other expenses. The economic classification can be problematic. For example, subsidies to public corporations or banks may be disguised as capital financing or hidden in special contractual pricing for goods and services. For further discussion of government finance statistics, see *About the data* for tables 4.12 and 4.14.

• **Goods and services** are all government payments in exchange for goods and services used for the production of market and nonmarket goods and services. Own-account capital formation is excluded. • **Compensation of employees** is all payments in cash, as well as in kind (such as food and housing), to employees in return for services rendered, and government contributions to social insurance schemes such as social security and pensions that provide benefits to employees. • **Interest payments** are payments made to nonresidents, to residents, and to other general government units for the use of borrowed money. (Repayment of principal is shown as a financing item, and commission charges are shown as purchases of services.) • **Subsidies and other transfers** include all unrequited, nonrepayable transfers on current account to private and public enterprises; grants to foreign governments, international organizations, and other government units; and social security, social assistance benefits, and employer social benefits in cash and in kind. • **Other expense** is spending on dividends, rent, and other miscellaneous expenses, including provision for consumption of fixed capital.

Data sources

Data on central government expenses are from the IMF's Government Finance Statistics database. Each country's accounts are reported using the system of common definitions and classifications in the IMF's *Government Finance Statistics Manual 2001*. See these sources for complete and authoritative explanations of concepts, definitions, and data sources.

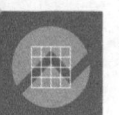 
	Taxes on income, profits, and capital gains		Taxes on goods and services		Taxes on international trade		Other taxes		Social contributions		Grants and other revenue	
	% of revenue		% of revenue		% of revenue		% of revenue		% of revenue		% of revenue	
	2000	2010	2000	2010	2000	2010	2000	2010	2000	2010	2000	2010
Afghanistan[a]	..	3	..	3	..	5	..	0	..	0	..	89
Albania[a]	14	..	43	..	9	..	1	..	17	..	17	..
Algeria	..	60	..	28	..	4	..	1	..	..	..	6
Angola	..	..	..	..	..	..	..	..	..	..	..	..
Argentina	13	..	28	..	14	..	15	..	20	..	11	..
Armenia[a]	10	19	43	43	3	4	10	8	13	13	20	15
Australia	67	65	18	23	2	2	2	0	..	..	11	10
Austria	24	23	24	23	0	0	4	5	41	42	7	7
Azerbaijan[a]	..	33	..	23	..	4	..	1	..	..	..	39
Bahrain	11	19	25	29	31	24	4	3	..	..	28	24
Bangladesh[a]	3	1	2	0	6	4	2	..	..	..	87	95
Belarus[a]	11	7	39	32	5	11	3	3	35	37	7	9
Belgium	37	35	24	25	..	..	2	1	34	36	2	4
Benin[a]	20	16	35	38	21	22	7	6	..	2	18	15
Bolivia	7	10	41	43	4	3	8	9	9	7	32	28
Bosnia and Herzegovina	2	6	28	45	18	0	5	0	34	39	13	10
Botswana[a]	..	..	..	..	..	..	..	..	..	..	..	..
Brazil[a]	25	30	34	33	4	2	8	2	25	26	5	6
Bulgaria[a]	11	16	38	45	2	1	1	0	27	23	20	16
Burkina Faso	18	15	37	36	13	11	2	2	..	..	30	36
Burundi[a]	18	..	38	..	17	..	1	..	6	..	19	..
Cambodia	6	10	30	35	22	14	0	0	..	..	42	41
Cameroon[a]	21	..	26	..	28	..	4	..	2	..	18	..
Canada[a]	54	53	16	15	3	1	..	..	19	23	8	8
Central African Republic[a]	..	..	..	..	..	..	..	..	..	..	..	..
Chad	..	..	..	..	..	..	..	..	..	..	..	..
Chile	22	27	47	45	6	1	2	8	7	6	16	13
China[a]	8	25	65	59	10	4	6	1	..	..	11	12
Hong Kong SAR, China	38	36	13	9	0	0	10	17	0	0	39	38
Colombia	28	21	32	32	6	6	7	5	0	0	32	36
Congo, Dem. Rep.[a]	10	12	14	14	14	14	20	0	..	..	41	60
Congo, Rep.[a]	7	..	15	..	5	..	0	..	3	..	76	..
Costa Rica	..	17	..	32	..	4	..	3	..	34	..	10
Côte d'Ivoire	18	15	18	20	46	33	3	8	8	6	7	18
Croatia[a]	9	7	46	46	6	1	1	2	32	35	5	8
Cuba	..	..	..	..	..	..	..	..	..	..	..	..
Cyprus	..	26	..	34	..	1	..	4	..	22	..	..
Czech Republic[a]	13	15	34	28	2	0	1	1	47	44	3	12
Denmark	37	45	42	36	..	..	6	5	6	3	9	..
Dominican Republic	..	22	..	53	..	9	..	4	..	3	..	9
Ecuador[a]	..	..	..	..	..	..	..	..	..	..	..	..
Egypt, Arab Rep.[a]	20	25	22	22	8	5	3	4	..	..	47	44
El Salvador	20	25	39	40	7	5	1	0	15	12	19	17
Eritrea	..	..	..	..	..	..	..	..	..	..	..	..
Estonia	13	8	38	39	0	..	..	..	35	36	..	..
Ethiopia[a]	14	..	10	..	26	..	1	..	0	..	49	..
Finland	26	20	32	32	0	..	2	2	29	31	12	15
France	26	22	25	23	0	0	3	4	41	45	5	..
Gabon	..	..	..	..	..	..	..	..	..	..	..	..
Gambia, The[a]	..	..	..	..	..	..	..	..	..	..	..	..
Georgia[a]	8	31	57	51	7	1	..	1	21	17	7	15
Germany	18	16	20	24	..	..	..	..	57	55	4	4
Ghana[a]	22	23	15	29	32	16	..	..	..	..	31	32
Greece	22	21	29	29	0	0	4	3	30	36	15	12
Guatemala[a]	24	29	60	56	12	7	1	2	2	3	6	4
Guinea[a]	6	..	3	..	48	..	2	..	1	..	40	..
Guinea-Bissau	..	..	..	..	..	..	..	..	..	..	..	..
Haiti	..	..	..	..	..	..	..	..	..	..	..	..

Central government revenues

	Taxes on income, profits, and capital gains		Taxes on goods and services		Taxes on international trade		Other taxes		Social contributions		Grants and other revenue	
	% of revenue		% of revenue		% of revenue		% of revenue		% of revenue		% of revenue	
	2000	2010	2000	2010	2000	2010	2000	2010	2000	2010	2000	2010
Honduras	15	20	44	40	6	4	1	2	12	13	22	21
Hungary	20	23	34	32	3	0	1	1	34	32	8	12
India[a]	27	47	29	23	19	13	0	0	0	0	25	16
Indonesia[a]	31	36	26	29	3	2	3	4	..	..	37	28
Iran, Islamic Rep.[a]	13	19	7	3	6	6	1	1	11	19	61	52
Iraq	..	..	..	..	..	..	..	..	..	..	..	..
Ireland	39	33	..	..	0	0	4	2	15	22	..	..
Israel	34	26	26	33	1	1	5	5	15	18	20	17
Italy	35	32	23	20	..	..	5	7	33	36	4	5
Jamaica	15	25	33	37	8	7	20	10	2	3	21	18
Japan	..	..	..	..	..	..	..	..	..	..	..	..
Jordan[a]	9	13	31	43	17	6	8	2	1	0	35	36
Kazakhstan[a]	24	24	40	20	5	10	7	0	0	..	24	46
Kenya[a]	29	41	41	40	15	11	0	1	0	..	15	7
Korea, Dem. Rep.	..	..	..	..	..	..	..	..	..	..	..	..
Korea, Rep.[a]	26	28	28	27	4	4	10	8	13	16	18	17
Kosovo	..	..	..	..	..	..	..	..	..	..	..	..
Kuwait[a]	0	1	0	0	2	1	0	0	..	..	98	98
Kyrgyz Republic[a]	14	21	61	37	3	9	0	..	..	..	22	34
Lao PDR	..	13	..	42	..	7	..	1	..	..	..	37
Latvia[a]	12	7	40	35	1	0	0	0	34	29	13	28
Lebanon	12	15	26	44	26	6	11	10	2	1	24	23
Lesotho[a]	17	17	12	12	41	57	0	3	..	..	29	11
Liberia[a]	..	28	..	15	..	39	..	1	..	..	..	18
Libya	..	..	..	..	..	..	..	..	..	..	..	..
Lithuania	11	6	44	37	1	..	0	0	36	39	8	18
Macedonia, FYR[a]	..	13	..	40	..	5	..	0	..	29	..	13
Madagascar	12	12	22	15	40	31	1	6	..	4	26	32
Malawi	..	..	..	..	..	..	..	..	..	..	..	..
Malaysia[a]	43	46	25	17	7	2	3	4	..	..	22	31
Mali	12	19	42	29	11	10	5	10	..	..	30	31
Mauritania	..	..	..	..	..	..	..	..	..	..	..	..
Mauritius	..	20	..	50	..	2	..	7	..	7	..	14
Mexico[a]	34	..	62	..	4	..	1	..	10	..	10	..
Moldova[a]	3	1	45	48	5	4	0	0	23	30	23	17
Mongolia[a]	12	27	36	29	7	6	1	2	18	13	26	23
Morocco[a]	22	26	30	36	11	6	3	6	13	13	22	14
Mozambique	..	..	..	..	..	..	..	..	..	..	..	..
Myanmar[a]	19	..	33	..	4	..	..	..	..	..	44	..
Namibia[a]	32	28	23	19	35	44	1	1	1	0	9	7
Nepal[a]	15	14	30	38	23	16	3	5	..	..	28	27
Netherlands	25	26	26	27	..	..	4	2	39	35	6	10
New Zealand	54	57	29	26	3	3	0	0	0	0	14	15
Nicaragua[a]	13	27	54	52	7	4	0	0	..	..	27	16
Niger	..	12	..	18	..	26	..	3	..	..	..	41
Nigeria[a]	..	1	..	2	..	..	..	..	..	..	..	97
Norway	28	30	28	24	0	0	1	1	18	20	25	24
Oman[a]	24	..	1	..	3	..	2	..	..	..	70	..
Pakistan[a]	19	25	30	31	11	8	8	5	..	..	32	32
Panama[a]	18	..	9	..	9	..	4	..	18	..	38	..
Papua New Guinea[a]	31	..	9	..	24	..	2	..	0	..	33	..
Paraguay[a]	11	13	37	47	11	9	3	1	7	7	30	23
Peru[a]	19	31	40	39	8	2	3	6	10	9	20	14
Philippines[a]	40	41	27	29	19	21	4	..	..	..	10	9
Poland	15	14	33	37	2	0	0	1	36	37	14	10
Portugal	25	23	32	31	0	0	2	2	30	33	..	..
Puerto Rico	..	..	..	..	..	..	..	..	..	..	..	..
Qatar[a]	..	40	..	..	..	3	..	..	..	..	..	57

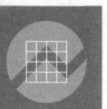

4.14 Central government revenues

	Taxes on income, profits, and capital gains		Taxes on goods and services		Taxes on international trade		Other taxes		Social contributions		Grants and other revenue	
	% of revenue		% of revenue		% of revenue		% of revenue		% of revenue		% of revenue	
	2000	2010	2000	2010	2000	2010	2000	2010	2000	2010	2000	2010
Romania	9	22	33	35	3	0	1	0	42	33	13	10
Russian Federation	5	2	28	21	9	26	0	0	37	20	20	31
Rwanda[a]	..	..	..	..	..	..	..	..	..	..	..	..
Saudi Arabia	..	..	..	..	..	..	..	..	..	..	..	..
Senegal[a]	21	..	34	..	30	..	3	..	..	..	12	..
Serbia[a]	..	9	..	45	..	4	..	0	..	34	..	8
Sierra Leone[a]	15	17	8	25	29	14	0	..	..	..	48	44
Singapore[a]	29	34	18	26	1	0	9	16	..	..	42	24
Slovak Republic	17	9	31	33	1	0	1	0	39	43	13	15
Slovenia[a]	13	10	34	34	2	0	3	0	39	42	9	14
Somalia	..	..	..	..	..	..	..	..	..	..	..	..
South Africa	52	53	33	32	3	3	3	2	2	2	7	8
South Sudan	..	..	..	..	..	..	..	..	..	..	..	..
Spain	27	23	25	20	0	..	0	0	41	51	..	6
Sri Lanka[a]	13	18	57	45	11	14	4	8	2	1	14	14
Sudan[a]	15	..	35	..	29	..	1	..	..	..	21	..
Swaziland[a]	24	..	13	..	50	..	4	..	..	..	9	..
Sweden	17	11	29	37	..	..	6	13	30	25	..	..
Switzerland[a]	14	24	22	26	1	6	3	3	41	36	19	5
Syrian Arab Republic[a]	30	..	21	..	11	..	6	..	0	..	32	..
Tajikistan[a]	3	..	55	..	14	..	1	..	20	..	7	..
Tanzania	..	..	..	..	..	..	..	..	..	..	..	..
Thailand	29	33	40	40	10	5	0	1	4	6	17	15
Timor-Leste	..	..	..	..	..	..	..	..	..	..	..	..
Togo	..	11	..	37	..	19	..	6	..	..	..	27
Trinidad and Tobago[a]	36	47	23	15	5	4	17	11	5	6	13	16
Tunisia[a]	20	27	37	31	11	6	4	4	17	21	10	10
Turkey[a]	..	24	..	51	..	1	..	8	..	..	..	16
Turkmenistan	..	..	..	..	..	..	..	..	..	..	..	..
Uganda[a]	10	22	29	47	22	10	0	0	..	..	39	22
Ukraine[a]	12	10	33	34	4	2	2	0	30	37	19	17
United Arab Emirates[a]	..	..	17	..	..	..	..	..	0	..	82	..
United Kingdom	38	36	30	28	..	..	8	7	20	23	4	6
United States	57	50	3	3	1	1	1	1	35	39	3	6
Uruguay[a]	15	18	34	40	3	4	8	2	29	30	12	7
Uzbekistan	..	..	..	..	..	..	..	..	..	..	..	..
Venezuela, RB[a]	27	..	25	..	7	..	4	..	4	..	34	..
Vietnam	..	..	..	..	..	..	..	..	..	..	..	..
West Bank and Gaza	..	2	..	21	..	11	..	0	..	0	..	66
Yemen, Rep.[a]	18	..	9	..	10	..	2	..	..	..	61	..
Zambia[a]	36	44	45	32	13	8	0	0	0	..	6	15
Zimbabwe[a]	43	..	23	..	20	..	2	..	3	..	9	..
World	**20 m**	**23 m**	**30 m**	**32 m**	**6 m**	**4 m**	**2 m**	**2 m**	**.. m**	**.. m**	**15 m**	**17 m**
Low income	..	..	..	..	..	..	..	..	..	..	..	..
Middle income	20	24	34	36	7	5	1	2	..	..	17	17
Lower middle income	18	23	32	33	13	7	1	1	..	..	20	18
Upper middle income	14	22	36	37	6	4	3	2	16	19	14	14
Low & middle income	18	21	32	36	9	6	2	1	..	..	20	18
East Asia & Pacific	25	33	30	29	9	6	3	1	..	..	24	28
Europe & Central Asia	10	8	37	40	6	4	0	0	30	30	17	16
Latin America & Carib.	18	26	40	39	6	4	4	2	9	9	16	16
Middle East & N. Africa	17	27	30	31	10	6	4	3	..	6	30	23
South Asia	17	19	30	27	15	10	4	3	..	0	26	30
Sub-Saharan Africa	..	..	..	..	..	..	..	..	..	..	..	..
High income	26	26	27	26	1	0	3	2	33	35	8	12
Euro area	25	23	25	27	0	0	3	3	35	37	6	7

Note: Components may not sum to 100 percent because of missing data or adjustment to tax revenue.
a. Data were reported on a cash basis and have been adjusted to the accrual framework.

Central government revenues | 4.14

About the data

The International Monetary Fund (IMF) classifies government revenues as taxes, grants, and property income. Taxes are classified by the base on which the tax is levied, grants by the source, and property income by type (for example, interest, dividends, or rent). The most important source of revenue is taxes. Grants are unrequited, nonrepayable, noncompulsory receipts from other government units and foreign governments or from international organizations. Transactions are generally recorded on an accrual basis.

The IMF's *Government Finance Statistics Manual 2001* describes taxes as compulsory, unrequited payments made to governments by individuals, businesses, or institutions. Taxes are classified in six major groups by the base on which the tax is levied: income, profits, and capital gains; payroll and workforce; property; goods and services; international trade and transactions; and other. However, the distinctions are not always clear. Taxes levied on the income and profits of individuals and corporations are classified as direct taxes, and taxes and duties levied on goods and services are classified as indirect taxes. This distinction may be a useful simplification, but it has no particular analytical significance except with respect to the capacity to fix tax rates. Direct taxes tend to be progressive, whereas indirect taxes are proportional.

Social security taxes do not reflect compulsory payments made by employers to provident funds or other agencies with a like purpose. Similarly, expenditures from such funds are not reflected in government expenses (see table 4.13). For further discussion of taxes and tax policies, see *About the data* for table 5.6. For further discussion of government revenues and expenditures, see *About the data* for tables 4.12 and 4.13.

Definitions

• **Taxes on income, profits, and capital gains** are levied on the actual or presumptive net income of individuals, on the profits of corporations and enterprises, and on capital gains, whether realized or not, on land, securities, and other assets. Intragovernmental payments are eliminated in consolidation. • **Taxes on goods and services** include general sales and turnover or value added taxes, selective excises on goods, selective taxes on services, taxes on the use of goods or property, taxes on extraction and production of minerals, and profits of fiscal monopolies. • **Taxes on international trade** include import duties, export duties, profits of export or import monopolies, exchange profits, and exchange taxes. • **Other taxes** include employer payroll or labor taxes, taxes on property, and taxes not allocable to other categories, such as penalties for late payment or nonpayment of taxes. • **Social contributions** include social security contributions by employees, employers, and self-employed individuals, and other contributions whose source cannot be determined. They also include actual or imputed contributions to social insurance schemes operated by governments. • **Grants and other revenue** include grants from other foreign governments, international organizations, and other government units; interest; dividends; rent; requited, nonrepayable receipts for public purposes (such as fines, administrative fees, and entrepreneurial income from government ownership of property); and voluntary, unrequited, nonrepayable receipts other than grants.

Data sources

Data on central government revenues are from the IMF's Government Finance Statistics database. Each country's accounts are reported using the system of common definitions and classifications in the IMF's *Government Finance Statistics Manual 2001.* The IMF receives additional information from the Organisation for Economic Co-operation and Development on the tax revenues of some of its members. See the IMF sources for complete and authoritative explanations of concepts, definitions, and data sources.

	Broad money		Claims on domestic economy		Claims on central government		Interest rate					
									%			
	annual % growth		Annual growth % of broad money		Annual growth % of broad money		Deposit		Lending		Real	
	2000	2010	2000	2010	2000	2010	2000	2010	2000	2010	2000	2010
Afghanistan	..	26.9	..	9.0	..	−6.0	..	..	..	15.7	..	11.6
Albania	12.0	12.5	0.9	4.9	4.8	0.2	8.3	6.4	22.1	12.8	17.0	9.0
Algeria	14.1	10.5	8.4	2.4	−11.6	−2.7	7.5	1.8	10.0	8.0	−11.7	−7.1
Angola[a]	303.7	14.0	..	..	−413.7	−13.9	39.6	12.8	103.2	22.5	−60.8	−3.2
Argentina[a]	1.5	33.1	..	..	−0.8	13.1	8.3	9.2	11.1	10.6	9.9	−4.2
Armenia	38.6	10.6	0.3	24.9	−5.7	8.3	18.1	9.0	31.6	19.2	33.4	9.2
Australia[a]	3.7	9.4	..	..	−1.8	0.2	5.1	4.2	9.3	7.3	6.6	7.2
Austria[b]	..	..	..	..	..	..	2.2	..	5.6	..	5.3	..
Azerbaijan	73.4	24.3	−23.9	12.9	15.4	8.2	12.9	11.6	19.7	20.7	6.4	8.5
Bahrain	10.2	10.5	..	..	−0.4	−0.5	5.8	1.2	11.6	7.2	−2.4	−3.0
Bangladesh	19.3	21.1	10.7	19.7	5.6	2.7	8.6	7.1	15.5	13.0	13.4	6.1
Belarus	219.3	31.9	59.9	79.2	22.2	−4.7	37.6	9.1	67.7	9.2	−41.2	−0.9
Belgium[b]	..	..	..	..	..	..	3.6	..	8.0	9.5	5.9	8.2
Benin[a]	26.0	7.1	..	..	0.6	−5.5	3.5	3.5	..	..	..	..
Bolivia	1.6	14.8	−1.3	9.6	3.1	−6.5	11.0	1.0	34.6	9.9	27.9	1.0
Bosnia and Herzegovina[a]	11.3	7.2	19.9	3.6	−0.4	2.3	14.7	3.2	30.5	7.9	1.3	6.6
Botswana	1.4	10.7	10.3	6.3	−56.2	20.2	9.4	5.6	15.5	11.5	15.4	−2.8
Brazil	19.7	15.4	8.3	20.7	13.5	4.9	17.2	8.9	56.8	40.0	47.7	30.4
Bulgaria	30.8	6.3	6.5	1.5	8.5	3.6	3.1	4.1	11.3	11.1	4.4	8.0
Burkina Faso[a]	7.5	19.3	..	..	6.6	3.4	3.5	3.5	..	..	..	..
Burundi	15.5	19.9	15.0	15.7	−22.6	5.3	..	..	15.8	12.4	2.3	4.3
Cambodia	26.9	21.3	5.4	14.8	−6.9	−0.4	6.8	1.3	..	..	..	..
Cameroon[a]	19.1	12.8	6.6	7.1	−12.3	3.2	5.0	3.3	22.0	15.0	18.6	12.7
Canada	6.6	15.1	3.6	23.3	2.4	4.7	3.5	0.1	7.3	2.6	3.0	−0.3
Central African Republic[a]	2.4	14.2	..	..	6.8	11.6	5.0	3.3	22.0	15.0	18.3	13.3
Chad[a]	19.4	26.1	..	..	15.1	8.7	5.0	3.3	22.0	15.0	15.9	9.4
Chile	9.1	10.6	4.1	2.1	4.0	0.4	9.2	1.8	14.8	4.8	9.8	−8.4
China[a]	12.3	18.9	..	..	0.0	0.3	2.3	2.8	5.9	5.8	3.7	−0.7
Hong Kong SAR, China[a]	9.3	7.4	..	..	0.4	0.6	4.8	0.0	9.5	5.0	13.6	4.5
Colombia	3.6	11.5	8.9	16.2	6.0	−0.7	12.1	3.7	18.8	9.4	−10.3	6.1
Congo, Dem. Rep.[a]	51.2	30.8	..	..	−1.6	−44.7	..	16.8	..	56.5	..	27.9
Congo, Rep.[a]	58.5	37.6	..	..	−11.7	−34.4	5.0	3.3	22.0	15.0	−17.0	14.4
Costa Rica	24.0	0.8	14.1	4.7	−0.2	0.2	13.4	5.3	24.9	17.1	16.7	8.6
Côte d'Ivoire[a]	−1.8	18.2	..	..	−7.6	4.7	3.5	3.5	..	..	..	..
Croatia	29.1	4.3	21.3	7.0	2.0	1.4	3.7	1.8	12.1	10.4	7.1	9.3
Cuba	..	..	..	..	..	..	..	..	..	..	..	..
Cyprus	10.4	19.8	11.1	35.6	0.1	3.5	6.5	3.4	8.0	6.7	4.0	2.0
Czech Republic	16.0	1.9	−11.0	2.1	2.6	1.9	3.4	1.1	7.2	5.9	5.6	7.1
Denmark	−12.1	−3.1	26.1	5.0	3.0	0.0	3.2	..	8.1	..	4.9	..
Dominican Republic	16.8	12.2	13.2	13.0	2.8	−0.1	17.7	4.9	26.8	12.1	18.6	6.7
Ecuador	47.0	18.6	−11.4	20.2	−28.1	−5.9	8.8	3.9	17.1	..	26.0	..
Egypt, Arab Rep.	11.6	12.4	4.1	3.9	7.7	2.5	9.5	6.2	13.2	11.0	7.9	0.8
El Salvador	1.6	−0.1	2.6	−0.4	2.3	2.0	9.3	..	14.0	..	10.5	..
Eritrea	17.3	15.6	3.7	1.6	25.7	12.6	..	..	..	..	..	..
Estonia	30.5	2.0	39.4	−8.6	−4.1	3.4	3.8	1.1	7.4	7.8	2.4	6.2
Ethiopia[a]	13.1	23.4	..	..	19.8	2.5	6.0	4.7	10.9	8.0	3.8	−17.1
Finland[b]	..	..	..	..	..	..	1.6	..	5.6	..	2.9	..
France[b]	..	..	..	..	..	..	2.6	1.5	6.7	..	5.0	..
Gabon[a]	18.3	19.2	..	..	−42.2	21.4	5.0	3.3	22.0	15.0	−4.8	9.3
Gambia, The[a]	34.8	13.7	..	..	2.7	15.4	12.5	14.6	24.0	27.0	19.6	17.2
Georgia	39.2	34.8	18.7	24.7	19.8	−2.0	10.2	9.2	32.8	24.2	26.8	14.3
Germany[b]	..	..	..	..	..	..	3.4	..	9.6	..	10.4	..
Ghana	54.2	31.9	7.5	13.0	32.9	11.7	28.6	17.1	..	..	..	..
Greece[b]	..	..	..	..	..	..	6.1	..	12.3	..	8.6	..
Guatemala	21.4	9.1	4.2	2.6	10.2	2.3	10.2	5.5	20.9	13.3	13.2	8.0
Guinea[a]	12.9	..	..	..	7.9	..	7.5	..	19.4	..	7.4	..
Guinea-Bissau[a]	60.7	24.4	..	..	16.2	9.4	3.5	3.5	..	..	..	..

Monetary indicators

	Broad money (annual % growth)		Claims on domestic economy (Annual growth % of broad money)		Claims on central government (Annual growth % of broad money)		Interest rate %					
							Deposit		Lending		Real	
	2000	2010	2000	2010	2000	2010	2000	2010	2000	2010	2000	2010
Haiti	20.3	26.1	12.3	−0.2	13.8	−9.0	12.1	0.7	31.4	17.5	18.3	11.5
Honduras	15.4	9.8	7.7	5.1	−2.6	1.4	15.9	9.8	26.8	18.9	−3.1	12.4
Hungary	12.6	4.2	14.5	5.0	−2.0	1.3	9.5	4.9	12.6	7.6	2.6	4.4
India[a]	15.2	17.8	9.9	15.8	4.7	5.3	..	..	12.3	12.2	8.5	12.6
Indonesia	16.6	15.4	7.2	17.1	17.2	−3.7	12.5	7.0	18.5	13.3	−1.7	4.8
Iran, Islamic Rep.[a]	22.4	27.7	..	..	−7.9	2.0	11.7	11.9	..	12.0	..	11.3
Iraq	..	31.2	..	8.1	..	14.4	..	6.1	..	14.3	..	−8.5
Ireland[b]	..	..	..	..	..	..	0.1	..	4.8	..	−2.2	..
Israel[a]	8.0	5.7	..	..	−4.8	1.3	8.6	1.6	12.9	4.5	11.1	3.4
Italy[b]	..	..	..	..	..	..	1.8	..	7.0	4.0	5.0	3.6
Jamaica	−7.0	5.8	9.1	−0.7	−2.3	−8.2	11.6	6.3	23.3	20.5	11.5	8.9
Japan	1.3	2.0	−5.4	−1.4	2.6	2.8	0.1	0.5	2.1	1.6	3.9	3.8
Jordan[a]	7.6	9.2	..	..	−1.2	0.4	7.0	3.5	11.8	9.0	12.2	2.6
Kazakhstan	45.0	13.3	32.2	7.1	−3.2	1.2	..	..	..	..	..	..
Kenya	4.9	22.4	4.7	14.3	−2.1	12.8	8.1	4.6	22.3	14.4	15.3	10.1
Korea, Dem. Rep.	..	..	..	..	..	..	..	..	..	..	..	..
Korea, Rep.[a]	25.4	14.9	..	..	−1.1	0.4	7.9	3.9	8.5	5.5	3.4	1.7
Kosovo	−12.2	13.5	12.1	10.9	−37.7	1.4	..	3.4	..	14.3	..	10.9
Kuwait	6.3	3.0	8.5	2.0	−7.4	−12.9	5.9	2.3	8.9	4.9	−9.7	2.5
Kyrgyz Republic[a]	11.7	33.2	..	..	7.8	−8.8	18.4	4.1	51.9	31.5	19.4	23.1
Lao PDR[a]	46.0	39.1	..	..	−17.6	1.5	12.0	3.0	32.0	22.6	5.5	12.0
Latvia	27.0	11.5	31.2	−18.1	7.8	2.4	4.4	1.9	11.9	9.6	7.4	12.2
Lebanon[a]	9.8	12.1	..	..	10.5	1.1	11.2	6.2	18.2	8.3	20.7	3.8
Lesotho	1.4	14.5	6.6	5.9	14.9	13.9	4.9	3.7	17.1	11.2	14.4	7.3
Liberia[a]	18.3	43.4	..	..	197.0	47.7	6.2	4.1	20.5	14.2	22.1	5.9
Libya[a]	3.1	−0.6	..	..	−10.4	−19.6	3.0	2.5	7.0	6.0	−9.6	57.8
Lithuania	16.5	8.4	14.4	−6.0	0.5	−0.6	3.9	4.8	12.1	8.4	11.1	12.6
Macedonia, FYR	22.2	12.1	2.7	6.3	−15.9	6.6	11.2	7.1	18.9	9.5	9.9	7.2
Madagascar[a]	17.2	9.7	..	..	0.1	−6.4	15.0	10.5	26.5	49.0	18.0	37.9
Malawi[a]	45.5	17.2	..	..	7.7	−13.1	33.3	3.6	53.1	24.6	17.3	15.7
Malaysia	10.0	7.3	5.5	8.1	2.1	−0.2	3.4	2.5	7.7	5.0	−1.1	−0.1
Mali[a]	12.5	12.2	..	..	−4.2	1.6	3.5	3.5	..	..	..	..
Mauritania[a]	..	15.5	..	..	..	12.6	9.4	8.0	25.6	17.0	23.9	−2.0
Mauritius	9.2	7.6	5.8	9.3	−4.7	1.0	9.6	8.4	20.8	8.9	18.3	7.2
Mexico	−4.5	12.8	10.1	8.7	3.5	0.8	8.3	1.2	16.9	5.3	4.3	0.9
Moldova	41.7	13.4	24.4	9.3	−5.7	−4.0	24.9	7.7	33.8	16.4	5.1	4.7
Mongolia	17.6	62.5	29.6	23.7	−7.1	−4.1	16.8	11.9	37.0	20.1	22.3	0.0
Morocco	8.4	7.9	4.0	8.8	3.6	0.3	5.2	3.7	13.3	..	14.0	..
Mozambique	38.3	22.8	11.9	18.3	6.9	−1.3	9.7	9.7	19.0	16.3	6.3	3.1
Myanmar[a]	42.4	42.5	..	..	24.9	32.6	9.8	12.0	15.3	17.0	12.5	8.1
Namibia	13.2	9.6	19.4	10.1	−4.0	7.1	7.4	5.0	15.3	9.7	−9.0	0.4
Nepal	18.8	9.6	−10.4	8.9	2.6	6.2	6.0	3.6	9.5	8.0	4.8	−4.8
Netherlands[b]	..	..	..	..	..	..	2.9	2.3	4.8	1.8	0.6	0.4
New Zealand[a]	1.5	8.4	..	..	−1.0	2.1	6.4	4.6	7.8	6.3	4.7	4.9
Nicaragua	9.4	21.7	7.0	4.8	10.0	3.9	10.8	3.0	18.1	13.3	8.8	10.1
Niger[a]	12.8	21.6	..	..	−13.8	0.8	3.5	3.5	..	..	..	..
Nigeria	48.1	9.3	5.8	−11.2	−43.0	24.0	11.7	6.5	21.3	17.6	−12.2	9.4
Norway[a]	8.7	..	..	..	−4.7	..	6.7	2.3	8.9	4.3	−5.8	11.4
Oman	6.0	11.3	1.1	16.1	9.5	−4.1	7.6	3.4	10.1	6.8	−8.3	40.4
Pakistan	12.1	15.1	2.0	2.3	2.6	10.9	..	8.1	..	14.0	..	1.9
Panama	9.3	11.1	−8.4	13.6	0.2	1.6	7.1	3.0	10.5	7.7	11.9	4.6
Papua New Guinea	5.0	10.2	1.2	9.3	−4.6	−6.6	8.5	1.4	17.5	10.4	13.1	18.1
Paraguay	2.8	19.0	1.7	27.2	4.7	−6.3	15.7	1.2	26.8	26.0	25.4	11.3
Peru[a]	−0.4	21.5	..	..	2.3	−3.4	9.8	1.5	30.0	19.0	4.9	3.3
Philippines	8.1	10.9	2.2	7.5	1.5	2.9	8.3	3.2	10.9	7.7	11.9	..
Poland	11.6	8.7	..	9.0	−5.8	1.2	14.2	..	20.0	..	1.8	..
Portugal[b]	..	..	..	..	..	..	2.4	5.2	..	..	..	..

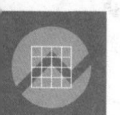

4.15 Monetary indicators

	Broad money		Claims on domestic economy		Claims on central government		Interest rate					
	annual % growth		Annual growth % of broad money		Annual growth % of broad money		Deposit		Lending		Real	
	2000	2010	2000	2010	2000	2010	2000	2010	2000	2010	2000	2010
Puerto Rico	..	..	..	..	..	..	..	..	..	..	..	..
Qatar	10.7	23.1	−1.7	21.6	−23.1	4.2	0.0	2.9	..	7.3	..	31.0
Romania	40.8	6.8	20.0	5.8	−1.1	8.0	33.1	7.3	53.9	14.1	6.7	10.1
Russian Federation	58.5	24.6	33.1	12.4	−18.0	9.7	6.5	6.0	24.4	10.8	−9.6	−0.5
Rwanda[a]	15.6	..	..	..	−11.4	..	10.1	7.1	17.0	16.7	20.6	14.3
Saudi Arabia[a]	4.5	5.2	..	..	−3.5	−5.4	..	..	..	..	..	..
Senegal[a]	10.8	13.7	..	..	−3.9	3.8	3.5	3.5	..	..	..	..
Serbia	160.8	13.1	−71.0	29.5	22.5	5.9	78.7	11.3	6.3	17.3	−40.1	7.6
Sierra Leone[a]	12.1	32.7	..	..	54.6	30.0	9.2	8.9	26.3	21.3	19.0	6.0
Singapore[a]	−2.0	8.6	..	..	−1.6	−4.9	1.7	0.2	5.8	5.4	2.1	5.9
Slovak Republic[b]	15.2	5.0	8.2	11.7	4.1	1.1	8.5	3.8	14.9	5.8	5.0	2.8
Slovenia[b]	..	..	..	..	..	..	10.0	1.4	15.8	5.9	10.0	2.9
Somalia	..	..	..	..	..	..	..	..	..	..	..	..
South Africa	7.2	6.9	−11.8	6.8	0.2	−0.2	9.2	6.5	14.5	9.8	5.2	1.6
South Sudan	..	..	..	..	..	..	..	..	..	..	..	..
Spain[b]	..	..	..	..	..	..	3.0	..	5.2	..	1.7	..
Sri Lanka[a]	12.9	15.8	..	..	12.5	−0.6	9.2	6.9	16.2	10.2	8.3	2.7
Sudan	36.9	25.4	16.9	10.7	33.9	12.5	..	..	..	..	..	..
Swaziland	−6.6·	7.9	16.9	5.0	1.7	26.0	6.5	3.9	14.0	9.8	13.8	3.4
Sweden	1.9	−8.5	8.5	9.5	2.4	−0.9	2.2	..	5.8	..	4.3	..
Switzerland[a]	−16.9	5.5	..	..	2.1	0.2	3.0	0.1	4.3	2.7	3.1	2.7
Syrian Arab Republic	19.0	13.5	−4.1	10.3	−6.1	1.9	4.0	6.2	9.0	9.9	−0.6	3.4
Tajikistan[a]	63.3	−3.6	..	..	36.6	−9.8	1.3	6.1	25.6	24.1	2.4	7.6
Tanzania	14.8	25.4	12.2	11.4	0.7	7.7	7.4	6.6	21.6	14.5	13.0	6.4
Thailand	4.9	10.9	6.2	10.7	0.5	−1.2	3.3	1.0	7.8	5.9	6.4	2.2
Timor-Leste	41.1	9.9	45.7	2.3	−36.8	−46.5	0.8	0.8	16.7	11.0	11.4	1.7
Togo[a]	15.4	16.3	..	..	−0.3	4.3	3.5	3.5	..	..	..	..
Trinidad and Tobago[a]	11.7	30.5	..	..	−13.2	25.3	8.2	1.5	16.5	9.3	3.2	4.6
Tunisia[a]	14.1	11.3	..	..	5.6	−1.2	..	..	..	..	..	..
Turkey	40.7	18.5	16.2	27.6	26.8	4.0	47.2	15.3	..	..	..	..
Turkmenistan[a]	83.3	..	..	..	−53.4	..	..	..	..	..	..	..
Uganda	18.1	37.8	8.2	20.7	29.4	14.0	9.8	7.7	22.9	20.2	10.6	10.2
Ukraine	44.5	22.7	30.9	2.1	−1.7	8.4	13.7	10.6	41.5	15.9	15.0	0.7
United Arab Emirates[a]	15.3	6.2	..	..	−9.6	2.6	6.2	..	9.7	..	−1.5	..
United Kingdom[a]	11.1	4.0	..	..	−2.4	2.9	4.5	..	6.0	0.5	5.3	−2.3
United States	8.1	−2.1	5.0	−1.5	0.5	0.6	..	..	9.2	3.3	6.9	2.4
Uruguay	9.5	22.1	45.1	11.3	−1.8	8.6	18.3	4.2	46.1	10.3	41.1	4.9
Uzbekistan	..	..	..	..	..	..	..	..	..	..	..	..
Venezuela, RB[a]	33.7	28.0	..	..	−6.4	−1.5	16.3	14.8	25.2	18.3	−3.3	−19.3
Vietnam[a]	35.4	29.7	..	..	−2.4	2.3	3.7	11.2	10.6	13.1	6.9	1.1
West Bank and Gaza	..	..	..	..	..	..	1.5	0.3	..	..	..	..
Yemen, Rep.[a]	25.3	11.8	..	..	−45.6	12.9	14.0	18.7	19.5	23.8	−3.1	−0.7
Zambia	73.8	29.9	−11.4	8.1	162.0	11.5	20.2	7.4	38.8	20.9	6.7	8.2
Zimbabwe[a]	45.7	..	..	..	29.5	..	50.2	121.5	68.2	579.0	67.8	605.4

a. Includes claims on the private sector only. b. As members of the European Monetary Union, these countries share a single currency, the euro.

About the data

Money and the financial accounts that record the supply of money lie at the heart of a country's financial system. There are several commonly used definitions of the money supply. The narrowest, M1, encompasses currency held by the public and demand deposits with banks. M2 includes M1 plus time and savings deposits with banks that require prior notice for withdrawal. M3 includes M2 as well as various money market instruments, such as certificates of deposit issued by banks, bank deposits denominated in foreign currency, and deposits with financial institutions other than banks. However defined, money is a liability of the banking system, distinguished from other bank liabilities by the special role it plays as a medium of exchange, a unit of account, and a store of value.

The banking system's assets include its net foreign assets and net domestic credit. Net domestic credit includes credit extended to the private sector and general government and credit extended to the nonfinancial public sector in the form of investments in short- and long-term government securities and loans to state enterprises; liabilities to the public and private sectors in the form of deposits with the banking system are netted out. Net domestic credit also includes credit to banking and nonbank financial institutions.

Domestic credit is the main vehicle through which changes in the money supply are regulated, with central bank lending to the government often playing the most important role. The central bank can regulate lending to the private sector in several ways—for example, by adjusting the cost of the refinancing facilities it provides to banks, by changing market interest rates through open market operations, or by controlling the availability of credit through changes in the reserve requirements imposed on banks and ceilings on the credit provided by banks to the private sector.

Monetary accounts are derived from the balance sheets of financial institutions—the central bank, commercial banks, and nonbank financial intermediaries. Although these balance sheets are usually reliable, they are subject to errors of classification, valuation, and timing and to differences in accounting practices. For example, whether interest income is recorded on an accrual or a cash basis can make a substantial difference, as can the treatment of nonperforming assets. Valuation errors typically arise for foreign exchange transactions, particularly in countries with flexible exchange rates or in countries that have undergone currency devaluation during the reporting period. The valuation of financial derivatives and the net liabilities of the banking system can also be difficult. The quality of commercial bank reporting also may be adversely affected by delays in reports from bank branches, especially in countries where branch accounts are not computerized. Thus the data in the balance sheets of commercial banks may be based on preliminary estimates subject to constant revision. This problem is likely to be even more serious for nonbank financial intermediaries.

Many interest rates coexist in an economy, reflecting competitive conditions, the terms governing loans and deposits, and differences in the position and status of creditors and debtors. In some economies interest rates are set by regulation or administrative fiat. In economies with imperfect markets, or where reported nominal rates are not indicative of effective rates, it may be difficult to obtain data on interest rates that reflect actual market transactions. Deposit and lending rates are collected by the International Monetary Fund (IMF) as representative interest rates offered by banks to resident customers. The terms and conditions attached to these rates differ by country, however, limiting their comparability. Real interest rates are calculated by adjusting nominal rates by an estimate of the inflation rate in the economy. A negative real interest rate indicates a loss in the purchasing power of the principal. The real interest rates in the table are calculated as $(i - P) / (1 + P)$, where i is the nominal lending interest rate and P is the inflation rate (as measured by the GDP deflator).

In 2009 the IMF began publishing a new presentation of monetary statistics for countries that report data in accordance with its *Monetary Financial Statistical Manual 2000*. The presentation for countries that report data in accordance with its *International Financial Statistics* (IFS) remains the same.

Definitions

• **Broad money** (IFS line 35L..ZK) is the sum of currency outside banks; demand deposits other than those of the central government; the time, savings, and foreign currency deposits of resident sectors other than the central government; bank and traveler's checks; and other securities such as certificates of deposit and commercial paper. Change in broad money is measured as the difference in end-of-year totals relative to the preceding year. Data for 2010 for countries reporting under the old presentation of monetary statistics and data for 2000 for all countries are based on money plus quasi money. • **Claims on domestic economy** (IFS line 32S..ZK) are gross credit from the financial system to households, nonprofit institutions serving households, nonfinancial corporations, state and local governments, and social security funds. Data for countries where claims on the domestic economy are not available are claims on the private sector (IFS line 32D..ZK or 32D.ZF) and are footnoted as such. • **Claims on central government** (IFS line 32AN..ZK) are loans to central government institutions less deposits. • **Deposit interest rate** is the rate paid by commercial or similar banks for demand, time, or savings deposits. • **Lending interest rate** is the rate charged by banks on loans to prime customers. • **Real interest rate** is the lending interest rate adjusted for inflation as measured by the GDP deflator.

Data sources

Data on monetary and financial statistics are published by the IMF in its monthly *International Financial Statistics* and annual *International Financial Statistics Yearbook*. The IMF collects data on the financial systems of its member countries. The World Bank receives data from the IMF in electronic files that may contain more recent revisions than the published sources. The discussion of monetary indicators draws from Caiola (1995). Also see the IMF's *Monetary and Financial Statistics Manual* (2000) for guidelines for the presentation of monetary and financial statistics. Data on real interest rates are derived from World Bank data on the GDP deflator.

Exchange rates and prices

	Official exchange rate		Purchasing power parity (PPP) conversion factor		Ratio of PPP conversion factor to market exchange rate	Real effective exchange rate	GDP implicit deflator		Consumer price index		Wholesale price index	
	local currency units to $		local currency units to international $			Index 2005 = 100	average annual % growth		average annual % growth		average annual % growth	
	2010	2011[a]	2000	2010	2010	2010	1990–2000	2000–10	1990–2000	2000–10	1990–2000	2000–10
Afghanistan	46.45	46.58	13.7	19.3	0.4	..	..	7.8	..	8.9	..	..
Albania	103.94	100.51	40.6	44.5	0.4	..	37.7	3.3	27.8	2.8	..	4.1
Algeria	74.39	72.94	25.1	40.3	0.5	102.4	18.5	8.3	17.3	3.4	..	4.0
Angola	91.91	93.74	2.8	66.9	0.7	..	739.4	36.1	711.0	36.7	..	..
Argentina	3.90	4.11	0.8	2.2	0.6	..	5.2	13.0	8.9	9.8	0.1	15.1
Armenia	373.66	372.50	164.8	207.3	0.6	126.2	212.5	4.6	70.5	4.3	..	2.4
Australia	1.09	0.97	1.3	1.5	1.3	115.2	1.4	3.9	2.1	2.9	1.1	3.4
Austria[b]	0.76	0.72	0.9	0.9	1.1	98.7	1.5	1.7	2.2	1.9	0.3	2.3
Azerbaijan	0.80	0.79	0.3	0.5	0.6	..	203.0	9.8	179.7	8.4	..	..
Bahrain	0.38	0.38	0.2	0.3	0.8	89.5	0.5	7.4	0.8	2.1	..	..
Bangladesh	69.65	74.15	21.3	28.1	0.4	..	4.1	5.4	5.5	6.8	..	..
Belarus	2,978.51	4,974.63	177.3	1,232.9	0.4	..	355.1	21.5	271.3	17.4	267.8	21.2
Belgium[b]	0.76	0.72	0.9	0.9	1.1	100.7	1.8	2.1	1.9	2.1	1.2	2.6
Benin	495.28	471.87	212.7	233.9	0.5	..	8.7	3.3	8.7	3.2	..	..
Bolivia	7.02	6.94	2.0	2.9	0.4	122.1	8.6	6.9	8.7	5.4	..	..
Bosnia and Herzegovina	1.48	1.41	0.7	0.8	0.5	..	4.1	3.8	..	3.3	..	..
Botswana	6.79	6.84	1.9	3.6	0.5	..	9.7	9.0	10.4	8.8	..	..
Brazil	1.76	1.67	1.0	1.7	1.0	..	211.8	8.1	199.5	6.6	204.9	9.3
Bulgaria	1.48	1.41	0.5	0.7	0.5	121.1	102.1	5.9	117.5	6.2	85.7	6.1
Burkina Faso	495.28	471.87	196.9	211.2	0.4	..	3.7	2.7	5.5	3.0	..	..
Burundi	1,230.75	1,261.07	255.8	535.3	0.5	113.3	13.4	10.7	16.1	9.4	..	..
Cambodia	4,184.92	4,058.50	1,232.7	1,516.7	0.4	..	4.4	4.9	6.6	6.2	..	..
Cameroon	495.28	471.87	256.8	248.1	0.5	101.1	6.3	2.1	6.5	2.5	..	..
Canada	1.03	0.99	1.2	1.2	1.2	111.8	1.5	2.5	1.7	2.1	2.7	1.3
Central African Republic	495.28	471.87	271.9	287.2	0.6	110.3	4.5	2.8	5.3	3.3	6.0	4.4
Chad	495.28	471.87	180.3	244.3	0.5	..	7.1	5.4	6.9	2.7	..	..
Chile	510.25	483.67	284.0	402.0	0.8	108.4	7.9	6.4	..	..	7.0	6.1
China	6.77	6.46	3.3	4.0	0.6	118.7	7.9	4.4	8.6	2.4	..	..
Hong Kong SAR, China	7.77	7.78	7.5	5.3	0.7	..	4.5	–1.1	5.9	0.6	0.6	0.2
Colombia	1,898.57	1,848.14	898.0	1,248.6	0.7	120.3	22.6	5.9	20.2	5.6	16.4	4.6
Congo, Dem. Rep.	905.91	919.49	26.0	519.9	0.6	1,025.3	964.9	26.7	930.2	26.9	..	..
Congo, Rep.	495.28	471.87	264.4	343.3	0.7	..	9.0	7.4	9.3	3.4	..	..
Costa Rica	525.83	505.66	173.9	349.6	0.7	121.8	15.9	10.1	15.6	10.8	14.1	12.5
Côte d'Ivoire	495.28	471.87	278.7	301.0	0.6	99.6	9.2	3.2	7.2	2.9	..	..
Croatia	5.50	5.34	3.7	3.9	0.7	105.9	90.0	3.9	86.3	2.9	69.8	3.1
Cuba	..	..	..	..	..	..	6.4	3.3	..	..	..	..
Cyprus[b]	0.76	0.72	0.7	0.7	0.9	102.3	4.3	3.1	3.7	2.7	2.8	3.8
Czech Republic	19.10	17.70	14.2	14.2	0.7	122.5	12.8	2.0	7.8	2.5	8.2	2.2
Denmark	5.62	5.37	8.4	7.9	1.4	102.0	1.6	2.5	2.1	2.0	1.1	2.4
Dominican Republic	36.88	38.11	8.8	20.5	0.6	97.4	9.8	12.6	8.7	13.4	..	..
Ecuador	..	..	0.3	0.5	0.5	96.7	4.4	8.0	37.1	6.3	..	7.6
Egypt, Arab Rep.	5.62	5.93	1.4	2.4	0.4	..	8.7	8.7	8.8	8.5	6.1	9.4
El Salvador	8.75	8.75	0.5	0.5	0.5	..	6.2	3.3	8.5	3.8	..	4.4
Eritrea	15.38	15.38	2.9	11.4	0.7	..	7.9	16.7	..	..	..	..
Estonia	11.81	0.72	7.1	8.2	0.7	..	53.7	5.4	21.6	4.3	8.1	3.4
Ethiopia	14.41	16.90	2.2	4.4	0.3	..	6.5	11.5	5.5	12.8	..	..
Finland[b]	0.76	0.72	1.0	0.9	1.2	98.3	1.9	1.2	1.5	1.5	0.9	2.1
France[b]	0.76	0.72	0.9	0.9	1.2	98.8	1.3	1.9	1.6	1.8	..	1.7
Gabon	495.28	471.87	248.7	284.7	0.6	101.3	7.0	4.9	4.6	2.1	..	..
Gambia, The	28.01	29.46	4.1	9.1	0.3	101.0	4.2	10.9	4.0	7.2	..	..
Georgia	1.78	1.69	0.6	0.9	0.5	118.5	356.7	6.9	24.7	7.0	..	6.6
Germany[b] *	0.76	0.72	1.0	0.8	1.1	97.3	1.8	1.0	2.1	1.6	0.4	2.3
Ghana	1.43	1.51	0.2	1.1	0.8	97.6	26.7	26.2	28.4	15.9	..	..
Greece[b]	0.76	0.72	0.7	0.7	0.9	106.7	9.2	3.2	9.0	3.3	3.6	4.2
Guatemala	8.06	7.79	3.8	4.8	0.6	..	10.4	5.5	10.1	7.1	..	..
Guinea	5,726.07	6,620.84	829.0	2,480.8	0.4	..	5.5	16.2	..	20.5	..	..
Guinea-Bissau	495.28	471.87	121.8	230.2	0.5	..	32.5	10.2	34.0	2.5	..	..

Exchange rates and prices

	Official exchange rate		Purchasing power parity (PPP) conversion factor		Ratio of PPP conversion factor to market exchange rate	Real effective exchange rate	GDP implicit deflator		Consumer price index		Wholesale price index	
	local currency units to $		local currency units to international $			Index 2005 = 100	average annual % growth		average annual % growth		average annual % growth	
	2010	2011a	2000	2010	2010	2010	1990–2000	2000–10	1990–2000	2000–10	1990–2000	2000–10
Haiti	39.80	40.52	8.9	24.1	0.6	..	18.1	14.2	21.9	15.2	..	..
Honduras	18.90	18.90	6.7	9.8	0.5	..	19.9	6.3	18.8	7.7	..	..
Hungary	207.94	201.06	107.9	130.2	0.6	106.1	20.0	5.0	20.3	5.5	16.8	3.7
India	45.73	46.67	13.2	18.8	0.4	..	8.1	5.9	9.1	6.0	7.4	5.3
Indonesia	9,090.43	8,770.43	2,801.1	6,190.8	0.7	..	15.8	11.1	13.7	8.7	15.4	10.9
Iran, Islamic Rep.	10,254.18	10,616.31	1,335.8	3,858.8	0.4	145.9	27.7	16.4	26.0	15.3	28.4	10.8
Iraq	1,170.00	1,170.00	501.8	842.5	0.7	..	..	11.1	97.6	21.0	..	..
Irelandb	0.76	0.72	1.0	0.9	1.1	100.2	3.7	1.7	2.3	2.8	1.6	-0.1
Israel	3.74	3.58	3.4	3.7	1.0	115.4	11.0	1.4	9.7	2.0	8.1	4.2
Italyb	0.76	0.72	0.8	0.8	1.1	99.4	3.8	2.3	3.7	2.2	2.9	2.6
Jamaica	87.20	85.89	25.7	59.2	0.7	..	24.8	11.5	23.5	11.9	..	..
Japan	87.78	79.81	154.8	111.5	1.3	102.7	0.0	-1.1	0.8	-0.1	-1.0	0.6
Jordan	0.71	0.71	0.4	0.6	0.8	..	3.2	6.5	3.5	4.6	..	8.7
Kazakhstan	147.36	146.62	36.5	109.8	0.8	..	204.7	15.1	67.8	8.8	16.3	12.6
Kenya	79.23	88.81	27.2	37.3	0.5	..	16.6	6.1	15.6	11.2	..	..
Korea, Dem. Rep.	..	..	..	..	..	..	..	..	..	..	..	..
Korea, Rep.	1,156.06	1,108.29	746.2	824.6	0.7	..	5.9	2.3	5.1	3.1	3.7	2.6
Kosovo	..	..	..	..	..	..	..	0.5	..	1.7	..	..
Kuwait	0.29	0.28	0.2	..	..	..	1.5	9.8	2.0	3.7	1.4	2.9
Kyrgyz Republic	45.96	46.14	10.0	17.4	0.4	..	110.6	8.6	23.3	7.4	35.6	11.2
Lao PDR	8,258.77	8,058.40	2,155.5	3,777.2	0.5	..	27.2	8.3	28.3	7.8	..	..
Latvia	0.53	0.50	0.3	0.4	0.7	..	48.0	8.1	29.2	6.3	12.0	7.0
Lebanon	1,507.50	1,507.50	909.2	988.7	0.7	..	19.0	3.1	..	..	..	..
Lesotho	7.32	7.26	2.7	4.7	0.6	106.1	9.7	8.0	5.9	7.6	..	..
Liberia	71.32	72.38	19.1	42.2	0.6	..	51.8	10.3	..	10.6	..	..
Libya	1.27	1.22	0.3	0.7	0.6	..	..	17.9	5.6	0.4	..	..
Lithuania	2.61	2.48	1.4	1.6	0.6	..	75.0	3.9	32.6	3.3	24.8	4.7
Macedonia, FYR	46.49	44.23	20.0	18.6	0.4	100.3	79.3	3.7	10.6	2.4	8.5	2.7
Madagascar	2,089.95	2,025.12	426.5	908.3	0.4	..	19.1	10.9	18.7	10.6	..	..
Malawi	150.49	155.78	15.6	58.6	0.4	101.1	33.6	15.8	33.8	11.7	..	..
Malaysia	3.22	3.06	1.7	1.8	0.6	108.8	4.1	3.8	3.6	2.4	3.4	4.6
Mali	495.28	471.87	227.0	280.0	0.6	..	7.0	4.5	5.2	2.5	..	..
Mauritania	275.89	281.12	71.1	148.0	0.5	..	8.7	10.7	6.1	7.1	..	..
Mauritius	30.78	28.71	12.5	17.1	0.6	..	6.3	6.0	6.9	6.2	..	..
Mexico	12.64	12.42	6.1	7.9	0.6	92.7	19.0	7.4	19.5	4.5	18.4	5.8
Moldova	12.37	11.74	3.0	6.5	0.5	126.6	119.6	10.8	21.4	10.4	..	..
Mongolia	1,357.06	1,265.52	259.3	756.5	0.6	..	56.3	14.7	35.7	9.1	..	..
Morocco	8.42	8.09	5.2	5.0	0.6	98.0	4.0	2.0	3.9	1.9	2.9	..
Mozambique	33.96	29.07	8.0	14.8	0.4	..	34.1	8.2	31.8	10.6	..	..
Myanmar	5.58	5.39	107.2	433.1	..	..	25.3	17.6	25.9	21.1	..	..
Namibia	7.32	7.26	3.6	6.0	0.8	..	11.1	7.3	..	6.1	..	..
Nepal	73.16	74.02	19.4	32.6	0.4	..	8.0	7.0	8.7	6.7	..	..
Netherlandsb	0.76	0.72	0.9	0.8	1.1	99.0	2.1	1.9	2.4	1.9	1.3	2.6
New Zealand	1.39	1.27	1.4	1.5	1.0	94.9	1.7	3.0	1.8	2.7	1.5	3.4
Nicaragua	21.36	22.42	5.2	8.3	0.4	104.3	42.4	7.8	..	8.8	..	..
Niger	495.28	471.87	221.5	243.4	0.5	..	6.0	3.3	6.1	2.9	..	..
Nigeria	150.30	153.90	29.0	77.2	0.5	117.9	29.5	13.7	32.5	12.4	..	..
Norway	6.04	5.60	9.1	9.0	1.5	102.8	2.7	4.6	2.2	1.9	1.6	8.4
Oman	0.38	0.38	0.2	0.3	0.7	..	0.1	8.5	..	3.2	..	..
Pakistan	85.19	86.34	16.2	31.8	0.4	103.4	11.1	9.2	9.7	8.8	10.4	9.8
Panama	1.00	1.00	0.6	0.6	0.6	..	3.6	2.6	1.1	2.7	1.0	3.8
Papua New Guinea	2.72	2.37	1.1	1.5	0.6	113.0	7.6	6.2	9.3	5.9	..	..
Paraguay	4,735.46	4,176.07	1,372.0	2,595.9	0.6	139.6	11.5	9.8	13.1	8.1	..	9.6
Peru	2.83	2.75	1.5	1.6	0.6	..	26.7	3.4	27.3	2.5	23.7	2.8
Philippines	45.11	43.31	19.4	24.3	0.5	126.8	9.4	4.7	7.7	5.4	6.3	5.9
Poland	3.02	2.96	1.8	1.9	0.6	104.7	23.2	2.7	25.3	2.6	19.8	2.7
Portugalb	0.76	0.72	0.7	0.6	0.9	99.9	5.2	2.5	4.5	2.5	..	2.5

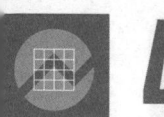

	Official exchange rate		Purchasing power parity (PPP) conversion factor		Ratio of PPP conversion factor to market exchange rate	Real effective exchange rate	GDP implicit deflator		Consumer price index		Wholesale price index	
	local currency units to $		local currency units to international $			Index 2005 = 100	average annual % growth		average annual % growth		average annual % growth	
	2010	2011ª	2000	2010	2010	2010	1990–2000	2000–10	1990–2000	2000–10	1990–2000	2000–10
Puerto Rico	..	..	..	..	..	..	3.0	4.3	..	..	..	..
Qatar	3.64	3.64	1.9	2.8	0.8	..	..	10.6	2.8	6.7	..	..
Romania	3.18	3.05	0.6	1.7	0.5	104.2	98.0	14.7	100.5	10.7	93.8	14.1
Russian Federation	30.37	29.38	7.3	15.9	0.5	125.9	161.5	15.1	99.1	12.1	99.8	14.7
Rwanda	583.13	600.31	142.5	265.5	0.5	..	14.3	10.4	16.2	8.9	..	..
Saudi Arabia	3.75	3.75	2.0	2.6	0.7	104.8	1.6	7.0	1.0	2.7	1.3	2.6
Senegal	495.28	471.87	259.3	264.9	0.5	..	6.0	2.7	5.4	2.2	..	..
Serbia	77.73	73.33	8.9	36.1	0.5	..	..	15.3	50.2	14.3	..	..
Sierra Leone	3,978.09	4,230.53	853.8	1,566.0	0.4	99.7	31.9	9.6	..	..	..	..
Singapore	1.36	1.26	1.2	1.0	0.7	111.3	1.4	1.4	1.7	1.6	–1.0	2.4
Slovak Republicᵇ	0.76	0.72	0.5	0.5	0.7	132.2	11.4	3.0	8.4	4.5	9.5	4.1
Sloveniaᵇ	0.76	0.72	0.5	0.6	0.9	..	29.4	3.7	12.0	3.9	9.1	3.7
Somalia	..	..	..	..	..	..	..	..	..	..	..	..
South Africa	7.32	7.26	3.1	5.0	0.7	101.2	9.9	7.2	8.7	5.8	7.7	6.7
South Sudan	..	..	..	..	..	..	..	..	..	..	..	..
Spainᵇ	0.76	0.72	0.7	0.7	1.0	103.7	3.9	3.4	3.8	2.9	2.4	3.1
Sri Lanka	113.06	110.57	24.7	52.9	0.5	..	9.1	10.6	9.9	10.9	8.1	12.2
Sudan	2.31	2.67	0.8	1.6	0.6	..	65.5	10.6	72.0	9.0	..	..
Swaziland	7.32	7.26	2.7	4.4	0.6	..	10.5	7.8	9.5	7.0	..	..
Sweden	7.21	6.49	9.1	9.0	1.3	95.5	2.2	1.7	1.9	1.5	2.3	3.2
Switzerland	1.04	0.89	1.9	1.5	1.5	107.5	1.1	1.2	1.6	0.9	–0.4	1.0
Syrian Arab Republic	11.23	11.23	17.4	25.6	0.6	..	7.9	7.3	6.4	6.3	4.7	4.5
Tajikistan	4.38	4.61	0.3	1.7	0.4	..	235.0	19.7	..	12.3	..	..
Tanzania	1,409.27	1,572.12	320.4	518.2	0.4	..	23.0	7.4	20.9	6.8	..	..
Thailand	31.69	30.49	16.0	17.1	0.5	..	4.2	3.2	4.9	2.9	3.8	5.6
Timor-Leste	1.00	1.00	0.5	0.7	0.7	..	..	5.3	..	5.2	..	..
Togo	495.28	471.87	255.9	259.6	0.5	98.1	7.0	2.4	8.5	2.9	..	..
Trinidad and Tobago	6.38	6.41	3.2	3.8	0.6	130.7	5.4	5.6	5.7	6.9	2.8	4.0
Tunisia	1.43	1.41	0.6	0.6	0.4	93.5	5.7	3.3	4.4	3.4	3.6	4.6
Turkey	1.50	1.67	0.3	1.0	0.6	..	81.7	14.1	79.9	15.6	75.2	15.3
Turkmenistan	..	..	0.6	1.4	0.5	..	408.2	12.6	..	..	..	..
Uganda	2,177.56	2,522.75	564.1	811.9	0.4	111.4	12.1	5.9	8.3	6.9	..	..
Ukraine	7.94	7.97	1.1	3.6	0.5	99.1	271.0	16.6	155.7	11.4	161.6	15.2
United Arab Emirates	3.67	3.67	2.1	3.1	0.8	..	2.2	8.2	..	..	..	..
United Kingdom	0.65	0.62	0.6	0.7	1.0	83.7	2.4	2.5	2.5	2.1	2.4	2.1
United States	1.00	1.00	1.0	1.0	1.0	91.4	2.0	2.5	2.7	2.6	1.2	4.0
Uruguay	20.06	19.31	9.8	16.5	0.8	137.2	32.6	7.9	33.9	8.8	27.2	12.7
Uzbekistan	..	..	91.3	705.2	0.4	..	245.8	24.0	..	..	..	..
Venezuela, RB	2.58	4.29	0.4	2.9	1.1	195.3	45.3	25.1	49.0	21.9	44.1	25.7
Vietnam	18,612.92	20,450.10	4,018.5	7,109.8	0.4	..	15.2	8.7	4.1	8.2	..	..
West Bank and Gaza	..	..	2.0	..	..	..	5.7	3.4	..	4.0	..	..
Yemen, Rep.	219.59	213.80	46.8	107.6	0.5	..	20.9	11.9	26.3	11.4	..	..
Zambia	4,797.14	4,860.67	1,082.7	3,847.2	0.8	126.0	52.1	15.9	57.0	15.2	101.4	..
Zimbabwe	..	..	..	..	..	..	–3.9	5.1	29.0	497.7	25.9	..

Note: The differences in the growth rates of the GDP deflator and consumer and wholesale price indexes are due mainly to differences in data availability for each of the indexes during the period.
a. Average for December or latest monthly data available. b. As members of the euro area, these countries share a single currency, the euro.

Exchange rates and prices

In a market-based economy, household, producer, and government choices about resource allocation are influenced by relative prices, including the real exchange rate, real wages, real interest rates, and other prices in the economy. Relative prices also largely reflect these agents' choices. Thus relative prices convey vital information about the interaction of economic agents in an economy and with the rest of the world.

The exchange rate is the price of one currency in terms of another. Official exchange rates and exchange rate arrangements are established by governments. Other exchange rates recognized by governments include market rates, which are determined largely by legal market forces, and for countries with multiple exchange arrangements, principal rates, secondary rates, and tertiary rates.

Official or market exchange rates are often used to convert economic statistics in local currencies to a common currency in order to make comparisons across countries. Since market rates reflect at best the relative prices of tradable goods, the volume of goods and services that a U.S. dollar buys in the United States may not correspond to what a U.S. dollar converted to another country's currency at the official exchange rate would buy in that country, particularly when nontradable goods and services account for a significant share of a country's output. An alternative exchange rate—the purchasing power parity (PPP) conversion factor—is preferred because it reflects differences in price levels for both tradable and nontradable goods and services and therefore provides a more meaningful comparison of real output. See table 1.1 for further discussion.

The ratio of the PPP conversion factor to the official exchange rate—the national price level or comparative price level—measures differences in the price level at the gross domestic product (GDP) level. The price level index tends to be lower in poorer countries and to rise with income.

The real effective exchange rate is a nominal effective exchange rate index adjusted for relative movements in national price or cost indicators of the home country, selected countries, and the euro area. A nominal effective exchange rate index is the ratio (expressed on the base 2005 = 100) of an index of a currency's period-average exchange rate to a weighted geometric average of exchange rates for currencies of selected countries and the euro area. For most high-income countries weights are derived from industrial country trade in manufactured goods. Data are compiled from the nominal effective exchange rate index and a cost indicator of relative normalized unit labor costs in manufacturing. For selected other countries the nominal effective exchange rate index is based on manufactured goods and primary products trade with partner or competitor countries. For these countries the real effective exchange rate index is the nominal index adjusted for relative changes in consumer prices; an increase represents an appreciation of the local currency. Because of conceptual and data limitations, changes in real effective exchange rates should be interpreted with caution.

Inflation is measured by the rate of increase in a price index, but actual price change can be negative. The index used depends on the prices being examined. The GDP deflator reflects price changes for total GDP. The most general measure of the overall price level, it accounts for changes in government consumption, capital formation (including inventory appreciation), international trade, and the main component, household final consumption expenditure. The GDP deflator is usually derived implicitly as the ratio of current to constant price GDP—or a Paasche index. It is defective as a general measure of inflation for policy use because of long lags in deriving estimates and because it is often an annual measure.

Consumer price indexes are produced more frequently and so are more current. They are also constructed explicitly, based on surveys of the cost of a defined basket of consumer goods and services. Nevertheless, consumer price indexes should be interpreted with caution. The definition of a household, the basket of goods, and the geographic (urban or rural) and income group coverage of consumer price surveys can vary widely by country. In addition, weights are derived from household expenditure surveys, which, for budgetary reasons, tend to be conducted infrequently in developing countries, impairing comparability over time. Although useful for measuring consumer price inflation within a country, consumer price indexes are of less value in comparing countries.

Wholesale price indexes are based on the prices at the first commercial transaction of commodities that are important in a country's output or consumption. Prices are farm-gate for agricultural commodities and ex-factory for industrial goods. Preference is given to indexes with the broadest coverage of the economy.

The least squares method is used to calculate growth rates of the GDP implicit deflator, consumer price index, and wholesale price index.

• **Official exchange rate** is the exchange rate determined by national authorities or the rate determined in the legally sanctioned exchange market. It is calculated as an annual average based on monthly averages (local currency units relative to the U.S. dollar). • **Purchasing power parity (PPP) conversion factor** is the number of units of a country's currency required to buy the same amount of goods and services in the domestic market that a U.S. dollar would buy in the United States. • **Ratio of PPP conversion factor to market exchange rate** is the result obtained by dividing the PPP conversion factor by the market exchange rate. • **Real effective exchange rate** is the nominal effective exchange rate (a measure of the value of a currency against a weighted average of several foreign currencies) divided by a price deflator or index of costs. • **GDP implicit deflator** measures the average annual rate of price change in the economy as a whole for the periods shown. • **Consumer price index** reflects changes in the cost to the average consumer of acquiring a basket of goods and services that may be fixed or may change at specified intervals, such as yearly. The Laspeyres formula is generally used. • **Wholesale price index** refers to a mix of agricultural and industrial goods at various stages of production and distribution, including import duties. The Laspeyres formula is generally used.

Data on official and real effective exchange rates and consumer and wholesale price indexes are from the International Monetary Fund's *International Financial Statistics*. PPP conversion factors and GDP deflators are from the World Bank's data files.

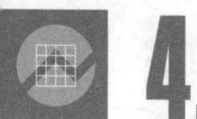

4.17 Balance of payments current account

	Goods and services				Net income		Net current transfers		Current account balance		Total reserves[a]	
	Exports		Imports		$ millions		$ millions		$ millions		$ millions	
	$ millions											
	2000	2010	2000	2010	2000	2010	2000	2010	2000	2010	2000	2010
Afghanistan	..	..	..	..	..	..	..	..	..	..	..	..
Albania	704	3,791	1,499	6,316	107	−101	533	1,223	−156	−1,403	646	2,541
Algeria	..	48,171	..	49,082	..	−1,319	..	2,632	..	402	13,556	170,461
Angola	8,188	51,452	5,739	35,421	−1,681	−8,172	28	−438	796	7,421	1,198	19,749
Argentina	31,277	81,251	33,108	67,992	−7,548	−9,938	399	−388	−8,981	2,932	25,152	52,208
Armenia	447	1,937	966	4,212	53	339	188	563	−278	−1,373	314	1,866
Australia	83,898	261,340	87,799	246,140	−10,814	−45,803	−47	−1,388	−14,763	−31,990	18,822	42,268
Austria	87,777	202,416	85,125	189,033	−2,259	737	−1,732	−2,658	−1,339	11,461	17,650	22,242
Azerbaijan	2,118	28,590	2,024	10,592	−335	−3,467	73	509	−168	15,040	680	6,409
Bahrain	7,176	17,880	5,132	13,095	−224	−2,373	−990	−1,642	830	770	1,605	..
Bangladesh	7,214	21,661	9,673	29,477	−266	−1,454	2,420	11,379	−306	2,109	1,516	11,175
Belarus	7,641	29,909	8,087	37,367	−47	−1,163	155	304	−338	−8,317	350	5,025
Belgium	206,988	366,855	195,511	363,040	4,475	10,958	−4,341	−8,423	11,611	6,349	12,272	26,779
Benin	528	1,446	708	2,234	−12	−33	111	172	−81	−649	459	1,200
Bolivia	1,470	6,840	2,078	6,159	−225	−889	387	1,081	−446	874	1,184	9,731
Bosnia and Herzegovina	1,580	6,221	4,157	9,819	590	331	1,591	2,258	−396	−1,008	497	4,411
Botswana	3,000	5,028	2,321	5,718	−351	−243	217	979	545	46	6,318	7,885
Brazil	64,584	233,736	72,444	244,360	−17,886	−39,486	1,521	2,788	−24,225	−47,323	33,015	288,575
Bulgaria	7,000	27,326	7,670	28,421	−323	−1,680	290	2,038	−703	−736	3,507	17,223
Burkina Faso	237	1,053	658	1,942	−20	−5	122	514	−319	−380	243	1,068
Burundi	53	181	150	607	−12	−11	59	136	−50	−301	38	332
Cambodia	1,826	6,887	2,263	7,879	−123	−533	425	646	−136	−879	611	3,817
Cameroon	2,668	5,645	2,501	6,408	−493	−239	109	146	−218	−856	220	3,643
Canada	329,252	462,349	288,093	493,120	−22,291	−15,968	754	−2,569	19,622	−49,307	32,427	57,151
Central African Republic	..	..	..	..	..	..	..	..	..	..	136	181
Chad	..	..	..	..	..	..	..	..	..	..	114	632
Chile	23,293	81,826	21,893	66,990	−2,856	−15,424	558	4,390	−898	3,802	15,055	27,827
China[†]	279,561	1,752,621	250,688	1,520,559	−14,666	30,380	6,311	42,932	20,518	305,374	171,763	2,913,712
Hong Kong SAR. China	243,127	500,447	235,589	487,850	1,125	3,644	−1,670	−3,443	6,993	12,798	107,560	268,743
Colombia	15,808	45,224	14,397	46,608	−2,289	−11,945	1,673	4,475	795	−8,855	9,006	28,076
Congo, Dem. Rep.	..	..	..	..	..	..	..	..	..	..	83	1,300
Congo, Rep.	2,628	..	1,194	..	−805	..	19	..	648	..	225	4,447
Costa Rica	7,750	13,662	7,297	14,723	−1,252	−748	93	370	−707	−1,439	1,318	4,630
Côte d'Ivoire	4,370	11,478	3,629	8,803	−653	−890	−330	−115	−241	1,670	674	3,624
Croatia	8,645	23,105	9,592	23,409	−466	−2,080	880	1,436	−533	−947	3,524	14,133
Cuba	..	..	..	..	..	..	..	..	..	..	..	..
Cyprus	5,019	9,745	5,142	11,235	−542	−1,267	177	−45	−488	−2,803	1,869	1,142
Czech Republic	35,858	137,665	37,550	130,932	−1,371	−13,198	373	472	−2,690	−5,992	13,142	42,483
Denmark	73,805	156,176	64,506	139,022	−4,023	5,771	−3,014	−5,792	2,262	17,134	15,696	76,510
Dominican Republic	8,964	11,697	10,852	17,462	−1,041	−1,788	1,902	3,118	−1,027	−4,435	632	3,501
Ecuador	5,906	19,610	4,927	22,651	−1,405	−1,054	1,352	2,310	926	−1,785	1,179	2,622
Egypt, Arab Rep.	16,864	48,831	22,895	59,862	888	−5,912	4,172	12,439	−971	−4,504	13,785	37,029
El Salvador	3,662	5,553	5,636	9,259	−253	−381	1,797	3,599	−431	−488	1,901	2,897
Eritrea	98	..	500	..	−1	..	299	..	−105	..	36	114
Estonia	4,784	16,169	4,965	14,771	−203	−1,067	86	341	−299	673	923	2,567
Ethiopia	992	4,644	1,621	9,911	−36	−64	678	4,905	13	−425	363	1,781
Finland	53,431	97,979	40,459	93,836	−1,724	2,523	−723	−2,207	10,526	4,459	8,410	9,547
France	380,260	662,123	366,239	720,573	19,425	48,892	−13,771	−34,941	19,674	−44,499	63,728	165,852
Gabon	3,498	..	1,656	..	−779	..	−63	..	1,001	..	194	1,736
Gambia, The	..	256	..	308	..	−8	..	113	..	52	109	202
Georgia	859	4,061	1,323	6,134	37	−363	250	1,098	−177	−1,337	116	2,264
Germany	627,879	1,541,139	626,519	1,362,052	−7,662	59,648	−25,976	−50,792	−32,279	187,943	87,497	215,978
Ghana	2,441	9,437	3,350	13,925	−108	−535	631	2,322	−387	−2,700	309	..
Greece	29,440	60,094	41,727	80,353	−885	−10,756	3,352	118	−9,820	−30,897	14,594	6,352
Guatemala	3,862	10,827	5,567	15,188	−210	−1,211	865	4,946	−1,050	−626	1,806	5,949
Guinea	734	1,534	872	1,800	−78	−77	75	17	−140	−327	168	..
Guinea-Bissau	67	155	92	289	−12	−11	26	98	−11	−48	67	156
Haiti	504	799	1,369	4,084	−9	22	760	3,097	−114	−166	183	1,337
[†]Data for Taiwan, China	171,909	314,339	164,874	285,177	4,468	13,447	−2,604	−2,710	8,899	39,899	110,464	401,148

	Goods and services ($ millions)				Net income ($ millions)		Net current transfers ($ millions)		Current account balance ($ millions)		Total reserves[a] ($ millions)	
	Exports		Imports									
	2000	2010	2000	2010	2000	2010	2000	2010	2000	2010	2000	2010
Honduras	3,850	6,764	4,681	9,881	−215	−598	538	2,760	−508	−955	1,319	2,701
Hungary	34,662	110,843	36,449	102,710	−2,575	−7,207	357	490	−4,004	1,417	11,217	44,988
India	59,932	349,264	73,075	440,277	−4,892	−12,926	13,434	52,158	−4,601	−51,781	41,059	300,480
Indonesia	70,622	174,840	56,002	153,537	−8,443	−20,291	1,816	4,630	7,992	5,643	29,353	96,211
Iran, Islamic Rep.	29,727	..	17,503	..	−200	..	457	..	12,481	..	..	..
Iraq	..	65,695	..	37,731	..	2,106	..	−2,936	..	27,133	7,882	50,642
Ireland	92,068	207,689	79,792	168,853	−13,547	−36,293	915	−1,589	−356	954	5,408	2,114
Israel	46,591	80,323	46,794	76,094	−8,323	−6,312	6,470	8,426	−2,056	6,342	23,281	70,907
Italy	297,030	546,949	286,526	586,410	−12,010	−11,410	−4,276	−21,144	−5,781	−72,015	47,201	158,478
Jamaica	3,589	4,004	4,427	6,454	−350	−495	821	2,010	−367	−934	1,054	2,501
Japan	528,751	871,533	459,660	796,674	60,401	133,291	−9,831	−12,395	119,660	195,755	361,639	1,096,069
Jordan	3,539	12,189	5,796	17,949	100	507	2,184	3,941	27	−1,312	3,441	13,633
Kazakhstan	10,341	65,086	8,970	43,268	−1,254	−18,325	249	−481	366	3,013	2,099	28,265
Kenya	2,776	8,900	3,763	13,543	−133	−155	921	2,286	−199	−2,512	898	4,321
Korea, Dem. Rep.	..	..	..	..	..	..	..	..	..	..	..	..
Korea, Rep.	209,589	547,006	192,970	516,332	−2,383	768	566	−3,229	14,803	28,214	96,251	292,143
Kosovo	..	..	..	..	..	..	..	..	..	..	..	846
Kuwait	21,301	74,689	11,372	32,682	6,699	7,818	−1,956	−13,003	14,672	36,822	7,779	24,805
Kyrgyz Republic	573	2,472	654	3,905	−82	−343	87	1,391	−76	−385	262	1,720
Lao PDR	506	2,257	578	2,324	−52	−83	116	179	−8	29	144	1,105
Latvia	3,229	12,800	3,813	13,025	17	85	195	871	−371	731	919	7,606
Lebanon	5,849	21,240	9,600	31,010	−868	76	78	785	−4,541	−8,909	8,475	44,476
Lesotho	269	900	1,044	2,515	467	532	237	661	−71	−421	418	..
Liberia	..	400	..	1,800	..	24	..	960	..	−416	0	372
Libya	12,210	49,345	5,024	30,686	−429	−30	−487	−1,828	6,270	16,801	13,730	106,144
Lithuania	5,109	24,849	5,833	25,245	−194	−828	243	1,758	−675	534	1,363	6,598
Macedonia, FYR	1,637	4,213	2,280	6,094	−70	−124	609	1,805	−103	−200	460	2,277
Madagascar	1,188	..	1,520	..	−42	..	113	..	−260	..	285	1,172
Malawi	437	1,399	629	2,105	−17	−110	135	253	−73	−563	247	325
Malaysia	112,370	231,714	94,350	189,499	−7,608	−8,142	−1,924	−6,783	8,488	27,290	28,651	106,528
Mali	644	2,128	927	2,812	−98	−457	126	486	−255	−655	382	1,344
Mauritania	393	..	471	..	−32	..	187	..	77	..	49	288
Mauritius	2,622	4,957	2,707	6,141	−16	202	64	183	−37	−800	914	2,619
Mexico	179,876	313,797	191,818	327,077	−13,795	−13,948	6,994	21,504	−18,743	−5,724	35,577	120,584
Moldova	641	2,292	972	4,581	22	487	211	1,319	−98	−484	222	1,718
Mongolia	614	3,394	771	3,869	−7	−599	94	187	−70	−887	202	2,288
Morocco	10,453	30,129	12,546	40,083	−864	−1,242	2,483	7,270	−475	−3,925	5,017	23,609
Mozambique	689	2,980	1,492	4,666	−192	−85	231	657	−764	−1,113	742	2,265
Myanmar	2,139	8,198	2,493	5,173	−133	−1,740	276	241	−212	1,527	286	..
Namibia	1,483	4,982	1,630	5,620	−98	−564	436	1,232	192	30	260	1,696
Nepal	1,282	1,574	1,790	5,887	37	94	340	4,092	−131	−128	987	2,925
Netherlands	254,590	576,108	238,810	513,539	−2,297	3,570	−6,219	−14,504	7,264	51,635	17,688	46,147
New Zealand	17,864	40,916	17,306	38,882	−3,202	−6,999	237	−29	−2,407	−4,994	3,952	16,723
Nicaragua	1,102	3,628	2,152	5,486	−296	−278	410	1,173	−936	−963	492	1,799
Niger	321	1,097	456	2,529	−16	−39	47	151	−104	−1,320	81	760
Nigeria	20,965	76,774	12,017	75,768	−3,148	−18,623	1,627	20,093	7,427	2,476	10,099	35,885
Norway	78,111	172,425	49,476	117,143	−2,305	872	−1,250	−4,711	25,079	51,444	27,922	52,798
Oman	11,770	38,362	6,351	24,400	−838	−3,162	−1,451	−5,704	3,129	5,096	2,460	13,025
Pakistan	10,119	28,062	12,148	40,021	−2,218	−3,187	4,162	13,778	−85	−1,368	2,087	17,256
Panama	7,833	18,402	8,122	19,882	−560	−1,859	177	477	−673	−2,862	723	2,714
Papua New Guinea	2,337	6,055	1,771	6,286	−210	−592	−5	190	351	−633	304	3,122
Paraguay	2,924	9,989	3,286	10,671	22	−502	177	542	−163	−641	772	4,167
Peru	8,510	39,521	9,648	34,809	−1,410	−10,053	1,001	3,026	−1,546	−2,315	8,676	44,215
Philippines	40,724	65,106	48,565	73,133	−30	347	5,643	16,604	−2,228	8,924	15,074	62,326
Poland	46,300	198,427	57,204	207,139	−731	−16,923	1,292	3,762	−10,343	−21,873	27,469	93,472
Portugal	34,102	72,125	47,262	87,411	−2,371	−10,423	3,342	2,858	−12,189	−22,850	14,262	20,937
Puerto Rico	..	..	..	..	..	..	..	..	..	..	..	..
Qatar	..	..	..	..	..	..	..	..	..	..	1,163	31,182

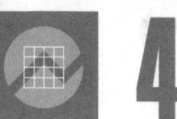

	Goods and services				Net income		Net current transfers		Current account balance		Total reserves[a]	
	$ millions				$ millions		$ millions		$ millions		$ millions	
	Exports		Imports									
	2000	2010	2000	2010	2000	2010	2000	2010	2000	2010	2000	2010
Romania	12,113	58,268	14,043	66,807	−285	−2,532	860	4,557	−1,355	−6,514	3,396	48,048
Russian Federation	114,598	445,539	61,091	323,070	−6,736	−48,615	69	−3,600	46,839	70,255	27,656	479,222
Rwanda	128	608	423	1,641	−15	−46	216	657	−94	−421	191	813
Saudi Arabia	82,259	261,832	52,932	174,204	479	7,044	−15,490	−27,921	14,317	66,751	20,847	459,313
Senegal	1,307	3,119	1,742	5,276	−111	−181	214	1,473	−332	−865	388	2,047
Serbia	..	13,351	..	19,689	..	−899	..	4,417	..	−2,819	517	13,308
Sierra Leone	55	423	250	879	−5	−49	88	185	−112	−320	49	409
Singapore	181,346	470,793	169,223	408,190	−784	−8,230	−1,095	−4,815	10,244	49,558	80,170	225,715
Slovak Republic	14,137	70,494	14,596	71,300	−355	−1,658	120	−544	−694	−3,009	4,376	2,156
Slovenia	10,696	30,489	11,385	30,360	26	−662	116	146	−548	−388	3,196	1,071
Somalia	..	..	..	..	..	..	..	..	..	..	..	..
South Africa	36,995	99,703	33,075	100,318	−3,184	−7,224	−926	−2,278	−191	−10,117	7,702	43,820
South Sudan	..	..	..	..	..	..	..	..	..	..	..	..
Spain	168,221	376,601	186,027	402,450	−6,849	−28,985	1,469	−9,508	−23,185	−64,342	35,608	31,872
Sri Lanka	6,378	10,776	8,105	15,282	−300	−572	983	3,660	−1,044	−1,418	1,131	7,195
Sudan	1,834	11,658	2,014	11,161	−575	−2,472	237	2,131	−518	157	138	1,036
Swaziland	1,240	2,063	1,438	2,625	51	−226	101	400	−46	−388	352	756
Sweden	111,275	225,662	97,042	196,830	−1,231	7,781	−3,142	−6,204	9,860	30,408	16,499	48,246
Switzerland	125,517	342,153	107,391	285,841	19,187	29,967	−4,483	−12,263	32,830	74,015	53,620	270,480
Syrian Arab Republic	6,845	19,606	5,390	19,409	−879	−1,514	485	949	1,061	−367	355	20,632
Tajikistan	768	1,512	928	3,329	−41	−79	186	1,513	−15	−383	94	..
Tanzania	1,361	6,388	2,050	8,975	−130	−216	391	824	−428	−1,978	974	3,905
Thailand	81,762	227,908	71,653	206,780	−1,381	−14,061	586	6,031	9,313	13,099	32,665	172,028
Timor-Leste	..	..	..	..	..	..	..	..	..	..	43	406
Togo	424	1,197	602	1,690	−29	−19	68	336	−140	−177	141	715
Trinidad and Tobago	4,844	9,940	3,709	7,356	−629	−997	38	27	544	1,614	1,403	9,692
Tunisia	8,607	22,236	9,311	24,351	−942	−1,925	825	1,935	−821	−2,104	1,871	9,764
Turkey	50,353	155,632	61,035	197,042	−4,002	−7,137	4,764	1,448	−9,920	−47,099	23,515	85,959
Turkmenistan	..	..	..	..	..	..	..	..	..	..	1,513	..
Uganda	663	3,474	1,409	6,099	−112	−305	499	1,190	−359	−1,740	808	2,706
Ukraine	19,522	69,255	17,947	73,239	−942	−2,009	848	2,975	1,481	−3,018	1,477	34,571
United Arab Emirates	..	..	..	..	..	..	..	..	..	..	13,632	42,785
United Kingdom	404,775	667,596	433,976	731,828	5,156	20,679	−14,756	−31,676	−38,800	−75,229	43,075	82,365
United States	1,072,780	1,837,576	1,449,535	2,337,607	19,179	165,224	−58,767	−136,095	−416,343	−470,902	128,400	488,928
Uruguay	3,660	10,555	4,193	9,743	−61	−1,093	27	122	−566	−160	2,776	7,656
Uzbekistan	..	..	..	..	..	..	..	..	..	..	1,242	..
Venezuela, RB	34,711	67,603	21,300	49,661	−1,388	−5,302	−170	−568	11,853	12,072	15,899	29,665
Vietnam	17,150	79,652	17,325	87,260	−451	−4,564	1,732	7,885	1,106	−4,287	3,417	12,467
West Bank and Gaza	1,012	1,224	3,270	5,008	628	808	639	2,239	−990	−737	..	..
Yemen, Rep.	4,008	9,329	3,294	11,017	−777	−1,812	1,399	2,291	1,337	−1,209	2,914	5,939
Zambia	872	7,725	1,312	5,650	−164	−1,893	14	432	−591	615	245	2,094
Zimbabwe	..	..	..	..	..	..	..	..	..	..	..	..
World	**7,977,777 t**	**18,856,365 t**	**7,950,280 t**	**18,328,230 t**	..	..	..	..	..	..	..	..
Low income	32,005	105,896	45,127	156,378	..	..	..	..	..	..	..	..
Middle income	1,592,025	5,719,672	1,495,508	5,389,112	..	..	..	..	..	..	..	..
Lower middle income	369,018	1,288,993	375,652	1,374,029	..	..	..	..	..	..	..	..
Upper middle income	1,224,283	4,435,558	1,121,580	4,021,226	..	..	..	..	..	..	..	..
Low & middle income	1,623,276	5,824,525	1,540,600	5,547,163	..	..	..	..	..	..	..	..
East Asia & Pacific	612,105	2,566,113	550,904	2,271,625	..	..	..	..	..	..	..	..
Europe & Central Asia	251,713	993,266	223,344	944,420	..	..	..	..	..	..	..	..
Latin America & Carib.	418,299	996,199	438,522	1,009,026	..	..	..	..	..	..	..	..
Middle East & N. Africa	..	..	122,648	384,516	..	..	..	..	..	..	..	..
South Asia	85,777	414,188	106,235	537,246	..	..	..	..	..	..	..	..
Sub-Saharan Africa	111,058	374,373	102,161	394,903	..	..	..	..	..	..	..	..
High income	6,357,262	13,051,331	6,409,545	12,801,007	..	..	..	..	..	..	..	..
Euro area	2,298,517	4,964,584	2,262,865	4,779,448	..	..	..	..	..	..	..	..

a. International reserves including gold valued at London gold price.

Balance of payments current account | 4.17

About the data

The balance of payments records an economy's transactions with the rest of the world. Balance of payments accounts are divided into two groups: the current account, which records transactions in goods, services, income, and current transfers, and the capital and financial account, which records capital transfers, acquisition or disposal of non-produced, nonfinancial assets, and transactions in financial assets and liabilities. The table presents data from the current account plus gross international reserves.

The balance of payments is a double-entry accounting system that shows all flows of goods and services into and out of an economy; all transfers that are the counterpart of real resources or financial claims provided to or by the rest of the world without a quid pro quo, such as donations and grants; and all changes in residents' claims on and liabilities to nonresidents that arise from economic transactions. All transactions are recorded twice—once as a credit and once as a debit. In principle the net balance should be zero, but in practice the accounts often do not balance, requiring inclusion of a balancing item, net errors and omissions.

Discrepancies may arise in the balance of payments because there is no single source for balance of payments data and therefore no way to ensure that the data are fully consistent. Sources include customs data, monetary accounts of the banking system, external debt records, information provided by enterprises, surveys to estimate service transactions, and foreign exchange records. Differences in collection methods—such as in timing, definitions of residence and ownership, and the exchange rate used to value transactions—contribute to net errors and omissions. In addition, smuggling and other illegal or quasi-legal transactions may be unrecorded or misrecorded. For further discussion of issues relating to the recording of data on trade in goods and services, see *About the data* for tables 4.4–4.7.

The concepts and definitions underlying the data in the table are based on the fifth edition of the International Monetary Fund's (IMF) *Balance of Payments Manual* (1993). That edition redefined as capital transfers some transactions previously included in the current account, such as debt forgiveness, migrants' capital transfers, and foreign aid to acquire capital goods. Thus the current account balance now reflects more accurately net current transfer receipts in addition to transactions in goods, services (previously nonfactor services), and income (previously factor income). Many countries maintain their data

collection systems according to the fourth edition of the *Balance of Payments Manual* (1977). Where necessary, the IMF converts such reported data to conform to the fifth edition (see *Primary data documentation*). Values are in U.S. dollars converted at market exchange rates.

Definitions

• **Exports** and **imports of goods and services** are all transactions between residents of an economy and the rest of the world involving a change in ownership of general merchandise, goods sent for processing and repairs, nonmonetary gold, and services. • **Net income** is receipts and payments of employee compensation for nonresident workers, and investment income (receipts and payments on direct investment, portfolio investment, and other investments and receipts on reserve assets). Income derived from the use of intangible assets is recorded under business services. • **Net current transfers** are recorded in the balance of payments whenever an economy provides or receives goods, services, income, or financial items without a quid pro quo. All transfers not considered to be capital are current. • **Current account balance** is the sum of net exports of goods and services, net income, and net current transfers. • **Total reserves** are holdings of monetary gold, special drawing rights, reserves of IMF members held by the IMF, and holdings of foreign exchange under the control of monetary authorities. The gold component of these reserves is valued at year-end (December 31) London prices ($386.75 an ounce in 1995 and $1,087.50 an ounce in 2009).

Data sources

Data on the balance of payments are published in the IMF's *Balance of Payments Statistics Yearbook* and *International Financial Statistics*. The World Bank exchanges data with the IMF through electronic files that in most cases are more timely and cover a longer period than the published sources. More information about the design and compilation of the balance of payments can be found in the IMF's *Balance of Payments Manual,* fifth edition (1993), *Balance of Payments Textbook* (1996), and *Balance of Payments Compilation Guide* (1995).

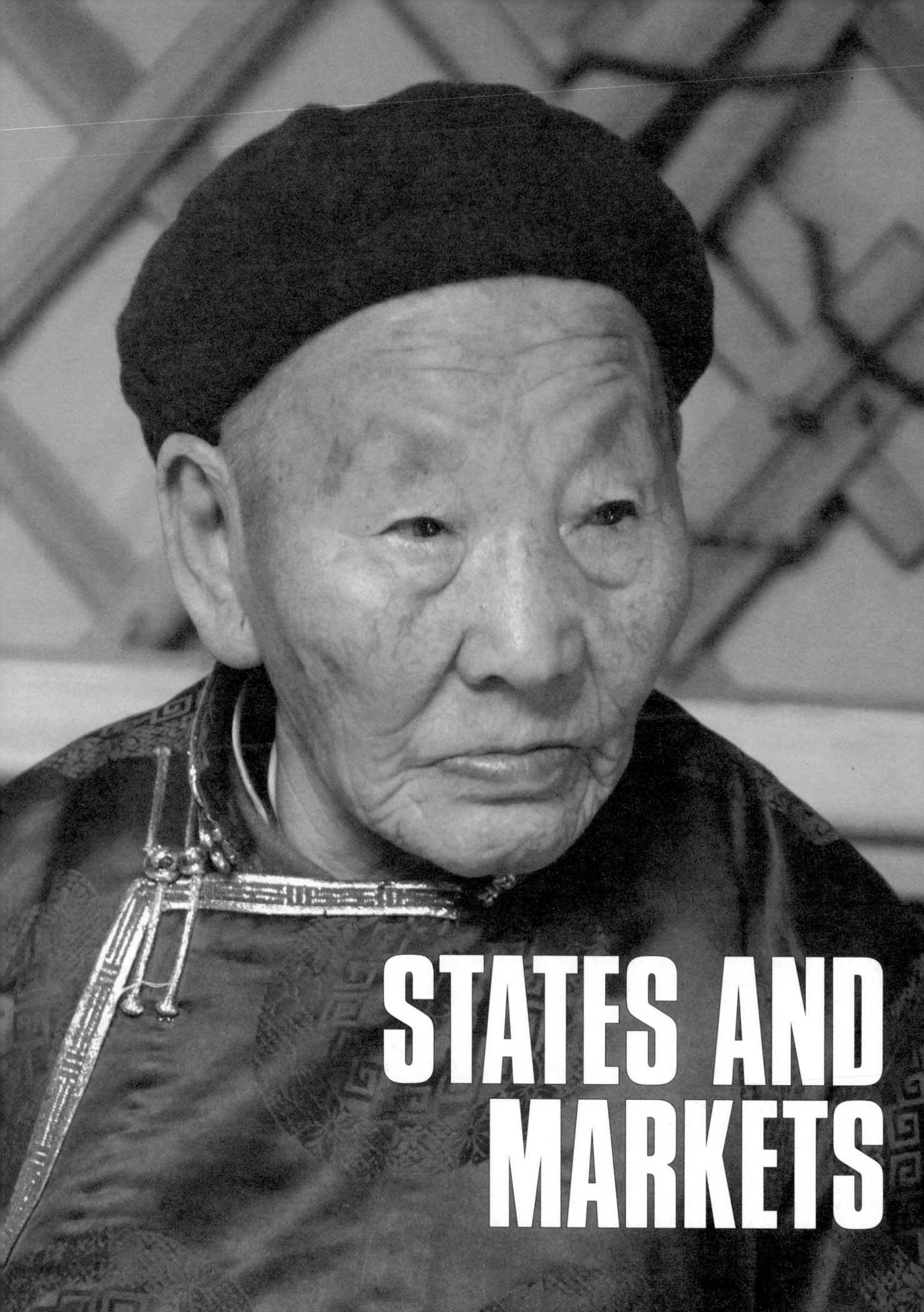

STATES AND MARKETS

States and markets includes indicators of private sector investment and performance, the role of the public sector in nurturing investment and growth, and the quality and availability of infrastructure essential for growth and development.

When private firms make investments, create jobs, and improve productivity, they promote growth and expand opportunities for people. Tables 5.1–5.6 cover private investment in infrastructure, the business environment, and the development of financial systems. Just as a vibrant private sector is essential for job creation and growth, so are capable governments and high-quality institutions essential for promoting growth, raising incomes, and reducing poverty. Tables 5.7–5.9 cover these functions of governments, from tax policies and public institutions to crime statistics, and military expenditures. Tables 5.10–5.12 cover infrastructure—the systems for delivering energy, transport, water and sanitation, and information and communication technology services to people. Table 5.13 covers innovation in science and technology.

World Development Indicators 2010 introduced a new table, continued this year as table 5.8, *Fragile situations,* with indicators for countries that have been identified as fragile or conflict-affected. *World Development Report 2011: Conflict, Security, and Development* (World Bank 2011d, p. xvi) defined fragility or fragile situations as "periods when states or institutions lack the capacity, accountability, or legitimacy to mediate relations between citizen groups and between citizens and the state, making them vulnerable to violence." The report provided a framework and practical recommendations on how to move beyond fragility and conflict to secure development. Its central message was that strengthening legitimate institutions and governance to provide citizens security, justice, and jobs is crucial to breaking cycles of violence and underdevelopment.

Although civil wars and wars between states are less common than in the past, insecurity remains a primary development challenge. Some 1.5 billion people live in areas affected by fragility, conflict, or large-scale organized criminal violence, and no fragile or conflict-affected country has achieved a single Millennium Development Goal. People in these countries are more than twice as likely to be undernourished as people in other developing countries, more than three times as likely to be unable to send their children to school, twice as likely to see their children die before age 5, and more than twice as likely to lack access to clean water.

A major episode of violence can wipe out an entire generation of economic progress. The average cost of a civil war is equivalent to more than 30 years of GDP growth for a medium-size developing country. *World Development Report 2011* found that countries and areas with the weakest institutional legitimacy (both formal and informal) and poor governance are the most vulnerable to violence and instability and the least able to respond to internal and external stresses.

The World Bank manages the State and Peace Building Fund, a multidonor trust fund that provides grants to scale up Bank engagement in fragile and conflict-affected countries; to promote cross-cutting, innovative approaches; and to foster strategic partnerships. As state-building and peace, security, and institution-building become central objectives for developing countries and the development community, new indicators are being developed to measure progress. The International Dialogue on Peacebuilding and Statebuilding, with more than 40 participating countries and eight international organizations (including the World Bank) is contributing to this work.

5.1 | Private sector in the economy

	Investment commitments in infrastructure projects with private participation[a]								Domestic credit to private sector	Businesses registered	
	\$ millions										
	Telecommunications		Energy		Transport		Water and sanitation		% of GDP	New	Entry density
	2000–05	2006–10	2000–05	2006–10	2000–05	2006–10	2000–05	2006–10	2010	2009	2009
Afghanistan	466.1	1,040.4	1.6	..	..	..	..	..	10.5	..	..
Albania	569.2	778.8	790.6	692.0	308.0	..	8.0	0.0	38.0	2,045	0.84
Algeria	3,422.5	2,162.0	962.0	2,320.0	120.9	269.0	510.0	1,572.0	15.6	10,544	0.44
Angola	278.7	1,663.0	45.0	9.4	..	53.0	..	..	20.3	..	..
Argentina	5,836.8	5,993.9	3,826.9	3,801.9	203.6	1,402.6	791.6	..	14.6	11,924	0.46
Armenia	317.1	586.7	74.0	127.0	63.0	715.0	0.0	0.0	26.5	2,698	1.28
Australia	..	..	..	..	..	..	..	..	131.1	89,960	6.38
Austria	..	..	..	..	..	..	..	..	122.4	3,228	0.58
Azerbaijan	355.6	1,407.8	375.2	..	..	..	..	0.0	18.3	5,314	0.93
Bahrain	..	..	..	..	..	..	..	..	79.6	..	..
Bangladesh	1,294.3	4,250.3	501.5	340.4	0.0	0.0	..	..	47.1	..	..
Belarus	735.4	2,638.7	..	2,500.0	..	4.0	..	..	44.8	5,508	0.80
Belgium	..	..	..	..	..	..	..	..	94.9	29,548	4.28
Benin	116.9	793.7	590.0	..	..	..	..	..	23.1	..	..
Bolivia	520.5	284.7	884.4	137.3	16.6	..	..	..	40.3	2,504	0.43
Bosnia and Herzegovina	0.0	1,102.5	..	908.6	..	..	..	..	66.0	1,896	0.58
Botswana	104.0	242.9	..	..	..	..	..	..	23.4	..	..
Brazil	41,053.8	40,063.0	26,034.6	52,825.6	3,156.5	23,527.7	1,234.4	1,581.0	57.0	315,645	2.38
Bulgaria	2,179.1	2,211.3	3,253.5	2,454.1	2.1	536.2	152.0	..	74.6	35,545	7.20
Burkina Faso	41.9	979.6	..	..	..	..	..	..	17.6	610	0.08
Burundi	53.6	0.0	..	..	..	..	..	..	25.5	..	..
Cambodia	136.1	446.7	82.1	2,452.3	125.3	40.1	..	..	27.6	2,003	0.22
Cameroon	394.4	934.4	91.8	908.0	0.0	..	..	0.0	11.9	..	..
Canada	..	..	..	..	..	..	..	..	128.2	174,000	7.56
Central African Republic	0.0	30.8	..	..	..	..	..	..	8.7	..	..
Chad	11.0	591.4	0.0	..	..	..	..	..	5.7	..	..
Chile	1,260.7	1,326.7	1,393.2	1,567.2	4,830.7	1,943.1	1,495.2	3.1	86.3	23,541	2.12
China	8,548.0	0.0	10,970.9	7,477.5	15,454.0	15,795.0	3,505.2	4,626.9	130.0	..	..
Hong Kong SAR, China	..	..	..	..	..	..	..	..	189.0	101,023	19.19
Colombia	1,570.9	6,347.9	351.6	1,080.9	1,497.4	4,461.4	314.3	305.0	43.5	31,132	1.07
Congo, Dem. Rep.	473.4	1,054.0	..	..	..	..	..	..	6.6	..	..
Congo, Rep.	61.8	407.7	..	..	..	735.0	0.0	..	5.5	..	..
Costa Rica	..	..	80.0	190.0	465.2	407.0	..	..	45.9	26,765	8.78
Côte d'Ivoire	134.9	1,204.4	0.0	0.0	176.4	..	..	0.0	18.1	..	..
Croatia	1,205.7	3,035.0	7.1	85.0	451.0	492.0	298.7	..	70.1	7,800	2.57
Cuba	60.0	0.0	116.0	60.0	0.0	..	600.0	..	..	..	..
Cyprus	..	..	..	..	..	..	..	..	283.6	16,101	20.30
Czech Republic	..	..	..	..	..	..	..	..	56.2	21,717	3.00
Denmark	..	..	..	..	..	..	..	..	223.5	16,519	4.57
Dominican Republic	393.0	220.1	1,306.6	0.0	898.9	948.9	..	..	22.7	12,881	2.13
Ecuador	357.8	2,003.3	302.0	129.0	695.0	766.0	510.0	..	30.8	..	..
Egypt, Arab Rep.	3,471.9	10,977.0	678.0	469.0	821.5	1,370.0	..	475.0	33.1	6,291	0.13
El Salvador	1,110.6	1,037.6	85.0	16.0	..	..	..	..	41.0	4,400	1.19
Eritrea	40.0	0.0	..	..	..	..	..	..	16.0	..	..
Estonia	..	..	..	..	..	..	..	..	97.2	7,199	8.10
Ethiopia	..	0.0	..	4.0	..	..	..	..	17.8	1,327	0.03
Finland	..	..	..	..	..	..	..	..	95.2	11,820	3.37
France	..	..	..	..	..	..	..	..	114.4	128,906	3.08
Gabon	26.6	403.8	0.0	0.0	177.4	3.9	..	..	8.2	3,490	4.27
Gambia, The	6.6	35.0	..	0.0	..	..	..	..	19.1	..	..
Georgia	201.3	722.0	40.0	634.2	..	573.0	..	435.0	32.4	7,226	2.32
Germany	..	..	..	..	..	..	..	..	107.8	64,840	1.19
Ghana	156.5	3,206.0	590.0	100.0	10.0	..	0.0	..	15.2	9,606	0.72
Greece	..	..	..	..	..	..	..	..	115.9	8,426	1.18
Guatemala	560.1	1,724.4	110.0	1,021.8	..	..	..	6.7	23.4	5,133	0.68
Guinea	50.6	313.2	..	..	..	159.0	..	..	..	..	..
Guinea-Bissau	9.7	107.2	..	..	..	..	..	..	6.2	..	..
Haiti	18.0	306.0	5.5	0.0	..	..	..	1.0	14.0	..	..

	Investment commitments in infrastructure projects with private participation[a]								Domestic credit to private sector	Businesses registered	
					$ millions						Entry
	Telecommunications		Energy		Transport		Water and sanitation		% of GDP	New	density
	2000–05	2006–10	2000–05	2006–10	2000–05	2006–10	2000–05	2006–10	2010	2009	2009
Honduras	135.0	1,001.0	358.8	250.0	120.0	..	207.9	..	50.2	..	..
Hungary	5,172.8	1,523.3	851.6	1,707.0	3,297.5	1,588.0	0.0	0.0	72.6	42,951	6.26
India	20,551.8	53,090.4	8,663.6	90,973.0	4,413.4	38,036.2	112.9	241.7	49.0	84,800	0.12
Indonesia	6,557.2	11,009.5	1,280.5	6,079.3	159.2	1,731.5	44.8	20.2	29.1	28,998	0.18
Iran, Islamic Rep.	695.0	1,992.0	650.0	..	..	..	..	..	36.7	..	..
Iraq	984.0	4,977.0	..	590.0	..	500.0	..	..	9.1	..	..
Ireland	..	..	..	..	..	..	..	..	215.0	13,188	4.67
Israel	..	..	..	..	..	..	..	..	95.7	19,758	4.46
Italy	..	..	..	..	..	..	..	..	122.0	68,508	1.78
Jamaica	612.0	157.9	201.0	210.0	565.0	..	..	..	24.8	2,003	1.16
Japan	..	..	..	..	..	..	..	..	169.3	105,698	1.28
Jordan	1,589.0	949.6	..	989.0	0.0	1,380.0	169.0	951.0	70.3	2,737	0.74
Kazakhstan	1,153.7	3,766.5	300.0	0.0	231.0	31.0	..	..	39.3	27,978	2.59
Kenya	1,434.0	3,465.8	..	437.7	..	404.0	..	..	33.8	17,896	0.85
Korea, Dem. Rep.	..	474.0	..	..	..	..	..	..	..	..	..
Korea, Rep.	..	..	..	..	..	..	..	..	100.8	60,039	1.72
Kosovo	..	385.1	..	..	..	..	0.0	..	37.3	141	0.12
Kuwait	..	..	..	..	..	..	..	..	82.4	..	..
Kyrgyz Republic	11.5	130.2	..	..	..	..	0.0	..	..	4,412	1.26
Lao PDR	87.7	135.0	1,250.0	5,285.0	1.5	1.5	..	..	20.4	..	..
Latvia	700.0	468.1	158.1	184.0	..	135.0	..	..	103.7	7,175	4.62
Lebanon	138.1	0.0	..	..	153.0	..	0.0	..	81.3	..	..
Lesotho	88.4	41.6	0.0	..	..	..	..	..	13.6	..	..
Liberia	70.3	88.8	..	170.0	..	120.0	..	..	16.0	..	..
Libya	..	..	..	..	..	..	..	..	10.9	..	..
Lithuania	993.0	548.2	514.3	464.1	..	..	..	..	66.4	5,399	2.18
Macedonia, FYR	706.6	575.4	..	655.0	..	295.0	..	..	45.3	8,074	5.63
Madagascar	12.6	436.8	0.0	17.8	61.0	17.5	..	..	11.7	724	0.07
Malawi	36.3	313.7	0.0	..	..	..	..	..	16.0	619	0.08
Malaysia	3,294.9	3,689.9	6,637.6	384.5	4,263.0	1,632.3	6,502.2	0.0	114.9	41,638	2.55
Mali	82.6	837.0	365.9	..	55.4	..	..	..	18.4	..	..
Mauritania	92.1	266.1	..	..	..	..	..	..	30.4	..	..
Mauritius	393.0	63.1	0.0	..	..	..	..	0.0	87.8	6,626	7.33
Mexico	18,758.0	16,290.6	6,749.3	2,282.7	2,970.4	12,651.5	523.7	1,096.8	24.6	44,084	0.61
Moldova	46.1	426.8	227.2	68.0	0.0	60.0	..	..	33.3	4,180	1.32
Mongolia	22.1	0.0	..	..	..	..	..	..	39.6	..	..
Morocco	6,139.5	3,673.6	1,049.0	..	200.0	200.0	..	..	68.7	26,166	1.28
Mozambique	123.0	236.2	1,205.8	..	334.6	0.0	..	0.0	25.8	..	..
Myanmar	..	..	..	556.1	..	..	..	..	4.7	..	..
Namibia	35.0	8.5	1.0	..	..	..	0.0	..	45.6	..	..
Nepal	109.3	26.0	15.1	34.1	..	..	..	0.0	55.6	..	..
Netherlands	..	..	..	..	..	..	..	..	199.3	35,100	3.10
New Zealand	..	..	..	..	..	..	..	..	149.0	47,897	17.08
Nicaragua	218.5	512.2	126.3	510.0	104.0	..	..	..	32.5	..	..
Niger	85.5	358.7	..	..	..	..	3.4	..	12.6	24	0.00
Nigeria	6,949.7	14,384.1	1,920.0	280.0	2,355.4	644.1	..	..	29.4	65,089	0.79
Norway	..	..	..	..	..	..	..	..	..	13,805	4.49
Oman	..	..	..	..	..	..	..	..	48.2	3,165	1.67
Pakistan	6,594.9	9,006.5	375.4	4,120.5	112.8	923.7	..	..	21.5	2,759	0.03
Panama	211.4	1,262.2	449.3	877.0	51.4	0.0	..	..	91.5	548	0.26
Papua New Guinea	..	150.0	..	..	..	..	..	..	31.8	..	..
Paraguay	199.0	636.4	..	..	..	..	..	..	37.8	..	..
Peru	2,241.4	3,191.1	2,498.9	2,191.0	522.5	3,289.6	152.0	119.8	24.3	51,151	2.65
Philippines	4,616.4	5,172.0	3,428.4	10,942.5	943.5	968.9	0.0	530.5	29.6	11,435	0.19
Poland	16,800.1	7,750.0	2,620.5	2,475.4	1,672.0	3,642.3	64.3	0.8	54.8	14,434	0.52
Portugal	..	..	..	..	..	..	..	..	191.0	27,759	3.92
Puerto Rico	..	..	..	..	..	..	..	..	..	..	..
Qatar	..	..	..	..	..	..	..	..	51.5	..	..

	Investment commitments in infrastructure projects with private participation[a] ($ millions)								Domestic credit to private sector	Businesses registered	
	Telecommunications		Energy		Transport		Water and sanitation		% of GDP	New	Entry density
	2000–05	2006–10	2000–05	2006–10	2000–05	2006–10	2000–05	2006–10	2010	2009	2009
Romania	3,906.9	4,996.4	1,240.8	6,288.7	..	116.8	116.0	41.0	46.1	56,698	3.66
Russian Federation	22,049.4	30,982.6	1,726.0	32,401.2	109.4	4,786.9	904.7	1,241.7	45.1	261,633	2.61
Rwanda	72.3	414.0	1.6	..	..	..	..	..	..	3,028	0.51
Saudi Arabia	..	..	..	..	..	..	..	..	47.6	..	..
Senegal	593.1	1,569.0	93.3	22.0	55.4	398.0	0.0	0.0	25.9	1,636	0.22
Serbia	563.5	3,024.1	..	..	..	..	0.0	..	51.5	9,715	1.94
Sierra Leone	48.8	149.2	..	1.2	..	130.0	..	..	10.4	..	..
Singapore	..	..	..	..	..	..	..	..	102.1	26,416	7.40
Slovak Republic	..	..	..	..	..	..	..	..	44.9	15,825	4.04
Slovenia	..	..	..	..	..	..	..	..	94.4	5,836	4.16
Somalia	13.4	0.0	..	..	..	..	..	..	..	..	..
South Africa	10,519.5	9,815.0	1,251.3	15.9	504.7	3,483.0	31.3	0.0	145.5	24,700	0.77
South Sudan	..	..	..	..	..	..	..	..	..	..	..
Spain	..	..	..	..	..	..	..	..	211.6	79,757	2.92
Sri Lanka	714.6	1,283.5	270.8	..	..	..	..	..	26.6	4,223	0.29
Sudan	747.7	2,226.3	..	..	..	30.0	..	120.7	11.6	..	..
Swaziland	27.7	63.3	..	..	..	..	..	..	23.0	..	..
Sweden	..	..	..	..	..	..	..	..	140.2	24,228	4.09
Switzerland	..	..	..	..	..	..	..	..	174.6	25,250	4.88
Syrian Arab Republic	583.0	372.7	..	..	..	82.0	..	..	22.5	..	..
Tajikistan	8.5	196.4	16.0	..	..	..	..	..	..	2,171	0.48
Tanzania	515.3	2,109.5	348.0	28.4	27.7	134.0	8.5	..	16.2	..	..
Thailand	5,602.7	3,526.0	4,693.3	6,641.4	939.0	..	524.7	18.8	116.6	27,520	0.59
Timor-Leste	0.0	0.0	..	..	..	..	..	..	15.6	..	..
Togo	0.0	67.0	657.7	190.0	..	..	..	..	23.0	125	0.04
Trinidad and Tobago	..	..	..	..	..	..	..	..	39.2	..	..
Tunisia	751.0	3,771.0	30.0	..	..	840.0	..	95.0	68.8	9,079	1.23
Turkey	12,788.6	13,751.7	5,854.8	13,504.2	3,203.6	4,471.2	..	..	44.0	44,472	0.87
Turkmenistan	20.0	202.5	..	..	..	..	..	..	..	..	..
Uganda	387.6	1,720.0	113.9	1,000.6	..	404.0	0.0	..	15.8	11,152	0.72
Ukraine	3,162.9	4,921.4	160.0	64.9	..	130.0	100.0	102.0	61.7	19,300	0.60
United Arab Emirates	..	..	..	..	..	..	..	..	72.5	..	..
United Kingdom	..	..	..	..	..	..	..	..	202.9	330,100	8.05
United States	..	..	..	..	..	..	..	..	202.2	..	..
Uruguay	114.2	200.2	330.0	..	251.1	..	368.0	..	23.0	4,664	2.08
Uzbekistan	285.6	2,046.8	..	..	..	25.0	0.0	..	..	14,428	0.78
Venezuela, RB	3,337.0	3,042.8	39.5	..	34.0	..	15.0	..	18.9	..	..
Vietnam	430.0	1,593.7	2,360.6	297.0	20.0	1,120.0	266.0	..	125.0	..	..
West Bank and Gaza	279.8	644.0	150.0	..	..	..	..	..	..	..	..
Yemen, Rep.	376.8	451.2	..	15.8	..	220.0	..	..	6.2	..	..
Zambia	208.3	1,077.0	3.0	..	15.6	..	..	0.0	11.5	5,509	0.88
Zimbabwe	72.0	644.0	..	..	..	..	..	..	..	..	..
World	.. s	.. s	.. s	.. s	.. s	.. s	.. s	.. s	134.8 w		
Low income	4,646.3	21,615.6	..	..	..	..	..	..	28.3		
Middle income	226,353.6	317,609.7	107,559.1	266,780.1	51,413.6	106,204.4	16,177.1	6,654.9	73.7		
Lower middle income	68,257.9	144,334.1	19,986.8	123,341.9	1,781.0	34,127.5	192.0	..	40.2		
Upper middle income	158,095.7	34,212.5	83,156.9	143,438.2	41,607.7	72,076.9	18,427.2	9,705.8	83.3		
Low & middle income	232,154.6	339,225.4	85,938.8	272,012.7	5,437.5	86,673.9	2,481.0	..	73.0		
East Asia & Pacific	29,380.1	4,662.0	30,710.4	40,115.6	21,905.4	20,538.0	10,842.9	5,196.4	116.3		
Europe & Central Asia	51,002.1	76,087.4	4,439.1	58,924.3	..	..	..	..	46.2		
Latin America & Carib.	78,935.4	85,698.9	45,347.6	67,445.3	16,419.9	49,397.7	2,516.1	..	41.9		
Middle East & N. Africa	13,435.4	29,970.1	..	..	..	..	..	..	35.0		
South Asia	29,784.3	68,726.2	9,828.0	95,669.0	4,526.2	39,437.9	112.9	241.7	45.7		
Sub-Saharan Africa	24,622.2	52,365.4	..	..	..	..	..	..	65.4		
High income	..	..	..	..	..	..	..	..	164.6		
Euro area	..	..	..	..	..	..	..	..	133.6		

a. Data refer to total for the period shown. Includes infrastructure projects with private sector participation that reached financial closure in 1990–2010.

Private sector development and investment—tapping private sector initiative and investment for socially useful purposes—are critical for poverty reduction. In parallel with public sector efforts, private investment, especially in competitive markets, has tremendous potential to contribute to growth. Private markets are the engine of productivity growth, creating productive jobs and higher incomes. And with government playing a complementary role of regulation, funding, and service provision, private initiative and investment can help provide the basic services and conditions that empower poor people—by improving health, education, and infrastructure.

Investment in infrastructure projects with private participation has made important contributions to easing fiscal constraints, improving the efficiency of infrastructure services, and extending delivery to poor people. Developing countries have been in the forefront, pioneering better approaches to infrastructure services and reaping the benefits of greater competition and customer focus.

The data on investment in infrastructure projects with private participation refer to all investment (public and private) in projects in which a private company assumes operating risk during the operating period or development and operating risk during the contract period. Investment refers to commitments not disbursements. Foreign state-owned companies are considered private entities for the purposes of this measure.

Investments are classified into two types: investments in physical assets—the resources a company commits to invest in expanding and modernizing facilities—and payments to the government to acquire state-owned enterprises or rights to provide services in a specific area or to use part of the radio spectrum.

The data are from the World Bank's Private Participation in Infrastructure (PPI) Project database, which tracks infrastructure projects with private participation in developing countries. It provides information on more than 4,800 infrastructure projects in 139 developing economies from 1984 to 2010. The database contains more than 30 fields per project record, including country, financial closure year, infrastructure services provided, type of private participation, investment, technology, capacity, project location, contract duration, private sponsors, bidding process, and development bank support. Data on the projects are compiled from publicly available information. The database aims to be as comprehensive as possible, but some projects—particularly those

involving local and small-scale operators—may be omitted because they are not publicly reported. The database is a joint product of the World Bank's Finance, Economics, and Urban Development Department and the Public-Private Infrastructure Advisory Facility. Geographic and income aggregates are calculated by the World Bank's Development Data Group. For more information, see http://ppi.worldbank.org/.

Credit is an important link in money transmission; it finances production, consumption, and capital formation, which in turn affect economic activity. The data on domestic credit to the private sector are taken from the banking survey of the International Monetary Fund's (IMF) *International Financial Statistics* or, when unavailable, from its monetary survey. The monetary survey includes monetary authorities (the central bank), deposit money banks, and other banking institutions, such as finance companies, development banks, and savings and loan institutions. Credit to the private sector may sometimes include credit to state-owned or partially state-owned enterprises.

Entrepreneurship is essential to the dynamism of the modern market economy, and a greater entry density of new businesses can foster competition and economic growth. The table includes data on business registrations from the 2008 and 2010 World Bank Group Entrepreneurship Survey, which includes entrepreneurial activity in more than 100 countries for 2000–09. Survey data are used to analyze firm creation, its relationship to economic growth and poverty reduction, and the impact of regulatory and institutional reforms. The 2010 survey improves on earlier surveys' methodology and country coverage for better cross-country comparability; the database will be updated in 2012. Data on total registered businesses were collected directly from national registrars of companies. For cross-country comparability, only limited liability corporations that operate in the formal sector are included. For additional information on sources, methodology, calculation of entrepreneurship rates, and data limitations see http://econ.worldbank.org/research/entrepreneurship.

• **Investment commitments in infrastructure projects with private participation** refers to infrastructure projects in telecommunications, energy (electricity and natural gas transmission and distribution), transport, and water and sanitation that have reached financial closure and directly or indirectly serve the public. Incinerators, movable assets, standalone solid waste projects, and small projects such as windmills are excluded. Included are operation and management contracts, concessions (operation and management contracts with major capital expenditure), greenfield projects (new facilities built and operated by a private entity or a public-private joint venture), and divestitures. Investment commitments are the sum of investments in physical assets and payments to the government. Investments in physical assets are resources the project company commits to invest during the contract period in new facilities or in expansion and modernization of existing facilities. Payments to the government are the resources the project company spends on acquiring government assets such as state-owned enterprises, rights to provide services in a specific area, or use of specific radio spectrums. • **Domestic credit to private sector** is financial resources provided to the private sector—such as through loans, purchases of nonequity securities, and trade credits and other accounts receivable—that establish a claim for repayment. For some countries these claims include credit to public enterprises. • **New businesses registered** are the number of limited liability corporations registered in the calendar year. • **Entry density** is the number of newly registered limited liability corporations per 1,000 people ages 15–64.

Data on investment commitments in infrastructure projects with private participation are from the World Bank's PPI Project database (http://ppi.worldbank.org). Data on domestic credit are from the IMF's *International Financial Statistics*. Data on business registration are from the World Bank's Entrepreneurship Snapshots (http://econ.worldbank.org/research/entrepreneurship).

	Survey year	Regulations and tax		Permits and licenses	Corruption	Crime	Informality	Gender	Finance	Infrastructure	Innovation	Trade	Workforce
		Time dealing with officials % of management time	Average number of times meeting with tax officials	Time required to obtain operating license days	Informal payments to public officials % of firms	Losses due to theft, robbery, vandalism, and arson % of sales	Firms formally registered when operations started % of firms	Firms with female participation in ownership % of firms	Firms using banks to finance investment % of firms	Value lost due to electrical outages % of sales	Inter-nationally recognized quality certification ownership % of firms	Average time to clear direct exports through customs days	Firms offering formal training % of firms
Afghanistan	2008	6.8	1.2	13.8	41.5	1.5	88.0	2.8	1.4	6.5	8.5	14.6	14.6
Albania	2007	18.7	3.9	21.2	57.7	0.5	89.4	10.8	12.4	13.7	24.6	1.9	19.9a
Algeria	2007	25.1	2.3	19.3	66.6	0.9	98.3	15.0	8.9	4.0	5.0	14.1	17.3a
Angola	2010	12.2	2.5	34.7	48.9	1.5	62.7	56.6	13.1	12.6	21.7	6.7	23.5
Argentina	2010	20.8	2.7	176.1	18.2	0.6	92.4	38.0	30.3	3.5	18.2	7.3	63.6
Armenia	2009	10.3	2.1	20.0	16.0	0.6	96.2	31.8	31.9	1.8	26.9	3.3	30.4
Australia		..	..	..	..	..	..	..	..	..	..	..	..
Austria		..	..	..	..	..	..	..	..	..	..	..	..
Azerbaijan	2009	3.0	2.1	15.8	52.2	0.3	85.1	10.8	19.0	1.8	18.2	1.9	10.5
Bahrain		..	..	..	..	..	..	..	..	..	..	..	..
Bangladesh	2007	3.2	1.3	6.0	85.1	0.1	..	16.1	24.7	10.6	7.8	8.4	27.2a
Belarus	2008	13.6	1.1	38.2	26.1	0.4	98.5	52.9	35.8	0.8	13.9	2.6	44.4
Belgium		..	..	..	..	..	..	..	..	..	..	..	..
Benin	2009	20.7	1.2	64.3	54.5	1.9	87.9	43.9	4.2	7.5	7.3	9.6	32.4
Bolivia	2010	28.5	1.6	37.3	17.6	0.8	72.4	41.3	27.8	2.5	22.4	12.4	57.1
Bosnia and Herzegovina	2009	11.2	1.0	21.4	10.3	0.4	98.6	32.8	59.7	1.9	30.1	1.3	66.5
Botswana	2010	10.2	1.0	27.2	7.3	1.5	93.9	55.3	32.8	3.7	21.3	6.2	51.9
Brazil	2009	18.7	1.2	83.5	11.9	1.7	95.8	59.3	48.4	3.0	25.7	15.9	52.9
Bulgaria	2009	10.6	2.2	20.8	22.4	0.5	98.5	33.9	34.7	1.6	19.9	4.2	30.7
Burkina Faso	2009	22.2	1.5	35.8	8.5	0.3	77.7	19.2	25.6	5.8	14.4	7.4	24.8
Burundi	2006	5.7	1.8	27.3	56.5	1.1	..	34.8	12.3	10.7	7.1	..	22.1a
Cambodia	2007	5.6	1.0	..	61.2	0.4	87.5	..	11.3	2.4	2.8	1.5	48.4a
Cameroon	2009	7.0	4.4	30.0	51.2	1.6	82.1	15.7	31.4	4.9	20.4	15.1	25.5
Canada		..	..	..	..	..	..	..	..	..	..	..	..
Central African Republic		..	..	..	..	..	..	..	..	..	..	..	..
Chad	2009	20.8	3.4	24.3	41.8	2.5	77.1	40.1	4.2	3.3	43.3	11.9	43.4
Chile	2010	9.9	2.9	68.5	0.7	0.8	96.1	29.6	44.8	1.3	22.1	10.8	57.5
China	2003	18.3	14.4	11.6	72.6	0.1	..	..	28.8	1.3	35.9	6.6	84.8
Hong Kong SAR, China		..	..	..	..	..	..	..	..	..	..	..	..
Colombia	2010	12.9	0.9	25.6	2.8	0.3	94.3	35.3	35.0	1.8	20.8	8.6	65.2
Congo, Dem. Rep.	2010	29.4	8.0	40.0	65.7	1.8	61.9	38.9	6.7	22.7	8.5	18.0	24.1
Congo, Rep.	2009	6.0	2.7	..	81.8	3.3	84.3	31.8	7.7	16.4	19.6	..	37.5
Costa Rica	2010	8.4	0.8	35.6	3.7	0.4	80.8	43.5	22.2	1.7	13.3	10.0	54.7
Côte d'Ivoire	2009	1.6	3.7	44.1	38.5	3.4	56.4	61.9	13.9	5.0	4.3	16.6	19.1
Croatia	2007	10.9	0.7	26.5	14.5	0.2	98.1	33.5	60.0	0.8	16.5	1.3	28.0a
Cuba		..	..	..	..	..	..	..	..	..	..	..	..
Cyprus		..	..	..	..	..	..	..	..	..	..	..	..
Czech Republic	2009	10.4	1.5	19.9	12.8	0.4	98.0	25.0	33.4	0.6	43.5	5.7	70.7
Denmark		..	..	..	..	..	..	..	..	..	..	..	..
Dominican Republic	2005	8.8	0.5	..	26.3	0.7	..	..	12.5	15.2	9.6	11.4	53.3
Ecuador	2010	22.5	0.8	30.0	11.8	1.0	85.1	24.1	17.0	3.9	9.7	18.2	65.9
Egypt, Arab Rep.	2008	8.8	3.4	42.7	15.2	3.0	17.9	34.0	5.6	3.2	21.1	6.2	21.7
El Salvador	2010	19.7	3.0	44.4	12.7	1.6	75.7	40.2	31.7	7.0	14.5	3.7	61.0
Eritrea	2009	0.5	0.2	..	0.0	0.0	100.0	4.2	11.9	0.2	15.1	9.6	26.1
Estonia	2009	5.5	0.4	8.3	3.7	0.9	97.4	36.3	41.5	0.5	21.2	1.8	69.3
Ethiopia	2006	3.8	1.1	11.4	12.4	1.4	..	30.9	11.0	0.9	4.2	4.3	38.2a
Finland		..	..	..	..	..	..	..	..	..	..	..	..
France		..	..	..	..	..	..	..	..	..	..	..	..
Gabon	2009	2.8	15.2	12.1	41.8	0.4	63.7	33.1	6.3	1.7	18.6	3.8	30.9
Gambia, The	2006	7.3	2.5	8.4	52.4	2.7	..	21.3	7.6	11.8	22.2	5.0	25.6a
Georgia	2008	2.1	0.6	11.8	14.7	0.7	99.6	40.8	38.2	1.4	16.0	3.8	14.5
Germany	2005	1.2	1.3	..	..	0.5	..	20.3	45.0	..	..	4.7	35.4
Ghana	2007	3.2	4.3	6.4	38.8	0.9	66.4	44.0	16.0	5.6	6.8	7.8	33.0a
Greece	2005	1.8	1.7	..	21.6	0.0	..	24.4	25.9	..	11.7	5.5	20.0
Guatemala	2010	10.2	2.7	41.1	6.3	1.3	90.0	44.2	26.6	2.8	11.9	4.7	51.9
Guinea	2006	2.7	2.8	13.0	84.8	2.0	..	25.4	0.9	14.0	5.2	4.3	21.1a
Guinea-Bissau	2006	2.9	3.4	30.4	63.1	1.1	..	19.9	0.7	5.3	8.4	5.6	12.4a
Haiti		..	..	..	..	..	..	..	..	..	..	..	..

	Survey year	Regulations and tax		Permits and licenses	Corruption	Crime	Informality	Gender	Finance	Infrastructure	Innovation	Trade	Workforce
		Time dealing with officials	Average number of times meeting with tax officials	Time required to obtain operating license	Informal payments to public officials	Losses due to theft, robbery, vandalism, and arson	Firms formally registered when operations started	Firms with female participation in ownership	Firms using banks to finance investment	Value lost due to electrical outages	Inter-nationally recognized quality certification ownership	Average time to clear direct exports through customs	Firms offering formal training
		% of management time		days	% of firms	% of sales	% of firms	% of firms	% of firms	% of sales	% of firms	days	% of firms
Honduras	2010	17.0	2.2	28.8	6.1	2.2	81.3	43.3	17.0	9.2	16.3	10.1	35.8
Hungary	2009	13.5	0.8	35.6	5.4	0.1	100.0	42.4	48.7	0.9	39.4	4.3	14.8
India	2006	6.7	2.6	..	47.5	0.1	..	9.1	46.6	6.6	22.5	15.1	15.9[a]
Indonesia	2009	1.6	0.2	21.1	14.9	0.4	29.1	42.8	11.7	2.2	2.9	2.3	4.7
Iran, Islamic Rep.		..	..	..	..	..	..	..	..	..	..	..	..
Iraq		..	..	..	..	..	..	..	..	..	..	..	..
Ireland	2005	2.3	1.3	..	8.3	0.3	..	41.6	37.4	1.5	17.2	2.6	73.2
Israel		..	..	..	..	..	..	..	..	..	..	..	..
Italy		..	..	..	..	..	..	..	..	..	..	..	..
Jamaica	2010	1.7	0.6	9.3	10.6	0.4	90.0	38.2	44.4	0.2	16.5	13.1	25.9
Japan		..	..	..	..	..	..	..	..	..	..	..	..
Jordan	2006	6.7	1.7	6.4	18.1	0.1	..	13.1	8.6	1.7	15.5	3.8	23.9[a]
Kazakhstan	2009	4.7	2.6	30.8	34.1	1.0	97.4	34.4	31.0	3.7	10.8	8.5	40.9
Kenya	2007	5.1	6.7	23.4	79.2	3.9	..	37.1	22.9	6.4	9.8	5.6	48.5[a]
Korea, Dem. Rep.		..	..	..	..	..	..	..	..	..	..	..	..
Korea, Rep.	2005	0.1	2.2	..	14.1	0.0	..	19.1	39.9	..	17.6	7.2	39.5
Kosovo	2009	9.8	4.5	18.8	7.5	0.3	89.2	10.9	25.3	17.1	7.9	1.7	24.6
Kuwait		..	..	..	..	..	..	..	..	..	..	..	..
Kyrgyz Republic	2009	4.9	2.1	18.0	47.8	0.3	95.9	60.4	17.9	10.5	16.2	15.8	29.7
Lao PDR	2009	1.2	4.4	13.6	39.8	0.3	93.5	39.4	0.0	4.3	7.2	7.5	11.1
Latvia	2009	9.7	1.5	11.5	13.4	0.3	98.5	46.3	37.3	1.1	18.2	1.9	43.4
Lebanon	2009	8.9	2.2	81.0	23.0	0.0	97.6	33.5	23.8	9.4	17.9	7.6	52.4
Lesotho	2009	5.6	1.8	16.4	28.1	2.9	86.8	18.4	32.7	6.7	24.7	5.4	42.5
Liberia	2009	7.5	6.5	16.0	55.4	2.8	73.8	53.0	10.1	2.9	2.4	..	17.0
Libya		..	..	..	..	..	..	..	..	..	..	..	..
Lithuania	2009	9.3	0.8	65.5	10.7	0.4	97.1	38.7	47.4	0.7	15.6	2.4	46.0
Macedonia, FYR	2009	14.5	3.0	33.8	16.9	0.7	99.2	36.4	47.0	5.9	21.5	2.5	19.0
Madagascar	2009	17.1	0.9	41.3	21.8	1.2	97.5	50.0	12.2	7.7	8.7	14.2	27.0
Malawi	2009	3.5	2.6	15.0	10.8	5.7	78.6	23.9	20.6	13.3	17.9	9.9	48.4
Malaysia	2007	7.8	2.1	22.4	..	1.0	53.0	13.1	48.6	3.0	54.1	2.7	50.1[a]
Mali	2010	2.0	1.2	41.0	19.4	0.5	79.2	58.3	29.3	4.1	24.8	12.9	32.1
Mauritania	2006	5.8	1.8	10.7	82.1	0.6	..	17.3	3.2	1.6	5.9	3.9	25.5[a]
Mauritius	2009	9.4	0.5	19.1	5.9	1.4	84.2	16.9	37.5	2.2	11.1	10.3	25.6
Mexico	2010	13.6	1.1	54.0	11.6	1.4	84.7	25.7	16.2	3.4	24.0	7.1	50.8
Moldova	2009	7.0	1.9	13.9	33.5	0.4	97.9	53.1	30.8	2.0	9.1	2.4	33.1
Mongolia	2009	12.1	2.0	43.5	33.4	0.6	90.1	52.0	26.5	0.8	16.7	18.6	61.2
Morocco	2007	11.4	0.9	3.4	13.4	0.0	86.0	13.1	12.3	1.3	17.3	1.8	24.7[a]
Mozambique	2007	3.3	1.9	35.2	14.8	1.8	85.9	24.4	10.5	2.4	18.7	10.1	22.1[a]
Myanmar		..	..	..	..	..	..	..	..	..	..	..	..
Namibia	2006	2.9	0.3	9.6	11.4	1.3	..	33.4	8.1	0.7	17.6	1.4	44.5[a]
Nepal	2009	6.5	1.3	14.5	15.2	0.9	94.0	27.4	17.5	27.0	3.1	5.6	8.8
Netherlands		..	..	..	..	..	..	..	..	..	..	..	..
New Zealand		..	..	..	..	..	..	..	..	..	..	..	..
Nicaragua	2010	20.2	1.5	17.6	8.3	2.2	74.0	61.9	21.9	18.2	15.5	4.7	47.2
Niger	2009	22.9	1.2	39.7	35.2	0.9	90.5	17.6	9.3	1.9	4.6	2.6	32.1
Nigeria	2007	6.1	3.0	12.1	40.9	4.1	..	20.0	2.7	8.9	8.5	7.5	25.7[a]
Norway		..	..	..	..	..	..	..	..	..	..	..	..
Oman		4.4	11.8	33.2	..	..	..	31.0	4.2	10.8	3.4	20.9	..
Pakistan	2007	1.9	1.5	10.2	48.0	0.4	..	6.7	9.7	9.2	9.6	2.6	6.7[a]
Panama	2010	33.3	0.8	66.3	30.5	0.3	99.7	24.7	1.2	2.1	22.5	7.6	11.0
Papua New Guinea		..	..	..	..	..	..	..	..	..	..	..	..
Paraguay	2010	20.7	1.0	81.3	17.5	1.3	98.7	51.6	30.1	1.4	15.0	21.7	54.9
Peru	2010	14.1	1.7	46.5	21.4	0.6	82.6	28.7	45.9	3.2	14.2	16.1	60.1
Philippines	2009	9.1	1.5	10.6	18.6	1.1	97.5	69.4	22.0	3.9	15.7	10.0	31.1
Poland	2009	12.8	0.6	14.6	14.7	0.5	99.3	47.9	40.7	1.9	17.3	6.0	60.9
Portugal	2005	1.1	1.6	..	14.5	0.2	..	50.8	24.4	..	12.7	7.2	31.9
Puerto Rico		..	..	..	..	..	..	..	..	..	..	..	..
Qatar		..	..	..	..	..	..	..	..	..	..	..	..

	Survey year	Regulations and tax		Permits and licenses	Corruption	Crime	Informality	Gender	Finance	Infrastructure	Innovation	Trade	Workforce
		Time dealing with officials % of management time	Average number of times meeting with tax officials	Time required to obtain operating license days	Informal payments to public officials % of firms	Losses due to theft, robbery, vandalism, and arson % of sales	Firms formally registered when operations started % of firms	Firms with female participation in ownership % of firms	Firms using banks to finance investment % of firms	Value lost due to electrical outages % of sales	Internationally recognized quality certification ownership % of firms	Average time to clear direct exports through customs days	Firms offering formal training % of firms
Romania	2009	9.2	2.3	23.7	22.2	0.3	98.7	47.9	37.3	2.2	26.1	2.0	24.9
Russian Federation	2009	19.9	1.6	57.4	39.6	0.8	94.7	33.1	30.6	1.2	11.7	4.6	52.2
Rwanda	2006	5.9	3.3	6.5	20.0	1.3	..	41.0	15.9	8.7	10.8	6.7	27.6[a]
Saudi Arabia	..	..	..	..	..	..	..	..	..	..	..	..	..
Senegal	2007	2.9	1.3	21.4	18.1	0.5	78.9	26.3	19.8	5.0	6.1	7.4	16.3[a]
Serbia	2009	12.2	1.4	28.0	21.4	0.6	95.0	28.8	42.8	1.3	21.8	1.6	36.5
Sierra Leone	2009	7.4	1.9	12.6	20.4	0.8	89.2	7.9	6.9	6.6	13.8	..	18.6
Singapore	..	..	..	..	..	..	..	..	..	..	..	..	..
Slovak Republic	2009	6.7	0.9	32.1	15.7	0.7	100.0	29.6	33.5	0.3	28.6	2.4	33.1
Slovenia	2009	7.3	0.3	56.1	5.8	0.4	99.9	42.2	52.2	0.5	28.0	2.2	47.5
Somalia	..	..	..	..	..	..	..	..	..	..	..	..	..
South Africa	2007	6.0	0.8	36.2	15.1	1.0	91.0	22.6	34.8	1.6	26.4	4.5	36.8[a]
South Sudan	..	..	..	..	..	..	..	..	..	..	..	..	..
Spain	2005	0.8	1.5	..	4.4	0.2	..	34.1	32.6	3.0	21.3	4.9	51.3
Sri Lanka	2004	3.5	4.9	49.5	16.3	0.5	..	..	26.2	..	..	7.6	32.6
Sudan	..	..	..	..	..	..	..	..	..	..	..	..	..
Swaziland	2006	4.4	1.4	24.0	40.6	1.3	..	28.6	7.7	2.5	22.1	2.1	51.0[a]
Sweden	..	..	..	..	..	..	..	..	..	..	..	..	..
Switzerland	..	..	..	..	..	..	..	..	..	..	..	..	..
Syrian Arab Republic	2009	12.2	2.3	169.2	83.8	0.8	..	14.4	20.7	8.6	7.4	5.1	38.3
Tajikistan	2008	11.7	1.4	22.6	44.6	0.3	92.7	34.4	21.4	15.1	16.7	20.4	21.1
Tanzania	2006	4.0	2.7	15.9	49.5	1.2	..	30.9	6.8	9.6	14.7	5.7	36.5[a]
Thailand	2006	0.4	1.0	32.1	..	0.1	..	..	74.4	1.5	39.0	1.3	75.3[a]
Timor-Leste	2009	3.8	0.9	16.6	19.4	2.7	91.8	42.9	1.6	7.6	2.2	..	49.7
Togo	2009	2.7	1.2	56.4	16.7	2.4	75.8	31.8	16.9	10.5	6.6	6.7	31.0
Trinidad and Tobago	..	..	..	..	..	..	..	..	..	..	..	..	..
Tunisia	..	..	..	..	..	..	..	..	..	..	..	..	..
Turkey	2008	27.1	1.3	36.0	18.0	0.4	94.1	40.7	51.9	2.8	30.0	5.2	28.8
Turkmenistan	..	..	..	..	..	..	..	..	..	..	..	..	..
Uganda	2006	5.2	2.4	9.3	51.7	1.0	..	34.7	7.7	10.2	15.5	3.2	35.0[a]
Ukraine	2008	11.3	2.1	31.0	31.8	0.6	95.8	47.1	32.1	4.4	13.0	3.4	24.8
United Arab Emirates	..	..	..	..	..	..	..	..	..	..	..	..	..
United Kingdom	..	..	..	..	..	..	..	..	..	..	..	..	..
United States	..	..	..	..	..	..	..	..	..	..	..	..	..
Uruguay	2010	11.6	1.0	108.0	8.1	0.3	94.6	23.1	13.7	0.3	10.8	6.2	48.6
Uzbekistan	2008	11.1	0.7	9.1	59.5	0.7	100.0	39.8	8.2	5.4	1.3	5.1	9.6
Venezuela, RB	2010	27.6	3.0	117.2	23.7	1.4	95.6	30.7	35.3	8.3	25.9	18.4	56.0
Vietnam	2009	4.6	0.9	15.9	52.5	0.3	87.5	59.2	21.5	3.6	16.7	4.2	43.6
West Bank and Gaza	2006	5.7	1.7	21.3	13.3	1.2	..	18.0	4.2	4.6	18.2	6.0	26.5[a]
Yemen, Rep.	2010	11.8	7.3	6.5	68.2	0.6	81.7	6.4	4.2	13.2	4.4	6.2	12.9
Zambia	2007	4.6	1.9	48.3	14.3	1.0	96.2	37.2	10.2	3.7	17.2	2.3	26.0[a]
Zimbabwe	..	..	..	..	..	..	..	..	..	..	..	..	..

Note: Enterprise surveys are updated several times a year; see www.enterprisesurveys.org for the most recent updates.
a. The sample was drawn from the manufacturing sector only.

About the data

The World Bank Enterprise Surveys gather firm-level data to benchmark the business environment of economies and assess how business environment constraints affect productivity and job creation. Standardized surveys are conducted all over the world, and data are available on more than 130,000 firms in 128 countries. The survey covers 11 dimensions of the business environment, including regulation, corruption, crime, informality, finance, infrastructure, and trade. For several countries firm-level panel data are also available, making it possible to track changes in the business environment over time.

Firms evaluating investment options, governments interested in improving business conditions, and economists seeking to explain economic performance have all grappled with defining and measuring the business environment. The firm-level data from Enterprise Surveys provide a useful tool for benchmarking economies across a large number of indicators measured at the firm level.

Most countries can improve regulation and taxation without compromising broader social interests. Excessive regulation may harm business performance and growth. For example, time spent with tax officials is a burden firms may face in paying taxes. The business environment suffers when governments increase uncertainty and risks or impose unnecessary costs and unsound regulation and taxation. Time to obtain licenses and permits and the associated red tape constrain firm operations.

In some countries doing business requires informal payments to "get things done" in customs, taxes, licenses, regulations, services, and the like. Such corruption can harm the business environment by distorting policymaking, undermining government credibility, and diverting public resources. Crime, theft, and disorder also impose costs on businesses and society.

In many developing countries informal businesses operate without formal registration. These firms have less access to financial and public services and can engage in fewer types of contracts and investments, constraining growth.

Equal opportunities for men and women contribute to development. Female participation in firm ownership and in management measures women's integration as decisionmakers.

Financial markets connect firms to lenders and investors, allowing firms to grow their businesses: creditworthy firms can obtain credit from financial intermediaries at competitive prices. But too often market imperfections and government-induced distortions limit access to credit and thus restrain growth.

The reliability and availability of infrastructure benefit households and support development. Firms with access to modern and efficient infrastructure—telecommunications, electricity, and transport—can be more productive. Firm-level innovation and use of modern technology may help firms compete.

Delays in clearing customs can be costly, deterring firms from engaging in trade or making them uncompetitive globally. Ill-considered labor regulations discourage firms from creating jobs, and while employed workers may benefit, unemployed, low-skilled, and informally employed workers will not. A trained labor force enables firms to thrive, compete, innovate, and adopt new technology.

The data in the table are from Enterprise Surveys implemented by the World Bank's Financial and Private Sector Development Enterprise Analysis Unit. All economies in East Asia and Pacific, Europe and Central Asia, Latin America and the Caribbean, Middle East and North Africa, and Sub-Saharan Africa (for 2009) and Afghanistan, Bangladesh, and India draw a sample of registered nonagricultural businesses, excluding those in the financial and public sectors. Samples for other economies are drawn only from the manufacturing sector and are footnoted in the table. Typical Enterprise Survey sample sizes range from 150 to 1,800, depending on the size of the economy. In each country samples are selected by stratified random sampling, unless otherwise noted. Stratified random sampling allows indicators to be computed by sector, firm size, and location and increases the precision of economywide indicators compared with alternative simple random sampling. Stratification by sector of activity divides the economy into manufacturing and retail and other services sectors. For medium-size and large economies the manufacturing sector is further stratified by industry. Firm size is stratified into small (5–19 employees), medium (20–99 employees), and large (more than 99 employees). Geographic stratification divides the national economy into the main centers of economic activity.

Definitions

- **Survey year** is the year in which the underlying data were collected. • **Time dealing with tax officials** is the average percentage of senior management's time that is spent in a typical week dealing with requirements imposed by government regulations. • **Average number of times meeting with tax officials** is the average number of visits or required meetings with tax officials. • **Time required to obtain operating license** is the average wait to obtain an operating license from the day applied for to the day granted. • **Informal payments to public officials** are the percentage of firms that answered positively to the question "Was a gift or informal payment expected or requested during a meeting with tax officials?" • **Losses due to theft, robbery, vandalism, and arson** are the estimated losses from those causes that occurred on establishments' premises as a percentage of annual sales. • **Firms formally registered when operations started** are firms formally registered when they started operations in the country. Firms not formally registered (the residual) are in the informal sector of the economy. • **Firms with female participation in ownership** are firms with a woman among the owners. • **Firms using banks to finance investment** are firms that invested in fixed assets during the last fiscal year that used banks to finance fixed assets. • **Value lost due to electrical outages** is losses that resulted from power outages as a percentage of annual sales. • **Internationally recognized quality certification ownership** is the percentage of firms that have an internationally recognized quality certification, such as International Organization for Standardization 9000, 9001, 9002, or 14000 or Hazard Analysis and Critical Control Points. • **Average time to clear direct exports through customs** is the average number of days to clear direct exports through customs. • **Firms offering formal training** are firms offering formal training programs for their permanent, full-time employees.

Data sources

Data on the business environment are from the World Bank Enterprise Surveys website (www.enterprisesurveys.org).

5.3 | Business environment: Doing Business indicators

	Starting a business			Registering property		Dealing with construction permits		Getting electricity	Enforcing contracts		Protecting investors	Resolving insolvency
	Number of procedures June 2011	Time required days June 2011	Cost % of per capita income June 2011	Number of procedures June 2011	Time required days June 2011	Number of procedures to build a warehouse June 2011	Time required to build a warehouse days June 2011	Time required days June 2011	Number of procedures June 2011	Time required days June 2011	Disclosure index 0–10 (least to most disclosure) June 2011	Time required years June 2011
Afghanistan	4	7	25.8	9	250	12	334	109	47	1,642	1	2.0
Albania	5	5	29.0	6	33	..	..	177	39	390	8	2.0
Algeria	14	25	12.1	10	48	19	281	159	45	630	6	2.5
Angola	8	68	118.9	7	184	11	321	48	46	1,011	5	6.2
Argentina	14	26	11.9	7	53	25	365	67	36	590	6	2.8
Armenia	3	8	2.9	3	7	18	79	242	49	440	5	1.9
Australia	2	2	0.7	5	5	15	147	81	28	395	8	1.0
Austria	8	28	5.2	3	21	13	194	23	25	397	3	1.1
Azerbaijan	6	8	2.7	4	11	30	212	241	39	237	7	2.7
Bahrain	7	9	0.7	2	31	12	43	90	48	635	8	2.5
Bangladesh	7	19	30.6	8	245	11	201	372	41	1,442	6	4.0
Belarus	5	5	1.3	2	10	13	140	254	29	275	7	5.8
Belgium	3	4	5.2	8	64	12	169	88	26	505	8	0.9
Benin	6	29	149.9	4	120	12	372	158	42	795	6	4.0
Bolivia	15	50	90.4	7	92	14	249	42	40	591	1	1.8
Bosnia and Herzegovina	12	40	17.0	7	33	18	181	125	37	595	3	3.3
Botswana	10	61	1.8	5	16	22	145	121	28	625	7	1.7
Brazil	13	119	5.4	13	39	17	469	34	45	731	6	4.0
Bulgaria	4	18	1.5	8	15	23	120	130	39	564	10	3.3
Burkina Faso	3	13	47.7	4	59	12	98	158	37	446	6	4.0
Burundi	9	14	116.8	5	94	22	135	188	44	832	8	..
Cambodia	9	85	109.7	7	56	21	652	183	44	401	5	6.0
Cameroon	5	15	45.5	5	93	11	147	67	43	800	6	3.2
Canada	1	5	0.4	6	17	12	73	168	36	570	8	0.8
Central African Republic	7	21	175.5	5	75	18	203	102	43	660	6	4.8
Chad	11	66	208.5	6	44	13	154	67	41	743	6	4.0
Chile	7	7	5.1	6	31	17	155	31	36	480	8	4.5
China	14	38	3.5	4	29	33	311	145	34	406	10	1.7
Hong Kong SAR, China	3	3	1.9	5	36	6	67	43	26	280	10	1.1
Colombia	9	14	8.0	7	15	8	46	165	34	1,346	8	1.3
Congo, Dem. Rep.	10	65	551.4	6	54	11	117	58	43	610	3	5.2
Congo, Rep.	10	160	85.2	6	55	14	186	129	44	560	6	3.3
Costa Rica	12	60	11.1	5	20	20	188	62	40	852	2	3.5
Côte d'Ivoire	10	32	132.6	6	62	18	583	33	33	770	6	2.2
Croatia	6	7	8.6	5	104	12	317	70	38	561	1	3.1
Cuba	..	..	..	..	..	..	..	..	..	..	..	..
Cyprus	6	8	13.1	6	42	9	677	247	43	735	8	1.5
Czech Republic	9	20	8.4	4	25	33	120	279	27	611	2	3.2
Denmark	4	6	0.0	3	16	5	67	38	35	410	7	1.0
Dominican Republic	7	19	18.2	7	60	14	216	87	34	460	5	3.5
Ecuador	13	56	28.8	9	16	16	128	89	39	588	1	5.3
Egypt, Arab Rep.	6	7	5.6	7	72	22	218	54	41	1,010	8	4.2
El Salvador	8	17	45.1	5	31	33	157	78	34	786	3	4.0
Eritrea	13	84	62.6	11	78	..	..	59	39	405	4	..
Estonia	5	7	1.8	3	18	13	148	111	35	425	8	3.0
Ethiopia	5	9	12.8	10	41	9	128	95	37	620	4	3.0
Finland	3	14	1.0	3	14	16	66	53	33	375	6	0.9
France	5	7	0.9	8	59	10	184	123	29	331	10	1.9
Gabon	9	58	17.3	7	39	13	201	160	38	1,070	6	5.0
Gambia, The	8	27	206.1	5	66	14	143	78	33	434	2	3.0
Georgia	2	2	4.3	1	2	9	74	97	36	285	9	3.3
Germany	9	15	4.6	5	40	9	97	17	30	394	5	1.2
Ghana	7	12	17.3	5	34	16	218	78	36	487	7	1.9
Greece	10	10	20.1	11	18	14	169	77	39	819	1	2.0
Guatemala	12	37	52.5	4	23	19	165	39	31	1,459	3	3.0
Guinea	12	40	118.0	6	59	29	287	69	49	276	6	3.8
Guinea-Bissau	9	9	49.8	8	210	12	170	455	40	1,715	6	..
Haiti	12	105	314.2	5	301	9	1,129	66	35	530	2	5.7

	Starting a business			Registering property		Dealing with construction permits		Getting electricity	Enforcing contracts		Protecting investors	Resolving insolvency
	Number of procedures	Time required days	Cost % of per capita income	Number of procedures	Time required days	Number of procedures to build a warehouse	Time required to build a warehouse days	Time required days	Number of procedures	Time required days	Disclosure index 0–10 (least to most disclosure)	Time required years
	June 2011	June 2011	June 2011	June 2011	June 2011	June 2011	June 2011	June 2011	June 2011	June 2011	June 2011	June 2011
Honduras	13	14	46.7	7	23	14	94	33	47	920	0	3.8
Hungary	4	4	7.6	4	17	29	102	252	35	395	2	2.0
India	12	29	46.8	5	44	34	227	67	46	1,420	7	7.0
Indonesia	8	45	17.9	6	22	13	158	108	40	570	10	5.5
Iran, Islamic Rep.	6	8	3.8	9	36	16	320	140	39	505	5	4.5
Iraq	11	77	115.7	5	51	13	187	47	51	520	4	..
Ireland	4	13	0.4	5	38	10	141	205	21	650	10	0.4
Israel	5	34	4.4	7	144	19	212	132	35	890	7	4.0
Italy	6	6	18.2	7	27	11	258	192	41	1,210	7	1.8
Jamaica	6	7	7.2	6	37	8	145	96	35	655	4	1.1
Japan	8	23	7.5	6	14	14	193	117	30	360	7	0.6
Jordan	7	12	13.9	7	21	17	70	43	38	689	5	4.3
Kazakhstan	6	19	0.8	4	40	32	189	88	36	390	9	1.5
Kenya	11	33	37.8	8	64	8	125	163	40	465	3	4.5
Korea, Dem. Rep.	..	..	..	..	..	..	..	..	..	..	..	..
Korea, Rep.	5	7	14.6	7	11	12	30	49	33	230	7	1.5
Kosovo	10	58	26.7	8	33	17	301	60	53	420	3	2.0
Kuwait	12	32	1.2	8	47	24	130	42	50	566	7	4.2
Kyrgyz Republic	2	10	3.5	4	5	12	142	337	38	260	8	4.0
Lao PDR	7	93	7.6	5	98	23	108	134	42	443	2	..
Latvia	4	16	2.6	5	18	23	205	108	27	369	5	3.0
Lebanon	5	9	67.1	8	25	19	219	75	37	721	9	4.0
Lesotho	7	40	24.9	6	101	12	510	140	40	785	2	2.6
Liberia	4	6	68.4	10	50	23	75	586	41	1,280	4	3.0
Libya	..	..	..	..	..	..	..	..	..	..	..	..
Lithuania	6	22	2.8	3	3	15	142	148	30	275	7	1.5
Macedonia, FYR	3	3	2.4	4	40	10	117	151	37	370	9	2.0
Madagascar	3	8	12.1	6	74	16	172	450	38	871	5	2.0
Malawi	10	39	90.9	6	69	18	200	244	42	312	4	2.6
Malaysia	4	6	16.4	5	48	22	260	51	29	425	10	1.5
Mali	4	8	90.5	5	29	11	179	120	36	620	6	3.6
Mauritania	9	19	48.3	4	49	18	119	75	46	370	5	8.0
Mauritius	5	6	3.6	4	22	16	136	91	36	645	6	1.7
Mexico	6	9	11.2	7	74	10	81	114	38	415	8	1.8
Moldova	7	9	9.1	5	5	27	291	140	30	352	7	2.8
Mongolia	7	13	2.9	5	11	19	208	156	32	314	5	4.0
Morocco	6	12	15.7	8	75	15	97	71	40	510	7	1.8
Mozambique	9	13	11.7	8	42	13	370	117	30	730	5	5.0
Myanmar	..	..	..	..	..	..	..	..	..	..	..	..
Namibia	10	66	17.2	7	39	12	139	55	33	270	5	1.5
Nepal	7	29	37.4	3	5	13	222	70	39	910	6	5.0
Netherlands	6	8	5.5	5	7	15	176	143	26	514	4	1.1
New Zealand	1	1	0.4	2	2	6	64	50	30	216	10	1.3
Nicaragua	8	39	107.9	8	49	16	218	70	37	409	4	2.2
Niger	9	17	114.4	4	35	12	326	120	39	545	6	5.0
Nigeria	8	34	70.6	13	82	15	85	260	40	457	5	2.0
Norway	5	7	1.8	1	3	11	250	66	34	280	7	0.9
Oman	5	8	3.1	2	16	14	174	62	51	598	8	4.0
Pakistan	10	21	11.2	6	50	11	222	206	46	976	6	2.8
Panama	6	8	9.9	8	32	17	113	35	31	686	1	2.5
Papua New Guinea	6	51	15.6	4	72	21	219	66	42	591	5	3.0
Paraguay	7	35	47.2	6	46	12	137	53	38	591	6	3.9
Peru	5	26	11.9	4	7	16	188	100	41	428	8	3.1
Philippines	15	35	19.1	8	39	30	85	50	37	842	2	5.7
Poland	6	32	17.3	6	152	30	301	143	37	830	7	3.0
Portugal	5	5	2.3	1	1	14	255	64	31	547	6	2.0
Puerto Rico	6	6	0.6	8	194	18	189	32	39	620	7	3.8
Qatar	8	12	8.3	7	13	17	70	90	43	570	5	2.8

5.3 Business environment: Doing Business indicators

	Starting a business			Registering property		Dealing with construction permits		Getting electricity	Enforcing contracts		Protecting investors	Resolving insolvency
	Number of procedures June 2011	Time required days June 2011	Cost % of per capita income June 2011	Number of procedures June 2011	Time required days June 2011	Number of procedures to build a warehouse June 2011	Time required to build a warehouse days June 2011	Time required days June 2011	Number of procedures June 2011	Time required days June 2011	Disclosure index 0–10 (least to most disclosure) June 2011	Time required years June 2011
Romania	6	14	3.0	8	26	16	287	223	31	512	9	3.3
Russian Federation	9	30	2.0	5	43	51	423	281	36	281	6	2.0
Rwanda	2	3	4.7	5	25	12	164	30	24	230	7	3.0
Saudi Arabia	3	5	5.9	2	2	9	75	71	43	635	9	1.5
Senegal	3	5	68.0	6	122	13	210	125	43	780	6	3.0
Serbia	7	13	7.8	6	11	19	279	131	36	635	7	2.7
Sierra Leone	6	12	93.3	7	86	20	238	137	39	515	6	2.6
Singapore	3	3	0.7	3	5	11	26	36	21	150	10	0.8
Slovak Republic	6	18	1.8	3	17	11	286	177	32	565	3	4.0
Slovenia	2	6	0.0	5	110	13	199	38	32	1,290	3	2.0
Somalia	..	..	..	..	..	..	..	..	..	..	..	..
South Africa	5	19	0.3	6	23	13	127	226	29	600	8	2.0
South Sudan	..	..	..	..	..	..	..	..	..	..	..	..
Spain	10	28	4.7	5	13	8	182	101	39	515	5	1.5
Sri Lanka	4	35	4.7	8	83	18	217	132	40	1,318	6	1.7
Sudan	10	36	31.4	6	9	16	270	70	53	810	0	2.0
Swaziland	12	56	29.2	9	21	13	95	137	40	972	2	2.0
Sweden	3	15	0.6	1	7	7	116	52	30	508	8	2.0
Switzerland	6	18	2.1	4	16	13	154	39	32	390	0	3.0
Syrian Arab Republic	7	13	17.1	4	19	23	104	71	55	872	7	4.1
Tajikistan	5	24	33.3	6	37	26	228	238	35	430	8	1.7
Tanzania	12	29	28.8	9	73	19	303	109	38	462	3	3.0
Thailand	5	29	6.2	2	2	8	157	35	36	479	10	2.7
Timor-Leste	10	103	4.5	..	..	19	238	63	51	1,285	3	..
Togo	7	84	177.2	5	295	12	309	74	41	588	6	3.0
Trinidad and Tobago	9	43	0.9	8	162	17	297	61	42	1,340	4	4.0
Tunisia	10	11	4.2	4	39	17	88	65	39	565	5	1.3
Turkey	6	6	11.2	6	6	24	189	70	36	420	9	3.3
Turkmenistan	..	..	..	..	..	..	..	..	..	..	..	..
Uganda	16	34	84.5	13	48	15	125	91	38	490	2	2.2
Ukraine	9	24	4.4	10	117	21	375	274	30	343	5	2.9
United Arab Emirates	7	13	5.6	1	2	14	46	55	49	537	4	5.1
United Kingdom	6	13	0.7	6	29	9	99	109	28	399	10	1.0
United States	6	6	1.4	4	12	15	26	68	32	300	7	1.5
Uruguay	5	7	24.9	8	66	27	234	48	41	720	3	2.1
Uzbekistan	6	14	6.4	12	78	25	243	117	42	195	4	4.0
Venezuela, RB	17	141	26.1	8	38	10	381	125	30	510	3	4.0
Vietnam	9	44	10.6	4	57	10	200	142	34	295	6	5.0
West Bank and Gaza	11	49	96.0	7	47	18	119	63	44	540	6	..
Yemen, Rep.	6	12	83.8	6	19	12	116	35	36	520	6	3.0
Zambia	6	18	27.4	5	40	14	196	117	35	471	3	2.7
Zimbabwe	9	90	148.9	5	31	12	614	125	38	410	8	3.3
World	**7 u**	**31 u**	**36.2 u**	**6 u**	**55 u**	**16 u**	**193 u**	**111 u**	**38 u**	**610 u**	**5 u**	**2.9 u**
Low income	8	33	106.0	6	86	15	260	167	39	662	5	3.7
Middle income	8	36	28.0	6	51	17	188	102	39	626	5	3.1
Lower middle income	8	34	40.9	6	66	16	181	98	40	662	4	3.3
Upper middle income	8	38	13.9	6	36	17	195	106	38	588	6	2.8
Low & middle income	8	35	46.3	6	60	16	205	117	39	634	5	3.2
East Asia & Pacific	8	39	26.4	5	80	17	172	98	37	548	5	3.2
Europe & Central Asia	6	16	8.0	6	29	21	214	168	37	390	7	2.8
Latin America & Carib.	9	57	40.8	7	56	14	221	66	40	699	4	3.1
Middle East & N. Africa	8	23	50.4	7	41	17	166	84	42	692	6	3.5
South Asia	7	23	21.6	6	103	16	222	145	43	1,075	5	3.4
Sub-Saharan Africa	8	34	80.8	6	66	15	212	138	39	657	5	3.4
High income	6	17	6.8	5	44	14	159	93	35	539	6	2.1
Euro area	6	12	5.4	5	32	12	210	111	32	600	6	1.7

Note: Regional aggregates differ from those reported on the Doing Business website because the regional aggregates reported on the Doing Business website include developed countries.

The economic health of a country is measured not only in macroeconomic terms but also by other factors that shape daily economic activity such as laws, regulations, and institutional arrangements. The Doing Business indicators measure business regulation, gauge regulatory outcomes, and measure the extent of legal protection of property, the flexibility of employment regulation, and the tax burden on businesses.

The table presents a subset of Doing Business indicators covering 7 of the 11 sets of indicators: starting a business, registering property, dealing with construction permits, getting electricity, enforcing contracts, protecting investors, and resolving insolvency. Table 5.5 includes Doing Business measures of getting credit, and table 5.6 presents data on paying business taxes.

The fundamental premise of the Doing Business project is that economic activity requires good rules and regulations that are efficient, accessible to all who need to use them, and simple to implement. Thus some Doing Business indicators give a higher score for more regulation, such as stricter disclosure requirements in related-party transactions, and others give a higher score for simplified regulations, such as a one-stop shop for completing business startup formalities.

In constructing the indicators, it is assumed that entrepreneurs know about all regulations and comply with them; in practice, entrepreneurs may not be aware of all required procedures or may avoid legally required procedures altogether. But where regulation is particularly onerous, levels of informality are higher, which comes at a cost: firms in the informal sector usually grow more slowly, have less access to credit, and employ fewer workers—and those workers remain outside the protections of labor law. The indicators in the table can help policymakers understand the business environment in a country and—along with information from other sources such as the World Bank's Enterprise Surveys—provide insights into potential areas of reform.

Doing Business data are collected with a standardized survey that uses a simple business case to ensure comparability across economies and over time—with assumptions about the legal form of the business, its size, its location, and nature of its operation. Surveys in 183 countries are administered through more than 9,000 local experts, including lawyers, business consultants, accountants, freight forwarders, government officials, and other professionals who routinely administer or advise on legal and regulatory requirements.

The Doing Business project encompasses two types of data: data from readings of laws and regulations and data on time and motion indicators that measure efficiency in achieving a regulatory goal. Within the time and motion indicators cost estimates are recorded from official fee schedules where applicable. The data from surveys are subjected to numerous tests for robustness, which lead to revision or expansion of the information collected.

The Doing Business methodology has limitations that should be considered when interpreting the data. First, the data collected refer to businesses in the economy's largest city and may not represent regulations in other locations of the economy. To address this limitation, subnational indicators are being collected for selected economies. These subnational studies point to significant differences in the speed of reform and the ease of doing business across cities in the same economy. Second, the data often focus on a specific business form—generally a limited liability company of a specified size—and may not represent regulation for other types of businesses such as sole proprietorships. Third, transactions described in a standardized business case refer to a specific set of issues and may not represent the full set of issues a business encounters. Fourth, the time measures involve an element of judgment by the expert respondents. When sources indicate different estimates, the Doing Business time indicators represent the median values of several responses given under the assumptions of the standardized case. Fifth, the methodology assumes that a business has full information on what is required and does not waste time when completing procedures.

• **Number of procedures for starting a business** is the number of procedures required to start a business, including interactions to obtain necessary permits and licenses and to complete all inscriptions, verifications, and notifications to start operations for businesses with specific characteristics of ownership, size, and type of production. • **Time required for starting a business** is the number of calendar days to complete the procedures for legally operating a business using the fastest procedure, independent of cost. • **Cost for starting a business** is normalized as a percentage of gross national income (GNI) per capita. It includes all official fees and fees for legal or professional services if they are required by law. • **Number of procedures for registering property** is the number of procedures required for a business to legally transfer property. • **Time required for registering property** is the number of calendar days for a business to legally transfer property. • **Number of procedures for dealing with construction permits to build a warehouse** is the number of interactions of a company's employees or managers with external parties, including government staff, public inspectors, notaries, land registry and cadastre staff, and technical experts apart from architects and engineers. • **Time required for dealing with construction permits to build a warehouse** is the number of calendar days to complete the required procedures for building a warehouse using the fastest procedure, independent of cost. • **Time required for getting electricity** is the number of calendar days required for a business to obtain a permanent electricity connection and supply. • **Number of procedures for enforcing contracts** is the number of independent actions, mandated by law or court regulation, that demand interaction between the parties to a contract or between them and the judge or court officer. • **Time required for enforcing contracts** is the number of calendar days from the time of the filing of a lawsuit in court to the final determination and payment. • **Disclosure index** measures the degree to which investors are protected through disclosure of ownership and financial information. Higher values indicate more disclosure. • **Time required to resolve insolvency** is the number of years from time of filing for insolvency in court until resolution of distressed assets and payment of creditors.

Data on the business environment are from the World Bank's Doing Business project (www.doingbusiness.org).

5.4 Stock markets

	Market capitalization				Market liquidity		Turnover ratio		Listed domestic companies		S&P/Global Equity Indices	
	$ millions		% of GDP		Value of shares traded % of GDP		Value of shares traded % of market capitalization		number		% change	
	2005	2011	2005	2010	2005	2010	2005	2011	2005	2011	2010	2011
Afghanistan	..	..	..	..	..	..	..	..	..	..	..	..
Albania	..	..	..	..	..	..	..	..	..	..	..	..
Algeria	..	..	..	..	..	..	..	..	..	..	..	..
Angola	..	..	..	..	..	..	..	..	..	..	..	..
Argentina	61,478	43,580	33.6	17.3	9.0	0.7	30.4	4.8	101	99	55.3[a]	–30.2[a]
Armenia	43	44	0.9	0.3	0.0	0.0	3.7	1.5	198	12		
Australia	804,074	1,198,164	115.4	128.5	88.5	108.0	78.0	94.0	1,643	1,922	12.5	–15.7
Austria	124,390	82,374	40.8	17.9	15.1	12.7	43.6	51.6	92	73	10.9	–35.8
Azerbaijan	..	..	..	..	..	..	..	..	..	..	..	..
Bahrain	17,364	17,152	129.0	82.2	5.3	4.2	4.6	1.5	47	44	10.0[a]	–14.4[a]
Bangladesh	3,035	23,546	5.0	15.6	1.7	14.6	31.5	92.6	262	216	37.6[a]	–42.3[a]
Belarus	..	..	..	..	..	..	..	..	..	..	..	..
Belgium	288,515	229,896	76.5	57.4	33.3	23.7	44.8	43.0	222	158	0.5	–15.1
Benin	..	..	..	..	..	..	..	..	..	..	..	..
Bolivia	2,200	4,125	23.0	17.2	0.0	0.1	0.1	0.4	36	40	..	..
Bosnia and Herzegovina	..	..	..	..	..	..	..	..	..	..	..	..
Botswana	2,437	4,107	23.8	27.4	0.4	0.9	1.8	3.6	18	23	–6.8[a]	–7.5[a]
Brazil	474,647	1,228,969	53.8	74.0	17.5	43.2	38.3	69.3	381	366	6.5	–24.4
Bulgaria	5,086	8,253	17.6	15.2	4.8	0.4	35.2	3.4	331	393	–15.2[a]	–22.1[a]
Burkina Faso	..	..	..	..	..	..	..	..	..	..	..	..
Burundi	..	..	..	..	..	..	..	..	..	..	..	..
Cambodia	..	..	..	..	..	..	..	..	..	..	..	..
Cameroon	..	..	..	..	..	..	..	..	..	..	..	..
Canada	1,480,891	1,906,589	130.6	137.0	74.5	86.6	63.6	74.8	3,721	3,932	22.0	–14.7
Central African Republic	..	..	..	..	..	..	..	..	..	..	..	..
Chad	..	..	..	..	..	..	..	..	..	..	..	..
Chile	136,446	270,289	115.4	160.6	16.0	25.5	14.9	18.6	245	229	47.2	–24.1
China	780,763	3,389,098	34.6	80.4	26.0	135.5	82.5	188.2	1,387	2,342	6.9	–21.7
Hong Kong SAR, China	693,486	889,597	390.1	481.0	165.4	711.7	43.3	157.6	1,020	1,472	21.3	–20.2
Colombia	46,016	201,296	31.4	72.3	4.3	8.0	17.9	13.3	114	79	44.1	–12.0
Congo, Dem. Rep.	..	..	..	..	..	..	..	..	..	..	..	..
Congo, Rep.	..	..	..	..	..	..	..	..	..	..	..	..
Costa Rica	1,478	1,443	7.4	4.0	0.1	0.1	1.7	2.6	19	9	..	..
Côte d'Ivoire	2,327	6,288	14.2	31.2	0.2	0.6	1.4	1.8	39	33	19.3[a]	–15.2[a]
Croatia	12,918	21,796	28.8	40.9	1.8	1.7	6.7	4.1	145	209	–0.4[a]	–30.3[a]
Cuba	..	..	..	..	..	..	..	..	..	..	..	..
Cyprus	6,583	2,853	38.7	29.5	2.4	2.7	7.1	10.0	144	117	..	–71.9[a]
Czech Republic	38,345	38,352	30.8	22.4	33.0	7.3	118.6	38.0	36	15	0.2	–15.0
Denmark	178,038	179,529	69.1	74.3	59.0	46.3	92.3	73.2	179	186	25.1	–17.3
Dominican Republic	..	..	..	..	..	..	..	..	..	..	..	..
Ecuador	3,214	5,779	8.7	9.1	0.4	0.2	5.0	1.9	32	41	9.7[a]	–9.6[a]
Egypt, Arab Rep.	79,672	48,683	88.8	37.7	28.3	17.0	43.0	33.5	744	231	11.5	–49.1
El Salvador	3,623	5,474	21.2	19.9	0.4	0.2	2.3	1.6	35	65	..	..
Eritrea	..	..	..	..	..	..	..	..	..	..	..	..
Estonia	3,495	1,611	25.1	11.8	17.8	1.7	51.1	12.6	15	15	56.0[a]	–23.3[a]
Ethiopia	..	..	..	..	..	..	..	..	..	..	..	..
Finland	209,504	143,081	107.0	49.6	139.7	42.8	139.1	133.5	134	121	10.7	–33.1
France	1,758,721	1,568,730	82.3	75.3	71.4	57.3	92.0	84.4	885	893	–9.9[b]	–19.5[b]
Gabon	..	..	..	..	..	..	..	..	..	..	..	..
Gambia, The	..	..	..	..	..	..	..	..	..	..	..	..
Georgia	355	796	5.5	9.1	0.6	0.0	13.6	0.2	257	135	..	..
Germany	1,221,250	1,184,459	44.1	43.6	63.7	42.8	146.0	134.5	648	670	7.4[c]	–16.6[c]
Ghana	1,661	3,097	15.5	11.3	0.6	0.3	3.2	4.1	30	36	94.1[a]	–22.8[a]
Greece	145,013	33,648	60.4	24.1	27.2	14.3	48.3	46.5	307	275	–43.8	–58.3
Guatemala	..	..	..	..	..	..	..	..	..	..	..	..
Guinea	..	..	..	..	..	..	..	..	..	..	..	..
Guinea-Bissau	..	..	..	..	..	..	..	..	..	..	..	..
Haiti	..	..	..	..	..	..	..	..	..	..	..	..

	Market capitalization				Market liquidity		Turnover ratio		Listed domestic companies		S&P/Global Equity Indices	
	$ millions		% of GDP		Value of shares traded % of GDP		Value of shares traded % of market capitalization		number		% change	
	2005	2011	2005	2010	2005	2010	2005	2011	2005	2011	2010	2011
Honduras	..	..	..	..	..	..	..	..	..	..	..	..
Hungary	32,576	18,773	29.5	21.5	21.7	20.6	78.0	83.9	44	52	–10.8	–35.3
India	553,074	1,015,370	66.3	93.6	52.0	61.2	92.2	56.3	4,763	5,112	18.7	–38.0
Indonesia	81,428	390,107	28.5	51.0	14.7	18.3	54.2	37.2	335	440	37.9	1.1
Iran, Islamic Rep.	38,724	107,249	20.2	19.1	4.3	5.2	19.1	20.7	420	347	..	..
Iraq	..	..	..	..	..	..	..	..	..	..	..	..
Ireland	114,134	35,363	56.1	16.3	31.8	8.1	56.7	45.3	53	48	–7.7	–1.5
Israel	120,114	144,970	89.5	100.3	44.6	61.4	55.5	64.7	572	576	7.4	–29.7
Italy	798,167	431,471	44.7	15.4	62.4	26.2	140.5	236.8	275	287	–17.4	–27.6
Jamaica	13,028	7,223	116.8	46.5	3.9	1.5	3.1	3.1	39	37	22.4[a]	28.4[a]
Japan	4,736,513	3,540,685	104.0	75.1	109.8	78.4	118.8	108.9	3,279	3,961	9.6[d]	–12.2[d]
Jordan	37,639	27,183	299.0	111.9	189.1	34.3	85.0	13.9	201	247	–8.6[a]	–16.2[a]
Kazakhstan	10,521	43,301	18.4	40.8	1.9	1.5	14.9	2.1	62	63	–1.0[a]	–36.4[a]
Kenya	6,384	10,203	34.1	46.0	2.7	3.5	9.8	7.1	47	58	33.8[a]	–31.6[a]
Korea, Dem. Rep.	..	..	..	..	..	..	..	..	..	..	..	..
Korea, Rep.	718,180	994,302	85.0	107.4	142.4	160.3	209.8	195.1	1,620	1,792	25.3	–10.9
Kosovo	..	..	..	..	..	..	..	..	..	..	..	..
Kuwait	130,080	100,869	161.0	87.6	116.4	63.9	94.3	19.4	143	206	29.1[a]	–21.4[a]
Kyrgyz Republic	42	165	1.7	1.7	0.5	0.2	34.1	2.7	8	34	..	..
Lao PDR	..	..	..	..	..	..	..	..	..	..	..	..
Latvia	2,527	1,076	15.8	5.2	0.6	0.1	4.6	4.4	45	32	39.4[a]	–17.3[a]
Lebanon	4,929	10,164	22.5	32.3	4.2	4.8	25.5	4.5	11	10	–8.7[a]	–22.2[a]
Lesotho	..	..	..	..	..	..	..	..	..	..	..	..
Liberia	..	..	..	..	..	..	..	..	..	..	..	..
Libya	..	..	..	..	..	..	..	..	..	..	..	..
Lithuania	8,183	4,075	31.5	15.6	2.9	0.8	10.1	5.0	43	33	44.0[a]	–16.1[a]
Macedonia, FYR	646	2,504	10.8	28.8	1.6	0.4	18.3	2.0	57	32	..	..
Madagascar	..	..	..	..	..	..	..	..	..	..	..	..
Malawi	230	1,384	8.4	26.7	0.3	0.4	4.1	3.9	9	13	..	..
Malaysia	181,236	395,083	131.4	172.6	36.2	37.9	26.9	32.0	1,020	941	35.1	–1.1
Mali	..	..	..	..	..	..	..	..	..	..	..	..
Mauritania	..	..	..	..	..	..	..	..	..	..	..	..
Mauritius	2,617	6,540	41.7	66.9	2.4	3.7	6.0	8.0	42	86	8.2[a]	–2.5[a]
Mexico	239,128	408,691	28.2	43.9	6.2	10.5	25.7	26.0	151	128	26.6	–14.8
Moldova	..	..	..	..	0.6	0.2	..	..	..	..	..	..
Mongolia	46	1,579	1.8	17.6	0.1	0.8	6.1	3.4	392	332	..	..
Morocco	27,220	60,088	45.7	76.2	7.0	11.8	15.9	9.8	56	75	13.1	–17.7
Mozambique	..	..	..	..	..	..	..	..	..	..	..	..
Myanmar	..	..	..	..	..	..	..	..	..	..	..	..
Namibia	415	1,152	5.7	9.7	0.1	0.2	1.5	1.2	13	7	24.2[a]	6.2[a]
Nepal	1,344	4,529	16.5	30.8	0.6	0.6	4.4	1.7	125	181	..	..
Netherlands	592,906	594,732	92.9	84.8	130.9	76.0	147.7	88.3	237	108	1.2	–16.4
New Zealand	43,409	71,657	39.1	52.9	15.7	14.2	40.0	39.6	154	144	5.2	–3.8
Nicaragua	..	..	..	..	..	..	..	..	..	..	..	..
Niger	..	..	..	..	..	..	..	..	..	..	..	..
Nigeria	19,356	39,270	17.2	26.3	1.7	2.7	11.5	9.2	214	196	20.3[a]	–29.5[a]
Norway	190,952	219,245	62.8	60.1	64.1	52.0	117.2	88.6	191	192	13.7	–18.1
Oman	15,269	19,719	49.4	36.9	10.4	12.4	29.8	12.9	96	136	12.2[a]	–14.1[a]
Pakistan	45,937	32,764	41.9	21.6	128.6	7.3	376.3	28.6	661	638	15.3[a]	–18.8[a]
Panama	5,074	10,682	32.8	40.9	0.5	0.7	1.8	0.6	24	21	12.8[a]	18.0[a]
Papua New Guinea	3,166	8,999	64.6	102.8	0.4	0.2	0.6	0.6	9	11	..	..
Paraguay	257	958	3.4	0.2	0.0	0.1	0.6	3.0	54	66	..	..
Peru	35,995	79,329	45.3	63.6	2.5	2.5	7.2	5.5	196	202	51.3	–21.3
Philippines	40,153	165,380	39.0	78.8	6.7	13.4	20.1	20.4	235	251	56.7	0.2
Poland	93,873	138,246	30.9	40.5	9.9	16.5	36.3	58.4	248	757	11.3	–33.4
Portugal	66,981	61,688	34.9	35.9	21.7	13.7	60.7	50.3	48	46	–16.6	–31.0
Puerto Rico	..	..	..	..	..	..	..	..	..	..	..	..
Qatar	87,316	125,413	202.9	89.4	65.2	25.9	40.0	18.6	31	42	27.7[a]	3.3[a]

	Market capitalization				Market liquidity		Turnover ratio		Listed domestic companies		S&P/Global Equity Indices	
	$ millions		% of GDP		Value of shares traded % of GDP		Value of shares traded % of market capitalization		number		% change	
	2005	2011	2005	2010	2005	2010	2005	2011	2005	2011	2010	2011
Romania	20,588	21,197	20.8	20.0	3.4	1.1	21.0	12.0	3,747	1,267	–6.6[a]	–18.2[a]
Russian Federation	548,579	796,376	71.8	67.9	20.9	54.0	39.0	127.3	296	327	21.7	–23.4
Rwanda	..	..	..	..	..	..	..	..	..	..	..	..
Saudi Arabia	646,104	338,873	204.7	81.3	349.7	46.7	231.7	84.6	77	150	9.0[e]	–3.9[e]
Senegal	..	..	..	..	..	..	..	..	..	..	..	..
Serbia	5,409	8,365	21.4	25.2	2.6	0.6	15.3	3.7	864	1,322	..	..
Sierra Leone	..	..	..	..	..	..	..	..	..	..	..	..
Singapore	316,658	308,320	256.4	177.3	97.0	135.1	40.4	74.8	685	462	18.4	–21.2
Slovak Republic	4,393	4,736	7.2	4.8	0.1	0.2	1.6	10.2	209	81	5.4[a]	3.0[a]
Slovenia	7,899	6,326	22.1	20.1	2.2	0.6	9.0	6.5	116	66	–20.3[a]	–30.7[a]
Somalia	..	..	..	..	..	..	..	..	..	..	..	..
South Africa	565,408	855,711	228.9	278.4	81.2	93.5	39.3	39.8	388	355	32.1	–17.4
South Sudan	..	..	..	..	..	..	..	..	..	..	..	..
Spain	960,024	1,030,951	84.9	83.2	137.8	96.7	163.9	128.9	3,300	3,241	–24.5	–16.8
Sri Lanka	5,720	19,437	23.4	40.2	4.7	6.7	24.3	25.1	239	253	84.6[a]	–23.0[a]
Sudan	..	..	..	..	..	..	..	..	..	..	..	..
Swaziland	197	..	7.8	..	0.0	..	0.0	..	6	5	..	..
Sweden	403,948	470,122	109.0	126.7	125.2	95.9	118.9	96.2	252	340	32.6	–18.5
Switzerland	938,624	932,207	252.0	232.9	237.1	164.7	100.1	85.9	263	246	11.0	–9.4
Syrian Arab Republic	..	..	..	..	..	..	..	..	..	..	..	..
Tajikistan	..	..	..	..	..	..	..	..	..	..	..	..
Tanzania	588	1,539	4.2	5.5	0.1	0.1	2.3	2.5	6	17	..	..
Thailand	124,864	268,489	70.8	87.2	50.6	68.4	73.9	85.1	504	545	52.1	–4.7
Timor-Leste	..	..	..	..	..	..	..	..	..	..	..	..
Togo	..	..	..	..	..	..	..	..	..	..	..	..
Trinidad and Tobago	16,972	14,725	106.2	59.0	3.9	0.7	3.7	1.2	37	37	0.8[a]	26.7[a]
Tunisia	2,876	9,662	8.9	24.1	1.4	3.8	16.5	11.0	46	57	11.7[a]	–13.4[a]
Turkey	161,537	201,817	33.4	41.8	41.7	57.4	154.9	162.7	302	362	21.4	–37.0
Turkmenistan	..	..	..	..	..	..	..	..	..	..	..	..
Uganda	103	7,727	1.1	10.5	0.0	0.1	3.1	..	5	8	..	..
Ukraine	24,976	25,558	29.0	28.6	0.8	1.5	3.6	14.1	221	195	53.8[a]	–36.3[a]
United Arab Emirates	225,568	93,767	124.9	35.2	79.2	9.2	89.6	15.9	79	104	–6.8[a]	–16.5[a]
United Kingdom	3,058,182	1,202,031	134.1	137.4	182.7	132.9	141.9	137.9	2,759	2,001	5.2[f]	–6.1[f]
United States	16,970,865	15,640,707	134.9	117.5	171.0	208.8	129.2	187.6	5,143	4,171	12.8[g]	0.0[g]
Uruguay	96	175	0.6	0.4	0.0	0.0	1.1	0.4	9	6	..	..
Uzbekistan	37	..	0.3	..	0.3	0.1	184.7	..	114	132	..	..
Venezuela, RB	5,017	5,143	3.4	1.0	0.2	0.0	4.5	0.9	50	36	..	..
Vietnam	461	18,316	0.9	19.2	0.2	16.2	24.8	29.5	33	301	0.5[a]	–26.8[a]
West Bank and Gaza	4,461	2,532	111.1	..	52.2	..	75.4	14.7	28	45	..	..
Yemen, Rep.	..	..	..	..	..	..	..	..	..	..	..	..
Zambia	989	4,009	13.8	17.4	0.2	1.6	2.0	..	15	20	17.4[a]	–1.3[a]
Zimbabwe	2,402	10,903	43.0	153.6	5.9	15.3	15.3	..	79	75	..	..
World	43,319,352 s	45,082,821s	96.6 w	88.7 w	105.7 w	106.4 w	116.3 w	133.4 w	50,936 s	49,553 s		
Low income	..	59,995	..	26.6	..	..	15.3	48.6	..	602		
Middle income	4,426,053	10,282,607	49.3	72.6	24.9	67.7	58.4	103.0	19,925	18,737		
Lower middle income	898,133	1,854,685	48.0	65.9	35.2	34.2	86.4	44.8	8,741	8,653		
Upper middle income	3,527,921	8,427,921	49.6	74.4	22.2	76.5	51.4	116.1	11,184	10,084		
Low & middle income	4,440,182	10,342,602	48.8	72.1	24.6	67.0	58.3	102.8	20,466	19,339		
East Asia & Pacific	1,212,704	4,638,422	40.1	79.9	25.6	113.3	68.4	154.3	3,931	5,181		
Europe & Central Asia	789,576	1,116,849	48.7	51.8	22.7	42.7	61.6	121.1	6,564	4,368		
Latin America & Carib.	1,028,157	2,274,194	40.5	57.6	9.9	22.9	28.4	46.4	1,504	1,446		
Middle East & N. Africa	135,018	265,561	36.8	34.6	7.2	7.5	39.3	19.4	1,531	1,012		
South Asia	609,110	1,095,645	58.8	81.9	55.7	52.6	111.6	55.4	6,050	6,400		
Sub-Saharan Africa	605,113	951,930	128.6	149.5	43.3	46.6	37.3	37.2	911	932		
High income	38,879,170	34,740,219	108.8	95.9	126.3	123.5	122.4	143.0	30,470	30,214		
Euro area	6,357,326	5,482,967	62.7	51.7	73.1	47.1	120.5	110.4	6,737	6,250		

a. Refers to the S&P Frontier BMI index. b. Refers to the CAC 40 index. c. Refers to the DAX index. d. Refers to the Nikkei 225 index. e. Refers to the Saudi Arabia country index. f. Refers to the FTSE 100 index. g. Refers to the S&P 500 index.

About the data

The development of an economy's financial markets is closely related to its overall development. Well functioning financial systems provide good and easily accessible information. That lowers transaction costs, which in turn improves resource allocation and boosts economic growth. Both banking systems and stock markets enhance growth, the main factor in poverty reduction. At low levels of economic development commercial banks tend to dominate the financial system, while at higher levels domestic stock markets tend to become more active and efficient relative to domestic banks.

Open economies with sound macroeconomic policies, good legal systems, and shareholder protection attract capital and therefore have larger financial markets. Recent research on stock market development shows that modern communications technology and increased financial integration have resulted in more cross-border capital flows, a stronger presence of financial firms around the world, and the migration of stock exchange activities to international exchanges. Many firms in emerging markets now cross-list on international exchanges, which provides them with lower cost capital and more liquidity-traded shares. However, this also means that exchanges in emerging markets may not have enough financial activity to sustain them, putting pressure on them to rethink their operations.

The indicators in the table are from Standard & Poor's Emerging Markets Data Base. They include measures of size (market capitalization, number of listed domestic companies) and liquidity (value of shares traded as a percentage of gross domestic product, value of shares traded as a percentage of market capitalization). The comparability of such indicators across countries may be limited by conceptual and statistical weaknesses, such as inaccurate reporting and differences in accounting standards. The percentage change in stock market prices in U.S. dollars for developing economies is from Standard & Poor's Global Equity Indices (S&P IFCI) and Standard & Poor's Frontier Broad Market Index (BMI). The percentage change for France, Germany, Japan, the United Kingdom, and the United States is from local stock market prices. The indicator is an important measure of overall performance. Regulatory and institutional factors that can affect investor confidence, such as entry and exit restrictions, the existence of a securities and exchange commission, and the quality of laws to protect investors, may influence the functioning of stock markets but are not included in the table.

Stock market size can be measured in various ways, and each may produce a different ranking of countries. Market capitalization shows the overall size of the stock market in U.S. dollars and as a percentage of GDP. The number of listed domestic companies is another measure of market size. Market size is positively correlated with the ability to mobilize capital and diversify risk.

Market liquidity, the ability to easily buy and sell securities, is measured by dividing the total value of shares traded by GDP. The turnover ratio—the value of shares traded as a percentage of market capitalization—is also a measure of liquidity as well as of transaction costs. (High turnover indicates low transaction costs.) The turnover ratio complements the ratio of value traded to GDP, because the turnover ratio is related to the size of the market and the value traded ratio to the size of the economy. A small, liquid market will have a high turnover ratio but a low value of shares traded ratio. Liquidity is an important attribute of stock markets because, in theory, liquid markets improve the allocation of capital and enhance prospects for long-term economic growth. A more comprehensive measure of liquidity would include trading costs and the time and uncertainty in finding a counterpart in settling trades.

S&P Indices, the source for all the data in the table, provides regular updates on 21 emerging stock markets and 36 frontier markets. S&P Indices maintains a series of indexes for investors interested in investing in stock markets in developing countries. The S&P/IFCI index, S&P Indices's leading emerging markets index, is designed to be sufficiently investable to support index tracking portfolios in emerging market stocks that are legally and practically open to foreign portfolio investment. The S&P Frontier BMI measures the performance of 36 smaller and less liquid markets. The S&P Frontier BMI country indexes aim to include all publicly listed equities representing an aggregate of at least 80 percent of the total market capitalization in each market, subject to the securities meeting size and liquidity thresholds defined by three market size tiers. These indexes are widely used benchmarks for international portfolio management. See www.standardandpoors.com for further information on the indexes.

Because markets included in Standard & Poor's emerging markets category vary widely in level of development, it is best to look at the entire category to identify the most significant market trends. And it is useful to remember that stock market trends may be distorted by currency conversions, especially when a currency has registered a significant devaluation.

About the data is based on Demirgüç-Kunt and Levine (1996), Beck and Levine (2001), and Claessens, Klingebiel, and Schmukler (2002).

Definitions

• **Market capitalization** (also known as market value) is the share price times the number of shares outstanding. • **Market liquidity** is the total value of shares traded during the period divided by gross domestic product (GDP). This indicator complements the market capitalization ratio by showing whether market size is matched by trading. • **Turnover ratio** is the total value of shares traded during the period divided by the average market capitalization for the period. Average market capitalization is calculated as the average of the end-of-period values for the current period and the previous period. • **Listed domestic companies** are the domestically incorporated companies listed on the country's stock exchanges at the end of the year. This indicator does not include investment companies, mutual funds, or other collective investment vehicles. • **S&P/Global Equity Indices** measure the U.S. dollar price change in the stock markets.

Data sources

Data on stock markets are from Standard & Poor's *Global Stock Markets Factbook 2011,* which draws on the Emerging Markets Data Base, supplemented by other data from Standard & Poor's. The firm collects data through an annual survey of the world's stock exchanges, supplemented by information provided by its network of correspondents and by Reuters. Data on GDP are from World Bank's national accounts data files.

5.5 Financial access, stability, and efficiency

	Getting credit		Financial access and outreach				Bank capital to asset ratio	Ratio of bank nonperforming loans to total gross loans	Domestic credit provided by banking sector	Interest rate spread	Risk premium on lending
	Strength of legal rights index 0–10 (weak to strong)	Depth of credit information index 0–6 (low to high)	per 1,000 adults Depositors with commercial banks	per 1,000 adults Borrowers from commercial banks	per 100,000 adults Commercial bank branches	per 100,000 adults Automated teller machines	%	%	% of GDP	Lending rate minus deposit rate percentage points	Prime lending rate minus treasury bill rate percentage points
	June 2011	June 2011	2010	2010	2010	2010	2010	2010	2010	2010	2010
Afghanistan	6	0	100	4	2.2	0.50	..	..	2.1	..	..
Albania	9	4	..	118	22.6	31.96	8.5	13.9	67.5	6.4	7.0
Algeria	3	3	346	23	5.2	6.07	..	..	−7.4	6.3	7.7
Angola	3	4	97	86	1.3	12.66	..	..	22.9	9.8	..
Argentina	4	6	702	285	13.3	42.45	11.9	1.8	29.2	1.4	..
Armenia	6	6	589	202	17.5	32.11	20.4	3.0	25.8	10.3	8.6
Australia	9	5	..	..	31.6	162.38	5.7	2.2	147.6	3.1	2.8
Austria	7	6	1,376	..	11.4	48.16	7.5	2.8	137.5	..	..
Azerbaijan	6	5	41	256	10.4	28.43	..	..	23.5	9.1	18.9
Bahrain	4	3	..	..	..	..	..	..	79.3	6.0	6.4
Bangladesh	7	2	418	81	6.9	1.93	6.5	11.2	65.9	5.9	..
Belarus	3	5	..	..	3.1	37.17	13.7	3.5	45.7	0.1	..
Belgium	7	4	..	..	48.0	86.37	5.0	2.8	117.1	..	8.9
Benin	6	1	..	..	..	..	..	..	18.1	..	..
Bolivia	1	6	..	..	..	..	8.4	2.2	49.4	8.9	9.8
Bosnia and Herzegovina	5	5	914	251	30.9	34.47	17.6	11.4	67.2	4.7	..
Botswana	7	4	496	238	8.6	..	..	..	9.4	5.9	..
Brazil	3	5	..	194	13.8	120.62	11.1	3.1	97.8	31.1	29.1
Bulgaria	8	6	1,958	421	91.2	80.53	10.5	11.9	71.0	7.1	8.6
Burkina Faso	6	1	..	..	..	..	..	..	16.4	..	..
Burundi	3	1	..	..	..	..	..	..	40.1	..	..
Cambodia	8	0	108	29	4.0	5.07	..	..	22.7	..	..
Cameroon	6	2	72	17	1.4	1.40	..	..	9.0	..	..
Canada	7	6	..	..	24.3	220.02	4.7	1.2	177.6	2.6	2.0
Central African Republic	6	2	3	1	0.6	..	..	..	18.8	..	..
Chad	6	2	24	3	0.6	0.36	..	..	9.3	..	..
Chile	6	5	2,134	310	17.6	62.51	8.3	2.7	90.3	3.0	..
China	6	4	..	..	..	..	6.1	1.1	146.4	3.1	..
Hong Kong SAR, China	10	5	..	..	23.6	..	12.3	0.8	199.0	5.0	4.7
Colombia	5	5	..	..	..	..	14.3	2.9	65.7	5.7	..
Congo, Dem. Rep.	3	0	..	..	..	..	..	..	1.0	39.7	..
Congo, Rep.	6	2	20	3	2.4	1.23	..	..	−16.4	..	..
Costa Rica	3	5	..	..	19.2	..	14.4	1.9	51.3	11.8	..
Côte d'Ivoire	6	1	..	..	..	..	..	..	25.1	..	..
Croatia	6	5	..	..	..	100.86	13.9	11.2	82.2	8.6	..
Cuba	..	..	..	..	..	..	..	..	..	..	..
Cyprus	9	0	..	..	151.5	87.58	5.9	5.6	315.8	..	..
Czech Republic	6	5	..	..	22.5	41.65	6.5	6.2	64.7	4.8	5.0
Denmark	9	4	..	..	41.1	63.55	5.5	4.1	215.3	..	..
Dominican Republic	3	6	..	..	..	..	9.3	2.9	39.6	7.3	..
Ecuador	3	6	..	..	..	..	8.9	3.5	26.4	..	..
Egypt, Arab Rep.	3	6	..	..	..	..	6.2	11.0	69.4	4.8	1.7
El Salvador	5	6	..	..	..	..	13.9	3.9	45.1	..	..
Eritrea	2	0	..	..	..	..	..	..	114.4	..	..
Estonia	7	5	1,993	542	19.3	88.09	9.3	5.4	97.6	6.7	..
Ethiopia	4	2	107	2	1.8	0.31	..	..	37.1	3.3	7.3
Finland	8	4	..	..	15.6	91.72	5.5	0.6	100.8	..	..
France	7	4	..	..	43.1	110.07	4.4	4.2	134.4	..	..
Gabon	6	2	95	46	4.7	8.62	11.3	9.9	10.2	..	..
Gambia, The	5	0	..	..	..	..	..	..	45.4	12.4	..
Georgia	8	6	697	377	18.6	42.34	16.9	12.5	33.8	15.0	14.7
Germany	7	6	..	..	17.6	116.80	4.3	3.3	132.0	..	..
Ghana	8	3	324	33	5.0	..	7.9	17.6	28.3	..	..
Greece	4	5	..	..	41.2	78.24	6.9	10.4	145.5	..	..
Guatemala	8	6	..	..	36.5	..	10.3	2.1	38.5	7.9	..
Guinea	6	0	..	..	..	..	..	..	..	..	..
Guinea-Bissau	6	1	..	..	..	..	..	..	7.7	..	..
Haiti	3	2	339	12	2.8	..	..	..	19.9	16.7	..

Financial access, stability, and efficiency

	Getting credit		Financial access and outreach				Bank capital to asset ratio	Ratio of bank nonperforming loans to total gross loans	Domestic credit provided by banking sector	Interest rate spread	Risk premium on lending
	Strength of legal rights index 0–10 (weak to strong)	Depth of credit information index 0–6 (low to high)	per 1,000 adults Depositors with commercial banks	Borrowers from commercial banks	per 100,000 adults Commercial bank branches	Automated teller machines	%	%	% of GDP	Lending rate minus deposit rate percentage points	Prime lending rate minus treasury bill rate percentage points
	June 2011	June 2011	2010	2010	2010	2010	2010	2010	2010	2010	2010
Honduras	8	6	..	..	..	..	..	..	52.3	9.0	..
Hungary	7	4	1,072	..	16.6	56.73	9.8	9.7	81.7	2.7	2.2
India	8	4	747	137	10.9	..	7.1	2.4	71.1	..	..
Indonesia	3	4	..	275	8.3	13.37	11.4	2.6	36.5	6.2	..
Iran, Islamic Rep.	4	4	..	..	26.6	30.95	..	..	37.2	0.1	..
Iraq	3	0	..	..	4.2	1.09	..	..	–2.1	8.3	8.0
Ireland	9	5	..	..	28.6	92.47	4.4	8.6	233.2	..	..
Israel	9	5	..	927	19.9	102.35	6.8	1.4	85.7	2.9	2.3
Italy	3	5	1,307	480	66.9	98.56	9.3	7.8	154.6	..	2.9
Jamaica	8	0	..	..	6.7	25.98	..	..	48.1	14.1	11.2
Japan	7	6	7,169	171	34.0	132.96	4.8	1.8	326.6	1.1	1.5
Jordan	4	2	..	..	18.1	..	10.5	7.9	96.0	5.5	..
Kazakhstan	4	5	874	..	3.3	62.75	10.9	23.8	45.4	..	..
Kenya	10	4	370	73	4.4	7.27	13.2	6.3	51.0	9.8	10.8
Korea, Dem. Rep.	..	..									
Korea, Rep.	8	6	4,522	..	18.6	250.29	7.6	1.9	103.2	1.7	..
Kosovo	8	5	770	54	17.5	22.86	..	4.4	17.8	10.9	..
Kuwait	4	4	..	..	..	..	12.6	8.9	84.0	2.6	4.3
Kyrgyz Republic	10	4	181	26	6.2	7.45	..	..		27.4	27.0
Lao PDR	4	0	44	4	2.6	4.33	..	..	26.1	19.6	14.6
Latvia	10	5	1,286	273	31.7	69.98	7.3	19.0	89.6	7.7	7.1
Lebanon	4	5	873	276	29.7	38.25	7.3	4.3	164.4	2.1	4.2
Lesotho	6	0	291	39	3.5	7.28	8.4	3.7	–6.2	7.5	5.0
Liberia	7	1	..	..	..	..	..	..	148.9	10.1	..
Libya	..	..	..	..	10.5	3.61	..	..	–65.9	3.5	..
Lithuania	5	6	..	..	27.3	55.29	8.9	19.7	64.6	3.6	–0.1
Macedonia, FYR	7	6	..	291	26.6	51.88	10.6	9.0	48.2	2.4	..
Madagascar	2	0	45	18	1.6	1.49	..	..	10.5	38.5	39.7
Malawi	7	0	..	..	..	..	..	..	28.4	21.0	17.5
Malaysia	10	6	1,458	280	10.4	46.38	9.1	3.4	132.2	2.5	2.4
Mali	6	1	..	..	..	..	..	..	12.5	..	..
Mauritania	3	1	..	32	4.3	..	..	..	52.9	9.0	8.5
Mauritius	6	3	465	2,168	23.0	1,009.32	7.3	2.8	110.8	0.5	..
Mexico	6	6	1,205	344	15.2	47.28	10.4	2.0	45.0	4.1	0.9
Moldova	8	4	1,197	38	10.3	143.38	16.0	13.3	37.2	8.7	9.2
Mongolia	6	4	1,339	706	53.6	..	..	..	29.9	8.2	..
Morocco	3	5	694	..	21.0	..	8.4	4.4	106.0	..	..
Mozambique	2	4	..	..	3.4	5.70	8.0	1.9	24.1	6.6	4.3
Myanmar	..	..	..	..	..	..	..	..	25.1	5.0	..
Namibia	8	5	624	213	7.6	30.49	8.4	2.0	48.4	4.7	3.3
Nepal	7	3	..	..	..	..	..	..	68.6	4.4	1.2
Netherlands	6	5	1,769	832	23.2	58.27	4.4	2.8	212.1	–0.6	..
New Zealand	10	5	..	..	34.7	72.75	..	..	157.8	1.7	3.5
Nicaragua	3	5	..	..	..	..	..	..	63.4	10.3	..
Niger	6	1	..	..	..	..	..	..	12.8	..	..
Nigeria	9	0	..	..	..	..	3.2	17.2	36.3	11.1	13.7
Norway	7	4	529	..	7.6	56.07	6.4	1.5	..	2.0	..
Oman	4	4	1,012	401	22.9	..	13.5	3.3	41.3	3.5	..
Pakistan	6	4	249	28	8.8	4.40	9.8	14.7	46.3	5.9	1.5
Panama	5	6	..	..	..	..	12.5	1.1	88.0	4.7	..
Papua New Guinea	5	3	178	23	1.8	5.25	..	..	35.7	9.1	5.8
Paraguay	3	6	..	..	..	..	9.4	1.3	32.5	24.8	..
Peru	7	6	436	139	49.5	25.21	9.5	2.6	18.0	17.4	..
Philippines	4	3	488	..	7.7	14.88	11.7	3.8	49.2	4.5	4.2
Poland	9	5	..	..	45.8	52.10	9.1	8.8	63.6	..	..
Portugal	3	4	2,806	413	75.9	197.05	6.4	3.3	209.2	..	..
Puerto Rico	8	5	..	..	..	..	..	..	..	..	..
Qatar	4	4	770	315	23.4	67.00	..	..	75.7	4.4	..

	Getting credit		Financial access and outreach				Bank capital to asset ratio	Ratio of bank nonperforming loans to total gross loans	Domestic credit provided by banking sector	Interest rate spread	Risk premium on lending
	Strength of legal rights index 0–10 (weak to strong)	Depth of credit information index 0–6 (low to high)	per 1,000 adults Depositors with commercial banks	Borrowers from commercial banks	per 100,000 adults Commercial bank branches	Automated teller machines	%	%	% of GDP	Lending rate minus deposit rate percentage points	Prime lending rate minus treasury bill rate percentage points
	June 2011	June 2011	2010	2010	2010	2010	2010	2010	2010	2010	2010
Romania	9	5	..	222	33.2	55.48	8.9	11.9	54.9	6.8	6.9
Russian Federation	3	5	..	..	..	76.58	14.0	8.2	38.6	4.8	..
Rwanda	8	6	218	29	2.2	0.81	11.4	10.8	..	9.6	9.2
Saudi Arabia	5	6	780	181	9.0	57.97	12.6	3.0	−0.2	..	..
Senegal	6	1	..	..	..	..	10.0	20.2	29.0	..	..
Serbia	8	5	..	186	10.2	47.43	19.7	16.9	57.8	6.0	3.1
Sierra Leone	7	0	190	12	2.9	0.43	17.5	15.6	18.4	12.3	4.0
Singapore	10	4	2,134	968	10.3	58.57	9.6	1.8	85.7	5.2	5.0
Slovak Republic	9	4	..	..	26.5	50.38	9.7	5.8	54.0	2.0	..
Slovenia	4	4	..	..	39.5	103.04	8.2	3.6	97.4	4.5	4.8
Somalia	..	..	..	..	..	..	..	..	..	..	..
South Africa	10	6	978	415	10.1	59.58	7.0	5.8	182.2	3.4	3.4
South Sudan	..	..	..	..	..	..	..	..	..	..	..
Spain	6	5	775	337	38.3	153.63	6.2	4.6	231.4	..	..
Sri Lanka	4	5	..	..	..	..	..	..	40.5	3.3	1.7
Sudan	4	0	..	..	..	..	..	..	20.5	..	..
Swaziland	6	5	455	185	5.7	21.43	12.2	8.0	17.2	5.9	3.1
Sweden	7	4	..	..	..	..	5.0	2.0	143.5	..	..
Switzerland	8	5	..	..	52.8	97.47	5.4	0.4	191.1	2.7	2.7
Syrian Arab Republic	1	2	220	67	3.8	7.35	..	..	47.7	3.7	..
Tajikistan	2	0	..	..	..	..	..	..	..	18.0	..
Tanzania	8	0	131	30	1.8	3.30	..	..	21.1	8.0	10.7
Thailand	5	5	1,120	237	11.2	77.69	11.3	3.9	135.5	4.9	4.5
Timor-Leste	2	3	..	..	..	..	..	..	−31.6	10.2	..
Togo	6	1	181	0	3.7	..	..	..	31.9	..	..
Trinidad and Tobago	8	4	..	..	..	..	..	..	32.4	7.8	8.4
Tunisia	3	5	..	148	16.6	20.84	..	12.1	73.7	..	..
Turkey	4	5	1,265	719	17.4	43.74	13.4	3.8	69.3	..	..
Turkmenistan	..	..	..	..	..	..	..	..	..	..	..
Uganda	7	4	192	18	2.5	3.58	13.9	2.1	17.1	12.5	15.2
Ukraine	9	4	3,220	..	2.3	76.13	14.6	15.3	78.6	5.3	..
United Arab Emirates	4	5	..	..	21.7	96.81	17.7	5.6	92.3	..	..
United Kingdom	10	6	..	..	25.5	64.58	5.4	4.0	222.6	..	0.0
United States	9	6	..	..	35.7	173.75	11.1	4.9	231.4	..	3.1
Uruguay	4	6	538	426	13.5	30.38	9.5	1.0	32.4	6.2	1.3
Uzbekistan	2	3	957	37	47.5	2.52	..	..	..	..	..
Venezuela, RB	1	0	..	..	..	..	9.9	3.4	22.6	3.5	..
Vietnam	8	5	..	..	3.3	17.64	..	..	135.8	1.9	2.0
West Bank and Gaza	1	3	543	68	10.3	13.68	..	..	..	..	..
Yemen, Rep.	3	2	101	2	2.0	2.75	..	..	19.3	5.2	2.9
Zambia	9	5	..	..	..	..	..	..	18.9	13.5	14.6
Zimbabwe	7	0	..	..	..	..	..	..	..	..	..
World	**5.9 u**	**3.2 u**	**.. w**	**.. w**	**13.7 w**	**44.00 w**	**9.4 m**	**4.0 m**	**167.9 w**	**6.2 m**	
Low income	5.8	1.3	..	..	..	..	..	..	37.2	11.4	
Middle income	5.5	3.3	..	167	12.2	29.02	10.2	3.9	90.8	6.3	
Lower middle income	5.3	2.8	..	..	5.6	9.77	..	..	57.1	8.7	
Upper middle income	5.7	3.7	..	238	16.6	47.36	10.4	3.7	100.5	5.8	
Low & middle income	5.6	2.8	..	..	8.1	18.23	..	3.9	90.0	7.3	
East Asia & Pacific	6.2	2.0	..	221	7.4	14.09	..	..	131.8	6.9	
Europe & Central Asia	6.5	4.7	894	212	18.1	44.89	13.6	12.2	50.8	6.9	
Latin America & Carib.	5.3	3.4	..	..	..	..	10.1	2.4	66.7	7.3	
Middle East & N. Africa	2.8	3.2	443	66	10.9	6.84	..	..	51.9	5.0	
South Asia	5.6	2.8	249	28	7.8	1.93	7.3	10.5	67.4	5.9	
Sub-Saharan Africa	5.8	1.8	167	27	2.7	..	..	..	81.6	9.7	
High income	6.9	4.3	..	..	23.9	90.08	6.8	4.1	205.6	..	
Euro area	6.4	4.1	..	..	24.9	91.72	6.2	4.4	156.1	..	

About the data

Access to finance can expand opportunities for all with higher levels of access and use of banking services associated with lower financing obstacles for people and businesses. A stable financial system that promotes efficient savings and investment is also crucial for a thriving democracy and market economy.

There are several aspects of access to financial services: availability, cost, and quality of services. The development and growth of credit markets depend on access to timely, reliable, and accurate data on borrowers' credit experiences. Access to credit can be improved by making it easy to create and enforce collateral agreements and by increasing information about potential borrowers' creditworthiness. Lenders look at a borrower's credit history and collateral. Where credit registries and effective collateral laws are absent—as in many developing countries—banks make fewer loans. Indicators that cover getting credit include the strength of legal rights index and the depth of credit information index.

The "unbanked" have to resort to informal services to manage their money—saving under the mattress, borrowing from family and friends, or using money lenders—that are usually less reliable and more costly than formal banking institutions. The table presents data on financial access covering depositors and borrowers and on outreach indicators such as the number of branches and automated teller machines. Data for these financial access and outreach indicators are from the International Monetary Fund's (IMF) Financial Access Survey database; this sources differs from that in the 2011 edition.

The size and mobility of international capital flows make it increasingly important to monitor the strength of financial systems. Robust financial systems can increase economic activity and welfare, but instability can disrupt financial activity and impose widespread costs on the economy. The ratio of bank capital to assets, a measure of bank solvency and resiliency, shows the extent to which banks can deal with unexpected losses. Capital includes tier 1 capital (paid-up shares and common stock), a common feature in all countries' banking systems, and total regulatory capital, which includes several types of subordinated debt instruments that need not be repaid if the funds are required to maintain minimum capital levels (tier 2 and tier 3 capital). Total assets include all nonfinancial and financial assets. Data are from internally consistent financial statements.

The ratio of bank nonperforming loans to total gross loans measures bank health and efficiency by identifying problems with asset quality in the loan portfolio. A high ratio may signal deterioration of the credit portfolio. International guidelines recommend that loans be classified as nonperforming when payments of principal and interest are 90 days or more past due or when future payments are not expected to be received in full.

Domestic credit provided by the banking sector as a share of GDP measures banking sector depth and financial sector development in terms of size. In a few countries governments may hold international reserves as deposits in the banking system rather than in the central bank. Since claims on the central government are a net item (claims on the central government minus central government deposits), the figure may be negative, resulting in a negative figure for domestic credit provided by the banking sector.

The interest rate spread—the margin between the cost of mobilizing liabilities and the earnings on assets—measures financial sector efficiency in intermediation. A narrow spread means low transaction costs, which reduces the cost of funds for investment, crucial to economic growth.

The risk premium on lending is the spread between the lending rate to the private sector and the "risk-free" government rate. Spreads are expressed as an annual average. A small spread indicates that the market considers its best corporate customers to be low risk; a negative value indicates that the market considers its best corporate clients to be lower risk than the government.

Definitions

• **Strength of legal rights index** measures the degree to which collateral and bankruptcy laws protect the rights of borrowers and lenders and thus facilitate lending. Higher values indicate that the laws are better designed to expand access to credit. • **Depth of credit information index** measures rules affecting the scope, accessibility, and quality of information available through public or private credit registries. Higher values indicate the availability of more credit information. • **Depositors with commercial banks** are deposit account holders at commercial banks and other resident banks functioning as commercial banks that are resident nonfinancial corporations (public and private) and households. For many countries data cover the total number of deposit accounts due to lack of information on account holders. The major types of deposits are checking accounts, savings accounts, and time deposits. • **Borrowers from commercial banks** are resident customers that are nonfinancial corporations (public and private) and households that obtained loans from commercial banks and other banks functioning as commercial banks. For many countries data cover the total number of loan accounts due to lack of information on loan account holders. • **Commercial bank branches** are retail locations of resident commercial banks and other resident banks that function as commercial banks that provide financial services to customers and are physically separated from the main office but not legally separated subsidiaries. • **Automated teller machines** are computerized telecommunications devices that provide clients of a financial institution access to financial transactions in a public place. • **Bank capital to asset ratio** is the ratio of bank capital and reserves to total assets. Capital and reserves include funds contributed by owners, retained earnings, general and special reserves, provisions, and valuation adjustments. • **Ratio of bank nonperforming loans to total gross loans** is the value of nonperforming loans (gross value of the loan as recorded on the balance sheet) divided by the total value of the loan portfolio (including nonperforming loans before the deduction of loan loss provisions). • **Domestic credit provided by banking sector** is all credit to various sectors on a gross basis, except to the central government, which is net. The banking sector includes monetary authorities, deposit money banks, and other banking institutions for which data are available. • **Interest rate spread** is the interest rate charged by banks on loans to prime customers minus the interest rate paid by commercial or similar banks for demand, time, or savings deposits. • **Risk premium on lending** is the interest rate charged by banks on loans to prime private sector customers minus the "risk-free" treasury bill interest rate at which short-term government securities are issued or traded in the market.

Data sources

Data on getting credit are from the World Bank's Doing Business project (www.doingbusiness. org). Data on financial access and outreach are from the IMF's Financial Access Survey database (http://fas.imf.org). Data on bank capital and nonperforming loans are from the IMF's Financial Soundness Indicators database (http://fsi.imf. org). Data on credit and interest rates are from the IMF's *International Financial Statistics*.

5.6 Tax policies

	Tax revenue collected by central government		Taxes payable by businesses						
	% of GDP		Number of payments	Time to prepare, file, and pay taxes hours	Profit tax	% of commercial profits			Total tax rate
						Labor tax and contributions	Other taxes		
	2005	2010	June 2011	June 2011	June 2011	June 2011	June 2011		June 2011
Afghanistan	6.3	8.3	8	275	0.0	0.0	36.4		36.4
Albania	17.3	..	44	371	8.7	25.0	4.8		38.5
Algeria	40.7[a]	34.9[a]	29	451	6.6	29.7	35.7		72.0
Angola	..	..	31	282	24.6	9.0	19.5		53.2
Argentina	14.2[a]	..	9	415	2.8	29.4	76.1		108.2
Armenia	14.3	16.9	34	500	16.8	23.0	1.1		40.9
Australia	24.7[a]	22.1[a]	11	109	26.0	20.4	1.3		47.7
Austria	20.1[a]	18.7[a]	14	170	15.0	34.8	3.4		53.1
Azerbaijan	..	15.9	18	225	12.9	24.8	2.2		40.0
Bahrain	1.4[a]	..	25	36	0.0	14.7	0.4		15.0
Bangladesh	8.2	8.6	21	302	25.7	0.0	9.2		35.0
Belarus	20.1	17.1	18	654	20.2	39.0	3.5		62.8
Belgium	26.0[a]	24.6[a]	11	156	5.2	50.4	1.7		57.3
Benin	15.5[a]	16.2[a]	55	270	14.8	27.3	23.9		66.0
Bolivia	16.2[a]	..	42	1,080	0.0	15.5	64.6		80.0
Bosnia and Herzegovina	20.7[a]	20.4[a]	40	422	7.1	12.6	5.3		25.0
Botswana	..	..	19	152	15.9	0.0	3.6		19.4
Brazil	16.7	15.6	9	2,600	22.4	40.9	3.8		67.1
Bulgaria	21.6	21.0	17	500	4.9	19.2	4.1		28.1
Burkina Faso	11.8[a]	13.0[a]	46	270	14.8	22.6	6.2		43.6
Burundi	..	..	24	274	37.4	7.8	1.0		46.2
Cambodia	7.9[a]	10.1[a]	39	173	18.9	0.1	3.5		22.5
Cameroon	..	..	44	654	29.9	18.3	0.9		49.1
Canada	13.7[a]	11.9[a]	8	131	9.3	12.6	6.8		28.8
Central African Republic	6.2	..	54	504	0.0	19.8	34.8		54.6
Chad	..	..	54	732	31.3	28.4	5.7		65.4
Chile	18.7[a]	17.8[a]	9	316	18.0	3.8	3.2		25.0
China	8.7	10.5	7	398	5.9	49.6	7.9		63.5
Hong Kong SAR, China	12.7[a]	12.8[a]	3	80	17.6	5.3	0.1		23.0
Colombia	12.8[a]	11.5[a]	9	193	18.9	28.8	27.1		74.8
Congo, Dem. Rep.	10.0	13.7	32	336	58.9	7.9	272.8		339.7
Congo, Rep.	6.2	..	61	606	18.1	32.5	15.4		65.9
Costa Rica	..	13.9[a]	31	246	18.9	29.5	6.6		55.0
Côte d'Ivoire	9.8[a]	16.6[a]	62	270	8.8	20.1	15.4		44.3
Croatia	20.0	18.8	17	196	11.5	19.4	1.5		32.3
Cuba	..	..	..	..	..	..	..		..
Cyprus	45.4[a]	25.8[a]	27	149	9.1	11.8	2.2		23.1
Czech Republic	15.6	13.9	8	557	7.5	38.4	3.2		49.1
Denmark	32.6[a]	34.3[a]	10	135	20.1	3.6	3.8		27.5
Dominican Republic	14.6[a]	13.1[a]	9	324	21.3	18.6	1.8		41.7
Ecuador	..	..	8	654	18.4	14.2	2.7		35.3
Egypt, Arab Rep.	14.1	14.1	29	433	13.0	27.1	3.6		43.6
El Salvador	12.5[a]	13.7[a]	53	320	16.5	17.2	1.3		35.0
Eritrea	..	..	18	216	8.8	0.0	75.8		84.5
Estonia	16.1[a]	17.4[a]	8	85	8.0	39.4	11.2		58.6
Ethiopia	8.8	..	19	198	26.8	0.0	4.3		31.1
Finland	22.6[a]	21.2[a]	8	93	13.7	24.2	1.2		39.0
France	22.4[a]	19.8[a]	7	132	8.2	51.7	5.7		65.7
Gabon	..	..	26	488	18.4	22.7	2.3		43.5
Gambia, The	..	..	50	376	6.1	12.8	264.6		283.5
Georgia	12.1	22.1	4	387	14.3	0.0	2.2		16.5
Germany	11.1[a]	12.2[a]	12	221	19.0	21.8	5.9		46.7
Ghana	21.3	12.6	33	224	18.4	14.7	0.5		33.6
Greece	20.3[a]	19.6[a]	10	224	13.4	31.7	1.4		46.4
Guatemala	11.2	10.3	24	344	25.9	14.3	0.7		40.9
Guinea	..	..	56	416	20.9	22.8	10.6		54.3
Guinea-Bissau	..	..	46	208	14.9	24.8	6.1		45.9
Haiti	..	..	46	184	24.1	12.4	4.3		40.8

	Tax revenue collected by central government		Taxes payable by businesses					
	% of GDP		Number of payments	Time to prepare, file, and pay taxes hours	Profit tax	Labor tax and contributions	Other taxes	Total tax rate
						% of commercial profits		
	2005	2010	June 2011	June 2011	June 2011	June 2011	June 2011	June 2011
Honduras	14.5[a]	14.8[a]	47	224	24.7	10.7	8.6	44.0
Hungary	20.3[a]	23.9[a]	13	277	14.8	34.1	3.5	52.4
India	9.9	9.5	33	254	24.7	18.2	19.0	61.8
Indonesia	12.5	10.9	51	266	23.7	10.6	0.1	34.5
Iran, Islamic Rep.	7.9	9.3	20	344	17.8	25.9	0.4	44.1
Iraq	..	..	13	312	14.9	13.5	0.0	28.4
Ireland	24.9[a]	21.2[a]	8	76	11.9	11.6	2.7	26.3
Israel	26.9[a]	24.3[a]	33	235	22.8	5.3	3.1	31.2
Italy	21.1[a]	22.9[a]	15	285	22.8	43.4	2.2	68.5
Jamaica	25.5[a]	21.0[a]	72	414	25.6	13.0	7.0	45.6
Japan	10.9[a]	8.7[a]	14	330	27.0	16.5	5.7	49.1
Jordan	24.4	15.3	25	116	13.0	12.4	2.3	27.7
Kazakhstan	17.1	8.9	7	188	15.9	11.2	1.6	28.6
Kenya	18.7	19.5	41	393	33.1	6.8	9.7	49.6
Korea, Dem. Rep.	..	..	..	..	..	..	..	..
Korea, Rep.	14.7	15.2	12	225	15.1	13.0	1.5	29.7
Kosovo	..	..	33	164	9.1	5.6	0.6	15.4
Kuwait	1.0	0.9	15	118	4.7	10.7	0.0	15.5
Kyrgyz Republic	14.2	15.6	52	210	6.2	19.5	43.4	69.0
Lao PDR	10.4	12.7	34	362	24.8	5.6	2.9	33.3
Latvia	15.1	12.8	7	290	6.1	27.2	4.7	37.9
Lebanon	14.9[a]	17.1[a]	19	180	6.1	24.1	0.0	30.2
Lesotho	46.6	59.8	21	324	13.1	0.0	3.0	16.0
Liberia	0.2	0.3	33	158	0.0	5.4	38.3	43.7
Libya	..	..	..	..	..	..	..	..
Lithuania	17.3[a]	13.4[a]	11	175	5.7	35.1	3.1	43.9
Macedonia, FYR	19.3	19.1	28	119	6.3	0.0	3.4	9.7
Madagascar	10.1[a]	13.0[a]	23	201	14.7	20.3	1.6	36.6
Malawi	..	..	19	157	23.6	1.1	3.5	28.2
Malaysia	15.4	14.3	13	133	17.0	15.6	1.4	34.0
Mali	15.7[a]	14.7[a]	59	270	10.8	34.3	6.6	51.8
Mauritania	..	..	37	696	0.0	17.6	50.7	68.3
Mauritius	..	18.5[a]	7	161	11.6	6.1	7.3	25.0
Mexico	..	..	6	347	24.5	26.8	1.4	52.7
Moldova	18.5	18.2	48	228	0.0	30.6	0.7	31.3
Mongolia	28.7	22.7	41	192	10.2	12.4	2.0	24.6
Morocco	22.0[a]	23.4[a]	17	238	25.2	22.7	1.8	49.6
Mozambique	..	..	37	230	27.7	4.5	2.1	34.3
Myanmar	3.9	..	..	..	..	..	..	..
Namibia	25.8	..	37	375	4.0	1.0	4.8	9.8
Nepal	9.2	13.3	34	326	17.2	11.3	3.0	31.5
Netherlands	22.6[a]	22.6[a]	9	127	20.9	18.1	1.5	40.5
New Zealand	30.8[b]	..	8	172	29.9	2.9	1.7	34.4
Nicaragua	16.7	18.3	42	207	24.5	20.3	22.0	66.8
Niger	10.1[b]	..	41	270	17.3	20.1	6.3	43.8
Nigeria	0.2	0.3	35	938	22.3	9.7	0.7	32.7
Norway	28.7[a]	26.9[a]	4	87	24.4	15.9	1.3	41.6
Oman	..	..	14	62	10.0	11.8	0.1	22.0
Pakistan	9.6	10.0	47	560	17.9	15.1	2.3	35.3
Panama	..	..	53	482	13.7	21.7	9.7	45.2
Papua New Guinea	..	..	33	194	22.0	11.7	8.6	42.3
Paraguay	11.8	13.1	35	387	9.6	18.6	6.7	35.0
Peru	13.5	14.5	9	309	26.6	11.0	3.1	40.7
Philippines	12.4	12.1	47	195	21.0	11.3	14.2	46.5
Poland	16.7[a]	16.3[a]	29	296	17.4	23.6	2.6	43.6
Portugal	20.6[a]	19.6[a]	8	275	15.1	26.8	1.5	43.3
Puerto Rico	..	..	16	218	28.3	14.4	20.5	63.1
Qatar	21.0	19.8	3	36	0.0	11.3	0.0	11.3

	Tax revenue collected by central government		Taxes payable by businesses					
	% of GDP		Number of payments	Time to prepare, file, and pay taxes hours	Profit tax	% of commercial profits		Total tax rate
						Labor tax and contributions	Other taxes	
	2005	2010	June 2011	June 2011	June 2011	June 2011	June 2011	June 2011
Romania	12.2[a]	17.9[a]	113	222	10.4	31.8	2.2	44.4
Russian Federation	16.6[a]	13.4[a]	9	290	8.9	32.1	5.8	46.9
Rwanda	..	..	18	148	21.2	5.7	4.4	31.3
Saudi Arabia	..	..	14	79	2.1	12.4	0.0	14.5
Senegal	..	..	59	666	14.8	24.1	7.0	46.0
Serbia	23.6	22.0	66	279	11.6	20.2	2.2	34.0
Sierra Leone	10.8	11.0	29	357	17.6	11.3	3.3	32.1
Singapore	11.8	13.8	5	84	6.5	15.9	4.7	27.1
Slovak Republic	14.9[a]	12.4[a]	31	231	7.2	39.6	2.0	48.8
Slovenia	20.5	17.1	22	260	14.1	18.2	2.4	34.7
Somalia	..	..	..	..	..	..	..	..
South Africa	26.9[a]	25.5[a]	9	200	24.4	4.1	4.6	33.1
South Sudan	..	..	..	..	..	..	..	..
Spain	12.9[a]	11.2[a]	8	187	1.2	36.7	0.7	38.7
Sri Lanka	13.7	13.3	71	256	26.7	16.9	61.6	105.2
Sudan	..	..	42	180	13.8	19.2	3.1	36.1
Swaziland	26.1	..	33	104	28.1	4.0	4.7	36.8
Sweden	22.6[a]	21.6[a]	4	122	15.7	35.5	1.6	52.8
Switzerland	10.3	10.9	19	63	8.9	17.5	3.6	30.1
Syrian Arab Republic	..	..	19	336	20.0	19.3	0.5	39.7
Tajikistan	9.8	..	69	224	0.0	28.5	56.0	84.5
Tanzania	..	..	48	172	20.1	18.0	7.3	45.5
Thailand	17.2[a]	16.0[a]	23	264	28.8	5.7	3.0	37.5
Timor-Leste	..	..	6	276	0.0	0.0	0.2	0.2
Togo	13.9[a]	15.8[a]	53	270	9.3	26.5	13.7	49.5
Trinidad and Tobago	26.4	26.2	39	210	21.6	5.8	1.8	29.1
Tunisia	18.9	20.1	8	144	15.2	25.2	22.5	62.9
Turkey	19.7[a]	20.5[a]	15	223	17.9	18.8	4.4	41.1
Turkmenistan	..	..	..	..	..	..	..	..
Uganda	11.8	12.2	32	213	23.3	11.3	1.1	35.7
Ukraine	17.1	16.4	135	657	12.2	43.3	1.6	57.1
United Arab Emirates	..	..	14	12	0.0	14.1	0.0	14.1
United Kingdom	27.2[a]	26.0[a]	8	110	23.1	11.0	3.2	37.3
United States	11.2[a]	9.3[a]	11	187	27.6	10.0	9.1	46.7
Uruguay	17.9	19.5	53	336	23.6	15.6	2.9	42.0
Uzbekistan	..	..	41	205	1.1	28.2	68.1	97.5
Venezuela, RB	15.5	..	70	864	6.9	18.0	38.5	63.5
Vietnam	..	..	32	941	17.2	22.6	0.3	40.1
West Bank and Gaza	..	..	27	154	16.2	0.0	0.6	16.8
Yemen, Rep.	..	..	44	248	20.0	11.3	1.5	32.9
Zambia	17.2	16.6	37	132	1.5	10.4	2.5	14.5
Zimbabwe	..	..	49	242	20.3	5.1	10.1	35.6
World	**15.4 w**	*13.5 w*	**29 u**	**277 u**	**16.0 u**	**16.2 u**	**12.6 u**	**44.8 u**
Low income	10.7	11.8	38	271	18.7	13.0	36.1	67.8
Middle income	12.9	13.0	32	327	16.5	15.5	9.2	41.1
Lower middle income	11.1	10.9	36	324	16.0	13.7	10.7	40.4
Upper middle income	13.5	13.4	26	330	17.0	17.3	7.5	41.9
Low & middle income	12.8	13.0	33	314	17.0	14.9	15.5	47.4
East Asia & Pacific	10.0	11.0	27	232	17.9	10.5	7.9	36.2
Europe & Central Asia	16.5	15.5	39	314	9.2	22.2	10.2	41.6
Latin America & Carib.	..	..	33	404	20.2	15.2	12.4	47.8
Middle East & N. Africa	18.7	17.5	24	253	15.5	19.1	6.0	40.6
South Asia	9.9	9.5	28	281	18.6	7.7	18.2	44.4
Sub-Saharan Africa	17.5	..	37	314	18.5	13.2	25.6	57.3
High income	16.0	13.6	15	169	13.0	20.2	4.2	37.4
Euro area	18.1	17.2	14	171	11.8	29.7	3.0	44.5

Note: Regional aggregates differ from those reported on the Doing Business website because the regional aggregates reported on the Doing Business website include developed countries.
a. Data were reported on a cash basis and have been adjusted to the accrual framework of the International Monetary Fund's *Government Finance Statistics Manual 2001*.

About the data

Taxes are the main source of revenue for most governments. The sources of tax revenue and their relative contributions are determined by government policy choices about where and how to impose taxes and by changes in the structure of the economy. Tax policy may reflect concerns about distributional effects, economic efficiency (including corrections for externalities), and the practical problems of administering a tax system. There is no ideal level of taxation. But taxes influence incentives and thus the behavior of economic actors and the economy's competitiveness.

The level of taxation is typically measured by tax revenue as a share of gross domestic product (GDP). Comparing levels of taxation across countries provides a quick overview of the fiscal obligations and incentives facing the private sector. The table shows only central government data, which may significantly understate the total tax burden, particularly in countries where provincial and municipal governments are large or have considerable tax authority.

Low ratios of tax revenue to GDP may reflect weak administration and large-scale tax avoidance or evasion. Low ratios may also reflect a sizable parallel economy with unrecorded and undisclosed incomes. Tax revenue ratios tend to rise with income, with higher income countries relying on taxes to finance a much broader range of social services and social security than lower income countries are able to.

The total tax rate payable by businesses provides a comprehensive measure of the cost of all the taxes a business bears. It differs from the statutory tax rate, which is the factor applied to the tax base. In computing business tax rates, actual tax payable is divided by commercial profit.

The indicators covering taxes payable by businesses measure all taxes and contributions that are government mandated (at any level—federal, state, or local), apply to standardized businesses, and have an impact in their income statements. The taxes covered go beyond the definition of a tax for government national accounts (compulsory, unrequited payments to general government) and also measure any imposts that affect business accounts. The main differences are in labor contributions and value added taxes. The indicators account for government-mandated contributions paid by the employer to a requited private pension fund or workers insurance fund but exclude value added taxes because they do not affect the accounting profits of the business—that is, they are not reflected in the income statement.

To make the data comparable across countries, several assumptions are made about businesses. The main assumptions are that they are limited liability companies, they operate in the country's most populous city, they are domestically owned, they perform general industrial or commercial activities, and they have certain levels of start-up capital, employees, and turnover. For details about the assumptions, see the World Bank's *Doing Business 2012.*

The Doing Business methodology on business taxes is consistent with the Total Tax Contribution framework developed by PwC, which measures the taxes that are borne by companies and that affect their income statements. However, PwC bases its calculation on data from the largest companies in the economy, while Doing Business focuses on a standardized medium-size company.

Definitions

• **Tax revenue collected by central government** is compulsory transfers to the central government for public purposes. Certain compulsory transfers such as fines, penalties, and most social security contributions are excluded. Refunds and corrections of erroneously collected tax revenue are treated as negative revenue. The analytic framework of the International Monetary Fund's (IMF) *Government Finance Statistics Manual 2001* (GFSM 2001) is based on accrual accounting and balance sheets. For countries still reporting government finance data on a cash basis, the IMF adjusts reported data to the GFSM 2001 accrual framework. These countries are footnoted in the table. • **Number of tax payments by businesses** is the total number of taxes paid by businesses during one year. When electronic filing is available, the tax is counted as paid once a year even if payments are more frequent. • **Time to prepare, file, and pay taxes** is the time, in hours per year, it takes to prepare, file, and pay (or withhold) three major types of taxes: the corporate income tax, the value-added or sales tax, and labor taxes, including payroll taxes and social security contributions. • **Profit tax** is the amount of taxes on profits paid by businesses. • **Labor tax and contributions** are the amount of taxes and mandatory contributions on labor paid by businesses. • **Other taxes** are the amounts paid by businesses for property taxes, turnover taxes, and other small taxes such as municipal fees and vehicle and fuel taxes. • **Total tax rate** is the amount of taxes and mandatory contributions payable by businesses in the second year of operation, expressed as a share of commercial profits. Taxes withheld (such as sales or value added tax or personal income tax) but not paid by businesses are excluded. For further details on the method used for assessing the total tax payable, see the World Bank's *Doing Business 2012.*

Data sources

Data on central government tax revenue are from print and electronic editions of the IMF's *Government Finance Statistics Yearbook*. Data on taxes payable by businesses are from *Doing Business 2012* (www.doingbusiness.org).

5.7 Military expenditures and arms transfers

	Military expenditures				Armed forces personnel				Arms transfers			
	% of GDP		% of central government expenditure		thousands		% of labor force		Trend indicator values 1990 $ millions			
									Exports		Imports	
	2005	2010	2005	2010	2005	2010	2005	2010	2005	2010	2005	2010
Afghanistan	1.6	1.8	8.7	4.6	27	307	0.4	3.4	..	..	42	407
Albania	1.3	1.6	6.2	..	23	15	1.6	1.0	..	..	42	13
Algeria	2.9	3.5	13.8	15.0	319	317	3.2	2.8	..	..	155	791
Angola	4.5	4.4	..	..	118	117	1.9	1.6	..	..	40	20
Argentina	0.9	0.9	5.2	..	102	104	0.6	0.6	2	..	3	17
Armenia	2.9	4.5	15.8	19.8	49	56	3.4	3.9	..	..	120	36
Australia	1.9	2.0	7.3	7.3	53	57	0.5	0.5	50	119	467	1,677
Austria	0.9	0.9	2.2	2.2	40	26	1.0	0.6	3	33	22	5
Azerbaijan	2.3	2.9	..	22.5	82	82	2.0	1.8	..	..	45	62
Bahrain	3.6	3.7	17.6	..	21	19	6.2	2.7	..	..	63	71
Bangladesh	1.2	1.2	12.4	10.2	252	221	0.4	0.3	..	..	9	45
Belarus	1.5	1.3	5.0	4.2	183	183	3.9	4.1	24	42	6	3
Belgium	1.1	1.1	2.5	2.5	37	36	0.8	0.7	161	7	0	30
Benin	1.1	1.0	8.1	6.8	8	7	0.3	0.2	..	..	2	0
Bolivia	1.9	1.6	7.2	..	70	83	1.7	1.8	..	..	1	1
Bosnia and Herzegovina	1.6	1.4	4.7	3.4	12	11	0.9	0.7	..	..	..	..
Botswana	2.9	2.7	..	..	11	11	1.2	1.0	..	..	8	10
Brazil	1.5	1.6	6.0	6.3	673	713	0.7	0.7	1	179	223	314
Bulgaria	2.4	1.4	7.6	6.3	85	65	2.5	1.9	66	14	149	17
Burkina Faso	1.2	1.5	10.2	12.4	11	11	0.2	0.2	..	..	19	2
Burundi	6.2	3.8	..	..	82	51	2.3	1.2	..	..	..	2
Cambodia	1.1	1.8	14.8	16.6	191	191	2.8	2.4	..	..	12	28
Cameroon	1.3	1.6	..	..	23	23	0.3	0.3	..	..	5	9
Canada	1.1	1.4	6.3	7.5	71	66	0.4	0.3	226	258	116	373
Central African Republic	1.1	2.6	12.3	..	3	3	0.2	0.2	..	..	9	0
Chad	1.0	3.0	..	..	35	35	0.9	0.8	..	..	9	17
Chile	3.6	3.2	20.0	15.5	116	104	1.7	1.3	..	133	460	434
China	2.1[a]	2.0[a]	15.3[a]	16.1[a]	3,755	2,945	0.5	0.4	303	1,423	3,536	559
Hong Kong SAR, China	..	..	..	..	..	..	..	..	..	..	..	..
Colombia	3.4	3.7	12.7	20.3	336	442	1.7	2.0	..	..	15	172
Congo, Dem. Rep.	2.3	1.4	10.5	10.2	65	159	0.3	0.6	..	..	17	25
Congo, Rep.	1.3	1.1	8.8	..	12	12	0.8	0.7	..	..	4	1
Costa Rica	..	..	..	..	10	10	0.5	0.4	..	0	..	..
Côte d'Ivoire	1.5	1.6	9.0	8.8	19	19	0.3	0.2	..	..	10	..
Croatia	1.6	1.7	4.7	4.6	31	22	1.6	1.1	..	..	8	10
Cuba	3.8	3.2	..	..	76	76	1.6	1.4	..	..	..	..
Cyprus	2.2	2.2	3.1	4.7	11	13	2.1	2.2	..	..	20	..
Czech Republic	2.0	1.3	5.4	3.6	28	29	0.5	0.5	66	3	621	73
Denmark	1.3	1.4	4.1	3.3	21	19	0.7	0.6	9	11	124	16
Dominican Republic	0.8	0.6	5.6	4.4	40	40	1.0	0.9	..	..	2	33
Ecuador	2.6	3.8	..	..	47	59	0.7	0.9	..	..	48	116
Egypt, Arab Rep.	2.9	2.0	10.4	6.9	799	836	3.3	3.1	..	..	641	681
El Salvador	0.6	0.6	3.6	3.0	16	33	0.7	1.3	..	..	9	4
Eritrea	20.9	..	..	..	202	202	9.3	7.8	..	..	69	..
Estonia	1.9	1.7	7.2	6.2	8	6	1.2	0.8	..	..	17	1
Ethiopia	2.8	1.1	18.6	..	183	138	0.5	0.3	..	..	240	..
Finland	1.4	1.5	3.9	3.8	31	25	1.2	0.9	27	34	99	72
France	2.5	2.3	5.4	5.3	359	342	1.2	1.1	1,724	834	60	120
Gabon	1.3	1.0	..	..	7	7	1.4	1.1	..	..	17	17
Gambia, The	0.6	..	..	..	1	1	0.1	0.1	..	..	5	..
Georgia	3.3	3.9	19.3	14.8	23	32	1.0	1.4	17	..	74	34
Germany	1.4	1.4	4.4	4.5	285	251	0.7	0.6	2,080	2,340	195	101
Ghana	0.6	0.4	2.6	2.4	7	16	0.1	0.1	..	..	0	6
Greece	2.9	3.1	6.9	6.3	168	150	3.3	2.8	13	..	389	703
Guatemala	0.4	0.4	2.9	3.1	48	34	1.0	0.6	..	..	..	0
Guinea	2.2	..	..	..	13	19	0.4	0.5	..	..	1	..
Guinea-Bissau	2.1	..	..	..	9	6	1.6	1.0	..	..	..	..
Haiti	..	..	..	..	5	0	0.1	0.0	..	..	..	..

Military expenditures and arms transfers

	Military expenditures				Armed forces personnel				Arms transfers			
	% of GDP		% of central government expenditure		thousands		% of labor force		Trend indicator values 1990 $ millions			
									Exports		Imports	
	2005	2010	2005	2010	2005	2010	2005	2010	2005	2010	2005	2010
Honduras	0.8	1.6	3.9	6.8	20	20	0.8	0.7	..	..	..	0
Hungary	1.4	1.0	3.4	2.5	44	35	1.0	0.8	82	..	13	18
India	2.7	2.4	18.3	16.0	3,047	2,626	0.7	0.6	19	4	1,059	3,337
Indonesia	1.1	1.0	6.9	7.1	582	582	0.5	0.5	8	..	32	198
Iran, Islamic Rep.	3.5	1.9	15.3	8.6	585	563	2.4	2.2	2	5	66	88
Iraq	3.6	6.0	..	..	227	802	3.6	10.6	..	..	165	464
Ireland	0.6	0.6	1.8	1.4	10	10	0.5	0.5	..	4	4	1
Israel	7.6	6.5	16.7	15.7	176	185	6.4	5.8	368	472	1,133	43
Italy	1.9	1.8	4.8	4.1	445	359	1.8	1.4	774	627	150	85
Jamaica	0.5	0.8	1.7	2.3	3	3	0.2	0.2	..	..	13	2
Japan	1.0	1.0	..	..	272	260	0.4	0.4	..	..	375	369
Jordan	4.8	5.2	13.5	20.1	111	111	8.0	7.1	17	88	35	114
Kazakhstan	1.0	0.9	5.7	5.5	101	81	1.3	0.9	12	..	42	57
Kenya	1.7	1.9	9.3	8.3	29	29	0.2	0.2	..	..	8	73
Korea, Dem. Rep.	..	..	..	..	1,295	1,379	9.2	9.5	40	..	5	1
Korea, Rep.	2.6	2.7	13.3	13.7	693	660	2.9	2.7	48	95	796	1,131
Kosovo	..	..	..	..	..	..	..	..	..	..	..	..
Kuwait	4.3	4.0	16.7	10.2	23	23	2.0	1.7	..	..	16	17
Kyrgyz Republic	3.1	3.6	20.0	18.9	18	20	0.8	0.8	92	14	3	..
Lao PDR	0.4	0.3	3.8	2.7	129	129	4.7	4.1	..	..	4	26
Latvia	1.7	1.1	5.9	3.0	5	5	0.4	0.4	..	..	7	15
Lebanon	4.4	4.2	16.7	14.0	85	79	6.5	5.4	..	..	1	60
Lesotho	2.5	2.7	5.9	3.1	2	2	0.2	0.2	..	..	1	..
Liberia	1.5	0.8	..	..	15	2	1.4	0.1	..	..	..	..
Libya	1.5	1.2	..	..	76	76	3.6	3.2	113	28	2	7
Lithuania	1.6	1.3	5.7	3.4	29	25	1.8	1.5	..	..	15	81
Macedonia, FYR	2.1	1.5	7.0	5.8	19	8	2.2	0.8	..	..	0	..
Madagascar	1.1	0.7	9.7	9.3	22	22	0.3	0.2	..	..	..	..
Malawi	1.2	..	..	..	7	5	0.1	0.1	..	..	..	2
Malaysia	2.3	1.5	12.3	7.8	135	134	1.2	1.1	..	0	49	411
Mali	2.3	1.9	15.0	13.3	12	12	0.3	0.3	..	..	13	9
Mauritania	3.1	3.8	..	..	21	21	2.2	1.9	..	..	7	4
Mauritius	0.2	0.2	..	..	2	2	0.4	0.3	..	..	6	..
Mexico	0.4	0.5	..	..	204	332	0.5	0.7	..	..	36	188
Moldova	0.4	0.3	1.4	0.9	10	8	0.7	0.6	18	20	..	..
Mongolia	1.2	0.9	4.9	3.3	16	17	1.5	1.5	..	..	..	13
Morocco	3.4	3.5	11.4	11.4	251	246	2.3	2.2	..	..	87	138
Mozambique	0.9	0.9	..	..	11	11	0.1	0.1	..	..	1	0
Myanmar	..	..	..	..	483	513	1.9	1.8	..	..	65	76
Namibia	2.6	3.3	10.3	..	15	15	1.9	1.6	..	..	72	14
Nepal	1.9	1.5	12.8	..	131	158	0.9	1.0	..	..	5	1
Netherlands	1.5	1.4	3.8	3.4	60	43	0.7	0.5	583	503	96	162
New Zealand	1.0	1.1	3.1	..	9	10	0.4	0.4	0	..	8	71
Nicaragua	0.7	0.7	4.0	3.4	14	12	0.7	0.5	..	..	..	..
Niger	1.0	0.9	10.6	..	10	11	0.2	0.2	..	..	14	1
Nigeria	0.6	1.0	12.1	10.8	161	162	0.4	0.3	..	..	14	189
Norway	1.6	1.6	4.9	4.5	47	24	1.9	0.9	12	141	14	205
Oman	11.8	9.6	..	..	46	47	5.1	3.9	1	..	164	36
Pakistan	4.0	3.2	27.6	18.5	921	946	1.8	1.6	22	..	406	2,580
Panama	..	..	..	..	12	12	0.8	0.7	..	..	..	5
Papua New Guinea	0.6	0.5	..	..	3	3	0.1	0.1	..	..	..	..
Paraguay	0.8	0.9	4.8	5.8	25	25	0.9	0.8	..	..	1	3
Peru	1.5	1.4	8.5	8.3	157	192	1.2	1.2	5	..	368	60
Philippines	0.8	0.8	4.9	4.8	147	166	0.4	0.4	4	..	14	8
Poland	1.9	1.9	5.3	5.1	162	121	0.9	0.7	17	8	95	142
Portugal	2.1	2.2	5.1	4.8	93	90	1.7	1.6	..	0	172	941
Puerto Rico	..	..	..	..	..	..	..	..	..	..	..	..
Qatar	2.5	2.3	12.1	15.4	12	12	2.3	0.9	6	..	11	20

	Military expenditures				Armed forces personnel				Arms transfers			
	% of GDP		% of central government expenditure		thousands		% of labor force		Trend indicator values 1990 $ millions			
									Exports		Imports	
	2005	2010	2005	2010	2005	2010	2005	2010	2005	2010	2005	2010
Romania	2.0	1.4	8.3	4.4	177	154	1.8	1.5	2	4	491	109
Russian Federation	3.7	4.0	18.7	14.1	1,452	1,430	2.0	1.9	5,134	6,039	5	19
Rwanda	1.7	1.4	..	..	53	35	1.2	0.7	..	..	3	13
Saudi Arabia	8.0	10.4	..	..	216	249	2.7	2.6	..	58	150	787
Senegal	1.4	1.6	..	..	19	19	0.4	0.3	..	..	15	4
Serbia	2.5	2.2	6.5	5.5	110	29	2.8	0.8	4	5	..	14
Sierra Leone	1.9	2.3	8.3	11.2	13	11	0.7	0.5	..	..	10	..
Singapore	4.4	3.8	33.9	28.2	167	148	7.4	5.3	3	27	537	1,078
Slovak Republic	1.7	1.1	4.9	3.7	20	16	0.8	0.6	7	8	4	8
Slovenia	1.4	1.6	3.6	3.8	12	12	1.2	1.2	..	..	2	73
Somalia	..	..	..	..	..	2	..	0.1	..	..	..	..
South Africa	1.5	1.2	5.1	4.1	56	77	0.3	0.4	26	80	262	183
South Sudan	..	..	..	..	..	140	..	..	..	..	37	1
Spain	1.0	1.1	4.2	3.6	220	223	1.0	1.0	108	513	339	313
Sri Lanka	2.6	2.8	13.1	19.3	200	223	2.5	2.6	..	..	33	5
Sudan	4.3	..	..	..	123	127	1.0	0.9	..	..	104	14
Swaziland	2.3	3.4	7.0	..	..	..	..	..	..	..	..	..
Sweden	1.5	1.2	..	..	29	21	0.6	0.4	538	806	82	35
Switzerland	0.9	0.9	4.9	4.8	109	25	2.6	0.6	246	137	164	34
Syrian Arab Republic	5.0	3.9	..	..	416	403	8.0	7.4	3	25	7	167
Tajikistan	2.2	..	15.8	..	13	16	0.5	0.6	..	..	13	..
Tanzania	1.0	1.0	..	..	28	28	0.1	0.1	..	..	9	9
Thailand	1.1	1.5	6.7	8.2	421	420	1.1	1.1	8	..	63	83
Timor-Leste	2.5	2.8	..	..	1	1	0.3	0.4	..	..	..	20
Togo	1.6	1.8	9.8	13.0	10	9	0.4	0.3	..	..	..	1
Trinidad and Tobago	..	..	..	..	3	4	0.4	0.6	..	..	6	45
Tunisia	1.5	1.2	5.6	4.5	47	48	1.4	1.2	..	..	168	2
Turkey	2.5	2.4	11.5	9.4	617	613	2.7	2.3	47	31	1,065	468
Turkmenistan	..	..	..	..	26	22	1.3	1.0	..	..	22	29
Uganda	2.4	1.7	14.4	15.3	47	47	0.4	0.3	..	..	9	1
Ukraine	2.8	2.7	7.7	7.0	273	215	1.2	0.9	290	201	..	..
United Arab Emirates	4.2	5.4	..	..	51	51	2.0	1.0	11	37	2,199	493
United Kingdom	2.4	2.6	5.9	5.7	217	174	0.7	0.5	1,039	1,054	27	518
United States	4.0	4.8	18.9	17.9	1,546	1,569	1.0	1.0	6,700	8,641	520	893
Uruguay	1.3	1.5	5.0	5.0	25	25	1.6	1.5	..	..	20	36
Uzbekistan	0.5	..	..	..	91	87	0.9	0.7	4	90	..	..
Venezuela, RB	1.4	0.9	5.6	..	82	115	0.7	0.9	7	40	23	365
Vietnam	1.9	2.2	..	..	495	522	1.1	1.0	12	..	328	515
West Bank and Gaza	..	..	..	..	56	56	7.1	5.7	..	..	2	4
Yemen, Rep.	4.9	4.4	..	..	138	138	2.6	2.1	..	..	306	7
Zambia	2.0	1.7	8.5	10.0	16	17	0.3	0.3	..	..	0	..
Zimbabwe	2.3	1.3	..	..	51	51	0.8	0.8	..	..	25	..
World	**2.5 w**	**2.6 w**	**10.8 w**	**10.0 w**	**28,539 s**	**27,994 s**	**0.9 w**	**0.9 w**	**.. s**	**.. s**	**20,973 s**	**24,960 s**
Low income	1.6	1.4	12.0	..	3,330	3,714	1.1	1.0	..	..	..	..
Middle income	2.1	2.0	12.5	12.3	19,030	18,527	0.9	0.8	..	..	10,757	13,328
Lower middle income	2.4	2.1	13.8	12.7	8,635	8,858	0.9	0.9	..	..	3,334	8,426
Upper middle income	2.0	2.0	12.3	12.4	10,395	9,669	0.8	0.7	6,188	7,020	7,423	4,902
Low & middle income	2.1	2.0	12.5	12.2	22,360	22,241	0.9	0.8	..	..	11,031	14,002
East Asia & Pacific	1.9	1.9	13.9	14.6	7,656	7,005	0.7	0.6	311	1,423	4,096	1,912
Europe & Central Asia	2.9	3.0	15.2	11.9	3,398	3,169	1.9	1.6	5,585	6,380	1,152	920
Latin America & Carib.	1.3	1.4	..	..	2,072	2,439	0.8	0.9	..	..	1,213	1,739
Middle East & N. Africa	3.2	3.3	12.5	..	3,123	3,611	3.3	3.5	..	..	1,639	2,523
South Asia	2.8	2.4	18.7	16.2	4,578	4,480	0.7	0.7	41	4	1,554	6,378
Sub-Saharan Africa	1.7	1.6	..	..	1,533	1,536	0.5	0.5	..	..	986	530
High income	2.6	2.9	10.5	10.0	6,179	5,753	1.1	1.0	14,880	16,758	9,942	10,958
Euro area	1.7	1.6	4.5	4.3	1,802	1,606	1.2	1.0	5,473	4,891	1,527	2,620

Note: For some countries data are partial or uncertain or based on rough estimates; see SIPRI (2011).

a. Estimates differ from official statistics of the government of China, which has published the following estimates: military expenditure as 1.4 percent of GDP in 2005 and 1.5 percent in 2009 and 7.3 percent of national government expenditure in 2005 and 6.5 percent in 2009 (see National Bureau of Statistics of China, www.stats.gov.cn).

About the data

Although national defense is an important function of government and security from external threats that contributes to economic development, high military expenditures for defense or civil conflicts burden the economy and may impede growth. Data on military expenditures as a share of gross domestic product (GDP) are a rough indicator of the portion of national resources used for military activities and of the burden on the economy. As an "input" measure military expenditures are not directly related to the "output" of military activities, capabilities, or security. Comparisons of military spending among countries should take into account the many factors that influence perceptions of vulnerability and risk, including historical and cultural traditions, the length of borders that need defending, the quality of relations with neighbors, and the role of the armed forces in the body politic.

Data on military expenditures are reported to the United Nations Office for Disarmament Affairs (UNODA) by about 60 governments. Data on military expenditures are not compiled using standard definitions and are often incomplete and unreliable due to countries' reluctance to disclose military information. Even in countries where the parliament vigilantly reviews budgets and spending, military expenditures and arms transfers rarely receive close scrutiny or full, public disclosure (see Ball 1984 and Happe and Wakeman-Linn 1994). However, the Stockholm International Peace Research Institute (SIPRI) has adopted a definition of military expenditure derived from the North Atlantic Treaty Organization's (NATO) former definition (in use until 2002; see *Definitions*). The data on military expenditures as a share of GDP are SIPRI estimates. Data on military expenditures as a share of central government expenditures use data on central government expenditures from the International Monetary Fund (IMF). Therefore the data in the table may differ from comparable data published by national governments.

SIPRI's primary source of military expenditure data is official data provided by national governments. These data are derived from budget documents, defense white papers, and other public documents from official government agencies, including government responses to questionnaires sent by SIPRI, the UNODA, or the Organization for Security and Co-operation in Europe. Secondary sources include international statistics, such as those of NATO and the IMF's *Government Finance Statistics Yearbook*. Other secondary sources include country reports of the Economist Intelligence Unit, country reports by IMF staff, and specialist journals and newspapers.

In the many cases where SIPRI cannot make independent estimates, it uses the national data

provided. Because of the differences in definitions and the difficulty in verifying the accuracy and completeness of data, data on military expenditures are not always comparable across countries. However, SIPRI puts a high priority on ensuring that the data series for each country is comparable over time. More information on SIPRI's military expenditure project can be found at www.sipri.org/contents/milap/.

Data on armed forces refer to military personnel on active duty, including paramilitary forces. Because data exclude personnel not on active duty, they underestimate the share of the labor force working for the defense establishment. Governments rarely report the size of their armed forces, so such data typically come from intelligence sources.

SIPRI's Arms Transfers Programme collects data on arms transfers from open sources. Since publicly available information is inadequate for tracking all weapons and other military equipment, SIPRI covers only what it terms *major conventional weapons*. Data cover the supply of weapons through sales, aid, gifts, and manufacturing licenses; therefore the term *arms transfers* rather than *arms trade* is used. SIPRI data also cover weapons supplied to or from rebel forces in an armed conflict as well as arms deliveries for which neither the supplier nor the recipient can be identified with acceptable certainty; these data are available in SIPRI's database.

SIPRI's estimates of arms transfers are designed as a trend-measuring device in which similar weapons have similar values, reflecting both the quantity and quality of weapons transferred. The estimated values do not reflect financial value (payments for weapons transferred) because reliable data on the value of the transfer are not available, and even when values are known, the transfer usually includes more than the actual conventional weapons, such as spares, support systems, and training, and details of the financial arrangements (such as credit and loan conditions and discounts) are usually not known.

Given these measurement issues, SIPRI's method of estimating the transfer of military resources includes an evaluation of the technical parameters of the weapons. Weapons for which a price is not known are compared with the same weapons for which actual acquisition prices are available (core weapons) or for the closest match. These weapons are assigned a value in an index that reflects their military resource value in relation to the core weapons. These matches are based on such characteristics as size, performance, and type of electronics, and adjustments are made for secondhand weapons. More information on SIPRI's Arms Transfers Programme is available at www.sipri.org/research/armaments/transfers.

Definitions

• **Military expenditures** are SIPRI data derived from NATO's former definition, (in use until 2002) which includes all current and capital expenditures on the armed forces, including peacekeeping forces; defense ministries and other government agencies engaged in defense projects; paramilitary forces, if judged to be trained and equipped for military operations; and military space activities. Such expenditures include military and civil personnel, including retirement pensions and social services for military personnel; operation and maintenance; procurement; military research and development; and military aid (in the military expenditures of the donor country). Excluded are civil defense and current expenditures for previous military activities, such as for veterans benefits, demobilization, and weapons conversion and destruction. This definition cannot be applied for all countries, however, since that would require more detailed information than is available about military budgets and off-budget military expenditures (for example, whether military budgets cover civil defense, reserves and auxiliary forces, police and paramilitary forces, and military pensions). • **Armed forces personnel** are active duty military personnel, including paramilitary forces if the training, organization, equipment, and control suggest they may be used to support or replace regular military forces. Reserve forces, which are not fully staffed or operational in peace time, are excluded. The data also exclude civilians in the defense establishment and so are not consistent with the data on military expenditures on personnel. • **Arms transfers** cover the supply of military weapons through sales, aid, gifts, and manufacturing licenses and are based on actual deliveries only. Weapons must be transferred voluntarily by the supplier, have a military purpose, and be destined for the armed forces, paramilitary forces, or intelligence agencies of another country. Data cover major conventional weapons such as aircraft, armored vehicles, artillery, radar systems and other sensors, missiles, and ships designed for military use as well as some major components such as turrets for armored vehicles and engines. Excluded are other military equipment such as most small arms and light weapons, trucks, small artillery, ammunition, support equipment, technology transfers, and other services.

Data sources

Data on military expenditures are from SIPRI's Military Expenditure Database (www.sipri.org/databases/milex). Data on armed forces personnel are from the International Institute for Strategic Studies' *The Military Balance 2012*. Data on arms transfers are from SIPRI's Arms Transfers Database (www.sipri.org/databases/armstransfers).

5.8 | Fragile situations

	International Development Association Resource Allocation Index 1–6 (low to high) 2010	Peacebuilding and peacekeeping — Operation name[a] December 2011	Troops, police, and military observers number December 2011	Battle-related deaths number 2000–10[c]	Intentional homicides per 100,000 people Combined source estimates[b] 2008	Military expenditures % of GDP 2010	Business environment — Survey year	Losses due to theft, robbery, vandalism, and arson % of sales	Firms formally registered when operations started % of firms
Afghanistan	2.6	UNAMA	15	35,460	2.4	1.8	2008	1.5	88.0
Angola	2.8		..	2,620	19.0	4.4	2010	1.5	62.7
Bosnia and Herzegovina	3.7		..	..	1.7	1.4	2009	0.4	98.6
Burundi	3.1	BNUB	1	6,413	21.7	3.8	2006	1.1	..
Central African Republic	2.8	BINUCA	4	544	29.3	2.6		..	..
Chad	2.4		..	4,238	15.8	3.0	2009	2.5	77.1
Comoros	2.5		..	..	12.2	..		..	..
Congo, Dem. Rep.	2.7	MONUSCO	18,928	6,348	21.7	1.4	2010	1.8	61.9
Congo, Rep.	2.9		..	167	30.8	1.1	2009	3.3	84.3
Côte d'Ivoire	2.7	UNOCI	10,999	809	56.9	1.6	2009	3.4	56.4
Eritrea	2.2		..	25,057	17.8	..	2009	0.0	100.0
Georgia	4.4		..	648	4.1[h]	3.9	2008	0.7	99.6
Guinea	2.8		..	647	22.5	..	2006	2.0	..
Guinea-Bissau	2.7	UNIOGBIS	17	0	20.2	..	2006	1.1	..
Haiti	2.9	MINUSTAH	11,611	244	6.9[h]	..		..	..
Iraq	..	UNAMI	361	24,088	2.0	6.0		..	..
Kiribati	3.0		..	..	7.3	..		..	..
Kosovo	3.4	UNMIK	16	..	..	..	2009	0.3	89.2
Liberia	2.9	UNMIL	9,206	2,427	10.1	0.8	2009	2.8	73.8
Marshall Islands	..		..	..	..	..		..	..
Micronesia, Fed. Sts.	..		..	..	0.9	..	2009	2.1	96.9
Myanmar	..		..	1,590	10.2	..		..	..
Nepal	3.3		..	9,418	2.8[i]	1.5	2009	0.9	94.0
Sierra Leone	3.3		..	156	14.9	2.3	2009	0.8	89.2
Solomon Islands	2.8	RAMSI	468	..	3.7	..		..	..
Somalia	..	UNPOS	6	7,574	1.5	..		..	..
Sudan	2.4		..	17,658	24.2	..		..	..
Timor-Leste	3.0	UNMIT	1,216	..	6.9	2.8	2009	2.7	91.8
Togo	2.9		..	..	10.9	1.8	2009	2.4	75.8
West Bank and Gaza	..		..	..	..	..	2006	1.2	..
Western Sahara[m]	..	MINURSO	228	..	..	..		..	..
Yemen, Rep.	3.2		..	259	4.2[i]	4.4	2010	0.6	81.7
Zimbabwe	2.0		..	..	14.3	1.3		..	..
Fragile situations	..		..	82,763 s	15.8 w	3.8 w			
Low income			..	..	17.5	1.4			

Note: The countries and territories with fragile situations in the table are primarily International Development Association-eligible countries and nonmember or inactive countries and territories that have a 3.2 or lower harmonized average of the World Bank's Country Policy and Institutional Assessment rating and the corresponding rating by a regional development bank or that have had a UN or regional peacebuilding and political mission (for example by the African Union, European Union, or Organization of American States) or peacekeeping mission (for example, by the African Union, European Union, North Atlantic Treaty Organization, or Organization of American States) during the last three years. This definition is pursuant to an agreement among the World Bank and other multilateral development banks at the start of the International Development Association 15 round in 2007. The list of countries and territories with fragile situations is imperfect and is used here to reflect a complex concept. The World Bank continues to work with partners and client countries to refine the concept.

a. UNAMA is United Nations Assistance Mission in Afghanistan, BNUB is United Nations Office in Burundi, BINUCA is United Nations Integrated Peacebuilding Office in the Central African Republic, MONUSCO is United Nations Organization Stabilization Mission in the Democratic Republic of the Congo, UNOCI is United Nations Operation in Côte d'Ivoire, UNIOGBIS is United Nations Integrated Peacebuilding Office in Guinea-Bissau, MINUSTAH is United Nations Stabilization Mission in Haiti, UNAMI is United Nations Assistance Mission for Iraq, UNMIK is Interim Administration Mission in Kosovo, UNMIL is United Nations Mission in Liberia, RAMSI is Regional Assistance Mission to Solomon Islands, UNPOS is United Nations Political Office for Somalia, UNMIT is United Nations Integrated Mission in Timor-Leste, and MINURSO is United Nations Mission for the Referendum in Western Sahara. b. Best estimate from the UN Office on Drug and Crime's Intentional Homicide Statistics database. The combined source estimate uses both public health and law enforcement and criminal justice sources. c. Total over the period. d. Data are for the most recent year available. e. Average over the period. f. Covers only Angola-secured territory. g. Covers children ages 10–14. h. Data are for 2010. i. Data are for 2009. j. Northern Sudan only. k. Figure represents the Internal Displacement Monitoring Centre's (IDMC) high estimate; the low estimates is 4,500,000. l. Includes Palestinian refugees under the mandate of the United Nations Relief and Works Agency for Palestine Refugees in the Near East, who are not included in data from the Office of the United Nations High Commissioner for Refugees. m. The designation Western Sahara is used instead of Former Spanish Sahara (the designation used on the maps on the inside front and back cover flaps) because it is the designation used by the UN operation established there by Security Council resolution 690/1991. Neither designation expresses any World Bank view on the status of the territory so-identified. n. Figure represents IDMC's high estimate; the low estimate is 570,000.

	Children in employment		Refugees		Internally displaced persons	Access to an improved water source	Access to improved sanitation facilities	Maternal mortality ratio		Under-five mortality rate	Depth of hunger	Primary gross enrollment ratio
								per 100,000 live births			kilocalories	
	Survey year	% of children ages 7–14	By country of origin 2010	By country of asylum 2010	number 2010	% of population 2010	% of population 2010	National estimates 2005–10[d]	Modeled estimates 2008	per 1,000 live births 2010	per person per day 2006–08[e]	% of relevant age group 2010
Afghanistan		..	3,054,709	6,434	352,000	50	37	..	1,400	149	..	97
Angola	2001	30.1[f]	134,858	15,155	..	51	58	..	610	161	320	124
Bosnia and Herzegovina	2006	10.6	63,004	7,016	113,400	99	95	3	9	8	140	88
Burundi	2005	11.7	84,064	29,365	100,000	72	46	620	970	142	390	156
Central African Republic	2000	67.0	164,905	21,574	192,000	67	34	540	850	159	300	93
Chad	2004	60.4	53,733	347,939	171,000	51	13	..	1,200	173	320	90
Comoros		..	368	..	..	95	36	..	340	86	300	104
Congo, Dem. Rep.	2000	39.8[g]	476,693	166,336	1,700,000	45	24	550	670	170	..	94
Congo, Rep.	2005	30.1	20,679	133,112	7,800	71	18	780	580	93	230	115
Côte d'Ivoire	2006	45.7	41,758	26,218	621,000	80	24	540	470	123	230	88
Eritrea		..	222,460	4,809	10,000	61	14	..	280	61	350	45
Georgia	2006	31.8	10,640	639	258,000	98	95	52	48	22	160	109
Guinea	1994	48.3	11,985	14,113	..	74	18	980	680	130	260	94
Guinea-Bissau	2006	50.5	1,127	7,679	..	64	20	410	1,000	150	250	123
Haiti	2005	33.4	25,892	3	..	69	17	630	300	165	420	..
Iraq	2006	14.7	1,683,579	34,655	2,800,000	79	73	84	75	39	..	..
Kiribati		..	33	..	..	..	..	..	..	49	180	113
Kosovo		..	..	..	18,300	..	..	..	..	..	..	..
Liberia	2007	37.4	70,129	24,743	..	73	18	990	990	103	330	96
Marshall Islands		..	..	..	..	94	75	..	..	26	..	102
Micronesia, Fed. Sts.		..	..	1	..	..	..	..	..	42	..	..
Myanmar		..	415,670	..	446,000	83	76	320	240	66	..	126
Nepal	1999	47.2	5,889	89,808	50,000	89	31	280	380	50	220	..
Sierra Leone	2007	14.9	11,275	8,363	..	55	13	860	970	174	340	125
Solomon Islands		..	75	..	..	..	..	..	100	27	190	..
Somalia	2006	43.5	770,154	1,937	1,500,000	29	23	1,000	1,200	180	..	..
Sudan	2000	19.1[j]	387,288	178,308	5,200,000[k]	58	26	1,100	750	103	240	73
Timor-Leste		..	8	1	400	69	47	560	370	81	260	117
Togo	2006	38.7	18,330	14,051	..	61	13	..	350	103	280	140
West Bank and Gaza		..	93,323	1,910,677[l]	160,000	85	92	..	..	22	190	91
Western Sahara[m]		..	..	..	..	..	..	..	..	..	..	..
Yemen, Rep.	2006	18.3	2,076	190,092	250,000	55	53	..	210	77	260	87
Zimbabwe	1999	14.3	24,089	4,435	1,000,000[n]	80	40	730	790	80	300	..
Fragile situations			7,848,793 s	3,237,459 s	14,328,500 s	65 w	41 w	..	650 w	120 w	271 w	102 w
Low income			5,650,811	1,873,979	7,113,000	65	37	..	590	108	281	104

About the data

The table focuses on countries and territories with fragile situations and highlights the links among weak institutions, poor development outcomes, fragility, and risk of conflict. Many of these countries and territories have weak institutions that are ill-equipped to handle economic shocks, natural disasters, and illegal trade or to resist conflict, which increasingly spills across borders. Organized violence, including violent crime, interrupts economic and social development through lost human and social capital, disrupted services, displaced populations, and reduced confidence for future investment. As a result, countries with fragile situations achieve lower development outcomes and make slower progress toward the Millennium Development Goals.

According to the Geneva Declaration on Armed Violence and Development, more than 526,000 people die each year because of the violence associated with armed conflict and large- and small-scale criminality. Recovery and rebuilding can take years, and the challenges are numerous: infrastructure to be rebuilt, persistently high crime, widespread health problems, education systems in disrepair, and unexploded ordnance to be cleared. Most countries emerging from conflict lack the capacity to rebuild the economy. Thus, capacity building is one of the first tasks for restoring growth and is linked to building peace and creating the conditions that lead to sustained poverty reduction. The World Bank and other international development agencies can help, but countries with

fragile situations have to build their own institutions tailored to their own needs. Peacekeeping operations in post-conflict situations have been effective in reducing the risks of reversion to conflict.

The countries and territories with fragile situations in the table are primarily International Development Association– eligible countries and nonmember or inactive countries or territories of the World Bank that have a 3.2 or lower harmonized average of the World Bank's Country Policy and Institutional Assessment rating and the corresponding rating by a regional development bank or that have had a UN or regional peacebuilding mission (for example, by the African Union, European Union, or Organization of American States) or peacekeeping mission (for example, by the

African Union, European Union, North Atlantic Treaty Organization [NATO], or Organization of American States) during the last three years. Peacebuilding and peacekeeping involve many elements—military, police, and civilian—working together to lay the foundations for sustainable peace. The list of countries and territories with fragile situations is imperfect and is used here to reflect a complex concept. The World Bank continues to work with partners and client countries to refine the concept.

An armed conflict is a contested incompatibility that concerns a government or territory where the use of armed force between two parties (one of them the government) results in at least 25 battle-related deaths in a calendar year. There were 30 active armed conflicts in 2010. This table presents data from the Uppsala Conflict Data Program (UCDP) Battle-Related Deaths Dataset (v.5 2011), which focuses on the incompatibility and lists the country, as well as the battle location and territory where battle-related deaths are reported. When more than one country is listed in the dataset, the assignment of battle-related deaths in the table is determined by the battle location. See country footnotes for additional details.

Data on intentional homicides are from the United Nations Office on Drugs and Crime (UNODC), which uses a variety of national and international sources on homicides—primarily criminal justice sources as well as public health data from the World Health Organization (WHO) and the Pan American Health Organization—and the United Nations Survey of Crime Trends and Operations of Criminal Justice Systems to present accurate and comparable statistics. The UNODC defines homicide as "unlawful death purposefully inflicted on a person by another person." This definition excludes deaths arising from armed conflict. For additional information, see the UNODC Homicide Statistics database at www.unodc. org/unodc/en/data-and-analysis/homicide.html.

Data on military expenditures reported by governments are not compiled using standard definitions and are often inconsistent across countries, incomplete, and unreliable. Even in countries where the parliament vigilantly reviews budgets and spending, military expenditures and arms transfers rarely receive close scrutiny or full public disclosure. Data are from the Stockholm International Peace Research Institute (SIPRI), which uses NATO's former definition of military expenditure (in use until 2002; see *Definitions*). Therefore, the data in the table may differ from comparable data published by national governments. For a more detailed discussion of military expenditures, see *About the data* for table 5.7.

Along with public sector efforts, private sector development and investment, especially in competitive markets, has tremendous potential to contribute to growth and poverty reduction. The World Bank's Enterprise Surveys review the business environment, assessing constraints to private sector growth and enterprise performance. Crime, theft, and disorder impose costs on businesses and society. And in many developing countries informal businesses operate without licenses. These firms have less access to financial and public services and can engage in fewer types of contracts and investments, constraining growth. The table presents data on the loss of sales due to theft, robbery, vandalism, and arson and on the percentage of firms operating informally. For further information on enterprise surveys, see *About the data* for table 5.2.

As the table shows, the human toll of armed violence across various contexts is severe. Additionally, in countries with fragile situations weak institutional capacity often results in poor performance and failure to meet expectations of effective service delivery. Failure to deliver water, health, and education services can weaken struggling governments. The table includes several indicators related to living conditions in fragile situations: children in employment, refugees, internally displaced persons, access to water and sanitation, maternal and under-five mortality, depth of hunger, and primary school enrollment. For more detailed information on these indicators, see *About the data* for table 2.6 (children in employment), table 6.14 (refugees), table 2.18 (access to improved water and sanitation), table 2.19 (maternal mortality), table 2.23 (under-five mortality), and table 2.12 (primary school enrollment).

• **International Development Association Resource Allocation Index** is from the Country Policy and Institutional Assessment rating, which is the average score of four clusters of indicators designed to measure macroeconomic, governance, social, and structural dimensions of development: economic management, structural policies, policies for social inclusion and equity, and public sector management and institutions (see table 5.9). Countries are rated on a scale of 1 (low) to 6 (high). • **Peacebuilding and peacekeeping** refer to operations that engage in peacebuilding (reducing the risk of lapsing or relapsing into conflict by strengthening national capacities for conflict management and laying the foundation for sustainable peace and development) or peacekeeping (providing essential security to preserve the peace where fighting has been halted and to assist in implementing agreements achieved by the peacemakers). UN peacekeeping operations are authorized by the UN Secretary-General and planned, managed, directed, and supported by the United Nations Department of Peacekeeping Operations and the Department of Field Support. The UN Charter gives the Security Council primary responsibility for maintaining international peace and security, including the establishment of a UN peacekeeping operation. • **Troops, police, and military observers in peacebuilding and peacekeeping** are people active in peacebuilding and peacekeeping as part of an official operation. Peacekeepers deploy to war-torn regions where no one else is willing or able to go to prevent conflict from returning or escalating. • **Battle-related deaths** are deaths of members of warring parties in battle-related conflicts. Typically, battle-related deaths occur in warfare involving the armed forces of the warring parties (battlefield fighting, guerrilla activities, and all kinds of bombardments of military units, cities, and villages). The targets are usually the military and its installations or state institutions and state representatives, but there is often substantial collateral damage of civilians killed in crossfire, indiscriminate bombings, and other military activities. All deaths—civilian as well as military— incurred in such situations are counted as battle-related deaths. • **Intentional homicides** are estimates of unlawful homicides purposely inflicted as a result of domestic disputes, interpersonal violence, violent conflicts over land resources, intergang violence over turf or control, and predatory violence and killing by armed groups. Intentional homicide does not include all intentional killing; the difference is usually in the organization of the killing. Individuals or small groups usually commit homicide, whereas killing in armed conflict is usually committed by fairly cohesive groups of up to several hundred members and is thus usually excluded. • **Military expenditures** are SIPRI data derived from NATO's former definition (in use until 2002), which includes all current and capital expenditures on the armed forces, including peacekeeping forces; defense ministries and other government agencies engaged in defense projects; paramilitary forces, if judged to be trained and equipped for military operations; and military space activities. Such expenditures include military and civil personnel, including retirement pensions and social services for military personnel; operation and maintenance; procurement; military research and development; and military aid (in the military expenditures of the donor country). Excluded are civil defense and current expenditures for previous military activities, such as for veterans benefits, demobilization, and weapons conversion and destruction. This definition cannot be applied to all countries, however, since the necessary detailed information is missing in some cases for military budgets and off-budget military expenditures (for example, whether military budgets cover civil defense, reserves and auxiliary forces, police and paramilitary forces, and military pensions). • **Survey year** is the year in which the underlying data were collected. • **Losses due to theft, robbery, vandalism, and arson** are the estimated losses from those causes that occurred on business establishment premises calculated as a percentage of annual sales. • **Firms formally registered when operations started** are firms formally registered when they started operations in the country. • **Children in employment** are children involved in any economic activity for at least one hour in the reference week of the survey. • **Refugees** are people who are recognized as refugees under the 1951 Convention Relating to the Status of Refugees or its 1967 Protocol, the 1969 Organization of African Unity Convention Governing the Specific Aspects of Refugee Problems in Africa, people recognized as refugees in accordance with the UN Refugee Agency (UNHCR) statute, people granted refugee-like humanitarian status, and people provided temporary protection. Asylum seekers—people who have applied for asylum or refugee status and who have not yet received a decision, or who are registered as asylum seekers—are excluded. Palestinian refugees are people (and their descendants) whose residence was Palestine between June 1946 and May 1948 and who lost their homes and means of livelihood as a result of the 1948 Arab-Israeli conflict. • **Country of origin** refers to the nationality or country of citizenship of a claimant. • **Country of asylum** is the country where an asylum claim was filed and granted. • **Internally displaced persons** are people or groups of people who have been forced or obliged to flee or to leave their homes or places of habitual residence, in particular as a result of armed conflict, or to avoid the effects of armed conflict, situations of generalized violence, violations of human rights, or natural or human-made disasters and who have not crossed an international border. • **Access to an improved water source** refers to people with reasonable access to water from an improved source, such as piped water into a dwelling, public tap, tubewell, protected dug well, and rainwater collection.

Reasonable access is the availability of at least 20 liters a person a day from a source within 1 kilometer of the dwelling. • **Access to improved sanitation facilities** refers to people with at least adequate access to excreta disposal facilities that can effectively prevent human, animal, and insect contact with excreta. Improved facilities range from protected pit latrines to flush toilets. • **Maternal mortality ratio** is the number of women who die from pregnancy-related causes during pregnancy and childbirth per 100,000 live births. National estimates are based on national surveys, vital registration records, and surveillance data or are derived from community and hospital records. Modeled estimates are based on an exercise by the WHO, United Nations Children's Fund (UNICEF), United Nations Population Fund (UNFPA), and the World Bank. See About the data for table 2.19 for further details. • **Under-five mortality rate** is the probability of a child born in a specific year dying before reaching age 5, if subject to the age-specific mortality rate of that year. The probability is derived from life tables and expressed as rate per 1,000 live births. • **Depth of hunger,** or the intensity of food deprivation, indicates how much people who are food-deprived fall short of minimum food needs in terms of dietary energy. It is measured by comparing the average amount of dietary energy that undernourished people get from the foods they eat with the minimum amount of dietary energy they need to maintain body weight and undertake light activity. Depth of hunger is low when it is less than 200 kilocalories per person per day and high when it is above 300. • **Primary gross enrollment ratio** is the ratio of total enrollment, regardless of age, to the population of the age group that officially corresponds to the primary level of education. Primary education provides children with basic reading, writing, and mathematics skills along with an elementary understanding of such subjects as history, geography, natural science, social science, art, and music.

Data sources

Data on the International Development Association Resource Allocation Index are from the World Bank Group's International Development Association database (www.worldbank.org/ida). Data on peacebuilding and peacekeeping operations are from the UN Department of Peacekeeping Operations. Data on battle-related deaths are from the UCDP Battle-Related Deaths Dataset (v.5-2011) 1989-2010. Data on intentional homicides are

from the UNODC's International Homicide Statistics database (www.unodc.org/unodc/en/data-and-analysis/homicide.html). Data on military expenditures are from SIPRI's Military Expenditure database (www.sipri.org/databases/milex). Data on the business environment are from the World Bank's Enterprise Surveys (www.enterprise-surveys.org). Data on children in employment are estimates produced by the Understanding Children's Work project based on household survey data sets made available by the International Labour Organization's International Programme on the Elimination of Child Labour under its Statistical Monitoring Programme on Child Labour, UNICEF under its Multiple Indicator Cluster Survey program, the World Bank under its Living Standards Measurement Study program, and national statistical offices (see table 2.6). Data on refugees are from the UNHCR's *Statistical Yearbook 2010,* complemented by statistics on Palestinian refugees under the mandate of the United Nations Relief and Works Agency for Palestine Refugees in the Near East as published on its website (www.unrwa.org). Data on internally displaced persons are from the Internal Displacement Monitoring Centre. Data on access to water and sanitation are from the WHO and UNICEF's *Progress on Drinking Water and Sanitation* (2012). National estimates of maternal mortality are from UNICEF's *The State of the World's Children 2009* and Childinfo and MEASURE DHS Demographic and Health Surveys by ICF International. Modeled estimates for maternal mortality are from WHO, UNICEF, UNFPA, and the World Bank's *Trends in Maternal Mortality: 1990–2008* (2010). Data on under-five mortality estimates by the UN Inter-agency Group for Child Mortality Estimation (which comprises UNICEF, WHO, the World Bank, United Nations Population Division, and other universities and research institutes) and are based mainly on household surveys, censuses, and vital registration data, supplemented by the World Bank's Human Development Network estimates based on vital registration and sample registration data (see table 2.23). Data on depth of hunger are from the Food and Agriculture Organization's Food Security Statistics database (www.fao.org/economic/ess/ess-fs/fs-data/ess-fadata/en/). Data on primary gross enrollment are from the United Nations Educational, Scientific, and Cultural Organization's Institute for Statistics.

	International Development Association Resource Allocation Index 1–6 (low to high)	Economic management 1–6 (low to high)				Structural policies 1–6 (low to high)			
		Macroeconomic management	Fiscal policy	Debt policy	Average	Trade	Financial sector	Business regulatory environment	Average
	2010	**2010**	**2010**	**2010**	**2010**	**2010**	**2010**	**2010**	**2010**
Afghanistan	2.6	3.5	3.0	2.5	3.0	3.0	2.0	2.5	2.5
Angola	2.8	3.0	3.0	3.0	3.0	4.0	2.5	2.0	2.8
Armenia	4.1	4.5	5.0	4.5	4.7	4.5	3.5	4.0	4.0
Azerbaijan	3.7	4.0	4.5	4.5	4.3	3.5	3.0	4.0	3.5
Bangladesh	3.5	4.0	4.0	4.0	4.0	3.0	3.5	3.5	3.3
Benin	3.5	4.0	3.0	3.5	3.5	4.0	3.5	3.5	3.7
Bhutan	3.9	4.5	4.5	4.5	4.5	3.0	3.0	3.5	3.2
Bolivia	3.7	4.0	4.0	4.5	4.2	5.0	3.5	2.5	3.7
Bosnia and Herzegovina	3.7	4.0	3.5	4.0	3.8	4.0	4.0	4.0	4.0
Burkina Faso	3.8	4.5	4.5	4.0	4.3	4.0	3.0	3.5	3.5
Burundi	3.1	3.5	3.5	3.0	3.3	4.0	2.5	2.5	3.0
Cambodia	3.4	4.5	4.0	3.5	4.0	4.0	2.5	3.5	3.3
Cameroon	3.2	4.0	3.5	3.0	3.5	3.5	3.0	3.0	3.2
Cape Verde	4.1	4.5	4.5	4.0	4.3	4.0	4.0	3.5	3.8
Central African Republic	2.8	3.5	3.5	3.0	3.3	3.5	2.5	2.0	2.7
Chad	2.4	2.5	2.5	2.5	2.5	3.0	2.5	2.0	2.5
Comoros	2.5	3.0	2.0	2.0	2.3	3.5	2.5	2.5	2.8
Congo, Dem. Rep.	2.7	3.5	3.5	3.0	3.3	3.0	2.0	2.0	2.3
Congo, Rep.	2.9	3.5	3.0	3.0	3.2	3.5	3.0	2.5	3.0
Côte d'Ivoire	2.7	3.5	2.5	2.0	2.7	4.0	3.0	3.0	3.3
Djibouti	3.2	3.5	3.0	2.5	3.0	4.0	3.0	3.5	3.5
Dominica	3.8	4.0	4.5	3.0	3.8	4.0	3.5	4.5	4.0
Eritrea	2.2	2.0	2.0	1.5	1.8	1.5	1.0	2.0	1.5
Ethiopia	3.4	3.5	4.0	3.5	3.7	3.0	3.0	3.5	3.2
Gambia, The	3.4	4.0	3.5	3.0	3.5	3.5	3.5	3.5	3.5
Georgia	4.4	4.5	4.5	5.0	4.7	6.0	3.5	5.5	5.0
Ghana	3.9	3.5	3.5	4.0	3.7	4.0	4.0	4.5	4.2
Grenada	3.8	3.5	3.0	3.0	3.2	4.5	4.0	4.5	4.3
Guinea	2.8	2.5	2.5	2.0	2.3	4.0	3.0	2.5	3.2
Guinea-Bissau	2.7	3.0	2.5	2.0	2.5	4.0	2.5	2.5	3.0
Guyana	3.4	3.5	3.5	4.0	3.7	4.0	3.5	3.0	3.5
Haiti	2.9	4.0	3.5	2.5	3.3	4.0	3.0	2.5	3.2
Honduras	3.6	3.5	3.5	4.0	3.7	4.5	3.0	3.5	3.7
India	3.7	4.5	3.5	4.0	4.0	3.5	4.0	3.5	3.7
Kenya	3.8	4.5	4.0	4.0	4.2	4.0	4.0	4.0	4.0
Kiribati	3.0	2.5	3.0	3.5	3.0	3.0	3.0	3.0	3.0
Kosovo	3.4	3.5	3.0	3.5	3.3	5.0	3.5	3.5	4.0
Kyrgyz Republic	3.7	4.5	4.0	4.0	4.2	5.0	3.0	3.5	3.8

About the data

The International Development Association (IDA) is the part of the World Bank Group that helps the poorest countries reduce poverty by providing concessional loans and grants for programs aimed at boosting economic growth and improving living conditions. IDA funding helps these countries deal with the complex challenges they face in meeting the Millennium Development Goals.

The World Bank's IDA Resource Allocation Index (IRAI), presented in the table, is based on the results of the annual Country Policy and Institutional Assessment (CPIA) exercise, which covers the IDA-eligible countries. The table does not include Myanmar and Somalia because they were not rated in the 2010 exercise even though they are IDA eligible. Country

assessments have been carried out annually since the mid-1970s by World Bank staff. Over time the criteria have been revised from a largely macroeconomic focus to include governance aspects and a broader coverage of social and structural dimensions. Country performance is assessed against a set of 16 criteria grouped into four clusters: economic management, structural policies, policies for social inclusion and equity, and public sector management and institutions. IDA resources are allocated to a country on per capita terms based on its IDA country performance rating and, to a limited extent, based on its per capita gross national income. This ensures that good performers receive

a higher IDA allocation in per capita terms. The IRAI is a key element in the country performance rating.

The CPIA exercise is intended to capture the quality of a country's policies and institutional arrangements, focusing on key elements that are within the country's control, rather than on outcomes (such as economic growth rates) that are influenced by events beyond the country's control. More specifically, the CPIA measures the extent to which a country's policy and institutional framework supports sustainable growth and poverty reduction and, consequently, the effective use of development assistance.

All criteria within each cluster receive equal weight, and each cluster has a 25 percent weight in the

	International Development Association Resource Allocation Index 1–6 (low to high)	Economic management 1–6 (low to high)				Structural policies 1–6 (low to high)			
		Macroeconomic management	Fiscal policy	Debt policy	Average	Trade	Financial sector	Business regulatory environment	Average
	2010	2010	2010	2010	2010	2010	2010	2010	2010
Lao PDR	3.3	4.0	4.0	3.0	3.7	3.5	2.0	3.0	2.8
Lesotho	3.5	4.0	3.5	4.0	3.8	3.5	3.0	3.0	3.2
Liberia	2.9	3.5	3.5	3.0	3.3	3.0	2.5	3.0	2.8
Madagascar	3.4	3.5	3.0	4.0	3.5	4.0	3.0	3.0	3.3
Malawi	3.3	3.0	3.5	3.0	3.2	3.5	3.0	3.0	3.2
Maldives	3.4	2.5	2.0	2.5	2.3	4.0	3.0	4.0	3.7
Mali	3.6	4.5	4.0	4.0	4.2	4.0	3.0	3.5	3.5
Mauritania	3.2	3.5	3.0	3.5	3.3	4.0	2.5	3.0	3.2
Moldova	3.7	3.5	3.5	4.0	3.7	4.5	3.5	3.5	3.8
Mongolia	3.4	3.5	3.0	3.5	3.3	4.5	2.5	3.5	3.5
Mozambique	3.7	4.5	4.5	4.5	4.5	4.5	3.5	3.0	3.7
Nepal	3.3	3.5	4.0	3.0	3.5	3.5	3.0	3.0	3.2
Nicaragua	3.7	4.0	4.0	4.5	4.2	4.5	3.0	3.5	3.7
Niger	3.4	4.0	3.5	4.0	3.8	4.0	3.0	3.0	3.3
Nigeria	3.4	4.0	4.0	4.5	4.2	3.5	3.5	3.5	3.5
Pakistan	3.1	2.5	2.5	3.5	2.8	3.5	3.5	3.5	3.5
Papua New Guinea	3.3	4.0	3.5	4.5	4.0	4.5	3.0	3.0	3.5
Rwanda	3.8	4.0	4.0	3.5	3.8	4.0	3.5	4.0	3.8
Samoa	4.1	4.0	4.0	5.0	4.3	5.0	4.0	3.5	4.2
São Tomé and Príncipe	3.0	3.0	3.0	2.5	2.8	4.0	2.5	2.5	3.0
Senegal	3.7	4.0	4.0	4.0	4.0	4.0	3.5	4.0	3.8
Sierra Leone	3.3	4.0	3.5	3.5	3.7	3.5	3.0	3.0	3.2
Solomon Islands	2.8	3.5	2.5	3.0	3.0	3.0	3.0	2.5	2.8
Sri Lanka	3.5	3.0	3.0	3.5	3.2	3.5	4.0	4.0	3.8
St. Lucia	3.8	4.0	3.5	3.5	3.7	4.0	3.5	4.5	4.0
St. Vincent & Grenadines	3.8	4.0	3.5	3.5	3.7	4.0	3.5	4.5	4.0
Sudan	2.4	3.5	3.0	1.5	2.7	2.5	2.5	2.5	2.5
Tajikistan	3.3	4.0	3.5	3.5	3.7	4.0	2.5	3.0	3.2
Tanzania	3.8	4.5	4.0	4.0	4.2	4.0	4.0	3.5	3.8
Timor-Leste	3.0	3.0	3.5	4.0	3.5	4.5	2.5	1.5	2.8
Togo	2.9	3.0	3.0	3.0	3.0	4.0	2.5	3.0	3.2
Tonga	3.5	3.0	3.0	2.5	2.8	5.0	3.5	3.0	3.8
Uganda	3.8	4.5	4.0	4.5	4.3	4.0	3.5	4.0	3.8
Uzbekistan	3.4	4.0	4.0	4.0	4.0	2.5	3.0	3.0	2.8
Vanuatu	3.4	4.0	3.5	4.5	4.0	3.0	3.0	3.5	3.2
Vietnam	3.8	4.0	4.5	4.0	4.2	3.5	3.0	3.5	3.3
Yemen, Rep.	3.2	3.5	3.0	3.0	3.2	4.5	2.5	3.5	3.5
Zambia	3.4	4.0	3.0	3.5	3.5	4.0	3.5	3.5	3.7
Zimbabwe	2.0	2.0	2.0	1.0	1.7	3.0	2.0	2.0	2.3

overall score, which is obtained by averaging the average scores of the four clusters. For each of the 16 criteria countries are rated on a scale of 1 (low) to 6 (high). The scores depend on the level of performance in a given year assessed against the criteria, rather than on changes in performance compared with the previous year. All 16 CPIA criteria contain a detailed description of each rating level. In assessing country performance, World Bank staff evaluate the country's performance on each of the criteria and assign a rating. The ratings reflect a variety of indicators, observations, and judgments based on country knowledge and on relevant publicly available indicators. In interpreting the assessment scores, it should be noted that the criteria are designed in a developmentally neutral manner. Accordingly, higher scores can be attained by a country that, given its stage of development, has a policy and institutional framework that more strongly fosters growth and poverty reduction.

The country teams that prepare the ratings are very familiar with the country, and their assessments are based on country diagnostic studies prepared by the World Bank or other development organizations and on their own professional judgment. An early consultation is conducted with country authorities to make sure that the assessments are informed by up-to-date information. To ensure that scores are consistent across countries, the process involves two key phases. In the benchmarking phase a small representative sample of countries drawn from all regions is rated. Country teams prepare proposals that are reviewed first at the regional level and then in a Bankwide review process. A similar process is followed to assess the performance of the remaining countries, using the benchmark countries' scores as guideposts. The final ratings are determined following a Bankwide review. The overall numerical IRAI score and the separate criteria scores were first publicly disclosed in June 2006.

See IDA's website at www.worldbank.org/ida for more information.

	Policies for social inclusion and equity 1–6 (low to high)						Public sector management and institutions 1–6 (low to high)					
	Gender equality	Equity of public resource use	Building human resources	Social protection and labor	Policies and institutions for environmental sustainability	Average	Property rights and rule-based governance	Quality of budgetary and financial management	Efficiency of revenue mobilization	Quality of public administration	Transparency, accountability, and corruption in the public sector	Average
	2010	2010	2010	2010	2010	2010	2010	2010	2010	2010	2010	2010
Afghanistan	2.0	3.0	3.0	2.5	2.5	2.6	1.5	3.5	3.0	2.0	2.0	2.4
Angola	3.5	2.5	2.5	2.5	3.0	2.8	2.0	2.5	2.5	2.5	2.5	2.4
Armenia	4.5	4.5	4.0	4.5	3.0	4.1	3.5	4.5	3.5	4.0	3.0	3.7
Azerbaijan	4.0	4.0	4.0	4.0	3.0	3.8	3.0	3.5	3.5	3.0	2.5	3.1
Bangladesh	4.0	3.5	4.0	3.5	3.0	3.6	3.0	3.0	3.0	3.0	3.0	3.0
Benin	3.5	3.5	3.5	3.0	3.5	3.4	3.0	3.5	3.5	3.0	3.5	3.3
Bhutan	4.0	4.0	4.5	3.5	4.5	4.1	3.5	3.5	4.0	4.0	4.5	3.9
Bolivia	4.0	4.0	4.0	3.5	3.5	3.8	2.5	3.5	4.0	3.0	3.5	3.3
Bosnia and Herzegovina	4.5	3.5	3.5	3.5	3.5	3.7	3.0	3.5	4.0	3.0	3.0	3.3
Burkina Faso	3.5	4.0	3.5	3.5	3.5	3.6	3.5	4.5	3.5	3.5	3.5	3.7
Burundi	4.0	3.5	3.5	3.0	3.0	3.4	2.5	3.0	3.0	2.5	2.0	2.6
Cambodia	4.0	3.5	3.5	3.0	3.0	3.4	2.5	3.5	3.0	2.5	2.0	2.7
Cameroon	3.0	3.0	3.5	3.0	3.0	3.1	2.5	3.0	3.5	3.0	2.5	2.9
Cape Verde	4.5	4.5	4.5	4.5	3.5	4.3	4.0	4.0	3.5	4.0	4.5	4.0
Central African Republic	2.5	2.5	2.5	2.0	3.0	2.5	2.0	3.0	2.5	2.5	2.5	2.5
Chad	2.5	2.0	2.5	2.5	2.0	2.3	2.0	2.0	2.5	2.5	2.0	2.2
Comoros	3.0	2.5	3.0	2.5	2.0	2.6	2.5	2.0	2.5	2.5	2.5	2.4
Congo, Dem. Rep.	2.5	3.0	3.5	2.5	2.5	2.8	2.0	2.5	2.5	2.0	2.0	2.2
Congo, Rep.	3.0	2.5	3.5	2.5	2.5	2.8	2.5	2.5	3.0	2.5	2.5	2.6
Côte d'Ivoire	2.5	2.0	2.5	2.5	2.5	2.4	2.0	2.5	3.5	2.0	2.0	2.4
Djibouti	3.0	3.0	3.5	3.5	3.5	3.3	2.5	3.0	3.5	2.5	2.5	2.8
Dominica	3.0	3.5	4.0	3.5	3.5	3.5	4.0	4.0	4.0	3.5	4.0	3.9
Eritrea	3.5	2.5	3.5	2.5	2.0	2.8	2.5	2.5	3.5	3.0	2.0	2.7
Ethiopia	3.0	4.5	4.0	3.5	3.0	3.6	3.0	3.5	3.5	3.5	2.5	3.2
Gambia, The	3.5	4.0	3.5	2.5	3.5	3.4	3.0	3.5	3.5	3.0	2.0	3.0
Georgia	4.5	4.5	4.5	4.5	3.0	4.2	3.5	4.0	4.5	4.0	3.5	3.9
Ghana	4.0	4.0	4.5	4.0	3.5	4.0	3.5	3.5	4.0	3.5	4.0	3.7
Grenada	4.5	3.5	4.0	3.5	4.0	3.9	3.5	4.0	3.5	3.5	4.0	3.7
Guinea	3.5	3.0	3.0	3.0	2.5	3.0	2.0	3.0	3.0	3.0	2.0	2.6
Guinea-Bissau	2.5	3.0	2.5	2.5	3.0	2.7	2.5	2.5	3.0	2.5	2.5	2.6
Guyana	3.5	3.5	4.0	3.0	3.0	3.4	3.0	3.5	3.5	2.5	2.5	3.0
Haiti	3.0	3.0	2.5	2.5	2.5	2.7	2.0	3.0	2.5	2.5	2.5	2.5
Honduras	4.0	4.0	4.0	3.0	3.5	3.7	3.0	3.5	4.0	3.0	3.0	3.3
India	3.5	4.0	4.0	3.5	3.5	3.7	3.5	3.5	4.0	3.5	3.5	3.6
Kenya	3.5	4.0	4.0	3.5	3.5	3.7	2.5	3.5	4.0	3.5	3.0	3.3
Kiribati	2.5	4.0	2.5	3.0	3.0	3.0	3.5	3.0	3.0	3.0	3.0	3.1
Kosovo	3.5	3.5	2.5	3.5	3.0	3.2	3.0	4.0	3.5	2.5	3.0	3.2
Kyrgyz Republic	4.5	3.5	3.5	3.5	3.0	3.6	2.5	3.5	3.5	3.0	2.5	3.0

Definitions

• **International Development Association Resource Allocation Index** is obtained by calculating the average score for each cluster and then by averaging those scores. For each of 16 criteria countries are rated on a scale of 1 (low) to 6 (high) • **Economic management** cluster: **Macroeconomic management** assesses the monetary, exchange rate, and aggregate demand policy framework. • **Fiscal policy** assesses the short- and medium-term sustainability of fiscal policy (taking into account monetary and exchange rate policy and the sustainability of the public debt) and its impact on growth. • **Debt policy** assesses whether the debt management strategy is conducive to minimizing budgetary risks and ensuring

long-term debt sustainability. • **Structural policies** cluster: **Trade** assesses how the policy framework fosters trade in goods. • **Financial sector** assesses the structure of the financial sector and the policies and regulations that affect it. • **Business regulatory environment** assesses the extent to which the legal, regulatory, and policy environments help or hinder private businesses in investing, creating jobs, and becoming more productive. • **Policies for social inclusion and equity** cluster: **Gender equality** assesses the extent to which the country has installed institutions and programs to enforce laws and policies that promote equal access for men and women in education, health, the economy, and

protection under law. • **Equity of public resource use** assesses the extent to which the pattern of public expenditures and revenue collection affects the poor and is consistent with national poverty reduction priorities. • **Building human resources** assesses the national policies and public and private sector service delivery that affect the access to and quality of health and education services, including prevention and treatment of HIV/AIDS, tuberculosis, and malaria. • **Social protection and labor** assess government policies in social protection and labor market regulations that reduce the risk of becoming poor, assist those who are poor to better manage further risks, and ensure a minimal level of welfare

	Policies for social inclusion and equity 1–6 (low to high)						Public sector management and institutions 1–6 (low to high)					
	Gender equality	Equity of public resource use	Building human resources	Social protection and labor	Policies and institutions for environmental sustainability	Average	Property rights and rule-based governance	Quality of budgetary and financial management	Efficiency of revenue mobilization	Quality of public administration	Transparency, accountability, and corruption in the public sector	Average
	2010	2010	2010	2010	2010	2010	2010	2010	2010	2010	2010	2010
Lao PDR	3.5	4.0	3.5	2.5	4.0	3.5	3.0	3.5	3.5	3.0	2.5	3.1
Lesotho	4.0	3.0	3.5	3.0	3.0	3.3	3.5	3.5	4.0	3.0	3.5	3.5
Liberia	2.5	3.5	2.5	2.5	2.5	2.7	2.5	2.5	3.5	2.5	3.0	2.8
Madagascar	3.5	4.0	3.5	3.5	3.5	3.6	3.0	2.5	3.5	3.5	2.5	3.0
Malawi	3.5	3.5	3.5	3.5	3.5	3.5	3.5	3.0	4.0	3.5	3.0	3.4
Maldives	4.0	4.0	4.0	3.5	4.0	3.9	3.5	3.0	4.5	3.5	3.0	3.5
Mali	3.5	4.0	3.5	3.5	3.0	3.5	3.5	3.5	3.5	3.0	3.5	3.4
Mauritania	4.0	3.5	3.0	2.5	3.0	3.2	3.0	3.0	3.5	3.0	2.5	3.0
Moldova	5.0	3.5	4.0	3.5	4.0	4.0	3.5	4.0	3.5	3.0	3.0	3.4
Mongolia	3.5	3.5	3.5	3.5	3.0	3.4	3.0	4.0	3.5	3.5	3.0	3.4
Mozambique	3.5	3.5	3.5	3.0	3.5	3.4	3.0	4.0	4.0	3.0	3.0	3.4
Nepal	4.0	4.0	4.0	3.0	3.5	3.7	2.5	2.5	3.5	3.0	2.5	2.8
Nicaragua	3.5	4.0	3.5	3.5	3.5	3.6	2.5	4.0	4.0	3.0	2.5	3.2
Niger	2.5	3.5	3.5	3.0	3.5	3.2	3.0	3.5	3.5	3.0	3.0	3.2
Nigeria	3.0	3.5	3.0	3.5	3.0	3.2	2.5	3.0	3.0	3.0	3.0	2.9
Pakistan	2.0	3.5	3.0	3.5	2.5	2.9	3.0	3.5	3.0	3.5	2.5	3.1
Papua New Guinea	2.5	4.0	2.5	3.0	2.0	2.8	2.0	3.0	3.5	3.0	3.0	2.9
Rwanda	4.0	4.5	4.5	3.5	3.5	4.0	3.5	4.0	3.5	4.0	3.5	3.7
Samoa	3.5	4.5	4.0	3.5	4.0	3.9	4.0	3.5	4.5	4.0	4.0	4.0
São Tomé and Príncipe	3.0	3.0	3.5	2.5	3.0	3.0	2.5	3.0	3.5	3.0	3.5	3.1
Senegal	3.5	3.5	3.5	3.0	3.5	3.4	3.5	3.5	4.0	3.5	3.0	3.5
Sierra Leone	3.0	3.5	3.5	3.5	2.5	3.2	2.5	3.5	3.0	3.0	3.0	3.0
Solomon Islands	3.0	2.5	3.0	2.5	2.0	2.6	3.0	2.5	3.0	2.0	3.0	2.7
Sri Lanka	4.0	3.5	4.5	3.5	3.0	3.7	3.5	4.0	3.5	3.0	3.0	3.4
St. Lucia	3.5	4.0	4.0	3.5	3.5	3.7	4.0	3.5	4.5	3.5	4.5	4.0
St. Vincent & Grenadines	4.0	3.5	4.0	3.5	3.5	3.7	4.0	3.5	4.0	3.5	4.0	3.8
Sudan	2.5	2.5	2.5	2.5	2.0	2.4	2.0	2.0	3.0	2.5	1.5	2.2
Tajikistan	4.0	3.5	3.0	3.5	3.0	3.4	2.5	3.5	3.0	3.0	2.0	2.8
Tanzania	3.5	4.0	3.5	4.0	3.5	3.7	3.5	3.5	4.0	3.0	2.5	3.3
Timor-Leste	3.5	3.0	3.0	2.5	2.5	2.9	2.0	3.0	3.0	2.5	3.0	2.7
Togo	3.0	2.5	3.0	3.0	2.5	2.8	2.5	3.0	3.0	2.0	2.5	2.6
Tonga	3.0	4.0	4.0	3.0	3.0	3.4	4.0	3.5	4.5	3.5	3.5	3.8
Uganda	3.5	4.0	3.5	3.5	4.0	3.7	3.5	3.5	3.5	3.0	2.5	3.2
Uzbekistan	4.0	4.0	4.0	3.5	3.5	3.8	2.5	3.5	3.5	3.0	1.5	2.8
Vanuatu	3.5	3.5	2.5	2.5	3.0	3.0	3.5	4.0	3.5	3.0	3.0	3.4
Vietnam	4.5	4.5	4.0	3.5	3.5	4.0	3.5	4.0	4.0	3.5	3.0	3.6
Yemen, Rep.	2.0	3.5	3.0	3.5	3.5	3.1	2.5	3.5	3.0	3.0	2.5	2.9
Zambia	3.5	3.5	4.0	3.0	3.5	3.5	3.0	3.5	3.5	3.0	2.5	3.1
Zimbabwe	2.5	2.0	1.5	1.0	2.0	1.8	1.5	2.0	3.5	2.0	1.5	2.1

to all people. • **Policies and institutions for environmental sustainability** assess the extent to which environmental policies foster the protection and sustainable use of natural resources and the management of pollution. • **Public sector management and institutions** cluster: **Property rights and rule-based governance** assess the extent to which private economic activity is facilitated by an effective legal system and rule-based governance structure in which property and contract rights are reliably respected and enforced. • **Quality of budgetary and financial management** assesses the extent to which there is a comprehensive and credible budget linked to policy priorities, effective financial management systems,

and timely and accurate accounting and fiscal reporting, including timely and audited public accounts. • **Efficiency of revenue mobilization** assesses the overall pattern of revenue mobilization—not only the de facto tax structure, but also revenue from all sources as actually collected. • **Quality of public administration** assesses the extent to which civilian central government staff is structured to design and implement government policy and deliver services effectively. • **Transparency, accountability, and corruption in the public sector** assess the extent to which the executive can be held accountable for its use of funds and for the results of its actions by the electorate, the legislature, and the judiciary and the

extent to which public employees within the executive are required to account for administrative decisions, use of resources, and results obtained. The three main dimensions assessed are the accountability of the executive to oversight institutions and of public employees for their performance, access of civil society to information on public affairs, and state capture by narrow vested interests.

Data sources

Data on public policies and institutions are from the World Bank Group's CPIA database (www. worldbank.org/ida).

	Roads				Railways			Ports	Air		
	Total road network km	Paved roads %	Passengers carried million passenger-km	Goods hauled million ton-km	Rail lines total route-km	Passengers carried million passenger-km	Goods hauled million ton-km	Port container traffic thousand TEU	Registered carrier departures worldwide thousands	Passengers carried thousands	Air freight million ton-km
	2000–09[a]	2000–09[a]	2000–09[a]	2000–09[a]	2000–10[a]	2000–10[a]	2000–10[a]	2010	2010	2010	2010
Afghanistan	42,150	29.3	232	6,575	..	..	..	..	..	..	..
Albania	18,000	39.0	197	2,200	423	32	46	87	10	920	0
Algeria	112,039	74.0	..	..	3,512	1,045	1,281	266	44	3,686	6
Angola	51,429	10.4	166,045	4,709	..	..	..	..	14	1,283	91
Argentina	231,374	30.0	..	..	25,023	6,979	12,025	2,018	100	10,030	178
Armenia	7,705	93.6	2,356	182	826	50	346	..	9	757	6
Australia	817,089	43.5	301,524	189,847	8,615	1,500	64,172	6,536	418	45,268	2,380
Austria	106,840	100.0	69,000	16	5,066	10,306	23,104	350	184	13,869	430
Azerbaijan	52,942	50.6	15,291	10,634	2,079	917	8,250	..	10	801	8
Bahrain	4,083	82.1	..	..	..	..	..	290	58	5,339	843
Bangladesh	239,226	9.5	..	..	2,835	7,305	710	1,356	12	2,177	85
Belarus	94,797	88.6	8,184	22,767	5,503	7,578	46,224	..	13	888	2
Belgium	153,872	78.2	131,470	36,174	3,578	10,493	5,439	10,985	143	7,263	1,274
Benin	19,000	9.5	..	..	758	..	36	278	..	..	..
Bolivia	80,294	7.9	..	..	2,866	313	1,060	..	36	1,916	14
Bosnia and Herzegovina	21,846	52.3	1,959	1,711	1,026	59	1,227	..	2	133	0
Botswana	25,798	32.6	..	..	888	94	674	..	8	290	0
Brazil	1,751,868	5.5	..	..	29,817	..	267,700	8,121	885	77,255	976
Bulgaria	40,231	98.4	13,839	17,742	4,098	2,100	3,061	143	31	2,243	2
Burkina Faso	92,495	4.2	..	..	622	..	..	..	4	254	0
Burundi	12,322	10.4	..	..	..	..	..	..	..	..	..
Cambodia	38,257	6.3	201	..	650	45	92	224	5	312	18
Cameroon	28,857	17.0	..	..	977	377	978	250	10	466	23
Canada	1,409,000	39.9	493,814	129,600	58,345	2,875	322,741	4,813	1,235	67,325	2,011
Central African Republic	24,307	..	..	..	..	..	..	..	..	..	..
Chad	40,000	0.8	..	..	..	..	..	..	..	..	..
Chile	78,425	22.5	..	..	5,352	840	4,032	3,172	109	10,234	1,400
China	3,860,823	53.5	1,351,144	3,718,882	66,239	791,158	2,451,185	129,611	2,391	267,691	17,441
Hong Kong SAR, China	2,050	100.0	..	..	..	..	..	23,699	151	25,383	7,970
Colombia	129,485	..	157	39,726	1,672	..	9,049	2,444	180	15,111	1,576
Congo, Dem. Rep.	153,497	1.8	..	..	3,641	37	193	..	..	..	..
Congo, Rep.	17,000	7.1	..	..	795	211	234	297	..	..	..
Costa Rica	39,039	26.0	27	1	..	..	..	1,013	49	1,747	20
Côte d'Ivoire	81,996	7.9	..	..	639	10	675	608	..	..	..
Croatia	29,343	90.5	3,438	9,429	2,722	1,742	2,618	137	26	1,641	2
Cuba	..	49.0	6,634	2,315	5,076	1,285	1,351	228	10	862	16
Cyprus	12,380	64.9	..	944	..	..	..	349	22	2,363	38
Czech Republic	130,573	100.0	88,352	44,955	9,569	6,553	13,592	..	94	7,103	23
Denmark	73,330	100.0	68,907	10,003	2,131	7,405	2,030	709	4[b]	519[b]	0[b]
Dominican Republic	12,600	49.4	..	..	..	..	..	1,383	..	..	..
Ecuador	43,670	14.8	11,819	1,193	..	..	..	1,222	50	4,461	115
Egypt, Arab Rep.	100,472	89.4	12,793	..	5,195	40,837	3,840	6,709	113	9,637	188
El Salvador	10,029	19.8	..	..	..	..	..	146	20	2,150	17
Eritrea	4,010	21.8	..	..	..	..	..	..	..	..	..
Estonia	58,382	28.6	2,453	5,249	787	248	6,261	152	11	809	1
Ethiopia	44,359	13.7	219,113	2,456	..	..	..	..	48	3,141	672
Finland	78,925	65.5	72,700	25,200	5,919	3,959	9,760	1,247	183	11,578	736
France	951,260	100.0	773,000	265,000	33,608	86,853	22,840	5,323	751	65,401	5,081
Gabon	9,170	12.0	..	..	810	111	2,238	136	1	96	2
Gambia, The	3,742	19.3	16	..	..	..	..	..	..	..	..
Georgia	20,329	94.1	5,724	611	1,566	655	6,228	226	6	328	15
Germany	643,969	100.0	949,306	427,300	33,708	78,582	105,794	14,625	1,086	112,399	9,245
Ghana	109,515	12.6	..	..	953	85	181	514	..	..	..
Greece	116,929	91.8	..	28,585	2,552	1,413	538	1,165	148	15,588	37
Guatemala	14,095	34.5	..	..	..	..	..	1,012	..	..	..
Guinea	44,348	9.8	..	..	..	..	..	..	..	..	..
Guinea-Bissau	3,455	27.9	..	..	..	..	..	..	..	..	..
Haiti	4,160	24.3	..	..	..	..	..	..	..	..	..

	Roads				Railways			Ports	Air		
	Total road network km	Paved roads %	Passengers carried million passenger-km	Goods hauled million ton-km	Rail lines total route-km	Passengers carried million passenger-km	Goods hauled million ton-km	Port container traffic thousand TEU	Registered carrier departures worldwide thousands	Passengers carried thousands	Air freight million ton-km
	2000–09[a]	2000–09[a]	2000–09[a]	2000–09[a]	2000–10[a]	2000–10[a]	2000–10[a]	2010	2010	2010	2010
Honduras	13,600	20.4	..	..	..	..	..	620	..	..	..
Hungary	197,519	38.0	20,449	35,373	7,893	5,398	1,000	..	118	11,829	8
India	4,109,592	49.5	..	..	63,974	903,465	600,548	9,753	630	64,144	1,720
Indonesia	476,337	56.9	..	..	3,370	14,344	4,390	8,371	405	35,321	660
Iran, Islamic Rep.	192,685	73.3	..	..	6,073	16,814	20,247	2,593	152	17,585	131
Iraq	40,988	84.3	..	..	2,025	54	121	..	..	..	..
Ireland	96,424	100.0	..	12,787	1,919	1,678	92	773	683	76,488	350
Israel	18,318	100.0	..	..	1,034	1,986	1,062	2,282	54	6,141	865
Italy	487,700	100.0	97,560	192,700	18,011	44,535	12,037	9,787	364	48,748	1,164
Jamaica	22,121	73.3	..	..	..	..	..	1,892	8	974	6
Japan	1,207,867	80.1	905,907	334,667	20,035	244,235	20,432	18,060	650	94,212	8,380
Jordan	7,878	100.0	..	..	294	..	353	619	39	2,972	219
Kazakhstan	96,846	88.5	110,475	66,254	14,202	15,448	213,174	..	27	2,426	48
Kenya	61,945	14.3	..	22	1,917	226	1,399	696	36	3,284	258
Korea, Dem. Rep.	25,554	2.8	..	..	..	..	..	..	1	84	7
Korea, Rep.	104,983	79.3	100,617	12,545	3,379	33,027	9,452	18,538	483	42,763	12,802
Kosovo	..	..	..	..	..	..	..	..	..	..	..
Kuwait	6,524	85.0	..	..	..	..	..	888	22	2,741	274
Kyrgyz Republic	34,000	91.1	6,745	912	417	99	738	..	5	270	1
Lao PDR	39,568	13.7	2,113	287	..	..	..	..	11	645	0
Latvia	69,148	20.9	14,625	8,115	1,897	79	17,164	257	66	4,466	23
Lebanon	6,970	..	..	..	..	..	..	949	17	1,600	43
Lesotho	5,940	18.3	..	..	..	..	..	..	..	..	..
Liberia	10,600	6.2	..	..	..	..	..	..	..	..	..
Libya	83,200	57.2	..	..	..	..	..	162	25	2,345	17
Lithuania	81,331	29.4	20,376	17,757	1,767	373	13,431	295	5	167	120
Macedonia, FYR	13,940	57.6	1,239	3,978	699	155	497	..	2	137	0
Madagascar	49,827	11.6	..	..	854	10	12	141	12	417	22
Malawi	15,451	45.0	..	..	797	44	33	..	3	172	4
Malaysia	98,722	81.3	..	..	1,665	1,527	1,384	18,247	240	26,255	2,451
Mali	22,474	24.6	..	..	733	196	189	..	..	..	..
Mauritania	11,066	26.8	..	..	728	47	7,566	66	1	154	0
Mauritius	2,066	98.0	..	..	..	..	..	445	12	1,268	179
Mexico	366,807	35.3	436,900	211,600	26,704	178	71,136	3,694	186	13,608	1,380
Moldova	12,779	85.8	2,268	2,714	1,157	399	927	..	6	455	1
Mongolia	49,250	3.5	1,215	782	1,814	1,220	10,287	..	8	417	3
Morocco	58,216	70.3	..	800	2,109	4,398	5,572	2,058	92	8,971	11
Mozambique	30,331	20.8	..	..	3,116	114	695	223	14	553	8
Myanmar	27,000	11.9	..	..	..	4,163	885	167	8	396	2
Namibia	42,100	14.7	47	591	..	..	..	256	9	488	0
Nepal	19,875	53.9	..	..	..	..	..	..	2	288	4
Netherlands	136,827	90.0	..	72,675	3,016	15,400	4,331	11,331	243	27,554	5,028
New Zealand	94,301	66.2	..	..	..	..	4,078	2,427	186	10,128	668
Nicaragua	21,975	11.6	133	..	..	..	..	68	..	..	..
Niger	18,948	20.7	..	..	..	..	..	..	..	..	..
Nigeria	193,200	15.0	..	..	3,528	174	77	90	17	1,555	1
Norway	93,853	80.7	64,014	16,109	4,114	2,674	2,092	331	3[b]	399[b]	0[b]
Oman	56,361	46.0	..	..	..	..	..	3,893	35	4,068	27
Pakistan	258,350	65.4	263,788	129,249	7,791	24,731	6,187	2,149	50	6,012	310
Panama	13,974	42.0	..	..	..	..	..	5,906	81	7,366	2
Papua New Guinea	19,600	3.5	..	..	..	..	..	269	20	1,158	26
Paraguay	31,531	50.8	..	..	..	..	..	7	6	606	0
Peru	126,500	13.9	..	..	2,020	76	900	1,534	68	6,130	248
Philippines	200,037	9.9	..	..	479	83	1	4,947	169	18,933	472
Poland	384,104	69.9	24,386	191,484	19,702	15,715	34,266	1,045	91	5,466	91
Portugal	82,900	86.0	..	35,808	2,843	3,718	1,932	1,610	171	11,124	375
Puerto Rico	26,677	95.0	..	10	..	..	..	1,526	..	..	..
Qatar	7,790	90.0	..	..	..	..	..	346	91	12,391	2,946

	Roads				Railways			Ports	Air		
	Total road network km	Paved roads %	Passengers carried million passenger-km	Goods hauled million ton-km	Rail lines total route-km	Passengers carried million passenger-km	Goods hauled million ton-km	Port container traffic thousand TEU	Registered carrier departures worldwide thousands	Passengers carried thousands	Air freight million ton-km
	2000–09[a]	2000–09[a]	2000–09[a]	2000–09[a]	2000–10[a]	2000–10[a]	2000–10[a]	2010	2010	2010	2010
Romania	198,817	30.2	12,805	20,878	13,620	5,248	9,134	557	66	3,996	5
Russian Federation	982,000	80.1	139,034	180,135	85,292	139,028	2,011,308	3,130	673	56,848	4,614
Rwanda	14,008	19.0	..	..	..	..	..	..	..	..	..
Saudi Arabia	221,372	21.5	..	..	1,020	337	1,748	5,313	163	18,998	1,336
Senegal	14,825	32.0	..	..	906	129	384	349	0	573	0
Serbia	44,334	63.2	4,169	1,184	4,058	658	3,868	..	18	1,059	2
Sierra Leone	11,300	8.0	..	..	..	..	..	..	0	24	9
Singapore	3,356	100.0	5,762	..	..	..	..	29,179	81	25,319	4,004
Slovak Republic	43,879	87.1	31,093	27,484	3,587	2,291	7,669	..	14	991	0
Slovenia	38,927	100.0	777	14,762	1,228	813	3,283	477	25	1,170	2
Somalia	22,100	11.8	..	..	..	..	..	..	..	..	..
South Africa	362,099	17.3	..	434	22,051	18,865	113,342	3,806	210	16,779	1,107
South Sudan	..	..	..	..	..	..	..	..	..	..	..
Spain	667,064	99.0	410,192	211,891	15,317	22,304	7,844	12,608	606	58,563	1,684
Sri Lanka	97,286	81.0	21,067	..	1,463	4,767	135	4,080	17	2,800	329
Sudan	11,900	36.3	..	..	4,508	34	766	439	6	602	13
Swaziland	3,594	30.0	..	..	300	0	776	..	..	..	..
Sweden	582,950	24.4	109,100	35,000	9,957	6,774	11,500	1,391	3[b]	363[b]	0[b]
Switzerland	71,371	100.0	95,090	16,734	3,543	17,609	8,725	99	220	21,477	1,275
Syrian Arab Republic	68,157	90.3	589	..	2,139	1,120	2,370	649	11	1,018	3
Tajikistan	27,767	..	8,591	5,013	621	33	808	..	5	951	5
Tanzania	103,706	6.7	8	7	2,600[c]	475[c]	728[c]	427	21	749	2
Thailand	180,053	98.5	..	..	4,429	8,037	3,161	6,649	122	20,303	3,133
Timor-Leste	..	..	..	..	..	..	..	..	..	..	..
Togo	11,652	21.0	..	..	..	..	..	..	..	..	..
Trinidad and Tobago	8,320	51.1	..	..	..	..	..	573	25	1,721	13
Tunisia	19,371	75.2	..	16,611	1,119	1,493	2,073	466	44	5,464	21
Turkey	362,660	88.7	212,464	176,455	9,594	5,491	11,030	5,547	400	51,590	1,101
Turkmenistan	24,000	81.2	..	..	3,115	1,811	11,992	..	3	399	6
Uganda	70,746	23.0	..	..	259	..	218	..	0	70	32
Ukraine	169,495	97.8	54,631	33,193	21,705	50,240	218,091	660	84	5,679	598
United Arab Emirates	4,080	100.0	..	..	..	..	..	15,174	261	42,555	10,126
United Kingdom	419,665	100.0	736,000	143,453	31,471	55,019	12,512	7,389	1,173	123,972	8,555
United States	6,545,839	67.4	7,874,329	1,889,923	228,513	9,518	2,468,738[d]	42,190	8,934[e]	707,426[e]	50,743[e]
Uruguay	77,732	10.0	2,588	..	2,993	15	284	672	19	744	0
Uzbekistan	81,600	87.3	56,674	21,038	4,227	2,905	22,282	..	24	2,167	166
Venezuela, RB	96,155	33.6	..	..	336	..	81	1,216	125	5,881	5
Vietnam	160,089	47.6	59,735	30,261	2,347	4,378	3,901	5,984	103	14,099	428
West Bank and Gaza	5,588	91.7	..	..	..	..	..	..	..	..	..
Yemen, Rep.	71,300	8.7	..	..	..	..	..	370	11	1,134	28
Zambia	66,781	22.0	..	..	1,273	183	..	..	4	62	..
Zimbabwe	97,267	19.0	..	..	2,583	..	1,580	..	5	302	12
World	64.9 m	.. m	.. m	.. s	2,134 m	4,532 m	538,284 s	28,078 s	2,595,449 s	189,325 s	
Low income	20.7	..	..	..	..	..	..	182	13,444	1,142	
Middle income	53.5	..	..	..	1,220	4,802	260,211	8,539	834,810	41,820	
Lower middle income	48.6	..	..	..	1,120	3,910	51,323	1,973	185,587	5,190	
Upper middle income	57.6	..	..	..	1,269	4,032	208,887	6,566	649,224	36,630	
Low & middle income	44.8	..	..	..	..	3,127	263,722	8,721	848,254	42,962	
East Asia & Pacific	30.7	..	..	..	4,248	3,384	174,467	3,572	388,023	24,716	
Europe & Central Asia	85.8	14,625	9,375	177,892	658	8,250	10,901	1,464	136,681	6,725	
Latin America & Carib.	22.5	..	..	..	..	..	36,495	1,974	160,869	5,967	
Middle East & N. Africa	75.2	..	..	..	1,493	2,222	15,441	547	54,412	668	
South Asia	53.9	..	..	..	24,731	6,187	17,396	719	75,735	2,453	
Sub-Saharan Africa	18.8	..	..	..	..	..	..	445	32,534	2,432	
High income	81.1	..	28,585	..	7,090	8,285	274,561	19,357	1,747,195	146,364	
Euro area	87.3	69,000	28,035	131,414	10,306	7,669	73,233	4,711	457,356	30,754	

a. Data are for the most recent year available in the period shown. b. Covers international nonscheduled carriers only. Total for scheduled international and domestic carriers for Scandinavian countries are 621,715 registered carrier departures worldwide, 48,916,632 passengers carried, and 583,140,000 ton-kilometers of air freight. c. Includes Tazara railway. d. Refers to class 1 railways only. e. Covers only carriers designated by the U.S. Department of Transportation as major and national air carriers.

About the data

Transport infrastructure—highways, railways, ports and waterways, and airports and air traffic control systems—and the services that flow from it are crucial to the activities of households, producers, and governments. Because performance indicators vary widely by transport mode and focus (whether physical infrastructure or the services flowing from that infrastructure), highly specialized and carefully specified indicators are required. The table provides selected indicators of the size, extent, and productivity of roads, railways, and air transport systems and of the volume of traffic in these modes as well as in ports. Indicators on traffic and congestion are presented in table 3.15, and indicators on logistics performance are presented in table 6.8.

Data for transport sectors are not always internationally comparable. Unlike for demographic statistics, national income accounts, and international trade data, the collection of infrastructure data has not been "internationalized." But data on roads are collected by the International Road Federation (IRF), and data on air transport by the International Civil Aviation Organization (ICAO).

National road associations are the primary source of IRF data. In countries where a national road association is lacking or does not respond, other agencies are contacted, such as road directorates, ministries of transport or public works, or central statistical offices. As a result, definitions and data collection methods and quality differ, and the compiled data are of uneven quality. Moreover, the quality of transport service (reliability, transit time, and condition of goods delivered) is rarely measured, though it may be as important as quantity in assessing an economy's transport system.

Unlike the road sector, where numerous qualified motor vehicle operators can operate anywhere on the road network, railways are a restricted transport system with vehicles confined to a fixed guideway. Considering the cost and service characteristics, railways generally are best suited to carry—and can effectively compete for—bulk commodities and containerized freight for distances of 500–5,000 kilometers, and passengers for distances of 50–1,000 kilometers. Below these limits road transport tends to be more competitive, while above these limits air transport for passengers and freight and sea transport for freight tend to be more competitive. The railways indicators in the table focus on scale and output measures: total route-kilometers, passenger-kilometers, and goods (freight) hauled in ton-kilometers.

Measures of port container traffic, much of it commodities of medium to high value added, give some indication of economic growth in a country. But when traffic is merely transshipment, much of the economic benefit goes to the terminal operator and ancillary services for ships and containers rather than to the country more broadly. In transshipment centers empty containers may account for as much as 40 percent of traffic.

The air transport data represent the total (international and domestic) scheduled traffic carried by the air carriers registered in a country. Countries submit air transport data to ICAO on the basis of standard instructions and definitions issued by ICAO. In many cases, however, the data include estimates by ICAO for nonreporting carriers. Where possible, these estimates are based on previous submissions supplemented by information published by the air carriers, such as flight schedules.

The data cover the air traffic carried on scheduled services, but changes in air transport regulations in Europe have made it more difficult to classify traffic as scheduled or nonscheduled. Thus recent increases shown for some European countries may be due to changes in the classification of air traffic rather than actual growth. For countries with few air carriers or only one, the addition or discontinuation of a home-based air carrier may cause significant changes in air traffic.

Definitions

• **Total road network** covers motorways, highways, main or national roads, secondary or regional roads, and all other roads in a country. • **Paved roads** are roads surfaced with crushed stone (macadam) and hydrocarbon binder or bituminized agents, with concrete, or with cobblestones. • **Passengers carried by road** are the number of passengers transported by road times kilometers traveled. • **Goods hauled by road** are the volume of goods transported by road vehicles, measured in millions of metric tons times kilometers traveled. • **Rail lines** are the length of railway route available for train service, irrespective of the number of parallel tracks. • **Passengers carried by railway** are the number of passengers transported by rail times kilometers traveled. • **Goods hauled by railway** are the volume of goods transported by railway, measured in metric tons times kilometers traveled. • **Port container traffic** measures the flow of containers from land to sea transport modes and vice versa in twenty-foot-equivalent units (TEUs), a standard-size container. Data cover coastal shipping as well as international journeys. Transshipment traffic is counted as two lifts at the intermediate port (once to off-load and again as an outbound lift) and includes empty units. • **Registered carrier departures worldwide** are domestic takeoffs and takeoffs abroad of air carriers registered in the country. • **Passengers carried by air** include both domestic and international passengers of air carriers registered in the country. • **Air freight** is the volume of freight, express, and diplomatic bags carried on each flight stage (operation of an aircraft from takeoff to its next landing), measured in metric tons times kilometers traveled.

Data sources

Data on roads are from the IRF's *World Road Statistics,* supplemented by World Bank staff estimates. Data on railways are from a database maintained by the World Bank's Transport, Water, and Information and Communication Technologies Department, Transport Division, based on data from the International Union of Railways. Data on port container traffic are from Containerisation International's *Containerisation International Yearbook* and the United Nations Conference on Trade and Development's UNCTADstat database (http://unctadstat.unctad.org). Data on air transport are from the ICAO's *Civil Aviation Statistics of the World* and ICAO staff estimates.

	Electric power			Telephones[a]							
			Access and use				Quality	Affordability and efficiency			
			Subscriptions per 100 people		International voice traffic minutes per person		Population covered by mobile cellular network %	$ per month			Mobile cellular and fixed-telephone subscriptions per employee
	Consumption per capita kWh	Transmission and distribution losses % of output	Fixed telephone	Mobile cellular	Fixed telephone	Mobile cellular network		Residential fixed-telephone tariff	Mobile cellular prepaid tariff	Telecommunications revenue % of GDP	
	2009	2009	2010	2010	2010	2010	2010	2010	2010	2010	2010
Afghanistan	..	..	0	38	..	..	75	..	..	..	..
Albania	1,747	21	10	142	46	201	98	6.4	25.8	4.7	1,151
Algeria	971	21	8	92	17	36	..	5.4	12.5	3.6	..
Angola	202	10	2	47	..	..	..	16.5	19.2	..	..
Argentina	2,759	15	25	142	44	..	..	3.8	30.7	3.2	..
Armenia	1,550	15	19	125	185	233	99	4.2	8.8	4.4	969
Australia	11,113	7	39	101	..	..	99	27.6	27.7	..	315
Austria	7,944	5	39	146	..	..	99	25.3	13.9	1.8	961
Azerbaijan	1,620	22	17	101	20	74	100	2.5	6.9	2.7	645
Bahrain	9,214	12	18	124	..	..	100	4.8	15.0	4.4	698
Bangladesh	252	2	1	46	..	..	..	1.3	2.0	..	..
Belarus	3,299	11	44	109	98	25	100	1.3	7.9	3.1	..
Belgium	7,903	5	43	112	..	..	100	31.4	40.2	2.6	907
Benin	91	..	2	80	12	52	90	9.0	13.0	5.4	3,146
Bolivia	558	11	9	72	84	..	..	23.7	11.3	7.3	..
Bosnia and Herzegovina	2,867	12	27	83	190	73	100	9.3	15.4	5.3	499
Botswana	1,503	79	7	118	113	..	99	18.7	13.2	3.5	4,031
Brazil	2,206	17	22	104	..	..	100	23.0	57.2	4.9	..
Bulgaria	4,401	11	30	135	70	84	100	12.5	30.6	3.2	543
Burkina Faso	..	..	1	35	..	..	..	10.9	21.2	..	2,306
Burundi	..	..	0	14	..	..	83	..	..	3.1	838
Cambodia	131	18	3	58	..	..	99	7.4	6.7	5.5	1,333
Cameroon	271	9	3	44	3	26	..	15.0	20.1	3.8	2,251
Canada	15,471	8	50	70	..	..	99	19.4	34.3	2.7	..
Central African Republic	..	..	0	22	0	12	55	10.1	12.9	2.9	..
Chad	..	..	0	24	..	..	..	16.7	15.4	..	..
Chile	3,283	11	20	116	30	9	100	25.0	23.7	..	646
China	2,631	5	22	64	9	..	99	4.7	6.0	2.0	1,254
Hong Kong SAR, China	5,925	13	62	195	1,463	504	100	8.5	1.4	3.5	1,066
Colombia	1,047	15	16	96	83	..	..	5.9	16.9	4.2	466
Congo, Dem. Rep.	104	5	0	18	0	7	50	..	..	4.9	5,538
Congo, Rep.	146	73	0	94	..	..	..	..	..	..	..
Costa Rica	1,813	11	32	65	141	77	70	6.9	3.4	2.1	498
Côte d'Ivoire	203	25	1	76	30	47	92	19.6	13.6	6.7	3,912
Croatia	3,712	16	42	144	248	66	100	17.0	17.1	4.6	945
Cuba	1,348	14	10	9	19	16	78	0.3	33.9	..	129
Cyprus	4,620	4	37	94	367	504	100	23.8	7.7	3.6	458
Czech Republic	6,114	5	23	137	90	80	100	26.8	28.1	3.4	778
Denmark	6,246	6	47	125	189	186	..	27.8	9.8	2.3	616
Dominican Republic	1,358	11	10	90	322	..	81	15.5	15.6	2.2	1,394
Ecuador	1,115	14	14	102	55	20	93	14.1	13.8	..	..
Egypt, Arab Rep.	1,549	11	12	87	11	22	100	2.9	7.0	3.2	1,217
El Salvador	845	12	16	124	..	..	..	10.2	9.5	3.5	2,748
Eritrea	51	12	1	4	6	18	90	..	..	3.2	149
Estonia	5,950	10	36	123	85	99	100	11.5	22.3	4.9	631
Ethiopia	46	10	1	8	6	4	..	1.0	4.1	1.5	604
Finland	15,242	4	23	156	..	..	100	16.8	13.1	2.7	708
France	7,488	6	54	97	288	74	99	26.6	48.6	2.3	789
Gabon	922	18	2	107	26	23	..	..	..	..	..
Gambia, The	..	..	3	86	..	..	..	2.4	6.3	..	..
Georgia	1,585	13	25	89	56	64	99	2.3	11.6	3.7	697
Germany	6,779	4	56	128	..	43	99	27.0	13.1	2.4	851
Ghana	265	23	1	71	10	60	77	7.3	7.4	3.7	3,764
Greece	5,540	5	46	109	185	114	100	23.8	38.5	3.0	804
Guatemala	548	14	10	126	..	..	..	5.6	7.8	..	..
Guinea	..	..	0	40	..	..	80	1.6	4.1	..	..
Guinea-Bissau	..	..	0	39	..	..	..	..	..	..	..
Haiti	36	51	1	40	..	..	..	..	..	..	..

	Electric power		Telephones[a]								
	Consumption per capita kWh	Transmission and distribution losses % of output	Access and use				Quality	Affordability and efficiency			
			Subscriptions per 100 people		International voice traffic minutes per person		Population covered by mobile cellular network %	$ per month		Telecom-munications revenue % of GDP	Mobile cellular and fixed-telephone subscriptions per employee
			Fixed telephone	Mobile cellular	Fixed telephone	Mobile cellular network		Residential fixed-telephone tariff	Mobile cellular prepaid tariff		
	2009	2009	2010	2010	2010	2010	2010	2010	2010	2010	2010
Honduras	678	22	9	125	39	197	..	6.3	8.9	6.2	..
Hungary	3,773	10	30	120	..	..	99	21.2	25.7	3.8	1,127
India	571	24	3	61	..	..	83	3.3	3.4	2.3	..
Indonesia	590	10	16	92	..	..	..	5.0	7.8	..	..
Iran, Islamic Rep.	2,238	17	36	91	..	..	..	0.2	3.6	..	..
Iraq	1,069	40	5	75	0	..	..	..	..	..	1,466
Ireland	6,034	8	46	105	..	..	99	26.3	37.3	2.5	534
Israel	6,608	3	43	130	413	..	100	15.7	34.1	4.0	..
Italy	5,271	7	36	150	..	..	99	25.6	29.8	2.1	1,341
Jamaica	1,902	7	10	118	119	978	..	11.6	12.0	5.4	..
Japan	7,819	5	32	95	..	..	100	26.4	55.9	3.0	1,304
Jordan	2,112	14	8	109	23	217	99	9.5	10.5	5.9	1,499
Kazakhstan	4,448	8	25	119	23	54	95	2.4	14.4	2.2	463
Kenya	147	16	1	62	1	23	89	14.2	10.8	6.3	2,546
Korea, Dem. Rep.	733	16	5	2	..	..	..	..	..	..	..
Korea, Rep.	8,980	4	58	104	24	45	100	5.3	14.4	4.6	703
Kosovo	..	..	..	..	..	..	..	..	..	..	..
Kuwait	17,610	12	21	161	..	..	100	8.6	7.8	..	..
Kyrgyz Republic	1,386	30	9	97	40	19	96	1.2	3.6	7.9	442
Lao PDR	..	..	2	65	..	..	80	4.0	6.3	3.8	1,283
Latvia	2,875	13	24	103	..	..	..	10.1	10.1	3.6	661
Lebanon	3,130	13	21	68	..	..	95	10.3	27.3	..	..
Lesotho	..	..	2	45	..	26	..	13.0	24.1	3.1	6,933
Liberia	..	..	0	39	..	52	..	..	..	..	..
Libya	4,170	14	19	172	..	..	98	..	..	..	..
Lithuania	3,431	7	22	149	49	61	100	13.1	9.6	2.7	..
Macedonia, FYR	3,442	17	20	105	165	86	100	11.9	23.4	5.7	329
Madagascar	..	..	1	37	1	6	..	18.2	15.4	2.8	3,203
Malawi	..	..	1	20	5	1	85	4.3	21.2	3.6	..
Malaysia	3,614	4	16	119	85	..	95	5.1	7.5	..	..
Mali	..	..	1	48	2	21	..	8.5	14.4	6.1	4,091
Mauritania	..	..	2	79	4	..	62	18.0	14.6	6.9	2,842
Mauritius	..	..	30	93	105	148	99	5.1	6.8	2.4	..
Mexico	1,943	16	18	81	159	..	100	18.9	17.4	3.0	918
Moldova	1,018	40	33	89	126	133	..	1.9	12.6	8.5	461
Mongolia	1,411	12	7	91	4	48	85	0.7	3.6	5.6	372
Morocco	756	12	12	100	66	63	98	21.3	33.1	4.7	2,770
Mozambique	453	9	0	31	..	9	32	12.4	17.0	3.9	2,430
Myanmar	104	16	1	1	..	..	..	0.9	12.8	..	83
Namibia	1,576	15	7	67	..	..	..	15.1	17.0	..	..
Nepal	91	31	3	31	..	..	35	3.1	2.7	..	981
Netherlands	6,896	4	44	115	..	84	98	22.4	33.2	2.3	..
New Zealand	9,346	7	43	115	..	..	97	34.1	47.2	3.2	600
Nicaragua	460	24	4	65	39	..	100	4.5	13.2	..	..
Niger	..	..	1	25	..	..	..	11.7	20.8	..	..
Nigeria	121	6	1	55	1	30	90	14.0	13.7	3.4	..
Norway	23,550	8	34	116	..	..	..	32.7	20.5	1.3	..
Oman	5,724	13	10	166	24	406	98	13.1	9.1	3.5	1,275
Pakistan	449	20	2	57	5	33	92	3.3	2.5	2.4	1,888
Panama	1,735	13	16	185	53	77	91	12.0	8.5	3.3	712
Papua New Guinea	..	..	2	28	..	..	..	4.5	23.3	..	..
Paraguay	1,056	6	6	92	41	21	94	6.8	8.6	4.0	..
Peru	1,136	8	11	100	..	..	97	14.6	43.2	2.9	2,512
Philippines	593	12	7	86	..	..	99	15.3	10.1	..	4,504
Poland	3,591	8	20	123	..	..	99	20.2	15.8	3.0	945
Portugal	4,815	8	42	143	..	121	99	25.3	22.9	4.5	1,507
Puerto Rico	..	..	22	74	..	..	68	..	..	..	411
Qatar	14,421	7	17	132	..	..	100	9.1	18.4	1.6	927

	Electric power		Telephones[a]								
	Consumption per capita kWh 2009	Transmission and distribution losses % of output 2009	Access and use				Quality	Affordability and efficiency			
			Subscriptions per 100 people		International voice traffic minutes per person		Population covered by mobile cellular network % 2010	$ per month		Telecom-munications revenue % of GDP 2010	Mobile cellular and fixed-telephone subscriptions per employee 2010
			Fixed telephone 2010	Mobile cellular 2010	Fixed telephone 2010	Mobile cellular network 2010		Residential fixed-telephone tariff 2010	Mobile cellular prepaid tariff 2010		
Romania	2,267	12	21	115	49	97	100	13.3	21.8	3.0	883
Russian Federation	6,136	11	32	168	..	..	..	6.2	9.2	2.8	820
Rwanda	..	..	0	33	0	15	96	13.2	13.9	3.0	3,892
Saudi Arabia	7,427	8	15	188	..	..	99	9.2	14.1	3.8	2,381
Senegal	196	17	3	67	12	101	90	10.3	12.7	9.9	3,710
Serbia	4,224	16	43	136	125	59	97	5.4	11.6	5.1	865
Sierra Leone	..	..	0	34	..	..	..	..	..	..	..
Singapore	7,949	5	39	145	..	..	100	8.2	8.1	4.0	..
Slovak Republic	4,925	3	20	109	170	109	100	20.4	38.2	3.0	688
Slovenia	6,103	5	44	104	81	117	100	17.9	20.8	3.6	552
Somalia	..	..	1	7	..	..	..	..	..	..	..
South Africa	4,532	10	8	101	..	..	..	25.0	23.3	..	..
South Sudan	..	..	..	..	..	..	..	..	..	..	..
Spain	6,006	3	44	112	163	..	100	27.0	53.2	2.7	923
Sri Lanka	408	15	17	83	..	..	98	4.9	1.9	..	1,524
Sudan	114	28	1	41	6	..	66	3.9	3.4	3.2	2,168
Swaziland	..	..	4	69	..	..	91	5.0	24.2	4.5	2,000
Sweden	14,142	7	53	116	..	..	99	25.5	17.2	1.6	813
Switzerland	8,021	6	56	122	..	..	100	29.4	57.0	3.2	599
Syrian Arab Republic	1,563	28	20	58	35	74	98	1.3	19.9	11.7	..
Tajikistan	1,985	17	5	86	..	..	..	0.9	1.8	..	..
Tanzania	86	19	0	47	0	7	85	8.8	9.7	..	..
Thailand	2,045	6	10	104	..	..	..	8.8	8.7	..	..
Timor-Leste	..	..	0	53	98	22	69	17.3	16.1	8.1	1,751
Togo	111	53	4	41	4	42	75	11.0	19.9	9.5	1,896
Trinidad and Tobago	5,662	2	22	141	..	..	100	19.5	12.1	2.8	1,862
Tunisia	1,311	13	12	105	21	52	100	2.5	10.0	3.9	1,130
Turkey	2,298	15	22	85	73	29	100	16.8	43.9	2.0	2,069
Turkmenistan	2,446	14	10	63	..	..	..	..	..	..	..
Uganda	..	..	1	38	..	..	100	8.8	12.2	4.3	2,046
Ukraine	3,200	12	28	118	..	..	100	3.0	7.5	4.0	..
United Arab Emirates	11,464	12	20	145	..	..	100	4.1	8.6	3.6	1,094
United Kingdom	5,692	7	54	130	..	..	100	21.0	31.0	4.5	..
United States	12,914	6	49	90	..	..	100	12.8	32.7	2.0	478
Uruguay	2,671	13	29	132	..	..	100	13.3	17.8	3.1	765
Uzbekistan	1,636	9	7	74	..	..	93	1.1	3.0	..	739
Venezuela, RB	3,152	27	25	97	46	..	..	1.7	22.3	3.3	1,490
Vietnam	918	10	19	177	..	..	..	2.4	5.4	7.1	..
West Bank and Gaza	..	..	9	45	..	..	..	..	..	..	..
Yemen, Rep.	219	24	4	46	20	61	84	1.1	8.1	3.3	1,273
Zambia	635	23	1	42	..	..	90	24.1	16.9	..	..
Zimbabwe	1,026	7	3	61	15	23	80	9.1	20.5	..	2,369
World	**2,803 w**	**8 w**	**17 w**	**78 w**	**.. w**	**.. w**	**93 w**	**11.3 m**	**14.4 m**	**2.7 w**	**887 m**
Low income	229	12	1	33	..	..	..	8.8	13.0	..	2,306
Middle income	1,675	11	14	78	..	..	92	7.1	12.6	3.2	1,044
Lower middle income	644	19	6	72	..	..	86	5.3	10.7	3.4	..
Upper middle income	2,714	9	22	84	30	..	99	9.8	14.9	2.4	765
Low & middle income	1,525	11	12	72	..	..	91	8.8	12.7	3.2	1,168
East Asia & Pacific	2,095	5	19	73	11	..	99	5.1	7.7	2.1	1,283
Europe & Central Asia	3,859	12	26	124	..	..	..	4.8	10.8	2.7	697
Latin America & Carib.	1,892	16	18	98	..	..	98	10.9	14.7	4.2	..
Middle East & N. Africa	1,497	18	16	86	17	..	..	4.1	11.5	..	1,131
South Asia	517	23	3	59	..	..	84	3.3	2.5	2.3	1,363
Sub-Saharan Africa	511	11	1	45	..	21	..	12.0	15.0	..	1,840
High income	9,064	6	44	111	..	..	100	21.2	22.3	2.6	784
Euro area	6,592	5	46	122	..	..	99	25.3	29.8	2.4	789

a. Data are from the International Telecommunication Union's (ITU) World Telecommunication/ICT Indicators database. Please cite the ITU for third-party use of these data.

About the data

The quality of an economy's infrastructure, including power and communications, is an important element in investment decisions for both domestic and foreign investors. Government effort alone is not enough to meet the need for investments in modern infrastructure; public-private partnerships, especially those involving local providers and financiers, are critical for lowering costs and delivering value for money. In telecommunications, competition in the marketplace, along with sound regulation, is lowering costs, improving quality, and easing access to services around the globe.

An economy's production and consumption of electricity are basic indicators of its size and level of development. Although a few countries export electric power, most production is for domestic consumption. Expanding the supply of electricity to meet the growing demand of increasingly urbanized and industrialized economies without incurring unacceptable social, economic, and environmental costs is one of the great challenges facing developing countries.

Data on electric power production and consumption are collected from national energy agencies by the International Energy Agency (IEA) and adjusted by the IEA to meet international definitions (for data on electricity production, see table 3.8). Electricity consumption is equivalent to production less power plants' own use and transmission, distribution, and transformation losses less exports plus imports. It includes consumption by auxiliary stations, losses in transformers that are considered integral parts of those stations, and electricity produced by pumping installations. Where data are available, it covers electricity generated by primary sources of energy—coal, oil, gas, nuclear, hydro, geothermal, wind, tide and wave, and combustible renewables. Neither production nor consumption data capture the reliability of supplies, including breakdowns, load factors, and frequency of outages.

Over the past decade new financing and technology, along with privatization and market liberalization, have spurred dramatic growth in telecommunications in many countries. With the rapid development of mobile telephony and the global expansion of the Internet, information and communication technologies are increasingly recognized as essential tools of development, contributing to global integration and enhancing public sector effectiveness, efficiency, and transparency. The table presents telecommunications indicators covering access and use, quality, and affordability and efficiency.

Access to telecommunication services rose on an unprecedented scale over the past 15 years. This growth was driven primarily by wireless technologies and liberalization of telecommunications markets, which have enabled faster and less costly network rollout. Developing countries' share of world mobile subscriptions rose from 53 percent in 2005 to 73 percent in 2010. And the number of short message service texts sent globally tripled between 2007 and 2010, from 1.8 trillion to 6.1 trillion. The International Telecommunication Union (ITU) estimates that there were 5.9 billion mobile subscriptions globally in 2011. No technology has ever spread faster around the world. Mobile communications have a particularly important impact in rural areas. The mobility, ease of use, flexible deployment, and relatively low and declining rollout costs of wireless technologies enable them to reach rural populations with low levels of income and literacy. The next billion mobile subscribers will consist mainly of the rural poor.

Access is the key to delivering telecommunications services to people. If the service is not affordable to most people, goals of universal usage will not be met. Two indicators of telecommunications affordability are presented in the table: fixed-telephone service tariff and prepaid mobile cellular service tariff. Telecommunications efficiency is measured by total telecommunications revenue divided by GDP and by mobile cellular and fixed-telephone subscriptions per employee.

Operators have traditionally been the main source of telecommunications data, so information on subscriptions has been widely available for most countries. This gives a general idea of access, but a more precise measure is the penetration rate—the share of households with access to telecommunications. During the past few years more information on information and communication technology use has become available from household and business surveys. Also important are data on actual use of telecommunications services. Ideally, statistics on telecommunications (and other information and communications technologies) should be compiled for all three measures: subscriptions, access, and use. The quality of data varies among reporting countries as a result of differences in regulations covering data provision and availability.

Definitions

• **Electric power consumption per capita** is the production of power plants and combined heat and power plants less transmission, distribution, and transformation losses and own use by heat and power plants, divided by midyear population. • **Electric power transmission and distribution losses** are losses in transmission between sources of supply and points of distribution and in distribution to consumers, including pilferage. • **Fixed-telephone subscriptions** are the sum of the active number of analog fixed-telephone lines, voice-over-IP subscriptions, fixed wireless local loop subscriptions, Integrated Services Digital Network voice-channel equivalents, and fixed public payphones. • **Mobile cellular telephone subscriptions** are subscriptions to a public mobile telephone service using cellular technology, which provide access to the public switched telephone network. Post-paid and prepaid subscriptions are included. • **International voice traffic** is the sum of international incoming and outgoing telephone traffic (in minutes) divided by total population. • **Population covered by mobile cellular network** is the percentage of people that live in areas served by a mobile cellular signal regardless of whether they use it. • **Residential fixed-telephone tariff** is the monthly subscription charge plus the cost of 30 three-minute local calls (15 peak and 15 off-peak). • **Mobile cellular prepaid tariff** is based on the Organisation for Economic Co-operation and Development's low-user definition, which includes the cost of monthly mobile use for 25 outgoing calls per month spread over the same mobile network, other mobile networks, and mobile to fixed-telephone calls and during peak, off-peak, and weekend times as well as 30 text messages per month. • **Telecommunications revenue** is the revenue from the provision of telecommunications services such as fixed telephone, mobile, and Internet divided by GDP. • **Mobile cellular and fixed-telephone subscriptions per employee** are telephone subscriptions (fixed telephone plus mobile) divided by the total number of telecommunications employees.

Data sources

Data on electricity consumption and losses are from the IEA's *Energy Statistics of Non-OECD Countries 2011, Energy Balances of Non-OECD Countries 2011,* and *Energy Statistics of OECD Countries 2011* and from the United Nations Statistics Division's *Energy Statistics Yearbook*. Data on telecommunications are from the ITU's World Telecommunication/ICT Indicators database and TeleGeography.

5.12 | The information society

	Daily newspapers	Households with television[a]	Personal computers and the Internet							Information and communications technology trade		
			Use		Quality		Affordability	Application		Goods		Services
			per 100 people		Fixed broadband Internet subscriptions[a] per 100 people	International Internet bandwidth[a] bits per second per capita	Fixed broadband Internet access tariff[a] $ per month	Secure Internet servers per million people		Exports % of total goods exports	Imports % of total goods imports	Exports % of total services exports
	per 1,000 people	%	Computers users[a]	Internet users[a]								
	2000–05[b]	2010	2010	2010	2010	2010	2010	December 2011		2010	2010	2010
Afghanistan	..	..	..	3.7	0.00	58	..	1		..	0.4	..
Albania	24	..	..	45.0	3.29	5,304	11	14		0.8	4.1	4.8
Algeria	..	98	..	12.5	2.54	1,015	15	1		0.0	3.0	3.5
Angola	2	38	..	10.0	0.10	63	133	3		..	..	5.4
Argentina	36	..	..	36.0	9.56	9,898	26	34		0.1	9.1	11.7
Armenia	8	97	..	44.0	2.75	3,411	32	28		0.8	4.7	16.8
Australia	155	..	..	75.9	24.15	31,392	37	2,006		1.0	10.6	4.9
Austria	311	..	77.8	72.7	23.86	53,635	26	996		3.9	5.8	6.2
Azerbaijan	16	100	38.6	46.7	5.08	4,524	12	5		0.0	3.5	4.0
Bahrain	..	..	72.0	55.0	5.36	7,924	27	118		0.9	4.4	..
Bangladesh	..	36	..	3.7	0.04	103	15	1		..	..	13.0
Belarus	81	98	..	32.1	17.55	7,060	18	12		0.5	2.4	8.8
Belgium	165	..	78.8	73.7	30.96	82,599	25	604		2.3	3.5	9.2
Benin	0	25	..	3.1	0.04	70	50	1		..	..	..
Bolivia	..	69	..	20.0	0.97	854	35	10		0.0	3.4	11.8
Bosnia and Herzegovina	..	97	..	52.0	8.18	8,138	14	20		0.1	2.9	..
Botswana	41	..	..	6.0	0.60	386	30	9		0.3	3.1	5.5
Brazil	36	98	44.1	40.7	6.81	5,130	17	54		1.0	9.5	2.0
Bulgaria	79	99	48.0	46.0	14.44	29,520	13	139		2.5	5.6	8.9
Burkina Faso	..	18	..	1.4	0.09	49	83	1		0.0	2.5	10.5
Burundi	..	..	..	2.1	0.00	2	..	0		0.4	5.8	..
Cambodia	..	60	..	1.3	0.25	354	47	3		0.1	2.5	5.5
Cameroon	..	33	..	4.0	0.01	16	80	1		0.0	2.6	3.6
Canada	175	99	..	81.3	29.71	43,955	26	1,369		2.8	8.4	11.4
Central African Republic	..	..	..	2.3	0.00	4	1,329	0		0.0	6.8	..
Chad	..	..	..	1.7	0.00	2	12	..		..	..	..
Chile	51	..	42.8	45.0	10.45	8,613	39	67		0.4	8.2	2.2
China	74	..	..	34.4	9.44	821	18	2		29.1	20.4	6.1
Hong Kong SAR, China	222	..	70.0	71.8	29.87	557,998	19	568		44.2	42.8	1.8
Colombia	23	91	43.1	36.5	5.60	3,739	35	21		0.1	9.6	6.2
Congo, Dem. Rep.	..	..	..	0.7	0.01	2	..	0		..	..	..
Congo, Rep.	..	38	..	5.0	0.00	2	..	1		..	..	..
Costa Rica	65	96	42.6	36.5	6.19	4,630	7	111		19.9	17.7	26.6
Côte d'Ivoire	..	..	..	2.6	0.04	203	40	1		0.2	3.3	11.0
Croatia	..	97	58.0	60.1	18.19	25,804	18	225		2.1	5.5	3.6
Cuba	65	..	..	15.9	0.03	35	1,753	0		..	..	..
Cyprus	..	100	57.2	53.0	17.63	27,380	21	1,121		9.1	4.8	2.3
Czech Republic	183	..	70.7	68.6	14.46	47,529	31	387		15.0	17.8	8.6
Denmark	353	98	89.9	88.8	37.72	126,194	44	2,185		3.6	7.9	..
Dominican Republic	39	86	..	39.5	3.63	4,029	19	20		2.3	4.8	4.5
Ecuador	99	85	37.5	29.0	1.37	2,394	20	20		0.1	6.3	..
Egypt, Arab Rep.	..	94	21.6	26.7	1.79	1,762	8	3		0.1	3.7	4.2
El Salvador	38	83	21.0	15.9	2.83	242	25	17		0.3	5.6	17.7
Eritrea	..	..	..	5.4	0.00	6	..	..		..	..	..
Estonia	191	99	75.6	74.2	25.10	17,164	21	534		7.8	9.5	8.9
Ethiopia	5	..	..	0.7	0.00	40	294	0		0.2	8.4	4.5
Finland	431	..	88.7	86.9	28.57	93,214	35	1,489		6.4	8.2	24.5
France	164	99	78.0	77.5	32.89	53,933	30	356		4.4	7.3	4.2
Gabon	..	..	..	7.2	0.27	3,767	..	8		0.0	3.5	..
Gambia, The	..	76	..	9.2	0.02	98	307	3		0.4	1.5	17.8
Georgia	4	94	..	26.3	5.70	5,615	39	19		0.2	5.3	2.2
Germany	267	95	85.4	82.5	31.90	61,142	39	1,026		5.1	9.2	9.1
Ghana	..	47	..	9.5	0.21	139	32	2		0.0	7.1	..
Greece	..	100	49.5	44.6	19.95	13,816	19	154		2.5	5.0	2.4
Guatemala	..	71	..	10.5	1.80	417	33	14		0.9	6.8	14.3
Guinea	..	..	..	1.0	0.01	15	800	0		0.0	5.2	21.6
Guinea-Bissau	..	..	..	2.5	0.00	1	..	1		..	..	..
Haiti	..	..	..	8.4	0.00	9	..	1		..	..	..

	Daily newspapers per 1,000 people 2000–05[b]	Households with television[a] % 2010	Personal computers and the Internet — Use per 100 people — Computers users[a] 2010	Use per 100 people — Internet users[a] 2010	Quality — Fixed broadband Internet subscriptions[a] per 100 people 2010	Quality — International Internet bandwidth[a] bits per second per capita 2010	Affordability — Fixed broadband Internet access tariff[a] $ per month 2010	Application — Secure Internet servers per million people December 2011	Goods Exports % of total goods exports 2010	Goods Imports % of total goods imports 2010	Services Exports % of total services exports 2010
Honduras	..	69	..	11.1	1.00	658	22	8	0.1	6.3	25.2
Hungary	217	99	67.1	65.2	19.56	6,500	21	220	25.6	21.3	8.5
India	71	60	..	7.5	0.90	437	5	3	2.0	6.6	47.0
Indonesia	..	72	..	9.9	0.79	292	22	3	5.1	8.6	7.4
Iran, Islamic Rep.	..	97	..	13.0	0.68	406	30	1	0.0	3.6	..
Iraq	..	98	13.5	2.5	0.00	2	..	0	..	..	0.6
Ireland	182	..	72.0	69.8	21.04	44,693	33	1,145	7.5	10.2	39.0
Israel	..	90	65.6	65.4	24.46	5,247	8	471	12.3	9.2	33.0
Italy	137	..	55.7	53.7	21.92	33,067	26	192	2.1	7.4	8.9
Jamaica	..	88	..	26.5	4.32	5,551	25	48	0.4	3.9	6.4
Japan	551	99	66.9	77.6	26.71	12,293	23	743	10.7	12.0	1.3
Jordan	..	98	56.0	38.9	3.24	2,481	19	25	1.3	4.3	..
Kazakhstan	..	87	..	33.4	8.74	2,868	13	6	0.1	2.9	2.4
Kenya	..	28	..	25.9	0.01	499	38	3	1.4	7.2	9.8
Korea, Dem. Rep.	..	..	..	0.0	0.00	..	..	0	..	..	..
Korea, Rep.	..	..	81.5	82.5	35.18	9,802	24	2,536	21.4	11.9	1.2
Kosovo	..	..	..	..	..	..	..	..	..	..	..
Kuwait	..	..	..	38.3	1.68	3,655	19	180	0.3	6.4	..
Kyrgyz Republic	1	..	..	19.6	0.28	55	55	3	0.6	2.7	3.3
Lao PDR	3	..	..	7.0	0.19	161	140	1	..	..	..
Latvia	154	..	69.7	71.5	19.42	21,438	13	205	5.8	6.4	6.2
Lebanon	54	..	..	31.0	4.73	591	23	41	7.1	2.8	3.0
Lesotho	..	..	..	3.9	0.02	12	51	0	20.9	2.7	4.5
Liberia	..	9	..	7.0	0.00	14	..	1	..	..	..
Libya	..	..	..	14.0	1.15	1,574	..	1	..	..	..
Lithuania	108	99	64.2	62.8	20.81	28,533	10	237	2.7	4.1	3.7
Macedonia, FYR	89	..	57.5	51.9	12.47	8,738	13	29	0.4	4.7	14.1
Madagascar	..	16	..	1.7	0.03	94	91	1	0.2	3.1	..
Malawi	..	..	..	2.3	0.03	1	562	0	0.4	5.2	..
Malaysia	109	..	..	56.3	7.32	6,443	20	54	34.0	29.8	7.0
Mali	..	31	..	2.7	0.02	50	50	1	0.1	2.6	23.2
Mauritania	..	25	..	3.0	0.19	81	24	2	..	0.9	..
Mauritius	77	97	35.8	28.7	6.18	2,646	16	117	1.1	5.1	3.8
Mexico	93	95	40.1	31.1	9.98	2,272	17	27	20.2	19.2	..
Moldova	..	93	42.4	40.1	7.55	26,390	6	20	0.7	3.9	22.7
Mongolia	20	89	..	12.9	2.60	6,237	8	14	..	..	2.0
Morocco	12	93	50.9	49.0	1.56	2,347	12	4	3.8	5.9	8.0
Mozambique	3	..	..	4.2	0.06	55	22	1	0.1	1.8	7.0
Myanmar	..	..	..	0.2	0.03	21	28	0	..	..	..
Namibia	28	42	..	6.5	0.42	287	95	20	0.5	4.0	1.7
Nepal	..	36	..	7.9	0.20	134	23	2	0.4	7.2	..
Netherlands	307	99	91.7	90.7	38.10	139,986	33	2,757	12.5	14.5	11.7
New Zealand	182	97	82.7	83.0	24.93	16,026	29	1,597	1.2	8.3	4.6
Nicaragua	..	66	..	10.0	0.82	864	34	10	0.1	4.8	..
Niger	0	10	0.9	0.8	0.02	19	60	0	0.3	1.9	12.8
Nigeria	..	41	..	28.4	0.06	32	53	2	0.0	6.6	..
Norway	516	..	93.8	93.3	35.26	102,270	49	1,822	1.4	7.5	9.5
Oman	..	..	..	62.0	1.63	3,786	31	53	0.1	3.1	..
Pakistan	50	68	..	16.8	0.31	435	14	1	0.2	3.3	6.6
Panama	65	92	..	42.7	7.84	9,096	17	143	9.6	9.6	4.8
Papua New Guinea	9	..	..	1.3	0.09	41	140	7	..	..	0.7
Paraguay	..	88	..	19.8	0.44	1,644	19	10	0.1	27.0	1.4
Peru	..	77	..	34.3	3.14	2,911	42	19	0.1	7.4	3.1
Philippines	79	74	..	25.0	1.85	2,681	22	8	35.6	31.6	12.6
Poland	114	..	65.4	62.5	12.99	23,570	18	270	9.5	9.7	6.4
Portugal	..	..	58.2	51.3	19.30	75,202	26	224	4.0	5.7	4.2
Puerto Rico	..	..	61.3	42.7	13.86	57,818	..	98	..	..	..
Qatar	..	95	84.6	81.6	8.19	13,930	55	126	0.0	4.3	..

	Daily newspapers	Households with television[a]	Personal computers and the Internet						Information and communications technology trade		
			Use		Quality		Affordability	Application	Goods		Services
					Fixed broadband Internet subscriptions[a] per 100 people	International Internet bandwidth[a] bits per second per capita	Fixed broadband Internet access tariff[a] $ per month	Secure Internet servers per million people	Exports % of total goods exports	Imports % of total goods imports	Exports % of total services exports
	per 1,000 people	%	Computers users[a]	Internet users[a]							
	2000–05[b]	2010	2010	2010	2010	2010	2010	December 2011	2010	2010	2010
Romania	70	..	45.9	40.0	13.90	20,571	5	54	8.4	9.3	18.0
Russian Federation	92	99	40.3	43.4	11.08	13,346	10	27	0.2	7.9	6.0
Rwanda	..	3	..	13.0	0.02	155	86	1	0.6	11.7	4.4
Saudi Arabia	..	..	..	41.0	5.45	11,584	27	22	0.1	7.2	..
Senegal	9	57	29.9	16.0	0.63	386	36	1	0.4	3.3	12.9
Serbia	..	..	54.5	43.1	11.77	20,241	15	29	1.6	4.2	9.2
Sierra Leone	..	10	..	0.3	..	29	..	1	..	..	..
Singapore	361	..	69.1	71.1	24.99	122,454	27	607	34.3	27.9	2.8
Slovak Republic	126	..	82.4	79.9	12.79	9,208	26	164	19.3	15.4	9.2
Slovenia	173	..	71.0	69.3	24.02	48,804	34	433	2.2	4.6	7.3
Somalia	..	..	..	1.2	0.00	..	..	0	..	..	..
South Africa	30	75	..	12.3	1.49	211	27	74	1.0	9.4	3.7
South Sudan	..	..	..	..	..	..	..	..	..	..	..
Spain	144	..	69.7	65.8	22.87	36,900	26	284	2.2	6.7	6.9
Sri Lanka	26	..	..	12.0	1.09	398	5	6	0.5	2.9	14.1
Sudan	..	..	..	10.2	0.38	305	23	0	0.0	3.3	25.8
Swaziland	24	..	..	9.0	0.15	52	875	15	..	..	9.0
Sweden	481	..	92.8	90.0	31.85	213,265	35	1,455	9.8	11.3	13.9
Switzerland	420	..	82.2	82.2	37.16	127,779	33	2,153	1.6	5.9	..
Syrian Arab Republic	..	..	..	20.7	0.33	280	22	0	0.0	1.1	1.9
Tajikistan	..	..	..	11.5	0.07	..	362	1	..	..	37.0
Tanzania	2	10	..	11.0	0.01	77	21	0	0.4	3.8	2.1
Thailand	..	97	30.9	21.2	4.61	2,296	19	17	18.9	14.2	..
Timor-Leste	..	..	..	0.2	0.04	28	99	3	..	..	..
Togo	2	..	..	5.4	0.06	230	166	2	0.2	5.1	18.6
Trinidad and Tobago	149	..	..	48.5	10.81	8,656	13	85	0.2	3.0	..
Tunisia	23	..	..	36.6	4.57	4,854	11	19	6.5	6.3	5.9
Turkey	..	..	41.0	39.8	9.73	7,601	19	143	1.8	4.5	1.6
Turkmenistan	9	..	..	2.2	0.01	77	..	0	..	..	..
Uganda	..	6	..	12.5	0.16	108	14	2	5.7	7.4	5.2
Ukraine	131	95	..	44.6	6.44	2,616	8	18	1.1	3.2	5.5
United Arab Emirates	..	96	74.0	78.0	10.47	13,991	41	180	2.0	4.5	..
United Kingdom	290	..	86.7	84.7	31.46	112,482	25	1,594	5.9	9.3	8.8
United States	193	..	..	74.2	27.71	29,093	20	1,562	10.5	14.2	4.6
Uruguay	..	94	49.1	47.9	10.95	11,004	19	70	0.1	6.4	8.2
Uzbekistan	..	..	..	19.4	0.32	53	200	0	..	..	..
Venezuela, RB	93	96	..	35.9	5.40	2,428	16	8	0.0	7.6	8.2
Vietnam	..	87	..	27.9	4.18	1,546	10	5	5.8	8.6	..
West Bank and Gaza	10	96	55.6	36.4	..	..	..	4	0.9	3.2	6.0
Yemen, Rep.	4	..	..	12.3	0.35	133	119	0	0.0	2.0	..
Zambia	5	27	..	10.1	0.08	39	59	2	0.0	2.3	8.0
Zimbabwe	..	..	..	11.5	0.26	35	406	1	0.0	3.6	..
World	**104 w**	**.. m**	**.. w**	**30.2 w**	**7.75 w**	**8,662 w**	**26 m**	**184 w**	**11.1 w**	**12.7 w**	**9.3 w**
Low income	..	..	..	5.6	0.05	93	55	1	..	..	..
Middle income	68	87	..	23.8	4.65	1,856	20	12	14.2	14.2	13.6
Lower middle income	..	72	..	13.5	1.04	656	32	3	8.3	10.4	27.9
Upper middle income	69	96	..	34.1	8.36	3,084	18	20	15.5	15.0	5.8
Low & middle income	65	84	..	21.5	4.05	1,628	23	10	14.1	14.0	13.5
East Asia & Pacific	74	..	..	29.8	7.18	992	22	4	26.2	21.3	7.1
Europe & Central Asia	..	..	40.9	39.3	9.12	9,777	13	48	1.2	5.5	5.9
Latin America & Carib.	64	87	..	34.0	6.59	4,062	23	36	10.3	14.0	..
Middle East & N. Africa	..	97	..	20.9	1.36	1,139	17	3	..	4.2	..
South Asia	68	48	..	8.1	0.73	394	14	2	1.6	5.7	43.8
Sub-Saharan Africa	..	26	..	11.3	0.18	116	52	6	0.5	7.0	..
High income	255	..	..	73.4	26.46	44,235	26	1,068	10.4	12.5	8.1
Euro area	201	..	73.7	71.2	27.65	53,594	26	647	5.2	8.2	10.7

a. Data are from the International Telecommunication Union's (ITU) World Telecommunication/ICT Indicators database. Please cite the ITU for third-party use of these data. b. Data are for the most recent year available.

About the data

The digital and information revolution has changed the way the world learns, communicates, does business, and treats illnesses. New information and communications technologies (ICT) offer vast opportunities for progress in all walks of life in all countries—opportunities for economic growth, improved health, better service delivery, learning through distance education, and social and cultural advances.

Comparable statistics on access, use, quality, and affordability of ICT are needed to formulate growth-enabling policies for the sector and to monitor and evaluate the sector's impact on development. Although basic access data are available for many countries, in most developing countries little is known about who uses ICT; what they are used for (school, work, business, research, government); and how they affect people and businesses. The global Partnership on Measuring ICT for Development is helping to set standards, harmonize information and communications technology statistics, and build statistical capacity in developing countries. For more information see www.itu.int/ITU-D/ict/partnership/.

Data on daily newspaper circulation are from United Nations Educational, Scientific, and Cultural Organization (UNESCO) Institute for Statistics surveys on newspaper statistics.

Estimates of households with television are derived from household surveys. Some countries report only the number of households with a color television set, and so the true number may be higher than reported.

Data on computer users, Internet users, and related indicators (broadband and bandwidth) are collected by national statistics offices through household surveys. Since survey questions and definitions differ, the estimates may not be strictly comparable across countries. In particular, in the "post-PC age" what constitutes a computer is becoming harder to define. Today's smartphones and tablets have computer power equivalent to that of yesterday's computers and provide a similar range of functions. Device convergence is thus rendering the conventional definition obsolete. Countries without surveys generally derive their estimates by multiplying subscriber counts reported by Internet service providers by a multiplier. This method may undercount actual users, particularly in developing countries, where many commercial subscribers rent out computers connected to the Internet or prepaid cards are used to access the Internet.

Broadband refers to technologies that provide Internet speeds of at least 256 kilobits a second of upstream and downstream capacity and includes digital subscriber lines, cable modems, satellite broadband Internet, fiber-to-home Internet access, Ethernet local access networks, and wireless area networks. Bandwidth refers to the range of frequencies available for signals. The higher the bandwidth, the more information that can be transmitted at one time. Reporting countries may have different definitions of broadband, so data are not strictly comparable.

The number of secure Internet servers, from the Netcraft Secure Server Survey, indicates how many companies conduct encrypted transactions over the Internet. The survey examines the use of encrypted transactions through extensive automated exploration, tallying the number of Web sites using a secure socket layer (SSL). The country of origin of more than a third of the 1.5 million distinct valid third-party certificates is unknown. Some countries, such as the Republic of Korea, use application layers to establish the encryption channel, which is SSL equivalent; these data are reported in the table.

Information and communication technology goods exports and imports are defined by the Working Party on Indicators for the Information Society and are reported in the Organisation for Economic Co-operation and Development's *Guide to Measuring the Information Society* (2005). Information and communication technology service exports data are based on the International Monetary Fund's (IMF) *Balance of Payments Statistics Yearbook* classification.

Definitions

• **Daily newspapers** are newspapers published at least four times a week that report mainly on events since the previous issue. The indicator is average circulation per 1,000 people. • **Households with television** are the percentage of households with a television set. • **Computer users** are individuals who have used a computer (in any location) in the last 12 months. Computers include desktop, portable, or handheld computers (such as a personal digital assistant) and exclude equipment with some embedded computing abilities (such as mobile phones or television sets). • **Internet users** are individuals who have used the Internet (in any location) with a device such as a computer, smartphone, or digital television in the last 12 months via a fixed or mobile network. The Internet provides access to the worldwide network. • **Fixed broadband Internet subscriptions** are the number of fixed broadband subscriptions with a digital subscriber line, cable modem, or other high-speed technology (excluding wireless). • **International Internet bandwidth** is the contracted capacity of international connections between countries for transmitting Internet traffic. • **Fixed broadband Internet access tariff** is the lowest sampled cost per 100 kilobits a second per month and are calculated from low- and high-speed monthly service charges. Monthly charges do not include installation fees or modem rentals. • **Secure Internet servers** are servers using encryption technology in Internet transactions. • **Information and communication technology goods exports** and **imports** include telecommunications, audio and video, computer and related equipment; electronic components; and other information and communication technology goods. Software is excluded. • **Information and communication technology services exports** include computer and communications services (telecommunications and postal and courier services) and information services (databases, data processes, software design and development, maintenance and repair, and news-related service transactions).

Data sources

Data on newspapers are compiled by the UNESCO Institute for Statistics. Data on televisions, computer users, Internet users, Internet broadband users and cost, and Internet bandwidth are from the ITU's World Telecommunication/ICT Indicators database and TeleGeography. Data on secure Internet servers are from Netcraft (www.netcraft.com) and official government sources. Data on information and communication technology goods trade are from the United Nations Conference on Trade and Development's UNCTADstat database (http://unctadstat.unctad.org). Data on information and communication technology services exports are from the IMF's Balance of Payments Statistics database.

	Research and development (R&D) full-time equivalent per million people		Scientific and technical journal articles	Expenditures for R&D	High-technology exports		Royalty and license fees $ millions		Patent applications filed[a,b]		Trademark applications filed[a,c]
	Researchers 2005–09[d]	Technicians 2005–09[d]	2009	% of GDP 2005–09[d]	$ millions 2010	% of manufactured exports 2010	Receipts 2010	Payments 2010	Residents 2010	Non-residents 2010	Total 2010
Afghanistan	..	..	12	..	..	..	..	..	..	..	..
Albania	147	38	8	0.15	9	0.9	1	12	..	361	2,920
Algeria	170	34	607	0.07	5	0.5	2	17	76	730	5,632
Angola	..	..	6	..	..	..	12	6	..	..	..
Argentina	1,046	207	3,655	0.52	1,635	7.5	119	1,541	801	4,781	69,565
Armenia	..	..	164	0.27	4	1.8	..	..	136	6	4,620
Australia	4,259	1,144	18,923	2.35	3,826	11.9	703	3,026	2,409	22,478	59,459
Austria	4,122	1,959	4,832	2.75	13,721	11.9	646	1,403	2,424	249	10,375
Azerbaijan	..	..	151	0.26	6	1.1	0	17	222	5	3,310
Bahrain	..	..	36	..	1	0.1	..	..	..	..	2,044
Bangladesh	..	..	260	..	134	1.2	1	18	66	276	10,231
Belarus	..	..	380	0.64	408	3.0	9	101	1,759	174	10,695
Belgium	3,491	1,406	7,218	1.96	32,227	10.5	2,138	1,904	620	140	25,799e
Benin	..	..	48	..	..	..	0	3	..	..	..
Bolivia	..	..	45	..	37	8.6	3	20	..	..	6,081
Bosnia and Herzegovina	197	71	64	0.02	71	2.6	15	5	56	9	4,730
Botswana	..	..	45	0.52	15	0.4	0	11	..	..	674
Brazil	696	560	12,306	1.08	8,122	11.2	397	2,850	2,705	19,981	125,654
Bulgaria	1,587	492	735	0.53	802	7.9	34	115	243	17	7,140
Burkina Faso	..	..	50	0.21	3	7.8	0	1	2	..	34
Burundi	..	..	3	..	1	8.5	..	..	..	..	..
Cambodia	..	..	27	..	5	0.1	0	6	..	..	2,866
Cameroon	..	..	145	..	14	4.9	0	12	..	..	..
Canada	4,335	1,740	29,017	1.95	23,966	14.1	3,813	8,665	4,550	30,899	45,220
Central African Republic	..	..	4	..	..	..	..	..	..	..	..
Chad	..	..	2	..	..	..	..	..	..	..	..
Chile	355	293	1,868	0.39	483	5.5	64	496	328	748	45,104
China	1,199	..	74,019	1.47	406,090	27.5	830	13,040	293,066	98,111	1,057,480
Hong Kong SAR, China	2,759	352	..	0.79	1,106	16.1	383	1,700	133	11,569	28,872
Colombia	157	..	608	0.16	425	5.1	56	362	133	1,739	25,990
Congo, Dem. Rep.	..	..	19	0.48	..	..	..	..	..	..	..
Congo, Rep.	..	..	18	..	..	..	..	..	..	..	..
Costa Rica	257	..	98	0.40	2,193	40.0	8	64	8	1,212	11,265
Côte d'Ivoire	70	..	56	..	126	8.2	0	21	..	..	..
Croatia	1,571	636	1,164	0.83	732	9.2	32	225	257	21	7,950
Cuba	..	..	222	0.49	..	..	..	..	59	172	1,397
Cyprus	752	216	195	0.46	140	37.1	8	31	4	4	2,381
Czech Republic	2,755	1,533	3,946	1.53	17,469	15.3	105	771	868	114	11,048
Denmark	6,390	2,628	5,306	3.02	8,291	14.2	..	..	1,626	142	5,788
Dominican Republic	..	..	6	..	102	2.9	..	63	..	..	6,453
Ecuador	106	31	68	0.26	145	8.4	..	54	4	690	16,195
Egypt, Arab Rep.	420	394	2,247	0.21	96	0.9	122	226	605	1,625	3,955
El Salvador	..	..	6	0.11	186	5.8	0	31	..	..	..
Eritrea	..	..	4	..	..	..	..	..	..	..	..
Estonia	3,210	627	518	1.44	721	9.1	20	60	84	13	3,140
Ethiopia	21	13	175	0.17	6	3.1	0	1	12	25	719
Finland	7,647	..	4,949	3.96	5,776	10.8	2,340	1,236	1,731	102	5,504
France	3,690	1,872	31,748	2.23	99,736	24.9	10,407	5,559	14,748	1,832	93,187
Gabon	..	..	18	0.64	7	3.0	..	..	..	..	..
Gambia, The	..	..	20	0.02	0	1.1	..	..	..	..	327
Georgia	..	..	129	0.18	11	1.8	5	7	179	180	4,301
Germany	3,780	1,329	45,003	2.82	158,507	15.3	14,384	13,051	47,047	12,198	74,339
Ghana	17	15	102	0.23	8	2.0	..	..	..	..	884
Greece	1,849	756	4,881	0.58	1,090	10.2	69	627	728	16	6,559
Guatemala	39	35	22	0.06	205	5.7	13	94	7	374	9,175
Guinea	..	..	3	..	0	0.1	0	1	..	..	..
Guinea-Bissau	..	..	6	..	..	..	..	0	..	..	6
Haiti	..	..	7	..	..	..	..	0	..	..	..

	Research and development (R&D)		Scientific and technical journal articles	Expenditures for R&D	High-technology exports		Royalty and license fees		Patent applications filed[a,b]		Trademark applications filed[a,c]
	full-time equivalent per million people					% of manu-factured exports	$ millions			Non-residents	Total
	Researchers 2005–09[d]	Technicians 2005–09[d]	2009	% of GDP 2005–09[d]	$ millions 2010	2010	Receipts 2010	Payments 2010	Residents 2010	residents 2010	2010
Honduras	..	..	6	..	12	1.3	..	30	..	..	7,403
Hungary	2,006	553	2,397	1.15	18,771	24.2	1,051	1,386	649	47	6,298
India	136	93	19,917	0.76	10,087	7.2	129	2,438	7,262	27,025	141,943
Indonesia	90	..	262	0.08	6,673	11.4	60	1,616	..	..	47,794
Iran, Islamic Rep.	751	..	6,313	0.79	584	4.5	..	..	..	..	3,096
Iraq	49	26	70	..	0	0.1	1,312	396	..	..	..
Ireland	3,373	742	2,799	1.77	21,232	21.2	2,252	37,823	733	59	3,769
Israel	..	..	6,304	4.27	7,979	14.7	849	860	1,450	5,856	8,614
Italy	1,690	..	26,755	1.27	26,366	7.2	3,603	6,986	8,814	903	4,387
Jamaica	..	..	51	..	3	0.6	5	36	..	..	1,708
Japan	5,189	597	49,627	3.45	122,047	18.0	26,680	18,769	290,081	54,517	124,726
Jordan	..	..	383	0.42	122	2.9	..	..	45	429	5,971
Kazakhstan	..	..	99	0.23	2,110	29.9	..	86	11	162	3,615
Kenya	56	63	291	0.42	100	5.7	54	18	77	120	4,321
Korea, Dem. Rep.	..	..	8	..	..	..	..	..	8,018	39	1,231
Korea, Rep.	4,947	825	22,271	3.36	92,856	28.7	3,146	8,965	131,805	38,296	129,486
Kosovo	..	..	..	..	..	..	..	..	..	..	..
Kuwait	152	35	214	0.11	16	0.5	..	..	..	..	..
Kyrgyz Republic	..	..	15	0.16	2	1.0	1	3	134	6	2,535
Lao PDR	..	..	12	..	..	..	..	..	..	..	..
Latvia	1,601	561	162	0.46	396	7.6	12	33	178	7	3,589
Lebanon	..	..	256	..	279	12.8	7	13	..	..	..
Lesotho	21	22	4	0.03	0	0.2	..	3	..	..	566
Liberia	..	..	0	..	..	..	..	..	..	..	612
Libya	..	..	34	..	..	..	..	..	..	..	..
Lithuania	2,541	445	388	0.84	1,190	10.6	1	35	108	6	4,351
Macedonia, FYR	472	82	57	0.23	40	2.9	7	18	34	406	3,436
Madagascar	46	25	35	0.15	5	1.0	..	..	9	34	1,773
Malawi	30	58	53	..	1	1.3	..	0	..	..	..
Malaysia	365	43	1,351	0.63	59,332	44.5	266	1,133	1,233	5,230	26,370
Mali	38	12	25	0.25	2	2.4	0	3	..	..	..
Mauritania	..	..	3	..	..	..	..	..	..	..	..
Mauritius	..	..	22	0.37	6	0.7	1	12	2	22	2,032
Mexico	347	183	4,128	0.37	37,657	16.9	..	..	951	13,625	94,457
Moldova	794	78	80	0.53	17	8.3	5	13	134	5	5,459
Mongolia	..	..	42	0.24	7	7.4	0	3	110	69	2,403
Morocco	661	61	391	0.64	897	7.7	4	30	152	882	11,030
Mozambique	16	35	29	0.21	1	1.3	0	4	18	22	891
Myanmar	..	..	10	..	..	..	..	..	..	..	..
Namibia	..	..	14	..	19	0.9	0	8	..	..	804
Nepal	..	..	56	..	4	0.6	..	..	..	..	1,132
Netherlands	2,818	1,131	14,866	1.84	59,510	21.3	5,491	3,707	2,575	279	..
New Zealand	4,324	886	3,188	1.17	548	9.0	183	669	1,585	5,051	17,124
Nicaragua	..	..	12	..	6	4.8	..	..	..	..	5,975
Niger	8	11	16	..	4	6.6	0	2	..	..	..
Nigeria	39	13	462	0.22	63	1.1	..	224	..	..	13,835
Norway	5,504	..	4,440	1.80	3,830	16.1	498	536	1,117	696	..
Oman	..	..	114	..	18	0.6	..	..	..	..	1,913
Pakistan	162	64	1,043	0.46	262	1.7	4	123	170	1,375	15,734
Panama	111	..	73	0.21	1	0.8	..	46	..	468	9,629
Papua New Guinea	..	..	17	..	..	..	..	..	1	45	612
Paraguay	75	..	11	0.06	32	6.6	254	3	18	347	22,102
Peru	..	..	159	..	252	6.6	3	197	39	261	23,120
Philippines	78	11	223	0.11	29,792	67.8	4	445	166	3,223	16,838
Poland	1,598	189	7,355	0.68	8,378	6.6	237	2,248	3,203	227	18,251
Portugal	4,308	383	4,157	1.66	1,213	3.4	41	548	499	46	19,636
Puerto Rico	668	..	..	0.49	..	..	..	..	..	..	..
Qatar	..	..	64	..	1	0.0	..	..	..	..	..

	Research and development (R&D) full-time equivalent per million people		Scientific and technical journal articles	Expenditures for R&D	High-technology exports		Royalty and license fees $ millions		Patent applications filed[a,b]		Trademark applications filed[a,c]
	Researchers 2005–09[d]	Technicians 2005–09[d]	2009	% of GDP 2005–09[d]	$ millions 2010	% of manufactured exports 2010	Receipts 2010	Payments 2010	Residents 2010	Non-residents 2010	Total 2010
Romania	895	185	1,367	0.48	4,249	10.9	466	453	1,382	36	12,063
Russian Federation	3,091	475	14,016	1.25	5,193	8.8	625	5,066	28,722	13,778	56,856
Rwanda	12	..	12	..	1	5.9	0	0	..	..	238
Saudi Arabia	..	..	710	0.08	201	0.7	..	..	288	643	..
Senegal	384	53	56	0.37	9	1.2	1	12	..	..	..
Serbia	1,060	224	1,173	0.89	..	..	39	156	290	39	7,005
Sierra Leone	..	..	3	..	..	..	1	0	..	..	676
Singapore	5,834	597	4,187	2.66	126,982	49.9	1,867	15,857	895	8,878	17,504
Slovak Republic	2,438	345	1,000	0.48	3,921	7.0	45	147	234	48	5,027
Slovenia	3,679	1,863	1,234	1.86	1,131	5.5	69	369	442	11	3,894
Somalia	..	..	1	..	..	..	..	..	..	..	..
South Africa	396	124	2,864	0.93	1,420	4.3	59	1,941	821	5,562	30,549
South Sudan	..	..	..	..	..	..	..	..	..	..	..
Spain	2,932	1,148	21,543	1.38	11,290	6.4	877	2,649	3,566	213	47,120
Sri Lanka	96	77	135	0.11	57	1.0	..	..	225	235	6,244
Sudan	..	..	63	0.29	10	29.4	3	11	3	13	1,026
Swaziland	..	..	8	..	1	0.1	0	16	..	..	659
Sweden	5,018	2,006	9,478	3.62	16,133	13.9	6,133	1,383	2,196	353	12,662
Switzerland	3,320	2,874	9,469	3.00	42,820	24.8	..	..	1,622	533	27,972
Syrian Arab Republic	..	..	72	..	86	1.8	1	37	..	..	2,362
Tajikistan	..	..	12	0.09	..	..	1	0	7	3	2,293
Tanzania	..	..	152	0.43	25	3.5	0	0	..	..	556
Thailand	316	140	2,033	0.21	34,156	24.0	153	3,084	1,214	723	37,656
Timor-Leste	..	..	..	..	..	..	..	..	..	..	..
Togo	38	18	7	..	0	0.1	..	5	..	..	..
Trinidad and Tobago	..	..	48	0.04	3	0.2	..	..	1	280	..
Tunisia	1,863	43	1,022	1.10	611	4.9	25	15	..	..	..
Turkey	804	122	8,301	0.85	1,714	1.9	..	816	2,555	177	8,241
Turkmenistan	..	..	1	..	..	..	..	..	..	..	2,245
Uganda	..	..	143	0.41	6	2.4	4	4	6	1	..
Ukraine	1,353	288	1,639	0.86	1,441	4.3	132	744	2,556	2,756	28,915
United Arab Emirates	..	..	265	..	50	3.2	..	..	..	..	..
United Kingdom	3,947	871	45,649	1.87	59,447	20.9	13,822	8,499	15,490	6,439	36,484
United States	4,673	..	208,601	2.79	145,498	19.9	105,583	33,450	241,977	248,249	281,867
Uruguay	346	..	246	0.66	79	5.8	0	17	23	761	5,730
Uzbekistan	..	..	139	..	..	..	..	..	370	262	4,863
Venezuela, RB	183	..	354	..	145	5.1	..	340	..	..	..
Vietnam	..	..	326	..	2,101	6.2	..	..	306	3,276	32,289
West Bank and Gaza	144	27	..	..	..	..	0	0	..	..	..
Yemen, Rep.	..	..	25	..	0	0.4	33	5	20	55	4,165
Zambia	43	67	35	0.34	4	1.0	..	1	..	..	765
Zimbabwe	..	..	56	..	9	0.8	..	..	..	..	..
World	**1,269 w**	**.. w**	**788,333 s**	**2.15 w**	**1,572,076 s**	**17.5 w**	**210,577 s**	**216,352 s**	**1,060,313 s**	**621,207 s**	**3,023,628 s**
Low income	..	..	1,561	..	..	3.1	62	56	..	..	..
Middle income	591	..	167,803	1.07	490,375	17.9	3,612	37,290	281,357	190,556	1,826,974
Lower middle income	..	..	28,049	0.61	46,413	11.0	665	6,170	11,816	44,547	352,071
Upper middle income	1,197	..	139,753	1.10	569,935	19.5	2,947	31,120	333,407	164,472	1,737,397
Low & middle income	574	..	169,364	1.07	527,339	17.8	3,674	37,346	289,428	191,053	1,850,304
East Asia & Pacific	1,199	..	78,373	1.47	..	28.7	1,049	18,196	304,113	110,671	1,222,061
Europe & Central Asia	2,006	329	29,089	0.96	17,622	6.7	1,352	7,678	36,143	17,415	187,119
Latin America & Carib.	482	346	23,970	0.65	51,633	10.9	970	6,291	4,216	40,206	466,522
Middle East & N. Africa	..	..	11,421	..	1,572	3.2	37	326	..	..	36,211
South Asia	129	86	21,432	0.75	..	6.7	142	2,578	7,519	27,500	172,509
Sub-Saharan Africa	..	..	5,079	0.58	2,570	2.8	124	2,277	..	..	..
High income	3,982	..	618,970	2.44	1,081,514	17.4	206,903	179,006	775,219	450,049	1,183,907
Euro area	3,119	1,355	171,873	2.09	439,190	14.9	42,900	76,676	72,951	14,959	305,982

a. Original information was provided by the World Intellectual Property Organization (WIPO). The International Bureau of WIPO assumes no responsibility with respect to the transformation of these data. b. Excludes applications filed under the auspices of the European Patent Office (150,961 by nonresidents) and the Eurasian Patent Organization (3,329 by nonresidents). c. Excludes applications filed under the auspices of the Office for Harmonization in the Internal Market (98,616). d. Data are for the most recent year available. e. Includes Luxembourg and the Netherlands.

About the data

The United Nations Educational, Scientific, and Cultural Organization (UNESCO) Institute for Statistics collects data on researchers, technicians, and expenditure on research and development (R&D) through its biennial R&D survey and from other international partners such as the Organisation for Economic Co-operation and Development (OECD), Eurostat, and the Network for Science and Technology Indicators—Ibero-American and Inter-American. The OECD's *Frascati Manual 2002* (OECD 2002) defines research and experimental development as "creative work undertaken on a systemic basis in order to increase the stock of knowledge, including knowledge of man, culture and society, and the use of this stock of knowledge to devise new applications." R&D covers basic research, applied research, and experimental development. Data on researchers and technicians in R&D are measured in both full-time equivalent and headcount but are shown in full-time equivalent only.

Scientific and technical article counts are from journals classified by the Institute for Scientific Information's Science Citation Index (SCI) and Social Sciences Citation Index (SSCI). Counts are based on fractional assignments; articles with authors from different countries are allocated proportionately to each country (see *Definitions* for fields covered). The SCI and SSCI databases cover the core set of scientific journals but may exclude some of local importance and may reflect some bias toward English-language journals.

R&D expenditures include expenditures from all sources for R&D performed within a country, including capital expenditures and current costs (wages and associated costs of researchers, technicians, and other supporting staff and other current costs, including noncapital purchases of materials, supplies, and minor equipment to support R&D such as utilities, reference materials, subscriptions to libraries and scientific societies, and materials for laboratories).

The method for determining high-technology exports was developed by the Organisation for Economic Co-operation and Development in collaboration with Eurostat. It takes a "product approach" (rather than a "sectoral approach") based on R&D intensity (expenditure divided by total sales) for groups of products from Germany, Italy, Japan, the Netherlands, Sweden, and the United States. Because industrial sectors specializing in a few high-technology products may also produce low-technology products, the product approach is more appropriate for international trade. The method takes only R&D intensity into account, but other characteristics

of high technology are also important, such as know-how, scientific personnel, and technology embodied in patents. Considering these characteristics would yield a different list (see Hatzichronoglou 1997).

A patent is an exclusive right granted for a specified period (generally 20 years) for a new way of doing something or a new technical solution to a problem—an invention. The invention must be of practical use and display a characteristic unknown in the existing body of knowledge in its field. Most countries have systems to protect patentable inventions. The Patent Cooperation Treaty (www.wipo.int/pct) provides a two-phase system for filing patent applications in 144 eligible countries (as of November 2011). International applications under the treaty provide for a national patent grant only—there is no international patent. The national filing represents the applicant's seeking of patent protection for a given territory, whereas international filings, while representing a legal right, do not accurately reflect where patent protection is sought. Resident filings are those from residents of the country concerned. Nonresident filings are from applicants abroad. For regional offices applications from residents of any member state of the regional patent convention are considered nonresident filings. Some offices (notably the U.S. Patent and Trademark Office) use the residence of the inventor rather than the applicant to classify filings.

A trademark is a distinctive sign identifying goods or services as produced or provided by a specific person or enterprise. A trademark protects the owner of the mark by ensuring exclusive right to use it to identify goods or services or to authorize another to use it. The period of protection varies, but a trademark can be renewed indefinitely for an additional fee. Detailed components of trademark filings, available on the *World Development Indicators* CD-ROM and at http://data.worldbank.org, include applications filed by direct residents (domestic applicants filing directly at a given national or regional intellectual property [IP] office); direct nonresident (foreign applicants filing directly at a given national or regional IP office); aggregate direct (applicants not identified as direct resident or direct nonresident by the national or regional office); and Madrid (designations received by the national or regional IP office based on international applications filed via the World Intellectual Property Organization–administered Madrid System). Data are based on information supplied to WIPO by IP offices in annual surveys, supplemented by data in national IP office reports. Data may be missing for some offices or periods.

Definitions

• **Researchers in research and development (R&D)** are professionals engaged in conceiving of or creating new knowledge, products, processes, methods, and systems and in managing the projects concerned. Postgraduate doctoral students (International Standard Classification of Education 1997 level 6) engaged in R&D are considered researchers. • **Technicians in R&D** and equivalent staff are people whose main tasks require technical knowledge and experience in engineering, physical and life sciences (technicians), and social sciences and humanities (equivalent staff). They engage in R&D by performing scientific and technical tasks involving the application of concepts and operational methods, normally under researcher supervision. • **Scientific and technical journal articles** are published articles in physics, biology, chemistry, mathematics, clinical medicine, biomedical research, engineering and technology, and earth and space sciences. • **Expenditures for R&D** are current and capital expenditures on creative work undertaken on a systematic basis to increase the stock of knowledge, including knowledge on humanity, culture, and society, and the use of knowledge to devise new applications. • **High-technology exports** are products with high R&D intensity, such as in aerospace, computers, pharmaceuticals, scientific instruments, and electrical machinery. • **Royalty and license fees** are payments and receipts between residents and nonresidents for authorized use of intangible, nonproduced, nonfinancial assets and proprietary rights (such as patents, copyrights, trademarks, and industrial processes) and for the use, through licensing, of produced originals of prototypes (such as films and manuscripts). • **Patent applications filed** are patent applications at a national or regional patent office; an international patent application (Patent Cooperation Treaty filing) provides a national patent grant only. • **Trademark applications filed** are applications to register a trademark with a national or regional IP office.

Data sources

Data on R&D are provided by the UNESCO Institute for Statistics. Data on scientific and technical journal articles are from the U.S. National Science Board's *Science and Engineering Indicators 2012*. Data on high-technology exports are from the United Nations Statistics Division's Commodity Trade (Comtrade) database. Data on royalty and license fees are from the International Monetary Fund's *Balance of Payments Statistics Yearbook*. Data on patents and trademarks are from the World Intellectual Property Organization (www.wipo.int/ipstats).

GLOBAL
LINKS

The world economy is bound together by trade in goods and services, financial flows, and movements of people. As economies develop, their links expand and grow more complex. The indicators in *Global links* measure the size and direction of these flows and document policy interventions, such as tariffs, trade facilitation, and aid flows.

During economic crises, declining trade and financing and changes in migration patterns in one country or region can transmit shocks to others. An example is the financial crisis that began in the United States in 2007 and spread rapidly to Europe. But the same links that transfer shocks also allow expansion into new markets and access to new sources of finance, reducing the impacts of shocks. In an increasingly multipolar world, developing countries are trading and investing more with each other, reducing their dependence on high-income economies. Evidence of this shift can be found in the tables of *Global links*.

Capital inflows rebounded strongly in 2010, especially in low- and middle-income economies, where combined net debt and equity inflows rose 37 percent, to $799 billion. Foreign direct investment (FDI) inflows rose 3 percent—with wide disparity across income groups. In high-income economies FDI inflows fell 7 percent, dragged down by a 13 percent drop in net inflows to the euro area. But inflows to the United States—the world's largest FDI recipient—surged. And low- and middle-income economies saw net FDI inflows jump 27 percent, to $514 billion, and their share of global FDI inflows increase to almost 36 percent, up from 29 percent in 2009. A better investment environment, corporate earnings revival, and increased developing country investment in extractive industries and infrastructure development in other developing countries fueled the rebound. China was a key driver, with net FDI inflows up 62 percent in 2010 (to $185 billion).

Portfolio equity flows recovered rapidly as the global financial crisis ebbed, particularly in emerging markets with good growth prospects. Low- and middle-income economies recorded a 19 percent increase (to $130 billion), underpinned by a 89 percent rise in net inflows to India. For high-income economies the story was mixed—particularly in the euro area, where net inflows rose 13 percent.

Debt-related flows to low- and middle-income economies from private creditors rose in 2010 to $111 billion, more than twice their 2009 level, underpinned by a resurgence of bond issuance by public and private sector borrowers. Similarly, net inflows from banks and other private creditors showed signs of recovery, rising 123 percent, to $44 billion, albeit from a low base of $20 billion in 2009. Net inflows from bilateral and multilateral creditors (loans and grants) fell 11 percent, due largely to the redirection of International Monetary Fund flows to countries in the euro zone.

Low- and middle-income economies' combined external debt rose $437 billion in 2010, to $4 trillion, but it remained within sustainable bounds, an average of 21 percent of gross national income and 69 percent of export earnings. Short-term external debt was the fastest growing component, rising 34 percent in 2010 compared with 6 percent for outstanding long-term external debt. Risks associated with a high proportion of short-term debt—25 percent of total debt stock at end-2010—were mitigated by international reserves equivalent to 137 percent of total outstanding external debt.

	Export volume	Import volume	Export value	Import value	Net barter terms of trade index
	average annual % growth	average annual % growth	average annual % growth	average annual % growth	2000 = 100
	2000–10	2000–10	2000–10	2000–10	2010
Afghanistan	9.9	4.4	20.1	11.0	146.5
Albania	15.0	11.6	20.2	17.5	95.3
Algeria	0.0	12.2	14.4	17.9	177.5
Angola	11.4	22.0	27.6	26.4	210.9
Argentina	5.9	11.7	11.9	14.6	126.6
Armenia	3.6	12.6	12.3	19.4	126.2
Australia	2.3	8.3	14.0	13.1	178.9
Austria	5.9	4.5	9.9	9.7	91.1
Azerbaijan	22.3	14.1	38.6	20.8	160.3
Bahrain	0.6	3.5	11.7	11.9	114.5
Bangladesh	11.4	5.0	13.0	13.3	59.0
Belarus	6.8	8.7	16.4	18.3	102.8
Belgium	2.5	3.0	9.7	10.1	100.8
Benin	6.6	7.1	15.5	16.2	103.5
Bolivia	9.4	8.2	21.2	13.7	152.4
Bosnia and Herzegovina	13.4	5.1	20.4	11.5	101.1
Botswana	3.5	5.7	7.1	11.6	84.7
Brazil	6.6	8.1	15.5	14.9	125.1
Bulgaria	7.9	9.3	18.0	18.4	108.8
Burkina Faso	11.8	7.9	19.3	14.5	120.9
Burundi	–3.1	9.7	7.9	15.8	153.1
Cambodia	12.7	9.3	15.0	15.3	75.9
Cameroon	–2.5	5.2	9.8	13.9	143.8
Canada	–0.9	2.5	4.9	6.4	119.9
Central African Republic	–4.3	6.6	–0.4	13.1	85.9
Chad	23.9	11.6	42.2	17.4	180.0
Chile	4.3	11.2	17.1	14.9	204.0
China[†]	20.5	15.0	22.4	20.9	77.4
Hong Kong SAR, China	6.7	6.6	7.8	8.3	96.0
Colombia	6.2	11.0	14.7	15.3	133.9
Congo, Dem. Rep.	10.1	14.9	20.9	21.8	137.9
Congo, Rep.	1.4	16.6	15.9	22.4	182.3
Costa Rica	7.3	6.8	7.0	9.2	78.2
Côte d'Ivoire	–0.1	5.1	11.6	13.7	161.6
Croatia	6.3	6.0	12.5	12.2	100.7
Cuba	0.5	8.9	11.2	12.4	..
Cyprus	0.3	5.5	5.7	10.9	103.5
Czech Republic	9.9	8.0	18.5	15.7	106.4
Denmark	2.1	2.9	8.3	8.7	106.6
Dominican Republic	–0.8	3.3	2.1	6.7	98.4
Ecuador	7.5	12.2	16.4	17.5	121.9
Egypt, Arab Rep.	9.0	10.2	23.5	17.9	152.4
El Salvador	2.6	3.4	4.8	6.6	91.3
Eritrea	–10.9	–3.8	–6.7	3.6	77.2
Estonia	3.3	4.1	13.3	11.4	144.4
Ethiopia	9.1	16.5	19.2	23.6	127.5
Finland	2.6	2.9	6.7	10.0	77.1
France	1.5	2.9	6.2	8.0	98.2
Gabon	0.1	7.2	14.4	11.9	195.8
Gambia, The	–3.7	0.9	2.7	8.4	93.3
Georgia	8.9	19.5	19.8	27.5	132.2
Germany	5.2	4.9	10.3	9.9	103.3
Ghana	5.2	9.2	17.2	16.3	175.4
Greece	0.8	1.2	9.1	10.3	92.7
Guatemala	7.9	5.1	12.4	10.5	92.6
Guinea	–0.2	2.8	8.5	9.6	110.2
Guinea-Bissau	1.8	7.9	9.0	17.5	83.5
Haiti	4.9	4.0	8.2	11.2	77.9
[†]Data for Taiwan, China	7.5	2.4	8.0	8.0	66.0

	Export volume	Import volume	Export value	Import value	Net barter terms of trade index
	average annual % growth 2000–10	average annual % growth 2000–10	average annual % growth 2000–10	average annual % growth 2000–10	2000 = 100 2010
Honduras	3.5	4.7	6.2	9.7	83.4
Hungary	10.5	7.6	15.1	12.8	95.4
India	11.4	19.5	19.9	24.2	127.2
Indonesia	0.8	6.5	11.0	14.4	127.3
Iran, Islamic Rep.	2.9	7.6	17.5	14.8	157.9
Iraq	1.7	9.2	16.8	15.1	184.3
Ireland	1.7	0.0	4.7	3.8	95.4
Israel	3.3	1.5	8.1	6.4	98.1
Italy	−0.1	0.4	8.1	9.1	99.0
Jamaica	0.0	0.0	4.0	7.7	70.7
Japan	5.2	1.8	6.3	8.0	67.8
Jordan	3.9	5.1	15.0	15.6	85.4
Kazakhstan	8.6	14.2	25.3	20.7	192.6
Kenya	5.1	8.9	12.2	17.1	91.7
Korea, Dem. Rep.	7.1	−1.7	13.5	7.5	77.0
Korea, Rep.	12.1	7.1	12.4	12.6	68.0
Kosovo	..	..	..	..	..
Kuwait	4.1	9.2	18.7	13.8	187.3
Kyrgyz Republic	7.7	16.4	16.8	26.0	107.6
Lao PDR	11.1	9.3	19.6	16.0	119.5
Latvia	9.6	7.3	20.5	17.1	105.2
Lebanon	13.4	4.4	20.6	12.1	95.5
Lesotho	12.8	7.3	13.5	12.0	66.2
Liberia	−7.4	4.5	0.5	10.4	146.7
Libya	4.2	13.5	19.4	20.8	162.5
Lithuania	12.7	10.7	21.0	18.3	103.8
Macedonia, FYR	6.2	6.0	13.4	14.3	89.1
Madagascar	1.5	8.6	4.8	15.2	76.3
Malawi	6.9	9.9	12.2	16.6	87.7
Malaysia	5.5	5.1	9.2	8.6	100.2
Mali	2.9	7.7	13.7	14.6	158.7
Mauritania	11.2	11.3	23.6	18.0	132.7
Mauritius	3.2	6.0	2.9	9.1	73.2
Mexico	2.9	3.4	7.0	6.8	104.5
Moldova	11.3	18.8	12.6	20.2	104.8
Mongolia	3.9	12.4	21.2	20.5	215.6
Morocco	0.6	8.1	10.9	15.4	134.2
Mozambique	10.0	7.3	19.1	14.6	108.9
Myanmar	7.4	0.3	17.3	7.6	110.2
Namibia	6.2	10.6	14.5	15.4	120.3
Nepal	−2.9	4.5	2.5	14.0	78.3
Netherlands	5.2	5.7	11.5	11.3	101.8
New Zealand	3.3	5.5	9.5	9.5	124.4
Nicaragua	9.5	5.6	12.9	10.7	81.7
Niger	4.0	14.4	16.4	21.2	150.1
Nigeria	3.0	13.9	18.4	20.3	186.9
Norway	−0.1	5.0	11.3	11.1	140.4
Oman	−0.2	11.1	14.8	17.1	193.1
Pakistan	5.8	4.6	9.6	16.8	51.9
Panama	0.0	9.7	1.7	13.7	87.5
Papua New Guinea	−1.1	6.0	14.0	15.1	150.4
Paraguay	14.8	16.1	19.1	19.9	102.9
Peru	7.2	9.8	20.6	17.4	152.5
Philippines	2.8	−0.1	3.4	4.9	68.6
Poland	10.0	7.4	19.8	16.5	101.9
Portugal	5.1	3.4	9.0	9.0	88.0
Puerto Rico	..	..	..	..	..
Qatar	8.1	23.0	23.3	27.9	187.8

6.1 Growth of merchandise trade

	Export volume	Import volume	Export value	Import value	Net barter terms of trade index
	average annual % growth	average annual % growth	average annual % growth	average annual % growth	2000 = 100
	2000–10	2000–10	2000–10	2000–10	2010
Romania	12.4	13.7	18.5	19.9	99.9
Russian Federation	3.6	16.8	17.7	21.1	197.3
Rwanda	1.0	17.0	18.3	23.4	234.4
Saudi Arabia	0.3	10.8	16.1	16.3	222.6
Senegal	1.1	5.7	9.3	14.4	98.9
Serbia	..	..	..	..	..
Sierra Leone	25.9	4.5	32.7	15.2	70.2
Singapore	10.2	7.5	12.0	11.4	83.2
Slovak Republic	17.1	13.8	21.7	19.6	90.0
Slovenia	11.2	8.6	15.5	14.5	89.3
Somalia	−0.2	4.0	7.7	11.6	106.2
South Africa	1.5	7.4	12.2	14.6	139.4
South Sudan	..	..	..	..	..
Spain	3.1	3.9	9.5	9.9	104.5
Sri Lanka	2.5	2.1	5.9	9.2	75.7
Sudan	8.0	17.0	23.5	22.1	196.8
Swaziland	−2.2	−0.9	5.0	5.8	110.1
Sweden	2.8	3.0	8.3	9.9	88.6
Switzerland	6.8	3.3	10.4	9.1	81.0
Syrian Arab Republic	0.7	11.7	12.5	19.2	139.5
Tajikistan	−1.0	9.3	7.0	18.9	96.8
Tanzania	7.0	12.3	18.2	19.9	139.2
Thailand	7.2	7.5	12.6	12.7	98.0
Timor-Leste	..	..	..	..	..
Togo	2.0	−2.2	10.1	12.4	30.7
Trinidad and Tobago	0.7	1.4	14.4	10.1	133.5
Tunisia	6.6	4.8	12.4	11.2	95.2
Turkey	10.4	9.2	17.4	17.0	91.8
Turkmenistan	−0.6	8.4	14.0	13.1	195.6
Uganda	13.0	8.9	21.7	15.7	111.1
Ukraine	4.7	9.9	15.1	18.7	118.9
United Arab Emirates	6.5	14.6	19.3	20.2	163.3
United Kingdom	0.4	2.0	4.9	6.1	103.3
United States	3.9	2.5	6.6	5.9	97.1
Uruguay	8.5	7.6	14.3	14.3	99.6
Uzbekistan	7.6	10.6	18.9	16.0	151.6
Venezuela, RB	−2.5	10.8	12.2	14.3	216.3
Vietnam	11.4	12.6	19.4	20.6	100.6
West Bank and Gaza	..	..	..	..	..
Yemen, Rep.	−4.1	9.7	9.7	18.2	149.6
Zambia	9.4	14.1	25.9	20.8	189.0
Zimbabwe	−4.9	−1.3	4.5	7.5	106.7

About the data

Data on international trade in goods are available from each country's balance of payments and customs records. While the balance of payments focuses on the financial transactions that accompany trade, customs data record the direction of trade and the physical quantities and value of goods entering or leaving the customs area. Customs data may differ from data recorded in the balance of payments because of differences in valuation and time of recording. The 2008 United Nations System of National Accounts and the fifth edition of the International Monetary Fund's (IMF) *Balance of Payments Manual* (1993) attempted to reconcile definitions and reporting standards for international trade statistics, but differences in sources, timing, and national practices limit comparability. Real growth rates derived from trade volume indexes and terms of trade based on unit price indexes may therefore differ from those derived from national accounts aggregates.

Trade in goods, or merchandise trade, includes all goods that add to or subtract from an economy's material resources. Trade data are collected on the basis of a country's customs area, which in most cases is the same as its geographic area. Goods provided as part of foreign aid are included, but goods destined for extraterritorial agencies (such as embassies) are not.

Collecting and tabulating trade statistics are difficult. Some developing countries lack the capacity to report timely data, especially landlocked countries and countries whose territorial boundaries are porous. Their trade has to be estimated from the data reported by their partners. (For further discussion of the use of partner country reports, see *About the data* for table 6.2.) Countries that belong to common customs unions may need to collect data through direct inquiry of companies. Economic or political concerns may lead some national authorities to suppress or misrepresent data on certain trade flows, such as oil, military equipment, or the exports of a dominant producer. In other cases reported trade data may be distorted by deliberate under- or over-invoicing to affect capital transfers or avoid taxes. And in some regions smuggling and black market trading result in unreported trade flows.

By international agreement customs data are reported to the United Nations Statistics Division, which maintains the Commodity Trade (Comtrade) and Monthly Bulletin of Statistics databases. The United Nations Conference on Trade and Development (UNCTAD) compiles international trade statistics, including price, value, and volume indexes, from national and international sources such as the IMF's International Financial Statistics database, the United Nations Economic Commission for Latin America and the Caribbean, the U.S. Bureau of Labor Statistics, Japan Customs, Bank of Japan, and UNCTAD's Commodity Price Statistics and Merchandise Trade Matrix. The IMF also compiles data on trade prices and volumes in its International Financial Statistics (IFS) database.

The growth rates and terms of trade in the table were calculated from index numbers compiled by UNCTAD.

The terms of trade index measures the relative prices of a country's exports and imports. There are several ways to calculate it. The most common is the net barter (or commodity) terms of trade index, or the ratio of the export price index to the import price index. When a country's net barter terms of trade index increases, its exports become more expensive or its imports become cheaper.

Definitions

• **Export** and **import volumes** are indexes of the quantity of goods traded. They are derived from UNCTAD's volume index series and are the ratio of the export or import value indexes to the corresponding unit value indexes. Unit value indexes are based on data reported by countries that demonstrate consistency under UNCTAD quality controls, supplemented by UNCTAD's estimates using the previous year's trade values at the Standard International Trade Classification three-digit level as weights. To improve data coverage, especially for the most recent periods, UNCTAD constructs a set of average price indexes at the three-digit product classification of the Standard International Trade Classification revision 3 using its Commodity Price Statistics database, international and national sources, and estimates by the UNCTAD secretariat and calculates unit value indexes at the country level using the current year's trade values as weights. • **Export** and **import values** are the current value of exports (free on board, f.o.b.) or imports (cost, insurance, and freight, c.i.f.), converted to U.S. dollars and expressed as a percentage of the average for the base period (2000). UNCTAD's export or import value indexes are reported for most economies. • **Net barter terms of trade index** is calculated as the percentage ratio of the export unit value indexes to the import unit value indexes, measured relative to the base year 2000.

Data sources

Data on trade indexes are from UNCTAD's annual *Handbook of Statistics*.

Direction of trade

	Low- and middle-income importers							High-income importers
	% of world trade, 2010							% of world trade, 2010
Source of exports	East Asia & Pacific	Europe & Central Asia	Latin America & Caribbean	Middle East & N. Africa	South Asia	Sub-Saharan Africa	Total	Total
High-income economies	9.2	2.6	3.5	1.4	1.6	1.0	19.3	47.6
European Union	1.2	1.9	0.7	0.7	0.3	0.5	5.3	26.1
Japan	1.6	0.1	0.3	0.0	0.1	0.1	2.1	3.0
United States	0.9	0.1	1.9	0.1	0.2	0.1	3.4	5.2
Other high-income economies	5.6	0.5	0.6	0.5	1.0	0.3	8.5	13.3
Low- and middle-income economies	3.3	1.9	2.0	0.9	1.2	0.9	10.5	20.9
East Asia & Pacific	1.9	0.5	0.7	0.3	0.6	0.4	4.4	10.8
China	0.7	0.5	0.6	0.3	0.4	0.3	2.8	7.8
Europe & Central Asia	0.3	1.1	0.0	0.3	0.1	0.0	1.8	2.9
Russian Federation	0.2	0.4	0.0	0.1	0.0	0.0	0.7	1.5
Latin America & Caribbean	0.6	0.1	1.1	0.1	0.1	0.1	2.0	3.6
Brazil	0.2	0.0	0.3	0.1	0.0	0.0	0.7	0.6
Middle East & N. Africa	0.2	0.1	0.0	0.2	0.2	0.1	0.8	1.4
Algeria	0.0	0.0	0.0	0.0	0.0	0.0	0.1	0.3
South Asia	0.2	0.1	0.1	0.1	0.1	0.1	0.6	1.2
India	0.2	0.0	0.0	0.1	0.1	0.1	0.5	0.9
Sub-Saharan Africa	0.1	0.0	0.1	0.0	0.2	0.2	0.9	1.1
South Africa	0.1	0.0	0.0	0.0	0.0	0.1	0.2	0.3
World	12.5	4.5	5.5	2.3	2.9	1.8	29.7	68.5

Nominal growth of trade

	Low- and middle-income importers							High-income importers
	average annual % growth, 2000–10							average annual % growth, 2000–10
Source of exports	East Asia & Pacific	Europe & Central Asia	Latin America & Caribbean	Middle East & N. Africa	South Asia	Sub-Saharan Africa	Total	Total
High-income economies	15.1	17.3	8.8	13.7	21.4	12.5	14.1	7.5
European Union	15.0	16.7	9.5	11.4	15.5	11.3	13.8	8.2
Japan	12.5	24.8	11.1	12.5	14.1	11.2	12.7	3.4
United States	12.1	14.0	7.2	12.9	21.1	13.2	9.4	5.2
Other high-income economies	16.5	21.0	13.4	20.1	25.7	15.0	17.4	8.2
Low- and middle-income economies	22.3	20.8	18.1	22.7	27.0	21.5	21.7	13.9
East Asia & Pacific	20.9	34.8	27.7	25.9	28.1	27.1	24.9	15.5
China	26.1	37.2	31.5	30.3	35.0	31.0	31.0	20.4
Europe & Central Asia	19.4	17.8	20.5	22.4	24.3	21.9	19.0	16.7
Russian Federation	17.4	15.8	21.0	19.8	20.5	14.0	16.9	16.4
Latin America & Caribbean	30.5	19.5	14.5	18.0	29.4	20.9	18.2	8.6
Brazil	31.8	20.4	16.6	21.8	25.6	22.4	20.9	12.1
Middle East & N. Africa	22.0	16.4	14.4	22.5	37.9	18.5	23.4	13.9
Algeria	32.5	11.2	8.6	19.0	64.1	15.9	16.0	14.3
South Asia	25.8	17.5	23.3	21.5	19.2	23.7	22.5	15.4
India	27.2	16.0	25.2	23.8	19.8	24.7	23.8	18.2
Sub-Saharan Africa	22.6	24.5	20.4	13.8	21.7	16.1	21.8	13.5
South Africa	31.2	23.9	12.3	19.5	29.0	13.8	19.8	12.4
World	16.5	18.6	11.4	16.6	23.5	15.8	16.3	9.1

About the data

The table provides estimates of the flow of trade in goods between groups of economies. The data are from the International Monetary Fund's (IMF) Direction of Trade database. All high-income economies and major developing economies report trade on a timely basis, covering about 85 percent of trade for recent years. Trade by less timely reporters and by countries that do not report is estimated using reports of trading partner countries and extrapolation. Because the largest exporting and importing countries are reliable reporters, a large portion of the missing trade flows can be estimated from partner reports. Partner country data may introduce discrepancies due to confidentiality, different exchange rates, overreporting of transit trade, inclusion or exclusion of freight rates and insurance, and different points of valuation and times of recording.

Most countries report their trade data in national currencies, which are converted into U.S. dollars using the IMF's published period average exchange rate (series rf or rh, monthly averages of the market or official rates) for the reporting country. Because imports are reported at cost, insurance, and freight (c.i.f.) valuations, and exports at free on board (f.o.b.) valuations, the IMF adjusts country reports of import values by dividing them by 1.10 to estimate equivalent export values. The accuracy of this approximation depends on the set of partners and the items traded. Other factors affecting the accuracy of trade data include lags in reporting, recording differences across countries, and whether the country reports trade according to the general or special system of trade. (For further discussion of the measurement of exports and imports, see *About the data* for tables 4.4 and 4.5.)

The regional trade flows in the table are calculated from current price values. The growth rates are in nominal terms; that is, they include the effects of changes in both volumes and prices.

Definitions

- **Merchandise trade** includes all trade in goods; trade in services is excluded. • **High-income economies** are those classified as such by the World Bank (see front cover flap). • **European Union** is defined as all high-income EU members: Austria, Belgium, Cyprus, Czech Republic, Denmark, Estonia, Finland, France, Germany, Greece, Hungary, Ireland, Italy, Luxembourg, Malta, the Netherlands, Portugal, Slovak Republic, Slovenia, Spain, Sweden, and the United Kingdom. • **Other high-income economies** include all high-income economies (both Organisation for Economic Co-operation and Development members and others) except the high-income European Union, Japan, and the United States. • **Low- and middle-income regional groupings** are based on World Bank classifications (see back cover flap) and may differ from those used by other organizations.

Data sources

Data on the direction and growth of merchandise trade were calculated using the IMF's Direction of Trade database. Regional and income group classifications are according to the World Bank classification of economies as of July 1, 2011, and are as shown on the cover flaps of this report.

6.3 High-income economy trade with low- and middle-income economies

	High-income economies		European Union		Japan		United States	
	2000	2010	2000	2010	2000	2010	2000	2010
Exports to low-income economies								
Total ($ billions)	**19.5**	**53.9**	**8.8**	**19.3**	**2.3**	**5.3**	**1.9**	**7.3**
% of total exports								
Food	11.8	9.8	13.8	12.0	0.5	0.3	27.5	15.1
Agricultural raw materials	2.5	2.1	2.1	2.1	1.3	1.4	7.2	4.5
Ores and nonferrous metals	1.0	0.9	0.6	0.7	0.5	1.1	0.4	0.5
Fuels	5.6	8.7	2.9	10.2	0.4	0.2	1.3	1.7
Manufactured goods	74.1	64.8	77.7	71.0	94.7	95.2	54.6	56.7
Miscellaneous goods	5.1	13.7	2.9	4.0	2.6	1.8	9.0	21.5
Imports from low-income economies								
Total ($ billions)	**19.6**	**45.9**	**10.5**	**23.9**	**1.1**	**1.5**	**5.6**	**11.7**
% of total imports								
Food	20.9	14.0	24.2	17.5	42.7	26.3	8.0	5.0
Agricultural raw materials	6.1	3.6	8.6	4.9	3.3	2.7	1.4	1.4
Ores and nonferrous metals	5.7	11.5	5.3	11.7	21.6	12.2	2.8	1.7
Fuels	2.9	7.6	0.4	2.5	1.1	0.0	3.3	22.8
Manufactured goods	62.8	58.1	59.4	61.8	30.8	58.5	83.6	67.5
Miscellaneous goods	1.6	5.2	2.2	1.6	0.5	0.2	0.9	1.6
Simple applied tariff rates on imports from low-income economies (%)[a]								
Average	**4.2**	**2.5**	**0.8**	**0.9**	**3.1**	**0.5**	**5.2**	**3.3**
Food	5.9	4.4	3.2	0.3	10.9	1.2	2.8	1.9
Agricultural raw materials	5.2	1.5	0.0	0.2	0.4	0.1	0.2	0.1
Ores and nonferrous metals	1.2	0.7	0.3	0.2	1.4	0.2	0.0	0.1
Fuels	3.2	1.5	0.0	1.2	0.0	0.0	0.0	0.2
Manufactured goods	4.0	2.3	0.5	1.1	1.9	0.4	5.8	3.8
Miscellaneous goods	0.6	0.8	0.1	0.2	0.0	0.0	0.0	0.1
Exports to middle-income economies								
Total ($ billions)	**737.3**	**2,225.7**	**252.8**	**846.5**	**107.1**	**314.4**	**216.6**	**436.2**
% of total exports								
Food	6.1	6.3	7.0	6.1	0.3	0.4	7.8	12.0
Agricultural raw materials	1.9	2.2	1.4	1.5	1.0	1.1	2.4	4.1
Ores and nonferrous metals	2.1	5.1	1.8	3.0	1.9	3.4	1.6	4.2
Fuels	3.9	6.9	2.2	3.8	0.5	1.5	3.1	9.6
Manufactured goods	81.5	74.3	83.4	82.0	93.5	89.5	80.3	61.3
Miscellaneous goods	4.3	5.3	4.3	3.5	2.8	4.1	4.9	8.8
Imports from middle-income economies								
Total ($ billions)	**1,231.2**	**3,446.5**	**362.3**	**1,229.0**	**136.2**	**318.9**	**453.1**	**1,004.2**
% of total imports								
Food	8.0	6.8	10.3	7.9	12.9	8.0	5.4	5.3
Agricultural raw materials	2.1	1.3	3.2	1.7	3.6	2.1	1.0	0.9
Ores and nonferrous metals	4.7	4.2	5.9	4.5	8.8	10.5	2.7	1.9
Fuels	17.0	20.5	24.2	26.4	16.4	18.3	15.5	20.3
Manufactured goods	65.9	64.4	53.1	56.8	56.9	59.5	72.8	69.2
Miscellaneous goods	2.3	2.9	3.3	2.7	1.5	1.6	2.6	2.4
Simple applied tariff rates on imports from middle-income economies (%)[a]								
Average	**5.1**	**3.7**	**2.5**	**1.6**	**2.7**	**2.3**	**3.4**	**2.5**
Food	8.8	6.0	10.4	3.2	12.9	7.1	3.7	2.9
Agricultural raw materials	2.7	2.1	0.5	0.4	1.1	0.5	0.4	0.4
Ores and nonferrous metals	1.8	1.4	0.9	0.8	0.1	0.1	0.3	0.4
Fuels	3.2	1.7	0.0	0.3	0.8	0.2	0.6	1.3
Manufactured goods	4.8	3.5	1.7	1.5	1.4	1.9	3.6	2.6
Miscellaneous goods	1.9	1.0	0.9	0.5	0.0	0.0	0.5	0.3

a. Includes ad valorem equivalents of specific rates.

About the data

Developing economies are becoming increasingly important in the global trading system. Since the early 1990s trade between high-income economies and low- and middle-income economies has grown faster than trade among high-income economies. The increased trade benefits consumers and producers. But as was apparent at the World Trade Organization's (WTO) Ministerial Conferences in Doha, Qatar, in October 2001; Cancun, Mexico, in September 2003; Hong Kong SAR, China, in December 2005; and Geneva, Switzerland, in December 2009 and December 2011, achieving a more pro-development outcome from trade remains a challenge. Doing so will require strengthening international consultation. After the Doha meetings, negotiations were launched on services, agriculture, manufactures, WTO rules, the environment, dispute settlement, intellectual property rights protection, and disciplines on regional integration. At the most recent negotiations in Geneva, Switzerland, trade ministers reaffirmed that development is a core element of the WTO's work and that the WTO needs to assist in further integrating developing countries into the multilateral trading system.

Trade flows between high-income and low- and middle-income economies reflect the changing mix of exports to and imports from developing economies. While food and primary commodities have continued to fall as a share of high-income economies' imports, manufactures as a share of goods imports from both low- and middle-income economies have grown. And trade between developing economies has grown substantially over the past decade, a result of their increasing share of world output and liberalization of trade, among other influences.

Yet trade barriers remain high. The table includes information about tariff rates by selected product groups. Applied tariff rates are the tariffs in effect for partners in preferential trade agreements such as the North American Free Trade Agreement. When these rates are unavailable, most favored nation rates are used. The difference between most favored nation and applied rates can be substantial. Simple averages of applied rates are shown because they are generally a better indicator of tariff protection than weighted average rates are.

The data on trade flows are from the United Nations Statistics Division's Commodity Trade (Comtrade) database. Partner country reports by high-income economies were used for both exports and imports. Because of differences in sources of data, timing, and treatment of missing data, the numbers in the table may not be fully comparable with those used to calculate the direction of trade statistics in tables 6.2 and 6.4 or the aggregate flows in tables 4.4, 4.5, and 6.1. Tariff data are from the United Nations Conference on Trade and Development's (UNCTAD) Trade Analysis and Information System database. For further discussion of merchandise trade statistics, see *About the data* for tables 4.4, 4.5, 6.1, 6.2, and 6.4, and for information about tariff barriers, see table 6.7.

Definitions

The product groups in the table are defined in accordance with SITC revision 2: **food** (0, 1, 22, and 4), **agricultural raw materials** (2 excluding 22, 27, and 28), **ores and nonferrous metals** (27, 28, and 68), **fuels** (3), **manufactured goods** (5–8 excluding 68), and **miscellaneous goods** (9). • **Exports** are all merchandise exports by high-income economies to low-income and middle-income economies as recorded in the United Nations Statistics Division's Comtrade database. Exports are recorded free on board (f.o.b.). • **Imports** are all merchandise imports by high-income economies from low-income and middle-income economies as recorded in the United Nations Statistics Division's Comtrade database. Imports include insurance and freight charges (c.i.f.). • **High-, middle-, and low-income economies** are those classified as such by the World Bank as of July 1, 2011 (see front cover flap). • **European Union** is defined as all high-income EU members: Austria, Belgium, Cyprus, Czech Republic, Denmark, Estonia, Finland, France, Germany, Greece, Hungary, Ireland, Italy, Luxembourg, Malta, the Netherlands, Poland, Portugal, Slovak Republic, Slovenia, Spain, Sweden, and the United Kingdom.

Data sources

Data on trade flows are from United Nations Statistics Division's Comtrade database. Data on tariffs are from UNCTAD's Trade Analysis and Information System database and are calculated by World Bank staff using the World Integrated Trade Solution system.

	Exports						Imports					
	% of total merchandise exports						% of total merchandise imports					
	To developing economies				To high-income economies		From developing economies				From high-income economies	
	Within region		Outside region				Within region		Outside region			
	2000	2010	2000	2010	2000	2010	2000	2010	2000	2010	2000	2010
East Asia & Pacific	8.9 w	12.4 w	7.3 w	16.6 w	83.3 w	70.3 w	11.7 w	16.3 w	8.5 w	18.5 w	78.1 w	62.8 w
Cambodia	7.4	6.1	0.2	2.3	91.6	91.6	39.7	55.4	1.0	2.1	58.5	42.5
China	4.9	7.0	8.9	19.0	86.2	73.7	7.8	9.6	10.4	18.0	78.4	63.4
Fiji	10.9	21.1	2.0	2.2	74.5	48.2	8.3	16.7	2.6	3.2	88.1	78.1
Indonesia	11.5	22.6	7.6	14.3	80.8	63.1	14.1	28.4	7.5	9.7	77.4	61.8
Korea, Dem. Rep.	7.5	50.8	43.9	36.7	48.6	12.5	34.9	62.3	32.9	30.3	32.3	7.4
Lao PDR	..	..	0.5	1.1	34.6	15.4	78.4	87.1	1.3	0.5	18.7	11.0
Malaysia	11.1	24.6	5.9	11.6	83.1	63.8	13.7	28.3	2.8	7.1	81.6	64.0
Mongolia	..	..	9.5	3.4	40.6	14.7	19.1	42.7	37.2	30.3	43.7	27.0
Myanmar	22.6	59.4	10.6	20.2	56.6	14.5	48.0	70.0	2.7	4.6	49.3	25.4
Papua New Guinea	9.0	12.1	0.1	1.5	58.5	48.0	11.2	19.8	1.8	1.1	85.8	77.9
Philippines	9.2	19.3	1.6	2.9	88.8	77.0	11.2	27.6	4.2	4.4	83.9	68.1
Thailand	15.0	29.1	6.2	11.8	78.3	58.5	15.9	26.5	7.2	7.3	74.8	64.8
Vietnam	22.6	22.3	6.1	8.3	70.6	69.4	20.2	38.8	4.6	6.7	74.4	54.5
Europe & Central Asia	24.7 w	20.7 w	9.6 w	14.0 w	63.0 w	56.6 w	31.3 w	25.6 w	11.8 w	14.7 w	57.9 w	52.5 w
Albania	3.9	10.7	0.0	7.4	96.0	81.9	14.0	16.1	2.7	10.6	83.3	73.3
Armenia	25.0	38.7	10.5	13.1	54.2	47.1	25.2	43.0	13.6	22.6	55.8	34.3
Azerbaijan	21.0	13.2	2.3	13.9	76.2	73.0	44.4	44.6	11.4	16.4	44.1	39.0
Belarus	72.2	60.3	7.5	11.9	20.0	26.8	71.8	61.0	3.2	11.1	23.8	24.4
Bosnia and Herzegovina	6.6	6.5	..	..	90.3	90.3	5.4	12.6	..	..	94.4	86.4
Bulgaria	29.0	29.9	5.3	7.1	56.6	61.2	36.1	36.4	6.0	7.3	56.0	55.7
Cyprus	..	..	35.1	21.1	52.9	66.9	..	..	20.3	14.9	79.7	83.3
Georgia	64.7	61.3	5.9	6.5	29.2	32.2	52.6	54.1	3.7	11.9	42.0	34.0
Kazakhstan	25.2	18.8	11.3	22.8	42.3	47.1	57.6	33.2	7.0	36.3	35.2	30.5
Kyrgyz Republic	45.3	80.9	..	..	43.1	7.0	59.1	29.2	10.1	63.5	30.8	7.2
Lithuania	33.2	37.6	1.2	1.6	65.5	60.8	34.1	43.2	3.9	4.4	60.5	52.4
Macedonia, FYR	31.7	27.7	1.0	3.2	67.1	55.9	36.5	34.1	4.1	11.5	59.4	54.0
Moldova	69.4	64.3	1.8	2.7	28.8	32.2	54.0	50.1	1.5	12.3	44.4	37.5
Romania	14.3	18.3	7.6	6.1	77.6	75.5	16.4	16.6	5.5	8.9	74.4	74.4
Russian Federation	21.6	14.1	10.1	12.0	68.1	60.3	36.8	13.3	10.5	26.6	52.5	58.1
Serbia	..	32.5	..	2.3	..	56.5	..	21.2	..	5.3	..	61.0
Tajikistan	56.2	46.9	..	..	41.0	4.7	91.2	65.3	..	..	5.8	14.5
Turkey	9.2	14.5	9.8	24.5	75.4	57.9	12.8	19.7	13.7	25.4	70.4	53.9
Turkmenistan	60.5	26.9	..	..	26.2	24.5	54.3	51.0	..	..	32.2	32.8
Ukraine	42.6	47.2	18.5	22.2	37.8	29.7	60.8	48.7	4.7	13.6	34.2	36.7
Uzbekistan	57.0	56.5	..	..	36.4	10.2	45.3	40.2	..	..	51.2	42.6
Latin America & Carib.	15.4 w	18.9 w	3.8 w	15.6 w	77.6 w	63.0 w	15.2 w	19.4 w	3.4 w	14.8 w	75.0 w	58.4 w
Argentina	48.1	41.9	14.5	26.0	35.6	30.3	34.3	39.9	9.9	19.3	53.5	36.5
Bolivia	44.5	64.4	1.0	3.7	53.4	31.5	51.2	73.3	4.5	4.4	44.1	22.2
Brazil	22.9	22.7	8.6	29.8	57.3	45.5	20.8	16.6	12.5	28.5	66.4	54.5
Chile	21.1	18.2	8.6	30.4	65.3	51.3	32.2	29.3	10.9	22.1	46.4	47.9
Colombia	27.2	25.0	1.2	8.3	70.7	66.1	28.0	27.4	3.9	18.4	66.8	51.0
Costa Rica	17.9	28.5	2.7	6.3	79.4	65.2	22.3	22.8	3.9	10.1	38.9	65.5
Cuba	8.8	21.6	31.9	35.2	59.4	43.2	40.3	47.4	12.7	21.8	47.0	30.8
Dominican Republic	3.9	24.9	0.7	3.0	95.3	65.3	20.7	25.2	3.0	8.5	76.2	63.8
Ecuador	31.4	39.8	3.0	7.4	62.1	52.4	41.4	37.6	3.7	11.9	51.5	49.6
El Salvador	27.7	42.8	0.9	1.1	70.8	56.1	30.8	40.3	2.0	7.1	64.2	52.6
Guatemala	40.4	43.3	2.7	3.7	56.4	52.7	36.2	33.8	2.6	10.7	60.2	54.5
Haiti	4.4	5.1	0.8	3.3	94.7	91.3	21.8	38.7	4.5	10.8	72.1	50.4
Honduras	24.3	29.5	0.8	3.4	69.7	67.1	31.9	40.6	3.5	6.6	62.8	52.8
Jamaica	3.5	10.1	2.5	6.8	93.5	81.8	15.3	24.8	3.4	7.4	78.3	65.3
Mexico	3.1	6.9	0.3	2.1	96.1	90.2	2.5	4.2	4.3	20.2	91.1	74.2
Nicaragua	30.5	20.3	0.0	1.4	64.0	77.9	45.8	52.7	0.0	9.5	42.6	37.5
Panama	22.3	20.3	0.4	7.5	70.3	70.0	30.6	21.3	1.4	7.5	55.2	42.9
Paraguay	74.5	67.8	1.9	13.7	20.7	17.3	49.5	46.1	12.5	37.2	38.0	16.5
Peru	18.0	18.4	11.6	21.9	68.8	59.7	38.0	32.3	8.1	21.1	53.1	46.5
Uruguay	53.9	43.5	9.7	24.6	35.4	29.0	51.7	48.1	12.3	23.7	35.6	28.0
Venezuela, RB	19.7	12.0	0.5	16.0	74.2	52.7	21.1	34.8	2.4	11.5	57.1	52.2

Direction of trade of developing economies

	Exports — % of total merchandise exports						Imports — % of total merchandise imports					
	To developing economies				To high-income economies		From developing economies				From high-income economies	
	Within region		Outside region				Within region		Outside region			
	2000	2010	2000	2010	2000	2010	2000	2010	2000	2010	2000	2010
Middle East & N. Africa	3.9 w	7.4 w	15.6 w	27.0 w	76.0 w	60.4 w	5.1 w	7.9 w	18.2 w	26.5 w	71.6 w	61.3 w
Algeria	1.4	3.2	15.3	14.7	83.4	82.1	1.4	2.9	16.7	28.2	81.8	68.2
Bahrain	..	..	13.6	11.4	24.4	17.1	..	..	12.8	26.4	86.7	73.0
Egypt, Arab Rep.	6.9	19.2	9.8	24.0	73.5	53.1	1.1	3.2	19.6	35.2	72.7	61.2
Iran, Islamic Rep.	1.4	1.3	22.8	42.3	63.3	40.9	0.9	0.5	30.1	24.7	68.3	73.2
Iraq	7.3	3.7	7.4	31.3	85.3	65.0	10.1	24.1	38.5	48.2	51.4	27.7
Jordan	22.8	30.1	35.9	25.6	38.9	42.9	18.0	10.0	18.1	28.0	61.0	61.9
Lebanon	17.8	39.6	13.0	14.4	68.2	45.1	7.9	15.5	20.1	26.6	70.6	56.0
Libya	3.5	3.3	7.5	13.7	89.1	83.0	12.1	13.4	10.0	29.5	77.7	57.0
Morocco	2.8	3.8	10.9	22.4	83.1	70.2	10.2	7.1	13.0	23.5	75.2	69.2
Syrian Arab Republic	8.7	49.5	12.5	6.6	75.9	43.9	3.6	18.4	23.6	35.7	54.5	45.9
Tunisia	7.5	11.3	5.6	9.5	83.2	79.2	6.6	7.4	9.4	16.6	82.4	74.7
Yemen, Rep.	0.5	2.2	56.3	70.2	40.4	26.8	4.4	4.0	22.9	39.6	70.1	55.4
South Asia	4.6 w	5.8 w	16.0 w	28.4 w	75.3 w	63.9 w	4.3 w	4.0 w	12.8 w	17.0 w	58.2 w	56.9 w
Afghanistan	42.4	52.6	18.2	16.7	39.4	30.6	27.3	28.4	35.5	26.9	37.2	44.7
Bangladesh	1.7	2.9	4.1	9.6	79.7	83.5	11.8	15.8	18.3	37.0	53.1	40.4
India	4.3	5.0	18.8	30.4	73.4	63.2	0.9	0.6	20.0	39.2	55.6	59.7
Nepal	42.9	65.9	..	..	55.3	27.8	37.4	57.5	..	..	40.5	15.1
Pakistan	4.6	12.4	14.3	27.2	80.6	58.5	2.7	6.3	22.3	36.0	74.7	57.0
Sri Lanka	3.5	7.4	10.5	16.4	79.9	65.5	10.6	25.7	16.7	32.3	64.2	39.8
Sub-Saharan Africa	10.5 w	12.4 w	14.7 w	32.2 w	63.2 w	53.5 w	12.0 w	13.0 w	18.2 w	31.0 w	70.0 w	50.0 w
Angola	0.2	3.7	25.0	54.1	74.7	42.1	19.8	7.3	13.8	31.8	66.2	60.7
Benin	10.7	29.9	65.9	57.1	23.4	13.0	22.2	7.7	15.8	57.5	61.5	34.8
Burkina Faso	22.0	13.7	0.0	43.0	76.5	39.2	31.0	43.4	11.7	10.8	52.6	37.3
Burundi	17.0	12.0	0.0	20.4	61.9	51.3	23.8	28.6	8.1	17.4	46.7	44.4
Cameroon	7.0	13.6	9.4	20.5	77.9	62.8	27.3	21.2	8.8	29.5	54.7	48.7
Central African Republic	1.5	10.2	7.9	40.7	90.7	49.1	12.2	12.3	7.0	11.2	57.0	55.3
Chad	6.0	0.4	..	..	82.3	82.2	13.7	19.2	..	..	81.7	45.4
Comoros	..	..	..	..	96.2	59.3	..	..	..	..	52.4	46.4
Congo, Dem. Rep.	2.2	25.7	0.4	48.3	97.2	25.8	43.2	50.3	6.8	18.8	49.4	30.8
Congo, Rep.	3.0	1.1	17.4	38.7	79.5	60.0	13.2	6.3	11.2	31.4	68.5	60.4
Côte d'Ivoire	27.5	30.6	10.4	13.0	50.2	51.6	28.1	29.1	13.1	28.0	46.2	34.7
Ethiopia	0.6	5.3	18.3	26.0	81.1	55.2	1.8	2.8	39.6	28.6	48.9	35.1
Gabon	1.1	2.4	9.3	28.1	83.7	55.8	4.8	10.9	3.4	18.8	90.6	68.3
Gambia, The	18.0	7.0	10.7	48.4	71.3	44.7	16.0	16.9	37.2	56.1	46.8	27.0
Ghana	5.3	10.7	11.6	24.4	74.8	52.8	22.1	24.9	15.7	33.5	61.3	40.7
Guinea	6.4	2.3	13.0	46.9	80.6	35.1	24.4	6.4	13.8	21.1	61.5	26.2
Guinea-Bissau	1.2	30.5	..	..	6.9	4.0	13.6	22.1	..	..	48.5	38.8
Kenya	40.0	37.4	18.7	15.6	39.6	38.2	8.4	12.3	16.0	38.4	75.0	48.3
Liberia	1.2	32.2	14.6	9.4	84.2	58.4	1.3	0.9	5.7	29.6	93.0	69.6
Madagascar	3.0	4.9	3.5	13.1	88.4	72.1	6.2	12.9	33.0	27.3	52.6	48.2
Malawi	15.6	22.3	14.7	28.1	69.2	49.1	71.8	61.8	6.9	16.0	20.0	21.5
Mali	6.4	6.6	40.5	41.5	50.7	43.9	26.0	30.9	7.5	12.5	32.7	28.1
Mauritania	20.4	14.4	8.3	44.4	70.2	40.0	4.4	4.7	21.0	33.5	65.8	51.9
Mauritius	7.6	14.6	0.9	4.6	91.5	80.8	18.3	11.5	26.8	48.6	54.9	39.8
Mozambique	36.0	25.9	7.0	8.3	36.7	64.0	51.8	38.1	7.4	15.9	28.6	39.6
Niger	48.5	77.6	0.5	5.6	51.0	16.7	13.2	21.1	5.8	29.8	80.5	49.1
Nigeria	7.0	9.6	22.3	25.1	70.4	64.3	4.1	4.9	20.1	28.5	75.2	49.6
Rwanda	7.3	58.4	16.1	21.2	42.6	19.7	33.9	50.1	5.4	12.7	37.6	36.1
Senegal	27.7	50.2	15.5	14.9	48.7	26.9	19.2	15.2	17.4	32.8	58.8	51.7
Sierra Leone	4.2	8.0	2.4	25.8	91.2	63.1	6.4	24.8	8.8	34.9	81.3	35.5
Somalia	4.0	4.1	21.2	23.9	74.9	71.9	13.4	8.8	50.9	64.8	24.7	13.7
South Africa	12.9	14.9	7.2	28.9	52.9	56.1	2.0	7.9	15.5	32.3	82.1	59.8
Sudan	0.2	1.6	50.6	78.6	49.2	19.7	3.5	7.4	36.6	49.6	59.9	39.2
Tanzania	18.2	19.6	17.8	33.3	63.1	38.4	20.2	16.6	21.1	42.1	58.6	37.1
Togo	40.4	63.2	30.2	25.2	25.1	11.2	22.1	13.6	12.1	34.1	62.6	50.9
Uganda	30.9	50.9	2.2	6.8	63.8	39.3	39.9	27.1	15.6	23.3	44.4	49.5
Zambia	41.8	19.1	1.8	21.5	49.8	59.4	69.0	63.6	3.7	9.6	26.4	26.8
Zimbabwe	17.4	47.3	8.9	23.1	29.4	29.4	49.6	69.2	6.3	13.0	33.0	13.6

Note: Bilateral trade data are not available for Timor-Leste, Kosovo, West Bank and Gaza, Botswana, Eritrea, Lesotho, Namibia, South Sudan, and Swaziland. Components may not sum to 100 percent because of trade with unspecified partners or with economies not covered by World Bank classification.

6.4 Direction of trade of developing economies

Developing economies are an increasingly important part of the global trading system. From 2009 to 2010 the volume of merchandise exports increased 14.5 percent globally and 12.9 percent in developing countries; the volume of merchandise imports increased 13.5 percent globally and 10.7 percent in developing countries. Trade between high-income economies and low- and middle-income economies has grown faster than trade between high-income economies. This increased trade benefits both producers and consumers in developing and high-income economies.

The table shows trade in goods between developing economies in the same region and other regions and between developing economies and high-income economies. Data on exports and imports are from the International Monetary Fund's (IMF) Direction of Trade database and should be broadly consistent with data from other sources, such as the United Nations Statistics Division's Commodity Trade (Comtrade) database. All high-income economies and major developing economies report trade data to the IMF on a timely basis, covering about 85 percent of trade for recent years. Trade data for less timely reporters and for countries that do not report are estimated using reports of trading partner countries. Therefore, data on trade between developing and high-income economies shown in the table should be generally complete. But trade flows between many developing economies—particularly those in Sub-Saharan Africa—are not well recorded, and the value of trade among developing economies may be understated. The table does not include some developing economies because data on their bilateral trade flows are not available. Data on the direction of trade between selected high-income economies are presented and discussed in tables 6.2 and 6.3.

At the regional level most exports from developing economies are to high-income economies, but the share of intraregional trade is increasing. Geographic patterns of trade vary widely by country and commodity. Larger shares of exports from oil- and resource-rich economies are to high-income economies.

The relative importance of intraregional trade is higher for both landlocked countries and small countries with close trade links to the largest regional economy. For most developing economies—especially smaller ones—there is a "geographic bias" favoring intraregional trade. Despite the broad trend toward globalization and the reduction of trade barriers, the relative share of intraregional trade increased for most economies between 1999 and 2010. This is due partly to trade-related advantages, such as proximity, lower transport costs, increased knowledge from repeated interaction, and cultural and historical affinity. The direction of trade is also influenced by preferential trade agreements that a country has made with other economies. Though formal agreements on trade liberalization do not automatically increase trade, they nevertheless affect the direction of trade between the participating economies. Table 6.6 illustrates the size of existing regional trade blocs that have formal preferential trade agreements.

Although global integration has increased, developing economies still face trade barriers when accessing other markets (see table 6.7).

- **Exports to developing economies within region** are the sum of merchandise exports from the reporting economy to other developing economies in the same World Bank region as a percentage of total merchandise exports by the economy. • **Exports to developing economies outside region** are the sum of merchandise exports from the reporting economy to other developing economies in other World Bank regions as a percentage of total merchandise exports by the economy. • **Exports to high-income economies** are the sum of merchandise exports from the reporting economy to high-income economies as a percentage of total merchandise exports by the economy. • **Imports from developing economies within region** are the sum of merchandise imports by the reporting economy from other developing economies in the same World Bank region as a percentage of total merchandise imports by the economy. • **Imports from developing economies outside region** are the sum of merchandise imports by the reporting economy from other developing economies in other World Bank regions as a percentage of total merchandise imports by the economy. • **Imports from high-income economies** are the sum of merchandise imports by the reporting economy from high-income economies as a percentage of total merchandise imports by the economy.

Data sources

Data on merchandise trade flows are published in the IMF's *Direction of Trade Statistics Yearbook* and *Direction of Trade Statistics Quarterly;* the data in the table were calculated using the IMF's Direction of Trade database. Regional and income group classifications are according to the World Bank classification of economies as of July 1, 2011, and are as shown on the cover flaps of this report.

	1970	1980	1990	1995	2000	2005	2006	2007	2008	2009	2010	2011
World Bank commodity price index												
(2005 = 100)												
Energy	11	87	45	32	60	100	115	120	156	105	128	153
Nonenergy commodities	138	134	87	92	81	100	122	139	156	130	154	171
Agriculture	155	157	94	104	88	100	110	124	146	136	151	170
Beverages	182	207	94	113	86	100	105	114	129	144	161	169
Food	165	163	94	100	86	100	108	128	159	142	150	171
Fats and oils	190	158	85	105	86	100	102	145	178	151	163	181
Grains	176	166	103	110	89	100	116	139	190	155	152	194
Other food	124	168	97	83	83	100	110	96	106	120	131	136
Raw materials	115	116	93	109	95	100	115	119	122	118	147	168
Timber	94	89	85	107	102	100	112	115	117	116	116	125
Other raw materials	138	144	102	111	87	100	119	123	128	121	182	215
Fertilizers	61	117	68	75	75	100	102	137	341	186	166	217
Metals and minerals	112	89	75	69	67	100	151	171	154	110	159	167
Base metals	125	97	81	76	71	100	162	171	142	109	150	157
Steel products[a]	..	77	76	71	61	100	95	90	133	112	110	117
Commodity prices												
(2005 prices)												
Energy												
Coal, Australian ($/mt)	29	53	41	37	29	48	48	61	109	66	88	98
Natural gas, Europe ($/mmBtu)	2	6	3	3	4	6	8	8	11	8	7	9
Natural gas, U.S. ($/mmBtu)	1	2	2	2	5	9	7	6	8	4	4	3
Natural gas, liquefied, Japan ($/mmBtu)	..	7	4	3	5	6	7	7	11	8	10	12
Petroleum, avg, spot ($/bbl)	4	48	24	16	32	53	63	66	83	56	70	85
Beverages (cents/kg)												
Cocoa	249	342	131	133	101	154	156	180	220	264	277	242
Coffee, Arabica	423	455	204	309	215	253	247	251	263	290	383	486
Coffee, robusta	337	426	122	257	102	111	146	176	198	150	154	196
Tea, avg., 3 auctions	308	218	213	138	210	165	183	188	207	249	255	238
Tea, Colombo auctions	231	146	194	132	201	184	187	232	238	287	291	266
Tea, Kolkata auctions	365	269	290	162	202	162	172	177	193	230	248	226
Tea, Mombasa auctions	327	238	154	121	227	148	191	153	189	230	227	221
Food												
Fats and oils ($/mt)												
Coconut oil	1,464	884	348	621	504	617	594	846	1,046	664	995	1,407
Copra[a]	829	594	239	407	341	414	394	559	697	439	664	941
Groundnut oil	1,395	1,127	997	920	799	1,060	950	1,245	1,821	1,083	1,243	1,615
Palm oil	959	766	300	583	347	422	468	719	810	625	798	915
Palm kernel oil[a]	..	..	..	..	496	627	569	818	965	640	1,049	1,341
Soybeans	431	389	255	241	237	275	263	354	447	400	398	440
Soybean meal	378	344	207	183	212	214	205	284	363	373	335	324
Soybean oil	1,056	784	463	580	378	545	586	812	1,075	776	890	1,057
Grains ($/mt)												
Barley	..	103	83	97	86	95	114	159	171	117	140	169
Maize	215	164	113	115	99	99	119	151	191	151	165	237
Rice, Thailand, 5%	466	539	280	298	227	286	298	301	555	508	433	442
Rice, Thailand, 25%[a]	..	..	270	276	193	265	271	282	289	419	391	412
Rice, Thailand, A1[a]	..	..	209	269	187	218	215	251	412	299	340	373
Rice, Vietnam, 5%[a]	..	..	..	..	..	258	255	284	485	..	380	418
Sorghum[a]	191	169	107	110	99	96	120	150	178	138	146	219
Wheat, Canada[a]	231	250	162	192	165	198	212	277	388	275	277	358
Wheat, U.S., soft red winter[a]	210	221	133	155	111	136	156	220	232	170	203	233
Wheat, U.S., hard red winter	202	227	140	164	128	152	188	235	279	205	198	257

	1970	1980	1990	1995	2000	2005	2006	2007	2008	2009	2010	2011
Commodity prices (continued)												
(2005 prices)												
Food (continued)												
Other food												
Bananas, U.S. ($/mt)	612	495	559	413	475	603	663	622	721	775	769	787
Beef (cents/kg)	481	362	265	177	216	262	249	240	268	241	297	329
Chicken meat (cents/kg)	..	99	112	114	147	163	149	159	159	173	168	157
Fishmeal ($/mt)[a]	726	662	426	459	462	731	1,142	1,084	968	1,125	1,494	1,251
Oranges ($/mt)	619	513	549	493	407	875	812	881	946	832	915	725
Shrimp, Mexico (cents/kg)[a]	..	1,511	1,106	1,401	1,696	1,034	1,002	930	913	865	890	971
Sugar, EU domestic (cents/kg)	41	64	60	64	62	67	63	63	60	48	39	37
Sugar, U.S. domestic (cents/kg)	61	87	53	47	48	47	48	42	40	50	70	68
Sugar, world (cents/kg)	30	83	29	27	20	22	32	20	24	37	42	47
Agricultural raw materials												
Cotton A Index (cents/kg)	249	271	188	197	146	122	124	129	134	126	202	271
Cotton, Memphis (cents/kg)	..	..	191	200	164	130	131	132	138	133	207	59
Logs, Cameroon ($/cu. m)[a]	159	330	355	315	308	334	312	351	450	386	380	394
Logs, Malaysian ($/cu. m)	159	257	183	237	213	203	234	247	250	263	246	318
Rubber, Singapore (cents/kg)	150	187	89	147	75	149	203	208	221	176	324	392
Rubber, TSR 20 (cents/kg)[a]	0	0	0	0	70	139	190	199	216	165	299	368
Rubber, US (cents/kg)[a]	170	213	106	168	93	166	226	228	243	196	342	421
Plywood (cents/sheet)[a]	380	359	367	542	502	509	583	590	551	517	504	494
Sawnwood, Malaysian ($/cu. m)	647	520	551	687	666	659	734	743	760	737	751	764
Sawnwood, Cameroon ($/cu. m)[a]	..	..	..	553	547	559	610	700	819	685	720	672
Tobacco ($/mt)[a]	3,967	2,986	3,508	2,453	3,332	2,790	2,906	3,054	3,066	3,880	3,812	3,641
Woodpulp ($/mt)[a]	654	704	842	792	744	635	684	706	701	562	768	732
Fertilizers ($/mt)												
Diammonium phosphate	199	292	177	201	173	247	255	398	826	296	443	503
Phosphate rock	41	61	42	32	49	42	43	65	295	111	109	150
Potassium chloride	116	152	101	109	137	158	171	184	487	577	294	354
Triple superphosphate	157	237	136	139	154	201	197	312	751	235	338	438
Urea	67	252	123	174	113	219	218	285	421	228	256	342
Metals and minerals												
Aluminum ($/mt)	2,050	1,910	1,695	1,676	1,734	1,898	2,516	2,430	2,198	1,523	1,924	1,953
Copper ($/mt)	5,219	2,863	2,752	2,724	2,030	3,679	6,580	6,557	5,943	4,711	6,672	7,181
Gold ($/toz)[a]	132	798	397	357	312	445	592	642	745	890	1,084	1,276
Iron ore, spot, cfr China ($/dmt)[a]	..	..	..	..	..	..	68	113	133	73	129	136
Lead (cents/kg)	112	119	84	59	51	98	126	238	179	157	190	195
Nickel ($/mt)	10,492	8,553	9,167	7,636	9,669	14,744	23,742	34,293	18,035	13,406	19,313	18,637
Silver (cents/toz)[a]	653	2,708	498	482	560	734	1,132	1,235	1,281	1,344	1,789	2,868
Tin (cents/kg)	1,354	2,201	629	577	608	738	860	1,339	1,581	1,242	1,807	2,119
Zinc (cents/kg)	109	100	157	96	126	138	321	299	160	151	191	178
MUV G-15 index (2005 = 100)	27	76	97	108	89	100	102	109	117	109	113	123
MUV G-5 index (2005 = 100)	26	74	93	109	91	100	102	106	114	107	110	115

Note: bbl = barrel, cu. m = cubic meter, dmtu = dry metric ton unit, kg = kilogram, mmBtu = million British thermal units, mt = metric ton, toz = troy ounce.
a. Series not included in the nonenergy index.

Primary commodity prices

Primary commodities—raw or partially processed materials that will be transformed into finished goods—are often developing countries' most important exports, and commodity revenues can affect living standards. Price data are collected from various sources, including international commodity study groups, government agencies, industry trade journals, and Bloomberg and Datastream. Prices are compiled in U.S. dollars or converted to U.S. dollars when quoted in local currencies.

The table is based on frequently updated price reports. Prices are those received by exporters when available, or the prices paid by importers or trade unit values. Annual price series are generally simple averages based on higher frequency data. The constant price series in the table are deflated by the manufactures unit value (MUV) index for the Group of Fifteen (G-15) countries (see below).

Commodity price indexes are calculated as Laspeyres index numbers; the fixed weights are the 2002–04 average export values for low- and middle-income economies (based on 2001 gross national income) rebased to 2005. Data for exports are from the United Nations Statistics Division's Commodity Trade Statistics (Comtrade) database Standard International Trade Classification (SITC) revision 3, the Food and Agriculture Organization's FAOSTAT database, the International Energy Agency database, BP's *Statistical Review of World Energy,* the World Bureau of Metal Statistics, and World Bank staff estimates.

Each index in the table represents a fixed basket of primary commodity exports over time. The nonenergy commodity price index contains 39 price series for 38 nonenergy commodities. Separate indexes are compiled for energy and steel products, which are not included in the nonenergy commodity price index.

The MUV G-15 index is a composite index of prices for manufactured exports from the 15 major (G-15) developed and emerging economies (Brazil, Canada, China, France, Germany, India, Italy, Japan, the Republic of Korea, Mexico, South Africa, Spain, Thailand, the United Kingdom, and the United States) to low- and middle-income economies, valued in U.S. dollars. For the MUV G-15 index, unit value indexes in local currency for each country are converted to U.S. dollars using market exchange rates and are combined using weights determined by the share of each country's exports to low- and middle-income countries in the base year (2005). The MUV G-5 index is a composite index of prices for manufactured exports from the five major (G-5) industrial

economies (France, Germany, Japan, the United Kingdom, and the United States) and is included in the table for comparison purposes.

• **Energy price index** is the composite price index for coal, petroleum, and natural gas, weighted by exports of each commodity from low- and middle-income countries. • **Nonenergy commodity price index** covers the 38 nonenergy primary commodities that make up the agriculture, fertilizer, and metals and minerals indexes. • **Agriculture** includes beverages, food, and agricultural raw materials. • **Beverages** include cocoa, coffee, and tea. • **Food** includes fats and oils, grains, and other food items. Fats and oils include coconut oil, copra, groundnut oil, palm oil, palm kernel oil, soybeans, soybean meal, and soybean oil. Grains include barley, maize, rice, sorghum, and wheat. Other food items include bananas, beef, chicken meat, fishmeal, oranges, shrimp, and sugar. • **Agricultural raw materials** include timber and other raw materials. Timber includes tropical hard logs and sawnwood. Other raw materials include cotton, natural rubber, and tobacco. • **Fertilizers** include phosphate, phosphate rock, potassium, and nitrogenous products. • **Metals and minerals** include base metals (aluminum, copper, lead, nickel, tin, and zinc) and iron ore. • **Steel products price index** is the composite price index for eight steel products based on quotations free on board (f.o.b.) Japan excluding shipments to the United States for all years and to China prior to 2002, weighted by product shares of apparent combined consumption (volume of deliveries) for Germany, Japan, and the United States. • **Commodity prices**—for definitions and sources, see "Commodity price data" (also known as the "Pink Sheet") at the World Bank Prospects for Development website (www.worldbank.org/prospects, click on Products). • **MUV G-15 index** is the manufactures unit value index for G-15 country exports to low- and middle-income economies.

Data on commodity prices and the MUV G-15 index are compiled by the World Bank's Development Prospects Group. Monthly updates of commodity prices are available at http://data.worldbank.org.

6.6 Regional trade blocs

	Year of creation	Year of entry into force of the most recent agreement	Type of most recent agreement[a]	Merchandise exports within bloc		Merchandise exports by bloc
				$ millions	% of total bloc exports	% of world exports
				2010	2010	2010
High-income and low- and middle-income economies						
APEC[b]	1989		None	4,868,838	67.5	47.3
EEA	1994	1994	EIA	3,519,827	68.7	33.6
EFTA	1960	2002	EIA	2,096	0.6	2.2
European Union	1957	1958	EIA, CU	3,356,310	67.3	32.7
NAFTA	1994	1994	FTA	955,598	48.7	12.9
SPARTECA	1981	1981	PTA	20,717	8.1	1.7
Trans-Pacific SEP	2006	2006	EIA, FTA	3,969	0.9	3.0
East Asia and Pacific and South Asia						
APTA	1975	1976	PTA	278,451	12.1	15.1
ASEAN	1967	1992	FTA	262,270	25.0	6.9
MSG	1993	1994	PTA	99	0.8	0.1
PICTA	2001	2003	FTA	308	2.6	0.1
SAARC	1985	2006	FTA	15,702	5.8	1.8
Europe, Central Asia, and Middle East						
Agadir agreement	2004		NNA	2,068	3.2	0.4
CEFTA	1992	1994	FTA	5,229	17.5	0.2
CEZ	2003	2004	FTA	18,065	4.0	2.9
CIS	1991	1994	FTA	68,596	12.9	3.5
Customs Union of Belarus, Kazakhstan, and Russian Federation	2010		CU	18,065	4.0	2.9
EAEC	1997	2000	CU	21,200	4.7	2.9
ECO	1985	2003	PTA	27,654	8.8	2.1
GCC	1981	2003[c]	CU	28,623	4.8	3.9
PAFTA	1997	1998	FTA	81,816	9.7	5.5
UMA	1989	1994[c]	NNA	3,926	2.9	0.9
Latin America and the Caribbean						
Andean Community	1969	1988	CU	7,825	8.5	0.6
CACM	1961	1961	CU	6,330	22.5	0.2
CARICOM	1973	1997	EIA	3,356	15.2	0.1
LAIA	1980	1981	PTA	128,829	15.9	5.3
MERCOSUR	1991	2005	EIA	44,239	15.7	1.9
OECS	1981	1981[c]	NNA	132	17.5	0.0
Sub-Saharan Africa						
CEMAC	1994	1999	CU	383	1.2	0.2
CEPGL	1976		NNA	81	1.5	0.0
COMESA	1994	1994	CU	8,158	7.7	0.7
EAC	1996	2000	CU	1,997	20.3	0.1
ECCAS	1983	2004[c]	NNA	483	0.6	0.6
ECOWAS	1975	1993	PTA	8,911	8.8	0.7
Indian Ocean Commission	1984	2005[c]	NNA	184	5.3	0.0
SADC	1992	2000	FTA	14,576	9.8	1.0
UEMOA	1994	2000	CU	2,250	14.6	0.1

Note: APEC is Asia Pacific Economic Cooperation, EEA is European Economic Area, EFTA is European Free Trade Association, NAFTA is North American Free Trade Agreement, SPARTECA is South Pacific Regional Trade and Economic Cooperation Agreement, Trans-Pacific SEP is Trans-Pacific Strategic Economic Partnership, APTA is Asia-Pacific Trade Agreement, ASEAN is Association of South East Asian Nations, MSG is Melanesian Spearhead Group, PICTA is Pacific Island Countries Trade Agreement, SAARC is South Asian Association for Regional Cooperation, CEFTA is Central European Free Trade Area, CEZ is Common Economic Zone, CIS is Commonwealth of Independent States, EAEC is Eurasian Economic Community, ECO is Economic Cooperation Organization, GCC is Gulf Cooperation Council, PAFTA is Pan-Arab Free Trade Area, UMA is Arab Maghreb Union, CACM is Central American Common Market, CARICOM is Caribbean Community and Common Market, LAIA is Latin American Integration Association, MERCOSUR is Southern Common Market, OECS is Organization of Eastern Caribbean States, CEMAC is Economic and Monetary Community of Central Africa, CEPGL is Economic Community of the Great Lakes Countries, COMESA is Common Market for Eastern and Southern Africa, EAC is East African Community, ECCAS is Economic Community of Central African States, ECOWAS is Economic Community of West African States, SADC is Southern African Development Community, UEMOA is West African Economic and Monetary Union. For regional bloc memberships, see the World Trade Organization's Regional Trade Agreements Information System (http://rtais.wto.org/UI/PublicMaintainRTAHome.aspx).
a. CU is customs union; EIA is economic integration agreement; FTA is free trade agreement; PTA is preferential trade agreement; and NNA is not notified agreement, which refers to preferential trade arrangements established among member countries that are not notified to the World Trade Organization (these agreements may be functionally equivalent to any of the other agreements). b. No preferential trade agreement c. Collected from the official website of the trade bloc.

About the data

Trade blocs are groups of countries that have established preferential arrangements governing trade between members. Although in some cases the preferences—such as lower tariff duties or exemptions from quantitative restrictions—may be no greater than those available to other trading partners, such arrangements are intended to encourage exports by bloc members to one another—sometimes called intraregional trade. Most countries are members of a regional trade bloc, and the surge of countries participating in such arrangements has continued unabated since the early 1990s. While trade blocs vary in structure, they all have the same objective: to reduce trade barriers among member countries. But effective integration requires more than reducing tariffs and quotas. Economic gains from competition and scale may not be achieved unless other barriers that divide markets and impede the free flow of goods, services, and investments are lifted. For example, many regional trade blocs retain contingent protections on intrabloc trade, including antidumping, countervailing duties, and "emergency protection" to address balance of payments problems or protect an industry from import surges. Other barriers include differing product standards, discrimination in public procurement, and cumbersome border formalities. In addition, becoming a member of a trade bloc can result in trade diversion, where a member switches from being a relatively efficient, low-cost producer outside a trade bloc to a less efficient, higher cost producer within a trade bloc. On a global scale this could lead to misallocated resources.

Membership in a regional trade bloc may reduce the frictional costs of trade, increase the credibility of reform initiatives, and strengthen security among partners. But making it work effectively is challenging. All economic sectors may be affected, and some may expand while others contract, so it is important to weigh the potential costs and benefits of membership. The table shows the value of intraregional merchandise trade (service exports are excluded) for

important regional trade blocs and the size of intraregional trade relative to each bloc's exports of goods and the share of the bloc's exports in world exports. Although the Asia Pacific Economic Cooperation has no preferential arrangements, it is included because of the volume of trade between its members.

The data on country exports are from the International Monetary Fund's (IMF) Direction of Trade database and should be broadly consistent with those from sources such as the United Nations Statistics Division's Commodity Trade Statistics (Comtrade) database. All high-income economies and major developing economies report trade to the IMF on a timely basis, covering about 85 percent of trade for recent years. Trade by less timely reporters and by countries that do not report is estimated using reports of trading partner countries. Therefore, data on trade between developing and high-income economies shown in the table should be generally complete. However, trade flows between many developing countries—particularly those in Sub-Saharan Africa—are not well recorded, and the value of trade among developing countries may be understated.

Membership in the trade blocs shown is based on the most recent information available (see Data sources). Other types of preferential trade agreements may have entered into force earlier than those shown in the table and may still be effective. Unless otherwise footnoted, information on the type of agreement and date of enforcement are based on the World Trade Organization's (WTO) list of regional trade agreements. Information on trade agreements not notified to the WTO was collected from the Global Preferential Trade Agreements database (box 6.6a) and from official websites of the trade blocs.

Some countries belong to more than one trade bloc, so shares of world exports exceed 100 percent. Exports include all commodity trade, which may include items not specified in trade bloc agreements. Differences from previously published estimates may be due to changes in membership or revisions in underlying data.

Definitions

• **Type of most recent agreement** includes customs union, under which members substantially eliminate all tariff and nontariff barriers among themselves and establish a common external tariff for nonmembers; economic integration agreement, which liberalizes trade in services among members and covers a substantial number of sectors, affects a sufficient volume of trade, includes substantial modes of supply, and is nondiscriminatory (in the sense that similarly situated service suppliers are treated the same); free trade agreement, under which members substantially eliminate all tariff and nontariff barriers but set tariffs on imports from nonmembers; preferential trade agreement, which is an agreement notified to the WTO that is not a free trade agreement, a customs union, or an economic integration agreement; and not notified agreement, which is a preferential trade arrangement established among member countries that is not notified to the World Trade Organization (the agreement may be functionally equivalent to any of the other agreements).
• **Merchandise exports within bloc** are the sum of merchandise exports by members of a trade bloc to other members of the bloc. They are shown both in U.S. dollars and as a percentage of total merchandise exports by the bloc. • **Merchandise exports by bloc** as a share of world exports are the bloc's total merchandise exports (within the bloc and to the rest of the world) as a share of total merchandise exports by all economies in the world.

Global Preferential Trade Agreement Database 6.6a

The Global Preferential Trade Agreement Database provides information on preferential trade agreements around the world, including agreements that have not been notified to the World Trade Organization (WTO). It is designed to help trade policymakers, scholars, and business operators better understand and navigate the world of preferential trade agreements. Updated regularly, the database currently covers more than 330 preferential trade agreements in their original language, which have been indexed by WTO criteria and can be downloaded as PDFs. Users can search by provision or keyword; compare provisions across multiple agreements; and sort agreements by membership, date of signature, in-force status, and other criteria. The database was developed jointly by the World Bank and the Center for International Business, Tuck School of Business at Dartmouth College. It was supported by the Multidonor Trust Fund for Trade and Development, with financing from the governments of Finland, Norway, Sweden, and the United Kingdom. The database is integrated with the World Integrated Trade Solution database and is part of the World Bank's Open Data initiative (http://wits.worldbank.org/gptad/).

Data sources

Data on merchandise trade flows are published in the IMF's *Direction of Trade Statistics Yearbook* and *Direction of Trade Statistics Quarterly;* the data in the table were calculated using the IMF's Direction of Trade database. Data on trade bloc membership are from World Bank (2000b), UNCTAD's *Trade and Development Report 2007,* WTO's Regional Trade Agreements Information System (http://rtais.wto.org/UI/PublicMaintainRTAHome.aspx), and the World Bank and the Center for International Business at the Tuck School of Business at Dartmouth College's Global Preferential Trade Agreements Database.

	Most recent year	Binding coverage	Simple mean bound rate	All products %					Primary products %		Manufactured products %	
				Simple mean tariff	Weighted mean tariff	Share of tariff lines with international peaks	Share of tariff lines with specific rates		Simple mean tariff	Weighted mean tariff	Simple mean tariff	Weighted mean tariff
Afghanistan	2008	..	..	6.2	6.4	4.4	0.7		7.0	6.7	6.1	6.3
Albania	2009	100.0	7.1	5.7	5.1	0.0	0.0		6.8	5.4	5.6	5.0
Algeria	2009	..	..	14.2	8.6	53.2	0.0		14.5	7.8	14.2	8.9
Angola	2009	100.0	59.2	7.4	7.4	23.4	0.6		11.6	13.9	6.8	5.9
Antigua and Barbuda	2009	97.9	58.7	13.8	14.6	49.4	0.1		17.2	14.8	13.1	14.5
Argentina	2010	100.0	31.9	11.4	6.2	24.3	0.0		7.5	1.6	11.9	7.0
Armenia	2008	100.0	8.5	3.7	2.3	0.0	0.4		5.6	2.2	3.5	2.4
Australia	2010	97.0	10.0	2.8	1.9	0.0	0.2		1.3	0.4	3.0	2.5
Azerbaijan	2009	..	..	8.3	3.9	46.5	2.3		9.5	3.8	8.1	4.0
Bahamas, The	2010	..	..	33.2	21.5	68.8	0.5		21.9	7.6	36.1	32.6
Bahrain	2009	73.6	34.8	4.4	3.6	0.3	0.2		7.0	6.9	4.0	3.1
Bangladesh	2008	15.9	169.9	13.9	13.0	38.0	0.9		16.3	8.8	13.6	14.0
Barbados	2007	97.8	78.1	15.1	14.8	44.9	1.0		26.3	21.9	13.4	12.3
Belarus	2010	..	..	6.7	2.1	4.5	14.0		6.3	0.9	6.8	3.4
Belize	2010	97.9	58.4	11.5	6.4	31.9	1.9		17.5	4.0	10.6	10.1
Benin	2010	39.5	28.7	13.3	15.4	50.2	0.0		15.5	12.4	12.9	17.0
Bermuda	2010	..	..	18.0	26.1	64.3	2.8		10.0	14.3	19.4	27.7
Bhutan	2007	..	..	18.2	17.8	50.7	0.0		43.5	44.9	15.5	16.0
Bolivia	2010	100.0	40.0	9.6	5.4	11.9	0.0		8.4	5.8	9.7	5.2
Bosnia and Herzegovina	2010	..	..	3.3	1.8	0.0	4.2		1.4	1.1	3.6	2.3
Botswana	2010	96.1	19.0	8.8	5.2	20.2	1.0		6.1	0.5	9.0	6.6
Brazil	2010	100.0	31.4	13.4	7.6	26.4	0.0		8.1	1.5	14.0	9.8
Brunei Darussalam	2010	95.3	24.1	3.8	4.1	20.8	1.2		0.2	0.1	4.4	5.0
Burkina Faso	2010	39.4	42.5	12.4	8.8	44.5	0.0		11.4	8.1	12.5	9.2
Burundi	2010	22.3	67.8	9.8	5.5	29.8	0.1		15.4	9.4	9.1	4.6
Cambodia	2008	100.0	19.1	12.4	9.9	19.7	0.0		13.8	11.8	12.2	9.6
Cameroon	2009	13.7	79.9	18.4	15.0	52.5	0.0		20.5	12.9	18.1	15.9
Canada	2010	99.7	5.2	2.9	0.9	6.5	3.4		1.7	0.3	3.2	1.1
Cape Verde	2010	100.0	15.8	14.7	11.6	44.3	0.0		16.2	12.2	14.4	11.0
Central African Republic	2007	62.5	36.0	17.5	13.6	47.4	0.1		18.9	13.8	17.3	13.3
Chad	2009	13.9	79.9	17.6	14.7	47.4	0.3		22.5	17.2	16.8	13.8
Chile	2010	100.0	25.1	4.9	4.0	0.0	0.0		4.4	2.7	4.9	4.8
China[†]	2010	100.0	10.0	7.7	4.0	11.2	0.2		8.1	1.8	7.7	5.6
Hong Kong SAR, China	2010	45.8	0.0	0.0	0.0	0.0	0.0		0.0	0.0	0.0	0.0
Macao SAR, China	2010	28.2	0.0	0.0	0.0	0.0	0.0		0.0	0.0	0.0	0.0
Colombia	2010	100.0	43.1	11.2	8.9	19.8	0.0		10.9	8.8	11.3	8.9
Comoros	2010	..	..	7.6	8.1	1.5	0.3		4.5	3.9	8.4	11.2
Congo, Dem. Rep.	2009	100.0	96.2	12.9	11.0	42.5	0.2		14.2	10.8	12.6	11.1
Congo, Rep.	2007	16.5	27.4	18.6	14.7	52.6	0.2		21.9	18.6	18.2	14.1
Costa Rica	2009	100.0	43.2	4.8	2.4	0.7	0.0		6.3	3.3	4.6	2.1
Côte d'Ivoire	2010	33.8	11.2	13.1	7.3	47.9	0.0		15.1	5.4	12.8	9.3
Croatia	2010	100.0	6.0	2.4	1.2	4.1	5.2		4.5	1.9	2.1	1.0
Cuba	2010	31.7	21.4	10.5	8.7	11.6	0.0		11.1	6.2	10.4	9.8
Cyprus	2010	100.0	4.2	1.9	1.6	1.9	7.8		2.5	0.5	1.9	2.3
Djibouti	2009	100.0	41.2	20.6	15.2	69.4	0.5		15.9	8.7	21.3	18.6
Dominica	2007	94.7	58.7	11.9	7.9	43.3	0.0		19.2	5.7	10.6	9.3
Dominican Republic	2010	100.0	34.9	8.3	6.1	30.1	0.0		11.8	4.6	7.8	6.9
Ecuador	2010	100.0	21.7	9.3	6.0	20.2	0.0		9.0	4.3	9.4	6.7
Egypt, Arab Rep.	2009	99.3	37.3	12.6	8.1	18.4	0.2		37.6	6.4	9.4	9.5
El Salvador	2010	100.0	36.9	5.1	5.5	1.9	0.0		8.4	7.4	4.7	4.3
Equatorial Guinea	2007	..	..	18.3	15.6	52.3	0.2		21.5	21.4	17.8	14.3
Eritrea	2006	..	..	9.6	5.4	22.4	0.0		9.2	3.5	9.6	7.2
Ethiopia	2010	..	..	18.1	10.5	55.6	0.0		19.7	5.1	18.0	13.2
European Union	2010	100.0	4.2	1.9	1.6	1.9	7.8		2.5	0.5	1.9	2.3
Fiji	2010	51.4	40.1	11.9	11.0	23.3	1.9		13.5	9.8	11.6	12.2
French Polynesia	2009	..	..	6.8	4.2	28.0	0.0		4.1	2.7	7.3	5.2
Gabon	2009	100.0	21.4	18.7	14.5	53.1	0.1		21.2	15.1	18.4	14.3
Gambia, The	2009	13.7	101.8	18.7	14.8	91.2	0.1		16.9	12.8	19.2	17.0
Georgia	2010	100.0	7.2	0.5	0.4	0.0	1.0		4.0	1.0	0.1	0.0
Ghana	2009	14.4	92.5	13.0	8.6	40.5	1.2		16.6	8.9	12.5	8.4
[†]Data for Taiwan, China	2010	100.0	6.0	5.3	2.5	6.0	1.7		8.4	2.0	4.8	2.9

	Most recent year	Binding coverage	Simple mean bound rate	Simple mean tariff	Weighted mean tariff	Share of tariff lines with international peaks	Share of tariff lines with specific rates	Simple mean tariff	Weighted mean tariff	Simple mean tariff	Weighted mean tariff
				All products %				Primary products %		Manufactured products %	
Grenada	2010	100.0	56.8	8.9	7.7	36.7	0.0	10.1	7.0	8.6	8.3
Guatemala	2010	100.0	42.3	4.1	2.4	16.0	0.0	4.8	1.7	4.0	2.8
Guinea	2010	38.6	20.3	13.5	11.9	56.1	0.0	15.6	13.9	13.2	10.2
Guinea-Bissau	2010	97.6	48.6	13.3	9.9	51.8	0.0	14.6	10.0	12.9	9.7
Guyana	2010	100.0	56.8	10.1	6.9	39.2	0.0	15.5	5.9	9.4	7.7
Haiti	2009	89.8	17.6	3.0	5.1	5.1	0.3	5.8	4.1	2.5	5.9
Honduras	2009	100.0	32.5	6.4	6.5	0.5	0.1	9.9	8.1	6.0	5.5
Iceland	2010	95.0	13.5	1.8	1.1	5.2	3.4	2.3	1.1	1.7	1.1
India	2009	74.5	50.2	11.5	8.2	10.4	4.7	20.1	7.5	10.3	8.3
Indonesia	2010	96.6	37.5	4.8	2.5	7.0	0.5	3.2	1.6	5.0	2.9
Iran, Islamic Rep.	2008	..	..	24.8	19.6	56.5	0.3	21.7	12.5	25.1	21.2
Iraq		..	..	..	..	..	..	..	..	..	..
Israel	2009	75.2	22.0	6.0	3.5	2.9	4.1	8.8	3.3	5.6	3.7
Jamaica	2010	100.0	49.7	8.4	7.5	42.6	0.0	13.9	6.1	7.7	8.9
Japan	2010	99.7	3.0	2.6	1.6	8.6	3.3	5.1	1.6	2.1	1.7
Jordan	2009	100.0	16.3	9.7	5.2	29.5	0.6	14.2	3.9	9.0	6.1
Kazakhstan	2010	..	..	6.4	3.4	19.6	16.4	6.1	0.9	6.4	4.0
Kenya	2010	15.2	95.3	12.1	9.2	36.6	0.1	16.0	12.6	11.7	6.7
Korea, Dem. Rep.		..	..	..	..	..	..	..	..	..	..
Korea, Rep.	2010	95.1	16.1	10.3	8.7	7.0	0.6	26.3	12.7	7.4	5.1
Kosovo		..	..	..	..	..	..	..	..	..	..
Kuwait	2009	99.9	100.0	4.1	4.1	0.0	0.3	3.4	3.0	4.2	4.4
Kyrgyz Republic	2010	99.9	7.5	3.3	2.3	1.8	1.7	4.5	0.9	3.1	3.6
Lao PDR	2008	..	..	9.3	13.2	20.4	0.1	16.0	14.2	8.4	12.6
Lebanon	2007	..	..	5.6	4.8	11.6	10.9	8.2	5.0	5.2	5.1
Lesotho	2010	100.0	78.9	9.5	10.5	21.6	1.4	9.2	1.6	9.5	10.9
Liberia		..	..	..	..	..	..	..	..	..	..
Libya	2006	..	..	0.0	0.0	0.0	0.0	0.0	0.0	0.0	0.0
Macedonia, FYR	2010	100.0	6.9	3.6	2.7	14.5	2.5	7.4	5.7	3.2	1.8
Madagascar	2010	30.5	27.3	10.6	7.7	38.3	0.2	12.6	3.3	10.3	8.9
Malawi	2010	32.0	75.9	11.7	6.6	42.7	0.3	13.4	6.0	11.5	6.8
Malaysia	2009	83.9	14.6	6.8	4.0	16.9	0.8	10.1	5.0	6.1	3.7
Maldives	2009	97.0	37.2	21.7	20.6	88.1	0.0	17.5	18.4	22.8	22.6
Mali	2010	40.5	28.9	12.8	8.4	47.9	0.0	12.8	7.9	12.8	8.7
Mauritania	2007	39.4	19.6	12.6	10.1	49.0	0.0	11.1	9.2	12.9	11.0
Mauritius	2010	17.7	98.3	2.0	1.1	10.4	8.7	1.2	0.4	2.1	1.6
Mayotte	2010	..	..	5.1	1.8	1.4	0.0	3.7	1.5	5.3	1.9
Mexico	2010	100.0	35.1	7.4	2.2	6.1	0.1	9.3	1.5	7.2	2.4
Moldova	2010	99.9	6.7	4.6	2.5	8.4	2.8	7.0	2.3	4.3	2.6
Mongolia	2009	100.0	17.5	4.9	5.1	0.1	0.0	5.1	5.4	4.9	4.9
Montenegro	2010	..	..	3.0	3.5	4.5	2.9	5.8	4.8	2.7	2.8
Morocco	2009	100.0	41.3	9.1	7.1	23.6	0.0	18.0	8.9	8.2	5.8
Mozambique	2010	14.0	97.4	7.7	4.8	23.9	0.1	8.7	4.7	7.5	4.7
Myanmar	2008	17.6	83.8	4.0	3.2	4.1	0.0	5.1	2.7	3.9	3.4
Namibia	2010	96.1	19.4	6.3	1.8	16.7	2.0	4.1	2.1	6.7	1.6
Nepal	2010	99.4	26.2	12.6	12.1	46.3	1.2	12.9	10.3	12.6	14.4
New Zealand	2010	100.0	10.0	2.5	1.6	0.0	2.9	1.4	0.4	2.6	2.1
Nicaragua	2010	100.0	41.7	4.2	2.3	16.2	0.0	5.6	2.8	4.0	1.9
Niger	2010	96.6	44.9	13.0	9.1	48.9	0.0	14.0	10.7	12.8	7.6
Nigeria	2010	19.5	119.4	10.9	10.6	34.9	0.0	11.8	9.1	10.7	10.8
Norway	2010	100.0	3.0	0.5	0.4	0.5	6.9	2.0	1.2	0.3	0.2
Oman	2009	100.0	13.9	3.7	3.2	0.3	0.2	5.0	3.3	3.5	3.2
Pakistan	2009	98.6	60.0	14.8	9.5	45.3	0.3	14.5	6.5	14.8	12.3
Palau	2010	..	..	2.7	1.0	1.3	6.6	0.7	0.1	3.3	3.1
Panama	2009	99.9	23.5	7.6	7.6	2.8	0.0	11.5	8.4	7.1	7.3
Papua New Guinea	2010	100.0	31.5	4.4	2.5	23.3	1.0	11.8	1.8	3.4	2.8
Paraguay	2010	100.0	33.5	8.1	3.7	18.3	0.0	5.8	0.8	8.2	4.8
Peru	2010	100.0	30.1	4.8	2.5	10.0	0.0	3.8	1.3	4.9	3.0
Philippines	2010	67.2	25.8	5.3	4.8	5.4	0.0	6.8	5.1	5.1	4.7
Puerto Rico		..	..	..	..	..	..	..	..	..	..

	Most recent year	Binding coverage	Simple mean bound rate	All products %				Primary products		Manufactured products	
				Simple mean tariff	Weighted mean tariff	Share of tariff lines with international peaks	Share of tariff lines with specific rates	% Simple mean tariff	Weighted mean tariff	% Simple mean tariff	Weighted mean tariff
Qatar	2009	100.0	16.0	4.2	3.8	0.2	0.2	5.1	4.0	4.1	3.8
Russian Federation	2010	..	..	6.0	3.8	17.4	15.4	5.8	3.4	6.0	3.9
Rwanda	2010	100.0	89.3	9.9	6.0	31.4	0.1	11.5	6.4	9.7	5.9
Saudi Arabia	2009	100.0	10.8	4.1	3.9	0.0	0.3	3.5	2.8	4.1	4.2
Senegal	2010	100.0	30.0	13.4	8.9	50.5	0.0	14.1	7.7	13.3	10.2
Serbia	2005[a]	..	..	8.1	6.0	17.8	0.0	10.9	4.5	7.8	6.8
Seychelles	2007	..	..	6.5	28.3	12.8	2.0	14.0	50.5	4.8	6.4
Sierra Leone	2004	100.0	47.4	..	..	..	..	..	..	..	..
Singapore	2010	69.6	7.0	0.0	0.0	0.0	0.1	0.0	0.0	0.0	0.0
Solomon Islands	2010	100.0	78.8	9.2	8.7	0.0	4.4	9.3	8.5	9.2	8.8
Somalia		..	..	..	..	..	..	..	..	..	..
South Africa	2010	96.1	19.4	7.6	4.4	17.9	1.8	5.4	1.9	7.9	5.7
South Sudan		..	..	..	..	..	..	..	..	..	..
Sri Lanka	2010	38.1	30.1	9.4	6.9	23.8	1.0	15.3	9.6	8.8	5.7
St. Kitts and Nevis	2010	97.8	76.1	9.6	10.5	36.1	0.5	9.9	7.0	9.6	11.8
St. Lucia	2007	99.6	61.9	9.6	9.0	39.9	0.0	12.7	4.9	9.1	12.2
St. Vincent & Grenadines	2007	99.7	62.5	11.3	8.4	44.4	0.5	15.1	7.8	10.6	8.6
Sudan	2010	..	..	13.3	14.8	28.3	0.1	16.6	10.9	12.9	15.8
Suriname	2010	27.6	18.1	11.6	11.9	36.2	0.1	18.3	15.0	10.4	10.4
Swaziland	2010	96.1	19.4	10.9	10.2	26.2	3.2	9.7	1.3	11.1	16.2
Switzerland	2010	99.8	0.0	0.0	0.0	0.0	26.9	0.0	0.0	0.0	0.0
Syrian Arab Republic	2010	..	..	6.7	6.1	27.6	0.0	6.5	6.1	6.7	6.1
Tajikistan	2010	..	..	4.4	5.9	8.2	0.8	3.5	1.1	4.5	7.8
Tanzania	2010	13.8	120.0	12.9	8.2	39.9	0.1	17.5	8.7	12.4	8.0
Thailand	2009	74.7	26.1	11.2	4.9	20.5	5.2	15.9	2.9	10.5	6.1
Timor-Leste		..	..	..	..	..	..	..	..	..	..
Togo	2010	14.3	80.0	12.8	14.2	47.3	0.0	14.4	12.4	12.6	14.9
Tonga	2010	100.0	17.6	10.9	7.2	65.6	0.3	11.9	5.1	10.6	9.0
Trinidad and Tobago	2008	100.0	55.8	8.7	10.0	43.6	0.5	16.6	3.1	7.6	17.4
Tunisia	2008	58.3	58.0	21.9	16.0	57.8	0.0	26.8	12.0	21.4	18.2
Turkey	2010	50.3	29.2	2.5	2.4	5.4	0.2	14.4	4.8	1.2	1.3
Turkmenistan	2002	..	..	5.4	2.9	14.8	3.2	14.7	12.6	3.8	1.1
Uganda	2010	16.1	73.5	12.1	8.2	37.5	0.2	15.7	8.8	11.6	7.9
Ukraine	2010	100.0	5.8	4.5	2.8	1.1	0.4	5.9	2.5	4.3	3.1
United Arab Emirates	2009	100.0	14.8	4.5	3.7	0.3	0.3	6.0	2.8	4.2	4.4
United States	2010	100.0	3.7	2.9	1.8	3.4	6.9	2.6	1.2	3.0	2.0
Uruguay	2010	100.0	31.6	9.6	3.6	29.3	0.0	5.6	1.1	10.0	5.3
Uzbekistan	2009	..	..	11.8	6.9	20.1	10.9	12.6	3.9	11.7	7.4
Vanuatu	2009	..	..	18.2	18.5	66.6	3.4	26.7	27.8	16.5	14.6
Venezuela, RB	2010	100.0	36.5	13.1	10.6	21.9	0.0	12.2	10.0	13.2	10.8
Vietnam	2010	100.0	11.5	7.1	5.7	23.6	0.5	8.6	6.0	6.9	5.6
West Bank and Gaza		..	..	..	..	..	..	..	..	..	..
Yemen, Rep.	2009	..	..	5.5	4.2	1.4	0.8	7.1	3.8	5.2	4.6
Zambia	2009	17.1	106.9	10.8	3.8	51.2	0.0	9.2	3.1	11.0	4.2
Zimbabwe	2007[b]	22.2	91.4	16.7	17.3	38.8	6.5	19.6	20.4	16.3	15.1
World		**78.3 w**	**31.2**	**6.9**	**3.1**	**15.0**	**2.0**	**9.0**	**2.7**	**6.6**	**3.3 w**
Low income		48.3	52.3	12.5	9.2	41.4	0.2	14.3	7.9	12.3	9.8
Middle income		87.7	32.9	8.5	5.0	20.1	0.8	10.8	3.4	8.2	5.7
Lower middle income		80.6	37.3	9.1	6.3	20.0	0.8	13.2	5.6	8.6	6.6
Upper middle income		90.3	29.3	8.3	4.6	20.7	0.8	9.3	2.7	8.1	5.5
Low & middle income		76.5	36.5	9.0	5.1	21.5	0.8	11.3	3.5	8.7	5.8
East Asia & Pacific		84.2	22.3	8.3	4.2	15.8	0.9	10.6	2.3	7.9	5.4
Europe & Central Asia		91.7	8.9	4.9	4.1	13.1	0.9	7.7	3.1	4.6	4.5
Latin America & Carib.		96.1	36.6	8.1	4.9	18.1	0.4	7.9	3.1	8.1	5.5
Middle East & N. Africa		99.9	30.4	10.6	7.4	25.0	0.0	17.2	6.8	9.7	7.8
South Asia		81.5	41.6	13.7	8.5	39.6	2.7	17.8	7.6	13.1	8.7
Sub-Saharan Africa		53.4	48.4	11.4	7.2	36.7	1.0	12.8	6.1	11.3	7.7
High income		90.3	17.3	3.6	2.2	5.0	4.2	6.4	2.4	3.1	2.1
OECD		89.6	7.4	3.3	2.2	5.1	5.4	7.1	2.6	2.6	2.0
Non-OECD		73.1	9.1	2.9	0.8	4.9	0.0	3.2	0.8	2.8	0.8

a. Includes Montenegro. b. Rates are most favored nation rates.

About the data

Poor people in developing countries work primarily in agriculture and labor-intensive manufactures, sectors that confront the greatest trade barriers. Removing barriers to merchandise trade could increase growth in these countries—even more if trade in services were also liberalized.

In general, tariffs in high-income countries on imports from developing countries, though low, are twice those collected from other high-income countries. But protection is also an issue for developing countries, which maintain high tariffs on agricultural commodities, labor-intensive manufactures, and other products and services.

Countries use a combination of tariff and nontariff measures to regulate imports. The most common form of tariff is an ad valorem duty, based on the value of the import, but tariffs may also be levied on a specific, or per unit, basis or may combine ad valorem and specific rates. Tariffs may be used to raise fiscal revenues or to protect domestic industries from foreign competition—or both. Nontariff barriers, which limit the quantity of imports of a particular good, include quotas, prohibitions, licensing schemes, export restraint arrangements, and health and quarantine measures. Because of the difficulty of combining nontariff barriers into an aggregate indicator, they are not included in the table.

Unless specified as most favored nation rates, the tariff rates used in calculating the indicators in the table are effectively applied rates. Effectively applied rates are those in effect for partners in preferential trade arrangements such as the North American Free Trade Agreement. The difference between most favored nation and applied rates can be substantial. Because more countries now report their free trade agreements, suspensions of tariffs, and other special preferences, this year's *World Development Indicators* includes effectively applied rates for most countries. All estimates are calculated using the most recent information, which is not necessarily revised every year. As a result, data for the same year may differ from data in last year's edition.

Three measures of average tariffs are shown: simple bound rates and the simple and the weighted tariffs. Bound rates are based on all products in a country's tariff schedule, while the most favored nation or applied rates are calculated using all traded items. Weighted mean tariffs are weighted by the value of the country's trade with each trading partner. Simple averages are often a better indicator of tariff protection than weighted averages, which are biased downward because higher tariffs discourage

trade and reduce the weights applied to these tariffs. Bound rates result from trade negotiations incorporated into a country's schedule of concessions and are thus enforceable.

Some countries set fairly uniform tariff rates across all imports. Others are selective, setting high tariffs to protect favored domestic industries. The share of tariff lines with international peaks provides an indication of how selectively tariffs are applied. The effective rate of protection—the degree to which the value added in an industry is protected—may exceed the nominal rate if the tariff system systematically differentiates among imports of raw materials, intermediate products, and finished goods.

The share of tariff lines with specific rates shows the extent to which countries use tariffs based on physical quantities or other, non–ad valorem measures. Some countries such as Switzerland apply mainly specific duties. To the extent possible, these specific rates have been converted to their ad valorem equivalent rates and have been included in the calculation of simple and weighted tariffs.

Data are classified using the Harmonized System at the six- or eight-digit level. Tariff line data were matched to Standard International Trade Classification (SITC) revision 2 codes to define commodity groups and import weights. Import weights were calculated using the United Nations Statistics Division's Commodity Trade Statistics (Comtrade) database. The table shows tariff rates for three commodity groups: all products, primary products, and manufactured products. Effectively applied rates at the six- and eight-digit product level are averaged for products in each commodity group. When an effectively applied rate is not available, the most favored nation rate is used instead.

Data are shown only for the last year for which complete data are available. EU member countries apply a common tariff schedule that is listed under European Union and are thus not listed separately.

Definitions

• **Binding coverage** is the percentage of product lines with an agreed bound rate. • **Simple mean bound rate** is the unweighted average of all the lines in the tariff schedule in which bound rates have been set. • **Simple mean tariff** is the unweighted average of effectively applied rates or most favored nation rates for all products subject to tariffs calculated for all traded goods. • **Weighted mean tariff** is the average of effectively applied rates or most favored nation rates weighted by the product import shares corresponding to each partner country. • **Share of tariff lines with international peaks** is the share of lines in the tariff schedule with tariff rates that exceed 15 percent. • **Share of tariff lines with specific rates** is the share of lines in the tariff schedule that are set on a per unit basis or that combine ad valorem and per unit rates. • **Primary products** are commodities classified in SITC revision 2 sections 0–4 plus division 68 (nonferrous metals). • **Manufactured products** are commodities classified in SITC revision 2 sections 5–8 excluding division 68.

Data sources

All indicators in the table were calculated by World Bank staff using the World Integrated Trade Solution system (http://wits.worldbank.org). Data on tariffs are from the United Nations Conference on Trade and Development's Trade Analysis and Information System database and the World Trade Organization's Integrated Data Base and Consolidated Tariff Schedules database. Data on global imports are from the United Nations Statistics Division's Comtrade database.

	Logistics Performance Index	Burden of customs procedures	Lead time		Documents		Liner Shipping Connectivity Index	Quality of port infrastructure	Freight costs to the United States
			days		number				1 kilogram DHL nondocument air package[a] $
	1–5 (worst to best) 2010	1–7 (worst to best) 2010–11[b]	To export 2010	To import 2010	To export June 2011	To import June 2011	0–100 (low to high) 2011	1–7 (worst to best) 2010–11	2012
Afghanistan	2.24	..	2.0	4.0	10	10	..	..	148.25
Albania	2.46	4.2	1.7	2.0	7	8	4.5	3.9	163.10
Algeria	2.36	2.8	4.6	7.1	8	9	31.1	3.0	162.00
Angola	2.25	2.7	6.0	8.0	11	8	11.3	2.3	162.00
Argentina	3.10	2.7	3.7	3.8	7	7	30.6	3.7	92.30
Armenia	2.52	2.9	..	..	5	8	..	2.7[c]	148.25
Australia	3.84	5.1	2.6	2.8	6	5	28.3	5.1	102.10
Austria	3.76	5.0	2.0	3.7	4	5	..	4.7[c]	142.10
Azerbaijan	2.64	3.5	7.0	3.0	8	10	..	4.1[c]	163.10
Bahrain	3.37	5.5	1.0	2.0	6	7	9.8	6.0	148.25
Bangladesh	2.74	3.4	1.4	1.4	6	8	8.2	3.4	102.10
Belarus	2.53	..	..	..	9	10	..	..	163.10
Belgium	3.94	4.6	1.7	1.6	4	5	88.5	6.5	116.75
Benin	2.79	3.7	3.0	7.0	7	8	12.7	3.9	162.00
Bolivia	2.51	3.0	15.0	28.3	8	7	..	3.1[c]	92.30
Bosnia and Herzegovina	2.66	3.4	2.0	2.0	8	9	..	1.7	163.10
Botswana	2.32	4.7	..	..	6	8	..	3.9[c]	162.00
Brazil	3.20	3.1	2.8	3.9	7	8	34.6	2.7	92.30
Bulgaria	2.83	3.5	2.0	3.9	5	6	5.4	3.8	142.10
Burkina Faso	2.23	4.0	4.0	14.0	10	10	..	3.7[c]	162.00
Burundi	2.29	2.9	..	..	9	10	..	3.0[c]	162.00
Cambodia	2.37	3.7	1.3	4.0	9	10	5.4	4.0	111.40
Cameroon	2.55	4.0	3.4	8.9	11	12	11.4	3.5	162.00
Canada	3.87	4.9	2.8	3.7	3	4	38.4	5.8	76.15
Central African Republic	..	..	..	..	9	17	..	..	162.00
Chad	2.49	2.8	74.0	35.0	8	11	..	2.7[c]	162.00
Chile	3.09	5.5	3.5	3.0	6	6	22.8	5.2	92.30
China	3.49	4.4	2.8	2.6	8	5	152.1	4.5	86.75
Hong Kong SAR, China	3.88	6.2	1.7	1.6	4	4	115.3	6.6	92.75
Colombia	2.77	4.0	7.0	7.0	5	6	27.3	3.4	92.30
Congo, Dem. Rep.	2.68	..	2.0	3.0	8	9	3.7	..	162.00
Congo, Rep.	2.48	..	..	..	11	10	10.8	..	162.00
Costa Rica	2.91	3.9	2.0	2.0	6	7	10.7	2.3	92.30
Côte d'Ivoire	2.53	3.9	1.0	1.0	10	9	17.4	4.9	162.00
Croatia	2.77	4.1	1.0	1.0	7	8	21.8	4.0	163.10
Cuba	2.07	..	..	..	..	..	6.6	..	80.30
Cyprus	3.13	4.9	1.0	2.0	5	7	17.1	5.1	142.10
Czech Republic	3.51	4.4	2.5	3.5	4	7	0.4	4.7[c]	142.10
Denmark	3.85	5.7	1.0	1.0	4	3	26.4	6.2	142.10
Dominican Republic	2.82	4.4	2.2	3.5	6	7	22.9	4.4	80.30
Ecuador	2.77	3.5	2.1	3.4	8	7	22.5	3.8	92.30
Egypt, Arab Rep.	2.61	4.1	1.3	3.1	8	9	51.2	4.0	148.25
El Salvador	2.67	3.9	2.0	2.0	8	8	12.0	3.8	92.30
Eritrea	1.70	..	3.0	3.0	10	12	4.0	..	162.00
Estonia	3.16	5.2	4.0	4.0	3	4	5.8	5.6	142.10
Ethiopia	2.41	3.5	5.0	6.0	7	9	..	3.9[c]	162.00
Finland	3.89	6.0	1.6	1.8	4	5	11.3	6.2	142.10
France	3.84	4.9	3.2	4.5	2	2	71.8	5.6	116.75
Gabon	2.41	..	4.3	13.0	7	8	8.0	..	162.00
Gambia, The	2.49	5.2	4.6	3.5	6	7	5.4	4.9	162.00
Georgia	2.61	4.9	..	..	4	4	3.8	4.2	163.10
Germany	4.11	4.7	3.6	2.4	4	5	93.3	6.1	116.75
Ghana	2.47	3.6	2.9	6.8	6	7	18.0	4.2	162.00
Greece	2.96	4.0	3.0	3.5	5	6	32.2	4.1	142.10
Guatemala	2.63	4.2	2.6	3.4	10	9	20.9	4.3	92.30
Guinea	2.60	..	3.5	3.9	7	9	6.2	..	162.00
Guinea-Bissau	2.10	..	..	..	6	6	4.1	..	162.00
Haiti	2.59	2.5	4.2	5.3	8	10	4.8	1.8	80.30

	Logistics Performance Index	Burden of customs procedures	Lead time		Documents		Liner Shipping Connectivity Index	Quality of port infrastructure	Freight costs to the United States
			days		number				1 kilogram DHL nondocument air package[a] $
	1–5 (worst to best) 2010	1–7 (worst to best) 2010–11[b]	To export 2010	To import 2010	To export June 2011	To import June 2011	0–100 (low to high) 2011	1–7 (worst to best) 2010–11	2012
Honduras	2.78	4.0	2.4	3.2	6	8	9.4	5.1	92.30
Hungary	2.99	4.5	3.5	5.0	6	7	..	4.0[c]	142.10
India	3.12	3.8	2.3	5.3	8	9	41.5	3.9	102.10
Indonesia	2.76	3.9	2.1	5.4	4	7	25.9	3.6	102.10
Iran, Islamic Rep.	2.57	3.5	2.6	28.3	7	8	30.3	3.9	148.25
Iraq	2.11	..	..	..	10	10	4.2	..	148.25
Ireland	3.89	5.2	1.0	1.0	4	4	5.9	5.2	116.75
Israel	3.41	4.7	2.0	2.0	5	4	28.5	4.2	148.25
Italy	3.64	4.0	2.6	3.0	4	4	70.2	3.9	116.75
Jamaica	2.53	3.7	10.0	10.0	6	6	28.2	5.3	80.30
Japan	3.97	4.7	1.0	1.0	3	5	67.8	5.2	124.90
Jordan	2.74	4.4	3.2	4.6	6	7	16.7	4.3	148.25
Kazakhstan	2.83	3.5	2.8	11.5	9	12	..	3.6[c]	163.10
Kenya	2.59	3.3	3.0	5.9	8	7	12.0	3.8	162.00
Korea, Dem. Rep.	..	..	..	..	..	..	..	..	111.40
Korea, Rep.	3.64	4.4	1.6	2.0	3	3	92.0	5.5	102.10
Kosovo	..	..	..	..	8	8	..	..	163.10
Kuwait	3.28	4.1	2.0	3.0	7	10	5.6	4.2	148.25
Kyrgyz Republic	2.62	2.8	2.0	..	8	9	..	1.5[c]	163.10
Lao PDR	2.46	..	..	..	9	10	..	..	111.40
Latvia	3.25	4.1	1.3	1.6	5	6	5.5	4.7	142.10
Lebanon	3.34	3.5	3.4	2.2	5	7	35.1	4.3	148.25
Lesotho	2.30	3.7	..	..	8	8	..	3.4[c]	162.00
Liberia	2.38	..	4.0	5.0	10	9	6.2	..	162.00
Libya	2.33	3.5	3.2	10.0	..	..	6.6	3.2	162.00
Lithuania	3.13	4.5	2.0	2.3	6	6	9.8	4.9	142.10
Macedonia, FYR	2.77	4.2	..	..	6	6	..	4.1[c]	163.10
Madagascar	2.66	3.4	..	..	4	9	7.7	3.3	162.00
Malawi	2.42	3.8	4.2	3.7	10	9	..	3.6[c]	162.00
Malaysia	3.44	5.0	2.6	2.8	6	7	91.0	5.7	102.10
Mali	2.27	4.1	5.0	4.0	6	9	..	3.7[c]	162.00
Mauritania	2.63	4.1	2.0	3.0	8	8	5.6	3.3	162.00
Mauritius	2.72	4.6	3.0	2.4	5	6	15.4	4.7	162.00
Mexico	3.05	4.1	2.1	2.5	5	4	36.1	4.0	51.15
Moldova	2.57	3.5	..	..	6	7	..	2.9	163.10
Mongolia	2.25	3.3	14.0	12.0	8	8	..	2.8[c]	111.40
Morocco	2.38	4.4	2.0	3.2	6	8	55.1	4.5	162.00
Mozambique	2.29	3.7	..	..	7	10	10.1	3.4	162.00
Myanmar	2.33	..	4.6	8.4	..	..	3.2	..	111.40
Namibia	2.02	4.1	3.0	3.0	9	7	12.0	5.5	162.00
Nepal	2.20	3.4	1.8	6.3	9	9	..	2.6[c]	111.40
Netherlands	4.07	5.2	1.8	1.9	4	5	92.1	6.6	116.75
New Zealand	3.65	5.8	1.3	1.6	7	5	18.5	5.5	102.10
Nicaragua	2.54	3.0	3.2	3.2	5	5	8.4	2.7	92.30
Niger	2.54	..	..	..	8	10	..	..	162.00
Nigeria	2.59	3.5	2.5	4.1	10	9	19.9	3.3	162.00
Norway	3.93	5.2	1.0	2.0	4	4	7.3	5.5	142.10
Oman	2.84	5.0	..	..	8	8	49.3	5.4	148.25
Pakistan	2.53	3.6	2.3	1.6	7	8	30.5	4.1	148.25
Panama	3.02	4.2	1.4	1.4	3	4	37.5	6.4	92.30
Papua New Guinea	2.41	..	..	..	7	9	8.8	..	111.40
Paraguay	2.75	3.9	1.0	4.0	8	10	0.0	3.4[c]	92.30
Peru	2.80	4.4	2.0	3.8	6	8	21.2	3.5	92.30
Philippines	3.14	3.0	1.8	5.0	7	8	18.6	3.0	102.10
Poland	3.44	4.4	3.0	3.6	5	5	26.5	3.4	142.10
Portugal	3.34	4.7	2.5	5.0	4	5	21.1	4.9	116.75
Puerto Rico	..	4.6	..	..	6	10	..	5.3	..
Qatar	2.95	4.8	3.8	2.3	5	7	3.6	5.4	148.25

	Logistics Performance Index	Burden of customs procedures	Lead time		Documents		Liner Shipping Connectivity Index	Quality of port infrastructure	Freight costs to the United States
			days		number				1 kilogram DHL nondocument air package[a] $
	1–5 (worst to best)	1–7 (worst to best)	To export	To import	To export	To import	0–100 (low to high)	1–7 (worst to best)	
	2010	2010–11[b]	2010	2010	June 2011	June 2011	2011	2010–11	2012
Romania	2.84	3.3	2.0	2.0	5	6	21.4	2.8	142.10
Russian Federation	2.61	2.8	4.0	2.9	8	10	20.6	3.7	163.10
Rwanda	2.04	5.3	..	..	8	8	..	3.2	162.00
Saudi Arabia	3.22	5.0	2.3	6.3	5	5	60.0	5.4	148.25
Senegal	2.86	4.7	1.4	2.7	6	5	12.3	4.5	162.00
Serbia	2.69[d]	3.7	2.0[d]	3.0[d]	6	6	..	2.7	163.10
Sierra Leone	1.97	..	2.0	32.0	7	7	5.4	..	162.00
Singapore	4.09	6.2	2.2	1.8	4	4	105.0	6.8	92.75
Slovak Republic	3.24	4.3	3.0	5.0	6	7	..	3.9[c]	142.10
Slovenia	2.87	5.0	1.0	2.0	6	8	21.9	5.2	142.10
Somalia	1.34	..	..	..	..	..	4.2	..	162.00
South Africa	3.46	4.2	2.3	3.3	8	8	35.7	4.7	162.00
South Sudan	..	..	..	..	..	..	..	..	..
Spain	3.63	4.5	4.0	7.1	6	7	76.6	5.8	116.75
Sri Lanka	2.29	4.4	1.3	2.5	6	6	41.1	4.9	102.10
Sudan	2.21	..	39.0	5.0	7	7	9.3	..	162.00
Swaziland	..	3.4	..	..	9	9	..	4.2	162.00
Sweden	4.08	5.8	1.0	2.6	3	3	30.0	6.0	142.10
Switzerland	3.97	5.1	2.6	2.6	4	5	1.9	5.2[c]	142.10
Syrian Arab Republic	2.74	2.9	2.5	3.2	8	9	16.8	3.4	148.25
Tajikistan	2.35	3.6	7.0	..	11	9	..	1.8[c]	163.10
Tanzania	2.60	3.6	3.2	7.1	6	6	11.5	3.3	162.00
Thailand	3.29	3.9	1.6	2.6	5	5	36.7	4.7	102.10
Timor-Leste	1.71	3.4	..	..	6	7	..	2.6	111.40
Togo	2.60	..	..	..	6	8	14.1	..	162.00
Trinidad and Tobago	..	3.0	..	..	5	6	17.9	3.9	80.30
Tunisia	2.84	4.6	1.7	7.0	4	7	6.3	4.6	162.00
Turkey	3.22	3.7	2.2	3.8	7	8	39.4	4.2	148.25
Turkmenistan	2.49	..	3.0	..	..	..	..	..	163.10
Uganda	2.82	4.4	5.5	14.0	7	9	..	3.7[c]	162.00
Ukraine	2.57	2.8	1.7	7.0	6	8	21.4	3.7	163.10
United Arab Emirates	3.63	5.6	2.5	2.0	4	5	62.5	6.2	148.25
United Kingdom	3.95	4.9	3.3	1.9	4	4	87.5	5.6	116.75
United States	3.86	4.3	2.8	4.0	4	5	81.6	5.5	..
Uruguay	2.75	4.2	3.0	3.0	9	9	24.4	5.1	92.30
Uzbekistan	2.79	..	1.4	2.0	10	11	..	..	163.10
Venezuela, RB	2.68	2.3	9.4	12.1	8	9	20.0	2.5	92.30
Vietnam	2.96	3.4	1.4	1.7	6	8	49.7	3.4	102.10
West Bank and Gaza	..	..	..	..	6	6	..	..	..
Yemen, Rep.	2.58	2.9	3.1	3.6	6	9	11.9	2.9	148.25
Zambia	2.28	4.1	9.2	4.0	6	8	..	4.0[c]	162.00
Zimbabwe	2.29	3.8	25.0	18.0	8	9	..	4.4[c]	162.00
World	**2.87[e] u**	**4.1 u**	**3.8[e] u**	**4.6[e] u**	**7 u**	**7 u**	**..**	**4.3 u**	
Low income	2.38	3.7	7.3	7.8	8	9	..	3.3	
Middle income	2.68	3.8	3.7	4.9	7	7	..	3.9	
Lower middle income	2.54	3.6	4.8	5.3	7	8	..	3.6	
Upper middle income	2.80	3.9	2.9	4.6	6	7	..	4.1	
Low & middle income	2.60	3.7	4.5	5.5	7	8	..	3.7	
East Asia & Pacific	2.73	3.8	3.6	4.9	7	7	..	3.8	
Europe & Central Asia	2.71	3.7	2.8	3.0	7	8	..	3.4	
Latin America & Carib.	2.74	3.7	3.9	5.5	6	7	..	3.8	
Middle East & N. Africa	2.60	3.7	2.7	7.2	7	8	..	3.9	
South Asia	2.49	3.7	1.9	3.3	8	9	..	3.8	
Sub-Saharan Africa	2.42	3.9	8.1	7.0	8	9	..	3.8	
High income	3.54	4.9	2.1	2.7	5	5	..	5.3	
Euro area	3.55	4.9	2.3	3.0	4	5	..	5.3	

a. Transportation charges only; excludes fuel, surcharges, duties, and taxes. b. Average of the 2010 and 2011 survey ratings. c. Landlocked country. d. Includes Montenegro. e. Aggregates are computed according to the World Bank classification of economies as of July 1, 2011, and may differ from data published in the original source.

Trade facilitation encompasses customs efficiency and other physical and regulatory environments where trade takes place, harmonization of standards and conformance to international regulations, and the logistics of moving goods and associated documentation through countries and ports. Though collection of trade facilitation data has improved over the last decade, data that allow meaningful evaluation, especially for developing economies, are lacking. Data on trade facilitation are drawn from research by private and international agencies. Most data are perception-based evaluations by business executives and professionals. Because of different backgrounds, values, and personalities, those surveyed may evaluate the same situation differently. Caution should thus be used when interpreting perception-based indicators. Nevertheless, they convey much needed information on trade facilitation.

The table presents data from Logistics Performance Surveys conducted by the World Bank in partnership with academic and international institutions and private companies and individuals engaged in international logistics. The Logistics Performance Index assesses performance across six aspects of the logistics environment (see *Definitions*), based on more than 5,000 country assessments by nearly 1,000 international freight forwarders. Respondents evaluate eight markets on six core dimensions. The markets are chosen based on the most important export and import markets of the respondent's country, random selection, and, for landlocked countries, neighboring countries that connect them with international markets. Scores for the six dimensions are averaged across all respondents and aggregated to a single score. Details of the survey methodology and index construction methodology are in Arvis and others (2010).

Data on the burden of customs procedures are from the World Economic Forum's Executive Opinion Survey. The 2011 round included more than 15,000 respondents from 142 countries. Sampling follows a dual stratification based on company size and sector of activity. Data are collected online, through in-person interviews, and through mail and telephone interviews. Responses are aggregated using sector-weighted averaging. Data are a two-year moving average. Respondents evaluated the efficiency of customs procedures in their country. The lowest value (1) rates the customs procedure as extremely inefficient, and the highest score (7) as extremely efficient.

The direct costs of cross-border trade include freight, customs, and storage fees. Indirect costs include the value of time to import or export and the risk of delay or loss of shipments. Long lead times and burdensome regulatory procedures may lower competitiveness. Data on lead time are from the Logistics Performance Index survey. Respondents provided separate values for the best case (10 percent of shipments) and the median case (50 percent of shipments). The data are exponentiated averages of the logarithm of single value responses and of mid-point values of range responses for the median case.

Data on the number of documents needed to export or import are from the World Bank's Doing Business surveys, which compile procedural requirements for exporting and importing a standardized cargo of goods by ocean transport from local freight forwarders, shipping lines, customs brokers, port officials, and banks. To make the data comparable across economies, several assumptions about the business and the traded goods are used (see www.doingbusiness.org).

Access to global shipping and air freight networks and the quality and accessibility of ports and roads affect logistics performance. The table shows two indicators related to trade and transport service infrastructure: the Liner Shipping Connectivity Index and the quality of port infrastructure rating. The Liner Shipping Connectivity Index captures how well countries are connected to global shipping networks. It is computed by the United Nations Conference on Trade and Development (UNCTAD) based on five components of the maritime transport sector: number of ships, their container-carrying capacity, maximum vessel size, number of services, and number of companies that deploy container ships in a country's ports. For each component a country's value is divided by the maximum value of each component in 2004, the five components are averaged for each country, and the average is divided by the maximum average for 2004 and multiplied by 100. The index generates a value of 100 for the country with the highest average index in 2004.

The quality of port infrastructure measures business executives' perception of their country's port facilities. Values range from 1 (extremely underdeveloped) to 7 (efficient). Respondents in landlocked countries were asked: "How accessible are port facilities (1 = extremely inaccessible; 7 = extremely accessible.)"

The costs of transport services are a crucial determinant of export competitiveness. The proxy indicator in the table is the shipping rates to the United States of an international freight moving business.

• **Logistics Performance Index** reflects perceptions of a country's logistics based on efficiency of customs clearance process, quality of trade- and transport-related infrastructure, ease of arranging competitively priced shipments, quality of logistics services, ability to track and trace consignments, and frequency with which shipments reach the consignee within the scheduled time. The index ranges from 1 to 5, with a higher score representing better performance. • **Burden of customs procedure** measures business executives' perceptions of their country's efficiency of customs procedures. Values range from 1 to 7, with a higher rating indicating greater efficiency. • **Lead time to export** is the median time (the value for 50 percent of shipments) from shipment point to port of loading. • **Lead time to import** is the median time (the value for 50 percent of shipments) from port of discharge to arrival at the consignee. • **Documents to export** and **documents to import** are all documents required per shipment by government ministries, customs authorities, port and container terminals, health and technical control agencies, and banks to export or import goods. Documents renewed annually and not requiring renewal per shipment are excluded. • **Liner Shipping Connectivity Index** indicates how well countries are connected to global shipping networks based on the status of their maritime transport sector. The highest value in 2004 is 100. • **Quality of port infrastructure** measures business executives' perceptions of their country's port facilities. Values range from 1 to 7, with a higher rating indicating better development of port infrastructure. • **Freight costs to the United States** is the DHL international U.S. inbound worldwide priority express rate for a 1 kilogram nondocument air package.

Data on the Logistics Performance Index and lead time to export and import are from Arvis and others (2010). Data on the burden of customs procedure and quality of port infrastructure ratings are from the World Economic Forum's *Global Competitiveness Report 2011–2012*. Data on number of documents to export and import are from the World Bank's Doing Business project (www.doingbusiness.org). Data on the Liner Shipping Connectivity Index are from UNCTAD's *Review of Maritime Transport* (2011). Freight costs to the United States are based on DHL's "DHL Rate and Transit Guide 2012" (2012).

	Total external debt		Long-term debt ($ millions)		Short-term debt			Total debt service	Present value of debt	
	$ millions	% of GNI	Public and publicly guaranteed	Private nonguaranteed	$ millions	% of total debt	% of total reserves	% of exports of goods and services and income[a]	% of GNI[a]	% of exports of goods and services and income[a]
	2010	2010	2010	2010	2010	2010	2010	2010	2010	2010
Afghanistan	2,297	..	2,076	..	102	4.4	..	..	6.5	21.1
Albania	4,736	40.5	2,972	1,133	573	12.1	22.6	11.1	29.5	87.6
Algeria	5,276	3.4	2,530	968	1,778	33.7	1.0	1.0	3.0	5.4
Angola	18,562	24.6	15,440	..	2,241	12.1	11.3	4.5	22.1	22.3
Argentina	127,849	36.1	67,331	25,514	35,005	27.4	67.1	16.7	37.5	150.3
Armenia	6,103	64.8	2,557	2,187	618	10.1	33.1	33.4	46.5	182.6
Australia	..	..	..	..	..	..	..	..	..	..
Austria	..	..	..	..	..	..	..	..	..	..
Azerbaijan	6,974	14.9	3,892	2,158	878	12.6	13.7	1.4	9.1	13.7
Bahrain	..	..	..	..	..	..	..	..	..	..
Bangladesh	24,963	22.8	21,371	..	2,974	11.9	26.6	4.7	16.2	84.3
Belarus	25,726	46.8	7,850	2,401	11,980	46.6	238.4	4.6	41.8	74.8
Belgium	..	..	..	..	..	..	..	..	..	..
Benin	1,221	18.4	1,134	..	32	2.7	2.7	..	12.8[b]	70.1[b]
Bolivia	5,267	27.8	2,806	2,358	103	2.0	1.1	9.3	17.4[b]	40.9[b]
Bosnia and Herzegovina	8,457	48.8	3,751	3,149	1,037	12.3	23.7	19.9	37.3	95.0
Botswana	1,709	11.6	1,352	..	357	20.9	4.5	1.5	8.7	18.9
Brazil	346,978	16.9	96,542	184,940	65,496	18.9	22.7	19.0	18.8	146.0
Bulgaria	48,077	104.8	4,466	28,238	15,373	32.0	89.3	14.2	94.9	159.1
Burkina Faso	2,053	23.3	1,925	..	0	0.0	0.0	..	18.6[b]	168.7[b]
Burundi	537	33.8	412	..	16	2.9	4.7	..	14.3[b]	151.5[b]
Cambodia	4,676	43.4	4,414	..	262	5.6	6.9	..	35.8	58.6
Cameroon	2,964	13.5	2,185	577	31	1.0	0.8	3.6	5.3[b]	19.1[b]
Canada	..	..	..	..	..	..	..	..	..	..
Central African Republic	385	19.2	218	..	77	19.9	42.3	..	12.4[b]	75.9[b]
Chad	1,733	25.7	1,708	..	8	0.5	1.3	..	28.3[b]	57.3[b]
Chile	86,349	45.9	12,929	47,541	25,879	30.0	93.0	15.2	47.7	98.9
China	548,551	9.3	90,180	110,847	347,524	63.4	11.9	3.3	10.1	31.2
Hong Kong SAR, China	..	..	..	..	..	..	..	..	..	..
Colombia	63,064	22.8	36,777	18,078	8,209	13.0	29.2	21.0	37.5	211.9
Congo, Dem. Rep.	5,774	47.1	4,957	..	494	8.6	38.0	3.8	27.0[b]	77.8[b]
Congo, Rep.	3,781	43.9	3,531	..	222	5.9	5.0	..	19.5[b]	19.2[b]
Costa Rica	8,849	26.8	3,725	2,693	2,431	27.5	52.5	7.7	26.8	59.1
Côte d'Ivoire	11,430	52.6	10,416	280	351	3.1	9.7	..	48.0[b]	88.2[b]
Croatia	..	..	..	..	..	..	..	..	..	..
Cuba	..	..	..	..	..	..	..	..	..	..
Cyprus	..	..	..	..	..	..	..	..	..	..
Czech Republic	..	..	..	..	..	..	..	..	..	..
Denmark	..	..	..	..	..	..	..	..	..	..
Dominican Republic	13,045	26.2	9,115	843	1,948	14.9	55.6	11.0	23.7	89.1
Ecuador	14,815	23.1	8,598	5,848	369	2.5	14.1	9.4	22.1	64.3
Egypt, Arab Rep.	34,844	16.2	31,641	54	3,149	9.0	8.5	6.0	15.2	46.0
El Salvador	11,069	53.2	6,394	3,569	1,105	10.0	38.1	19.0	46.5	177.1
Eritrea	1,010	48.2	1,003	..	7	0.7	6.3	..	33.8[b]	731.6[b]
Estonia	..	..	..	..	..	..	..	..	..	..
Ethiopia	7,147	24.1	6,545	..	314	4.4	..	..	13.3[b]	106.7[b]
Finland	..	..	..	..	..	..	..	..	..	..
France	..	..	..	..	..	..	..	..	..	..
Gabon	2,331	20.3	2,158	..	174	7.5	10.0	..	18.7	16.2
Gambia, The	470	63.3	395	..	44	9.4	21.9	7.2	29.5[b]	72.6[b]
Georgia	9,238	80.4	4,081	3,143	963	10.4	42.6	18.1	65.0	183.9
Germany	..	..	..	..	..	..	..	..	..	..
Ghana	8,368	27.2	5,727	0	2,249	26.9	..	3.4	17.5[b]	61.0[b]
Greece	..	..	..	..	..	..	..	..	..	..
Guatemala	14,340	35.9	5,527	7,218	1,595	11.1	26.8	14.3	31.7	117.6
Guinea	2,923	69.1	2,752	..	123	4.2	..	5.6	53.6[b]	145.2[b]
Guinea-Bissau	1,095	124.8	963	..	128	11.7	81.6	..	14.6[b]	86.6[b]
Haiti	492	7.3	479	..	0	0.0	0.0	15.7	4.3[b]	31.7[b]

External debt | 6.9

	Total external debt		Long-term debt		Short-term debt			Total debt service	Present value of debt	
			$ millions					% of exports of goods and services and income[a]		% of exports of goods and services and income[a]
			Public and publicly guaranteed	Private nonguaranteed			% of total reserves		% of GNI[a]	
	$ millions	% of GNI			$ millions	% of total debt				
	2010	2010	2010	2010	2010	2010	2010	2010	2010	2010
Honduras	4,168	28.2	2,798	942	398	9.6	14.7	7.6	14.0[b]	26.9[b]
Hungary	..	..	..	..	..	..	..	..	..	..
India	290,282	16.9	106,205	127,629	56,448	19.4	18.8	5.6	17.7	79.4
Indonesia	179,064	26.1	91,024	56,785	31,255	17.5	32.5	16.6	28.2	102.0
Iran, Islamic Rep.	12,570	..	6,411	0	6,159	49.0	..	2.0	3.3	..
Iraq	..	..	..	..	..	..	..	..	..	..
Ireland	..	..	..	..	..	..	..	..	..	..
Israel	..	..	..	..	..	..	..	..	..	..
Italy	..	..	..	..	..	..	..	..	..	..
Jamaica	13,865	104.2	7,593	4,307	1,180	8.5	47.2	27.9	102.2	221.3
Japan	..	..	..	..	..	..	..	..	..	..
Jordan	7,822	27.9	6,504	..	1,310	16.7	9.6	4.9	25.9	51.2
Kazakhstan	118,723	94.3	3,842	105,844	9,037	7.6	32.0	71.4	89.1	154.7
Kenya	8,400	26.9	6,978	0	1,005	12.0	23.3	4.4	19.6	71.8
Korea, Dem. Rep.	..	..	..	..	..	..	..	..	..	..
Korea, Rep.	..	..	..	..	..	..	..	..	..	..
Kosovo	342	6.0	342	..	0	0.0	0.0	1.6	4.2	24.8
Kuwait	..	..	..	..	..	..	..	..	..	..
Kyrgyz Republic	3,984	89.2	2,442	1,171	195	4.9	11.3	21.9	37.8[b]	66.0[b]
Lao PDR	5,559	79.0	2,939	2,610	0	0.0	0.0	..	65.4	210.8
Latvia	39,555	164.3	6,891	18,428	12,723	32.2	167.3	76.4	129.1	260.0
Lebanon	24,293	60.7	20,213	500	3,482	14.3	7.8	19.1	67.1	98.4
Lesotho	726	28.4	698	..	0	0.0	..	1.9	17.1	23.6
Liberia	228	28.3	184	..	0	0.0	..	1.3	11.7[b]	13.8[b]
Libya	..	..	..	..	..	..	..	..	..	..
Lithuania	29,602	83.0	11,664	12,468	5,469	18.5	80.0	34.3	68.7	107.1
Macedonia, FYR	5,804	65.1	1,865	1,885	2,054	35.4	90.2	15.2	57.0	118.4
Madagascar	2,295	26.6	1,981	3	214	9.3	18.3	2.6	20.8[b]	60.2[b]
Malawi	922	18.5	715	..	61	6.6	18.7	..	15.7[b]	63.4[b]
Malaysia	81,497	35.4	25,795	20,626	35,076	43.0	32.9	5.2	35.7	33.1
Mali	2,326	26.1	2,271	..	6	0.3	0.5	2.5	16.5[b]	57.6[b]
Mauritania	2,461	67.0	2,174	..	237	9.6	82.4	..	68.4[b]	126.1[b]
Mauritius	1,076	11.0	972	100	3	0.3	0.1	2.4	8.5	15.2
Mexico	200,081	19.5	111,467	49,600	39,013	19.5	32.4	9.8	18.0	60.5
Moldova	4,615	73.5	817	1,906	1,564	33.9	91.1	12.8	65.5	135.9
Mongolia	2,444	44.3	1,795	221	230	9.4	10.1	5.0	33.1	57.9
Morocco	25,403	28.1	21,015	2,589	1,800	7.1	7.6	10.7	23.4	67.1
Mozambique	4,124	43.8	2,960	..	975	23.6	43.0	2.9	20.9[b]	65.6[b]
Myanmar	6,352	..	4,395	..	1,956	30.8	..	..	..	..
Namibia	..	..	..	..	..	..	..	..	..	..
Nepal	3,702	23.4	3,527	..	61	1.6	2.1	10.5	19.9[b]	150.6[b]
Netherlands	..	..	..	..	..	..	..	..	..	..
New Zealand	..	..	..	..	..	..	..	..	..	..
Nicaragua	4,786	76.9	2,668	1,255	697	14.6	38.7	14.3	36.8[b]	70.7[b]
Niger	1,127	20.5	972	0	94	8.4	12.4	..	10.5[b]	53.2[b]
Nigeria	7,883	4.5	4,686	..	3,197	40.6	8.9	0.4	3.2	7.4
Norway	..	..	..	..	..	..	..	..	..	..
Oman	..	..	..	..	..	..	..	..	..	..
Pakistan	56,773	31.3	43,202	2,544	2,291	4.0	13.3	15.2	24.1	158.8
Panama	11,412	45.8	10,421	991	0	0.0	0.0	5.7	43.7	54.7
Papua New Guinea	5,822	62.9	1,030	4,400	392	6.7	12.6	12.9	54.9	79.1
Paraguay	4,938	25.3	2,369	1,421	1,147	23.2	27.5	4.6	25.7	47.7
Peru	36,271	24.6	20,027	10,189	6,055	16.7	13.7	16.7	24.9	88.9
Philippines	72,337	36.2	44,641	21,402	6,295	8.7	10.1	18.4	34.6	99.6
Poland	..	..	..	..	..	..	..	..	..	..
Portugal	..	..	..	..	..	..	..	..	..	..
Puerto Rico	..	..	..	..	..	..	..	..	..	..
Qatar	..	..	..	..	..	..	..	..	..	..

	Total external debt		Long-term debt ($ millions)		Short-term debt			Total debt service	Present value of debt	
	$ millions 2010	% of GNI 2010	Public and publicly guaranteed 2010	Private nonguaranteed 2010	$ millions 2010	% of total debt 2010	% of total reserves 2010	% of exports of goods and services and income[a] 2010	% of GNI[a] 2010	% of exports of goods and services and income[a] 2010
Romania	121,505	76.4	20,557	60,826	25,029	20.6	52.1	31.2	58.1	170.9
Russian Federation	384,740	26.9	162,924	183,059	38,756	10.1	8.1	12.8	24.7	72.1
Rwanda	795	14.2	766	..	14	1.8	1.7	2.3	11.5[b]	102.7[b]
Saudi Arabia	..	..	..	..	..	..	..	..	..	..
Senegal	3,677	28.5	3,155	308	0	0.0	0.0	..	20.0[b]	67.3[b]
Serbia	32,222	84.3	9,477	17,912	2,798	8.7	21.0	30.9	67.1	201.2
Sierra Leone	778	40.8	661	..	4	0.5	1.0	2.6	22.8[b]	115.1[b]
Singapore	..	..	..	..	..	..	..	..	..	..
Slovak Republic	..	..	..	..	..	..	..	..	..	..
Slovenia	..	..	..	..	..	..	..	..	..	..
Somalia	2,942	..	1,990	..	780	26.5	..	..	..	..
South Africa	45,165	12.7	17,753	15,107	12,305	27.2	28.1	4.9	14.7	45.4
South Sudan	..	..	..	..	..	..	..	..	..	..
Spain	..	..	..	..	..	..	..	..	..	..
Sri Lanka	20,452	41.8	16,449	919	1,773	8.7	24.6	13.0	36.6	156.1
Sudan	21,846	39.1	14,444	0	7,012	32.1	676.7	4.2	70.2[b]	339.2[b]
Swaziland	616	17.2	385	..	231	37.5	30.5	..	19.5	26.3
Sweden	..	..	..	..	..	..	..	..	..	..
Switzerland	..	..	..	..	..	..	..	..	..	..
Syrian Arab Republic	4,729	8.2	4,171	0	558	11.8	2.7	..	7.9	23.1
Tajikistan	2,955	53.1	1,806	927	122	4.1	..	44.8	42.4	145.9
Tanzania	8,664	37.7	5,572	1,224	1,515	17.5	38.8	3.0	22.8[b]	84.7[b]
Thailand	71,263	23.4	11,357	21,434	38,471	54.0	22.4	4.8	24.2	31.2
Timor-Leste	..	..	..	..	..	..	..	..	..	..
Togo	1,728	61.1	1,534	..	61	3.5	8.5	..	13.9[b]	34.9[b]
Trinidad and Tobago	..	..	..	..	..	..	..	..	..	..
Tunisia	21,584	51.1	14,609	1,996	4,979	23.1	51.0	10.4	47.5	77.1
Turkey	293,872	40.4	93,088	117,035	78,123	26.6	90.9	36.7	39.4	165.0
Turkmenistan	422	2.1	359	7	55	13.0	..	..	2.2	2.5
Uganda	2,994	17.9	2,671	..	314	10.5	11.1	1.8	7.1[b]	33.1[b]
Ukraine	116,808	85.9	16,246	59,858	26,459	22.7	76.5	40.7	75.0	144.0
United Arab Emirates	..	..	..	..	..	..	..	..	..	..
United Kingdom	..	..	..	..	..	..	..	..	..	..
United States	..	..	..	..	..	..	..	..	..	..
Uruguay	11,347	29.0	9,704	93	1,550	13.7	20.2	12.4	30.6	101.6
Uzbekistan	7,404	19.0	3,426	3,741	238	3.2	..	..	18.1	45.3
Venezuela, RB	55,572	14.3	37,086	3,060	15,426	27.8	52.0	..	..	..
Vietnam	35,139	36.5	28,145	..	6,949	19.8	55.7	1.7	28.9	37.1
West Bank and Gaza	..	..	..	..	..	..	..	..	..	..
Yemen, Rep.	6,324	..	5,933	..	313	5.0	5.3	2.8	15.2	44.4
Zambia	3,689	25.8	1,309	794	1,191	32.3	56.9	1.9	12.0[b]	26.6[b]
Zimbabwe	5,016	71.8	3,686	378	843	16.8	..	..	110.3	275.3
World	..	..	..	..	..	..	..	..	..	..
Low income	116,593	28.5	95,929	3,703	12,806	11.0	19.0	..	..	..
Middle income	3,959,705	20.8	1,486,657	1,388,971	1,023,572	25.8	18.3	..	..	..
Lower middle income	1,021,016	24.7	518,320	308,804	163,917	16.1	21.9	..	..	..
Upper middle income	2,938,688	19.7	968,337	1,080,167	859,655	29.3	17.7	..	..	..
Low & middle income	4,076,298	21.0	1,582,586	1,392,674	1,036,378	25.4	18.3	..	..	..
East Asia & Pacific	1,013,971	13.5	306,774	238,402	468,525	46.2	13.8	..	..	..
Europe & Central Asia	1,273,418	43.0	366,663	627,496	234,232	18.4	31.1	..	..	..
Latin America & Carib.	1,038,725	21.7	457,714	370,470	208,277	20.1	32.3	..	..	..
Middle East & N. Africa	143,595	14.1	113,766	6,106	23,528	16.4	5.3	..	..	..
South Asia	400,596	19.2	194,376	131,428	63,879	15.9	18.7	..	..	..
Sub-Saharan Africa	205,992	20.0	143,293	18,772	37,936	18.4	21.8	..	..	..
High income	..	..	..	..	..	..	..	..	..	..
Euro area	..	..	..	..	..	..	..	..	..	..

a. The numerator refers to 2010, whereas the denominator is a three-year average of 2008–10 data. b. Data are from debt sustainability analyses for low-income countries and include the effects of traditional relief, debt relief under the Heavily Indebted Poor Country Initiative, and relief under the Multilateral Debt Relief Initiative. Present value estimates for these countries are for public and publicly guaranteed debt only.

External indebtedness affects a country's credit-worthiness and investor perceptions. Data on external debt are gathered through the World Bank's Debtor Reporting System (DRS). Indebtedness is calculated using loan-by-loan reports submitted by countries on long-term public and publicly guaranteed borrowing and information on short-term debt collected by the countries or from creditors through the reporting systems of the Bank for International Settlements (BIS). These data are supplemented by information from major multilateral banks and official lending agencies in major creditor countries and by estimates by World Bank and International Monetary Fund (IMF) staff.

Currently, 129 developing countries report to the DRS. Nonreporting countries might have outstanding debt with the World Bank, other international financial institutions, or private creditors.

Debt data, normally reported in the currency of repayment, are converted into U.S. dollars to produce summary tables. Stock figures (amount of debt outstanding) are converted using end-of-period exchange rates, as published in the IMF's *International Financial Statistics*. Flow figures are converted at annual average exchange rates. Projected debt service is converted using end-of-period exchange rates. Debt repayable in multiple currencies, goods, or services and debt with a provision for maintenance of the value of the currency of repayment are shown at book value.

A country's external debt burden, both debt outstanding and debt service, affects its creditworthiness and vulnerability. The table shows total external debt relative to a country's size—gross national income (GNI). While data related to public and publicly guaranteed debt are reported to the DRS on a loan-by-loan basis. Aggregate data on long-term private nonguaranteed debt are reported annually and are reported by the country or estimated by World Bank staff for countries where this type of external debt is known to be significant. Estimates are based on national data from the World Bank's *Quarterly External Debt Statistics*.

The DRS encourages debtor countries to voluntarily provide information on their short-term external obligations. By its nature, short-term external debt is difficult to monitor: loan-by-loan registration is normally impractical, and monitoring systems typically rely on information requested periodically by the central bank from the banking sector. The World Bank regards the debtor country as the authoritative source of information on its short-term debt.

Where such information is not available from the debtor country, data are derived from BIS data on international bank lending based on time remaining to original maturity. The data are reported based on residual maturity, but an estimate of short-term external liabilities by original maturity can be derived by deducting from claims due in one year those that have a maturity of between one and two years. However, BIS data include liabilities reported only by banks within the BIS reporting area. The results should thus be interpreted with caution. Because short-term debt poses an immediate burden and is particularly important for monitoring vulnerability, it is compared with total debt and foreign exchange reserves, which are instrumental in providing coverage for such obligations.

Total debt service is contrasted with countries' ability to obtain foreign exchange through exports of goods, services, income, and workers' remittances.

The present value of external debt provides a measure of future debt service obligations. It is calculated by discounting the debt service (interest plus amortization) due on long-term external debt over the life of existing loans. Short-term debt is included at face value. The discount rate on long-term debt depends on the currency of repayment and is based on commercial interest reference rates established by the Organisation for Economic Co-operation and Development. Loans from the International Bank for Reconstruction and Development (IBRD), credits from the International Development Association (IDA), and obligations to the IMF are discounted using a special drawing rights reference rate. When the discount rate is greater than the loan interest rate, the present value is less than the nominal sum of future debt service obligations.

Debt ratios are used to assess the sustainability of a country's debt service obligations, but no absolute rules determine what values are too high. Empirical analysis of developing countries' experience and debt service performance shows that debt service difficulties become increasingly likely when the present value of debt reaches 200 percent of exports. Still, what constitutes a sustainable debt burden varies by country. Countries with fast-growing economies and exports are likely to be able to sustain higher debt levels.

• **Total external debt** is debt owed to nonresident creditors and repayable in foreign currencies, goods, or services by public and private entities in the country. It is the sum of long-term external debt, short-term debt, and use of IMF credit. Debt repayable in domestic currency is excluded. • **Long-term debt** is debt that has an original or extended maturity of more than one year. It has three components: public, publicly guaranteed, and private nonguaranteed debt. • **Public and publicly guaranteed debt** is the long-term external obligations of public debtors, including the national government and political subdivisions (or an agency of either) and autonomous public bodies, and the external obligations of private debtors that are guaranteed for repayment by a public entity. • **Private nonguaranteed debt** is the long-term external obligations of private debtors that are not guaranteed for repayment by a public entity. • **Short-term debt** is debt owed to nonresidents having an original maturity of one year or less and interest in arrears on long-term debt and on the use of IMF credit. • **Total reserves** are holdings of monetary gold, special drawing rights, reserves of IMF members held by the IMF, and holdings of foreign exchange under the control of monetary authorities. • **Total debt service** is the sum of principal repayments and interest actually paid in foreign currency, goods, or services on long-term debt, interest paid on short-term debt, and repayments (repurchases and charges) to the IMF. • **Exports of goods and services and income** are the total value of exports of goods and services, receipts of compensation of nonresident workers, and investment income from abroad. • **Present value of debt** is the sum of short-term external debt plus the discounted sum of total debt service payments due on public, publicly guaranteed, and private nonguaranteed long-term external debt over the life of existing loans.

Data on external debt are mainly from reports to the World Bank through its DRS from member countries that have received IBRD loans or IDA credits, with additional information from the files of the World Bank, the IMF, the African Development Bank and African Development Fund, the Asian Development Bank and Asian Development Fund, and the Inter-American Development Bank. Summary tables of the external debt of developing countries are published annually in the World Bank's *Global Development Finance,* on its *Global Development Finance* CD-ROM, and in its Global Development Finance database.

6.10 Global private financial flows

	Equity net flows			Debt flows	
	Foreign direct investment		Portfolio equity	$ millions	
	$ millions	Net inflow % of GDP	$ millions	Bonds	Commercial bank and other lending
	2010	2010	2010	2010	2010
Afghanistan	76	0.4	..	0	0
Albania	1,110	9.4	8	398	−35
Algeria	2,291	1.4	..	0	−398
Angola	−3,227	−3.8	0	0	−1,553
Argentina	7,055	1.9	−208	−1,660	−2,477
Armenia	570	6.1	0	0	703
Australia	30,576	2.7	9,974	..	..
Austria	−25,636	−6.8	−385	..	..
Azerbaijan	563	1.1	1	0	2,021
Bahrain	156	..	1,653	..	..
Bangladesh	917	0.9	0	0	−11
Belarus	1,403	2.6	1	1,777	702
Belgium	72,914	15.5	−1,837	..	..
Benin	111	1.7	..	0	0
Bolivia	622	3.2	0	0	−359
Bosnia and Herzegovina	232	1.4	0	−25	−913
Botswana	265	1.8	18	0	−1
Brazil	48,506	2.3	37,684	24,086	19,981
Bulgaria	2,355	4.9	9	0	−1,820
Burkina Faso	37	0.4	..	0	−2
Burundi	1	0.1	0	0	0
Cambodia	783	7.0	0	0	0
Cameroon	−1	0.0	0	0	−32
Canada	23,587	1.5	17,775	..	..
Central African Republic	72	3.6	..	0	0
Chad	781	10.3	..	0	−2
Chile	15,095	7.1	1,748	4,867	3,813
China	185,081	3.1	31,357	11,112	2,066
Hong Kong SAR, China	71,066	31.7	18,534	..	..
Colombia	6,914	2.4	1,351	972	4,302
Congo, Dem. Rep.	2,939	22.4	..	0	−4
Congo, Rep.	2,816	23.7	..	0	−24
Costa Rica	1,466	4.1	0	0	313
Côte d'Ivoire	418	1.8	..	0	−58
Croatia	408	0.7	112	..	..
Cuba	86	..	..	..	..
Cyprus	1,886	8.2	440	..	..
Czech Republic	6,720	3.5	287	..	..
Denmark	−7,697	−2.5	7,262	..	..
Dominican Republic	1,626	3.1	0	645	−85
Ecuador	167	0.3	0	−6	−3
Egypt, Arab Rep.	6,386	2.9	1,724	1,500	19
El Salvador	−6	0.0	0	0	131
Eritrea	56	2.6	..	0	0
Estonia	1,539	8.0	15	..	..
Ethiopia	288	1.0	0	0	647
Finland	7,072	3.0	1,980	..	..
France	33,672	1.3	−8,442	..	..
Gabon	170	1.3	..	−23	189
Gambia, The	37	4.6	0	0	6
Georgia	817	7.0	−20	250	100
Germany	46,127	1.4	−1,991	..	..
Ghana	2,527	8.1	0	0	251
Greece	430	0.1	−1,459	..	..
Guatemala	881	2.1	0	0	−88
Guinea	101	2.3	0	0	4
Guinea-Bissau	9	1.0	..	0	0
Haiti	150	2.2	0	0	0

	Equity net flows			Debt flows	
	Foreign direct investment		Portfolio equity $ millions	$ millions	
	$ millions	Net inflow % of GDP		Bonds	Commercial bank and other lending
	2010	**2010**	**2010**	**2010**	**2010**
Honduras	797	5.2	0	0	30
Hungary	−42,283	−32.9	−143	..	..
India	24,159	1.4	39,972	10,339	12,971
Indonesia	13,371	1.9	2,132	2,329	3,563
Iran, Islamic Rep.	3,617	..	..	0	−1,084
Iraq	1,426	1.7	..	..	..
Ireland	27,085	13.1	152,236	..	..
Israel	5,152	2.4	−612	..	..
Italy	9,594	0.5	3,826	..	..
Jamaica	228	1.6	0	1,007	146
Japan	−1,359	0.0	40,328	..	..
Jordan	1,701	6.2	−20	733	2
Kazakhstan	10,677	7.2	131	−1,053	7,156
Kenya	186	0.6	33	0	8
Korea, Dem. Rep.	38	..	..	..	..
Korea, Rep.	−150	0.0	23,026	..	..
Kosovo	481	8.7	0	0	0
Kuwait	81	..	−815	..	..
Kyrgyz Republic	438	9.5	−18	0	97
Lao PDR	279	3.8	54	0	−14
Latvia	369	1.5	9	0	−4,045
Lebanon	4,280	11.0	163	−396	5
Lesotho	117	5.5	0	0	0
Liberia	453	45.9	0	0	0
Libya	1,784	..	0	..	..
Lithuania	748	2.1	37	2,458	−3,897
Macedonia, FYR	207	2.3	−4	0	36
Madagascar	860	9.9	..	0	−1
Malawi	140	2.7	..	0	0
Malaysia	9,167	3.9	..	2,024	2,017
Mali	148	1.6	..	0	−1
Mauritania	14	0.4	..	0	−11
Mauritius	431	4.4	−40	0	27
Mexico	19,792	1.9	641	13,338	643
Moldova	193	3.3	6	0	119
Mongolia	1,455	23.5	680	−75	151
Morocco	1,241	1.4	132	1,327	77
Mozambique	789	8.2	0	0	71
Myanmar	910	..	..	0	−546
Namibia	796	6.5	4	..	..
Nepal	88	..	..	0	0
Netherlands	−15,597	−2.0	11,327	..	..
New Zealand	701	..	−298	..	..
Nicaragua	508	7.8	0	0	−63
Niger	947	17.1	..	0	−7
Nigeria	6,049	3.1	2,161	0	−33
Norway	11,747	2.8	1,993	..	..
Oman	2,333	..	703	..	..
Pakistan	2,022	1.1	524	−1,200	−227
Panama	2,350	8.8	0	−150	0
Papua New Guinea	29	0.3	..	0	2,418
Paraguay	345	1.9	0	0	426
Peru	7,328	4.7	87	4,635	971
Philippines	1,713	0.9	503	2,712	3,767
Poland	9,104	1.9	7,875	..	..
Portugal	1,476	0.7	−1,628	..	..
Puerto Rico	..	..	..	..	..
Qatar	5,534	..	..	..	..

	Equity net flows			Debt flows	
	Foreign direct investment		Portfolio equity	$ millions	
	$ millions	Net inflow % of GDP	$ millions	Bonds	Commercial bank and other lending
	2010	**2010**	**2010**	**2010**	**2010**
Romania	2,941	1.8	−25	−929	−858
Russian Federation	43,288	2.9	−4,808	14,900	−6,734
Rwanda	42	0.8	21	0	0
Saudi Arabia	21,560	5.0	..	..	..
Senegal	237	1.8	..	0	−63
Serbia	1,340[a]	3.5	84	0	312
Sierra Leone	87	4.6	0	0	0
Singapore	38,638	18.5	3,559	..	..
Slovak Republic	553	0.6	25	..	..
Slovenia	366	0.8	169	..	..
Somalia	112	..	..	0	0
South Africa	1,224	0.3	5,826	1,422	795
South Sudan	..	..	..	..	..
Spain	24,658	1.8	−4,790	..	..
Sri Lanka	478	1.0	−1,049	1,000	72
Sudan	2,064	3.3	1	0	0
Swaziland	136	3.7	5	0	0
Sweden	5,847	1.3	5,474	..	..
Switzerland	21,707	4.1	−7,210	..	..
Syrian Arab Republic	1,469	2.5	..	0	..
Tajikistan	16	0.3	0	0	50
Tanzania	433	1.9	3	0	137
Thailand	9,679	3.0	2,606	1,730	−452
Timor-Leste	280	39.9	..	..	..
Togo	41	1.3	..	0	0
Trinidad and Tobago	549	2.7	..	..	..
Tunisia	1,401	3.2	−26	0	−550
Turkey	9,084	1.2	3,468	5,961	−8,310
Turkmenistan	2,083	10.4	..	0	−39
Uganda	817	4.8	−70	0	0
Ukraine	6,495	4.7	290	3,089	6,892
United Arab Emirates	3,948	1.3	..	..	..
United Kingdom	52,968	2.3	−11,488	..	..
United States	236,226	1.6	172,376	..	..
Uruguay	1,627	4.2	−12	−93	7
Uzbekistan	822	2.1	..	0	534
Venezuela, RB	1,209	0.3	10	1,141	−264
Vietnam	8,000	7.5	2,383	981	129
West Bank and Gaza	..	..	..	..	..
Yemen, Rep.	56	0.2	0	0	−1
Zambia	1,041	6.4	101	0	−21
Zimbabwe	105	1.4	..	0	289
World	**1,430,438 s**	**2.3 s**	**779,547 s**	**.. s**	**.. s**
Low income	13,017	3.4	−31	0	733
Middle income	501,236	2.6	129,690	111,383	43,393
Lower middle income	90,233	2.1	49,598	22,252	29,824
Upper middle income	411,003	2.8	80,092	89,130	13,569
Low & middle income	514,253	2.6	129,660	111,383	44,126
East Asia & Pacific	231,299	3.1	39,715	20,813	13,127
Europe & Central Asia	86,991	2.8	−840	27,091	−7,863
Latin America & Carib.	117,368	2.4	41,302	48,776	27,376
Middle East & N. Africa	25,688	2.7	1,973	3,164	−1,933
South Asia	27,923	1.3	39,447	10,139	12,751
Sub-Saharan Africa	24,984	2.3	8,063	1,400	669
High income	916,185	2.1	649,887	..	..
Euro area	395,004	3.3	359,369	..	..

a. Includes Montenegro.

About the data

Private financial flows—equity and debt—account for the bulk of development finance. Equity flows comprise foreign direct investment (FDI) and portfolio equity. Debt flows are financing raised through bond issuance, bank lending, and supplier credits. Data on equity flows are based on balance of payments data reported by the International Monetary Fund (IMF). FDI data are supplemented by staff estimates using data from the United Nations Conference on Trade and Development and official national sources.

The internationally accepted definition of FDI (from the fifth edition of the IMF's *Balance of Payments Manual* [1993]), includes three components: equity investment, reinvested earnings, and short- and long-term loans between parent firms and foreign affiliates. Distinguished from other kinds of international investment, FDI is made to establish a lasting interest in or effective management control over an enterprise in another country. A lasting interest in an investment enterprise typically involves establishing warehouses, manufacturing facilities, and other permanent or long-term organizations abroad. Direct investments may take the form of greenfield investment, where the investor starts a new venture in a foreign country by constructing new operational facilities; joint venture, where the investor enters into a partnership agreement with a company abroad to establish a new enterprise; or merger and acquisition, where the investor acquires an existing enterprise abroad. The IMF suggests that investments should account for at least 10 percent of voting stock to be counted as FDI. In practice many countries set a higher threshold. Many countries fail to report reinvested earnings, and the definition of long-term loans differs among countries.

FDI data do not give a complete picture of international investment in an economy. Balance of payments data on FDI do not include capital raised locally, an important source of investment financing in some developing countries. In addition, FDI data omit nonequity cross-border transactions such as intrafirm flows of goods and services. For a detailed discussion of the data issues, see the World Bank's *Global Development Finance.*

Statistics on bonds, bank lending, and supplier credits are produced by aggregating transactions of public and publicly guaranteed debt and private nonguaranteed debt. Data on public and publicly guaranteed debt are reported through the Debtor Reporting System by World Bank member economies that have received loans from the International Bank for Reconstruction and Development or credits from the International Development Association. The reports are cross-checked with data from market sources that include transactions data. Information on private nonguaranteed bonds and bank lending is collected from market sources when data are not reported to the Debtor Reporting System.

Data on equity flows are shown for all countries for which data are available. Debt flows are shown only for 129 developing countries that report to the Debtor Reporting System; nonreporting countries may also receive debt flows.

The volume of global private financial flows reported by the World Bank generally differs from that reported by other sources because of differences in sources, classification of economies, and method used to adjust and disaggregate reported information. In addition, particularly for debt financing, differences may also reflect how some installments of the transactions and certain offshore issuances are treated.

Definitions

• **Foreign direct investment** is net inflows of investment to acquire a lasting interest in or management control over an enterprise operating in an economy other than that of the investor. It is the sum of equity capital, reinvested earnings, other long-term capital, and short-term capital, as shown in the balance of payments. Net inflows are new investments less disinvestments. • **Portfolio equity** includes net inflows from equity securities other than those recorded as direct investment and including shares, stocks, depository receipts, and direct purchases of shares in local stock markets by foreign investors • **Bonds** are securities issued with a fixed rate of interest for a period of more than one year. They include net flows through cross-border public and publicly guaranteed and private nonguaranteed bond issues. • **Commercial bank and other lending** includes net commercial bank lending (public and publicly guaranteed and private nonguaranteed) and other private credits.

Data sources

Data on equity and debt flows are compiled from a variety of public and private sources, including the World Bank's Debtor Reporting System, the IMF's International Financial Statistics and Balance of Payments databases, and Dealogic. These data are also published annually in the World Bank's *Global Development Finance,* on its *Global Development Finance* CD-ROM, and in the Global Development Finance database.

	Total		International financial institutions						
	$ millions		World Bank		$ millions IMF		Regional development banks[a]		
	From bilateral sources	From multilateral sources[a]	IDA	IBRD	Concessional	Non-concessional	Concessional	Non-concessional	Other institutions
	2010	2010	2010	2010	2010	2010	2010	2010	2010
Afghanistan	0.0	77.8	8.4	..	8.6	..	64.9	..	4.5
Albania	−7.1	102.5	15.1	3.1	−12.1	−0.2	..	1.9	82.3
Algeria	−142.4	−2.3	..	−0.5	..	..	..	..	−1.7
Angola	3,372.3	1.5	−0.7	..	..	524.2	3.0	−0.4	−0.5
Argentina	−249.8	788.3	..	46.2	..	..	..	609.9	136.7
Armenia	64.9	109.5	20.3	52.4	35.5	127.4	22.3	8.7	5.9
Australia	..	..	..	..	..	..	..	..	..
Austria	..	..	..	..	..	..	..	..	..
Azerbaijan	147.7	310.4	35.9	101.2	−14.7	..	5.1	33.6	134.6
Bahrain	..	..	..	..	..	..	..	..	..
Bangladesh	−112.3	352.1	83.5	..	−45.6	0.0	75.0	166.1	27.6
Belarus	1,589.5	33.6	..	35.7	..	668.3	..	−2.1	..
Belgium	..	..	..	..	..	..	..	..	..
Benin	19.2	144.2	78.3	..	16.2	..	40.1	..	25.7
Bolivia	45.8	297.4	44.0	0.0	..	..	86.2	29.7	140.8
Bosnia and Herzegovina	65.5	277.4	97.2	25.7	..	237.4	..	58.6	100.7
Botswana	−13.6	−24.8	−0.5	6.5	..	..	−1.8	−3.0	−26.0
Brazil	3,615.0	5,069.6	..	3,511.7	..	..	..	951.3	589.8
Bulgaria	−52.6	−8.6	..	−69.9	..	..	..	−11.8	73.0
Burkina Faso	16.5	228.4	66.6	..	20.2	..	63.4	..	98.5
Burundi	..	33.9	17.8	..	20.1	..	1.6	..	14.4
Cambodia	262.7	50.6	9.0	..	..	..	35.1	..	6.6
Cameroon	34.8	119.4	80.6	−5.4	0.0	..	50.3	−9.7	3.6
Canada	..	..	..	..	..	..	..	..	..
Central African Republic	−0.1	5.1	5.0	..	13.2	..	0.0	..	0.1
Chad	−4.1	17.9	−16.0	..	−11.1	..	3.8	..	30.2
Chile	36.9	−44.8	−0.7	−25.8	..	..	..	−18.3	..
China	−123.3	828.7	−348.4	195.6	..	..	..	1,033.3	−51.8
Hong Kong SAR, China	..	..	..	..	..	..	..	..	..
Colombia	−81.8	1,094.1	−0.7	937.2	..	..	−1.6	188.0	−28.7
Congo, Dem. Rep.	−23.4	−15.8	17.5	..	18.9	..	17.5	−38.1	−12.7
Congo, Rep.	−42.4	−11.2	1.5	..	1.8	..	−0.2	−8.3	0.2
Costa Rica	10.1	527.6	−0.2	512.3	..	..	−8.2	18.6	5.0
Côte d'Ivoire	−36.3	−81.3	−0.9	−24.9	44.4	..	−2.2	−32.5	−5.0
Croatia	..	..	..	..	..	..	..	..	..
Cuba	..	..	..	..	..	..	..	..	..
Cyprus	..	..	..	..	..	..	..	..	..
Czech Republic	..	..	..	..	..	..	..	..	..
Denmark	..	..	..	..	..	..	..	..	..
Dominican Republic	362.0	470.1	−0.7	116.2	..	382.9	−21.2	359.5	16.2
Ecuador	890.3	826.1	−1.1	−85.5	..	..	−26.7	64.0	455.4
Egypt, Arab Rep.	−1,015.2	772.7	−44.1	693.6	..	..	−6.0	140.5	−11.2
El Salvador	−44.4	365.8	−0.8	345.5	..	..	−23.2	26.0	18.3
Eritrea	−4.1	0.1	−0.5	..	..	..	3.7	..	−3.1
Estonia	..	..	..	..	..	..	..	..	..
Ethiopia	510.7	472.1	384.7	..	122.4	..	80.8	−6.7	13.3
Finland	..	..	..	..	..	..	..	..	..
France	..	..	..	..	..	..	..	..	..
Gabon	15.9	−7.4	..	5.6	..	..	−0.2	2.6	−15.4
Gambia, The	6.5	18.5	1.9	..	3.0	..	2.3	..	14.3
Georgia	36.1	294.0	52.9	72.8	−21.5	296.9	38.3	118.7	11.2
Germany	..	..	..	..	..	..	..	..	..
Ghana	357.9	427.0	304.8	..	124.4	..	130.0	0.0	−7.1
Greece	..	..	..	..	..	..	..	..	..
Guatemala	−14.6	631.0	..	260.0	..	..	−18.3	320.8	68.5
Guinea	−9.0	−11.0	0.0	..	−10.2	..	6.3	−4.6	−12.7
Guinea-Bissau	..	−2.5	−1.0	..	15.7	−8.1	−2.4	..	0.8
Haiti	121.4	42.3	−35.9	..	124.8	..	69.5	..	8.8

Net official financial flows

	Total		World Bank		IMF		Regional development banks[a]		Other institutions
	$ millions				$ millions				
	From bilateral sources	From multilateral sources[a]	IDA	IBRD	Concessional	Non-concessional	Concessional	Non-concessional	
	2010	2010	2010	2010	2010	2010	2010	2010	2010
Honduras	2.4	388.9	108.7	..	−1.6	..	101.0	36.1	143.2
Hungary	..	..	..	..	..	..	..	..	..
India	826.1	4,575.8	231.5	2,795.2	..	..	..	1,440.1	97.2
Indonesia	−8.2	1,367.1	110.0	1,177.4	..	..	66.1	13.6	0.0
Iran, Islamic Rep.	−289.5	73.4	..	64.2	..	..	..	..	..
Iraq	..	..	..	..	..	..	..	..	..
Ireland	..	..	..	..	..	..	..	..	..
Israel	..	..	..	..	..	..	..	..	..
Italy	..	..	..	..	..	..	..	..	..
Jamaica	32.1	835.2	..	180.6	..	778.1	−4.2	559.8	99.1
Japan	..	..	..	..	..	..	..	..	225.0
Jordan	13.1	153.9	−2.6	−68.5	..	−3.9	..	..	51.3
Kazakhstan	−195.0	1,436.1	..	1,283.0	..	..	−0.2	101.9	51.3
Kenya	40.4	223.3	132.4	..	−25.5	..	83.7	−2.4	9.6
Korea, Dem. Rep.	..	..	..	..	..	..	..	..	..
Korea, Rep.	..	..	..	..	..	..	..	..	..
Kosovo	..	−16.3	..	−16.3	..	..	..	..	..
Kuwait	..	..	..	..	..	..	..	..	..
Kyrgyz Republic	101.3	7.7	5.4	..	12.4	..	−8.5	2.3	8.5
Lao PDR	57.3	−31.2	−12.6	..	−5.5	..	−11.1	0.2	−7.6
Latvia	−17.6	1,086.1	..	117.6	..	409.6	..	−1.8	970.3
Lebanon	−71.8	−26.3	..	3.0	..	−19.4	..	..	−29.3
Lesotho	0.6	20.9	22.3	−0.7	4.4	..	−1.6	..	0.9
Liberia	3.7	−3.7	−1.7	..	13.6	..	−2.1	0.0	..
Libya	..	..	..	..	..	..	..	..	..
Lithuania	..	446.0	..	−3.1	..	..	..	−4.9	454.0
Macedonia, FYR	0.0	85.4	−8.2	61.6	..	..	..	−5.8	37.9
Madagascar	68.9	106.4	74.6	..	−1.7	..	12.5	..	19.3
Malawi	22.8	44.8	33.8	..	21.2	..	4.9	−2.1	8.2
Malaysia	−599.4	−69.9	..	−38.5	..	..	..	−21.5	−10.0
Mali	42.9	230.6	151.3	..	5.9	..	65.5	..	13.8
Mauritania	97.6	249.4	38.7	..	33.7	..	9.9	−8.1	209.0
Mauritius	110.7	136.8	−0.6	−3.0	..	..	−0.2	153.9	−13.3
Mexico	464.4	3,580.4	..	2,255.6	..	..	..	1,299.1	25.7
Moldova	−6.8	48.8	59.4	−17.8	113.6	61.0	..	−3.1	10.2
Mongolia	11.6	20.2	17.3	..	−4.6	23.4	0.5	..	2.3
Morocco	504.5	625.7	−1.4	69.2	..	..	−1.1	160.3	398.7
Mozambique	7.8	237.6	157.7	..	21.4	..	68.4	..	11.4
Myanmar	−103.6	−0.8	..	..	..	..	0.0	..	−0.8
Namibia	..	..	..	..	..	..	..	..	..
Nepal	−4.2	−11.1	−32.6	..	39.4	..	15.8	..	5.7
Netherlands	..	..	..	..	..	..	..	..	..
New Zealand	..	..	..	..	..	..	..	..	..
Nicaragua	−3.1	215.0	36.2	..	19.5	..	97.3	43.7	37.4
Niger	14.7	64.1	14.1	..	4.9	..	16.4	..	33.7
Nigeria	−28.7	866.5	975.4	−70.8	..	..	21.9	−65.2	5.1
Norway	..	..	..	..	..	..	..	..	..
Oman	..	..	..	..	..	..	..	..	..
Pakistan	−8.4	439.4	204.9	−127.1	−264.6	1,633.8	87.5	148.2	126.0
Panama	87.2	188.1	..	−14.8	..	..	−5.6	214.9	−6.5
Papua New Guinea	−21.9	−2.1	4.6	−10.6	..	..	−5.5	13.1	−3.8
Paraguay	−62.9	142.4	−1.5	−25.0	..	..	−11.3	140.4	43.3
Peru	−841.9	−527.3	..	118.9	..	..	..	−755.5	109.3
Philippines	−292.0	−179.9	−6.9	58.9	..	..	−41.1	−203.2	12.5
Poland	..	..	..	..	..	..	..	..	..
Portugal	..	..	..	..	..	..	..	..	..
Puerto Rico	..	..	..	..	..	..	..	..	..
Qatar	..	..	..	..	..	..	..	..	..

	Total		International financial institutions						
	$ millions		World Bank		IMF		Regional development banks[a]		
	From bilateral sources	From multilateral sources[a]	IDA	IBRD	Concessional	Non-concessional	Concessional	Non-concessional	Other institutions
	2010	2010	2010	2010	2010	2010	2010	2010	2010
Romania	84.4	3,374.6	..	−74.6	..	5,664.3	4.7	−51.5	3,496.0
Russian Federation	−297.2	−659.5	..	−596.4	..	..	..	−61.1	−2.1
Rwanda	17.1	36.0	9.4	..	−0.1	..	14.8	..	11.9
Saudi Arabia	..	..	..	..	..	..	..	..	..
Senegal	68.0	204.8	108.5	..	48.9	..	63.0	−12.7	46.2
Serbia	142.5	708.5	16.4	172.0	..	457.6	..	181.4	326.2
Sierra Leone	6.1	55.5	32.1	..	40.7	..	14.9	..	8.6
Singapore	..	..	..	..	..	..	..	..	..
Slovak Republic	..	..	..	..	..	..	..	..	..
Slovenia	..	..	..	..	..	..	..	..	..
Somalia	0.0	0.0	0.0	..	..	..	0.0	0.0	0.0
South Africa	..	872.8	..	363.1	..	..	..	509.8	..
South Sudan	..	..	..	..	..	..	..	..	..
Spain	..	..	..	..	..	..	..	..	..
Sri Lanka	1,002.8	293.8	82.9	..	−11.7	608.5	18.0	184.6	8.3
Sudan	471.9	65.9	0.0	..	..	−5.8	0.0	0.0	65.9
Swaziland	0.9	−19.8	−0.3	−5.2	..	..	−1.4	−7.8	−5.1
Sweden	..	..	..	..	..	..	..	..	..
Switzerland	..	..	..	..	..	..	..	..	..
Syrian Arab Republic	−309.3	98.3	−1.5	0.0	0.0	0.0	0.0	0.0	99.8
Tajikistan	83.7	129.8	10.7	..	59.8	..	33.0	−0.9	17.1
Tanzania	143.5	817.7	650.0	..	29.9	..	138.6	−1.0	30.2
Thailand	−352.5	−21.2	−3.4	−1.7	..	..	..	−4.8	−11.3
Timor-Leste	..	..	..	..	..	..	..	..	..
Togo	36.7	20.9	−22.0	..	43.6	..	−2.0	..	34.7
Trinidad and Tobago	..	..	..	..	..	..	..	..	..
Tunisia	83.8	547.3	−1.9	76.4	..	..	..	103.6	369.3
Turkey	174.9	3,657.1	−5.9	2,094.3	..	−2,170.8	..	..	1,533.7
Turkmenistan	−75.8	−2.9	..	−1.4	..	..	..	..	−1.5
Uganda	25.5	421.2	323.0	..	−0.3	..	92.0	0.0	6.3
Ukraine	−148.3	−6.1	..	−84.7	..	3,433.3	..	−11.9	90.5
United Arab Emirates	..	..	..	..	..	..	..	..	..
United Kingdom	..	..	..	..	..	..	..	..	..
United States	..	..	..	..	..	..	..	..	..
Uruguay	−20.6	−175.0	..	−42.0	..	..	−1.8	−408.4	279.2
Uzbekistan	72.7	106.3	32.1	−27.6	..	..	36.3	55.0	10.5
Venezuela, RB	−78.7	895.0	..	..	..	..	..	425.5	469.4
Vietnam	588.6	1,924.7	800.9	700.0	−37.9	..	171.4	170.3	82.0
West Bank and Gaza	..	..	..	..	..	..	..	..	..
Yemen, Rep.	−15.2	148.6	28.2	..	26.0	..	..	..	120.4
Zambia	59.3	70.6	29.9	..	55.3	..	51.7	−3.2	−7.9
Zimbabwe	18.7	−0.2	0.0	−0.1	−4.0	..	0.0	−0.1	0.0
World	.. s	.. s	.. s	.. s	.. s	.. s	.. s	.. s	.. s
Low income	1,525.0	3,790.5	2,155.6	−0.1	559.7	−8.1	1,008.3	112.5	434.0
Middle income	10,366.5	41,745.3	3,190.5	17,081.8	143.2	13,125.0	986.7	8,277.1	11,723.0
Lower middle income	5,826.9	14,764.8	3,365.2	5,803.1	163.2	6,702.9	1,026.0	2,747.0	1,839.5
Upper middle income	4,539.6	26,980.5	−174.8	11,278.7	−20.0	6,422.2	−39.2	5,530.1	9,883.5
Low & middle income	11,891.5	45,535.8	5,346.1	17,081.7	702.8	13,116.9	1,995.0	8,389.7	12,157.0
East Asia & Pacific	−498.0	3,926.3	589.6	2,081.2	−38.5	23.4	230.9	1,012.0	12.7
Europe & Central Asia	1,760.8	11,516.2	334.3	3,121.8	172.9	9,184.9	130.9	408.2	7,408.4
Latin America & Carib.	4,312.3	15,755.4	163.8	8,090.7	146.7	1,161.0	276.8	4,120.5	2,659.8
Middle East & N. Africa	−1,234.4	2,401.1	−24.0	837.3	22.7	−23.2	−5.4	404.3	1,179.7
South Asia	1,841.2	5,802.0	594.6	2,668.1	−272.4	2,247.8	301.2	1,960.1	266.3
Sub-Saharan Africa	5,709.6	6,134.8	3,687.8	282.7	671.5	523.1	1,060.6	484.6	630.0
High income	..	..	..	..	..	..	..	..	..
Euro area	..	..	..	..	..	..	..	..	..

a. Aggregates include amounts for economies not specified elsewhere.

The table shows concessional and nonconcessional financial flows from official bilateral sources and the major international financial institutions. The international financial institutions fund nonconcessional lending operations primarily by selling low-interest, highly rated bonds backed by prudent lending and financial policies and the strong financial support of their members. Funds are then on-lent to developing countries at slightly higher interest rates with 15- to 20-year maturities. Lending terms vary with market conditions and institutional policies.

Concessional flows from international financial institutions are credits provided through concessional lending facilities. Subsidies from donors or other resources reduce the cost of these loans. Grants are not included in net flows. The Organisation for Economic Co-operation and Development's (OECD) Development Assistance Committee (DAC) defines concessional flows from bilateral donors as flows with a grant element of at least 25 percent; they are evaluated assuming a 10 percent nominal discount rate.

World Bank concessional lending is done by the International Development Association (IDA) based on gross national income (GNI) per capita and performance standards assessed by World Bank staff. The cutoff for IDA eligibility, set at the beginning of the World Bank's fiscal year, has been $1,175 since July 1, 2011, measured in 2010 U.S. dollars using the *World Bank Atlas* method (see *Users guide*). In exceptional circumstances IDA extends temporary eligibility to countries above the cutoff that are undertaking major adjustments but are not creditworthy for International Bank for Reconstruction and Development (IBRD) lending. Exceptions are also made for small island economies. The IBRD lends to creditworthy countries at a variable base rate of six-month LIBOR plus a spread, either variable or fixed, for the life of the loan. The rate is reset every six months and applies to the interest period beginning on that date. Although some outstanding IBRD loans have a low enough interest rate to be classified as concessional under the DAC definition, all IBRD loans in the table are classified as nonconcessional. Lending by the International Finance Corporation, the Multilateral Investment Guarantee Agency, and the International Centre for Settlement of Investment Disputes is excluded.

The International Monetary Fund (IMF) makes concessional funds available through its Extended Credit Facility (which replaced the Poverty Reduction and Growth Facility in 2010), the Standby Credit Facility,

and the Rapid Credit Facility. Eligibility is based principally on a country's per capita income and eligibility under IDA. Nonconcessional lending from the IMF is provided mainly through Stand-by Arrangements, the Flexible Credit Line, and the Extended Fund Facility. The IMF's loan instruments have changed over time to address the specific circumstances of its members.

Regional development banks also maintain concessional windows. Their loans are recorded in the table according to each institution's classification and not according to the DAC definition.

Data for flows from international financial institutions are available for 129 countries that report to the World Bank's Debtor Reporting System. Nonreporting countries may have net flows from other international financial institutions.

• **Total net official financial flows** are disbursements of public or publicly guaranteed loans and credits, less repayments of principal. • **IDA** is the International Development Association, the concessional arm of the World Bank Group. • **IBRD** is the International Bank for Reconstruction and Development, the founding and largest member of the World Bank Group. • **IMF** is the International Monetary Fund, which provides concessional lending through its Extended Credit Facility, Standby Credit Facility, and Rapid Credit Facility and nonconcessional lending through credit to members, mainly for balance of payments needs. • **Regional development banks** are the African Development Bank, which serves Africa, including North Africa; the Asian Development Bank, which serves South and Central Asia and East Asia and Pacific; the European Bank for Reconstruction and Development, which serves Europe and Central Asia; and the Inter-American Development Bank, which serves the Americas. • **Concessional** financial flows are disbursements through concessional lending facilities. • **Nonconcessional** financial flows are all disbursements that are not concessional. • **Other institutions,** a residual category, includes such institutions as the Caribbean Development Fund, Council of Europe, European Development Fund, Islamic Development Bank, and Nordic Development Fund.

Data on net financial flows from international financial institutions are from the World Bank's Debtor Reporting System and published in the World Bank's *Global Development Finance 2012,* on its *Global Development Finance* CD-ROM, and in its Global Development Finance database.

	Net official development assistance				Aid dependency ratios			
			$ millions			Net official development assistance		
	Total $ millions	Per capita $	Grants	Technical cooperation	% of GNI	% of gross capital formation	% of imports of goods, services, and income	% of central government expense
	2010	2010	2010	2010	2010	2010	2010	2010
Afghanistan	6,374	185	5,476	982	42.0	227.0	..	80.2
Albania	357	112	160	101	2.9	11.1	5.0	..
Algeria	319	9	74	185	0.1	0.3	..	..
Angola	239	13	207	42	0.3	1.9	0.5	..
Argentina	127	3	36	69	0.0	0.2	0.2	
Armenia	526	170	159	32	3.5	10.9	7.0	15.9
Australia								
Austria								
Azerbaijan	232	26	84	53	0.3	1.8	1.1	..
Bahrain	..	..	..	..	..	..	..	
Bangladesh	1,226	8	1,082	218	1.3	5.8	4.6	..
Belarus	98	10	105	37	0.3	0.6	0.4	0.8
Belgium								
Benin	682	79	462	92	10.4	40.4	..	69.7
Bolivia	725	74	527	133	3.6	20.2	9.5	..
Bosnia and Herzegovina	414	110	214	138	2.9	15.2	4.9	7.3
Botswana	279	141	141	21	1.1	2.9	2.5	..
Brazil	337	2	413	237	0.0	0.2	0.2	..
Bulgaria	..	..	..	..	..	..	..	
Burkina Faso	1,083	68	766	125	12.1	..	..	99.6
Burundi	561	69	525	74	39.8	..	102.2	
Cambodia	721	52	453	186	6.9	37.7	8.7	58.1
Cameroon	648	34	358	155	2.4		8.0	
Canada								
Central African Republic	242	56	241	17	13.1	..	..	
Chad	561	51	453	40	7.3	17.6	..	..
Chile	79	5	83	65	0.1	0.4	0.2	0.4
China	1,129	1	459	960	0.0	0.0	0.0	..
Hong Kong SAR, China	..	..	..	..	..	..	..	
Colombia	1,059	23	669	141	0.3	1.3	1.5	1.7
Congo, Dem. Rep.	2,357	37	5,480	234	27.8	..	..	189.1
Congo, Rep.	283	72	1,574	24	15.2	44.3	..	..
Costa Rica	109	24	75	29	0.3	1.3	0.6	
Côte d'Ivoire	2,402	124	646	54	3.9	26.9	..	
Croatia	169	38	106	39	0.3	1.0	0.6	0.7
Cuba	115	10	96	33	..	..	..	
Cyprus	..	..	..	..	..	..	..	
Czech Republic	..	..	..	..	..	..	..	
Denmark								
Dominican Republic	119	12	197	41	0.4	2.1	0.9	..
Ecuador	208	15	166	81	0.3	1.0	0.6	..
Egypt, Arab Rep.	999	13	655	165	0.3	1.4	0.9	0.9
El Salvador	276	45	331	59	1.4	10.1	2.9	6.4
Eritrea	144	28	147	7	7.7	..	..	
Estonia	..	..	..	..	..	..	..	
Ethiopia	3,819	47	2,628	264	11.9	55.3	35.3	..
Finland								
France								
Gabon	77	52	56	41	0.9	3.1	..	..
Gambia, The	127	76	94	9	16.3	57.8	36.6	
Georgia	907	206	377	122	5.5	27.5	9.1	20.4
Germany								
Ghana	1,582	66	920	123	5.5	24.2	11.7	
Greece								
Guatemala	376	27	297	119	1.0	6.6	2.4	..
Guinea	214	22	167	62	5.1	23.6	11.3	..
Guinea-Bissau	147	99	270	18	16.0	..	..	..
Haiti	1,120	114	3,496	269	..	183.4	75.1	..

Aid dependency

	Net official development assistance				Aid dependency ratios			
	Total $ millions	Per capita $	$ millions Grants	Technical cooperation	% of GNI	Net official development assistance % of gross capital formation	% of imports of goods, services, and income	% of central government expense
	2010	2010	2010	2010	2010	2010	2010	2010
Honduras	456	61	279	55	3.9	16.3	5.5	16.0
Hungary	..	..	..	..	..	..	..	..
India	2,500	2	1,007	283	0.2	0.5	0.6	1.1
Indonesia	1,047	4	851	520	0.2	0.6	0.8	1.4
Iran, Islamic Rep.	92	1	78	73	..	..	..	..
Iraq	2,791	90	1,881	126	2.8	..	..	..
Ireland								
Israel	..	..	..		..		..	..
Italy								
Jamaica	149	55	152	15	1.0	4.8	2.0	..
Japan								
Jordan	740	125	762	73	3.4	22.6	5.2	13.4
Kazakhstan	298	18	186	50	0.2	0.6	0.3	0.9
Kenya	1,776	45	1,228	153	5.2	24.4	11.8	22.6
Korea, Dem. Rep.	65	3	72	5	..	..	..	..
Korea, Rep.								
Kosovo	781	433	318	275	10.3	35.0	..	..
Kuwait	..	..	..	..	..	..	..	..
Kyrgyz Republic	313	58	296	58	8.7	28.4	8.6	36.8
Lao PDR	419	69	281	110	6.0	21.9	16.9	52.8
Latvia	..	..	..	..	..	..	..	..
Lebanon	580	138	343	90	1.2	3.5	1.4	..
Lesotho	122	57	219	12	10.1	35.7	9.0	..
Liberia	513	134	1,698	30	176.8	..	78.7	..
Libya	41	7	12	9	..	..	0.0	..
Lithuania	..	..	..	..	..	..	..	..
Macedonia, FYR	192	94	97	68	2.0	7.6	2.8	..
Madagascar	444	22	307	67	5.5	..	..	..
Malawi	771	53	880	85	20.6	82.2	..	..
Malaysia	143	5	50	49	0.0	0.0	0.0	0.0
Mali	984	66	741	128	12.3	..	..	..
Mauritania	373	111	120	53	10.2	36.6	..	..
Mauritius	155	122	73	20	1.3	5.7	2.0	5.7
Mexico	184	2	286	112	0.0	0.2	0.1	..
Moldova	244	68	241	54	7.5	34.1	9.7	23.0
Mongolia	371	137	189	96	5.4	12.0	6.7	18.4
Morocco	930	29	424	291	1.1	3.1	2.4	3.6
Mozambique	2,012	88	1,443	171	20.8	86.2	39.9	..
Myanmar	356	7	339	57	..	..	5.1	..
Namibia	326	145	194	44	2.1	9.1	4.0	..
Nepal	854	29	684	125	..	..	13.7	..
Netherlands								
New Zealand								
Nicaragua	773	135	316	98	10.0	34.9	10.9	47.8
Niger	469	31	589	105	13.6	..	..	..
Nigeria	1,657	11	827	198	1.2	..	2.2	..
Norway								
Oman	154	57	18	3	..	..	−0.1	..
Pakistan	2,769	16	2,743	232	1.6	11.1	6.9	9.7
Panama	65	19	27	18	0.5	1.8	0.6	..
Papua New Guinea	412	61	221	313	5.5	30.4	7.4	..
Paraguay	148	23	104	53	0.6	2.9	0.9	3.8
Peru	441	15	327	173	−0.2	−0.7	−0.6	−1.0
Philippines	309	3	429	212	0.3	1.3	0.7	1.6
Poland	..	..	..	..	..	..	..	..
Portugal								
Puerto Rico	..	..	..		..	..	..	..
Qatar	..	..	..		..		..	..

6.12 | Aid dependency

	Net official development assistance				Aid dependency ratios			
	Total $ millions	Per capita $	$ millions			Net official development assistance			
			Grants	Technical cooperation	% of GNI	% of gross capital formation	% of imports of goods, services, and income	% of central government expense
	2010	2010	2010	2010	2010	2010	2010	2010
Romania	..	..	..	..	..	..	..	..
Russian Federation	..	..	..	..	..	..	..	..
Rwanda	934	91	848	153	18.5	..	60.9	..
Saudi Arabia	..	..	..	..	..	..	..	..
Senegal	1,016	84	449	195	7.2	24.8	..	..
Serbia	614	84	444	127	1.7	7.4	3.1	4.3
Sierra Leone	448	78	301	75	24.9	158.2	50.6	..
Singapore	..	..	..	..	..	..	..	..
Slovak Republic	..	..	..	..	..	..	..	..
Slovenia	..	..	..	..	..	..	..	..
Somalia	662	73	470	30	..	..	..	..
South Africa	1,075	22	841	161	0.3	1.1	0.9	..
South Sudan	..	..	..	..	..	..	..	..
Spain								
Sri Lanka	703	34	332	78	1.2	4.2	3.6	..
Sudan	2,351	55	1,760	228	3.7	14.2	14.9	..
Swaziland	56	54	90	8	2.6	15.3	3.0	..
Sweden								
Switzerland								
Syrian Arab Republic	208	10	203	119	0.2	1.2	0.6	..
Tajikistan	408	60	267	40	7.7	33.4	12.6	..
Tanzania	2,933	67	1,814	214	12.9	42.0	31.7	..
Thailand	−78	−1	167	115	0.0	0.0	0.0	0.0
Timor-Leste	216	197	144	149	10.8	..	..	..
Togo	499	84	455	52	14.9	..	..	92.1
Trinidad and Tobago	7	5	3	2	0.0	..	..	..
Tunisia	503	48	142	162	1.3	4.7	2.1	4.6
Turkey	1,362	19	340	154	0.1	0.7	0.5	0.6
Turkmenistan	40	8	24	20	0.2	0.4	..	..
Uganda	1,785	55	1,189	105	10.3	42.8	26.9	..
Ukraine	666	14	338	239	0.5	2.3	0.8	..
United Arab Emirates	..	..	..	..	..	..	..	..
United Kingdom								
United States								
Uruguay	50	15	30	24	0.1	0.7	0.4	0.4
Uzbekistan	190	7	70	53	0.6	2.2	..	..
Venezuela, RB	66	2	36	19	0.0	0.1	0.1	..
Vietnam	3,732	43	656	378	2.9	7.1	3.2	..
West Bank and Gaza	2,817	697	2,345	169	..	..	..	..
Yemen, Rep.	558	24	523	63	2.3	18.3	5.2	..
Zambia	1,267	100	706	72	6.4	25.2	12.1	32.9
Zimbabwe	736	59	669	78	10.6	1,860.4	..	..
World	**126,968 s**	**19 w**	..	..	**0.2 w**	**0.9 w**	**0.6 w**	..
Low income	36,252	46	..	..	9.6	40.9	24.6	..
Middle income	54,621	11	..	..	0.3	0.8	0.9	..
Lower middle income	40,510	16	..	..	0.9	3.0	2.6	..
Upper middle income	13,151	5	..	..	0.1	0.2	0.3	..
Low & middle income	126,593	22	95,651	19,564	0.7	2.0	2.1	..
East Asia & Pacific	10,165	5	..	..	0.1	0.3	0.4	..
Europe & Central Asia	8,087	20	..	..	0.2	1.0	0.7	..
Latin America & Carib.	9,036	16	..	..	0.2	1.0	0.9	..
Middle East & N. Africa	13,383	41	..	..	0.9	..	3.1	..
South Asia	14,591	9	..	..	0.7	2.3	2.7	..
Sub-Saharan Africa	44,582	54	..	..	4.3	18.8	9.9	..
High income	374	0	..	..	0.0	0.0	0.0	..
Euro area	..	..	..	..	..	..	..	..

Note: Regional aggregates include data for economies not listed in the table. World and income group totals include aid not allocated by country or region—including administrative costs, research on development issues, and aid to nongovernmental organizations. Thus regional and income group totals do not sum to the world total.

About the data

The flows of official and private financial resources from the members of the Development Assistance Committee (DAC) of the Organisation for Economic Co-operation and Development (OECD) to developing economies are compiled by DAC, based principally on reporting by DAC members using standard questionnaires issued by the DAC Secretariat.

DAC exists to help its members coordinate their development assistance and to encourage the expansion and improve the effectiveness of the aggregate resources flowing to recipient economies. In this capacity DAC monitors the flow of all financial resources, but its main concern is official development assistance (ODA). Grants or loans to countries and territories on the DAC list of aid recipients have to meet three criteria to be counted as ODA. They are provided by official agencies, including state and local governments, or by their executive agencies. They promote economic development and welfare as the main objective. And they are provided on concessional financial terms (loans must have a grant element of at least 25 percent, calculated at a discount rate of 10 percent). The DAC Statistical Reporting Directives provide the most detailed explanation of this definition and all ODA-related rules.

This definition excludes nonconcessional flows from official creditors, which are classified as "other official flows," and aid for military and anti-terrorism purposes. Transfer payments to private individuals, such as pensions, reparations, and insurance payouts, are in general not counted. In addition to financial flows, ODA includes technical cooperation, most expenditures for peacekeeping under UN mandates and assistance to refugees, contributions to multilateral institutions such as the United Nations and its specialized agencies, and concessional funding to multilateral development banks.

Flows are transfers of resources, either in cash or in the form of commodities or services measured on a cash basis. Short-term capital transactions (with one year or less maturity) are not counted. Repayments of the principal (but not interest) of ODA loans are recorded as negative flows. Proceeds from official equity investments in a developing country are reported as ODA, while proceeds from their later sale are recorded as negative flows.

The table shows data on ODA for aid-receiving countries. The data cover loans and grants from DAC member countries, multilateral organizations, and non-DAC donors. They do not reflect aid given by recipient countries to other developing countries. As a result, some countries that are net donors (such as Saudi Arabia) are shown in the table as aid recipients (see table 6.13a).

The table does not distinguish types of aid (program, project, or food aid; emergency assistance; or post-conflict peacekeeping assistance), which may have different effects on the economy.

Ratios of aid to gross national income (GNI), gross capital formation, imports, and government spending provide measures of recipient country dependency on aid. But care must be taken in drawing policy conclusions. For foreign policy reasons some countries have traditionally received large amounts of aid. Thus aid dependency ratios may reveal as much about a donor's interests as about a recipient's needs. Ratios are generally much higher in Sub-Saharan Africa than in other regions, and they increased in the 1980s. High ratios are due only in part to aid flows. Many African countries saw severe erosion in their terms of trade in the 1980s, which, along with weak policies, contributed to falling incomes, imports, and investment. Thus the increase in aid dependency ratios reflects events affecting both the numerator (aid) and the denominator (GNI).

Because the table relies on information from donors, it is not necessarily consistent with information recorded by recipients in the balance of payments, which often excludes all or some technical assistance—particularly payments to expatriates made directly by the donor. Similarly, grant commodity aid may not always be recorded in trade data or in the balance of payments. Moreover, DAC statistics exclude aid for military and antiterrorism purposes.

The nominal values used here may overstate the real value of aid to recipients. Changes in international prices and exchange rates can reduce the purchasing power of aid. Tying aid, still prevalent though declining in importance, also tends to reduce its purchasing power. Tying requires recipients to purchase goods and services from the donor country or from a specified group of countries. Such arrangements prevent a recipient from misappropriating or mismanaging aid receipts, but they may also be motivated by a desire to benefit donor country suppliers.

The aggregates refer to World Bank classifications of economies and therefore may differ from those of the OECD.

Definitions

• **Net official development assistance** is flows (net of repayment of principal) that meet the DAC definition of ODA and are made to countries and territories on the DAC list of aid recipients. • **Net official development assistance per capita** is net ODA divided by midyear population. • **Grants** are legally binding commitments that obligate a specific value of funds available for disbursement for which there is no payment requirement. • **Technical cooperation** is the provision of resources whose main aim is to augment the stock of human intellectual capital, such as the level of knowledge, skills, and technical know-how in the recipient country (including the cost of associated equipment). Contributions take the form mainly of the supply of human resources from donors or action directed to human resources (such as training or advice). Also included are aid for promoting development awareness and aid provided to refugees in the donor economy. Assistance specifically to facilitate a capital project is not included. • **Aid dependency ratios** are calculated using values in U.S. dollars converted at official exchange rates. Imports of goods, services, and income refer to international transactions involving a change in ownership of general merchandise, goods sent for processing and repairs, nonmonetary gold, services, receipts of employee compensation for nonresident workers, and investment income. For definitions of GNI, gross capital formation, and central government expense, see *Definitions* for tables 1.1, 4.8, and 4.10.

Data sources

Data on financial flows are compiled by OECD DAC and published in its annual statistical report, *Geographical Distribution of Financial Flows to Developing Countries*, and in its annual *Development Co-operation Report*. Data are available electronically on the OECD DAC *International Development Statistics* CD-ROM and at www.oecd.org/dac/stats/idsonline. Data on population, GNI, gross capital formation, imports of goods and services, and central government expense used in computing the ratios are from World Bank and International Monetary Fund databases.

	Total $ millions	United States	EU institutions	Germany	United Kingdom	France	Japan	Netherlands	Spain	Canada	Norway	Other DAC donors $ millions
	2010	**2010**	**2010**	**2010**	**2010**	**2010**	**2010**	**2010**	**2010**	**2010**	**2010**	**2010**
Afghanistan	5,701.3	2,893.4	285.0	469.8	234.8	58.6	745.7	59.2	60.8	267.1	120.2	506.8
Albania	301.6	30.1	75.0	35.4	0.9	4.3	2.4	4.0	4.8	0.0	2.5	142.2
Algeria	194.7	8.6	51.8	10.2	2.2	69.8	15.5	0.2	9.5	−0.5	1.0	26.5
Angola	174.0	54.8	24.4	7.1	16.7	4.1	37.6	−2.7	5.5	0.7	13.2	12.7
Argentina	149.4	3.9	8.0	21.9	0.5	13.5	73.8	0.5	23.0	1.0	0.1	3.2
Armenia	238.8	91.6	33.4	16.7	0.5	4.5	77.5	1.2	0.3	0.0	3.6	9.7
Australia												
Austria												
Azerbaijan	81.2	35.9	20.8	15.9	0.9	5.1	−11.0	0.0	0.1	0.0	3.4	10.2
Bahrain	..	..	..	..	..	..	..	..	..	..	..	..
Bangladesh	1,071.6	124.7	188.7	65.1	228.3	−3.0	24.2	78.0	5.5	86.1	16.9	257.2
Belarus	96.0	27.2	15.2	18.0	0.4	4.1	1.4	0.0	0.3	0.0	2.2	27.2
Belgium												
Benin	461.8	98.9	122.8	34.7	0.0	48.8	29.1	31.3	1.1	6.4	0.1	88.7
Bolivia	521.4	86.1	64.7	42.5	0.1	12.2	54.2	46.9	69.0	19.0	5.9	120.8
Bosnia and Herzegovina	348.2	28.3	105.1	30.0	9.7	3.5	2.2	14.3	20.2	0.4	18.2	116.4
Botswana	145.4	77.0	39.3	2.4	1.1	6.5	10.7	0.0	0.0	1.5	0.6	6.3
Brazil	632.3	24.4	21.3	247.5	40.7	46.6	−62.7	0.4	26.4	7.1	245.4	35.2
Bulgaria	..	..	..	..	..	..	..	..	..	..	..	..
Burkina Faso	619.9	62.1	164.1	52.5	0.1	63.8	41.6	51.4	12.3	30.8	0.8	140.4
Burundi	413.8	43.5	131.2	29.5	20.1	15.2	39.1	19.1	1.2	4.7	19.5	90.8
Cambodia	544.8	84.7	27.3	41.3	26.0	26.6	147.5	1.3	23.1	8.2	4.7	154.3
Cameroon	340.7	18.0	74.2	90.5	1.0	82.1	42.0	0.2	9.0	7.2	0.4	16.0
Canada												
Central African Republic	197.6	20.5	84.8	3.1	3.0	24.5	8.1	2.0	3.3	1.4	0.0	46.9
Chad	386.9	134.6	101.9	20.1	2.9	40.7	13.8	4.9	7.8	11.7	1.7	47.1
Chile	173.4	13.3	16.2	71.8	0.7	10.1	15.9	0.3	11.3	2.7	13.1	18.2
China	745.4	86.5	42.6	321.5	86.7	316.7	−192.7	4.0	1.4	9.0	22.6	47.1
Hong Kong SAR, China	..	..	..	..	..	..	..	..	..	..	..	..
Colombia	840.7	424.0	53.7	45.3	2.6	160.3	−26.2	26.3	56.2	22.6	14.2	61.8
Congo, Dem. Rep.	2,750.9	277.9	364.3	77.1	250.8	13.5	80.0	420.5	306.2	26.5	28.3	905.9
Congo, Rep.	1,247.5	21.4	32.2	9.4	78.8	909.4	6.0	0.0	0.5	21.9	0.6	167.4
Costa Rica	94.2	0.7	4.2	21.9	0.8	4.8	63.7	3.4	5.2	0.7	0.5	−11.8
Côte d'Ivoire	504.5	76.3	66.9	92.6	26.0	138.5	81.3	5.5	−7.6	6.9	1.7	16.5
Croatia	142.2	0.2	105.4	22.5	1.1	3.8	1.9	0.2	0.4	0.0	3.5	3.3
Cuba	112.4	16.4	24.9	2.5	0.4	2.7	5.2	0.1	42.8	5.7	1.1	10.6
Cyprus	..	..	..	..	..	..	..	..	..	..	..	..
Czech Republic	..	..	..	..	..	..	..	..	..	..	..	..
Denmark												
Dominican Republic	172.5	35.5	80.7	0.9	0.1	1.0	−1.9	0.2	49.9	1.3	0.3	4.6
Ecuador	160.8	33.0	24.7	27.8	0.0	0.5	−5.2	0.5	55.3	1.4	3.1	19.7
Egypt, Arab Rep.	502.8	52.7	136.9	104.5	9.0	140.1	−17.7	11.0	7.2	8.9	0.7	49.7
El Salvador	291.1	151.3	52.5	17.1	−48.8	3.3	8.8	0.1	85.5	2.0	1.1	18.2
Eritrea	70.8	0.9	37.1	1.1	5.5	0.7	9.9	0.5	0.2	0.0	9.6	5.4
Estonia	..	..	..	..	..	..	..	..	..	..	..	..
Ethiopia	2,164.3	875.3	237.6	96.5	407.0	13.3	93.9	53.2	39.5	140.4	32.6	175.1
Finland												
France												
Gabon	96.9	1.5	13.1	−1.3	0.2	58.1	24.8	0.0	0.2	0.1	0.0	0.3
Gambia, The	56.0	6.5	22.7	0.6	2.0	0.4	17.2	0.0	4.0	0.5	0.1	2.1
Georgia	504.7	202.2	154.7	82.0	3.4	6.2	6.5	3.2	0.1	0.0	10.0	36.4
Germany												
Ghana	1,005.2	208.1	105.6	58.2	166.6	33.8	70.0	72.9	14.3	114.2	3.6	158.1
Greece												
Guatemala	390.3	105.0	37.4	13.5	0.2	3.3	41.2	19.6	92.9	10.3	9.4	57.6
Guinea	164.1	21.7	72.4	13.3	0.0	36.0	10.8	0.0	2.1	2.2	0.0	5.6
Guinea-Bissau	70.4	6.5	16.6	1.3	0.1	1.8	16.1	0.0	8.3	0.5	0.0	19.1
Haiti	2,612.1	1,106.9	284.3	43.6	26.2	144.1	72.0	19.2	155.8	458.9	66.8	234.6

Distribution of net aid by Development Assistance Committee members

| | Ten major DAC donors | | | | | | | | | | | |
	Total $ millions 2010	United States 2010	EU institutions 2010	Germany 2010	United Kingdom 2010	France 2010	Japan 2010	Netherlands 2010	Spain 2010	Canada 2010	Norway 2010	Other DAC donors $ millions 2010
Honduras	339.0	102.9	58.5	14.1	25.3	1.4	16.0	0.3	69.1	17.6	1.5	32.4
Hungary	..	..	..	..	..	..	..	..	..	..	..	..
India	2,313.5	57.4	94.3	396.9	650.3	2.8	981.1	2.5	11.4	7.9	24.0	84.8
Indonesia	1,093.5	180.3	105.5	−12.6	26.9	262.5	61.1	34.1	−10.6	10.9	41.9	393.6
Iran, Islamic Rep.	76.1	1.6	3.4	45.8	0.0	14.2	−7.1	3.4	0.2	0.1	7.3	7.3
Iraq	2,059.3	1,622.9	54.1	36.9	31.0	9.6	144.4	2.6	0.4	6.3	7.7	143.5
Ireland												
Israel	..	..	..	..	..	..	..	..	..	..	..	..
Italy												
Jamaica	104.5	−3.6	106.4	−6.2	3.9	−0.4	−2.1	−2.9	0.5	4.1	0.1	4.7
Japan												
Jordan	544.4	371.6	129.9	39.4	2.6	6.2	−50.9	1.0	9.2	7.1	0.4	27.9
Kazakhstan	112.7	68.1	17.4	13.6	0.3	4.1	−1.8	0.4	0.1	0.1	4.3	6.2
Kenya	1,260.5	565.9	101.6	79.8	105.2	123.4	36.7	17.6	8.3	25.9	13.4	182.6
Korea, Dem. Rep.	42.6	5.4	14.8	2.5	0.4	0.7	0.0	0.1	0.0	0.0	2.5	16.2
Korea, Rep.												
Kosovo	558.2	101.0	279.3	30.6	9.5	1.7	1.1	3.2	0.1	0.0	24.2	107.5
Kuwait	..	..	..	..	..	..	..	..	..	..	..	..
Kyrgyz Republic	182.9	56.0	24.4	25.3	7.3	1.5	23.2	0.6	0.9	2.0	6.3	35.6
Lao PDR	301.9	12.8	16.0	24.8	0.1	15.0	121.5	0.1	0.0	0.6	2.6	108.5
Latvia	..	..	..	..	..	..	..	..	..	..	..	..
Lebanon	316.9	84.1	53.4	28.1	4.0	59.7	3.2	1.0	23.4	5.3	9.3	45.7
Lesotho	168.4	57.5	74.3	5.0	4.8	−1.4	8.8	0.0	0.0	0.4	1.1	17.9
Liberia	793.4	131.4	90.9	50.1	25.6	232.0	134.3	40.0	1.8	1.1	22.8	63.3
Libya	18.4	6.6	1.1	3.5	1.6	3.8	0.1	0.1	0.2	0.0	..	1.5
Lithuania	..	..	..	..	..	..	..	..	..	..	..	..
Macedonia, FYR	150.1	20.4	55.1	14.1	1.2	2.9	23.1	2.3	0.4	0.0	7.5	23.2
Madagascar	254.5	77.0	40.1	13.1	−0.3	84.0	9.6	0.0	0.3	1.9	13.0	15.7
Malawi	725.5	126.3	208.3	41.9	148.0	−1.0	69.5	0.0	0.6	16.5	64.7	50.5
Malaysia	−13.7	18.6	1.2	11.2	−0.8	1.0	−53.2	0.2	0.1	0.0	0.8	7.2
Mali	782.4	197.9	98.5	60.3	0.1	77.6	38.3	56.1	28.4	96.0	16.0	113.2
Mauritania	130.9	11.4	25.3	7.7	0.0	32.2	14.6	0.0	34.7	0.5	0.6	4.0
Mauritius	126.0	0.5	67.9	−0.2	5.5	54.0	−2.9	0.0	0.0	0.0	0.3	0.8
Mexico	428.6	205.6	7.5	35.5	9.4	205.8	−46.7	−0.3	5.3	1.4	0.1	5.0
Moldova	228.4	19.4	138.0	8.7	14.5	6.4	0.9	5.6	0.1	0.2	3.0	31.7
Mongolia	232.1	47.2	13.4	29.1	0.8	5.0	53.9	8.8	−0.3	8.3	1.7	64.2
Morocco	822.3	47.7	223.4	38.9	3.2	254.4	121.2	1.1	90.6	3.1	0.0	38.6
Mozambique	1,549.7	277.9	192.3	76.9	104.4	38.1	62.9	81.8	43.9	82.0	73.7	515.7
Myanmar	304.1	31.3	55.9	18.3	44.2	2.0	46.8	2.7	0.0	0.6	21.7	80.5
Namibia	222.1	117.2	10.8	24.0	0.6	0.4	40.6	1.6	8.5	0.5	−3.0	20.9
Nepal	521.9	51.9	46.2	42.0	105.2	−3.2	81.2	0.0	0.2	11.8	47.2	139.4
Netherlands												
New Zealand												
Nicaragua	416.2	54.5	21.9	27.7	7.3	1.0	34.4	26.3	106.2	12.5	18.5	106.1
Niger	531.6	102.6	150.8	22.6	3.2	50.0	25.2	2.8	25.9	53.7	3.5	91.4
Nigeria	909.5	445.9	60.3	39.0	264.6	8.9	23.9	9.1	0.5	12.6	14.1	30.7
Norway												
Oman	7.6	2.9	0.0	1.0	0.9	0.8	1.5	0.4	0.0	0.0	0.0	0.0
Pakistan	2,586.5	1,196.8	172.3	142.1	298.5	14.4	207.9	52.1	22.7	101.9	83.1	294.8
Panama	125.3	11.9	1.5	1.4	0.0	0.1	101.8	0.0	5.9	0.5	2.4	−0.3
Papua New Guinea	490.8	2.3	50.1	0.8	1.0	0.2	22.2	0.0	0.2	0.1	1.8	412.2
Paraguay	97.4	28.0	29.9	5.4	0.0	0.1	−3.7	0.0	21.8	0.5	1.0	14.4
Peru	−288.2	130.6	25.8	51.9	1.3	10.1	−711.6	0.3	118.1	22.2	3.8	59.5
Philippines	505.0	114.8	51.9	26.3	0.6	189.4	−87.7	0.4	27.0	16.7	17.6	148.1
Poland	..	..	..	..	..	..	..	..	..	..	..	..
Portugal												
Puerto Rico	..	..	..	..	..	..	..	..	..	..	..	..
Qatar												

6.13 Distribution of net aid by Development Assistance Committee members

	Total $ millions 2010	Ten major DAC donors — $ millions										Other DAC donors $ millions 2010
		United States 2010	EU institutions 2010	Germany 2010	United Kingdom 2010	France 2010	Japan 2010	Netherlands 2010	Spain 2010	Canada 2010	Norway 2010	
Romania	..	..	..	..	..	..	..	..	..	..	..	..
Russian Federation	..	..	..	..	..	..	..	..	..	..	..	..
Rwanda	652.1	140.6	104.4	48.3	106.2	4.1	22.8	39.4	1.8	58.7	4.4	121.5
Saudi Arabia	..	..	..	..	..	..	..	..	..	..	..	..
Senegal	618.4	101.4	84.1	23.1	0.9	157.2	55.2	30.0	45.6	56.7	0.3	64.0
Serbia	603.2	57.9	290.1	126.3	5.4	14.0	5.2	3.8	0.4	0.8	20.2	79.2
Sierra Leone	279.9	29.8	80.3	13.3	84.8	0.3	12.2	1.1	1.9	33.0	3.0	20.1
Singapore	..	..	..	..	..	..	..	..	..	..	..	..
Slovak Republic	..	..	..	..	..	..	..	..	..	..	..	..
Slovenia	..	..	..	..	..	..	..	..	..	..	..	..
Somalia	435.5	59.4	127.1	12.5	62.3	3.5	29.1	9.3	5.9	4.4	31.6	90.5
South Africa	974.7	529.5	153.1	39.5	39.3	47.6	7.1	36.1	1.1	16.5	24.7	80.1
South Sudan	..	..	..	..	..	..	..	..	..	..	..	..
Spain												
Sri Lanka	433.8	26.1	48.1	−6.4	−8.5	45.1	155.4	3.6	−0.7	11.5	29.0	130.6
Sudan	1,793.4	726.4	284.2	39.2	119.1	10.1	119.1	57.6	23.0	108.3	116.7	189.9
Swaziland	52.6	23.6	21.5	−0.6	0.0	0.2	4.4	0.0	0.0	0.8	1.6	1.3
Sweden												
Switzerland												
Syrian Arab Republic	95.7	6.9	51.6	45.9	2.0	23.1	−54.7	0.1	6.1	0.1	1.3	13.4
Tajikistan	201.2	45.9	36.6	34.7	12.5	0.2	43.4	0.6	0.0	0.7	3.2	23.3
Tanzania	1,848.1	457.4	192.6	134.5	240.9	21.3	104.6	59.2	3.2	111.6	124.0	398.8
Thailand	−76.1	47.2	24.1	−23.2	7.2	−13.6	−143.5	0.3	0.6	−0.6	0.3	25.3
Timor-Leste	272.7	27.3	14.6	9.4	0.0	0.1	27.7	0.0	6.0	1.1	7.8	178.7
Togo	301.7	4.0	48.9	8.8	−0.1	168.0	7.5	17.6	1.6	23.1	0.1	22.1
Trinidad and Tobago	4.1	1.3	0.6	0.4	0.2	0.5	0.1	0.0	0.1	0.3	0.0	0.6
Tunisia	447.6	−3.3	92.3	23.9	2.5	126.8	35.9	−0.7	158.0	−2.9	0.0	15.1
Turkey	1,029.7	6.4	295.2	−10.3	3.8	88.4	543.5	0.3	56.0	−2.6	0.1	49.0
Turkmenistan	17.0	8.4	5.7	1.8	0.1	0.1	−0.9	0.0	0.0	0.0	0.6	1.4
Uganda	1,162.0	378.1	128.9	40.9	179.3	1.8	71.2	36.7	4.3	5.7	71.5	243.6
Ukraine	545.6	140.2	153.0	89.1	0.8	21.5	53.2	0.1	0.3	20.2	3.8	63.4
United Arab Emirates	..	..	..	..	..	..	..	..	..	..	..	..
United Kingdom												
United States												
Uruguay	40.0	1.2	7.1	0.8	0.1	1.2	11.4	0.1	8.4	0.5	0.1	9.4
Uzbekistan	90.8	13.4	6.5	25.0	1.2	2.3	7.0	0.0	0.2	0.0	0.3	34.9
Venezuela, RB	43.4	8.6	5.9	7.0	1.1	6.9	3.1	0.1	8.2	0.4	0.1	2.0
Vietnam	1,866.5	93.1	41.9	96.4	82.2	242.4	807.8	21.2	16.0	25.0	20.2	420.3
West Bank and Gaza	2,069.2	720.8	441.1	104.6	97.6	69.3	78.6	33.7	97.6	65.1	109.5	251.4
Yemen, Rep.	322.8	45.4	40.7	82.1	63.9	7.0	26.7	26.5	1.1	2.6	0.4	26.4
Zambia	685.5	225.1	92.5	33.3	79.3	0.8	46.1	36.1	0.2	8.7	54.1	109.3
Zimbabwe	630.8	175.2	109.5	33.1	108.0	3.0	18.9	11.1	3.6	9.3	24.5	134.6
World	**103,174.7 s**	**26,586.4 s**	**12,428.0 s**	**8,035.5 s**	**8,016.8 s**	**7,786.7 s**	**7,331.1 s**	**4,644.2 s**	**3,998.9 s**	**3,919.6 s**	**3,560.9 s**	**16,866.6 s**
Low income	29,779.4	8,672.4	4,003.4	1,708.5	2,544.1	1,313.1	2,186.9	1,117.1	763.8	1,583.6	848.0	5,038.5
Middle income	41,152.0	10,211.0	6,373.5	3,372.7	2,351.5	4,952.3	3,460.9	724.8	1,637.4	844.5	1,103.9	6,119.4
Lower middle income	29,587.9	7,602.4	3,681.5	1,899.4	2,088.0	2,899.8	3,710.9	519.5	868.2	696.2	671.5	4,950.4
Upper middle income	10,377.3	2,549.0	2,088.8	1,312.3	254.1	1,954.3	−252.0	178.7	715.0	107.2	410.5	1,059.4
Low & middle income	102,918.5	26,581.7	12,301.2	8,011.3	8,014.4	7,778.5	7,326.1	4,643.7	3,978.6	3,918.5	3,557.5	16,807.2
East Asia & Pacific	7,875.1	1,032.2	530.7	565.1	281.2	1,221.0	973.2	73.1	88.4	116.2	151.5	2,842.4
Europe & Central Asia	5,556.1	979.9	1,754.1	664.7	72.5	173.7	780.3	41.4	97.7	37.0	120.8	834.1
Latin America & Carib.	9,201.1	2,720.6	1,268.2	912.0	179.2	664.2	−311.4	223.2	1,369.9	807.1	434.2	933.9
Middle East & N. Africa	8,009.6	3,006.8	1,441.4	622.9	229.7	859.7	335.8	80.1	462.6	123.5	150.0	697.3
South Asia	12,867.1	4,383.0	850.7	1,127.7	1,510.9	115.4	2,277.8	200.0	108.8	498.1	324.5	1,470.1
Sub-Saharan Africa	32,263.2	7,637.2	4,788.9	1,736.0	3,003.3	3,526.9	1,694.5	1,313.7	912.0	1,512.0	945.2	5,193.7
High income	256.2	4.7	126.9	24.3	2.4	8.2	5.0	0.5	20.3	1.0	3.5	59.4
Euro area	..	..	..	..	..	..	..	..	..	..	..	..

Note: Regional aggregates include data for economies not specified elsewhere. World and income group totals include aid not allocated by country or region.

About the data

The table shows net bilateral aid to low- and middle-income economies from members of the Development Assistance Committee (DAC) of the Organisation for Economic Co-operation and Development (OECD). DAC has 24 members—23 individual economies and 1 multilateral institution (European Union institutions).

The table is based on donor country reports of bilateral programs, which may differ from reports by recipient countries. Recipients may lack access to information on such aid expenditures as development-oriented research, stipends and tuition costs for aid-financed students in donor countries, and payment of experts hired by donor countries. Moreover, a full accounting would include donor country contributions to multilateral institutions, the flow of resources from multilateral institutions to recipient countries, and flows from countries that are not members of DAC.

Data in the table exclude DAC members' multilateral aid (contributions to the regular budgets of the multilateral institutions). However, projects executed by multilateral institutions or nongovernmental organizations on behalf of DAC members are classified as bilateral aid (since the donor country effectively controls the use of the funds) and are included in the data reported in the table.

The data include aid to some countries and territories not shown in the table and aid to unspecified economies recorded only at the regional or global level. Aid to countries and territories not shown in the table has been assigned to regional totals based on the World Bank's regional classification system. Aid to unspecified economies is included in regional totals and, when possible, income group totals. Aid not allocated by country or region—including administrative costs, research on development, and aid to nongovernmental organizations—is included in the world total. Thus regional and income group totals do not sum to the world total.

Some of the aid recipients shown in the table are also aid donors. Development cooperation activities by non-DAC members have increased in recent years and in some cases surpass those of individual DAC members. Some non-DAC donors report their development cooperation activities to DAC on a voluntary basis, but many do not yet report their aid flows to DAC. See table 6.13a for a summary of ODA from non-DAC countries.

Definitions

- **Net aid** refers to net bilateral official development assistance that meets the DAC definition of official development assistance and is made to countries and territories on the DAC list of aid recipients.
- **Other DAC donors** are Australia, Austria, Belgium, Denmark, Finland, Greece, Ireland, Italy, the Republic of Korea, Luxembourg, New Zealand, Portugal, Sweden, and Switzerland.

Official development assistance from non-DAC donors, 2006–10   6.13a

Net disbursements ($ millions)

	2006	2007	2008	2009	2010
OECD members (non-DAC)					
Czech Republic	161	179	249	215	228
Hungary	149	103	107	117	114
Iceland	42	48	48	34	29
Poland	297	363	372	375	378
Slovak Republic	55	67	92	75	74
Turkey	714	602	780	707	967
Arab countries					
Kuwait	158	110	283	221	211
Saudi Arabia	2,025	1,551	4,979	3,134	3,480
United Arab Emirates	783	2,426	1,266	834	412
Other donors					
Israel[a]	90	111	138	124	145
Taiwan, China	513	514	435	411	381
Thailand	74	67	178	40	10
Others[b]	121	188	343	385	808
Total	5,181	6,329	9,271	6,672	7,235

Note: The above table does not reflect aid provided by several major emerging non–Organisation for Economic Co-operation and Development (OECD) donors, as information on their aid has not been disclosed. a. Data are supplied by and under the responsibility of the relevant Israeli authorities. The use of such data by the OECD is without prejudice to the status of the Golan Heights, East Jerusalem, and Israeli settlements in the West Bank under the terms of international law. b. Includes Cyprus, Estonia, Latvia, Liechtenstein, Lithuania, Malta, Romania, the Russian Federation, and Slovenia.

Data sources

Data on financial flows are compiled by OECD DAC and published in its annual statistical report, *Geographical Distribution of Financial Flows to Aid Recipients*, and its annual *Development Co-operation Report*. Data are available electronically on the DAC's *International Development Statistics* CD-ROM and at www.oecd.org/dac/stats/idsonline.

6.14 Movement of people across borders

	Net migration	International migrant stock	Emigration of tertiary educated population to OECD countries	Refugees		Workers' remittances and compensation of employees	
			% of tertiary educated population ages 25 and older	thousands		$ millions	
	thousands	thousands		By country of origin	By country of asylum	Received	Paid
	2005–10	2010	2000	2010	2010	2010	2010
Afghanistan	−381	91	22.6	3,054.7	6.4	..	..
Albania	−48	89	17.5	14.8	0.1	1,156	24
Algeria	−140	242	9.5	6.7	94.1	2,044[a]	46
Angola	82	65	3.7	134.9	15.2	82	716
Argentina	−200	1,449	2.8	0.6	3.3	641	993
Armenia	−75	324	8.9	17.5	3.3	996	157
Australia	1,125	4,711	2.7	0.0	21.8	4,840[a]	3,776[a]
Austria	160	1,310	13.5	0.0	42.6	3,220	3,453
Azerbaijan	53	264	1.8	16.8	1.9	1,432	961
Bahrain	448	315	5.1	0.1	0.2	..	1,642
Bangladesh	−2,908	1,085	4.4	10.0	229.3	10,852	9
Belarus	−50	1,090	3.2	5.7	0.6	376	105
Belgium	200	975	5.5	0.1	17.9	10,178	4,040
Benin	50	232	8.7	0.4	7.1	248[a]	88
Bolivia	−165	146	5.8	0.6	0.7	1,088	104
Bosnia and Herzegovina	−10	28	20.3	63.0	7.0	1,905	54
Botswana	19	115	5.1	0.1	3.0	100	102
Brazil	−500	688	2.0	1.0	4.4	4,000	1,198
Bulgaria	−50	107	9.6	2.6	5.5	1,387	25
Burkina Faso	−125	1,043	2.6	1.1	0.5	95[a]	100
Burundi	370	61	9.3	84.1	29.4	28	1
Cambodia	−255	336	21.5	16.3	0.1	369	215
Cameroon	−19	197	17.3	15.0	104.3	195	54
Canada	1,098	7,202	4.7	0.1	165.5	..	..
Central African Republic	5	80	7.3	164.9	21.6	..	..
Chad	−75	388	9.1	53.7	347.9	..	..
Chile	30	320	6.0	1.2	1.6	3	5
China	−1,884[b]	686[b]	3.8	199.7[c]	301.0	53,038[a]	1,754
Hong Kong SAR, China	176	2,742	29.6	0.0	0.2	347	433
Colombia	−120	110	10.4	395.6	0.2	4,058	112
Congo, Dem. Rep.	−24	445	14.9	476.7	166.3	..	..
Congo, Rep.	50	143	28.2	20.7	133.1	15[a]	102
Costa Rica	76	489	7.1	0.4	19.5	552	271
Côte d'Ivoire	−360	2,407	6.2	41.8	26.2	179	754
Croatia	10	700	24.6	65.9	0.9	1,315	164
Cuba	−190	15	28.8	7.5	0.4	..	..
Cyprus	44	154	34.2	0.0	3.4	146	404
Czech Republic	240	453	8.5	0.8	2.4	1,122	1,812
Denmark	90	484	7.8	0.0	17.9	633	3,184
Dominican Republic	−140	434	22.4	0.2	0.6	3,369	29
Ecuador	−120	394	9.5	0.9	121.2	2,569	81
Egypt, Arab Rep.	−347	245	4.7	6.9	95.1	7,725	255
El Salvador	−292	40	31.7	5.0	0.0	3,449	23
Eritrea	55	16	35.2	222.5	4.8	..	..
Estonia	0	182	9.9	0.2	0.0	322	94
Ethiopia	−300	548	9.8	68.8	154.3	225	27
Finland	73	226	7.2	0.0	8.7	826	437
France	500	6,685	3.5	0.1	200.7	15,629	5,264
Gabon	5	284	14.6	0.2	9.0	..	..
Gambia, The	−14	290	67.8	2.2	8.4	116	58
Georgia	−150	167	2.8	10.6	0.6	806	50
Germany	550	10,758	5.8	0.2	594.3	11,338	15,908
Ghana	−51	1,852	44.7	20.2	13.8	136	..
Greece	154	1,133	12.2	0.1	1.4	1,499	1,932
Guatemala	−200	59	23.9	5.7	0.1	4,229	21
Guinea	−300	395	4.7	12.0	14.1	60	43
Guinea-Bissau	−10	19	27.7	1.1	7.7	48	17[a]
Haiti	−240	35	83.4	25.9	0.0	1,499	135

	Net migration	International migrant stock	Emigration of tertiary educated population to OECD countries	Refugees		Workers' remittances and compensation of employees	
			% of tertiary educated population ages 25 and older	thousands		$ millions	
	thousands	thousands		By country of origin	By country of asylum	Received	Paid
	2005–10	2010	2000	2010	2010	2010	2010
Honduras	−100	24	24.8	1.3	0.0	2,649	12
Hungary	75	368	12.8	1.4	5.4	2,265	1,265
India	−3,000	5,436	4.3	17.8	184.8	54,035	3,888
Indonesia	−1,293	123	2.9	16.9	0.8	6,916	2,840
Iran, Islamic Rep.	−186	2,129	14.3	68.8	1,073.4	1,181[a]	..
Iraq	−150	83	10.9	1,683.6	34.7	71	32[a]
Ireland	100	899	33.7	0.0	9.1	601	1,751
Israel	274	2,940	7.8	1.3	25.5	1,411	3,739
Italy	1,999	4,463	9.7	0.1	56.4	6,803	12,201
Jamaica	−100	30	84.7	1.1	0.0	2,011	314
Japan	270	2,176	1.2	0.2	2.6	1,802	4,474
Jordan	203	2,973	7.4	2.3	2,455.7[d]	3,641	495
Kazakhstan	7	3,079	1.2	3.6	4.4	291	3,021
Kenya	−189	818	38.5	8.6	402.9	1,777[a]	61
Korea, Dem. Rep.	0	37	..	0.9	..	..	..
Korea, Rep.	−30	535	7.5	0.6	0.4	8,708	11,385
Kosovo	..	..	..	..	..	932	146
Kuwait	278	2,098	7.1	1.0	0.2	..	11,770
Kyrgyz Republic	−132	223	0.9	2.7	2.5	1,275[a]	297
Lao PDR	−75	19	37.2	8.4	..	41	8
Latvia	−10	335	8.5	0.7	0.1	614	43
Lebanon	−13	758	43.9	15.9	435.1[d]	7,558	3,737
Lesotho	−20	6	4.1	0.0	..	746	19
Liberia	300	96	44.3	70.1	24.7	27[a]	1
Libya	−20	682	4.3	2.3	7.9	17[a]	1,361
Lithuania	−35	129	8.4	0.5	0.8	1,575	538
Macedonia, FYR	2	130	29.4	7.9	1.4	388	23
Madagascar	−5	38	7.7	0.3	..	..	..
Malawi	−20	276	20.9	0.2	5.7	..	..
Malaysia	84	2,358	10.5	0.6	81.5	1,301	6,528
Mali	−101	163	14.8	3.7	13.6	436[a]	167
Mauritania	10	99	8.6	37.7	26.7	..	..
Mauritius	0	43	56.0	0.0	..	226[a]	13
Mexico	−1,805	726	15.5	6.8	1.4	22,048	..
Moldova	−172	408	4.1	6.2	0.1	1,370	117
Mongolia	−15	10	7.4	1.7	0.0	277	169
Morocco	−675	49	18.6	2.3	0.8	6,423	62
Mozambique	−20	450	22.6	0.1	4.1	132	80
Myanmar	−500	89	3.9	415.7	..	133[a]	..
Namibia	−1	139	3.4	1.0	7.3	15	16
Nepal	−100	946	4.0	5.9	89.8	3,468	32
Netherlands	50	1,753	9.6	0.1	75.0	3,834	12,923
New Zealand	65	962	21.8	0.0	2.3	843	1,167
Nicaragua	−200	40	30.2	1.4	0.1	823	..
Niger	−28	202	5.5	0.8	0.3	88	22[a]
Nigeria	−300	1,128	10.5	15.6	8.7	10,045[a]	48
Norway	171	485	6.2	0.0	40.3	680	4,045
Oman	153	826	0.4	0.1	0.1	39	5,704
Pakistan	−2,000	4,234	12.7	40.0	1,900.6	9,690	19
Panama	11	121	16.7	0.1	17.1	231	248
Papua New Guinea	0	25	27.8	0.1	9.7	15	323
Paraguay	−40	161	3.8	0.1	0.1	673	..
Peru	−725	38	5.8	5.8	1.1	2,534	122
Philippines	−1,233	435	13.6	1.0	0.2	21,423	62
Poland	56	827	14.3	1.8	15.6	7,614	1,575
Portugal	150	919	19.0	0.0	0.4	3,540	1,406
Puerto Rico	−145	324	..	..	..	..	..
Qatar	857	1,305	2.1	0.1	0.1	..	..

	Net migration	International migrant stock	Emigration of tertiary educated population to OECD countries	Refugees		Workers' remittances and compensation of employees	
			% of tertiary educated population ages 25 and older	thousands		$ millions	
	thousands	thousands		By country of origin	By country of asylum	Received	Paid
	2005–10	2010	2000	2010	2010	2010	2010
Romania	–100	133	11.3	3.9	1.0	3,883	355
Russian Federation	1,136	12,270	1.4	111.9	4.9	5,264	18,796
Rwanda	15	465	31.7	114.8	55.4	92	71
Saudi Arabia	1,056	7,289	0.9	0.7	0.6	236	27,069
Senegal	–133	210	17.2	16.3	20.7	1,346	144[a]
Serbia	0	525	..	183.3	73.6	3,351[a]	70
Sierra Leone	60	107	49.2	11.3	8.4	58	6
Singapore	722	1,967	14.5	0.1	0.0	..	..
Slovak Republic	37	131	14.3	0.2	0.5	1,591	70
Slovenia	22	164	11.0	0.0	0.3	309	158
Somalia	–300	23	34.5	770.2	1.9	..	..
South Africa	700	1,863	7.4	0.4	57.9	1,119	1,372
South Sudan	..	..	..	..	..	..	..
Spain	2,250	6,378	4.2	0.0	3.8	10,507	12,227
Sri Lanka	–250	340	28.2	141.1	0.2	4,155	545
Sudan	135	753	6.8	387.3	178.3	1,974[a]	1[a]
Swaziland	–6	40	5.4	0.0	0.8	109	11
Sweden	266	1,306	4.5	0.0	82.6	688	695
Switzerland	183	1,763	9.6	0.0	48.8	2,619	21,668
Syrian Arab Republic	–56	2,206	6.2	18.5	1,483.2[d]	1,646[a]	214[a]
Tajikistan	–296	284	0.6	0.6	3.1	2,254	856
Tanzania	–300	659	12.1	1.1	109.3	25	127
Thailand	492	1,157	2.2	0.4	96.7	1,764	..
Timor-Leste	–50	14	16.5	0.0	0.0	..	..
Togo	–5	185	16.5	18.3	14.1	333[a]	72[a]
Trinidad and Tobago	–20	34	78.9	0.3	0.0	120[a]	..
Tunisia	–20	34	12.6	2.2	0.1	1,970	13
Turkey	–50	1,411	5.8	146.8	10.0	874	175
Turkmenistan	–54	208	0.4	0.7	0.1	..	..
Uganda	–135	647	36.0	6.4	135.8	915	602
Ukraine	–40	5,258	4.3	25.1	3.0	5,607	24
United Arab Emirates	3,077	3,293	0.7	0.4	0.5	..	..
United Kingdom	1,020	6,452	17.1	0.2	238.2	7,532	3,528
United States	4,955	42,813	0.5	3.0	264.6	5,277	51,597
Uruguay	–50	80	9.0	0.2	0.2	103	7
Uzbekistan	–518	1,176	0.8	8.8	0.3	..	..
Venezuela, RB	40	1,007	3.8	6.7	201.5	143	805
Vietnam	–431	69	27.0	338.7	1.9	8,260[a]	..
West Bank and Gaza	–90	1,924	12.0	93.3	1,910.7[d]	1,151[a]	9[a]
Yemen, Rep.	–135	518	6.0	2.1	190.1	1,240	337
Zambia	–85	233	16.4	0.2	47.9	44	68
Zimbabwe	–900	372	13.1	24.1	4.4	..	..
World	..[e] s	213,397[f] s	5.4 w	15,369.9[d,g] s	15,369.9[d] s	449,197 s	303,799 s
Low income	–6,818	11,158	11.8	5,650.8	1,874.0	24,553	3,088
Middle income	–16,342	70,369	6.8	4,518.3	11,535.2	300,725	55,580
Lower middle income	–12,613	31,148	8.0	3,223.5	6,412.2	161,464	11,579
Upper middle income	–3,729	39,220	6.1	1,294.8	5,123.0	139,262	44,001
Low & middle income	–23,160	81,527	7.1	10,169.1	13,409.2	325,278	58,668
East Asia & Pacific	–5,221	5,434	7.0	1,002.3	492.0	93,957	11,945
Europe & Central Asia	–595	27,681	3.5	637.2	140.8	36,037	25,865
Latin America & Carib.	–5,088	6,569	10.6	470.4	373.8	57,275	4,603
Middle East & N. Africa	–1,628	11,957	10.5	1,905.3	7,795.9	34,700	6,566
South Asia	–8,622	12,175	5.3	3,344.6	2,411.2	82,209	4,687
Sub-Saharan Africa	–2,006	17,710	12.6	2,809.5	2,195.6	21,101	5,002
High income	22,906	131,871	4.1	79.4	1,960.7	123,919	245,131
Euro area	6,336	36,317	7.1	1.0	1,023.9	71,976	82,745

a. World Bank estimates. b. Includes Taiwan, China. c. Includes Tibetans, who are listed separately by the UN Refugee Agency (UNHCR). d. Includes Palestinian refugees under the mandate of the United Nations Relief and Works Agency for Palestine Refugees in the Near East (UNRWA), who are not included in data from the UNHCR. e. World totals computed by the United Nations sum to zero, but because the aggregates refer to World Bank definitions, regional and income group totals do not. f. World totals are computed by the World Bank and include only economies covered by *World Development Indicators*, so data may differ from what is published by the United Nations Population Division. g. Includes refugees without specified country of origin and Palestinian refugees under the mandate of the UNRWA, so regional and income group totals do not sum to the world total.

Movement of people, most often through migration, is a significant part of global integration. Migrants contribute to the economies of both their host country and their country of origin. Yet reliable statistics on migration are difficult to collect and are often incomplete, making international comparisons a challenge.

The United Nations Population Division provides data on net migration and migrant stock. Because data on migrant stock is difficult for countries to collect, the United Nations Population Division takes into account the past migration history of a country or area, the migration policy of a country, and the influx of refugees in recent periods when deriving estimates of net migration. The data to calculate these estimates come from a variety of sources, including border statistics, administrative records, surveys, and censuses. When there is insufficient data, net migration is derived through the difference between the overall population growth rate and the rate of natural increase (the difference between the birth rate and the death rate) during the same period. Such calculations are usually made for intercensal periods. The estimates are also derived from the data on foreign-born population—people who have residence in one country but were born in another country. When data on the foreign-born population are not available, data on foreign population—that is, people who are citizens of a country other than the country in which they reside—are used as estimates.

For countries with information on the international migrant stock for at least two points in time, interpolation or extrapolation was used to estimate the international migrant stock on July 1 of the reference years. For countries with only one observation, estimates for the reference years were derived using rates of change in the migrant stock in the years preceding or following the single observation available. A model was used to estimate migrants for countries that had no data.

One negative effect of migration is "brain drain"—emigration of highly educated people. The table shows data on emigration of people with tertiary education, drawn from Docquier, Marfouk, and Lowell (2007), which analyzes skilled migration using data from censuses and registers of Organisation for Economic Development and Co-operation (OECD) countries and provides data disaggregated by gender for 1990 and 2000.

The table also shows data on refugees because they are an important part of migrant stock. The refugee data refer to people who have crossed an international border to find sanctuary and have been granted refugee or refugee-like status or temporary protection. Asylum seekers—people who have applied for asylum or refugee status and who have not yet received a decision or who are registered as asylum seekers—and internally displaced people—who are often confused with refugees—are not included. Unlike refugees, internally displaced people remain under the protection of their own government, even if their reason for fleeing was similar to that of refugees. Palestinian refugees are people (and their descendants) whose residence was Palestine between June 1946 and May 1948 and who lost their homes and means of livelihood as a result of the 1948 Arab-Israeli conflict.

Registrations, together with other sources—including estimates and surveys—are the main sources of refugee data. There are difficulties in collecting accurate statistics. Many refugees may not be aware of the need to register or may choose not to do so, and administrative records tend to overestimate the number of refugees because it is easier to register than to de-register. The UN Refugee Agency (UNHCR) collects and maintains data on refugees, except for Palestinian refugees residing in areas under the mandate of the United Nations Relief and Works Agency for Palestine Refugees in the Near East (UNRWA). Registration is voluntary, and estimates by the UNRWA are not an accurate count of the Palestinian refugee population. The table shows estimates of refugees collected by the UNHCR, complemented by estimates of Palestinian refugees under the UNRWA mandate. Thus, the aggregates differ from those published by the UNHCR.

Workers' remittances and compensation of employees are from the International Monetary Fund's (IMF) *Balance of Payments Statistics Yearbook.* The IMF data are supplemented by World Bank staff estimates for missing data for countries where workers' remittances are important. The data reported here are the sum of three items defined in the fifth edition of the IMF's *Balance of Payments Manual:* workers' remittances, compensation of employees, and migrants' transfers.

- **Net migration** is the net total of migrants (immigrants less emigrants, including both citizens and noncitizens) during the period. Data are five-year estimates. • **International migrant stock** is the number of people, including refugees, born in a country other than that in which they live. • **Emigration of tertiary educated population to OECD countries** is the stock of emigrants ages 25 and older with at least one year of tertiary education who reside in an OECD country other than that in which they were born. • **Refugees** are people recognized as refugees under the 1951 Convention Relating to the Status of Refugees or its 1967 Protocol, the 1969 Organization of African Unity Convention Governing the Specific Aspects of Refugee Problems in Africa; recognized as refugees in accordance with the UNHCR statute; granted refugee-like humanitarian status; or provided temporary protection. Asylum seekers and internally displaced people are excluded. • **Country of origin** refers to the nationality or country of citizenship of a claimant. • **Country of asylum** is the country where an asylum claim was filed and granted. • **Workers' remittances and compensation of employees,** received and paid, are current transfers by migrant workers and wages and salaries earned by nonresident workers. Remittances are classified as current private transfers from migrant workers resident in the host country for more than a year, irrespective of their immigration status, to recipients in their country of origin. Migrants' transfers are defined as the net worth of migrants who are expected to remain in the host country for more than one year that is transferred to another country at the time of migration. Compensation of employees is the income of migrants who have lived in the host country for less than a year.

Data sources

Data on net migration are from the United Nations Population Division's *World Population Prospects: The 2010 Revision.* Data on international migration stock are from the United Nations Population Division's *Trends in Total Migrant Stock: The 2008 Revision.* Data on migration of tertiary educated population are from Docquier, Lowell, and Marfouk (2009). Data on refugees are from the UNHCR's *Statistical Yearbook 2010,* complemented by statistics on Palestinian refugees under the mandate of the UNRWA as published on its website. Data on remittances are from the IMF's *Balance of Payments Statistics Yearbook* supplemented by World Bank staff estimates.

	International tourists				Inbound tourism expenditure				Outbound tourism expenditure			
	thousands				$ millions		% of exports		$ millions		% of imports	
	Inbound		Outbound									
	2000	2010	2000	2010	2000	2010	2000	2010	2000	2010	2000	2010
Afghanistan	..	..	..	..	..	..	..	..	..	..	..	..
Albania	317[a,b]	2,417[a,b]	..	3,443	398	1,780	56.6	47.0	290	1,454	19.3	23.0
Algeria	866[a,c]	..	1,006	..	102[d]				193[e]			
Angola	51	425	..	..	34[e]	726	0.4	1.4	146	275	2.5	0.8
Argentina	2,909	5,325	4,953	5,307	3,195	5,629	10.2	6.9	5,460	6,375	16.5	9.4
Armenia	45	..	111	..	52	456	11.6	23.5	56	466	5.8	11.1
Australia	4,931[a,b]	5,885[a,b,e]	3,498	7,111	13,016	..	15.5	..	8,780	..	10.0	..
Austria	17,982[f]	22,004[f]	7,528	9,882	11,382	20,931	13.0	10.3	7,001	12,215	8.2	6.5
Azerbaijan	..	1,280	1,326	3,176	68	792	3.2	2.8	138	856	6.8	8.1
Bahrain	2,420	..	..	..	854	2,163	11.9	12.1	425	684	8.3	5.2
Bangladesh	199	..	1,128	..	50[d]	103[d]	0.7	0.5	471	835	4.9	2.8
Belarus	60	119	1,289	415	188	662	2.5	2.2	247	738	3.1	2.0
Belgium	6,457[f]	7,186[f]	7,932	10,170	6,592[d]	11,431	..	3.1	9,429[d,e]	20,558	..	5.7
Benin	96	199	..	..	77	134	14.6	..	50	97	7.1	..
Bolivia	319	807	201	708	101	339	6.9	5.0	116	421	5.6	6.8
Bosnia and Herzegovina	171[f]	365[f]	..	..	246	668	15.6	10.7	92	244	2.2	2.5
Botswana	1,104	2,145	..	..	227	222	7.6	4.4	209	26	9.0	0.5
Brazil	5,313	5,161	3,228	5,305	1,969	6,181	3.0	2.6	4,548	19,340	6.3	7.9
Bulgaria	2,785	6,047	2,337	3,676	1,364	4,035	19.5	14.8	764	1,382	10.0	4.9
Burkina Faso	126[g]	274[g]	..	..	23	..	9.7	..	30	..	4.6	..
Burundi	29[c]	..	28	..	1	2	2.6	1.2	14[d]	35	9.3	5.8
Cambodia	..	2,399	41	505	345	1,412	18.9	20.5	52	268	2.3	3.4
Cameroon	277[g]	..	..	..	132	171	4.9	3.0	241	265	9.6	4.1
Canada	19,627	16,097	19,182	28,678	13,035	18,281	4.0	4.0	15,125	36,677	5.3	7.4
Central African Republic	11[h]	..	..	..	5[e]	..	..	..	33[e]	..	..	..
Chad	43[g]	..	27	..	14[e]	..	..	..	56[e]	..	..	..
Chile	1,742	2,766	1,830	3,348	1,179	2,413	5.1	2.9	904	2,339	4.1	3.5
China	31,229	55,664	10,473	57,386	17,318	50,154	6.2	2.9	14,169	59,840	5.7	3.9
Hong Kong SAR, China	8,814	20,085	..	84,442	8,198[e]	27,028[e]	3.4	5.4	12,502[d,e]	17,461[d,e]	5.3	3.6
Colombia	557	..	1,235	..	1,313	2,797	8.3	6.2	1,452	2,368	10.1	5.1
Congo, Dem. Rep.	103	..	..	..	..	..	..	..	..	..	..	..
Congo, Rep.	19[g]	..	..	..	12	..	0.5	..	59	..	4.9	..
Costa Rica	1,088	2,100	381	662	1,477	2,189	19.1	16.0	551	534	7.6	3.6
Côte d'Ivoire	..	..	..	..	53	..	1.2	..	291	..	8.0	..
Croatia	5,831[f]	9,111[f]	..	1,873	2,871	8,209	33.2	35.5	634	853	6.6	3.6
Cuba	1,741[h]	2,507[h]	139	251	1,948[e]	2,396[e]	..	..	..	..	..	..
Cyprus	2,686	2,173	503	1,067	2,137	2,416	42.6	24.8	543	1,436	10.6	12.8
Czech Republic	..	8,185	..	6,429	2,973[d]	8,017	8.3	5.8	1,276[d]	4,166	3.4	3.2
Denmark	3,535[f]	8,744[f]	5,011	..	3,671[d]	5,704[e]	5.0	3.7	4,669[d]	9,082[d]	7.2	6.5
Dominican Republic	2,978[c,h]	4,125[c,h]	360	401	2,860[d]	4,209[d]	31.9	36.0	440	542	4.1	3.1
Ecuador	627[a,b]	1,047[a,b]	520	899	451	786	7.6	4.0	416	862	8.4	3.8
Egypt, Arab Rep.	5,116	14,051	2,964	..	4,657	13,633	27.6	27.9	1,206	2,696	5.3	4.5
El Salvador	795	1,150	923	..	437	646	11.9	11.6	219	280	3.9	3.0
Eritrea	70[a,c]	84[a,c]	..	..	36[e]	..	36.8	..	..	..	..	..
Estonia	1,220	2,120	1,800	955	657	1,412	13.7	8.7	253	719	5.1	4.9
Ethiopia	136[c]	..	..	..	205	1,434	20.7	30.9	80	143[d]	4.9	1.4
Finland	2,714	3,670	5,914	6,633	2,035	4,362	3.8	4.5	2,293	5,202	5.7	5.5
France	77,190	77,148	19,886	21,609	38,534	56,654	10.1	8.6	26,703	46,227	7.3	6.4
Gabon	155[h]	..	168	..	99	..	2.8	..	183	..	11.1	..
Gambia, The	79	91	..	..	..	38	..	14.9	..	11[d]	..	3.6
Georgia	387[a]	2,033[a]	315	2,089	107	738	12.5	18.2	129	328	9.8	5.3
Germany	18,983[f]	26,875[f]	74,400	..	24,943	49,133	4.0	3.2	57,601	91,208	9.2	6.7
Ghana	399[c]	..	..	..	357	706	14.6	7.5	162	882	4.8	6.3
Greece	13,096	15,007	..	..	9,262	12,579	31.5	20.9	4,564	2,874	10.9	3.6
Guatemala	826[a]	1,876[a]	488	1,136	498	1,378	12.9	12.7	216	1,033	3.9	6.8
Guinea	33[h]	..	..	..	8	2	1.1	0.1	13	17	1.5	0.9
Guinea-Bissau	..	..	..	..	..	..	..	..	..	..	..	..
Haiti	140[h]	..	..	..	128[d]	167[d]	25.4	20.9	173	431	12.6	10.6

	International tourists				Inbound tourism expenditure				Outbound tourism expenditure			
	thousands				$ millions		% of exports		$ millions		% of imports	
	Inbound		Outbound									
	2000	2010	2000	2010	2000	2010	2000	2010	2000	2010	2000	2010
Honduras	471	896	274	429	263	652	6.8	9.6	198	406	4.2	4.1
Hungary	..	9,510	11,065	16,082	3,809	6,346	11.0	5.7	1,722	2,867	4.7	2.8
India	2,649[b]	5,776[b]	4,416	12,988	3,598	14,673	6.0	4.2	3,686	13,746	5.0	3.1
Indonesia	5,064	7,003	2,205	6,235	4,975[d]	7,618	7.0	4.4	3,197[d]	8,432	5.7	5.5
Iran, Islamic Rep.	1,342	..	2,286	..	677	..	2.3	..	671	..	3.8	..
Iraq	78[a]	1,518[a]	..	..	2[d]	..	..	..	9[d]	..	..	..
Ireland	6,646	..	3,783	..	3,517	8,071	3.8	3.9	2,626	7,798	3.3	4.6
Israel	2,417[b]	2,803[b]	3,530	4,269	4,611	5,474	9.9	6.8	3,733	4,433	8.0	5.8
Italy	41,181	43,626	21,993	29,823	28,706	40,058	9.7	7.3	18,169	33,053	6.3	5.6
Jamaica	1,323[c,h]	1,922[c,h]	..	..	1,577	2,095	43.9	52.3	238	235	5.4	3.6
Japan	4,757[a,b]	8,611[a,b]	17,819	16,637	5,970	15,356	1.1	1.8	42,643	39,306	9.3	4.9
Jordan	1,580[c]	4,557[c]	1,625	2,917	935	4,018	26.4	33.0	387	1,605	6.7	8.9
Kazakhstan	1,471	3,393	1,247	..	403	1,236	3.9	1.9	483	1,437	5.4	3.3
Kenya	899	1,469	..	..	500	1,620	18.0	18.2	156	212[d]	4.1	1.6
Korea, Dem. Rep.	..	..	..	..	..	..	..	..	..	..	..	..
Korea, Rep.	5,322[a,c]	8,798[a,c]	5,508	..	8,527	13,805	4.1	2.5	7,945	19,695	4.1	3.8
Kosovo	..	..	..	..	..	..	..	..	..	..	..	..
Kuwait	78[g]	207[g]	1,236	..	394	510	1.8	0.7	2,852	7,419	25.1	22.7
Kyrgyz Republic	59	1,316	47	1,296	20	336	3.5	13.6	28	398	4.3	10.2
Lao PDR	191	1,670	..	..	114[d]	385[d]	22.5	17.1	8	215[d]	1.4	9.3
Latvia	509	1,373	2,596	3,332	172	963	5.3	7.5	281	771	7.4	5.9
Lebanon	742	2,168	..	..	742	8,174	..	38.5	..	5,080	..	16.4
Lesotho	..	414	..	..	18[d]	34[d]	6.7	3.8	12	..	1.1	..
Liberia	..	..	..	..	..	12[d]	..	3.0	..	134	..	7.4
Libya	..	..	..	..	84	170	0.7	0.3	495	2,184	9.9	7.1
Lithuania	1,083	1,507	3,632	1,411	430	1,097	8.4	4.4	261	786	4.5	3.1
Macedonia, FYR	224[f]	262[f]	..	..	88	209	5.4	5.0	58	141	2.5	2.3
Madagascar	160[h]	196[h]	..	..	152	633	12.8	..	139	110[d]	9.1	..
Malawi	228	746	..	..	29	..	6.6	..	53	..	8.4	..
Malaysia	10,222	24,577	30,532	..	5,873	18,315	5.2	7.9	2,543	7,943[d]	2.7	4.2
Mali	86[g,h]	169[g]	..	..	47	296	7.3	..	66	235	7.1	..
Mauritania	30	..	..	..	..	..	..	..	..	..	..	..
Mauritius	656	935	163	212	732	1,585	27.9	32.0	203	423	7.5	6.9
Mexico	20,641[c]	22,260[c]	11,079	14,395	9,133	12,417	5.1	4.0	6,365	9,075	3.3	2.8
Moldova	18	8	32	117	57	233	8.9	10.2	86	329	8.8	7.2
Mongolia	137	457	..	..	43	288	7.0	8.5	54	319	7.0	8.2
Morocco	4,278[c]	9,288[c]	1,508	..	2,280	8,176	21.8	27.1	506	1,879	4.0	4.7
Mozambique	..	..	..	..	74[d]	230	10.7	7.7	122	285	8.2	6.1
Myanmar	208	311	..	..	195	92	9.1	1.1	30[d]	54	1.2	1.0
Namibia	656	984	..	..	193[d]	560[d]	13.0	11.2	86[d]	145	5.3	2.6
Nepal	464	603	155	765	219	378	17.1	24.0	109	528	6.1	9.0
Netherlands	10,003[f]	10,883[f]	13,896	18,430	11,285	18,690	4.4	3.2	13,649	19,772	5.7	3.9
New Zealand	1,780	2,492	1,283	2,026	2,272[d]	4,907[d]	12.7	12.0	1,235[d]	3,038[d]	7.1	7.8
Nicaragua	486	1,011[c]	486	908	129[d]	309[d]	11.7	8.5	126	323	5.9	5.9
Niger	50	..	..	..	23[d]	..	7.2	..	32	..	7.0	..
Nigeria	813	..	..	..	186	738	0.9	1.0	610	8,379	5.1	11.1
Norway	3,104	4,767	2,394	..	2,521	5,083	3.2	2.9	4,893	13,971	9.9	11.9
Oman	571[g]	1,048[g]	..	..	377	1,251	3.2	3.3	629[d]	1,768	9.9	7.2
Pakistan	557	..	..	..	551	998	5.4	3.6	574	1,370	4.7	3.4
Panama	484	1,324	216	392	628	2,552	8.0	13.9	241	575	3.0	2.9
Papua New Guinea	58	..	52	..	7[d]	2[d]	0.3	0.0	50[d]	138	2.8	2.2
Paraguay	289[b]	465	175	313	88	243	3.0	2.4	154	269	4.7	2.5
Peru	800	2,299	730	2,058	861	2,741	10.1	6.9	641	1,646	6.6	4.7
Philippines	1,992[c]	3,520[c]	1,670	..	2,334	3,228	5.7	5.0	1,841	4,253	3.8	5.8
Poland	17,400	12,470	56,677	42,760	6,128	9,986	13.2	5.0	3,417	9,100	6.0	4.4
Portugal	5,599[f]	6,756[f]	..	..	6,027	12,969	17.7	18.0	2,754	4,691	5.8	5.4
Puerto Rico	3,341[h]	3,679[h]	1,259	1,357	2,388[e]	3,598[e]	..	..	1,333[e]	1,723[e]	..	..
Qatar	378[g,i]	1,866[g,i]	..	..	128	..[e]	..	..	307[d,e]	..	..	..

6.15 | Travel and tourism

	International tourists				Inbound tourism expenditure				Outbound tourism expenditure			
	thousands				$ millions		% of exports		$ millions		% of imports	
	Inbound		Outbound									
	2000	2010	2000	2010	2000	2010	2000	2010	2000	2010	2000	2010
Romania	5,264[a]	..	6,388	..	394	1,653	3.3	2.8	447	1,897	3.2	2.8
Russian Federation	21,169[a]	22,281[a]	18,371	39,323	3,429[d]	13,379	3.0	3.0	8,848[d]	29,993	14.5	9.3
Rwanda	..	666	..	..	27	218[d]	21.1	35.9	35	94	8.3	5.7
Saudi Arabia	6,585	10,850	..	7,233	..	7,655	..	2.9	..	22,803	..	13.1
Senegal	..	..	..	..	152	..	11.6	..	125	..	7.2	..
Serbia	..	683	..	..	..	951	..	7.1	..	1,106	..	5.6
Sierra Leone	16[h]	39[f,h]	13	76	10[d]	26[d]	18.2	6.1	35	22	13.8	2.5
Singapore	6,062	9,161	4,444	7,342	5,142[d]	14,181[d]	2.8	3.0	4,535[d]	16,770[d]	2.7	4.1
Slovak Republic	1,053[f]	..	..	..	441	2,335	3.1	3.3	341	2,146	2.3	3.0
Slovenia	1,090[f]	1,869[f]	1,965	2,874	1,016	2,735	9.5	9.0	544	1,377	4.8	4.5
Somalia	..	..	..	..	..	..	..	..	..	..	..	..
South Africa	5,872	8,074	3,834	5,165	3,338	10,308	9.0	10.3	2,684	8,139	8.1	8.1
South Sudan	..	..	..	..	..	..	..	..	..	..	..	..
Spain	46,403	52,677	4,100	..	32,656	58,810	19.4	15.6	7,710	22,800	4.1	5.7
Sri Lanka	400[b]	654[b]	524	1,122	388	1,044	6.1	9.7	383	828	4.7	5.4
Sudan	38	..	..	..	5[d]	94[d]	0.3	0.8	55[d]	1,116[d]	2.7	10.0
Swaziland	281[i]	868[g]	..	1,141	24	51	1.9	2.5	32	87	2.2	3.3
Sweden	3,828[f]	4,951[f]	10,147	13,042	4,825	13,316	4.3	5.9	8,959	14,878	9.2	7.6
Switzerland	7,821[g]	8,628[g]	12,240	..	8,988	17,847	7.2	5.2	7,360	13,317	6.9	4.7
Syrian Arab Republic	2,100[c,f]	8,546	3,863	6,259	1,082[d]	6,308	15.8	32.2	669[d]	1,598	12.4	8.2
Tajikistan	..	..	6	..	..	32	..	2.1	..	18[d]	..	0.5
Tanzania	459	783	..	..	381	1,279	28.0	20.0	369	861	18.0	9.6
Thailand	9,579[c]	15,936	1,909	5,451	9,935	23,407	12.2	10.3	3,218	6,582	4.5	3.2
Timor-Leste	..	40	..	..	..	21	..	..	..	72	..	..
Togo	60[g]	..	..	..	11	..	2.6	..	15	..	2.5	..
Trinidad and Tobago	399[h]	..	..	..	371	..	7.7	..	190	..	5.1	..
Tunisia	5,058[b]	6,903[b]	1,632	2,250	1,977	3,477	23.0	15.6	310	611	3.3	2.5
Turkey	9,586	27,000	5,284	11,002	7,636[d]	24,784	15.2	15.9	1,713[d]	5,451	2.8	2.8
Turkmenistan	3	..	78	..	..	..	..	..	..	..	..	..
Uganda	193	946	153	324	165[d]	762	24.9	21.9	..	389	..	6.4
Ukraine	6,431	21,203	13,422	17,180	563	4,696	2.9	6.8	561	4,134	3.1	5.6
United Arab Emirates	3,907[c,i]	..	..	..	1,063[e]	8,577[e]	..	..	3,019[e]	11,818[e]	..	..
United Kingdom	23,212	28,295	56,837	55,562	29,978	39,945	7.4	6.0	47,009	60,291	10.8	8.2
United States	51,238	59,791	61,327	..	120,912	165,777	11.3	9.0	91,473	109,975	6.3	4.7
Uruguay	1,968	2,353	667	1,027	827	1,607	22.6	15.2	381	534	9.1	5.5
Uzbekistan	302	975	217	1,610	63[e]	121[d,e]	..	..	..	..	..	..
Venezuela, RB	469	..	954	..	469	672	1.4	1.0	1,647	2,196	7.7	4.4
Vietnam	2,140[a]	..	..	..	..	..	..	..	..	..	..	..
West Bank and Gaza	310[g]	522[g]	..	..	283[d]	..	28.0	..	316	..	9.7	..
Yemen, Rep.	73	536	..	..	73[d]	622[d]	1.8	6.7	127	252	3.9	2.3
Zambia	457	815	..	..	67[d]	125[d]	7.7	1.6	102	128	7.8	2.3
Zimbabwe	1,967[a]	2,239[a]	..	650	125[e]	634[e]	..	..	..	..	..	..
World	**681,151 t**	**941,666 t**	**730,907 t**	**.. t**	**572,408 t**	**1,111,919 t**	**7.4 w**	**5.9 w**	**531,843 t**	**996,273 t**	**6.8 w**	**5.4 w**
Low income	7,122	16,234	..	..	3,304	11,469	11.0	11.2	2,837	7,086	6.0	4.3
Middle income	196,996	360,007	179,453	370,724	112,754	304,678	7.2	5.5	82,078	261,770	5.6	4.8
Lower middle income	39,368	98,178	45,422	86,323	26,019	77,617	7.7	6.8	17,992	65,963	5.0	4.7
Upper middle income	157,416	261,779	124,379	..	86,796	227,263	7.0	5.2	64,076	196,511	5.8	4.8
Low & middle income	207,153	380,843	196,477	409,004	115,911	315,502	7.2	5.6	84,837	269,032	5.6	4.8
East Asia & Pacific	62,673	117,829	51,581	..	42,855	109,418	7.0	4.3	26,308	91,275	4.8	4.1
Europe & Central Asia	52,830	106,138	59,247	114,685	16,274	60,832	6.5	6.1	15,983	56,988	7.2	5.9
Latin America & Carib.	47,146	64,289	29,567	43,711	30,617	53,813	6.9	5.2	25,096	50,734	5.7	5.0
Middle East & N. Africa	21,987	53,132	18,577	..	12,902	48,730	12.9	20.9	5,237	23,279	5.5	6.8
South Asia	4,839	9,330	7,137	20,157	5,152	18,026	6.0	4.3	5,333	17,625	5.0	3.3
Sub-Saharan Africa	17,703	31,646	..	..	8,000	24,873	7.2	7.0	7,133	32,518	6.9	6.9
High income	470,103	558,474	481,718	..	456,489	796,198	7.4	6.0	446,402	730,544	7.1	5.7
Euro area	254,371	282,908	179,060	..	181,607	307,946	8.4	6.2	155,713	275,992	7.1	5.8

Note: Aggregates are based on World Bank country classifications and differ from those of the World Tourism Organization. Regional and income group totals include countries not shown in the table for which data are available.

a. Arrivals of nonresident visitors at national borders. b. Excludes nationals residing abroad. c. Includes nationals residing abroad. d. Expenditure of travel-related items only; excludes passenger transport items. e. Data are from national sources. f. Arrivals in all types of accommodation establishments. g. Arrivals in hotels and similar establishments. h. Arrivals in hotels only. i. Arrivals by air only.

About the data

Tourism is defined as the activities of people traveling to and staying in places outside their usual environment for no more than one year for leisure, business, and other purposes not related to an activity remunerated from within the place visited. The social and economic phenomenon of tourism has grown substantially over the past quarter century.

Statistical information on tourism is based mainly on data on arrivals and overnight stays along with balance of payments information. These data do not completely capture the economic phenomenon of tourism or provide the information needed for effective public policies and efficient business operations. Data are needed on the scale and significance of tourism. Information on the role of tourism in national economies is particularly deficient. Although the World Tourism Organization reports progress in harmonizing definitions and measurement, differences in national practices still prevent full comparability.

The usual environment of an individual is a key concept in tourism statistics and is defined as the geographical area within which an individual conducts regular life routines. This concept excludes travelers who commute regularly between their place of usual residence and place of work or study or who frequently visit places within their current life routine—for instance, homes of friends or relatives; shopping centers; and religious, health care, or other facilities a substantial distance away or in a different administrative area.

The data in the table are from the World Tourism Organization, a United Nations agency. The data on inbound and outbound tourists refer to the number of arrivals and departures, not to the number of people traveling. Thus a person who makes several trips to a country during a given period is counted each time as a new arrival. Unless otherwise indicated in the footnotes, the data on inbound tourism show the arrivals of nonresident tourists (overnight visitors) at national borders. When data on international tourists are unavailable or incomplete, the table shows the arrivals of international visitors, which include tourists, same-day visitors, cruise passengers, and crew members.

Sources and collection methods for arrivals differ across countries. In some cases data are from border statistics (police, immigration, and the like) and supplemented by border surveys. In other cases data are from tourism accommodation establishments. For some countries number of arrivals is limited to arrivals by air and for others to arrivals staying in hotels. Some countries include arrivals of nationals residing abroad while others do not. Caution should thus be used in comparing arrivals across countries.

The World Tourism Organization is improving its coverage of tourism expenditure data, using balance of payments data from the International Monetary Fund (IMF) supplemented by data from individual countries. These data, shown in the table, include travel and passenger transport items as defined in the IMF's *Balance of Payments Manual,* 5th edition. When the IMF does not report data on passenger transport items, expenditure data for travel items are shown.

Tourism can be either domestic or international. The table shows data relevant to international tourism, where the traveler's country of residence differs from the visiting country. International tourism consists of inbound and outbound tourism.

The aggregates are calculated using the World Bank's weighted aggregation methodology (see *Statistical methods*) and differ from the World Tourism Organization's aggregates.

Definitions

• **International inbound tourists** (overnight visitors) are tourists who travel to a country other than that in which they usually reside, and outside their usual environment, for a period not exceeding 12 months and whose main purpose in visiting is other than an activity remunerated in the country visited. When number of tourists are not available, data on visitors, which include tourists, same-day visitors, cruise passengers, and crew members, are shown. • **International outbound tourists** are departures that people make from their country of usual residence to any other country for any purpose other than an activity remunerated in the country visited. • **Inbound tourism expenditure** is expenditures by international inbound visitors, including payments to national carriers for international transport and any other prepayment made for goods or services received in the destination country. They may include receipts from same-day visitors, except when these are important enough to justify separate classification. For some countries they do not include receipts for passenger transport items. Their share in exports is calculated as a ratio to exports of goods and services (all transactions between residents of a country and the rest of the world involving a change of ownership from residents to nonresidents of general merchandise, goods sent for processing and repairs, nonmonetary gold, and services). • **Outbound tourism expenditure** is expenditures of international outbound visitors in other countries, including payments to foreign carriers for international transport. These expenditures may include those by residents traveling abroad as same-day visitors, except when these are important enough to justify separate classification. For some countries they do not include expenditures for passenger transport items. Their share in imports is calculated as a ratio to imports of goods and services (all transactions between residents of a country and the rest of the world involving a change of ownership from nonresidents to residents of general merchandise, goods sent for processing and repairs, nonmonetary gold, and services).

Data sources

Data on visitors and tourism expenditure are from the World Tourism Organization's *Yearbook of Tourism Statistics* and *Compendium of Tourism Statistics 2011*. Data in the table are updated from electronic files provided by the World Tourism Organization. Data on exports and imports are from the IMF's *Balance of Payments Statistics Yearbook* and data files.

PRIMARY DATA DOCUMENTATION

As a major user of socioeconomic data, the World Bank recognizes the importance of data documentation to inform users of differences in the methods and conventions used by primary data collectors—usually national statistical agencies, central banks, and customs services—and by international organizations, which compile the statistics that appear in the World Development Indicators database. These differences may give rise to significant discrepancies over time both within countries and across them. Delays in reporting data and the use of old surveys as the base for current estimates may further compromise the quality of data reported here.

The tables in this section provide information on sources, methods, and reporting standards of the principal demographic, economic, and environmental indicators in *World Development Indicators*. Additional documentation is available from the World Bank's Bulletin Board on Statistical Capacity at http://data.worldbank.org.

The demand for good-quality statistical data is ever increasing. Statistics provide the evidence needed to improve decisionmaking, document results, and heighten public accountability. The need for improved statistics to monitor the Millennium Development Goals and the parallel effort to support a culture of results-based management has stimulated a decade-long effort to improve statistics. The results has been impressive, but more needs to done.

Thus a new action plan for statistics, "Statistics for Transparency, Accountability, and Results: A Busan Action Plan for Statistics," was endorsed by the Busan Partnership for Effective Development Cooperation at the Fourth High-level Forum for Aid Effectiveness held November 29–December 1, 2011, in Busan, Republic of Korea. This new action plan builds on the progress made under the first global plan to improve national and international statistics, the 2004 Marrakech Action Plan for Statistics from 2004, but goes beyond it in many ways. The main objectives of the new plan are to integrate statistics into decisionmaking, promote open access to statistics within government and for all other uses, and increase resources for statistical systems, both for investment in new capacity and for maintaining current operations.

	Currency	National accounts						Balance of payments and trade			Government finance	IMF data dissem-ination standard
		Base year	Reference year	System of National Accounts	SNA price valuation	Alternative conversion factor	PPP survey year	Balance of Payments Manual in use	External debt	System of trade	Accounting concept	
Afghanistan	Afghan afghani	2002/03			VAB				Actual	G	C	G
Albania	Albanian lek	[a]	1996	[b]	VAB		2005	BPM5	Actual	G	C	G
Algeria	Algerian dinar	1980			VAB			BPM5	Actual	S	B	G
American Samoa	U.S. dollar									S		
Andorra	Euro									S		
Angola	Angolan kwanza	1997			VAP	1991–96	2005	BPM5	Actual	S		G
Antigua and Barbuda	East Caribbean dollar	2006			VAB			BPM5		G		G
Argentina	Argentine peso	1993		[b]	VAB	1971–84	2005	BPM5	Actual	S	C	S
Armenia	Armenian dram	[a]	1996	[b]	VAB	1990–95	2005	BPM5	Actual	S	C	S
Aruba	Aruban florin	1995						BPM5		S		
Australia	Australian dollar	[a]	2009	[b]	VAB		2005	BPM5		G	C	S
Austria	Euro	2005		[b]	VAB		2005	BPM5		S	C	S
Azerbaijan	New Azeri manat	[a]	2003	[b]	VAB	1992–95	2005	BPM5	Actual	G	B	G
Bahamas, The	Bahamian dollar	2006		[b]	VAB			BPM5		G	B	G
Bahrain	Bahraini dinar	1985			VAP		2005	BPM5		G	B	G
Bangladesh	Bangladeshi taka	1995/96		[b]	VAB		2005	BPM5	Actual	G	C	G
Barbados	Barbados dollar	1974			VAB			BPM5		G	B	G
Belarus	Belarusian rubel	[a]	2000	[b]	VAB	1990–95	2005	BPM5	Actual	G	C	S
Belgium	Euro	2005		[b]	VAB		2005	BPM5		S	C	S
Belize	Belize dollar	2000		[b]	VAB			BPM5	Actual	G	B	G
Benin	CFA franc	1985			VAP	1992	2005	BPM5	Actual	S	B	G
Bermuda	Bermuda dollar	1996			VAB			BPM5		G		
Bhutan	Bhutanese ngultrum	2000		[b]	VAB			BPM5	Actual	G	C	G
Bolivia	Bolivian Boliviano	1990		[b]	VAB	1960–85	2005	BPM5	Actual	G	C	G
Bosnia and Herzegovina	Bosnia and Herzegovina convertible mark	[a]	1996	[b]	VAB		2005	BPM5	Actual	S	C	
Botswana	Botswana pula	1993/94		[b]	VAB		2005	BPM5	Actual	G	B	G
Brazil	Brazilian real	2000		[b]	VAB		2005	BPM5	Actual	G	C	S
Brunei Darussalam	Brunei dollar	2000			VAP		2005			S		G
Bulgaria	Bulgarian lev	[a]	2002	[b]	VAB	1978–89, 1991–92	2005	BPM5	Actual	S	C	S
Burkina Faso	CFA franc	1999			VAB	1992–93	2005	BPM5	Actual	G	B	G
Burundi	Burundi franc	1980			VAB		2005	BPM5	Preliminary	S	C	G
Cambodia	Cambodian riel	2000			VAB		2005	BPM5	Actual	S	C	G
Cameroon	CFA franc	2000		[b]	VAB		2005	BPM5	Actual	S	B	G
Canada	Canadian dollar	2005		[b]	VAB		2005	BPM5		G	C	S
Cape Verde	Cape Verde escudo	1980			VAP		2005	BPM5	Actual	G	C	G
Cayman Islands	Cayman Islands dollar									G		
Central African Republic	CFA franc	2000			VAB		2005	BPM5	Preliminary	S	B	G
Chad	CFA franc	1995		[b]	VAB		2005	BPM5	Actual	S		G
Channel Islands	Pound sterling	2007, 2003	2007	[b]	VAB							
Chile	Chilean peso	2003		[b]	VAB		2005	BPM5	Actual	S	C	S
China	Chinese yuan	2000		[b]	VAP	1978–93	2005	BPM5	Preliminary	S	B	G
Hong Kong SAR, China	Hong Kong dollar		2009	[b]	VAB		2005	BPM5		G	C	S
Macao SAR, China	Macao pataca		2009		VAB		2005	BPM5		G	C	G
Colombia	Colombian peso	2005		[b]	VAB	1992–94	2005	BPM5	Actual	G	B	S
Comoros	Comorian franc	1990			VAP		2005		Actual	S		
Congo, Dem. Rep.	Congolese franc	1987			VAB	1999–2001	2005	BPM4	Estimate	S	C	G
Congo, Rep.	CFA franc	1978			VAP	1993	2005	BPM5	Estimate	S	C	G
Costa Rica	Costa Rican colon	1991		[b]	VAB		2005	BPM5	Actual	S	C	S
Côte d'Ivoire	CFA franc	1996			VAP		2005	BPM5	Estimate	S	C	G
Croatia	Croatian kuna	[a]	2000	[b]	VAB		2005	BPM5		G	C	S
Cuba	Cuban peso	1990			VAB					S		
Curaçao	Netherlands Antilles guilder											

PRIMARY DATA DOCUMENTATION

	Latest population census	Latest demographic, education, or health household survey	Source of most recent income and expenditure data	Vital registration complete	Latest agricultural census	Latest industrial data	Latest trade data	Latest water withdrawal data
Afghanistan	1979	MICS, 2003; Special Survey, 2010	IHS, 2008			2010	2010	2000
Albania	2001	DHS, 2008/09	LSMS, 2008	Yes	1998	2010	2010	2000
Algeria	2008	MICS, 2006	IHS, 1995		2001	2009	2010	2000
American Samoa	2010			Yes	2007		2009	
Andorra	1989			Yes			2006	
Angola	1970	MICS, 2001; MIS, 2006/07	IHS, 2000		1964–65	2010	1991	2000
Antigua and Barbuda	2011			Yes	2007	2010	2010	1990
Argentina	2010		IHS, 2010	Yes	2007	2010	2010	2000
Armenia	2001	DHS, 2005	IHS, 2010	Yes		2010	2010	2006
Aruba	2010			Yes			2010	
Australia	2006		ES/BS, 1994	Yes	2011	2010	2010	2000
Austria	2011		IS, 2000	Yes	2010	2010	2010	2000
Azerbaijan	2009	DHS, 2006	ES/BS, 2008	Yes		2010	2010	2005
Bahamas, The	2010					2006	2010	
Bahrain	2010			Yes		1995	2010	2003
Bangladesh	2011	DHS, 2007	IHS, 2010		2008	2010	2007	2008
Barbados	2010			Yes		2005	2010	2000
Belarus	2009	MICS, 2005	ES/BS, 2009	Yes	1994	2010	2010	2000
Belgium	2011		IHS, 2000	Yes	1999–2000	2009	2010	2007
Belize	2010	MICS, 2006	ES/BS, 1999			2008	2010	2000
Benin	2002	DHS, 2006	CWIQ, 2003		2011–12	2005	2006	2001
Bermuda	2010			Yes			2009	
Bhutan	2005	MICS, 2010	IHS, 2007		2008	2009	2010	2008
Bolivia	2001	DHS, 2008	IHS, 2008		2008	2010	2010	2000
Bosnia and Herzegovina	1991	MICS, 2006	LSMS, 2007	Yes		2010	2010	2009
Botswana	2011	MICS, 2000	ES/BS, 2003		1993	2010	2010	2000
Brazil	2010	DHS, 1996	LFS, 2009		2006	2010	2011	2006
Brunei Darussalam	2001			Yes		2008	2006	1994
Bulgaria	2011		ES/BS, 2007	Yes	2010	2010	2010	2009
Burkina Faso	2006	MICS, 2006	CWIQ, 2009		2010	2006	2010	2000
Burundi	2008	MICS, 2005	CWIQ, 2006			2005	2010	2000
Cambodia	2008	DHS, 2010	IHS, 2008		2012	2010	2010	2006
Cameroon	2005	MICS, 2006	PS, 2007		1984	2007	2010	2000
Canada	2011		LFS, 2000	Yes	2011	2007	2010	2000
Cape Verde	2010	DHS, 2005	ES/BS, 2007	Yes	2004	2009	2010	
Cayman Islands	2010			Yes				
Central African Republic	2003	MICS, 2006	PS, 2008		1985	2006	2009	2000
Chad	2009	DHS, 2004	PS, 2002/03		2011	2008	1995	2000
Channel Islands	2001							
Chile	2002		IHS, 2009	Yes	2007	2010	2010	2000
China	2010	NSS, 2007	IHS, 2008		2007	2010	2010	2005
Hong Kong SAR, China	2006			Yes		2010	2010	
Macao SAR, China	2011			Yes		2009	2010	
Colombia	2006	DHS, 2010	IHS, 2010		2001	2010	2010	2000
Comoros	2003	MICS, 2000	IHS, 2004			2009	2007	1999
Congo, Dem. Rep.	1984	MICS, 2010	1-2-3, 2005/06		1990	2009	1986	2000
Congo, Rep.	2007	AIS, 2009; DHS, 2005	CWIQ/PS, 2005		1985–86	2010	2005	2002
Costa Rica	2011	RHS, 1993	LFS, 2010	Yes	1973	2010	2010	2000
Côte d'Ivoire	1998	MICS, 2006	IHS, 2008		2001	2010	2010	2000
Croatia	2011		ES/BS, 2008	Yes	2003	2010	2011	2009
Cuba	2002	MICS, 2006		Yes		2008	2006	2000
Curaçao								

	Currency	National accounts					Balance of payments and trade			Government finance	IMF data dissemination standard
		Base year	Reference year	System of National Accounts	SNA price valuation	Alternative conversion factor	PPP survey year	Balance of Payments Manual in use	External debt	System of trade	Accounting concept	
Cyprus	Euro	a	2000		VAB		2005	BPM5		G	C	S
Czech Republic	Czech koruna	2000	1995	b	VAB		2005	BPM5		S	C	S
Denmark	Danish krone	2005		b	VAB		2005	BPM5		S	C	S
Djibouti	Djibouti franc	1990			VAB		2005	BPM5	Actual	G		G
Dominica	East Caribbean dollar	2006		b	VAB			BPM5	Actual	S		G
Dominican Republic	Dominican peso	1991			VAB			BPM5	Actual	G	C	G
Ecuador	U.S. dollar	2000		b	VAB		2005	BPM5	Actual	G	B	S
Egypt, Arab Rep.	Egyptian pound	1991/92			VAB		2005	BPM5	Actual	G	C	S
El Salvador	U.S. dollar	1990			VAB			BPM5	Actual	S	C	S
Equatorial Guinea	CFA franc	2000			VAB	1965–84	2005			G		
Eritrea	Eritrean nakfa	1992			VAB			BPM4	Actual			
Estonia	Estonian kroon	2000		b	VAB	1987–95	2005	BPM5		S	C	S
Ethiopia	Ethiopian birr	1999/2000		b	VAB		2005	BPM5	Actual	G	B	G
Faeroe Islands	Danish krone				VAB			BPM5		G		
Fiji	Fijian dollar	2005			VAB		2005	BPM5	Actual	G	B	G
Finland	Euro	2005		b	VAB		2005	BPM5		G	C	S
France	Euro	a	2005	b	VAB		2005	BPM5		S	C	S
French Polynesia	CFP franc									S		
Gabon	CFA franc	1991			VAP	1993	2005	BPM5	Actual	S		G
Gambia, The	Gambian dalasi	1987			VAB		2005	BPM5	Actual	G	C	G
Georgia	Georgian lari	a	1996	b	VAB	1990–95	2005	BPM5	Actual	G	C	S
Germany	Euro	2005		b	VAB		2005	BPM5		S	C	S
Ghana	New Ghanaian cedi	2006			VAB	1973–87	2005	BPM5	Actual	G	B	G
Gibraltar	Gibraltar pound											
Greece	Euro	a	2005		VAB		2005	BPM5		S	C	S
Greenland	Danish krone									G		
Grenada	East Caribbean dollar	2006			VAB			BPM5	Actual	S	B	G
Guam	U.S. dollar									G		
Guatemala	Guatemalan quetzal	2001		b	VAB			BPM5	Actual	S	B	G
Guinea	Guinean franc	1996			VAB		2005	BPM5	Estimate	S	B	G
Guinea-Bissau	CFA franc	2005			VAB		2005	BPM5	Estimate	G		G
Guyana	Guyana dollar	2006			VAB			BPM5	Actual	S		G
Haiti	Haitian gourde	1986/87			VAB	1991		BPM5	Actual	G		G
Honduras	Honduran lempira	2000		b	VAB	1988–89		BPM5	Actual	S	C	G
Hungary	Hungarian forint	a	2005	b	VAB		2005	BPM5		S	C	S
Iceland	Iceland krona	2005			VAB		2005	BPM5		G	C	S
India	Indian rupee	2004/05		b	VAB		2005	BPM5	Actual	G	C	S
Indonesia	Indonesian rupiah	2000			VAP		2005	BPM5	Actual	S	B	S
Iran, Islamic Rep.	Iranian rial	1997/98			VAB	1980–2002	2005	BPM4	Actual	S	C	
Iraq	Iraqi dinar	1997			VAB	1997, 2004	2005	BPM5				G
Ireland	Euro	2005		b	VAB		2005	BPM5		G	C	S
Isle of Man	Pound sterling	2005	2003									
Israel	Israeli new shekel	2005		b	VAP		2005	BPM5		S	C	S
Italy	Euro	2005		b	VAB		2005	BPM5		S	C	S
Jamaica	Jamaican dollar	2003			VAB			BPM5	Actual	G	C	G
Japan	Japanese yen	2005			VAB		2005	BPM5		G	C	S
Jordan	Jordanian dinar	1994			VAB		2005	BPM5	Actual	G	B	S
Kazakhstan	Kazakh tenge	a	2000	b	VAB	1987–95	2005	BPM5	Actual	G	C	S
Kenya	Kenyan shilling	2001		b	VAB		2005	BPM5	Actual	G	B	G
Kiribati	Australian dollar	2006			VAB			BPM5		G		G
Korea, Dem. Rep.	Democratic People's Republic of Korean won							BPM4				
Korea, Rep.	Korean won	2005		b	VAB		2005	BPM5		G	C	S
Kosovo	Euro								Actual			G
Kuwait	Kuwaiti dinar	1995			VAP		2005	BPM5		S	B	S
Kyrgyz Republic	Kyrgyz som	a	1995	b	VAB	1990–95	2005	BPM5	Actual	S	C	S
Lao PDR	Lao kip	1990			VAB		2005	BPM5	Preliminary	S		G
Latvia	Latvian lats	2000		b	VAB	1987–95	2005	BPM5	Actual	S	C	S
Lebanon	Lebanese pound	1997			VAB		2005	BPM5	Actual	G	B	G

	Latest population census	Latest demographic, education, or health household survey	Source of most recent income and expenditure data	Vital registration complete	Latest agricultural census	Latest industrial data	Latest trade data	Latest water withdrawal data
Cyprus	2001			Yes		2008	2010	2009
Czech Republic	2011	RHS, 1993	IS, 1996	Yes	2010	2010	2010	2007
Denmark	2011		ITR, 1997	Yes	2010	2010	2010	2009
Djibouti	2009	MICS, 2006	PS, 2002			2007	2009	2000
Dominica	2011			Yes		2010	2010	2004
Dominican Republic	2010	DHS, 2007	IHS, 2010		1971	2010	2010	2000
Ecuador	2010	RHS, 2004	LFS, 2010		2012	2010	2010	2000
Egypt, Arab Rep.	2006	DHS, 2008	ES/BS, 2008	Yes	2010	2010	2010	2000
El Salvador	2007	RHS, 2008	IHS, 2009	Yes	2007–08	2010	2010	2000
Equatorial Guinea	2002			.		2009		2000
Eritrea	1984	DHS, 2002				2009	2005	2004
Estonia	2000		ES/BS, 2004	Yes	2010	2009	2011	2007
Ethiopia	2007	DHS, 2005	ES/BS, 2005		2001–02	2010	2011	2002
Faeroe Islands	2011			Yes			2009	
Fiji	2007		ES/BS, 2009	Yes	2009	2010	2010	2000
Finland	2010		IS, 2000	Yes	2010	2010	2010	2005
France	2006c		ES/BS, 1994/95	Yes	2010	2009	2010	2007
French Polynesia	2007			Yes			2010	
Gabon	2003	DHS, 2000	CWIQ/IHS, 2005		1974–75	2010	2010	2000
Gambia, The	2003	MICS, 2005/06	IHS, 2003		2001–02	2010	2010	2000
Georgia	2002	MICS, 2005; RHS, 2005	IHS, 2009	Yes	2004	2010	2010	2005
Germany	2011		IHS, 2000	Yes	2010	2010	2010	2007
Ghana	2010	DHS, 2008	LSMS, 2006		2011	2010	2010	2000
Gibraltar	2001			Yes				
Greece	2011		IHS, 2000	Yes	2009	2009	2010	2007
Greenland	2010			Yes			2007	
Grenada	2011			Yes	2011	2010	2009	2005
Guam	2010			Yes				
Guatemala	2002	RHS, 2002	LSMS, 2006	Yes	2008	2010	2010	2000
Guinea	1996	DHS, 2005	CWIQ, 2007		2000–01	2010	2008	2000
Guinea-Bissau	2009	MICS, 2010	CWIQ, 2002		1988	2002	2005	2000
Guyana	2002	DHS, 2009	IHS, 1998			2010	2010	2000
Haiti	2003	DHS, 2005/06	IHS, 2001		2009		1997	2000
Honduras	2001	DHS, 2005/06	IHS, 2009		2013	2010	2009	2000
Hungary	2001		ES/BS, 2007	Yes	2007	2010	2010	2007
Iceland	d			Yes	2010	2009	2010	2005
India	2011	DHS, 2005/06	IHS, 2010		2011	2010	2010	2010
Indonesia	2010	DHS, 2007	IHS, 2011		2003	2010	2010	2000
Iran, Islamic Rep.	2006	DHS, 2000	ES/BS, 2005	Yes	2003	2007	2010	2004
Iraq	1997	MICS, 2006	IHS, 2007		2011	2003	2009	2000
Ireland	2011		IHS, 2000	Yes	2010	2009	2010	2000
Isle of Man	2006			Yes				
Israel	2009		ES/BS, 2001	Yes	1981		2010	2004
Italy	2012		ES/BS, 2000	Yes	2010	2010	2010	2000
Jamaica	2011	MICS, 2005	LSMS, 2007		2007	2010	2010	2000
Japan	2010		IS, 1993	Yes	2010	2009	2011	2001
Jordan	2004	DHS, 2009	ES/BS, 2010		2007	2010	2010	2005
Kazakhstan	2009	MICS, 2006	ES/BS, 2009	Yes		2010	2009	2000
Kenya	2009	DHS, 2008/09; MIS, 2010	IHS, 2005/06		1977–79	2010	2010	2003
Kiribati	2005					2009	2009	
Korea, Dem. Rep.	2009	MICS, 2010						2005
Korea, Rep.	2010		ES/BS, 1998	Yes	2000	2010	2010	2002
Kosovo	1981		IHS, 2009			2010		
Kuwait	2010	FHS, 1996		Yes	1970	2003	2009	2002
Kyrgyz Republic	2009	MICS, 2005/06	ES/BS, 2010	Yes	2002	2010	2010	2000
Lao PDR	2005	MICS, 2006	ES/BS, 2008		2010–11	2010	1975	2005
Latvia	2011		IHS, 2008	Yes	2010	2010	2010	2000
Lebanon	1970	MICS, 2000		Yes	2010	2010	2010	2005

	Currency	Base year	Reference year	System of National Accounts	SNA price valuation	Alternative conversion factor	PPP survey year	Balance of Payments Manual in use	External debt	System of trade	Accounting concept	IMF data dissemination standard
Lesotho	Lesotho loti	1995		[b]	VAB		2005	BPM5	Actual	G	C	G
Liberia	Liberian dollar	1992			VAP		2005	BPM5	Actual	S	B	G
Libya	Libyan dinar	1999			VAB	1986		BPM5		G		G
Liechtenstein	Swiss franc				VAB					S		
Lithuania	Lithuanian litas	2000		[b]	VAB	1990–95	2005	BPM5	Actual	G	C	S
Luxembourg	Euro		2005		VAB		2005	BPM5		S	C	S
Macedonia, FYR	Macedonian denar	1997	1995	[b]	VAB		2005	BPM5	Actual	S		S
Madagascar	Malagasy ariary	1984			VAB		2005	BPM5	Actual	S	C	G
Malawi	Malawi kwacha	1994			VAB		2005	BPM5	Actual	G		G
Malaysia	Malaysian ringgit	2000			VAP		2005	BPM5	Estimate	G	B	S
Maldives	Maldivian rufiyaa	2003			VAB		2005	BPM5	Actual	G	C	G
Mali	CFA franc	1987			VAB		2005	BPM5	Actual	S	B	G
Malta	Euro	2005			VAB		2005	BPM5		G	C	S
Marshall Islands	U.S. dollar	2004			VAB					G		
Mauritania	Mauritanian ouguiya	2004			VAB		2005	BPM4	Actual	S		G
Mauritius	Mauritian rupee	2006			VAB		2005	BPM5	Actual	G	C	G
Mayotte	Euro									G		
Mexico	Mexican peso	2003		[b]	VAB		2005	BPM5	Actual	G	C	S
Micronesia, Fed. Sts.	U.S. dollar	2004			VAB					G		
Moldova	Moldovan leu	[a]	1996	[b]	VAB	1990–95	2005	BPM5	Actual	G	C	S
Monaco	Euro									S		
Mongolia	Mongolian tugrik	2005		[b]	VAB		2005	BPM5	Actual	G	C	G
Montenegro	Euro	2000		[b]	VAB		2005	BPM5	Actual	S		G
Morocco	Moroccan dirham	1998			VAB		2005	BPM5	Actual	S	C	S
Mozambique	New Mozambican metical	2003			VAB	1992–95	2005	BPM5	Actual	S		G
Myanmar	Myanmar kyat	2005/06			VAP			BPM5	Estimate	G	C	
Namibia	Namibian dollar	2004/05		[b]	VAB		2005	BPM5		G	B	G
Nepal	Nepalese rupee	2000/01			VAB		2005	BPM5	Actual	G	C	G
Netherlands	Euro	[a]	2005	[b]	VAB		2005	BPM5		S	C	S
New Caledonia	CFP franc									S		
New Zealand	New Zealand dollar	2005/06			VAB		2005	BPM5		G	C	
Nicaragua	Nicaraguan gold cordoba	1994		[b]	VAB	1965–95		BPM5	Actual	G	B	G
Niger	CFA franc	1987			VAP	1993	2005	BPM5	Actual	S	B	G
Nigeria	Nigerian naira	2002			VAB	1971–98	2005	BPM5	Actual	G	B	G
Northern Mariana Islands	U.S. dollar											
Norway	Norwegian krone	[a]	2005	[b]	VAB		2005	BPM5		G	C	S
Oman	Rial Omani	1988			VAP		2005	BPM5		G	B	G
Pakistan	Pakistani rupee	1999/2000		[b]	VAB		2005	BPM5	Actual	B	B	G
Palau	U.S. dollar	1995			VAB					S		
Panama	Panamanian balboa	1996		[b]	VAB			BPM5	Actual	S	C	G
Papua New Guinea	Papua New Guinea kina	1998			VAB	1989		BPM5	Actual	G	B	G
Paraguay	Paraguayan guarani	1994			VAP		2005	BPM5	Actual	S	B	G
Peru	Peruvian new sol	1994			VAB	1985–90	2005	BPM5	Actual	S	C	S
Philippines	Philippine peso	2000			VAP		2005	BPM5	Actual	G	B	S
Poland	Polish zloty	[a]	2005	[b]	VAB		2005	BPM5		S	C	S
Portugal	Euro	2005		[b]	VAB		2005	BPM5		S	C	S
Puerto Rico	U.S. dollar	1954			VAP					G		
Qatar	Qatari riyal	2001			VAP		2005			S	B	G
Romania	New Romanian leu	[a]	2005	[b]	VAB	1987–89, 1992	2005	BPM5	Actual	S	C	S
Russian Federation	Russian ruble	2000		[b]	VAB	1987–95	2005	BPM5	Preliminary	G	C	S
Rwanda	Rwandan franc	1995			VAP	1994	2005	BPM5	Actual	G	C	G
Samoa	Samoan tala	2002			VAB			BPM5	Actual	S		
San Marino	Euro	1995	2000	[b]	VAB						C	G
São Tomé and Príncipe	São Tomé and Príncipe dobra	2001			VAP		2005	BPM4	Actual	S		G

PRIMARY DATA DOCUMENTATION

	Latest population census	Latest demographic, education, or health household survey	Source of most recent income and expenditure data	Vital registration complete	Latest agricultural census	Latest industrial data	Latest trade data	Latest water withdrawal data
Lesotho	2006	DHS, 2009/10	ES/BS, 2002/03		2010	2010	2008	2000
Liberia	2008	DHS, 2007; MIS, 2009	CWIQ, 2007			2008	1985	2000
Libya	2006	MICS, 2000			2001	2008	2004	2000
Liechtenstein	2010			Yes				
Lithuania	2011		ES/BS, 2008	Yes	2010	2009	2010	2007
Luxembourg	2011			Yes	2010	2010	2010	1999
Macedonia, FYR	2010	MICS, 2005	ES/BS, 2009	Yes	2007	2010	2009	2007
Madagascar	1993	DHS, 2008/09	PS, 2010		2004	2009	2010	2000
Malawi	2008	DHS, 2010	LSMS, 2004/05		2006–07	2010	2010	2000
Malaysia	2010		ES/BS, 2009	Yes	2012	2010	2010	2005
Maldives	2011	DHS, 2009	IHS, 2004	Yes		2010	2010	2008
Mali	2009	DHS, 2006; Special, 2010	IHS, 2010			2007	2010	2000
Malta	2005			Yes	2010	2009	2010	2002
Marshall Islands	2011							
Mauritania	2000	MICS, 2007	IHS, 2008			2010	2010	2000
Mauritius	2011			Yes		2010	2010	2003
Mayotte	2007			Yes			2009	
Mexico	2010	ENPF, 1995	LFS, 2010		2007	2010	2010	2008
Micronesia, Fed. Sts.	2000		IHS, 2000			1983		
Moldova	2004	DHS, 2005	ES/BS, 2010	Yes	2011	2010	2010	2000
Monaco	2008			Yes				
Mongolia	2010	MICS, 2010	LSMS, 2007/08	Yes	2011	2010	2007	2005
Montenegro	2011	MICS, 2005/06	ES/BS, 2008	Yes	2010	2010		
Morocco	2004	MICS, 2006	ES/BS, 2007		2012	2010	2010	2000
Mozambique	2007	DHS, 2003; AIS, 2009	ES/BS, 2008		2009–10	2010	2010	2000
Myanmar	1983	MICS, 2000			2010–11	2010	2001	2000
Namibia	2001	DHS, 2006/07; HIV/MCH SPA, 2009	ES/BS, 2004		1996–97	2010	2008	2000
Nepal	2001	MICS, 2010	LSMS, 2010		2011–12	2010	2010	2005
Netherlands	2011		IHS, 1999	Yes	2010	2010	2010	2008
New Caledonia	2009			Yes		1997	2010	
New Zealand	2006		IS, 1997	Yes	2012	2006	2010	2002
Nicaragua	2005	RHS, 2006/07	LSMS, 2005		2011	2010	2010	2000
Niger	2001	DHS, 2006	CWIQ/PS, 2008		2005–07	2003	2010	2000
Nigeria	2006	DHS, 2008	IHS, 2010		2007	2006	2010	2000
Northern Mariana Islands	2010							
Norway	2001		IS, 2000	Yes	2010	2010	2010	2006
Oman	2010	FHS, 1995			1978–79	2004	2010	2003
Pakistan	1998	MICS, 2010	IHS, 2008		2000	2010	2010	2008
Palau	2010			Yes		2007		
Panama	2010	LSMS, 2003	LFS, 2010		2011	2010	2010	2000
Papua New Guinea	2000	DHS, 1996	IHS, 1996			2010	2005	2005
Paraguay	2002	RHS, 2004	IHS, 2010		2008	2010	2011	2000
Peru	2007	DHS, 2007/08	IHS, 2010		2012	2010	2010	2000
Philippines	2010	DHS, 2008	ES/BS, 2009	Yes	2012	2010	2010	2009
Poland	2011		ES/BS, 2009	Yes	2010	2010	2010	2009
Portugal	2011		IS, 1997	Yes	2009	2010	2010	2002
Puerto Rico	2010	RHS, 1995/96		Yes	2007	2010		2005
Qatar	2010			Yes	2000–01		2009	2005
Romania	2011	RHS, 1999	LFS, 2009	Yes	2010	2010	2010	2009
Russian Federation	2010	RHS, 1996	IHS, 2009	Yes	2006	2010	2010	2001
Rwanda	2002	DHS, 2007/08	IHS, 2011		2008	2009	2010	2000
Samoa	2006	DHS, 2009			2009	2010	2010	
San Marino	2010			Yes				
São Tomé and Príncipe	2001	DHS, 2008/09	PS, 2000/01		2011	2005	2010	1993

	Currency	Base year	Reference year	System of National Accounts	SNA price valuation	Alternative conversion factor	PPP survey year	Balance of Payments Manual in use	External debt	System of trade	Accounting concept	IMF data dissemination standard
Saudi Arabia	Saudi Arabian riyal	1999			VAP		2005	BPM5		S		G
Senegal	CFA franc	1999	1987	b	VAB		2005	BPM5	Actual	G	B	G
Serbia	New Serbian dinar	a	2002	b	VAB		2005	BPM5	Actual	S	C	G
Seychelles	Seychelles rupee	1986			VAP			BPM5	Actual	G	C	G
Sierra Leone	Sierra Leonean leone	1990		b	VAB		2005	BPM5	Actual	S	B	G
Singapore	Singapore dollar	2005		b	VAB		2005	BPM5		G	C	S
Sint Maarten	Netherlands Antilles guilder											
Slovak Republic	Euro	2005		b	VAB		2005	BPM5		S	C	S
Slovenia	Euro	a	2005	b	VAB		2005	BPM5		S	C	S
Solomon Islands	Solomon Islands dollar	2004			VAB			BPM5	Actual	S		G
Somalia	Somali shilling	1985			VAB	1977–90			Estimate			
South Africa	South African rand	2005		b	VAB		2005	BPM5	Preliminary	G	C	S
South Sudan	South Sudanese Pound											
Spain	Euro	2005		b	VAB		2005	BPM5		S	C	S
Sri Lanka	Sri Lankan rupee	2002			VAP		2005	BPM5	Actual	G	B	G
St. Kitts and Nevis	East Caribbean dollar	2006		b	VAB			BPM5	Actual	S	C	G
St. Lucia	East Caribbean dollar	2006			VAB			BPM5	Actual	S		G
St. Martin	Euro											
St. Vincent & Grenadines	East Caribbean dollar	2006			VAB			BPM5	Actual	S	B	G
Sudan	Sudanese pound	1981/82e	1996		VAB		2005	BPM5	Actual	G	B	G
Suriname	Suriname dollar	1990		b	VAB			BPM5		G		G
Swaziland	Swaziland lilangeni	2000			VAB		2005	BPM5	Actual	G	B	G
Sweden	Swedish krona	a	2005		VAB		2005	BPM5		G	C	S
Switzerland	Swiss franc	2005			VAB		2005	BPM5		S	C	S
Syrian Arab Republic	Syrian pound	2000			VAB	1970–2010	2005	BPM5	Actual	S	C	G
Tajikistan	Tajik somoni	a	2000	b	VAB	1990–95	2005	BPM5	Actual	G	C	G
Tanzania	Tanzanian shilling	a	2001		VAB		2005	BPM5	Actual	G		G
Thailand	Thai baht	1988			VAP		2005	BPM5	Actual	S	C	S
Timor-Leste	U.S. dollar	2000			VAP					G		
Togo	CFA franc	1978			VAP		2005	BPM5	Actual	S	B	G
Tonga	Tongan pa'anga	2000/01			VAB			BPM5	Actual	G		G
Trinidad and Tobago	Trinidad and Tobago dollar	2000		b	VAB			BPM5		S	C	G
Tunisia	Tunisian dinar	1990			VAB		2005	BPM5	Actual	G	C	S
Turkey	New Turkish lira	1998			VAB		2005	BPM5	Actual	S	B	S
Turkmenistan	New Turkmen manat	a	2007	b	VAB	1987–95, 1997–2007		BPM4	Estimate	G		
Turks and Caicos Islands	U.S. dollar									G		
Tuvalu	Australian dollar				VAP					G		
Uganda	Ugandan shilling	2001/02			VAB		2005	BPM5	Actual	G	B	G
Ukraine	Ukrainian hryvnia	a	2003	b	VAB	1987–95	2005	BPM5	Actual	G	C	S
United Arab Emirates	U.A.E. dirham	2007			VAP			BPM5		G	B	G
United Kingdom	Pound sterling	2005		b	VAB		2005	BPM5		G	C	S
United States	U.S. dollar	a	2005		VAB		2005	BPM5		G	C	S
Uruguay	Uruguayan peso	2005			VAB		2005	BPM5	Actual	G	C	S
Uzbekistan	Uzbek sum	a	1997	b	VAB	1990–95		BPM4	Actual	G		
Vanuatu	Vanuatu vatu	2006			VAB			BPM5	Estimate	G	C	G
Venezuela, R.B.	Venezuelan bolivar fuerte	1997			VAB		2005	BPM5	Actual	G	C	G
Vietnam	Vietnamese dong	1994		b	VAP	1991	2005	BPM5	Preliminary	G		G
Virgin Islands (U.S.)	U.S. dollar	1982								G		
West Bank and Gaza	Israeli new shekel	1997			VAB			BPM5		S	B	G
Yemen, Rep.	Yemeni rial	1990			VAP	1990–96	2005	BPM5	Actual	G	B	G
Zambia	Zambian kwacha	1994			VAB	1990–92	2005	BPM5	Preliminary	S	B	G
Zimbabwe	U.S. dollar	2009			VAB	1991, 1998	2005	BPM4	Actual	G	C	G

PRIMARY DATA DOCUMENTATION

	Latest population census	Latest demographic, education, or health household survey	Source of most recent income and expenditure data	Vital registration complete	Latest agricultural census	Latest industrial data	Latest trade data	Latest water withdrawal data
Saudi Arabia	2010	Demographic survey, 2007			2010	2010	2010	2006
Senegal	2002	DHS, 2005; MIS, 2008/09	PS, 2005		2011–12	2010	2011	2002
Serbia	2011	MICS, 2005/06	IHS, 2009	Yes	2012	2010	2008	2009
Seychelles	2010		IHS, 2007	Yes	2011	2009	2008	2005
Sierra Leone	2004	DHS, 2008	IHS, 2003		1984–85	2003	2002	2000
Singapore	2010	General household, 2005		Yes		2010	2010	
Sint Maarten								
Slovak Republic	2011		IS, 2009	Yes	2001	2010	2010	2007
Slovenia	2011		ES/BS, 2004	Yes	2010	2010	2010	2009
Solomon Islands	2009				2012	2009	2007	
Somalia	1987	MICS, 2006			1990	1982		2003
South Africa	2001	DHS, 2003	ES/BS, 2009		2012	2010	2010	2000
South Sudan	2008							
Spain	2001		IHS, 2000	Yes	1999	2009	2010	2008
Sri Lanka	2001	DHS, 2006/07	ES/BS, 2007	Yes	2012	2010	2010	2005
St. Kitts and Nevis	2011			Yes		2010	2008	
St. Lucia	2010		IHS, 1995	Yes		2010	2008	2005
St. Martin								
St. Vincent & Grenadines	2011			Yes		2010	2010	1995
Sudan	2008	MICS, 2010	ES/BS, 2009			2010	2009	2000 f
Suriname	2004	MICS, 2006	ES/BS, 1999	Yes	2008	2009	2010	2000
Swaziland	2007	MICS, 2010	ES/BS, 2010		2003	2010	2007	2000
Sweden	d		IS, 2000	Yes	2010	2010	2010	2007
Switzerland	2010		ES/BS, 2000	Yes	2008	2010	2010	2000
Syrian Arab Republic	2004	MICS, 2006	ES/BS, 2004		2014	2002	2008	2005
Tajikistan	2010	MICS, 2005	LSMS, 2009		2013	2010	2000	2000
Tanzania	2002	DHS, 2010	ES/BS, 2007		2007–08	2010	2011	2002
Thailand	2010	MICS, 2005/06	IHS, 2009		2013	2010	2010	2007
Timor-Leste	2010	DHS, 2009/10	LSMS, 2007		2012	2000	2005	2004
Togo	2010	MICS, 2010	CWIQ, 2006		2011–12	2005	2010	2002
Tonga	2006			Yes	2011–12	2010	2010	
Trinidad and Tobago	2011	MICS, 2006	IHS, 1992	Yes	2004	2010	2010	2000
Tunisia	2004	MICS, 2006	IHS, 2005/06		2004	2010	2010	2001
Turkey	2000	DHS, 2003	LFS, 2008		2001	2010	2010	2003
Turkmenistan	1995	MICS, 2006	LSMS, 1998	Yes	2004	2000	2000	2000
Turks and Caicos Islands	2001			Yes			2009	
Tuvalu	2002					2008	2008	
Uganda	2002	DHS, 2006; MIS, 2009/10	PS, 2009		2008	2010	2010	2002
Ukraine	2001	DHS, 2007	ES/BS, 2009	Yes	2011	2010	2010	2000
United Arab Emirates	2010				2012	2010	2009	2005
United Kingdom	2011		IS, 1999	Yes	2010	2010	2010	2006
United States	2010	CPS (monthly)	LFS, 2000	Yes	2007	2010	2010	2005
Uruguay	2004		IHS, 2010	Yes	2011	2010	2009	2000
Uzbekistan	1989	MICS, 2006	ES/BS, 2003	Yes		2010		2000
Vanuatu	2009	MICS, 2007			2007	2009	2007	
Venezuela, R.B.	2001	MICS, 2000	IHS, 2009	Yes	2007	2007	2010	2000
Vietnam	2009	MICS, 2006	IHS, 2008	Yes	2011	2010	2009	2005
Virgin Islands (U.S.)	2010			Yes	2007			
West Bank and Gaza	2007	PAPFAM, 2006	IHS, 2009		1971		2008	
Yemen, Rep.	2004	MICS, 2006	ES/BS, 2005		2002	2010	2009	2005
Zambia	2010	DHS, 2007	IHS, 2006		1990	2010	2010	2000
Zimbabwe	2002	DHS, 2005/06	IHS, 2003		1960	2010	2010	2002

Note: For explanation of the abbreviations used in the table, see notes following the table.
a. Original chained constant price data are rescaled. b. Country uses the 1993 System of National Accounts methodology. c. Register based. d. Rolling. e. Reporting period switch from fiscal year to calendar year from 1996. Pre-1996 data converted to calendar year.

• **Base year** is the base or pricing period used for constant price calculations in the country's national accounts. Price indexes derived from national accounts aggregates, such as the implicit deflator for gross domestic product (GDP), express the price level relative to base year prices. • **Reference year** is the year in which the local currency, constant price series of a country is valued. The reference year is usually the same as the base year used to report the constant price series. However, when the constant price data are chain linked, the base year is changed annually, so the data are rescaled to a specific reference year to provide a consistent time series. When the country has not rescaled following a change in base year, World Bank staff rescale the data to maintain a longer historical series. To allow for cross-country comparison and data aggregation, constant price data reported in *World Development Indicators* are rescaled to a common reference year (2000) and currency (U.S. dollars). • **System of National Accounts** identifies countries that use the 1993 System of National Accounts (1993 SNA), the terminology applied in *World Development Indicators* since 2001, to compile national accounts. Although more countries are adopting the 1993 SNA, many still follow the 1968 SNA, and some low-income countries use concepts from the 1953 SNA. • **SNA price valuation** shows whether value added in the national accounts is reported at basic prices (VAB) or producer prices (VAP). Producer prices include taxes paid by producers and thus tend to overstate the actual value added in production. However, VAB can be higher than VAP in countries with high agricultural subsidies. See *About the data* for tables 4.1 and 4.2 for further discussion of national accounts valuation. • **Alternative conversion factor** identifies the countries and years for which a World Bank–estimated conversion factor has been used in place of the official exchange rate (line rf in the International Monetary Fund's [IMF] *International Financial Statistics*). See *Statistical methods* for further discussion of alternative conversion factors. • **Purchasing power parity (PPP) survey year** is the latest available survey year for the International Comparison Program's estimates of PPPs. See *About the data* for table 1.1 for a more detailed description of PPPs. • **Balance of Payments Manual in use** refers to the classification system used to compile and report data on balance of payments items in table 4.17. BPM4 refers to the 4th edition of the IMF's *Balance of Payments Manual* (1977), and BPM5 to the 5th edition (1993). • **External debt** shows debt reporting status for 2010 data. *Actual* indicates that data are as reported, *preliminary* that data are based on reported or collected information but include an element of

staff estimation, and *estimate* that data are World Bank staff estimates. • **System of trade** refers to the United Nations general trade system (G) or special trade system (S). Under the general trade system goods entering directly for domestic consumption and goods entered into customs storage are recorded as imports at arrival. Under the special trade system goods are recorded as imports when declared for domestic consumption whether at time of entry or on withdrawal from customs storage. Exports under the general system comprise outward-moving goods: (a) national goods wholly or partly produced in the country; (b) foreign goods, neither transformed nor declared for domestic consumption in the country, that move outward from customs storage; and (c) nationalized goods that have been declared for domestic consumption and move outward without being transformed. Under the special system of trade, exports are categories a and c. In some compilations categories b and c are classified as re-exports. Direct transit trade—goods entering or leaving for transport only—is excluded from both import and export statistics. See *About the data* for tables 4.4, 4.5, and 6.2 for further discussion. • **Government finance accounting concept** is the accounting basis for reporting central government financial data. For most countries government finance data have been consolidated (C) into one set of accounts capturing all central government fiscal activities. Budgetary central government accounts (B) exclude some central government units. See *About the data* for tables 4.12, 4.13, and 4.14 for further details. • **IMF data dissemination standard** shows the countries that subscribe to the IMF's Special Data Dissemination Standard (SDDS) or General Data Dissemination System (GDDS). S refers to countries that subscribe to the SDDS and have posted data on the Dissemination Standards Bulletin Board at http://dsbb.imf.org. G refers to countries that subscribe to the GDDS. The SDDS was established for member countries that have or might seek access to international capital markets to guide them in providing their economic and financial data to the public. The GDDS helps countries disseminate comprehensive, timely, accessible, and reliable economic, financial, and sociodemographic statistics. IMF member countries elect to participate in either the SDDS or the GDDS. Both standards enhance the availability of timely and comprehensive data and therefore contribute to the pursuit of sound macroeconomic policies. The SDDS is also expected to improve the functioning of financial markets. • **Latest population census** shows the most recent year in which a census was conducted and in which at least preliminary results have been released. The preliminary results

from the very recent censuses could be reflected in timely revisions if basic data are available, such as population by age and sex, as well as the detailed definition of counting, coverage, and completeness. Countries that hold register-based censuses produce similar census tables every 5 or 10 years. Germany's 2001 census is a register-based test census using a sample of 1.2 percent of the population. A rare case, France has been conducting a rolling census every year since 2004; the 1999 general population census was the last to cover the entire population simultaneously (www.insee.fr/en/recensement/page_accueil_rp.htm). • **Latest demographic, education, or health household survey** indicates the household surveys used to compile the demographic, education, and health data in section 2. AIS is HIV/AIDS Indicator Survey, CPS is Current Population Survey, DGHS is Demographic and General Health Survey, DHS is Demographic and Health Survey, ENPF is National Family Planning Survey (Encuesta Nacional de Planificacion Familiar), FHS is Family Health Survey, LSMS is Living Standards Measurement Survey, MICS is Multiple Indicator Cluster Survey, MIS is Malaria Indicator Survey, NSS is National Sample Survey on Population Change, PAPFAM is Pan Arab Project for Family Health, RHS is Reproductive Health Survey, and SPA is Service Provision Assessments. Detailed information for AIS, DHS, MIS, and SPA are available at www.measuredhs.com/aboutsurveys; for MICS at www.childinfo.org; and for RHS at www.cdc.gov/reproductivehealth/surveys. • **Source of most recent income and expenditure data** shows household surveys that collect income and expenditure data. Names and detailed information on household surveys can be found on the website of the International Household Survey Network (www.surveynetwork.org). Core Welfare Indicator Questionnaire Surveys (CWIQ), developed by the World Bank, measure changes in key social indicators for different population groups—specifically indicators of access, utilization, and satisfaction with core social and economic services. Expenditure survey/budget surveys (ES/BS) collect detailed information on household consumption as well as on general demographic, social, and economic characteristics. Integrated household surveys (IHS) collect detailed information on a wide variety of topics, including health, education, economic activities, housing, and utilities. Income surveys (IS) collect information on the income and wealth of households as well as various social and economic characteristics. Labor force surveys (LFS) collect information on employment, unemployment, hours of work, income, and wages. Living Standards Measurement Studies (LSMS), developed by the World Bank, provide a comprehensive picture of household welfare and the factors that affect it; they typically incorporate data collection at the individual, household, and community levels. Priority surveys (PS) are a light monitoring survey, designed by the World Bank, for collecting data from a large number of households cost-effectively and quickly. Income tax registers (ITR) provide information on a population's income and allowance, such as gross income, taxable income, and taxes by socioeconomic group. 1-2-3 surveys (1-2-3) are implemented in three phases and collect sociodemographic and employment data, data on the informal sector, and information on living conditions and household consumption. • **Vital registration complete** identifies countries that report at least 90 percent complete registries of vital (birth and death) statistics to the United Nations Statistics Division and reported in Population and Vital Statistics Reports. Countries with complete vital statistics registries may have more accurate and more timely demographic indicators than other countries. • **Latest agricultural census** shows the most recent year in which an agricultural census was conducted and reported to the Food and Agriculture Organization of the United Nations. • **Latest industrial data** show the most recent year for which manufacturing value added data at the three-digit level of the International Standard Industrial Classification (ISIC, revision 2 or 3) are available in the United Nations Industrial Development Organization database. • **Latest trade data** show the most recent year for which structure of merchandise trade data from the United Nations Statistics Division's Commodity Trade (Comtrade) database are available. • **Latest water withdrawal data** show the most recent year for which data on freshwater withdrawals have been compiled from a variety of sources. See About the data for table 3.5 for more information.

Exceptional reporting periods

In most economies the **fiscal year** is concurrent with the calendar year. Exceptions are shown in the table at right. The ending date reported here is for the fiscal year of the central government. Fiscal years for other levels of government and reporting years for statistical surveys may differ.

The **reporting period for national accounts data** is designated as either calendar year basis (CY) or fiscal year basis (FY). Most economies report their national accounts and balance of payments data using calendar years, but some use fiscal years. In World Development Indicators fiscal year data are assigned to the calendar year that contains the larger share of the fiscal year. If a country's fiscal year ends before June 30, data are shown in the first year of

the fiscal period; if the fiscal year ends on or after June 30, data are shown in the second year of the period. Balance of payments data are reported in World Development Indicators by calendar year.

Economies with exceptional reporting periods

Economy	Fiscal year end	Reporting period for national accounts data
Afghanistan	Mar. 20	FY
Australia	Jun. 30	FY
Bangladesh	Jun. 30	FY
Botswana	Jun. 30	FY
Canada	Mar. 31	CY
Egypt, Arab Rep.	Jun. 30	FY
Ethiopia	Jul. 7	FY
Gambia, The	Jun. 30	CY
Haiti	Sep. 30	FY
India	Mar. 31	FY
Indonesia	Mar. 31	CY
Iran, Islamic Rep.	Mar. 20	FY
Japan	Mar. 31	CY
Kenya	Jun. 30	CY
Kuwait	Jun. 30	CY
Lesotho	Mar. 31	CY
Malawi	Mar. 31	CY
Myanmar	Mar. 31	FY
Namibia	Mar. 31	CY
Nepal	Jul. 14	FY
New Zealand	Mar. 31	FY
Pakistan	Jun. 30	FY
Puerto Rico	Jun. 30	FY
Sierra Leone	Jun. 30	CY
Singapore	Mar. 31	CY
South Africa	Mar. 31	CY
Swaziland	Mar. 31	CY
Sweden	Jun. 30	CY
Thailand	Sep. 30	CY
Uganda	Jun. 30	FY
United States	Sep. 30	CY
Zimbabwe	Jun. 30	CY

Revisions to national accounts data

National accounts data are revised by national statistical offices when methodologies change or data sources improve. National accounts data in World Development Indicators are also revised when data sources change. The following notes, while not comprehensive, provide information on revisions from previous data.

• **Antigua and Barbuda.** Based on official government statistics, national accounts data have been revised for 2000 onward; the new base year is 2006.

• **Azerbaijan.** National accounts historical expenditure series in constant prices have been revised in

line with State Statistical Committee data that were not previously available. • **Botswana.** The Central Statistical Office has revised national accounts series for 2004 onward. • **Dominica.** Based on official government statistics, national accounts data have been revised for 2000 onward; the new base year is 2006. • **Grenada.** Based on official government statistics, national accounts data have been revised for 2000 onward; the new base year is 2006. • **Hungary.** Based on data from the Organisation for Economic Co-operation and Development, national accounts data have been revised for 1991 onward. • **Macedonia.** Based on official statistics, national accounts data have been revised for 2003 onward. • **Maldives.** The Department of National Planning has revised national accounts data for 2000 onward; the new base year is 2003. • **Mauritania.** Based on official government statistics, data have been revised for 1991 onward; the new base year for constant price series is 2004. • **Philippines.** National accounts data have been revised for 1998 onward. Because intellectual property products are now reported as a part of gross fixed capital formation, gross domestic product (GDP) in current prices averages 4 percent higher than previous estimates. • **Puerto Rico.** Based on data from the Instituto de Estadísticas de Puerto Rico, national accounts data have been revised for 2001 onward. • **Serbia.** The Statistical Office has improved the methodology of national accounts data for 2003 onward. Specifically, the classification of sectors has been revised, and GDP is now calculated using chain linked volumes in 2005 prices. • **Singapore.** National accounts time series have been replaced with official government statistics. • **St. Kitts and Nevis, St. Lucia, and St. Vincent and the Grenadines.** Based on official government statistics, national accounts data have been revised for 2000 onward; the new base year is 2006. • **Swaziland.** The Central Statistical Office has revised national accounts data for 1990 onward. • **Syria.** The Central Bureau of Statistics has revised national accounts data for 2003 onward. • **Tunisia.** Based on data from the Central Bank and its Statistical Bulletin, national accounts data have been revised for 1997 onward. • **Uganda.** The Bureau of Statistics has revised national accounts series for 1998 onward; the new base year for constant price series is 2001/02. • **United Arab Emirates.** The National Bureau of Statistics has revised national accounts data for 2001 onward; the new base year is 2007. • **Uruguay.** The Central Bank has revised national accounts data for 2006 onward. • **Yemen.** Based on official government statistics and International Monetary Fund data, national accounts data have been revised for 1990 onward.

STATISTICAL METHODS

This section describes some of the statistical procedures used in preparing *World Development Indicators*. It covers the methods employed for calculating regional and income group aggregates and for calculating growth rates, and it describes the *World Bank Atlas* method for deriving the conversion factor used to estimate gross national income (GNI) and GNI per capita in U.S. dollars. Other statistical procedures and calculations are described in the *About the data* sections following each table.

Aggregation rules

Aggregates based on the World Bank's regional and income classifications of economies appear at the end of most tables. The countries included in these classifications are shown on the flaps on the front and back covers of the book. Most tables also include the aggregate euro area. This aggregate includes the member states of the Economic and Monetary Union (EMU) of the European Union that have adopted the euro as their currency: Austria, Belgium, Cyprus, Estonia, Finland, France, Germany, Greece, Ireland, Italy, Luxembourg, Malta, Netherlands, Portugal, Slovak Republic, Slovenia, and Spain. Other classifications, such as the European Union and regional trade blocs, are documented in *About the data* for the tables in which they appear.

Because of missing data, aggregates for groups of economies should be treated as approximations of unknown totals or average values. Regional and income group aggregates are based on the largest available set of data, including values for the 158 economies shown in the main tables, other economies shown in table 1.6, and Taiwan, China. The aggregation rules are intended to yield estimates for a consistent set of economies from one period to the next and for all indicators. Small differences between sums of subgroup aggregates and overall totals and averages may occur because of the approximations used. In addition, compilation errors and data reporting practices may cause discrepancies in theoretically identical aggregates such as world exports and world imports.

Five methods of aggregation are used in *World Development Indicators*:

- For group and world totals denoted in the tables by a *t*, missing data are imputed based on the relationship of the sum of available data to the total in the year of the previous estimate. The imputation process works forward and backward from 2000. Missing values in 2000 are imputed using one of several proxy variables for which complete data are available in that year. The imputed value is calculated so that it (or its proxy) bears the same relationship to the total of available data. Imputed values are usually not calculated if missing data account for more than a third of the total in the benchmark year. The variables used as proxies are GNI in U.S. dollars, total population, exports and imports of goods and services in U.S. dollars, and value added in agriculture, industry, manufacturing, and services in U.S. dollars.
- Aggregates marked by an *s* are sums of available data. Missing values are not imputed. Sums are not computed if more than a third of the observations in the series or a proxy for the series are missing in a given year.
- Aggregates of ratios are denoted by a *w* when calculated as weighted averages of the ratios (using the value of the denominator or, in some cases, another indicator as a weight) and denoted by a *u* when calculated as unweighted averages. The aggregate ratios are based on available data, including data for economies not shown in the main tables. Missing values are assumed to have the same average value as the available data. No aggregate is calculated if missing data account for more than a third of the value of weights in the benchmark year. In a few cases the aggregate ratio may be computed as the ratio of group totals after imputing values for missing data according to the above rules for computing totals.
- Aggregate growth rates are denoted by a *w* when calculated as a weighted average of growth rates. In a few cases growth rates may be computed from time series of group totals. Growth rates are not calculated if more than half the observations in a period are missing. For further discussion of methods of computing growth rates see below.
- Aggregates denoted by an *m* are medians of the values shown in the table. No value is shown if more than half the observations for countries with a population of more than 1 million are missing.

Exceptions to the rules occur throughout the book. Depending on the judgment of World Bank analysts, the aggregates may be based on as little as 50 percent of the available data. In other cases, where missing or excluded values are judged to be small or irrelevant, aggregates are based only on the data shown in the tables.

Growth rates

Growth rates are calculated as annual averages and represented as percentages. Except where noted, growth rates of values are computed from constant price series. Three principal methods are used to calculate growth rates: least squares, exponential endpoint, and geometric endpoint. Rates of change from one period to the next are calculated as proportional changes from the earlier period.

Least squares growth rate. Least squares growth rates are used wherever there is a sufficiently long time series to permit a reliable calculation. No growth rate is calculated if more than half the observations in a period are missing. The least squares growth rate, r, is estimated by fitting a linear regression trend line to the logarithmic annual values of the variable in the relevant period. The regression equation takes the form

$$\ln X_t = a + bt$$

which is the logarithmic transformation of the compound growth equation,

$$X_t = X_o (1 + r)^t.$$

In this equation X is the variable, t is time, and $a = \ln X_o$ and $b = \ln (1 + r)$ are parameters to be estimated. If b^* is the least-squares estimate of b, then the average annual growth rate, r, is obtained as $[\exp(b^*) - 1]$ and is multiplied by 100 for expression as a percentage. The calculated growth rate is an average rate that is representative of the available observations over the entire period. It does not necessarily match the actual growth rate between any two periods.

Exponential growth rate. The growth rate between two points in time for certain demographic indicators, notably labor force and population, is calculated from the equation

$$r = \ln(p_n/p_0)/n$$

where p_n and p_0 are the last and first observations in the period, n is the number of years in the period, and ln is the natural logarithm operator. This growth rate is based on a model of continuous, exponential growth between two points in time. It does not take into account the intermediate values of the series. Nor does it correspond to the annual rate of change measured at a one-year interval, which is given by $(p_n - p_{n-1})/p_{n-1}$.

Geometric growth rate. The geometric growth rate is applicable to compound growth over discrete periods, such as the payment and reinvestment of interest or dividends. Although continuous growth, as modeled by the exponential growth rate, may be more realistic, most economic phenomena are measured only at intervals, in which case the compound growth model is appropriate. The average growth rate over n periods is calculated as

$$r = \exp[\ln(p_n/p_0)/n] - 1.$$

World Bank Atlas method

In calculating GNI and GNI per capita in U.S. dollars for certain operational purposes, the World Bank uses the *Atlas* conversion factor. The purpose of the *Atlas* conversion factor is to reduce the impact of exchange rate fluctuations in the cross-country comparison of national incomes.

The *Atlas* conversion factor for any year is the average of a country's exchange rate (or alternative conversion factor) for that year and its exchange rates for the two preceding years, adjusted for the difference between the rate of inflation in the country and that in Japan, the United Kingdom, the United States, and the euro area. A country's inflation rate is measured by the change in its GDP deflator.

The inflation rate for Japan, the United Kingdom, the United States, and the euro area, representing international inflation, is measured by the change in the "SDR deflator." (Special drawing rights, or SDRs, are the International Monetary Fund's unit of account.) The SDR deflator is calculated as a weighted average of these countries' GDP deflators in SDR terms, the weights being the amount of each country's currency in one SDR unit. Weights vary over time because both the composition of the SDR and the relative exchange rates for each currency change. The SDR deflator is calculated in SDR terms first and then converted to U.S. dollars using the SDR to dollar *Atlas* conversion factor. The *Atlas* conversion factor is then applied to a country's GNI. The resulting GNI in U.S. dollars is divided by the midyear population to derive GNI per capita.

When official exchange rates are deemed to be unreliable or unrepresentative of the effective exchange rate during a period, an alternative estimate of the exchange rate is used in the *Atlas* formula (see below).

The following formulas describe the calculation of the *Atlas* conversion factor for year t:

$$e_t^* = \frac{1}{3}\left[e_{t-2}\left(\frac{p_t}{p_{t-2}} \Big/ \frac{p_t^{S\$}}{p_{t-2}^{S\$}} \right) + e_{t-1}\left(\frac{p_t}{p_{t-1}} \Big/ \frac{p_t^{S\$}}{p_{t-1}^{S\$}} \right) + e_t \right]$$

and the calculation of GNI per capita in U.S. dollars for year t:

$$Y_t^{\$} = (Y_t/N_t)/e_t^*$$

where e_t^* is the *Atlas* conversion factor (national currency to the U.S. dollar) for year t, e_t is the average annual exchange rate (national currency to the U.S. dollar) for year t, p_t is the GDP deflator for year t, $p_t^{S\$}$ is the SDR deflator in U.S. dollar terms for year t, $Y_t^{\$}$ is the *Atlas* GNI per capita in U.S. dollars in year t, Y_t is current GNI (local currency) for year t, and N_t is the midyear population for year t.

Alternative conversion factors

The World Bank systematically assesses the appropriateness of official exchange rates as conversion factors. An alternative conversion factor is used when the official exchange rate is judged to diverge by an exceptionally large margin from the rate effectively applied to domestic transactions of foreign currencies and traded products. This applies to only a small number of countries, as shown in *Primary data documentation*. Alternative conversion factors are used in the *Atlas* methodology and elsewhere in *World Development Indicators* as single-year conversion factors.

CREDITS

1. World view

Section 1 was prepared by a team led by Eric Swanson. Eric Swanson wrote the introduction with input from Neil Fantom, Shota Hatakeyama, Masako Hiraga, Wendy Huang, Hiroko Maeda, Johan Mistiaen, Sulekha Patel, William Prince, Evis Rucaj, and Emi Suzuki and with valuable suggestions from Jose Alejandro Quijada, Sachin Shahria, Jos Verbeek, and participants of the *Global Monitoring Report 2012* seminar series. Bala Bhaskar Naidu Kalimili coordinated tables 1.1 and 1.6. Shota Hatakeyama, Masako Hiraga, Hiroko Maeda, and Johan Mistiaen prepared tables 1.2 and 1.5, and Mahyar Eshragh-Tabary, Shota Hatakeyama, Masako Hiraga, Buyant Erdene Khaltarkhuu, and Hiroko Maeda prepared table 1.3. Wendy Huang prepared table 1.4 with input from Azita Amjadi. Signe Zeikate of the World Bank's Economic Policy and Debt Department provided the estimates of debt relief for the Heavily Indebted Poor Countries Debt Initiative and Multilateral Debt Relief Initiative.

2. People

Section 2 was prepared by Shota Hatakeyama, Masako Hiraga, Hiroko Maeda, and Sulekha Patel in partnership with the World Bank's Human Development Network and the Development Research Group in the Development Economics Vice Presidency. Masako Hiraga, Sulekha Patel, and Johan Mistiaen wrote the introduction with valuable input and comments from Eric Swanson. Emi Suzuki prepared the demographic estimates and projections. The poverty estimates at national poverty lines were compiled by the Global Poverty Working Group, a team of poverty experts from the Poverty Reduction and Equality Network, the Development Research Group, and the Development Data Group. Shaohua Chen and Prem Sangraula of the World Bank's Development Research Group prepared the poverty estimates at international poverty lines. Lorenzo Guarcello and Furio Rosati of the Understanding Children's Work project prepared the data on children at work. Other contributions were provided by Emi Suzuki (health and nutrition); Montserrat Pallares-Miralles and Carolina Romero Robayo (vulnerability and security); Theo door Sparreboom and Alan Wittrup of the International Labour Organization (labor force); Amelie Gagnon, Said Ould Voffal, and Weixin Lu of the United Nations Educational, Scientific, and Cultural Organization Institute for Statistics (education and literacy); the World Health Organization's Chandika Indikadahena (health expenditure), Charu Garg (national health account), Monika Bloessner and Mercedes de Onis (malnutrition and overweight), Teena Kunjument (health workers), Jessica Ho (hospital beds), Rifat Hossain (water and sanitation), and Hazim Timimi (tuberculosis); Leonor Guariguata of the International Diabetes Federation (diabetes); and Colleen Murray of the United Nations Children's Fund (health). Eric Swanson provided valuable comments and suggestions on the introduction and at all stages of production.

3. Environment

Section 3 was prepared by Mahyar Eshragh-Tabary in partnership with the Environment Department of the Sustainable Development Vice Presidency of the World Bank. Mahyar Eshragh-Tabary wrote the introduction with input from Neil Fantom and Eric Swanson and with valuable suggestions from Jane Ebinger, Tim Herzog, Glenn-Marie Lange, and Soong Sup Lee. Esther G. Naikal and William Prince also contributed to the section. Other contributors include Kirk Hamilton; Carola Fabi and Edward Gillin of the Food and Agriculture Organization of the United Nations; Ricardo Quercioli and Karen Treanton of the International Energy Agency; Laura Battlebury of the World Conservation Monitoring Centre; Gerhard Metchies and Armin Wagner of German International Cooperation; and Craig Hilton-Taylor and Caroline Pollock of the International Union for Conservation of Nature. The World Bank's Environment Department devoted substantial staff resources.

4. Economy

Section 4 was prepared by Bala Bhaskar Naidu Kalimili in close collaboration with the Sustainable Development and Economic Data Team of the World Bank's Development Data Group and with valuable suggestions from Liu Cui and William Prince. Bala Bhaskar Naidu Kalimili wrote the introduction with valuable suggestions from Eric Swanson. Azita Amjadi and Esther G. Naikal also contributed to the section. The national accounts data for low- and middle-income economies were gathered by the World Bank's regional staff through the annual Unified Survey. Maja Bresslauer, Mahyar Eshragh-Tabary, Bala Bhaskar Naidu Kalimili, Buyant Erdene Khaltarkhuu, and Maurice Nsabimana updated, estimated, and validated the databases for national accounts. The team is grateful to Eurostat, the International Monetary Fund, Organisation for Economic Co-operation and Development, United Nations Industrial Development Organization, and World Trade Organization for access to their databases.

5. States and markets

Section 5 was prepared by Buyant Erdene Khaltarkhuu in partnership with the World Bank's Financial and Private Sector Development Network, Poverty Reduction and Economic Management Network, and Sustainable Development Network; the International Finance Corporation; and external partners. David Cieslikowski and Buyant Erdene Khaltarkhuu wrote the introduction with input from Eric Swanson. Other contributors include Ada Karina Izaguirre (privatization and infrastructure projects); Leora Klapper (business registration); Federica Saliola and Joshua Wimpey (Enterprise Surveys); Carolin Geginat and Frederic Meunier (Doing Business); Alka Banerjee, Trisha Malinky, and Michael Orzano (Standard & Poor's global stock market indexes); Oya Pinar Ardic Alper (financial access); Gary Milante, Holly Benner, and Kenneth Anya (fragile situations); Satish Mannan (public policies and institutions); James Hackett of the International Institute for Strategic Studies (military personnel); Sam Perlo-Freeman of the Stockholm International Peace Research Institute (military expenditures and arms transfers); Christian Gonzalez of the International Road Federation, Narjess Teyssier and Zubair Anwar of the International Civil Aviation Organization, and Hélène Stephan and Marc Juhel (transport); Jane Degerlund of Containerisation International and Vincent Valentine of the United Nations Conference on Trade and Development (ports); Azita Amjadi (high-tech exports); Vanessa Grey, Esperanza Magpantay, and Susan Teltscher of the International Telecommunication Union; Torbjörn Fredriksson and Rémi Lang of the United Nations Conference on Trade and Development (information and communication technology goods trade); Martin Schaaper of the United Nations Educational, Scientific, and Cultural Organization Institute for Statistics (research and development, researchers, and technicians); and Ryan Lamb of the World Intellectual Property Organization (patents and trademarks).

6. Global links

Section 6 was prepared by Wendy Huang and Evis Rucaj with valuable input from Uranbileg Batjargal and in partnership with the Financial Data Team of the World Bank's Development Data Group, Development Research Group (trade), Development Prospects Group (commodity prices and remittances), International Trade Department (trade facilitation), and external partners. Malvina Pollock and Evis Rucaj wrote the introduction with substantial input from Eric Swanson. Azita Amjadi (trade and tariffs) and Rubena Sukaj (external debt and financial data) provided substantial input on the data and tables. Other contributors include Frédéric Docquier (emigration rates); Flavine Creppy and Yumiko Mochizuki of the United Nations Conference on Trade and Development and Mondher Mimouni of the International Trade Centre (trade); Cristina Savescu (commodity prices); Jeff Reynolds and Joseph Siegel of DHL (freight costs); Yasmin Ahmad and Elena Bernaldo of the Organisation for Economic Co-operation and Development (aid); Ibrahim Levent, Hiroko Maeda, and Maryna Taran (external debt); Sanket Mohapatra and Ani Rudra Silwal (remittances); and Teresa Ciller of the World Tourism Organization (tourism). Ramgopal Erabelly, Shelley Lai Fu, and William Prince provided valuable technical assistance.

Other parts of the book

Jeff Lecksell of the World Bank's Map Design Unit coordinated preparation of the maps on the inside covers. William Prince prepared *Users guide*. Eric Swanson wrote *Statistical methods*. Maja Bresslauer, Federico Escaler, and Buyant Erdene Khaltarkhuu, prepared *Primary data documentation*. Alison Kwong prepared *Partners* and *Index of indicators*.

Database management

William Prince coordinated management of the World Development Indicators database, with assistance from Liu Cui. Operation of the database management system was made possible by Ramgopal Erabelly and Shelley Fu in the Data and Information Systems Team under the leadership of Reza Farivari.

Design, production, and editing

Azita Amjadi and Alison Kwong coordinated all stages of production with Communications Development Incorporated, which provided overall design direction, editing, and layout, led by Meta de Coquereaumont, Bruce Ross-Larson, and Christopher Trott and assisted by Rob Elson. Elaine Wilson created the cover and graphics and typeset the book. Joseph Caponio provided production assistance. Peter Grundy, of Peter Grundy Art & Design, designed the report.

Client services

The Development Data Group's Client Services and Communications Team (Federico Escaler, Alison Kwong, Beatriz Prieto-Oramas, Maryna Taran, Jomo Tariku, and Vera Wen) contributed to the design and planning and helped coordinate work with the Office of the Publisher under the leadership of Azita Amjadi.

Administrative assistance, office technology, and systems development support

Awatif Abuzeid, Elysee Kiti, Premi Ratham Raj, and Estela Zamora provided administrative assistance. Jean-Pierre Djomalieu, Gytis Kanchas, and Nacer Megherbi provided information technology support. Ramvel Chandrasekaran, Ugendran Machakkalai, Shanmugam Natarajan, Atsushi Shimo, and Malarvizhi Veerappan provided software support on the Development Data Platform application.

Publishing and dissemination

The Office of the Publisher, under the direction of Carlos Rossel, provided valuable assistance throughout the production process. Denise Bergeron, Dina Towbin, Stephen McGroarty, and Nora Ridolfi coordinated printing and supervised marketing and distribution. Merrell Tuck-Primdahl of the Development Economics Vice President's Office managed the communications strategy.

World Development Indicators CD-ROM

Software preparation and testing was managed by Vilas Mandlekar with the assistance of Ramgopal Erabelly, Parastoo Oloumi, and William Prince. Systems development was undertaken by the Data and Information Systems Team led by Reza Farivari. William Prince coordinated user interface design and overall production and provided quality assurance, with assistance from Jomo Tariku.

World Development Indicators mobile applications

Software preparation and testing was managed by Vilas Mandlekar and Shelley Fu with assistance from Azita Amjadi, Prashant Chaudhari, Ying Chi, Liu Cui, Ghislaine Delaine, Ramgopal Erabelly, Federico Escaler, Buyant Erdene Khaltarkhuu, Maurice Nsabimana Parastoo Oloumi, Beatriz Prieto Oramas, William Prince, Virginia Romand, Jomo Tariku, and Vera Wen. Systems development was undertaken in the Data and Information Systems Team led by Reza Farivari. William Prince provided data quality assurance.

Open Data and online access

Coordination of the Open Data website (http://data.worldbank.org) was provided by Neil Fantom. Design, programming, and testing were carried out by Reza Farivari and his team: Azita Amjadi, Ramvel Chandrasekaran, Ying Chi, Federico Escaler, Shelley Fu, Buyant Erdene Khaltarkhuu, Ugendran Machakkalai, Shanmugam Natarajan, Atsushi Shimo, Sun Hwa Song, Lakshmikanthan Subramanian, Maryna Taran, Jomo Tariku, Malarvizhi Veerappan, and Vera Wen. William Prince coordinated production and provided quality assurance. Support from the Corporate Communications Unit in External Affairs was provided by a team including George Gongadze and Jeffrey McCoy. The multilingual web team was led by James Edward Rosenberg.

Client feedback

The team is grateful to the many people who have taken the time to provide feedback and suggestions, which have helped improve this year's edition. Please contact us at data@worldbank.org.

BIBLIOGRAPHY

African Union and United Nations Economic Commission for Africa. 2005. "Transport and the Millennium Development Goals in Africa." Background document for the meeting of experts preceding the meeting of African transport ministers on the role of transport in achieving the Millennium Development Goals, April 4–5, Addis Ababa.

Anderson, Kym, Marianne Kurzweil, Will Martin, Damiano Sandri, and Ernesto Valenzuela. 2008. "Measuring Distortions to Agricultural Incentives, Revisited." Policy Research Working Paper 4612. World Bank, Development Research Group, Washington, D.C.

Arvis, Jean-François, Monica Alina Mustra, Lauri Ojala, Ben Shepherd, and Daniel Saslavsky. 2010. *Connecting to Compete 2010: Trade Logistics in the Global Economy: The Logistics Performance Index and Its Indicators.* Washington, D.C.: World Bank, International Trade Department.

Ball, Nicole. 1984. "Measuring Third World Security Expenditure: A Research Note." *World Development* 12 (2): 157–64.

Bates, Bryson, Zbigniew Kundzewicz, Shaohong Wu, and Jean Palutikof, eds. 2008. *Climate Change and Water.* Technical Paper IV. Geneva: Intergovernmental Panel on Climate Change.

Beck, Thorsten, and Ross Levine. 2001. "Stock Markets, Banks, and Growth: Correlation or Causality?" Policy Research Working Paper 2670. World Bank, Development Research Group, Washington, D.C.

Caiola, Marcello. 1995. *A Manual for Country Economists.* Training Series 1, Vol. 1. Washington, D.C.: International Monetary Fund.

CDIAC (Carbon Dioxide Information Analysis Center). n.d. Online database. [http://cdiac.ornl.gov/home.html]. Oak Ridge National Laboratory, Environmental Sciences Division, Oak Ridge, Tenn.

Chen, Shaohua, and Martin Ravallion. 2011. "The Developing World is Poorer than We Thought, but No Less Successful in the Fight against Poverty." *Quarterly Journal of Economics* 125 (4): 1577–1625.

Chomitz, Kenneth M., Piet Buys, and Timothy S. Thomas. 2005. "Quantifying the Rural-Urban Gradient in Latin America and the Caribbean." Policy Research Working Paper 3634. World Bank, Development Research Group, Washington, D.C.

CIESIN (Center for International Earth Science Information Network). 2005. Gridded Population of the World. Columbia University and Centro Internacional de Agricultura Tropical. [http://sedac.ciesin.columbia.edu/gpw/].

———. 2007. "National Aggregates of Geospatial Data: Population, Landscape and Climate Estimates, v.2 (PLACE II)." Columbia University, Earth Institute, Palisades, N.Y.

CIIFAD (Cornell International Institute for Food, Agriculture and Development). n.d. "The System of Rice Intensification." [http://ciifad.cornell.edu/sri/index.html]. Ithaca, N.Y.

Claessens, Stijn, Daniela Klingebiel, and Sergio L. Schmukler. 2002. "Explaining the Migration of Stocks from Exchanges in Emerging Economies to International Centers." Policy Research Working Paper 2816. World Bank, Washington, D.C.

Containerisation International. 2010. *Containerisation International Yearbook 2010.* London: Informa Maritime and Transport.

Corrao, Marlo Ann, G. Emmanuel Guindon, Namita Sharma, and Dorna Fakhrabadi Shokoohi. 2000. *Tobacco Control Country Profile.* Atlanta, Ga.: American Cancer Society.

Dealogic. n.d. M&A Analytics. Online database. [www.dealogic.com].

Demirgüç-Kunt, Asli, and Ross Levine. 1996. "Stock Market Development and Financial Intermediaries: Stylized Facts." *World Bank Economic Review* 10 (2): 291–321.

De Onis, Mercedes, and Monika, Blössner. 2003. "The WHO Global Database on Child Growth and Malnutrition: Methodology and Applications." *International Journal of Epidemiology* 32: 518–26.

De Onis, Mercedes, Adelheid W. Onyango, Elaine Borghi, Cutberto Garza, and Hong Yang. 2006. "Comparison of the World Health Organization (WHO) Child Growth Standards and the National Center for Health Statistics/WHO International Growth Reference: Implications for Child Health Programmes." *Public Health Nutrition* 9 (7): 942–47.

Development Committee (Joint Ministerial Committee of the Boards of Governors of the Bank and the Fund on the Transfer of Real Resources to Developing Countries). 2011. "Operationalizing the 2011 World Development Report: Conflict, Security, and Development." Development Committee, Washington, D.C.

DHL. 2012. "DHL Rate and Transit Guide 2012." Bonn, Germany.

Docquier, Frédéric, B. Lindsay Lowell, and Abdeslam Marfouk. 2009. "A Gendered Assessment of Highly Skilled Emigration." *Population and Development Review* 35 (2): 297–322.

Docquier, Frédéric, and Abdeslam Marfouk. 2006. "International Migration by Educational Attainment (1990–2000) – Release 1.1." In Caglar Ozden and Maurice Schiff, eds., *International Migration, Remittances and Development.* New York: Palgrave Macmillan.

Eurostat (Statistical Office of the European Communities). n.d. *Demographic Statistics.* [http://epp.eurostat.ec.europa.eu/portal/page/portal/eurostat/home/]. Luxembourg.

———. n.d. National Accounts database. Luxembourg. [http://epp.eurostat.ec.europa.eu/portal/page/portal/balance_of_payments/data/database]. Paris.

———. Various years. *Statistical Yearbook.* Luxembourg.

Fankhauser, Samuel. 1995. *Valuing Climate Change: The Economics of the Greenhouse.* London: Earthscan.

FAO (Food and Agriculture Organization of the United Nations). 2001. "Global Estimates of Gaseous Emissions of NH3, NO and N2O from Agricultural Land, 2001." Food and Agriculture Organization of the United Nations, Rome.

———. 2003. "How the World Is Fed." In *Agriculture, Food and Water.* Rome: Food and Agriculture Organization.

———. 2007. *Coping with Water Scarcity: Challenge of the Twenty-First Century.* Report for World Water Day 2007. Rome: Food and Agriculture Organization.

——. 2008a. "Climate Change Adaptation and Mitigation in the Food and Agriculture Sector." Technical background document from the expert consultation, March 5–7, Rome.

——. 2008b. "Climate Change and Food Security: A Framework Document." Food and Agriculture Organization, Rome.

——. 2009a. "2050: A Third More Mouths to Feed." Press release, September 23. Food and Agriculture Organization, Rome.

——. 2009b. "More People Than Ever Are Victims of Hunger." Press release, June 19. Food and Agriculture Organization, Rome.

——. 2010a. *Global Forest Resources Assessment 2010.* Rome: Food and Agriculture Organization.

——. 2010b. "Water and Poverty: An Issue of Life and Livelihoods." [www.fao.org/nr/water/issues/scarcity.html]. Rome.

——. n.d. AQUASTAT. [www.fao.org/nr/water/aquastat/data/query/index.html]. Rome.

——. n.d. FAOSTAT. http://faostat.fao.org.

——. n.d. Food Security Statistics database. [www.fao.org/economic/ess/food-security-statistics/]. Rome.

——. Various years. *The State of Food Insecurity in the World.* Rome: Food and Agriculture Organization.

Faurès, Jean-Marc, Jippe Hoogeveena, and Jelle Bruinsmab. 2004. "The FAO Irrigated Area Forecast for 2030." Food and Agriculture Organization, Rome.

Fredricksen, Birger. 1993. *Statistics of Education in Developing Countries: An Introduction to Their Collection and Analysis.* Paris: United Nations Educational, Scientific, and Cultural Organization.

Froese, R., and D. Pauly, eds. n.d. FishBase database. [www.fishbase.org]. Manila.

g7+. 2011. " The g7 and the International Dialogue on Statebuilding and Peacebuilding." [www.g7plus.org/dialogue-state-peace-building/]. Dili.

Geneva Declaration. 2011. *Global Burden of Armed Violence.* Geneva: Geneva Declaration.

Global Transport Knowledge Partnership. 2008. "Transport and the Millennium Development Goals." [www.gtkp.com]. Geneva.

GTZ (Deutsche Gesellschaft für Technische Zusammenarbeit). 2005. "Why Transport Matters: Contributions of the Transport Sector towards Achieving the Millennium Development Goals." Deutsche Gesellschaft für Technische Zusammenarbeit, Eschborn, Germany.

Hamilton, Kirk, and Michael Clemens. 1999. "Genuine Savings Rates in Developing Countries." *World Bank Economic Review* 13 (2): 333–56.

——. 2006. *Where Is the Wealth of Nations? Measuring Capital for the 21st Century.* Washington, D.C.: World Bank.

Hamilton, Kirk, and Eduardo Ley. 2010. "Measuring National Income and Growth in Resource-Rich, Income-Poor Countries." Economic Premise 28. World Bank, Poverty Reduction and Economic Management Network, Washington, D.C.

Hamilton, Kirk, and Giovanni Ruta. 2008. "Wealth Accounting, Exhaustible Resources and Social Welfare." *Environmental and Resource Economics* 42 (1): 53–64.

Hanushek, A. Eric. 2002. *The Long-Run Importance of School Quality.* NBER Working Paper 9071. Cambridge, Mass.: National Bureau of Economic Research.

Hanushek, A. Eric, and Wössman, Ludger. 2007. *Education Quality and Economic Growth.* Washington, D.C.: World Bank.

Happe, Nancy, and John Wakeman-Linn. 1994. "Military Expenditures and Arms Trade: Alternative Data Sources." Working Paper 94/69. International Monetary Fund, Policy Development and Review Department, Washington, D.C.

Hatcher, Jeffrey. 2009 "Securing Tenure Rights and Reducing Emissions from Deforestation and Degradation (REDD): Costs and Lessons Learned." Social Development Paper 120. World Bank, Development Research Group, Washington, D.C.

Hatzichronoglou, Thomas. 1997. "Revision of the High-Technology Sector and Product Classification." STI Working Paper 1997/2. Organisation for Economic Co-operation and Development, Directorate for Science, Technology, and Industry, Paris.

Hausman, Warren H., Hau L. Lee, and Uma Subramanian. 2005. "Global Logistics Indicators, Supply Chain Metrics, and Bilateral Trade Patterns." Policy Research Working Paper 3773. World Bank, Development Research Group, Washington, D.C.

Heston, Alan. 1994. "A Brief Review of Some Problems in Using National Accounts Data in Level of Output Comparisons and Growth Studies." *Journal of Development Economics* 44 (1): 29–52.

Hettige, Hemamala, Muthukumara Mani, and David Wheeler. 1998. "Industrial Pollution in Economic Development: Kuznets Revisited." Policy Research Working Paper 1876. World Bank, Development Research Group, Washington, D.C.

Hinz. Richard P., Montserrat Pallares-Miralles, Carolina Romero, and Edward Whitehouse. 2011. "International Patterns of Pension Provision II: Facts and Figures of the 2000s." Social Protection Discussion Paper. World Bank, Washington, D.C.

ICAO (International Civil Aviation Organization). 2011. *Civil Aviation Statistics of the World.* Montreal: International Civil Aviation Organization.

ICF International. Various years. *Demographic and Health Surveys.* [www.measuredhs.com]. Calverton, Md.: ICF International.

IEA (International Energy Agency). 2009. "World Energy Outlook 2009 Fact Sheet: Why Is Our Current Energy Pathway Unsustainable?" International Energy Agency, Paris.

——. 2010. *World Energy Outlook 2010.* Paris: International Energy Agency.

——. n.d. Carbon Dioxide Emissions (CO_2) from Fuel Combustion database. Paris.

——. Various years. *Energy Balances of Non-OECD Countries.* Paris: International Energy Agency.

——. Various years. *Energy Balances of OECD Countries.* Paris: International Energy Agency.

BIBLIOGRAPHY

——. Various years. *Energy Statistics of Non-OECD Countries.* Paris: International Energy Agency.

——. Various years. *Energy Statistics of OECD Countries.* Paris: International Energy Agency.

ILO (International Labour Organization). 2009a. *Guide to the New Millennium Development Goals Employment Indicators.* Geneva: International Labour Office.

——. 2009b. Resolution concerning statistics of child labour. Resolution II, Rpt. ICLS/18/2008/IV/FINAL, 18th International Conference of Labour Statisticians, Geneva.

——. 2010. *Accelerating Action Against Child Labour.* Geneva: International Labour Office.

——. Various years. *Key Indicators of the Labour Market.* Geneva: International Labour Office.

——. Various years. *Yearbook of Labour Statistics.* Geneva: International Labour Office.

IMF (International Monetary Fund). 1977. *Balance of Payments Manual.* 4th ed. Washington, D.C.: International Monetary Fund.

——. 1993. *Balance of Payments Manual.* 5th ed. Washington, D.C.: International Monetary Fund.

——. 1995. *Balance of Payments Compilation Guide.* Washington, D.C.: International Monetary Fund.

——. 1996. *Balance of Payments Textbook.* Washington, D.C.: International Monetary Fund.

——. 2000. *Monetary and Financial Statistics Manual.* Washington, D.C.: International Monetary Fund.

——. 2001. *Government Finance Statistics Manual.* Washington, D.C.: International Monetary Fund.

——. 2004. *Compilation Guide on Financial Soundness Indicators.* Washington, D.C.: International Monetary Fund.

——. 2008. *Monetary and Financial Statistics Compilation Guide.* Washington, D.C.: International Monetary Fund.

——. 2009a. *Global Financial Stability Report.* Washington, D.C.: International Monetary Fund.

——. 2009b. *World Economic Outlook: Sustaining the Recovery.* Washington, D.C.: International Monetary Fund.

——. n.d. Financial Access Survey database. [http://fas.imf.org]. Washington, D.C.

——. n.d. Financial Soundness Indicators database. [fsi.imf.org]. Washington, D.C.

——. Various issues. *Direction of Trade Statistics Quarterly.* Washington, D.C.: International Monetary Fund.

——. Various issues. *Government Finance Statistics Yearbook.* Washington, D.C.: International Monetary Fund.

——. Various issues. *International Financial Statistics.* Washington, D.C.: International Monetary Fund.

——. Various years. *Balance of Payments Statistics Yearbook. Parts 1 and 2.* Washington, D.C.: International Monetary Fund.

——. Various years. *Direction of Trade Statistics Yearbook.* Washington, D.C.: International Monetary Fund.

——. Various years. *International Financial Statistics Yearbook.* Washington, D.C.: International Monetary Fund.

Internal Displacement Monitoring Centre. 2011. *Internal Displacement: Global Overview of Trends and Developments in 2010.* Geneva: Internal Displacement Monitoring Centre.

International Diabetes Federation. Various years. *Diabetes Atlas.* Brussels: International Diabetes Federation.

International Institute for Strategic Studies. 2012. *The Military Balance 2012.* London: Oxford University Press.

International Trade Centre, UNCTAD (United Nations Conference on Trade and Development), and WTO (World Trade Organization). n.d. The Millennium Development Goals database. [www.mdg-trade.org]. Geneva.

International Working Group of External Debt Compilers. 1987. *External Debt Definitions.* Washington, D.C.: International Working Group of External Debt Compilers.

Inter-Secretariat Working Group on National Accounts. 1993. *United Nations Systems of National Accounts.* New York.

IPCC (Intergovernmental Panel on Climate Change). 2007. *Climate Change 2007: The Physical Science Basis. Contribution of Working Group I to the Fourth Assessment Report of the Intergovernmental Panel on Climate Change.* Cambridge, U.K.: Cambridge University Press.

IRF (International Road Federation). 2011. *World Road Statistics 2011.* Geneva: International Road Federation.

ITU (International Telecommunication Union). n.d. World Telecommunication/ICT Indicators database. Geneva: International Telecommunication Union.

IUCN (International Union for Conservation of Nature). 2011. *2011 IUCN Red List of Threatened Species.* Gland, Switzerland: International Union for Conservation of Nature.

Karl, T.R., N. Nicholls, and J. Gregory. 1997. "The Coming Climate." *Scientific American* 276: 78–83.

Kattenberg, A., F. Giorgi, H. Grassl, G.A. Meehl, J.F.B. Mitchell, R.J. Stouffer, T. Tokioka, A.J. Weaver, and T.M.L. Wigley, 1996. "Climate Models: Projections of Future Climate." In J.T. Houghton, L.G.M. Filho, B.A. Callander, N. Harris, A. Kattenberg, and K. Maskell, eds., *Climate Change 1995: The Science of Climate Change.* Cambridge, UK: Cambridge University Press.

Kundzewicz, Zbigniew W., and Luis José Mata. 2007. "Freshwater Resources and Their Management." In S. Solomon, D. Qin, M. Manning, Z. Chen, M. Marquis, K.B. Averyt, M. Tignor and H. L. Miller, eds., *Climate Change 2007: Climate Change Impacts, Adaptation and Vulnerability. Working Group II Contribution to* the Fourth Assessment Report of the Intergovernmental Panel on Climate Change. Cambridge, U.K.: Cambridge University Press.

Kunte, Arundhati, Kirk Hamilton, John Dixon, and Michael Clemens. 1998. "Estimating National Wealth: Methodology and Results." Environmental Economics Series 57. World Bank, Environment Department, Washington, D.C.

Luxembourg Income Study. n.d. Online database. [www.lisproject.org]. Luxembourg.

Meehl, G. A., C. Covey, T. Delworth, M. Latif, B. McAvaney, J. F. B. Mitchell, R. J. Stouffer, and K. E. Taylor. 2007. "The WCRP CMIP3 Multi-Model Dataset: A New Era in Climate Change Research." Bulletin of the American Meteorological Society 88: 1383–94.

Mitchell, T. D., T. R. Carter, P. D. Jones, M. Hulme, M. New, M. 2003. "A Comprehensive Set of High-Resolution Grids of Monthly Climate for Europe and the Globe: the Observed Record (1901-2000) and 16 Scenarios (2001-2100)." Working Paper 55. Tyndall Centre for Climate Change Research, Norwich, U.K.

Morgenstern, Oskar. 1963. On the Accuracy of Economic Observations. Princeton, N.J.: Princeton University Press.

Netcraft. 2011. "Netcraft Secure Server Survey." [www.netcraft.com].

Njinkeu, Dominique, John S. Wilson, and Bruno Powo Fosso. 2008. "Expanding Trade within Africa: The Impact of Trade Facilitation." Policy Research Working Paper 4790. World Bank, Development Research Group, Washington, D.C.

OECD (Organisation for Economic Co-operation and Development). 2002. Frascati Manual: Proposed Standard Practice for Surveys on Research and Experimental Development, 6th edition. Paris: Organisation for Economic Co-operation and Development.

——. 2005. Guide to Measuring the Information Society. DSTI/ICCP/ISS (2005)/6. Paris: Organisation for Economic Co-operation and Development.

——. 2008a. The Paris Declaration on Aid Effectiveness and the Accra Agenda for Action. Paris: Organisation for Economic Co-operation and Development. [www.oecd.org/dataoecd/11/41/34428351.pdf].

——. 2008b. A Profile of Immigrant Populations in the 21st Century: Data from OECD countries. Paris.

——. 2009. Agricultural Policies in OECD Countries: Monitoring and Evaluation. Paris: Organisation for Economic Co-operation and Development.

——. 2010a. OECD Economic Surveys: China 2010. Paris: Organisation for Economic Co-operation and Development.

——. 2010b. Restoring Fiscal Sustainability: Lessons for the Public Sector. Paris: Organisation for Economic Co-operation and Development.

——. 2011. "International Dialogue on Peacebuilding and Statebuilding: Civil Society Input to the Monrovia Meeting." [www.oecd.org/dataoecd/39/42/48153591.pdf]. Paris.

——. n.d. Creditor Reporting System database. [http://stats.oecd.org/Index.aspx?DatasetCode=CRSNEW]. Paris.

——. n.d. International Direct Investment database. [http://stats.oecd.org]. Paris.

——. n.d. International Trade by Commodity Statistics. [http://stats.oecd.org]. Paris.

——. n.d. Monthly Statistics of International Trade. [http://stats.oecd.org]. Paris.

——. n.d. National Accounts Statistics database. Paris.

——. n.d. Producer and Consumer Support Estimates. Online database. [www.oecd.org/tad/support/psecse]. Paris.

——. n.d. Trade in Services database. [http://stats.oecd.org]. Paris.

——. Various issues. Main Economic Indicators. Paris: Organisation for Economic Co-operation and Development.

——. Various years. Geographical Distribution of Financial Flows to Developing Economies. Paris: Organisation for Economic Co-operation and Development.

——. Various years. National Accounts. Vol. 1, Main Aggregates. Paris: Organisation for Economic Co-operation and Development.

——. Various years. National Accounts. Vol. 2, Detailed Tables. Paris: Organisation for Economic Co-operation and Development.

——. Various years. OECD Health Data. Paris: Organisation for Economic Co-operation and Development.

OECD (Organisation for Economic Co-operation and Development) DAC (Development Assistance Committee). 1996. Shaping the 21st Century: The Contribution of Development Cooperation. Paris: Organisation for Economic Co-operation and Development.

——. n.d.. International Development Statistics. [www.oecd.org/dac/stats/idsonline]. Paris.

——. Various years. Development Cooperation Report. Paris: Organisation for Economic Co-operation and Development.

——. Various years. Geographical Distribution of Financial Flows to Developing Economies. Paris: Organisation for Economic Co-operation and Development.

——. Various years. International Development Statistics. CD-ROM. Paris: Organisation for Economic Co-operation and Development.

OFDA (Office of U.S. Foreign Disaster Assistance)/CRED (Center for Research on the Epidemiology of Disaster). n.d. International Disaster Database. [www.emdat.be.] Brussels.

Ozden, Caglar, Christopher R. Parsons, Maurice Schiff and Terrie L. Walmsley. 2011. "Where on Earth Is Everybody? The Evolution of Global Bilateral Migration 1960–2000." World Bank Economic Review.

Pandey, Kiran D., Piet Buys, Kenneth Chomitz, and David Wheeler. 2006a. "Biodiversity Conservation Indicators: New Tools for Priority Setting at the Global Environmental Facility." World Bank, Development Economics Research Group and Environment Department, Washington, D.C.

Pandey, Kiran D., David Wheeler, Bart Ostro, Uwe Deichmann, Kirk Hamilton, and Katie Bolt. 2006b. "Ambient Particulate Matter Concentrations in Residential and Pollution Hotspots of World Cities: New Estimates Based on the Global Model of Ambient Particulates (GMAPS)." World Bank, Development Economics Research Group and Environment Department, Washington, D.C.

Pandey, Kiran D., Katharine Bolt, Uwe Deichmann, Kirk Hamilton, Bart Ostro, and David Wheeler. 2006c. "The Human Cost of Air Pollution: New Estimates for

BIBLIOGRAPHY

Developing Countries." World Bank, Development Research Group and Environment Department, Washington, D.C.

PARIS21 (The Partnership in Statistics for Development in the 21st Century). 2009a. *Dakar Declaration On The Development Of Statistics.* Paris: Organisation for Economic Co-operation and Development. [www.paris21.org/sites/default/files/DDDS-en.pdf].

——. 2009b. *PARIS21 at Ten: Improvements in statistical capacity since 1999.* Paris: Organisation for Economic-Coperation and Development. [www.paris21.org/sites/default/files/P21-at-10.pdf].

Partnership on Measuring ICT for Development. 2008. *The Global Information Society: A Statistical View.* Santiago: United Nations.

Patterson, Neil, Marie Montanjees, John Motala, and Colleen Cardillo. 2004. "Foreign Direct Investment: Trends, Data Availability, Concepts, and Recording Practices." International Monetary Fund, Washington D.C.

Porta, Emilio, Gustavo Arcia, Kevin Macdonald, Sergiy Radyakin, and Michael Lokshin. 2011. *Assessing Sector Performance and Inequality in Education.* World Bank: Washington D.C.

PwC, International Finance Corporation, and World Bank. 2011. *Paying Taxes 2012: The Global Picture.* London and Washington, D.C. [www.pwc.com/payingtaxes].

RAMSI (Regional Assistance Mission to Solomon Islands). 2012. "Fact Sheets." [www.ramsi.org]. Honiara.

Ratha, Dilip, and William Shaw. 2007. "South–South Migration and Remittances." Working Paper 102. World Bank, Washington, D.C.

Ravallion, Martin, and Shaohua Chen. 1996. "What Can New Survey Data Tell Us about the Recent Changes in Living Standards in Developing and Transitional Economies?" Policy Research Working Paper 16943. World Bank, Development Research Group, Washington, D.C.

Ravallion, Martin, Shaohua Chen, and Prem Sangraula. 2009. "Dollar a Day Revisited." *World Bank Economic Review* 23 (2): 163–84.

Ravallion, Martin, Gaurav Datt, and Dominique van de Walle. 1991. "Quantifying Absolute Poverty in the Developing World." *Review of Income and Wealth* 37(4): 345–61.

Ruggles, Robert. 1994. "Issues Relating to the UN System of National Accounts and Developing Countries." *Journal of Development Economics* 44 (1): 77–85.

Ryten, Jacob. 1998. "Fifty Years of ISIC: Historical Origins and Future Perspectives." ECA/STAT.AC. 63/22. United Nations Statistics Division, New York.

SIPRI (Stockholm International Peace Research Institute). n.d. Arms Transfers database. [www.sipri.org/databases/armstransfers]. Solna, Sweden.

——. n.d. Military Expenditure database. [www.sipri.org/databases/milex]. Solna, Sweden.

Smith, Kimberly, Talita Yamashiro Fordelone, and Felix Zimmermann. 2010. "Beyond the DAC: Welcome Role of Other Providers of Development Co-operation." OECD Development Co-operation Directorate, Paris.

Smith, Lisa, and Laurence Haddad. 2000. "Overcoming Child Malnutrition in Developing Countries: Past Achievements and Future Choices." 2020 Brief 64. International Food Policy Research Institute, Washington, D.C.

SPC (Secretariat of the Pacific Community). n.d. Online Statistics and Demography. [www.spc.int]. Nouméa.

Srinivasan, T. N. 1994. "Database for Development Analysis: An Overview." *Journal of Development Economics* 44 (1): 3–28.

Standard & Poor's. 2000. *The S&P Emerging Market Indices: Methodology, Definitions, and Practices.* New York: Standard & Poor's.

——. 2012. *Global Stock Markets Factbook 2011.* New York: Standard & Poor's.

Takle, Eugene, and Don Hofstrand. 2008. "Global Warming: Agriculture's Impact on Greenhouse Gas Emissions." *Ag Decision Maker,* April.

UCDP (Uppsala Conflict Data Program)/PRIO (Peace Research Institute Oslo). 2011. Armed Conflict Dataset v.4-2011, 1946–2010. [www.pcr.uu.se/research/ucdp/datasets/ucdp_prio_armed_conflict_dataset/]. Uppsala, Sweden.

UNAIDS (Joint United Nations Programme on HIV/AIDS) and WHO (World Health Organization). Various years. *Global Report: UNAIDS Report on the Global AIDS Epidemic.* Geneva: Joint United Nations Programme on HIV/AIDS.

UNCTAD (United Nations Conference on Trade and Development). 2001. *Electronic Commerce and Development Report 2001.* New York and Geneva: United Nations Conference on Trade and Development.

——. 2007. *Trade and Development Report 2007: Regional Cooperation for Development.* New York and Geneva: United Nations Conference on Trade and Development.

——. 2008. *Trade and Development Report 2008: Commodity Prices, Capital Flows and the Financing of Investment.* New York and Geneva: United Nations Conference on Trade and Development.

——. 2009a. *UNCTAD Training Manual on Statistics for FDI and the Operations of TNCs, Volumes I, II, and III.* Geneva: United Nations Conference on Trade and Development.

——. 2009b. *Transport Newsletter.* Issue 43.

——. 2010. *Review of Maritime Transport 2011.* Geneva: United Nations Conference on Trade and Development.

——. n.d. Transnational Corporations Statistics database. [www.unctad.org/Templates/Page.asp?intItemID=3159&lang=1]. Geneva.

——. n.d. UNCTADStat. Information Economy. [http://unctadstat.unctad.org]. Geneva.

——. n.d. UNCTADStat Maritime Transport. [http://unctadstat.unctad.org]. Geneva.

——. Various years. *Handbook of Statistics.* New York and Geneva: United Nations Conference on Trade and Development.

——. Various years. *World Investment Report.* Geneva: United Nations Conference on Trade and Development.

UNCTAD (United Nations Conference on Trade and Development) and UNEP (United Nations Environment Programme). 2008. *Organic Agriculture and Food Security in Africa.* UNCTAD-UNEP Capacity Building Task Force on Trade, Environment and Development. New York: United Nations.

Understanding Children's Work (UCW). n.d. Online database. [www.ucw-project. org]. Rome.

UNDP (United Nations Development Programme). 1990. *Human Development Report 1990.* New York: Oxford University Press.

———. 2005. *Human Development Report 2005: International Cooperation at a Crossroads: Aid, Trade and Security in an Unequal World.* New York: United Nations Development Programme.

———. 2006. *Asia-Pacific Human Development Report 2006: Trade on Human Terms: Transforming Trade for Human Development in Asia and the Pacific.* Colombo: Macmillan India Ltd.

UNEP (United Nations Environment Programme) and WCMC (World Conservation Monitoring Centre). 2011. Species database. [www.unep-wcmc-apps.org/ species/dbases/about.cfm]. Nairobi.

UNESCO (United Nations Educational, Scientific, and Cultural Organization). 1997. *International Standard Classification of Education.* Paris: United Nations Educational, Scientific, and Cultural Organization.

———. 2009. *World Water Development Report 3: Water in a Changing World.* 2009. Paris: United Nations Educational, Scientific, and Cultural Organization.

———. 2010. *UNESCO Science Report 2010.* Paris: United Nations Educational, Scientific, and Cultural Organization.

———. Various years. *EFA Global Monitoring Report.* Paris: United Nations Educational, Scientific, and Cultural Organization.

UNESCO (United Nations Educational, Scientific, and Cultural Organization) Institute for Statistics. n.d. Online database. [www.uis.unesco.org]. Montreal.

———. Various years. *Global Education Digest.* Paris.

UNHCR (Office of the United Nations High Commissioner for Refugees). Various years. *Statistical Yearbook.* Geneva: Office of the United Nations High Commissioner for Refugees.

UNICEF (United Nations Children's Fund). Various years. Multiple Indicator Cluster Surveys. [www.childinfo.org]. New York.

———. Various years. *The State of the World's Children.* New York: Oxford University Press.

UNICEF (United Nations Children's Fund), WHO (World Health Organization), World Bank, and United Nations Population Division. 2010. "Levels and Trends of Child Mortality in 2010: Estimates Developed by the UN Inter-Agency Group for Child Mortality Estimation." Working Paper. United Nations, New York.

UNIDO (United Nations Industrial Development Organization). Various years. *International Yearbook of Industrial Statistics.* Vienna: United Nations Industrial Development Organization.

UNIFEM (United Nations Development Fund for Women). 2005. *Progress of the World's Women.* New York: United Nations Development Fund for Women.

UN Inter-agency Group for Child Mortality Estimation. n.d. Child Mortality Estimation Info database. [www.childmortality.org]. New York.

———. 2011. *Levels and Trends in Child Mortality: Report 2011.* New York.

UNISDR (United Nations International Strategy for Disaster Reduction). Various years. *Progress Reports.* Geneva.

United Nations. 1990. *International Standard Industrial Classification of All Economic Activities,* Third Revision. Statistical Papers Series M, No. 4, Rev. 3. New York: United Nations.

———. 1992. "Kyoto Protocol to the United Nations Framework Convention on Climate Change. United Nations, New York.

———. 2009a. "Copenhagen Accord." December 18. United Nations Framework Convention on Climate Change, Copenhagen.

———. 2009b. "Fact Sheet: Stepping Up International Action on Climate Change: The Road to Copenhagen. United Nations Framework Convention on Climate Change, New York.

United Nations Department of Peacekeeping Operations. n.d. "Current Operations." [www.un.org/en/peacekeeping/currentops.shtml]. New York.

United Nations Population Division. 2009. *Trends in Total Migrant Stock: 2008 Revision.* New York: United Nations, Department of Economic and Social Affairs.

———. 2011. *World Population Prospects: The 2010 Revision.* New York: United Nations, Department of Economic and Social Affairs.

———. Various years. *World Urbanization Prospects.* New York: United Nations, Department of Economic and Social Affairs.

United Nations Statistics Division. 2010. "Implementation of Population Census Topics in the 2010 Round." [http://unstats.un.org/unsd/demographic/ sources/census/2010_phc/census_clock/TopicsPerCountry.pdf]. New York.

———. n.d. Comtrade database. New York.

———. n.d. *International Standard Industrial Classification of All Economic Activities, Third Revision.* [http://unstats.un.org/unsd/cr/registry/]. New York.

———. n.d. National Accounts Official Country Data database. New York.

———. n.d. World Energy Data Set. New York: United Nations.

———. Various issues. *Monthly Bulletin of Statistics.* New York: United Nations.

———. Various issues. *Population and Vital Statistics Report.* New York: United Nations.

———. Various years. *Demographic Yearbook.* New York: United Nations.

———. Various years. *International Trade Statistics Yearbook.* New York: United Nations.

———. Various years. *Energy Statistics Yearbook.* New York: United Nations.

———. Various years. *National Accounts Statistics: Main Aggregates and Detailed Tables. Parts 1 and 2.* New York: United Nations.

———. Various years. *National Income Accounts.* New York: United Nations.

———. Various years. *Statistical Yearbook.* New York: United Nations.

University of California, Berkeley, and Max Planck Institute for Demographic Research. n.d. Human Mortality Database. [www.mortality.org or www. humanmortality.de]. Berkeley, Calif., and Rostock, Germany.

UNODC (United Nations Office on Drugs and Crime). n.d. International Homicide Statistics database. [www.unodc.org/unodc/en/data-and-analysis/homicide. html]. Vienna.

BIBLIOGRAPHY

Uppsala University. 2011. Battle-Related Deaths Dataset v.5 2011, 1989–2010. Uppsala University, Sweden.

USAID (U.S. Agency for International Development). 2007. "Calculating Tariff Equivalents for Time in Trade." U.S. Agency for International Development, Washington, D.C.

U.S. Bureau of Mines. n.d. Cement Manufacturing Data Set. Washington, D.C.

U.S. Census Bureau. n.d. International Data Base (IDB). [www.census.gov/ipc/www/idb/]. Washington, D.C.

U.S. Centers for Disease Control and Prevention. Various years. *International Reproductive Health Surveys.* [www.cdc.gov/reproductivehealth/Surveys/]. Atlanta, Ga.

U.S. National Science Board. 2012. *Science and Engineering Indicators 2012.* Arlington, Va.: National Science Foundation.

Vandermoortele, Jan. 2009. "Taking the MDGs Beyond 2015: Hasten Slowly." European Association for Development Research and Training Institutes, Bonn, Germany.

Watkins, Kevin. 2008. *The Millennium Development Goals: Three Proposals for Renewing the Vision and Reshaping the Future.* Paris: United Nations Educational, Scientific, and Cultural Organization.

WHO (World Health Organization). 2008a. *Health Metrics Network Framework and Standards for Country Health Information Systems.* Geneva: World Health Organization.

———. 2008b. "Measuring Health System Strengthening and Trends: A Toolkit for Countries." World Health Organization, Geneva.

———. 2008c. *Worldwide Prevalence of Anemia 1993–2005.* Geneva: World Health Organization.

———. 2011. *WHO Report on the Global Tobacco Epidemic 2011: Implementing Smoke-Free Environments.* Geneva: World Health Organization.

———. n.d. Global Atlas of the Health Workforce. [http://apps.who.int/globalatlas/]. Geneva.

———. n.d. Global Database on Child Growth and Malnutrition. [www.who.int/nutgrowthdb]. Geneva.

———. n.d. Health Statistics and Health Information Systems [www.who.int/healthinfo/global_burden_disease/estimates_country/en/index.html]. Geneva.

———. n.d. Mediacenter factsheets. [www.who.int/mediacentre/factsheets]. Geneva.

———. n.d. National Health Account database. [www.who.int/nha/en/]. Geneva.

———. n.d. Topics [www.who.int/topics]. Geneva.

———. Various years. *World Health Report.* Geneva: World Health Organization.

———. Various years. *World Health Statistics.* Geneva: World Health Organization.

———. Various years. *Global Tuberculosis Control Report.* Geneva: World Health Organization.

WHO (World Health Organization) and UNICEF (United Nations Children's Fund). 2003. *Antenatal Care in Developing Countries: Promises, Achievements, and Missed Opportunities.* Geneva: World Health Organization.

———. 2012. *Progress on Drinking Water and Sanitation.* Geneva: World Health Organization.

———. Various years. WHO-UNICEF estimates of national immunization coverage database. [www.who.int/immunization_monitoring/routine/immunization_coverage/en/index4.html]. Geneva.

WHO (World Health Organization), UNICEF (United Nations Children's Fund), UNFPA (United Nations Population Fund), and World Bank. 2010. *Trends in Maternal Mortality 1990–2008: Estimates Developed by WHO, UNICEF, UNFPA, and the World Bank.* Geneva: World Health Organization.

WIPO (World Intellectual Property Organization). 2011. *World Intellectual Property Indicators.* Geneva: World Intellectual Property Organization.

World Bank. 1990. *World Development Report 1990: Poverty.* Washington, D.C.: World Bank.

———. 1992. *Poverty Reduction Handbook.* Report no. 10730. Washington, DC: World Bank.

———. 2000a. *Making Transition Work for Everyone: Poverty and Inequality in Europe and Central Asia.* Washington, D.C.: World Bank.

———. 2000b. *Trade Blocs.* New York: Oxford University Press.

———. 2001. *World Development Report 2000/2001: Attacking Poverty.* New York: Oxford University Press.

———. 2002. *Global Economic Prospects 2002: Making Trade Work for the World's Poor.* Washington, D.C.: World Bank.

———. 2007a. *Healthy Development: The World Bank Strategy for Health, Nutrition, and Population Results.* Washington, D.C.: World Bank.

———. 2007b. *Sanitation and Water Supply: Improving Services for the Poor.* IDA at Work. Washington, D.C.: World Bank, Sustainable Development Network.

———. 2008a. "Brazil Country Partnership Strategy 2008–2011." World Bank, Latin America and the Caribbean Region, Washington, D.C.

———. 2008b. "Improving Trade and Transport for Landlocked Developing Countries: World Bank Contributions to Implementing the Almaty Programme of Action: A Report for the Mid-Term Review October 2008." World Bank, International Trade Department, Washington, D.C.

———. 2008c. "Safe, Clean, and Affordable . . . Transport for Development: The World Bank Group's Transport Business Strategy for 2008–2012." World Bank, Transport Sector Board, Washington, D.C.

———. 2008d. *World Development Report 2009: Reshaping Economic Geography.* Washington, D.C.: World Bank.

———. 2009a. *Africa's Development in a Changing Climate: Act Now, Act Together, Act Differently.* Washington, D.C.: World Bank.

———. 2009b. "Air Freight: A Market Study with Implications for Landlocked Countries." Transport Paper 26. World Bank, Washington, D.C.

———. 2009c. *Development Outreach.* October.

———. 2009d. *Energy: Improving Services for the Poor.* IDA at Work. Washington, D.C.: World Bank, Sustainable Development Network.

———. 2009e. "Infrastructure Financing Gap Endangers Development Goals." Press release, April 23. World Bank, Washington, D.C.

———. 2009f. "Private Activity in Infrastructure Down, But Still Around Peak Levels." Private Participation in Infrastructure Data Update Note 28. World Bank, Washington, D.C.

———. 2009g. *Protecting Progress: The Challenge Facing Low-Income Countries in the Global Recession*. Washington, D.C.: World Bank.

———. 2009h. "Reduced Emissions and Enhanced Adaptation in Agricultural Landscapes." *Agriculture and Rural Development Notes*, Issue 50.

———. 2009i. "World Bank to Invest $45 Billion in Infrastructure to Help Create Jobs and Speed Crisis Recovery." Press release, April 23. World Bank, Washington, D.C.

———. 2009j. *World Development Report 2010: Development and Climate Change*. Washington, D.C.: World Bank.

———. 2009k. *Information and Communications for Development: Extending Reach and Increasing Impact*. Washington, D.C.: World Bank.

———. 2010a. *Global Economic Prospects 2010: Crisis, Finance, and Growth*. Washington, D.C.: World Bank.

———. 2010b. *The World Bank's Country Policy and Institutional Assessment: An IEG Evaluation*. Washington, D.C.: World Bank.

———. 2010c. "The World Bank Group Entrepreneurship Snapshots." [http://go.worldbank.org/C8Q8EGTTH0]." Washington, D.C.

———. 2011a. *Doing Business 2012*. Washington, D.C.: World Bank.

———. 2011b. "Fragility and Conflict: Supporting Peace and Development in Situations of Fragility and Conflict." World Bank, Washington, D.C.

———. 2011c. *The Changing Wealth of Nations: Measuring Sustainable Development in the New Millennium*. Washington, D.C.: World Bank.

———. 2011d. *World Development Report 2011: Conflict, Security, and Development*. [http://wdr2011.worldbank.org/]. Washington, D.C.

———. 2012. *Global Economic Prospects 2012: Uncertainties and Vulnerabilities*. Washington, D.C.: World Bank.

———. n.d. Enterprise Surveys Online. [www.enterprisesurveys.org]. Washington, D.C.

———. n.d. Entrepreneurship Snapshots. [http://econ.worldbank.org/research/entrepreneurship]. Washington, D.C.

———. n.d. National Global Health Expenditure database. [www.who.int/nha/expenditure_database/en/]. Geneva.

———. n.d. Performance Assessments and Allocation of IDA Resources database. [www.worldbank.org/ida]. Washington, D.C.

———. n.d. PovcalNet online database. [http://iresearch.worldbank.org/PovcalNet]. Washington, D.C.

———. n.d. Private Participation in Infrastructure Database. [http://ppi.worldbank.org/]. Washington, D.C.

———. n.d. World Trade Indicators Online database. [www.worldbank.org/wti]. Washington, D.C.

———. Various issues. *Commodity Market Review*. Washington, D.C.: World Bank, Development Prospects Group

———. Various issues. *Commodity Price Data*. Washington, D.C.: World Bank, Development Prospects Group.

———. Various issues. *Migration and Development Briefs*. Washington, D.C.: World Bank, Development Prospects Group.

———. Various years. *Global Development Finance: External Debt of Developing Countries*. Washington, D.C.: World Bank.

———. Various years. *World Development Indicators*. Washington, D.C.: World Bank.

———. Various years. *World Debt Tables*. Washington, D.C.: World Bank.

World Bank and Center for International Business, Tuck School of Business at Dartmouth Colleges. n.d. Global Preferential Trade Agreements database. [http://wits.worldbank.org/gptad/]. Washington, D.C.

World Bank and IFPRI (International Food Policy Research Institute). 2006. *Agriculture and Achieving the Millennium Development Goals*. Report 32729-GLB. Washington, D.C.: World Bank.

World Bank and IMF (International Monetary Fund). 2007. *Global Monitoring Report 2007: Millennium Development Goals: Confronting the Challenges of Gender Equality and Fragile States*. Washington, D.C.: World Bank.

———. 2008. *Global Monitoring Report 2008: MDGs and the Environment*. Washington, D.C.: World Bank.

———. 2009. *Global Monitoring Report 2009: A Development Emergency*. Washington, D.C.: World Bank.

———. 2011. "Heavily Indebted Poor Countries (HIPC) Initiative and Multilateral Debt Relief Initiative (MDRI)—Status of Implementation." Washington, D.C.

———. n.d. Quarterly Public Sector Debt database. [http://databank.worldbank.org/ddp/home.do?Step=12&id=4&CNO=3009]. Washington, D.C.

World Economic Forum. 2011. *The Global Competitiveness Report 2011–2012*. Geneva: World Economic Forum.

World Tourism Organization. Various years. *Compendium of Tourism Statistics*. Madrid: World Tourism Organization.

———. Various years. *Yearbook of Tourism Statistics*. Vols. 1 and 2. Madrid: World Tourism Organization.

WTO (World Trade Organization). n.d. Regional Trade Agreements Gateway. [www.wto.org/english/tratop_e/region_e/region_e.htm]. Geneva.

———. n.d. Regional Trade Agreements Information System. Online database. [http://rtais.wto.org/]. Geneva.

———. Various years. *Annual Report*. Geneva.

INDEX OF INDICATORS

References are to table numbers.

INDEX OF INDICATORS

D

DAC (Development Assistance Committee)—see Aid

Death rate, crude 2.1

    See also Mortality rate

Debt, external

    as share of GNI 6.9

    debt service

        total, as share of exports of goods and services and income 6.9

    long-term

        private nonguaranteed 6.9

        public and publicly guaranteed 6.9

    present value

        as share of GNI 6.9

        as share of exports of goods and services and income 6.9

    short-term

        as share of total debt 6.9

        as share of total reserves 6.9

        total 6.9

Debt flows

    bonds 6.10

    commercial banks and other lending 6.10

    See also Private financial flows

Deforestation, average annual 3.4

Demand—see Consumption; Imports; Exports; Savings

Density—see Population, density

Dependency ratio—See Population, age dependency ratio

Development assistance—see Aid

Disaster risk reduction progress score—see Resilience

Disease—see Health risks

Distribution of income or consumption—see Income distribution

E

Economic management (Country Policy and Institutional Assessment)

    debt policy 5.9

economic management cluster average 5.9

fiscal policy 5.9

macroeconomic management 5.9

Education

    children out of school

        male and female 2.12

        poorest and richest wealth quintile 2.15

    cohort survival rate

        to grade 5, male and female 2.13

        to last grade of primary education, male and female 2.13

    completion rate, primary

        male and female 2.14, 2.15

        poorest and richest wealth quintiles 2.15

        total 1.2, 2.14

    enrollment ratio

        girls to boys enrollment in primary and secondary education 1.2

        gross

            by level 2.12

            primary 5.8

            secondary 2.4

        net

            by level 2.12

            primary, adjusted 2.12

    intake ratio, gross

        first grade of primary education 2.13

        grade 1 .... 2.15

    primary participation rate, gross 2.15

    public expenditure on

        as share of GDP 2.11

        as share of GNI 4.11

        as share of total government expenditure 2.11

        per student, as share of GDP per capita, by level 2.11

    pupil–teacher ratio, primary 2.11

    repeaters, primary, male and female 2.13

    teachers, primary, trained 2.11

    transition to secondary school, male and female 2.13

    unemployment by level of educational attainment 2.5

    years of schooling, average, poorest and richest wealth quintiles 2.15

Electricity

    access to 3.8

    business lost due to outages 5.2

    consumption 5.11

    production

        total 3.8

        sources 3.8

INDEX OF INDICATORS

INDEX OF INDICATORS

INDEX OF INDICATORS

INDEX OF INDICATORS

INDEX OF INDICATORS

INDEX OF INDICATORS

INDEX OF INDICATORS